The U.S. Environmental Protection Agency

Is seeking men and women to help to Protect Public Health and the Environment

The U.S. Environmental Protection Agency brings together people from diverse backgrounds to improve and preserve the quality of public health and the environment. While that vital mission will endure, changing environmental challenges continue to emerge that require new, creative, and innovative solutions. Crafting these solutions collaboratively is EPA's primary business.

U.S. Environmental Protection Agency
Visit our website for more information: http://www.epa.gov
Job Information: http://www.usajobs.opm.gov/a9epa.htm
National Hispanic Outreach Strategy: http://www.epa.gov/hispanicoutreach

The U.S. Environmental Protection Agency is an Equal Opportunity Employer

You've got a degree and a head full of ideas. Will anybody listen?

We're all ears. For diverse points of view. Divergent outlooks. Different answers. If that sounds appealing, then listen to this. At State Farm, you can choose from any of a variety of careers in the expanding financial services arena, with competitive salaries, excellent benefits and great opportunities for professional advancement. What else do you need to hear?

Contact State Farm Human Resources at **jobopps.corpsouth@statefarm.com** for information about current positions. Or visit our website at **statefarm.com**.™

Get there with State Farm.

Contents

Indice

The ability to perform magic isn't part of Beverly Cole's job description, but maybe it should be. As Director of the Minority and Women Business Enterprise Program (MWBE) for The Walt Disney Company, her customers often need vendors with a rather *unique* set of skills.

For example, where would you begin to look for qualified minority and women-owned business entrepreneurs whose capabilities might include: building the Lion King's parade float; maintaining the beautiful foliage and landscaping throughout DISNEYLAND® Park; or creating mannequins for the Disney Store?

Beverly and her seven-person team, based in Burbank, turned first to the extensive database of The Walt Disney Company – and made very successful matches. With more than 13 years in service, the MWBE Program has matched hundreds of women and minority-owned firms with opportunities to provide their goods and services to Disney businesses which include: theme parks, resorts, film and television, consumer products, interactive CD's, games, and books for adults and children.

The ever-growing and ever-changing, dynamic world of Disney keeps the MWBE team

members constantly on the move in search of potential suppliers to meet their customers' needs. Their search takes them to trade shows, economic development events, and related community affairs. It leads to developing special internship programs, partnering with others in the entertainment industry, and supporting minority organizations and other associations, such as the National Minority Supplier Development Council, the National Association of Women Business Owners, as well as building relationships with Asian-, Latino/Hispanic-, African-American and other ethnic business associations.

With lots of hard work and a magic touch for business matchmaking, the MWBE team continues to make dreams come true for minority and women entrepreneurs who can deliver high-quality products and services (from advertising to zucchini) at competitive prices.

For details about the MWBE Program, call or write to: Beverly Cole, Director, MWBE Program, The Walt Disney Company, (Ref Code: HY98), 500 S. Buena Vista Street, Burbank, CA 91521-7270, (818) 972-5180.

**Beverly Cole, Director
Minority and Women Business
Enterprise Program**

The ᗯᗩᒪ丅 𝒟𝐼𝒮𝒩𝐸𝒴 Company®

Diversity Means Business At The WALT DISNEY Company.®

The Orlando area is known for its magic, from the NBA to the attractions of the WALT DISNEY WORLD® Resort. But Tom Flewellyn knows that making magic often requires a lot of hard work behind the scenes.

Tom is Director of Minority Business Relations (MBR) for the WALT DISNEY WORLD® Resort. He drives a multi-million dollar effort to ensure that the 43 square-mile complex works with a diverse base of suppliers and contractors throughout the region.

Thanks to MBR, in recent years minority- and women-owned business enterprises (MWBEs) have participated in a number of major construction projects for the WALT DISNEY WORLD® Resort. For example Construct Two Construction Managers, Inc.

served as construction manager and joint venture partner for Disney's Coronado Springs Resort – our largest East Coast convention hotel, which opened in 1997. This relationship resulted in millions of dollars of MWBE contracts.

The success of Tom and his team in reaching out to the minority business community exemplifies the dedication of all Cast Members to do what it takes to make everyone feel welcome at WALT DISNEY WORLD®.

To learn more about our commitment to diversity in contracting, write to: Minority Business Relations, WALT DISNEY WORLD® Resort, (Ref. Code: HY98), P.O. Box 10,000, Lake Buena Vista, FL 32830.

**Tom Flewellyn
Director, Minority Business Relations**

ᗯᗩᒪ丅 𝒟𝐼𝒮𝒩𝐸𝒴 World® Resort

The Walt Disney Company and its subsidiaries and affiliated companies are equal opportunity employers. We encourage diversity in all aspects of our business.

A N U A R I O
H I S P A N O
H I S P A N I C
Y E A R B O O K

Publisher
Juan Ovidio Zavala
Editor
Angela E. Zavala
Associate Publisher
John Zavala
Contributing Editors
Thomas A. Brunton
Aimée Winegar
Production
Andrew William Eberhard
Stephen J. Winegar
Corporate Marketing
Evelyn Day
Government Affairs & Circulation
Jess Quintero
Marketing & PR
Ramón Palencia-Calvo
Advertising Sales
Tony Barajas
Patricia Ortiz
Research
Omar A. Ruiz
Neil A. Salas
Research Assistant
Delie Minaie
Cover Design
Omar A. Ruiz

Representatives

Argentina
Avda. Callao 1630
(1024) Buenos Aires
Tel.: 54-1-801-4785

Paraguay
Damián Amaro
Ricardo Odriozola 982
Asunción, Paraguay
Tel/Fax: (595-21) 660-958

Trademark Nº 1699991
Library of Congress Card: Nº 87-64 1284
Call Main Nº: HD 2346.u 52 W 352
ISBN: 0-9656545-0-8
ISSN: 1067-330X

Printed in USA

Get Your Copy

The ▓▓▓▓ ▓▓▓▓▓▓ is distributed to federal, state and local government offices, Latin American countries, international organizations, embassies, consulates and diplomatic missions, information centers, companies and corporations, high schools and universities, voluntary health organizations, and Hispanic organizations and publications.

To obtain a copy, send a check or money order for $25.00 (or $30.00 drawn on a U.S. bank for international postage) payable to TIYM Publishing Co., Inc.

VISA / Mastercard / American Express Accepted

Obtenga su copia

El ▓▓▓▓ ▓▓▓▓ ▓▓▓▓ se envía a oficinas federales, estatales y locales, países latinoamericanos, organismos internacionales, misiones diplomáticas y consulares, centros de información, empresas privadas y públicas, universidades y escuelas, agencias voluntarias de salud, y organizaciones y publicaciones hispanas.

Si usted desea recibirlo, envíe un cheque o giro postal por US $25,00 (US$30,00 sobre banco estadounidense en caso de correo internacional) a nombre de TIYM Publishing Co., Inc.

Se acepta VISA / Mastercard / American Express

ANUARIO HISPANO - HISPANIC YEARBOOK

is an annual publication of
TIYM Publishing Company, Inc.
Angela E. Zavala, *President & CEO*
An 8(a) Certified Company
DUNS: 161904669

Headquarters:

6718 Whittier Ave., # 130
McLean, Virginia 22101 USA
Tel.: (703) 734-1632
Fax: (703) 356-0787
E-mail: TIYM@aol.com
Web Site: http://www.tiym.com
AnuarioHispano.com
HispanicYearbook.com

The Meaning of TIYM

TIYM, the commercial name of the publishing company of the ▓▓▓▓▓ ▓▓▓▓▓▓▓, recalls its roots in Argentina. Nineteen years ago, Dr. Juan Ovidio Zavala and Angela Elizalde Zavala left Argentina and their publishing company named TIYM. The acronym stood for "Transporte Integrado y Masivo" (integrated and large-scale transportation), and the company published a monthly periodical for the transportation business field entitled TODOTRANSPORTE ("ALLTRANSPORT"). In Argentina, TIYM continues to focus on the real-life issues of transportation and planning, while its US operations have concentrated on reference materials and issues concerning the Hispanic community in the United States.

VERIFIED
AUDIT CIRCULATION

Para nosotros
no existen calles
sin salida.

El dicho "volvió a nacer" va perfectamente con Antonio Rivera. Es que hasta hace un par de años, era un pandillero en las calles de Detroit. Conoció la cárcel y conoció la muerte de cerca. Por suerte también conoció a Frank Venegas, presidente y CEO de Ideal Steel & Builders' Supplies, Inc., un importante proveedor minoritario de Ford Motor Company. Así fue como Antonio tuvo una segunda oportunidad.

Frank Venegas creció en el mismo barrio que Antonio. Como dueño de Ideal Steel no olvida sus comienzos. Gracias a la ayuda de los Programas para Proveedores Minoritarios de Ford Motor Company pudo lograr muchos de sus sueños como empresario. "Parte de lo que tengo se lo debo a Ford", comenta. En Ford Motor Company no sólo construimos vehículos, también producimos relaciones duraderas.

Ford Motor Company

Frank Venegas, presidente y CEO
de Ideal Steel & Builders' Supplies, Inc.

www.ford.com

Letter from the Editor
Carta de la editora

From left to right: Diana Jones, First Lady of the US Marine Corps, Angela Zavala and Evelyn Day. In the background a painting of the 26th Commandant of the US Marine Corps, Louis Hugh Wilson.

December, 2000

We enter a new millennium almost 3,000 years since Plato decreed that democracy presented the best system for human beings to live together. Although we can disagree about the achievements, this nation continues to be the closest to the "philosopher's perfect society."

For more than 15 years, the ANUARIO HISPANO-HISPANIC YEARBOOK has focused on the Hispanic community, primarily within the United States. Now, with the YEARBOOK's presence on the Internet- www.AnuarioHispano.com and www.HispanicYearbook.com –the entire online world has free and full access to our information for and about Hispanics and Latinos. Hopefully, the "Internet Edition" will serve as a gateway to the thousands of Hispanic organizations, publications, and media in the US and Puerto Rico.

We also understand the importance and influence of other minority communities, and in our efforts to progress and expand the TIYM organization, we have formed a partnership with African-American leaders. This year, TIYM will launch an annual publication directed to the African American community, conceptually similar to the HISPANIC YEARBOOK, called the AFRICAN-AMERICAN YEARBOOK. This new resource guide will present a unique collection of information in the areas of business, health, and education.

Finally, we invite you to visit Scholar$ite (www.scholarsite.com), a web site consisting of more than 600,000 financial aid opportunities for every type of student. Scholar$ite represents many years of research in the area of scholastic financial aid, and we encourage you to utilize this free service, which does not require users to enter personal data. You will also have an opportunity to win the $1,000 monthly Scholarship Giveaway.

Until next year,

Angela E. Zavala

Angela E. Zavala
Editor

Entramos al nuevo milenio sumando casi 3000 años desde que Platon afirmara que la mejor forma de convivencia entre los seres humanos era la democracia. Aunque los logros son discutibles, este país sigue siendo el más cercano a "la ciudad perfecta del filósofo".

Durante quince años, el ANUARIO HISPANO-HISPANIC YEARBOOK se dirigió a la comunidad hispana localizada principalmente en los Estados Unidos. A partir de su inclusión en Internet- www.AnuarioHispano.com y www.HispanicYearbook.com –el mundo conectado al Internet tiene acceso gratis y completo a nuestra información para y sobre hispanos y latinos. Con optimismo, la "edición de Internet" será una puerta abierta a las miles de organizaciones, publicaciones y medios hispanos en los Estados Unidos y Puerto Rico.

Nosotros también comprendemos la importancia y la gravitación de las otros comunidades minoritarias, y en nuestro esfuerzo por el progreso y crecimiento de la organización de TIYM, hemos creado una alianza con líderes Africano-Americanos. En el año corriente TIYM lanzará una publicación similar a este ANUARIO, dirigida a la comunidad Africana-Americana y se llamará AFRICAN-AMERICAN YEARBOOK. Esta nueva fuente informativa presentará un material singular en las áreas de negocios, salud y educación.

Finalmente, invitamos a visitar Scholar$ite (www.scholarsite.com), un sitio que contiene más de 600.000 oportunidades de ayuda financiera para cada sector de estudiantes. Scholar$ite representa muchos años de investigación en las areas de ayuda financiera para los estudiantes y nosotros alentamos a nuestros lectores a utilizar este servicio que es gratuito y que no requiere los datos personales de quienes lo procuren. Además, usted tendrá la oportunidad de ganar los $1.000 que mensualmente Scholar$ite regala.

Hasta el próximo año.

This way to $17 billion in opportunity.

Dressing for success does not guarantee success, but the Department of Defense (DoD), Office of Small and Disadvantaged Business Utilization (SADBU) can put you on the right path. From Mentor/Protégé partnerships to funding for innovative research ideas you will find the fuel needed to ignite your firm and compete for defense contracts. The DoD SADBU office has what your business is missing. For more information on the programs listed below (and others) visit www.acq.osd.mil/sadbu or call (800) 553-1858.

SADBU
It's what your business is missing.

Women Owned
Small Business

Mentor Protégé

SBIR
Small Business
Innovative Research

Historically Black
Colleges and Universities

" Oportunidad ... "

"...to be treated fairly."*

"...to develop and advance."

"...to work with people who respect each other as important individuals."

"...to be part of a company that recognizes each individual as absolutely fundamental to its overall success."

Our approach is simple: Satisfied people satisfy Customers. At MBNA America® Bank, you'll work alongside terrific people with a variety of different backgrounds, skills, and talents in an environment rich with advancement opportunity. By being part of a company that respects your individual perspective and supports your ongoing development with comprehensive on-the-job education, you'll have all the tools you need to succeed.

Explore the opportunities available to individuals at MBNA.® Call toll-free or visit our Web site for more information.

1-877-ONE-MBNA
www.mbnacareers.com

*When calling, please reference source code **NPOH1SYB***

Or forward a resumé to:
MBNA America
1100 N. King St.
Wilmington, DE 19884-0241

MBNA is the leading issuer of affinity credit cards, offering a variety of financial services products to people across the nation and in the international marketplace. We have a strong commitment to our people, our Customers, and the many communities in which we do business. And that means building a company that reflects the diversity of these groups. We accomplish that by seeking out talented and enthusiastic people who like other people, a strategy that allows our people to grow and our company to prosper.

We invite you to learn more about us online at www.mbna.com.

What kind of world will we leave to our kids?

How hard will their lives be? How will they learn, shop, entertain? Where will they work? In a completely interconnected world, will they be, at last, completely liberated to be themselves?

At IBM, we are obsessed by these questions. Because we believe that every action we take today affects what will be possible for our kids, the world's kids. Every e-business we create, every solution we invent, every customer we touch today lays a foundation for what comes next.

Want to invent that world?
Explore your options at:

www.ibm.com

Una
Ventana Abierta
a tus *Sueños*

At Bank One, we take the time to get to know you, so we can offer financial solutions as unique as your dreams. Whether it's a new home, educating your children or that new car you've always wanted, we will work with you to help make your dreams a reality, opening a window to a world of possibilities.

1·888·BANK·ONE
www.bankone.com

AMERIC⬡S FINEST

FBI Special Agent Maria Fernandez

Maria Fernandez has been an FBI Special Agent for six years. In her own words, Special Agent Fernandez tells us what working for the FBI is really like.

On career satisfaction:

"Being a Special Agent of the FBI is, in itself, a rewarding experience. The everyday challenges of the job and variety of the work contribute to career satisfaction. Especially knowing that what I am doing may make a difference in other people's lives."

On her most rewarding case:

"Having worked in several different investigative areas, I would have to say that each investigation has its own distinct merits and sense of reward. Every investigation that you bring to a successful conclusion has its own unique feeling of satisfaction."

On doing good for the community:

"Community service and the FBI are synonymous with each other in that a Special Agent is a public servant of the community by simply doing their job. Whether making the streets a safer place to live, or speaking at a college career fair, an FBI agent has an active role in the community in which he or she lives."

On why others should consider a career at the FBI:

"A career in the FBI is for those who enjoy the diversity and challenge of matching wits with criminal minds ranging from the drug dealers to the international terrorists. The diversity is what makes a career with the FBI such a rewarding experience, you can have it all, as long as you enjoy meeting challenges."

FBI

Are you interested in a career with the FBI? Right now, we're looking for men and women, across the country, to become FBI Special Agents. Among the basic qualifications: a college degree, availability for assignment anywhere in the Bureau's jurisdiction, must be at least 23 years of age and not more than 36, and be in excellent physical condition. Interested candidates should forward resumes to: FBI Headquarters, Dept.: HY 2001, 935 Pennsylvania Ave., N.W., Room PA-1301-200, Washington, D.C. 20535. Only those candidates determined to be best qualified will be contacted to proceed in the selection process. An equal opportunity employer. For additional employment opportunities with the FBI, please visit our website: **www.fbi.gov**

Special People. Special Agents

At Prudential, diversity completes the picture of success.

Grace Torres
Vice President,
Mutual Fund Administration

Emilio Egea
Vice President,
Human
Resources–
Diversity

Jose Gener
Vice President,
Global Asset
Management
Operations

Jimmie
Gonzalez
Vice President,
Guaranteed
Products,
Operations
& Systems

Rolando
Torres
Vice President,
Human
Resources

How we picture diversity.

At Prudential, we embrace many points of view from a wide range of backgrounds—because a wider perspective helps us create better products and services. That's why we strive to understand cultural priorities that can help us design programs and services tailored to our customers' needs. And why creating a welcoming environment for all our employees is a key measurement of management performance.

www.prudential.com

 Prudential

United States Coast Guard
JOIN THE TEAM!

ACTIVE DUTY ❂ RESERVE ❂ AUXILIARY ❂ CIVILIAN
(MILITARY)   (MILITARY)   (VOLUNTEERS)   (FEDERAL)

1790

USCG Compass Program:
The Coast Guard's
Community Outreach
Initiative

For more information about
U.S. Coast Guard & Coast Guard Reserve
Opportunities call:
1-877-NOW-USCG
or visit **www.uscg.mil/job**

DESTINO:

BESO DE BIENVENIDA

A CASA

Ser recibido después de un largo viaje de negocios. Nosotros sabemos lo imp
es para Usted. Es por ello que ofrecemos más de 4,500 vuelos diarios con des
de 250 ciudades, viajando con US Airways,® US Airways Express,® US Airways S
MetroJetsm de US Airways. Nosotros le brindamos la libertad de regresar a ca
Usted lo desee. Llame al 1-800-428-4322 o visite *usairways.com*. Y haga plan
próximo beso de bienvenida a casa.

≡ U·S AIRWAYS

LET

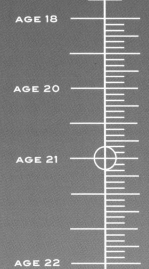

RICHARD BETANCOURT

AGE 18 ——— THE JOURNEY BEGINS

ATTENDS SAN DIEGO ST. UNIVERSITY,
MAJORS IN COMPUTER SCIENCE

AGE 20 ——— LIFEGUARDS PART-TIME TO HELP
PAY FOR SCHOOL

LEARNS OF NAVY BACCALAUREATE DEGREE
COMPLETION PROGRAM (BDCP), RECEIVES
$1600 A MONTH FROM PROGRAM

AGE 21 ——— USES MONEY TO PAY FOR SCHOOL,
BOOKS AND A REALLY COOL CAR

MOVES OUT OF PARENT'S HOUSE
INTO HIS OWN APARTMENT

MAKES DEAN'S LIST AGAIN,
EARNS A NAVY PROMOTION

AGE 22 ——— THE JOURNEY CONTINUES

[JUNIOR, FUTURE NAVAL OFFICER]

SPRINT...MAKING THE CONNECTION.

The world has become increasingly smaller and connected in

ways just a few short years ago seemed virtually impossible. As a

telecommunications provider, Sprint's commitment to people,

technology and the future remains unsurpassed. We are

connecting your world today, and into the future.

Isn't that the point of contact?

1-800-755-5719   www.sprint.com

The point of contact[SM]

ScholarＳite

www.scholarsite.com

Each year, many thousands of available scholarship dollars go unclaimed and unused because students don't know how to find them. This free, bilingual site allows students to quickly and accurately search for financial aid opportunities without entering personal information. The database is continuously updated and contains the latest information on scholarships, grants, fellowships, awards and many other types of financial help. Don't waste time! Go to www.scholarsite.com and find the financial aid you've been looking for. Good luck!

Scholar$ite offers a $1,000 monthly Scholarship Giveaway!

Produced by:

NAVY INTERNATIONAL PROGRAMS OFFICE

An Open Door to Education and Opportunity

I was appointed as Deputy Director of the Navy International Programs Office in March 1997. In this position, I am responsible for developing, planning and implementing the Department of the Navy's

"After 30 years with the Department of the Navy, I can truly say the rewards have been great and the challenges stimulating."

International Programs, including all Navy government-to-government sales of equipment and services, and disclosures of technology to foreign nations. I manage a work force of 160 military and civilians and a budget excess of $50 million per year. I have lectured extensively to government agencies, both military and civilian, in areas related to diversity, social change, gender, and race relations.

I serve my country proudly and share in its concepts of freedom and democracy.

The United States government has provided me ample opportunity for education and experience, and has enabled me to grow as a person and achieve success.

I offer you hope for your future. An investment in the best government in the world is an

Gibson G. LeBoeuf
Deputy Director
Navy International Programs Office

investment in yourself and your family. And, your potential in the Defense community is unlimited and vital.

For intern career opportunities in the Department of the Navy, please phone (717) 605-3980 or fax (717) 605-1980 E-mail: navyintern@fmso.navy.mil URL: www.navyintern.cms.navy.mil

DIVERSITY ®

For employment information, please contact:
Rey Gonzalez, Asst. Vice President, Diversity Initiatives
McDonald's Corporation • 2915 Jorie Blvd. Dept. 147 • Oak Brook, IL 60523

is proud to encourage diversity among its associates and MBE's.
se enorgullece en promover diversidad entre sus asociados y MBE's.

US Population as of April 1st 2000

La población de EUA al 1 de abril del año 2000

Area	April 1, 2000	April 1, 1990	State Rank as of April 1, 2000	State Rank as of April 1, 1990
Alabama	4,447,100	4,040,587	23	22
Alaska	626,932	550,043	48	49
Arizona	5,130,632	3,665,228	20	24
Arkansas	2,673,400	2,350,725	33	33
California	33,871,648	29,760,021	1	1
Colorado	4,301,261	3,294,394	24	26
Connecticut	3,405,565	3,287,116	29	27
Delaware	783,600	666,168	45	46
District of Columbia	572,059	606,900	(NA)	(NA)
Florida	15,982,378	12,937,926	4	4
Georgia	8,186,453	6,478,216	10	11
Hawaii	1,211,537	1,108,229	42	41
Idaho	1,293,953	1,006,749	39	42
Illinois	12,419,293	11,430,602	5	6
Indiana	6,080,485	5,544,159	14	14
Iowa	2,926,324	2,776,755	30	30
Kansas	2,688,418	2,477,574	32	32
Kentucky	4,041,769	3,685,296	25	23
Louisiana	4,468,976	4,219,973	22	21
Maine	1,274,923	1,227,928	40	38
Maryland	5,296,486	4,781,468	19	19
Massachusetts	6,349,097	6,016,425	13	13
Michigan	9,938,444	9,295,297	8	8
Minnesota	4,919,479	4,375,099	21	20
Mississippi	2,844,658	2,573,216	31	31
Missouri	5,595,211	5,117,073	17	15
Montana	902,195	799,065	44	44
Nebraska	1,711,263	1,578,385	38	36
Nevada	1,998,257	1,201,833	35	39
New Hampshire	1,235,786	1,109,252	41	40
New Jersey	8,414,350	7,730,188	9	9
New Mexico	1,819,046	1,515,069	36	37
New York	18,976,457	17,990,455	3	2
North Carolina	8,049,313	6,628,637	11	10
North Dakota	642,200	638,800	47	47
Ohio	11,353,140	10,847,115	7	7
Oklahoma	3,450,654	3,145,585	27	28
Oregon	3,421,399	2,842,321	28	29
Pennsylvania	12,281,054	11,881,643	6	5
Rhode Island	1,048,319	1,003,464	43	43
South Carolina	4,012,012	3,486,703	26	25
South Dakota	754,844	696,004	46	45
Tennessee	5,689,283	4,877,185	16	17
Texas	20,851,820	16,986,510	2	3
Utah	2,233,169	1,722,850	34	35
Vermont	608,827	562,758	49	48
Virginia	7,078,515	6,187,358	12	12
Washington	5,894,121	4,866,692	15	18
West Virginia	1,808,344	1,793,477	37	34
Wisconsin	5,363,675	4,891,769	18	16
Wyoming	493,782	453,588	50	50
Total Resident Pop.[1]	281,421,906	248,709,873	(NA)	(NA)
Northeast	53,594,378	50,809,229	(NA)	(NA)
Midwest	64,392,776	59,668,632	(NA)	(NA)
South	100,236,820	85,445,930	(NA)	(NA)
West	63,197,932	52,786,082	(NA)	(NA)
Puerto Rico	3,808,610	3,522,037	(NA)	(NA)
Total Resident Population, including Puerto Rico	285,230,516	252,231,910	(NA)	(NA)

[1] Includes the population of the 50 states and the District of Columbia. NA Not applicable.
NOTE: Consistent with the January 1999 U.S. Supreme Court ruling (Department of Commerce v. House of Representatives, 525 U.S. 316, 119 S. Ct. 765 (1999)), these resident population counts do not reflect the use of statistical sampling to correct for overcounting or undercounting.
Source: U.S. Department of Commerce, U.S. Census Bureau. Internet Release date: December 28, 2000

[1] Incluyendo la población de los 50 estados y el Distrito de Columbia. NA No aplicable.
NOTA: De acuerdo con el veredicto de la Corte Suprema de los EUA de enero de 1999 (Department of Commerce v. House of Representatives, 525 U.S. 316, 119 S. Ct. 765 (1999)), los recuentos de la población residente no reflejan el uso de muestras estadísticas para corregir recuentos de más o recuentos de menos.
Fuente: Departamento de Comercio de los EUA, Oficina del Censo de los EUA. Fecha de difusión en Internet: 28 de diciembre del 2001

How Many We Were. How Many We Are. How Many Will We Be?
Cuantos fuimos. Cuantos somos. ¿Cuántos seremos?

Year	US Population	Increase	%	Hispanic Population	Increase	%	Observations
1950	150,697,361	—	—	—	—		1. The methodology is not compatible with the one used at the present time. Hispanic origin was identified by the surname, but it did not represent a socioeconomic sector.
1960	178,464,236	27,766,875	15.5	—	—		
1970	200,255,151	21,790,915	10.8	9,294,509	—		
1980	226,542,199	26,287,048	11.6	14,609,000	5,314,491	36.3	2. A new methodology to inform and evaluate is established.
1990	248,709,873	22,167,674	8.9	22,379,000	7,770,000	34.7	
2000	281,421,906	32,712,033	11.6	35,305,818	12,926,818	36.6	3. For the first time, the population of Puerto Rico is included in the total population of U.S.A.

PROJECTIONS

Year	US Population	Increase	%	Hispanic Population	Increase	%	Observations
2010	310,910,000	29,488,094	9.48	47,662,854	12,357,036	25.9	1. The population projections for US are based on publications from the Census Bureau.
2020	354,642,000	43,732,000	12.3	64,344,852	16,681,998	25.9	2. The estimated percentage for Hispanic immigration to the US is explained by the economic progress of US and the decline of the economies of Central and South America.
2030	409,604,000	54,962,000	13.4	86,865,550	22,520,698	25.9	
2040	475,949,000	66,345,000	13.9	115,807,750	28,942,200	24.9	
2050	552,757,000	76,808,000	13.8	156,340,462	40,532,712	25.9	3. These figures signify that, in the year 2050, Hispanics will make up more than 1/4 of the total US population.

Source: U.S. Census Bureau

Hispanic Families
Las familias hispanas

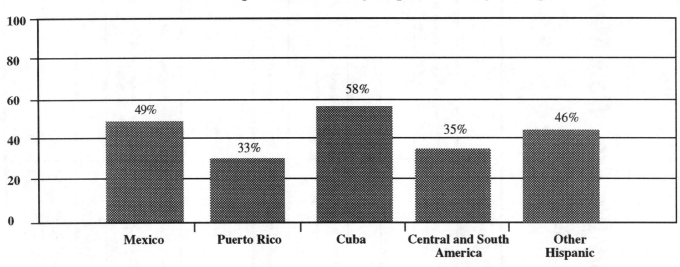

Percent Owner-Occupied Households by Hispanic Country of Origin

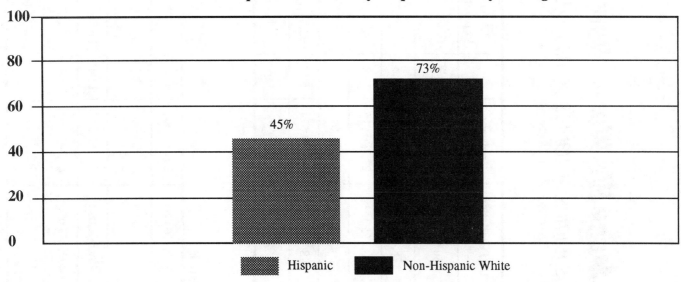

Percent Owner-Occupied Households by Hispanic Country of Origin

Source: U.S. Census Bureau (Press-Release/www/2000)

Family Households by Type and Hispanic Origin

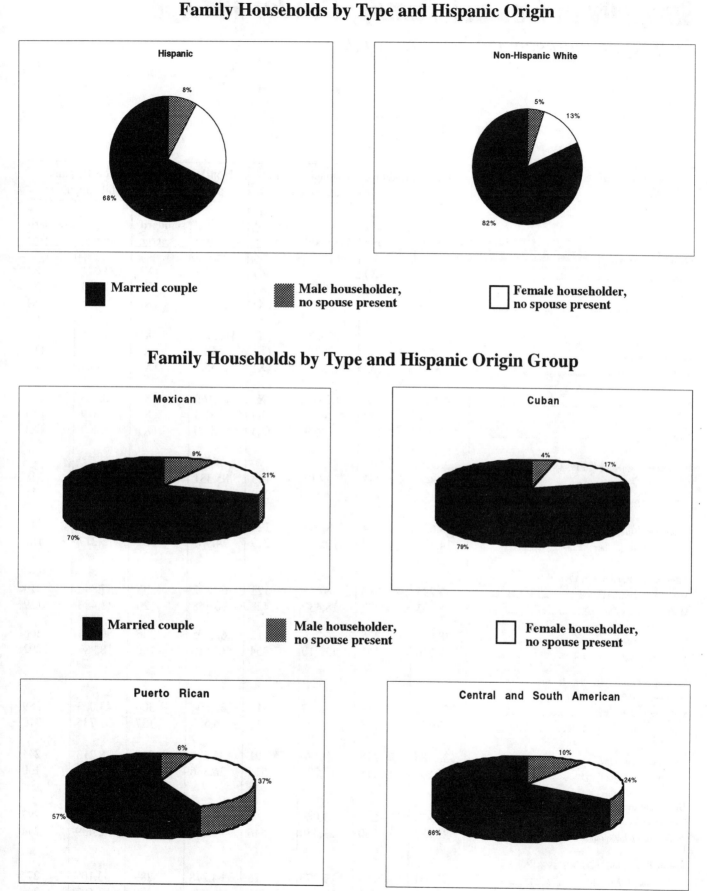

Hispanic

8%

68%

Non-Hispanic White

5%

13%

82%

■ **Married couple**

▨ **Male householder, no spouse present**

□ **Female householder, no spouse present**

Family Households by Type and Hispanic Origin Group

Mexican

9%

21%

70%

Cuban

4%

17%

79%

■ **Married couple**

▨ **Male householder, no spouse present**

□ **Female householder, no spouse present**

Puerto Rican

6%

37%

57%

Central and South American

10%

24%

66%

Source: U.S. Census Bureau (Press-Release/www/2000)

Summary of Income: Family, Gender and Age
Síntesis de ingresos: familia, sexo y edad

(Numbers in thousands)

Characteristic	Total Population		Hispanic-origin population (1)		Non-Hispanic population		Non-Hispanic White population	
	Estimate	One standard error	Estimate	One standard error	Estimate	One standard error	Estimate	One standard error
Gender and Age								
Total	271,743	(X)	31,689	(X)	240,054	(X)	193,074	(X)
Percent	100.0	(X)	100.0	(X)	100.0	(X)	100.0	(X)
Median age (years)	34.9	(X)	26.1	(X)	36.1	(X)	37.5	(X)
Males	132,764	(X)	15,879	(X)	116,885	(X)	94,705	(X)
Percent of total	48.9	(X)	50.1	(X)	48.7	(X)	49.1	(X)
Median age (years)	33.8	(X)	25.3	(X)	35.2	(X)	36.6	(X)
Females	138,979	(X)	15,810	(X)	123,169	(X)	98,368	(X)
Percent of total	51.1	(X)	49.9	(X)	51.3	(X)	50.9	(X)
Median age (years)	35.8	(X)	26.9	(X)	37.0	(X)	38.4	(X)
Total Money Earnings in 1998 [2]								
Males with income	94,948	353	9,617	123	85,331	349	71,707	338
Median income (dollars)	26,492	128	17,257	238	27,712	215	29,862	211
Females with income	98,694	354	8,405	121	90,289	352	74,106	341
Median income (dollars)	14,430	102	10,862	219	14,907	109	15,217	127
Total Money Earnings in 1998 [2]								
Males with earnings	77,295	343	8,443	121	68,852	335	57,896	319
Median earnings (dollars)	28,755	233	18,430	422	30,468	120	31,486	129
Females with earnings	68,846	335	6,240	112	62,605	326	50,834	306
Median earnings (dollars)	17,716	161	12,910	354	18,510	169	18,987	202
Earnings of Full-Time Year-Round Workers in 1998 [2]								
Males with earnings	56,951	318	6,147	112	50,804	306	43,023	289
Median earnings (dollars)	35,345	133	22,285	317	36,523	137	37,735	310
Females with earnings	38,785	278	3,476	91	35,309	268	28,213	244
Median earnings (dollars)	25,862	118	19,221	517	26,386	122	26,879	130
Household Income in 1998								
Total Households	103,874	292	9,060	68	94,814	297	78,577	297
Median income (dollars)	38,885	230	28,330	546	40,251	197	42,439	244
Family Household Income in 1998 [3]								
Total Family Households	71,551	294	7,273	75	64,278	289	53,107	276
Median income (dollars)	46,737	241	29,608	568	48,972	278	51,607	260

Characteristic	Population originating in Mexico		Population originating in Puerto Rico		Population originating in Cuba		Population originating in Central & South America		Populations of other Hispanic origins	
	Estimate	One standard error	Estimate	One standard error	Estimate	One standard error	Estimate	One standard error	Estimate	One standard error
Gender and Age										
Total	20,652	151	3,039	94	1,370	65	4,536	111	2,091	79
Percent	100.0	(X)	100.0	(X)	100.0	(X)	100.0	(X)	100.0	(X)
Median age (years)	24.2	0.34	27.5	1.08	41.3	1.72	29.9	0.72	28.3	1.64
Males	10,594	110	1,437	65	658	45	2,178	78	1,013	55
Percent of total	51.3	0.62	47.3	1.63	48.0	2.42	48.0	1.33	48.4	1.96
Median age (years)	24.0	0.46	25.6	1.48	41.0	2.29	28.7	1.14	24.6	2.16
Females	10,058	110	1,602	68	713	46	2,358	80	1,078	56
Percent of total	48.7	0.62	52.7	1.61	52.0	2.40	52.0	1.32	51.6	1.94
Median age (years)	24.5	0.50	29.5	1.44	41.5	2.51	30.8	0.89	31.1	1.88
Total Money Income in 1998 [2]										
Males with income	6,265	112	848	51	510	40	1,387	64	606	43
Median income (dollars) ..	16,799	315	18,699	1,670	18,751	2,497	18,455	837	18,740	1,808
Females with income	4,864	104	1,011	55	512	40	1,345	62	674	45
Median income (dollars) ..	10,644	292	10,392	850	10,312	1,158	11,917	482	10,814	1,006
Total Money Earnings in 1998 [2]										
Males with earnings	5,624	109	658	45	397	35	1,273	62	490	39
Median earnings (dollars) .	17,395	386	22,711	1,769	22,864	2,825	18,961	908	21,146	1,980
Females with earnings	3,751	95	643	44	295	30	1,097	57	454	37
Median earnings (dollars) .	11,995	275	16,444	1,255	20,673	2,330	13,309	825	14,832	1,815
Earnings of Full-Time Year-Round Workers in 1998 [2]										
Males with earnings	4,023	99	483	39	305	31	974	54	363	34
Median earnings (dollars) .	21,478	347	28,687	1,576	29,023	3,120	22,189	1,121	26,592	2,689
Females with earnings	1,994	74	365	34	184	24	670	45	263	29
Median earnings (dollars) .	17,480	543	23,224	1,737	25,337	1,527	17,748	1,111	23,432	2,680
Household Income in 1998										
Total Households	5,525	76	1,025	42	539	31	1,287	46	685	35
Median income (dollars) ..	27,361	537	26,365	1,483	32,375	2,760	31,636	1,243	30,463	2,426
Family Household Income in 1998 [3]										
Total Family Households ..	4,612	74	765	37	402	27	1,002	42	492	30
Median income (dollaras) .	27,883	636	28,953	1,597	39,530	3,543	32,676	1,866	35,264	2,922

Note: (X) Not applicable.

(1) Hispanic refers to people whose origins are Mexican, Puerto Rican, Cuban, South or Central American, or other Hispanic/Latino, regardless of race.

(2) People 15 years old and over.

(3) Includes families in group quarters.

SOURCE: U.S. Census Bureau, Ethnic and Hispanic Statistics Branch, Population Division.

Internet Release Date: March 8, 2000

Hispanics: *65 Years or Over and 18 Years or Less*

Hispanos: 65 años o más y de 18 años o menos

Age 65 and Over by Hispanic Origin as a Percent of Population

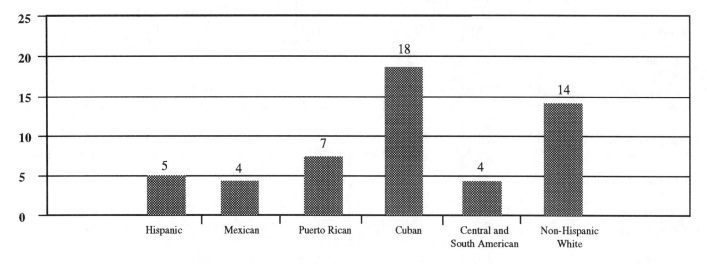

Under Age 18 by Hispanic Origin as a Percent of Population

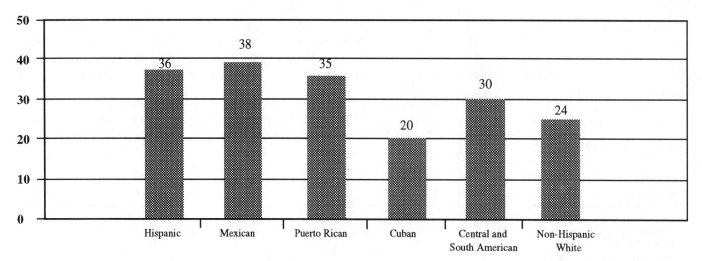

Source: U.S. Census Bureau (Press-Release/www/2000)

AnuarioHispano.**com**

Percentage of Hispanic Population With Income of $50,000 or More

Por ciento de la población hispana con ingresos de $50.000 ó mayores

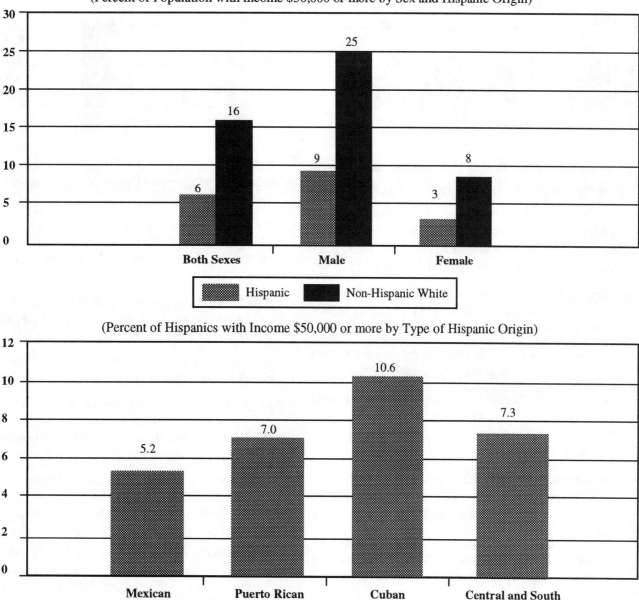

(Percent of Population with income $50,000 or more by Sex and Hispanic Origin)

Legend: Hispanic / Non-Hispanic White

(Percent of Hispanics with Income $50,000 or more by Type of Hispanic Origin)

Source: U.S. Census Bureau (Press-Release/www/2000)

Poverty and Hispanics
La pobreza y los hispanos

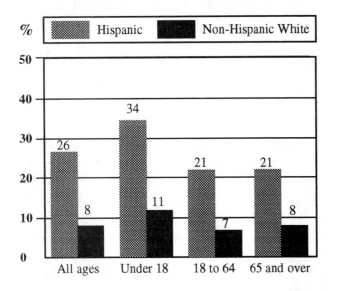

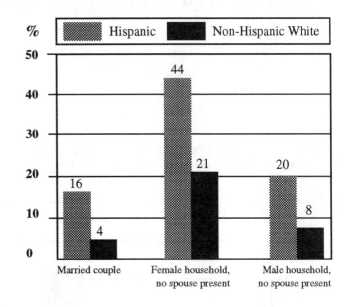

In September of 2000, the US Census Bureau published data of interest to the Hispanic population, such as the following:

- The poverty rate dropped from 12.7% in 1998 to 11.8% in 1999, the lowest rate since 1979. In 1999, 32.3 million were poor, down from 34.5 million in 1998.

- Even though it dropped (from 18.9% to 16.9%), the poverty rate for people under age 18 is still much higher than the general rate.

- On the other hand, the poverty rate for people 65 years and older is lower than the general rate (9.7%).

- The poverty rate for African-Americans fell to a record low of 23.6% in 1999. However, their poverty rate is still about three times the poverty rate for white non-Hispanics (7.7%).

- For Hispanics, even though the poverty rate declined to 22.8%, it is still very high, and is more than two times the poverty rate for Asians and Pacific Islanders (10.7%).

- The poverty rate for American Indians and Alaska Natives is 25.9%, which is the highest, but not very different from African-Americans and Hispanics.

En septiembre del 2000, el US Census Bureau difundió interesantes datos al respecto, como los siguientes:

- El índice general de pobreza de toda la población cayó del 12,7% en 1998 al 11,8% en 1999, el más bajo nivel desde 1979. (Es decir, en 1999 había 32,3 millones de pobres en los EEUU.)

- Aunque descendiendo (del 18,9% al 16,9%), el índice de pobreza de los menores de 18 años siguió siendo muy superior al promedio general.

- En cambio, los mayores de 65 años ostentan menor proporción de pobreza: 9,7%.

- La proporción de pobres afroamericanos -a pesar de descender a su más bajo nivel histórico del 23,6% en 1999- aún así triplicó la de los caucásicos no hispanos, que fue del 7,7%.

- Asimismo y aunque también descendió del 25,6% en 1998 al 22,8%, la pobreza entre los hispanos siguió siendo muy elevada y más que duplicó la de los asiáticos y de islas del Pacífico, que fue del 10,7%.

- El lamentable récord del mayor índice de pobreza lo siguen ostentando los Indios Americanos y los nativos de Alaska, con un 25,9%, que no obstante resulta bastante similar al de hispanos y afroamericanos.

- Geographically, nearly 40% of the poor live in large or main cities. The remaining population is distributed in the metropolitan suburbs and in the rural areas.

- The nation's number of Hispanic poor declined significantly between 1996 and 1997, while their real median household income increased significantly, according to reports released by the Commerce Department's Census Bureau.

- The decline in poverty rates for Hispanics accounted for a significant share of the decrease in the overall poverty rate between 1996 and 1997.

- Overall, the number of poor and the poverty rate for people of Hispanic origin, who may be of any race, dropped to 8.3 million (27.1%) in 1997, down from 8.7 million (29.4%) in 1996.

- Hispanic families also experienced a decline in their poverty rate in 1997, from 26.4% in 1996 to 24.7%. Hispanic households had a 4.5% increase in their real median income between 1996 and 1997, from $25,477 to $26,628. Meanwhile, the real per capita income of Hispanics rose during the same period, from $10,279 to $10,773, an increase of 4.8%.

- Hispanic households experienced their third consecutive year of rising income, going from $27,043 in 1997 to $28,330 in 1998, a 4.8% increase.

- Hispanic per-capita income rose 4.5% between the same period, from $10,941 to $11,434.

- The poverty rate for Hispanics declined during the same period, from 27.1% to 25.6%.

- Poverty rates and the number of poor declined for every racial and ethnic group. Poverty rates have fallen below or equaled the lowest rate ever recorded for each group except whites non-hispanics. The poverty rate for Hispanics declined from 25.6% in 1998 to 22.8% in 1999, statistically similar to the lowest rates recorded for this group (1972-74 and 1976-79).

We have been focusing on the positive side of the statistics—observing as the numbers indicate that the poverty indices have decreased; however, the numbers reveal some other negative aspects of the current situation:

- A higher proportion of Hispanics are in poverty than non-hispanic whites.

- Approximately one of every three Hispanic children under age 18 lives in poverty.

- Respecto de la localización geográfica, se determinó que -a comienzos del siglo XXI- cerca del 40% de los pobres vive en las grandes ciudades. El resto se distribuye en los suburbios de las áreas metropolitanas y en las zonas rurales.

- La cantidad de hispanos pobres declina en forma significativa entre los años 1996 y 1997, mientras que su real ingreso medio crece, también en forma remarcable, de acuerdo a los informes de la oficina de censos del Dpto. de Comercio de los Estados Unidos de América.

- La baja en los índices de pobreza de los hispanos es un factor significativo en la baja de los índices de pobreza en general entre los años 1996 y 1997.

- En números, el índice de pobreza para personas de origen hispano, que pueden ser de cualquier raza, cayó de 8,7 millones (29,4% de esa población) en 1996 a 8,3 millones (27,1%) en 1997.

- También bajó el índice de pobreza de las familias hispanas durante esos años, del 26,4% de 1996 al 24,7% de 1997: los hogares de origen hispano también tuvieron un crecimiento en sus ingresos medios del 4,5% entre 1996 y 1997. Mientras que el ingreso medio de hispanos era de $10.279 en el '96, y creció a $10.773 en el '97 (un incremento de 4,8%).

- Los hogares de origen hispano experimentaron su tercer año consecutivo de aumento en sus ingresos, elevados de $27.043 en 1997 a $28.330 en el '98, un aumento del 4,8%.

- También aumentó el ingreso "per-capita" de los hispanos, que fue de $10.941 a $11.434, o sea, un aumento del 4,5%.

- El índice de pobreza de los hispanos cayó durante este periodo, del 27,1% al 25,6%.

- Esos índices de pobreza y el número de personas pobres baja en todos los grupos étnicos y raciales.

Tales índices disminuyen de tal forma que igualan, o superan los records históricos más bajos en todos los grupos, con excepción de los blancos no-hispanos.

El índice de pobreza de los hispanos bajó del 25,6% del '98 al 22,8% en el '99, lo que no es estadísticamente diferente de los índices más bajos registrados para este grupo (años 1972-74 y 1976-79).

Hasta acá, estamos viendo el lado positivo, desde el momento que, como indican los números, los índices de pobreza bajan, pero también se revelan otros aspectos de la realidad que son desfavorables.

- Hay una mayor proporción de hispanos que viven en la pobreza que de blancos no-hispanos en esa situación.

- Aproximadamente, uno de cada tres hispanos menor de 18 años, vive en la pobreza.

Source: U S Bureau of the Census, Current Population Survey

Size of Family Unit	Weighted average threshold	Related children under 18 years								
		None	One	Two	Three	Four	Five	Six	Seven	Eight
One person (unrelated individual)....	8,501									
Under 65 years....................	8,667	8,667								
65 years and over.................	7,990	7,990								
Two people...........................	10,869									
Householder under 65 years........	11,214	11,156	11,483							
Householder 65 years and over......	10,075	10,070	11,440							
Three people........................	13,290	13,032	13,410	13,423						
Four people........................	17,029	17,184	17,465	16,895	16,954					
Five people........................	20,127	20,723	21,024	20,380	19,882	19,578				
Six people.........................	22,727	23,835	23,930	23,436	22,964	22,261	21,845			
Seven people.......................	25,912	27,425	27,596	27,006	26,595	25,828	24,934	23,953		
Eight people.......................	28,967	30,673	30,944	30,387	29,899	29,206	28,327	27,412	27,180	
Nine people or more................	34,417	36,897	37,076	36,583	36,169	35,489	34,554	33,708	33,499	32,208

- Nearly one fourth of all Hispanic households are in poverty.

For the purposes of our review, it may be useful to describe the steps taken by the authorities to measure poverty.

The US Census Bureau uses a set of money income thresholds that vary by family size and composition to detect who is poor. If a family's total income is less than that family's threshold, then that family, and every individual in it, is considered "poor."

The poverty thresholds do not vary geographically, but they are updated annually for inflation using the Consumer Price Index (CPI). The official definition of poverty considers money income before taxes and does not include capital gains and non-cash benefits, such as Medicaid and food stamps.

Poverty is not defined for people living in military barracks or in institutional groups quarters, or for unrelated individuals under age 15 (such as foster children). They are excluded from the poverty universe, that is, they are considered neither as "poor" nor as "non-poor."

- Cerca de la cuarta parte de todos los hogares de origen hispano son pobres.

A esta altura del informe conviene describir los pasos que dan las autoridades para medir la pobreza.

La oficina de censo de EEUU usa una cantidad de dinero como parámetro que varía según el número de personas que componen la familia. Si el ingreso total de una familia es inferior a ese parámetro, entonces esa familia, y cada individuo que la compone, es considerado "pobre".

El parámetro de pobreza no varía en razón de la ubicación geográfica, pero es actualizado anualmente a causa de la inflación, usando el "Indice de Precios del Consumidor". La definición oficial de "pobreza" tiene encuenta el ingreso de dinero antes de los impuestos, y no incluye los beneficios que no son dinero en efectivo, tales como beneficios médicos y estampas de alimentos.

La pobreza no es definida para personas en barracas militares o cuando las personas se encuentran en cantones institucionales, ni para menores de 15 años que no tienen parentezco con las personas con las que viven, como son los hijos adoptivos. Estos son excluidos del mundo de la pobreza, lo que quiere decir que no son considerados "pobres" ni "no pobres".

It is important to make clear that the US Census Bureau and the World Bank use different methods to measure poverty.
The US Census Bureau considers people with daily income lower than $18 poor, while the World Bank considers those people with less than $1 as poor.

Recalcamos que los índices de pobreza aplicados en Estados Unidos y los tenido en cuenta por el Banco Mundial con respecto al resto del mundo son distintos. Para la oficina de Censos son pobres en EUA las personas con un ingreso diario inferior de 18 dólares. Para el Banco Mundial son pobres quienes no ingresan un dólar por día.

Income of $10,000 or Less
Ingresos de $10.000 ó menores

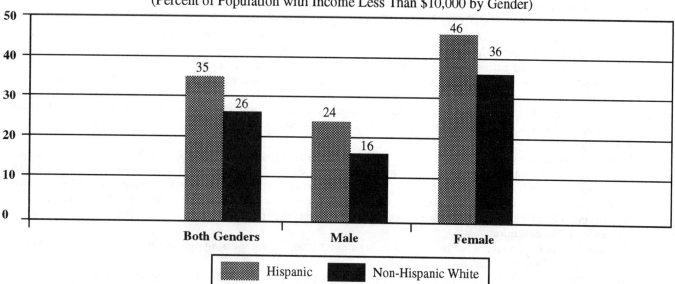

(Percent of Population with Income Less Than $10,000 by Gender)

	Hispanic	Non-Hispanic White
Both Genders	35	26
Male	24	16
Female	46	36

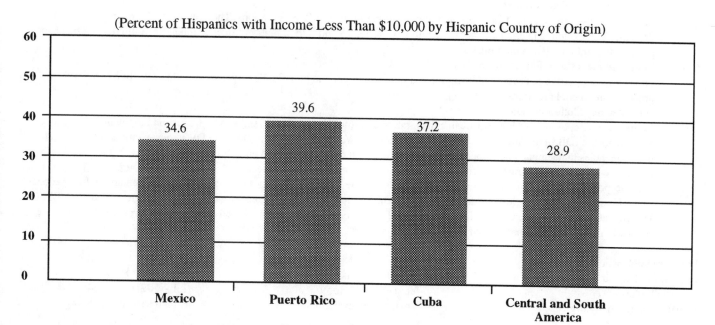

(Percent of Hispanics with Income Less Than $10,000 by Hispanic Country of Origin)

Mexico	Puerto Rico	Cuba	Central and South America
34.6	39.6	37.2	28.9

Source: U.S. Census Bureau (Press-Release/www/2000)

Over 500 million people live in Latin America and the Caribbean. Of this total, about 60 percent, or 3 out of 5 are people younger than age 30. The vast majority of these young people will grow up during a time of social, economic, technological, and political changes that will affect them profoundly. Such changes and the growth in the number of young people will have far-reaching implications for governments, economies, communities, and the environment. The future of the region has never been so heavily dependent on a single generation. The Inter-American Development Bank (IDB) recognizes the special role young people should play in the grand project of building a region of stable democracies, sustainable economies and societies based on equity. Thus, the IDB created the Youth Development and Outreach Program in 1995 to respond more effectively to the needs of young people in the region and promote their participation and leadership in the development process. This program is managed by the Special Programs Section (SPE) in the Office of External Relations.

* The Youth Development and Outreach Program envisions an Interamerican region where the voices and actions of young people are valued in all sectors of society as critical resources in the social, political and economic processes.
* The Youth Development and Outreach Program is an Inter-American Development Bank initiative that promotes the development and active participation of Latin American and Caribbean youth in the development process with emphasis on participation and leadership, entrepreneurial development, technology, community service, cultural development and environmental conservation.
* The Program establishes alliances with the public and private sectors, non-governmental organizations and youth themselves in order to create a space for the voices and actions of young people in the development process.

The Program has four main goals:
Advocate youth development and participation as an integral part of development.
Empower young people to become involved in their personal development and that of their communities.
Mainstream youth development and participation throughout IDB operations.
Promote inter-organizational partnerships to advance youth development and participation.
The Youth Development and Outreach Program carries out its activities through the following six main lines of action:

* **Capacity Building**
Creates training initiatives and projects that develop the managerial, entrepreneurial and leadership skills of youth, so that they become the actors of development instead of the subjects of development.

* **Youth Network**
Manages a regional network of IDB youth delegates established during a youth forum in Israel in 1995. This is a growing network of more than 8000 young leaders and social entrepreneurs actively engaged in socio-economic activities serving as catalysts in their communities and countries. By facilitating communication among youth both at the national and regional level, this network is having an effect on both policy and programs throughout the region. The IDB's Youth Development and Outreach Program supports the network through technical and financial assistance, and information exchange.

* **Outreach and Communications**
Creates public awareness among the general public, government agencies, and the non-profit and private sectors on the contributions and value of youth participation and development.
Develops communication tools and promotes best practices and model programs of youth development through conferences, audiovisual materials, publications, television programming, press articles, a monthly youth newsletter, an Internet website, and the creation of project-specific databases.

* **Intra-Agency Mainstreaming**
Seeks to mainstream youth development and participation throughout IDB operations. The Youth Development and Outreach Program has developed internal alliances with other departments and IDB Country Offices to integrate youth development and participation into the IDB's mission.

* **Policy Advocacy and Formulation**
Promotes a supportive policy environment for youth development and participation by disseminating effective policies, best practices and model programs.

* **Inter-Agency Collaboration**
Promotes the importance of Interamerican collaboration and inter-agency partnerships to better respond to the needs of youth. Represents the IDB in the Inter-American Working Group on Youth Development (IAWGYD), a consortium of international donor agencies that supports new approaches to positive youth development and participation in Latin America and the Caribbean. The IAWGYD exchanges information on best practices, jointly mobilizes technical and financial resources, collaborates on specific projects and advocates for effective youth policies. The IAWGYD includes the Inter-American Foundation, International Youth Foundation, Pan American Health Organization, Global Meeting of Generations, Organization of American States, UNESCO, United Nations Youth Unit, United States Agency for International Development, United States Peace Corps, Emerging Leaders Network, Youth Service America, and the IDB.

For more information:

Fabian Koss, Youth Liaison
Tel.: (202) 623-3097
E-mail: fabiank@iadb.org
Website:

Marta Estarellas
Tel.: (202) 623-1559
E-mail: martae@iadb.org

Sarika Seki Hussey
Tel.: (202) 623-3164
E-mail:sarikah@iadb.org

http://www.iadb.org/exr/mandates/youth.htm(English)   http://www.iadb.org/exr/mandates/joven.htm(Spanish)

Youth Development and Outreach Program, Special Programs Section, Office of External Relations
Inter-American Development Bank, 1300 New York Avenue, N.W., Washington, DC 20577 Fax: (202) 623-1402

Children and Families Below the Poverty Level in the US

Niños y familias por debajo de la línea de pobreza en EUA

(Percent of people under age 18)

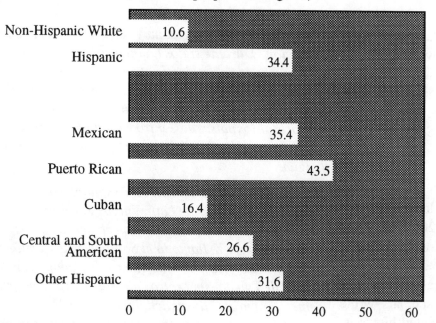

Non-Hispanic White	10.6
Hispanic	34.4
Mexican	35.4
Puerto Rican	43.5
Cuban	16.4
Central and South American	26.6
Other Hispanic	31.6

Excludes unrelated individuals under 15 years

(Percent of families)

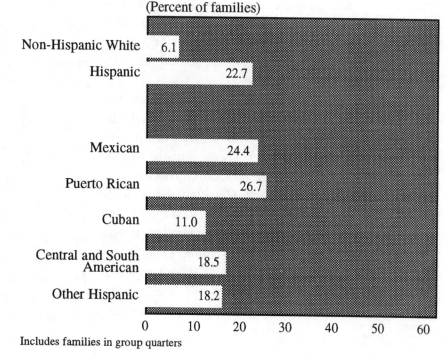

Non-Hispanic White	6.1
Hispanic	22.7
Mexican	24.4
Puerto Rican	26.7
Cuban	11.0
Central and South American	18.5
Other Hispanic	18.2

Includes families in group quarters

Source: U.S. Census Bureau (Press-Release/www/2000)

The Spanish Language
La lengua española

Spanish is a dynamic, ever-developing language. Over the centuries it has adopted and borrowed words and grammatical structures from many other language groups. Spanish is one of the world's most widely spoken languages; it is the official language of Spain and almost every country in Central and South America. Many people in North America speak it as a first or second language.

The creation of a standardized Spanish language based on the Castilian dialect began in the 1200s with King Alfonso X, who was called the Learned-King of Castile and Leon. He and his court of scholars adopted the city of Toledo, a cultural center in the central highlands, as the base of their activities. There, scholars wrote original works in Castilian and translated histories, chronicles, and scientific, legal, and literary works from other languages (principally Latin, Greek, and Arabic). Alfonso X also adopted Castilian for administrative work and all official documents and decrees.

The Castilian dialect of Spanish gained wider acceptance during the reign of the Catholic monarchs Isabella of Castile and Ferdinand of Aragón, who completed the reconquest of Spain in 1492 by pushing the Moors from their last stronghold in the southern city of Granada. Isabella and Ferdinand made Castilian the official dialect in their kingdom. In the same year the Moors were defeated, an important book appeared: Antonio de Nebrija's *Arte de la lengua castellana* (The Art of the Castilian Language). It was the first book to study and attempt to define the grammar of a European language. Today Spanish is spoken and written by 400 million people.

El español es una lengua muy dinámica, siempre en evolución. Durante siglos ha incorporado palabras y estructuras gramaticales de otros idiomas. El español es uno de los lenguajes más hablados a lo ancho del mundo, siendo el idioma oficial de España y de la mayoría de los países de Centro y Sudamérica. Muchos lo hablan en Norteamérica como primera o segunda lengua.

La estructuración de un lenguaje español - basado en un dialecto derivado del Latín Vulgar y originado en la región de Castilla (el castellano) - comenzó en el siglo XII con Alfonso X, llamado el Sabio, rey de Castilla y de León. El y su corte de ilustrados adoptaron la ciudad de Toledo - un centro cultural en la alta meseta central- como base de sus actividades. Allí, los eruditos escribieron trabajos originales en castellano y tradujeron historias, crónicas y obras científicas, legales y literarias de otros idiomas (principalmente del latín, griego y árabe). Alfonso X también adoptó el castellano para el trabajo administrativo, decretos y todos los documentos oficiales.

El dialecto castellano del español ganó su amplia aceptación durante el reinado de los monarcas Isabel de Castilla y Fernando de Aragón, llamados los Católicos, quienes completaron la reconquista de España en 1492 acorralando a los moros en su última fortaleza, la sureña ciudad de Granada. Isabel y Fernando hicieron del castellano el dialecto oficial de su reino. En el mismo año en que los moros fueron derrotados, un importante libro se editó: "Arte de la Lengua Castellana" de Antonio de Nebrija. Este fue el primer libro para estudiar e intentar definir la gramática de un lenguaje europeo. Hoy lo hablan y escriben 400 millones de personas.

Report on Visas and Citizenship in the US

Informe sobre visas y ciudadanía en EUA

OBJETIVO:

Orientar a la comunidad hispana sobre el marco jurídico vigente para ingresar, transitar, residir, estudiar, trabajar y eventualmente obtener la ciudadanía en los EUA.

VISA:

En el caso de los EUA, la autorización (visa) que se concede a los extranjeros para ingresar al país, se otorga con una finalidad y una duración determinadas, que se detallan y asientan en una hoja del pasaporte del solicitante. El trámite se informa y se inicia en la embajada o consulado del exterior que corresponda al domicilio de quien lo requiere y, en el caso de trámites de extensión o cambios, pueden continuarse en la oficina del Servicio de Inmigración y Nacionalización (INS) correspondiente al domicilio de quien ya se encuentra en los EUA, la cual ha habilitado la línea telefónica gratuita 1-800-5283 que -en inglés o español-contesta consultas las 24 hs todos los días. Además en el sitio INTERNET: http://www.ins.gov toda información sobre el tema está disponible y actualizada.

LIMITACIONES:

No se otorgará visa a quienes se les detecte enfermedades infectocontagiosas o serios desórdenes de conducta; que pertenezcan o hayan pertenecido a movimientos políticos totalitarios, subversivos o terroristas; a condenados por crímenes o tráfico de drogas o por haber entrado ilegalmente a los EUA, etc. De todos modos, si alguien incluido en alguna limitación quiere pedir excepción, las mismas son consideradas.

NO INMIGRANTE:

(Es el extranjero que desea radicarse sólo **transitoriamente** en los EUA) La aprobación de estas visas puede extenderse a la esposa/o e hijos solteros menores de 21 años, por un plazo máximo que debe ser respetado y, si las prórrogas no son concedidas, el extranjero y su familia deben abandonar en tiempo los EUA, bajo pena de ser expulsados y/o de prohibírseles entrar nuevamente. Las visas de no inmigrante comprenden -entre otras que se pueden plantear- las siguientes actividades:

1-N) **Funcionarios diplomáticos y consulares**, de otras naciones y de organismos internacionales, como las Naciones Unidas, la OEA, la NATO, etc. y sus empleados acreditados. Las visas suelen regir lo que duran las misiones.

2-N) **Tripulaciones** de barco o avión. Su vigencia depende de si desembarcan o permanecen a bordo, pero se suelen dar por 29 días.

3-N) **Empleados de compañías multinacionales** que son trasladados a la sede de EUA, siempre que el postulante acredite un año mínimo de antigüedad en la misma y la solicitud no exceda los 3 años de duración.

4-N) **Representantes de medios de prensa extranjeros**. Se dan por un año, son renovables y también dependen del medio solicitante y de la reciprocidad del país de origen.

5-N) **Visitantes por intercambio**: Deben responder a programas en desarrollo, aprobados previamente por el Departamento de Estado (DOS) o por el Servicio de Inmigración y Naturalización (INS). Se informan en los consulados, hay muchos vigentes, varían según el país del solicitante y la mayoría permite trabajar remunerativamente en las especialidades ofrecidas, que alcanzan a estudiantes avanzados, maestros, profesionales varios (especialmente médicos que no deben rendir equivalencia si no atienden pacientes) y también pueden ser exclusivamente culturales o de observación.

6-N) **Estudiantes**: El postulante debe acreditar principalmente haber sido aceptado como estudiante en la sede de EUA de un reconocido instituto de enseñanza (incluye los post-grados universitarios), así como disponer de fondos o becas para solventar la estadía, aunque luego se suelen conceder permisos para que el estudiante trabaje en EUA para completar el pago de los estudios, si así lo recomienda la institución educativa. Suelen caducar el mismo día en que finaliza el curso pero -como casi toda visa de EUA.- son prorrogables fundadamente.

7-N) **Trabajadores temporarios**: En este ítem se continúa el propósito de radicación definitiva de la mayoría de los extranjeros, que suelen comenzar con una visa de turista o estudiante. Hay tareas que necesitan -además de una oferta de empleo- aprobación consecuente del Departamento de Trabajo (DOL) de EUA, como las de graduados profesionales, oficios especializados y trabajadores comunes temporarios o estacionales; además hay otras que sólo exigen una oferta o un plan de trabajo, de quienes acrediten extraordinaria habilidad en las ciencias, artes, educación, negocios, atletismo, etc.

8-N) **Novia/o y sus hijos**: Se concede a solicitud de un ciudadano/a de EUA. y sólo para contraer matrimonio con él/ella en un plazo de 90 días.

9-N) **Comerciantes** e **industriales**: La visa se facilita si existe un tratado de reciprocidad con el país del solicitante. Incluye compra de maquinarias y repuestos; tecnología y asesoramiento; asistencia a conferencias y seminarios; visitas a empresas locales, etc. Se suelen otorgar por un año y prorrogarse.

10-N) **Turistas**, llamados visitantes de placer, representan la inmensa mayoría de quienes ingresan a los EUA (casi 50 millones en el 2000). Cabe señalar que las visas que otorgan los consulados de los países de origen, no siempre aseguran el ingreso: durante el mismo año se les impidió la entrada a casi 1 millón de personas con visas vigentes, en los puntos de ingreso y por funcionarios de inmigración que -con el poder burocrático o la información que disponen- determinaron que no tenían buenos antecedentes, o fondos suficientes, o que no respondieron bien el interrogatorio o el cuestionario escrito, etc. Los mismos funcionarios fijan el plazo de estadía de cada viajero, generalmente de 3 a 6 meses, aunque luego pueden gestionarse prórrogas.

Sobre los dos últimos rubros, se ha ratificado la vigencia de un régimen especial piloto, que beneficia a una veintena de países (con relativa baja emigración a los EUA) cuyos ciudadanos no deben solicitar visa previa para tales fines; los dos únicos países hispanos de la lista son Argentina y España.

INMIGRANTE:

Es el extranjero que solicita visa para residir **permanentemente** en los EUA. La misma -que se conoce como "green card"- puede solicitarse fundada en preferencias por razones familiares, de empleo, de antecedentes personales y hasta encomendada al azar de una lotería. La mayoría de las categorías tiene límites legales de cantidad anual que puede otorgarse, que se indica en cada caso:

Preferencias familiares:

1-I) Inmediata relación (IR): esposa/o, viuda/o e hijos solteros menores de 21 años, de ciudadano estaunidense; padres de ciudadano de EUA mayor de 21 años. Se conceden inmediatamente, sin limitación de cuotas anuales.

2-I) Primera preferencia (F1): hijos solteros de ciudadanos de EUA y sus hijos, si los tuvieran. Se conceden 23.400 visas por año.

3-I) Segunda preferencia (F2): esposa/o e hijos solteros de extranjeros con residencia permanente legal.(114.000 visas anuales)

4-I) Tercera preferencia (F3): hijos casados de ciudadanos de EUA y sus esposas/os e hijos menores. (23.400 visas por año)

5-I) Cuarta preferencia (F4): hermanos de ciudadanos (mayores de 21 años) de EUA, y sus esposas/os e hijos menores. (65.000 visas por año)

Estas preferencias siempre registran atrasos considerables en su otorgamiento, que actualmente resultan de varios años en las dos últimas.

Preferencias de empleo

6-I) **Primera preferencia (E1)**: Personas de extraordinaria habilidad (no se requiere título académico) en ciencias, artes, educación, negocios o deportes, con documentación que demuestre reconocimiento nacional o internacional en el campo de su desempeño. Los postulantes pueden solicitar esta visa sin necesidad de tener un ofrecimiento de trabajo en los EUA. En la misma categoría -pero en un segundo nivel- se seleccionan profesores o investigadores universitarios con tres años de experiencia y reconocimiento internacional, que deberán presentar en la solicitud una oferta de trabajo en los EUA. Finalmente, se consideran también E1 a gerentes y ejecutivos de empresas multinacionales de EUA, las cuales deberán iniciar la solicitud. En este nivel se otorgan 40.000 visas por año y -dado los requisitos- no hay prácticamente espera.

7-I) **Segunda preferencia (E2)**: Profesionales universitarios o personas de excepcional habilidad en ciencias, artes o negocios, de menor trascendencia que los de E1 y el trámite lo debe iniciar una empresa de EUA que ofrezca el trabajo, que además necesitará la certificación del DOL. Se limita a 40.000 visas por año, pero puede ampliarse con las no ocupadas de la categoría anterior.

8-I **Tercera preferencia (E3)**: Trabajadores especializados o profesionales que no califiquen en E1 o E2, pero cuyo trabajo requiera al menos 2 años de entrenamiento o experiencia; o trabajadores cuya labor requiera menos entrenamiento pero que resulte -comos las anteriores E3- aprobada por el DOL y a solicitadud de un empleador de EUA. También se prevén 40.000 visas por año para este grupo, más las no utilizadas de los dos anteriores.

9-I) **Cuarta preferencia (E4):** Se consideran inmigrantes especiales a los de esta categoría, que incluye a ciertos empleados del gobierno y de las fuerzas armadas de EUA en el exterior, de la Compañía del Canal de Panamá, de organizaciones internacionales y -la más requerida entre las 10.000 visas otorgadas por año en E4- al clasificado como trabajador religioso, que debe demostrar su condición y prepararse para una demora en esa visa, estimada actualmente en 10 años, por la gran demanda pendiente.

10-I) **Quinta preferencia (E5):** Esta nueva categoría facilita a los inversores de todo el mundo su radicación en los EUA Dependiendo del lugar donde se establezcan, se otorgarán 10.000 visas anuales a quienes, con una inversión de entre 500.000 y 1.000.000 de dólares, den empleo full-time a -por lo menos- 10 ciudadanos o residentes legales de EUA (sin contarse el inversor ni su familia) y previa autorización de varios organismos, según el rubro.

Visa de Inmigrante por Lotería

Un máximo de 55.000 visas se otorgan anualmente a personas que se inscriban en este programa y que son seleccionadas al azar, pero teniendo en cuenta cuotas determinadas en países con baja proporción de emigración a los EUA, según lo determina cada año el DOS e informan luego las embajadas y consulados en el exterior y, dentro de EUA, el INS.

CIUDADANIA:

Luego de 5 años de haber obtenido la residencia permanente por empleo o lotería, o luego de 3 por razones familiares, el inmigrante puede solicitar la ciudadanía de EUA, que se otorga cumplimentando varios requisitos, como un examen (que demuestre un mínimo conocimiento oral y escrito del idioma inglés, con excepciones según la edad del residente) sobre historia, legislación general y forma de gobierno de los EUA; tener buenos antecedentes durante el periodo de residencia y prestar un juramento de lealtad y renuncia a otra nacionalidad. Ser ciudadano implica poder entrar y salir libremente de los EUA. (los extranjeros residentes tienen limitaciones de ausentismo); poder dar residencia a ciertos parientes extranjeros (padres, hijos, hermanos, esposa/o); el derecho a votar y a ser candidato a cualquier cargo público (menos presidente o vice de la nación) en elecciones primarias o generales. Cabe señalar que manifestando reservas religiosas -antes de prestar juramento- es posible eximirse de ser convocado para eventuales servicios en las fuerzas armadas, aunque no para servicios civiles comunitarios que se resuelvan obligatorios.

ASILADOS-REFUGIADOS:

Especial consideración merecen los extranjeros que pretenden radicarse por razones **políticas** en los EUA. Al comienzo del 2001, cientos de miles de hispano-americanos (salvadoreños, guatemaltecos, hondureños, nicaragüenses y cubanos) vieron defraudadas sus pretensiones, al sancionarse una legislación que favorece la regularización por razones **familiares**. Esta postergación también involucra a ciudadanos de otro origen, como Liberia, India, China, Haití, etc. y es poco probable que el problema - por su magnitud y controversia (se cree que muchos refugiados lo son por razones sólo **económicas**)- se resuelva en un corto plazo.

The Origin of Hispanics
Origen de los hispanos

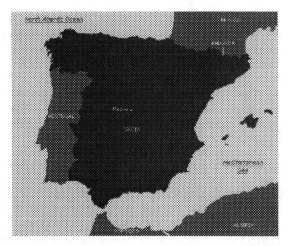

Hispania was the name given by the Phoenicians to the peninsula furthest west of the European continent. Philologists have since determined that the name signified "land of rabbits," possibly because of the abundance of those mammals, mainly in the Mediterranean regions of the peninsula. Now the area is known as the Iberian Peninsula, and includes the territories of Andorra, Spain, and Portugal.

The first inhabitants of those territories, the original Iberians, apparently arrived from North Africa about 20,000 years ago as part of a community that also expanded north toward what are today the republics of Chechnya and Georgia in the Caucasus region, the area considered to be the homeland of the Caucasian race.

In Hispania, the Iberians established themselves primarily in the region of Old Castille, leaving testimony of their presence with primitive paintings such as those in the caves of Altamira, near the city of Santander. During the entire Stone Age, and practically until the arrival of the Phoenicians, the Iberians occupied the entire territory of the peninsula which was almost as inaccessible as an island, due to the difficulty of passage through the Pyrenees.

During the eighth century BC, the Phoenicians—who had established themselves twelve centuries earlier along the entire Mediterranean coast and had founded Cádiz (the oldest port in Europe) on the Atlantic—allied with Carthage. To avoid being expelled, the Phoenicians allowed the Carthaginians to found Cartagena (the new Carthage) in what is today Murcia, and together the two peoples initiated the Hispanic fishing tradition.

During the sixth century BC, Hispania was the site of a double invasion: from the North through Germany and France arrived the Celts; from the South swarmed the Greeks. The former crossed the Pyrenees near the borders of the Basques, believed to have been another Caucasian tribe already established at an unknown date. The Celts integrated themselves as the Celtibera community, from which most of the Galicians and Portuguese descend. The Greeks remained on the Mediterranean coast, assimilated the Phoenician monetary system and Carthaginian war tactics, and spread their plantations of olive trees and vineyards as well as their philosophy and theater. They founded cities such as Malaga and Barcelona.

From the second century BC to approximately 400 AD, the Romans dominated Hispania, leaving behind 600 years of cultural influence, especially Roman judicial law and the Latin language which—with modifications from the incorporation of words from regional dialects as well as the passage of centuries—became the Spanish language, the most important derivative of Latin, used today by 400 million people.

After the defeat of the western Roman Empire, the conquerors

Hispania fue el nombre con que los fenicios designaron la península más extrema del oeste del continente europeo. Los filólogos interpretan que el nombre dado significaba "tierra de conejos" y que habría sido sugerido por la abundancia de estos mamíferos, sobre todo en las zonas aledañas al Mediterraneo. En la Europa de hoy se conoce como península Ibérica y corresponde a los territorios de Andorra, España y Portugal.

Precisamente los íberos fueron los primeros habitantes de esas tierras y habrían arribado desde el norte de Africa hace unos 20.000 años, como parte de una comunidad, que también se expandió hacia donde hoy están las repúblicas de Chechenia y de Georgia, en el Caúcaso, y que se considera originaria de la raza llamada blanca.

Los íberos de Hispania se radicaron principalmente en la zona de Castilla la Vieja y -en las grutas de Altamira, cerca de la ciudad de Santander- dejaron testimonios de su presencia con sus pinturas rupestres. Durante toda la edad de piedra y prácticamente hasta la llegada de los fenicios los íberos dispusieron de toda la península, que por su difícil acceso a través de los Pirineos, puede considerarse casi una isla.

En el siglo VIII AC, los fenicios, que se establecieron desde 2 siglos antes sobre toda la costa del Mediterráneo y habían fundado Cádiz (el más antiguo puerto de Europa) sobre el Atlántico se aliaron con Cartago y, para no ser expulsados, aceptaron que éstos fundaran Cartagena (la nueva Cartago) en lo que hoy es Murcia y juntos comienzan la tradición pesquera hispánica.

En el siglo VI AC, Hispania recibe una doble invasión: por el norte (desde Alemania y Francia) los celtas y por el sur, los griegos. Los primeros cruzan los Pirineos, bordeando el pueblo vasco -que se supone otra tribu caucásica ya radicada con fecha incierta- y se integran como la comunidad celtíbera, de la que desciende la mayoría de gallegos y portugueses. Los griegos se quedan en la costa mediterránea, asimilan el sistema monetario fenicio, las tácticas guerreras de los cartagineses y difunden sus cultivos del olivo y del viñedo, también la filosofía y el teatro, fundando ciudades como Málaga y Barcelona.

Desde el siglo II AC hasta el IV de nuestra era, los romanos dominaron Hispania, dejando también un vasto legado cultural de 600 años, especialmente su derecho judicial y el latín que -con modificaciones debidas a los aportes de dialectos regionales y a los siglos transcurridos- se transformó en el idioma español, el más importante derivado de esa lengua, en la que hoy se comunican más de 400 millones de personas.

Derrotado el Imperio Romano de Occidente, los vencedores comienzan a invadir sus provincias y los godos y vándalos llegan a

began to invade the empire's provinces. The Goths and Vandals arrived in Hispania in the year 408 AD. They totaled more than 200,000 men and remained in the peninsula for three centuries. The invading tribes spread out, the Visigoths (Goths from the East) and in Andalusia (from Vandalucia) settled the Vandals. It is believed that their legacy includes the breeding of ranch cattle, the art of bullfighting, and the flamenco dances, which were also influenced by the gypsies (from Egyptians), the nomadic tribes that still today inhabit the Costa del Sol.

During the seventh century AD, Islamic Arabs invaded the peninsula, and were stopped only by the cold weather of the North. From this region, 500 years later, El Cid initiated the Christian reconquest of Hispania. The kingdom of Portugal was established in the twelfth century, with a disconnection that would become definitive, particularly with the imposition of a separate Latin dialect. Spanish and Portuguese, however, remain more similar than dissimilar, and one can move almost immediately from one to another much more easily, for example, than one can transfer between the Basque and Catalan languages spoken elsewhere in the peninsula.

It was not until the close of the fifteenth century AD that the kings of Castille and Aragon—also called the Catholic Kings—united and expelled the Arabs and all other non-Christians. The Catholic Kings definitively transformed Hispania into Spain, and in 1492 they financed the greatest expedition in the history of humanity: the voyage which culminated in the discovery of America. Although certain episodes of the conquest have been questioned, the colonization was essentially characterized by its civilizing integration: most Latin Americans have both Hispanic immigrants and pre-Columbian aborigines or Africans as ancestors.

At the dawn of the new millennium, and for the purpose of comparison, we should recall that when the thirteen original colonies of North America declared their independence from England on July 4, 1776, the territory involved was limited to the area bounded by the Great Lakes to the North, the Atlantic Ocean to the East, the peninsula of Florida to the South, and the Espiritu Santo River (the Mississippi River) to the West. The thirteen colonies represented less than 25% of the current continental United States. At the same time, Hispanic sovereignty in North America, employed either directly from Spain or through the Viceregency of Mexico, extended more than 3.2 square kilometers, or more than 30% of the total area of the United States. Furthermore, an area similar in size to the original English colonies was controlled by the French as the French Louisiana (named for Louis XIV). In other words, a little more than two centuries ago, most of US continental territory was under Latino control.

The Hispanic heritage in the United States is more than historically significant. Its geographic and ethnic influences are revealed in every atlas, but it is also felt in some of the oldest traditions of this nation, such as that of the archetypal cowboy, which does not have any Anglo-Saxon antecedents, but is rather a derivative of the Spanish landowners who relocated to Mexico and all of Latin America.

As Hispanics, these references are not intended to simply remind "Americans" (for whom—*noblesse oblige*—we have nothing but gratitude for their hospitality as well as for the cultural and professional possibilities of the US) of our origins; this review of Hispanic origins is fundamentally for the community represented by the ANUARIO HISPANO-HISPANIC YEARBOOK. Let us reflect with respect and humility on the pride and confidence that a past with such civilized lineage brings us. In all of our actions—at work, as well as socially and with our families—we can and should live up to that tradition. Many centuries of great history support us and demand that we be exemplary.

Hispania en el año 408. Suman más de 200.000 hombres y se quedan 3 siglos (en gran parte los visigodos -godos del este- y en Andalucía -de Vandalucía- los vándalos). Se estima que su herencia comprende la cría de hacienda, el llamado arte del toreo y los bailes flamencos, estos últimos en influencia recíproca con los gitanos (de egiptanos), las tribus nómadas que aún hoy habitan la Costa del Sol.

Durante el siglo VII invaden la península los árabes islámicos, a quienes sólo los detiene el frío del norte, región desde donde y sólo 500 años más tarde, el Mío Cid pudo iniciar la reconquista cristiana de Hispania, que quedó obviamente influida para siempre por lo arábigo (en arquitectura, en su cocina, en arítmetica). También en el siglo XII se conforma el reino de Portugal, en una separación que –salvo durante Felipe II- resultaría definitiva, especialmente porque se impone otro dialecto del latín, más afín al celtíbero. De todos modos, el portugués y el español son idiomas muy afines y casi inmediatos de asimilar mutuamente (mucho más, por ejemplo, que el vascuence o el catalán que se hablan en otras regiones de la península).

Finalmente, casi en el final del siglo XV, se unen los reyes de Castilla y Aragón, llamados Los Católicos, expulsan a los árabes y a todos los que se declaran de otro credo religioso, transforman Hispania definitivamente en España y financian en 1492 la expedición más importante en la historia de la Humanidad, que culminara con el descubrimiento definitorio de América. Cuestionables por episodios de la conquista, sus corrientes colonizadoras se caractizaron cabalmente por su integración humana: la mayoría de los latinoamericanos tiene como ancestros comunes a inmigrantes hispanos y aborígenes precolombinos o africanos.

En estos comienzos del siglo XXI y a propósito de este informe, se puede recordar que cuando los EUA declarararon su independencia el 4 de julio de 1776 lo hicieron sobre el territorio de 13 estados. Sus límites eran los grandes lagos al norte, el océano Atlántico al este, la península de Florida al sur y el río del Espíritu Santo (hoy Missisipi) al oeste, los cuales representaban menos del 25% de su actual superficie. En la misma época y sobre la geografía actual de EUA, el dominio hispano (de España o del virreinato de Méjico) era sobre un territorio de más de 3,2 millones de km cuadrados, es decir el 30% del área total de los EUA del presente. Esto sin tener en cuenta la región -hoy norteamericana- de la Luisiana (por Luis XIV) francesa, también con una superficie similar a la suma de todos los estados fundadores. Es decir, que hace poco más de 2 siglos estaba bajo dominio latino la mayor parte del territorio de los EUA.

La tradición hispana en esta nación no es simplemente histórica. También es geográfica y con la toponimia aborigen se revelan mayoritarias en los atlas. También comprende costumbres muy enraizadas: por ejemplo, el arquetípico cowboy no tiene antecedentes anglosajones y es fiel reflejo del hacendado español que luego se radicó en México y en toda Latinoamérica.

Como hispanos, estas referencias no pretenden ser solamente recordatorias para los estadounidenses (para quienes -nobleza obliga- no tenemos otro sentir que agradecimiento por su hospitalidad y posibilidades culturales y de trabajo) sino fundamentalmente para la comunidad que el AHHY representa. Que todos reflejemos -con respeto y humildad- el orgullo y la confianza que nos brinda un pasado de muy civilizados linajes. En todo acto -tanto en el trabajo como en lo familiar y social- podemos y debemos ser dignos de esa tradición. Muchos siglos de grandes epopeyas históricas nos respaldan, pero también nos obligan a ser ejemplares.

Occupations: Hispanics and Non-Hispanic Whites
Ocupación: hispanos y blancos no hispanos

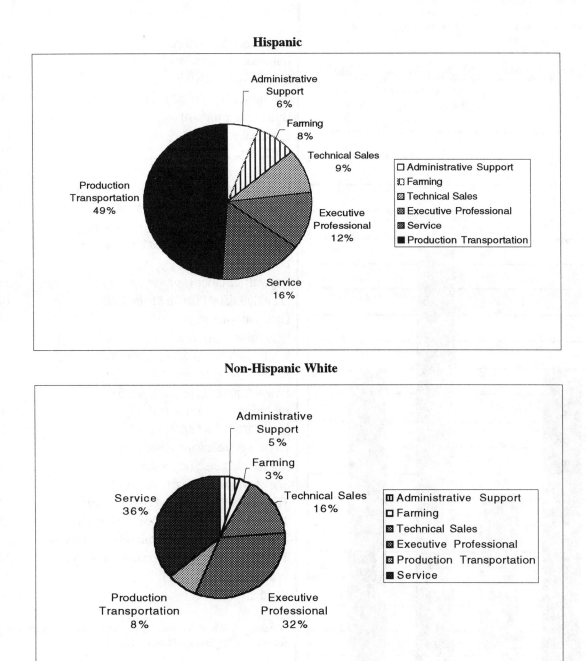

Hispanic

Administrative
Support
6%

Farming
8%

Technical Sales
9%

Production
Transportation
49%

Executive
Professional
12%

Service
16%

- ☐ Administrative Support
- Farming
- Technical Sales
- Executive Professional
- Service
- Production Transportation

Non-Hispanic White

Administrative
Support
5%

Farming
3%

Technical Sales
16%

Service
36%

Production
Transportation
8%

Executive
Professional
32%

- Administrative Support
- ☐ Farming
- Technical Sales
- Executive Professional
- Production Transportation
- Service

Source: U.S. Census Bureau (Press-Release/www/2000)

Occupations of Hispanics and Unemployment

Ocupación de hispanos y desempleo

Unemployment January 2001
Desocupación Enero 2001

The civilian labor force of 15,540,000 Hispanics includes both the employed and unemployed, according to the definition of the Department of Labor . To obtain the percent of the unemployment rate, we divided the number of unemployed (927,000) by the civilian labor force (15,540,000) to get 6.0%.

La fuerza de trabajo de 15.540.000 hispanos incluye ocupados y desocupados de acuerdo al Departamento de Trabajo de los Estados Unidos. Para obtener el porcentaje de desempleo se dividió el número de desocupados (927.000) por el total de la fuerza de trabajo (15.540.000) y dió un 6%.

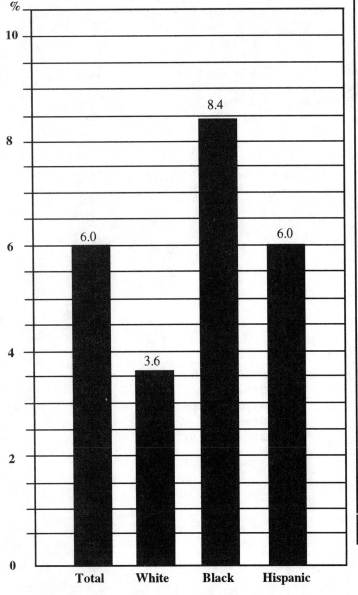

Source: U.S. Dept. of Labor   (Numbers in thousands. *Números en miles)*

OCCUPATIONS OF HISPANICS IN THE U.S. *Ocupaciones de los hispanos en E.U.A.**	%
Auto mechanic (*mecánico*)	13.8
Bartender (*cantinero*)	12.9
Brickmason (*albañil*)	17.0
Bus driver (*chofer de bus*)	9.3
Butcher (*carnicero*)	34.5
Cab driver (*taxista*)	16.2
Child care (*niñera*)	21.5
Cleaner (*personal de limpieza*)	33.9
PC programmer (*programador de PC*)	3.8
Systems analyst (*analista de sistemas*)	3.4
Data entry keyer (*cargador datos PC*)	10.9
Data PC repairer (*técnico en PC*)	6.3
Dentist (*dentista*)	3.3
Drywall installer (*inst. de paneles*)	32.2
Dental assistant (*asistente dental*)	10.4
Dietitian (*dietista*)	4.6
Economist (*economista*)	1.9
Editor, reporter (*editor, reportero*)	2.7
Janitor (*mantenimiento*)	22.1
Lawyer, judge (*abogado, juez*)	4.0
Librarian (*bibliotecario*)	4.8
Mail carrier (*cartero*)	5.6
Physician (*médico y afines*)	4.8
Registered nurse (*enfermera*)	3.3
Social worker (*asistente social*)	7.4
Teacher college & university (*profesor*)	4.2
Teacher elementary school (*maestro*)	5.3
Telephone installer (*instalador telefónico*)	6.9
Telephone operator (*operador telefónico*)	12.2
Waiter (*mesero, mozo*)	10.2
Welder (*soldador*)	14.9

Percent of total in each sector.   (*Porcentaje del total en cada sector*)
Source: U.S. Department of Labor , January 2000

Hispanic Professional: You Are In Demand!

Profesional hispano: ¡usted está en demanda!

TIYM Publishing Co., Inc. is in permanent contact with recruiters from Fortune 500 companies, government agencies, educational institutions, small businesses and other organizations. At the moment, there is great demand for bilingual Hispanic professionals.

If you are interested in making yourself available for these attractive positions, please fill out the following form or send us your resume. You should know that TIYM guarantees your privacy and will only provide your information if you are interested in the position.

High-Level Executives, Educators, Administrators, Consultants, Managers
Please Respond Quickly!

We are currently receiving requests from the following industries and sectors. Please circle the one(s) you have experience or knowledge in:

Advertising	Banking	Defense	Education	Government
High Tech	Import/Exp.	Info. Systems	Media	Publishing
Retail	Telecomm.	Transportation	Sports	Languages
Tourism	Art	Other _____		

_____   _____
NAME   LAST NAME

_____
ADDRESS   CITY   STATE   ZIP CODE

_____   _____   _____
TELEPHONE   FAX   E-MAIL

_____
DEGREE

_____
EXPERIENCE

_____
LANGUAGES

Send to:
TIYM Publishing Co., Inc.
6718 Whittier Ave., #130 McLean, VA 22101 USA
Phone: (703) 734-1632 Fax: (703) 356-0787
E-mail: TIYM@aol.com Web Site: http://www.TIYM.com

Hispanics in the Nation's Legislative Branch

Los hispanos en el Poder Legislativo de la Nación

ANIBAL ACEVEDO VILA

Aníbal Acevedo Vilá was born on February 13, 1962 in Hato Rey, Puerto Rico. He graduated from Colegio San José, High School in 1979. In 1982, he obtained a B.A. in Political Science, graduating Magna Cum Laude from University of Puerto Rico. In 1985, he graduated Magna Cum Laude from the University of Puerto Rico, School of Law, where he was elected Vice President of the Student Council and Editor of the Law Review.

After passing the Puerto Rican Bar, Acevedo Vilá worked for a year as law clerk for Supreme Court Judge Federico Hernández Denton. He obtained his Master of Law from Harvard Law School in 1987. During 1987 and 1988 he worked as law clerk for the Honorable Levin Campbell, Chief Justice of the Federal Court of Appeals for the first Circuit Court in Boston, Massachusetts.

In January 1989, he was recruited by Governor Rafael Hernandez Colon as Advisor on Legislative Affairs. He was responsible for writing, analyzing and evaluating some of the most important legislation of this period, specifically laws relating to education and municipal reform.

He ran first for an elective office in 1992, following his father's (former Senator Salvador Acevedo) footsteps, after being nominated in a primary process in which 14 candidates participated. He was elected Representative At Large for Popular Democratic Party (PDP).

In July 1996, at the PDP General Assembly, Acevedo Vilá was appointed to an At Large Position as a representative at large in that years general election. In 1997, his PDP colleagues elected him House Minority in that year's general election.

In December 1997, the former President of the PDP, Hector Luis Acevedo appointed Aníbal Acevedo Vilá as elected President of the PDP. He defended the Commonwealth status, both in Puerto Rico and the United States, and participated in diverse state and federal forums and activities in support of this status option.

In 1999, at the conclusion of his term as President of the PDP, Acevedo Vilá was elected Vice President of the PDP. After winning a primary in 1999, Acevedo Vilá was elected Puerto Rico's Resident Commissioner in Washington, DC in November 2000.

Acevedo Vilá is married to Luisa Gándara and has two children, Gabriela and Juan Carlos. He is the author of "En Honor a la Verdad, a compilation of speeches," on issues regarding Puerto Rico's democracy and self-determination.

JOE BACA

Congressman Joe Baca was elected to the United States Congress on November 16, 1999 in a special election. He is the first Latino Congressman to serve from the Inland Empire. He serves on the Agriculture and Science Committees. Immediately after being sworn in, Congressman Baca supported federal legislation to:

- Bring more high-quality teachers to schools, decrease class sizes, double funding for after school programs, and bring accountability to low-performing schools.
- Fund more police officers to ensure safe streets and keep crime down.
- Strengthen public health infrastructure and provide prevention and treatment service.

Joe Baca served in the California Legislature for seven years. His career in Sacramento was one of the historic firsts. After his election to the California State Assembly in 1992, Mr. Baca was elected Speaker pro Tempore of the Assembly—the first Latino since California joined the Union in 1850. From January 1997 through December 1998, he was the third ranking leader of the Assembly serving as Assistant Speaker pro Tempore and the Speaker's Federal Government Liaison. He also served as a member of Rules.

As Assistant Speaker pro Tempore, Mr. Baca shared the responsibility of presiding over Assembly floor sessions.

He was elected to the California State Senate on November 3, 1998, where he served on the Rules Committee, which is responsible for confirming Governor's appointments; the Veterans Affairs Committee; Public Employment and Retirement; Energy, Utilities and Communications; Local Government; and Governmental Organizations.

Mr. Baca is a Vietnam War-era veteran, serving as a paratrooper from 1966-68, leaving with the rank of specialist E-4. Before coming to Sacramento, Mr. Baca earned his bachelor's degree in sociology from the Cali-

fornia State University-Los Angeles. Later, he worked for 15 years in community relations with GTE. In 1989, he and his wife, Barbara, began their own business as partners in InterstateWorld Travel in San Bernardino. They have four children, Joe Jr., Jeremy, Natalie, and Jennifer

XAVIER BECERRA

Representative Xavier Becerra (D-California) was first elected to represent California's 30th Congressional District in November 1992. The district is located in the City of Los Angeles. Some of the communities represented include: Atwater Village, Boyle Heights, Chinatown, Cypress Park, Eagle Rock, Hollywood, Echo Park, El Sereno, Elysian Park, Elysian Valley, Glassell Park, Highland Park, Koreatown, Lincoln Heights, Montecito Heights, Monterey Hills, Mount Washington and Silver Lake.

Rep. Becerra currently serves on the House Ways and Means Committee. As a member of this committee, he handles issues such as trade, tax policy and oversight of the Internal Revenue Service (IRS). Through his participation on the panel's Subcommittee on Health, Rep. Becerra plays a critical role in formulating policy on such issues as Medicare and access to health care.

In 1980, Rep. Becerra earned his Bachelor of Arts in Economics from Stanford University. He was awarded his Juris Doctor from Stanford Law School in 1984.

Rep. Becerra is married to Dr. Carolina Reyes (Stanford '81, Harvard '87), an assistant professor in the department of obstetrics and gynecology at George Washington University. The couple has three daughters: Clarisa, Olivia and Natalia.

HENRY BONILLA

Congressman Henry Bonilla is married to Deborah Knapp. They have two children, Alicia, age 12 and Austin, age 9. Rep. Bonilla was born in San Antonio, attended South San Antonio High School and earned a Bachelor of Journalism degree from the University of Texas at Austin in 1976.

Most of Henry Bonilla's professional career has been in television news. Having started as a reporter in San Antonio, he later became a producer for WABC, the flagship station of

the ABC network, in New York, then Assistant News Director for WTAF in Philadelphia, returning to KENS-TV in San Antonio in 1986 as Executive Producer/News. In 1989, Henry assumed the role of Executive Producer for Public Affairs at KENS, a position that involved heading up civic and community projects on behalf of the television station.

Henry believes the most pressing issues affecting the 23rd District and the nation are burdensome federal regulations, and government waste and spending. He has emerged as a leader in the fight to protect private property rights and to reduce the federal burden on small business. Seven military bases are located in or near his district; he has been active in defense issues and keeping our military strong.

LINCOLN DIAZ-BALART

Lincoln Diaz-Balart was born in Cuba in 1954, and fled the country along with his family upon the arrival of communism in 1959. He went to public elementary schools in South Florida and attended high school at the American School of Madrid, Spain. Subsequently, he received a degree in international relations from New College of the University of South Florida, in Sarasota, and also obtained a diploma in British politics in Cambridge, England. Rep. Diaz-Balart served as student government president in both high school and college. He received his law degree from Ohio's Case Western Reserve University.

In 1992, Rep. Diaz-Balart was elected to the United States House Representatives from Florida's 21st Congressional District, which encompasses much of western Miami-Dade County. He served as a member of the House Foreign Affairs Committee during his first term, leading fights against the relaxation of sanctions on the Cuban dictatorship, working to maintain the special U.S. -Israel relationship and striving to protect United States national security.

After being reelected to Congress without opposition in 1994, Lincoln Diaz-Balart became the first Hispanic in U.S. history to be named to the powerful Rules Committee. The Rules Committee, composed of only nine members of the majority party and four from the minority, decides which legislation may reach the House Floor and what amendments may be debated. Diaz-Balart was named Vice-Chairman of the Sub-Committee on the Rules of the House.

Congressman Diaz-Balart lives in Miami with his wife, Cristina, and their two sons, Lincoln (age 15) and Daniel (age 13).

CHARLES A. GONZALEZ

Charles A. Gonzalez was elected to the United States Congress on November 3, 1998, and took office on January 6, 1999, in Washington D.C. Gonzalez has been appointed to serve on the Committee on Banking and Financial Services and the Committee on Small Business. Gonzalez is a graduate of Edison High School in San Antonio, the University of Texas at Austin, and St. Mary's University School of Law, also in San Antonio, Texas.

Gonzalez has served as an elementary school

teacher, a lawyer in private practice (1972-1982), a Municipal Court Judge for 9 years (1989-1997), resigning in 1997 to seek the Office of United States Congressman, 20th District Texas.

While serving as Judge of the 57th District Court, Gonzalez was instrumental in developing a model for mediation as an alternative to lengthy and costly litigation.

During his career, Gonzalez has been involved in many civic activities in San Antonio.

Gonzalez and his wife, Becky Whetsone, have three children, Leo Gonzalez, Benjamin Schmidt and Casey Schmidt.

LUIS V. GUTIERREZ

During his first three terms in the U.S. House, Congressman Luis V. Gutierrez has worked to establish himself as an effective legislator and energetic spokesman on behalf of his constituents.

During his third term, Rep. Gutierrez has continued to be a leader in the fight to protect immigrants. In Chicago, his citizenship workshops have now helped more than 15,000 individuals who wish to become naturalized. As chair of the Hispanic Caucus' Task Force on Naturalization and Citizenship, Congressman Gutierrez taught his colleagues how to replicate the Gutierrez citizenship workshops in Los Angeles, New York, Miami, and other cities. Gutierrez testified before a House Committee to oppose legislation that would wipe-out the Constitutional provision that allows all children born on U.S. soil to automatically qualify for citizenship.

Rep. Gutierrez was born in Chicago in 1953. He graduated from Northeastern Illinois University in 1975 and worked as a teacher, social worker, and community activist until his 1986 election as Alderman from the city's 26th ward. In the Chicago City Council, he led the fight for affordable housing, tougher ethics rules, and a law to ban discrimination based on sexual orientation. He was elected to the U.S. House in 1992 and reelected in 1994 and 1996.

He and his wife Soraida have two daughters, Omaira and Jessica.

RUBEN HINOJOSA

Congressman Rubén Hinojosa, a longtime businessman and native of the Lower Rio Grande Valley of South Texas, was elected to serve as the U.S. Representative for the 15th Congressional District of Texas in November 1996.

Congressman Hinojosa currently serves on two House committees: Education and the Workforce Committee, and Small Business. His appointment to the Education and the Workforce Committee as well as his appointment to chair the Congressional Hispanic Caucus' Education Task Force were critical to the success of his first major legislative initiative: the Higher Education for the Twenty-first Century Act. This legislation directly affects Hispanic Serving Institutions throughout the nation, by significantly increasing funding for curriculum development, academic instruction, and libraries.

Not only has Congressman Hinojosa aspired

to work for Valley residents in Washington, he has brought Washington to the Rio Grande Valley, South Texas area during his first term. He invited many high-profile leaders to the 15th Congressional District in order that they might speak directly with residents about their needs and concerns. Among them were President Clinton, Vice-President Gore, Secretary of Agriculture Dan Glickman, Secretary of Education Richard Riley, Deputy Secretary of Commerce Robert Malletk, Small Business Administrator Aida Alvarez, and Minority Leader Richard Gephardt. Congressman Hinojosa has also accompanied the President on two delegations to South America.

BOB MENENDEZ

The son of Cuban immigrants, Robert Menendez was born in New York City on January 1, 1954. Along with thousands of other Cuban-Americans, the Menendez family eventually settled down in the nation's most densely populated community per square mile-Union City, New Jersey.

After graduating high school, Menendez turned down a prestigious scholarship to Columbia University in order to pursue his interest in local community activism and urban affairs. He attended St. Peter's College in New Jersey, N.J. In February of 1991, Menendez became New Jersey's first Hispanic State Senator in the state's history. And in November of 1992, Bob Menendez became the very first Hispanic from New Jersey to be elected to the United States House of Representatives to serve the 13th Congressional District.

Today, Congressman Menendez not only represents a major voice for the people of North and Central New Jersey, he is a major voice for urban areas throughout his state and nation. Now serving his third term in the House of Representatives, he has been selected to serve on the influential Transportation & Infrastructure Committee where he works on the Surface Transportation and Water Resources Subcommittees. In addition, he was appointed to the prestigious International Relations Committee where he is both the ranking member on the Africa Subcommittee and a member of the Western Hemisphere Subcommittee.

House Democratic Leader Dick Gephardt and David Bonior, House Democratic Whip, chose Menendez to serve in the leadership position of Chief Deputy Whip, one of only four members afforded that honor.

Congressman Menendez is married to Jane Jacobsen-Menendez, an urban education administrator. They have two children, Alicia and Robert, Jr.

GRACE F. NAPOLITANO

Grace Flores Napolitano, Democratic U.S. Representative-elect for California's 34th Congressional District, is finishing her third and final two-year term in the State Assembly. Congresswoman Napolitano represents communities in the Southeast and San Gabriel regions of Los Angeles County. She was overwhelmingly elected to her first term in the House of Representatives with 68% of the vote on No-

vember 3, 1998. She was sworn-in as a member of the 106th Congress on January 6, 1999.

As a member of the California State Assembly, representing the 58th District, since 1992, Rep. Napolitano was elected by her female colleagues as Chair of the California Women's Legislative Caucus, 1993-94. She also served as Vice-Chair of the Latino Legislative Caucus. Rep. Napolitano has served as the founding Chair of the Assembly Standing Committee on International Trade and Development. In this role she has worked aggressively to create jobs by facilitating access to foreign markets for California exports. She has also served on the Assembly committees on Consumer Protection, Government Efficiency and Economic Development; Local Government; Public Safety and Transportation.

Congresswoman Napolitanois married to Frank Napolitano, retired restaurateur and community activist. They reside in Norwalk and have five children and 12 grandchildren.

SOLOMON ORTIZ

Congressman Solomon Ortiz was born June 3, 1937 in Robstown, Texas. He is a Methodist, and is divorced with two children: Yvette and Solomon, Jr.

A summary of Rep. Ortiz's public service includes his election in 1964 as Nueces County Constable; his election in 1968 and 1972 as Nueces County Commissioner; his election in 1976 and 1980 as Nueces County Sheriff; and his election in 1982 to the 98th United States Congress. He has been re-elected each subsequent Congress to date.

Congressman Ortiz served in the military from 1960-62 as a Specialist 4th Class, United States Army Military Policeman and investigator in Verdun, France.

Among the honors Congressman Ortiz has attained for community and public achievement are:

• 1980, Boss of the Year (American Businesswomen Association)
• 1981, Man of the Year (International Order of Foresters) -1986, Conservation Legislator of the Year (Sportsman Clubs of Texas)
• 1987, Tree of Life Award (Jewish National Fund)
• 1990, Who's Who Among Hispanic Americans
• 1991, Leadership Award (Latin American Management Association)
• 1991, Doctorate of Humane Letters from Southeastern University (Honorary)
• 1992, 1994, National Security Leadership Award (American Security Council)
• 1992, National Government Hispanic Business Advocate (U.S. Hispanic Chamber of Commerce)
• 1994, Outstanding Achievement Award (American Logistics Association)
• 1996, Minuteman Award (Texas National Guard Association)
• 1997, Man of the Year (National Association of Foreign Trade Zones)

ED PASTOR

In the 105th Congress, Ed Pastor is serving his sixth year in Congress and was recently reappointed to serve on the House Appropriations Committee. He had also served on this committee during the 103rd Congress. During this term, he will be on two Subcommittees: the Subcommittee of Energy and Water Development and the Subcommittee of Transportation. Rep. Pastor is also serving on the Committee on Standards of Official Conduct and the Democratic Steering and Policy Committee.

An Arizona native, Ed Pastor was born in the mining community of Claypool on June 28, 1943. The oldest of three children, he attended public school in Miami, Arizona. He was the first member of his family to attend college, graduating from Arizona State University with a bachelor of arts degree in chemistry in 1966. He was also the first in his family to attend law school, earning his Juris doctorate from ASU in 1974.

Congressman Pastor is married to Verma Mendez Pastor, former director of Bilingual Education for the Arizona Department of Education, who currently is program director for WestEd, an education research laboratory. The couple has two daughters, Yvonne and Laura, and one granddaughter, Alexis.

SILVESTRE REYES

Congressman Silvestre Reyes (D-Texas) was elected to represent the 16th District of Texas in November 1996. The 16th District lies within the El Paso county boundary and is ideally and centrally located in the Sun Belt region of our country, across from the Mexican city of Juarez, Chihuahua. The City of El Paso sits along the Rio Grande River, the fifth longest river in North America. With its more than 700,000 residents, El Paso County is the largest border community in the United States and approximately 66.5 percent of the district's voting age population is Hispanic.

Silvestre Reyes, a Vietnam veteran, has devoted his life to public service since 1969. For five of those years, Rep. Reyes served in Dallas as an assistant Regional Commissioner for the U.S. Immigration and Naturalization Service, where he had direct responsibility for administering a budget program exceeding $100 million for a thirteen state area.

Rep. Reyes, age 52, grew up in Canutillo, Texas just 5 miles outside the city limits. He is married to Carolina Gaytan Reyes and they have three children: Monica, age 27, Rebecca, age 25 and Silvestre Jr., age 22. Congressman Reyes holds an Associates Degree from El Paso Community College and attended the University of Texas at Austin and El Paso.

CIRO D. RODRIGUEZ

Elected to the Texas House of Representatives in 1987, then-Representative Rodriguez held the chairmanship of the important Local and Consent Calendar Committee. He served on the Public Health Committee and the Higher Education Committee, and presided as a vice-chairman of the Legislative Study Group, a coalition of progressive Texas House mem-

bers.

Congressman Rodriguez attended San Antonio College and later received his BA in Political Science from St. Mary's University in San Antonio. He received his MSW from Our Lady of the Lake University. He and his wife of more than 20 years, Carolina Peña, have one daughter, Xochil Daria.

From 1975 through 1987, Mr. Rodriguez served as a board member of the Harlandale Independent School District, worked as an educational consultant for the Intercultural Development Research Association, and worked as a caseworker with the Department of Mental Health and Mental Retardation. From 1989 through 1996, he taught at Our Lady of the Lake University's Worden School of Social Work.

ILEANA ROS-LEHTINEN

The first Hispanic woman elected to the United States Congress, Ileana Ros-Lehtinen was born in Havana, Cuba on July 15, 1952, and came to the United States with her family fleeing communist aggression when she was seven years old. She earned her Bachelor's and Master's degrees from Florida International University. Ros-Lehtinen began her career as an educator and founded a private elementary school in South Florida.

Rep. Ros-Lehtinen served four years in the Florida House of Representatives and then became a State Senator. As a state legislator, she achieved the creation of the Florida Pre-Paid College Tuition Program. Following the death of Claude Pepper, she won a special Congressional election by beating 10 opponents to represent South Miami Beach, Little Havana, Coral Gables, Key Biscayne, and suburban Miami.

Rep. Ros-Lehtinen has also been active on the domestic front primarily on issues concerning education and children.

As a member of the Speaker's Task Force for a Drug Free America, she fights to ensure that there is a decrease in demand and supply of drugs and an increase in accountability. Moreover, as an ardent supporter and leader in the area of victims' rights, she has proposed a Constitutional amendment to protect the rights of those who have been victims of crimes.

LUCILLE ROYBALL-ALLARD

Congresswoman Lucille Roybal-Allard is the first Mexican-American woman elected to Congress. She was elected by California's 33rd Congressional District in 1992 and handily won re-election in 1994 and 1996 with more than 80% of the vote. In 1997, the Congresswoman again made history when she was elected as Chair of the 29 member California Democratic Congressional Delegation. Most recently, recognizing her objectivity and strong judgment, House Minority Leader Richard Gephardt appointed Congresswoman Roybal-Allard to the House Select Committee on U.S. National Security and Military/Commercial Concerns with the People's Republic of China. This 9-member committee is charged with investigating the transfer of missile technology to China. Recognizing that the next census is one of the most critical issues facing Latinos, the Congressional Hispanic Caucus appointed

Congresswoman Roybal-Allard to lead the fight for a fair and accurate 2000 Census as the Chair of the Task Force on Census Outreach and Education

Prior to her election to Congress, Roybal - Allard represented the 56th Assembly District in the California State Assembly for three terms. Born and raised in Boyle Heights, the Congresswoman is the eldest daughter of Lucille Besserra Roybal and retired Congressman Edward R. Roybal, who served as a Member of Congress for 30 years. The 1965 graduate of the California State University at Los Angeles, is married to Edward T. Allard, III, and is the mother of two adult children, Lisa Marie and Ricardo Olivarez.

LORETTA SANCHEZ

Loretta Sanchez has lived most of her life in central Orange County, California. She was elected to Congress in November, 1996 defeating long-term incumbent, Robert K. Dornan. Previously Loretta was a businesswoman in Santa Ana, specializing in assisting public agencies with financial matters, including cost-benefit analysis, strategic planning and capital acquisition.

She is on the Executive Committee of the Hispanic Caucus, and also sits on the Hispanic Caucus Task Force on Education. She has become a member of the Blue Dog Democrats, which are a group of moderate Democrats who attempt to find mainstream solutions to major fiscal and social issues. She is a member of the Democratic Caucus, and she sits on the Caucus' Education Task Force. She is a member of the bipartisan Woman's Caucus. She is the Past-President of the National Society of Hispanic MBAs, a member of the Los Amigos of Orange County, and the Anaheim Assistance League. She earned a Bachelor's Degree in Economics from Chapman University, where she was recognized as Student of the Year at graduation. She holds an MBA in Finance from American University in Washington, D.C. Congresswoman Sanchez is married to Stephen Brixey, a securities trader, and their families have called Anaheim home for over half a century.

JOSÉ E. SERRANO

José E. Serrano (Democrat-Liberal), was born in Mayaguez, Puerto Rico on October 24, 1943. In 1950, his family moved to the South Bronx where he attended public schools. Congressman Serrano served in the 172nd Support Battalion, Fort Wainright, Alaska, in the U.S. Army Medical Corps.

Prior to his election to Congress, Mr. Serrano had a distinguished sixteen-year career in the New York State Assembly, including six years as chairman of the Education Committee.

Serrano is the architect of the "English-Plus" Resolution, which expresses the sense of Congress that the Government should pursue policies to encourage the use and learning of various languages to protect national interests and civil rights. In 1996, Serrano introduced the resolution as a substitute to an English-only measure on the House floor, for which he gained the support of 178 Members. During

the first session of the 105th Congress, Serrano became the Ranking Democrat on the Appropriations Committee's Subcommittee on Legislative Branch and third ranking Democratic member on its Subcommittee on Agriculture, Rural Development, Food and Drug Administration and Related Agencies. Serrano has vehemently fought against measures proposed by Republicans which would balance the budget on the backs of poor working families, children, the ill, the elderly, and immigrants.

HILDA L. SOLIS

Senator Hilda L. Solis is a trailblazer and champion of working families. She has demonstrated a rare willingness to take on tough issues by authoring landmark legislation in the areas of domestic violence, labor, environmental protection, education and crime, and most recently welfare reform.

She has been a strong advocate for women's rights and a leading author of measures pertaining to women's health, restraining orders, and spousal rape. She co-chaired the successful initiative to raise the minimum wage for working families in California. In addition, she has become an aggressive fighter against the proliferation of illegal methamphetamine drugs in our neighborhoods. She has authored legislation to increase penalties against criminals who sell and produce illegal "meth" and successfully obtained state funding to buy two anti-meth mobile enforcement vehicles that will be used by Los Angeles drug enforcement teams. As a member of the Senate Budget Committee, she has led efforts to fund health insurance for children of the working poor and increased state funding for programs that encourage at-risk youth to stay in school

Senator Hilda L. Solis was elected to 24th Senatorial District in November of 1994 and was re-elected with an overwhelming majority in 1998. Upon her election, Senator Solis made history by becoming the first Latina to ever serve in the State Senate. Prior to being elected to the upper house of the Legislature, Senator Solis served in the Assembly from 1992 through 1994, where she represented the 57th Assembly District. Senator Solis is the Chairperson of the Senate Budget and Fiscal Review Subcommittee on Health, Human Services, Labor and Veterans' Affairs; the Senate Industrial Relations Committee; and the Senate Subcommittee on Asia Trade and Commerce. She is a member of Budget and Fiscal Review, Energy, Utilities and Communications; Environmental Quality; Health and Human Services; and Natural Resources and Wildlife Committees.

Before seeking public office, Hilda established an exemplary record of public service. After earning her Bachelor of Arts degree at Cal Poly Pomona and her Masters at USC, Solis served as Editor-in-Chief for the White House Office of Hispanic Affairs during the Carter Administration. She also served as a management analyst for the U.S. Office of Management and Budget in Washington, D.C. She was also a two-term member of the Rio Hondo Community College Board of Trustees (1985-1992). In 1991, Supervisor Gloria Molina appointed her to serve on the Los Angeles County Insurance Comission.

NYDIA M. VELAZQUEZ

Congresswoman Nydia M. Velázquez is the first Puerto Rican woman elected to the United States House of Representatives. She was first elected to Congress in 1992 to represent the 12th district of New York. In 1994, she was re-elected with 92 percent of the vote.

Born March 28, 1953, in Yabucoa, Puerto Rico, Nydia Velázquez and her twin sister were among nine children raised by Doña Carmen Luisa Velázquez and Don Benito Velázquez.

Nydia Velázquez was the first person in her family to receive a high school diploma. She entered the University of Puerto Rico in Rio Piedras at the age of 16, and graduated Magna Cum Laude in 1974, with a Bachelor's degree in Political Science.

After earning a Master's degree in Political Science from New York University in 1976, she joined the faculty of Hunter College at the City University in 1981 as an adjunct professor of Puerto Rican studies.

In 1983, Ms. Velázquez served as Special Assistant to U.S. Representative Edolphus Towns, and the following year became the first Latina appointed to serve on the New York City Council. In 1986, Velázquez served as the Director of the Department of Puerto Rican Community Affairs in the United States.

ROBERT A. UNDERWOOD

Robert A. Underwood ws born July 13, 1948 in Tamuning, Guam. He received a Bachelor of Arts degree in History in 1969 and a Master of Arts in History in 1971. He has attended California State University in Los Angeles, and John F. Kennedy High School in Tumon, Guam. He is married to the former Loraine Aguilar and they have five children: Sophia, Roberto, Ricardo, Ramon, Raphael

Underwood was elected to the 103rd Congress in 1992, to the 104th Congress in 1994, and to the 105rth Congress, 1996.

From 1976 to 1992, Underwood served the University of Guam as: Academic Vice-President; Dean of the College of Education; Associate Professorin the College of Education; Director, Project BEAM (Bilingual Education Assistance for Micronesia); Director, Bilingual Bicultural Training Program Faculty, Bilingual Bicultural Training Program. He also served as chair of the Political Status Ed. Coord. Commission (1991); on the Chamorro Language Commission (1977-1991); on the Guam Historic Preservation Review Board (1978-1990); as a member of the Advisory Panel, Guam Council for the Arts and Humanities, (1987); and as an Advisor, Guam, Pacific Festival of the Arts (1985). He is a founding member of the Organization of People for Indigenous Rights (OPI-R). In 1982 he served on the Guam Commission on Self-Determination Task Force on Free Association/Independence. In 1981 he was active in the National Advisory Council on Bilingual Bicultural Assn. In 1979 he was elected to the Territorial Board of Education. He was a founding member of PARA'-PADA.

The 2000 Census
El Censo del 2000

Government officials aren't the only ones who will be using Census 2000 data come 2001. People from many walks of life use census data to advocate for causes, research markets, target advertising, locate pools of skilled workers, prevent diseases, even rescue disaster victims.

When Hurricane Andrew hit south Florida in 1992, for example, census information aided the rescue effort by providing relief workers with estimates of the number of people missing in each block, as well as detailed maps of whole neighborhoods that had been obliterated.

Senior citizen groups often draw on statistics from the census to support their desire for community centers. The census can show that the population of elderly residents near a proposed center is plentiful and increasing. When county commissioners digest this supporting data, they often cannot argue with the clear evidence that a new senior citizen center is needed.

As businesses try to determine if the market for a new product is large enough or if the product will be accessible to consumers, one source of vital statistics is the census. It shows, on a local, regional or national basis, how many men, women and children live in a specific area, breaking out the data by age and ethnic origin, sex and race, home owners versus renters. Census numbers help businesses reduce their financial risk and broaden their markets.

Nonprofit organizations often use census numbers to estimate the number of potential volunteers in communities across the nation. Developers analyze census data before deciding where to locate a new shopping mall. Male/female distribution will be considered by a dating service before deciding to advertise in an area, and income levels will be reviewed by an expensive clothing store before investing in a new outlet.

Los funcionarios del gobierno no son las únicas personas que usarán los datos del Censo 2000 en 2001. Todo tipo de personas usa los datos del censo para apoyar causas, investigar mercados, enfocar publicidad, localizar concentraciones de trabajadores calificados, prevenir enfermedades e incluso rescatar a víctimas de desastres.

Por ejemplo, cuando el huracán Andrew azotó el sur de la Florida en 1992, la información del censo ayudó en el esfuerzo de rescate proporcionando a los trabajadores que llevaban auxilio, estimados del número de personas extraviadas en cada manzana, así como mapas detallados de vecindarios completos que habían sido arrasados.

Los grupos de ciudadanos de edad avanzada a menudo se basan en las estadísticas del censo para apoyar sus necesidades de centros comunitarios. El censo puede mostrar que el número de residentes de edad avanzada cerca de un centro propuesto es alto y que está aumentando. Cuando los comisionados del condado asimilan estos datos de apoyo, a menudo no pueden argüir en contra de la evidencia clara de que se necesita un nuevo centro para ciudadanos de edad avanzada.

El censo es una fuente de estadísticas vitales para los comercios al intentar determinar si el mercado para un nuevo producto es lo suficientemente grande o si el producto será accesible para los clientes. El censo muestra, sobre una base local, regional o nacional, cuántos hombres, mujeres y niños viven en un lugar específico, clasificando los datos por edad y origen étnico, sexo y raza, o si se trata de propietarios o arrendatarios. Las cifras del censo ayudan a los comercios a reducir su riesgo financiero y a ampliar sus mercados.

Las organizaciones sin fines de lucro a menudo usan las cifras del censo para estimar el número de voluntarios potenciales en las comunidades de toda la nación. Los promotores inmobiliarios analizan los datos del censo antes de decidir dónde ubicar un nuevo centro comercial. Una agencia de contactos para parejas toma en consideración la distribución de hombres y mujeres antes de decidir anunciarse en un lugar, y una tienda de ropa cara considera los niveles de ingreso antes de invertir en un nuevo local.

Census statistics help determine where to build more roads (add lanes, install stoplights or decrease speed limits, too) and hospitals (or free health clinics) and child-care centers. They also help identify which communities need more federal help for job training, Head Start or the Women, Infants and Children (WIC) Program, which provides dairy and other nutritional supplements to new and nursing mothers and their children.

In a June 1998 symposium in Houston, Texas, on Census 2000, President Clinton pointed out the importance of census data in creating a bipartisan majority for higher funding for the WIC program.

"People know that it makes good sense to feed babies and take care of them and provide for them when they're young," the president said. "But the funds, once appropriated, can only flow where they're needed if there is an accurate count of where the kids are. So, ironically, no matter how much money we appropriate for WIC, unless we actually can track where the children are, the program will be less than fully successful."

At the symposium, Dr. Judith Craven, president of the United Way of the Texas Gulf Coast in Houston, spoke about how census data help determine where the most acute social service problems in the community are and where the money the United Way raises from private sources each year for health and human services will be distributed.

"Traditionally, we have been one of the major funders of community planning and analysis," Craven said. As her agency tries to leverage the $64 million it raised in 1997, "it's essential ... that we have accurate data in order to distribute those dollars to those that are most in need — and in a fair and equitable way."

Dr. Mary desVignes-Kendrick, health director for the city of Houston, told the symposium that "accurate census data is critical to public health. It is not possible for us to do public health without it."

DesVignes-Kendrick, who is immediate past president of the National Association of County and City Health Officials, which represents 3,000 local health departments throughout the country, said the census "gives us the denominators for calculating birth rates, death rates, disease incidents and prevalence within the community.

"Any national, state, or local data that you hear about, such as the adolescent birth rate has decreased by X percent — this is generally based on denominators supplied by the census," she said. "For us to target interventions in a population, to know whether we're having any impact, to measure that impact, it is very important to have accurate census data."

Las estadísticas del censo ayudan a determinar dónde construir más carreteras (también añadir carriles, instalar semáforos o reducir los límites de velocidad) y hospitales (o clínicas de salud gratuitas) y centros de cuidado infantil. También ayudan a identificar cuáles comunidades necesitan más ayuda federal para capacitación laboral o para los programas Head Start o WIC (para mujeres, infantes y niños), el cual proporciona suplementos nutricionales lácteos y de otros tipos a las madres nuevas y lactantes, así como a sus hijos.

En junio de 1998, en un simposio en Houston, Texas acerca del Censo 2000, el Presidente Clinton señaló la importancia de los datos del censo en la creación de una mayoría bipartidista para conseguir más fondos para el programa WIC.

"La gente sabe que tiene mucho sentido alimentar a los bebés y cuidar de ellos y satisfacer sus necesidades cuando son jóvenes", dijo el presidente. "Pero los fondos, una vez que se apropian, sólo pueden aplicarse donde se necesitan si hay un conteo acertado de dónde están los niños. Así que, irónicamente, sin importar cuánto dinero apropiemos para WIC, a menos que en efecto podamos ubicar dónde están los niños, el programa no tendrá un éxito completo".

En el simposio, la Dra. Judith Craven, presidenta de United Way de la costa del Golfo de Texas en Houston, habló acerca de cómo los datos del censo ayudan a determinar dónde están los problemas de servicios sociales más agudos en la comunidad y dónde se distribuirá el dinero que recauda United Way de fuentes privadas cada año para servicios humanos y de salud.

"Tradicionalmente, hemos sido una de las principales fuentes de financiamiento de la planificación y del análisis comunitarios", dijo Craven. Al intentar su agencia aprovechar los $64 millones que recaudó en 1997, "es necesario... que tengamos datos acertados para distribuir esos dólares a aquéllos con mayor necesidad, y de una manera justa y equitativa".

La Dra. Mary desVignes-Kendrick, directora de salud de la ciudad de Houston, dijo a los asistentes al simposio que "los datos acertados del censo son cruciales para la salud pública. No nos es posible procurar la salud pública sin ellos".

DesVignes-Kendrick, quien es la anterior presidenta de la National Association of County and City Health Officials (asociación nacional de funcionarios de salud de los condados y las ciudades), la cual representa a 3,000 departamentos locales de salud en todo el país, dijo que el censo "nos brinda los denominadores para calcular las tasas de natalidad, las tasas de mortalidad, y las incidencias y la permanencia de enfermedades en la comunidad.

"Todo dato nacional, estatal o local del que usted se entere, tal como el que la tasa de natalidad entre los adolescentes ha disminuido en un X por ciento, se basa por lo general en los denominadores proporcionados por el censo", dijo. "Para identificar intervenciones en la población, para saber si estamos logrando un efecto, para medir ese efecto, es muy importante que tengamos datos acertados del censo".

Census Products
Los productos del Censo

100-Percent Data Products.
Productos ciento por ciento estadísticos.

CENSUS 2000 REDISTRICTING DATA SUMMARY FILE
Planned Release Date: Mar-Apr 1, 2001
Contents: State Population Counts for legislative redistricting.
Media: Internet, CD-ROM, DVD if appropriate.
Lowest Geographic Level: Blocks.

Census 2000 Redistricting Data Summary File
Mar-Abr 1, 2001
Recuento de la población por estado y por legislative
redistricting.
Difusión: Internet, CD-ROM, DVD si es apropiado.
Mínimo nivel geográfico: Barrios.

DEMOGRAPHIC PROFILE
Planned Release Date: Jun-Sep 2001
Contents: Population totals and selected population and housing characteristics in a single table.
Media: Internet, CD-ROM, DVD if appropriate, paper.
Lowest Geographic Level: Places, Census tracts (Internet only).

Demographic Profile
Jun-Sep 2001
Totales poblacionales y determinadas características de vivienda y
población en la misma tabla.
Difusión: Internet, CD-ROM, DVD si es apropiado e informe escrito.
Mínimo nivel geográfico: Ciudades y areas del Censo (solo para la versión
en Internet).

CONGRESSIONAL DISTRICT DEMOGRAPHIC PROFILE
Planned Release Date: Jun-Sep 2001
Contents: Population totals and selected population and housing characteristics in a single table for Congressional Districts only.
Media: Internet, CD-ROM, DVD if appropriate, paper.
Lowest Geographic Level: Congressional Districts of the 106th Congress.

Congressional District Demographic Profile
Jun-Sep 2001
Totales poblacionales y determinadas características de vivienda y
población en la misma tabla por Distritos Congresionales unicamente.
Difusión: Internet, CD-ROM, DVD si es apropiado e informe escrito.
Mínimo nivel geográfico: Distritos Congresionales del 106° Congreso.

RACE AND HISPANIC OR LATINO SUMMARY FILE ON CD-ROM.
Planned Release Date: Jul 2001
Media: CD-ROM.
Lowest Geographic Level: Places.

Race and Hispanic or Latino Summary File on CD-ROM
Jul 2001
Difusión: CD-ROM.
Mínimo nivel geográfico: Ciudades.

SUMMARY FILE 1 (SF 1)
Planned Release Date for States: Jun-Sep 2001
Advance national: Nov-Dec 2001
Final National: May-Jun 2002
Contents:
1. Population counts for 63 race categories and Hispanic or Latino.
2. Population counts for many detailed race and Hispanic or Latino categories, and American Indian and Alaska Native tribes.
3. Selected population and housing characteristics.

(Urban/rural data are on the final national file; this is the only difference from the advance national file).
Media: Internet; CD-ROM; DVD if appropriate.
Lowest Geographic Level: 1. Blocks; 2. Census tracts;
3. Blocks/Census tracts

Summary File 1 (SF 1)
Estados: Jun-Sep 2001
Avance nacional: Nov-Dic 2001
Final nacional: May-Jun 2002
1. Recuentos de población pora 63 razas e Hispanos o Latinos.
2. Recuentos de población para muchas razas específicas e Hispanos o
Latinos, Nativo-americano y tribus nativas de Alaska.
3. Determinadas características de población y vivienda.
(La información urbano/rural se encuentran en el apartado "final nacional";
esta es la única diferencia con el informe "avance nacional").
Difusión: Internet, CD-ROM, DVD si es apropiado.
Mínimo nivel geográfico: 1. Barrios; 2. Areas del Censo;
3. Barrios/areas del Censo.

SUMMARY FILE 2 (SF 2)
Planned Release Date for States: Sep-Dec 2001
Advance national: Mar-Apr 2002
Final National: Jun-Jul 2002
Contents: Population and housing characteristics iterated for many detailed race and Hispanic or Latino categories, and American Indian and Alaska Native tribes.
(Urban/rural data are on the final national file; this is the only difference from the advance national file).
Media: Internet; CD-ROM; DVD if appropriate.
Lowest Geographic Level: Census tracts.

Summary File 2 (SF 2)
Estados: Sep-Dic 2001
Avance nacional: Mar-Abr 2002
Final nacional: Jun-Jul 2002
Determinadas características de población y vivienda son explicadas para
muchas razas específicas e Hispanos o Latinos, Nativo-americano y tribus
nativas de Alaska.
(La información urbano/rural se encuentran en el apartado "final nacional";
esta es la única diferencia con el informe "avance nacional").
Difusión: Internet, CD-ROM, DVD si es apropiado.
Mínimo nivel geográfico: Areas del Censo.

QUICK TABLES
Planned Release Date for States: Apr-Dec 2001
National: Nov 2001-Apr 2002
Contents: Table shells with population and housing characteristics where the user can specify a geographic area and a population group.
Media: Internet; CD-ROM; DVD if appropriate.
Lowest Geographic Level: Census tracts.

Quick Tables
Estados: Abr-Dic 2001
Nacional: Nov 2001-Abr 2002
Tablas con características de población y vivienda donde el usuario puede detallar areas geográficas y grupos poblacionales.
Difusión: Internet, CD-ROM, DVD si es apropiado.
Mínimo nivel geográfico: Areas del Censo.

GEOGRAPHIC COMPARISON TABLES
Planned Release Date forStates: Apr 2001-Jan 2002
National: Dec 2001-Aug 2002
Contents: Population and housing characteristics for a list of geographic areas (e.g., all counties in a state).
Media: Internet; CD-ROM; DVD if appropriate.
Lowest Geographic Level: Places.

Geographic Comparison Tables
Estado: Abr 2001-Ene 2002
Nacional: Dic 2001-Ago 2002
Características poblacionales y de vivienda para una serie de areas geográficas (ejemplo: todos los condados en un estado).
Difusión: Internet, CD-ROM, DVD si es apropiado.
Mínimo nivel geográfico: Ciudades.

ADVANCED QUERY FUNCTION
Planned Release Date: Sep-Dec 2001 (Release subject to policy decisions on access and confidentiality).
Contents: User specifies contents of tabulations from full microdata file. Includes safeguards against disclosure of identifying information about individuals and housing units.
Media: Internet.
Lowest Geographic Level: User defined down to block groups.

Advanced Query Function
Sep-Dic 2001
(Difusión sujeta a las decisiones de política sobre acceso y confidencialidad).
El usuario especifica los contenidos de tabulaciones desde Full microdata file.
Incluye protección contra revelación o identificación de información sobre particulares y unidades de vivienda.
Difusión: Internet.
Mínimo nivel geográfico: User defined down to block groups.

CENSUS 2000: SUMMARY POPULATION AND HOUSING CHARACTERISTICS
Planned Release Date: Jan-Nov 2002
Media: Internet, paper (printed report).
Lowest Geographic Level: Places.

Census 2000: Summary Population and Housing Characteristics
Ene-Nov 2002
Difusión: Internet, informe escrito.
Mínimo nivel geográfico: Ciudades.

CENSUS 2000: POPULATION AND HOUSING UNIT TOTALS
Planned Release Date:2003
Media: Internet, paper (printed report with selected historical counts).
Lowest Geographic Level: Places.

Census 2000: Population and Housing Unit Totals
2003
Difusión: Internet, informe escrito con determinados hechos históricos.

Mínimo nivel geográfico: Ciudades.

Sample Data Products.
Productos de muestras estadísticas.

DEMOGRAPHIC PROFILE
Planned Release Date: Dec 2001-Mar 2002
Contents: Demographic, social, economic, and housing characteristics presented in three separate tables.
Media: Internet, CD-ROM, DVD if appropriate, paper.
Lowest Geographic Level: Places, Census tracts (Internet only).

Demographic Profile
Dic 2001-Mar 2002
Características demográficas, sociales y económicas presentadas en tres tablas individuales.
Difusión: Internet, CD-ROM, DVD si es apropiado e informe escrito.
Mínimo nivel geográfico: Ciudades, areas del Censo (solo versión en Internet).

CONGRESSIONAL DISTRICT DEMOGRAPHIC PROFILE
Planned Release Date: Dec 2001-Mar 2002
Contents: Demographic, social, economic, and housing characteristics presented in three separate tables for Congressional Districts only.
Media: Internet, CD-ROM, DVD if appropriate, paper.
Lowest Geographic Level: Congressional Districts of the 106th Congress.

Congressional District Demographic Profile
Dic 2001-Mar 2002
Características demográficas, sociales y económicas presentadas en tres tablas individuales por Distritos Congresionales unicaménte.
Difusión: Internet, CD-ROM, DVD si es apropiado e informe escrito.
Mínimo nivel geográfico: Distritos Congresionales del 106° Congreso.

SUMMARY FILE 3 (SF 3)
Planned Release Date: Jun-Sep 2002
Contents:
1. Population counts for ancestry groups.
2. Selected population and housing characteristics.
Media: Internet; CD-ROM; DVD if appropriate.
Lowest Geographic Level: 1. Census tracts; 2. Block groups/Census tracts.

Summary File 3 (SF 3)
Jun-Sep 2002
1. Recuentos de población por grupos de antepasado.
2. Características determinadas de población y vivienda.
Difusión: Internet, CD-ROM, DVD si es apropiado.
Mínimo nivel geográfico: 1.-Areas del Censo, 2.-Grupos de barrios/areas del Censo.

SUMMARY FILE 4 (SF 4)
Planned Release Date: Oct 2002-Feb 2003
Contents: Population and housing characteristics for many detailed race and Hispanic or Latino categories, American Indian and Alaska Native tribes, and ancestry groups.
Media: Internet, CD-ROM, DVD if appropriate.
Lowest Geographic Level: Census tracts.

Summary File 4 (SF 4)
Oct 2002-Feb 2003
Determinadas características de población y vivienda son explicadas para muchas razas específicas e Hispanos o Latinos, Nativo-americano, tribus nativas de Alaska y grupos de antepasados.
Difusión: Internet, CD-ROM, DVD si es apropiado.
Mínimo nivel geográfico: Areas del Censo.

QUICK TABLES
Planned Release Date: Jun 2002-Feb 2003
Contents: Table shells with population and housing characteristics where the user can specify a geographic area and a population group.

Media: Internet; CD-ROM; DVD if appropriate.
Lowest Geographic Level: Census tracts.

Quick Tables
Jun 2002-Feb 2003
Tablas con características de población y vivienda donde el usuario puede detallar areas geográficas y grupos poblacionales.
Difusión: *Internet, CD-ROM, DVD si es apropiado.*
Mínimo nivel geográfico: *Areas del Censo.*

GEOGRAPHIC COMPARISON TABLES
Planned Release Date: Jul 2002-Jan 2003
Contents:Population and housing characteristics for a list of geographic areas (e.g., all counties in a state).
Media: Internet, CD-ROM, DVD if appropriate.
Lowest Geographic Level: Places.

Geographic Comparison Tables
Jul 2002-Ene 2003
Características poblacionales y de vivienda para una serie de areas geográficas (ejemplo: todos los condados en un estado).
Difusión: Internet, CD-ROM, DVD si es apropiado.
Mínimo nivel geográfico: Ciudades.

PUBLIC USE MICRODATA SAMPLE (PUMS) FILES.
Planned Release Date For 1-percent sample: 2002
Planned Release Date For 5-percent sample: 2003
Contents:
1. 1-percent sample (information for the nation and states, as well as substate areas where appropriate).
2. 5-percent sample (information for state and sub-state areas).
Media: CD-ROM; DVD if appropriate.
Lowest Geographic Level: 1. Super Public Use Microdata Areas (Super-PUMAs) of 400,000+; 2. PUMAs of 100,000+.

Public Use Microdata Sample (PUMS) Files
Para muestras al 1 por ciento: 2002
Para muentràs al 5 por ciento: 2003
1. *Muestras al 1 por ciento (información nacional y estatal, así como areas sub-estatales en donde sea apropiado).*
2. *Muestras al 5 por ciento (información estatal y areas sub-estatales).*
Difusión: *Internet, CD-ROM, DVD si es apropiado.*
Mínimo nivel geográfico: *1. Super Public Use Microdata Areas (Super-PUMAs) of 400,000+; 2. PUMAs of 100,000+.*

ADVANCED QUERY FUNCTION
Planned Release Date: Dec 2002-Mar 2003 (Release subject to policy decisions on access and confidentiality).
Contents: User specifies contents of tabulations from full microdata file. Includes safeguards against disclosure of identifying information about individuals and housing units.
Media: Internet.
Lowest Geographic Level: User defined down to census tracts.

Advanced Query Function
Dic 2002-Mar 2003 (Difusión sujeta a las decisiones de política sobre acceso y confidencialidad).
El usuario especifica los contenidos de tabulaciones desde Full microdata file.
Incluye protección contra revelación o identificación de información sobre particulares y unidades de vivienda.
Difusión: *Internet.*
Mínimo nivel geográfico: *User defined down to census tracts.*

CENSUS 2000: SUMMARY SOCIAL, ECONOMIC, AND HOUSING CHARACTERISTICS
Planned Release Date: 2003
Media: Internet, paper (printed report).
Lowest Geographic Level: Places.

Census 2000: Summary Social, Economic, and Housing Characteristics
2003

Difusión: *Internet, informe escrito.*
Mínimo nivel geográfico: *Ciudades.*

CONGRESSIONAL DISTRICT DATA SUMMARY FILE
Planned Release Date: 2003
Contents: 100-percent and sample data for the redistricted 108th Congress.
Media: Internet, CD-ROM, DVD if appropriate.
Lowest Geographic Level: Census tracts within Congressional Districts.

Congressional District Data Summary File
2003
Ciento por ciento y muestras estadísticas para el redistricted Congreso 108°.
Difusión: *Internet, CD-ROM, DVD si es apropiado.*
Mínimo nivel geográfico: *Areas del Censo dentro de los Distritos del Congreso*

GENERAL INFORMATION
Census 2000 data products are designed to meet a variety of data needs for different segments of the data user community. The data products described here provide a summary of the general tabulation and publication program for the 50 states, the District of Columbia, and Puerto Rico (which is treated as a state equivalent for each data product).

Please note that constraints with staffing and budget, federal guidelines regarding the tabulation of data by race and ethnicity, data processing, or other considerations may result in changes to the types of data products prepared or the timing of their release. For more information on Census 2000 data products, please call Customer Services on 301-457-4100 or contact Louisa Miller (Population Division) on 301-457-2073.
Source: U.S. Census Bureau, Population Division, Decennial Programs Coordination Branch. Maintained By: Laura K. Yax (Population Division). Created: August 23, 2000. The Planned Release Date refers to the first medium of release.

Aviso
Los productos estadísticos del Censo 2000 están diseñados para satisfacer una variedad de necesidades estadísticas para los diferentes segmentos de la comunidad usuaria de estadísticas. Los productos estadísticos descritos proporcionan un resumen del programa de tabulacion y publicación para los 50 estados, el Distrido de Columbia y Puerto Rico (el cual es tratado como cualquier otro estado para cada producto estadístico).

Restricciones con personal y presupuesto, pautas federales en referencia a la tabulación de las estadísticas por raza y grupo étnico, proceso de las estadísticas o otras consideraciones, pude resultar en cambios sobre los tipos de productos estadísticos preparados o el tiempo de difusión. Para más información sobre productos del Censo 2000 llamar al Servicio de atención al cliente al (301) 457-4100 o contactar a Louisa Miller (Population Division) en el (301) 457-2073. Fuente: U.S. Census Bureau, Population Division, Decennial Programs Coordination Branch. Mantenido por: Laura K. Yax (Population Division). Creado: 23 de Agosto del 2000. La Fecha de Emisión Planeada se refiere al primer medio de emisión.

Hispanics: Distribution, Origin
Hispanos: distribución, origen

On page 24 of the 2000 ░░░░░ ░░░░░-HISPANIC YEARBOOK, we had included a report on the origin of Hispanic Americans. Below, we have reproduced a graphic representation, but not the figures. The figures in the report corresponded to the 1990 U.S. census, and those provided below have been extracted from the "Current Population Survey" (CPS). These numbers should not be expected to coincide with the figures from the 2000 Census, from which the state-by-state figures are included on page 22.

By February 2001, the Office of the Census had not published figures for racial or cultural groups, much less subtotals for subgroups.

A final commentary. On page 23 appears a chapter entitled "How many we were...." This section was originally published in the 1995 edition of the ░░░░ ░░░░░-HISPANIC YEARBOOK, because we believed that the figures published about the Hispanic population in the U.S. were questionable. We maintained that there were two groups that were not included. The first was the population of the Territory of Puerto Rico, with the argument that they had a census office of their own. The second was the group of undocumented persons, because the official census form did not include a method for including them. We continued researching and the Census expressed (1995), that they had estimated approximately 4,000,000 undocumented residents, of which 60% were considered to be Hispanic. This figure was presented on page 8 of the 1995 HISPANIC YEARBOOK.

The 2000 Census has changed the previous criterion and has included the population of Puerto Rico at 3,808,610. However, the census naturally did not include the undocumented population, and those persons can only be counted using other methods. The ░░░░░ ░░░░░-HISPANIC YEARBOOK estimates that the figure for undocumented residents of the U.S. cannot be lower than 4.5 million.

En la página 24 del ░░░░░ ░░░░░-HISPANIC YEARBOOK 2000 habíamos incluido un informe sobre el origen de los hispanos-americanos. Aquí reproducimos la graficación pero no las cifras. Los números anteriores correspondían al censo 1990 y los que aquí damos son extraídos de "Current Population Survey (CPS)". Estos números debe presumirse que no coincidirán con las cifras del Censo del 2000, cuyas cantidades por estado, damos en la página 22.

Hasta la fecha la Oficina del Censo no ha revelado las cantidades por grupos raciales o culturales y mucho menos la subdivisión de esas cantidades Marzo 19, 2001.

Y un último comentario. En la página 23 figura un capítulo titulado "Cuantos fuimos...". Esta nota se originó en el ░░░░░ ░░░░░-HISPANIC YEARBOOK 1995 porque nosotros creíamos que la cifra que se daba sobre la población hispana en Estados Unidos, era cuestionable. Sosteníamos que había dos cantidades, que no se incluían. Una, la población del Estado Libre Asociado de Puerto Rico, argumentando que ellos tenían oficina de censos propia y otra, los indocumentados, porque no está incluida esa condición en el formulario del censo. Seguimos analizando y el Censo nos manifestó (1995), que habían realizado una estimación de alrededor de 4.000.000 de indocumentados de los cuales consideraban que el 60% eran hispanos. Esto consta en la página 8 del HISPANIC YEARBOOK 1995.

En el Censo 2000, cambiando el anterior criterio, se ha incluido la población del Estado Asociado de Puerto Rico que es de 3.808.610 pero naturalmente no se ha incluido la de los indocumentados que solo puede lograrse por otros sistemas de cálculos. El ░░░░░ ░░░░░-HISPANIC YEARBOOK estima que la cifra no puede ser menor de 4.500.000.

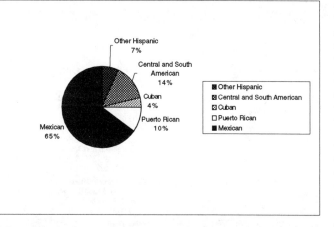

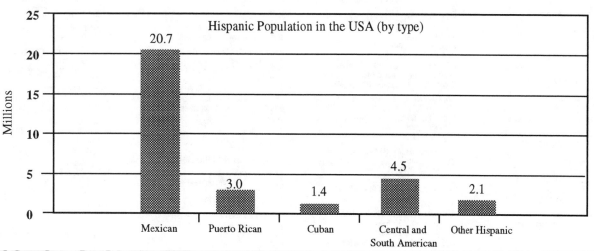

Source: U.S. Census Bureau (Press-Release/www/2000)

Hispanic Companies
Empresas hispanas

The following list presents contact information, in alphabetical order, on the largest Hispanic-owned businesses. (The size of the business is based on annual revenues.)

La siguiente lista presenta información (para tomar contacto), en órden alfabético, sobre las mayores empresas hispanas. (El tamaño de la empresa está basado en el ingreso anual.)

A

A.L.L. MASONRY CONSTRUCTION COMPANY
1414 West Willow Street
Chicago , IL 60622
CEO: Mr. Luis Puig
(773) 489-1280 Fax: (773) 489-0360

A.M. CAPEN'S CO.
1255 Liberty Avenue
Hillside , NJ 07205
CEO: Mr. Camilo Fernandez
(908) 351-1520 Fax: (908) 351-9235

A & N QUALITY PRODUCTS
2155 S. Valley Road
Denver , CO 80222
CEO: Mr. Alvin K. Lucero
(303) 639-5525 Fax: (303) 639-5700

A.R. ALVAREZ ENTERPRISES
800 IH 10 West, Suite 1150
San Antonio, TX 78230
CEO: Mr. Anthony Alvarez
(210) 342-1900 Fax: (210) 342-6900

A. RUIZ CONSTRUCTION CO.
1601 Courtland Avenue
San Francisco, CA 94110
CEO: Mr. Antonio Ruiz
(415) 647-4010 Fax: (415) 285-9243

A&D FIRE PROTECTION, INC.
11465 Woodside Avenue, 1st Floor
Santee, CA 92071
CEO: Mr. Andrew Otero
(619) 448-1962 Fax: (619) 448-5425
Email: andcorp1@aol.com

A&R JANITORIAL
5234 W. 25th Street
Cicero, IL 60804
CEO: Ms. Deborah Pintor
(708) 656-8300

ABC SECURITY SERVICE, INC.
1840 Embarcado
Oakland, CA 94606
CEO: Ms. Ana Chretien
(510) 436-0666 Fax: (510) 436-0826

ADVANCED TESTING TECHNOLOGIES, INC.
Corporate Headquarters
110 Ricefield Ln.
Hauppauge, NY 41788
CEO: Mr. Hector M. Gavilla
(631) 231-8777 Fax: (631) 231-7174
Email: atti@attinet.com
Web: http://www.attinet.com

Fairfax Office
3915 Old Lee Highway, Suite 23B
Fairfax, VA 22030
(703) 383-9388 Fax: (703) 383-9389

Warner Robins Office
127 Osigian Blvd.
Warner Robins, GA 31088
(912) 953-6356 Fax: (912) 953-6494

San Antonio Office
310 South Saint Mary's, Suite 2310
San Antonio, TX 78205
(210) 225-5007 Fax: (210) 225-5008

Oklahoma Office
3000 Tower Drive, Suite 205
Oklahoma City, OK 73115
(405) 670-0384 Fax: (405) 670-0388

Hanscom Office
Bldg. 1704, Room 206
Hanscom AFB, MA 01731
(781) 377-2656 Fax: (781) 377-4624

Ogden Office
2485 Grant Avenue, Suite 300
Ogden, UT 84401
(801) 627-6568 Fax: (801) 627-8640

ADVANCIA CORPORATION
800 Research Parkway, Suite 250
Oklahoma City, OK 73104
CEO: Mr. Randy Alvarado
(405) 996-3000 Fax: (405) 996-3100
Email: info@advancia.com
Web: http://www.advancia.com

AGUIRRE INTERNATIONAL
Corporate Headquarters
480 E. 4th Avenue, Unit A
San Mateo, CA 94401
CEO: Dr. Edward Aguirre
(650) 373-4900 Fax: (650) 348-0260
Email: aguirre@aiweb.com
Web: http://www.aguirreinternational.com
East Coast Office
4630 Montgomery Avenue, Suite 600
Bethesda, MD 20814
CEO: Dr. Edward Aguirre
(301) 654-8800 Fax: (301) 654-9120
Email: aguirre@aiweb.com
Web: http://www.aguirreinternational.com

AIB FINANCIAL GROUP, INC.
2500 NW 79th Avenue
Miami, FL 33122
CEO: Mr. Jose M. Alvarez
(305) 715-0000 Fax: (305) 715-0044

AIR FLOW SHEET METAL, INC.
21220 Commerce Point
Walnut, CA 91789
CEO: Mr. Augie D. Juarez
(909) 468-2600 Fax: (909) 468-2606

AJ CONTRACTING
470 Palm Avenue, South, 4th Floor
New York, NY 10016
CEO: Mr. Leonard Bass
(212) 889-9100 Fax: (212) 889-8889

AJT & ASSOCIATES, INC.
Corporate Headquarters
8910 Astronaut Blvd.
Cape Canaveral, FL 32920
CEO: Mr. Alfredo Teran
(321) 783-7989
Web: http://www.ajt-assoc.com

Huntsville Operations
6767 Madison Pike NW., Suite 294
Huntsville, AL 35806
(256) 971-1622

Orlando Sales Office
7131 Grand National Drive, Suite 104
Orlando, FL 32819
(407) 903-5870

Miami Lab
8304 NW., South River Drive
Medley, FL 33166
(305) 888-8330

Research & Development Facility
8900 Astronaut Blvd.
Cape Canaveral, FL 32920
(321) 799-1852

ALAMO TRAVEL GROUP
9000 Wurzbach
San Antonio, TX 78240
CEO: Ms. Patricia Stout
(210) 593-0084 Fax: (210) 696-2022
Email: alamotv1@satx.net

ALGUS ENTERPRISES, INC.
5959 NW., 35th Avenue
Miami, FL 33142
CEO: Mr. Gus Lima
(305) 634-2300
(800) 887-1484
Email: guslima@algus.net
Web: http://www.aidatamall.com

ALL AMERICAN CONTAINERS, INC.
Corporate Headquarters
11825 N.W. 100th Rd., Bldg. 1
Miami, FL 33178
CEO: Ms. Remedios Diaz-Oliver
(305) 887-0797 Fax: (305) 888-4133
Email: info@americancontainers.com
Web: http://www.americancontainers.com

Tampa Branch
2400 Gelman Place
Tampa, FL 33619
(813) 248-2023 Fax: (813) 248-1059

American Packaging of Puerto Rico Br.
Royal Industrial Park Bldg., D-4 Bo. Palmas
Cantano, PR 00962
(787) 275-2670 Fax: (787) 275-2673

ALL STAR FORD-MERCURY INC.
2929 S Loop 256
Palestine, TX 75801
CEO: Mr. Fernando Varela
(903) 729-2171
Email: fvarela@allstarford.com
Web: http://www.allstarfordmercury.com

ALMAN ELECTRIC, INC.
7677 Hunnicut Road
Dallas , TX 75228
CEO: Mr. Joe Alcantar
(214) 388-1800 Fax: (214) 388-1818

ALVAREZ LINCOLN MERCURY INC.
8051 Auto Drive
Riverside, CA 92504
CEO: Mr. Ramon Alvarez
(909) 687-1212 Fax: (909) 687-1288
Email: bdd@alvarezlincoln-mercury.com
Web: http://www.alvarezlincoln-mercury.com

AMERICAN DATA & COMPUTER PRODUCTS, INC.
6107-D Memorial Highway
Tampa, FL 33615-4564
CEO: Mr. Robert Castro Jr.
(813) 884-0767/0584 Fax: (813) 886-2802
Email: info@adcpi.com
Web: http://www.adcpi.com

AMERICAN FASTENERS CORP.
7323 NW. 66th Street
Miami , FL 33166
CEO: Mr. Manny Benitez
(305) 885-1717 Fax: (305) 477-5278
Email: mannyb@amerifast.com
Web: http://www.amerifast.com

AMI MECHANICAL, INC.
12141 Pensylvania Street
Thorton, CO 80241
CEO: Mr. Manuel Gonzales
(303) 280-1401 Fax: (303) 280-9931

AMVEST SECURITIES, INC.
1395 E. Dublin Granville Road, Suite 203
Columbus, OH 43229
CEO: Mr. Ralph Martinez
(614) 431-2004

ANALYTICAL COMPUTER SERVICES
Corporate Office
11500 Northwest Freeway, Suite 320
Houston, TX 77092
CEO: Mr. Frank Trifilio
(713) 681-0039 Fax: (713) 681-0057
Web: http://www.acsbuy.com

Operations/Technical
4202 Directors Row, Suite 100
Houston, TX 77092
(713) 290-2230 Fax: (713) 681-0056

Dallas Office
1321 Valwood Parkway
Carrollton, TX 75006
(972) 247-4227 Fax: (972) 448-8784

Austin Office
7801 N. Lamar Suite E-182
Austin, TX 78752
(512) 459-0455 Fax: (512) 459-0266

ANASTEEL & SUPPLY CO.
2145 Plastered Bridge Road, NE.
Atlanta, GA 30324
CEO: Ms. Ana Cablik
(404) 873-1244 Fax: (404) 876-6585

ANCICARE PPO INC.
Corporate Headquarters
3700 Lakeside Drive, Suite 401
Miramar, FL 33027
CEO: Mr. Michael Cabrera
(954) 441-7600
(800) 414-4MRI Fax: (954) 441-0398
Email: eramallo@ancicare.com
Web: http://www.ancicare.com

ANCIRA ENTERPRISES
6111 Bandera Road
San Antonio, TX 78238
CEO: Mr. Ernesto Ancira Jr.
(210) 681-4900 Fax: (210) 681-5541
Email: g.ancira@worldnet.att.net
Web: http://www.ancira.com

ANDES CHEMICAL CORPORATION
10850 NW., 30th Street
Miami, FL 33172
CEO: Mr. Fernando Espinosa
(305) 591-5601 Fax: (305) 591-5607
Email: fernando.espinosa@andeschem.com
Web: http://www.andeschem.com

ANPESIL DISTRIBUTION SERVICES
1273 Imperial Way
Thorofare, NJ 08086
CEO: Mr. Juan V. Gallicchio
(856) 384-0080 Fax: (856) 384-6173

APACHE CONSTRUCTION CORPORATION
P.O. Box 12312
Albuquerque, NM 87195
CEO: Mr. Mariano Chavez & Mr. Paul Chavez
(505) 877-7978 Fax: (505) 877-5301

APEX OFFICE PRODUCTS, INC.
Corporate Headquarters
5209 N. Howard Avenue
Tampa, FL 33603
CEO: Mr. Aurelio Llorente Jr.
(813) 871-2010 Fax: (813) 875-9059
Email: jrapex@aol.com
Web: http://www.apexofficeproducts.com

APS INTERNATIONAL
120 2nd st.
San Francisco , CA 94105
CEO: Mr. Erick Vargas
(415) 496-1949 Fax: (415) 392-0128
Web: http://www.apsint.com

ARANDA TOOLING, INC.
15301 Springdale Street
Huntington Beach, CA 92649
CEO: Mr. Pedro Aranda
(714) 379-6565 Fax: (714) 379-6570
Email: dan.aranda@arandatooling.com
Web: http://www.arandatooling.com

ARCOM ELECTRONICS, INC.
1500 McCandless Drive
Milpitas, CA 95035
CEO: Mr. Armando Garcia
(408) 452-0678 Fax: (408) 586-5306
Email: inquiry@arcom.com
Web: http://www.arcom.com

ARROYO PROCESS EQUIPMENT, INC.
13750 Automobile Blvd.
Clearwater, FL 33762
CEO: Mr. Frank Arroyo Sr.
(727) 573-5294 Fax: (727) 573-0217
Web: http://www.arroyoprocess.com

ASG RENAISSANCE
Fairlane Plaza North
290 Town Center Drive, Suite 624
Dearborn, MI 48126
CEO: Ms. Beth Ardisana
(313) 336-3770 Fax: (313) 336-3094
Email: infor@asgren.com
Web: http://www.asgren.com

Southfield Town Center
3000 Town Center, Suite 2237
Southfield, MI 48075
(248) 353-0890 Fax: (248) 358-4499

ATLANTIC GRAPHIC SERVICES, INC.
57 Plain Street
Clinton, MA 01510
CEO: Mr. Ariel Schmidt
(978) 368-1262 Fax: (978) 365-6945

AZF AUTOMOTIVE GROUP, INC.
190 NW., 42nd Avenue
Miami, FL 33126
CEO: Mr. Motta-Domenech
(305) 477-2425 Fax: (305) 477-2930
Web: http://www.zonafranca-auto.com

AZTEC COMPANY
954 North Batavia
Orange, CA 92867
CEO: Mr. Eric Berge
(714) 744-8276

AZTEC MANUFACTURING CORPORATION
15378 Oakwood Dr.
Romulus, MI 48174
CEO: Mr. Francis Lopez
(734) 942-7433 Fax: (734) 942-9499
Email: flopez@aztecmfgcorp.com
Web: http://www.aztecmfgcorp.com

AZTECA CONSTRUCTION
3871 Security Park Drive
Rancho Cordova, CA 95742
CEO: Mr. Rafael Martin
(916) 351-0202 Fax: (916) 351-9270

AZTECH CONTRACTING, INC.
2856 Jhonson Ferry Road
Marietta, GA 30062
CEO: Ms. Helen Barrios
(770) 642-3955 Fax: (770) 642-3950

B

BARCON CORPORATION
P.O. Box 370
Miami, AR 85539
CEO: Mr. Fred Barcon
(520) 425-5426 Fax: (520) 425-5193

BARRI ELECTRIC CO., INC.
1485 Bayshore Blvd.
San Francisco, CA 94124
CEO: Mr. Ernest Ulibarri
(415) 570-2261 Fax: (415) 468-7191

BEAM RADIO, INC.
220 NW., 2nd Avenue, Unit 3
Miami, FL 33172
CEO: Mr. Manny Junior
(305) 477-2326

BERMELLO, AJAMIL & PARTNERS, INC.
2601 South Bayshore Drive
Miami, FL 33133
CEO: Mr. Willy Bermello
(305) 859-2050 Fax: (305) 859-7835
Email: info@bamiami.com
Web: http://www.bamiami.com

BERND GROUP INC.
P.O. Box 2245
Dunedin, FL 34697
CEO: Ms. Pilar Bernd
(727) 733-0122 Fax: (727) 736-2251

BIRD ROOFING & WATERPROOFING, INC.
633 East Ventura Blvd.
Oxnard, CA 93030-1701
CEO: Mr. Tony Reyes
(805) 278-1611 Fax: (805) 278-1601
Email: frances@birdroofing.com
Web: http://www.birdroofing.com

BMI FINANCIAL GROUP, INC.
Corporate Headquarters
1320 S Dixie Hwy., 6th Floor
Coral Gables, FL 33146
CEO: Mr. Anthony Cieria
(305) 443-2898 Fax: (305) 442-8486
Email: bminb@bmicos.com
Web: http://www.bmicos.com

BORBON, INC.
7312 Wallnut Avenue
Buena Park, CA 90620
CEO: Mr. David Morales
(714) 994-0170 Fax: (714) 994-0641

BORRELL FIRE SYSTEMS, INC.
4101 North Florida
Tampa, FL 33603
CEO: Mr. Jim Flores
(813) 237-2727 Fax: (813) 237-6565

BOYETT CONSTRUCTION, INC.
6th South Linden Avenue, Suite 3
South San Francisco, CA 94080
CEO: Mr. Vernon H. Boyett
(650) 873-7006 Fax: (650) 873-7133

BRTRC, INC.
8260 Willow Oaks Corporate Drive, Suite 800
Fairfax, VA 22031
CEO: Mr. Gerardo Sanz
(703) 204-9277
(800) 307-9277 Fax: (703) 204-9447
Email: business@brtrc.com
Web: http://www.brtrc.com

BURT AUTOMOTIVE NETWORK
5200 S. Broadway
Englewood, CO 80110
CEO: Mr. Lloyd G. Chavez
(303) 761-0333 1-800-535-BURT
Fax: 303-789-6211
Email: autos@burt.com
Web: http://www.burt.com

BURTIN CORPORATION
West Coast Office
2550 S. Garnsey
Santa Ana, CA 92707
CEO: Mr. Carlos Burtin
(714) 850-1370 ext.227 Fax: (714) 850-0437
Web: http://www.urethaneburtin.com

East Coast Office
100 Enterprise Dr.
Cartersville, GA 30120
(770) 387-2525 Fax: (770) 387-9945

BUSINESS TRAVEL ADVISORS
3750 NW., 87th Avenue, Suite 100
Miami, FL 33178
CEO: Mr. Sergio L. Barrera
(305) 594-2929
(800) 237-2929 Fax: (305) 593-0473
Web: http://www.bta-fl.com

C

C-PAK SEAFOOD, INC.
742 East 66th Street
San Francisco, CA 93001
CEO: Mr. Benjamin Gonzales
(323) 231-7077 Fax: (323) 231-7170

CABACO, INC.
Sierra Vista Operations
1849 Paseo San Luis
Sierra Vista, AZ 85635
CEO: Mr. James S. Arellano
(520) 459-3193 Fax: (520) 459-2250
Email: jarellano@cabaco.com
Web: http://www.cabaco.com
Yuma Operations
255 W. 24th Street, Suite 3
Yuma , AZ 85364
CEO: Mr. James S. Arellano
(520) 726-6560 Fax: (520) 726-5254
Email: mluckie@cabaco.com
Web: http://www.cabaco.com

CAL INC.
2040 Peabody Road, Suite 400
Vacaville, CA 95687
CEO: Mr. David Esparza
(707) 446-7996 Fax: (707) 446-4906
Web: http://www.cal-inc.com

CANO CONTAINER CORPORATION
2300 Raddant Road, Suite A
Aurora, IL 60504
CEO: Mr. Juventino Cano
(630) 585-7500 Fax: (630) 585-7501
Email: CC@canocontainer.com
Web: http://www.canocontainer.com

CAPE ENVIRONMENTAL MANAGEMENT, INC.
Georgia Office
2302 Parklake Drive, Suite 200
Atlanta, GA 30345
CEO: Mr. Fernando J. Rios
(770) 908-7200 Fax: (770) 908-7219
Web: http://www.capeenv.com

Illinois Office
91 Noll Street
Waukegan, IL 60085
(847) 336-4341 Fax: (847) 336-4971

Florida Office
5796 Hoffner Avenue, Suite 607
Orlando, FL 32822
CEO: Mr. Fernando J. Rios
(407) 275-2900 Fax: (407) 275-2985

Kansas City Office
14113 West 72 Terrace
Shawnee, KS 66216
(913) 248-1278 Fax: (913) 248-1279

California Office
3631 S. Harbor Blvd., Suite 130
Santa Ana, CA 92704
(714) 427-6160 Fax: (714) 427-6161

Pennsylvania Office
486 Thomas Jones Way, Suite 260
Exton, PA 19341
(610) 594-8606 Fax: (610) 594-8609

New York Office
71 South Central Avenue
Valley Stream, NY 11580
(516) 568-2730 Fax: (516) 568-2693

CAPITOL TRAVEL AGENCY, INC.
3099 West 4th Avenue
Hialeah, FL 33012
CEO: Mr. William Gonzales
(305) 884-5323
(800) 848-0329
Fax: (305) 884-5396
Email: capitol-travel@msn.com
Web: http://www.capitol-travel.com

CAPRI HOMES CORPORATION
735 N. Thorton Avenue
Orlando, FL 32803
CEO: Mr. Mario Prieto
(407) 228-4645 Fax: (407) 228-4648

CAPTREE CHEMICAL CORPORATION
605 Albany Avenue
Amityville, NY 11701
CEO: Mr. Ernest P. Gonzales
(516) 841-0200
(800) 899-2725 Fax: (516) 841-5370
Email: patg@captreegroup.com
Web: http://www.captreegroup.com

Puerto Rico Warehouse
P.O. Box 270287
San Juan , PR 00927-0287
(787) 775-0485 Fax: (787) 775-0466

CARFEL, INC.
6900 N.W. 77th Ct.
Miami, FL 33166
CEO: Mr. George Felbenkreis
(305) 592-2760 Fax: (305) 592-8495
Web: http://www.bryco.com

CARLSON ADVANCE TRAVEL
601 Broadway, Suite 211
Denver, CO 80203
CEO: Ms. Ramona Martinez
(303) 260-7081 Fax: (303) 260-7082
Email: advancetravel@worldnet.att.net
Web: http://www.carlsontravel.com

CARTER CUSTOM CARPETS, INC.
75 Eden Valley Road
Rome, GA 30161
CEO: Mr. Eugenio Barnet-Cortina
(706) 235-8657 Fax: (706) 378-1001
Web: http://www.cartercarpets.com

CASA HERRERA, INC.
2655 North Pine Street
Pomona, CA 91767
CEO: Mr. Alfred Herrera
(909) 392-3930 Fax: (909) 392-0231
Email: sheilas@casaherrera.com
Web: http://www.casaherrera.com

CASAS INTERNATIONAL BROKERAGE, INC.
Main Office
10030 Marconi Drive, Otay Mesa
San Diego, CA 92154-7202
CEO: Ms. Sylvia Casas-Jolliffe
(619) 661-6162 Fax: (619) 661-6800
Web: http://www.casasinternational.com

Calexico Office
2380 Martin Luther King Avenue
Calexico, CA 92231
(760) 357-5911 Fax: (760) 357-5912

CASEY LUNA FORD-MERCURY, INC.
19381 North Business Loop
Belen, NM 87002
CEO: Mr. Casey Luna
(505) 864-4414 Fax: (505) 864-9713
Email: kclunasha@aol.com
Web: http://www.caseylunafordmerc.com

CCI INCORPORATED
Corporate Headquarters
277 S. Washington Street, Suite 120
Alexandria, VA 22314
CEO: Mr. Paul Chase

(703) 739-9330 Fax: (703) 739-9355
Email: solutions@ccicorp.com
Web: http://www.ccicorp.com
San Diego Regional Office
4355 Ruffin Rd., Suite 320
San Diego, CA 92123
CEO: Mr. Paul Chase
(619) 874-3356
Email: solutions@ccicorp.com
Web: http://www.ccicorp.com

Washington, DC Regional Office
300 E Street, SW., Room 8J69
Washington, DC 20546
(202) 358-1742

Jacksonville Regional Office
35 Industrial Loop N, Suite 190
Orange Park, FL 32073
(904) 264-6686

Patuxent River, MD Regional Office
46915 S. Shangri La Drive
Lexington Park, MD 20653
(301) 866-0078

Cherry Point, NC Regional Office
322 E. Main Street, Suite 4
Havelock, NC 28532
(252) 447-9526

Elizabeth City, NC Regional Office
P.O. Box 2647
Elizabeth City, NC 27906
(252) 334-5217

Arlington, VA Regional Office
1601 N. Kent Street, Plaza C, Suite 909
Arlington, VA 22209
(703) 276-7336

Norfolk, VA Regional Office
154B Rosemont Road
Virginia Beach, VA 23452
(757) 431-2550

Springfield, VA Regional Office
8600 L-1 Morrisette Drive, Lower Level
Springfield, VA 22152
(703) 644-8414

CENTINEL BANK OF TAOS
Main Office
512 Paseo del Pueblo Sur
Taos, NM 87571
CEO: Ms. Rebeca Romero
(505) 758-6700 Fax: (505) 758-6772
Email: centinel@centinelbank.com
Web: http://www.centinelbank.com

MotorBank
508 Paseo del Pueblo Norte
Taos, NM 87571
(505) 758-6788 or (505) 758-6789

Northside Office
707 Paseo del Pueblo Norte
Taos, NM 87571
(505) 758-6721

Questa Office
P.O. Box 761, #1 State Road 38
Questa, NM 87556
(505) 586-0577

Red River Office
320 East Main Street
P.O. Box 960
Red River, NM 87558
(505) 754-2351

Las Vegas Office
2609 7th Street
Las Vegas, NM 87701
(505) 426-9199

CHAVEZ SHEET METAL CO.
1001 W. 42nd Avenue
Denver , CO 80211
CEO: Mr. Robert A. Chavez
(303) 455-9387 Fax: (303) 455-0527

**CHICAGO CONTRACT CLEANING &
SUPPLY CO.**
5115 N. Ravenswood
Chicago, IL 60640
CEO: Ms. Lucia Chavez De Hollister
(773) 271-7200 Fax: (773) 271-1452

CISCO BROS. CORP.
Manufacturing Plant and Showroom
1933 W. 60th Street
Los Angeles, CA 90047
CEO: Mr. Francisco Pineda
(323) 778-8612 Fax: (323) 778-9073

Email: cisco@ciscobrothers.com
Web: http://www.ciscobrothers.com
High Point Showroom
300 W. Broad Avenue
High Point , NC 27262
(336) 887-4022

San Francisco Showroom
1355 Market Street
San Francisco, CA 94103
(415) 436-0131

CISCO ELECTRICAL SUPPLY CO.
P.O. Box 12367
Columbus, OH 43212
CEO: Mr. Francisco Muguruza
(614) 299-6606 Fax: (614) 299-2378

CLASSIC CONTAINERS, INC.
400 S. Rockefeller Avenue
Ontario, CA 91761
CEO: Mr. Manny Hernandez
(909) 390-6422
(909) 390-6423 Fax: (909) 390-6428
Email: mannysr@classiccontainers.com
Web: http://www.classiccontainers.com

CNC ENGINEERING CO.
17 Corporate Plaza
Newport Beach, CA 92662
CEO: Mr. Clement N. Calvillo
(949) 644-1505 Fax: (949) 644-2191

COBE CHEM LABS
8616 Slauson Avenue
Pico Rivera, CA 90660
CEO: Mr. Sergio Quiñones
(562) 942-2426 Fax: (562) 942-9985
Email: sales@cobechem.com
Web: http://www.cobechem.com

COLONIAL PRESS INTERNATIONAL
3690 NW., 50th Street
Miami, FL 33142
(305) 633-1581 Fax: (305) 638-3545

COLSA CORPORATION
6726 Odyssey Drive
Huntsville, AL 35806
CEO: Mr. George Williams
(256) 922-1512 Fax: (256) 922-9126
Email: webmaster@colsa.com

COMMUNICATIONS PRODUCTS INC.
7301 East, 90th Street, Suite 111
Indianapolis, IN 46256
CEO: Mr. Cliff Arellano
(317) 595-7860 Fax: (317) 842-0278
Web: http://www.comprod.com

COMMUNITY ASPHALT CORPORATION
14005 NW 186th Street
Hialeah, FL 33018
CEO: Mr. Jose Fernandez
(305) 829-0700 Fax: (305) 829-8772

COMPLAS, INC.
255 Airport Circle
Corona , CA 92880
CEO: Ms. Monica E. Garcia
(909) 371-5009 Fax: (909) 371-6997
Email: MonicaEG@aol.com
Web: http://www.complasinc.com

**COMPREHENSIVE ENVIRONMENTAL
SERVICES, INC. (CES)**
457 River Drive
Garfield, NJ 07026
CEO: Mr. Roque Schipilliti
(973) 478-5755 Fax: (973) 478-5551
Email: central@cesenv.com
Web: http://www.cesenv.com

COMPUTING TECHNOLOGIES, INC.
Corporate Headquarters
3028 Javier Road, Suite 400
Fairfax, VA 22031
CEO: Mr. Manuel Sosa Jr.
(703) 280-8800 Fax: (703) 280-8804
Email: cotsinfo@cots.com
Web: http://www.cots.com

Quantico Office
265 South Fraley Blvd.
Dumfries, VA 22026
703) 221-7655 Fax: (703) 221-7504
Web: http://www.cots-q.com

Tampa Office
2909 Bay-to-Bay Blvd., Suite 202
Tampa, FL 33629
(813) 837-4515 Fax: (813) 837-5195
Web: http://www.cots-t.com

CONNECTS ONE COMMUNICATIONS
150 South Arroyo Pkwy.
Pasadena, CA 91105
CEO: Mr. Robert Boladin
(626) 771-2021 Fax: (626) 844-2872

**CONTINENTAL BINDER & SPECIALTY
CORP.**
Main Plant
407 West Compton Blvd.
Gardena, CA 90248-1703
CEO: Mr. Andrew H. Lisardi
(310) 324-8227
(800) USA-BUYS Fax: (310) 715-6740
Email: sales@continentalbinder.com
Web: http://www.continentalbinder.com

Arizona Regional Office
3625 North 16th Street, Suite 118
Phoenix , AZ 85016
(602) 222-2463 Fax: (602) 222-1119

Colorado Regional Office
2765 South Colorado Blvd., Suite 216
Denver , CO 80222
(303) 691-2222 Fax: (303) 758-0209

Texas Regional Office
5719 Kenwick Street
San Antonio, TX 78238
(210) 522-1011 Fax: (210) 522-9828

CONTINENTAL ENVELOPE CO., INC.
404 Tonnelle Avenue
Jersey City, NJ 07306
CEO: Mr. Jose M. Perez
(201) 656-7800 Fax: (201) 656-8026

CONTOUR COMPUTER SERVICES, INC.
46221 Landing Pkwy.
Fremont, CA 94538
CEO: Mr. Henry J. Martinez
(510) 440-8177 Fax: (510) 440-8008
Web: http://www.contour.com

CONTRACT INTERIORS
950 Laidlaw Avenue
Cincinnatti, OH 45237
CEO: Mrs. Deni TaTo
(513) 641-3700 Fax: (513) 641-0744

CORDOBA CORPORATION
Corporate Headquarters
800 Wilshire Blvd., Suite 1300
Los Angeles, CA 90017
CEO: Mr. George L. Pla
(213) 895-0224 Fax: (213)895-6677
Email: vpla@cordobacorp.com
Web: http://www.cordobacorp.com

Sacramento Office
400 Capital Mall, Suite 1850
Sacramento, CA 95814
(916) 772-1465 Fax: (916) 999-9999
Email: kmiddleton@cordobacorp.com

Oakland Office
1300 Clay Street, Suite 840
Oakland, CA 94612
(510) 208-0200 Fax: (510) 208-0206
Email: vruiz@cordobacorp.com

CORDOVA BOLT, INC.
5601 Dolly Avenue
Buena Park, CA 90621
CEO: Mr. Moses Cordova
(714) 739-7500 Fax: (714) 994-2661
Web: http://www.cordovabolt.com

CORELLA ELECTRIC WIRE AND CABLE, INC.
Corporate Office
3200 North Central Avenue, Suite 2550
Phoenix, AZ 85012
CEO: Mr. John Corella
(602) 274-5709 Fax: (602) 265-4202

COREV AMERICA, INC.
11620 Brittmoore Park Drive
Houston, TX 77041
CEO: Mr. Mauricio Pineda
(713) 937-3437 Fax: (713) 937-9765
Email: mauri@corev.com
Web: http://www.corev.com

CORNEJO & SONS, INC.
P.O. Box 16204
Wichita, KS 67216
CEO: Mr. Ron Cornejo
(316) 522-5100 Fax: (316) 522-8187

CORPORATE SYSTEMS GROUP, INC.
Miami Office
7255 Corporate Center Drive
Miami, FL 33126

CEO: Mr. Anthony X. Siva
(305) 913-8800 or (305) 507-1188
(888) 507-4CSG Fax: (305) 913-8855
Web: http://www.csgserv.com

Boca Raton Office
6531 Park of Commerce, Suite C180
Boca Raton, FL 33487
(561) 999-0073/(888) 485-5CSG
Fax: (561) 999-0074

COSTA ENTERPRISES INC.
6630 Patterson Pass, Suite A
Livermore, CA 94550
CEO: Mr. Jose Munoz
(925) 606-6495 Fax: (925) 606-8732

**CREATIVE ASSOCIATES INTERNATIONAL,
INC.**
5301 Wisconsin Avenue, NW., Suite 700
Washington, DC 20015
CEO: M. Charito Kruvant
(202) 966-5804 Fax: (202) 363-4771
Email: creative@caii-dc.com
Web: http://www.caii-dc.com

CRISTINA FOODS, INC.
1056 W. Lake Street
Chicago, IL 60607
CEO: Mr. Cesar A. Dovalina Jr.
(312) 829-0360 Fax: (312) 829-0408

CSI CARDENAS, INC.
42265 Yearego
Sterling Heights, MI 48314
CEO: Mr. Curtis Cardenas
(810) 726-1700 Fax: (810) 726-1440

CSR GROUP
139 Chestnut Street
Nutley , NJ 07110
CEO: Mr. Francisco J. Salas
(973) 667-1600 Fax: (973) 667-6461
Web: http://www.csrgroup.com

CSSI, INC.
Corporate Headquarters
600 Maryland Avenue, SW., Suite 890
Washington, DC 20024
CEO: Ms. Cindy Castillo
(202) 863-2175
Email: info@cssiinc.com
Web: http://www.cssiinc.com

**CUIDADO CASERO HOME HEALTH
SERVICES, INC.**
600 Six Flags Drive
Arlington, TX 76011
CEO: Ms. Carmen Santiago
(817) 640-0646 Fax: (817) 652-9659
Email: cuidadocasero@aol.com

D

DAVID L. AMADOR, INC.
762 N. Loren Avenue
Azusa , CA 91702
CEO: Mr. David L. Amador
(626) 334-2011 Fax: (626) 969-8406

DAVID MONTOYA CONSTRUCTION, INC.
P.O. Box 10254
Albuquerque, NM 87184
CEO: Mr. David Montoya
(505) 898-6330 Fax: (505) 898-4331

DAVILA PHARMACY, INC.
1423 Guadalupe
San Antonio, TX 78207
CEO: Mr. Rodolfo Davila
(210) 226-5293 Fax: (210) 224-9257

DAVILA PLUMBING
5309 Bandera Road
San Antonio, TX 78238
CEO: Mr. Tony Davila
(210) 684-9640 Fax: (210) 684-1753

DELGADO ERECTORS INC.
14233 Dante
Dolton, IL 60419
CEO: Mr. Dominic Delgado
(708) 841-9095 Fax: (708) 841-9365

DENEBA SOFTWARE
1150 NW. 72nd Avenue
Miami, FL 33126
CEO: Mr. Manny Menendez
(305) 596-5644 Fax: (305) 273-9069
Email: sales@deneba.com
Web: http://www.deneba.com

DESERT SUN MOTORS
2600 N. White Sands Blvd.
Alamogordo, NM 88310
CEO: Mr. Bobby Martinez
(505) 437-7530 Fax: (505) 434-2097
Web: http://www.desertsunmotors.com

DEVELOPMENT ASSOCIATES, INC.
1730 North Lynn Street
Arlington, VA 22209
CEO: Mr. Leveo V. Sanchez
(703) 276-0677 Fax: (703) 276-0432
Email: devassoc@devassoc1.com
Web: http://www.devassoc1.com

DGR ASSOCIATES, INC.
1002 N. Scott Avenue
Belton, MO 64012
CEO: Ms. Belinda A. Davis
(816) 322-4452 Fax: (816) 322-8014

DIAZ FOODS WHOLESALE
5500 Bucknell Drive
Atlanta, GA 30336
CEO: Mr. Rene Diaz
(404) 344-5421
(800) 394-4639 Fax: (404) 344-3003
Email: DiazFoods@DiazFoods.com
Web: http://www.diazfoods.com

DIEZ MANAGEMENT SYSTEMS, INC.
12724 Directors Loop
Lake Ridge, VA 22192
CEO: Mr. Roberto Diez
(703) 494-9745 Fax: (703) 494-8946
Email: rdiez@erols.com
Web: http://www.diezmanagement.com

DIXIE NUMERICS LLC
P.O. Box 337
Forest Park, GA 30298
CEO: Mr. Rod Suarez
(404) 366-7427

DYNAMIC SYSTEMS, INC.
Corporate Headquarters
120 W. Bellevue, Suite 10
Pasadena, CA 91105
CEO: Mr. Carlos A. Stygar
(626) 795-4101 Fax: (626) 683-2767
Web: http://www.dynasys.com

27281 Las Rambles, Suite 200
Mission Viejo, CA 92691
(949) 367-5119 Fax: (949) 367-5111

350 Ward Avenue, Suite 106
Honolulu, HI 96814
(808) 585-2882 Fax: (800) 886-3828

E

E & M CONCRETE CONSTRUCTION, INC.
P.O. Box 50512
Oxnard, CA 93030
CEO: Mr. Edmundo Mendez
(805) 658-2888 Fax: (805) 650-9428
Email: emc@jetlink.net
Web: http://www.emconcrete.com

EAGLE BRANDS, INC.
3201 NW 72nd Avenue
Miami, FL 33122
CEO: Mr. Carlos De La Cruz
(305) 594-6971 Fax: (305) 477-6122

EBCO INC.
1371 Brummel Avenue
Elk Grove Village, IL 60007
CEO: Mr. Bill Bernardo
(847) 956-7700 Fax: (847) 364-0364
Web: http://www.ebco-inc.com

EL DORADO COMMUNICATIONS, INC.
1980 Post Oak Blvd., Suite 1500
Houston, TX 77056
CEO: Mr. Thomas H. Castro
(713) 993-8000 Fax: (713) 993-8054

EL DORADO FURNITURE
Headquarters
4200 NW 157th Street
North Miami, FL 33054
CEO: Mr. Manuel Capo
(305) 624-2400
Web: http://www.eldoradofurniture.com

EL PASO FAIRVIEW FOODS, INC.
7231 Brogan Drive
El Paso, TX 79915
CEO: Mr. Al Garcia
(915) 772-2720 Fax: (915) 772-2748

ELAN INTERNATIONAL
620 NewPort Center Drive, 11th Floor
NewPort Beach, CA 92660
CEO: Ms. Lucia De Garcia
(949) 721-6644 Fax: (949) 653-9855

ELECTRIC MACHINERY ENTERPRISES
P.O. Box 9658
Tampa, FL 36674
CEO: Mr. Jaime Jurado
(813) 238-5010 Fax: (813) 238-4900

EMERGENCY 24, INC.
National Headquarters
4179 W. Irving Park Road
Chicago, IL 60641-2906
CEO: Mr. Dante Monteverde
(773) 777-0707
(800) 877-EM24 Fax: (773) 286-1992
Email: info@emergency24.com
Web: http://www.emergency24.com

Los Angeles Office
2721 Saturn Street
Brea, CA 92821-6705
(714) 792-0300
(800) 444-EM24 Fax: (714) 792-2869

Detroit Office
25300 Evergreen
Southfield, MI 48075
(248) 357-5797
(800) 359-EM24 Fax: (248) 357-0918

Washington, DC Office
8607 2nd Avenue, Suite 305
Silver Spring, MD 20910
(301) 588-3700
(800) 776-EM24 Fax: (301) 565-3062

EMPIRE MAINTENANCE CO., INC.
Corporate Headquarters
624 South Palm Avenue
Alhambra, CA 91803
CEO: Mr. Ruben Garcia
(626) 289-8755
(323) 283-6123 Fax: (626) 281-4263
Web: http://www.empiremaintenance.com

Southern California
9187 Chesapeake Drive
San Diego, CA 92123
(619) 715-1574 Fax: (619) 715-1579

Southern California
841 West Fairmont Drive, Suite 4
Tempe, CA 85282
(602) 967-1201 Fax: (602) 967-1271

EVERGLADE STEEL CORPORATION
P.O. Box 667510
Miami, FL 33166-7510
CEO: Mr. Orlando Gomez
(305) 591-9460 Fax: (305) 592-1037

EXPRESS TRAVEL OF MIAMI, INC.
6351 Sunset Drive
South Miami, FL 33143
CEO: Ms. Olga Ramudo
(305) 341-1200 Fax: (305) 341-1211
Web: http://www.expresstravelmia.com

F. GAVIÑA & SONS, INC.
2369 E. 51st Street
Vernon, CA 90058
CEO: Mr. Pedro Gaviña
(323) 582-0671
Email: sales@gavina.com
Web: http://www.gavina.com

F.R. ALEMAN & ASSOCIATES, INC.
10305 NW. 41st Street, Suite 200
Miami, FL 33178
CEO: Mr. Frank R. Aleman
(305) 591-8777 Fax: (305) 599-8749
Email: fraaino@gate.net

F&L CONSTRUCTION INC.
8095 W., 21st Lane
Hialeah Garden, FL 33016
CEO: Mr. Julio Batista
(305) 362-7277 Fax: (305) 362-3424

FALCON INTERNATIONAL BANK
Main Bank
5219 McPherson Road
Laredo, TX 78041
CEO: Mr. Adolfo E. Gutierrez
(956) 723-2265
Web: http://www.falconbank.com

Downtown Branch
801 Matamoros
Laredo, TX 78041
(956) 723-9855

FAR WEST MEATS
7759 Victoria Ave.
Highland, CA 92346
CEO: Mr. Thomas Serrato III
(909) 305-1047 Fax: (909) 394-7415
Email: sales@farwestmeats.com
Web: http://www.farwestmeats.com

FARMA INTERNATIONAL
9501 Old South Dixie Hwy.
Miami, FL 33156-2820
CEO: Mr. George Medina
(305) 670-4416 Fax: (305) 670-4417
Email: farma1@aol.com
Web: http://www.farmainternational.com

FASTEEL, INC.
7379 Pagedale Industrial Ct.
St. Louis, MO 63133
CEO: Mr. Richard D. Ruiz
(314) 726-1500
(800) 536-5880 Fax: (314) 726-4744
Web: http://www.fasteel.com

FIELD LINING SYSTEMS, INC.
6970 NW. Grand Avenue
Glendale, AZ 85301
CEO: Mr. Phillip Ramos
(623) 842-1255
(888) 382-9301 Fax: (623) 930-1766
(888) 382-9302
Web: http://www.fieldliningsystems.com

FLORIDA LUMBER CO.
2431 NW., 20th Street
Miami, FL 33142
CEO: Mr. Ignacio Perez
(305) 635-6412 Fax: (305) 633-4054
Email: info@floridalumber.com
Web: http://www.floridalumber.com

FORCE 3, INC.
2147 Priest Bridge Drive, Suite 1
Crofton, MD 21114
CEO: Mr. Rocky D. Cintron
(301) 261-0204 Fax: (410) 721-5624
Email: rocky@force3.com
Web: http://www.force3.com

FORTUN INSURANCE
365 Palarmo Avenue
Coral Gables, FL 33134
CEO: Mr. Hector D. Fortun
(305) 445-3535 Fax: (305) 447-9478
Web: http://www.fortuninsurance.com

FOURTH GENERATION SERVICES, INC.
4700 Rochester Road
Troy, MI 48098
CEO: Mr. Juan Vazquez
(248) 680-9400
(248) 524-9600 Fax: (248) 680-9403
Web: http://www.4serv.com

FRED LOYA INSURANCE AGENCY, INC.
1800 Lee Trevino, Suite 201
El Paso, TX 79936
CEO: Mr. Fred Loya Jr.
(915) 590-5692 Fax: (800) 387-8220
Email: customerservice@visionmga.com
Web: http://www.fredloyainsurance.com

FRU-VEG MARKETING, INC.
2300 NW., 102 Avenue
Miami, FL 33172
CEO: Ms. Conchita Espinosa
(305) 591-7766 Fax: (305) 591-7665
Email: fruveg@gate.net
Web: http://www.fruveg.com

FUENTEZ SYSTEMS CONCEPTS INC.
Corporate Headquarters
2460 Remount Road, Suite 102
N. Charleston, SC 29406
CEO: Mr. Brian Alderson

(843) 745-9496 Fax: (843) 566-9372
Email: Balderson@fuentez.com
Web: http://www.fuentez.com

California Office
6160 Fairmont Avenue, Suite A
San Diego, CA 92120
(619) 280-7477 Fax: (619) 280-6585

Virginia Office
7426 Alban Station Road, Suite A-100
Springfield, VA 22150
(703) 455-1791 Fax: (703) 455-1799

Virginia Office
1801-P Sara Drive
Norfolk, VA 23320
(757) 366-4080 Fax: (757) 366-9041

Virginia Office
600 Water Street, Suite F
Charlottesville, VA 22320
(804) 295-7357 Fax: (804) 455-1799

West Virginia Office
1 Discovery Place, Suite 2
Martinsburg, WV 25401
304) 263-0163 ext.201 Fax: (304) 263-0702

FUTURE PACKAGING INC.
1500 Duane Avenue
Santa Clara, CA 95054
CEO: Mr. Rufino Vega
(408) 988-5444 Fax: (408) 986-8682

G

G.M. CONSTRUCTION, INC.
6002 N. Michigan Road
Indianapolis, IN 46228
CEO: Mr. Charles J. Garcia
(317) 254-3240 Fax: (317) 254-3250
Email: gmconinc@aol.com

GANCEDO LUMBER CO.
4300 NW., 30th Avenue
Miami, FL 33147
CEO: Mr. Martin Perez
(305) 836-7030 Fax: (305) 836-8032

GARCIA & ASSOCIATES, INC.
418 Oak Street
Bakersfield, CA 93304
CEO: Mr. Robert Garcia Jr.
(661) 325-9207 Fax: (661) 325-8935
Email: info@garciainsurance.com
Web: http://www.garciainsurance.com

GATEWAY CHEVROLET MOTOR CO., INC.
15000 E. Firestorm Blvd.
La Mirada, CA 90638
CEO: Mr. Mike Padilla
(562) 220-2300 Fax: (714) 562-0428

GATOR INDUSTRIES, INC.
1000 SE 8th Street
Hialeah, FL 33010
CEO: Mr. Guillermo Miranda
(305) 888-5000 Fax: (305) 888-3869
Web: http://www.gatorindustries.com

GC MICRO CORPORATION
Corporate Headquarters
25 Leveroni Court
Novato, CA 94949
CEO: Ms. Belinda Guadarrama
(415) 883-8838 Fax: (415) 883-9393
Web: http://www.gcmicro.com

GCI INFORMATION SERVICES, INC.
7927 Jones Branch Drive, Suite 400
McLean , VA 22102
CEO: Mr. Arthur F. Garcia,Jr
(703) 287-0200 Fax: (703) 506-0847
Web: http://www.gvi-info.com

GEMINI ASSOCIATES, INC.
Corporate Office
27126A Paseo Espada, Suite 1605
San Juan Capistrano, CA 92675
CEO: Mr. Robert L. Manciet
(949) 240-9200
(714) 479-0010 Fax: (949) 240-0302
(714) 479-0011
Web: http://www.federalsales.com

GEOLOGICS CORPORATION
5285 Shawnee Road, Suite 210
Alexandria, VA 22312
CEO: Mr. Fernando Arroyo
(703) 750-4000 Fax: (703) 750-4010
Web: http://www.geologics.com

GOLDEN GATE AIR FREIGHT, INC.
1809 Sabre Street
Hayward, CA 94545
CEO: Mr. John R. Cardenas
(510) 785-5720
(800) 638-6638 Fax: (510) 786-3277
Email: ggaf@ggaf.com
Web: http://www.ggaf.com

GONZALES LABOR SYSTEMS, INC.
Corporate Office
3008-A W. Division Street
Arlington, TX 76012
CEO: Mr. Cruz Gonzales
(817) 261-5005
(877) 261-5005 Fax: (817) 261-0466
Email: mail@gls-temps.com
Web: http://www.glstemps.com

Fort Worth Office
1523 Jacksboro Hwy.
Fort Worth, TX 76106
(817) 626-9880 Fax: (817) 626-9888

Dallas Office
1499 Regal Row
Dallas, TX 75247
(214) 638-5601 Fax: (214) 638-1674

Garland Office
1436 Buckingham
Garland, TX 75042
(972) 205-0909 Fax: (972) 205-0783

Terrell Office
306 N. Adelaide
Terrell, TX 75160
(972) 524-4080 Fax: (972) 563-2651

GONZALEZ DESIGN GROUP
Corporate Headquarters
29401 Stephenson Highway
Madison Heights, MI 48071
CEO: Mr. Rick Gonzalez
(248) 548-6010 Fax: (248) 548-3160
Email: gonzalez@gonzalez-group.com
Web: http://www.gonzalez-group.com

GOVERNMENT MICRO RESOURCES, INC.
7203 Gateway Court
Manassas, VA 20109
CEO: Mr. Humberto A. Pujals
(703) 330-1199 Fax: (703) 330-9646
Web: http://www.gmri.com

GOYA FOODS, INC.
100 Seaview Drive
Secaucus, NJ 07096
CEO: Mr. Joseph A. Unanue
(201) 348-4900 Fax: (201) 348-6609
Web: http://www.goya.com

GRACIOUS HOME
Corporate Office
51220, 3rd Avenue
New York, NY 10021
CEO: Mr. Natan Wekselbam
(212) 517-6300 Fax: (212) 249-1534
Email: eastside@gracioushome.com
Web: http://www.gracioushome.com

Westside Store
1992 Broadway, at 67th Street
New York, NY 10023
(212) 231-7800 Fax: (212) 875-9976
Email: westside@gracioushome.com

Eastside Store
1217 & 1220 3rd Avenue, at 70th Street
New York, NY 10021
(212) 517-6300 Fax: (212) 249-1534
Email: eastside@gracioushome.com

GROWERS FORD TRACTOR CO.
8501 NW., 58th Street
Miami, FL 33166
CEO: Mr. Norberto Lopez
(305) 592-7890 Fax: (305) 477-1659
Email: sales@growersford.com
Web: http://www.growersford.com

2695 Davie Road
Davie, FL 33314
CEO: Mr. Norberto Lopez
(954) 916-1020 Fax: (954) 916-0080

GSC INDUSTRIES
6727 Guion Road
Indianapolis , IN 46268
CEO: Mr. Manuel T. Gonzales
(317) 290-9400 Fax: (317) 290-0543
Web: http://www.gscind.com

GSE CONSTRUCTION
1020 Shannon Court
Livermore, CA 94550
CEO: Mr. Orlando Gutierrez
(925) 447-0292 Fax: (925) 447-0962
Email: gseconstruction@msn.com
Web: http://www.gseconstruction.com

GTC, INC.
216 W. Florence Avenue
Inglewood, CA 90301
CEO: Mr. Albert Barrios
(310) 673-8422 Fax: (310) 672-2905

GULF TILE DISTRIBUTORS OF FLORIDA, INC.
2318 W. Columbus Drive
Tampa, FL 33607
CEO: Mr. Frank J. Garcia
(813) 251-8807 Fax: (813) 251-8911

GUS MACHADO FORD, INC.
1200 West 49th Street
Hialaeh, FL 33012
CEO: Mr. Gus Machado
(305) 822-3211 Fax: (305) 820-2505
Web: http://www.gusmachadoford.com

GUTIERREZ-PALMENBERG, INC.
Corporate Office
2922 West Clarendon Avenue
Phoenix, AZ 85017
CEO: Mr. Gilbert T. Gutierrez
(602) 234-0696 Fax: (602) 234-0699
Web: http://www.gpieng.com

H

H & H FOODS
1/2 Mile East Expressway 83
Mercedes, TX 78570
CEO: Mr. Liborio Hinojosa
(956) 565-6363 Fax: (956) 565-4108
Email: hfoods@rgv.net
Web: http://www.rgv.net/hhfoods/

HAMILTON BANCORP, INC.
Corporate Headquarters, Doral Branch
3750 N.W. 87 Avenue
Miami, FL 33178
CEO: Mr. Eduardo A. Masferrer
(305) 717-5500 Fax: (305) 717-5556
Email: doral_mgr@hamiltonbank.com
Web: http://www.hamiltonbank.com

Airport Branch
3901 N.W. 7th Street
Miami, FL 33126
(305) 649-3901 Fax: (305) 541-7825
Email: airport_mgr@hamiltonbank.com

Brickell Branch
1000 Brickell Avenue
Miami, FL 33131
(305) 530-3800 Fax: (305) 530-3918
Email: brickell_mgr@hamiltonbank.com

West Palm Beach
2090 Palm Beach Lakes Blvd.
West Palm Beach, FL 33880
(561) 683-8787 Fax: (561) 683-5598
Email: wpalm_mgr@hamiltonbank.com

Tampa Branch
2203 N. Lois Avenue
Tampa , FL 33607
(813) 876-2500 Fax: (813) 872-0652
Email: tampa_mgr@hamiltonbank.com

Winter Haven Branch
1120 1st Street South
Winter Haven, FL 33880
(941) 294-7567 Fax: (941) 293-5012
Email: winter_mgr@hamiltonbank.com

Sarasota Branch
1790 Main Street
Sarasota, FL 34236
(941) 954-7747 Fax: (941) 954-4332
Email: sarasota_mgr@hamiltonbank.com

Puerto Rico Branch
416 Ponce de Leon Avenue
San Juan , PR 00918
(787) 753-0700 Fax: (787) 753-9315
Email: sanjuan_mgr@hamiltonbank.com

Weston Branch
2700 Commerce Pkwy.
Weston, FL 33331
(954) 217-2150 Fax: (954) 217-2155
Email: weston_mgr@hamiltonbank.com

HARVARD CUSTOM MANUFACTURING
3714 Bluestein Drive, Suite 600
Austin, TX 78721
CEO: Mr. Manny Chavez
(512) 478-6900 Fax: (512) 478-6909
Email: tgraves@harvardgrp.com
Web: http://www.harvardgrp.com

HEDGES CONSTRUCTION CORPORATION
4405 Mall Blvd., Suite 100
Union City, GA 30291
CEO: Mr. Thomas A. Kalb
(770) 969-5522 Fax: (770) 969-6364
Web: http://www.hedgescorp.com

HERMAN-MILES TRUCKING, INC.
10 Leigh Fisher Blvd.
El Paso , TX 79906
CEO: Mr. Joe Wardy
(915) 779-7762
(800) 288-8463
Email: info@hermanmiles.com
Web: http://www.hermanmiles.com

HERNANDEZ COS. INC.
3734 E. Anne Street
Phoenix, AZ 85040
CEO: Mr. Chris Hernandez
(602) 438-7825 Fax: (602) 438-6558
Email: herco@dancris.com
Web: http://www.hernandezcompanies.com

HERNANDEZ ENGINEERING
17625 El Camino Real, Suite 200
Houston, TX 77058
CEO: Mr. Miguel Hernandez
(281) 280-5159 Fax: (281) 480-7525
Web: http://www.hernandez-eng.com

HERNANDEZ ENTERPRISES, INC.
901 Indiana, Suite 580
Wichita, TX 76301
CEO: Mr. Joe Hernandez
(940) 723-9116 Fax: (940) 723-9128

HISPANIC MANAGEMENT SERVICES CO.
P.O. Box 5809
Takoma Park, MD 20913
CEO: Ms. Isabel Martinez
(202) 882-8934 Fax: (202) 726-1299
Email: hmsdc@aol.com
Web: http://www.hmsdc.com

HJ FORD
Arlington Center
1111 Jeff Davis Hwy., Suite 808
Arlington, VA 22202
CEO: Mr. Don Jorge Alducin
(703) 416-6500 Fax: (703) 416-6501
Web: http://www.hjford.com

Dayton Center
2940 Presidential Drive, Suite 250
Fairborn, OH 45324
(937) 427-1300 Fax: (937) 427-2958

Lexington Park Center
22300 Exploration Drive, Suite 100
Lexington Park, MD 20653
(301) 866-6400 Fax: (301) 866-6401

Mechanicsburg Center
940 Century Drive
Mechanicsburg, PA 17055
(717) 795-5990 Fax: (717) 795-5994

HOLMAN'S INC.
Corporate Headquarters
6201 Jefferson St., NE
Albuquerque, NM 87109
CEO: Mr. Tony Trujillo
(505) 343-0007 Fax: (505) 343-3562
Email: info@holmans.com
Web: http://www.holmans.com

Los Alamos Office
114 Central Park Square
Los Alamos, NM 87544
(505) 661-3552 Fax: (505) 662-4310

Tempe Office
1320 South Priest Dr., Suite 102
Tempe, AZ 85281
(480) 967-0032 Fax: (480) 967-8726
Email: AZ-info@holmans.com

HONSHY ELECTRIC CO., INC.
7345 SW. 41st Street
Miami, FL 33155
CEO: Mr. Manuel G. Diaz
(305) 264-5500 Fax: (305) 266-3159

HURLEN CORPORATION
9841 Bell Ranch Drive
Santa Fe Springs, CA 90670
CEO: Mr. I. Jay Hurtado
(562) 941-5330 Fax: (562) 941-4750
Email: info@hurlen.com
Web: http://www.hurlen.com

HUSCO INTERNATIONAL
World Headquarters
W.239 N. 218 Pewaukee Road
Waukesha, WI 53188
CEO: Mr. Augustin A. Ramirez
(262) 547-0261 Fax: (262) 513-4514
Email: HUSCO Webmaster@huscointl.com
Web: http://www.huscointl.com

European Headquarters
6 Rivington Road
Runcon, Cheshire WA, 3DT England
(44) 192-8701888 Fax: (44) 192-8710813

Pacific Rim Headquarters
Rm. 301-302, #5, Lane 31, Yazhi Road,
Xinzhuang
Shanghai, 201100, P.R. China
(86) 21-64132064 Fax: (86) 21-64137582
Email: China Sales@public1.sta.net.cn

I

IDEAL DAIRY
P.O. Box 1357
Perth Amboy, NJ 08862
CEO: Mr. Rafael Mendez
(732) 442-6337 Fax: (732) 442-8227
Web: http://www.idealdairy.com
http://www.tropicalcheese.com

IDEAL STEEL AND BUILDERS' SUPPLIES, INC.
10068 Industrial Drive
Hamburg, MI 48139
CEO: Mr. Frank Venegas, Jr.
(810) 231-1722 Fax: (810) 231-9568
Web: http://www.idealsteel.com

IKE BEHAR APPAREL & DESIGN
Ike Behar Store
12801 W. Sunrise Blvd.
Saw Grass Mills Mall, Suite 1047
Sunrise, FL 33323
CEO: Mr. Isaac Behar
(954) 846-9369 Fax: (954) 846-1109
Email: custserv@ikebehar.com
Web: http://www.ikebehar.com

Corporate Office
13955 NW., 60th Avenue
Miami Lakes, FL 33014
(305) 557-5212 Fax: (305) 557-5232

INCORE CONSTRUCTION, INC.
P.O. Box 790189
San Antonio, TX 78279
CEO: Mr. Frank Casias
(210) 494-7721 Fax: (210) 491-0322

INDOTRONIX INTERNATIONAL CORPORATION (IIC)
331 Main Mall
Poughkeepsie, NY 12601
CEO: Mr. Babu Mandava
(914) 473-1137 Fax: (914) 473-1197
Web: http://www.iic.com

INDUSTRIAL COMPONENTS
2250 NW 102 Ave.
Miami, FL 33172
CEO: Mr. Abelardo Gomez
(305) 477-0387 Fax: (305) 594-7332

INFORMATICS CORPORATION
Headquarters
1933 Jadwin Avenue, Suite 210
Richland, WA 99352
CEO: Mr. Arnold Whipple Lara
(509) 946-9900 Fax: (509) 946-9800
Email: Arnold_Whipple@informaticscorp.com
Web: http://www.informaticscorp.com

Northwest Division
14240 Interurban Avenue, So., Suite 216
Seattle, WA 98168
(206) 444-4414 Fax: (206) 444-4418
Email: Raoul_Mebane@informaticscorp.com

Vancouver Office
400 E. Evergreen Blvd., Suite 218
Vancouver, WA 98660
(360) 695-6102 Fax: (360) 695-7384
Email: Don_McCormick@informaticscorp.com

Denver Office
9035 Wadsworth Parkway Suite 3840
Westminster, CO 80030
(303) 424-8676 Fax: (303) 424-9046
Email: Mike_Cappello@informaticscorp.com

San Antonio Office
8610 Broadway Suite 420
San Antonio, TX 78217
(210) 804-4325 Fax: (210) 832-0018
Email: David_Rhodes@informaticscorp.com

Oak Ridge Office
574-A Oak Ridge Turnpike
Oak Ridge, TN 37830
(865) 482-8900 Fax: (865) 482-1745
Email: John_Wagoner@informaticscorp.com

INSURANCE MARKETERS, INC.
141 Almeria
Coral Gables, FL 33134
CEO: Mr. Evarist Milian Jr.
(305) 442-9507 Fax: (305) 447-8527
Email: info@insurancemrkt.com
Web: http://www.insurancemrkt.com

INTEGRATED TELECOMMUNICATIONS, INC.
P.O. Box 608
Spring, TX 77383
CEO: Mr. Charlie Castillo Jr.
(281) 449-3410

INTERAMERICA TECHNOLOGIES CORPORATION
Corporate Office
8150 Leesburg Pike, Suite 1400
Vienna, VA 22182
CEO: Mr. Juan J. Gutierrez
(703) 893-3514 Fax: (703) 893-1741
Email: sales@hg.interamerica.com
Web: http://www.interamerica.com
Congressional Sales
330 Pennsylvania Avenue, SE
Washington, DC 20003
CEO: Mr. Juan J. Gutierrez
(202) 547-7450 Fax: (202) 544-8110
Email: sales@ch.interamerica.com
Web: http://www.interamerica.com

INTERAMERICAN BANK
Main Branch
9190 Coral Way
Miami, FL 33165
CEO: Mr. Agustin C. Velasco
(305) 223-1434
Web: http://www.interamericanbank.com

West Miami Branch
1350 Red Road
Miami, FL 33144
(305) 261-1415

Kendall Branch
12855 SW., 88th Street
Miami, FL 33186
(305) 380-0990

Hialeah Branch
4090 West 12th Avenue
Hialeah, FL 33012
(305) 824-0001

INTERAMERICAN TRADING & PRODUCTS CORP.
P.O. Box 402427
Miami Beach, FL 33140
CEO: Mr. Claudio Feuermann
(305) 885-9666 Fax: (305) 885-0402

INTERNATIONAL BANCSHARES CORPORATION
1200 San Bernardo Avenue
Laredo, TX 78040
CEO: Mr. Dennis E. Nixon
(956) 722-7611 Fax: (956) 726-6616
(956) 726-6637

INTRA-AMERICAN FOUNDATION & DRILLING CO. INC.
502 W. Watkins
Phoenix, AZ 85003
CEO: Mr. Salvador H. Altamirano
(602) 256-2843 Fax: (602) 253-6860

IQ MANAGEMENT CORPORATION
9001 Braddock Road, Suite 300
Springfield, VA 22151
CEO: Mr. Luis Quinonez
(703) 425-4900 Fax: (703) 425-4930
Email: services@iqmanagement.com
Web: http://www.iqmanagement.com

J

J.L. PATTERSON & ASSOCIATES, INC.
Main Office
725 Town & Country Road, Suite 100
Orange, CA 92868
CEO: Ms. Jacqueline L. Patterson
(714) 835-6355 Fax: (714) 835-6671
Email: macanas@jlpatterson.com
Web: http://www.jlpatterson.com
Regional Office
1800-112th Avenue NE, Suite 210W
Bellevue, WA 98004
(425) 688-8694 Fax: (425) 646-7569

J.L. STEEL, INC.
P.O. Box 1910
Roanoke, TX 76262
CEO: Mr. Oscar Trevino Jr.
(817) 430-2410 Fax: (817) 491-3831
Email: oscar@jlsteel.com
Web: http://www.cyberramp.net/~jlsitx/

J.R. INC
9223 Business Lane
Converse, TX 78109
CEO: Mr. Jesse Rodriguez
(210) 658-6364 Fax: (210) 658-0329

J&R FERNANDEZ INC.
245 N. Mountain View Avenue
Pomona, CA 91767
CEO: Mr. Jorge Fernandez
(909) 629-7279 Fax: (909) 620-1109

JARDON & HOWARD TECHNOLOGIES, INC.
5514 Lake Howell Road
Winter Park, FL 32792
CEO: Mr. James E. Jardon II
(407) 657-2727 Fax: (407) 657-5233
Web: http://www.jht.com

JAY AUTOMOTIVE SPECIALTIES, INC.
701 North Street
Berlin, PA 15530
CEO: Mr. John Sotomayor
(814) 267-4151
(800) 838-7703 Fax: (814) 267-3841
(800) 811-0410
Web: http://www.j-auto-specialties.com

JESS DIAZ TRUCKING, INC.
P.O. Box 367
La Miranda, CA 90638
CEO: Mr. Dimas Diaz
(714) 522-4800

JJJ FLOOR COVERING
4831 Passons Blvd., Unit A
Pico Rivera, CA 90660
CEO: Mr. Jose Gutierrez
(562) 692-9008 Fax: (562) 692-5979

K

K & M ENGINEERING AND CONSULTING CORPORATION
2001 L Street, NW., Suite 500
Washington, DC 20036
CEO: Mr. Michael Kappaz
(202) 728-0390 Fax: (202) 872-9174
Email: marketing@mailer.kmec.com
Web: http://www.kmec.com

KELL MUÑOZ WIGODSKY ARCHITECTS, INC.
800 NW. Loop 410, Suite 700, N. Tower
San Antonio, TX 78216
CEO: Mr. Henry R. Muñoz III
(210) 349-1163 Fax: (210) 525-1038
Email: kmw@kmw-architects.com
Web: http://www.kmw-architects.com

KFOURY CONSTRUCTION GROUP, INC.
11307 Sunset Hills Road
Reston, VA 20190-5231
CEO: Mr. Jorge Kfoury
(703) 736-1000 Fax: (703) 736-0736
Email: jKfoury@Kfoury.com
Web: http://www.Kfoury.com

KING TACO RESTAURANTS INC.
3421 East 14th Street
Los Angeles, CA 90023
CEO: Mr. Raul O. Martinez
(323) 266-3585 Fax: (323) 266-6565

KOHLY CONSTRUCTION
12227 SW., 131st Avenue
Miami, FL 33186

CEO: Mr. Gene Kohly
(305) 255-2624 Fax: (305) 255-1913

KROSSLAND CONSTRUCTION COMPANY
P.O. Box 45
Columbus, KS 66725
CEO: Mr. Ivan Krossland
(316) 429-1414 Fax: (316) 429-1412

L

L. MILTON CONSTRUCTION CORPORATION
3711 SW., 27th Street
Miami, FL 33134
CEO: Mr. Lazaro Milton
(305) 444-8326
(800) 304-9032 Fax: (305) 444-9642

L&M TECHNOLOGIES, INC.
4209 Balloon Park Road, NE.
Albuquerque, NM 87109-5802
CEO: Mr. Fred Mondragon
(505) 343-0200 Fax: (505) 343-0300
Email: fred@lmtechnologies.com
Web: http://www.lmtechnologies.com

LA AMAPOLA, INC.
7223 S. Compton Avenue
Los Angeles, CA 90001
CEO: Mr. Carlos B. Galvan
(323) 587-7118 Fax: (323) 587-2889

LA PIZZA LOCA INC.
Corporate Office
7920 Orange Thorpe Avenue, Suite 202
Buena Park, CA 90620
CEO: Mr. Alex Maruelo
(714) 670-0934 Fax: (714) 670-7849

LA REINA, INC.
P.O. Box 3042
El Centro, CA 92244
CEO: Mr. Mauro Robles
(760) 352-9182 Fax: (760) 352-9182

LA ROSA DEL MONTE EXPRESS INC.
1133-35 Tiffany Street
Bronx, NY 10459
CEO: Mr. Hiram Rodriguez
(718) 991-3300 Fax: (718) 893-1948

LA TORTILLA FACTORY
3635 Standish Avenue
Santa Rosa , CA 95407
CEO: Mr. Carlos Tamayo
(707) 586-4000
(800) 446-1516
Email: isabelg@latortillafactory.com
Web: http://www.latortillafactory.com

LASER ELECTRIC, INC.
2789 West Alameda Avenue, Unit B
Denver , CO 80219
CEO: Mr. Jose Berumen
(303) 922-5456 Fax: (303) 922-8939
Web: http://www.laserelecinc.com

LION PLASTICS, INC.
167 Fornelius Avenue
Clifton, NJ 07015
CEO: Mr. Diego De Leon
(973) 471-2071 Fax: (973) 471-0147

LOIEDERMAN ASSOCIATES, INC.
Corporate Headquarters
1390 Piccard Drive
Rockville, MD 20850
CEO: Mr. Jim Soltesz
(301) 948-2750 Fax: (301) 948-9067
Web: http://www.loiederman.com
Lanham Office
4407 Forbes Blvd.
Lanham , MD 20706
(301) 794-7555 Fax: (301) 794-7656
Frederick Office
7 North Market Street
Frederick, MD 21701
(301) 696-1240 Fax: (301) 831-4865
Waldorf Office
6E Industrial Park Drive
Waldorf, MD 20607
CEO: Mr. Jim Soltesz
(301) 870-2166 Fax: (301) 870-2884

LOPEZ FOODS, INC.
9500 NW 4th Street
Oklahoma City, OK 73127

CEO: Mr. John C. Lopez
(405) 789-7500 Fax: (405) 499-0114
Web: www.lopezfoods.com

LOS RANCHOS RESTAURANTS, INC.
125 SW. 107th Avenue
Miami, FL 33174
CEO: Mr. Julio Somoza
(305) 229-7002 Fax: (305) 229-7006

LOU SOBH PONTIAC BUICK GMC, INC.
2473 Pleasant Hill Road
Duluth, GA 30096
CEO: Mr. Lou Sobh
(770) 232-0099 Fax: (770) 232-2695
Web: http://www.lousobh.com

LOVE CHRYSLER, PLYMOUTH
4331 South Staples
Corpus Christi, TX 78411
CEO: Ms. Marion Luna Brem
(361) 991-5683 Fax: (361) 991-2351
Email: lovechry@aol.com
Web: http://www.lovechryslerplymouth.com

LUGO CONSTRUCTION INC.
6423 Pacific Highway East
Fife, WA 98424
CEO: Mr. Adrian Lugo
(253) 838-7655 Fax: (253) 874-0307
Web: http://www.lugoconst.com

LUNA BACARDI GROUP
Corporate Headquarters
1625 17th Street, Unit #7
Santa Monica, CA 90404
CEO: Mr. Gregorio M. Bennett
(310) 314-5252 Fax: (310) 314-5262
Web: http://www.lunabacardi.com

M

MAC AEROSPACE CORPORATION
14301-I Sullyfield Circle
Chantilly, VA 20151-1630
CEO: Mr. Javier Rodriguez
(703) 502-8300 Fax: (703) 502-8303
Web: http://www.macaero.com

MAC ENTERPRISES
1801 Howard Street
Detroit, MI 48216
CEO: Mr. Dan Hess
(313) 963-6114 Fax: (313) 963-6217

MACK SALES OF SOUTH FLORIDA, INC.
Miami
6801 NW 74th Avenue
Miami, FL 33166
CEO: Mr. Alfredo Pernas
(305) 883-8506 Fax: (305) 883-5125
Email: apernas@macksales.com
Web: http://www.macksales.com
Pompano Beach
1490 NW 22nd Street
Pompano Beach, FL 33069
(954) 984-9494 Fax: (954) 984-9493
Riviera Beach
7151 Industrial Drive
S. Riviera Beach, FL 33404
(561) 842-6225 Fax: (561) 863-6836

MACRO-Z-TECHNOLOGY CO.
4761 Lincoln Avenue
Cypress, CA 90630
CEO: Mr. Brian Zatica
(714) 821-9596

MAGIC VALLEY CONCRETE, INC.
P.O. Box 1941
Mission, TX 78572
CEO: Mr. Rufino Garza
(956) 581-7429 Fax: (956) 581-1083

MALACO INTERNATIONAL INC.
1990 N. California Blvd., Suite 608
Walnut Creek, CA 94596
CEO: Mr. Peter Llama
(925) 280-8710 Fax: (925) 280-4580

MANUFACTURED CONCRETE, LTD.
17910 IH-10 West, Suite 300
San Antonio, TX 78257
CEO: Mr. Carlos Cerna
(210) 690-1705 Fax: (210) 690-1755
Web: http://www.manco-satx.com

MARIMON BUSINESS SYSTEMS, INC.
Houston Office
1500 North Post Oak, Suite 100

Houston, TX 77055
CEO: Ms. Yolanda B. Marimon
(713) 686-6601 Fax: (713) 686-6676
Email: marimon@marimoninc.com
Web: http://www.marimoninc.com

Dallas-Ft. Worth Metroplex
8001 Jetstar, Suite 175
Irving, TX 75063
(972) 929-4445
(972) 717-1300 Fax: (972) 929-4446

San Antonio & Austin Office
1077 Central Parkway, Suite 150
San Antonio, TX 78232
(210) 495-9494 Fax: (210) 495-9660

MARINA SQUARE AUTO CENTER
1152 Marina Blvd.
San Leandro, CA 94577
(510) 638-4000
Web: http://www.marinaauto.com

MARISA INDUSTRIES, INC.
2965 Lapeer Road
Auburn Hills , MI 48326
CEO: Mr. Jesse M. Lopez
(248) 475-9600 Fax: (248) 475-9908
Email: arbelaez@marisaind.com
Web: http://www.marisaind.com

MARKET DEVELOPMENT, INC.
600 B Street, Suite 1600
San Diego, CA 92101-4506
CEO: Ms. Loretta H. Adams
(619) 232-5628 Fax: (619) 232-0373
Email: info@mktdev.tnsofres.com
Web: http://www.mktdev.tnsofres.com

MARMAN U.S.A.
P.O. Box 22829
Tampa , FL 33622-2829
(813) 286-2503

MARTINEZ & TUREK, INC.
300 South Cedar Avenue
Rialto, CA 92376-9102
CEO: Mr. Larry Martinez
(909) 820-6800 Fax: (909) 873-3735
Web: http://www.martinezandturek.com

MAST DISTRIBUTORS, INC.
710-2 Union Parkway
Ronkonkoma, NY 11779
CEO: Mr. Jaime Santiago
(516) 471-4422
(800) 645-4420 Fax: (516) 471-2040
Web: http://www.mastd.com

MASTEC, INC.
3155 NW. 77th Avenue
Miami, FL 33122
CEO: Mr. Joel-Tomás Citron
(305) 599-1800 Fax: (305) 406-1960
Email: services@mastec.com
Web: http://www.mastec.com

MBE ELECTRIC, INC.
9920 Arlington Avenue
Riverside, CA 92503
CEO: Mr. Peter Mendoza
(909) 352-2490 Fax: (909) 352-1288

MCA COMMUNICATIONS, INC.
525 Northville
Houston, TX 77037
CEO: Mr. Richard Cortez
(281) 591-2434 Fax: (281) 591-6228
Email: mca@mcacom.com
Web: http://www.mcacom.com

MCBA, INC.
1500 Perimeter Parkway, Suite 400
Huntsville, AL 35806
CEO: Mr. John Harkins
(256) 890-2000 Fax: (256) 722-5710
Email: mcba@mcba.com
Web: http://www.mcba.com

MCBRIDE AND ASSOCIATES
5555 McLeod Road, NE
Albuquerque, NM 87109
CEO: Ms. Teresa McBride
(505) 837-7500 (800) 829-9409
Fax: (505) 837-7501
Email: tmcbride@mcbride.com
Web: http://www.mcbride.com

MCDONALD'S CORPORATION
Ocean Side Franchise
P.O. Box 1580
Ocean Side, CA 92051

CEO: Ms. Erni Sandoval
(760) 967-7775 Fax: (760) 967-5841

MCLEAN CARGO SPECIALISTS, INC.
1310 Rankin Road
Houston, TX 77073-4802
CEO: Mr. Angel F. Jimenez
(281) 443-2777 Fax: (281) 443-3777
Email: mclean@mclean-cargo.com
Web: http://www.mclean-cargo.com

MCO TRANSPORT, INC.
Wilmington Office
3301 Hwy., 421 North
P.O. Box 1320
Wilmington, NC 28402
CEO: Mr. Danny McComas
(910) 763-4531
Web: http://www.mcotransport.com

Charleston Office
3639 Sieberling Road
P.O. Box 70208
Charleston, SC 29415
(843) 552-0528

Savannah Office
6037 Commerce Court
P.O. Box 7088
Garden City, GA 31408
(912) 966-0277

Brunswick Office
1400 West Ninth Street,
Administrative Bldg., Gate 1
Brunswick, GA 31512
(912) 264-6167

MDP CONSTRUCTION, INC.
7712 Eastwood Road
Colorado Springs, CO 80919
CEO: Ms. Maria D. Perez
(719) 599-4543 Fax: (719) 260-6276

MECHANICAL HEATING SUPPLY, INC.
461 Timpson Place
Bronx, NY 10455
CEO: Mr. Frank Rivera
(718) 402-9765 Fax: (718) 585-1682

MED-NATIONAL, INC.
1010 Central Parkway South
San Antonio, TX 78232-5021
CEO: Ms. Blanca Flores Welborn
(210) 490-4515
(800) 725-6364 Fax: (210) 490-5742
Email: info@mednational.com
Web: http://www.mednational.com

MENENDEZ FINANCIAL & INSURANCE SERVICES
555 5th Street, Suite 300
Santa Rosa, CA 95401
CEO: Mr. Michael J. Menendez
(707) 578-0675 Fax: (707) 578-4245
Web: http://www.menendezfinancial.com

MERCEDES ELECTRIC SUPPLY, INC.
8550 NW, South River Drive
Miami, FL 33166
CEO: Ms. Mercedes C. La Porta
(305) 887-5550 Fax: (305) 887-8761
Email: info@mercedeselectric.com
Web: http://www.mercedeselectric.com

METRO FORD
9000 N.W. 7th Ave.
Miami, FL 33150
CEO: Mr. Lombardo Pérez
(305) 751-9711 Fax: (305) 757-4819
Email: metroford@metroford.com
Web: http://www.metroford.com

METRO PACKAGING & IMAGING
101 Moonachie Avenue
Moonachie, NJ 07074
CEO: Mr. Manuel De Torres
(201) 935-1450 Fax: (201) 935-7868

MEVATEC CORPORATION
1525 Perimeter Parkway, Suite 500
Huntsville, AL 35806
CEO: Ms. Nancy E. Archuleta
(256) 890-8000
Email: tom_houser@mevatec.com
Web: http://www.mevatec.com

MIKE LOZANO FORD MERCURY, INC.
P.O. Box 506
Floresville, TX 78114
CEO: Mr. Mike Lozano
(830) 216-4040 Fax: (830) 216-4388

MILAM & COMPANY PAINTING
1313 Herkimer
Houston, TX 77008
CEO: Mr. David Milam
(713) 869-0225 Fax: (713) 869-9528

MOLINA HEALTHCARE, INC.
One Goldenshore Drive
Long Beach, CA 90802
CEO: Mr. J. Marino Molina
(562) 435-3666 Fax: (562) 437-7235

MOLZEN-CORBIN & ASSOCIATES
2701 Miles Road
Albuquerque, NM 87106
CEO: Mr. Del Archuleta
(505) 242-5700 Fax: (505) 242-0673

MOUNTAIN POWER ELECTRICAL CONTRACTORS
P.O. Box 27043
Tucson, AZ 85726
CEO: Mr. Frank Siqueiros
(520) 294-1131
Email: mountainpower@aol.com

MOUNTAIN VISTA BUILDERS, INC.
1400 North Zaragosa
El Paso, TX 79936
CEO: Mr. Edward Santamaria
(915) 855-4690 Fax: (915) 855-3795
Email: info@mountainvista.com
Web: http://www.mountainvista.com

MURRIETTA CIRCUITS
4761 E. Hunter Avenue
Anaheim, CA 92807
CEO: Mr. Al Murrieta
(714) 970-2430 Fax: (714) 970-2406
Email: sales@murrietta.com
Web: http://www.murrieta.com

MÚSICA MÚSICA
Bosque de los Frailes, 12 Fray Inigo St.
Guaynabo, PR 00969
CEO: Mr. Francisco Famadas
(787) 789-6819 Fax: (787) 272-5306
Email: frankie@post.harvard.edu

N

NATIONAL WATER PURIFIERS CORP.
1065 E. 14th Street
Hialeah, FL 33010
CEO: Ms. Judith Garcia
(305) 887-7065 Fax: (305) 887-6209

NAVARRO DISCOUNT PHARMACIES
5959 NW 37th Avenue
Miami, FL 33142
CEO: Mr. Jose Navarro
(305) 633-3000 Fax: (305) 633-7755
Web: http://www.navarropharmacies.com

NEMESIS DISTRIBUTORS, INC.
2400 NW., 94th Avenue
Miami, FL 33172
CEO: Ms. Yolanda Caraballo
(305) 477-8822 Fax: (305) 477-8222

NEWVENTURE TECHNOLOGIES CORPORATION
176 South Road
Enfield, CT 06082-9854
CEO: Mr. Miguel Garcia
(860) 253-7000 Fax: (860) 253-5005
Email: info@ntc1.com
Web: http://www.ntc1.com

NORSAN GROUP
5060 N. Royal Atlanta Dr., Suite 30
Tucker , GA 30084
CEO: Mr. Norberto Sanchez
(770) 414-5026 Fax: (770) 414-5839
Web: http://www.fronteramexmexgrill.com

NORTHEAST CONSTRUCTION, INC.
100 Highway 70
Lakewood, NJ 08701
CEO: Mr. Juan Gutierrez
(732) 364-8200
(800) 879-8204 Fax: (732) 370-1926
Web: http://www.northeastconstruction.org

NORTHTOWNE CHEVROLET
7640 Lewis Avenue
Temperance, MI 48182
CEO: Mr. Martin Cumba
(734) 847-6711 Fax: (734) 847-3633

NORTHWESTERN MEAT, INC.
2100 Northwest 23rd Street
Miami, FL 33142
CEO: Mr. Elpidio Nuñez
(305) 633-8112 Fax: (305) 633-6907
Email: numeat@gate.net
Web: http://www.numeat.com

NUMET MACHINING
60 Old South Avenue
Stratford, CT 06615
CEO: Mr. Antonio Neto
(203) 375-4995 Fax: (203) 378-9840

O

OCEAN MAZDA
850 NW Le Jeune Road
Miami, FL 33126
CEO: Mr. Eugenio Dosal
(305) 460-7200 Fax: (305) 460-7222
Web: http://www.oceanmazda.com

OCEAN TECHNICAL SERVICES, INC.
1140 Peters Road
Harvey, LA 70058
CEO: Mr. Esteban Fernandez
(504) 364-1572
(800) 783-7442 Fax: (504) 362-5949
Email: beverly@oceantech.com
Web: http://www.oceantech.com

OFFICE SOLUTIONS BUSINESS PRODUCTS AND SERVICES, INC.
23303 La Palma Avenue
Yorba Linda, CA 92887
CEO: Mr. Robert Mairena
(714) 692-7412 Fax: (714) 692-7409
Email: sales@officesol.com
Web: http://www.officesol.com

OFFSHORE TRADERS, INC.
4828 SW., 72nd Avenue
Miami, FL 33155
CEO: Mr. Robert G. Weller
(305) 666-4001 Fax: (305) 666-2742

OFICINA LATINO AMERICANA DE NEGOCIOS
571 W. 173rd St.
New York, NY 10032
CEO: Ms. Velkis Coiscou
(212) 568-5540 Fax: (212) 928-1099

OMEGA RESEARCH, INC.
8700 W. Flagler Street, Suite 250
Miami, FL 33174
CEO: Mr. William R. Cruz & Ralph L. Cruz
(305) 485-7000 Fax: (305) 485-7300
Email: sean.davis@omegaresearch.com
Web: http://www.omegaresearch.com

OMNI METAL FINISHING, INC.
11665 Coley River Cir.
Fountain Valley, CA 92708
CEO: Mr. Victor M. Salazar
(714) 979-9414 Fax: (714) 662-5949
Email: victor@omnimetal.com
Web: http://www.omnimetal.com

ONESOURCE DISTRIBUTORS, INC.
Corporate Office
6154 Nancy Ridge Drive
San Diego, CA 92121
CEO: Mr. Robert Zamarripa
(858) 452-9001 Fax: (858) 546-0638
Web: http://www.1soucedist.com

OPERATIONAL TECHNOLOGIES CORPORATION
Corporate Office
Mail: 4100 NW Loop 410, Suite 230
San Antonio, TX 78229-4253
CEO: Mr. Robert Tokerud
(210) 731-0000 Fax: (210) 731-0008
Email: carl@otcorp.com
Web: http://www.otcorp.com

OPERATIONAL TECHNOLOGIES CORPORATION
Midwest Regional Office
Mail: 1370 North Fairfield Rd., Suite A
Beaver Creek, OH 45432
CEO: Mr. Robert Tokerud
(937) 429-0022 Fax: (937) 429-0066
Email: evermule@otcorp.com
Web: http://www.otcorp.com

Southeast Regional Office
Mail: 683 Emory Valley Rd., Suite B
Oak Ridge, TN 37830

(423) 483-8020 Fax: (423) 483-2800
Email: cpotter@otcorp.com

Alamo Downs Facility
Mail: 6900 Alamo Downs Pkwy., Suite 120
San Antonio, TX 78238
(210) 523-2020 Fax: (210) 523-1554
Email: dlucas@otcorp.com

Gulf Coast Regional Office
Mail: 3837 Plaza Tower Drive, Suite B
Baton Rouge, LA 70816
(225) 292-0035 Fax: (225) 293-1552
Email: csims@otcorp.com

Northeast Regional Office
Mail: 1248 Route 28A
Cataumet, MA 02534
(508) 563-0199 Fax: (508) 563-0198
Email: elfewins@otcorp.com

ORANGE COAST ELECTRIC SUPPLY CO., INC.
1021 Duryea
Irvine, CA 92614
CEO: Mr. Jim Espinosa
(949) 263-8900 Fax: (949) 263-6735
Email: sales@oces.com
Web: http://www.oces.com

ORIGINAL IMPRESSIONS, INC.
12900 SW., 89th Court
Miami, FL 33176-5803
CEO: Mr. Roland Garcia
(305) 233-1322 Fax: (305) 251-1190
Web: http://www.originalimpressions.com

ORION INTERNATIONAL TECHNOLOGIES, INC.
2201 Buena Vista Dr., SE, Suite 211
Albuquerque, NM 87106
CEO: Mr. Miguel Rios, Jr.
(505) 998-4000
Email: info@orionint.com
Web: http://www.orionint.com

P

PACIFIC ACCESS
3079 Kilgore Road
Rancho Cordova, CA 95670
CEO: Ms. Julie Pulos
(800) 648-6161 Fax: (916) 852-3870
Email: info@pacificaccess.net
Web: http://www.pacacc.com

PACIFIC MARINE YACHTS
Coporate Office
50 Francisco Street, Suite 120
San Francisco, CA 94133
CEO: Ms. Marti Cornejo-McMahon
(415) 788-9100 Fax: (415) 788-5445
Email: info@pacificmarineyachts.com
Web: http://www.pacificmarineyachts.com

PAMTOURS INTERNATIONAL OF NEW YORK, INC.
60 East 42nd Street, Suite 1045
New York, NY 10165
CEO: Mr. Alvaro F. Peña Jr.
(212) 949-8717 Fax: (212) 949-8727
Email: pamtoursny@aol.com
Web: http://www.pamtours.com

PAN AMERICAN EXPRESS, INC.
5002 Riverside Drive
Laredo, TX 78041
CEO: Mr. Arturo Volpe
(956) 723-4848
(800) 874-7197 Fax: (956) 723-9979
Email: panamex@panamex-zero.com
Web: http://www.panamex-zero.com

Zero Motor Freight, Inc.
P.O. Box 33940
San Antonio, TX 78265
(210) 661-4151
(800) 531-5335 Fax: (210) 660-0800

PAN AMERICAN HOSPITAL
5959 Northwest 7th Street
Miami, FL 33126
CEO: Mr. Roberto Tejidor
(305) 264-1000 Fax: (305) 265-6403
Web: www.pahnet.org

PANAMERICAN BANK
1300 South El Camino Real, Suite 320
San Mateo, CA 94402
CEO: Mr. Lawrence Grill
(650) 345-1800 Fax: (650) 349-8504

PAQUITO & SONS, INC.
Island Systems & Design
1517 Railroad Street
Glendale, CA 91204
CEO: Mr. Carlos Gonzales
(818) 244-8186 Fax: (818) 244-8150
Web: http://www.islandsys.net

Island Systems & Design/ Corporate Office
225 Yellow Place
Rockledge, FL 32955
(407) 638-9966 Fax: (407) 638-9977

PAUL J. SIERRA CONSTRUCTION, INC.
912 W. Martin Luther King Blvd.
Tampa, FL 33603
CEO: Mr. Paul J. Sierra
(813) 228-6661 Fax: (813) 223-5328
Web: http://www.sierraconstruction.com

PAUL YOUNG AUTO-MALL CO.
P.O. Box 2965
Laredo, TX 78044
CEO: Mr. Paul Young
(956) 727-1192 Fax: (956) 727-7842

PB INC.
4615 Hawkins Street, NE
Albuquerque, NM 87109
CEO: Mr. Christofer M. Pacheco
(505) 345-1000
Email: cpacheco@pbincorporated.com
Web: http://www.pbincorporated.com

PCNET, INC.
100 Technology Drive
Trumbull, CT 06611-1395
CEO: Mr. Camilo Soto
(203) 452-8500 Fax: (203) 452-8696
Email: teric@pcnet-inc.com
Web: http://www.pcnet-inc.com

PDS
Arizona Branch
3030 N. Central Ave., Suite 1404
Phoenix, AZ 85012
(602) 279-7377 Fax: (602) 279-7451
Web: http://www.pdsinc.com

Fair Oaks Branch
7806 Madison Avenue
Fair Oaks, CA 95628
(916) 967-7373 Fax: (916) 967-7343

Edwards Branch
P.O. Box 595
Edwards, CA 93523
(805) 258-8744

Colorado Branch
1155 Kelly Johnson Blvd., Suite 111
Colorado Springs, CO 80920
(719) 590-4105 Fax: (719) 590-7262

Omaha Branch
1004 Farnam, Suite 203
Omaha, NE 68102
(402) 344-4204 Fax: (402) 344-4104

Albuquerque Branch
6400 Uptown Blvd., NE, Suite 300W
Albuquerque, NM 87110
(505) 875-1270 Fax: (505) 875-1421

Rochester Branch
31 Erie Canal Dr., Ste. F1
Rochester, NY 14626
(716) 225-7850 Fax: (716) 225-7843

Bellevue Branch
10900 NE 8th Street, Suite 460
Bellevue, WA 98004
(877) 451-3336 Fax: (425) 451-2288

El Paso Branch
4150 Rio Bravo, Suite 135
El Paso, TX 79902
CEO: Mr. Marty Loya
(915) 532-0006 Fax: (915) 532-0664

Layton Branch
1572 N. Woodland Park Dr., Suite 510
Layton, UT 84041
(801) 779-2070 Fax: (801) 779-2075

PERERA CONSTRUCTION & DESIGN, INC.
8480 Utica Avenue
Rancho Cucamonga, CA 91730
CEO: Mr. Henry Perera
(909) 484-6350 Fax: (909) 484-3439

PHARMED GROUP CORPORATION
3075 NW. 107th Avenue
Miami, FL 33172

CEO: Mr. Carlos M. de Cespedes
(305) 592-2324 Fax: (305) 591-9643
Web: http://www.pharmed.com

PHILLIPS MAY CO.
4861 Sharp Street
Dallas, TX 75247
CEO: Mr. Gilbert May
(214) 631-3331 Fax: (214) 630-5607

PHYSICIANS HEALTHCARE PLANS, INC.
2333 Ponce De Leon Blvd., Suite 303
Coral Gables, FL 33134
CEO: Mr. Miguel B. Fernandez
(305) 441-9400 Fax: (305) 441-2294
Email: PHPI@is.phpi.com
Web: http://www.phpi.com

PLASTEC USA
7752 NW 74th Avenue
Miami, FL 33166
CEO: Mr. Hector Soza
(305) 887-6920 Fax: (305) 883-8254
Web: http://www.plastecusa.com

PLUMBING TODAY INC.
17624 15th Avenue, SE., Suite 101
Bothell, WA 98012
CEO: Ms. Barbara Rendon
(425) 481-1837 Fax: (425) 987-9451

PMA CONSULTANTS LLC
Corporate Office
226 W. Liberty Street
Ann Arbor, MI 48104
CEO: Mr. Gui Ponce De Leon
(734) 769-0530 Fax: (734) 663-9561
Web: http://www.pma-a2.com
Boston Regional Office
253 Summer Street, Suite 400
Boston, MA 02210
CEO: Mr. Gui Ponce De Leon
(617) 443-4515 Fax: (617) 443-4553
Web: http://www.pma-a2.com

Chicago Regional Office
333 West Wacker Drive, Suite 860
Chicago, IL 60606
(312) 920-0404 Fax: (312) 920-0405

Detroit Regional Office
One Woodward Avenue, Suite 1400
Detroit, MI 48226
(313) 963-8863 Fax: (313) 963-8918

Houston Regional Office
6750 West Loop South, Suite 500
Houston, TX 77401
(713) 662-8578 Fax: (713) 662-8571

Lansing Regional Office
120 N. Washington Square, Suite 260
Lansing, MI 48933
(517) 482-9401 Fax: (517) 482-9407

New York Regional Office
1285 Avenue of the Americas, 35th Floor
New York, NY 10019
(212) 554-4386 Fax: (212) 554-4089

Orlando Regional Office
5850 T.G. Lee Blvd., Suite 260
Orlando, FL 32822
(407) 859-5537 Fax: (407) 859-5765

Phoenix Regional Office
3800 N. Central Avenue, Suite 570
Phoenix, AZ 85012
(602) 277-7307 Fax: (602) 277-2827

Portland Regional Office
1001 SW. Fifth Avenue, Suite 1100
Portland, OR 97204
(503) 674-2745 Fax: (503) 674-5456

PMR CONSTRUCTION, INC.
4320 Alison NE.
Albuquerque, NM 87109
CEO: Mr. Paul Rivera
(505) 344-5267 Fax: (505) 345-0238

PRE-CON PRODUCTS
240 W. Los Angeles Avenue
Simi Valley, CA 93065
CEO: Mr. David Zarraonandia
(805) 527-0841 Fax: (805) 579-0544

PRIBUSS ENGINEERING INC.
690 Potrero Avenue
San Francisco, CA 94110
CEO: Mr. Ballardo Chamorro
(415) 282-1500 Fax: (415) 282-7504

PRIORITY ONE SERVICES, INC.
6600 Fleet Drive
Alexandria, VA 22310

CEO: Mr. Jose Figueroa
(703) 971-5505 Fax: (703) 719-6773
Web: http://www.priorityoneservices.com

PRODUCTIVE DATA SYSTEMS
Corporate Headquarters
6160 S. Seracuse Way, Suite 300
Greenwood Village, CO 80111
CEO: Mr. Joseph Martinez
(303) 220-7165 Fax: (303) 220-7425

PROFESSIONAL BUILDING MAINTENANCE CO.
8523 Lankershim
Sun Valley, CA 91352
CEO: Mr. Fernando Real
(818) 771-1100 Fax: (818) 771-1107

PROFESSIONAL & SCIENTIFIC ASSOCIATES, INC.
Virginia Office
6066 Leesburg Pike, Suite 200
Falls Church, VA 22041
CEO: Ms. Lily Fernandez Richardson
(703) 852-2900 Fax: (703) 852-2901
Email: info@psava.com
Web: http://www.psava.com

Georgia Office
2635 Century Parkway, Suite 990
Atlanta, GA 30345
(404) 633-6869 Fax: (404) 633-5756

PROFTECH CORPORATION
200 Clearbrook Road
Elmsford , NY 10523
CEO: Mr. Jose R. Montiel
(914) 347-3000 Fax: (914) 347-3900
Email: admin@proftech.com
Web: http://www.proftech.com

PROJECT ADVISERS CORPORATION
Corporate Headquarters
3050 SW., US 1
Miami, FL 33155
CEO: Ms. Linda Murphy-Barrera
(305) 266-5920 Fax: (305) 262-9468
Web: http://www.projectadvisers.com

PRONTO POST, INC.
5300 NW. 163 Street
Hialeah, FL 33014
CEO: Mr. Mike Vazquez
(305) 621-7900 Fax: (305) 620-9252
Email: mike@prontopost.com
Web: http://www.prontopost.com

PROTEC, INC.
6935 NW., 50th Street
Miami, FL 33166
CEO: Mr. Alfredo Sotolongo
(305) 594-3684 Fax: (305) 477-2514

PS ENERGY GROUP, INC.
2957 Clairmont Road, Suite 510
Atlanta, GA 30329
CEO: Ms. Livia Whisenhunt
(404) 321-5711 Fax: (404) 321-3938
Email: info@psenergy.com
Web: http://www.psenergy.com

PUENTE CONCESSIONS, INC.
P.O. Box 613136
Dallas-Forth Worth Airport, TX 75261-3136
CEO: Ms. Gina Puente-Brancato
(972) 574-4351 Fax: (972) 574-4353

PUENTES BROTHERS, INC.
1660 Salem Industrial Drive, NE
Salem , OR 97303
CEO: Mr. George J. Puentes
(503) 370-9710 Fax: (503) 370-4482
Web: http://www.donpancho.com

PUMA CONSTRUCTION CO., INC.
2814 Isleta SW
Albuquerque, NM 87105
CEO: Mr. Ralph Leon Torres
(505) 873-3189 Fax: (505) 873-3188

Q

QA SYSTEMS, INC.
6620 Manor Road
Austin, TX 78723
CEO: Mr. Marco Gutierrez
(512) 637-6100 Fax: (512) 637-8811
Email: duken@qasystems.com
Web: http://www.qasystems.com

QUALIFIED MECHANICAL CONTRACTORS, INC.
1001 S. Euclid Avenue
Tucson, AZ 85719
CEO: Mr. Santiago Nieto
(520) 624-8988 Fax: (520) 624-3716
Web: http://www.qualifiedmechanical.com

QUALITY SOLUTIONS, INC.
104 Barrows Place
De Soto, TX 75115
CEO: Mr. Manuel G. Guerrero
(972) 230-1230 Fax: (972) 223-9510

QUANTUM TECHNOLOGY SERVICES, INC.
Corporate Headquarters
1980 N. Atlantic Avenue, Suite 707
Cocoa Beach, FL 32931
CEO: Mr. Freddie Garcia
(407) 868-0288
Web: http://www.qtsi.com

R

R.F.G. FINANCIAL
1522 E. 4th Street
Santa Ana, CA 92701
(714) 560-8830 Fax: (714) 560-8840

RAM ENTERPRISES, INC.
24940 Avenue Tibbits
Valencia, CA 91355
CEO: Ms. Maricela Monstein
(661) 257-0800
(800) 890-4999 Fax: (661) 257-7750
Web: http://www.rament.com

RAMOS OIL COMPANIES, INC.
P.O. Box 401
West Sacramento, CA 95691
CEO: Mr. William Ramos
(530) 661-1200 Fax: (916) 371-0635

RAPID SUPPLY, INC.
23281 Telegraph Road
Southfield, MI 48034
CEO: Mr. Curtis E. Cardenas
(248) 352-1016 Fax: (248) 352-0072
Email: arcadesys@aol.com

RC ALUMINUM INDUSTRIES, INC.
2805 N.W. 75 Avenue
Miami, FL 33122
CEO: Mr. Raul Casares
(305) 592-1515 Fax: (305) 592-2184
Web: http://www.rcalum.com

REED CANDLE CO.
1531 W. Poplar
San Antonio, TX 78207
CEO: Sister Schodts Reed
(210) 734-4243 Fax: (210) 734-2342

REEF BRAZIL
9660 Chesapeake
San Diego , CA 92123
CEO: Mr. Santiago Aguerre
(858) 514-3600 Fax: (858) 514-3620
Web: http://www.reefbrazil.com

REFRICENTER, INC.
7101 NW 43rd Street
Miami, FL 33166
CEO: Mr. Cirilo Hernandez
(305) 477-8880 Fax: (305) 599-9323

REYNOSA CONSTRUCTION INC.
P.O. Box 3008
Amarillo, TX 79116
CEO: Ms. Cira Reynosa
(806) 373-3171 Fax: (806) 374-3808

RHO INDUSTRIES
5625 FM96 West, Suite 406
Houston, TX 77069
CEO: Mr. Jorge De La Riva
(281) 880-6263 Fax: (281) 880-5354

RICHARD ELECTRICS SUPPLYING, INC.
7281 NW., 8th Street
Miami, FL 33126
CEO: Mr. Julio Gonzales
(305) 266-8000 Fax: (305) 266-7192

RIO GRANDE STEEL, INC.
P.O. Box 5178
McAllen, TX 78502
CEO: Mr. Hector Maldonado
(956) 702-4434 Fax: (956) 702-4434

RIOJAS ENTERPRISES, INC.
10 E. Cambridge Circle Drive, Suite 120

Kansas City, KS 66103
CEO: Mr. Carlos Riojas
(913) 281-1600 Fax: (913) 281-2468
Email: riojas@kcnet.com
Web: http://www.riojas-able.com

RMPERSONNEL, INC.
4707 Montana
El Paso, TX 79903
CEO: Ms. Ceci Miles Mulvihill
(915) 565-7674 Fax: (915) 565-7687
Email: info@RMPersonnel.com
Web: http://www.rmpersonnel.com

ROBERT E. RIVERA CONSTRUCTION CO.
HCR 69 Box 735
Santa Rosa, NM 88435
CEO: Mr. Robert E. Rivera
(505) 472-3885 Fax: (505) 472-3892
Email: whitegriego@aol.com

RODY TRUCK CENTER
2479 NW., 36th Street
Miami, FL 33142
CEO: Mr. Rody Gomez
(305) 638-3583 Fax: (305) 638-0957

ROGER & SONS CONSTRUCTION, INC.
P.O. Box 358
East Chicago, IN 46312
CEO: Mr. Rogelio Zepeda Sr.
(219) 397-8819 Fax: (219) 397-1010
Email: cze42188@aol.com
Web: http://www.nebsnow/rogerandsons.com

ROSENDIN ELECTRIC, INC.
Corporate Headquarters
880 Mabury Road
San Jose, CA 95133
CEO: Mr. Tom Sorley
(408) 286-2800 Fax: (408) 793-5001
Email: TSorley@rosendin.com
Web: http://www.rosendin.com

San Fracisco Branch
440 9th Street
San Francisco, CA 94103
(415) 575-1600

Los Angeles Branch
140 Oregon Street
El Segundo, CA 90245
(310) 322-8000

Arizona Branch
2452 W. Birchwood Ave., #101
Mesa, AZ 85202
(602) 921-4022

Oregon Branch
2501 N.W. 229th Street
Hillsboro, OR 97124
(503) 201-3570

ROSES SOUTHWEST PAPERS, INC.
1701 2nd Street, SW.
Albuquerque, NM 87102
CEO: Mr. Robert Espat Jr.
(505) 842-0134 Fax: (505) 242-0342
Web: http://www.rosessouthwest.com

ROWLAND COFFEE ROASTERS, INC.
8080 NW, 58th Street
Miami , FL 33166
CEO: Mr. Jose Angel Souto
(305) 594-9039 Fax: (305) 594-7603
Web: http://www.cafepilon.com

RUIZ FOOD PRODUCTS, INC.
501 South Alta Avenue
Dinuba, CA 93618
CEO: Mr. Ricardo Alvarez
(559) 591-5510 Fax: (559) 591-6329
Web: http://www.elmontorey.com

RW GARCIA COMPANY
345 Phelan Avenue
San Jose , CA 95112
CEO: Mr. Robert W. Garcia
(408) 287-4616 Fax: (408) 287-7724
Web: http://www.rwgarcia.com

Tampa Office

6002 Benjamin Road
Tampa, FL 33634
C(813) 886-3590 Fax: (813) 888-8064

S

S3, LTD.
2387 Court Plaza Drive, Suite 200
Virginia Beach, VA 23456
CEO: Mr. William Casanova

(757) 321-8000 Fax: (757) 321-8099
Email: mail@3ltd.com
Web: http://www.s3ltd.com/s3ltd_frontpage.html

SAN ANTONIO PRESS, INC.
300 Arbor
San Antonio, TX 78207
CEO: Mr. Jose H. Medellin
(210) 224-2653 Fax: (210) 224-8132
Email: webmaster@sanantoniopressinc.com

SANDOVAL DODGE
955 South Valley Drive
Las Cruces, NM 88005
CEO: Mr. Rudy Sandoval
(505) 882-2442 Fax: (505) 524-7724

SAPPER CONSTRUCTION COMPANY
9148 Birch Street
Spring Valley, CA 91977
CEO: Mr. David Sapper
(619) 465-7222 Fax: (619) 465-7227
Email: flexpave@sapper.com
Web: http://www.sapper.com

SAV-ON PLATING CO.
15523 Illinois Avenue
Paramount, CA 90723
CEO: Ms. Carmen Carcedo
(310) 635-9797
Email: joseph@savonplating.com

SBS, INC.
4720 Esco Drive
Fort Worth, TX 76140
CEO: Mr. John Pereda
(817) 572-4029
(800) 793-7727 Fax: (817) 483-4625
Email: sales@sprayboothsystems.com
Web: http://www.sprayboothsystems.com

SCION STEEL, INC.
23800 Blackstone
Warren , MI 48089
CEO: Mr. Charlie Hurches
(800) 288-2127 Fax: (810) 755-4064
Web: http://www.scionsteel.com

SEDANO'S SUPERMARKETS
Store
9875 SW 40 Street
Miami, FL 33175
CEO: Mr. Manuel Herran
(305) 559-0479 Fax: (305) 559-4414
Web: http://www.sedanos.com

Store
3950 West 12 Avenue
Hialeah, FL 33012
(305) 556-6477 Fax: (305) 556-6479

Store
4040 East 4th Avenue
Hialeah, FL 33013
(305) 825-1725 Fax: (305) 825-1748

Corporate Headquarters
3925 Palm Avenue
Hialeah, FL 33012
(305) 824-1034 Fax: (305) 556-6981

SERVICE ELECTRIC CO., INC.
3716 Commercial NE
Albuquerque, NM 87107
CEO: Mr. Sam Alderete
(505) 345-1955 Fax: (505) 345-0593

SHERIKON, INC.
Corporate Headquarters
14500 Avion Parkway, Suite 200
Chantilly, VA 20151-1108
CEO: Ms. Carol Cloer
(800) 899-0123 Fax: (703) 803-3730
Email: info@sherikon.com
Web: http://www.sherikon.com

Orlando, FL Branch
12249 Science Drive, Suite 140
Orlando, FL 32826
(407) 281-8587 Fax: (407) 281-0008

Silver Spring, MD Branch
8601 Georgia Avenue, Suite 900
Silver Spring, MD 20910-3440
(301) 588-1700 Fax: (301) 588-1047

Crystal City, VA Branch
2711 Jefferson Davis Highway, Suite 500
Arlington, VA 22202
(703) 281-8587 Fax: (407) 281-0008

Los Alamitos, CA Branch
4332 Ceritos Avenue, Suite 106
Los Alamitos, CA 90720
(714) 828-5344 Fax: (714) 828-1271

New Orleans, LA Branch
1600 Canal Street, Suite 508
New Orleans, LA 70112
(504) 539-9496 Fax: (504) 539-9497

Harrisburg, PA Branch
355 N. 21st Street, Suite 204
Camp Hill, PA 17011
(717) 541-1168 Fax: (717) 541-0903

Skyline, VA Branch
5202 Leesburg Pike, Suite 310
Falls Church, VA 22041
(703) 824-7890 Fax: (703) 824-7881

San Diego, CA Branch
9449 Balboa Avenue, Suite 111
San Diego, CA 92123
(858) 569-7789 Fax: (858) 569-7940

Frederick, MD Branch
92 Thomas Johnson Drive, Suite 130
Frederick, MD 21702
(301) 698-2686 Fax: (301) 698-9894

San Antonio, TX Branch
8610 N. New Braunfels, Suite 100
San Antonio, TX 78217
(210) 824-1100 Fax: (210) 824-1774

Stafford, VA Branch
235 Garrisonville Road, Suite 202
Stafford, VA 22554
(540) 659-9992 Fax: (540) 657-9933

Orlando, FL Branch
12249 Science Drive, Suite 140
Orlando, FL 32826
(407) 281-8587 Fax: (407) 281-0008

Pasadena, CA Branch
145 North Altadena Blvd.
Pasadena, CA 91107
(626) 449-1593 Fax: (626) 449-3950

Aransas Pass, TX Branch
Redfish Bay Terminal, Ocean Dr. at Beasley
Aransas Pass, TX 78336
(512) 758-3103 Fax: (512) 758-0845

SILVER EAGLE DISTRIBUTORS
1000 Park of Commerce Blvd.
Homestead, FL 33035
CEO: Mr. Ramon Oyarzun
(305) 230-2337

SILVESTRI CONSTRUCTION
1961 Rice Road
Ojai, CA 93023
CEO: Mr. Joe Silvestri
(805) 649-1486 Fax: (805) 649-5725

SITE PERSONNEL SERVICES, INC.
Corporate Office
16550 W. Lisbon Road
Menomonee Falls , WI 53051
CEO: Mr. David Aragon
(262) 783-5181 Fax: (262) 783-7905
Web: http://www.sitepersonnel.com
Fox Valley Office
2602 American Drive
Appleton , WI 54915
CEO: Mr. David Aragon
(262) 739-6443 Fax: (262) 739-1311
Web: http://www.sitepersonnel.com
Ohio Valley Office
10979 Reed Hartman Hwy., Suite 1030
Cincinnatti, OH 45242
CEO: Mr. David Aragon
(513) 793-7696 Fax: (513) 793-8027
Web: http://www.sitepersonnel.com
Florida Office
2402 Cleveland Street
Tampa, FL 33609
CEO: Mr. David Aragon
(813) 253-2213 Fax: (813) 253-2417
Web: http://www.sitepersonnel.com

Chicago Office
117 W. Harrison Bldg., Suite s-625
Chicago, IL 60605
(312) 922-7547 Fax: (312) 922-7590

Minnesota Office
8030 Old Cedar Avenue, Suite 219
Minneapolis, MN 55425
(612) 854-4113 Fax: (612) 854-4672

Colorado Office
4646 Bedford Court
Boulder, CO 80301
303) 530-1446 Fax: (303) 530-1590

Michigan Office
3040 Charlevoix Drive SE., Suite 101

Grand Rapids, MI 48456
(616) 949-3387 Fax: (414) 783-7905

SKYLINE FORD
8630 East R.L. Thorton Freeway I-30
Dallas, TX 75228
CEO: Mr. Fred Salinas
(214) 327-4500 Fax: (214) 319-2318
Email: slawson@skylineford.com
Web: http://www.skylineford.com

SKYNET WORLWIDE EXPRESS
3301 NW., 93rd Avenue
Miami, FL 33172
CEO: Mr. Albert P. Hernandez
(305) 477-0996 Fax: (305) 477-0998
Web: http://www.skynetmia.com

SOLAR TOURS
Corporate Headquarters
1629 K Street NW., Suite 604
Washington, DC 20006
CEO: Ms. Maria Checa
(202) 861-5864 Fax: (202) 452-0905
Email: headquarters@solartours.com
Web: http://www.solartours.com

Florida Office
8460 South Tamiami Trail
Sarasota, FL 34238
(941) 966-1664 Fax: (941) 966-9586
Email: sarasota@solartours.com

Western USA Sales Support
9851 NE., 26th Street
Bellevue, WA 98004
(425) 462-9883 Fax: (425) 462-9880
Email: headquarters@solartours.com

SOLARES FLORIDA CORPORATION
7625 NW, 54th Street
Miami, FL 33166
CEO: Mr. Alberto E. Solares
(305) 592-0593 Fax: (305) 592-0400
Email: sales@solaresflorida.com
Web: http://www.solaresflorida.com

SOLVENTS AND CHEMICALS, INC.
4704 Shank Road
Pearland, TX 77584
CEO: Mr. Baizan
(281) 485-5377 Fax: (281) 485-6129

SOMERSET CAPITAL GROUP, LTD.
1087 Broad Street, Suite 201
Bridgeport, CT 06604
CEO: Mr. Pedro E. Wasmer
(203) 394-6182 Fax: (203) 394-6192
Email: somerset@somersetcapital.com
Web: http://www.somersetcapital.com

SONAG CO., INC.
5510 W. Florist Avenue
Milwaukee, WI 53218
CEO: Mr. Brian Ganos
(414) 393-9911 Fax: (414) 393-9902

SOURCE DIVERSIFIED, INC.
Corporate Office
22961 Triton Way, Suite G
Laguna Hills , CA 92653
CEO: Mr. Alfred Ortiz
(949) 380-4891
(800) 210-7484 Fax: (949) 380-9243
Web: http://www.sourced.com

SOUTH VALLEY AUTO PLAZA
905 Broadway
King City, CA 93930
CEO: Mr. Vincent Lopez
(831) 385-4865 Fax: (831) 385-3324
Email: vlopez@southvalleyautoplaza.com
Web: http://www.southvalleyautoplaza.com

SOUTHERN AUTOMOTIVE GROUP
2282 Crain Highway
Waldorf, MD 20601
CEO: Mr. Agustin F. Otero
(301) 843-1234
(800) 448-6537 Fax: (301) 843-2631
Email: southernauto@erols.com
Web: http://www.southernauto.com

SOUTHWEST ENTERTAINMENT, INC.
5415 Bandera Road, Suite 504
San Antonio, TX 78238-1959
CEO: Mr. Nelson I. Balido
(210) 523-2616
(800) 683-7389 Fax: (210) 684-6300
Web: http://www.sweonline.com

SOUTHWESTERN CONTROLS CORPORATION
Corporate Headquarters
6720 Sands Point Drive
Houston, TX 77074-3789
CEO: Mr. Russell Church
(713) 777-2626
(800) 444-9368 Fax: (713) 988-1521
Email: mailw@swcontrols.com
Web: http://www.swcontrols.com

Dallas Office
8808 Sovereign Row
Dallas, TX 75247-4618
(214) 638-4266
(800) 444-9367 Fax: (214) 638-0209

Tulsa office
9912-B East 45th Place
Tulsa, OK 74146-4752
(918) 663-6777
(800) 444-9369 Fax: (918) 663-5422

San Antonio Office
859 Isom Road
San Antonio, TX 78216-4035
(210) 340-4111
(800) 658-1570 Fax: (210) 340-4121

SOZA & COMPANY, INC.
Corporate Headquarters
8550 Arlington Blvd.
Fairfax, VA 22031
CEO: Mr. William Soza
(703) 560-9477 Fax: (703) 573-9026
Email: jim_goodridge@soza.com
Web: http://www.soza.com

Management Consulting
2735 Hartland Road
Falls Church, VA 22043
(703) 560-8324 Fax: (703) 560-2082

Rockville Office
c/o Netcomm, Inc.
6000 Executive Blvd., Suite 600
Rockville, MD 20852
(301) 770-6990 Fax: (301) 770-6992
Falls Church Office-HUD Contract

Falls Church Office
2777b Hartland Road
Falls Church, VA 22043
(703) 560-9532 Fax: (703) 560-3285

Fairfax Branch-Presearch Bldg.
8500 Executive Park Avenue
Fairfax, VA 22031
(703) 560-6551 Fax: (703) 560-6640

West Virginia Office
1116-Y Winchester Avenue
Martinsburg, WV 25401
(304) 263-8188 Fax: (304) 263-8777

North Carolina Office
905 Halstead Blvd., Suite 24
Elizabeth City, NC 27909
(252) 338-2511

Connecticut Office
214 Thames Street
Groton, CT 06340
(860) 405-0184 Fax: (860) 405-0469

Houston Office
1100 Louisiana, Suite 4560
Houston, TX 77002-5219
(713) 659-7602 Fax: (713) 659-7627

Colorado Office
1726 Cole Blvd., Bldg. 22, Suite 250
Golden, CO 80401

Puerto Rico Office
Capital Center Bldg., South Tower, Suite 704
San Juan, PR 00918

SPECTRUM IMAGING SYSTEMS
Customer Service & Support Center
1314 East Yandell
El Paso, TX 79902
CEO: Mr. Marcelo Plesant
(915) 533-5511 Fax: (915) 533-3925
Web: http://www.spectrumimagingsystems.com

Las Cruces, NM Branch
318 N. Downtown Mall
Las Cruces, NM 88001
(505) 526-6602 Fax: (505) 526-9787

Showroom & Administrative Office
5900 Gateway East
El Paso, TX 79905
(915) 781-2000 Fax: (915) 781-2100

SPILLIS CANDELA & PARTNERS, INC.
800 Douglas Entrance
Coral Gables, FL 33134
CEO: Mr. Hilario Candela
(305) 444-4691 Fax: (305) 447-3580
Web: http://www.scpmiami.com

STANDARD GLASS & MIRROR
P.O. Box 230070
Houston, TX 77223
CEO: Mr. Bennie Romero Jr.
(713) 640-2233 Fax: (713) 640-2244
Email: romerosplace@msn.com

STAR HUMAN RESOURCES GROUP, INC.
2036 East Camelback Road
Phoenix, AZ 85016
CEO: Mr. Charlie Shoumaker
(602) 956-4200 Fax: (602) 956-4238
Web: http://www.starbridge.com

STAR PAVING CO.
P.O. Box 12333
Albuquerque, NM 87195
CEO: Mr. Joe Cruz
(505) 877-0380 Fax: (505) 877-6655

STATURE CONSTRUCTION
2323 West Shepherd, Suite 1430
Houston, TX 77019
CEO: Mr. Tom Thibodeau
(713) 521-9344 Fax: (713) 521-9388

STEVE'S EQUIPMENT SERVICE, INC.
Facilities & Administrative Offices
1400 Powin Road
West Chicago, IL 60185
CEO: Mr. Steve Martines
(630) 231-4840 Fax: (630) 231-4945
Web: http://www.sesequip.com

Facilities
6915 W. Chicago Avenue
Gary, IN 46406
(219) 949-9595 Fax: (219) 949-3533

STEVE'S HOMETOWN MOTORS INC.
602 Hwy. 95
Weiser, ID 83672
CEO: Mr. Stephen Dominguez
(208) 549-3310
(800) 658-5080
Web: http://www.hometownmotors.com

STRUCTURAL ENGINEERING ASSOCIATES, INC.
3838 NW Loop 410
San Antonio, TX 78229
CEO: Mr. Jesse S. Covarrubias
(210) 735-9202 Fax: (210) 735-2074

SUN BAY CONTRACTING, INC.
4865 Haygood Road
Virginia Beach, VA 23455
CEO: Mr. Joe Guenther
(757) 557-0100 Fax: (757) 557-6896

SUN CONSTRUCTION, INC.
4004 Mark Dabling
Colorado Springs, CO 80907
CEO: Mr. Floyd G. Abeyta
(719) 533-4004 Fax: (719) 533-4003

SUN EAGLE CORPORATION
461 N. Dean Avenue
Chandler, AZ 85226
CEO: Mr. Martin Alvarez
Email: info@suneaglecorporation.com
Web: http://www.suneaglecorporation.com

SUNSTRAND ELECTRIC CO., INC.
1616 Berkley
Elgin, IL 60123
CEO: Mr. Eugene Aguirre
(847) 742-0266 Fax: (847) 742-0268
Web: http://www.sunstrand.com

SUPERIOR SERVICES, INC.
1505 N. Chestnut Avenue
Fresno, CA 93703
CEO: Ms. Sheila Guarderas
(559) 277-8020 Fax: (559) 458-0539
Email: ssi10451@worldnet.att.net

SUPERIOR TANK COMPANY, INC.
12450 Los Nietos Road
Santa Fe Springs, CA 90670
CEO: Mr. J.E. Marquez
(562) 946-8804 Fax: (562) 941-1722
Web: http://www.superiortank.com

SUPERMIX, INC.
4300 SW., 74th Avenue
Miami, FL 33155-7520

CEO: Mr. Jose Cancio
(305) 262-3250 Fax: (305) 267-0698
Web: http://www.supermix.com

SUPPLYSOURCE, INC.
Main Office
2605 Reach Road, P.O. Box 3553
Williamsport, PA 17701
CEO: Ms. Ray Thompson
(570) 327-1500
(800) 633-8753 Fax: (570) 327-1244
Email: info@officesupplysource.com
Web: http://www.officesupplysource.com

139 Stewart Road
Wilkes-Barre, PA 18706
(570) 824-4050

521 Napoleon Street
Johnstown , PA 15901
(814) 535-8271

1040 Benner Pike
State College, PA 16801
(814) 237-9155

SUPREME INTERNATIONAL CORPORATION
3000 N.W. 107th Avenue
Miami, FL 33172
CEO: Mr. George Feldenkreis
(305) 592-2830 Fax: (305) 594-2307
Email: financial@supreme.com
Web: http://www.supreme.com

SURAM TRADING COPORATION
2655 LeJeune Road, Suite 1006
Coral Gables, FL 33134
CEO: Mr. Guido Adler
(305) 448-7165 Fax: (305) 445-7185
Email: gadler@suram.com
Web: http://www.suram.com

SYMVIONICS, INC.
Corporate Office
3280 East Foothill Blvd., Suite 200
Pasadena, CA 91107
CEO: Mr. Lawrence Barraza
(626) 585-0115 Fax: (626) 585-0427
Web: http://www.symvionics.com

San Diego Office
674 Via De La Valle Suite 208
Solana, CA 92075
(619) 793-9483 Fax: (619) 793-3686

LA AFB
2400 South Pacific Avenue, Bldg. 37
San Pedro, CA 90731
(310) 363-8340 Fax: (310) 363-8368

Palmdale
190 Sierra Court, Suite C-4
Palmdale, CA 93550
(661) 273-7003 Fax: (661) 273-7144

Northrop
Military Aircraft Division, One Hornet Way
El Segundo, CA 90245
(619) 793-9483 Fax: (619) 793-3686

NFESC Port Hueneme
1100 23rd Avenue
Port Hueneme, CA 93043
(805) 982-1546 Fax: (805) 982-1602

Gilbert
1025 N. McQueen Road Suite 155
Gilbert, AZ 85233
(480) 633-5630 Fax: (480) 633-5632

SYMVIONICS, INC. (CONTINUED)
Pensacola
4051-G Barrancas Avenue PMB #104
Pensacola, FL 32507
(850) 452-7034 Fax: (850) 452-2014

Niceville
1813 John Sims Parkway Suite 104
Niceville, FL 32578
(850) 897-3311 Fax: (850) 897-2201

Eglin AFB
46 OSS/OSXR, 505 N. Barrancas Avenue, Bldg.
104 Room 310
Eglin AFB, FL 32542-6818
(850) 882-8709 Fax: (850) 882-2354

Charleston
222 West Coleman Blvd., Suite 202
Mt. Pleasant, SC 29464
(843) 881-5559 Fax: (843) 881-9359

Alexandria
2121 Eisenhower Avenue, Suite 200
Alexandria, VA 22314
(703) 549-8330 Fax: (703) 549-8120

Norfolk
1300 Diamond Springs Rd., Suite 206
Virginia Beach, VA 23455
(757) 363-1777 Fax: (757) 363-2529

Dayton
1312 Research Park Drive
Dayton, OH 45432
(937) 426-4504 Fax: (937) 426-5928

Washington Navy Yard
1322 Patterson Avenue, Suite 1000
Attn: Code HSG-BH (Symvionics)
Washington, DC 20374-5065
(202) 685-9377 Fax: (202) 685-1674

Sterling Software
14450 Trinity Blvd., Suite 150
Ft. Worth, TX 76155
(817) 354-4335 Fax: (817) 354-4466

Lackland AFB
PSC 3, Box 5796, 1500 Shaw Dr.
Lackland AFB, TX 78236
(805) 982-1546 Fax: (805) 982-1602

SYTECH CORPORATION
6121 Lincolnia Road, Suite 200
Alexandria, VA 22312
CEO: Mr. Jose Diaz
(703) 941-7887 Fax: (703) 941-7997
Web: http://www.sytechcorp.com

T

T&G CORPORATION
7131 Grand Nation Drive, Suite 106
Orlando, FL 32819
CEO: Mr. Ricardo Gonzalez
(407) 352-4443 Fax: (407) 352-0778
Email: info@t-and-g.com
Web: http://www.t-and-g.com

TAMIAMI AUTOMOTIVE GROUP
8250 SW H Street
Miami, FL 33144
CEO: Mr. Carlos Planas
(305) 513-4776 Fax: (305) 262-6114

TC ENTERPRISES
6000 Indian School Road, NE
Albuquerque, NM 87160
CEO: Ms. Elizabeth Pohl
(505) 883-8233 Fax: (505) 883-6275
Email: mainoffice@tce/abq.com

TCG, INC.
4100 Rio Bravo, Suite 202
El Paso, TX 79902
CEO: Ms. Olga Mapula
(915) 532-1171 Fax: (915) 544-6840
Email: email@tcg-ep.com
Web: http://www.tcg-ep.com

TDF CORPORATION
1515 - 5th Avenue, Suite 310
Moline, IL 61265
CEO: Ms. Claudia F. Fabela
(309) 797-1030 Fax: (309) 797-0142
Web: http://www.tdfcorporation.com

TEAM ONE SERVICES INC.
Corporate Headquarters
10850 Wilshire Blvd., Suite 350
Los Angeles, CA 90024
CEO: Mr. Frank Moran
(800) 767-0606 Fax: (310) 475-9221
Web: http://www.teamonejobs.com

South Bay Office
18726 S. Western, Suite 206
Torrance, CA 90248
(310) 243-6833 Fax: (310) 323-9098

Ontario Office
1777 S. Vintage Avenue
Ontario, CA 91761
(909) 974-0209 Fax: (909) 974-0409

TECHNISERV DATA SYSTEMS, INC.
1560 Teaneck Road
Teaneck, NJ 07666
CEO: Mr. Lutfi Mansoor
(201) 837-0032 Fax: (201) 837-0504
Email: info@techniservdata.com
Web: http://www.techniservdata.com

TECHNOLOGY INTEGRATION GROUP
Corporate Headquarters
7810 Trade Street
San Diego, CA 92121
CEO: Mr. Bruce Geier
(858) 566-1900 Fax: (858) 566-8794
Email: info@tig.com
Web: http://www.tig.com

Phoenix Office
5090 North 40th Street, Suite 180
Phoenix, AZ 85018
(602) 840-5696 Fax: (602) 840-5655

Northern California Office
3478 Buskirk Avenue, Suite 1013
Pleasant Hill, CA 94523
(877) 519-7568 Fax: (925) 256-4029

North Los Angeles Office
100 East Huntington Drive
Monrovia , CA 91016
(800) 908-4363 Fax: (626) 821-1841

Los Angeles Office
4281 Katella Avenue, Suite 100
Los Alamitos , CA 90720
(714) 995-4155 Fax: (714) 893-7777

Irvine Office
23 Mauchly, Suite 115
Irvine, CA 92618
(949) 753-1933 Fax: (949) 753-1997

Torrance Office
1860 Carson Street, Suite 104
Torrance, CA 90501
(310) 320-4934 Fax: (310) 320-4646

TIG Technical Training
7830 Trade Street
San Diego, CA 92121
(858) 566-1900 ext.6000 (858) 566-8794

Denver Office
6886 South Yosemite Street
Englewood, CO 80112
(303) 741-9123 Fax: (303) 741-9801

Las Vegas Office
2915 West Charleson Blvd., Suite 11
Las Vegas, NV 89102
(702) 222-0152 Fax: (702) 222-0267

Albuquerque Office
4421 McLeod NE, Suite B
Albuquerque, NM 87109
(505) 830-8280 Fax: (505) 872-9279

Salt Lake City
4931 South 900 East, Bldg. E, Suite 200
Salt Lake City, UT 84117
(801) 269-9100 Fax: (801) 269-9799

Seattle Office
1606 148th Avenue SE, Suite 100
Bellevue, WA 98007
(425) 747-2633 Fax: (425) 747-4409

Orlando Office
1503 West Smith Street
Orlando, FL 32804
(407) 428-6266 Fax: (407) 648-8780

Honolulu Office
660 Ala Moana Blvd.
Honolulu, HI 96813
(808) 524-6652
(800) 848-2397 Fax: (808) 536-2845

Philadelphia Office
308 Commerce Drive, Suite 100
Exton, PA 19341
(610) 280-7688 Fax: (610) 280-7843

TECNICO CORPORATION
Baltimore Office
4701 Belle grove Rd., Suite C
Baltimore , MD 21225
CEO: Mr. Rafael Torrech III
(410) 609-2055 Fax: (410) 609-5057
Email: dstoermer@tecnicocorp.com
Web: http://www.tecnicocorp.com

Chesapeake Office
831 Industrial Avenue
Chesapeake, VA 23324-2614
(757) 545-4013 Fax: (757) 545-4925

Mobile, Alabama Office
7611 Lake Road South, Bulding 307
Mobile, AL 36605
(334) 443-9900 Fax: (334) 443-9050

National City Office
100 W. 35th Street, Suite J&K
National City, CA 91950
(619) 426-7385 Fax: (619) 426-7387

Panama City Office
7518 McElvey Road
Panama City, FL 32408
(850) 236-0080 Fax: (858) 236-0035

TEI ENGINEERS & PLANNERS
300 Primera Blvd.
Lake Mary, FL 32746
CEO: Mr. Andréz E. Núñez, Jr.
(407) 805-0355 Fax: (407) 805-0227
Web: http://www.tei-fl.com

TEJAS OFFICE PRODUCTS, INC.
1225 W. 20th Street
Houston, TX 77008
CEO: Mr. Lupe Fraga
(713) 864-6004 Fax: (713) 864-3933
Web: http://www.tejasoffice.com

TELACU INDUSTRIES, INC.
5400 East Olympic Blvd., Suite 300
Los Angeles, CA 90022
CEO: Mr. Michael D. Lizarraga
(323) 721-1655 Fax: (323) 724-3372
Email: telacu@telacu.com
Web: http://www.telacu.com

TELEVENTAS SHOPPING NETWORK
Electronics-E
7500 NW., 25th Street Bay 7
Miami, FL 33122
CEO: Mr. Abbey Fiallo
(305) 471-8111 Fax: (305) 471-8195
Web: http://www.electronics-e.com

TELEVIDEO SAN DIEGO
4783 Ruffner Street
San Diego, CA 92111
CEO: Mr. David Stepp
(858) 268-1100 Fax: (619) 268-1790
Email: sales@televideosd.com
Web: http://www.televideosd.com

TELEXPORT, INC.
750 18th Street
Hialeah, FL 33010
CEO: Mr. Danilo Alonso
(305) 887-5197 Fax: (305) 885-4950
Web: http://www.teilighting.com

THE CENTECH GROUP, INC.
4600 North Fairfax Drive, Suite 400
Arlington, VA 22203
CEO: Mr. Fernando Galavis
(703) 525-4444 Fax: (703) 525-2349
Email: marketing@centechgroup.com
Web: http://www.centechgroup.com

THE COMMUNITIES GROUP
1012 N Street, NW
Washington, DC 20001
CEO: Mr. Jaime Bordenave
(202) 667-3002 Fax: (202) 667-3035
Web: http://www.thecommunitiesgroup.com

THE DIAL GROUP
14522 E. Whittier Blvd.
Whittier, CA 90605
CEO: Mr. Douglas Lopez
(562) 945-1071 Fax: (562) 698-1145
Web: http://www.dialworks.com

Dial Med
14613 E. Whittier Blvd., Suite 210
Whittier, CA 90605
CEO: Mr. Douglas Lopez
(562) 464-0295 Fax: (562) 464-0299

1033 E. Imperial Hwy., Suite E10
Brea, CA 92821
(714) 671-1726 Fax: (714) 671-2169

350 S. Figueroa Street, Suite 475
Los Angeles, CA 90071
(213) 620-0608 Fax: (213) 620-0826

THE MILES GROUP, INC.
4950 Gateway East
El Paso, TX 79905
CEO: Mr. Danny Miles & Mr. Michael Miles
(915) 778-3636 Fax: (915) 778-7401
Email: info@milesgroup.com
Web: http://www.milesgroup.com

THE OAKS GROUP
3100 Wilcrest Drive, Suite 360

Houston, TX 77042
(713) 430-1999 Fax: (713) 430-1955
Web: http://www.oaksgroup.com

THE PLAZA GROUP
2500 Tanglewild, Suite 470
Houston, TX 77063
CEO: Mr. Randy Velrade
(713) 266-0707 Fax: (713) 266-8660

THE RELATED GROUP OF FLORIDA, INC.
2828 Coral Way, Penthouse One
Miami, FL 33145
CEO: Mr. Jorge Perez
(305) 460-9900 Fax: (305) 460-9911
Web: www.relatedgroup.com

THE TREVINO GROUP
1616 West 22nd Street
Houston, TX 77088
CEO: Mr. Dale Trevino
(713) 863-8333 Fax: (713) 863-8522

THE VPM FUNDING COMPANY
Corporate Headquarters
1888 Sherman Street, Suite 200
Denver, CO 80203
CEO: Mr. Tony Gallegos
(800) 730-3750 Fax: (800) 863-7284
Email: vpmfunding@earthlink.net
Web: http://www.vpmfunding.com

THREE PLUS, INC.
P.O. Box 248
Kenner, LA 70063
CEO: Ms. Miriam Seiglie
(504) 469-1213 Fax: (504) 469-1219

TIRE GROUP INTERNATIONAL, INC.
6695 NW., 36th Avenue
Miami, FL 33147
CEO: Mr. Antonio R. Gonzales
(305) 696-0096 Fax: (305) 696-5926
Web: http://www.tiregroup.com

TITAN RUBBER & SUPPLY CO.
232 Commercial Street
San Jose, CA 95112
CEO: Mr. Dave Rodriguez
(408) 998-8205 Fax: (408) 998-8249

TRADE LITHO, INC.
5301 NW., 37th Avenue
Miami, FL 33142
CEO: Mr
(305) 63...
(800) 367-5871 Fax: (305) 633-2848
Email: info@trade-litho.com
Web: http://www.trade-litho.com

TRAMEX TRAVEL
4505 Spicewood Springs Road, Suite 200
Austin, TX 78759
CEO: Mr. Juan Portillo
(512) 343-2201 Fax: (512) 343-0022
Web: http://www.tramex.com

TRANDES CORPORATION
Corporate Office
4601 Presidents Drive, Suite 360
Lanham, MD 20706
CEO: Mr. James A. Brusse
(301) 459-0200 Fax: (301) 459-1069
Web: http://www.trandes.com

San Diego Office
9630 Ridgehaven Ct., Suite A
San Diego, CA 92123
(619) 268-4930 Fax: (619) 268-4603

Norfolk Electronic Maintenance Center
4600 Village Avenue
Norfolk, VA 23502
(757) 857-5225 Fax: (757) 857-5696

Vallejo Office
1422 Springs Road, Suite A
Vallejo, CA 94591
(707) 648-2445 Fax: (707) 648-1035

TRANEX, INC.
2350 Executive Circle
Colorado Springs, CO 80906
CEO: Mr. Troy Valdez
(719) 576-7994 Fax: (719) 576-1503
Email: tranexs@att.global.net
Web: http://www.tranexinc.com

TRANS-NATIONAL MOTOR CARS, INC.
1827 N. Keystone Street
Burbank, CA 91504
CEO: Mr. Marc A. Castro

(818) 559-3325 Fax: (818) 559-3405
Email: ebmw@pacbell.com
Web: http://www.ebmwsales.com

TRI-COR INDUSTRIES, INC.
2900 Eisenhower Ave., 5th Fl.
Alexandria, VA 22314
CEO: Mr. Louis Gonzalez
(703) 682-2000 Fax: (703) 682-2001
Email: sales@tricor.net
Web: http://www.tricorind.com

Kansas City Branch
9229 Ward Parkway, Suite 104
Kansas City, MO 64114
(800) 711-9335 Fax: (816) 523-3968

Fort Worth Branch
307 West 7th Street, Suite 1716
Fort Worth, TX 76102
(817) 877-4669 Fax: (817) 877-4199

O'Fallon Branch
5 Eagle Center, Suite 8
O'Fallon, IL 62269
(618) 632-9804 Fax: (618) 632-9805

St. Louis Branch
2300 Millpark Drive, Suite 104
Maryland Heights, MO 63044
(314) 428-8005 Fax: (314) 428-5540

Denver Branch
445 Union Blvd., Suite 124
Lakewood, CO 80228
(303) 914-8313 Fax: (303) 914-0859

San Antonio Branch
2929 Mossrock, Suite 108
San Antonio, TX 78230
(210) 348-9836 Fax: (210) 348-9838

Oklahoma City Branch
5600 Liberty Parkway, Suite 700E
Midwest City, OK 73110
(405) 741-2394 Fax: (405) 741-2396

Davenport Branch
1019 Mound Street, Suite 204
Davenport, IA 52803
(319) 326-1983 Fax: (319) 326-2031

Salt Lake City Branch
880 West Heritage Park Blvd., Suite 100-C
North Layton, UT 84041
(801) 825-6855 Fax: (801) 825-7299

TRINET COMMUNICATIONS, INC.
Warehouse and Distribution Facility
6567 Brisa Street
Livermore, CA 94450
CEO: Mr. Jon Fernandez
(925) 294-1720 Fax: (925) 449-9063
Email: sales@trinet-mail.com
Web: http://www.trinetcommunications.com

Denver Facility
15965 E. 32nd Avenue, Suite F
Aurora, CO 80011
(303) 343-2010 Fax: (303) 343-2770

Dallas Facility
1821 Diplomat Drive
Dallas, TX 75234
(972) 852-0538 Fax: (972) 852-0542

Milwaukee Office
W249 S6075 Deerfield Circle
Waukesha, WI 53189
(262) 970-7164

Palm City Office
3131 Southwest Martindowns Blvd., Suite 369
Palm City, FL 34990
(561) 219-8294

TSN INC.
4001 Salazar Way P.O. Box 679
Frederick, CO 80530
CEO: Mr. Israel Salazar
(303) 530-0600 Fax: (303) 530-1919

TUBE AMERICA, INC.
6550 Bingle Road
Houston, TX 77092
CEO: Ms. Cosme J. Salazar
(713) 690-9990 Fax: (713) 690-9991

U

UGETAPPROVED.COM
1650 Hotel Circle North #215
San Diego, CA
CEO: Mr. Gary Acosta
(800) 809-1952 Fax: (619) 209-4755
Email: info@ugetapproved.com

Web: http://www.209.126.134.58/company/about.htm

UNALITE ELECTRIC & LIGHTING CORPORATION
58-18 37th Avenue
Woodside , NY 11377
CEO: Mr. Israel Bulbank
(718) 898-5100 Fax: (718) 898-7957

UNI BORING CO., INC.
2280 W. Grand River
Howell, MI 48843
CEO: Mr. Facundo Bravo
(517) 548-0500 Fax: (517) 548-1336
Email: ubci@uniboring.com
Web: http://www.uniboring.com

UNITED BUILDING MAINTENANCE, INC.
165 Easy Street
Carol Stream, IL 60188
CEO: Mr. James S. Cabrera
(630) 653-4848 Fax: (630) 653-0660
Web: http://www.ubm-usa.com

225 West Randolph
Chicago, IL 60606
(312) 727-3754 Fax: (312) 629-8758

UNITED PUMPING SERVICE, INC.
14016 E. Valley Blvd.
City of Industry, CA 91746
CEO: Mr. Eduardo Perry Sr.
(626) 961-9326 Fax: (626) 961-3799
(626) 336-7734
Web: http://www.unitedpumping.com

UPPER VALLEY MATERIAL, INC.
7301 W. Expressway 83
Mission , TX 78572
CEO: Mr. Ramiro J. Flores & Mr. Rufino Garza
(956) 580-2502 Fax: (956) 585-8675

V

VALLEY FENCE CO.
Division of Apache Construction Corporation
1933 Coors Blvd., SW.
Albuquerque, NM 87121
CEO: Mr. Mariano Chavez & Mr. Paul Chavez
(505) 877-7978
(505) 877-1815 Fax: (505) 877-5301

VALOR INSURANCE CORPORATION
10556 NW., 26th Street, Suite D101
Miami, FL 33172
CEO: Mr. Jack Valor
(305) 406-1112 Fax: (305) 406-1121

VALVERDE CONSTRUCTION, INC.
10936 Shoemaker Avenue
Santa Fe Springs, CA 90670
CEO: Mr. Joe A. Valverde
(562) 906-1826 Fax: (562) 906-1918
Email: rosev@valverdeconst.com
Web: http://www.valverdeconst.com

VARIO CONSTRUCTION CO.
207 S. Villa Avenue
Villa Park, IL 60181
CEO: Mr. Carlos E. Vargas
(630) 834-4604 Fax: (630) 833-4175

VICTOR BUICK GMC INC.
2525 Wardlow Road
Corona, CA 92882
CEO: Mr. Victor Covarrubias
(909) 737-2552 Fax: (909) 737-7866
Web: http://www.victorbuickgmc.com

VISTA TECHNOLOGIES, INC.
Corporate Headquarters
2309 Renard Place, SE, Suite 202
Albuquerque, NM 87106
CEO: Mr. Armando De La Paz
(505) 764-8770 Fax: (505) 764-8772
Email: okell@vistatechnologies.com
Web: http://www.vistatechnologies.com

South East Office
5001 Technology Drive
Huntsville, AL 35805
(256) 726-4701 Fax: (256) 726-4740
Email: jstracha@vistatechnologies.com

South West Office
7700 Alabama, Suite C
El Paso, TX 79904
(915) 751-6014 Fax: (915) 757-3399
Email: jdelapaz@vistatechnologies.com

South West Office
10500 Hwy. 281 N., Suite 107
San Antonio, TX 78216
(210) 494-4282 Fax: (210) 348-7088
Email: rparker@vistatechnologies.com

VISTACOLOR CORPORATION, LTD.
3401 NW., 36th Street
Miami, FL 33142
CEO: Mr. J.E. Serrano
(305) 635-2000 Fax: (305) 635-1985
Email: vista@shadow.net
Web: http://www.vistacolor.com

VITERI CONSTRUCTION MANAGEMENT, INC.
11841 Canon Blvd.
Newport News, VA 23606
CEO: Mr. Carlos Viteri
(757) 873-0406 Fax: (757) 873-3488
Web: http://www.members.tripod.com/viericonstruction

W.G. VALENZUELA DRYWALL, INC.
4085 North Highway Drive
Tucson , AZ 85705
CEO: Mr. William G. Valenzuela
(520) 887-5652 Fax: (520) 887-8404

WASHINGTON CONSULTING GROUP, INC.
6707 Democracy Blvd., Suite 1010
Bethesda, MD 20817
CEO: Mr. Armando Chapelli, Jr.
(301) 581-3300 Fax: (301) 571-2010
Email: bmpiper@washcg.com
Web: http://www.washcg.com

WEST COAST SAMPLES, INC.
14450 Central Avenue
Chino, CA 91710
CEO: Mr. Larry Barrios Jr.
(909) 464-1616 Fax: (909) 465-9982
Email: lbarrios@wcsample.com
Web: http://www.wcsample.com

WESTERN SWITCHES & CONTROLS, INC.
2400 Pullman Street
Santa Ana, CA 92705
CEO: Mr. Leo Alonzo
(949) 252-1144
(800) 454-8144 Fax: (949) 252-9199
Web: http://www.westernswitches.com

WINDWARD SEAFOODS
2699 South Bayshore Drive, Suite 800C
Coconut Grove, FL 33133
CEO: Mr. Rafael Puga
(305) 860-5444 Fax: (305) 860-5333
Email: info@windwardseafoods.com
Web: http://www.windwardseafoods.com

WOLFBERG ALVAREZ & PARTNERS
5960 SW 57th Avenue
Miami, FL 33143
CEO: Mr. Julio E. Alvarez
(305) 666-5474 Fax: (305) 669-9875
Email: lcastellon@wolfbergalvarez.com
Web: http://www.wolfbergalvarez.com

WR CHAVEZ CONSTRUCTION, INC.
12125 Kear Place, Suite A
Poway, CA 92064-7133
CEO: Mr. Willy Chavez
(858) 375-2100 Fax: (858) 375-2109
Web: http://www.wrchavez.com

WWCOT, INC.
Main Office
3130 Wilshire Blvd., Sixth Floor
Santa Monica, CA 90403
CEO: Mr. Adrian O. Cohen
(310) 828-0040 Fax: (310) 453-9432
Email: info@wwcot.com
Web: http://www.wwcot.com

Inland Empire
3890 11th Street, Suite 212
Riverside, CA 92501
(909) 682-0470 Fax: (909) 682-1801

Y

YUCAHU, INC.
18 E. 116th St., 2nd Floor
New York, NY 10029
CEO: Mr. Alvin D. Gonzalez
(917) 460-9045 Fax: (212) 427-0875
Email: yucahu@consultant.com

Z

Z-SPANISH RADIO NETWORK, INC.
1436 Auburn Blvd.
Sacramento, CA 95815
CEO: Mr. Amador Bustos
(916) 646-4000 Fax: (916) 646-3230
Email: zcorpoffice@zspanish.com
Web: http://www.zspanish.com

ZERIMAR CORPORATION
1355 Vander Way
San Jose, CA 95112
CEO: Ms. Slivia L. Ramirez
(408) 977-3145 Fax: (408) 977-3146
Email: Zerimar@zerimar.com
Web: http://www.zerimar.com

USAJOBS
THE FEDERAL GOVERNMENT'S EMPLOYMENT INFORMATION SYSTEM

THE DOOR TO A WORLD OF OPPORTUNITY, ON YOUR TERMS.

DON'T WAIT FOR OPPORTUNITY TO KNOCK:
TAKE CHARGE OF YOUR CAREER WITH USAJOBS.

H BY:

- Job type
- Career field
- Location
- Salary range
- Education requirements
- Work experience

.USAJOBS.opm.gov

Telephone System
-3000 or TDD (478) 744-2299
companies charge for long-distance calls.

h Screen Computer Kiosks
government locations nationwide.

E

T INFORMATION,

RE, ALWAYS UP-TO-DATE

OPM UNITED STATES OFFICE OF PERSONNEL MANAGEMENT

USDA United States
Department of
Agriculture

USDA: The People's Department

USDA le ofrece un mundo de oportunidades.

The mission of the U.S. Department of Agriculture is to enhance the quality of life for the American people by supporting production agriculture; ensuring a safe, affordable, nutritious, and accessible food supply; caring for agricultural, forest, and range lands; supporting rural communities' sound development; providing economic opportunities for farm and rural residents; expanding global markets for agricultural and forest products and services; and working to reduce hunger in America and throughout the world.

Careers With a
Difference

Because USDA is one of the Government's largest civilian employers, we offer unparalleled career choices in areas such as management, business and industry, and science and technology.

Visit us on the web:
www.usda.gov

LLEGAMOS A MÁS COMUNIDADES
DE LAS QUE SE IMAGINA.

Todos los días, American Airlines vuela a cientos de ciudades. Pero también llega a comunidades hispanas de una manera distinta.

¿Cómo? Contribuyendo y estando presente en eventos locales y nacionales que promueven la educación y la salud, los deportes,

el desarrollo empresarial, y muchas otras actividades que benefician a niños y adultos. Este apoyo se realiza, en parte, gracias a la

ayuda y colaboración que ofrecen los empleados de American en diversas comunidades.

American Airlines se siente orgullosa de apoyar a nuestra comunidad hispana.

AmericanAirlines®
American *Eagle®*

MÁS ESPACIO. SÓLO EN AMERICAN AIRLINES*
PARA MÁS INFORMACIÓN, VISITE A'A.COM®

miembro de oneworld

United States Secret Service

Some things are worth DEFENDING...
your country is one of them

The U.S. Secret Service protects our nation's highest elected officials, critical infrastructure, and the integrity of our nation's financial systems.

We are seeking qualified individuals with diverse skills and backgrounds who are interested in a challenging career with our federal law enforcement agency.

For more information, contact your local U.S. Secret Service Field Office or call:

www.treas.gov/usss

1-888-813-USSS

The United States Secret Service is an Equal Opportunity Employer

Federal & State Employment Offices
Oficinas de empleos federales y estatales

An extensive list of Federal and State Hispanic Employment Program and Equal Employment Opportunity offices, listed by state and agency.

Una lista extensa de oportunidades de empleo en agencias federales y estatales, por estados y agencias.

ALABAMA

AGRICULTURE, DEPARTMENT OF

SOUTHEAST REGION
Carolyn King, HEPM
1504-C Hwy 31 South
Bay Minette, AL 36507
(334) 937-3297
Carolyn.King@al.usda.gov

EQUAL EMPLOYMENT OPPORTUNITY COMMISSION

BIRMINGHAM DISTRICT OFFICE
Cynthia G. Pierre, Director
1130 22nd St., S, #2000
Birmingham, AL 35205
(205) 731-0082

NAVY, DEPARTMENT OF THE

USMC RECRUITING STATION
Maj Mark Costeloo, Commanding Officer
2853 Fairlane Dr. #64, Bldg. G
Montgomery, AL 36116-1698
(334) 223-7575

POSTAL SERVICE

ALABAMA DISTRICT
Brenda A. Johnson, Div. Dev.Field Spec.
351 24th St., N
Birmingham, AL 35203-9989
(205) 521-0256

TRANSPORTATION, DEPT. OF

U.S. COAST GUARD
Eastwood Festival
7001 Crestwood Blvd., #612
Birmingham, AL 35210-2332
(205) 592-8923
blee@cgrc.uscg.mil
www.gocoastguard.com

U.S. COAST GUARD
Mobile Festival Centre
3725 Airport Blvd. #148
Mobile, AL 36608-1633
(334) 441-5171/72
chowie@cgrc.uscg.mil
www.gocoastguard.com

U.S. COAST GUARD
400 Eastern Blvd., #207
Montgomery, AL 36117-2043
(334) 279-3130/29/4880
jgooch@cgrc.uscg.mil
www.gocoastguard.com

ALASKA

AGRICULTURE, DEPARTMENT OF

FOREST SERVICE
Jovita Luster, HEPM
P.O. Box 21628,
709 W 9th St., Federal Office Bldg.
Juneau, AK 99802
(907) 586-7844
jluster@fs.fed.us

FOREST SERVICE
Sandra Herrera, EEO Specialist
P.O. Box 21628
709 W 19th St., Federal Office Bldg.
Juneau, AK 99802-1628
sherrera@fs.fed.gov

WEST REGION
Rhoda Portis, HEPM
351 W Park Hwy., #100
Wasilla, AK 99654
(907) 373-1062
rpostis@ak.nrcs.usda.gov

INTERIOR, DEPARTMENT OF THE

NATIONAL PARK SERVICE
Darwin Aho, Human Resources Manager
2525 Gambell St.
Anchorage, AK 99503
(907) 257-2580

POSTAL SERVICE

ANCHORAGE DISTRICT
Lori McDonald, Div. Dev.Field Spec.
P.O. Box 19940
Anchorage, AK 99519-9400
(907) 266-3245

TRANSPORTATION, DEPT. OF

U.S. COAST GUARD
800 Diamond Blvd., Space 3-205
Anchorage, AK 99515-1515
(907) 271-2447/49
mharrington@cgrc.uscg.mil
www.gocoastguard.com

ARIZONA

AGRICULTURE, DEPARTMENT OF

WEST REGION
Daniel Tafoya, HEPM
Leslie Canyon Rd., Rt 1 Box 226,
Douglas Field Office
Douglas, AZ 85607-9716
(520) 364-2001x3
Daniel.Tafoya@az.usda.gov

EQUAL EMPLOYMENT OPPORTUNITY COMMISSION

PHOENIX DISTRICT OFFICE
Charles D. Burtner, Director
3300 N Central Ave., #690
Phoenix, AZ 85012-9688
(602) 640-5000

INTERIOR, DEPARTMENT OF THE

BUREAU OF INDIAN AFFAIRS
Doris Tauchin, Budget Assistant
P.O. Box 127
Tuba City, AZ 86045
(520) 283-2294

BUREAU OF INDIAN AFFAIRS
Merle Zunigha, Personnel Officer
400 N 5th St.
Phoenix, AZ 85001
(602) 379-6739

NAVY, DEPARTMENT OF THE

USMC RECRUITING STATION
1 N 1st St., 3rd Floor
Phoenix, AZ 85004
(602) 256-7819

POSTAL SERVICE

ARIZONA DISTRICT
Pascual J. Torres, Hispanic Prog. Spec.
1441 E Buckeye Rd., #236
Phoenix, AZ 85034-4128
(602) 253-8301

PHOENIX DISTRICT
Aida Murrieta-Penn, Div. Dev. Field Spec.
4949 E Van Buren, #113
Phoenix, AZ 85026-9422
(602) 223-3649

STATE OF ARIZONA

GOVERNOR'S OFFICE
Erika Quintero, Outreach Specialist
1700 W Washington Ave. #156
Phoeniz, AZ 85007
(602) 542-3711

TRANSPORTATION, DEPT. OF

U.S. COAST GUARD
826 N Central Ave.
Phoenix, AZ 85004-2003
(602) 379-3834
wnash@cgrc.uscg.mil
www.gocoastguard.com

ARKANSAS

AGRICULTURE, DEPARTMENT OF

SOUTH CENTRAL REGION
Rose Webb, HEPM
700 W Capitol Ave., Fedd. Bldg. #3416
Little Rock, AR 72201
(501) 301- 3174
rose.webb@ar.usda.gov

EQUAL EMPLOYMENT OPPORTUNITY COMMISSION

LITTLE ROCK AREA OFFICE
Kay Klugh, Director
425 W Capitol Ave., #625
Little Rock, AR 72201
(501) 324-5060

THE DEPARTMENT OF JUSTICE IS SEEKING HISPANIC MEN AND WOMEN

- **ATTORNEYS**
- **CRIMINAL INVESTIGATORS**
- **SPECIAL AGENTS**
- **CORRECTIONAL OFFICERS**
- **IMMIGRATION INSPECTORS**
- **CLERK TYPISTS**
- **SECRETARY STENOGRAPHERS**
- **PARALEGAL SPECIALISTS**
- **DEPUTY U.S. MARSHALS**
- **BORDER PATROL AGENTS**
- **COMPUTER SPECIALISTS/SCIENTIST**
- **AND MANY OTHER ADMINISTRATIVE AND**
- **TECHNICAL POSITIONS**

The Department of Justice employs over 120,000 persons throughout the Nation, foreign countries, and U.S. Territories. Through its thousands of lawyers, investigators, agents and support staffs, the Department plays a key role in protecting agaisnt crime; in ensuring healthy competition of business; in safeguarding the consumer; and in enforcing civil rights, drug, and immigration laws. The Department also plays a significant role in protecting citizens thorugh its efforts in areas of prosecution and rehabilitation of offenders. Moreover, the Department represents the Government in legal matters generally, rendering legal advice and opinions upon request to the President and to the heads of executive departments and agencies.

For more information about career opportunities, visit our web site or you can also write to the address listed below. Indicate the type of position you are seeking, and the desired geographical location you are interested in applying to:

Write to: **U.S. Department of Justice**
Hispanic Employment Program
950 Pennsylvania Avenue, N.W.
Room 7643
Washington, D.C. 20530
www.USDOJ.GOV/JMD/EEOS

The Department of Justice is an Equal Opportunity Employer

NAVY, DEPARTMENT OF THE

USMC RECRUITING STATION
Staff Sgt.Howard Googh, Op. Chief
100 S Main St., #500
Little Rock, AR 72201-2603
(501) 324-5498
googhhe@8mcd.usmc.mil

STATE OF ARKANSAS

DEPARTMENT OF FINANCE AND ADMINISTRATION
Beth Perdue, Mgr. of Human Resources
1000 Center St.
Little Rock, AR 72203
(501) 371-6009

TRANSPORTATION, DEPT. OF

U.S. COAST GUARD
Ashley Square Shopping Center
9112 N Rodney Parham Rd.
Little Rock, AR 72205-1648
(501) 217-9446/8219/8719
rrankin@cgrc.uscg.mil
www.gocoastguard.com

CALIFORNIA

AGRICULTURE, DEPARTMENT OF

FOREST SERVICE
Gladys Evans, HEPM
800 Buchanan St., West Bldg.
Albany, CA 94710-0011
(510) 559-6308
gevans@fs.fed.gov

FOREST SERVICE
Sandra Stasenka, HEPM
630 Sansome St.
San Francisco, CA 94111
(415) 705-2558
sstasenka@fs.fed.us

FOREST SERVICE
Larry Sandoval, Equal Employment Mgr.
2550 Riverside Dr.
Susanville, CA 96130
(505) 257-2151
isandoval@fs.fed.gov

FOREST SERVICE
Lori Tapia-Piozet, Director of Civil Rights
1323 Club Dr.
Vallejo, CA 94592
(707) 562-8752
ltapiapiozet@fs.fed.gov

FOREST SERVICE
Genie Ott Mendiola, SEPM Specialist
875 N Humboldt
Willows, CA 95988
(530) 934-7724
gmendiola@fs.fed.gov

LOCKEFORD PLANT MATERIALS CENTER
Tish Espinosa, West Region HEPM
P.O. Box 68
21001 N Elliot Rd.
Lockeford, CA 95233
(209) 727-3129x13
tish.espinosa@ca.usda.gov

CITY OF LOS ANGELES

L.A. UNIFIED SCHOOL DISTRICT
450 N Grand Ave., #C-102
Los Angeles, CA 90012
(800) 832-2452
www.teachinla.com

COMMERCE, DEPARTMENT OF

MAYOR'S OFFICE OF ECON. DEV.
Diane Castaño Sallee, Director
City Hall East, 8th Fl.
Los Angeles, CA 90012
(213) 847-6200

ENERGY, DEPARTMENT OF

DOE BERKELEY SITE OFFICE
Ken Rivera, HEPM
1 Cyclotron Rd., MS 90-1023
Berkeley, CA 94720
(510) 486-6343
Krivera@lbl.gov

ENVIRONMENTAL PROTECTION AGENCY

HUMAN RESOURCES OFFICE, REGION 9
Karen Nelson, Outreach Coordinator
75 Hawthorne St., PMD-12
San Francisco, CA 94105
(415) 744-1541

EQUAL EMPLOYMENT OPPORTUNITY COMMISSION

FRESNO LOCAL OFFICE
David Rodríguez, Director
1265 W Shaw Ave., #103
Fresno, CA 93711
(209) 487-5793

LOS ANGELES DISTRICT OFFICE
Olophius Perry, Director (Acting)
255 E Temple St., 4th Fl.
Los Angeles, CA 90012
(213) 894-1000

OAKLAND LOCAL OFFICE
Joyce A. Hendy, Director
1301 Clay St., #1170-N
Oakland, CA 94612-5217
(510) 637-3230

SAN DIEGO AREA OFFICE
Walter D. Champe, Director
401 B St., #1550
San Diego, CA 92101
(619) 557-7235

SAN FRANCISCO DISTRICT OFFICE
Susan L. McDuffie, Director
901 Market St., #500
San Francisco, CA 94103
(415) 356-5100

SAN JOSE LOCAL OFFICE
Dequese Cooper, Director
96 N 3rd St., #200
San Jose, CA 95112
(408) 291-7352

INTERIOR, DEPARTMENT OF THE

BUREAU OF LAND MANAGEMENT
Keith Arnold, Personnel Officer
2800 Cottage Way (CA946)
Sacramento, CA 95825
(916) 978-4464

BUREAU OF RECLAMATION
Tyrone Long, Personnel Mgmt. Specialist
Federal Office Bldg., 2800 Cottage Way
Sacramento, CA 95825
(916) 978-5482

GEOLOGICAL SURVEY, WESTERN REGION
345 Middlefield Rd., M/S 612
Menlo Park, CA 94025
(650) 329-4109

NATIONAL PARK SERVICE
Marsha Lee Human Resources Manager
600 Harrison St., #600
San Francisco, CA 94101
(415) 427-1316

LABOR, DEPARTMENT OF

EMPLOYMENT AND TRAINING ADMINISTRATION
Jacqueline Roberts Regional Director
71 Stevenson St., #1015
San Francisco, CA 94105-2970
(415) 975-4680

NAVY, DEPARTMENT OF THE

12TH MARINE CORPS DISTRICT
3074 Hochmoth Ave.
San Diego, CA 92140-5191
(619) 542-5510

MARINE CORPS RECRUITMENT DEPOT
1600 Henderson Ave., #248
San Diego, CA 92140-5001
(619) 524-8807

SPAWAR SYSTEMS COMMAND (CODE 00A-HR)
Cheryl Givens-Hayes, Command Deputy
EEO Officer
4301 Pacific Hwy.
San Diego, CA 92110
(858) 537-0218
givens@spawar.navy.mil

USMC RECRUITING STATION
620 Central Ave., Blbg. 2E, Fed. Ctr
Alameda, CA 94501-3406
(510) 865-7966

USMC RECRUITING STATION
2302 Martin St., #400
Irvine, CA 92612-1449
(949) 261-8807

USMC RECRUITING STATION
5051 Rodeo Rd., #2061
Los Angeles, CA 90016-4794
(213) 294-1968

USMC RECRUITING STATION
Bldg. 546, Vernon Ave.
Moffet Federal Airfield
Mountain View, CA 94043

USMC RECRUITING STATION
3870 Rosin Ct. #110
Sacramenrto, CA 95834-1633
(916) 646-6980

USMC RECRUITING STATION
2221 Camino del Rio, South #212
San Diego, CA 92108-3610
(619) 688-1515

POSTAL SERVICE

LONG BEACH DISTRICT
Maggie Pulido-Lara, Hispanic Prog. Spec.
11721 183rd St.
Artesia, CA 90701-9998
(562)-924-3747

LONG BEACH DISTRICT
Letty Sevilla-Scott, Div. Dev. Field Spec.
13031 W Jefferson Blvd.
Inglewood, CA 90311-9202
(310) 301-1224

LOS ANGELES DISTRICT
Gilbert Martínez, Hispanic Prog. Spec.
7001 S Central Ave., #105
Los Angeles, CA 90052-4200
(323) 586-2991

LOS ANGELES DISTRICT
Melody Nelson
Diversity Development Field Specialist
7001 South Central Ave.
Los Angeles, CA 90052-4200
(323) 586-1330

LOS ANGELES DISTRICT
Manuel Lopez, Div. Dev. Field Spec.
7001 S Central Ave.
Los Angeles, CA 90052-4200
(323) 586-4474

OAKLAND DISTRICT
Elmira A. Walton, Div. Dev. Field Spec.
1675 Seventh St., #306
Oakland, CA 94615-9512
(510) 874-8665

OAKLAND DISTRICT
Kelly M. Sotelo, Hispanic Prog. Spec.
1675 Seventh St.
Oakland, CA 94615-9512
(510) 874-8645

PACIFIC AREA OFFICE
Henrietta Clark Goldsby, Div. Dev. Field Spec.
400 Oyster Point Blvd.
South San Francisco, CA 94099-4001
(650) 635-3133

SACRAMENTO DISTRICT
Linda H. Gregory, Div. Dev. Field Spec.
3775 Industrial Blvd.
West Sacramento, CA 95799-0067
(916) 373-8604

SACRAMENTO DISTRICT
Margarita Ramirez Palmer, Hisp. Prog. Spec.
3775 Industrial Blvd., #3019
West Sacramento, CA 95799-9994
(916) 373-8705

SAN DIEGO DISTRICT
Edward G. Carmona, Hisp. Prog. Spec.
P.O. Box 19001
San Bernardino, CA 92423-9001
(909) 335-4366

SAN DIEGO DISTRICT
Alicia Allgood, Div. Dev. Field Spec.
11251 Rancho Carmel Dr., #341
San Diego, CA 92199-9461
(619) 674-2713

SAN DIEGO DISTRICT
Hector Baca, Hispanic Prog. Specialist
11251 Rancho Carmel Dr.
San Diego, CA 92199-9002
(619) 674-0256

SAN FRANCISCO DISTRICT
David Minamide, Div. Dev. Field Spec.
P.O. Box 884210
San Francisco, CA 94188-4210
(415) 550-5775

SAN FRANCISCO DISTRICT
Abel E. Sánchez, Hispanic Prog. Spec.
P.O. Box 885050
San Francisco, CA 94188-5348
(415) 550-5710

SAN JOSE DISTRICT
Jeanie Lew, Div. Dev. Field Spec.
1750 Lundy Ave.
San Jose, CA 95101-7062
(408) 437-6952

SAN JOSE DISTRICT
Rose Canela, Hispanic Prog. Specialist
1750 Lundy Ave.
San Jose, CA 95101-7081
(408) 437-6940

SANTA ANA DISTRICT
Norma Diaz, Div. Dev. Field Spec.
15421 Gale Ave.
City of Industry, CA 91747-9347
(626) 855-6354

SANTA ANA DISTRICT
Christina Hurtado, Hispanic Prog. Spec.
15421 Gale Ave.
City of Industry, CA 91715-9347
(626) 855-6351

VAN NUYS DISTRICT
Tyrone Washington, Div. Dev. Field Spec.
28201 Franklin Pkwy.
Santa Clarita, CA 91383-9994
(661) 775-7055

VAN NUYS DISTRICT
Alex Hernandez, Hispanic Prog. Spec.
28201 Franklin Pkwy.
Santa Clarita, CA 91383-9994
(661) 775-7057

VAN NUYS DISTRICT
Guadalupe N. Contraras, Hispanic Prog. Spec.
28201 Franklin Pkwy.
Santa Clarita, CA 91383-9994
(661) 775-7056

STATE OF CALIFORNIA

EMPLOYMENT DEV. DEPARTMENT
Josephine R. DeLeon, Chief
P.O. Box 826880, MIC-49
Sacramento, CA 94280-0001
(916) 654-8434

TRANSPORTATION, DEPT. OF

U.S. COAST GUARD
11149 183rd St
Cerritos, CA 90703-5415
(562) 402-6244
bmelton@cgrc.uscg.mil
www.gocoastguard.com

U.S. COAST GUARD
1090 E Washington St., #A
Colton, CA 92324-8180
(909) 783-2772/2807
wcampbell@cgrc.uscg.mil
www.gocoastguard.com

U.S. COAST GUARD
Victoria Place Shopping Center
3220 S Broadway St., Unit A-4
Eureka, CA 95501-3854
(707) 268-2471
kclark@cgrc.uscg.mil
www.gocoastguard.com

U.S. COAST GUARD
5050 Sunrise Blvd., Building C/5
Fair Oaks, CA 95628-4942
(916) 962-3942
mgirard@cgrc.uscg.mil
www.gocoastguard.com

U.S. COAST GUARD
1490 W Shaw St., #A
Fresno, CA 93711
(559) 221-6600/80
rcruikshank@cgrc.uscg.mil
www.gocoastguard.com

U.S. COAST GUARD
4202 S Victora Ave.
Oxnard, CA 93035
(805) 984-6893/9284
cthomson@cgrc.uscg.mil
www.gocoastguard.com

U.S. COAST GUARD
Point Loma Plaza
3663 E Midway Dr.
San Diego, CA 92110-3224
(619) 226-8222/31
rwashington@cgrc.uscg.mil
www.gocoastguard.com

U.S. COAST GUARD
3381 Stevens Creek Blvd.
San Jose, CA 95117-1070
(408) 246-8724
ybutler@cgrc.uscg.mil
www.gocoastguard.com

U.S. COAST GUARD
Menlo Plaza
14410 Washington Ave., #118
San Leandro, CA 94578
(510) 352-8992
blovellette@cgrc.uscg.mil
www.gocoastguard.com

U.S. COAST GUARD
12113 Santa Monica Blvd., #201
West Los Angeles, CA 90025
(310) 447-0883/0682
dmoore@cgrc.uscg.mil
www.gocoastguard.com

TREASURY, DEPARTMENT OF THE

CUSTOMS SERVICE
Anna Morales, Hispanic Prog. Manager
1 World Trade Center, #723
Long Beach, CA 90831
(562) 980-3115 x119

INTERNAL REVENUE SERVICE
Deborah Zipp, Hispanic Prog. Manager
1650 Mission Street, Room 508
San Francisco, CA 94103
(415) 575-7083

COLORADO

AGRICULTURE, DEPARTMENT OF

FOREST SERVICE
Mary E. McDonough, HEPM
240 W Prospect Rd.
Fort Collins, CO 80525-2098
(970) 498-1167/1295
mmcdonough/rmrs/usdafs@fsnotes

FOREST SERVICE
Angela Baca, HEPM
P.O. Box 25127
Lakewood, CO 80225
(303) 275-5343
abaca@fs.fed.us

FOREST SERVICE
Bob Gonzales, HEPM, Facilities Engineer
Lakewood, CO 80225
(303) 275-5197
bgonzalea@fs.fed.gov

NORTH PLAINS REGION
Olivia Romero, HEPM
655 Parfet St., #E200C
Lakewood, CO 80215-5517
(303) 236-2903x250
oromero@co.nrcs.usda.gov

AIR FORCE, DEPARTMENT OF THE

HEADQUARTERS AIR FORCE SPACE COMMAND
Margret M. Waldie, HEPM
150 Vandenberg St., #1150
Peterson AFB, CO 80914-4550
(719) 554-5395

HEADQUARTERS UNITES STATES AIR FORCE ACADEMY
Lorraine Boddie, HEPM
8034 Edgerton Dr., #100
USAF Academy, CO 80840-2215
(719) 333-7201

COMMERCE, DEPARTMENT OF

OCEANIC & ATMOSPHERIC RESEARCH
Tony Tafoya, EEO Officer
325 Broadway, Bldg. 22
Boulder, CO 80303
(303) 497- 6731

EDUCATION, DEPARTMENT OF

HUMAN RESOURCES DEPARTMENT
Mary Kelly, Regional Officer
Regional Office, Federal Bldg.
1244 Speer Blvd., #353
Denver, CO 80204
(303) 844-3864

ENERGY, DEPARTMENT OF

DOE DENVER REGIONAL OFFICE
Steve Palomo, HEPM
1617 Cole Blvd., Bldg. 17
Golden, CO 80002
(303) 275-4838
Steve_palomo@nrel.gov

GOLDEN FIELD OFFICE
Victor V. Candelaria, HEPM
1617 Cole Blvd.
Golden, CO 80401
(303) 275-4717
Victor_candelaria@nrel.gov

ROCKY FLATS FIELD OFFICE
Harold Armenta, HEPM
P.O. Box 928
Golden, CO 80402-0928
(303) 966-4760
Harold.armenta@rf.doe.gov

ROCKY FLATS FIELD OFFICE
Anna Martínez, HEPM
P.O. Box 928
Golden, CO 80402-0928
(303) 966-5881
Anna.martinez@rf.doe.gov

WESTERN AREA POWER ADMIN.
Richard L. Gallegos, HEPM
Bldg. CSO, #353A, MS-A0300
Lakewood, CO
(720) 962-7044
Gallegos@wapa.gov

WESTERN AREA POWER ADMIN.
Josephine Quijas, HEPM
P.O. Box 281213
12155 W Alameda Pkwy.
Lakewood, CO 80228-8213
(720) 962-7035
Quijas@wapa.gov

ENVIRONMENTAL PROTECTION AGENCY

REGION 8
Barbara Barron, HEPM
999 18th Street, #300, Mail Code: 8PWMS
Denver, CO 80202
(303) 312-6617

EQUAL EMPLOYMENT OPPORTUNITY COMMISSION

DENVER DISTRICT OFFICE
Francisco J. Flores, Jr., Director
303 E 17th Ave., # 510
Denver, CO 80203
(303) 866-1300

INTERIOR, DEPARTMENT OF THE

BUREAU OF RECLAMATION
Laurie Johnson, Manager
P.O. Box 25007, Denver Federal Center
Denver, CO 80225-0007
(303) 445-2654

BUREAU OF RECLAMATION
Roger Molinar, Diversity Prog. Manager
Denver Federal Center Bldg., #369D
Denver, CO 80225-0007
(303) 445-3133
rmolinar@do.usbr.gov

INTERIOR, DEPARTMENT OF THE

GEOLOGICAL SURVEY, CENTRAL REGION
P.O. Box 25046
Denver Federal Center, M/S 612
Denver, CO 80225-0046
(303) 236-5900x361

MINERALS MGMT. SERVICE
Susan Hester, Chief Personnel Manager
P.O. Box 25165. M/S 2720
Denver, CO 80225
(303) 275-7312

NATIONAL PARK SERVICE
John Crowley, Human Resources Mgr.
P.O. Box 25287, 12795 W Alameda Pkwy.
Denver, CO 80225
(303) 969-2506

LABOR, DEPARTMENT OF

EMPLOYMENT AND TRAINING ADMINISTRATION
Patricia Putnins, Assoc. Reg. Dir. (Acting)
1999 Broadway, #1720
Denver, CO 80202-5716
(303) 844-1630

NAVY, DEPARTMENT OF THE

USMC RECRUITING STATION
1600 Sherman St., #500
Denver, CO 80203-9860
(303) 832-2532

POSTAL SERVICE

COLORADO/WYOMING DIST.
Corally I. Power-Brugueras, Hisp. Prog. Spec.
1501 Wynkoop St., # 220
Denver, CO 80266-9702
(303) 454-4149

DENVER DISTRICT
Jay Kubokawa, Div. Dev. Field Spec.
Terminal Annex, 1501 Wynkoop St. # 220
Denver, CO 80266-3001
(303) 454-4217

WESTERN AREA OFFICE
Monica Y. Vital, Div. Dev. Field Spec.
One Park Pl., #1000
Denver, CO 80299-1000
(303) 391-5009

TRANSPORTATION, DEPT. OF

U.S. COAST GUARD
Pinnacle Shopping Center
550 E Thornton Pkwy., #174
Thornton, CO 80229-2135
(303) 252-0919/1037/1360
ddietrich@cgrc.uscg.mil
www.gocoastguard.com

CONNECTICUT

POSTAL SERVICE

CONNECTICUT DISTRICT
Kathleen A. Felsted, Div. Dev. Field Spec.
24 Research Pkwy.
Wallingford, CT 06492-9032
(203) 949-3129

NORTHEAST AREA OFFICE
Roberta G. Strange, Div. Dev. Field Spec.
6 Griffin Rd. N
Windsor, CT 06006-7110
(860) 285-7012

NORTHEAST AREA OFFICE
Juan L. Cruz, Hispanic Prog. Specialist
6 Griffin Rd. N
Winsor, CT 06006-7050
(860) 285-7110

TRANSPORTATION, DEPT. OF

U.S. COAST GUARD
William Cotter Building #G-5
135 High St
Hartford, CT 06103-1111
(860) 240-4259/60
rschultz@cgrc.uscg.mil
www.gocoastguard.com

U.S. COAST GUARD
Route 1, 260 S Frontage Rd.
New London, CT 06320-2641
(860) 444-4947/48/49
knuzzolilli@cgrc.uscg.mil
www.gocoastguard.com

DELAWARE

AGRICULTURE, DEPARTMENT OF

EAST REGION
Georgia Brock, HEPM
1203 College Park Dr., #101
Dover, DE 19904-8713
(302) 678-4160
jan.georgia.brock@de.usda.gov

TRANSPORTATION, DEPARTMENT OF

U.S. COAST GUARD
1169 S DuPont Highway
Dover, DE 19901-4423
(302) 736-0176/5623
fburgess@cgrc.uscg.mil
www.gocoastguard.com

DISTRICT OF COLUMBIA

AGENCY FOR INTERNATIONAL DEVELOPMENT

EQUAL OPPORTUNITY OFFICE
Gladys Fry, HEPM
1300 Pennsylvania Ave., NW, #2.09-084-Ronald Reagan Bldg.
Washington, DC 20523-0001
(202) 712-5272
gfry@usaid.gov

AGRICULTURE, DEPARTMENT OF

ADMINISTRATION
Nancy S. Robinson, USDA HEPM
1400 Independence Ave. SW, #313-W, Whitten Bldg.
Washington, DC 20250
(202) 720-4654
Nancy.Robinson@usda.gov
www.usda.gov

ADMINISTRATION
Pam Carter, HEPM
1400 Independence Ave., SW, #S-313-W, Whitten Bldg.
Washington, DC 20250
(202) 720-2874
Pcarter@usda.gov

AGRICULTURAL MARKETING SERVICE
Joseph E. Soles, EEO Specialist
1400 Independence Ave.SW #3074
S Bldg.
Washington, DC 20250
(202) 720-2702
Joseph.soles@usda.gov

FARM AND FOREIGN AGRICULTURAL SERVICES
Heather Escobar, HEPM
1400 Independence Ave. SW #3051
S Bldg.
Washington, DC 20250
(202) 690-5886
Heather.Escobar@usda.gov
www.usda.gov

FARM AND FOREIGN AGRICULTURAL SERVICES
Doretha Frierson, HEPM
1280 Maryland Ave., SW
Portals Bldg., #580-B
Washington, DC 20250-0509
(202) 401-7186
Doretha_Frierson@fsa.usda.gov

FARM AND FOREIGN AGRICULTURAL SERVICES
Roger Mireles, HEPM
1400 Independence Ave., SW, #5503
S Bldg.
Washington, DC 20250
(202)720-1314
mireles@fas.usda.gov

FOREST SERVICE
Jesus Cota, HEPM
P.O. Box 96090
Washington, DC 20090-6090
(202) 205-1595
jcota@fs.fed.gov

NATURAL RESOURCES AND ENVIRONMENT
Mary Lou Martinez, HEPM
201 14th & Independence Ave., SW
4th Fl., Sidney Yates Bldg.
Washington, DC 20350
(202) 205-0558
Mmartinez/wo@fs.fed.usda.gov

OFFICE OF CIVIL RIGHTS
Gilbert Fandate, Deputy Dir. for Emp.
300 7th St., SW, M/S 9406
Reporters Bldg.
Washington, DC 20250
(202) 401 7653
www.usda.gov

OFFICE OF CIVIL RIGHTS
Deborah Shipman, HEPM
14th & Independence Ave., SW, #0623
Washington, DC 20250
(202) 720-1735
debbieshipman@gipsadc.usda.gov
www.usda.gov

OFFICE OF INSPECTOR GENERAL
Mary Ward, HEPM
1400 Independence Ave. SW #26-E
Whitten Bldg.
Washington, DC 20250
(202) 720-6001
Mward@oig.usda.gov

OFFICE OF OPERATIONS
Sheila Milburn, Human Resource Liaison
1400 Independence Ave. SW
#1575--South Bldg.
Washington, DC 20250
(202) 720-3937
www.usda.gov

RESEARCH, EDUCATION AND ECONOMICS
Susan Dixon, HEPM
1400 Independence Ave. SW #3552
S Bldg.
Washington, DC 20250
(202) 690-0372
sdixon@ars.usda.gov

RESEARCH, EDUCATION AND ECONOMICS
Jenny Grover, HEPM
1400 Independence Ave. SW #3913
S Bldg.
Washington, DC 20250
(202) 690-0005/833-8361
igrover@csree.usda.gov

RESEARCH, EDUCATION AND ECONOMICS
Nydia R. Suárez, HEPM
1800 M St., NW
Washington, DC 20036
(202) 694-5259
Nrsuarez@usda.gov

RESEARCH, EDUCATION AND ECONOMICS
Rafael Sánchez, HEPM
1400 Independence Ave. SW #4116
S Bldg.
Washington, DC 20036
(202) 720-8257
Rafael.Sanchez@usda.gov

RURAL DEVELOPMENT
Jacqueline Micheli, HEPM
1400 Indepence Ave. SW, Stop 0703
Washington, DC 20250-0703
(202) 692-0099
jmicheli@rdmail.rural.usda.gov
www.usda.gov

AIR FORCE, DEPARTMENT OF THE

11 WING
Margaret Wilson, HEPM
1460 Air Force Pentagon
Washinton, DC 20030-1460
(703) 607-3534

11 WING
1460 Air Force Pentagon
Washington, DC 20330-1460
(703) 697-9336

HEADQUARTERS UNITED STATES AIR FORCE
Mary Young, HEPM
1040 Air Force Pentagon
Washington, DC 20330-1040
(703) 693-2699

ARMY, DEPARTMENT OF THE

CORPS OF ENGINEERS
Gonzallas Williams, EEO Officer
441 G St., NW, Attn: CEEO
Washington, DC 20134-1000
(202) 761-8705

HQ ARMY
Deborah Muse, Director. of EEO
105 Army Pentagon, #5A532
Washington, DC 20310-0105
(703) 697-1008

PERSONNEL & EMPLOYMENT SVCS., WASHINGTON
Tracy Richardson, Spec. Emph. Prog. Mgr.
Pentagon, CPAC, PSD, #1A881-6800
Army Pentagon
Washington, DC 20310-6800
(703) 588-1472
richatc@hqda.army.mil

CENTRAL INTELLIGENCE AGENCY

DIVERSITY PLANS & PROGRAMS
Linda Sarfaty, HEPM
Washington, DC 20505
(703) 482-2019

COMMERCE, DEPARTMENT OF

Jorge E. Ponce, Diversity Prog. Manager
14th St. & Constitution Ave. NW #6003
Washington, DC 20230
jponce@doc.gov

INTERNATIONAL TRADE ADMINISTRATION
Tina James, Recruitment Manager
14th & Constitution Ave. NW #7417
Washington, DC 20230
(202) 482-3301
www.ita.doc.gov

OFFICE OF THE INSPECTOR GENERAL
Ausma Karlsons, HEPM
14th St. & Constitution Ave. NW #H-7713
Washington, DC 20230
(202) 482-4948
akarlsons@doc.gov

PATENT AND TRADEMARK OFFICE
Eloisa Done, HEPM
2011 Crystal Dr., #608
Washington, DC 20231
(703) 305-8292
eloisa.done@uspto.gov

US & FOREIGN COMMERCIAL SERVICE
Dorothy Maetin, Diversity Specialist
14th & Constitution Ave. NW # 3227
Washington, DC 20230
(202) 482-2001

COMMISSION ON CIVIL RIGHTS

HUMAN RESOURCES DEPARTMENT
Myrna Hernandez, Human Res. Spec.
624 9th St. NW #510
Washington, DC 20425
(202) 376-8364
www.usccr.gov

CORPORATION FOR NATIONAL SERVICE

EO OFFICE
Nancy Voss, Director
1201 New York Ave., NW
Washington, DC 20525
(202) 606-5000x309

DEFENSE, DEPARTMENT OF

ARMED FORCES-INSTITUTE OF PATHOLOGY
Florabel G. Mullick, MD, HEPM
14th St. & Alaska Ave. NW,
Bldg. 54 #1097
Washington, DC 20306-6000
(202) 782-2503

DEFENSE INTELLIGENCE AGENCY
Nilda Figueroa, HEPM
Attn: TWX
Washington, DC 20340
(202) 231-4742

OFFICE OF DASN
Louisa Ruiz, Diversity Manager
321 Sommers Ct. NW #40103
Washington, DC 20393-5451
(202) 764-0767
ruiz.louisa@hq.navy.mil
www.army.mil

DEFENSE, DEPARTMENT OF

OFFICE OF THE SECRETARY OF DEFENSE
Clairborne D. Hauthton,
Director for Civilian Equal Opportunity
4000 Defense Pentagon, #3A272
Washington, DC 20301-4000
(703) 695-0107
haughtoc@pr.osd.mil

DISTRICT OF COLUMBIA

CONSUMER & REGULATORY AFFAIRS
Cleo Smith, Mgmt.& Program Analyst
941 N. Capitol St., NE
Washington, DC 20002
(202) 442-4400
www.dcra.org

DC OFFICE OF PERSONNEL
Milou Carolan, Director
441 4th St. NW, #320 South
Washington, DC 20001
(202) 442-9600

DEPT. OF HUMAN SERVICES
Tasha Stewart, Director
2700 M. L. King Ave. SE, 801 East Bldg.
Washington, DC 20032
(202) 373-5372

FIRE DEPARTMENT
Frederica Smith, EEO Officer
1923 Vermont Ave. N.W., # 201 South
Washington, DC 20001
(202) 673-3320

MULTICULTURAL SERVICE DIVISION
Marco Esparza, Social Worker
1536 U St. NW
Washington, DC 20009
(202) 671-1224

OFFICE OF BILIGUAL EDUCATION
Mary Ellen Gallegos, Director
4301 Upshur St. NW, 3rd Fl.,
Washington, DC 20011
(202) 576-8850

OFFICE OF EMERGENCY MANAGEMENT AGENCY
Peter G. LaPorte, Director
2000 14th St. NW, 8th Fl.
Washington, DC 20009
(202) 727-3151

OFFICE OF HUMAN RIGHTS
Charles F. Holman, III, Director
441 4th St. NW # 970 North
Washington, DC 20001
(202) 727-3900

OFFICE OF INSPECTOR GENERAL
Grace Price, Administration Officer
717 14th St., # 500
Washington, DC 20005
(202) 727-2540

EDUCATION, DEPARTMENT OF

EEO OFFICE
James R. White, Director EEO
400 Maryland Ave. SW #2W228,
FOB-6, M/S 4550
Washington, DC 20202
(202) 401-3560

HUMAN RESOURCES GROUP
Clarissa Lara, Hisp. Outreach Prog. Mgr.
400 Maryland Ave., SW, #2E300
Washington, DC
(202) 260-8267
om_diversity_recruitment@ed.gov

WHITE HOUSE INITIATIVE ON EDUCATIONAL EXCELLENCE FOR HISPANIC AMERICANS
Sarita Brown, Executive Director
400 Maryland Ave, SW #5E100
Washington, DC 20202
(202) 401-1411

EMPLOYMENT AND TRAINING ADMINISTRATION

OFFICE HUMAN RESOURCES
Merfil Cuesta, HEPM
200 Constitution Ave., NW, #S5214
Washington, DC 20210
(202) 693-3412

ENERGY, DEPARTMENT OF

ENERGY INFORMATION ADMINISTRATION, EI-20
Barbara Hall, HEPM
1000 Independence Ave., SW, 4A-149
Washington, DC 20585
(202) 586-4484
Bhall@eia.doe.gov

ENVIRONMENTAL MGMT., EM-22
Margaret Fernández, HEPM
1000 Independence Ave., SW
Washington, DC 20585
(202) 586-5821
Margaret.fernandez@em.doe.gov

FOSSIL ENERGY, FE-422
Casimiro Izquierdo, HEPM
1000 Independence Ave., SW, #3G-070
Washington, DC 20585
(202) 586-9353
casimiro.izquierdo@hq.doe.gov

HQ HEPM, MA-3
Jeffrey Vargas, HEPM
1000 Independence Ave., SW, #4D-025
Washington, DC 20585
(202) 586-3039
Jeffrey.vargas@hq.doe.gov

OFFICE OF CHIEF FINANCIAL OFFICER, CR-10
Ruth Fulwood, HEPM
1000 Independence Ave., SW, #4A-149
Washington, DC 20585
(202) 586-3464
ruth.fulwood@hq.doe.gov

OFFICE OF CIVIL RIGHTS AND DIVERSITY
Emma López-Cardona, DOE Nat'l HEPM
1000 Independence Ave. SW #1E-278/8
Washington, DC 20585
(202) 586-7601
emma.lopez-cardona@hq.doe.gov

OFFICE OF SCIENCE SC-5
Bill Valdez, HEPM
1000 Independence Ave. SW #3H-051
Washingron, DC 20585
(202) 586-9942
bill.valdez@science.doe.gov

SECURITY AND EMERGENCY OPERATIONS
Juan M. Castro, HEPM
1000 Independence Ave. SW #6E-050
Washington, DC 20585
(202) 586-9706
Juan.castro@hq.doe.gov

ENVIRONMENTAL PROTECTION AGENCY

OFFICE OF CIVIL RIGHTS
Ann Goode, Director
1200 Pennsylvania Ave. NW, MC 1201-A
Washington, DC 20460
(202) 564-7272

OFFICE OF HUMAN RESOURCES AND ORGANIZATIONAL SVCS.
Daiva Balkus, Director
1200 Pennsylvania Ave. NW, MC 3610-A
Washington, DC 20460
(202) 564-4606

EQUAL EMPLOYMENT OPPORTUNITY COMMISSION

WASHINGTON FIELD OFFICE
Tulio L. Diaz, Jr., Director
1400 L St., NW, #200
Washington, DC 20005
(202) 275-7377

EXEC. OFFICE OF THE PRESIDENT

OFFICE OF ADMINISTRATION
Cassin Gordon, Assoc. Director for EEO
725 17th St., NW, #2200, New Exec. OB
Washington, DC 20503
(202) 395-3996

EXPORT-IMPORT BANK OF THE U.S.

EEO AND DIVERSITY PROG. OFFICE
811 Vermont Ave. NW, #753
Washington, DC 20571
(202) 565-3591

HUMAN RESOURCES
Dennis Heins, Director of Personnel
811 Vermont Ave. NW, #771
Washington, DC 20571
(202) 565-3316

FEDERAL COURTS ADMINISTRATIVE OFFICE

EMPLOYEE RELATIONS OFFICE
Trudi M. Morrison, Chief, Emp. Rel. Office
1 Columbus Cir. NE, #5-265
Washington, DC 20544
(202) 502-1380

FEDERAL DEPOSIT INSURANCE CORPORATION

OFFICE OF DIVERSITY AND ECONOMIC OPPORTUNITY
Rolando Esparza, EEO Specialist
801 17th St. NW #1240
Washington, DC 20434-0001
(202) 416-2451
resparza@fdic.gov

FEDERAL ELECTION COMMISSION

EEO OFFICE
Patricia Brown, EEO Officer
999 E St., NW, #436
Washington, DC 20463
(202) 694-1228

FEDERAL HOUSING FINANCE BOARD (FHFB)

DEPT. OF HUMAN RESOURCES
Bob Stanton, Human Resources Officer
1777 F Street, NW, 1st Fl.
Washington, DC 20006
(202) 408-2517

FEDERAL MARITIME COMMISSION

GENERAL COUNSEL OFFICE
Alice Blackman, Director of EEO
800 N. Capitol St., NW, #1018
Washington, DC 20573-0001
(202) 523-5740
aliceb@fmc.gov

FEDERAL MEDIATION & CONCILIATION SERVICE

HUMAN RESOURCES
Bill Carlisle, Director
2100 K St. NW, 7th Fl.
Washington, DC 20427
(202) 606-5460

FEDERAL RESERVE BOARD

EEO
Juana Montgomery, Hisp.Prog. Coord.
20th & Constitution Ave., NW, MS 94
Washington, DC 20551
(202) 452-2642
www.federalreserve.gov

FEDERAL RETIREMENT THRIFT INVESTMENT BOARD

PERSONNEL OFFICE
Leonard Sese, Director of Personnel
1250 H St., NW. #200
Washington, DC 20005
(202) 942-1600

FEDERAL TRADE COMMISSION

HUMAN RESOURCES
Elliott Davis, Director
600 Pennsylvania Ave. NW #144
Washington, DC 20580
(202) 326-2022

GENERAL ACCOUNTING OFFICE

INFORMATION TECHNOLOGY
Yvonne Sanchez, Chairperson,
Hispanic Employee Council
441 G St. NW, #4R36
Washington, DC 20548
(202) 512-6274

PHYSICAL INFRASTRUCTURE
Ivonne Pufahl, Hispanic Liaison
441 G St. NW, #2T23
Washington, DC 20548
(202) 512-2313

RECRUITMENT OFFICE
Sally Jaggar, Acting Director
441 G St. NW, #1165
Washington, DC 20548
(202) 512-6388

GENERAL SERVICES ADMIN.

PERSONNEL POLICY & PLANNING DIVISION
Irene De La Torre, HEPM
1800 F St., NW #G126
Washington, DC 20405
(202) 501-1580
www.gsa.gov

GOVERNMENT PRINTING OFFICE

SMALL & DISADVANTAGED BUSINESS OFFICE
Robert Freeman, Director
732 N Capitol St. NW, #C-897
Washington, DC 20401
(202) 512-1365
rfreeman@gpo.gov

HEALTH AND HUMAN SERVICES, DEPARTMENT OF

Sandra Aguilar, Deputy Director of
Operations and Government Affairs
HHH Bldg
200 Independence Ave. SW, 600E
Washington, DC 20201
(202) 401-5631

ADMINISTRATION FOR CHILDREN AND FAMILIES
Carl Montoya, HEPM
330 C St. SW #2124
Washington, DC 20447
(202) 205-8557
www.hhs.gov/progorg/ohr/jobs

EEO PROGRAMS GROUP
Bonita V. White, Esq., Director
HHH Bldg., #536E,
200 Independence Ave., SW
Washington, DC 20201
(202) 690-6555
bwhite@os.dhhs.gov

HEADQUARTERS OFFICE
Martin D. Levy, HHS HEPM
HHH Bldg., Rm 536-E
200 Independence Ave., SW
Washington, DC 20201
(202) 690-6660
mlevy@os.dhhs.gov

OFFICE OF THE SECRETARY, EEO
Barbara Barski, Program Manager
Hubert H. Humphrey Bldg.
200 Independence Ave. SW, #510-B
Washington, DC 20201
(202) 619-1564
bbarski@os.dhhs.gov

HOUSING AND URBAN DEVELOPMENT, DEPT. OF

OFFICE OF EEO
Robert Walker, Diversity Manager
451 7th St. SW #2106
Washington, DC 20410
(202) 708-5921

INTERIOR, DEPARTMENT OF THE

BUREAU OF LAND MANAGEMENT
Gloria Inniss , EEO Manager
1849 C. St., NW, M/S 302LS
Washington, DC 20240
(202) 452-5090
www.blm.gov

BUREAU OF RECLAMATION
Carmen Maymi
1849 C St.NW. Room 7060-MIB
Washington, DC 20240-0001
(202) 208-4157

EEO OFFICE
Melody Stith, Director
1849 C St., NW, M/S 5214
Washington, DC 20240
(202) 208-5693

GEOLOGICAL SURVEY
Lynne Sendejo, HEPM
250 Sunrise Valley Dr., #1B418, M/S 602
Washington, DC 20240
(703) 648-4868
www.usgs.gov

NATIONAL CAPITAL REGION
Karrie Serrell, Spec. Emph. Prog. Mgr.
1100 Ohio Dr., SW
Washington, DC 20242
(202) 619-7224

NATIONAL PARK SERVICE
William Nieto, Jr., HEPM
1100 Ohio Dr. SW, Room #105
Washington, DC 20240
(202) 619-7020

NATIONAL PARK SERVICE
Lynn Smith, Employment Officer
1849 C St., NW
Washington, DC 20240
(202) 208-4649

NATIONAL PARK SERVICE
Adele Singer, Personnel Specialist
1849 C St. NW, #2328
Washington, DC 20240
(202) 208-4649

NATIONAL PARK SERVICE
Kerrie Ferrell, Spec. Emphasis Prog. Mgr.
1100 Ohio Dr., SW
Washington, DC 20242
(202) 619-7233

OFFICE OF SURFACE MINING
Diane Wood, HEPM
1951 Constitution Ave., NW, Rm. 138
Washington, DC 20240
(202) 208-5897

OFFICE OF SURFACE MINING
James Joiner, EO Officer
1951 Constitution Ave., NW, #138
Washington, DC 20240
(202) 208-5897

INTERNATIONAL BROADCASTING BUREAU

OFFICE OF EE & CIVIL RIGHTS
Delia Johnson, Director
301 4th St., SW, M/S-858
Washington, DC 20237
(202) 619-5157
djohnson@ibb.gov
www.ibb.gov

JUSTICE, DEPARTMENT OF

EXECUTIVE OFFICE FOR U. S. ATTORNEYS
Sheila J. Washington, EEO Specialist
600 E St., NW, #2300
Washington, DC 20530
(202) 514-3111
www.usdoj.gov/usao/eouse.html

FED. BUREAU OF INVESTIGATION
Kathelin Koch, Chief
935 Pennsylvania Ave., NW Rm. 7901
Washington, DC 20535
(202) 324-4128

FED. BUREAU OF INVESTIGATION
Gloria Lalka, HEPM
935 Pennsylvania Ave., NW, #7901
Washington, DC 20535-0001
(202) 324-4136

FED. BUREAU OF INVESTIGATION
Calvin Shivers, EEO Specialist
935 Pennsylvania Ave., NW
Washington, DC 20535-0001
(202) 324-3674
www.fbi.gov/employment.htm

FEDERAL BUREAU OF PRISONS
Wanda Hunt, EEO Officer
320 1st St. NW #700
Washington, DC 20534
(202) 514-6165

**IMMIGRATION AND
NATURALIZATION SERVICE**
Kathy Lane, EEO Program Manager
425 I St. NW #1122
Washington, DC 20536
(202) 514-1246

MARSHALS SERVICE
Dolores Witcher, EEO Specialist
1735 Jefferson Davis Hwy.
Crystal Square 3, #103
Arlington, VA 22202
(202) 307-9495

**OFFICE OF THE ASSISTANT
ATTORNEY GENERAL**
Lori Bledsoe, EEO Officer
810 7th St. NW #6109
Washington, DC 20531
(202) 307-5933

**OFFICES BOARDS AND
DIVISIONS**
Carmen Mendez, Program Manager
950 Pennsylvania Ave. NW #7647
Washington, DC 20530
(202) 616-4800

LABOR, DEPARTMENT OF

BUREAU OF LABOR STATISTICS
Dorothy Wigglesworth, EO Officer
2 Massachusetts Ave., NE, #4280
Washington, DC 20212
(202) 606-6606

**EMPLOYMENT STANDARDS
ADMINISTRATION**
Kate Durrell, Director
200 Constitution Ave. NW, #C-3315
Washington, DC 20210
(202) 693-0024

HUMAN RESOURCES
Ivonne Cervoni, HEPM
200 Constitution Ave., NW, #C-5516
Washington, DC 20210
(202) 219-6532

INTERNATIONAL LABOR AFFAIRS
Ana Maria Valdes, HEPM
200 Constitution Ave. NW #S5325
Washington, DC 20210
(202) 219-6201
www.dol.gov/dol.ilab

**OCCUPATIONAL SAFETY &
HEALTH ADMINISTRATION**
Betty Gills-Robinson, Director
200 Constitution Ave. NW #N-3315
Washington, DC 20210
(202) 693-2150

OFFICE OF CIVIL RIGHTS
Linda Blumner, EEO Specialist
200 Constitution Ave. NW #N-4123
Washington, DC 20210
(202) 219-6362

OFFICE OF INSPECTOR GENERAL
Leroy J. Sandoval , HEPM
200 Constitution Ave. NW #S5522
Washington, DC 20210
(202) 693-5162

**OFFICE OF THE ASST. SECRETARY
FOR ADMIN. AND MGMT.**
Viviana Rodriguez-Bernstein,
Personnel Management Specialist
200 Constitution Ave. NW #N5454
Washington, DC 20210
(202) 219-6741 ext:109

**OFFICE OF THE ASST. SECRETARY
FOR ADMIN. AND MGMT.**
Milton Blount, EEO Manager
200 Constitution Ave. NW #S-1514
Washington, DC 20210
(202) 693-4031

LIBRARY OF CONGRESS

HUMAN RESOURCES
James Madison
101 Independence Ave., SE Bldg.,
#LM-107
Washington, DC 20540
(202) 707-5627

MERIT SYSTEM PROTECTION BOARD

EEO OFFICE
Carolyn Smith, EEO Specialist
1120 Vermont Ave., NW
Washington, DC 20419
(202) 653-6180

METROPOLITAN POLICE DEPT.

OFFICE OF POLICE RECRUITING
Jeffrey Moore, Director
#6 DC Village Lane SW, Bldg. 1A
Washington, DC 20032
(202) 645-0445

NATIONAL AERONAUTICS AND SPACE ADMINISTRATION (NASA)
Miguel Torres HEPM
300 E St., SW
Washington, DC 20546
(202) 358-0937
mtorres@hq.nasa.gov

NATIONAL ENDOWMENT FOR THE ARTS

HUMAN RESOURCES
Maxine Jefferson, Director
1100 Pennsylvania Ave., NW, #627
Washington, DC 20506
(202) 682-5470
www.arts.endow.gov

NATIONAL ENDOWMENT FOR THE HUMANITIES

ADMINISTRATOR SERVICES
Willie McGhee, EEO Officer
1100 Pennsylvania Ave., NW, #202
Washington, DC 20506
(202) 606-8233

HUMAN RESOURCES
Timothy Connelly, Director
1100 Pennsylvania Ave. NW #418
Washington, DC 20506
(202) 606-8656

NATIONAL LABOR RELATIONS BOARD

OFFICE OF EO
Robert Poindexter, Director
1099 14th St. NW #9600
Washington, DC 20570
(202) 273-3891

NATIONAL MEDIATION BOARD

ARBITRATION SERVICES
Roland Watkins, Director/HEPM
1301 K St. NW #250 East
Washington, DC 20572
(202) 692-5055

NAVY, DEPARTMENT OF THE

**CHIEF OF NAVAL OPERATION
(NO9BE)**
Deborah McCormick , Comm. Dep. EEO Off.
2000 Pentagon
Washington, DC 20350-2000
(703) 697-8203
mccormick.deborah.@hq.navy.mil

CIVILIAN PERSONNEL /EEO
Betty S. Welch, DASN
Pentagon, #4E789
Washington, DC 20350-1000
(703) 695-2633
welch.betty@hq.navy.mil

**COMPUTER & TELECOMM.
COMMAND**
Issac Oliver, Command Dep. EEO Officer
AND (BUMED) Washington Navy
Yard~1014 N St. SE #1
Washington, DC 20374-5050
(202) 433-0712
oliver.issac@hrow.navy.mil

MILITARY SEALIFT COMMAND
Wanda Watson-Young, Comm. Dep. EEO Off.
914 Charles Morris Ct., SE
Washington, DC 20398
(202) 685-5988
wanda.watson-young@msc.navy.mil

**NAVAL CRIMINAL
INVESTIGATIVE SERVICE HQ**
Jackie Hoffman, Comm. Dep. EEO Off.
716 Sicard St. SE #2000
Washington, DC 20388-5380
(202) 433-9140
jhoffman@ncis.navy.mil

**NAVAL FACILITIES ENGINEERING
COMMAND**
Jacqueline L. Hayes, Comm. Dep. EEO Off.
1322 Patterson Ave. SE
Washington Navy Yard
Washington, DC 20374-5065
(202) 685-9099
hayesjl@navfac.navy.mil

OFFICE OF NAVAL INTELLIGENCE
Patricia Proctor, Comm. Dep. EEO Off.
4251 Suitland Rd., #2A129
Washington, DC 20359-5720
(301) 669-5119
proctor@nmic.navy.mil

**SECRETARIAT/HQ HUMAN
RESOURCES OFFICE**
Rhonda L. McGee, Comm. Dep. EEO Off.
2 Navy Annex, #2052
Washington, DC 20370-5240
(703) 693-0202
mcgee.rhonda@hq.navy.mil

**SECRETARIAT/HQ HUMAN
RESOURCES OFFICE**
Rhonda L. McGee, Asst. Comm. Dep. EEO Off.
2 Navy Annex, #2052
Washington, DC 20370-5240
(703) 693-0243
cheek.kay@hq.navy.mil

NUCLEAR REGULATORY COMM.

OFFICE OF HUMAN RESOURCES
Henry Rubin, Recruitment Manager
Mail Stop O3E17A
Washington, DC 20555
(301) 415-1374

OFFICE OF MANAGEMENT AND BUDGET
Cynthia Vallina, HEPM
725 17th St., NW, Rm. 8025
Washington, DC 20503
(202) 395-3634

OFFICE OF PERSONNEL MGMT.

HUMAN RESOURCES, EEO
Melissa Rodriguez, HEPM/ EEO Spec.
1900 E Street, NW, #1469
Washington, DC 20415
(202) 606-1786
mmrodig@opm.gov

OVERSEAS PRIVATE INVESTMENT CORPORATION

HUMAN RESOURCES MGMT.
Rick Cooley, HEPM
1100 New York Ave., NW
Washington, DC 20527
(202) 336-8529

PEACE CORPS

MINORITY RECRUITMENT I
Wilfredo Sauri, Director
1111 20th St., NW, 6th Fl.
Washington, DC 20526
(202) 692-1819

POSTAL SERVICE

CAPITAL DISTRICT
Olivia J. Mallory, Div. Dev. Field Spec.
900 Brentwood Rd., NE
Washington, DC 20066-7400
(202) 636-1485

SECURITIES AND EXCHANGE COMMISSION

EEO OFFICE
Deborah Balducchi, Director
450 5th St. NW, Mail Stop 3-12
Washington, DC 20549
(202) 942-0040
www.sec.gov

SMALL BUSINESS ADMIN.

OFFICE OF EEO
M. Farrok Sait, Acting Officer EEO
409 3rd St., SW, Room #6400
Washington, DC 20416
(202) 205-6750

OFFICE OF EEO AND CIVIL RIGHTS
Mary Ann Fresco, HEPM
409 3rd St., SW, 6th Fl.
Washington, DC 20416
(202) 205-7148

OFFICE OF PERSONNEL
José Mendez, Recruitment Officer
409 3rd St., SW, #4200
Washington, DC 20416
(202) 205-6178

SMITHSONIAN INSTITUTION

OFFICE OF EQUAL EMPLOYMENT OPPORTUNITY & MINORITY AFFAIRS
Paula Fletemeyer, Spec. Emph. Prog. Mgr.
750 9th St. NW #8100
Washington, DC 20560-0901
(202) 275-0145

OFFICE OF HUMAN RESOURCES AND RECRUITMENT
Betty Pricher, Chief Exec. Res. Branch
750 9th St. NW #6100, MRC 912
Washington, DC 20560-0912

TRANSPORTATION, DEPT. OF

BUREAU OF TRANSPORTATION STATISTICS
Cynthia Roscoe, National HEPM
400 7th St., SW, #3430, M/S K-5
Washington, DC 20590
(202) 366-8088
cynthia.roscoe@bts.gov

FEDERAL AVIATION ADMIN.
Myrna Rivera, National HEPM
800 Independence Ave. SW #1030,
M/S ACR-6
Washington, DC 20591
(202) 267-9928
myrna.rivera@faa.gov
www.dot.gov

FEDERAL HIGHWAY ADMIN.
National HEPM
400 7th St. SW #3118, M/S HNG44
Washington, DC 20590
(202) 366-2226
jose.garcia@fhwa.dot.gov

FEDERAL RAILROAD ADMIN.
Brenda Moscoso, National HEPM
1120 Vermont Ave., #0711
Washington, DC 20590
(202) 493-6282
brenda.moscoso@fra.dot.gov

FEDERAL TRANSIT ADMIN.
Michael Virts, National HEPM
400 7th St., SW, #9100, M/S TCR-1
Washington, DC 20590
(202) 366-0814
michael.virts@fta.dot.gov

MARITIME ADMINISTRATION
Edna Brown, National HEPM
400 7th St. SW #7301, M/S MAR-318
Washington, DC 20590
(202) 366-4146
edna.brown@marad.dot.gov

NATL. HIGHWAY SAFETY ADMIN.
Phyllis D. Alston, National HEPM
400 7th St. SW #6128, M/S NOA-20
Washington, DC 20590
(202) 366-8046
palston@nhtsa.dot.gov

OFFICE OF INSPECTOR GENERAL
Leslie McBroom, National HEPM
400 7th St. SW #7107, M/S JM-20
Washington, DC 20590
(202) 366-1438
leslie.a.mcbroom@oig.dot.gov

OFFICE OF THE SECRETARY
Harry Salinas, Departmental HEPM
400 7th St. SW #1030 M/S DOCR (S-32)
Washington, DC 20590
(202) 366-4121
harry.salinas@ost.dot.gov

SURFACE TRANSPORTATION BD.
Frank Jacobs, National HEPM
1925 K St. NW #880
Washington, DC 20423
(202) 565-1692
jacobsf@stb.dot.gov

TRANS. ADMIN. SVC. CTR.
Frances Brown, National HEP Manager
400 7th St. SW., #2225, M/S SVC-190
Washington, DC 20590
(202) 366-5809
frances.brown@tasc.dot.gov

U.S. COAST GUARD
National HEPM
2100 Second St. SW #2510 M/S HSC (t-4c)
Washington, DC 20593-0001
(202) 493-7705
daniel.mendez@uscg.dot.gov

TREASURY, DEPT. OF THE

BUREAU OF ALCOHOL, TOBACCO AND FIREARMS
Carmen-Nydia Olmeda
650 Massachusetts Ave. NW #8210
Washington, DC 20226
(202) 927-8815
cnolmeda@atfhq.atf.treas.gov

BUR. OF ENGRAVING & PRINTING
Idalia Noriega-O'Brien, Hisp. Prog. Mgr.
14th & C St., SW Rm. 639-17 PD
Washington, DC 20228
(202) 874-3537
idalia.obrien@bep.treas.gov

COMPTROLLER OF THE CURRENCY
Cindy Petitt, Director
250 E. St., SW Mail Stop 4-13
Washington, DC 20219
(202) 874-5540

COMPTROLLER OF THE CURRENCY
Irene Sandate, SEP Manager
250 E. St., SW Mail Stop 2-6, 4th Fl.
Washington, DC 20219
(202) 874-5360
irene.sandate@occ.treas.gov

CUSTOMS SERVICE
Sophia Thornton, Office of EEO, Director
1300 Constitution Ave. NW #3.2A
Washington, DC 20229
(202) 927-0210

CUSTOMS SERVICE
Darren Goebels, AEP Manager
1300 Constitution Ave. NW #3.2A
Washington, DC 20229
(202) 927-0220
darren.w.goebels@customs.treas.gov

DEPARTMENTAL OFFICES
Sandra Heaton, Director
1500 Pennsylvania Ave., NW Rm. 1136 MT
Washington, DC 20220
(202) 622-0831
sandra.heaton@treas.sprint.com

FINANCIAL MGMT. SERVICE
Vanessa Rini-Lopez, Recruitment
Coordinator, HEPM
PG Center II, #106, 3700 East West Hwy.
Hyattsville, MD 20782
(202) 874-6287
vanessa.rini-lopez@fms.treas.gov
www.fms.treas.gov

INTERNAL REVENUE SERVICE
Yolanda Lopez, Servicewide HEPM
111 Constitution Ave., NW Rm. 2326
Washington, DC 20224
(202) 622-9447
yolanda.Lopez@m1.irs.gov
www.irs.gov

INTERNAL REVENUE SERVICE EEO
Charles D. Fowler, III
National Director, EEO and Diversity
1111Constitution Ave., NW. #2422
Washington, DC 20224
(202) 622-5400
Charles.d.Fowler@m1.irs.gov
www.irs.gov

INTERNAL REVENUE SERVICE EEO
Denise Fayne, Deputy National Director
1111 Constitution Ave., NW. #2422
Washington, DC 20224
(202) 622-5400
Denise.Fayne@m1.irs.gov
www.irs.gov

INTERNAL REVENUE SERVICE
Patrice Jones-Brown, SEP Manager
1111 Constitution Ave. NW. #2422
Washington, DC 20224
(202) 622-6789
jones-brown.patrice@irs.treas.gov
www.irs.gov

MINT
Jerry Folks, SEP Manager
633 3rd St., NW 7th Floor
Washington, DC 20220
(202) 874-9444
jerry.folks@usmint.treas.gov

OFFICE OF THE INSPECTOR GENERAL
Bobbie Sisselberger, SEP Manager
740 15th Street, Suite 510
Washington, DC 20220
(202) 927-5767
bobbie.sisselberger@oig.treas.gov

OFFICE OF THRIFT SUPERVISION
Barbara Davis, Hispanic Prog. Manager
1700 G St. NW, 2nd Fl.
Washington, DC 20552
(202) 906-6977
barbara.davis@ots.treas.gov

OFFICE OF THRIFT SUPERVISION
Douglas Mason, Sr. Contract Spec. &
Advoc., Outreach Program
1700 G Street, N.W., 3rd Floor
Washington, DC 20552
(202) 906-7624
douglas.mason@ots.treas.gov

SECRET SERVICE
Manny Velasquez, HEP Manager
950 H St., NW #7910
Washington, DC 20223
(202) 406-5946
lvelasquez@usss.treas.gov

VETERANS AFFAIRS, DEPT. OF

DIVERSITY MANAGEMENT & EEO
José Marrero, National HEPM
810 Vermont Ave., NW, RC 06-A
Washington, DC 20420
(202) 273-5839

WASHINGTON METRO TRANSIT AUTHORITY

HUMAN RESOURCES
Katrina Wiggins, Director
600 5th St., NW, #7F
Washington, DC 20001
(202) 962-2314

WHITE HOUSE

OFFICE OF MANAGEMENT AND BUDGET
725 17th St., NW, #8026
Washington, DC 20503
(202) 395-4708

PUBLIC LIAISON
Abel Guerrera, Hispanic Liaison
Old Executive Office Bldg., #121
Washington, DC 20502
(202) 456-2930

FLORIDA

AGRICULTURE, DEPARTMENT OF

SOUTHEAST REGION
Roy Herrera, HEPM
P.O. Box 248
La Belle, FL 33975-0248
(863) 674-4160
Roel.Herrera@fl.usda.gov

EQUAL EMPLOYMENT OPPORTUNITY COMMISSION

MIAMI DISTRICT OFFICE
Federico Costales Director
One Biscayne Tower
2 S Biscayne Blvd., #2700
Miami, FL 33131
(305) 536-4491

TAMPA AREA OFFICE
Manuel Zurita, Director
501 E Polk St., #1020
Tampa, FL 33602
(813) 228-2310

NATIONAL AERONAUTICS AND SPACE ADMINISTRATION (NASA)

EMPLOYEE SERVICES
Stacy Gregg, Recruit. & College Relations
Mail Code BAB-Kennedy Space Center
Kennedy Space Center, FL 32899
(321) 867-3620

NAVY, DEPARTMENT OF THE

CHIEF OF NAVAL ED. & TRAINING
Cheryl Lawson, Comm. Dep. EEO Officer
Naval Air Station, 386 S Ave.
Pensacola, FL 32508-5124
(850) 452-4875
cheryl-e.lawson@smtp.cnet.navy.mil

USMC RECRUITING STATION
8011 Phillips Hwy., #4
Jacksonville, FL 32256-7405
(904) 448-8880

USMC RECRUITING STATION
5886 S Semoran Blvd., Air Bus. Center
Orlando, FL 32822-4817
(407) 249-5870

USMC RECRUITING STATION
7820 Peters Rd., #105-9, Blvd. E
Plantation, FL 33324-4006
(954) 452-0663

POSTAL SERVICE

CENTRAL FLORIDA DISTRICT
Erica Mann, Hispanic Program Specialist
P.O. Box 999994
Mid Florida, FL 32799-9994
(407) 333-8460

CENTRAL FLORIDA DISTRICT
Annie P. Seabrooks, Div. Dev. Field Spec.
P.O. Box 999237
Mid Florida, FL 32799-9237
(407) 333-4892

NORTH FLORIDA DISTRICT
Mary L. Moore, Div. Dev. Field Spec.
P.O. Box 40005
Jacksonville, FL 32203-0005
(904) 858-6575

SOUTH FLORIDA DISTRICT
Dorothy Johnson, Div. Dev. Field Spec.
2200 NW 72nd Ave., #204
Miami, FL 33152-9461
(305) 470-0622

SOUTH FLORIDA DISTRICT
Jacinto Acebal, Hispanic Prog. Specialist
2200 NW 72 Ave. #210
Miami, FL 33152-9416
(305) 470-0619

SUNCOAST DISTRICT
Regla M. Watts, Div. Dev. Field Spec.
2203 N Lois Ave., #1070
Tampa, FL 33607-7170
(813) 354-6023

TRANSPORTATION, DEPT. OF

U.S. COAST GUARD
10601 San Jose Blvd., #215
Jacksonville, FL 32257
(904) 232-1561/2702/4595
mmilliken@cgrc.uscg.mil
www.gocoastguard.com

U.S. COAST GUARD
Royal Oaks Plaza Center
15466 NW 77th Ave.
Miami Lakes, FL 33016
(305) 819-0875
tkanzig@cgrc.uscg.mil
www.gocoastguard.com

U.S. COAST GUARD
Colonial Corners
5600 W Colonial Dr., #109
Orlando, FL 32808-7646
(407) 292-5381
jlocklair@cgrc.uscg.mil
www.gocoastguard.com

U.S. COAST GUARD
Ormond Interchange Conplex
1568 W Granada Blvd.
Ormond Beach, FL 32174
(904) 672-2945
ddepietro@cgrc.uscg.mil
www.gocoastguard.com

U.S. COAST GUARD
Willow Lake
1714 W 23rd St., #C
Panama City, FL 32405-2928
(850) 763-1950
tfomby@cgrc.uscg.mil
www.gocoastguard.com

U.S. COAST GUARD
Bayview Shopping Center
11022 4th St. N
St. Petesburg, FL 33716-2945
(727) 579-3849
mwahlers@cgrc.uscg.mil
www.gocoastguard.com

GEORGIA

AGRICULTURE, DEPARTMENT OF

FOREST SERVICE
Lori Johnston, HEPM
1720 Peachtree Rd., NW
Atlanta, GA 30367
(404) 347-0111
ljohnston@fs.fed.us

SOUTHEAST REGION
Delores Almand, Acting HEPM
355 E Hancock Ave.
Athens, GA 30601-2769
(706) 546-2270
Delores.Almand@ga.usda.gov

SOUTHEAST REGION
Ramiro Cordero, HEPM
1213 Vada Rd.
Bainbridge, GA 31717-3266
(912) 246-8282
Ramiro.Cordero@gabainbrid.fsc.usda.gov

AIR FORCE, DEPT. OF THE

HEADQUARTERS AIR FORCE RESERVE COMMAND
Rick DuPree, HEPM
155 2nd St.
Robins AFB, GA 31098-1635
(912) 327-1339

ARMY, DEPARTMENT OF THE

US ARMY FORCES COMMAND, EEO PROGRAMS
Armando Canales, Director
1777 Hardee Ave. SW
Ft. McPherson, GA 30330-1062
(404) 464-5740

CENTERS FOR DISEASE CONTROL & PREVENTION

HUMAN RESOURCES
Mr. Carlos Alonso, Diversity Coordinator
4770 Buford Highway, Mail Stop K06
Atlanta, GA 30341-3724
(770) 488-1805

ENERGY, DEPARTMENT OF

SOUTHEASTERN POWER ADMIN.
Carol M. Franklin, HEPM
2 Public Square
Elberton, GA 30635-2496
(706) 213-3813
Carolf@sepa.fed.us

SOUTHEASTERN POWER ADMIN.
Joel W. Seymour, HEPM
2 Public Square
Elberton, GA 30635-2496
(706) 213-3810
Joels@sepa.doe.gov

ENVIRONMENTAL PROTECTION AGENCY

HUMAN RESOURCES OFFICE, REGION 4
Steve Prince, Director
61 Forsyth Street, SW
Atlanta, GA 30303-3104
(404) 562-8132

EQUAL EMPLOYMENT OPPORTUNITY COMMISSION

ATLANTA DISTRICT OFFICE
Bernice Williams-Kimbrough Director
100 Alabama St., SW, #4R30
Atlanta, GA 30303
(404) 562-6800

SAVANNAH LOCAL OFFICE
Lyn Jordan, Director
410 Mall Blvd., #G
Savannah, GA 31406-4821
(912) 652-4234

FEDERAL RESERVE BOARD

EEO
Frank J. Craven, VP of Human Resources
104 Marietta St., NW
Atlanta, GA 30303-2713
(404) 521-8500

INTERIOR, DEPARTMENT OF THE

GEOLOGICAL SURVEY, SE REGION
3850 Holcomb Bridge Rd., #160
Norcross, GA 30092
(770) 409-7750

NATIONAL PARK SERVICE
Gwen Evans, Spec. Emph. Prog. Manager
100 Alabama St., SW, 1924 Building
Atlanta, GA 30303
(404) 562-3103x562

LABOR, DEPARTMENT OF

ATLANTA REGIONAL OFFICE
Mike Watt, Personnel Manager Specialist
61 Forsyth St., SW, #6B50
Atlanta, GA 30303
(404) 562-2008

EMPLOYMENT AND TRAINING ADMINISTRATION
Don Scott, Regional Director
61 Forsyth St. SW, #6T95
Atlanta, GA 30303
(404) 562-2395

NAVY, DEPARTMENT OF THE

USMC RECRUITING STATION
6855 Jimmy Carter Blvd., #2600
Norcross, GA 30071-1251
(770) 246-0001

POSTAL SERVICE

SOUTH GEORGIA DISTRICT
Alberta Lawson, Div. Dev. Field Spec.
451 College St.
Macon, GA 31213-9800
(912) 752-8494

SMALL BUSINESS ADMIN.

DISASTER PERSONNEL OFFICE-DISASTER AREA 2
Rhonda Alderman, Personnel Officer
1 Baltimore Pl., #300
Atlanta, GA 30308
(404) 347-3771

SOCIAL SECURITY ADMIN.

ATLANTA REGION
Janet Keith, Director
61 Forsyth St. SW., 22T-64
Atlanta, GA 30303
(404) 562-1387

TRANSPORTATION, DEPT. OF

U.S. COAST GUARD
410 Mall Blvd.
Savannah, GA 31406

(912) 352-9714/9760
cwaterfield@cgrc.uscg.mil
www.gocoastguard.com

U.S. COAST GUARD
Northlake Tower Festival Shopping Ctr.
3983 Lavista Rd., #189
Tucker, GA 30084
(770) 934-9686/87/7406
sjohnson@cgrc.uscg.mil
www.gocoastguard.com

TREASURY, DEPARTMENT OF THE

FEDERAL LAW ENFORCEMENT TRAINING CENTER
Luz Sánchez, Hispanic Program Manager
Facilities Management Division (FAC)
Building 200
Glynco, GA 31524
(912) 267-2839
Lsanchez@fletc.treas.gov

FEDERAL LAW ENFORCEMENT TRAINING CENTER
Bill Jamison, AEP Manager
Building 29
Glynco, GA 31524
(912) 261-3766
bjamison@fletc.treas.gov

GUAM

TRANSPORTATION, DEPT. OF

U.S. COAST GUARD
Baltej Pavillion
415 Chalan, San Antonio Rd.
Tamuning, Guam 96911
(671) 647-6156/67/81
cjones@cgrc.uscg.mil
www.gocoastguard.com

HAWAII

AGRICULTURE, DEPARTMENT OF

WEST REGION
Terri Souza, HEPM
USDA-FSA 300 Ala Moana Blvd., #5-112
Honolulu, HI 96850
(808) 541-2600x141
Theresa.Souza@hi.usda.gov

AIR FORCE, DEPARTMENT OF THE

HEADQUARTERS PACIFIC AIR FORCES
Dennis Nagatani, HEPM
25 E St., #D208
Hickam AFB, HI 96853-5411
(808) 449-5863

EQUAL EMPLOYMENT OPPORTUNITY COMMISSION

HONOLULU LOCAL OFFICE
Timothy A. Riera, Director
P.O. Box 50082
300 Ala Moana Blvd., #7-127
Honolulu, HI 96850-0051
(808) 541-3120

NAVY, DEPARTMENT OF THE

PACIFIC FLEET (CODE N01CP)
Maureen Kleintop, Comm. Dep. EEO Off.
250 Makalapa Dr.
Pearl Harbor, HI 96860-7000
(808) 471-9393
kleintmu@cpf.navy.mil

POSTAL SERVICE

HONOLULU DISTRICT
Anette Goo, Div. Dev. Field Specialist
3600 Aolele St., #M-4
Honolulu, HI 96820-3695
(808) 423-3642

TRANSPORTATION, DEPT. OF

U.S. COAST GUARD
Pearl Ridge Mall, Phase III
98-151 Pali Moni St., #106
Aiea, HI 96701
(808) 486-8677/487-1152
thopkins@cgrc.uscg.mil
www.gocoastguard.com

IDAHO

AGRICULTURE, DEPARTMENT OF

FOREST SERVICE
Joe Encinas, HEPM
Idaho Panhandle National Forests
Coeur d'Alene, ID 83814
(208) 769-3060
jencinas@fs.fed.us

WEST REGION
Matin Pena, HEPM
1630 3rd Ave. W
Payette, ID 83661-2999
(208) 642-4049
martin.pena@id.usda.gov

ENERGY, DEPARTMENT OF

IDAHO OPERATIONS OFFICE
José Elizondo, HEPM
850 Energy Dr., #1225
Idaho Falls, ID 83404
(208) 526-0965
Elizonjl@id.doe.gov

INTERIOR, DEPARTMENT OF THE

BUREAU OF LAND MGMT.
Paula Reed, Personnel Mgmt. Specialist
3833 S. Development Ave.
Boise, ID 83705
(208) 387-5498
http://www.nifc.gov

BUREAU OF RECLAMATION
Max Gallegos
1150 N. Curtis Rd. #100
Boise, ID 83706-1234
(208) 378-5144

TRANSPORTATION, DEPT. OF

U.S. COAST GUARD
Overland Park
6907 Overland Rd.
Boise, ID 83709-1908
(208) 376-7685
jschultz@cgrc.uscg.mil
www.gocoastguard.com

ILLINOIS

AGRICULTURE, DEPARTMENT OF

MIDWEST REGION
Rich Stewart, HEPM
301 E North St
Cambridge, IL 61238
(309) 937-5263
Rich.Stewart@il.usda.gov

AIR FORCE, DEPARTMENT OF THE

HEADQUARTERS AIR MOBILITY COMMAND
Pat Wessel HEPM
100 Heritage Dr., #106
Scott AFB, IL 62225-5002
(618) 229-7901

EDUCATION, DEPARTMENT OF

REGION V PERSONNEL OFFICE (IL, IN, MI, MN, OH, WI)
Garland M. Clegget, Regional Officer
6130 South Wolcott
Chicago, IL 60636
(773) 535-9575

ENERGY, DEPARTMENT OF

CHICAGO OPERATIONS OFFICE
Yvette Collazo, Chair, HEPM Adv. Coun.
9800 S Cass Ave.
Argonne, IL 60439
(630) 252-2102
yvette.collazo@ch.doe.gov

CHICAGO OPERATIONS OFFICE
Frank Gines, HEPM
9800 S Cass Ave., (ARG)
Argonne, IL 60439
(630) 252-4182
Frank.gines@ch.doe.gov

ENVIRONMENTAL PROTECTION AGENCY

HUMAN RESOURCES OFFICE, REGION 5
Jeniffer Lang, Director
77 West Jackson Blvd.
Chicago, IL 60604-3507
(312) 886-0539

EQUAL EMPLOYMENT OPPORTUNITY COMMISSION

CHICAGO DISTRICT OFFICE
John P. Rowe, Director
500 W Madison St., #2800
Chicago, IL 60661
(312) 353-2713

FEDERAL RESERVE BOARD

CHICAGO DISTRICT OFFICE
Human Resources Offices
230 S La Salle St.
Chicago, IL 60604-1413
(312) 322-5322

LABOR, DEPARTMENT OF

EMPLOYMENT AND TRAINING ADMINISTRATION
Stephen Garlington, Regional Director
Federal Bldg., #676, 230 S Dearborn St.
Chicago, IL 60604
(312) 353-7237

LABOR, DEPARTMENT OF

OFFICE OF THE SOLICITOR
Rafael Alvarez, HEPM
230 S Dearborn St., 8th Fl.
Chicago, IL 60604
(312) 353-1144
www.dol.gov/dol/sol

NAVY, DEPARTMENT OF THE

USMC RECRUITING STATION
1700 S Wolf Rd.
Des Plaines, IL 60018-5912
(847) 803-6061

POSTAL SERVICE

CENTRAL ILLINOIS DISTRICT
Sharon T. Murphy, Div. Dev. Field Spec.
6801 W 73rd St.
Bedford Park, IL 60499-9311
(708) 563-7343

CENTRAL ILLINOIS DISTRICT
José L. Aguilar, Hispanic Prog. Specialist
6801 W 73rd St., #224
Bedford Park, IL 60499-8902
(708) 563-7872

CHICAGO DISTRICT
Jaime Claudio Jr., Hispanic Prog. Spec.
433 West Harrison St.
Chicago, IL 60607-9994
(312) 983-8014

CHICAGO DISTRICT
Mehlanie Spears, Div. Dev. Field Spec.
433 West Harrison St., 4th Fl.
Chicago, IL 60607-9998
(312) 983-8039

GREAT LAKES AREA OFFICE
Susan R. Barela, Div. Dev. Field Spec.
244 Knollwood Dr., 2nd Fl.
Bloomingdale, IL 60117-3050
(630) 539-8338

NORTHERN ILLINOIS DISTRICT
Marquetta Tisdell, Div. Dev. Field Spec.
500 E. Fullerton Ave.
Carol Stream, IL 60199-9998
(630) 260-5203

NORTHERN ILLINOIS DISTRICT
Eduardo Cuevas, Hispanic Prog. Spec.
500 E Fullerton
Carol Stream, IL 60199-9994
(630) 260-5213

RAILROAD RETIREMENT BOARD

EO OFFICE
Candice Gabriel, Director
844 Rush St., 8th Fl., #844
Chicago, IL 60611
(312) 751-4943

STATE OF ILLINOIS

DEPARTMENT OF COMMERCE AND COMMUNITY AFFAIRS
Victoria Benn-Rochelle, EEO/Aff. Action Off.
620 E. Adams St.
Springfield, IL 62701
(217) 524-2997

TRANSPORTATION, DEPT. OF

U.S. COAST GUARD
10503 S Western Ave.
Chicago, IL 60643-2527
(773) 239-3856
dholder@cgrc.uscg.mil
www.gocoastguard.com

U.S. COAST GUARD
Foot of Washington St.
East Peoria, IL 61611-2039
(309) 698-0372
tshull@cgrc.uscg.mil
www.gocoastguard.com

U.S. COAST GUARD
Crest Creek Center
1011 A West Ogden Ave.
Naperville, IL 60563-2912
(630) 579-0063
mjenkins@cgrc.uscg.mil
www.gocoastguard.com

U.S. COAST GUARD
7225 Caldwell Ave.
Niles, IL 60714-4524
(847) 647-0184/4060
dholder@cgrc.uscg.mil
www.gocoastguard.com

INDIANA

AGRICULTURE, DEPARTMENT OF

MID. REGION
Alicia Love, HEPM
6960 S Gray Rd., #C
Indianapolis, IN 46237
(317) 780-1765
Alicia.Love@in.usda.gov

EQUAL EMPLOYMENT OPPORTUNITY COMMISSION

INDIANAPOLIS DISTRICT OFFICE
Danny G. Harter, Director
101 W Ohio St., #1900
Indianapolis, IN 46204-4203
(317) 226-7212

NAVY, DEPARTMENT OF THE

USMC RECRUITING STATION
9152 Kent Ave., #C-200
Indianapolis, IN 46216-2036
(317) 554-0510

POSTAL SERVICE

GREATER INDIANA DISTRICT
McDowell Barbara, Div. Dev. Field Spec.
P.O. Box 9855
3939 Vincennes Rd.
Indianapolis, IN 46298-9855
(317) 870-8562

TRANSPORTATION, DEPT. OF

U.S. COAST GUARD
Metroplex Center
8255 Craig St., #130
Indianapolis, IN 46250-4583
(317) 596-0833
rmoorhouse@cgrc.uscg.mil
www.gocoastguard.com

IOWA

AGRICULTURE, DEPARTMENT OF

MIDWEST REGION
Pedro Ramos, Jr., HEPM
22659 Filbert Ave.
Onawa, IA 51040-9301
(712) 423-2624
pedro.ramos@ia.usda.gov

NAVY, DEPARTMENT OF THE

USMC RECRUITING STATION
4725 Marle Hay, #209
Des Moines, IA 50322
(515) 252-9871

POSTAL SERVICE

HAWKEYE DISTRICT
Mattie L. Darling, Div. Dev. Field Spec.
P.O. Box 185610
Des Moines, IA 50318-5610
(515) 251-2124

TRANSPORTATION, DEPT. OF

U.S. COAST GUARD
Swanson Depot
8830 Swanson Blvd., #K
Clive, IA 50325-6910
(515) 226-0235/0240/0253
jlawson@cgrc.uscg.mil
www.gocoastguard.com

U.S. COAST GUARD
Old Town Mall
901 E Kimberly Rd., #20
Davenport, IA 50807-1622
(319) 388-2002/2013/2029
kmachovec@cgrc.uscg.mil
www.gocoastguard.com

KANSAS

AGRICULTURE, DEPARTMENT OF

NORTH PLAINS
James Pena, Regional HEPM
524 S Main St.
Ulysses, KS 67860-2621
(316) 356-1726
james.pena@ks.usda.gov

ENVIRONMENTAL PROTECTION AGENCY

HUMAN RESOURCES OFFICE, REGION 7
Thomas Phillips, Director
901 N 5th St.
Kansas City, KS 66101
(913) 551-7407

EQUAL EMPLOYMENT OPPORTUNITY COMMISSION

KANSAS CITY AREA OFFICE
George R. Dixon, Director
400 State Ave., #905
Kansas City, KS 66101
(913) 551-5655

KENTUCKY

AGRICULTURE, DEPARTMENT OF

SOUTHEAST REGION
Edward Turner, HEPM
530 Noel Ave.
Hopkinsville, KY 42240-1361
(270) 885-8692
eturner@ky.usda.gov

EQUAL EMPLOYMENT OPPORTUNITY COMMISSION

LOUISVILLE AREA OFFICE
Marcia Hall-Craig, Director
600 Dr. Martin Luther King Jr. Pl. #268
Louisville, KY 40202
(502) 582-6082

NAVY, DEPARTMENT OF THE

USMC RECRUITING STATION
600 Martin Luther King Jr. Place, #221
Louisville, KY 40202-2269
(502) 582-6608

POSTAL SERVICE

KENTUCKIANA DISTRICT
Laura A. Larimore, Div. Dev. Field Spec.
P.O. Box 31050
Louisville, KY 40231-1050
(502) 473-4217

TRANSPORTATION, DEPT. OF

U.S. COAST GUARD
3111 Fern Valley Road, #112
Louisville, KY 10213-3535
(502) 969-4006/3929
kjohnson@cgrc.uscg.mil
www.gocoastguard.com

LOUISIANA

EQUAL EMPLOYMENT OPPORTUNITY COMMISSION

NEW ORLEANS DISTRICT OFFICE
Patricia T. Bivins, Director
701 Loyola Ave., # 600
New Orleans, LA 70113-9936
(504) 589-2329

INTERIOR, DEPARTMENT OF THE

MINERALS MANAGEMENT SVC.
Sarah Schlumbrecht, Pers. Staff. Class. Spec.
1201 Elmwood Park Blvd., M/S 2620
New Orleans, LA 70123
(504) 736-2884

NAVY, DEPARTMENT OF THE

8TH MARINE CORPS DISTRICT
Bldg. 10, Naval Support Activity
New Orleans, LA 70142-5200
(504) 678-2364

COMMANDER NAVAL RESERVE FORCE (N01D2)
Angie C. Salayton, Comm. Dep. EEO Off.
4400 Dauphine St.
New Orleans, LA 70146-5000
(504) 678-1986
salayon@cnrf.nola.nav.ymil

USMC RECRUITING STATION
4400 Dauphine St., 602-2-C
Naval Support Station
New Orleans, LA 70146-0800
(504) 678-5659

POSTAL SERVICE

LOUISIANA DISTRICT
Hedy H. Duplessis, Div. Dev. Field Spec.
701 Loyola Ave., #10021
New Orleans, LA 70113-9813
(504) 589-1283

TRANSPORTATION, DEPT. OF

U.S. COAST GUARD
East Point Shopping Center
9820 Lake Forest Blvd., #N
New Orleans, LA 70127-3077
(504) 589-6264/72
jkeller@cgrc.uscg.mil
www.gocoastguard.com

MAINE

AGRICULTURE, DEPARTMENT OF

EAST REGION
Keith O. Roble, HEPM
99 Fort Fairfield Rd.
Presque Isle, ME 04769
(207) 764-4153
kroble@me.nrcs.usda.gov

POSTAL SERVICE

MAINE DISTRICT
Elaine P. Edwards, Div. Dev. Field Spec.
380 Riverside St.
Portland, ME 04103-7000
(207) 828-8400

TRANSPORTATION, DEPT. OF

U.S. COAST GUARD
Brighton Ave. Plaza
1041 Brighton Ave. Plaza
Portland, ME 04101-1042
(207) 761-4307/3921
jsullivan@cgrc.uscg.mil
www.gocoastguard.com

MARYLAND

AGRICULTURE, DEPARTMENT OF

EAST REGION
E.J. Fanning, HEPM
92 Thoman Johnson Dr., #230
Frederick, MD 21702-4300
(301) 695-2803
edward.fanning@md.usda.gov

FOOD SAFETY
Noemí Hyman, HEPM
5601 Sunnyside Ave.
Beltsville, MD 20705
(301) 504-7751
Noemi.Hyman@dchqexsl.hqnet.usda.gov

MARKETING AND REGULATORY PROGRAMS
Ardahlia Short, HEPM
4700 River Rd., #5C09, Civil Rights
Enforcement and Compliance
Riverdale, MD 20737
(301) 734-8153
ardahlia.g.short@usda.gov

NATURAL RESOURCES AND ENVIRONMENT
J. Xavier Montoya, HEPM
5601 Sunnyside Ave.
Beltsville, MD 20705-5472
(301) 504-2187
Xavier.Montoya@usda.gov

ARMY, DEPARTMENT OF THE

BALTIMORE DISTRICT CORPS OF ENGINEERS
Marie Jonson, EEO Officer
10 S Howard St., #9500
Baltimore, MD 21203-1715
(410) 962-4556

COMMERCE, DEPARTMENT OF

BUREAU OF THE CENSUS
Patricia Galloway, Acting Chief
Rm 3071-34700, Silver Hill Rd.
Suitland, MD 20746
(301) 457-2853

NATIONAL INSTITUTE OF STANDARDS AND TECHNOLOGY
Sol del Ande Eaton, Diversity Prog. Mgr.
TB 415/Room 118
Gaithersburg, MD 20899-0001
(301) 975-5481
so.eaton@nist.gov
www.nist.gov

NATIONAL INSTITUTE OF STANDARDS & TECHNOLOGY
Alvin C. Lewis, Director of Civil Rights
100 Bureau Dr., M/S1030
Gaithersburg, MD 20899-1030
(301) 975-2037
lewis@nist.gov

NATIONAL OCEANIC & ATMOSPHERIC ADMIN.
Jerry Beat, HEPM
1305 East-West Hwy., SSMC4/12222, CR
Silver Spring, MD 20910
(301) 713-0500x139

CONSUMER PRODUCT SAFETY COMMISSION

OFFICE OF EEO & MINORITY ENTERPRISE
Felipa Coleman, Director
4330 E West Hwy., # 712
Bethesda, MD 20814
(301) 504-0570
info@cpsc.gov

DEFENSE, DEPARTMENT OF

NATIONAL IMAGERY AND MAPPING AGENCY
Bea Oviedo, HEPM
4600 Sangamore Rd., M/S D119
Bethesda, MD 20816-5003
(301) 227-7870
oviedob@nima.mil

NATIONAL SECURITY AGENCY
Tonya Young, HEPM
Fort George Meade, MD 20755
(301) 688-6961
ajkmbuc@fggm.osis.gov

EQUAL EMPLOYMENT OPPORTUNITY COMMISSION

BALTIMORE DISTRICT OFFICE
James L. Lee, Director
City Crescent Bldg., 10 S Howard St., 3rd Fl.
Baltimore, MD 21201
(410) 962-3932

HEALTH AND HUMAN SERVICES, DEPARTMENT OF

DRUG EVALUATION & RESEARCH
Gloria Sundaresan, EEO Specialist
5600 Fishers Ln., HDF-12
Rockville, MD 20852
(301) 594-5427

FOOD AND DRUG ADMIN.
Janet Yellin , HEPM
5600 Fishers Ln. Rm. 8-72, HF-16
Rockville, MD 20857
(301) 827-2427
jyellin@oc.fda.gov
www.fda.gov

FOOD AND DRUG ADMIN.
Jo Ann Crowder, Spec. Emph. Prog. Mgr.
Parklawn Bldg.
5600 Fishers Ln. Rm. 8-72, HF-16
Rockville, MD 20857
(301) 827-4839
jcrowder@oc.FDA.gov
www.fda.gov

HEALTH CARE FINANCING ADMIN.
Ivette Blanc, HEPM
North Bldg., Rm. N2-22-17
7500 Security Blvd.
Baltimore, MD 21244-1850
(410) 786-0018
lblanc@hcfa.gov

HEALTH CARE FINANCING ADMINISTRATION
Ramon Suris-Fernandez, Director
7500 Security Blvd. #N2-22-17
Baltimore, MD 21244
(410) 786-5110
rsurisfernandez@hcfa.gov

HEALTH CARE FINANCING ADMINISTRATION
Leslie Knight, Hispanic Emp. Manager
7500 Security Blvd. #N2-22-17
Baltimore, MD 21244
(410) 786-5124
lknight@hcfa.gov

HEALTH CARE FINCANCING ADMIN.
Lesley Knicht
Office of Equal Opp. & Civil Rights
7500 Security Blvd., #N2-22-17
Baltimore, MD 21244-1850
(410) 786-5112
www.hcfa.gov

HEALTH RESOURCES AND SERVICES ADMINISTRATION
Darío Prieto, HEPM
5600 Fishers Ln. #14-A27
Rockville, MD 20857
(301) 443-0331
Dprieto@HRSA.gov
www.hrsa.dhhs.gov

INDIAN HEALTH SERVICE
Vaughn Arkie, HEPM
#16A-14, Parklawn Bldg.
5600 Fishers Ln.
Rockville, MD 20857
(301) 443-2700

PROGRAM SUPPORT CENTER
Kay Tockman, HEPM
5600 Fishers Lane, #16A-54
Rockville, MD 20857
(301) 443-1144

SUBSTANCE ABUSE & MENTAL HEALTH SERVICES ADMIN.
Ann Ambler, Special Emphasis Mgr.
Parklawn Bldg.
5600 Fishers Ln., #16C-24
Rockville, MD 20857
(301) 443-4447
www.samhsa.gov

SUBSTANCE ABUSE & MENTAL HEALTH SERVICES ADMIN.
Sharon Lynn Holmes, Director
5600 Fishers Ln., #10-85
Rockville, MD 20857
(301) 443-4447
Sholmes1@SAMHSA.GOV

MINORITY HEALTH RESOURCE CENTER, OFFICE OF

José T. Carneiro, Project Director
5515 Security Ln., #101
Rockville, MD 20852
(301) 230-7874

MONTGOMERY COUNTY GOVERNMENT

MINORITY AND MULTI-CULTURAL AFFAIRS
Betty Valdes, Hispanic Affairs Liaison
Executive Office Bldg.
101 Monroe St.
Rockville, MD 20850
(240) 777-0017

MONTGOMERY COUNTY DEPARTMENT OF POLICE

Brian Walker, Recruitment Officer
2350 Research Boulevard, #203
Rockville, MD 20850
(240) 773-5310

NATIONAL AERONAUTICS AND SPACE ADMINISTRATION (NASA)

Dan Krieger, HEPM
Mail Code 120, Goddard Space Flight Ctr.
Greenbelt, MD 20771
(301) 286-7913

NAVY, DEPARTMENT OF THE

NAVAL AIR SYSTEMS COMMAND
Harry Carter, Comm. Deputy EEO Officer
Code HRO 7.3.4 Bldg 1489, Unit
7--22095 Fortin Circle
Patuxent River, MD 20670-1139
(301) 342-3746
carterhl.nimitz@navair.navy.mil

NAVAL SECURITY GROUP COMMAND
Lucinda T. Marshall, Comm. Dep. EEO Off.
9800 Savage Rd., Code G14
Fort George D. Mead, MD 20755-6000
(240) 373-3006
ltmarsh@hqcnsq.navy.mil

USMC RECRUITING STATION
6845 Deerpath Rd., Doesey Business Ctr.
Baltimore, MD 21227-6221
(410) 379-0806

USMC RECRUITING STATION
5112 Pegasus Ct.
Frederick, MD 21704
(301) 660-2025

POSTAL SERVICE

BALTIMORE DISTRICT
Thomasine A. Adams, Div. Dev. Field Spec.
900 E. Fayette St., #327
Baltimore, MD 21233-9989
(410) 347-4265

SOCIAL SECURITY ADMIN.

CENTER FOR PERSONNEL POLICY AND STAFFING
6401 Security Blvd., #G-120,
W High Rise Bldg
Baltimore, MD 21235
(410) 965-4506

TRANSPORTATION, DEPT. OF

U.S. COAST GUARD
6499 Baltimore National Park
Catonsville, MD 21228-3904
(410) 747-3963
dburton@cgrc.uscg.mil
www.gocoastguard.com

U.S. COAST GUARD
613 Hunderford Dr.
Rockville, MD 20850
(301) 610-7631
stennyson@cgrc.uscg.mil
www.gocoastguard.com

U.S. COAST GUARD
Court Plaza Unit 7
1506 S. Salisbury Blvd.
Salisbury, MD 21801
(410) 543-2621
bcole@cgrc.uscg.mil
www.gocoastguard.com

TREASURY, DEPARTMENT OF THE

FINANCIAL MANAGEMENT SVC.
Steve Lopez, HEP Manager
PG Center Bldg. 2, Rm. 137
3700 East-West Hwy.
Hyattsville, MD 20782
(202) 874-7126
stephen.lopez@fms.treas.gov

FINANCIAL MANAGEMENT SVC.
Jerome Thomas, Hisp. Program Manager
Prince Georges Center II Rm. 137
Hyattsville, MD 20782
(202) 874-8330

INTERNAL REVENUE SERVICE
Beverly Cournoyer, Chief Employment
Baltimore District, 31 Hopkins Plz., #706
Baltimore, MD 21201
(410) 230-6327

MASSACHUSETTS

AGRICULTURE, DEPARTMENT OF

EAST REGION (MA, CT, RI)
Kristina Wiley, HEPM
451 West St.
Amherst, MA 01002-4351
(413) 253-4363
Kristina.Wiley@ma.usda.gov

EDUCATION, DEPARTMENT OF

**REGION I PERSONNEL
OFFICE~(CN, ME, MA, NH, RI, VT)**
Thomas J. Hibino, Director
540 McCormack Courthouse, #222
Boston, MA 02109-4557
(617) 220-9667

ENVIRONMENTAL PROTECTION AGENCY

**HUMAN RESOURCES OFFICE,
REGION 1**
Laurel Seneca, Director
One Congress Street, #1100
Boston, MA 02203-02114
(617) 918-1980

EQUAL EMPLOYMENT OPPORTUNITY COMMISSION

BOSTON AREA OFFICE
Robert L. Sanders, Director
JFK Federal Bldg., 2400 Government
Center, #475, E Tower
Boston, MA 02114
(617) 565-3200

LABOR, DEPARTMENT OF

**EMPLOYMENT AND TRAINING
ADMINISTRATION**
Marcus Gray, Regional Director
JFK Federal Center Bldg., #E-350
Boston, MA 02203
(617) 565-2179

NAVY, DEPARTMENT OF THE

USMC RECRUITING STATION
105 East St.
Chicopee Falls, MA 01020-3400
(413) 594-2230

POSTAL SERVICE

BOSTON DISTRICT
Lillian J. Buckley, Div. Dev. Field Spec.
25 Dorchester Ave., #2002C
Boston, MA 02205-9431
(617) 654-5933

MIDDLESEX-CENTRAL DISTRICT
Carol A. Dallocco, Div. Dev. Field Spec.
74 Main St.
North Reading, MA 01889-9998
(978) 664-7652

SPRINGFIELD DISTRICT
Deborah A. Woods, Div. Dev. Field Spec.
190 Fiberloid St
Springfield, MA 01152-9400
(413) 785-6431

SOCIAL SECURITY ADMIN.

BOSTON REGION
Geraldine Hamlin, EEO Manager
JFK Federal Bldg., #1900
Boston, MA 02203
(617) 565-2879

TRANSPORTATION, DEPT. OF

**RESEARCH & SPECIAL
PROGRAMS ADMINISTRATION**
María Caminos-Medina, National HEPM
55 Broadway, #1128, M/S DTS-802
Cambridge, MA 02142
(617) 494-2340
caminos@volpe.dot.gov

U.S. COAST GUARD
44 Winter St., 4th Fl.
Boston, MA 02108-4710
(617) 565-8656
jhinson@cgrc.uscg.mil
www.gocoastguard.com

U.S. COAST GUARD
New Federal Office Building
1550 Main St., Rm. 110
Springfield, MA 01103-1422
(413) 785-0324
lsantos@cgrc.uscg.mil
www.gocoastguard.com

MICHIGAN

AGRICULTURE, DEPARTMENT OF

MIDWEST REGION
Teresa Moore, HEPM
3001 Coolidge Rd.,#250
East Lansing, MI 48823
Teresa.Moore@mi.usda.gov

EQUAL EMPLOYMENT OPPORTUNITY COMMISSION

DETROIT DISTRICT OFFICE
James R. Neely, Jr., Director
477 Michigan Ave., #865
Detroit, MI 48226-9704
(313) 226-4600

NAVY, DEPARTMENT OF THE

USMC RECRUITING STATION
6545 Mercantile Way, #12
Lansing, MI 48933
(517) 882-5050

USMC RECRUITING STATION
580 Kirts Blvd., #307
Troy, MI 48084
(248) 269-9207

POSTAL SERVICE

DETROIT DISTRICT
Alzana Braxton, Div. Dev. Field Spec.
1401 W Fort St., 10th Fl.
Detroit, MI 48233-9998
(313) 226-8131

GREATER MICHIGAN DISTRICT
Eugenia C. Halliburton, Div. Dev. Field Spec.
4800 Collins Rd.
Lansing, MI 48924-9750
(517) 337-8836

ROYAL OAK DISTRICT
Margaret M. Perez, Div. Dev. Field Spec.
800 S Mill St.
Clio, MI 48420-9998
(810) 686-0811

TRANSPORTATION, DEPT. OF

U.S. COAST GUARD
650 S. Harbor Dr.
Grand Haven, MI 49417-1752
(616) 850-2585
rcrawford@cgrc.uscg.mil
www.gocoastguard.com

U.S. COAST GUARD
2515 E. Jolly Rd., #1
Lansing, MI 48910
(517) 377-1719
tkimberling@cgrc.uscg.mil
www.gocoastguard.com

U.S. COAST GUARD
Malberry Plaza
26097 John R. Rd.
Madison Heights, MI 48071-3607
(248) 582-8364
kmyers@cgrc.uscg.mil
www.gocoastguard.com

MINNESOTA

AGRICULTURE, DEPARTMENT OF

MIDWEST REGION
Chris Borden, HEPM
1400 West Main
Albert Lea, MN 56007
(507) 835-4631
Chris.Borden@nm.usda.gov

EQUAL EMPLOYMENT OPPORTUNITY COMMISSION

MINNEAPOLIS AREA OFFICE
Bobbie Carter, Director
330 S 2nd Ave., #430
Minneapolis, MN 55401-2224
(612) 335-4040

NAVY, DEPARTMENT OF THE

USMC RECRUITING STATION
Bishop Henry Whipple Federal Bldg.,
#450, 1Federal Bldg.
Ft. Sneling, MN 55111

POSTAL SERVICE

NORTHLAND DISTRICT
Andrew Fisher, Div. Dev. Field Spec.
P.O. Box 645001
St. Paul, MN 55164-5001
(612) 293-3716

TRANSPORTATION, DEPT. OF

U.S. COAST GUARD
5192 Central Ave. NE
Columbia Height, MN 55421-1825
(612) 334-4000
rcolby@cgrc.uscg.mil
www.gocoastguard.com

U.S. COAST GUARD
1201 Minnesota Ave.
Duluth, MN 55802-2492
(218) 720-5229
tshourds@cgrc.uscg.mil
www.gocoastguard.com

MISSISSIPPI

AGRICULTURE, DEPARTMENT OF

SOUTHEAST REGION
Nancy Lazenby, HEPM
747 Industrial Park Rd., NE
Brookhaven, MS 39601
(601) 833-5539
Nancy.Lazenby@ms.usda.gov

EQUAL EMPLOYMENT OPPORTUNITY COMMISSION

JACKSON AREA OFFICE
Benjamin Bradley, Director
100 W Capitol St., #207
Jackson, MS 39269
(601) 965-4537

NAVY, DEPARTMENT OF THE

**COMMANDER NAVAL
METEOROLOGY AND
OCEANOGRAPHY COMMAND**
Diddy Kirby, Command Deputy EEO Off./
Director Human Resources Programs
1020 Balch Blvd.
Stennis Space Center, MS 39529-5005
(228) 688-5790
kirby@cnmoc.navy.mil

POSTAL SERVICE

MISSISSIPPI DISTRICT
Mae L. Johnson, Div. Dev. Field Spec.
1461 Lakeover Rd., P.O. Box 99987
Jackson, MS 39205-9987
(601) 351-7251

TRANSPORTATION, DEPT. OF

U.S. COAST GUARD
4229 Lakeland Dr.
Flowood, MS 39208-8947
(601) 933-4901
bbennick@cgrc.uscg.mil
www.gocoastguard.com

MISSOURI

AGRICULTURE, DEPARTMENT OF

MIDWEST REGION
Michael Squires, HEPM
P.O. Box 199
Marble Hill, MO 63764
(573) 236-2028
Mike.Squires@mo.usda.gov

NATIONAL INFORMATION TECHNOLOGY CENTER
William Morales, Computer Spec./Listserv
8930 Ward Parkway
Kansas City, MO 64114
(816) 823-2409
william.morales@usda.gov

COMMERCE, DEPARTMENT OF

NOAA, CENTRAL ADMINISTRATIVE SUPPORT CTR.
Martha McBroome, Director
601 E. 12th Street, #1737
Kansas City, MO 64106
(816) 426-2050

DEFENSE, DEPARTMENT OF

NATIONAL IMAGERY AND MAPPING AGENCY
Helen Alexander, HEPM
3200 S Second St.
St. Louis, MO 63118
(314) 263-4234

EQUAL EMPLOYMENT OPPORTUNITY COMMISSION

ST. LOUIS DISTRICT OFFICE
Lynn Bruner, Director
Robert A. Young Bldg.
1222 Spruce St., #8.100
St. Louis, MO 63103
(314) 539-7800

FEDERAL RESERVE BOARD

HUMAN RESOURCES
Esther George, Vice President
925 Grand Ave.
Kansas City, MO 64198-0001
(816) 881-2463

LABOR, DEPARTMENT OF

EMPLOYMENT AND TRAINING ADMINISTRATION
Tom Deuschle, Assoc. Regional Director
1100 Main St. #1000
Kansas City, MO 64105-2112
(816) 426-3661x290

NAVY, DEPARTMENT OF THE

9TH MARINE CORPS DISTRICT
3805 E 155 St., Bldg. 710
Kansas City, MO 64147-1309
(816) 843-3903

USMC RECRUITING STATION
10302 NW Prairie View Rd.
Kansas City, MO 64153-1350
(916) 891-7577

USMC RECRUITING STATION
1222 Spruce St., #1031
St. Louis, MO 63103-2817
(314) 331-4550

POSTAL SERVICE

GATEWAY DISTRICT
Glenda Fields, Div. Dev. Field Spec.
1720 Market St., # 2024
St. Louis, MO 63155-9756
(314) 436-3868

MID-AMERICA DISTRICT
Rita Hamilton, Div. Dev. Field Spec.
315 W Pershing Rd., #576
Kansas City, MO 64108-9403
(816) 374-9131

MIDWEST AREA OFFICE
Margaret Sumner, Div. Dev. Field Spec.
P.O. Box 66609
St. Louis, MO 63166-6609
(314) 692-5527

SOCIAL SECURITY ADMIN.

KANSAS CITY REGION
Wanda McIntosh, Director
601 E 12th St., #436
Kansas City, MO 64106
(816) 936-5707

TRANSPORTATION, DEPT. OF

U.S. COAST GUARD
6228 NW Barry Rd. & I-29
Kansas City, MO 64154
(816) 746-9924
tmorrison@cgrc.uscg.mil
www.gocoastguard.com

U.S. COAST GUARD
5445 Telegraph Rd., #125
St. Louis, MO 63129-3500
(314) 845-0807
jpeoples@cgrc.uscg.mil
www.gocoastguard.com

MONTANA

AGRICULTURE, DEPARTMENT OF

FOREST SERVICE
Mike Wong, HEPM
P.O. Box 7669, Federal Bldg.
Missoula, MT 59807
(406) 329-3107
mwong@fs.fed.us

NORTH PLAINS REGION
Jose Valadez, HEPM
10 E Babcock St., #443, Federal Bldg.
Bozeman, MT 59715-4704
(406) 587-6761
Jose.Valadez@mt.usda.gov

INTERIOR, DEPARTMENT OF THE

BUREAU OF INDIANS AFFAIRS
Sharon Limberhand, Personnel Officer
316 N 26th St.
Billings, MT 59101
(406) 247-7956

BUREAU OF RECLAMATION
Sue McCannel, Personnel Officer
P.O. Box 36900
Billings, MT 59107-6900
(406) 247-7614

TRANSPORTATION, DEPT. OF

U.S. COAST GUARD
Butte Plaza Mall, 3100 Harrison Ave.
Butte, MT 59701-3652
(406) 494-3556
schadwell@cgrc.uscg.mil
www.gocoastguard.com

NEBRASKA

AGRICULTURE, DEPARTMENT OF

NORTH PLAINS REGION
Ralph Arauza, HEPM
1245 Lincoln St.
Blair, NE 68008-2164
(402) 426-4644x108
Ralph.Arauza@ne.usda.gov

NORTH PLAINS REGION
Maureen Lnenicka, HEPM
100 Centennial Mall North, Federal
Bldg., #153, MS 41
Lincoln, NE 68508
(402) 437-5016
Maureen.Lnenicka@mssc.nrcs.usda.gov

INTERIOR, DEPARTMENT OF THE

NATIONAL PARK SERVICE
Carol Solnosky, Personnel Mgmt. Spec.
1709 Jackson St.
Omaha, NE 68102
(402) 221-3415

POSTAL SERVICE

CENTRAL PLAINS DISTRICT
Benito L. Alba, Div. Dev. Field Spec.
P.O. Box 249510
Omaha, NE 68124-9510
(402) 255-3931

STATE OF NEBRASKA

EQUAL OPPORTUNITY COMMISSION
Alfonza Whitaker, Executive Director
P.O. Box 94934
Lincoln, NE 68509-4934
(402) 471-2024

TRANSPORTATION, DEPT. OF

U.S. COAST GUARD
2758 S. 129th Ave.
Omaha, NE 68144
(402) 334-0607
pvojchehoske@cgrc.uscg.mil
www.gocoastguard.com

NEVADA

AGRICULTURE, DEPARTMENT OF

WEST REGION
Sylvia Nieto, HEPM
USDA-RD, 2357-A Renaissance Dr.
Las Vegas, NV 89119-6150
(702) 262-9047x112
Sylvia.Nieto@nv.usda.gov

ENERGY, DEPARTMENT OF

NEVADA OPERATIONS OFFICE
Elaine Jiménez, Secretary
HEPM Advisory Council
P.O. Box 98515
Las Vegas, NV 89193-8518
(702) 295-1484
jimenez@nv.doe.gov

ENVIRONMENTAL PROTECTION AGENCY

HUMAN RESOURCES OFFICE
Sheron Johnson, Director
P.O. Box 98516
Las Vegas, NV 89193-8516
(702) 798-2413

INTERIOR, DEPARTMENT OF THE

BUREAU OF RECLAMATION
Bob Johnson, Office Director
P.O. Box 61470
Boulder City, NV 89006-1740
(702) 293-8492

POSTAL SERVICE

LAS VEGAS DISTRICT
Patricia Diggins, Hispanic Prog. Spec.
1001 E Sunset Rd.
Las Vegas, NV 89199-9421
(702) 361-9485

STATE OF NEVADA

DEPARTMENT OF EMPLOYMENT TRAINING AND REHABILITATION
Chris Anastassatos, Personnel Officer
500 E 3rd St.
Carson City, NV 89713
(775) 684-3923

TRANSPORTATION, DEPT. OF

U.S. COAST GUARD
Tropicana Gardens
3510 E. Tropicana Blvd.
Las Vegas, NV 89122-7341
(702) 898-2226
rharris@cgrc.uscg.mil
www.gocoastguard.com

NEW HAMPSHIRE

HOUSING AND URBAN DEVELOPMENT, DEPARTMENT OF

NEW HAMPSHIRE STATE OFFICE
Robert A. Grenier
Comm. Builder/Comm. Resource Rep.
275 Chestnut St., 5th Fl.
Manchester, NH 03101-2487
(603) 666-7510
Robert_Grenier@hud.gov
www.hud.gov/local/man

NAVY, DEPARTMENT OF THE

USMC RECRUITING STATION
875 Greenland Rd., #A-9
Portsmouth, NH 03801-4123
(603) 436-0890

POSTAL SERVICE

NEW HAMPSHIRE DISTRICT
Harry Figueroa, Div. Dev. Field Spec.
955 Goffs Falls Rd.
Manchester, NH 03103-9994
(603) 644-3890

NEW JERSEY

AGRICULTURE, DEPARTMENT OF

EAST REGION
Arsenio A. Cruz, HEPM
UCAP, 51 Gibralltar Dr., #2E
Morris Plains, NJ 07950
(973) 538-1552x3
Arsenio.Cruz@nj.usda.gov

EQUAL EMPLOYMENT OPPORTUNITY COMMISSION

NEWARK AREA OFFICE
Corrado Gigante, Director
1 Newark Ctr., 21st Fl.
Newark, NJ 07102-5233
(973) 645-6383

NAVY, DEPARTMENT OF THE

USMC RECRUITING STATION
485A US Route 1 South
Woodbridge Corporate Pl.
Iselin, NJ 08830
(732) 750-9408

POSTAL SERVICE

CENTRAL NEW JERSEY DISTRICT
Suzanne R. Hutchinson, Div. Dev. Field Spec.
21 Kilmer Rd., #322
Edison, NJ 08899-9998
(908) 819-3675

NORTHERN NEW JERSEY DIST.
Florina Cordero, Div. Dev. Field Spec.
494 Broad St.
Newark, NJ 07102-9300
(973) 468-7203

SOUTH JERSEY DISTRICT
Deborah L. Lewis, Div. Dev. Field Spec.
P.O. Box 9001
Bellmawr, NJ 08099-9001
(609) 933-4454

TRANSPORTATION, DEPT. OF

U.S. COAST GUARD
Rodino Federal Building, Rm 1434A
970 Broad St.
Newark, NJ 07102
(973) 645-2635
jblatche@cgrc.uscg.mil
www.gocoastguard.com

U.S. COAST GUARD
Plaza 9, 1333 New Rd.
Northfield, NJ 08225-1202
(609) 484-8260
dpierce@cgrc.uscg.mil
www.gocoastguard.com

NEW MEXICO

AGRICULTURE, DEPARTMENT OF

FOREST SERVICE
Chuck Sheldon, HEPM
517 Gold Ave. SW
Albuquerque, NM 87102
(505) 842-3344
csheldon@fs.fd.us

WEST REGION
Richard Montoya, HEPM
117 North Silver
Grants, NM 87020
(505) 287-4045
Richard.Montoyanm.usda.gov

COMMERCE, DEPARTMENT OF

NEW MEXICO NATIVE AMERICAN BUSINESS DEVELOPMENT CTR.
Michael Peacock, Director
123 4th St., SW
Albuquerque, NM 87103
(505) 889-9092

ENERGY, DEPARTMENT OF

ALBUQUERQUE OPERATIONS OFFICE
Donald J. García, HEPM
P.O. Box 5400
Albuquerque, NM 87185
(505) 845-5878
Dgarcia@doeal.gov

ALBUQUERQUE OPERATIONS OFFICE
Doris Sandoval, HEPM
P.O. Box 5400
Albuquerque, NM 87185
(505) 845-5673
Dsandoval@doeal.gov

EQUAL EMPLOYMENT OPPORTUNITY COMMISSION

ALBUQUERQUE DISTRICT OFFICE
Georgia M. Marchbanks, Enforcement Mgr.
505 Marquette, NW, # 900
Albuquerque, NM 87102
(505) 248-5201

INTERIOR, DEPARTMENT OF THE

BUREAU OF INDIAN AFFAIRS
Karen Chicharello, Personnel Officer
615 1st St. NW, #201
Albuquerque, NM 87102
(505) 346-7571

NAVY, DEPARTMENT OF THE

USMC RECRUITING STATION
5338 Montgomery Blvd. NE #300
Albuquerque, NM 87100
(505) 248-5270

POSTAL SERVICE

ALBUQUERQUE DISTRICT
Mickie Bourguet de Silva, Hisp. Prog. Spec.
500 Marquette Ave., NW, #912
Albuquerque, NM 87102-9994
(505) 346-8783

ALBUQUERQUE DISTRICT
Karen M. Harger, Div. Dev. Field Spec.
500 Marquette Ave., NW, #900
Albuquerque, NM 87102-9994
(505) 346-8809

STATE OF NEW MEXICO

ENERGY, MINERALS & NATURAL RESOURCES
Faye Barela, Personnel Officer
1220 S Saint Francis St.
Santa Fe, NM 87505
(505) 476-3375

TRANSPORTATION, DEPT.OF

U.S. COAST GUARD
Fiesta Del Norte
6001 San Mateo Blvd. NE, #B-2A
Albuquerque, NM 87109-3348
(505) 883-5396
rsteiner@cgrc.uscg.mil
www.gocoastguard.com

NEW YORK

AGRICULTURE, DEPARTMENT OF

EAST REGION
Luis Hernandez, HEPM
200 Nevada Ave.
Staten Island, NY 10306
(718) 667-2165
Luis.Hernandez@ny.usda.gov

ARMY, DEPARTMENT OF THE

U.S. MILITARY ACADEMY AT WESTPOINT, CIVILIAN PERSONNEL OFFICE
Michael Heller, Director
Bldg 626, #104
Westpoint, NY 10996
(845) 938-3039

EDUCATION, DEPARTMENT OF

REGION II
Secretary Regional Representative
75 Park Place
New York, NY 10007
(212) 264-7005

ENERGY, DEPARTMENT OF

SCHENECTADY NAVAL REACTORS
Calvert Bowie, HEPM
P.O. Box 1069
Schenectady, NY 12301
(518) 395-6373
Bowiec@kapl.doe.gov

ENVIRONMENTAL PROTECTION AGENCY

HUMAN RESOURCES OFFICE, REGION 2
John Henderson, Director
290 Broadway, 28th Fl.
New York, NY 10007-1866
(212) 637-3550

EQUAL EMPLOYMENT OPPORTUNITY COMMISSION

BUFFALO LOCAL OFFICE
Elizabeth Cadle, Director
6 Fountain Plaza, #350
Buffalo, NY 14202
(716) 551-4441

NEW YORK DISTRICT OFFICE
Spencer H. Lewis, Jr., Director
7 Trade World Ctr., 18th Fl.
New York, NY' 10048-1102
(212) 748-8500

FEDERAL RESERVE BOARD

HUMAN RESOURCES
Robert Scrivani, Vice President
33 Liberty St.
New York, NY 10045-0001
(212) 720-6040

LABOR, DEPARTMENT OF

EMPLOYMENT AND TRAINING ADMINISTRATION
Joseph A. Semansky
Regional Director
201 Varick St., #897
New York, NY 10014-4811
(212) 337-2282

NAVY, DEPARTMENT OF THE

1ST MARINE CORPS DISTRICT
605 Stewart Ave.
Garden City, NY 11530-4761
(516) 228-5630

USMC RECRUITING STATION
111 W Huron St., #205-FOB
Buffalo, NY 14202-2391
(716) 551-4916

USMC RECRUITING STATION
605 Stewart Ave.
Garden City, NY 11530-4761
(516) 228-3679

USMC RECRUITING STATION
Watervliet Arsenal, Bldg. 40-3, 2nd Fl.
Watervliet, NY 12189-4050
(518) 266-6124

POSTAL SERVICE

ALBANY DISTRICT
Josephine D. Grimes, Div. Dev. Field Spec.
30 Old Karner Rd.
Albany, NY 12288-9291
(518) 452-2219

LONG ISLAND DISTRICT
Diane Nannery, Div. Dev. Field Spec.
1377 Motor Pkwy., P.O. Box 7700
Hauppauge, NY 11760-9997
(516) 582-7478

NEW YORK CITY DISTRICT
Evette Corchado, Div. Dev. Field Spec.
421 8th Ave., #3517
New York, NY 10199-5610
(212) 330-3935

NEW YORK METRO AREA
Guillermina C. Colón, Hisp. Prog. Spec.
142-02 20th Ave., # 318
Flushing, NY 11351-0600
(718) 321-5806

NEW YORK METRO AREA OFFICE
Hector J. Borges, Div. Dev. Field Spec.
1200 William St., #303
Buffalo, NY 14240-9431
(716) 846-2484

TRIBORO DISTRICT
Judith N. Matzio, Div. Dev. Field Spec.
142-02 20th Ave.
Flushing, NY 11351-9998
(718) 321-5081

WESTCHESTER DISTRICT
Enid M. Samuels, Div. Dev. Field Spec.
1000 Westchester Ave.
White Plains, NY 10610-9411
(914) 697-7102

WESTERN NEW YORK DISTRICT
Donna C. Biro, Div. Dev. Field Spec.
1200 William St., #303
Buffalo, NY 14240-9431
(716) 846-2484

SMALL BUSINESS ADMIN.

**DISASTER PERSONNEL OFFICE-
DISASTER AREA 1**
Luane Boushe, Personnel Officer
360 Rainbow Blvd., S, 3rd Fl.
Niagara Falls, NY 14303-1192
(716) 282-4612

**REGIONAL PERSONNEL OFFICE,
REGION II (NY, NJ, PR, VI)**
26 Federal Plz., #31-08
New York, NY 10278
(212) 264-3254

TRANSPORTATION, DEPT. OF

**ST. LAWRENCE SEAWAY
DEVELOPMENT CORPORATION**
Rhonda Worden, National HEPM
180 Andrews St.
Massena, NY 13662-0520

(315) 764-3208
slsdcsec@northnet.org

U.S. COAST GUARD
Louden Plaza, 324 Northern Blvd.
Albany, NY 12204-1028
(518) 465-6182
gepps@cgrc.uscg.mil
www.gocoastguard.com

111 W. Huron St., Rm 225
Buffalo, NY 14202-2370
(716) 551-4177
dwestbrook@cgrc.uscg.mil
www.gocoastguard.com

U.S. COAST GUARD
Battery Park Building, Rm. 115A
New York, NY (212) 668-7036
(212) 668-7866
pfunderburk@cgrc.uscg.mil
www.gocoastguard.com

U.S. COAST GUARD
Shop City Shopping Center, 386 Grant
Ave.
Syracuse, NY 13206
(315) 437-6135
jwells@cgrc.uscg.mil
www.gocoastguard.com

U.S. COAST GUARD
Wantagh Plaza, 747 Wantagh Ave.
Wantagh, NY 11793-3133
(516) 796-3340
cewing@cgrc.uscg.mil
www.gocoastguard.com

U.S. COAST GUARD
398 Central Park Ave.
White Plains, NY 10606
(914) 686-8975
kgateling@cgrc.uscg.mil
www.gocoastguard.com

NORTH CAROLINA

AGRICULTURE, DEPARTMENT OF

FOREST SERVICE
Laura Lipe, HEPM
P.O. Box 2680
Asheville, NC 28802
(704) 257-4287
llipe@fs.fed.gov

SOUTHEAST REGION
Milton Cortez, HEPM
4405 Bland Rd., #205
Raleigh, NC 27609-6293
(919) 873-2171
Milton.Cortez@nc.usda.gov

COMMERCE, DEPARTMENT OF

**NATIVE AMERICAN BUSINESS
DEVELOPMENT CENTER,
CHEROKEE OFFICE**
Ronald Blythe, Director
70 Woodfin Place, #305
Asheville, NC 28801
(828) 252-2516

ENVIRONMENTAL PROTECTION
AGENCY

**HUMAN RESOURCES OFFICE
(MD-29)**
Mary Day, Director
79 TW Alexander Dr., 4201 Bldg., #105
Research Triangle Park, NC 27709
(919) 541-3072

EQUAL EMPLOYMENT
OPPORTUNITY COMMISSION

CHARLOTTE DISTRICT OFFICE
Reuben Daniels, Jr., Director
129 W Trade St., #400
Charlotte, NC 28202
(704) 344-6682

GREENSBORO LOCAL OFFICE
Patricia B. Fuller, Director
801 Summit Ave.
Greensboro, NC 27405-7813
(336) 333-5174

RALEIGH AREA OFFICE
Richard E. Walz, Director
1309 Annapolis Dr.
Raleigh, NC 27608-2129
(919) 856-4064

NAVY, DEPARTMENT OF THE

USMC RECRUITING STATION
5000 Falls of Neuse Rd., #404
Raleigh, NC 27609-5408
(919) 790-3039

POSTAL SERVICE

GREENSBORO DISTRICT
René Stutts, Div. Dev. Field Spec.
P.O. Box 27499
Greensboro, NC 27498-9000
(336) 668-1268

MID CAROLINAS DISTRICT
Susan M. McHenry, Div. Dev. Field Spec.
2901 S Interstate 85, Service Rd.
Charlotte, NC 28228-9982
(704) 424-4440

TRANSPORTATION, DEPT. OF

U.S. COAST GUARD
Sugar Creek Professional Building
537 W. Sugar Creek Rd.
Charlotte, NC 28213-6159
(704) 598-2424
jcarter@cgrc.uscg.mil
www.gocoastguard.com

U.S. COAST GUARD
2702 S. Elm-Eugene St.
Greensboro, NC 27406-3625
(336) 275-4951
kporter@cgrc.uscg.mil
www.gocoastguard.com

U.S. COAST GUARD
2917 Brentwood Rd.
Raleigh, NC 27604-2464
(919) 878-4303
dlane@cgrc.uscg.mil
www.gocoastguard.com

U.S. COAST GUARD
Corner Shopping Center
1616 Shipyard Blvd., #15
Wilmington, NC 28412
(910) 791-2593
ndennis@cgrc.uscg.mil
www.gocoastguard.com

NORTH DAKOTA

AGRICULTURE, DEPARTMENT OF

NORTH PLAINS REGION
Jackie Henderson, HEPM
P.O. Box 1458
Bismarck, ND 58502
(701) 530-2077
jackie.henderson@nd.usda.gov

TRANSPORTATION, DEPT. OF

U.S. COAST GUARD
412 Broadway, #1
Fargo, ND 58102
(701) 235-0954
dlemmon@cgrc.uscg.mil
www.gocoastguard.com

OHIO

AGRICULTURE, DEPARTMENT OF

MIDWEST REGION
Barry Cavanna, HEPM
426 West Liberty
Wooster, OH 44691-4835
(303) 262-2836
Barry.Cavanna@oh.usda.gov

AIR FORCE, DEPARTMENT OF THE

**HEADQUARTERS AIR FORCE
MATERIAL COMMAND**
Pamela Sotherland, HEPM
4375 Chidlaw Rd., #N208
Wright-Patterson AFB, OH 45433-5008
(937) 527-4137

ENERGY, DEPARTMENT OF

OHIO FIELD OFFICE
Ronald Berry, HEPM
P.O. Box 3020
Miamisburg, OH 45343-2030
(937) 865-4836
Ronald.berry@ohio.doe.gov

ENVIRONMENTAL PROTECTION
AGENCY

HUMAN RESOURCES OFFICE
Sandra Bowman, Dir. of Human Res.
26 West Martin Luther King Drive
Cincinnati, OH 45268
(513) 569-7801

EQUAL EMPLOYMENT
OPPORTUNITY COMMISSION

CINCINNATI AREA OFFICE
Wilma L. Javey, Director
525 Vine St., #810
Cincinnati, OH 45202-3122
(513) 684-2851

CLEVELAND DISTRICT OFFICE
Michael C. Fetzer, Director
1660 W. 2nd. St., #850
Cleveland, OH 44113-1454
(216) 522-2001

FEDERAL RESERVE BOARD

HUMAN RESOURCES
Elizabeth Robinson, Asst. Vice Pres.
1455 E. Sixth St.
Cleveland, OH 44114
(216) 579-2000

JUSTICE, DEPARTMENT OF

**FEDERAL BUREAU OF
INVESTIGATION**
Annette Nowak, Special Agent Recruiter
1240 E.9th Street, Rm. 3005
Cleveland, OH 44199
(216) 622-6890
www.fbi.gov

NAVY, DEPARTMENT OF THE

USMC RECRUITING STATION
7261 Engle Rd., #110
Middleburg Heights, OH 44130-3479
(440) 243-4010

POSTAL SERVICE

AKRON DISTRICT
Veronica Cook, Div. Dev. Field Spec.
580 Grant St.
Akron, OH 44320-9431
(330) 996-9676

CINCINNATI DISTRICT
John Jamison, Div. Dev. Field Spec.
3055 Crescentville Rd., #205
Cincinnati, OH 45235-5908
(513) 733-7110

CLEVELAND DISTRICT
Gloria M. Jennings, Div. Dev. Field Spec.
2200 Orange Ave., #239
Cleveland, OH 44101-9431
(216) 443-4235

COLUMBUS DISTRICT
Deborah O'Neal, Div. Dev. Field Spec.
850 Twin River Dr.
Columbus, OH 43216
(614) 722-9629

STATE OF OHIO

ATTORNEY'S GENERAL OFFICE
Alethea Botts, Director
30 E Broad St., 16th Fl.
Columbus, OH 43215-3428
(614) 466-8911

TRANSPORTATION, DEPT. OF

U.S. COAST GUARD
7255 Dixie Hwy.
Cincinnati, OH 45014-8504
(513) 942-3145
kriggs@cgrc.uscg.mil
www.gocoastguard.com

U.S. COAST GUARD
6064 Huntley Rd.
Columbus, OH 43229-2508
(614) 431-0270
jmccoy@cgrc.uscg.mil
www.gocoastguard.com

90

U.S. COAST GUARD
912 Great Northern Mall
North Olmstead, OH 44070-3394
(440) 437-4400
khinderliter@cgrc.uscg.mil
www.gocoastguard.com

OKLAHOMA

AGRICULTURE, DEPARTMENT OF

SOUTHCENTRAL REGION
Cathy Holguin, HEPM
601 SE Fifth
Guyman, OK 73942-9804
(560) 336-7379x115
Catherine.Holguin@ok.usda.gov

COMMERCE, DEPARTMENT OF

**OKLAHOMA NATIVE AMERICAN
BUSINESS DEVELOPMENT CENTER**
Denise Dowell, Director
616 S. Boston, #304
Tulsa, OK 74119
(918) 592-1113

ENERGY, DEPARTMENT OF

SOUTHWESTERN POWER ADMIN.
Carlos E. Valencia, HEPM
P.O. Box 1619, Routing Code: SWPA-3300
Tulsa, OK 74101
(918) 595-6707
Valencia@swpa.gov

EQUAL EMPLOYMENT
OPPORTUNITY COMMISSION

OKLAHOMA AREA OFFICE
Joyce Davis Powers, Director
210 Park Ave., #1350
Oklahoma City, OK 73102
(405) 231-4911

INTERIOR, DEPARTMENT OF THE

BUREAU OF INDIAN AFFAIRS
Jeannie Cooper, Personnel Officer
P.O. Box 368
Anadarko, OK 73005
(405) 247-6673x218

NAVY, DEPARTMENT OF THE

USMC RECRUITING STATION
5924 NW 2nd St., #1000
Oklahoma City, OK 73127
(405) 787-3869

POSTAL SERVICE

OKLAHOMA DISTRICT
Eugene Talley, Div. Dev. Field Spec.
3030 NW Expressway St., #1042
Oklahoma City, OK 73125-9807
(405) 553-6217

TRANSPORTATION,
DEPARTMENT OF

U.S. COAST GUARD
Westernview Center, 719 S. Western
Oklahoma City, OK 73139
(405) 231-4483
tbiggerstaff@cgrc.uscg.mil
www.gocoastguard.com

OREGON

AGRICULTURE, DEPARTMENT OF

FOREST SERVICE
Randy Avart, HEPM
P.O. Box 3623
Portland, OR 97208-3623
(503) 808-2650
ravart@fs.fed.us

WEST REGION
Michelle Richwine, HEPM
625 SE Salmon Ave.,#4
Redmond, OR 97756-9580
(541) 923-4358x116
Michelle.Richwine@or.usda.gov

ENERGY, DEPARTMENT OF

**BONNEVILLE POWER
ADMINISTRATIOON**
Libby R. Herrera, HEPM
P.O. Box 3621
Portland, OR 97208-3621
(503) 230-5588
Lrherrera@bpa.gov

INTERIOR, DEPARTMENT OF THE

BUREAU OF INDIAN AFFAIRS
Danielle Dutt, Personnel Officer
911 NE 11th Ave.
Portland, OR 97232-4169
(503) 231-6709

BUREAU OF LAND MGMT.
Carolyn Robinson-Ware, EEO Manager
1515 SW 5th Ave., 9th Fl.
Portland, OR 97201
(503) 952-6341

NAVY, DEPARTMENT OF THE

USMC RECRUITING STATION
1220 SW 3rd Ave., #519, Fed. Bldg.
Portland, OR 97204-2888
(503) 326-3025

POSTAL SERVICE

PORTLAND DISTRICT
Diversity Development Field Specialist
715 NW Hoyt St., #2007
Portland, OR 97208-8098
(503) 294-2392

STATE OF OREGON

OFFICE OF THE GOVERNOR
Raleigh Lewis, Director
155 Cottage St., NE
Salem, OR 97310
(503) 373-1224

PENNSYLVANIA

AGING, DEPARTMENT OF

PERSONNEL OFFICE
Kathy McFadden, Personnel Analyst
555 Walnut St, 5th Fl.
Forum Place
Harrisburg, PA 17101
(717) 783-3126

AGRICULTURE, DEPARTMENT OF

EAST REGION
Juan Carlos Hernandez, HEPM
1432 Route 266
Indiana, PA 15701-1464
(724) 463-8547x106
Juancarlos.Hernandez@paindiana.fsc.usda.gov

FOREST SERVICE
Will McWilliams, HEPM
100 Matsonford Rd.
5 Radnor Corporate Center, #200
Radnor, PA 19087-4585
(610) 975-4075
wmcwilliams@fs.fed.us

FOREST SERVICE
Dave Lombardo, HEPM
P.O. Box 847
222 Liberty St.
Warren, PA 16365
(814) 723-5150
dlombardo@fs.fed.us

COMMERCE, DEPARTMENT OF

MBDA DISTRICT OFFICE
600 Arch St., Rm. 10128
Philadelphia, PA 19106
(215) 861-3597

COMMONWEALTH OF
PENNSYLVANIA

**COMMUNITY AND ECONOMIC
DEVELOPMENT, DEPT. OF**
Connie Franklin, Director
Commonwealth Keystone Bldg.
400 North St.
Harrisburg, PA 17120
(717) 720-1430

**COMMUNITY AND ECONOMIC
DEVELOPMENT, DEPT. OF**
Cheryl Chase, Personnel Analyst
DCDE, Commonwealth Keystone
Bldg.400 North St.
Harrisburg, PA 17120
(717) 787-6857

CORRECTIONS, DEPARTMENT OF
Rafael Chieke, Director
P.O. Box 598
Camp Hill, PA 17001-0598
(717) 975-4905

**DEPARTMENT OF PUBLIC
WELFARE**
Robert Lane, Jr., Director
H & W Building, #521
Harrisburg, PA 17105
(717) 787-3336

GOVERNORS CABINET
Kevin Hoffman, Personnel Director
333 Market St., 16th Fl.
Harrisburg, PA 17101
(717) 787-4129

**GOVERNORS EXECUTIVE OFFICE
OF ADMINISTRATION**
Denise Motley-Brownlee, Director
Finance Building, #508 B
Harrisburg, PA 17120
(717) 783-1130

INSURANCE DEPARTMENT
Tracey Pontius, Director
Strawberry Sq., #1326
Harrisburg, PA 17120
(717) 787-6469

LABOR AND INDUSTRY, DEPT. OF
Stella Spells, Director
L & I Bldg., #514
Harrisburg, PA 17120
(717) 787-1182

PENNSYLVANIA LIQUOR CONTROL BOARD
Graciela Alvarado-Engle, EO Specialist
Northwest Office Bldg., #403-A
Harrisburg, PA 17124
(717) 705-6958

PUBLIC TV NETWORK COMMISSION
Jane Staver, Director
P.O. Box 397
24 Northeast Dr.
Hershey, PA 17033
(717) 533-3548

SECURITIES COMMISSION
Joe Shepard, Director
Eastgate Office Bldg., 2nd Fl.,1010 N. 7th St.
Harrisburg, PA 17102-1410
(717) 787-8061

TURNPIKE COMMISSION
Joanne Gitto Davis, Director
P.O. Box 67676
Harrisburg, PA 17106
(717) 939-9551x4140

EDUCATION, DEPARTMENT OF

OFFICE OF PERSONNEL
Susan Shatto, Equal Opportunity Specialist
333 Market St., 11th Fl., Harristown 2
Harrisburg, PA 17126-0333
(717) 705-2672

ENERGY, DEPARTMENT OF

FEDERAL ENERGY TECHNOLOGY CENTER
Nancy Vargas, HEPM
P.O. Box 10940
Pittsburgh, PA 15236
(412) 892-4654
Vargas@fetc.doe.gov

PITTSBURG NAVAL REACTORS
Ed Rose, HEPM
P.O. Box 109
West Mifflin, PA 15122-0109
(412) 476-7204
Roseev@bettis.gov

ENVIRONMENTAL PROTECTION AGENCY

HUMAN RESOURCES MGMT. BRANCH, REGION 3
Angela Mosby, Chief
1650 Arch St. Mail Code 3PM40
Philadelphia, PA 19103-2029
(215) 814-5331

EQUAL EMPLOYMENT OPPORTUNITY COMMISSION

PHILADELPHIA DISTRICT OFFICE
Marie M. Tomasso, Director
21 S 5th St., #400
Philadelphia, PA 19106-2515
(215) 451-5800

PITTSBURGH AREA OFFICE
Eugene V. Nelson, Director
Liberty Ctr., 1001 Liberty Ave., #300
Pittsburgh, PA 15222-4187
(412) 644-3444

GENERAL SERVICES, DEPT. OF

OFFICE OF EO
Annette A. Watson, Director
Finance Bldg., #402C
Harrisburg, PA 17120
(717) 787-9995

INTERIOR, DEPARTMENT OF THE

NATIONAL PARK SERVICE
Dolores Dyer, Spec. Emph. Prog. Mgr.
200 Chesnut St., 3rd Fl.
Philadelphia, PA 19106
(215) 597-7067

LABOR, DEPARTMENT OF

EMPLOYMENT AND TRAINING ADMINISTRATION
Lynn Intrepidi, Regional Director
170 S Independence Mall West, The Curtis Center, #815
Philadelphia, PA 19106-3315
(215) 861-5501

MILITARY VETERANS AFFAIRS, DEPARTMENT OF

BUREAU OF ADMINISTRATIVE SERVICES
John Cutler, Director
Ft. Indiantown Gap, Building P-0-47
Annville, PA 17003
(717) 861-8796

NAVY, DEPARTMENT OF THE

4TH MARINE CORPS DISTRICT
Bldg. 54, Suite 3, P.O. Box 806
New Cumberland, PA 17070-0806
(717) 770-4708

NAVAL SUPPLY SYSTEMS COMMAND
Crystal Kerns, Comm.Dep. EEO Officer
5450 Carlisle Pike, P.O. Box 2020
Mechanicsburg, PA 17055-0788
(717) 605-5335
Crystal.a.kerns@navsup.navy.mil

USMC RECRUITING STATION
Harrisburg, Bldg. 54, #5
New Cumberland, PA 17070-5006
(717) 770-6646

USMC RECRUITING STATION
1000 Liberty Ave., #1552
New Federal Bldg.
Pittsburgh, PA 15222-4179
(412) 395-6345

PENNSYLVANIA BOARD OF PROBATION AND PAROLE
LeDelle Ingram, EO Specialist
1101 S Front St., #5600
3101 N. Front St., #308
Harrisburg, PA 17104-2522
(717) 787-6897

PENNSYLVANIA FISH AND BOAT COMMISSION
Luis Kauffman, Personnel Officer
1601 Elmerton Ave.
Harrisburg, PA 17110
(717) 705-7800

PENNSYLVANIA GAME COMM.
Jane Peyton, Personnel Analyst
2001 Elmerton Ave.
Harrisburg, PA 17110-9797
(717) 787-7836

PENNSYLVANIA HISTORICAL AND MUSEUM COMMISSION

DIVISION OF PERSONNEL SVCS.
George C. Spiess, Chief
P.O. Box 1026
State Museum Building, Room 509
Harrisburg, PA 17108-1026
(717) 772-1223

PENNSYLVANIA HUMAN RELATIONS COMMISSION
Dr. Iris Cooley, Personnel Officer
101 S. Second St., #308
Executive House
Harrisburg, PA 17105
(717) 783-8270

PENNSYLVANIA MILK MARKETING BOARD
Tim Moyer, Personnel Analyst
Agriculture Bldg., #110
Harrisburg, PA 17110
(717) 787-4194

PENNSYLVANIA PUBLIC SCHOOL EMPLOYMENT RETIREMENT SYSTEM

HUMAN RESOURCES DIVISION
Gary Banks, Director
5 N. 6th St., #106
Harrisburg, PA
(717) 787-8540

PENNSYLVANIA STATE POLICE COMMISSION
Sgt. Marcenia M. Robinson, EEO Officer
1800 Elmerton Ave.
Harrisburg, PA 17110
(717) 787-7220

POSTAL SERVICE

ALLEGHENY AREA OFFICE
Diversity Development Field Specialist
5315 Campbells Run Rd., #125
Pittsburgh, PA 15277-7000
(412) 494-2598

ERIE DISTRICT
Wendy Nelson-Smith, Div. Dev. Field Spec.
1314 Griswold Plaza., #202
Erie, PA 16501-9700
(814) 878-0031

HARRISBURG DISTRICT
Bobbi Reid, Div. Dev. Field Spec.
1425 Crooked Hill Rd.
Harrisburg, PA 17107-0041
(717) 257-5380

LANCASTER DISTRICT
Sonia E. Loza, Div. Dev. Field Spec.
1000 W Valley Rd., 2nd Fl., #2011
Southeastern, PA 19399-7601
(610) 964-6485

PHILADELPHIA DISTRICT
Awilda Casiano, Div. Dev. Field Spec.
P. O. Box 7237
Philadelphia, PA 19101-7237
(215) 895-8040

PITTSBURGH DISTRICT
Clarissa Scott-Jones, Div. Dev. Field Spec.
1001 California Ave., #2062B
Pittsburg, PA 15291
(412) 359-7510

SOCIAL SECURITY ADMIN.

PHILADELPHIA REGION
Hanna Aufschauer, EEO Specialist
P.O. Box 8788
Philadelphia, PA 19101
(215) 597-1694

STATE, DEPARTMENT OF
Harold Conrad, Personnel Analyst
North Office Building, Room 309
Harrisburg, PA 17120
(717) 787-6604

STATE EMPLOYEES' RETIREMENT SYSTEM

OFFICE OF HUMAN RESOURCES
Deborah Facciolo, Personnel Officer
30 N. 3rd St., 5th Fl.
Harrisburg, PA 17108-1147
(717) 783-8085

TRANSPORTATION, DEPT. OF

U.S. COAST GUARD
Union Court, 4337A Union Deposit Rd.
Harrisburg, PA 17111-2883
(717) 561-0972
bsanger@cgrc.uscg.mil
www.gocoastguard.com

U.S. COAST GUARD
Haverford Avenue Shops
7567 Haverford Ave.
Philadelphia, PA 19151
(215) 473-8497
crowland@cgrc.uscg.mil
www.gocoastguard.com

U.S. COAST GUARD
7206 McKnight Rd., # 104
Pittsburgh, PA 15237-3510
(412) 369-2870
mrychorcewicz@cgrc.uscg.mil
www.gocoastguard.com

TREASURY, DEPARTMENT OF THE

Joseph Djardin, Dir. of Human Resources
105 Finance Building
Harrisburg, PA 17120
(717) 787-5979

IRS
Barbara Hatter, Administrative Officer
Strawberry Sq., 11th Fl.
Harrisburg, PA 17128-1100
(717) 783-3682

PUERTO RICO

AGRICULTURE, DEPARTMENT OF

CARIBBEAN AREA
Carlos Hernandez, HEPM
P.O. Box 5100
San German, PR 00683-5100
(787) 264-1912x7796
chernandez@sg.inter.edu

FOREST SERVICE
Maria Correa, HEPM
P.O. Box 25000
Rio Piedras, PR 00928-5000

UPR Experimental Station Grounds, Botanical Garden
Rio Piedras, PR 00928
(787) 766-5335
mcorreas@fs.fed.gov

NAVY, DEPARTMENT OF THE

USMC RECRUITING SUB-STATION
Buchanan Office Ctr., #104,
Carr165, Km. 0.6. Pueblo Viejo
Guaynabo, PR 00968
(787) 782-1115

OFFICE OF PERSONNEL MANAGEMENT

SAN JUAN SERVICE CENTER
Luis Rodriguez, Director
Torre de Plaza Las Americas,
#1114–525 FD Roosevelt Ave.
San Juan, PR 00918-8026
(787) 766-5620

POSTAL SERVICE

CARIBBEAN DISTRICT
Lourdes Lopez, Div. Dev. Field Spec.
P. O. Box 360806
San Juan, PR 00936-0806
(787) 767-3234

TRANSPORTATION, DEPT. OF

U.S. COAST GUARD
USCG Air Station Borinquen
260 Guard Rd.
Ramey, PR 00603
(787) 890-8400
plopez@cgrc.uscg.mil
www.gocoastguard.com

U.S. COAST GUARD
100 Gran Bulevar Los Paseos, #102
San Juan, PR 00926
(787) 723-6129
arodriguez@cgrc.uscg.mil
www.gocoastguard.com

RHODE ISLAND

POSTAL SERVICE

SE NEW ENGLAND DISTRICT
Mary Hahnen, Div. Dev. Field Spec.
24 Corliss St.
Providence, RI 02904-9994
(401) 276-6905

STATE OF RHODE ISLAND

EO OFFICE
A. Vincent Igliozzi, Administrator
1 Capitol Hill
Providence, RI 02908
(401) 222-3090

TRANSPORTATION, DEPT. OF

U.S. COAST GUARD
380 Westminister Mall
Providence, RI 02903-3246
(401) 421-1291
cbrewis@cgrc.uscg.mil
www.gocoastguard.com

SOUTH CAROLINA

AGRICULTURE, DEPT. OF

SOUTHEAST REGION
Donna Ray, HEPM
394 Hwy. 28 Bypass
Abbeville, SC 29620
(864) 459-5419
Donna.Ray@sc.usda.gov

SOUTHEAST REGION
Delores Stevenson, Regional HEPM
1835 Assembly St., #950
Columbia, SC 29201
(803) 253-3920
dstevenson@sc.nr.cs.usda.gov

ENERGY, DEPARTMENT OF

SAVANNAH RIVER OPERATIONS OFFICE
Roberto González, Co-Chair,
HEPM Advisory Council
P.O. Box A
Aiken, SC 29802
(803) 725-7681
roberto.gonzalez@srs.gov

SAVANNAH RIVER OPERATIONS OFFICE
Alejandro Baez, HEPM
P.O. Box A
Aiken, SC 29802
(803) 725-8926
Alejandro.baez@srs.gov

EQUAL EMPLOYMENT OPPORTUNITY COMMISSION

GREENVILLE LOCAL OFFICE
John E. Smith, Director
Wachovia Bank Bldg., 15 S Main St., #530
Greenville, SC 29601
(864) 241-4400

NAVY, DEPARTMENT OF THE

6TH MARINE CORPS DISTRICT
P.O. Box 19201, Bldg. 10, Mexico St.
Parris Island, SC 29905-9201
(843) 228-3027

USMC RECRUITING STATION
9600 Two Notch Rd.
Columbia, SC 29223-4379
(803) 788-4620

POSTAL SERVICE

GREATER SOUTH CAROLINA DIST.
Leonora J. Jordon, Div. Dev. Field Spec.
P. O. Box 929801
Columbia, SC 29292-9801
(803) 926-6429

SOUTH CAROLINA STATE WIDE

MINORITY BUSINESS DEVELOPMENT CENTER
Gwen Bullock, Director
2111 Bull St.
Columbia, SC 29201
(803) 779-5905

TRANSPORTATION, DEPT. OF

U.S. COAST GUARD
1650 Sam Rittenberg Blvd., #1
Charleston, SC 29407-4933
(843) 766-7315
jmonsanto@cgrc.uscg.mil
www.gocoastguard.com

U.S. COAST GUARD
Capitol Center Shopping Center
201 Columbia Mall Blvd.
Columbia, SC 29223
(803) 699-7230
gleeth@cgrc.uscg.mil
www.gocoastguard.com

SOUTH DAKOTA

AGRICULTURE, DEPARTMENT OF

NORTH PLAINS REGION
Mike Stirling, HEPM
1530 Samco Rd., #4
Rapid City, SD 57702-3364
(605) 343-1643
Michael.Stirling@sd.usda.gov

INTERIOR, DEPARTMENT OF THE

BUREAU OF INDIAN AFFAIRS
Loretta Webster, EEO Manager
115 4th Ave., SE
Aberdeen, SD 57401
(605) 226-7466

POSTAL SERVICE

DAKOTA DISTRICT
Lorrie Papka, Div. Dev. Field Spec.
P.O. Box 7560
Souix Falls, SD 57117-7560
(605) 333-2786

STATE OF SOUTH DAKOTA

PERSONNEL BUREAU
Bob Sahr, Attorney
500 E Capitol Ave.
Pierre, SD 57501
(605) 773-3148

TENNESSEE

AGRICULTURE, DEPARTMENT OF

SOUTHEAST REGION
Hugh Jackson, HEPM
286 E. Main St.
Gallatin, TN 37066
(615) 452-3838
Hugh.Jackson@tn.usda.gov

ENERGY, DEPARTMENT OF

OAK RIDGE OPERATIONS OFFICE
Leon F. Duquella, HEPM
P.O. Box 2001
Oak Ridge, TN 37831
(865) 576-9649
Duquellalf@oro.doe.gov

OAK RIDGE OPERATIONS OFFICE
Jorge Ferrer, HEPM
P.O. Box 2001
Oak Ridge, TN 37831
(865) 576-6638
Ferrer@oro.doe.gov

EQUAL EMPLOYMENT OPPORTUNITY COMMISSION

MEMPHIS DISTRICT OFFICE
Walter S. Grabon, Director
1407 Union Ave., # 621
Memphis, TN 38104
(901) 544-0115

NASHVILLE AREA OFFICE
Sarah Smith, Director
50 Vantage Way, # 202
Nashville, TN 37228-9940
(615) 736-5820

NAVY, DEPARTMENT OF THE

BUREAU OF NAVAL PERSONNEL
Jimmy Lee, Jr., Command Deputy EEO Officer
5720 Integrity Dr., Code PERS-08
Millington, TN 38055
(901) 874-3023
pooe@bupers.navy.mil

USMC RECRUITING STATION
2519 Perimeter Place Dr.
Nashville, TN 37214-3681
(615) 736-7141

POSTAL SERVICE

TENNESSEE DISTRICT
Sheila Baskins, Div. Dev. Field Spec.
811 Royal Pkwy.
Nashville, TN 37229-9971
(615) 872-5693

STATE OF TENNESSEE

PERSONNEL DEPARTMENT
Rose Wilson, Director, Affirmative Action
Div.
505 Deadericks St.–James K. Polk Bldg.,
2nd Fl.
Nashville, TN 37243-0635
(615) 741-4845

TENNESSEE VALLEY AUTHORITY

EMPLOYMENT SERVICES
400 W. Summit Hill Dr.
Knoxville, TN 37902
(888) 975-4882

TRANSPORTATION, DEPARTMENT OF

U.S. COAST GUARD
The Market at Bell Forge
5308 Mount View Rd., #C
Antioch, TN 37013-2307
(615) 731-3408
rprice@cgrc.uscg.mil
www.gocoastguard.com

U.S. COAST GUARD
5811 Lee Hwy.
Chattanooga, TN 37421-3542
(423) 485-8307
smacy@cgrc.uscg.mil
www.gocoastguard.com

U.S. COAST GUARD
Plaza at the Commons,
120 S. Peters Rd., #14
Knoxville, TN 37923-5200
(423) 690-7219
mmcnair@cgrc.uscg.mil
www.gocoastguard.com

U.S. COAST GUARD
Timber Creek Shopping Center
2830 Coleman Rd.
Memphis, TN 38128
(901) 380-9873
mjenkins@cgrc.uscg.mil
www.gocoastguard.com

TEXAS

AGRICULTURE, DEPARTMENT OF

SOUTH CENTRAL REGION
Zaragoza Rodriguez, III, HEPM
P.O. Box 1006
Zapata, TX 78076-1006
(956) 765-6911
Zaragoza.Rodriguez@tx.usda.gov

AIR FORCE, DEPARTMENT OF THE

HEADQUARTERS AIR EDUCATION AND TRAINING COMMAND
Norman W. Shultze, HEPM
1851 First St W, #1
Randolph AFB, TX 78150-4308
(210) 652-7977

HEADQUARTERS AIR FORCE PERSONNEL OFFICE
550 C St., W, #57
Randolph AFB, TX 78150-4759
(800) 699-4473

HEADQUARTERS AIR INTELLIGENCY AGENCY
Beverly Hernandez, HEPM
321 Hoff St.
San Antonio, TX 78243-7129
(210) 977-2716x206

RANDOLPH AFB
Irene Reyes, HEPM
550 D St., E., #1
Randolph AFB, TX 78150
(210) 652-6224

ARMY, DEPARTMENT OF THE

MEDICAL COMMAND, EEO OFFICE
Delia Ramirez Trimble, Director
ATTN: MCEE
2050 Worth Rd.
Ft. Sam Houston, TX 78234-6020
(210) 221-8170

COMMERCE, DEPARTMENT OF

NATIONAL WEATHER SERVICE
Joe Villescac, HEPM
2090 Airport Rd.
New Braunfels, TX 78130
(830) 606-3600

EDUCATION, DEPARTMENT OF

REGION VI PERSONNEL OFFICE (AK, LA, NM, OK, TX)
Bob Wise, Personnel Mgmt. Specialist
1999 Bryant St., #2110
Dallas, TX 75201-6817
(214) 767-3651

ENERGY, DEPARTMENT OF

STRATEGIC PETROLEUM RESERVE
Jorge Aguiñaga, HEPM
P.O. Box 2276
Freeport, TX 77542-2276
(979) 230-2201
jorge.aguinaga@spr.doe.gov

ENVIRONMENTAL PROTECTION AGENCY

HUMAN RESOURCES OFFICE, REGION 6
1445 Ross Ave., M/C 6MD-AP
Dallas, TX 75202-2733
(214) 665-6544

EQUAL EMPLOYMENT OPPORTUNITY COMMISSION

DALLAS DISTRICT OFFICE
Thelma H. Taylor, Director
207 S Houston St., 3rd Fl.
Dallas, TX 75202-4726
(214) 655-3355

EL PASO AREA OFFICE
Roberto Calderon, Director
The Commons, Bldg. C # 100
4171 N Mesa St.
El Paso, TX 79902
(915) 832-4001

HOUSTON DISTRICT OFFICE
H. Joan Ehrlich, Director
Mickey Leland Federal Bldg.
1919 Smith St., 7th Fl.
Houston, TX 77002-8049
(713) 209-3320

SAN ANTONIO DISTRICT OFFICE
Pedro M. Esquivel, Director
5410 Fredericksburg Rd., #200
San Antonio, TX 78229-3555
(210) 281-7600

FEDERAL RESERVE BOARD

HUMAN RESOURCES
Bob Williams, Vice President
2200 North Pearl St.
Dallas, TX 75201-2272
(214) 922-5270

INTERIOR, DEPARTMENT OF THE

NATIONAL PARK SERVICE
Karen Steed, Personnel Specialist
2202 Roosevelt Ave.
San Antonio, TX 78210
(210) 534-8833

JUSTICE, DEPARTMENT OF

ATTORNEY'S OFFICE
Tina Gomez, HEPM
601 NW Loop 410, suite 600
San Antonio, TX 78216-5597
(210) 384-7100

IMMIGRATION AND NATURALIZATION SERVICE
Alfredo N. Martínez, HEPM
P.O.Box 179
700 Zaragoza St.
Laredo, TX 78042-0179
(956) 726-2200

IMMIGRATION AND NATURALIZATION SERVICE
Felipa Salazar, HEPM
8940 Four Winds Dr.
San Antonio, TX 78239
(210) 967-7004

IMMIGRATION AND NATURALIZATION SERVICE, BORDER PATROL
Cynthia Garcia, Personnel Specialist
2301 S Main St.
McAllen, TX 78503
(956) 984-3800

LABOR, DEPARTMENT OF

EMPLOYMENT AND TRAINING ADMINISTRATION
Jose de Olivares, Regional Director
525 Griffin St., #403
Dallas, TX 75202
(214) 767-2114

NAVY, DEPARTMENT OF THE

USMC RECRUITING STATION
207 S Houston St., #146
Dallas, TX 75202-4703
(214) 655-3482

USMC RECRUITING STATION
701 San Jacinto St.
Houston, TX 77002-3622
(713) 718-4284

USMC RECRUITING STATION
1265 Buck Rd., #MC. Fort Sam Houston
San Antonio, TX 78234-5034
(210) 295-1008

POSTAL SERVICE

DALLAS DISTRICT
Gail Lofton, Div. Dev. Field Spec.
951 W Bethel Rd.
Coppell, TX 75099-9852
(972) 393-6665

FORT WORTH DISTRICT
Linda Brantley, Div. Dev. Field Spec.
4600 Mark IV Pkwy.
Fort Worth, TX 76161-9998
(817) 870-8133

FORT WORTH DISTRICT
Vickie Magallon, Hispanic Prog. Spec.
4600 Mark IV Pkwy.
Ft. Worth, TX 76161-9100
(817) 317-2705

HOUSTON DISTRICT
Diversity Development Field Specialist
401 Franklin St., Annex Bldg.
Houston, TX 77201-9421
(713) 226-3938

HOUSTON DISTRICT
John Martinez, Hispanic Prog. Spec.
1002 Washington Ave., #228B
Houston, TX 77202-9421
(713) 226-3186

RIO GRANDE DISTRICT
Alice Orta, Hispanic Program Specialist
1 Post Office Dr.
San Antonio, TX 78284-9425
(210) 368-5563

SAN ANTONIO DISTRICT
Martin Cantu, Div. Dev. Field Spec.
1 Post Office Dr.
San Antonio, TX 78284-9997
(210) 368-5512

SOUTHWEST AREA OFFICE
Tom M. Claunch, Div. Dev. Field Spec.
P. O. Box 225428
Dallas, TX 75222-5428
(214) 819-8605

SMALL BUSINESS ADMIN.

DISASTER PERSONNEL OFFICE-DISASTER AREA 3
Kandye Wells, Personnel Officer
4400 Amon Carter Blvd., #102
Ft. Worth, TX 76155
(817) 684-5600

SOCIAL SECURITY ADMIN.

DALLAS REGION
Emerson Lattimore, Director
1301 Young St.
Dallas, TX 75202
(214) 767-3036

STATE OF TEXAS

OFFICE OF THE GOVERNOR
Liana Ptomey, Acting Dir. of Human Res.
P.O. Box 12428
Austin, TX 78711
(512) 463-1740

TEXAS WORKFORCE COMMISSION
Jan Thomas, Director
101 E 15th St., #230
Austin, TX 78778-0001
(512) 463-2314

TRANSPORTATION, DEPT. OF

U.S. COAST GUARD
1030 W. Arkansas Ln., #308
Arlington, TX 76013
(817) 265-1345
nbreen@cgrc.uscg.mil
www.gocoastguard.com

U.S. COAST GUARD
Wind Chase Shopping Center
2033 Airline Rd., #E-4
Corpus Christi, TX 78412
(361) 993-6977
ddelgado@cgrc.uscg.mil
www.gocoastguard.com

U.S. COAST GUARD
9100 Viscount Blvd., #E
El Paso, TX 79925
(915) 591-6741
ewitherspoon@cgrc.uscg.mil
www.gocoastguard.com

U.S. COAST GUARD
701 San Jacinto
Houston, TX 77002
(713) 718-4268
ccalloway@cgrc.uscg.mil
www.gocoastguard.com

U.S. COAST GUARD
8347 Perrin Beitel River Oaks Plaza
San Antonio, TX 78218
(210) 590-9760
bcrawford@cgrc.uscg.mil
www.gocoastguard.com

TREASURY, DEPT. OF THE

BUEAU OF ENGRAVING AND PRINTING
Martin Muñoz, HEPM
9000 Blue Mound Rd.
Ft. Worth, TX 76131
(817) 847-3959
munoz.martin@bep.treas.gov

VETERANS AFFAIRS, DEPT. OF

VETERANS ADMINISTRATION HOSPITAL
Nick Villanueva, HEPM
3600 Memorial Blvd.
Kerrville, TX 78028
(830) 792-2580

UTAH

AGRICULTURE, DEPARTMENT OF

FOREST SERVICE
Cindy Quintana, HEPM
324 25th St., #2309
Federal Bldg, HR&S
Ogden, UT 84404
(801) 625-5242
cquintana@fs.fed.us

WEST REGION
Gaylene Howard, HEPM
85 S First E
Tremonton, UT 84337
(435) 257-5403x16
Gaylene.Howard@ut.usda.gov

COMMERCE, DEPARTMENT OF

SALT LAKE CITY SBA
Stan Nakano, Director
125 S State St.
Salt Lake City, UT 84138
(801) 524-3209

INTERIOR, DEPARTMENT OF THE

BUREAU OF RECLAMATION
Ann Gold, Human Resources Officer
125 S State St., Room 6107.
Salt Lake City, UT 84138-1102
(801) 524-3656

NAVY, DEPARTMENT OF THE

USMC RECRUITING STATION
1279 W 2200 S, #A
West Valley City, UT 84119-1471
(801) 954-0400

POSTAL SERVICE

SALT LAKE CITY DISTRICT
Jo Vicknair Jeppson, Div. Dev. Field Spec.
1760 W 2100 South
Salt Lake City, UT 84199-2922
(801) 974-2922

STATE OF UTAH

DEPARTMENT OF COMMUNITY AND ECONOMIC DEVELOPMENT
Leti Medina, Director
324 S. State St. #500
Salt Lake City, UT 84114
(801) 538-8755

TRANSPORTATION, DEPT. OF

U.S. COAST GUARD
Roy Shopping Center
5639 S. 1900 W., #302
Roy, UT 84041-2301
(801) 525-1904
mwalker@cgrc.uscg.mil
www.gocoastguard.com

VERMONT

AGRICULTURE, DEPARTMENT OF

EASTERN REGION
Charles Mitchell, HEPM
RR#4, Box 932, Professional Dr.
Morrisville, VT 05661
(802) 888-4965
Charles.Mitchell@vt.usda.gov

VIRGINIA

AGRICULTURE, DEPARTMENT OF

FOOD, NUTRITION & CONSUMER SERVICE
Carmen Nordlund, HEPM
3101 Park Center Dr., #1006
Alexandria, VA 22302
(703) 305-2620
Carmen.Nordlund@fns.usda.gov

SOUTH CENTRAL REGION
Holly Martien, HEPM
3737 Government St.
Alexandria, VA 71302
(318) 473-7753
Holly.Martien@nrcs.usda.gov

SOUTHEAST REGION
Jaime Valentin, HEPM
1934 Deyerle Ave., #B
Harrisonburg, VA 22801
(540) 433-2853/2901
Jaime.Valentin@va.usda.gov

AIR FORCE, DEPARTMENT OF THE

HQ AIR COMBAT COMMAND
Phyllis Bibb, HEPM
114 Douglas St., #214
Langley AFB, VA 23665-2773
(757) 764-7720

ARLINGTON COUNTY GOVERNMENT

DEPARTMENT OF HUMAN RESOURCES
Hilaria Helman, Pers. Analyst/Outreach Spec.
2100 Clarendon Blvd., # 511
Arlington, VA 22201
(703) 228-3506

ARMY, DEPARTMENT OF THE

EEO AGENCY
Yolanda Maldonado Echeverria
Dir., Hispanic Employment Programs
1941 Jefferson Davis Hwy.
Crystal Mall-4, #207
Arlington, VA 12202-4508
(703) 607-1976
yolanda.maldonado@army.mil
www.army.mil

FORT BELVOIR
Augustin Bill, HEPM
9725 Belvoir Rd., Bldg. 1000
Ft. Belvoir, VA 22060
(703) 805-5388

FORT BELVOIR
Oliver Allen, Director
9725 Belvoir Rd., Bldg. 1000
Ft. Belvoir, VA 22060
(703) 805-3034

FORT MYER, EEO OFFICE
Mae Bullock, Chief EEO Office
Bldg 203, #215
Fort Myer, VA 22211-5050
(703) 696-3544

HQ, U. S. ARMY MATERIAL COMMAND
Frances Cruz, Equal Employment Specialist
5001 Eisenhower Ave.
Alexandria, VA 22333-0001
(703) 617-3763

MILITARY TRAFFIC MGMT. COMMAND
Ana Colon, EEO Officer
200 Stovall St., #12F71
Alexandria, VA 22332-5000
(703) 428-2105

COMMERCE, DEPARTMENT OF

PATENT & TRADEMARK OFFICE
Carl Dolder, Recruitment Manager
2011 Crystal Park 1, Crystal Dr.
Arlington, VA 22202
(703) 305-8231

PATENT & TRADEMARK OFFICE
Mary Bowman, Recruitment Specialist
2011 Crystal Park 1, Crystal Dr.
Arlington, VA 22202
(703) 305-8313

DEFENSE, DEPARTMENT OF

DEFENSE COMMISSARY AGENCY
Karen Swindell
1300 E Ave.
Fort Lee, VA 23801-1000
(703) 734-8620
swindell@hqlee.deca.mil

DEFENSE CONTRACT AUDIT AGENCY HDQRTS.
Steve Hernandez, HEPM
8725 John G. Kingman Rd. #2135
Ft. Belvoir, VA 22060-6219
(703) 767-2302
steve.hernandez@dcaa.mil

DEFENSE INFORMATION SYSTEMS AGENCY
Renata Penn
701 S. Courthouse Rd.
Arlington, VA 22204-2199
(703) 607-6459
pennr@ncr.disa.mil

DEFENSE SECURITY SERVICE
Carlynn Marsh, HEPM
1340 Braddock Pl.
Dulles, VA 22304
(703) 325-5344
carlynn.marsh@mail.dss.mil

DEFENSE THREAT REDUCTION AGENCY/ADR
Rey Ovalle, Jr., HEPM
45045 Aviation Dr.
Dulles, VA 20166
(703) 810-4459
reyovalle@dtra.mil

DOD DEPENDENT SCHOOLS
Jerald Bloom, Director, EEO
4040 N. Fairfax Dr.
Arlington, VA 22203-1635
jbloom@odedodea.edu

HEADQUARTERS, DEFENSE CONTRACT AUDIT AGENCY
Evelyn Pi, HPM
John J. Kingman Rd., #2135
Fort Belvoir, VA 22060
(703) 767-2219
evelyn.pi@dcaa.mil

HEADQUARTERS, DEFENSE LOGISTICS AGENCY
George Korolevich, HEPM
8725 John J. Kingmann Rd., #2533
Ft. Belvoir, VA 22060
(703) 767-6100
jorge_korolevich@hq.dla.mil

NATIONAL GUARD BUREAU
Felton Page, HEM
4501 Ford Ave., #380
Alexandria, VA 22302
(703) 756-8950
pagef@ngb.ang.af.mil

OFFICE OF THE INSPECTOR GENERAL
Matthew Johnson, Director of EEO
400 Army Navy Dr., #520
Arlington, VA 22202
(703) 604-9708
mjohnson@dodig.osd.mil

WASHINGTON HEADQUARTER SERVICES
Renee Coates, Assistant Director
1777 N. Kent St.
Arlington, VA 22209
(703) 588-0451
coater@osd.pentagon.mil
www.pentagon.mil

EQUAL EMPLOYMENT OPPORTUNITY COMMISSION

NORFOLK AREA OFFICE
Herbert Brown, Director
World Trade Ctr., 101 W Main St., #4300
Norfolk, VA 23510
(757) 441-3470

RICHMOND AREA OFFICE
Gloria L. Underwood, Director
3600 W Broad St., #229
Richmond, VA 23230
(804) 278-4651

FAIRFAX COUNTY PUBLIC SCHOOLS

RECRUITMENT OFFICE
Terri Czarniak, Recruitment Specialist
6815 Edsall Rd.
Springfield, VA 22151
(703) 750-8519

INTERIOR, DEPARTMENT OF THE

BUREAU OF LAND MANAGEMENT
Heddy Lozano, HEPM
7450 Boston Blvd.
Springfield, VA 22153
(703) 440-1500

FISH & WILDLIFE SERVICE
Pedro De Jesus, EEO Manager
4401 N. Fairfax Dr., #300, WEBB
Arlington, VA 22203
(703) 358-2552

GEOLOGICAL SURVEY, HQ & EASTERN REGION
National Center, M/S 601
12201 Sunrise Valley Dr.
Reston, VA 20192
(703) 648-7432

JEFFERSON NATIONAL FOREST
Mick Michelsen, Personnel Manager
5162 Valleypointe Pkwy.
Roanoke, VA 24019
(540) 265-5100

MINERALS MANAGEMENT SVC.
Patricia Callis, Chief
381 Elden St., Atrium Bldg., M/S 0400
Herndon, VA 22070
(703) 787-1313

MINERALS MANAGEMENT SVC.
Sandra Streets, Chief Personnel Manager
Mail Stop 2200, 381 Elden St.
Herndon, VA 20170
(703) 787-1423

MINERALS MANAGEMENT SVC.
Rosa Thomas, EEO Specialist
381 Elden St., M/S 290
Herndon, VA 20170
(703) 787-1313

JUSTICE, DEPARTMENT OF

DEPARTMENT OF CORRECTIONS
Tom Garten, Human Resources Officer
6900 Atmore Dr.
Richmond, VA 23225
(804) 674-3507

DRUG ENFORCEMENT ADMIN.
Carmen Robles, EEO Manager
600 Army-Navy Dr., #E11275
Arlington, VA 22202
(202) 307-8889

MARSHALS SERVICE
Jeff Cahall, Employment Officer
600 Army-Navy Dr.
Arlington, VA 22202-4210
(202) 307-9600

LABOR, DEPARTMENT OF

MINE SAFETY AND HEALTH ADMINISTRATION
Michael Thompson, Director
4015 Wilson Blvd., BT3, #431
Arlington, VA 22203
(703) 235-8262

MINE SAFETY AND HEALTH ADMINISTRATION
Ellen Gee, HEPM
4015 Wilson Blvd., BT3, #605
Arlington, VA 22203
(703) 235-8262
www.msha.gov/jobs.htm

NATIONAL CREDIT UNION ADMINISTRATION

EEO PROGRAMS OFFICE
Marilyn Gannon, Director
1775 Duke St., #3019
Alexandria, VA 22314
(703) 518-6325

NATIONAL SCIENCE FOUNDATION

OFFICE OF EQUAL OPPORTUNITY PROGRAMS
Ana A. Ortiz, Program Manager
4201 Wilson Blvd., #1080
Arlington, VA 22230
(703) 292-8020
www.nsf.gov

NAVY, DEPARTMENT OF THE

ATLANTIC FLEET (CODE N-15)
Nona Jordan, Comm. Deputy EEO Officer
1562 Mitcsher Ave., #250
Norfolk, VA 23511-2487
(757) 836-0497
jordannj@clf.navy.mil

ATLANTIC FLEET (CODE N-1513)
Pat Hugh (Asst.), Comm. Dep. EEO Officer
1562 Mitcsher Ave., #250
Norfolk, VA 23511-2487
(757) 836-0494
hughespj@clf.navy.mil

HQ USMC
Howard E. Matthews, Jr., CDEEO Officer
3280 Rusell Rd.
Quantico, VA 22134-5103
(703) 784-9380/81
howard-e-mathews@manpower.usmc.mil

MILITARY SEALIFT COMMAND
Laudess M. Scales (Asst.), CDEEO Off.
P.O. Box 120 Code 00E
Virginia Beach, VA 23458-0120
(757) 417-4266
laudess.scales@ms.c.navy.mil

NAVAL SEA SYSTEMS COMMAND
Veronica D. Cruz, CDEEO Officer
Code Sea 09B52, NC3, RM 11N14, 2531 Jefferson Davis Hwy.
Arlington, VA 22212-5161
(703) 607-1660
cruzvd@navsea.navy.mil

NAVY INTERNAL PROGRAMS DIV.
Gibson G. LeBoeuf, Deputy Director
1111 Jeff Davis Hwy., #701E
Arlington, VA 22202-1111
(703) 604-0019
leboeuf.gibson@hq.navy.mil

OFFICE OF NAVAL RESEARCH
James Richardson, Chief/CDEEO Officer
800 N Quincy St., Code 00DE
Arlington, VA 22217-5660
(703) 696-4266
richarj@orn.navy.mil

USMC RECRUITING STATION
9210 Arboretum Parkway, #220
Richmond, VA 23236-3472
(804) 272-0518

PERSONNEL MANAGEMENT, OFFICE OF

NORFOLK SERVICE CENTER
F. Alan Nelson, Director
Federal Building, 200 Granby St., #500
Norfolk, VA 23510-1886
(757) 441-3373

POSTAL SERVICE

MID-ATLANTIC AREA OFFICE
Carmen I. Villarreal, Div. Dev. Field Spec.
2800 S Shirlington Rd.
Arlington, VA 22205-7050
(703) 824-5082

NORTHERN VIRGINIA DISTRICT
Young Chung, Div. Dev. Field Spec.
8409 Lee Hwy.
Merrifield, VA 22081-9998
(703) 698-6614

RICHMOND DISTRICT
Laverne Wiggins, Div. Dev. Field Spec.
P.O. Box 2873
Norfolk, VA 23501-9315
(757) 629-2259

SELECTIVE SERVICE SYSTEM

EEO OFFICE
Richard S. Flahavan, EEO Officer
1515 Wilson Blvd., #400
Arlington, VA 22209-2425
(703) 605-4100

TRANSPORTATION, DEPARTMENT OF

U.S. COAST GUARD
Huntington Gateway Shopping Plaza
5950 Richmond Hwy
Alexandria, VA 22303-1855
(703) 960-5923
wharris@cgrc.uscg.mil
www.gocoastguard.com

U.S. COAST GUARD
1011 Eden Way N., #A
Chesapeake, VA 23320-2768
(757) 312-0514
jhoesli@cgrc.uscg.mil
www.gocoastguard.com

U.S. COAST GUARD
Oak Hill Shopping Center
3131 Mechanicsville Turnpike
Richmond, VA 23223
(804) 771-8635
hfreeland@cgrc.uscg.mil
www.gocoastguard.com

WASHINGTON

AGRICULTURE, DEPARTMENT OF

WEST REGION
Martin Rodriguez, HEPM
200 Cheyne Rd
Zillah, WA 98953
(509) 829-3003
martin.rodriguez@wa.usda.gov

COMMERCE, DEPARTMENT OF

NATIONAL OCEANIC ATMOSPHERIC ADMIN.
Elizabeth Blas, Personnel Mgmt. Special
Western Administrative Support
Center~7600 Sand Point Way, NE
Seattle, WA 98115-6349
(206) 526-6057

EDUCATION, DEPARTMENT OF

HUMAN RESOURCES OFFICE
Ike Gilbert, Human Resources Officer
Jackson Federal Bldg.
915 2nd Ave., Rm 3388
Seattle, WA 98174
(206) 220-7813

ENERGY, DEPARTMENT OF

RICHLAND OPERATIONS OFFICE
Paul Hernández, HEPM
P.O. Box 550, MS A5-52
Richland, WA 99352
(509) 376-2209
Paul_r_hernandez@rl.gov

RICHLAND OPERATIONS OFFICE
Mary F. Jarvis, HEPM
P.O. Box 550, A5-15
Richland, WA 99352
(509) 376-2256
Mary_f_jarvis@rl.gov

ENVIRONMENTAL PROTECTION AGENCY

HUMAN RESOURCES OFFICE, REGION 10
Thomas Davison, Director
1200 6th Ave., Mail Code OMP-162
Seattle, WA 98101
(206) 553-2957

EQUAL EMPLOYMENT OPPORTUNITY COMMISSION

SEATTLE DISTRICT OFFICE
Jeanette M. Leino, Director
Federal Office Bldg., 909 1st Ave., #400
Seattle, WA 98104-1061
(206) 220-6883

HEALTH AND HUMAN SERVICES, DEPARTMENT OF

CENTER FOR DISEASE CONTROL & PREVENTION, NATIONAL INSTITUTE OF OCCUPATIONAL SAFETY & HEALTH
Karen Rogge, Personnel Assistant
315 E Montgomery Ave.
Spokane, WA 99207
(509) 354-8110

LABOR, DEPARTMENT OF

EMPLOYMENT AND TRAINING ADMINISTRATION
Ernest Priestley, Assoc. Regional Director
1111 Third Ave., #800
Seattle, WA 98101-3212
(206) 553-7938x8057

NAVY, DEPARTMENT OF THE

USMC RECRUITING STATION
4735 E Marginal Way, South,
Fed. Ctr. South
South Seattle, WA 98134-2379
(206) 767-9569

POSTAL SERVICE

SEATTLE DISTRICT
Carol V. Peoples-Proctor,
Diversity Development Field Specialist
415 First Ave.
North Seattle, WA 98109-8872
(206) 442-6293

SEATTLE DISTRICT
Pedro A. Rodriguez, Hisp. Prog. Spec.
415 First Ave.
North Seattle, WA 98109-9997
(206) 442-6203

STATE OF WASHINGTON

SOCIAL AND HEALTH SERVICES, DEPARTMENT OF
Jim Ruiz, Diversity Program Mgr.
P.O. Box 45600
Olympia, WA 98504-5600
(360) 725-2551

TRANSPORTATION, DEPT. OF

U.S. COAST GUARD
10505 Aurora Ave. N., #002
Seattle, WA 98133-8811
(206) 523-0793
mstocks@cgrc.uscg.mil
www.gocoastguard.com

U.S. COAST GUARD
11516-A E. Sprague Ave.
Spokane, WA 99206-2134
(509) 927-0993
mebrown@cgrc.uscg.mil
www.gocoastguard.com

U.S. COAST GUARD
Tacoma Office Mall Building
4301 S. Pine St., #102
Tacoma, WA 98409-7264
(253) 476-5939
pswofford@cgrc.uscg.mil
www.gocoastguard.com

U.S. COAST GUARD
8109 F NE Vancouver Mall Dr.
Vancouver, WA 98662-6422
(360) 699-1047
tcox@cgrc.uscg.mil
www.gocoastguard.com

U.S. COAST GUARD
Plaza 2, 1200 Chesterly Dr., #110
Yakima, WA 98902-7338
(509) 452-1356
llawton@cgrc.uscg.mil
www.gocoastguard.com

WEST VIRGINIA

AGRICULTURE, DEPARTMENT OF

EAST REGION
Walter Salamacha, HEPM
418 Goff Mountain Rd., #102
Cross Lanes, WV 25313
(304) 776-5256
Walter.Salamacha@wvcrosslan.fsc.usda.gov

HIGHWAYS & TRANSPORTATION, DEPARTMENT OF

HUMAN RESOURCES DEPT.
Drema Smith, Admin. Services Manager
1900 Kanawha Blvd., Bldg. 5, #949
Charleston, WV 25305
(304) 558-3111

INTERIOR, DEPARTMENT OF THE

NATIONAL PARK SERVICE
Magaly M. Green, EEO Manager
P.O. Box 50
Harpers Ferry, WV 25425
(304) 535-6003

NAVY, DEPARTMENT OF THE

USMC RECRUITING STATION
Charleston, Heritage Plaza, Rt. 34
Hurricane, WV 25526
(304) 346-6456

POSTAL SERVICE

APPALACHIAN DISTRICT
Lora M. Moles, Div. Dev. Field Spec.
P.O. Box 59000
Charleston, WV 25350-9000
(304) 561-1269

TRANSPORTATION, DEPT. OF

U.S. COAST GUARD
410 Beckley Crossing Shopping Center
Beckley, WV 25801-7109
(304) 253-4625
wmartin@cgrc.uscg.mil
www.gocoastguard.com

TREASURY, DEPARTMENT OF THE

BUREAU OF PUBLIC DEBT
Judy Shawver, HEPM
200 3rd St., #102
Parkersburg, WV 26101
(304) 480-7944

BUREAU OF PUBLIC DEBT
Patty Adams, SEP Manager
200 3rd St., #307
Parkersburg, WV 26106
(304) 480-7944
padams@bpd.treas.gov

WISCONSIN

AGRICULTURE, DEPARTMENT OF

MIDWEST REGION
Rosabeth Sais, Regional HEPM
2820 Waalton Commons W, #123
Madison, WI 53718-6797
(608) 224-3036
Rosabeth.Sais@mw.nrcs.usda.gov

MIDWEST REGION
Kent Pena, HEPM
6515 Watts Rd., #200
Madison, WI 53719-2726
(608) 276-8732x274
Kent.Pena@wi.usda.gov

EQUAL EMPLOYMENT OPPORTUNITY COMMISSION

MILWAUKEE DISTRICT OFFICE
Chester V. Bailey , Director
310 W Wisconsin Ave., #800
Milwaukee, WI 53203-2292
(414) 297-1111

NAVY, DEPARTMENT OF THE

USMC RECRUITING STATION
310 Wisconsin Ave., #480
Milwaukee, WI 53203-2216
(414) 297-1399

POSTAL SERVICE

MILWAUKEE DISTRICT
Terri Jordan, Div. Dev. Field Spec.
P.O. Box 5027
Milwaukee, WI 53201-5027
(414) 287-1836

STATE OF WISCONSIN

DEPARTMENT OF EMPLOYMENT RELATIONS
Greg Jones, Administrator
Affirmative Action Division
P.O. Box 7855
Madison, WI 53707-7855
(608) 266-5709

TRANSPORTATION, DEPT. OF

U.S. COAST GUARD
Woodland Court
3953 S. 76th St.
Milwaukee, WI 53220-2320
(414) 321-4220
aalicea@cgrc.uscg.mil
www.gocoastguard.com

WYOMING

AGRICULTURE, DEPARTMENT OF

NORTH PLAINS REGION
Norm Vigil, HEPM
P.O. Box 217
Baggs, WY 82321-0271
(307) 383-2550
Norman.Vigil@wy.usda.gov

STATE OF WYOMING

EMPLOYMENT SECURITY COMMISSION
Greg Chocas, Manager
Division of Employment Resources
851 Warner Ct., #120
Casper, WY 82601
(307) 234-4591

Private Sector Employment Opportunities

Oportunidades de empleo en el sector privado

This section contains a comprehensive listing of private companies with the contact person for each Department of Human Resources or Equal Employment Opportunity Office.

Esta sección contiene una lista de empresas privadas, con el nombre de la persona que usted debe contactar en el Departamento de Recursos Humanos o en la oficina de EEO.

3M
3M Center, 224-1N-04
St. Paul, MN 55144-1000
Mr. Jim Anderson, Purchasing Manager
(651) 733-7587 Fax: (651) 733-3572

A. J. WRIGHT
350 Commerce Dr.
Fall River, MA 02720
(508) 730-2027 Fax: (508) 730-5216

A. J. WRIGHT (HEADQUARTERS)
550 Cochituate Road
Framingham, MA 01701
(508) 390-4000 Fax: (508) 390-4011

A PUBLIC AFFAIRS FIRM
7407 Gabsby Square #10
Alexandria, VA 22315
Roger Rivera, President
(703) 922-2438 Fax: (703) 922-3761

ADVANTICA & DENNYS
203 E. Main St.
Spartanburg, SC 29319
Deanna Banister, Director
(864) 597-8427 Fax: (864) 597-8243

AERO SIMULATION INC.
9220 Palm River Rd., #105
Tampa, FL 33619-4426
Jill Fernandez, Human Resources Mgr.
(813) 628-4447 Fax: (813) 628-8404

AEROJET
P.O. Box 1322
Sacramento, CA 95813
Russ Barnes, Employee Relations Mgr.
(916) 355-3269 Fax: (916) 355-2379

AETNA RETIREMENT SERVICES
151 Farmington Ave.
Hartford, CT 06156
(860) 272-1237

AIR LIQUIDE AMERICA CORP.
2700 Post Oak Blvd. #1800
Houston, TX 77056
Kristy Carlson, Director
(715) 402-2277 Fax: (713) 624-8030

AIRBORNE EXPRESS
145 Hunter Dr.
Wilmington, OH 45177-9390
Howard L. Moore, Recruitment Mgr.
(937) 382-5591 Fax: (937) 383-3838

ALCOA
15 W. South Temple, #1600
Salt Lake City, UT 84101
Mr. Greg Coronado, EEO Manager
(801) 933-4000 Fax: (801) 933-4012

ALLIANT TECHSYSTEMS, INC
TCCAAP, Bldg. 103, MN29-3688
New Brighton, MN 55112
(612) 639-3861

ALLSTATE INSURANCE COMPANY
2775 Sanders Rd., #A1
Northbrook, IL 60062-6127
Iris Chester, Director
(847) 402-1142

ALMA CONSULTANT SERVICES
5130 North 24th Street
Arlington, VA 22207
Alma Riojas Esparza, President
(703) 241-0835

AMERADA HESS CORPORATION
1 Hess Plaza
Woodbridge, NJ 07095
Walter Vertreace, Corporate EEO Mgr.
(908) 750-6408 Fax: (732) 750-6807

AMERICAN AIRLINES
4333 Amon Carter Blvd., MD-5106
Fort Worth, TX 76155
Mary Lanch, Director
(817) 963-1146 Fax: (817) 967-4380

AMERICAN ASSOCIATION OF HEALTH PLANS
1129 20th St. NW #600
Washington, DC 20036
Juli Anne Harkins, Program Manager
(202) 778-3271 Fax: (202) 361-1477

AMERICAN EXPRESS CORPORATION
200 Vessey St.
New York, NY 10285
Murray Coon, Campus Recruiting
(212) 640-6309

AMERICAN NATIONAL CAN CORP
8770 W. Bryn Mawr Ave.
Chicago, IL 60631-3542
Joe Steffan, Recruiter
(733) 399-3000

AMERICAN PRESIDENT LINES LTD.
8410 Amelia St.
Oakland, CA 94621
(510) 872-8000

AMERITECH CORP.
30 S. Wacker Dr., 35th Fl.
Chicago, IL 60606-7402
Fax: (312) 750-5977

AMERITECH INTERNATIONAL
225 W. Randolph Rd., 18th Fl.
Chicago, IL 60606
Brian Stating, Director
(312) 609-6004

AMGEN, INC.
One Amgen Ctr. Dr.
Thousand Oaks, CA 91320
Edward Garnett, Vice President
(805) 447-1000

AMOCO CORPORATION
200 E. Randolph Dr., Mail Code 3408
Chicago, IL 60601
Jane Drasites, Diretor
(312) 856-6111

AMR GLOBAL SERVICES
4255 AMON Carter Blvd.
Fort Worth, TX 76155
Kitty Villa Franco, Human Resources Rep.
(817) 963-9167

AMTRAK
60 Massachusetts Ave., NE
Washington, DC 20002
Roscoe A. Swann Jr., Director,
Minority Business Development
(202) 906-3600 Fax: (202) 906-2889

ANHEUSER-BUSCH, INC.
One Busch Place
St. Louis, MO 63118
Ron Kratzer, Sr. Employment Rep.
(314) 577-0701 Fax: (314) 865-9069

APACHE CORPORATION
2000 Post Oak Blvd., #100
Houston, TX 77056-4400
Matt Watson, Human Resources Mgr.
(713) 296-6000 Fax: (713) 296-6479

APPLE COMPUTER, INC.
1 Infinite Loop
Cupertino, CA 95014
Oliver Krevet, Supplier Diversity &
Development Program Specialist
(408) 974-2852 Fax: (408) 974-5691

ARAMARK UNIFORM SERVICES
115 N. First St.
Burbank, CA 91512
Gloria Hailes, Director
(818) 973-3601

AT&T CORPORATION
1200 Peachtree St., #7071
Atlanta, GA 30309
AT&T Resume Scanning Center
(800) 562-7288

ATLANTIC RICHFIELD CO. (ARCO)
515 S. Flower Street
Los Angeles, CA 90071-2295
Mr. William Holland, Work Force
Diversity & Development Dir.
(213) 486-3511 Fax: (213) 486-1270

AVIS
900 Old Country Road
Gardencity, NY 11530
Sam Ojofeitimi, Mgr., College Relations
(516) 222-3235 Fax: (516) 222-6677

AVON PRODUCTS, INC.
1251 Ave. of the Americas
New York, NY 1001910025
Fiona McLennan
(212) 282-7537 Fax: (212) 282-6550

BALTIMORE GAS & ELECTRIC
2900 Lord Baltimore Dr.
Baltimore, MD 21203-1472
(410) 597-6873 Fax: (410) 597-6871

BANK OF AMERICA
401 N. Tryon Street, NC1-021-02-17
Charlotte, NC 28255
(704) 386-6300

BANK ONE
1717 Main St., 4th Fl.
Dallas, TX 75201
John Muñoz
(214) 290-2464

BATH IRON WORKS
700 Washington St.
Bath, ME 04530
(207) 442-1756 Fax: (207) 442-1156

BAXTER INTERNATIONAL, INC.
1 Baxter Pkwy.
Deerfield, IL 60015
Staffing Manager
Fax: (847) 948-2964

BECHTEL CORPORATION
50 Beale St.
San Francisco, CA 94105-1895
E. Dave Rainwater, Program Manager
(415) 768-4834 Fax: (415) 768-9038

BELLSOUTH CORPORATION
1155 Peachtree St., NE, #13G07
Atlanta, GA 30309-3610
(404) 329-9455 Fax: (404) 249-3245

BLOCKBUSTER VIDEO
8320 S. Madison
Burr Ridge, IL 60521
Ellen Wullbradt, Director
(630) 794-5862

THE BOEING COMPANY
(800) 525-2236

BOISE CASCADE CORPORATION
One Jefferson Square
Boise, ID 83728
John Holleran, Director
(208) 384-6161

BOOZ ALLEN & HAMILTON
8283 Greensboro Drive
McLean, VA 22102
Brian Parks, Director
(703) 377-0188

BORDEN
180 East Broad St.
Columbus, OH 43215
(614) 225-4000 Fax: (614) 220-6553

BOY SCOUTS OF AMERICA HDQTRS.
1325 W. Walnut Hill Ln.
Irving, TX 75015-2079
(972) 580-2000 Fax: (972) 580-7895

BRISTOL-MYERS SQUIBB COMPANY
Plainsboro, NJ 08543-4500
(609) 897-4921

BURGER KING
17777 Old Cutler Rd.
Miami, FL 33157
Eli Ruiz, Director
(305) 378-3000 Fax: (305) 378-3516

BURLINGTON INDUSTRIES, INC.
3330 W. Friendly
Greensboro, NC 27410
Mr. Tony Michaels, Human Resources Rep.
(336) 379-2355

CATERPILLAR, INC.
100 NE Adams Street
Peoria, IL 61629-1490
Brian Bailer
(309) 675-5923 Fax: (309) 675-6476

THE CENTERCORE GROUP, INC.
1355 W. Front Street
Plainfield, NJ 07063
R.C. Thorton, Human Resources Dir.
(908) 561-7662 Fax: (908) 754-8493

CENTEX CONSTRUCTION COMPANY
P.O. Box 299009
Dallas, TX 75229-9009
Mr. David Preston, Vice Pres. of Admin.
(214) 357-1891 Fax: (214) 902-6391

CHASE BANK OF TEXAS
Houston, TX 77252
Douglas Monroe, Director
(713) 216-4865

CHASE MANHATTAN BANK
270 Park Ave., 44th Fl.
New York, NY 10017
Ednid Winn, Prog. Dir.
(212) 270-6410 Fax: (212) 270-7544

CHASE MANHATTAN BANK
55 Water St., 2nd. Fl.
New York, NY 10041
(212) 638-6881

CHASE MANHATTAN BANK
4 Chase Metro Tech. Ctr., Ground Fl.
Brooklyn, NY 11245
(718) 753-3400

CHEM-NUCLEAR SYSTEMS
140 Stoneridge Dr.
Columbia, SC 29210
Mr. JoDell Balch, Human Resources Mgr.
(803) 758-1817 Fax: (803) 799-4470

CHEVY CHASE BANK
7700 Old Georgetown Rd.
Bethesda, MD 20814
Russ Mcnish, Dir. of Human Resources
(301) 907-5600 Fax: (301) 907-4733

CIRCUIT CITY STORES
9954 Mayland Dr.
Richmond, VA 23233
(804) 527-4000 Fax: (804) 527-4086

CITIBANK
1775 Pennsylvania Ave., NW
Washington, DC 20006
Human Resources Dept.
(202) 429-7760

CITIBANK/CITICORP
1101 Pennsylvania Ave. NE
Washington, DC 20004
John Murphy, Human Resources,
Mid-Atlantic Group
(202) 879-6891 Fax: (202) 508-4512

COCA COLA COMPANY
Atlanta, GA 30301
Lee Perrett, Mgr.
(404) 676-2121 Fax: (404) 515-8221

COCA COLA USA
Atlanta, GA 30301
(404) 676-2121 Fax: (404) 515-8221

COLGATE-PALMOLIVE COMPANY
909 River Rd.
Piscataway, NJ 08855-1343
Mgr., Staffing & Recruiting Officer
(732) 878-7500

COMPAQ COMPUTER CORPORATION
P.O. Box 692000 Mail Stop 110415
Houston, TX 77269-2000
Ms. Terri Alexander, Human Resources/
Corporate Diversity Director
(281) 514-2119 Fax: (281) 514-9107

COMPUTER SCIENCES CORPORATION
29 Sawyer Rd.
Waltham, MA 02453
Bob Chamney
(781) 647-0116 Fax: (781) 894-0418

COMPUWARE CORPORATION
31440 Northwestern Hwy.
Farmington Hills, MI 48334
(800) 267-4884 Fax: (877) 873-6784

CONNER BROS. CONSTRUCTION CO.
P.O. Box 3070
Auburn, AL 36831-3070
Carol Elrod, Human Resources
Administrative Assistant
(334) 821-1470 Fax: (334) 821-8534

CONSOLIDATED EDISON
4 Irving Place
New York, NY 10003
Loretta Vancore, Human Resources Rep.
(212) 460-2014

COORS BREWING COMPANY
311 10th St.
Golden, CO 80401
Larry Moore, Manager
(303) 277-2611

COUNTER TECHNOLOGY, INC.
4733 Bethesda Ave., #200
Bethesda, MD 20814
Director of Human Resources
(301) 907-0127 Fax: (301) 907-6997

DAIMLER CHRYSLER
(248) 512-2187

DEAN WITTER
5 World Trade Center, 6th Fl.
New York, NY 10048
Bernice Jee, Vice President
(212) 392-3786

DELL COMPUTER CORP.
1 Dell Way
Round Rock, TX 78682
Ms. Bradie Speller, Senior Human
Resource Manager
(512) 728-6940 Fax: (512) 728-2046

DHL WORLDWIDE EXPRESS
333 Twin Dolphin Dr.
Redwood City, CA 94065
(650) 802-4664

DIAMOND SHAMROCK
(210) 592-2000

DISCOVER CARD SERVICES, INC.
2500 Lake Cook Rd.
Riverwoods, IL 60015
(847) 405-1109 Fax: (847) 405-4688

DIVERSITY WORKS, INC.
1554 Dranesville Rd.
Herndon, VA 20170
Francine DeFerreire-Kemp, CEO
(703) 834-3611 Fax: (703) 733-0742

DOW CHEMICAL
2301 Brozosport Blvd.
Freeport, TX 77541
Debra Fowler, Global Implementation Ldr.
(979) 238-9823 Fax: (979) 238-0480

DUPONT
Nemours Bldg., Rm. 12420
1007 Market St.
Wilmington, DE 19898
Lew Shoemaker, Mgr.
(302) 774-3275

E.I. DU PONT DE NEMOURS & CO.
1007 Market Street
Wilmington, DE 19898
Lou Shumacker, Human Resource Rep.
(302) 774-3275

EASTMAN KODAK CO.
343 State St.
Rochester, NY 14650-0517
(716) 724-4000

EDISON ELECTRIC INSTITUTE
701 Pennsylvania Ave. NW, 5rd Floor
Washington, DC 20004-2696
Jennifer Vick
(202) 508-5000 Fax: (202) 508-5503

EDISON ELECTRIC INSTITUTE
701 Pennsylvania Ave. NW
Washington, DC 20004-2696
Karen Bernard, Director
(202) 508-5488 Fax: (202) 508-5186

EL ECHO DE VIRGINIA
101 W. Plumbe St. 4 Fl.
Norfolk, VA 23510
Augusto Ratti-Angulo, Dir. Human Res.
(757) 625-1341 Fax: (757) 625-1327

EQUITY RESEARCH CORP.
5 Thomas Circle, NW
Washington, DC 20005
Miriam I. Cruz, President
(202) 387-3331 Fax: (202) 797-1344

EXXON COMPANY, USA
Houston, TX 77210-4692
Alfredo "AL" Pena, Mgr., Supplier Dev.
(713) 656-7618 Fax: (713) 656-1733

FNMA (FANNIE MAE)
3900 Wisconsin Ave., NW
Washington, DC 20016-2899
Francis Jordan, Director
(202) 752-4811

FEDERAL EXPRESS
2605 Nonconnah Blvd., #135
Memphis, TN 38132-2611
Theresa Williamson, Diversity Programs
(901) 922-1227

FIRST VIRGINIA BANK
6400 Arlington Blvd.
Falls Church, VA 22042
Lynn Wilber
(703) 241-4672

FLUOR DANIEL
100 Fluor Daniel Dr.
Greenville, SC 29607
Diane Richardson
(864) 281-4400

FORD MOTOR COMPANY WORLDWIDE
Allan Park, MI 48101
(888) 621-1723 Fax: (313) 337-2967

**FOSTER WHEELER ENVIRONMENTAL
CORP.**
1940 E Deere Ave., #200
Santa Ana, CA 92204
(949) 756-7561 Fax: (714) 444-5500

FRESQUEZ AND ASSOCIATES
405 14th St., #208
Oakland, CA 94612
Ernesto Fresquez, President
(925) 283-0295 Fax: (925) 274-1875

FRITO LAY
(972) 334-7000

GEC-MARCONI HAZELTINE
450 E. Pulaski Rd., Mail Stop 1-54
Greenlawn, NY 11740-1606
Doreen Cassidy, Human Resources Rep.
(516) 262-8624

GENERAL DYNAMICS CORP.
3190 Fairview Park Dr.
Falls Church, VA 22042-4523
(703) 876-3000 Fax: (703) 876-3550

GENERAL ELECTRIC
Fax: (513) 583-7340

GENERAL MOTORS CORP.
100 Renaissance Center
Detroit, MI 48265
(313) 556-5000 Fax: (313) 556-9165

GIANT FOOD, INC.
6300 Chair Sheriff Rd.
Landover, MD 20785
Henry Hailstock, Mgr., Minority Affairs
(301) 341-4100

GIRLS SCOUTS OF AMERICA HDQTRS.
420 Fifth Ave.
New York, NY 10018-2798
DeAngela Webb, Mgr., Emp. Rel. & Recruit.
(212) 852-8000 Fax: (212) 852-6514

GOODYEAR TIRE & RUBBER CO.
1144 E. Market St.
Akron, OH 44316-0001
Ms. Sally Ann Bamer, Mgr.
(330) 796--2121

GOYA FOODS, INC.
100 Seaview Dr.
Secaucus, NJ 07096
Carmen Ieccio, Human Resources Dept.
(201) 348-4900 Fax: (201) 348-3004

H.B.O.
1100 Ave. of the Americas
New York, NY 10036
Bernadette Aulestia, Manager., Hisp. Mkts.
(212) 512-5108

H-E-B GROCERY COMPANY
San Antonio, TX 78283-3999
(210) 938-5222 Fax: (210) 938-5583

HALLIBURTON/BROWN & ROOT
P.O. Box 3
Houston, TX 77001-0003
Diana Thomas, Diversity Manager
(713) 676-7733 Fax: (713) 676-4470

HALLMARK CARDS
Mail Drop 112, P.O. Box 419580
Kansas City, MO 64141
Felisha Moore, Director
(816) 545-3021 Fax: (816) 274-4299

HECHINGER CO.
1801 McCormik Dr.
Landover, MD 20785
Linda Harris, Human Resources Dept.
(301) 883-4500 Fax: (301) 925-9640

HELLER FINANCIAL
500 West Monroe
Chicago, IL 60661
Margarita Cruz
(312) 441-7010

HERMAN HOSPITAL
6410 Fannin #716
Houston, TX 77030-1501
Ed Muraski, Director
(713) 704-6655 Fax: (713) 704-5599

HEWLETT PACKARD CORP.
3000 Hanover St., M.Stop 20 APP
Palo Alto, CA 94304-1181
(650) 852-8473 Fax: (650) 852-8138

HILTON HOTELS CORPORATION
Heritage Sq. Twr., 14835 LBJ Freeway, #535
Dallas, TX 75244
Diana Jones, Liaison
(972) 701-3700 Fax: (972) 720-3611

HISPANNABELLE COMMUNICATIONS
2712 W. 40th
Lorraine, OH 44053
AnnaBelle Droz-Berrios, President
(216) 282-1854

HOFFMANN-LA ROCHE, INC.
340 Kingsland St.
Nutley, NJ 07110-1199
Bradley Smith, Dir., Human Resources
(973) 235-5000

HOMEGOOD'S DISTRIBUTION CENTER
71 Hampden Road
Mansfield, MA 02048
(508) 337-3381 Fax: (508) 261-2833

HOMEGOOD'S HOME OFFICE
Division of TJX Companies
492-6 Old Connecticut Path
Framingham, MA 01701
(508) 390-3886 Fax: (508) 390-3850

HONEYWELL, INC.
27401 4th Ave., South
Minneapolis, MN 55440
Ms. Karen Owak, Staffing Representative
(612) 951-0192 Fax: (612) 951-0199

**HONEYWELL TECHNOLOGY
SOLUTIONS, INC.**
7000 Columbia Gateway Dr.
Columbia, MD 21046
Cynthia English, Director
(410) 964-7521 Fax: (410) 964-7498
brunsos@clmmp001.atscallied.com

HOUSEHOLD FINANCE CORPORATION
961 Weigel Dr.
Elmhurst, IL 60126
Lynn Littlefied
(630) 617-7000

HUGHES ELECTRONICS
P.O. Box 92919, Bldg. S10 S368
Los Angeles, CA 90009
Carol Wilson, Human Resources Rep.
(310) 364-6693

HURRICANE ISLAND OUTWARD BOUND
1900 Eagle Dr.
Baltimore, MD 21207
Denise M. Scotland, Div. Coordinator
(410) 448-1721 ext 218 Fax: (410) 298-3822

HYATT HOTELS CORPORATION
200 W Madison
Chicago, IL 60606
(312) 750-1234

IBM
4800 Falls of the Neuse
Raleigh, NC 27609
Rene Cabrera, Recruiter, HR Staffing Svcs.
(800) 964-4473 Fax: (800) 262-2494

INTELLISYS TECHNOLOGY CORP.
12015 Lee Jackson Hwy.
Fairfax, VA 22033
Ms. Divya Katyal, Finance Manager
(703) 385-9134

INTER-AMERICAN MEDIA CORP.
575 Madison Ave., #1006
New York, NY 10022
Rafael Bonnelly, President
(212) 605-0382 Fax: (212) 605-0383

**INTERNATIONAL BUSINESS
RESOURCES, INC.**
1400 E. College Dr.
Cheyenne, WY 82007-3299
(304) 635-6654

INTERNATIONAL CONSULTING CORP.
Princeton, NJ 08542
Juliana Arenas, Exec. Dir.
(609) 940-2035

INTERNATIONAL PAPER CO.
6400 Poplar Ave.
Memphis, TN 38197

Carol L. Roberts, V.P. of People Dev.
(901) 763-6000 Fax: (901) 763-6055

IT CORP
2790 Mosside Blvd.
Monroeville, PA 15146
Susan Caruso, Human Resources Mgr.
Fax: (412) 858-3973

ITT CORPORATION
1919 West Cook Rd.
Ft. Wayne, IN 46801
Mr. James Beeson, Recruiting Manager
(219) 451-6000 Fax: (219) 451-6124

JC PENNEY CO.
6501 Legacy Dr.
Plano, TX 75024
Corporate Personnel
(972) 431-2300

JC PENNEY DISTRICT OFFICE
6564 Loisdale Ct., #300
Springfield, VA 22150
Keith Kinchiner, Personnel Manager
(703) 313-9701

JOHNSON & JOHNSON
Johnson & Johnson Pl.
New Brunswick, NJ 08973
Shelly Carpenter, Dir. of Human Resources
(908) 524-3712

K-MART INTERNATIONAL HDQTRS.
3100 W. Big Beaver Rd.
Troy, MI 48084
Lynn Marie Siciliano, Mgr., Recruitment
& Staffing
(248) 643-1000

**KAISER FOUNDATION HEALTH PLAN,
INC.**
100 South Los Robles#304
Pasadena, CA 91188
Julia Garcia, Hispanic Director
(818) 564-3535

KELLOGG COMPANY
One Kellogg Sq.
Battle Creek, MI 49016-3599
Veolis Bowers, Dir., Emp. & Recruiting
(616) 961-2004

KFC HEADQUARTERS
1441 Gardiner Ln.
Louisville, KY 40213
Walt Simon, Franchising Dept.
(502) 456-8300

KINNEY SHOE CORPORATION
233 Broadway
New York, NY 10279-0099
Sharon Orlopp, Dir., Fair Emp. Practice
(212) 720-4123

KRAFT GENERAL FOODS
250 North St.
White Plains, NY 10625
Patti Paladino-Connally, Dir., Equal
Employment Opportunities
(914) 335-2500

KRAFT GENERAL FOODS, INC.
Kraft Court, GV532
Glenview, Il 60025
Luis Nieto, Director of Ethnic Marketing
(847) 646-7774

LEER ASTRONICS
3400 Airport Ave.
Santa Monica, CA 90405
Marylin Conderan, Human Resources Mgr.
(310) 915-6000

LEVI STRAUSS & COMPANY
Levi's Plaza, 1155 Battery St.
San Francisco, CA 94111
Jeannea Macauley, Mgr., Employment
(415) 544-7446

LIBERTY MUTUAL INSURANCE GROUP/ BOSTON
175 Berkeley St.
Boston, MA 02117
Lynne Jeffries
(617) 357-9500 Fax: (617) 338-6963

LITTON INDUSTRIES, INC.
21240 Burbank Blvd.
Woodland Hills, CA 91367
Mr. Doug Peters, Corporate EEO Dir.
(818) 598-5008

LOCKHEED MARTIN
P.O. Box 3504
Sunnyvale, CA 94088-3504
Vanessa Williams, Work Force Div. Mgr.
(408) 742-8346 Fax: (408) 743-2118

LOCKHEED-MARTIN
Sandia National Laboratories
Albuquerque, NM 87185
Ed Gullick
(505) 844-2559 Fax: (505) 844-6636

LOCKHEED-MARTIN
232 Strawbridge Drive
Moorestown, NJ 08057-0927
Natalie Gregory
(609) 866-6519 Fax: (609) 866-6510

LOCKHEED-MARTIN
86 S. Cobb Dr.
Marietta, GA 30063-0510
Mr. Jerry Kirby, Aeronautical Systems
(770) 494-8176 Fax: (770) 494-1500

LOCKHEED-MARTIN
Denver, CO 80201
Mr. Herbert Watkins, LM Astronautics
(303) 971-5304 Fax: (303) 971-2191

LOCKHEED-MARTIN
LM Stennis Operations, Bldg. 1100
Rm. 1012
Stennis Space Center, MS 39529
Danielle Frank
(228) 688-3501 Fax: (228) 688-1313

LOCKHEED-MARTIN
Livermore, CA 94551-0969
David Rosenzweig
(510) 294-3341 Fax: (510) 294-2006

LOS ALAMOS NATIONAL LABORATORY
Los Alamos, NM 87545

Shelly Melton, Resumé Center
(505) 665-2117 Fax: (505) 667-6446

LOTUS DEVELOPMENT CORP.
55 Cambridge Pkwy.
Cambridge, MA 02142
Christine Leonardo, Recruiting Special.
(617) 693-8084

LUCENT TECHNOLOGIES
283 King George Rd., Rm. B2-C76
Warren, NJ 07059
Employment Manager
(908) 559-5000

THE MARMAXX GROUP
Division of TJX Companies, Inc.
770 Cochituate Road
Framingham, MA 01701
(860) 277-0111 Fax: (508) 390-2486

MARRIOTT CORPORATION
One Marriott Dr., #935.51
Washington, DC 20058
Kristy Godbold, Director, Staffing &
Employment Mktg.
(301) 380-1200 Fax: (301) 380-2111

MARSHALLS BRIDGEWATER
701 North Main St.
Bridgewater, VA 22812
(540) 828-5161 Fax: (540) 828-5198

MARSHALLS DECATUR
2300 Miller Rd.
Decatur, GA 30035
(770) 808-4703 Fax: (770) 808-4724

MARSHALLS REGION 1 OFFICE
Executive Place V
60 Mall Rd., #300
Burlington, MA 01803
(781) 273-4033 Fax: (781) 229-9924

MARSHALLS REGION 2 OFFICE
677 Exton Commons
Exton, PA 19341
(610) 524-7705 Fax: (610) 524-1625

MARSHALLS REGION 3 OFFICE
12801 West Sunrise Blvd.
Sunrise, FL 33323
(954) 858-1768 Fax: (954) 846-8753

MARSHALLS REGION 4 OFFICE
31 W 001 North Ave., #101
West Chicago, IL 60185
(630) 876-0155 Fax: (630) 876-0188

MARSHALLS REGION 6 OFFICE
424 Executive Court North, #A
Suisun, CA 94585
(707) 864-8044 Fax: (707) 864-8088

MARSHALLS WOBURN
83 Commerce Way
Woburn, MA 01801
(781) 932-2100 Fax: (617) 932-2298

MARY KAY CORPORATE
16251 Dallas Parkway, Box 799045
Dallas, TX 75379
(800) MARY KAY

MBNA AMERICA
1100 N. King Street
Wilmington, DE 19884-0244
S. Moore, AVP
(302) 432-3308 Fax: (302) 432-3925

MCDONALD'S CORPORATION
1 McDonald's Plaza
Oak Brook, IL 60523
(630) 623-3000

MCI
1200 S. Hayes St.
Arlington, VA 22202
Human Resources
(703) 414-4497

MCI TELECOMMUNICATIONS CORP.
1801 Pennsylvania Ave., NW
Washington, DC 20006
Colleeen Lee, Dir. of Staffing Services
(202) 887-3052 Fax: (202) 887-3205

MCKESSON CORP.
1 Post Street, 31st Fl.
San Francisco, CA 94104
Ms. Kara Halvorsen, Staffing & Work
Force Planning Director
(415) 983-9087 Fax: (415) 983-8900

METRO-NORTH COMMUTER RAILROAD
347 Madison Avenue
New York, NY 10017
Employment Dept. WW

METROPOLITAN LIFE INSURANCE
501 U.S. Hwy. 22
Bridgewater, NJ 08807-2437
Diana Soltis, Human Resources
(908) 253-2514 Fax: (908) 253-2788

MILLER BREWING COMPANY
3939 W. Highland Blvd.
Milwaukee, WI 53201
Tom Gavinski, Human Resources
(414) 931-2614 Fax: (414) 931-3497

MITRE CORP.
202 Burlington Rd.
Bedford, MA 01730
Deb Lane, Corporate Recruitment Mgr.
(781) 271-2265

MOBIL OIL CORPORATION
3225 Gallows Rd.
Fairfax, VA 22037
William Butler, Mgr., EEO Relations
(703) 846-3781

MONSANTO
800 N. Lindbergh Blvd., #B2A
St. Louis, MO 63167
(314) 694-3489

MOTOROLA, INC.
9980 Carroll Canyon Rd.
San Diego, CA 92131
Mr. Daryl Smith, Human Resource Mgr.
(800) 445-3620 Fax: (619) 530-8317
Q11820@email.mot.com

MPS PERSONNEL SERVICES, INC.
23361 El Toro Rd., #107
Lake Forest, CA 92630

Arlene Duarte de Bersentes,
Employment Specialist
(949) 770-2728 Fax: (949) 770-1509

MUTUAL OF OMAHA
Mutual of Omaha Plaza
Omaha, NE 68175
(402) 342-7600 Fax: (402) 351-3026

NATIONAL HISPANIC ANSWERING SERVICE
1405 Caitlin Ct.
Silver Spring, MD 20904
Ana Calleja, Dir. of Marketing
(301) 625-2020 Fax: (301) 625-1715

NATIONSBANK
6610 Rockledge Dr.
Bethesda, MD 20817
(800) 254-0800

NCN NETWORK CORP.-NATIONAL CONSULTANTS NETWORK
Sacramento, CA 95834-0792
Peter Francci, Public Relations Exec.
(916) 564-0810

NEC AMERICA
8 Corporate Center Drive
Melville, TN 11747
Mark Janiak, Human Resources Mgr.
(631) 753-7010 Fax: (631) 753-7141

NESTLÉ USA, INC.
800 N. Brand Blvd.
Glendale, CA 91203
Human Resources Dept.
(818) 549-6000

NEW YORK LIFE INSURANCE COMPANY
51 Madison Ave., Rm. 151
New York, NY 10010
Karen O'Sullivan, Human Res. Dept.
(212) 576-5995 Fax: (212) 447-4213

NIKE, INC.
One Bowerman Dr.
Beaverton, OR 97005
Cheryl Nickerson
(800) 891-6453 Fax: (888) 767-9855

NORDSTROM
1501 5th Ave.
Seattle, WA 98101
Diane Chesterfield, Mgr., Corporate
Human Resources
(206) 628-2111

NORTHROP GRUMMAN
Century Park East, MS 122-CC
Los Angeles, CA 90067
Gloria Rodriguez, Human Resources
(310) 553-6262 Fax: (310) 556-4510

NORTHWEST AIRLINES
5101 Northwest Drive
St. Paul, MN 55111
Human Resources Manager
(612) 726-3600

NUCLEAR ENERGY INSTITUTE
1776 I Street NW #400
Washington, DC 20006
K. Parson
(202) 739-8000 Fax: (202) 533-0136

NYNEX
1095 Ave. of the Americas, 2nd Fl.
New York, NY 10036
(212) 302-4636

ORACLE CORP.
500 Oracle Pkwy. M/S LGN-2
Redwood Shores, CA 94065
Jane Conley, Diversity Manager
(650) 506-7000 Fax: (650) 506-7395

PACIFIC BELL
666 Folson St.
San Francisco, CA 94107
Management Employment
(415) 542-8926

PACIFIC GAS AND ELECTRIC
P.O. Box 770000, N3Y
San Francisco, CA 94177
Catherine Moore, Corp. Commun.
(415) 973-5195
www.pge.com/005_career/

PACIFIC GAS & ELECTRIC CO.
201 Mission, 15th Fl.
San Francisco, CA 94177
Barbara Williams, Dir., Human Res.
(415) 973-7000

PACKARD BELL
1 Packard Bell Way, MS 150-14
Sacramento, CA 95828
Mr. Bill Warwick, Employment Director
Fax: (916) 388-5459

PEPSI COLA COMPANY
Somers, NY 10589-0902
(914) 767-6000 Fax: (914) 767-1214

PFIZER, INC. (NORTHEAST REGION)
235 E. 42nd St., M/S 4-32
New York, NY 10047
(212) 573-2323

PFIZER, INC. (SOUTHEAST REGION)
4360 N. E. Expressway
Doraville, GA 30340
Steve Smith, Distribution Center
(404) 448-6666

PFIZER, INC. (SOUTHWEST REGION)
502 Fountain Pkwy.
Grand Prairie, TX 75050
Larry Holden, Regional Personnel Mgr.
(972) 647-0222

PFIZER, INC. (WEST COAST REGION)
16700 Redhill Ave.
Irvine, CA 92714
Brooks Walker, Distribution Center
(714) 250-3260

PHILIP MORRIS COMPANIES, INC.
120 Park Ave., 18th Fl.
New York, NY 10017
Helen Abril, Public Programs
(212) 880-3469

PHILIP MORRIS INTERNATIONAL-LATIN AMERICA
800 Westchester Ave.
Rye Brook, NY 10573-1301
Mr. Philip Gambaccini, Mgr.
(914) 335-5000

PITNEY BOWES
1 Elmcroft Rd.
Stamford, CT 06926-0700
Susan L. Johnson, Director, Corp. Div.
(800) 948-8488 Fax: (203) 351-6811

PIZZA HUT
9111 E. Douglas
Wichita, KS 10589
Human Resources
(316) 767-6000

PLANNED PARENTHOOD FEDERATION OF AMERICA
810 7th Ave.
New York, NY 10019
Desiree Bunch, Vice President of Human Resources
(212) 261-4644

POLAROID CORPORATION
784 Memorial Dr.
Cambridge, MA 02139
(781) 386-2000 Fax: (781) 386-9703

PROCTER & GAMBLE
Cincinnati, OH 45201-0599
Human Resources
(513) 983-1100

PROCTOR AND GAMBLE
P.O. Box 5999
Cincinnati, OH 45201
Glenna F. Anderson, Recruiting Mgr.
(800) 543-7691 Fax: (513) 983-6758
anderson.gf.1@pg.com

PRUDENTIAL INSURANCE COMPANY OF AMERICA
Prudential Plaza (18P)
Newark, NJ 07102
Selchar Ramaswamy, Director, Office of Equal Opportunity
(973) 802-2187 Fax: (973) 367-8445

PYA/MONARCH, INC.
5501 Fulton Industrial Blvd.
Atlanta, GA 30336
Cathy Wofford, Human Resource Mgr.
(404) 346-1400 Fax: (404) 346-6398

RATNER
2815 Hartland Rd
Falls Church, VA 22043
Glen Goldmark, Dir. Human Resources
(703) 698-7090

RAYTHEON-SYSTEMS, INC.
Dallas, TX 75266-0023
John Bell, Director of Staffing
(972) 272-0515

REEBOK INTERNATIONAL, LTD.
1895 JW Foster Blvd.
Canton, MA 02021
Adrienne Williams, Diversity Dev.
(781) 401-5000

REVLON
625 Madison Ave., 8th Fl.
New York, NY 10022
(212) 527-4000

REYNOLDS METALS CORPORATION
6603 West Broad St.
Richmond, VA 23230
Mary Ann Wince, Manager
(804) 281-2000

RIGGS NATIONAL BANK OF DC
1512 Connecticut Ave. NW
Washington, DC 20036
(301) 887-4400 Fax: (202) 835-5616

ROBERT A. TOIJO FOUNDATION
1211 Preservation Pkwy.
Oakland, CA 94612
(510) 763-5771

ROCKWELL
(949) 221-7647 Fax: (888) 815-1923

RYDER SYSTEM
3600 N. W. 82nd Ave.
Miami, FL 33166
C. Robert Campbell, Sr. V. P., Human Resources
(305) 593-3726 Fax: (305) 500-5909

S.I.R., INC.
P.O. Box 10206
Zephyr Cove, NV 89998
Mr. Raymond C. Ramos, Vice President
(775) 588-2226 Fax: (775) 588-2226

SAFETY-KLEEN CORPORATION
1301 Gervais St., #300
Columbia, SC 29201
Sarah Heilman, Human Resources Asst.
(803) 933-4376 Fax: (803) 933-4357

SCROOGE'S DELIGHT
115 Utah NE, #5
Albuquerque, NM 87108
Lee Shuster
(505) 268-4800 Fax: (505) 268-4800

SEARS, ROEBUCK AND CO.
3333 Beverly Rd., E2-113B
Hoffman Estates, IL 60179
Bob Wery, Director, College Relations
(847) 286-4728

SHELL OIL COMPANY
910 Louisiana St., #952
Houston, TX 77252-2463
Donald Young, Human Resources Rep.
(713) 241-4278

SILICON GRAPHICS, INC.
2011 N. Shoreline Blvd.
Mountain View, CA 94043-1389
Deborah Dagit, Diversity Programs Dir.
(650) 933-2734 Fax: (650) 932-0912

SMITHKLINE-BEECHAM
One Franklin Plz.
Philadelphia, PA 19101-7929
(215) 751-4000

SONY PICTURES ENTERTAINMENT
10202 W. Washington Blvd.
Culver City, CA 90232

Jeffrey Wallace
(310) 244-4000

SOUTHLAND CORPORATION/ 7-ELEVEN
Box 711
Dallas, TX 75221-0711
Fran Eichorst, Mgr., Corp. Personnel
(800) 255-0711

SOZA AND COMPANY, LTD.
8550 Arlington Blvd.
Fairfax, VA 22031
(703) 560-9477 Fax: (703) 573-9026

SPRINT CORPORATION
2330 Shawnee Mission Pkwy.
Westwood, KS 66205
Ms. Vickie Smith, Fair Employment Practices Director

ST. PAUL FEDERAL BANK FOR SAVINGS
6645 W. North Ave.
Oakpark, IL 60302
(773) 804-2454 Fax: (773) 804-2454

STATE FARM INSURANCE COMPANIES
P.O. Box 2315
Bloomington, IL 61712-2315
Debb Dressler, Assist. Dir., Home Office Personnel Rel.
(309) 735-1723

STONE CONTAINER CORPORATION
150 N. Michigan Ave.
Chicago, IL 60601-7508
Ms. Linda Giardini, Personnel Manager
(312) 346-6600 Fax: (312) 649-4294

STORAGE TECHNOLOGIES CORPORATION
2270 S. 88th Street
Louisville, CO 80028-3246
Ms. Annie Fulmer, AA/EEO Specialist
(303) 673-4837 Fax: (303) 673-7389

SUN MICROSYSTEMS, INC.
Dept. EEJ, Mail Stop PAL1-404
2550 Garcia Ave.
Mountain View, CA 94039-1100
Catherine Lee, Strategic Cultural Initiatives Group
(415) 960-1300

SUN MICROSYSTEMS, INC.
901 San Antonio Rd.
Palo Alto, CA 94303
Vicky Yee, Corporate Diversity Mgr.
(650) 336-0798 Fax: (650) 336-0425

SUNTRUST BANK
14401Sweitzer Ln.
Laurel, MD 20707
Muriel Garr, Representative
(301) 497-3586 Fax: (301) 497-3585

T.J. MAXX, CENTRAL REGIONAL OFFICE-CRO
9100 South Hills Blvd., #201
Broadview Heights, OH 44147
(440) 546-7497 Fax: (440) 546-6453

T.J. MAXX CHARLOTTE
14300 Carowinds Blvd.
Charlotte, NC 28273
(704) 588-9222 Fax: (704) 583-7743

T.J. MAXX EVANSVILLE
3301 Maxx Rd.
Evansville, IN 47711-2905
(812) 424-0932 Fax: (812) 465-4852

T.J. MAXX LAS VEGAS
4100 E Lone Mountain Rd.
North Las Vegas, NV 89031
(702) 643-4033 Fax: (702) 643-2436

T.J. MAXX MID-ATLANTIC REGIONAL OFFICE-MARO
1300 Route 73, #308
MT. Laurel, NJ 08054
(609) 787-1071 Fax: (609) 787-1084

T.J. MAXX MID-SOUTH REGIONAL OFFICE-MSRO
950 Herndon Pkwy., #250
Herndon, VA 20170
(703) 481-5337 Fax: (703) 689-2503

T.J. MAXX MID-WEST REGIONAL OFFICE-MWRO
Crossroads Commerce III, 3501 W
Algonquin Rd., #330
Rolling Meadows, IL 60008
(847) 818-1734 Fax: (847) 394-0259

T.J. MAXX NORTHEAST REGIONAL OFFICE-NERO
200 Friberg Pkwy, #1004
Westboro, MA 01581
(508) 366-5696 Fax: (508) 366-7798

T.J. MAXX PACIFIC REGIONAL OFFICE-PRO
2151 Michelson Dr., #200
Irvine, CA 92612-1311
(949) 752-8716 Fax: (949) 752-0140

T.J. MAXX SOUTHEAST REGIONAL OFFICE-SERO
1600 Parkwood Circle, #610
Atlanta, GA 30339
(770) 980-1114 Fax: (770) 980-1972

T.J. MAXX WORCESTER
135 Goddard Memorial Dr.
Worcester, MA 01603
(508) 797-8667 Fax: (508) 791-0911

TACO BELL
17901 Von Karman Ave., 2nd Fl.
Irvine, CA 92714
Michael Kearns, Mgr., Corp. Staffing
(949) 863-4500

TELCORDIA TECHNOLOGIES
6 Corporate Pl.
Piscataway, NJ 08854
Carol Cole, Director
(973) 829-3410 Fax: (973) 829-2093

TENNECO GAS
Houston, TX 77252-2511
Human Resources Dept.

TEXACO, INC.
Houston, TX 77251-1404
(713) 752-8000

TEXAS INSTRUMENTS
P.O. Box 655474 M/S 238
Dallas, TX 75251
Mr. Roger Coker, Staffing Manager
(972) 480-4900 Fax: (972) 480-2535

TGI FRIDAY'S, INC.
P.O. Box 805062
Dallas, TX 75244
Diana Smith, Selective Support Consult.
(972) 450-5193 Fax: (972) 450-3644

TIME WARNER, NY
277 S. Washington St.
Old Alexandria, VA 22314
(703) 838-7160 Fax: (703) 838-7160

TJX COMPANIES, INC. HDQTRS.
770 Cochituate Rd.
Framingham, MA 01701
(508) 390-2915 Fax: (508) 390-2828

TMP WORLDWIDE
10635 Santa Monica Blvd., Suite #360
Los Angeles, CA 90025
(310) 441-0922

TOM BROWN & COMPANY, INC.
1090 Vermont Ave., N.W. #800
Washington, DC 22070-0684
(202) 393-7755

TOYOTA MOTOR SALES, USA, INC.
19001 S. Western Ave.
Torrance, CA 90509
, Staffing Dept.
(310) 618-4000 Fax: (310) 618-7816

TOYS "R" US
461 From Rd.
Paramus, NJ 07652
(201) 599-8808 Fax: (201) 262-8112

THE TRAVELERS COMPANIES
Hartford, CT 06183-7060
(860) 277-0111 Fax: (860) 277-1970

TRW
1900 Richmond Rd.
Cleveland, OH 44124
D. Bradford Neary, Human Res. Director
(216) 291-7000 Fax: (216) 291-7321

TURNER CONSTRUCTION COMPANY
375 Hudson St.
New York, NY 10014
Mr. Bruce Rughven, Hum. Res. Director
(212) 229-6024

U.S. STEEL (USX CORP.)
600 Grant St., #2514-D
Pittsburgh, PA 15219-2749
Eugene E. Harris, Dir. of Human Res.
(412) 433-6767 Fax: (412) 433-6762

U.S. WEST
2005 South 5th St., #110
Minneapolis, MN 55402
Gary Verke, Manager Staffing
(612) 663-0881

U.S. WEST
3033 N. 3rd St., Rm.101
Phoenix, AZ 85012
Call to apply
(602) 235-8888

U.S. WEST
1801 California, Suite 200
Denver, CO 80202
Sherry Ziegler, Staffing Manager
(303) 896-0583 Fax: (303) 896-7788

U.S. WEST
1600 7th Avenue, #2110
Seattle, WA 98191
Sanita Paul, Manager of Staffing
(206) 345-6132 Fax: (206) 345-5403

U.S. WEST
421 SW Oak St., Rm.130
Portland, OR 97204
Chas Fleenor, Manager of Staffing
(503) 464-1872

UNIDYNE CORPORATION
3835 E. Princess Anne Rd.
Norfolk, VA 23502
Ms. Susan Shawkey, Emp. Coordinator
(757) 855-8037 Fax: (757) 853-0924

UNION CARBIDE
39 Old Ridgebury Rd., Rm. G2356
Danbury, CT 06817
Eileen Devlin, Human Resources Rep.
(203) 794-6213

UNISYS CORPORATION
8008 W. Park Drive
McLean, VA 22102
David Boddie
(703) 556-5235 Fax: (703) 556-5695

UNITED AIRLINES
Chicago, IL 60666
Jim Houser, Mgr., Professional Employ.
(847) 700-4000

UNITED PARCEL SERVICE
55 Glenlake Pkwy, NE
Atlanta, GA 30328
Fred Fernandez, Dir. EEO & Div.
(404) 828-6000

UNITED PARCEL SERVICE
55 Glenlake Parkway
Atlanta, GA 30328
Steven Jones, Recruiter
(404) 828-6286

UNITED TECHNOLOGIES CORP.
1 Financial Plaza, 4th Fl.
Hartford, CT 06101
Yvette Bowden, Work Force Div. Dir.
(860) 728-7000 Fax: (860) 728-6562

UNITED WAY OF AMERICA
701 N. Fairfax St.
Alexandria, VA 22314-2045
(703) 836-7100 Fax: (703) 683-5811

USAIR, INC.
Crystal Park Four, 2345 Crystal Dr.
Arlington, VA 22227
Dorinda K. Short, Manager
(703) 872-7000 Fax: (703) 872-7410

WALTER KAITZ FOUNDATION
1388 Sutter St. #800
San Francisco, CA 94109
(415) 749-6980 Fax: (415) 749-6985

WANG LABORATORIES, INC.
600 Tech Park Drive
Billerica, MA 01821
Mary Beth McKinneon, Corporate
Diversity & Compliance Director
(978) 967-5000 Fax: (978) 967-5771

WASHINGTON GAS
Springfield, VA 22151
(703) 750-5814

THE WASHINGTON POST
1150 15th St. NW
Washington, DC 20071
Carl Williams, Director of Personnel
(202) 334-5656

WASTE MANAGEMENT FEDERAL SERVICES, INC.
3900 S. Wadsworth Blvd., #620
Lakewood, CO 80235
Gloria Laurence, Human Res. Admin.
(303) 914-2211

THE WELLA CORPORATION
524 Grand Avenue
Englewood, NJ 07631
Beth Jones
(201) 569-1020

WILLIAM KENDALL & ASSOC.
50 E. St. SE

Washington, DC 20003
(202) 546-2600

WINNERS' DISTRIBUTION CENTER
Division of TJX Companies, Inc.
55 West Drive
Brampton, Ontario, Canada LGT 4A1
(905) 451-7200 Fax: (905) 451-4877

WINNERS
Division of TJX Companies, Inc.
6715 Airport Rd., #500
Mississauga, Ontario, Canada L4V 1Y2
(905) 405-8000 Fax: (905) 405-1848

WORLD DATA, INC.
1015 18St., #710
Washington, DC 20036
Robert Dick, Director
(202) 785-6800 Fax: (202) 785-8850

XEROX CORPORATION
800 Long Ridge Rd.
Stamford, CT 06904
Ms. Julie Baskin Brooks, Manager of
Diversity Strategy & Programs
(203) 968-3637 Fax: (203) 968-4462

ZENECA, INC.
P.O. Box 15437
1800 Concord Pike
Wilmington, DE 19850-5438
Darla Wilson, Manage Staff Programs
(302) 886-3000 Fax: (302) 886-5148

Public Sector Minority Business Opportunities

Oportunidades para los negocios minoritarios en el sector público

ALABAMA

DEFENSE, DEPT. OF

U.S. ARMY ENGINEER & SUPPORT CENTER
4820 University Square
Huntsville, AL 35807-4301
(256) 895-1050
Judy Griggs, Deputy for Small Business
www.hnd.usace.army.mil

NATIONAL AERONAUTICS & SPACE ADMINISTRATION

MARSHALL SPACE FLIGHT CENTER
Mail Code GP-16
Huntsville, AL 35812
(256) 544-0254
Stanley McCall, Small Business Specialist
stan.e.mccall@msfc.nasa.gov

VETERANS AFFAIRS, DEPT. OF

V.A. MEDICAL CENTER
700 South 19th Street,
Birmingham, AL 35233
(205) 933-4493
Suzanne L. Jené, Small Business Specialist

ALASKA

VETERANS AFFAIRS, DEPT. OF

V. A. MEDICAL CENTER
2925 De Barr Road
Anchorage, AK 99508-2989
(907) 257-6933
Kenneth Carleton, Small Business Specialist

ARIZONA

COMMERCE, DEPT. OF

MINORITY-WOMEN BUSINESS ENTERPRISES
3800 N Central, #1650
Phoenix, AZ 85012
(800) 542-5684
Delia Garcia, Director

DEFENSE, DEPT. OF

CECOM ACQUISITION CENTER, SW OPERATIONS
CECOM Acquisition Center
SW Operations Office
ATT: AMSEL-AC-CC-S-SB.
Greeley Hall, #3214
Fort Huachuca, AZ 85613-6000
(520) 538-7870
Michael P. Dean, Small Business Advisor
http://cissb.hqisec.army.mil/sba.htm

VETERANS AFFAIRS, DEPT. OF

V. A. MEDICAL CENTER
650 East Indian School Rd.
Phoenix, AZ 85012
(602) 222-6402
Rich Hague, Small Business Specialist

3601 South 6th Ave.
Tucson, AZ 85723
(520) 629-4623
James Waterman, Small Business Specialist

ARKANSAS

VETERANS AFFAIRS, DEPT. OF

ARKANSAS VETERANS HEALTHCARE SYSTEM
1100 North College
Fayetteville, AR 72703
(501) 443-5035
Donna Lenz, Small Business Specialist

CALIFORNIA

COMMERCE, DEPT. OF

MINORITY BUSINESS DEVELOPMENT AGENCY
9660 Flair Dr., #455
El Monte, CA 91731
(626) 453-8636 Fax: (626) 453-8640
Rodolfo Guerr, Minority Business Specialist

San Francisco Regional Office
221 Main St., #1280
San Francisco, CA 94105
(415) 744-3001 Fax: (415) 744-3061
Melda C. Cabrera, Director

DEFENSE, DEPT. OF

AIR FORCE FLIGHT TEST CENTER
5 South Wolfe Ave., Bldg. 2800, #2
Edwards AFB, CA 93524-1185
(661) 277-3604
Judith K. Vaughn, Small Business Specialist

DEFENSE CONTRACT MANAGEMENT COMMAND WEST
18901 S Wilmington, Bldg. DHZ
Carston, CA 90746
(800) 222-2556
E. Renee Deavens, Small Business Specialist

FLEET & INDUSTRIAL SUPPLY CENTER SAN DIEGO
937 N Harbor Dr.
San Diego, CA 92132-0060
(619) 532-3439
James W. Conrad, Small Business Specialist

NAVAL AIR WARFARE CENTER
Naval Air Warfare Center
Code 00K000D
One Administration Circle
China Lake, CA 93555-6100
(760) 939-2712
Lois Herrington, Deputy for Small Business
www.nawcwpns.navy.mil/~contract/sbo_p.htm

SPACE AND SYSTEMS MISSILE CENTER
155 Discoverer Blvd. #2017
El Segundo, CA 90245-4692
(310) 363-2855
Charles Willett, Small Business Specialist

ENERGY, DEPT. OF

LAWRENCE BERKELEY NATIONAL LABORATORY
1 Cyclotron Rd., Mail Stop 937-200
Berkeley, CA 94720
(510) 486-4506
David Chen, Small Business Liaison Office

OAKLAND OPERATIONS OFFICE
1301 Clay St., #700N
Oakland, CA 94612-5208
(510) 637-1897
Aundra Richards, Small Business Prog. Mgr.
www.oak.doe.gov

ENVIRONMENTAL PROTECTION AGENCY

REGION IX OSDBU
75 Hawthorne St. (PMD-1)
San Francisco, CA 94105
(415) 744-1628
Joe Ochab, Program Coordinator

GENERAL SERVICES ADMINISTRATION

PACIFIC RIM REGION
450 Golden Gate Ave., 5th Floor
San Francisco, CA 94102
(415) 522-2700
Carol Honore/Lori Falkenstron
Enterprise Development, Team Leader

LOS ANGELES MINORITY BUSINESS OPPORTUNITY COMMITTEE (LAMBOC)

Mayor's Office of Economic Development
200 N Main Street, 8th Fl.
City Hall East
Los Angeles, CA 90012
(213) 847-2670
Diane Castaño Sallee, Director

NATIONAL AERONAUTICS & SPACE ADMINISTRATION

DRYDEN FLIGHT RESEARCH CENTER
P.O. Box 273
Mail Code D-1422
Edwards, CA 93523-0273
(661) 276-3343
Robert Medina
www.dfrc.nasa.gov/Procure/procure.html

JET PROPULSION LABORATORY
Mail Code 249-113
Pasadena, CA 91109
(818) 354-5722
Margo Kuhn
Business Opportunities Office Manager
www.jpl.nasa.gov

UNITED STATES POSTAL SERVICE

PACIFIC AREA
400 Oyster Point Blvd.
South San Francisco, CA 94099-4400
(650) 635-3200
Henrietta Clark-Goldsby, Diversity Dev. Spec.

VETERANS AFFAIRS, DEPT. OF

NETWORK BUSINESS CENTER
5901 East 7th St.
Long Beach, CA 90822
(562) 494-5533
Ralph Tillman, Small Business Specialist

V.A. OUTPATIENT CLINIC
351 East Temple St.
Los Angeles, CA 90012-3328
(562) 494-5533
Ralph Tillman, Small Business Specialist

V.A. MEDICAL CENTER
4150 Clement St.
San Francisco, CA 94121
(925) 372-2046
Karen Pridmore, Small Business Specialist

COLORADO

COMMERCE, DEPT. OF

MINORITY BUSINESS DEVELOPMENT COUNCIL
930 W 7th Ave.
Denver, CO 80204
(303) 623-5660 Fax: (303) 623-9015
Sarah Fuentes, Minority Business Specialist

ENERGY, DEPT OF

GOLDEN FIELD OFFICE
1617 Cole Blvd.
Golden, CO 80401
(303) 275-4700
Mary Hart Ford, Small Business Specialist

WESTERN AREA POWER ADMINISTRATION
12155 W. Alameda Pkwy.
Lakewood, CO 80228
(720) 962-7154
Judy Madsen, Procurement Analyst
www.wapa.gov

ENVIRONMENTAL PROTECTION AGENCY

REGION VII OSDBU
999 18th St., #500
Denver, CO 80202-2405
(303) 312-6862
Maurice Velasquez

GENERAL SERVICES ADMINISTRATION

ROCKY MOUNTAIN REGION
P.O. Box 25006
Denver Federal Complex Center Bldg. 41, #240
Denver, CO 80225-0006
(303) 236-7409
Pennie Strada, Small Business Team Leader

HOUSING & URBAN DEVELOPMENT, DEPT. OF

WESTERN SERVICE CENTER
633 17th St.,8th Floor (8AAC)
Denver, CO 80202-3607
(303) 672-5281
Nancy Paulette, Senior Procurement Analyst

UNITED STATES POSTAL SERVICE

WESTERN AREA
1745 Stout St., #600
Denver, CO 80299-4000
(303) 313-5009
Monica Vital, Diversity Coordinator

VETERANS AFFAIRS, DEPT. OF

V.A. MEDICAL CENTER
1055 Clermont St.
Denver, CO 80220
(303) 393-2852
Pat Amidon, Small Business Specialist

V.A. SOUTHERN COLORADO HEALTH CARE SYSTEM CENTER
County Road 15
Ft. Lyon, CO 81038
(719) 384-3146
John Apodaca, Small Business Specialist

V.A. MEDICAL CENTER
2121 North Ave.
Grand Junction, CO 81501
(970) 263-5004
Denise Boren, Small Business Specialist

CONNECTICUT

VETERANS AFFAIRS, DEPT. OF

V.A. MEDICAL CENTER
950 Campbell Ave.
West Haven, CT 06514
(203) 937-3079
Bruce Fortuna
Small Business Specialist

DELAWARE

COMMERCE, DEPT. OF

MINORITY BUSINESS CENTER
800 N French St., 6th Floor
Wilmington, DE 19801
(302) 571-4093
Thomas Moyer

VETERANS AFFAIRS, DEPT. OF

V.A. MEDICAL CENTER
1601 Kirkwood Highway
Wilmington, DE 19805
(302) 633-5371
Toni Wilson, Small Business Specialist

DISTRICT OF COLUMBIA

BOARD OF GOVERNORS OF THE FEDERAL RESERVE SYSTEMS
20th & Constitution Ave.
Washington, DC 20551
(202) 452-2458
Carlos Gutierrez, Small Business Coordinator
www.frv.gov

ADMINISTRATIVE SERVICES DIVISION

OFFICE OF FINANCIAL MGMT.
1155 21st St. NW, 10th Floor
Washington, DC 20581
(202) 418-5180
Emory Bebill, Acting Director

OFFICE OF ADMINISTRATIVE SERVICES
1155 21st St. NW, 10th Floor
Washington, DC 20581
(202) 418-5170
Karen Dyson, Director

AGRICULTURE, DEPT. OF

FARM SERVICE AGENCY
1400 Independence Ave. SW, #6962
Mail Stop 0567
Washington, DC 20250-0567
(202) 720-7349
Scott Cook, OSDBU Coordinator

FOOD & SAFETY INSPECTION SERVICE
1400 Independence Ave., #2925
Washington, DC 20250-3700
(202) 720-9352
Ramona Swann
Procurement & Property Branch Chief

FOREST SERVICE
P.O. Box 96090
Rosslyn Plaza E, #706
Washington, DC 20090-6090
(202) 205-1661
Rudy Watley, OSDBU Coordinator

OFFICE OF SMALL AND DISADVANTAGED BUSINESS
1400 Independence Ave. SW #1566
Washington, DC 20250-9501
(202) 720-7117
Mike Green, Deputy Director

RURAL DEVELOPMENT
1400 Independence Ave. SW
Washington, DC 20250
(202) 720-4581
Cindy Buck, OSDBU Coordinator

AIR FORCE, DEPT. OF THE

OFFICE OF SMALL AND DISADVANTAGED BUSINESS
1060 Air Force Pentagon
Washington, DC 20330-1060
(703) 696-1103
Anthony DeLuca, Director

ARMY, DEPT. OF THE

OFFICE OF SMALL AND DISADVANTAGED BUSINESS
Office of the Secretary of the Army
106 Army Pentagon
Washington, DC 20310-0106
(703) 697-2868
Tracy Pinson, Director

COMMERCE, DEPT. OF

MINORITY BUSINESS DEVELOPMENT AGENCY
14th & Constitution Ave. NW, #5055
Washington, DC 20230
(202) 482-5061

OFFICE OF SMALL AND DISADVANTAGED BUSINESS
14th & Constitution Ave. NW, #H-6411
Washington, DC 20230
(202) 482-1472
T.G. García, Director

PATENT & TRADEMARK OFFICE
2011 Crystal Dr., #810 Box 6
Washington, DC 20231
(703) 305-8008
Helen Hensley, Small Business Liaison
www.uspto.gov

CORPORATION FOR NATIONAL SERVICE

OFFICE OF SMALL AND DISADVANTAGED BUSINESS
1201 New York Ave. NW, #6100
Washington, DC 20525
(202) 606-5000
Simon Wooded, Contract Specialist

DEFENSE, DEPT. OF

MILITARY SEALIFT COMMAND
Charles Morris Ct. SE, Washington Navy Yard
Washington, DC 20398-5540
(202) 685-5025
Sylvester Rainey, Small Business Specialist
www.msc.navy.mil

U.S. ARMY CORPS OF ENGINEERS
20 Massachusetts Ave. NW
Washington, DC 20314-1000
(202) 761-0725
Bernard Ford, Small Business Specialist
www.usace.army.mil

EDUCATION, DEPT. OF

OFFICE OF SMALL AND DISADVANTAGED BUSINESS
600 Independence Ave. SW
Washington, DC 20202-0521
(202) 708-9820
Viola Jaramillo, Director

ENERGY, DEPT. OF

OFFICE OF SMALL AND DISADVANTAGED BUSINESS
1000 Independence Ave. SW, 5B148
Washington, DC 20585
(202) 586-7377
Sarah Summerville, Deputy Director

ENVIRONMENTAL PROTECTION AGENCY

OFFICE OF SMALL AND DISADVANTAGED BUSINESS
1200 Pennsylvania Ave. NW, Code 1230A
Washington, DC 20460
(202) 564-4100
Jeanette L. Brown, Director

EXECUTIVE OFFICE OF THE PRESIDENT

OFFICE OF ADMINISTRATION /GENERAL SERVICES
725 17th St. NW, #5013
Washington, DC 20503
(202) 395-7669 Fax: (202) 395-1155
Thelma B Toler, Small Business Specialist

FEDERAL DEPOSIT INSURANCE CORPORATION

MINORITY & WOMEN OWNED BUSINESS
Office of Equal Opportunity
Washington, DC 20429
(202) 416-2489
Velda Fludd, MWOB Specialist

FEDERAL TRADE COMMISSION

OFFICE OF SMALL AND DISADVANTAGED BUSINESS
600 Pennsylvania Ave., NW, #706
Washington, DC 20580
(202) 326-2258
Jean Sefchick, Chief of Procurement

GENERAL SERVICES ADMINISTRATION

FEDERAL PROCUREMENT DATA CENTER
7th & D St. SW, #5652
Washington, DC 20407
(202) 401-1529

Jack Finley, Deputy Director
www.fpds.gsa.gov

NATIONAL CAPITAL REGION
7th & D St. SW, #1050
Washington, DC 20407
(202) 708-5804
Algeon Gaither, Director
www.gsa.gov

OFFICE OF ENTERPRISE DEVELOP.
18th & F St. NW, #6029
Washington, DC 20405
(202) 501-1021 Fax: (202) 208-5938
Diedra L. Ford, Associate Director

HEALTH & HUMAN SERVICES, DEPT. OF

OFFICE OF SMALL AND DISADVANTAGED BUSINESS
200 Independence Ave. SW, #517D
Washington, DC 20201
(202) 690-7300
Debby Ridgely, Director

HOUSING AND URBAN DEVELOPMENT, DEPT. OF

HEADQUARTER OFFICE OF PROCUREMENTS & CONTRACTS
451 7th St. SW, #5256
Washington, DC 20410
(202) 708-1290
Antoinette Henry, Small Business Specialist

OFFICE OF SMALL AND DISADVANTAGED BUSINESS
451 7th St. SW, #3130
Washington, DC 20410
(202) 708-1428
Joe Piljay
Small Business Specialist

INTERIOR, DEPT. OF THE

BUREAU OF INDIAN AFFAIRS
1849 C. St. NW
Mail Stop 2626
Washington, DC 20240
(202) 208-2825 Fax: (202) 219-4071
David Brown, Division Chief

OFFICE OF SMALL AND DISADVANTAGED BUSINESS
1849 C St. NW, #5070
Washington, DC 20240
(202) 208-3493
Robert W Faitful, Director

INTERNATIONAL TRADE COMMISSION

500 E St. SW, #511C
Washington, DC 20436
(202) 205-3403
Ruben Mata, Hispanic Program Manager

JUSTICE, DEPT. OF

BUREAU OF PRISONS
320 1st St. NW # 500
Washington, DC 20534
(202) 616-6150
Ron Williams, Small Business Specialist

FEDERAL BUREAU OF INVESTIGATION
935 Pennsylvania Ave. NW, #1B105
Washington, DC 20525-0001
(202) 324-2280
Doreen Williams, Small Business Specialist
www.fbi.gov

FEDERAL PRISON INDUSTRIES
400 1st St. NW, 7th Floor, Resources Division
Washington, DC 20534
(202) 305-7333
Rhonda Robinson, Small Business Specialist
www.unicor.gov

IMMIGRATION & NATURALIZATION SERVICE
425 I St. NW, #2208
Washington, DC 20536
(202) 305-1270
Rosmary Goldberg, Small Business Advisor
www.ins.usdoj.gov

OFFICE OF SMALL AND DISADVANTAGED BUSINESS
1331 Pennsylvania Ave. NW, #1010
Washington, DC 20530
(202) 616-0521
Joseph Brian, Director
www.usdoj.gov/jmd/pss/home_osd.htm

LABOR, DEPT. OF

EMPLOYMENT & TRAINIG ADMINISTRATION
200 Constitution Ave. NW, #S4203
Washington, DC 20210
(202) 219-5000
John Steenbergen, Small Business Specialist

OCCUPATIONAL SAFETY & HEALTH ADMINISTRATION
200 Constitution Ave. NW, #3419
Washington, DC 20210
(202) 219-5000
Dennis A. Sprouse, Small Business Specialist

PROCUREMENT SERVICES CENTER
200 Constitution Ave. NW, #N5416
Washington, DC 20210
(202) 219-4631
Daniel Murphy, Director

SMALL BUSINESS PROGRAMS OFFICE
200 Constitution Ave. NW, #C2318
Washington, DC 20210
(202) 219-5000
June M. Robinson, Director

MINORITY BUSINESS DEVELOPMENT AGENCY

OFFICE OF SMALL AND DISADVANTAGED BUSINESS
1110 Vermont Ave. NW
Washington, DC 20005
(202) 606-4000
Calvin Jenkins, Director

NATIONAL AERONAUTICS & SPACE ADMINISTRATION

OFFICE OF SMALL AND DISADVANTAGED BUSINESS
300 E St. SW, Code K
Washington, DC 20546-0001
(202) 358-2088
Ralph C. Thomas III, Asst. Admin.
www.hq.nasa.gov/office/codek

NAVY, DEPT. OF THE

OFFICE OF SMALL AND DISADVANTAGED BUSINESS UTILIZATION
720 Kennon St. SE #207
Washington Navy Yard, DC 20374
(202) 685-6485
Nancy Tarrant

NUCLEAR REGULATORY COMMISSION

OFFICE OF SMALL AND DISADVANTAGED BUSINESS
Mail Stop T-2F18
Washington, DC 20555
(301) 415-7380
Irene P. Little, Dir.

OFFICE OF PERSONNEL MGMT.

OFFICE OF SMALL BUSINESS ADMIN.
1900 E St. NW #5315
Washington, DC 20415
(202) 606-1000
Janice R. Liachance, Dir. of Personnel Mgmt.

OFFICE OF THE COMPTROLLER OF THE CURRENCY

ACQUISITIONS AND PROCUREMENT BRANCH
250 E St. SW, Mail Stop 4-13
Washington, DC 20219
(202) 874-5040
Anthony Cooch, Contract Specialist

STATE, DEPT. OF

OFFICE OF SMALL AND DISADVANTAGED BUSINESS
S/SDBU. SA-6, #633
Washington, DC 20522-0602
(703) 875-6822
Durie White, Operations Director

TRANSPORTATION, DEPT. OF

ACQUISITION SERVICES
SVC-180 400 7th St. SW, #5106
Washington, DC 20590
(202) 366-6699
Dan Telep, Small Business Purchasing Dir.

COAST GUARD, OFFICE OF CONTRACT SUPPORT
2100 2nd St. SW, #ET5212
Washington, DC 20593-0001
(202) 267-2499
Mary Kim, Small Business Specialist

FEDERAL AVIATION ADMINISTRATION
800 Independence Ave. SW #715
Washington, DC 20591
(202) 267-8862
Inez.C. Williams, Director, Small Business Liaison Office
www.faa.gov/sbo

FEDERAL RAILROAD ADMINISTRATION
400 7th St. SW, Mail Stop 50
Washington, DC 20590
(202) 493-6131
Dana Hicks, Purchasing Agent

FEDERAL TRANSIT ADMINISTRATION
400 7th St. SW, #9102
Washington, DC 20590
(202) 366-4018
Arthur Lopez, Office of Civil Rights Director

NATIONAL HIGHWAY TRAFFIC SAFETY ADMIN.
400 7th St. SW #5301
Washington, DC 20590
(202) 366-9887
Margaret Bryant, Contracting Officer
www.nhtsa.gov

OFFICE OF SMALL AND DISADVANTAGED BUSINESS
400 7th St. SW, #9414
Washington, DC 20590
(202) 366-1930

TASC
400 7th St. SW, #5106
Washington, DC 20590
(202) 366-4968
Cynthia R. Blackmon, Small Business Specialist

TREASURY, DEPT. OF THE

BUREAU OF ALCOHOL, TOBACCO AND FIRE ARMS
650 Massachusetts Ave. NW, #3290
Washington, DC 20226
(202) 927-8332 Fax: (202) 927-8688
Jackie Barber, Small Business Specialist

BUREAU OF ENGRAVING & PRINTING
14th & C St. SW, #708A-06
Washington, DC 20228
(202) 874-3153
Donna Harrison, Small Business Specialist
www.bep.treas.gov

CUSTOMS SERVICE
1300 Constitution Ave. NW, #4216
Washington, DC 20229
(202) 927-0278 Fax: (202) 927-1190
William Bickelman, Small Business Specialist

OFFICE OF SMALL AND DISADVANTAGED BUSINESS
1500 Pennsylvania Ave. NW
1310 G St. NW, #400 West
Washington, DC 20220
(202) 622-0530
Kevin Boschears, Director

OFFICE OF THRIFT SUPERVISION
1700 G St. NW, 3rd Fl.
Washington, DC 20552
(202) 906-7624
Douglas Mason, Small Business Specialist

PROCUREMENT ADMINISTRATIVE SERVICES
1700 G St. NW, 3rd Floor
Washington, DC 20552
(202) 906-6666 Fax: (202) 906-6303
John Connors, Director

SECRET SERVICE
950 H St. NW, #6700
Washington, DC 20223
(202) 406-6940 Fax: (202) 406-6801
Robert Petrosky, Small Business Specialist

U.S. MINT
633 3rd St. NW
Washington, DC 20220
(202) 354-7827
Jill Daly, Small Business Specialist

UNITED STATES POSTAL SERVICE

475 L'Enfant Plaza, SW. #3821
Washington, DC 20260
(202) 268-6566
Benjamin Ocasio
Diversity Policies and Planning Manager

CORPORATE SUPPLIER DIVERSITY
475 L'Enfant Plaza, SW. #3821
Washington, DC 20260-5616
(202) 268-6578
Evelyn Hill, Mgr.

VETERANS AFFAIRS, DEPT. OF

VETERANS BENEFITS ADMINISTRATION
810 Vermont Ave., N.W.
Washington, DC 20420
(202) 273-6818
Yvonne White
Small Business Specialist

V.A. MEDICAL CENTER
50 Irving St., N.E.
Washington, DC 20422
(202) 745-8413
Joan Van Middlesworth
Small Business Specialist

FLORIDA

COMMERCE, DEPT. OF

MBDA DISTRICT OFFICE
51 SW 1st Ave., #1314, Box 25
Miami, FL 33130
(305) 536-5054
Rudy Suarez, District Officer

MBDC TAMPA/ST. PETERSBURG
102 E. 7th Ave.
Tampa, FL 33602
(813) 274-5522 Fax: (813) 274-5544
George A. Davis, Manager

DEFENSE, DEPT. OF

45TH SPACE WING
1201 Edward H. White II St.
Patrick AFB, FL 32925-3237
(321) 494-2207
Linda Sherod, Small Business Specialist
www.pafb.af.mil/45SW/45bc/Sbindex.htm

AIR ARMAMENT CENTER, AAC
205 West D Ave., #449
Eglin AFB, FL 32542-6863
(850) 882-2843
Ralph K. Frangioni, Small Business Specialist
http://eglinpk.eglin.af.mil

U.S. SPECIAL OPERATIONS
7701 Tampa Point Blvd.
Tampa, FL 33621-5323
(813) 828-7515
Craig Bowers, Small Business Specialist
www.socom.mil

NATIONAL AERONAUTICS & SPACE ADMINISTRATION

KENNEDY SPACE CENTER
Mail Code OP
Kennedy Space Center, FL 32899
(321) 867-7353
David A. Wansley, Small Business Specialist
www.ksc.nasa.gov

VETERANS AFFAIRS, DEPT. OF

V.A. MEDICAL CENTER
1201 NW 16th St.
Miami, FL 33125
(305) 324-3281
Gwendolyn Moore, Small Business Specialist

V.A. MEDICAL CENTER
13000 Bruce B. Downs Blvd.
Tampa, FL 33612
(813) 972-7502

V.A. MEDICAL CENTER
P.O.Box 33207
7305 North Military Trail
West Palm Beach, FL 33410-6400
(561) 882-6511
Stacy Malott-Hennes, Small Business Specialist

GEORGIA

COMMERCE, DEPT. OF

MINORITY BUSINESS DEV. AGENCY
401 W Peachtree St. NW, #1715
Atlanta, GA 30308-3516
(404) 730-3300
Robert Henderson, Regional Director

DEFENSE, DEPT. OF

U.S. FORCES COMMAND
1777 Hardee Ave.
Atlanta, GA 30330-1062
(404) 464-6223
Jerry L. Blaydes, Small Business Specialist
www.forscom.army.mil/contract/default.htm

ENVIRONMENTAL PROTECTION AGENCY

REGION IV OSDBU
61 Forsyth St.
Atlanta, GA 30303
(404) 562- 8110
Rafael Santa Maria

FEDERAL EMERGENCY MANAGEMENT AGENCY

REGION IV
303 Chamblee Tucker Rd.
Atlanta, GA 30341
(770) 220-5264
Helen Housand, Contracting Officer

GENERAL SERVICES ADMINISTRATION

SOUTHEAST SUNBELT REGION
401 W Peachtree St.
Atlanta, GA 30365-2550
(404) 331-5103
Patricia Geisinge, Small Business Deputy
www.gsa.gov

HEALTH & HUMAN SERVICES, DEPT. OF

CENTER FOR DISEASE CONTROL
2420 Brandy Wine Rd.
Atlanta, GA 30341
(770) 488-2806
Curtis L. Bryant, Small Business Specialist
www.cdc.gov

HOUSING & URBAN DEV., DEPT. OF

SOUTHEAST/SOUTHWEST SERVICE CTR.
5 Point Plaza BOD 40, Mariatta St.
Atlanta, GA 30303-3388
(404) 730-2705
Kimberlee Lewis, Small Business Specialist

MINORITY BUSINESS DEVELOPMENT AGENCY

ATLANTA REGIONAL OFFICE
401 W. Peachtree St. #1715
Atlanta, GA 30308
(404) 730-3300
Robert Henderson, Regional Director

TREASURY, DEPT. OF THE

FEDERAL LAW TRAINING CENTER
120 Chapel Crossing Rd. Bldg. 94
Glynco, GA 31524
(912) 267-2289 Fax: (912) 267-2567
John Richardson, Chief of Procurement Div.

UNITED STATES POSTAL SERVICE

SOUTHEAST AREA
P.O. Box 599390
Duluth, GA 30026-9390
(770) 717-2992
Veverly Allen-Stokes, Diversity Dev. Specialist

VETERANS AFFAIRS, DEPT. OF

V.A. MEDICAL CENTER
1670 Clairmont Rd., NE
Decatur (Atlanta), GA 30033
(404) 728-4826
Paul Dixon, Small Business Specialist

HAWAII

COMMERCE, DEPT. OF

HONOLULU MBDC
1132 Bishop St., #1000
Honolulu, HI 96813-3652
(808) 933-0776

VETERANS AFFAIRS, DEPT. OF

V.A. MEDICAL & REGIONAL OFFICE CENTER
P.O.Box 50188
Honolulu, HI 96850
(925) 372-2046
Karen Pridmore
Small Business Specialist

IDAHO

ENERGY, DEPT. OF

IDAHO OPERATIONS OFFICE
850 Energy Dr., Mail Stop1221
Idaho Falls, ID 83405
(208) 526-3737
Trudy Thorne
Small Business Specialist

VETERANS AFFAIRS, DEPT. OF

V.A. MEDICAL CENTER
500 West Fort St.
Boise, ID 83702-4598
(208) 422-1131
Carol Grant Barr
Small Business Specialist

ILLINOIS

COMMERCE, DEPT. OF

MBOC CHICAGO
U.S. Dept. of Agriculture-Food & Nut. Serv.
77 W Jackson Blvd., 20th Floor
Chicago, IL 60604
(312) 353-6664
Theodore Bell, Regional Administrator

MBDA REGIONAL OFFICE
55 E Monroe St., #1406
Chicago, IL 60603
(312) 353-0182
Carlos Guzman, Regional Dir.

ENERGY, DEPT.OF

CHICAGO OPERATIONS OFFICE
9800 S Cass Ave.
Argonne, IL 60439
(630) 252-2711
Larry Thompson, Small Business Prog. Mgr.

ENVIRONMENTAL PROTECTION AGENCY

REGION V OSDBU
77 W Jackson Blvd.
Chicago, IL 60604-3507
(312) 353-5677
Robert I. Richardson, Program Manager

FEDERAL EMERGENCY MANAGEMENT AGENCY

REGION V
175 W Jackson Blvd., 4th Floor
Chicago, IL 60604
(312) 408-5513
Catherine McNamara, Contracting Officer

GENERAL SERVICES ADMIN.

GREAT LAKES REGION
230 S Dearborn St., #3718 Mail Stop 37-5
Chicago, IL 60604
(312) 353-5383
Maureen Cruz, Business Specialist

VETERANS AFFAIRS, DEPT. OF

V.A. NATIONAL ACQUISITION CENTER, MEDICAL EQUIPMENT & PHARMACEUTICAL PRODUCTS
P.O. Box 76
Hines, IL 60141
(708) 786-5144
Phil Naas, Small Business Specialist
www.va.gov

V.A. CHICAGO HEALTH CARE SYSTEM
333 East Huron St.
Chicago, IL 60611
(414) 902-5407
Michael Cunningham, Small Business Specialist

INDIANA

COMMERCE, DEPT. OF

GARY MBDC
504 Broadway St., #328
Gary, IN 46402
(219) 885-7407
Jeff Williams, Exec. Dir.

INDIANAPOLIS MBD
402 N. Washington St.
Indianapolis, IN 46204
(317) 232-3061
Elena Cooper, Director

IOWA

VETERANS AFFAIRS, DEPT. OF

V.A. MEDICAL CENTER
1481 West 10th St.
Des Moines, IA 50310-5774
(515) 699-5886
Connie Mabley, Small Business Specialist

V.A. MEDICAL CENTER
6 West Highway
Iowa City, IA 52240
(319) 339-7144

KANSAS

VETERANS AFFAIRS, DEPT. OF

V.A. MEDICAL CENTER
4101 South Fourter St.
Leavenworth, KS 66048
(913) 758-4281
Marcus A. Clayton, Small Business Specialist

KENTUCKY

COMMERCE, DEPT. OF

LOUISVILLE MBDC
609 W Main St., 3rd Floor
Louisville, KY 40202
(502) 589-6232
Toni Cardell, Director

VETERANS AFFAIRS, DEPT. OF

V.A. MEDICAL CENTER
800 Zorn Ave.
Louisville, KY 40202
(502) 895-6116
Peggy Hall, Small Business Specialist

LOUISIANA

COMMERCE, DEPT. OF

BATON ROUGE MBDC
7455 E. Industrial Ave.
Baton Rouge, LA 70805
(225) 924-0186
Barry Kelly, Consultant

ENERGY, DEPT. OF

STRATEGIC PETROLEUM RESERVES
900 Commerce Rd. East
New Orleans, LA 70123
(504) 734-4000
Henry Gaffney, Small Business Specialist

VETERANS AFFAIRS, DEPT. OF

V.A. MEDICAL CENTER
1601 Perdido St.
New Orleans, LA 71101-4295
(504) 589-5280
Denise Smith, Small Business Specialist

MARYLAND

AGRICULTURE, DEPT. OF

AGRICULTURAL RESEARCH SERVICES
5601 Sunnyside Ave.
Beltsville, MD 20705
(301) 504-1725
Teresa Stephens, OSDBU Coordinator
www.usda.gov/da/smallbuis.html

ANIMAL & PLANT HEALTH INSPECTION SERVICE
4700 River Rd., Unit 81
Riverdale, MD 20737-1238
(301) 734-6178
Noripa Wallace, OSDBU Coordinator

AIR NATIONAL GUARD

2701 Eastern Blvd.
Baltimore, MD 21220
(410) 391-5122
Ms. Dana Dowell, Contracting Officer

ARMY, DEPT. OF THE

ABERDEEN PROVING GROUND
Aberdeen Proving Ground-Bldg. E-4455
Aberdeen, MD 21005
(410) 278-1549
Mr. John Rasmussen, Small Business Office

COMMERCE DEPT. OF

BUSINESS RESOURCE CENTER
3 W Baltimore St.
Baltimore, MD 21201
(410) 605-0990 Fax: (410) 605-0995

CENSUS BUREAU
4700 Silver Hill Rd.
Suitland, MD 20746
(301) 457-1864
Jackie Wilson, Small Business Liaison
www.census.gov

NATIONAL INSTITUTE OF STANDARDS & TECHNOLOGY
Room B128, Bldg. 301
Gaithersburg, MD 20899-0001
(301) 975-6343 Fax: (301) 963-7732
Henry M. Levy, Small Business Specialist

NIST Stop 2000.
100 Bureau Dr
Gaithersburg, MD 20899-2000
(301) 975-4517
Norman Taylor, Program Manager
Small Business Innovation Research Program
www.nist gov/sbir

Route 270/Quince Orchard Rd.
Bldg.301, #B152.
Gaithersburg, MD 20899
(301) 975-6302
Nicolas D'Ascoli, Small Purchasing Grp. Leader

NATIONAL OCEANIC & ATMOSPHERIC ADMINISTRATION

1305 East-West Highway, #7604
Code OFA-514
Silver Spring, MD 20910-3281
(301) 713-0851
Lawrence Frazier, Chief of Small Business Purchasing

HEALTH & HUMAN SERVICES, DEPT. OF

AGENCY FOR HEALTH CARE POLICY & RESEARCH
2101E Jefferson St., #601
Rockville, MD 20852
(301) 594-1445
Sherry Baldwin, Small Business Prog. Manager

FOOD & DRUG ADMINISTRATION
5630 Fishers Lane, #2017
Rockville, MD 20857
(301) 827-7034
Joan Stanard, Small Business Prog. Manager
jstanard@oc.fda.gov

HEALTH CARE FINANCING ADMINISTRATION
7500 Security Blvd. Code C2-21-15
Baltimore, MD 21244-1850
(410) 786-5166
Joann Day, Small Business Manager

HEALTH RESOURCES & SERVICES ADMINISTRATION
5600 Fishers Lane Parklawn, Bldg. #14A-27
Rockville, MD 20857
(301) 443-5636
Ann H. Linkins, Small Business Prog. Manager

INDIAN HEALTH SERVICE
12300 Twinbrook Parkway, #450-A
Rockville, MD 20852
(301) 443-1480
Myrna Mooney, Small Business Prog. Manager

NATIONAL INSTITUTES OF HEALTH
6100 Executive Blvd., #6D05 , Mail Stop 7540
Bethesda, MD 20892-7540
(301) 496-9639
Diana Mukitarian
www.nih.gov

PROGRAM SUPPORT CENTER
5600 Fishers Lane, Parklawn Bldg. 5C-26
Rockville, MD 20857
(301) 443-1715
Linda Danley, Small Business Prog. Manager

SOCIAL SECURITY ADMINISTRATION
P.O. Box 7696
Baltimore, MD 21207
(410) 965-9457 Fax: (410) 965-2965
Wanda B. Eley, Small & Disadvantaged Bus. Spec.

SUBSTANCE ABUSE & MENTAL HEALTH SERVICES
5600 Fishers Lane. Parklawn Bldg. #1085
Rockville, MD 20857
(301) 443-4447
Vivian Kim, Small Business Program Manager

NATIONAL AERONAUTICS & SPACE ADMINISTRATION

GODDARD SPACE FLIGHT CENTER
Mail Code 213.0
Greenbelt, MD 20771
(301) 286-4726
Rosa Acevedo
http://procurement.nasa.gov

NUCLEAR REGULATORY COMMISSION

OFFICE OF SMALL BUSINESS AND CIVIL RIGHTS
11545 Rockville Pike, Mail Stop #T2F18
Rockville, MD 20852
(301) 415-7382

TREASURY, DEPT OF THE

INTERNAL REVENUE SERVICE
6009 Oxon Hill Road #700
Oxon Hill, MD 20754
(202) 283-1199
Jodie Paustian, Small Business Specialist
www.irs. gov

VETERANS AFFAIRS, DEPT. OF

V.A. MEDICAL CENTER
10 North Green St.
Baltimore, MD 21201
(410) 605-7163
Andrea O'Connor, Small Business Specialist

MASSACHUSETTS

COMMERCE, DEPT. OF

MBDA NEW ENGLAND DISTRICT OFFICE
10 Causeway St., #418
Boston, MA 02222-1041
(617) 565-6850
R.K. (Shelly) Schwartz, Director
www.mbda.gov

DEFENSE, DEPT. OF

**DEFENSE CONTRACT MANAGEMENT
COMMAND EAST**
495 Summer St.
Boston, MA 02210-2184
(800) 321-1861
Stephen T. Shea, Director of Small Business

**U.S. ARMY SOLDIERS SYSTEMS
COMMAND**
Kansas St.
Natick, MA 01760-5008
(508) 233-4995
Phil G. Haddad Jr., Small Business Specialist

**GENERAL SERVICES
ADMINISTRATION**

NEW ENGLAND REGION
10 Causeway St., #901
Boston, MA 02222
(617) 565-8100
Rosemary Coffey, Small Business Center Dir.

**HOUSING & URBAN
DEVELOPMENT, DEPT. OF**

**NORTHEAST/MIDWEST SERVICE
CENTER**
10 Causeway St., #365
Boston, MA 02222-1092
(617) 565-6788
John Karwowski, Small Business Specialist

TRANSPORTATION, DEPT. OF

**VOLPE NATIONAL TRANSPORTATION
SYSTEMS CENTER, DTS-85**
55 Broadway
Kendall Square, Rm. 2104
Cambridge, MA 02142-1093
(617) 494-2389
Laura Dione, Small Business Specialist

VETERANS AFFAIRS, DEPT. OF

V.A. MEDICAL CENTER
150 South Huntington Ave.
Boston, MA 02130
(617) 232-9500 ext. 5538
Michael Kennison

MICHIGAN

DEFENSE, DEPT. OF

**U.S. ARMY TANK, AUTOMOTIVE &
ARMAMENTS COMMAND**
AMSTA CS-CB
Warren, MI 48397-5000
(810) 574-8874
Patricia Redding, Small Business Specialist
www.tacom.army.mil

TREASURY, DEPT. OF THE

**INTERNAL REVENUE SERVICE-DETROIT
COMPUTING CENTER**
985 Michigan Ave.
Detroit, MI 48226
(313) 234-1908
Wenda Hollenbeck, Small Business Specialist

VETERANS AFFAIRS, DEPT. OF

V.A. MEDICAL CENTER
4646 John R
Detroit, MI 48201
(313) 576-1000 ext. 3356
Debbie Fischer, Small Business Specialist

MINNESOTA

VETERANS AFFAIRS, DEPT. OF

V.A. MEDICAL CENTER
One Veterans Dr.
Minneapolis, MN 55417
(612) 725-2176
Janice Severs, Small Business Specialist

MISSISSIPPI

**NATIONAL AERONAUTICS & SPACE
ADMINISTRATION**

JOHNSON C. STENNIS SPACE CENTER
Mail Code DA30
Stennis Space Center, MS 39529-6000
(228) 688-3681
Jane Johnson

VETERANS AFFAIRS, DEPT. OF

V.A. MEDICAL CENTER
400 Veterans Blvd.
Biloxi, MS 39531
(228) 385-5729
Kenneth W. Johns, Small Business Specialist

MISSOURI

GENERAL SERVICES ADMINISTRATION

HEARTLAND REGION
1500 E Bannister Rd., #1161
Kansas City, MO 64131
(816) 926-7203
Lois Phillips, Business Specialist
www.r6.gsa.gov/obss

VETERANS AFFAIRS, DEPT. OF

V.A. MEDICAL CENTER
800 Stadium Road
Columbia, MO 65201
(913) 758-4281
Marcus A Clayton, Small Business Specialist

MONTANA

VETERANS AFFAIRS, DEPT. OF

V.A. MEDICAL CENTER
Ft. Harrison, MT 59636
(406) 447-7905
John Worster, Small Business Specialist

NEBRASKA

VETERANS AFFAIRS, DEPT. OF

V.A. MEDICAL CENTER
4101 Woolworth Ave.
Omaha, NE 68105
(402) 449-0613

NORTH CAROLINA

COMMERCE, DEPT. OF

BUSINESS RESOURCE CENTER
200 N College St., #2000
Charlotte, NC 28202
(704) 344-9797
April M. Gonzalez, Director

RALEIGH/DURHAM MBDC
205 Sayeteville St. Mall, #200
Raleigh, NC 27601
(919) 833-6122

VETERANS AFFAIRS, DEPT. OF

V.A. MEDICAL CENTER
1100 Tunnel Rd.
Asheville, NC 28805
(704) 299-5830
Djuna Roberts, Small Business Specialist

NEVADA

ENERGY, DEPT. OF

NEVADA OPERATIONS OFFICE
P.O. Box 98518
Las Vegas, NV 89193-8518
(702) 295-2792
Angela L. Avery, Small Business Specialist
www.nv.doe.gov

VETERANS AFFAIRS, DEPT. OF

V.A. MEDICAL CENTER
1703 West Charleston Blvd.
Las Vegas, NV 89102
(562) 494-5533
Ralph Tillman, Small Business Specialist

NEW HAMPSHIRE

DEFENSE, DEPT. OF

**NAVAL SHIPYARD PURCHASING
DIVISION**
Code 530.SB
Portsmouth, NH 03801-2590
(207) 438-2233
Michael Levesque, Small Business Specialist

VETERANS AFFAIRS, DEPT. OF

V.A. MEDICAL CENTER
718 Smyth Rd.
Manchester, NH 03104
(603) 626-6582

NEW JERSEY

COMMERCE, DEPT. OF

**MIDDLESEX/SOMMERSET/HUNTERDON
MBDC**
390 George St., #401
New Brunswick, NJ 08901
(732) 249-5511

DEFENSE, DEPT. OF

**U.S. ARMY ARMAMENT RESEARCH &
ENGINEERING CENTER (TACOM ARDEC)**
Picatinny Arsenal
New Jersey, NJ 07860-5000
(973) 724-4106
Rick Burdett, Small Business Specialist
www.pica.army.mil

**U.S. ARMY COMMUNICATIONS-
ELECTRONIC COMMAND**
HQ-CECOM
ATTN:AMSEL-SB
Fort Monmouth, NJ 07703-5005
(732) 532-4511
Joe Brady, Small Business Specialist
acbop.monmouth.army.mil

VETERANS AFFAIRS, DEPT. OF

V.A. MEDICAL CENTER
385 Tremont Ave.
East Orange, NJ 07019
(718) 584-9000 ext. 4332
Rufino Villaluz, Small Business Specialist

NEW MEXICO

COMMERCE, DEPT. OF

STATEWIDE NEW MEXICO MBDC
718 Central SW
Albuquerque, NM 87102
(505) 843-7114 Fax: (505) 242-2030
Anna Muller, Director

DEFENSE, DEPT. OF

U.S. ARMY WHITE SANDS MISSILE RANGE
ATTN: STEWS-SBA
White Sands, NM 88002-5031
(505) 678-1401
Luis Sosa, Small Business Specialist

ENERGY, DEPT. OF

ALBUQUERQUE OPERATIONS OFFICE
P.O. Box 5400
Albuquerque, NM 87117
(505) 845-6182
Lillian Retallack, Small Business Specialist
www.doeal.gov

VETERANS AFFAIRS, DEPT. OF

V.A. MEDICAL CENTER
2100 Ridgecrest Dr., S.E.
Albuquerque, NM 87108
(505) 256-2712
Deborah Heckman
Small Business Specialist

NEW YORK

COMMERCE, DEPT. OF

MBDC MANHATTAN
51 Madison Ave., #2212
New York, NY 10010
(212) 947-5351

MBDA REGIONAL OFFICE
26 Federal Plaza, #3720
New York, NY 10278
(212) 264-3262
Heyward Dazenport

MBDC ROCHESTER
350 North St.
Rochester, NY 14605
(716) 546-5556
Beverly Jackson, Director

MBDC WILLIAMSBURG/BROOKLYN
12 Heyward St.
Brooklyn, NY 11211
(718) 522-5620
Deborah Charnas, Project Director

ENERGY, DEPT. OF

**SCHENECTADY NAVAL REACTORS
OFFICE**
P.O. Box 1069
Schenectady, NY 12301-1069
(518) 395-6375
Marie Z. Pastor, Small Business Liaison

**ENVIRONMENTAL PROTECTION
AGENCY**

REGION II OSDBU
290 Broadway
New York, NY 10007-1866
(212) 637-3417
Otto Salamon, Management Specialist

**FEDERAL EMERGENCY
MANAGEMENT AGENCY**

REGION II
26 Federal Plaza, #1307
New York, NY 10278
(212) 225-7292
María Pizarro, Contracting Officer

TREASURY, DEPT. OF THE

**INTERNAL REVENUE SERVICE-NORTH
ATLANTIC REGION**
90 Church St., #811
New York, NY 10008
(212) 264-2733
Deborah Paulin-Foster, Small Business Spec.

UNITED STATES POSTAL SERVICE

NEW YORK METRO AREA
142-02 20th Ave.
Flushing, NY 11351-0600
(718) 321-5723
Guillermina Colón, Hispanic Program Specialist

VETERANS AFFAIRS, DEPT. OF

V.A. MEDICAL CENTER
130 West Kingsbridge Rd.
Bronx, NY 10468
(718) 584-9000 ext. 4332
Rufino Villaluz, Small Business Specialist

OHIO

COMMERCE, DEPT. OF

MBDC COLUMBUS
4335 Donlyn Court
Columbus, OH 43232
(614) 575-2250

MBDC DAYTON
1 Chamber Plz.
Dayton, OH 45402
(937) 226-1444
Sarah Dunnigan

NATIONAL AERONAUTICS & SPACE ADMINISTRATION

GLENN RESEARCH CENTER
Mail Code 500-313
Cleveland, OH 44135
(216) 433-2786
Carl Silski, Small Business Specialist
www.lerc.nasa.gov/Other-Groups/procure/home.htm

VETERANS AFFAIRS, DEPT. OF

V.A. MEDICAL CENTER
3200 Vine St.
Cincinatti, OH 45220
(937) 262-5960
Judith Blasingame, Small Business Specialist

V.A. MEDICAL CENTER
10701 East Boulevard
Cleveland, OH 44106
(440) 838-6068
Wanda Mims, Small Business Specialist

OKLAHOMA

COMMERCE, DEPT. OF

OKLAHOMA CITY MBDC
3017 N MLK Ave.
Oklahoma City, OK 73111
(405) 424-0082 •
Shany Raschidi, Director

VETERANS AFFAIRS, DEPT. OF

V.A. MEDICAL CENTER
921 NW 13th St.
Oklahoma City, OK 73104
(405) 270-0501 ext. 5110
Denny Drennan, Small Business Specialist

OREGON

VETERANS AFFAIRS, DEPT. OF

V.A. MEDICAL CENTER
3710 SW U.S. Veterans
Portland, OR 97207
(503) 402-2865
Small Business Specialist

PENNSYLVANIA

DEFENSE, DEPT. OF

FLEET & INDUSTRIAL SUPPLY CENTER. PHILADELPHIA DETACHMENT
700 Robbins Ave., Bldg. 2B
Philadelphia, PA 19111-5093
(215) 697-9664
Jim McGinley, Small Business Specialist

NAVAL INVENTORY CONTROL POINT
Code P0061
700 Robbins Ave., Bldg. 1
Philadelphia, PA 19111-5098
(215) 697-4950
Nina Evans, Small Business Specialist

NAVY INVENTORY CONTROL POINT
Code 006 5450 Carlisle Pike
Mechanicsburg, PA 17055-0788
(800) 309-1357
Helen Katz, Small Business Specialist
www.navicp.navy.mil

GENERAL SERVICES ADMINISTRATION

MID-ATLANTIC REGION
100 Penn Square East, #829
Philadelphia, PA 19107
(215) 656-5525
Helena Kock, Procurement Analyst
www.tse.r3.gsa.gov

TREASURY, DEPT. OF THE

INTERNAL REVENUE SERVICE-MID ATLANTIC REGION
615 Chestnut St.
Philadelphia, PA 19106
(800) 829-1040
Paul Maher, Small Business Specialist

UNITED STATES POSTAL SERVICE

ALLEGHENY AREA
1 Marquis Plaza
5315 Campbell Run Rd.
Pittsburgh, PA 15277-7000
(412) 494-2598
Betty Davis, Diversity Development Specialist

VETERANS AFFAIRS, DEPT. OF

V.A. MEDICAL CENTER
Highland Dr.
Pittsburgh, PA 15206
(412) 365-5435
Neal P. Delaney, Small Business Specialist

PUERTO RICO

COMMERCE, DEPT. OF

MBDC PUERTO RICO
P.O. Box 363631
San Juan, PR 00936-3631
(787) 753-8484
Teresa Berries, Project Director

VETERANS AFFAIRS, DEPT. OF

V.A. MEDICAL CENTER
One Veterans Plaza
San Juan, PR 00927-5800
(843) 577-5011 ext. 7210
Eliza Cruz, Small Business Specialist

RHODE ISLAND

DEFENSE, DEPT. OF

NAVAL UNDERSEA WARFARE CENTER
ATTN: David Rego Code 00SB. Bldg. 11
Newport, RI 02841-1708
(401) 832-1766
David Rego, Deputy for Small Business

VETERANS AFFAIRS, DEPT. OF

V.A. MEDICAL CENTER
830 Chalkstone Ave.
Providence, RI 02908
(401) 457-3035
James M. Gunn, Small Business Specialist

SOUTH CAROLINA

COMMERCE, DEPT. OF

BUSINESS RESOURCE CENTER
284 King St.
Charleston, SC 29401
(843) 937-0011
Gwen Bullock, Director

COLUMBIA MBDC
2111 Bull St.
Columbia, SC 29201
(803) 779-5905
Gwen Bullock, Director

DEFENSE, DEPT. OF

NAVAL FACILITIES ENGINEERING COMMAND, SOUTHERN DIVISION, CODE 09J
P.O.Box 190010
North Charleston, SC 29419-9010
(843) 820-5935
Kristine Pennaegeo, Small Business Specialist
www.efdsouth.navfac.navy.mil

ENERGY, DEPT. OF

SAVANNAH RIVER OPERATION OFFICE
P.O. Box A
Aiken, SC 29802
(803) 725-8123
Angela Sistrunk, Small Business Program Manager

VETERANS AFFAIRS, DEPT. OF

V.A. MEDICAL CENTER
109 Bee Street
Charleston, SC 29403
(803) 577-5011 ext. 7210
Linda S. Alderson, Small Business Specialist

TENNESSEE

COMMERCE, DEPT. OF

MBDA-BUSINESS RESOURCE CENTER
3401 West End Ave., #110
Nashville, TN 37203
(615) 794-4088

MBDC MEMPHIS
283 N. Bellevue
Memphis, TN 38105
(901) 726-5353
Gary Rowe, Director

MBDC NASHVILLE
223 8th Ave. N. #205
Nashville, TN 37203
(615) 255-0432
Marilyn Robinson, Director

STATE OF TENNESSEE

ECONOMIC & COMMUNITY DEV. DEPT.
312 8th Ave. N.
Nashville, TN 37243
(615) 741-2545
John Birdsong, Dir. Min. Bus. Enterprise Dev.

VETERANS AFFAIRS, DEPT. OF

V.A. MEDICAL CENTER
1030 Jefferson Ave.
Memphis, TN 38104
(901) 577-7227
Florence Winfield, Small Business Specialist

TEXAS

COMMERCE, DEPT. OF

CMBC CORPUS CHRISTI
226 Enterprise Pkwy. #112
Corpus Christi, TX 78405
(361) 883-1809
John Longoria, Project Director

MBDC HOUSTON
2900 Woodridge St., #310
Houston, TX 77087
(713) 644-0821

MBDC SAN ANTONIO
1222 N Main St., #750
San Antonio, TX 78212
(210) 558-2480

DEFENSE, DEPT. OF

SAN ANTONIO AIR LOGISTICS CENTER
303 Tinker Dr. Suite 1 Kelly AFB
San Antonio, TX 78241-5921
(210) 925-6918
Vangie Flugmeire, Small Business Specialist
WWW.kelly-afb.org

ENVIRONMENTAL PROTECTION AGENCY

REGION VI OSDBU
1445 Ross Ave., #1200
Dallas, TX 75202-2733
(214) 665-7406
Debora N. Bradford

FEDERAL EMERGENCY MANAGEMENT AGENCY

REGION VI, CONTRACTING DIVISION
800 N Loop 288
Denton, TX 76209
(940) 898-5312
Barbara Journeli, Contracting Officer

GENERAL SERVICES ADMINISTRATION

GREATER SOUTHWEST REGION
819 Taylor St., 1E13A
Fort Worth, TX 76102
(817) 978-3284
Willie Heath, Small Business Liaison Director

MINORITY BUSINESS DEVELOPMENT AGENCY

DALLAS REGIONAL OFFICE
1100 Commerce St., #7B-23
Dallas, TX 75242
(214) 767-8001
Johnigohart

NATIONAL AERONAUTICS & SPACE ADMINISTRATION

JOHNSON SPACE CENTER
Mail Code BA
Houston, TX 77058
(281) 483-4157
Deborah Johnson, Small Business Advocate

SPACE STATION PROGRAM
Mail Code BG3 Masa
NASA-Johnson Space Center
Houston, TX 77058
(281) 244-8196
Kenneth Martindale, Small Business Specialist
www.procure.msfc.nasa.gov/nasa_ref.html

TREASURY, DEPT. OF THE

INTERNAL REVENUE SERVICE-MID-STATES REGION
4050 Alpha Rd., 9th Floor-SWRO 1430
Dallas, TX 75244-4203
(972) 308-1972
Larry Roberts, Small Business Specialist

UNITED STATES POSTAL SERVICE

SOUTHWEST AREA
7800 N. Stemmons Freeway #700
Dallas, TX 75247-4217
(214) 819-7109
Barbara Reagor, Supplier Diversity Specialist

VETERANS AFFAIRS, DEPT. OF

V.A. MEDICAL CENTER
4500 South Lancaster Rd.
Dallas, TX 75216
(214) 857-0001
Robert Thomale Jr., Small Business Specialist

V.A. MEDICAL CENTER
7400 Merton Minter Blvd.
San Antonio, TX 78284
(210) 617-5152
Frank Caraballo, Small Business Specialist

UTAH

VETERANS AFFAIRS, DEPT. OF

V.A. MEDICAL CENTER
500 Foothill Blvd.
Salt Lake City, UT 84148
(801) 584-1201
Brenda Alverson, Small Business Specialist

VERMONT

VETERANS AFFAIRS, DEPT. OF

V.A. MEDICAL & REGIONAL OFFICE CENTER
North Hartland Rd.
White River Junction, VT 05009
(802) 296-5101
Suzanne Rybcyzk, Small Business Specialist

Fairfax County Chamber of Commerce
8230 Old Courthouse Rd., Suite 350
Vienna, VA 22182
Tel: (703) 749-0400 Fax: (703) 749-9075
Judy Gray, President & CEO

VIRGINIA

AGRICULTURE, DEPT. OF

FOOD & NUTRITION SERVICE
3101 Park Center Dr., 2nd Fl.
Alexandria, VA 22302
(703) 305-2250
Patricia Palmer, OSDBU Coordinator
www.usda.gov/fcs/contract.html

COMMERCE, DEPT. OF

HAMPTON ROADS MBDC
420 Bank St.
Norfolk, VA 23510
(757) 825-2957

PATENT AND TRADEMARK OFFICE
2011 Crystal Dr. #810
Arlington, VA 22202
(703) 305-8152 Fax: (703) 305-8294
Helen Hensley, Procurement Analyst & Small
Business Liaison Officer

DEFENSE, DEPT. OF

**DEFENSE ADVANCED RESEARCH
PROJECTS AGENCY**
3701 N Fairfax Dr.
Arlington, VA 22203-1714
(703) 696-2379
Connie Jacobs, Deputy Director
www.darpa.mil

DEFENSE COMMISSARY AGENCY
1300 E Ave.
Fort Lee, VA 23801-1800
(804) 734-8721
Crosby Johnson, Executive Director for Support
www.deca.mil/default.htm

DEFENSE FUEL SUPPLY CENTER
8725 John J. Kingman Rd., #4943
Fort Belvoir, VA 22060-6222
(703) 767-9400
Kathy S. Williams, Small Business Specialist
www.dfsc.dla.mil

DEFENSE LOGISTICS AGENCY
8725 John J. Kingman Rd.
ATTN: DAS Suite 2533
Fort Belvoir, VA 22060-6221
(703) 767-1650
Lloyd C. Alderman
www.dla.mil

FLEET & INDUSTRIAL SUPPLY CENTER
Bldg. 143. 1968 Gilbert St. #600
Norfolk, VA 23511-3392
(757) 443-1435
Linda Owen, Deputy for Small Business

**NAVAL FACILITIES ENGINEERING COMMAND,
ATLANTIC DIVISION, CODE 09W**
1510 Gilbert St.
Norfolk, VA 23511-2699
(757) 322-8222
Susan M. Kranes, Small Business Specialist

NAVAL SURFACE WARFARE CENTER
17320 Dahlgren Rd.
Dahlgren, VA 22448-5100
(540) 653-4806
James Howard, Small Business Specialist
www.nswc.navy.mil

**OFFICE OF SMALL AND
DISADVANTAGED BUSINESS**
1777 N. Kent St.
Arlington, VA 22209
(703) 588-8631
Robert L. Neal, Jr., Director
www.acq.osd.mil/sadbu

**U.S. ARMY TRAINING & DOCTRINE
COMMAND**
ATCS-B Bldg.105, #104
Fort Monroe, VA 23651-5000
(757) 727-3291
Thomas Kobezak, Associate Director

DEFENSE SPECIAL WEAPON
AGENCY

**OFFICE OF SMALL AND
DISADVANTAGED BUSINESS**
6801 Telegraph Rd.
Alexandria, VA 22310-3398
(703) 325-5021
Bill Burks, Small Business Specialist

GEORGE MASON UNIVERSITY

**PROCUREMENT TECHNICAL
ASSISTANCE CENTER**
7960 Donegan Dr., Bldg. B-Sudley N
Manassas, VA 22110
(703) 330-5458
Amy Erwin, Associate Director

INTERIOR, DEPT. OF THE

**U.S. FISH & WILDLIFE SERVICE-
BUSINESS UTILIZATION DEVELOPMENT**
4401 N Fairfax Dr., Rm. 212B
Arlington, VA 22203
(703) 358-1899
James McKoy, Jr., Acting Specialist

JUSTICE, DEPT. OF

DRUG ENFORCEMENT ADMINISTRATION
700 Army Navy Dr., # W-5142
Arlington, VA 22202
(202) 307-7812
Burdette Burton, Small Business Specialist

U.S. MARSHALS SERVICE
CS-3, #1118 600 Army-Navy Dr.
Arlington, VA 22202
(202) 307-9349
Elizabeth Howard, Small Business Specialist

NATIONAL AERONAUTICS & SPACE
ADMINISTRATION

LANGLEY RESEARCH CENTER
Mail Code 144
Hampton, VA 23681-2199
(757) 864-2456
Vernon Vann, Small Business Specialist
www.larc.nasa.gov/procurement/home-
page.html

NATIONAL SCIENCE FOUNDATION

**OFFICE OF SMALL AND
DISADVANTAGED BUSINESS
UTILIZATION**
4201 Wilson Blvd., #590
Arlington, VA 22230
(703) 292-8330
Donald Senich

TRANSPORTATION, DEPT. OF

**U.S. COAST GUARD, MAINTENANCE &
LOGISTICS COMMAND**
300 E Main St., #8000
Norfolk, VA 23510-9107
(757) 628-4103
Peter Frechette, Small Business Specialist

VETERANS AFFAIRS, DEPT. OF

V.A. MEDICAL CENTER
100 Emancipation Dr.
Hampton, VA 23667
(757) 728-3113
Nancy Bailey, Small Business Specialist

WASHINGTON

COMMERCE, DEPT. OF

NORTHWEST NABDC
934 North 143rd St.
Seattle, WA 98133
(206) 365-7735
Mario Gonzalez, Director

SEATTLE MBDC
155 NE 100th Ave., #401
Seattle, WA 98125
(206) 353-7347

DEFENSE, DEPT. OF

**FLEET & INDUSTRIAL SUPPLY CENTER.
PUGET SOUND**
467 W St., Code 04
Bremerton, WA 98312-5100
(360) 476-7300
Peggy Williams, Small Business Specialist

ENERGY, DEPT. OF

RICHLAND OPERATIONS OFFICE
P.O. Box 550 MSAN A7-80
Richland, WA 99352
John Perez, Small Business Specialist
www.hanford.gov

TRANSPORTATION, DEPT. OF

**COAST GUARD, FACILITIES DESIGN &
CONSTRUCTION CENTER**
915 2nd Ave., #2664
Seattle, WA 98174-1011
(206) 220-7426

VETERANS AFFAIRS, DEPT. OF

V.A. MEDICAL CENTER
1660 South Columbian Way
Seattle, WA 98108
(206) 764-2146
María Losoya
Small Business Specialist

WEST VIRGINIA

STATE OF WEST VIRGINIA

**MINORITY & SMALL BUSINESS
DEVELOPMENT AGENCY**
950 Kanawtha Blvd. E
Charleston, WV 25301
(304) 558-2960
Hazel Palmer, Dir.

TREASURY, DEPT. OF THE

**INTERNAL REVENUE SERVICE
MARTINSBURG COMPUTING CENTER**
P.O. Box 1208 CPU
Martinsburg, WV 25401
(304) 264-5507
Linda Miller, Small Business Specialist

VETERANS AFFAIRS, DEPT. OF

V.A. MEDICAL CENTER
200 Veterans Ave.
Beckley, WV 25801
(304) 255-2121 ext. 4133
Kathy Hymes, Small Business Specialist

WISCONSIN

COMMERCE, DEPT. OF

MILWAUKEE MBDC
1442 N Farwell Ave., #500
Milwaukee, WI 53202
(414) 289-3422

VETERANS AFFAIRS, DEPT. OF

CONTRACT SERVICE CENTER
5000 West National Ave., Bldg.
Milwaukee, WI 53295-0005
(414) 902-5407
Michael Cunningham, Small Business Spec.

WYOMING

VETERANS AFFAIRS, DEPT. OF

V.A. MEDICAL CENTER
1898 Fort Rd.
Sheridan, WY 82801
(307) 778-7326
Bob Baker, Small Business Specialist

Private Sector Minority Business Opportunities

Oportunidades para los negocios minoritarios en el sector privado

This section contains a listing of private companies offering minority business development opportunities.

Esta sección contiene una lista de empresas privadas, que ofrecen oportunidades de negocios para empresas minoritarias.

3COM
5400 Bayfront Plaza
Santa Clara, CA 95054-5003
Laurie Valdez, Supplier Diversity Mgr.
(408) 326-5033 Fax: (408) 326-3299
www.3com.com/partners/index.html

3M
P.O. Box 33327
St. Paul, MN 55144-1000
Jim Anderson, Purchasing Manager/
Minority Supplier and Development
Fax: (612) 736-7174

ABBOTT LABORATORIES
200 Abbott Park Rd. D. 548, AP34
Abott Park, IL 60064-6193
W.J. Stewart, M/WBE Business Dev.
(847) 937-5052 Fax: (847) 937-5691

AERO SIMULATION INC.
9220 Palm River Rd., #105
Tampa, FL 33619
Shane Hall, Purchasing Manager
(813) 628-4447 Fax: (813) 628-8404

AEROJET (A GENCORP CO.)
P.O. Box 13222
Sacramento, CA 95813-6000
W.A. Ashbaugh, Director, Material
(916) 355-4000 Fax: (916) 351-8667

AEROSPACE CORPORATION, THE
P.O. Box 92957
Los Angeles, CA 90009-2957
Michael J. Cryderman, SBLO
(310) 366-1198 Fax: (310) 336-5703

AEROTHEM CORPORATION
580 Clyde Ave.
Mountain View, CA 94043-2212
Donald Kwong, Subcontractor Admin.
(650) 254-2591 Fax: (650) 964-8349

AETNA- RETIREMENT SERVICES
151 Farmington Ave. TNAI
Harford, CT 06156
(860) 616-2600

AIL SYSTEMS
254 E. Ave. K-4
Lancaster, CA 93535
(661) 723-3886 Fax: (661) 948-7003

ALARIS MEDICAL SYSTEMS
10221 Wateridge Circle
San Diego, CA 92121-2733
Cynthia Wessel, Sourcing Manager
(858) 458-7000 Fax: (858) 458-7760

ALLIANT TECHSYSTEMS
600 2nd St., NE
Hopkins, MN 55343
Steve Brandt, SBLO
(612) 931-5157 Fax: (612) 931-5865

ALLIED-SIGNAL, INC.
Morristown, NJ 07962-1057
Material Resources Small/Min. Bus.
(201) 455-3677

ALUMINIUM COMPANY OF AMERICA (ALCOA)
Pittsburg, PA 15219
Business Dev.
(412) 553-4913

AMERADA HESS CORPORATION
1 Hess Plaza
Woodbridge, NJ 07095
Corporate Purchasing
(908) 750-6592

AMERICAN AIRLINES
P.O. Box 619616
DFW Airport, TX 75261-9616
Fred Kahl, Coord., Minority Vendor Dev.
(817) 963-2620 Fax: (817) 931-6947

AMERICAN EXPRESS COMPANY
777 American Expressway
Ft. Lauderdale, FL 33337
Teresa Applegate, Senior Manager
(954) 503-3077

AMERICAN PRESIDENT LINES LTD.
8410 Amelia St.
Oakland, CA 94621
(510) 272-8865

AMERITECH
30 S. Wacker Dr., 35th Fl.
Chicago, IL 60606
(312) 750-5977

AMERITECH SERVICES
722 N. Broadway, 10th Fl.
Milwaukee, WI 53202
(414) 678-2713

AMERITECH SERVICES
2000 W. Ameritech Ctr. Dr.
Hoffman Estates, IL 60196-1025
Debra Jennings Johnson
(847) 248-2249

AMOS TUCK SCHOOL OF BUSINESS
100 Tuck Hall
Hanover, NH 03755-9050
(603) 646-2300

AMTRAK
60 Massachusetts Ave. NE www-113
Washington, DC 20002
Roscoe A. Swann, Jr., Director
(202) 906-3600 Fax: (202) 906-2689

ANHEUSER-BUSCH, INC.
One Busch Place
St. Louis, MO 63118
Floyd E. Lewis, Dir.,Corporate Affairs
(314) 577-2230 Fax: (314) 577-2905

APPLE
1 Infinite Loop MS-72PM
Cupertino, CA 95014
Oliver Krevet, Supplier Diversity &
Development Program Specialist
(408) 974-2852 Fax: (312) 616-0139

ARAMARK
115 N. First St.
Burbank, CA 91510
(818) 973-3532

AT&T
P.O. Box 25000
Greensboro, NC 27420-5000
Relations MWBE Prog.
(800) 322-MWBE

AVERSTAR
23 Fourth Ave.
Burlington, MA 01803-3303
Dick Prussman, SBLO
(781) 221-6990 Fax: (781) 221-6991

AVON PRODUCTS, INC.
9 W. 57th St., 20th Fl.
New York, NY 10019
(212) 265-8150

BALL AEROSPACE & TECHNOLOGY CORPORATION
P.O. Box 1062
Boulder, CO 80306
Teressa Pederson, SBLO
(303) 939-5955 Fax: (303) 939-4999

BALTIMORE GAS & ELECTRIC
290 Lord Baltimore Dr.
Baltimore, MD 21203-1472
Harold Williams, Procurement Opp. Prog.
(410) 597-6873

BANK OF AMERICA
333 South Beaudry Ave. #4231
Los Angeles, CA 90017
Joyce Tabak, VP, Min./Women's Bus.
Prog. Admin.
(213) 345-1495

BANK ONE SERVICES CORPORATION
P. O. Box 71
Arizona Corporate Purchasing, A546
Phoenix, AZ 85001-0071
Lupe Barto, Officer
(214) 290-2583 Fax: (214) 290-7697

BATH IRON WORKS
700 Washington St.
Bath, ME 04530
(207) 442-1756 Fax: (207) 442-1156

BECTON DICKINSON & COMPANY
1 Becton Dr.
Franklin Lakes, NJ 07417-1883
Harry Hamme, Mgr., Purchasing Svcs.
(201) 847-7164 Fax: (410) 316-4251

BELLSOUTH CORPORATION
675 W. Peachtree St., NE, Rm. 31C 500
Atlanta, GA 30375
Judith M. Tyler, Mgr., Small Business Prog.
(404) 420-6400 Fax: (404) 872-1326

THE BOEING COMPANY
M/C 14-51
Seattle, WA 98124-2207
Nick Sena, Dir., Co. Supplier Diversity
(425) 266-1825

THE BOEING COMPANY
P.O. Box 2515 M/C 110-SC71
2201 Seal Beach Blvd. M/C 110-SC71
Seal Beach, CA 90740-8250
Barbara Taylor, Mgr., Supplier Diversity
(562) 797-5812 Fax: (562) 797-5713

THE BOEING COMPANY
P.O. Box 516
63166 M/C S100 3204
St. Louis, MO
Gary Eisenhart, Manager
(314) 232-4242 Fax: (314) 232-4388

BOISE CASCADE CORPORATION
P. O. Box 50
1111W. Jefferson St.
Boise, ID 83728-0001
(208)384-6470

BOOZ, ALLEN & HAMILTON
8283 Greensboro Dr.
McLean, VA 22102
John Grindle, Small Bus. Administrator
(703) 902-5251 Fax: (703) 902-3351

BORDEN, INC.
180 E. Broad St.
Columbus, OH 43215
(614) 225-4075

BP
200 E. Randolph Dr. M/C 1803
Chicago, IL 60601-7125
Debra Jennings-Johnson, Dir., Supp. Div.
(312) 856-3640 Fax: (312) 616-0139

BRISTOL-MYERS SQUIBB CORPORATION
Plainsboro, NJ 08543-4500
(609) 897-4921

BURGER KING
17777 Old Cutler Rd.
Miami, FL 33157
Mike Alonso, Franchise Sales
(305) 378-3187

BURLINGTON INDUSTRIES
Greensboro, NC 27420
Gary Lyon, Manager
(919) 379-2146 Fax: (336) 379-4953

C.E. WYLIE CONSTRUCTION CORPORATION
3777 Ruffin Rd.
San Diego, CA 92123-1811
Sharon Wylie, M/WBE Coordinator
(619) 571-4911 Fax: (619) 571-4911

CADBURY SCHWEPPES PLC
6 High Ridge Park
Stamford, CT 06905
Tom Hamiton, Dir., World Sourcing
(203) 968-7636 Fax: (203) 968-7573

CATERPILLAR INC.
100 Adams St. NE
Peoria, IL 61629-1490
Karl Stach, Procurement Manager
(309) 494-1383

CENTEX CONSTRUCTION CORPORATION
1050 Monroe Dr.
Dallas, TX 75229-9009
David Preston, Vice President
(214) 357-1891 Fax: (214) 902-6339

CHADWICK'S OF BOSTON, LTD.
35 United Dr.
West Bridgewater, MA 02379
Maureen Peters, Purchasing Mgr.
(508) 583-8110 Fax: (508) 583-6314

CHASE MANHATTAN BANK
270 Park Ave., 44th Fl.
New York, NY 10017
Ednid Winn, Program Dir.
(212) 270-4268

CHASE MANHATTAN BANK
One Chase Manhattan Plaza, 20th Fl.
New York, NY 10081
John Tumminello, Recruiting Mgr.
(212) 552-7224

CHEVRON CORPORATION
575 Market St., 17th Fl.
San Francisco, CA 94105
Audree Brichi, Mgr. of Small Business
(415) 894-7700 Fax: (925) 842-4503

CHRYSLER CORPORATION
7500 Maehr Rd.
Auburn Hills, MI 76705-1647
Joseph E. Harris, Executive Special
Supplier Relations
(810) 576-6102
www2.chryslercorp.com

CINCOM SYSTEMS INC.
2300 Montana Ave.
Cincinnati, OH 45211-3898
Thomas M. Nies, SBLO
(513) 612-2480 Fax: (513) 662-2300

CIRCUIT CITY STORES
9950 Mayland Drive
Richmond, VA 23233
(804) 527-4000 x 4397

CISCO SYSTEMS
170 W.Tasman Dr.
San Jose, CA 95134
Diane Thelan, SBLO/MBE Outreach
(408) 526-4503

CITIBANK
1101 Pennsylvania Ave. NW #1100
Washington, DC 20004
Ernest Skinner, Community Dev. Dir.
(202) 859-6870 Fax: (202) 879-6888

COASTAL GOVERNMENT SERVICES
3104 Croasdaile Dr.
Durham, NC 27712
L. Kelly Brann, CFO
(919) 383-6934 Fax: (919) 309-1402

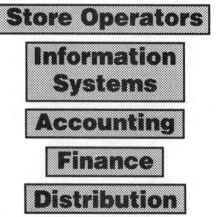

COCA-COLA COMPANY
P.O. Drawer 1734
Atlanta, GA 30301
Ivette McNell, Mgr.
(404) 676-2121

COMPAQ
200 Forester St. M/S MR01 3/D1
Marlboro, MA 01752-3085
Daniel Dean, Supplier Div. Prog. Mgr.
(508) 467-2759 Fax: (508) 467-7128

COMPUTER DATA SYSTEMS, INC.
1 Curie Ct.
Rockville, MD 20850-4389
James Hollister, SBLO
(301) 921-7000 Fax: (301) 921-0795

COMPUTER SCIENCE CORPORATION
3190 Fairview Park Dr.
Falls Church, VA 22042-4516
Addie Olsen, SBLO
(703) 876-3095 Fax: (703) 876-3530

CON EDISON
4 Irving Place, #12075
New York,, NY 10003
Joy Crichlow, Dir., Min. Business Prog.
(212) 460-3076 Fax: (334) 821-8534

**CONNER BROS. CONSTRUCTION
CORPORATION, INC.**
P.O. Box 3070
Auburn, AL 36831-3070
Ron Burke, Estimator
(334) 821-1470 Fax: (334) 821-8534

**CONRAIL (CONSOLIDATED RAIL
CORPORATION)**
2001 Market St., Rm. 7B
Philadelphia, PA 19103
Paul Jones, Mgr., Min. Vendor Prog.
(215) 209-5080

CONSTRUCTION CORPORATION, INC.
P.O. Box 8270
Tyler, TX 75711
Tanya Gilbert, SBLO
(903) 597-1500 Fax: (903) 597-0567

**CONTRACTORS PAVING
CORPORATION, INC.**
121 Chestnut Ave.
Virginia Beach, VA 23452
Ed Manley, Vice-President
(757) 340-7582 Fax: (757) 340-4582

COORS BREWING COMPANY
Mail #CE110
Golden,,, CO 80401
Yvette Hyman, Logistics Mgr.
(303) 277-3818

DEERE & COMPANY
1 John Deere Pl.
Moline, IL 61265-1373
Tad Birdit, Administrator, Government
and Internal Programs
(309) 765-5525 Fax: (309) 765-4584

DELL COMPUTER
1 Dell Way

Round Rock, TX 78682
Doug Edgar, SBLO
(512) 338-4400 Fax: (512) 283-1111

DOMINION VIRGINIA POWER
Richmond, VA 23261
(877) 244-0459

DOW CHEMICAL
1776 Building Dow Chemical
Corporation
Midland, MI 48674-1776
P.W. Tower, SBLO
(517) 636-1000

**DR. PEPPER/SEVEN-UP COMPANIES,
INC.**
Dallas, TX 75265-5086
Minority Affairs
(972) 360-7000

DUKE POWER COMPANY
P.O. Box 1004
Charlotte, NC 28201-1004
Charles Grobusky, Coord., Min./
Women's Bus.
(704) 382-4281

DUPONT SOURCING
Chestnut Run Plz., HR-1091
Wilmington, DE 19880-0723
(302) 774-1684

**DUTRA CONSTRUCTION
CORPORATION, INC.**
1000 Point San Pedro Rd.
San Rafael, CA 94901
Lanie Abendroth, SBLO
(415) 458-5466 Fax: (415) 458-5474

DYNCORP AEROSPACE TECHNOLOGY
2000 Edmund Halley Dr.
Reston, VA 20191-3400
Michelle Germanie, SBLO
(703) 715-4451 Fax: (703) 715-4422

DYNCORP AEROSPACE TECHNOLOGY
6500 W. Freeway #600
Fort Worth, TX 76116
Cheryl Dial, Purchasing Manager
(817) 737-1548 Fax: (817) 737-1606

E G & G WASC, INCORPORATED
1396 Piccard Dr.
Rockville, MD 20850
Larry Richardson, Socio-economic
Liaison Officer
(301) 840-3147

E.I. DU PONT DE NEMOUS & COMPANY
1007 Market St. M/S CSB-7609
Wilmington, DE 19898
Bill Blue, Sourcing Manager
(302) 996-1808 Fax: (302) 773-5974
www.dupont.com/corp/whatsnew/
releases/95archive

E-SYSTEMS, INC.
Dallas, TX 75266-0023
Barbara Osborn, Officer, Small Bus. Liais.
(972) 205-7202

EASTMAN KODAK CORPORATION
343 State St.
Rochester, NY 14650-0517
(716) 781-5567

EBASCO SERVICES, INC.
2 World Trade Ctr.
New York, NY 10048-0752
Mary L. Boyd-Foy, Corporate Mgr.
(212) 839-1218

EL ECHO TRANSLATIONS
600 W. 25th St.
Norfolk, VA 23517
Augusto Ratti-Angulo, President
(800) 908-2828

EL ECO DE VIRGINIA
600 W. 25th St.
Norfolk, VA 23517
Augusto Ratti-Angulo, President
(757) 625-1341

EDISON ELECTRIC INSTITUTE
701 Pennsylvania Ave., NW
Washington, DC 20004-2696
Randy Ihara, External Prog.
(202) 508-5585

EDS
13600 EDS Dr.
Herndon, VA 22071
Randy Gamble, VP Managing Dir. of
Fin. Systems & Electronic Commerce
(703) 742-1841

EG &G WASC, INC
3604 Collins Serry Rd. #200
Morgantown, WV 26505-2353
Kathy Clinton, Socio-Economic Liais.
Officer
(304) 599-5941 Fax: (304) 599-8904

**ELECTRONIC DATA SYSTEMS
CORPORATION**
5400 Legacy Dr. M/S H1-IF-22
Plano, TX 75024
Pheebe Elder, Supp. Diversity Program
(972) 605-4150 Fax: (972) 605-5185

ENERGY SERVICES, INC.
New Orleans, LA 70113
(504) 569-4744

EXXON COMPANY
Houston, TX 77210-4692
Alfredo "AL" Pena, Mgr., Supplier Dev.
(713) 656-7618 Fax: (713) 656-1733

FNMA (FANNIEMAE)
3900 Wisconsin Ave. NW
Washington, DC 20016-2899
Min. & Women-Owned Business
(202) 752-3775

FEDERAL EXPRESS
2605 Nonconnah Blvd., #135
Memphis, TN 38132-2611
William Shotwell, Dir. of Corp. Diversity
(901) 922-3636 Fax: (901) 922-3954

FIRST UNION BANK
301 S. Tryon St.
Charlotte, NC 28288-0842
Isa Powell, Coord., Minority/Women's
Bus. Enterprise
(704) 344-2420

FLUOR DANIEL
100 Fluor Daniel Dr.
Greensville, SC 29607
(864) 281-4400

FORD MOTOR COMPANY
5111 Auto Club Dr.
Dearborn, MI 48121
Ray Jansen, Minority Supplier Develop.
(313) 594-7338 Fax: (313) 845-4713

**FOSTER WHEELER ENVIRONMENTAL
CORPORATION**
10900 Eight St. NE, #1300
Bellevue, WA 98004-4405
Julie Clayton, Small Bus. Liason Coord.
(425) 482-7600 ext.7612 Fax: (425)
482-7652

FREDDIE MAC
8200 Jones Branch Dr.
McLean, VA 22102
(703) 902-7700

FRITO-LAY, INC.
Dallas, TX 75266-0634
Bob Gonzales
(972) 334-5940

FUJITSU NETWORK COMUNICATIONS
2801 Telecom Pkwy.
Richardson, TX 75082
Havier Fernandez, Manager, National
Diversity Initiative
(972) 455-3000 Fax: (858) 455-3590

GENERAL ATOMIC
P.O. Box 85608
San Diego, CA 92186-5608
Larry Boysen, SBLO
(619) 455-3422 Fax: (619) 455-3545

GENERAL ELECTRIC
1 Newman Way-Mail Drop A-86
Cincinnati, OH 45215
Mark Miller, Small Bus. Liaison Office
(513) 243-3612 Fax: (513) 786-4671

GENERAL MOTORS CORPORATION
30400 Mound Rd. Bldg. 18
MC 480-108-103
Warren, MI 48090-9015
J. David Allen, Dir. Min. Business Dev.
(313) 556-5000 Fax: (313) 556-5108

**GOODYEAR TIRE & RUBBER
CORPORATION**
1144 East Market St.
Akron, OH 44316-0001
Anita Fullum, Manager
(330) 796-7606

GOVCON INC.
2400 Research Blvd., #250
Rockville, MD 20850
Raj Khera
(301) 921-4700

GOVERNMENT TECHNOLOGY SERVICES, INC.
4100 Lafayette Ctr. Dr.
Chantilly, VA 22021
Darlin Fredisks, Events Coord.
(703) 631-3333, ext. 2096

GRAND CANYON MINORITY SUPPLIER DEVELOPMENT COUNCIL
323 W. Roosevelt, #101
Phoenix, AZ 85003
Joe Castillo, Executive Director
(602) 495-9950 Fax: (602) 495-9943

GRANITE CONSTRUCTION COMPANY
P.O. Box 50024
Watsonville, CA 95077
Charles A. May, SBLO
(831) 724-1011/722-2716
Fax: (831) 728-7570

GTE CORPORATION
5615 Highpoint Dr.
Irving, TX 75062-3957
Supplier Diversity Hotline
(800) 347-1508 Fax: (972) 751-5605

GTE SPACENET CORPORATION
1700 Old Meadow Rd.
McLean, VA 22102
Jim Stevenson, Small/Min. Business Prog.
(703) 848-1000 Fax: (703) 848-1010

HALLIBURTON/BROWN & ROOT
P.O. Box 3
Houston, TX 77001-0003
Deanie Veselka, Mgr., Supplier Div. Prog.
(713) 676-5989 Fax: (713) 676-5997

HALLMARK CARDS, INC.
P. O. Box 419580
2501 McGee
Kansas City, MO 64141-6580
Jerry Mcquin, Mgr., Min.Supplier Dev.
(816) 274-3903 Fax: (816) 274-8008
gmcque1@hallmark.com

HARKINS BUILDERS, INC.
12301 Old Columbia Pike
Silver Spring, MD 20904
Robert LaFollette, Estimator
(301) 622-9000 Fax: (301) 680-4299

HEALTH NET
3400 Data Dr.
Rancho Cordova, CA 95670-7956
Donna Clausen, Buyer, Supplier Div. Prog.
(916) 631-5000

HENSEL PHELPS CONSTRUCTION
2415 Campus Dr. #100
Irvine, CA 92612
Richard Faris
(949)852-0111 Fax: (949)852-0218

HERCULES, INC.
1313 N. Market St. Hercules Plaza
Wilmington, DE 19894-0001
Janet Gray, Mgr., Energy and Support Svcs.
(302) 594-6411 Fax: (302) 594-6664

HERSHEY'S CHOCOLATE
One E. Chocolate Ave.
Hershey, PA 17033
Paul Smith, Mgr.
(717) 534-7044

HEWLETT-PACKARD
3000 Hanover St.
Palo Alto, CA 94304-1181
Jo Ann Butler, Corporate Business Diversity Program Manager
(650) 857-2643 Fax: (650) 852-2920

HOLMES & NARVER, INC.
999 Town and Country Rd.
Orange, CA 92868
Lawrence S. Boval, COO
(714) 567-2505 Fax: (714) 567-2649

HOMEGOODS
Division Of The TJX Companies, Inc.
492-6 Old Connecticut Path
Framingham, MA 01701
Anita Bonelli, Purchasing and Supplies Supervisor
(508) 390-3875 Fax: (508) 390-3963

HONEYWELL, INC.
2701 Fourth Ave. South M/S 12-2128
Minneapolis, MN 55408
Thomas Minor, Supplier Div. Manager
(612) 951-1000

HONEYWELL INTERNATIONAL
Mail Code 1/G20
Route 46
Teterboro, NJ 07608
(201) 393-2545 Fax: (201) 393-6800

HOOPER BECHTEL JACOBS COMPANY LLC
P.O. Box 4699
K1330 Mail Stop 7596
Oak Ridge, TN 37831
Freda H. Hooper, Supplier Advocate Mgr.
(423) 241-1288 Fax: (423) 241-9330

HUGHES ELECTRONICS CORPORATION
P.O. Box Bldg. C01 M/S B145
Los Angeles, CA 90080-0028
Benita Fortner, Corporate SBLO
(310) 847-2312

HUNT BUILDING CORPORATION
4401 N. Mesa #201
El Paso, TX 79902
Linda Moore, SBA Liaison Officer
(915) 533-1122 Fax: (915) 533-0119

HUNTINGTON MEDICAL RESEARCH INSTITUTES
99 W. El Molino
Pasadena, CA 91101
Frank Davis, Business Manager
(626) 795-4343 Fax: (626) 795-5774

IBM CORPORATION
9000 South Rita Rd.
Tucson, AZ 85744
Jevette Jenkins, Buyer, Facilities and Contract Svcs.
(800) 426-4968 Fax: (520) 799-4966

IN SPANISH
333 46 E Ave. # 116
New York, NY 10017
Margarita Leño-Friedman
(212) 490 3919

INTERNATIONAL BUSINESS MACHINES INC. (IBM)
Route 100, Mail Drop 2277
Somers, NY 10589
Phyllis McCarley, Prog. Mgr., Minority Supplier Progs.
(914) 766-2697 Fax: (914) 766-2856

INTERNATIONAL BUSINESS RESOURCES, INC.
1400 E. College Dr.
Cheyenne, WY 82007-3299
Carlos Angel, President
(307) 635-6654

INTERNATIONAL FRANCHISE ASSOCIATION
1350 New York Ave. NW #900
Washington, DC 20005
Marcel Portman, Vice President
(202) 628-8000 Fax: (202) 628-0812

IT CORPORATION
2790 Mosside Blvd.
Monroeville, PA 15146
Debra Borkovich, Corporate SBLO
(800) 444-9586 Fax: (412) 858-3946

ITT CORPORATION
P.O. Box 731
M/S 575
Fort Wayne, IN 46801
Bill Slabach, SBLO
(219) 451-5598 Fax: (219) 451-5628
www.ittind.com/defns/home-fo1.htm
www.ittfsc.com

JC PENNEY COMPANY
Dallas, TX 75301-8122
Susan Maxwell, Mgr.Diversity Dev.
(972) 431-4339 Fax: (972) 431-4896

JOHNSON & JOHNSON
One Johnson & Johnson Plz.
New Brunswick, NJ 08933
(732) 524-0400 Fax: (908) 247-5309

K-MART CORPORATION
3100 W. Big Beaver Rd.
Troy, MI 48084
Richard Cocert, Director
(248) 643-5238 Fax: (248) 637-1771

KAISER PERMANENTE
1950 Franklin
Oakland, CA 94612-3610
Jerilyn Gleaves, Analyst
(510) 596-6110 Fax: (510) 873-5048

KFC
P. O. Box 32070
Louisville, KY 40232-2070
Matt Beeson, Sr. Dir., Strategic Sourcing
(800) 225-5532

KRAFT GENERAL FOODS
3 Lakes Dr.
Glennville, IL 60093-2753
Charles Reid, Dir., Diversity Mgmt.
(847) 646-2000

KRAFT GENERAL FOODS
1 Kraft Court
Glenview, IL 60025
Boris Oglosbille, Director
(847) 646-7774 Fax: (847) 646-0392

LANDMARK CONSTRUCTION
710 N. Plankinton Ave.
Milwaukee, WI 53203-2404
Donald Mantz, President
(414) 274-2800 Fax: (414) 274-2711

LEAR ASTRONICS
3400 Airport Ave.
Santa Monica, CA 90405
Shari Steger, SBLO
(310) 915-6753 Fax: (310) 915-8382

LEVI STRAUSS & COMPANY
Levi's Plaza, 1155 Battery Street
San Francisco, CA 94111
Minority Supplier Development
(415) 501-6000 Fax: (415) 501-3939

LITTON SYSTEMS, INC.
960 Industrial Rd.
San Carlos, CA 94070-4194
Richard L. Greeno, SBLO
(650)591-8411 Fax: (650) 594-9612

LOCKHEED MARTIN
M/S DC9804
Denver, CO 80201
Bob Gartner, SBLO
(303) 971-5775 Fax: (303) 971-2191

LOCKHEED MARTIN
6801 Rockledge Dr.
Bethesda, MD 20817
Charles Mathis, Corporate Director
(301) 897-6000 Fax: (301) 897-6441

LOCKHEED MARTIN
9201 Corporate Blvd.
Rockville, MD 20850
Kent Miller, SBLO
(301) 640-3891 Fax: (301) 460-4055

LOCKHEED MARTIN
P.O. Box 2002
Oak Ridge, TN 37831-9501
Robert Waters, SBLO
(423) 576-2090 Fax: (432) 576-3664

LOCKHEED MARTIN
300 Frank W. Burr Blvd.
Teaneck, NJ 07666
Peter Reyes, SBLO
(201) 996-7021 Fax: (201) 692-0971

LOS ANGELES MINORITY BUSINESS OPPORTUNITY COMMITTEE (LAMBOC)
200 N. Main Street, 8th Floor
City Hall East
Los Angeles, CA 90012
Diane Castaño Sallee
(213) 847-2670 Fax: (213) 473-5649

LUCENT TECHNOLOGIES
P.O. Box 20046
Greensboro, NC 27420
(336) 279-3655 Fax: (336) 279-4953

LUFKIN, DIVISION OF COOPER HAND TOOLS
P.O. Box 728
Apex, NC 27502
Van Milton, Purchasing Mgr.
(919) 387-2385 Fax: (919) 387-2370

MARMAXX GROUP
Division Of The TJX Companies, Inc.
770 Cochituate Rd.
Framingham, MA 01701
Debbie Messier, Mgr. of Purchasing
(508) 390-2329 Fax: (508) 390-2350

MCDONALD'S CORPORATION
1 Kroc Dr., Dept. #147
Oak Brook, IL 60523
Lee Erins, Director, Diversity Dev.
(630) 623-5268

MCDONNELL DOUGLAS AEROSPACE
M/C 1003292
St. Louis, MO 63166
Anna L. Richards, Socio-Economic Exec.
(314) 232-0232 (206) 655-4323

MCI TELECOMMUNICATIONS CORPORATION
701 S. 12th St.
Arlington, VA 22202
Vernestine Davis
(703) 341-6283 Fax: (703) 341-7282

McKESSON BIOSERVICES
14665 Rothgeb Dr.
Rockville, MD 20850
Joan O'Brien, SBLO
(301) 838-9315 Fax: (301) 838-9320

McKESSON CORPORATION
1 Post St. 28th Floor
San Francisco, CA 94104-5295
Brenda Peach, SBLO
(415) 983-8338 Fax: (415) 983-8343

MERCK & COMPANY, INC.
One Merck Dr.
Whitehouse Station, NJ 08889-0100
Larry French
(732) 594-4000

METROPOLITAN LIFE
501 US Hwy. 22
Bridgewater, NJ 08807-2438
(908) 253-1335 Fax: (903) 253-2958

MICROSOFT CORPORATION
1 Microsoft Way
Redmond, WA 98052-6399
Melvin Henderson-Rubio, Prog. Mgr.
(425) 936-4099

MILLER BREWING COMPANY
3939 W. Highland Blvd.
Milwaukee, WI 53201-0482
(414) 931-4451 Fax: (414) 931-2324

MISSISSIPPI SPACE SERVICES
Bldg. 2204
Stennis Space Center, MS 39529-6000
Beverly Nurock, Sr. Contracts Specialist
(228) 688-2010 Fax: (228) 688-2517

MITRE CORPORATION
1820 Dolly Madison Blvd.
Mc Lean, VA 22102-3481
(703) 883-6583

MOBIL OIL CORPORATION
3225 Gallows Rd.
Fairfax, VA 22037
Eugene Renna, President
(703) 846-3000

MONTGOMERY WATSON AMERICAS
1340 Treat Blvd., #300
Walnut Creek, CA 94596
David Leishman, Procurement Manager
(925) 274-5800 Fax: (925) 274-5858

MOTOROLA
1301 East Algonquin Rd., SH5
Schaumburg, IL 60196
Nam Kelly, Supplier Diversity Manager
(847) 576-6485 Fax: (847) 538-2279

NABISCO FOODS GROUP
7 Campus Dr., Plaza 1, Fl. 1
Parsippany, NJ 07054
Ron LeGrand, Dir., Min. Affairs &
Business Development
(973) 682-5000

NAI DIRECT
572 US Route 130
Hightstown, NJ 08520
(609) 448-4700

NATIONAL MINORITY SUPPLIER DEVELOPMENT COUNCIL
15 W. 39th St., 9th Fl.
New York, NY 10018
Harriet Michel, President
(212) 944-2430 Fax: (212) 719-9611

NATIONAL SEMICONDUCTOR CORPORATION
3875 Kifer Rd. W
Santa Clara, CA 95051
(408) 721-5250 Fax: (408) 720-9574

NATIONSBANK
1801 K St. NW, 2nd Fl.
Washington, DC 20006-1396
Patricia Warr, Assist. Vice Pres.
(202) 955-8756

NCR
1700 S. Patterson Blvd. WHQ3
Dayton, OH 45479
Silvia B., Director, Supplier Div. Prog.
(937) 445-1672 Fax: (937) 445-1672

NESTLÉ USA, INC.
800 N. Brand Blvd.
Glendale, CA 91203
Donna Marshall, Mgr., Min. Vending Prog.
(818) 549-6000 Fax: (818) 549-5840

NIKE, INC.
Beaverton, OR 97005
(503) 671-6453 Fax: (503) 671-6300

NORTHROP GRUMMAN CORPORATION
1840 Century Park E.
Los Angeles, CA 90067-2199
Lisa Pollack, SBLO
(310) 201-3023/553-2076
Fax: (310) 201-3000

OCEANEERING INTERNATIONAL INC.
501 Prince George`s Blvd.
Upper Marlboro, MD 20774
Robert McCauley, Purchasing Mgr./SBLO
(301) 249-2457 Fax: (301)249-4022

OLIN CHEMICAL CORPORATION
427 N. Shamrock St.
East Alton, IL 62024-1197
Gregory A. Smith, Small and
Disadvantaged Business Programs
(618) 258-2817 Fax: (618) 258-2861

PACIFIC BELL
San Ramon,, CA 94583
Minority / Women's Bus. Develop.
(510) 823-0470

PACIFIC GAS & ELECTRIC CORPORATION
San Francisco, CA 94177
(415) 973-7000

PEPSI-COLA COMPANY
One Pepsi Way
Somers, NY 10589
(914) 767-6000 Fax: (914) 767-7761

PFIZER, INC.
235 E. 42nd St., 9th Fl.
New York, NY 10017
(212) 573-2323

PHILIP MORRIS COMPANIES, INC.
New York, NY 10017-5592
(212) 878-2457 Fax: (212) 970-5542

PHP FAMILY HEALTH CARE CORPORATION
3041 Olcott St.
Santa Clara, CA 95054
John Wetherell, SBLO
(408) 727-5775 Fax: (408) 727-0182

PITNEY BOWES, INC.
1 Elmcroft Rd. Mail Stop 64-15
Stamford, CT 06926-0700
Henry Hernandez, Director, Business
Diversity Development Programs
(203) 356-5000 Fax: (203) 351-6961

POLAROID CORPORATION
400 Boston Post Rd.
Wayland, MA 01778
(781) 386-2000

POTOMAC ELECTRIC POWER COMPANY (PEPCO)
Washington, DC 20006
Norman Carter, Mgr.
(202) 872-2000 Fax: (202) 872-2032

PRAXAIR, INC.
P.O. Box 44
Tonawanda, NY
Kim Smith, Purchasing Agent
(716) 879-7834 Fax: (716) 879-2344

PRC
1500 PRC Dr. Mail Stop 5S5
McLean, VA 22102-5050
(703) 556-1000 Fax: (703) 556-1534

PROCTER & GAMBLE COMPANY
1 Procter & Gamble Plz.
Cincinnati, OH 45202
(513) 983-1100 Fax: (513) 983-2642

RALPH'S GROCERY COMPANY
Compton, CA 90220
(310) 605-4663

RAYTHEON AIRCRAFT
555 Industrial Dr. South
Madison, MS 39110-9073
(601) 856-2274 Fax: (601) 853-8006

RAYTHEON SYSTEMS
7700 Arlington Blvd.
Falls Church, VA 22042-2900
J. B. Flanagan, SBLO
(703) 849-1565 Fax: (703) 206-0240

REEBOK INTERNATIONAL LTD.
100 Technology Ctr. Dr.
Stoughton, MA 02072
Adrian Williams
(781) 401-5000 Fax: (781) 401-4951

RICOH COPIERS
5 Dedrick Pl.
West Caldwell, NJ 07006
Garry R. Kappmeier, Mgr., Min. Vend. Prog.
(973) 808-7544 Fax: (973) 808-7643

RJ REYNOLDS TOBACCO COMPANY
401 N. Main St.
Winston-Salem, NC 27102
(336) 741-5000

ROCKWELL
4311 Jamboree Rd.
Newport Beach, CA 92660
Jim Hudson, Mgr., Corp. Small Bus. Prog.
(949) 221-7647 Fax: (949) 221-7281

RUBBERMAID, INC.
Wooster, OH 44691
(330) 264-6464

RYDER SYSTEM, INC.
3600 NW 82nd Ave.
Miami, FL 33166
(305) 593-3726

SAFEGUARD BUSINESS SYSTEMS
455 Maryland Dr.
Fort Washington, PA 19034
(215) 641-5032

SAFETY-KLEEN, INC.
902 S. Main St.
Saukville, WI 53080-2118
Phil Bail, SBLO
(262) 268-6716 Fax: (262) 268-6761

SEARS, ROEBUCK & CO.
3333 Beverly Rd., EC-224B
Hoffman State, IL 60179
Carol Marten, Director
(847) 286-6108

SHELL OIL COMPANY
P.O. Box 77252
1 Shell Plaza
Houston, TX 77252
Kieth Jones, Mgr., Supplier Div. Prog.
(713) 241-1844 Fax: (713) 241-8949

SIKORSKY AIRCRAFT
P.O. Box 9727
6900 Main St.
Stratford, CT 06615-9127
Larry Wooton, SBLO
(800) 544-4243 Fax: (203) 383-8628

SILICON GRAPHICS
2011 N. Shoreline Blvd. M/S 231720
Mountain View, CA 94043
(650) 933-3042 Fax: (650) 932-0551

**SMALL BUSINESS CAPITAL
DEVELOPMENT GROUP**
1900 L St. NW #302
Washington, DC 20036
Dewey Thomas, Jr., Pres.
(202) 833-3882 Fax: (202) 785-9199

SMITHKLINE-BEECHAM
One Franklin Plaza
Philadelphia, PA 19102
(800) 366-8900 Fax: (610) 293-3419

SONY MUSIC ENTERTAINMENT, INC.
550 Madison Ave.
New York, NY 10022-3211
(212) 833-8000

**SOUTH FLORIDA WATER
MANAGEMENT DISTRICT**
West Palm Beach, FL 33406
Carolin Williams
(561) 687-6335 Fax: (561) 687-6397

SOUTHERN CALIFORNIA EDISON
P.O. Box 600
Rosemead, CA 91771
(800) 427-2200 Fax: (626) 302-5325

**SOUTHERN CALIFORNIA GAS
COMPANY**
555 W. 5th St, ML 18E1
Los Angeles,, CA 90013
(800) 427-2200

**SOUTHLAND CORPORATION/
7 ELEVEN**
Dallas, TX 75221-0711
Janey Camacho, Consumer Hisp. Affair Mgr.
(214) 828-7011 Fax: (214) 828-7512
www.7-eleven.com

SPRINT CORPORATION
903 East 104St.
Kansas City, MO 64131-5409
Terry Smelcer, Mgr., Supplier Diversity
(913) 624-6000 Fax: (816) 854-5804

STATE FARM INSURANCE
8491 South Old Kings Rd.

Jacksonville, FL 32217
Elisabeth Winckler
(904) 886-2695

STONE CONTAINER CORPORATION
150 N. Michigan Ave.
Chicago, IL 60601
Deborah Jurgenson, Corporate Buyer,
Supplier Diversity Program.
(312) 580-3574 Fax: (312) 649-4294

STORAGE TECHNOLOGY CORP.
1 Storage Tek Dr.
Louisville , Co 80028
Faith A. Magill, Subcontracting Admin.
(303) 673-5151 Fax: (303) 673-4945

SVERDRUP
13723 Riverport Dr.
Maryland Heights, MO 63043
Gabrielle M. Mack, Dir., Div. & M/WBE
(314) 436-7600 Fax: (314)770-5120

SYSCO FOOD SERVICES
P.O. Box 310
Ocoee, FL 34761-0310
Don Kermmoade, Vice Pres., Marketing
and Merchandising
(407) 877-1417 Fax: (407) 656-8977

TACO BELL
17901 Von Karman
Irvine, CA 92614
Dal Holden
(949) 863-4730

TEXACO
Bellaire, TX 77402-2550
Pat Richards, Corp. Coord.
(713) 666-8000

TEXAS INSTRUMENTS
P O. Box 660199
M/S 8603
Dallas, TX 75266
Richard Stouffer, Director, Minority/
Women Business Development
(800) 336-5236 Fax: (972) 480-7564

THE TJX COMPANIES, INC.
770 Cochituate Road
Framingham, MA 01701
Mike Brogan, Mgr.
(508) 390-2556 Fax: (508) 390-2680

TOM BROWN & COMPANY
1090 Vermont Ave. NW #800
Washington, DC 20005
Tom Brown, President
(202) 393-7755 Fax: (703) 318-7177

TOM BROWN & COMPANY
620 Herndon Pkwy., #200
Herndon, VA 22070-0684
Tom Brown, President
(703) 318-8181

TOWILL, INC.
5075 Commercial Circle, Ste. F
Concord, CA 94520
(925) 682-6976 Fax: (925) 682-6390

TRW
1 Space Park
Redondo Beach, CA 90278-1071
Kit NcNamara, Small Bus. Program
Administrator
(310) 812-4617 Fax: (310) 813-5599

**TURNER CONSTRUCTION
CORPORATION**
4601 N. Fairfax Dr. #900
Arlington, VA 22203
Deborah H. Cook, SBLO
(703) 841-5239 Fax: (703) 841-5209

UNIDYNE CORPORATION
3835 Princess Anne Rd.
Norfolk, VA 23502
Bobbi Brown, Manager, Material/SBLO
(757) 855-8037 Fax: (757) 853-3046

UNITED DEFENSE LP
4800 E. River Rd.
Minneapolis, MN 55421
Marv Kolling, Small and Disadvantaged
Business Liason
(763) 572-6802 Fax: (612) 571-3089

UNYSIS CORPORATION
8008 W. Park Dr.
McLean, VA 22102
Murray J. Schooner, Director,
Socio-Economic Business Development
(703)556-5000 Fax: (703) 620-1442

VIAD CORP
1850 N. Central Ave.
Phoenix, AZ 85077-2452
Angela Phoenix, Corporate
Communication Mgr.
(602) 207-5608 Fax: (602)207-5900

WALT DISNEY ATTRACTIONS
P.O. Box 10,000
Lake Buena Vista, FL 32830-1000
Thomas Flewellyn, Director
(407) 828-4136

WASHINGTON GAS
6801 Industrial Rd.
Springfield, VA 22151
Denitra Byrum, Analyst
(703) 750-7509 Fax: (703) 750-4424

**WESTINGHOUSE ELECTRIC
CORPORATION**
Baltimore, MD 21203
Darleen Eathly, Mgr., Socio-economic
Programs
(410) 765-8269

XEROX CORPORATION
800 Philips Rd., Bldg., 205-99P
Webster, NY 14580
Dan Robinson, Mgr.
(716) 422-2295 Fax: (716) 231-5895

YELLOW FREIGHT SYSTEM
10990 Roe Ave.
Overland Park, KS 66211
Barbara Adams, Dir.Purchasing
(913) 344-3000

The United States Department of Defense
Committed to Opportunities for Small Disadvantaged Businesses

As a critical component of our nation's industrial base, the U.S. Department of Defense (DoD) is committed to developing and maintaining opportunities for Small, Small Disadvantaged, and Women-Owned Businesses to achieve economic growth and prosperity. This commitment is demonstrated through a number of resources and program that foster and encourage full participation in the DoD procurement process.

Office of Small and Disadvantaged Business Home Page (www.sadbu.com)
> The Office of Small and Disadvantaged Business Utilization (OSADBU) Home Page is an on-line resource for a variety of information on procurement, subcontracting, and many other topics. Many of the publications can be downloaded to a personal computer.

Women-Owned Small Business Website (www.sadbu/wosb.com)
> This site provides assistance to Women-Owned Small Businesses seeking procurement opportunities with the DoD and other Government Agencies. Features include technical assistance, procurement guides, lists of trade association, and useful information about identifying potential sources for future prime and subcontracting opportunities.

Mentor-Protégé Program (www.sadbu/mentor-protégé.com)
> The Mentor-Protégé Program (MPP) provides incentives for major DoD contractors to assist Small Disadvantaged Businesses by providing training, technical resources, and subcontracting opportunities. For more information, call the toll-free information hotline: (800)-553-1858.

Small Business Innovation Research (SBIR) and Small Business Technology Transfer (STTR) programs (www.sadbu/sbir)
> The SBIR program provides more than a half a billion dollars each year in funding for early stage research and development (R&D) at small technology companies. These are designed to meet DoD needs and present the potential for commercialization in the private sector or other public sector markets. The DoD's SBIR program is a part of a larger SBIR program administered by 10 Federal Agencies.

> Similar in structure to SBIR program, the STTR program funds cooperative R&D projects involving a small business with one of the following entities: a university, a federally-funded R&D center, or a non-profit research institution. The DoD's STTR program is part of a larger federal STTR program administered by five federal agencies.

> For more information about SBIR and STTR programs, call SBA general program information line at (202) 205-6450, or the toll-free DoD SBIR/STTR Help Desk: (800)-382-4634.

Procurement Technical Assistance Centers (PTAC): www.dla.mil/ddas/procurem.htm
> Almost 100 Procurement Technical Assistance Centers are available throughout the country. Each center provides in-depth counseling to small business concerns at minimal or no cost. The counseling ranges from marketing and finance, to contracting and electronic commerce. For a listing of PTAC centers in your state, visit the Website at www.dla.mil/ddas/procurem.htm

Historically Underutilized Business Zone (HUB Zone) Program
> To provide federal contracting assistance for qualified small business concerns located in HUB Zones in an effort to increase employment opportunities, investment, and economic development in such areas.

The Comprehensive Subcontracting Plan (CSP) Program
> The DoD Comprehensive Subcontracting Plan Test Program initiated to determine whether or not the negotiation and administration of comprehensive ("company-wide") small business subcontracting plans, rather than individual small business subcontracting plans, will reduce administrative burdens on contractors while enhancing subcontracting opportunities for small business concerns owned and controlled by socially and economically disadvantaged individuals under DoD contracts.

The Historically Black College and Universities and Minority Institutions (HBCU/ MI) Program
> The Department of Defense (DoD) Small and Disadvantaged Business Utilization (SADBU) office (HBCU/ MI) program gives technical assistance to enable participating minority institutions to enhance their ability to participate in a multitude of DoD initiatives, educational programs, research and development efforts, and other selected contract/grant opportunities.

Women Owned
Small Business

SBIR

Small Business
Innovative Research

The United States Department
(DoD)
Small and Disadvantaged Business Utili

DoD is committed to opportunities for small disadvantaged bu
is demonstrated through a wide variety of programs, such as SB
WOSB, CSP, HBCU/MI, HUBZones and the Mentor-Pr

Top 500 Hispanic Businesses for 20

65. MEVATEC - Nancy E. Archuleta, C

108. Technico Corp.22 - Rafael Torrech,

135. Excel Professional Services Inc. - Annette Q

161. HJ Ford Associates Inc. - Don Jorge Ald

191. Vista Technologies Inc. - Armando

212. Diez Software Services - Robert

269. Cape Environmental Management Inc. -

408. Wendy Lopez & Associates Inc. - W

467. Fiore Industries Inc. - Bill A.

Source: Hispanic Business Magazine, Jan

We have been fortunate to team with aggre
such as Mentor-Protégé Program participant
500 Hispanic Businesses for 2000. We cong
to working with growing Hispanic businesse
our men and women in uniform!

Robert L. Neal, Jr., Director, SADBU

SADBU has what your business is missi
www.sadbu.com

USCG Compass Prog
The Coast Guard
Community Outre
Initiative

Gente Normal,
Héroes Diarios.

U.S. COAST GUARD & COAST GUARD RESERVE

se buscan héroes.

Si eres bilingüe y deseas más información
sobre las oportunidades del U.S. Coast Guard
y la Reserva del Coast Guard llama al:

1-877-NOW-USCG

o visita **www.uscg.mil/jobs**

Marine Corps
Infantería de Marina

A MESSAGE FROM THE COMMANDANT OF THE MARINE CORPS

During the United States' ascendancy in the often-turbulent events of the last century, Marines were ever-present, exerting influence far beyond the expected of a Corps so few in number. Marines protected America's interests, struggled against foes who attempted to do our country harm, and remained at the forefront of the nation's efforts to maintain global peace and stability. From the defense of the Peking Legation to operations in Kosovo, the 20th century witnessed Marines " in ev'ry clime and place," helping the United States grow from a fledging world power to the only remaining superpower. In two World Wars, the corps marched to victory against powerful enemies. In Korea, Vietnam and Kuwait, Marines fought valiantly for our friends who sought to live in peace. In hundreds of distant lands, from Nicaragua to Lebanon to Somalia, Marines restored and maintained order, aided people in distress, provided protection for the weak, and upheld the values that have come to define our country and distinguish it on the world stage.

The Americans who accomplished these noble deeds came from communities throughout our great land. Many of these heroes were of Hispanic descent. In 1968, Sergeant Alfredo Gonzales earned our nation's highest military award, the Medal of Honor, for his heroic actions while serving as a platoon commander in Vietnam. Like him, Hispanic Marines have consistently exemplified the qualities of honor, courage, and commitment we work so hard to develop in every Marine. In total, thirteen other Hispanic Marines have earned the Medal of Honor. Their heroic achievements epitomize the dedicated, faithful service of the many thousands of Hispanic Americans in our Marine Corps and, indeed, all the military services.

As you consider your plans for the future, I urge you to consider how you will "give something back" to our great nation. Whether it is through military service or leadership in the community, your civic involvement is instrumental to our collective efforts to achieve America's full promise. I wish you the very best. May God bless you!

J.L. JONES
General, U.S. Marine Corps

The Enlisted Marine and The Marine Officer

El enlistado y el Oficial de la Infantería Marina

The Enlisted Marine

The United States Marine Corps is the nation's Force in Readiness. The Marines respond on a moment's notice to any contingency facing our nation, from humanitarian assistance to combat. They are tough and trained to provide instant action from the air, land, and sea.

The Marine Corps combines air and ground units into a unique and capable fighting force called the Marine Air-Ground Task Force (MAGTF). It has capabilities unlike any other single military service.

MAGTF operations provide the nation with an unmatched combination of air, land, and sea forces. The foundation for MAGTF operations is built upon expeditionary readiness and operations, combined arms and sea-based forcible entry. They define a force that has the flexibility to be employed anywhere to accomplish the entire range of military missions, either independently or as part of a joint warfighting team. Being able to quickly deploy forces to distant areas of operation with the precise capabilities necessary to accomplish the mission is the Marine Corps' forte.

That's what MAGTF operations are all about, using the right size force with the right set of skills to get the job done rapidly with the appropriate amount of force re-quired. To accomplish this, MAGTF operations rely upon scalable task organizations, building upon whatever force is "first on the scene" until the capabilities necessary to accomplish the mission are available. This unique building-block approach conserves both Marine combat power and scarce defense resources.

Since MAGTF operations depend so much on the ability to be first on the scene, Marine Expeditionary Units (MEU) are among the most highly trained elements of the Marine Corps and carry a designator of Special Operations Capable (SOC). To earn this designation, each MEU undergoes an intensive 26-week standardized pre-deployment training program. Pro-

gressive improvements and unit skills allow the MEU to execute a full range of conventional operations from humanitarian assistance to combat. It takes special individuals to be trained for these tasks and special training to transform civilians into Marines.

High school graduates can excel through enlistment as Marines. After they take off their graduation cap to wear a Marine cover, they'll find they've stepped into the elite. Marine standards are tough — beyond those set for all services by the Department of Defense.

Marines seek the highest quality young men and women. They enlist high school graduates, 17-28 years of age, who are physically, mentally and morally sound. They seek out

those who are on the right path — who have stayed away from drug abuse and criminal backgrounds. If someone qualifies, the Marines may offer him or her the chance to be transformed into a Marine.

That's just what they get — a chance. Earning the title Marine isn't an easy mark. Those who enlist attend the toughest training in the military today — Marine Corps recruit training. Going through this rite of passage, they're trained, pushed and honed physically and mentally. They learn the Marine ethos and core values. They find their inner strengths and learn what it means to be part of an elite team.

No matter what their occupation, every Marine attends 12 weeks of boot camp and four weeks of Marine Combat Training. Afterwards, their training continues in one of many occupational fields. They may find themselves as an infantryman, military policeman, a computer network administrator or an air traffic controller. Photography, writing, map reading, microwave technology, and intelligence gathering are just a few of the many Marine Military Occupational Specialties (MOS). All Marines receive regular pay, medical and dental care, meals, housing and thirty days of paid vacation per year.

Once they've become a Marine and decided college might be in their future, the Marine Corps provides financial assistance. The Corps offers Marines many educational programs that are discussed later in this article.

Just like earning the title Marine, pride is something every Marine earns. The pride that comes from being a Marine stays with them the rest of their lives. The pride of belonging to the Marine Corps is instilled in everyone who wears the uniform.

Marines develop a highly spirited drive to excel at everything they do. Marine training teaches the moral courage to do what everyone knows is right. Marines are self-starters. They are independent people who take charge of their lives. They believe in themselves and in getting the job done!

Marines seek out challenges at every opportunity. Challenges make life exciting and worthwhile. When faced with awesome challenges, it takes more than strength alone to conquer such adversities. Learning to solve difficult problems requires using imagination and initiative. Developing the ability to adapt quickly to changing situations is a Marine trademark. Through recruit training, a Marine's mettle is tempered to withstand the stresses of future challenges.

The Marine Officer

Leading Marines is not an easy task. It takes special leaders to make Marine missions a success.

In many companies, it takes years to prove someone's leadership ability. The Marines give officer candidates as little as 10 weeks. They're looking for men and women who are tough, smart and determined — who believe they can be leaders.

College freshmen or sophomores may start the climb to a Marine Corps commission through the Platoon Leaders Class (PLC), which consists of two six-week summer training sessions, at the Officer Candidates School (OCS) in Quantico, Va. Juniors may begin their training with a 10-week session. A student's academic studies continue with no interruption during the school year and they incur no obligation to accept a commission under PLC.

College graduates attend one ten-week training session at OCS. Upon successful completion of training at OCS, all candidates are commissioned second lieutenants and attend The Basic School (TBS), also at Quantico. New officers spend six months polishing their leadership skills and learning offensive and defensive ground combat tactics.

Once officers complete TBS, they must decide on one of more than 36 occupational specialties in which they'll receive training based upon their qualifications and class standing. As early as their freshman year, the Marines can guarantee applicants a chance to become an aviator if fully qualified.

If someone has been accepted to an accredited law school, they delay TBS training until they graduate, and continue training with their Officer Selection Officer as part of the PLC Law program.

As an officer of Marines, they receive competitive pay, promotional opportunities, medical and dental care and thirty days of paid vacation each year. The travel is tremendous and there are opportunities to be assigned at many Marine Corps bases around the United States or overseas.

Educational Opportunities

Oportunidades de educación

The strength of the Marine Corps has always been the individual Marine. In that tradition all Marines find that their personal and educational development go hand-in-hand with their growth as Marines. If they have the interest and determination to pursue educational goals, while on active duty or after their enlistment, the Marine Corps has educational programs to assist.

The first step in the continuing education process is a career in the Marine Corps. With programs at over 100 vocational schools, Marines gain valuable skills and train to become a specialist or technician in over 300 jobs in various occupational fields.

Marines have the opportunity to complete an Apprenticeship Program, earn college credits, or even receive a commission as an officer of Marines. When they earn the title United States Marine, they also earn the opportunity to set and fulfill new goals and ambitions. To assist them, every Marine Corps command has an educational services officer who helps them take advantage of the educational programs available.

The Montgomery GI Bill

The Montgomery GI Bill provides up to $23,400 towards a college degree or technical education at any college, university or technical school approved by the Veterans Administration. It's an outstanding opportunity for Marines to further their education or training.

Recruits are automatically enrolled during their first month of recruit training, unless they choose not to participate. Once their decision is made, it cannot be changed. While enrolled in the program, $100 per month is automatically deducted from their pay for 12 months for a total of $1,200.

Upon completion of their service requirements they can draw up to $650 a month for 36 months while enrolled as a full-time student. If they choose to enroll as a part-time student while fulfilling their service requirement, they can draw on their accumulated funds at a reduced rate.

Marine College Fund

The Marine College Fund (MCF) takes the MGIB and adds additional dollars for a total of $50,000 towards a college education. Qualified Marines are paid a maximum of $1,389 a month for 36 months.

To qualify for the MCF, an applicant must score in the upper half of the military written entrance examination and sign up for the MGIB. Marines do not make contributions to MCF, however, MGIB participation still requires a $1,200 contribution.

Tuition Assistance

While on active duty, Marines may attend part time classes after working hours using Tuition Assistance (TA) that pays 75% of the tuition. The total TA per year is $3,500; so on a four-year enlistment a Marine has $14,000 to use while on active duty.

Professional Military Education

The military is a profession just like any other. Just as doctors, lawyers, teachers and airline pilots must continue their education process to maintain their skills, Marines must participate in Professional Military Education (PME). This includes Marine Corps Institute (MCI)

courses, resident training programs, and the Commandant's Reading Program to enhance Marines professionally as they advance in rank.

MCI offers over 180 skill courses to further a Marine's knowledge of leadership, skill, or occupation. Each program is set up like a correspondence course with requirements and a certificate upon completion, but scheduling and participation are flexible to the needs of the individual Marine.

There is no limit to your participation, and while these programs are designed for application in your military career, 40 percent of each course counts as college credits approved by the American Council of Education. In addition, completion of MCI courses can earn Marines points that count toward promotion.

The second leg of PME are the resident programs that focus on developing the noncommissioned officer, staff noncommissioned officer, and company and field grade officer in leadership and staff functions. Programs range from the Corporals Course for corporals to the War College for lieutenant colonels and colonels.

The final PME leg is the Commandant's Reading Program, a list of books selected to expand the understanding of historical and present day military strategy and tactics. The list is divided into rank specific groups based upon content and scope.

Broadened Opportunity for Officer Selection and Training

Enlisted Marines, with the rank of lance corporal or above, may qualify for the Broadened Opportunity for Officer Selection and Training (BOOST) program.

If selected, they will attend a ten-month prep school. It is designed to help them acquire the academic disciplines needed to complete a college degree and possibly an appointment to the United States Naval Academy, a Naval Reserve Officer Training Corps (NROTC) Scholarship or acceptance into the Marine Corps Enlisted Commissioning Education Program (MECEP).

Naval Academy Prep Program

This program helps outstanding enlisted Marines embark on officer careers by aiding their preparation for the rigorous college curriculum of the United States Naval Academy.

MECEP

Marine corporals or above may apply for MECEP. If accepted, they will attend a college of their choice where an NROTC program resides. Applicants can choose other colleges or universities that do not have NROTC units if their institution has an agreement with the local NROTC unit to support students. Upon obtaining a bachelor's degree and OCS graduation, the Marine will be commissioned a second lieutenant.

NROTC

The NROTC Scholarship program is open to any high school senior, regular or reserve enlisted Marine who meets the eligibility requirements.

Marines selected will attend one of more than 60 colleges and universities hosting an NROTC unit. They will be transferred to the nearest Marine Corps command and be temporarily released from their active duty obligation.

The scholarship pays for tuition, cost of textbooks, and fees of an instructional nature and a subsistence allowance of $200 per month for a maximum of 40 academic months. Upon completion, they will receive a commission as a second lieutenant.

Continuing Education

Transfers and moving are a regular part of life in the Marine Corps. So is the opportunity for personal improvement. That is why the Marine Corps has developed programs to help Marines continue their studies or training without losing credits.

Each program is fully accredited and makes advanced education available and easily accessible. In addi-

tion, most Marine Corps bases offer Marines the opportunity to take various courses on base.

National institutions with top reputations administer continuing education curriculums. In many cases, colleges will grant Marines credit for certain military training and approved military correspondence study. They can also receive credit for assignments completed in the line of duty.

Apprenticeship Program

Marines can take advantage of an outstanding trade program and earn "journeyman" status. The Apprenticeship Program is sanctioned by the Department of Labor and is excellent for Marines to gain documented experience in their field. To qualify, they must be on active duty and in an MOS. With formal training, documented work experience, and the required number of hours on the job, the Department of Labor grants Marines a Certificate of Completion and "journeyman" status.

A Marine's apprenticeship training not only benefits them while they're active in the Marine Corps, it also gives them experience that will put them ahead in their trade after retirement or once they leave the Corps.

Staff Degree Completion Program

This program provides staff noncommissioned officers an opportunity to keep pace with new technologies, and to pursue a bachelor's degree or other personal and professional educational goal that fulfills Marine Corps requirements.

Other Educational Assistance

The Marine Corps offers many educational opportunities designed to help you reach your full potential. SAT, ACT, and CLEP exams for college/university admissions and college credit are administered free through testing centers located on base.

Equivalency for Technical School Training helps Marines receive civilian school credit for military training. Basic Skills Education Program is offered during on duty time in academic skills related to enhancing performance in MOSs.

Service members Opportunity Colleges

Marine (SOCMAR) is the Marine Corps' degree program that, from virtually anywhere in the world, can help Marines get the college degree they are seeking. In the two-year program, accredited colleges offer associate degrees on or at locations accessible from Marine Corps installations worldwide.

With the four-year program, Marines can have their bachelor's degree. Over 30 colleges and universities have joined together in a network so that each member college accepts credits from the others. This guarantees Marines the opportunity to continue advancement toward their degree whether they are at home, in a remote location, or at sea.

For more information on the Marine Corps or Marine Corps opportunities, please contact the nearest Marine recruiting office, or dial 1-800-MARINES or visit their web site at **http://www.MARINES.com**

District Recruiting Headquarters

1st Marine Corps District Public Affairs Officer
605 Stewart Ave.
Garden City, NY 11530-4761
(516) 228-5640/1/2 Fax: (516) 228-5794

4th Marine Corps District Public Affairs Officer
Building 54, Suite 3, P.O. Box 806
New Cumberland, PA 17070-0806
(717) 770-4647 Fax: (717) 770-4684

6th Marine Corps District Public Affairs Officer
P.O. Box 19021
Parris Island, S.C. 29905-9201
(843) 228-2614 Fax: (843) 228-3383

8th Marine Corps District Public Affairs Officer
Building 10, Naval Support Activity
New Orleans, LA 70142-5100
(504) 678-2356 Fax: (504) 678-2347

9th Marine Corps District Public Affairs Officer
3805 E 155th St. Dyes Hall
Kansas City, KS 66147
(816) 843-3927/8 Fax: (816) 843-3984

12th Marine Corps District Public Affairs Officer
3704 Hochmuth Ave.
San Diego, CA 92140-5191
(619) 542-5517 Fax: (619) 542-5520

We're your headquarters for federal government travel. Our domestic and international routes on US Airways,®
US Airways Express,® US Airways Shuttle® and MetroJet℠ by US Airways offer more than 1,000 contract
fares to federal government agencies. In addition, you can experience Envoy Class,® our award-winning
business class, on all transatlantic flights. To make your mission possible, call your contracted travel agency
or US Airways at 1-800-428-4322.

≡ U·S AIRWAYS

NAVY

La Armada

Navy Recruiting and the Navy Recruiting Command

Our seas and coastlines are protected by the highly trained, motivated Sailors of the United States Navy. Everyday, Sailors are involved in missions that take them to the farthest reaches of the world. Whether it's preparing the ship for a cruise to the Mediterranean Sea, or standing watch on the bow of an aircraft carrier as F/A 18's are launching before your eyes, the Navy is always moving.

For those assigned to the Navy Recruiting Command, the mission is simple, to recruit the best and the brightest men and women to meet the Navy's needs for Sailors. Navy Recruiting Command is dedicated to recruiting highly qualified people for today's Navy. We are actively hiring. The Navy currently has nearly 60,000 new jobs available for men and women annually in more than 60 different career fields. The number of jobs available is expected to remain the same in the foreseeable future.

Men and women in today's Navy work daily with some of the most sophisticated equipment on the market, getting experience that cannot be matched by most civilian employers. Navy technical training is followed by immediate hands on experience in the workplace. To compete in the work force of the future, young people need-on-the-job technical training, and the Navy provides that.

Many Navy career opportunities are in highly technical fields such as aviation, electronics, computer systems and nuclear propulsion with guaranteed training in state-of-the art Navy technical schools.

While getting the experience of a lifetime working in the Navy, Sailors and officers also have the opportunity to complete an undergraduate or graduate degree through the Tuition Assistance Program. Tuition Assistance covers up to 75 percent of tuition costs for service members on active duty. The Navy also assists with education after leaving the active service. For those who qualify, the Montgomery G. I. Bill provides up to $14,676 for college education for Navy veterans. When combined with the Navy College Fund, up to $50,000 is available in college benefits.

The Navy College Program (NCP) offers a flexible way to earn an advanced education, at little or no cost to Sailors. There is no application fee, no minimum test score required for admission, and no tuition deposit required. The NCP allows you to pursue a degree tailored to your specific area of expertise, helping you enhance your current skill set. A wide variety of tutoring and assistance is readily available, and the Navy will issue transcripts for you, assuring that college credits have been earned.

Tech Prep is currently available at colleges across the nation. Tech Prep gives high school juniors and seniors the opportunity to earn up to 15 semester hours of college credits. Upon graduation, students attend community college to earn additional 15 credits and then enter active duty. From basic training designated technical schools, Sailors will have completed requirements for an associate's degree in Electronics Engineering Technology or Manufacturing Technology.

The Navy has great programs for those who want to complete their college degree before entering the service. The Naval Academy is a fully subsidized, four-year undergraduate educational program, in which students are paid a monthly Navy salary while obtaining their degrees.

Naval Reserve Officers' Training Corps Scholarship Program, for those who qualify, provides a scholarship package like no other, followed by a commission as a naval officer. For those selected, the program offers tuition and other financial benefits up to $80,000 in college costs at more than 60 of the country's leading colleges and universities. Two, three and four-year scholarships are offered, and participants also receive monthly cash allowances.

For talented young people who need assistance in meeting all of the academic requirements for the Academy or NROTC, the Navy offers the Broadened Opportunity for Officer Selection and Training Program (BOOST) and the Naval Academy Preparatory School (NAPS). Young men and women who qualify embark on a rigorous curriculum to develop the skills necessary to succeed in college. Armed with that base, BOOST and NAPS students continue their education while developing the skills necessary to become future leaders of the Navy.

Being a leader in today's Navy takes more than a good education. It takes dedication and commitment. Equal opportunity in the Navy guarantees that the best qualified individuals will be where they are needed the most.

Equal opportunity goes beyond the Navy's insistence on fair treatment for all within each command. With the repeal of the combat exclusion law, new opportunities are open for women in the Navy, including a variety of shipboard jobs aboard carriers and combatants and in aviation squadrons. Now, approximately 97% of Navy enlisted and officer career fields and the associated technical training are open to women.

The Navy has many opportunities for everyone. From aviation to information technology, the Navy has a job for you.

Navy medicine is a special world- a high-tech world of adventure and opportunities in health care delivery with an exciting lifestyle. Recruiting tomorrow's Navy medical team continues to present special challenges in attracting health professionals who are in demand by the civilian sector. Navy medicine offers a professional life with steady advancement, variety and challenge - a career in which medical skills play a vital role in the future of our nation.

At no other time in our history has the Navy been able to boast about a higher quality of recruits, both men and women, than it can today. The technology demands of the high-tech fleet require top-notch recruits with strong math and science backgrounds. The Navy remains committed to maintaining high entrance standards for applicants, ensuring that new recruits can "hit the deck plates running." Staying in school and getting an education are some of the points the Navy stresses.

Naval service is an excellent way to prepare for the future. High-tech training on state-of-the art equipment and opportunities to further your education are just a few of the "perks" offered by the Navy.

If you or anyone you know is interested in learning more about the Navy and what the Navy can offer you, contact your local Navy recruiter.

TIYM Congratulates the USO on their 60th Anniversary as they continue to "Deliver America" to the men and women in uniform

USO Hosted a Gala to Celebrate 60 Years of Service

On Sunday, February 4, 2001, the legendary USO (United Service Organizations) which "Delivers America" to United States service men and women serving around the globe celebrated its 60th anniversary with a gala at the Washington Hilton & Towers in Washington, DC. This Congressionally chartered organization is best known for bringing a "Touch of Home" to the American military by providing morale, welfare and recreation-type services since World War II.

To commemorate the sixty years of service, the USO gala was full of celebrity entertainment and military fanfare, which included special recognition of a "hero" from each branch of the Armed Forces, including a special tribute to a crew member of the USS COLE. In addition, members of the Joint Chiefs of Staff, other senior representatives of the Department of Defense, top government officials, corporate leaders and members of Congress attend. Special guest Janet Cohen, wife of former Secretary of Defense William Cohen and Ross Perot also attended the black tie event.

The USO presentation its most prestigious honor, the "Spirit of Hope" Award, to the United Services Automobile Association (USAA) and Frau Helga Haub, of the Great Atlantic Pacific Tea Company, in recognition of their years of advocacy for the men and women of the Armed Forces.

Entertainment for the gala was provided by renowned country/gospel group "The Oak Ridge Boys" and newcomer country singer Craig Morgan. Legendary pop icon Carole King was the headliner for the black-tie event, and Ruth Pointer sang the national anthem. Alex Trebek, host of the popular game show *Jeopardy!* served as Master of Ceremonies.

The USO is chartered by Congress as a non-profit charitable corporation, and is not a part of the United States Government. It is endorsed by the President of the United States, the Congress and the Secretary of Defense. Each President has been the Honorary Chairman of the USO since its inception.

The USO serves our Armed Forces through a network of more than 115 USO Centers at major airports, overseas cyber cafes, mobile canteens, family centers and a program of celebrity entertainment and handshake tours to America's military worldwide.

For 60 years, the United Service Organizations (USO) has "Delivered America" to America's military personnel – America's finest. The USO is a Congressionally chartered, nonprofit organization, and is not a government agency. The USO is supported by World Partners AT&T, USAA, Nicorette/NicoDerm CQ, BAE SYSTEMS and Yahoo!, corporate donors such as Northwest Airlines, General Dynamics, and Anheuser-Busch, the United Way and Combined Federal Campaign (CFC-0600), as well as contributions from individuals. For more information on contributing to the USO, please call 1-800-876-7469 or visit our Web site at www.uso.org.

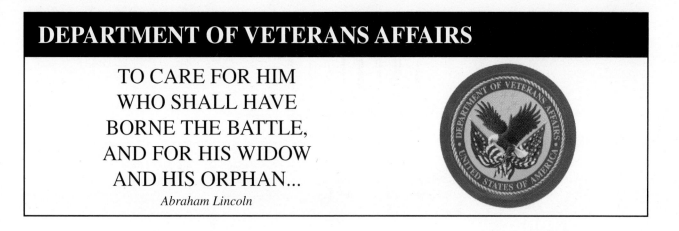

National Internship Program

The Hispanic Association of Colleges and Universities (HACU) National Internship Program works with the Department of Veterans Affairs (VA) to recruit well-qualified, motivated college students into VA. The Department's internship program provides a quality, professional, learning experience that helps students make educated career choices. VA also supports Histori- cally Black Colleges and Universities (HBCUs), People With Disabilities Program, and the Washington Intern- ship for Native Stu- dents (WINS).

From Left to right: Yvonne Ballasteros, University of California, Los Angeles, Marianne Carreras-Paz, University of Indiana, and Zoe Santiago, University of Puerto Rico

For additional information on internship opportunities, please visit www.hacu.net, http://www.hacu.net/, www.nafeo.org, http://www.nafeo.org/, or call the American University WINS Program office at (202) 895-4967.

For information on VA's People With Disabilities Internship Program, contact the Office of Diversity Management and EEO at (202) 273-5888.

AFRICAN
AMERICAN
YEARBOOK

March 27, 2001

Ms. Angela E. Zavala
President & CEO
TIYM Publishing Co., Inc.
6718 Whittier Ave., #130
McLean, VA 22101

Dear Ms. Zavala:

I would like to congratulate you on the 15th anniversary of this publication, the ANUARIO HISPANO-HISPANIC YEARBOOK. I want to also express my most sincere appreciation and gratitude for this publication, as it has enhanced my knowledge and understanding of the Hispanic community and its contribution to the United States. As a non-Hispanic, the ANUARIO HISPANO-HISPANIC YEARBOOK is an invaluable resource that has a permanent place in my reference library. I have also made sure that I share this resource with my friends, both personal and professional.

On a different note, I want to thank you for inviting me to participate, as Publisher, in the creation of the AFRICAN-AMERICAN YEARBOOK . We will continue the tradition of excellence established by the ANUARIO HISPANO-HISPANIC YEARBOOK, by sharing our culture, history, resources, and information about African Americans and our continuing contributions to American Society.

The AFRICAN-AMERICAN YEARBOOK will provide African Americans with exclusive content not presently found in any one source. We will improve and grow with the experiences of the ANUARIO HISPANO-HISPANIC YEARBOOK and present accurate, reliable, and relevant data and information. The ANUARIO HISPANO-HISPANIC YEARBOOK and the AFRICAN-AMERICAN YEARBOOK are unique tools that will research and develop much needed material, in the areas of business, education, and health. I am humbled and honored to be a part of this collaboration.

A special thanks to the TIYM Publishing Co., Inc. family.

Sincerely,

Samuel E. Miller
Publisher

TIYM Publishing Co., Inc.
6718 Whittier Avenue, Suite 130 • McLean, VA 22101 • (703) 734-1632 • Fax: (703) 356-0787 • E-mail: tiym@aol.com
http://www.tiym.com

US Trade with Latin America and the Caribbean
Intercambio comercial de EUA con América Latina y el Caribe

(US Billions; Total Exports F.A.S.; General Imports Customs Value)

Countries	1992 Exp	1992 Imp	1992 BOT	1993 Exp	1993 Imp	1993 BOT	1994 Exp	1994 Imp	1994 BOT	1995 Exp	1995 Imp	1995 BOT	1996 Exp	1996 Imp	1996 BOT	1997 Exp	1997 Imp	1997 BOT	1998 Exp	1998 Imp	1998 BOT	1999 Exp	1999 Imp	1999 BOT
Argentina	3.22	1.25	1.97	3.77	1.5	2.57	4.46	1.72	2.74	4.18	1.76	2.42	4.51	2.27	2.23	5.81	2.28	3.53	5.88	2.23	3.65	4.94	2.59	2.35
Bolivia	.22	.16	.06	.22	.19	.03	.184	.26	-.076	.213	.262	-.049	.26	.27	-.005	.29	.23	.06	.41	.24	.17	.29	.22	.07
Brazil	5.75	7.60	-1.85	6.05	7.47	-1.42	8.10	8.68	-.58	11.43	8.82	2.61	12.7	8.77	3.94	15.91	9.62	6.29	15.14	10.10	5.04	13.20	11.31	1.88
Chile	2.46	1.38	1.08	2.59	1.46	1.13	2.77	1.82	.95	3.61	1.93	1.68	4.13	2.26	1.87	4.36	2.29	2.07	3.97	2.45	1.52	3.07	2.95	.12
Colombia	3.28	2.83	.45	3.23	3.03	.202	4.06	3.17	.89	4.62	3.75	.87	4.71	4.42	.29	5.19	4.73	.46	4.81	4.65	.16	3.55	6.25	-2.69
Ecuador	.99	1.34	-.35	1.10	1.39	-.299	1.19	1.72	-.53	1.53	1.92	-.39	1.25	1.95	-.69	1.52	2.05	-.53	1.68	1.75	-.07	.90	1.82	-.91
Mexico	40.50	35.20	5.30	41.58	39.91	1.67	50.84	49.49	1.35	46.29	61.68	-15.39	56.8	74.29	-17.50	71.38	85.93	-14.55	78.77	94.62	-15.85	86.90	109.72	-22.81
Paraguay	.41	.03	.38	1.07	.753	.318	.787	.080	.707	.992	.055	.937	.91	.042	.85	.91	.04	.87	.78	.03	.75	.51	.04	.46
Peru	1.00	.73	.27	3.52	4.89	-1.36	1.40	.841	.586	1.77	1.03	.74	1.77	1.26	.51	1.95	1.77	.18	2.06	1.98	.08	1.69	1.92	-.23
Uruguay	.23	.26	-.03	.253	.265	-.012	.310	.167	.143	.395	.167	.228	.48	.26	.22	.54	.22	.32	.59	.25	.34	.49	.19	.29
Venezuela	5.44	8.18	-2.74	4.59	8.13	-3.54	4.03	8.37	-4.33	4.64	9.72	-5.08	4.74	13.17	-8.42	6.60	13.47	-6.87	6.51	9.18	-2.67	5.35	11.33	-5.98
Bahamas	.71	.60	.11	.704	.328	.376	.684	.202	.482	.661	.156	.505	.72	.16	.56	.81	.15	.66	.81	.14	.67	.84	.19	.64
Barbados	.12	.03	.09	.145	.034	.111	.161	.034	.126	.185	.037	.148	.22	.041	.18	.28	.04	.24	.28	.03	.25	.30	.05	.24
Belize	.11	.05	.06	.135	.053	.082	.115	.05	.064	.099	.052	.047	.11	.068	.04	.11	.07	.04	.12	.06	.06	.13	.08	.05
Cayman Islands	.28	.01	.27	.164	.034	.129	.202	.052	.149	.180	.018	.162	.21	.016	.19	.27	.02	.25	.42	.01	.41	.36	.01	.35
Costa Rica	1.35	1.41	-.06	1.542	1.541	.008	1.87	1.64	.222	1.73	1.84	-.11	2.02	1.97	.05	2.02	2.32	-.30	2.29	2.74	-.46	2.38	3.96	-1.58
Dominican Republic	2.10	2.37	-.27	2.34	2.67	-.322	2.79	3.09	-.291	3.01	3.39	-.38	3.57	3.87	-.30	3.92	4.32	-.40	3.94	4.44	-.5	4.10	4.28	-.18
El Salvador	.74	.38	.36	.873	.487	.385	.931	.609	.322	1.11	.812	.298	1.27	1.07	.20	1.40	1.34	.06	1.51	1.43	.08	1.51	1.59	-.08
Guatemala	1.20	1.08	.12	1.312	1.194	.117	1.35	1.28	.069	1.64	1.52	.12	1.67	1.61	.06	1.73	1.99	-.26	1.93	2.07	-.14	1.81	2.26	-.45
Guyana	.11	.10	.01	.112	.090	.031	.109	.098	.011	.141	.107	.034	.13	.10	.027	.14	.11	.032	.14	.13	.01	.14	.12	.02
Haiti	.20	.10	.10	.228	.154	.074	.204	.058	.145	.550	.129	.421	.47	.14	.33	.49	.18	.31	.54	.27	.27	.61	.30	.31
Honduras	.81	.78	.03	.898	.913	-.015	1.01	1.09	-.085	1.27	1.44	-.17	1.64	1.79	-.15	2.01	2.36	-.35	2.31	2.54	-.23	2.36	2.71	-.34
Jamaica	.93	.59	.34	1.11	.719	.396	1.06	.746	.318	1.42	.847	.573	1.49	.83	.65	1.41	.73	.68	1.30	.75	.55	1.29	.67	.61
Leeward & Windward Is.	.34	.07	.27	.065	.016	.049	N/A	N/A	N/A	N/A	N/A	N/A	N/A	N/A	N/A	N/A	N/A	N/A	.70	.08	.62	N/A	N/A	N/A
Neth. Antilles	.76	.85	-.09	.519	.396	.122	.521	.425	.095	.504	.288	.216	.68	.34	.34	.71	1.19	-.48	1.10	.77	.33	.59	.38	.21
Nicaragua	.18	.06	.12	.150	.128	.021	.185	.167	.018	.249	.238	.011	.35	.34	.03	.34	.09	.25	.33	.04	.29	.37	.49	-.12
Panamá	1.10	.25	.85	1.18	.279	.907	1.27	.322	.954	1.38	.307	1.07	1.38	.34	1.03	1.53	.36	1.17	1.75	.31	1.44	1.74	.36	1.37
Suriname	.14	.04	.10	.114	.058	.056	.121	.043	.078	.189	.100	.089	.22	.096	.12	.18	.09	.09	.18	.10	.08	.14	.12	.02
Trinidad & Tobago	.44	.84	-.40	.528	.802	-.274	.540	1.113	-.572	.689	.968	-.279	.66	1.31	-.64	.83	1.13	-.30	.98	.97	.01	.78	1.28	-.50
Turks & Caicos	.03	.00	.03	.021	.004	.017	.029	.004	.024	.033	.005	.028	.04	.005	.038	.05	.005	.04	.06	.005	.0	.09	.006	.08
US Trade with World	448.16	532.6	-84.50	465.0	580.65	-115.56	512.6	663.25	-150.6	584.74	743.44	-158.70	625.07	795.28	-170.21									

Notes: 1) Total figures and percentage changes are calculated from actual, not rounded data.   2) Caribbean Basin includes Central America, Caribbean Islands, Guyana and Suriname.   3) 1996 from January to December

Source: US Dept. of Commerce Bureau of the Census–Foreign Trade Division

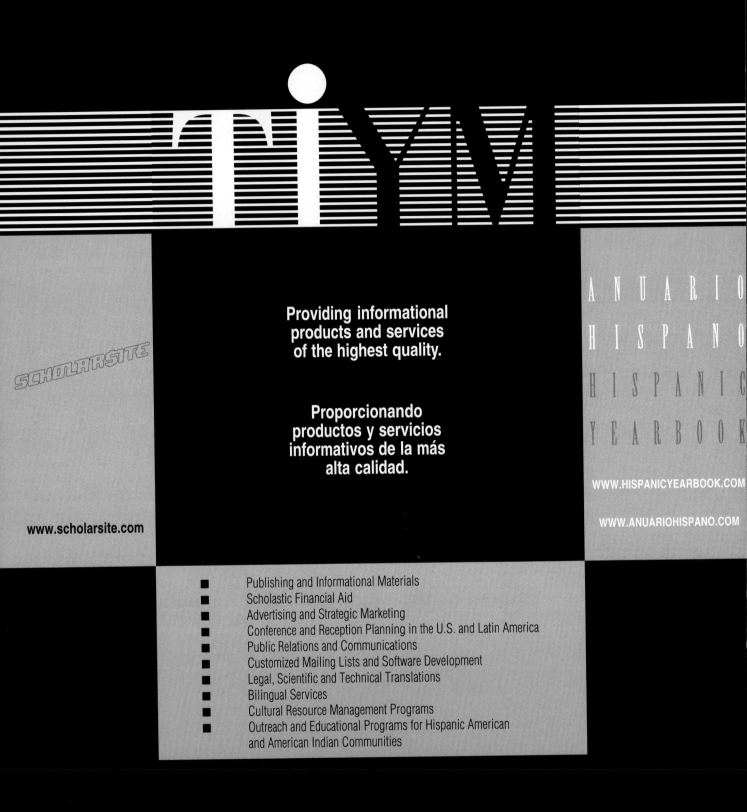

TiYM

Providing informational products and services of the highest quality.

Proporcionando productos y servicios informativos de la más alta calidad.

ANUARIO HISPANO
HISPANIC YEARBOOK

WWW.HISPANICYEARBOOK.COM

WWW.ANUARIOHISPANO.COM

SCHOLARSITE

www.scholarsite.com

- Publishing and Informational Materials
- Scholastic Financial Aid
- Advertising and Strategic Marketing
- Conference and Reception Planning in the U.S. and Latin America
- Public Relations and Communications
- Customized Mailing Lists and Software Development
- Legal, Scientific and Technical Translations
- Bilingual Services
- Cultural Resource Management Programs
- Outreach and Educational Programs for Hispanic American and American Indian Communities

TIYM Publishing Co., Inc.
6718 Whittier Avenue, Suite 130 McLean, VA 22101
(703) 734-1632 Fax: (703) 356-0787 TIYM@aol.com

WWW.TIYM.COM

Hispanic- and woman -owned
8(a) certified

Selective Service System
El Sistema de Servicio Selectivo

This is the name of the federal government agency that keeps a list of names for any national emergency requiring military conscription. It was created on September 16, 1940 through Law No. 783 during Franklin Roosevelt's presidency. The Selective Service System is an independent agency within the Executive Branch of the federal government. The Director of the Selective Service is appointed by the President and confirmed by the Senate.

The legislation that regulates this agency is the Selective Military Service Act. Pursuant to this law, the Selective Military Service System fulfills a dual role: that of providing human resources (untrained) to the Armed Forces in times of emergency, pursuant to the specifications established by the Department of Defense, and that of administering the alternative service program for conscientious objectors.

Conscription systems were used during the Civil War and again during the First World War. In both cases, the process was dismantled at the end of the hostilities. In 1940, before the United States entered the Second World War, the first obligatory military service during peacetime in the history of our nation was carried out in response to growing tension worldwide. In this manner, the system met human resource needs for wartime purposes quickly and without conflict following the attack on Pearl Harbor. At the end of the war, the obligatory military service law was allowed to expire but was reinstated as a result of the Cold War. From 1948 to 1973, men were recruited during peacetime as well as during times of conflict to fill vacancies in the Armed Forces made up exclusively of volunteers, in case an emergency mandated that Congress authorize the resumption of incorporation orders.

The registry was suspended in early 1975 and the Selective Service System entered into a more pronounced "reserve" phase. In late 1979, a series of "revitalization" attempts were made with the purpose of recovering the system's capacity of rapid mobilization in case of emergency. Later, in the summer of 1980, the obligation to register entered into effect once more. Currently, young men must do so within 30 days of turning 18.

The Selective Military Service Act, along with its Regulation, provides that the agency's structure include a national headquarters and offices in every state. In addition, there is another office for each of the following locations: New York City, the District of Columbia, Guam, Puerto Rico, the Mariana Islands, and the Virgin Islands. The Act and the Regulation provide for the creation of local boards that are assigned according to the county or the corresponding political subdivisions. There is also a provision that establishes a National Appeals Board and other boards that cover the same areas corresponding to the federal judicial districts. These boards oversee cases involving people who disagree with the local boards' mandates.

Así se llama la agencia del gobierno federal que mantiene la lista de nombres para cualquier emergencia nacional que requiera conscripción militar. Fue creada el 16 de septiembre de 1940 por la ley nº 783 durante la presidencia de Franklin Roosevelt. El Sistema del Servicio Selectivo es un organismo independiente dentro del Poder Ejecutivo del gobierno federal. El Director del Servicio Selectivo es nombrado por el Presidente y confirmado por el Senado.

La legislación que regula este organismo es el Acta del Servicio Militar Selectivo. De acuerdo con esta ley, el Sistema del Servicio Militar Selectivo cumple una doble misión: la de proveer recursos humanos (sin adiestrar) a las Fuerzas Armadas en momentos de emergencia, de acuerdo con las especificaciones establecidas por el Departamento de Defensa y la de administrar el programa alternativo de servicio para los contradictores de conciencia.

Durante la Guerra Civil se utilizaron sistemas de conscripción y nuevamente durante la Primera Guerra Mundial. El mecanismo, en ambas instancias, fue desmontado al final de las hostilidades. En 1940, antes de que los Estados Unidos entraran en la Segunda Guerra Mundial, se llevó a cabo el primer servicio militar obligatorio en tiempos de paz en la historia de nuestra nación, en respuesta a la creciente tensión mundial. De este modo, el sistema pudo cubrir las necesidades de recursos humanos para tiempos de guerra de una manera rápida y sin conflictos, después del ataque a Pearl Harbor. Al final de la guerra se permitió que la ley del servicio militar obligatorio caducase, pero a consecuencia de la Guerra Fría la misma fue repuesta. Desde 1948 hasta 1973, tanto en tiempos de paz como en períodos de conflicto, se reclutaron hombres para llenar vacantes en las Fuerzas Armadas integradas exclusivamente por voluntarios, en caso de que una emergencia hiciera necesario que el Congreso autorizara una reanudación de las incorporaciones.

El registro se suspendió a principios de 1975 y el Sistema del Servicio Selectivo entró en una fase más pronunciada de "reserva". A fines de 1979 se iniciaron una serie de tentativas de "revitalización" con el propósito de recuperar la capacidad del sistema para una rápida movilización en caso de emergencia. Después, en el verano de 1980 se puso en vigor nuevamente la obligación de registrarse. En la actualidad, los jóvenes deben hacerlo dentro de los 30 días de haber cumplido los 18 años.

El acta del Servicio Militar Selectivo, junto con su Reglamento, dispone que la estructura del organismo incluya una sede a nivel nacional y sedes en cada Estado. Además, una para los siguientes lugares: la ciudad de Nueva York, el Distrito de Columbia, Guam, Puerto Rico, las Islas Marianas y las Islas Vírgenes. El Acta y el Reglamento disponen la creación de juntas locales, asignadas con arreglo al Condado o a las correspondientes subdivisiones políticas. Existe también una disposición creando una Junta Nacional de Apelación y otras juntas que cubren las mismas áreas que corresponden a los distritos judiciales federales. Estas juntas atienden los casos de personas que están en desacuerdo con el dictamen de las juntas locales.

The Selective Service System has 200 full-time employees, the majority of whom are civilians, and who are incorporated pursuant to the rules dictated by the Personnel Administration Office (formerly the United States Civil Service Commission). There are approximately 20 Armed Forces Reserve officers in active service assigned to the Selective Service. These officers serve as the link with the Armed Forces and administer the Reserve Forces Program for the Selective Service. These reserve forces are made up of approximately 450 Reserve and National Guard officials who are assigned to the Selective Service for monthly exercises and for two two-week annual training sessions in active service. In case of emergency, these officers can be called to active service in order to increase the number of full-time staff.

The current structure of the agency consists of the National Headquarters, the Data Administration Center, and three Regional Offices. The state and local offices were closed in 1976 and will only be reopened if citizens are incorporated again.

In case of mobilization, the Selective Service reserve forces officials will be called to active service in order to establish state offices and offices in predetermined locations; local and appeals boards will be activated at the same time. There will be a lottery to determine the order of calling and incorporation orders will be issued following the order of the lottery, using Western Union's telegram service. The first priority will consist of the group of men turning 20 within the corresponding calendar year. Those who are registered and who receive incorporation orders should appear at the Processing Station for examination; this way, they will possibly be incorporated to the military service or they may present a request for deferment, postponement or exemption. Such requests will be considered by the Area Office or the Local Board pursuant to the nature of the request. The agency's mobilization plans are made in order to satisfy the Defense Department's needs.

Section 3 of the Selective Military Service Act contains the registry of "all male United States citizens and all other people of the male sex residing in the United States" whose age falls within the established limits. This Section excludes from the registry "all foreigners legally admitted in the United States as non-immigrants." The status of non-immigrant applies to those who have been legally admitted with student, tourist, diplomatic corps or trade affairs or mission visas and their respective families. A foreigner who remains here illegally is not legally admitted as a non-immigrant and consequently cannot be exempted.

Foreigners who reside in the United States are not necessarily those who have been admitted for permanent residence. Parolees, refugees, and those requesting political asylum reside in the United States and therefore must register. A foreigner who does not reside in the United States, even if he has permanent resident status, does not need to register until he moves to or resides in the country. Those who hold citizenship in the United States and elsewhere must register, no matter where they live, by virtue of their United States nationality.

All foreigners or persons with dual nationality have the same right as any other enrollee to request a deferment, postponement or exemption from service, or may declare themselves conscientious objectors if obligatory military service is in effect. There are also some special provisions that are not within the reach of other enrollees; these provisions take into consideration the country in which the man holds citizenship or the duration of his residency in the United States.

A foreigner must have resided in the United States for a year before being able to be admitted to the United States Armed Forces. This

El Sistema del Servicio Selectivo cuenta con 200 empleados con dedicación total, que son mayormente civiles, incorporados con arreglo a las reglas dictadas por la Oficina de Administración del Personal (anteriormente Comisión del Servicio Civil de los Estados Unidos). Hay aproximadamente 20 oficiales de la Reserva de las Fuerzas Armadas en servicio activo, asignados al Servicio Selectivo. Los mismos sirven de enlace con las Fuerzas Armadas y administran el Programa de Fuerzas de Reserva del Servicio Selectivo. Estas fuerzas de reserva se componen de aproximadamente 450 oficiales de la Reserva y de la Guardia Nacional que están asignados al Servicio Selectivo para sus ejercicios mensuales, y para sus dos sesiones anuales de entrenamiento de dos semanas de duración en servicio activo. En caso de una emergencia, se puede convocar a estos oficiales a servicio activo, para aumentar el personal con dedicación total.

La estructura actual del organismo está compuesta de su Sede Nacional, el Centro de Administración de Datos y tres Sedes Regionales. Las oficinas estatales y locales fueron cerradas en 1976, y su reapertura se producirá solamente si se comienza nuevamente a incorporar los ciudadanos.

En caso de movilización, los oficiales de la fuerza de reserva del Servicio Selectivo serán convocados a servicio activo para establecer las sedes estatales y las oficinas de área en ubicaciones predeterminadas; al mismo tiempo se activarán las Juntas locales y de Apelación. Se llevará a cabo un sorteo para determinar el orden de la convocatoria, y se emitirán órdenes de incorporación siguiendo el orden del sorteo, vía telegrama postal de la Western Union. La primera prioridad consistirá en el grupo de hombres que cumplan 20 años dentro del correspondiente año calendario. Las personas inscritas que reciban órdenes de incorporación deben presentarse a la Estación de Procesamiento para ser examinados; de esta manera podrán ser posiblemente incorporados al servicio militar, presentar un pedido de prórroga, aplazamiento o exención al mismo. Tales pedidos serán considerados por la Oficina del Area o por la Junta Local según la naturaleza del pedido. Los planes de movilización del organismo están trazados para satisfacer las necesidades del Departamento de Defensa.

La Sección 3 del Acta del Servicio Militar Selectivo dispone el registro de "todo ciudadano estadounidense varón y de toda otra persona del sexo masculino residente en los Estados Unidos" cuya edad esté dentro de los límites establecidos. A continuación, en esta Sección se excluye del registro a "todo extranjero legalmente admitido en los Estados Unidos como no inmigrante". El estado de no inmigrante les corresponde a aquellos que han sido legalmente admitidos bajo visas de estudiante, de turista, miembros del cuerpo diplomático o de asuntos o misiones de comercio y sus respectivas familias. Un extranjero que permanece ilegal no está legalmente admitido como no inmigrante y consecuentemente no puede acogerse a la extención.

Los extranjeros que residen en los Estados Unidos no son necesariamente aquellos que han sido admitidos para residir en forma permanente. Aquellos que están bajo el régimen de libertad condicional, los refugiados y quienes han solicitado asilo político residen en los Estados Unidos y por ende deben registrarse. Un extranjero que no resida en los Estados Unidos, aunque tenga el estatus de residente en forma permanente, no tiene que registrarse hasta que se mude o resida en el mismo. Las personas que poseen nacionalidad estadounidense y de otro país deben registrarse, sin consideración en donde residan, en virtud de su nacionalidad estadounidense.

Todo extranjero o persona con doble nacionalidad tiene el mismo derecho que cualquier otro inscrito a solicitar una prórroga, aplazamiento o exención del servicio, o de contradictor de conciencia, en caso de que exista servicio militar obligatorio. Hay también algunas disposiciones especiales que no están al alcance de otros inscritos, que toman en consideración el país de donde el hombre es ciudadano o la duración de su residencia en los Estados Unidos.

Un extranjero debe haber residido en los Estados Unidos durante un año antes de poder ser admitido a las Fuerzas Armadas Estadounidenses. Este período

yearlong period does not have to consist of twelve consecutive months but can be comprised of more than one period of residency. If a foreigner left the United States before being issued an incorporation order, he will be exempt from the service while he resides outside the country. A foreigner who registered when required to do so and who later acquired the status of one of the groups exempt from obligatory military service can be exempt from military service.

The United States has treaties or agreements with certain countries that provide that their citizens or nationals may be exempt from military service in the United States. A foreigner who makes such a request and who is exempt under this provision is automatically limited to obtaining United States citizenship and, if he leaves the United States, will not be admitted again as a permanent resident. If a foreigner has served a minimum of twelve months in the armed forces of a country with which the United States has signed a treaty of mutual defense activity, he has the right to the same classification as any other man who has complied with military service in the United States. People with dual nationality can be exempt from military service in the United States if the other country in which they hold citizenship has signed a treaty or agreement that includes such an exemption.

In the case of obligatory military service, requests for classification based on the condition of foreigner or dual nationality will be determined in an administrative fashion by the Area Office. Such appeals are based on documentary evidence and generally do not require a personal appearance by the enrollee.

In the case of all other registered persons, the final determination of the fitness of anyone who has not been deferred or exempt should be made by the Armed Forces. The country in which the foreigner holds citizenship could likely have to do with his fitness for service, depending on the nature of the conflict and the role that country has played in the conflict. Inscription is very easy. The card received must be returned by mail or the person can go to the post office and fill out a form there. In any case, the process takes just a few minutes and can also be done on the Internet. If the person you know is in the hospital or in prison when he turns 18, he still must register. He has a period of 30 days in which to do so after leaving the hospital or prison. For more information on registration, contact the Office of Public Affairs: (703) 235 2053.

Non-compliance with the obligation to register will prevent the violator from the following:
a) obtaining work in the federal government;
b) obtaining job training provided by the federal government;
c) obtaining federal government student loans;
d) obtaining employ in the Postal Service;
e) joining a vocational program headed by the federal government.

Congress has adopted three measures that are linked to registration in the Selective Service with accessibility to certain federal benefits. The legislative intent was to increase public awareness regarding the obligation to register and to ensure that those who receive federal funds have complied with the law. Student aid and job training benefits have come to be known as the "Salomon Amendments," named for Representative Gerald Salomon (Republican from New York), who presented the bill. Public Law 97-252, signed September 8, 1982, provides that those who are eligible for the Selective Service should have complied in registering with the service before receiving student financial aid with the change in Chapter IV of the Higher Education Act. This provision includes the famous Pell Grants and Guaranteed Student Loans. The applicants are asked to sign a statement that they have complied with the registration requirement since this is part of the application form for financial aid.

de un año no tiene que estar constituido por 12 meses consecutivos; puede estar en más de un período de residencia. Si un extranjero partió de los Estados Unidos antes de que se le haya emitido una orden de incorporación, estará exento del servicio mientras resida fuera del mismo. Un extranjero que se haya registrado cuando se le exigió que lo hiciera, y adquirió más tarde estado dentro de uno de los grupos que están exentos del servicio militar obligatorio, puede estar exento del servicio militar.

Los Estados Unidos tienen tratados o acuerdos con ciertos países que disponen que los ciudadanos o nativos de esos países puedan estar exentos del servicio militar en los EEUU. Un extranjero que así lo solicite y que esté exento bajo esta disposición está automáticamente limitado a obtener la ciudadanía norteamericana y si abandona los Estados Unidos, no volverá a ser admitido como residente permanente. Si un extranjero ha servido un mínimo de 12 meses en las fuerzas armadas de un país con el cual los Estados Unidos ha suscripto un tratado de actividades en defensa mutua, tiene derecho a la misma clasificación que la de cualquier otro hombre que haya cumplido servicio militar en los Estados Unidos. Las personas que tienen doble nacionalidad pueden quedar exentas del servicio militar en los Estados Unidos si el otro país en el que tienen ciudadanía ha suscrito un tratado o acuerdo que incluya tal exención.

En el caso del servicio militar obligatorio, los pedidos de clasificación basados en la condición de extranjeros o en la de doble nacionalidad, serán determinados en forma administrativa por la Oficina del Area. Tales apelaciones se basan en evidencia documental y generalmente no se requiere una presentación personal por parte del inscrito.

En el caso de todas las otras personas inscriptas, la determinación final de la aptitud de cualquiera que no haya sido prorrogado o exento deberá ser hecha por les Fuerzas Armadas. El país de donde el extranjero es ciudadano, bien podría tener que ver en su aptitud para el servicio, dependiendo de la naturaleza del conflicto y del papel que el país de donde él es ciudadano, haya cumplido en el conflicto. La inscripción es muy fácil. Todo lo que tiene que hacerse es regresar la tarjeta que le ha llegado por correo, o ir a la oficina de correos y llenar uno de los formularios ahí mismo. De cualquier forma, el proceso toma sólo unos cuantos minutos, y puede efectuarse también a través del Internet. Y si la persona que usted conoce está en el hospital o en prisión cuando cumple los 18 años, de todos modos tendrá que inscribirse. Tiene un plazo de 30 días después de salir del hospital o de la prisión. Para mayor información sobre la inscripción deberá llamarse a la Oficina de Asuntos Públicos: (703) 235-2053.

El no cumplimiento de esta obligación de inscripción, le impedirá al infractor:
a) obtener trabajo en el gobierno federal;
b) obtener capacitación de trabajo proporcionada por el gobierno federal;
c) obtener préstamos estudiantiles del gobierno federal;
d) obtener empleo en el Servicio Postal;
e) incorporarse a un programa vocacional propiciado por el gobierno federal.

El Congreso ha adoptado tres medidas que se vinculan a la inscripción en el Servicio Selectivo con accesibilidad a ciertos beneficios federales. La intención legislativa fue la de incrementar la conciencia pública acerca de la obligación de inscribirse y de asegurar que quienes reciben fondos federales han cumplido con la ley. La ayuda para estudiantes y los beneficios de adiestramiento laboral han pasado a ser conocidos como las "Enmiendas de Salomón", en reconocimiento al Representante Gerald Salomón (Republicano de Nueva York), que presentó los proyectos de ley. La Ley Pública 97-252, firmada el 8 de septiembre de 1982, dispone que las personas elegibles para el Servicio Selectivo deben haber cumplido con la inscripción de éste antes de recibir asistencia financiera para estudiantes con el cambio del Capítulo IV del Acta de Educación Superior. En esta disposición están incluidas las famosas "Pell Grants" y los "Guaranteed Student Loans". A los solicitantes se les pide que firmen una declaración que muestre que han cumplido con el requisito de la inscripción, ya que es parte del formulario de la solicitud de ayuda financiera.

On behalf of the entire production team, we are proud to bring the Pioneer Living Series to PBS... a 9-part series for multicultural audiences, especially America's immigrants, refugees and everyone arriving to our shores from other lands...a series promoting integration, inclusiveness, and individual effort as a means to achieving the American Dream. Hosted by Noriyuki "Pat" Morita.

Student guides, videos and transcripts available from Pioneer Living Corp.,

info@pioneerliving.com
Tel. 410-374-3117
www.pioneerliving.com
Program information:
www.pbs.org/pioneerliving

The agreement between the Department of Education and the Selective Service System, signed in January 1986, provided a computerized count of Pell Grant applicants and beneficiaries with the registry of Selective Service enrollees. The Department of Education will be provided the names of those suspected of evading registration so that this body can take the appropriate measures to resolve the case. Public Law 97-300, signed October 13, 1982, amended the Job Training Protection Act (JTPA) and imposed similar obligations for those requesting job training. The basic provisions in this amendment also require registration as a condition on the rights to benefits.

The Selective Service and the Department of Labor are trying to assist applicants in obtaining the necessary proof to request job training benefits. Those men who have not yet registered may turn in the registration forms at the majority of the training centers since the registration is part of their application process. Those who have lost their proof of registration (Letter of Admission to the Selective Service) can obtain a duplicate by contacting the Selective Service by letter (Selective Service System, Registration Information Office, P.O. Box 94638, Palatine, IL 60094-4638) or by calling, toll-free, (847) 688 6888. This service is at the disposal of any person who needs registration verification.

On November 8, 1985, President Reagan signed Public Law 99-145, also known as the Thurmond Amendment to the Law for the Authorization of Defense Costs. This law, proposed by Senator Strom Thurmond, Republican from South Carolina, prevents those men who did not register with the Selective Service, and who were obligated to do so, from being appointed to federal posts. This law is also valid for those men who request temporary employ during the summer with a federal agency or department.

The purpose of this legislation is twofold. First, it increases public awareness regarding obligatory registration and second, it ensures that those who receive federal funds have complied with the law.

El acuerdo entre el Departamento de Educación y el Sistema de Servicio Selectivo, suscrito en enero de 1986, dispuso un conteo computarizado de los solicitantes y beneficiarios de los "Pell Grants" con el archivo de inscritos en el Servicio Selectivo. Al Departamento de Educación se le proveerán los nombres de los sospechosos que evadieron la inscripción para que éste tome las medidas adecuadas para resolver el caso. La Ley Pública 97-300 del 13 de octubre de 1982, enmendó el Acta de Cooperación para la Capacitación Laboral (JTPA, por sus siglas en inglés) e impuso obligaciones similares a quienes solicitaran capacitación laboral. Las disposiciones básicas de esta enmienda también exigen la inscripción como condición para tener derecho a los beneficios.

El Servicio Selectivo y el Departamento del Trabajo están tratando de asistir a los solicitantes en la obtención de la prueba necesaria para solicitar los beneficios de capacitación laboral. Los varones que no se han registrado aún, pueden entregar los formularios de inscripción en la mayor parte de los centros de capacitación ya que el registro forma parte del proceso de su solicitud. Los varones que hayan perdido la evidencia de inscripción (Carta de Admisión del Servicio Selectivo) pueden obtener un duplicado poniéndose en contacto con el Servicio Selectivo por carta o llamando sin ningún costo, al teléfono 1-847-688-6888. Este servicio está a disposición de cualquier persona que necesite de una verificación de inscripción.

El 8 de noviembre de 1985, el Presidente Reagan firmó la Ley Pública 99-145 normalmente conocida como la Enmienda de Thurmond a la Ley de Autorización de Gastos para Defensa. Esta ley, propuesta por el Senador Strom Thurmond, republicano de Carolina del Sur, impide el nombramiento en cargos federales a los varones que estando obligados a inscribirse en el Servicio Selectivo no lo hicieron. Esta ley también tiene validez para los jóvenes que soliciten empleo temporario durante el verano con un organismo o departamento federal.

Esta legislación tiene doble intención. Primero, la de incrementar la conciencia pública acerca del registro obligatorio y segundo, asegurar que quienes reciban fondos federales, hayan cumplido con la ley.

Hispanic Embassies in the US
Embajadas hispanas en EUA

ARGENTINA

Embassy of the Argentine Republic
Chancery: 1600 New Hampshire Ave. NW
Washington, DC 20009
Tel: (202) 238-6400
Fax: (202) 332-3171
http://athea.ar/cwash/home
E-mail: aln@atina.ar
E-mail: mjr@atina.ar

National Holiday:
National Day, May 25

Ambassador E. and P.
His E., Guillermo GONZALEZ;
Mrs. Adriana Posse de Gonzalez

Minister (Deputy Chief of Mission)
Mr. Ricardo E. LAGORIO;
Mrs. Alejandra M.R.G. de Lagorio

Minister (Commercial)
Mrs. Cecilia BARRIOS BARON;
Mr. David T. Hollywood

Minister (Cultural)
Mr. Rodolfo A. CERVINO;
Mrs. Ana María Curia de Cerviño

Minister (Financial)
Mrs. Noemí C.E. LA GRECA

Minister (Agricultural)
Mr. José Domingo MOLINA;
Mrs. Mary Alice Troast**

Minister (Political)
Mr. Jorge Alberto OSELLA;
Mrs. Graciela García Moris de Osella

Counselor (Political)
Mr. Diego Javier TETTAMANTI;
Mrs. Alejandra María Ruiz de Tettamanti

Counselor
Mr. Jose Luis SUTERA

Counselor (Commercial)
Mrs. Marta Victoria DE JONG

Counselor (Political)
Mrs. Patricia ESPADA;
Mr. Nelson F. Espada

Counselor (Consular Affairs)
Mr. Alejandro CASIRO;
Mrs. Hyo Shin Kim de Casiro

First Secretary (Intelligence Service)
Mrs. María José CASSINA;
Mr. Rubén Darío Ronchetti

Second Secretary
Mr. Marcelo A. MASSONI;

Mrs. María Catalina Olivero

Third Secretary
Mr. Mariano ENRICO

Attaché (Administrative)
Mrs. Graciela ABREU

Attaché (Administrative)
Mr. Luis Ángel BARBERO;
Mrs. Rosa Álvarez de Barbero

Attaché (Administrative)
Mrs. Silvia S. SPAGNOLO;
Mr. Roger Armand Do Rosario

Military Attaché
Major Gral. Daniel M. REIMUNDES;
Mrs. Silvia Tarraf de Reimundes

Assistant Attaché
Lieutenant Colonel German Pedro TAGNI;
Mrs. Roxana Claudia Flammini

Assistant Military Attaché
Colonel Rafael J. BARNI;
Mrs. Maria Rosa Palacios de Barni

Assistant Military Attaché
Lieutenant Colonel Enrique A. NUNEZ;
Mrs. Mariana Valeria Rozados

Naval Attaché
Rear Admiral Jorge Oscar Pedro LOPEZ;
Mrs. Alicia I. den Dulk de Lopez

Assistant Naval Attaché
Captain Guillermo O. IGLESIAS;
Mrs. Cecilia Ines Bouilly

Assistant Naval Attaché
Captain Felix MEDICI;
Mrs. Laura G. Garcia Martinez de Medici

Assistant Naval Attaché
Lieutenant Commander Rubén Eduardo GALLIUSSI;
Mrs. Míriam Graciela Galliussi

Air Force Attaché
Major General Dante A. ASLA;
Mrs. Irene Bongiovanni de Asla

Assistant Air Attaché
Colonel Humberto Héctor Hugo FERNÁNDEZ;
Mrs. María de los Angeles Torassa

Assistant Air Force Attaché
Colonel Ricardo D. GIBSON;
Mrs. Beatriz C. Ricci de Gibson

Assistant Air Attaché

Lieutenant Colonel Julio César GIMÉNEZ;
Mrs. Susana Gloria Giménez

Assistant Air Attaché
Lieutenant Colonel Fernando Luis MASSERINI;
Mrs Liliana Noemi Malavassi

Accounting Section
1811 Q Street, NW
Washington, DC 20009
Tel: (202) 238-6473

Consular Section
1811 Q Street, NW
Washington, DC 20009
Tel: (202) 238-6460/6463

Cultural Section
1811 Q Street, NW
Washington, DC 20009
Tel: (202) 238-6464

Financial Office
1901 L Street, NW, #606
Washington, DC 20036
Tel: (202) 466-3021

Military Attaché Office
1810 Connecticut Ave. NW
Washington, DC 20009
Tel: (202) 667-4900

Naval Attaché Office
630 Indiana Ave. NW
Washington, DC 20004
(202) 626-2100

Air Attaché Office
2405 I Street, NW
Washington, DC 20037
Tel: (202) 452-8500

BOLIVIA

Embassy of the Republic of Bolivia
Chancery: 3014 Massachusetts Ave. NW
Washington, DC 20008
Tel: (202) 483-4410
Fax: (202) 328-3712
http://www.embassy.org/embassies/bo.html

National Holiday:
Independence Day, August 6

Ambassador E. and P.
Her E., Marlene FERNANDEZ DEL GRANADO;

Mr. Scott Bartlett**

Minister-Counselor (Deputy Chief of Mission)
Mr. Erich KUHN POPPE;
Mrs. Ana Maria Carpio de Kuhn

Minister-Counselor
Mr. Enrique Javier VARFA DELOS;
Mrs. Carmina Iloka Banzer de Vargas

Counselor and Consul General
Ms. Carolina TOLEDO CANDEO

Counselor (Political)
Mr. Juan Francisco ROQUE

First Secretary (Legal)
Mr. Rolando Javier VISCARRA VALDIVIA;
Mrs. Maria Cecilia Wilde de Vargas

First Secreaty (Commercial)
(Vacant)

First Secretary
Mrs. Maria Rosario SIAN

Second Secretary
Ms. Neiza Fabiola SOLIZ RECKLING

Third Secretary and Consular Agent
Mr. Fernando GRANDY CAVERO;
Mrs. Dabeyva Valda

Attaché (Cultural)
Ms. Neiza Fabiola SOLIZ RECKLING

Attaché (Civil)
Ms. Lilian R. ROCHA PELAEZ

Military Administrative Secretary
Mrs. Aida Casanovas VALDIVIA

Attaché (Police)
Mr. Rafael VARGAS BARRIENTOS;
Mrs. Daisy Torrez De Vargas

Military Attaché
Colonel Cesar LÓPEZ;
Mrs. Carmen López

Naval Attaché
Captain Ismael SCHABIB;
Mrs. Vania Schabib

Air Attaché
Colonel Rafael SANDOVAL;
Mrs. Yeni Sandoval

Assistant Military Attaché
Captain Oscar ROMERO

Assistant Air Attaché
Colonel Johnny VERA;
Mrs. Maria Rene Claure

Military, Naval, & Air Attaché Office
3014 Massachusetts Ave. NW
Washington, DC 20008
Tel: (202) 232-4805,4807, and 4808

Information updated from Diplomatic List (Summer 1999 United States Department of State)

•• American Nationality

BRAZIL

Brazilian Embassy
Chancery: 3006 Massachusetts Ave. NW
Washington, DC 20008
Tel: (202) 238-2700
Fax: (202) 238-2827
http://www.brasilemb.org/
E-mail: webmaster@brasilemb.org

National Holiday:
Independence Day, Sept. 7

Ambassador E. and P.
His E., Rubens BARBOSA;
Mrs. Maria Ignez Correa Barbosa

Minister-Counselor (Deputy Chief of Mission)
Mr. Regis P. ARSLANIAN;
Mrs. María Beatriz Arslanian

Minister-Counselor
Mr. Paulo Roberto ALMEIDA;
Mrs. Carmen Licia P. Almeida

Counselor
Mr. Renato Assumpcao FARIA

Counselor
Mr. Marcos V.P. GAMA;
Mrs. Claudia Nunes P. Gama

Counselor
Mr. Luis Henrique S. LOPES;
Mrs. Dora S. Lopes

Counselor
Mr. Sergio E. BATH;
Mrs. Rosana Bath

First Secretary
Mr. Julio G. BITELLI;
Mrs. Lysolette M. Bitelli

First Secretary
Mr. Luis Balduino CARNEIRO;
Mrs. Agnes D. Balduino

First Secretary
Mr. Antonio LUZ;
Mrs. Adriana Luz

First Secretary
Mr. Francisco C. Soares LUZ;
Mrs. Ivana Panizzi Luz

First Secretary
Ms. Ana Maria MORALES

First Secretary and Consul
Mrs. Wanja Campos Da NOBREGA;
Mr. Aldemo García Junior

First Secretary
Mr. Luis Claudio Villafance G. SANTOS;
Mrs. Daniella Xavier V.G. Santos

Second Secretary
Mr. Raphael AZEREDO;
Mrs. Vanessa De Andrade Azeredo

Second Secretary
Mr. Carlos FRANCA;
Mrs. Ana María de Leao Franca

Second Secretary
Mr. Mauricio Carvalho LYRIO;
Mrs. Paula Alves de Souza

Second Secretary
Ms. María Elisa R. MAIA

Second Secretary
Mr. Bernardo PARANHOS VELLOSO;
Mrs. Deborah Paranhos Velloso

Second Secretary
Mrs. Paula Alves De SOUZA;
Mr. Mauricio Carvalho Lyrio

Second Secretary
Mr. Renato Mosca De SOUZA;
Mrs. Luciana Duarte Paiva Arantes

Second Secretary
Mr. Philip YANG;
Mrs. Patricia Vanzella

Attaché
Ms. Andrea AZEVEDO

Attaché
Mrs. María Ester G. CARVALHO;
Mr. Ary Mamede Cruzeiro

Attaché
Ms. Sonia Reis Da COSTA

Attaché
Mrs. Keila EVANGELISTA;
Mr. Joao Sergio Carneiro

Attaché
Mr. Orlando HENRIQUES;
Mrs. María Luz Carretero

Attaché
Mr. Dival LARA;
Mrs. Angela M. B. Lara

Attaché and Vice Consul
Mr. Mauricio Souza LEITE;
Mrs. María S. Apostolova

Attaché
Mr. Celso Ricardo Hottum MEIRA;
Mrs. Alice María Reis Meira

Attaché
Mr. José Menache NEISTEIN

Attaché
Mr. Joao Amancio QUEIROZ NETO;
Mrs. Victoria M. Ferreira De Queiroz

Attaché
Mr. Fabiano Rubio SCARANO;
Mrs. Marta Guedes da C. Scarano

Attaché
Mrs. Elgeni Lopes STRZELESKI;
Mr. Rogerio Strzeleski

Attaché
Mr. Jose Raúl TEIXEIRA;
Mrs. Yara S. Jorge Teixeira

Military Attaché
Major General Rui Alves CATAO;
Mrs. Vera Leda de Arruda Catao

Naval Attaché
Rear Admiral Alvaro Luiz PINTO;
Mrs. Sonia M. C. Pinto

Defense & Air Attaché
Major General Américo SOARES FILHO

Assistant Military Attaché
Colonel Antonio Luiz Da Costa BURGOS

Assistant Military Attaché
Colonel Joao Leri De Araujo SOARES;
Mrs. María Joana Marques Soares

Assistant Naval Attaché
Captain Paulo Pedro Moreira ALMEIDA

Assistant Naval Attaché
Captain Carlos Vinicius De MIRANDA;
Mrs. Lucia Regina A. Miranda

Assistant Air Attaché
Colonel Aprigio E. M. AZEVEDO;
Mrs. Regina Helene F.A. Azevedo

Assistant Air Attaché
Colonel Antonio Jose Faria Dos SANTOS;
Mrs. Andrea G. Nogueira dos Santos

Brazilian Aeronautical Commission
1701 22nd Street, NW
Washington, DC 20008
Tel: (202) 483-4031

Brazilian Army Commission
4632 Wisconsin Ave. NW
Washington, DC 20016
Tel: (202) 244-5010

Brazilian Naval Commission
5130 MacArthur Boulevard, NW
Washington, DC 20016-3344
Tel: (202) 244-3950

CHILE

Embassy of the Republic of Chile
Chancery: 1732 Massachusetts Ave. NW
Washington, DC 20036
Tel: (202) 785-1746
Fax: (202) 887-5579
http://www.embassy.org/embassies/cl.html
http://www.chileinfo.com
E-mail: echile@radix.net

National Holiday:
Independence Day, Sept. 18

Ambassador E. and P.
His E., Andrés BIANCHI;
Mrs. Liliam Urdinola Uribe

Minister-Counselor (Deputy Chief of Mission)
Mr. Daniel G. CARVALLO;
Mrs. Jackeline Pinto

Minister-Counselor
Mr. Jose Gabriel ZEPEDA;
Mrs. Rina D. Monroy

Counselor and Consul
Mr. José Miguel MENCHACA;
Mrs. María Constanza Fernández

Counselor (Technical)
Colonel Hector HENRIQUEZ;
Mrs. Pamela Solange Gana

Counselor (Agricultural)
Mr. Eduardo Alejandro SANTOS

Counselor
Mr. Guillermo ANGUITA;
Mrs. Cecilia M. Rademacher

First Secretary
Mr. Rene Mauricio HURTADO;
Mrs. Milagros Nancy Montesinos Arce

First Secretary
Mr. Roberto ARAOS;
Mrs. Ana Luisa LAZCANO

First Secretary (Commercial)
Mr. Roberto E. MATUS;
Mrs. Consuelo Olavarria

Second Secretary
Mr. Oscar J. FUENTES;
Mrs. Isabel Margarita Hurtado

Third Secretary and Consul
Mr. Bernardo J. DEL PICO

Third Secretary
Mr. Marcos Manuel CORREA;
Mrs. Cecilia Beatriz Diaz

Third Secretary
Mr. Andres LAMOLIATTE;
Mrs. Elisabeth Ursula Brauchle**

Third Secretary
Ms. Beatriz De LA FUENTE

Attaché (Press)
Mrs. Eliana JIMENEZ

Attaché (Cultural)
Mrs. Ana María PALMA

Attaché (Laboral)
Mr. Jorge CASTILLO

Attaché (Civil)
Mrs. María Hilda Bolvaran de PINCUS;
Mr. Pedro E. Pincus**

Attaché (Tourism)
Ms. Maria Soledad CABELLO

Defense and Military Attaché
Brigadier General Eduardo A. JARA;
Mrs. Ana Luisa Zuazagoitia

Naval Attaché
Rear Admiral Alfredo Mario GIULIANO;
Mrs. Elisa de Lourdes Correa

Air Attaché
Major General Ricardo Fernando ORTEGA;
Mrs. Denise X. Benard

Assistant Military Attaché
Colonel Ricardo E. BAHAMONDES;
Mrs. Ana María Asencio

Assistant Military Attaché
Colonel Victor M. BORQUEZ;
Mrs. Alexandra H. Hulse

Assistant Naval Attaché
Captain Sergio E. ROBINSON;
Mrs. Monserrat P. Garachena

Assitant Air Attaché
Colonel Mario R. GONZALEZ;
Mrs. Gina S. Frugone

Air Attaché Office
1029 Vermont Ave. NW, #1100
Washington, DC 20005
Tel: (202) 872-1334

Military Attaché Office
2174 Wisconsin Ave. NW
Washington, DC 20007
Tel: (202) 785-2083

Naval Attaché Office
1875 Connecticut Ave. NW, #700
Washington, DC 20009
Tel: (202) 667-7790

COLOMBIA

Embassy of Colombia
Chancery: 2118 Leroy Pl., NW
Washington, DC 20008
Tel: (202) 387-8338
Fax: (202) 232-8643
http://www.colombiaemb.org
E-Mail: emwas@colombiaemb.org

National Holiday:
Independence Day, July 20

Ambassador E. and P.

His .E., Luis Alberto MORENO;
MRS. Gabriela Febres Cordero

Minister (Deputy Chief of Mission)
Mr. Juan Esteban ORDUZ;
Mrs. María Lucía Del Castillo

Minister-Counselor (Commercial)
(Vacant)

Minister-Counselor
Mrs. María Claudia GÓMEZ;
Mr. Mauricio Camargo

Minister-Counselor (Trade)
Mr. Felipe JARAMILLO

Counselor (Deputy Director)
Ms. Mariana PACHECO

Counselor
Mr. Francisco J. ECHEVERRI;
Mrs. Elizabeth Marian Winger**

Counselor
Ms. Adriana MENDOZA

Counselor
Mr. Julio Andrés JIMENEZ;

First Secretary (Press)
Mrs. Claudia MORALES;
Mr. Rafael Nieto

Second Secretary (Commercial)
Mr. Alfonso LIEVANO;
Mrs. Isabel Lievano

Second Secretary
Mrs. Ana María PUJANA;
Mr. Miguel Ceballos

Third Secretary
Mr. Francisco Alberto GONZÁLEZ;
Mrs. Ruth Mery Ariza Lemus

Third Secretary
Ms. Johanna C. PETERS

Third Secretary (Cultural)
Mr. Assad Jose JATER;

Attaché (Police)
Colonel Marino ESCOBAR;
Mrs. Ligia Escobar

Assistant Attaché (Police)
Captain Raúl Fernando LÓPEZ;
Mrs. Mónica Fernanda Lizarazo

Defense Attaché
General Mario Fernando ROA;
Mrs. Irma Salgado

Military Attaché
Colonel Gustavo RODRIGUEZ;
Mrs. María Elena Herrera

Naval Attaché
Captain Alfonso DIAZ;
Mrs. Luz Elena Garcia

Assistant Military Attaché
Colonel Gustavo MATAMOROS;
Mrs. Claudia Marcela Galvis

Assistant Air Attaché
Colonel Javier PINZON;
Mrs. Beatriz Galarza

Commercial Attaché Office
1701 Pennsylvania Ave. NW, #560
Washington, DC 20006
Tel: (202) 463-6679

COSTA RICA

Embassy of Costa Rica
Chancery: 2114 S Street, NW

Washington, DC 20008
Tel: (202) 234-2945
Fax: (202) 265-4795
http://www.embassy.org/embassies/cr.html
http://www.costarica-embassy.org
E-mail: embassy@costarica-embassy.org

National Holiday:
Independence Day, Sept. 15

Ambassador E. and P.
His E., Jaime DAREMBLUM;
Mrs. Gina Daremblum

Minister-Counselor (Deputy Chief of Mission) and Consul General
Mrs. Erika HARMS

Minister-Counselor (Economic)
Mrs. Irene ARGUEDAS

Minister-Counselor (Political)
Ms. Jessica CLARK

Minister-Counselor (Cultural)
Mr. Sabino MORERA

Counselor (Administrative)
Mrs. Rocio ECHEVERRI

First Secretary
Ms. Nella GIL

Second Secretary (Tourism)
Ms. Pamela TREJOS

Attache and Vice Consul
Mr. Manuel NUÑEZ

Consular Office
2112 S. Street, NW
Washington, DC 20008
Tel: (202) 328-6628

CUBA

Embassy of Switzerland
Cuban Interests Section
2630 16th Street, NW
Washington, DC 20009
Tel: (202) 797-8518
Fax: (202) 797-8521
http://www.embassy.org/embassies/cu.html
E-mail: cubaseccion@igc.apc.org

Chief of Interests Section
Mr. Fernando REMÍREZ de ESTENOZ;
Mrs. Patricia Semidey Gonzalez

First Secretary (Consul)
Mr. José Anselmo LOPEZ PERERA

First Secretary
Mr. Fernando GARCIA BIELSA

First Secretary
Ms. Olga del C. FERNANDEZ RIOS

First Secretary
Mr. Gustavo R. MACHIN GOMEZ

First Secretary
Mr. Luis M. FERNANDEZ RODRIGUEZ

First Secretary
Ms. Josefina VIDAL FERREIRO

First Secretary
Mr. Oscar J. REDONDO TOLEDO

First Secretary (Vice Consul)
Mr. Orlando ACOSTA FAZ

First Secretary (Administrative Affairs)

Mr. Richard DARLINGTON EBANKS

First Secretary
Mr. Sergio MARTINEZ GONZALEZ

Third Secretary
Mr. José Luis NOA MONTERO

Third Secretary (Vice Consul)
Mr. Florentino BATISTA GONZALEZ

Third Secretary
Mr. Osvaldo DIAZ GARCIA

Attaché
Mr. Emilio PAGÁN FUENTES;
Mrs. Rosa Hechavarria Stable

Attaché
Mr. Noel TOCABENS PEREZ

Embassy of Switzerland, Cuban Annex
2639 16th Street, NW
Washington, DC 20009
Tel: (202) 797-8609
Fax: (202) 986-7283

DOMINICAN REPUBLIC

Embassy of the Dominican Republic
Chancery: 1715 22nd Street, NW
Washington, DC 20008
Tel: (202) 332-6280
Fax: (202) 265-8057
http://www.domrep.org
E-mail: embdomrepusa@msn.com

National Holiday:
Independence Day, Feb. 27

Ambassador E. and P.
His E., Roberto SALADIN SELIN;
Mrs. Bertha D. Nin de Saladin

Minister-Counselor (Cultural)
Mr. Leon BOSCH;
Mrs. Altagracia V. Santana de Bosch

Minister-Counselor (Consular)
Mr. Andrés BELGUETE;

Counselor
Mr. Francisco A. CARABALLO;
Mrs. Laura Amelia Yaryura De Caraballo

Minister Counselor (Commercial)
Mrs. Judith MARCANO

First Secretary
Mrs. Angelica M. ESPINAL DE APOLINAR

Counselor
Mrs. Germania Altagracia GASKILL;
Mr. Gilford Gaskill**

First Secretary
Mrs. Rosa GIRALDEZ

Defense, Military, Naval, and Air Attaché
Mayor General Andrés APOLINAR DISLA

ECUADOR

Embassy of Ecuador
Chancery: 2535 15th Street NW
Washington, DC 20009
Tel: (202) 234-7200
Fax: (202) 265-6385
http://www.ecuador.org
http://www.embassy.org/embassies/ec.html

E-mail: mecuawaa@erols.com

National Holiday:
Independence Day, August 10

Ambassador E. and P.
Her E., Ivonne A-BAKI;
Dr. Samy Baki

Minister (Deputy Chief of Mission)
Mr. Carlos JATIVA;
Mrs. Roció de Játiva

Counselor
Mr. Teodoro MALDONADO

First Secretary
Mrs. Sylvia BERMEO;
Mr. José V. Troya

Second Secretary
Mr. Diego RAMÍREZ;
Mrs. Mónica de Ramírez

Second Secretary
Mr. Alejandro DÁVALOS;
Mrs. María Patricia de Dávalos

Second Secretary
Mr. Juan Manuel ESCALANTE;
Mrs. Carla de Escalante

Third Secretary
Mrs. Pilar CORNEJO;
Mr. Carlos Cornejo

Attaché (Administrative-Financial)
Ms. Lucia GUERRA

Cultural Attaché
Mr. Jorge SAADE;
Mrs. Gina de Saade

Military Attaché
Colonel Robert TANDAZO;
Mrs. Ena Regalado de Tandazo

Naval Attaché
Captain Jose OLMEDO M.;
Mrs. Margoth de Olmedo

Air Attaché
Colonel Juan FAINI;
Mrs. María Antonieta Faini

Assistant Military Attaché
Colonel Eduardo VERGARA;
Mrs. Ived Cobo de Vergara

Assistant Naval Attaché
Commander Fernando PUENTE V.;
Mrs. Cecilia de Puente

Assistant Naval Attaché
Commander Carlos VALLEJO G.;
Mrs. Rommy de Vallejo

Assistant Naval Attaché
Commander Guillermo AYALA P.;
Mrs. Sonia de Ayala

Assistant Air Attaché
Colonel Alfredo OCHOA;
Mrs. Edith de Ochoa

Consular Affairs Office
2535 15th Street, NW
Washington, DC 20009
Tel: (202) 234-7166
Fax: (202) 265-9325

Military Attaché Office
2535 15th Street, NW
Washington, DC 20009
Tel: (202) 234-0647
Fax: (202) 745-0887

Naval Attaché Office
2535 15th Street, NW

Washington, DC 20009
Tel: (202) 328-6958
Fax: (202) 332-7954

Air Attaché Office
2535 15th Street, NW
Washington, DC 20009
Tel: (202) 234-0601
Fax: (202) 265-0936

EL SALVADOR

Embassy of El Salvador
Chancery: 2308 California Street, NW
Washington, DC 20008
Tel: (202) 265-9671
http://www.elsalvador.org
E-mail: cbartoli@elsalvador.org

National Holiday:
Independence Day, Sept. 15

Ambassador E. and P.
His E., René A. LEÓN

Minister-Counselor (Deputy Chief of Mission)
Mrs. Carmen TOBAR

Minister-Counselor
Ms. Lina Maria CALDERON

Counselor (Administrative)
Mrs. Grace M. AWAD

Counselor (Press and Public Affairs)
Mrs. Claudia Nuset DE BARTOLINI;
Mr. Frank Paul Bartolini**

Counselor (Community Affairs)
Mrs. Vilma HERRERA AMAROLI

Counselor (Political)
Mrs. Johana HILL

Counselor (Political)
Mr. Luis APARICIO BERMUDEZ;
Mrs. Carmen de Aparicio

Counselor (Trade and Investment Promotion)
Mr. Werner M. ROMERO

Counselor (Economic)
Mr. Enilson SOLANO;
Mrs. Claudia Rivera

Counselor (Systems)
Mr. Carlos CORTEZ MONTES

First Secretary and Consul General
Mr. Juan A. ACEVEDO;
Mrs. Ana Eugenia Sandoval de Acevedo

First Secretary
Mrs. Dora María DE AGUILAR;
Mr. José M. Aguilar

Second Secretary and Vice Consul
Mrs. María Isabel ROSALES LAGUARDIA

Attaché (Commercial)
Mr. Francisco Javier CALLEJA;
Mrs. Maureen Calleja**

Attaché (Cultural)
Mrs. Mirian Etelinda VARGAS CASTILLO

Defense, Military, Naval and Air Attaché
Colonel Ricardo ABREGO;
Mrs. Linda Marisel Abrego

Consular Affairs Office
1424 16th Street, NW, #200

Washington, DC 20036
Tel: (202) 331-4032

Counselor for Economic, Financial, & Commercial Affairs Office
2308 California Street, NW
Washington, DC 20008
Tel: (202) 265-9671,9672

Defense Attaché Office
2308 California Street, NW
Washington, DC 20008

EQUATORIAL GUINEA

Embassy of Equatorial Guinea
Chancery: 1712 I Street NW, # 410,
Washington, DC 20006
Tel: (202) 296-4174
Fax: (202) 296-4195

National Holiday:
Independence Day, Oct. 12

Ambassador (Chief of Mission)
Pastor Micha ONDO BILE

GUATEMALA

Embassy of Guatemala
Chancery: 2220 R Street NW
Washington, DC 20008
Tel: (202) 745-4952
Fax: (202) 745-1908
http://www.guatemala-embassy.org
E-mail: info@guatemala-embassy.org

National Holiday:
Independence Day, Sept 15

Ambassador E. and P.
His E., Ariel RIVERA IRIAS;
Mrs. Marta Marina Rivera

Minister-Counselor (Deputy Chief of Mission)
Mr. Manuel Estuardo ROLDÁN;
Mrs. Carina Faillace Roldán

Attaché (Cultural)
Mrs. María Z. LANDIS

Counselor (Economic and Financial)
Mr. Lionel VALENTÍN MAZA

Counselor (Legal)
Dr. Rodrigo VIELMAN

Third Secretary
Mr. Jorge Eduardo CONTRERAS

Third Secretary
Miss María Candelaria HERNÁNDEZ

Third Secretary
Mrs. Betty MARROQUIN

Third Secretary
Miss Ana C. VILLACORTA

Attaché (Commercial)
Miss Ana María González

Defense, Military, Naval and Air Attaché
(Vacant)

Commercial Attaché Office
2220 R Street NW
Washington, DC 20008

Consular Section Office
2220 R Street, NW
Washington, DC 20008

Defense, Military, Naval, and Air Attaché Office
2220 R Street, NW
Washington, DC 20008
Tel: (202) 232-2226

HONDURAS

Embassy of Honduras
Chancery: 3007 Tilden St. NW, #4-M
Washington, DC 20008
Tel: (202) 966-7702
Fax: (202) 966-9751
http://www.hondurasemb.org
E-mail: embhondu@aol.com

National Holiday:
Independence Day, Sept. 15

Ambassador E. and P.
His E., Hugo NOE PINO;
Vivian de Noe Pino

Minister-Counselor (Deputy Chief of Mission)
Mr. José Benjamín ZAPATA;
Mrs. Susan Mary Zapata

Minister
Mr. Ramón CUSTODIO;
Mrs. Mei Ling Lavecchia**

Minister (Political)
Mr. Salvador E. RODEZNO;
Mrs. Elizabeth R. Rodezno**

Counselor (Political)
Mr. David HERNÁNDEZ;
Mrs. Xochitl Noemí Salgado Álvarez

Counselor (Tourism)
Mr. Sergio MONCADA

Counselor
Ms. Rina MENJIVAR

First Secretary (Consular)
Mrs. Yolanda MEMBRENO

First Secretary
Ms. Cynthia MCKECHNIE

Defense, Military, Naval and Air Attaché
Colonel Efraín GUTIERREZ ARDÓN

Consular Section
1612 K Street, NW, #310
Washington, DC 20005
Tel: (202) 223-0185
Fax: (202) 223-0202

MEXICO

Embassy of Mexico
Chancery: 1911 Pennsylvania Ave. NW
Washington, DC 20006
Tel: (202) 728-1600
Fax: (202) 728-1698
http://www.quicklink.com/mexico
http://www.embassyofmexico.org
E-mail: mexembusa@aol.com

National Holiday:
Independence Day, Sept. 16

Ambassador E. and P.
His E., Juan Jose BREMER MARTINO

Minister (Deputy Chief of Mission)
Mr. Jorge Castro VALLE KUEHNE

Minister (Environment)
Mr. Mario Gilberto AGUILAR-SÁNCHEZ

Minister (Consular)
Mr. Juan Carlos CUE VEGA

Minister (Migration)
Mr. Alvaro RODRIGUEZ TIRADO;
Mrs. María S. Carreño de Rodríguez

Minister (Attorney General's Office)
Mr. Alejandro DIAZ DE LEON;
Mrs. María O. Nava

Minister (Trade)
Mr. Javier MANCERA;
Mrs. Cecilia Autrique

Minister (Economic)
Mr. Alfredo Guillermo PHILLIPS GREENE;
Mrs. Mónica A. Collantes de Phillips

Minister (Cultural)
Mr. Ignacio DURAN;
Mrs. Lucero Duran

Minister (Press)
Mr. José A. ZABALGOITIA TREJO;
Mrs. Lucía Villalobos Barragan

Minister (Ambassador's Office)
Mr. José Ignacio MADRAZO;
Mrs. Margarita Otaduy

Minister (Economic)
Mrs. María E. ESPINOSA LOYA DE HOUDE;
Mr. Michel Joseph P. Houde

Counselor (Trade)
Mrs. Alma América ALFARO-SIERRA;
Mr. José Luis Tapis Nava

Counselor (Trade)
Miss Luz María DE LA MORA

Counselor (Commercial)
Mr. Arturo Luis Germán JESSEL PÉREZ;
Mrs. María D. Sandoval de Jessel

Counselor (Political)
Mr. Fernando MARTÍNEZ ZURITA REED;
Mrs. Teresita Arellano de Martínez Z.

Counselor (Attorney General's Office)
Mr. Miguel A. MÉNDEZ BUENOS AIRES;
Mrs. Elma Alicia Oviedo Galdeano

Counselor (Legal)
Mr. Rodolfo QUILANTAN ARENAS;
Mrs. Patricia Lourdes Tapia de Quilantan

Counselor (Administrator)
Mr. Carlos Alberto RABAGO SALDÍVAR;
Mrs. Mariana Patricia Valdés de Rabago

Counselor (Financial)
Mr. Jesús RODRÍGUEZ MONTERO;
Mrs. Erendira Dávalos de Rodríguez

Counselor (Cultural)
Mrs. Luz Estela SANTOS de BRUCK

Counselor (Hispanic Affairs)
Mr. Carlos GONZÁLEZ GUTIÉRREZ;
Mrs. Alina Flores Soto

Counselor (Political)
Mr. Juan Rodrigo LABARDINI FLORES;
Mrs. Norma Libia Ramírez de Labardini

Counselor (Political)
Mrs. Mabel GÓMEZ OLIVER DE DOMÍNGUEZ;
Mr. Manuel Domínguez Menéndez

Counselor (Agricultural and Forestry)
Mr. Marco A. MARTÍNEZ-MUÑOZ;
Mrs. María A. Obregón Santacilia de Martínez

Counselor (Trade)
Mr. Raúl URTEAGA-TRANI;
Mrs. Julia Urteaga

Counselor (Trade)
Mr. Raúl VALLEJO LARA;
Mrs. Patricia Villafuerte de Vallejo

Counselor (Trade)
Mr. Ricardo VERA RYAN;
Mrs. Magali Jacheet

Counselor (Customs and Revenue)
Mr. José Martín GARCIA;
Mrs. Patricia Gómez

First Secretary (Deputy Chief of Mission Office)
Mr. Eduardo BACA CUENCA;
Mrs. Yarla Itzel Urrutia de Baca

First Secretary (Trade)
Mr. Bryan Andrew ELWOOD SALIDO;
Mrs. Adriana Sanchez de Tagle

First Secretary (Border Affairs)
Mr. Ricardo PINEDA ALBARRÁN;
Mrs. Silvia Esther Cruz Palma

First Secretary (Trade)
Mrs. Marcia SAN ROMAN

First Secretary (Deputy Chief of Mission Office)
Mr. Juan Carlos MENDOZA SÁNCHEZ;
Mrs. Alejandrina Díaz de Mendoza

Second Secretary (Personnel)
Mr. Rodrigo ENCALADA

Second Secretary (Migration)
Ms. María Elena ALCARAZ

Second Secretary (Legal)
Mrs. María CORTINA

Second Secretary (Cultural)
Mr. Juan Manuel SALDIVAR

Third Secretary (Political)
Ms. Leslie MARTÍNEZ

Attaché (Archives)
Mr. Juan Carlos CARRILLO CABRERA;
Mrs. Yolanda Gallegos Rodriguez

Attaché (Office of the Deputy Chief of Mission)
Mrs. Lea CORTI;
Mr. Jesús Arturo García

Attaché (Office of the Deputy Chief of Mission)
Mrs. Mercedes ESQUIVEL DE ANTUNES;
Mr. Joao de Deus Barbosa Antunes

Attaché (Office of the Ambassador)
Mrs. Martha DUARTE

Attaché (Press)
Mrs. Liliana GONZÁLEZ

Defense, Military, and Air Attaché
Brigadier General Gilberto HERNANDEZ-ANDREU;
Mrs. Beatriz Rodríguez

Jane S. Pennewell
Personal Image Consultant
Tel: (703) 442-9188
Jane@JPimageconsulting.com

1831 Opalocka Drive
McLean, VA 22101
Fax: (703) 883-1997
www.JPimageconsulting.com

Naval Attaché
Rear Admiral José Santiago VALDEZ-ALVAREZ;
Mrs. Laura Isabel Olivares

Consular Office
2827 16th Street, NW
Washington, DC 20009
Tel: (202) 736-1000/11/12
Fax: (202) 797-8458

Trade Office
1911 Pennsylvania Avenue, NW
Washington, DC 20006
Tel: (202) 728-1700
Fax: (202) 728-1712

Agricultural Office
1911 Pennsylvania Avenue, NW
Washington, DC 20006
Tel: (202) 728-1723
Fax: (202) 728-1728

NAFINSA Office
1615 L Street, NW, #310
Washington, DC 20005
Tel: (202) 338-9010
Fax: (202) 338-9244

Military and Air Defense Office
1911 Pennsylvania Avenue, NW
Washington, DC 20006
Tel: (202) 728-1740
Fax: (202) 728-1745

Naval Office
1911 Pennsylvania Avenue, NW
Washington, DC 20006
Tel: (202) 728-1760
Fax: (202) 728-1767

NAFTA Office
1911 Pennsylvania Avenue, NW
Washington, DC 20006
Tel: (202) 728-1719
fax: (202) 728-1712

Revenue and Customs Office
1911 Pennsylvania Avenue, NW
Washington, DC 20006
Tel: (202) 728-1621
Fax: (202) 728-1664

NICARAGUA

Embassy of the Republic of Nicaragua
Chancery: 1627 New Hampshire Ave. NW
Washington, DC 20009
Tel: (202) 939-6570
Fax: (202) 939-6542
http://members.aol.com/embanic1/
E-mail: ambanic@amdyne.net
E-mail: Embanic-prensa@amdynd.net

National Holiday:
Independence Day, Sept. 15

Ambassador E. and P.
His E., Alfonso Ortega Urbina;
Mrs. Norma Guerrero de Ortega

Minister-Counselor
Mr. Harold Rivas

Counselor (Economic and Cooperation)
Mr. Jorge WONG-VALLE

Counselor (Press)
Mrs. Magda M. SOBALVARRO-OCHOA

First Secretary (Cultural and Administrative Affairs)
Mrs. Mana Teresa TEFEL

Counselor (Trade, Commerce and Immigration Affairs)
Mr. Mauricio RIVAS

PANAMA

Embassy of the Republic of Panama
Chancery: 2862 McGill Terrace NW
Washington, DC 20008
Tel: (202) 483-1407
Fax: (202) 483-8413

National Holiday:
Independence Day, Nov. 3

Ambassador E. and P.
His E., Gullermo FORD;
Mrs. Pilar de Ford

Minister-Counselor
Mr. Germán BRAVO

General Consul
Mr. Francisco J. MORALES

Consul Attaché
Mrs. Mylene MARRONE RUIZ

Attaché (Protocol)
Mr Carlos GONZÁLEZ

Commercial Officer
Mrs. Angela VELÁSQUEZ

Administrative Attaché
Mrs. Aida De ARAUJO

Commercial Attaché
Mr. Carlos GONZALEZ

Administrative Officer
(Vacant)

Legal Counselor
Ms. María Alejandra TULIPANO

Legal Attaché
Ms. Maruquel ICAZA P.

Cultural Officer
Mrs. Noris ALDERSON

PARAGUAY

Embassy of Paraguay
Chancery: 2400 Massachusetts Ave. NW
Washington, DC 20008
Tel: (202) 483-6960/61/62
Fax: (202) 234-4508
http://www.embassy.org/embassies/py.html
http://www.proparaguay.gov.py
E-mail: embapar@erols.com

National Holiday:
Independence Day, May 15

Ambassador E. and P.
Her E., Leila RACHID De COWLES;
Mr. Frank Cowles

Minister
Mr. Marcial BOBADILLA;
Mrs. Norma de Bobadilla

Counselor
Mr. Jose Maria IBANEZ;
Mrs. Rosana de Ibáñez

First Secretary
Ms. María Leticia CASATI

First Secretary
Ms. Liz HAYDEE CORONEL

Second Secretary
Mr. Enrique RAMIREZ;
Mrs. Susana de Ramírez

Third Secretary
Ms. María Alexandra MIRANDA

Consul
Mr. Fernando FRONCIANI

Consular Attaché
Ms. Analissa VERDUN GRASSI

Consular Attaché
Mr. Ruben RAMOS

Defense Attaché
General Luis GARCIA
Mrs. Norma de Garcia

Commercial and Economic Affairs Office
2400 Massachusetts Avenue, NW
Washington, DC 20008
Tel: (202) 483-6960/62

Defense Attaché
2400 Massachusetts Avenue, NW
Washington, DC 20008

Press and Information Affairs
2400 Massachusetts Avenue, NW
Washington, DC 20008
Tel: (202) 483-6960/62

Visa and Consular Affairs
2400 Massachusetts Avenue, NW
Washington, DC 20008
Tel: (202) 483-6960/62

PERU

Embassy of Peru
Chancery: 1700 Massachusetts Ave. NW
Washington, DC 20036
Tel: (202) 833-9860 to 69
Fax: (202) 659-8124
http://www.peruemb.org
http://www.embassy.org/embassies/
pe.html
E-mail: hescuder@lepruwash.com
E-mail: lepruwash@aol.com

National Holiday:
Independence Day, July 28

Ambassador E. and P.
His E., Alfonso RIVERO
MONSALVE;
Mrs. Maria Isabel de Rivero

Minister (Deputy Chief of Mission)
Mr. Claudio de la PUENTE
RIBEYRO;
Mrs. Diana Cunliffe

Minister and Consul General
Mr. Luis SANDOVAL

Minister
Mr. Néstor POPOLIZIO BARDALES

Minister-Counselor
Mr. Daúl MATUTE MEJIA

Minister-Counselor (Political, Military and Narcotics)
Mr. Néstor POPOLIZIO BARDALES

Minister-Counselor (Economic and Financial)
Mr. Carlos HERRERA RODRIGUEZ;
Mrs. Veronique Miclea Herrera

Minister-Counselor (Economic)
Mr. Alfredo VALENCIA PAZ;
Mrs. Julia de Valencia

Counselor (Political, Environment, Scientific & Juridical)
Ms. María Elvira VELÁZQUEZ
RIVAS-PLATA

Counselor (Political)
Mr. Jorge RAFFO CARBAJAL

First Secretary (Political and Congressional)
Ms. Cecilia GALARRETA BAZAN

First Secretary (Political, Military and Narcotics)
Mr. Ignacio HIGUERAS HARE;
Mrs. Ena de Higueras

First Secretary (Commercial)
Roberto RODRIGUEZ ARNILLAS;
Mrs. Roxana Rodriguez

Third Secretary
Mr. Rodolfo CORONADO MOLINA

Attaché (Civil)
(Vacant)

Attaché (Cultural)
Mrs. Elvira VELÁZQUEZ

Attaché (Police)

(Vacant)

Military Attaché
Brigadier General Fernando de
VILLENA GALLARDO;
Mrs. Rosa I. de Villena

Naval Attaché
Rear Admiral César Humberto
CHAVEZ JONES

Air Attaché
Lieutenant General Guillermo Dante
CACEDA BENVENUTO;
Mrs. Carmen Caceda

Assistant Attaché (Police)
Mr. Domingo CARRILLO;
Mrs. Angelica Carrillo

Assistant Attaché (Police)
Major Miguel PALOMINO;
Mrs. Rorio Ursula Balvin de Palomino

Assistant Military Attaché
Colonel Jorge ALA LUNA;
Mrs. Doris Ala Luna

Assistant Military Attaché
Colonel Antonio REBAZA ARMAS;
Mrs. Edita Rebaza

Assistant Military Attaché
Lieutenant Colonel Juan R. YABAR

Assistant Naval Attaché
Captain Roberto Ángel BALAREZO;
Mrs. Gladys Marietta Balarezo

Assistant Naval Attaché
Lieutenant Commander Victor
Augusto CHICHIZOLA

Assistant Air Attaché
Colonel José L. COLLANTES;
Mrs. Maritsa Collantes

Assistant Air Attaché
Major General Ruben MIMBELA;
Mrs. Marilia Mimbela

Air Attaché Office
2141 Wisconsin Avenue, NW, #A-350
Washington, DC 20007
Tel: (202) 333-1528
Fax: (202) 337-6240

Consulate General Office
1625 Massachusetts Avenue, NW, 6th
Floor
Washington, DC 20036
Tel: (202) 883-9868/9869

Joint Fight Against Drugs Office
1511 K Street, NW, #717
Washington, DC 20005
Tel: (202) 737-5484

Military Attaché Office
2141 Wisconsin Avenue, NW, #F
Washington, DC 20007
Tel: (202) 342-8127/30
Fax: (202) 333-7417

Naval Commissioner and Attaché Office
2141 Wisconsin Avenue, NW; #J
Washington, DC 20007
Tel: (202) 337-6670/72
Fax: (202) 337-7954

SPAIN

Embassy of Spain
Chancery: 2375 Pennsylvania Ave. NW
Washington, DC 20037
Tel: (202) 452-0100 & (202) 728-2340
Fax: (202) 833-5670
http://www.spainemb.org
E-mail: Infspw@erols.com

National Holiday:
October 12

Ambassador E. and P.
His. E., Javier RUPEREZ;
Mrs. Rakela Cerovic

Minister (Deputy Chief of Mission)
Mr. Agustin NUNEZ;
Mrs. María Isabel Vicandi Plaza

Minister (Cultural)
Mr. Juan M.R. DE TERREROS;
Mrs. Carmen Fuente Salavador

Counselor (Economic and Commercial)
Mr. Jose Alberto ARCONA
OLIVERA;
Mrs. María Transito Abrain Rodriguez

Counselor (Juridical)
Mr. David BELTRAN;
Mrs. María del Carmen Argüelles

Counselor
Mr. Javier CARBAJOSA;
Mrs. María Jesús Murciego

Counselor (Agriculture, Fisheries and Food)
Mr. Luis María ESTERUELAS;
Mrs. Juliana Burke

Counselor (Education)
Mr. Gonzalo GÓMEZ DACAL;
Mrs. María Del Carmen Cid Fernández

Counselor
Mr. Juan Ignacio SELL

Counselor (Commercial)
Mr. Francisco GUERRA;
Mrs. Isabel Carbonell

Counselor and Consul General
Mr. Rafael JOVER;
Mrs. María Dolores de Villanueva

Counselor
Mr. Juan Antonio M. BURGOS

Counselor (Economic and Commercial)
Mr. Manuel MORENO;
Mrs. Estela Garcia

Counselor (Labor)
Mr. Eliseu ORIOL PAGES;
Mrs. Montserrat Puiggali Torrento

Counselor (Economic and Administrative)
Mr. Darío POLO

Counselor (Financial)
Mr. Enrique SÁNCHEZ BLANCO;
Mrs. Lourdes Gómez Gil Aizpurua

Counselor (Information)
Mr. Florentino SOTOMAYOR;
Mrs. María Teresa Suárez

Counselor
Mr. Felipe DE LA MORENA;
Mrs. Patricia Almudena Bernar

Attaché (Information)
Mr. Alberto BARCIELA

Attaché
Mrs. Paloma CONDE

Attaché
Mr. Juan HIDALGO CUESTA;
Mrs. María Dolores Martín Moreno

Attaché (Consular)
Mr. Cándido MONTALVO;
Mrs. Christine Marín

Attaché (Agricultural)
Mr. Alfonso PINO

Attaché
Mr. Gonzalo PIZARRO;
Mrs. María Alina Cuervo Arango Pulin

Attaché (Administrative)
Mr. José A. RIERA;
Mrs. María Pía De-Luca

Attaché (Comercial)
Ms. Adela RODRIGUEZ

Defense Attaché
Major General Miguel CAMPINS;
Mrs. Aurora Vargas

Defense Cooperation Attaché
Lieutenant Colonel José Luis
CEBALLOS;
Mrs. María Pilar de Diego

Military Attaché
Colonel Carlos I. SANTOS;
Mrs. María del Carmen Alonso Poncela

Naval Attaché
Captain José Manuel PALENCIA;
Mrs. María Dolores Calvo Agras

Air Attaché
Colonel Carlos SEBASTIA
CAMARASA;
Mrs. María Teresa Rodero Garcia

Assistant Defense Cooperation Attaché
Major Rafael de LUCAS;
Mrs. Estilita Gomez-Rodriguez

Assistant Defense Cooperation Attaché
Mr. Juan Carlos SANCHA;
Ms. Paloma Oria de Rueda

Assistant Defense Cooperation Attaché
Major Jose Luis SANCHEZ;
Ms. Begona Corujo

Agricultural Office
2375 Pennsylvania Avenue, NW
Washington, DC 20037
Tel: (202) 728-2339
Fax: (202) 728 2320

Air Attaché
4801 Wisconsin Avenue, NW, 3rd Floor
Washington, DC 20016
Tel: (202) 244-8843

Consular Office
2375 Pennsylvania Avenue, NW
Washington, DC 20037
Tel: (202) 728-2330
Fax: (202) 728-2302

Cultural Office
2375 Pennsylvania Avenue, NW
Washington, DC 20037
Tel: (202) 728-2334
Fax: (202) 728-2312

Defense Attaché
4801 Wisconsin Avenue, NW, 4th Floor
Washington, DC 20016
Tel: (202) 244-0093

Defense Cooperation Attaché
4801 Wisconsin Avenue, NW, 4th Floor
Washington, DC 20016
Tel: (202) 364-2257

Economic and Commercial Affairs Office
2558 Massachusetts Avenue, NW
Washington, DC 20008
Tel: (202) 265-8600 & 8601
Fax: (202) 265-9478

Education Office
2375 Pennsylvania Avenue, NW
Washington, DC 20037
Tel: (202) 728-2335
Fax: (202) 728-2313

Financial Office
2375 Pennsylvania Avenue, NW
Washington, DC 20037
Tel: (202) 728-2338
Fax: (202) 728-2318

Information Office
2375 Pennsylvania Avenue, NW
Washington, DC 20037
Tel: (202) 728-2332
Fax: (202) 728-2308/10

Labor and Social Affairs Office
2375 Pennsylvania Avenue, NW
Washington, DC 20037
Tel: (202) 728-2331
Fax: (202) 728-2304

Military Attaché
4801 Wisconsin Avenue, NW, 3rd Floor
Washington, DC 20016
Tel: (202) 244-6161

Naval Attaché
4801 Wisconsin Avenue, NW, 3rd Floor
Washington, DC 20016
Tel: (202) 244-2166/67

URUGUAY

Embassy of Uruguay
Chancery: 2715 M Street NW
Washington, DC 20007
Tel: (202) 331-1313/14/15/16
Fax: (202) 331-8142
http://www.embassy.org/uruguay
Email: uruguay@erols.com

National Holiday:
Independence Day, Aug. 25

Ambassador E. and P.
His E., Hugo FERNANDEZ-FAINGOLD;
Mrs. Ana María Renna-Valdez

Minister (Deputy Chief of Mission)
Dr. Carlos A. MORA;
Mrs. Odette Susanne Le Moyne de Mora

Minister (Financial)
Mr. Carlos STENERI;
Mrs. Mercedes B. de Steneri

Minister-Counselor
Dr. Nelson Yemil CHABEN;
Dr. Brenda Cabrera-Sosa de Chabén

Minister-Counselor (Commercial)
Mrs. Enriqueta SUZACQ;
Mr. Julio de la Paz

Counselor
Mr. Marion BLANCO

First Secretary
Dr. Eduardo A. ROSENBROCK;
Mrs. Silvana Sapriza-Carrasco

First Secretary (Consul)
Mr. Mario LIORI;
Mrs. María del Rosario Gonzales de Liori

Second Secretary
Mr. Alejandro GAROFALI;
Mrs. Irma Hummel de Garofali

Defense and Military Attaché
General Tomás MEDINA;
Mrs. Delia Piriz

Assistant Military Attaché
Colonel Carlos DIAZ;
Mrs. María Cristina Diaz

Naval Attaché
Captain Juan FERNÁNDEZ;
Mrs. Liliana Castelo

Air Attaché
Colonel José PINON;
Mrs. Ana Perujo

Financial Affairs Office
1025 Connecticut Ave. NW, #902
Washington, DC 20036
Tel: (202) 223-9833

Military, Naval, and Air Attaché Office
1825 K Street, NW, #701
Washington, DC 20006
Tel: (202) 466-3177

Uruguay Trade Bureau
1030 15th Street, NW #760
Washington, DC 20005
Tel: (202) 789-8225

VENEZUELA

Embassy of the Republic of Venezuela
Chancery: 1099 30th Street, NW
Washington, DC 20007
Tel: (202) 342-2214
Fax: (202) 342-6820
http://www.embavenez-us.org
E-mail: despacho@embavenez-us.org

National Holiday:
Independence Day, July 5

Ambassador E. and P.
His E., Alfredo TORO HARDY

Minister-Counselor (Deputy Chief of Mission)
Ms. Evelyn HOROWITZ

Minister-Counselor
Mrs. Sandra FRANCO DE PICO

Minister-Counselor (Petroleum Affairs)
Mr. Jorge IRSAY

Minister-Counselor (Petroleum Affairs)
Mr. Efraín PICO PONTE

Counselor
Mr. Rafael QUEVEDO

Counselor
Mr. Antonio RANGEL

Counselor (Press Office)
Fermin LARES

Counselor
Ms. Irama BALZA DE GODOY

First Secretary
Ms. Marie BORREGALES

First Secretary
Mrs. Ana PÉREZ YEPEZ

Second Secretary
Mr. Omar José TOURON UNDA;

Third Secretary
Ms. Adriana ALEMAN

Petroleum Attaché
Mr. Manuel IRIBARREN

Administrative Attaché
Ms. Miriam PEREZ LOBO

Cultural Attaché
Mrs. Carolina MARQUEZ DE MASSIANI

Attaché
Ms. Dominga DELGADO

Attaché
Ms. Zulay AHUMADA

Defense Attaché
Major General Wladimir FILATOV RIABKOV

Defense Assistant
Colonel José CADENA RODRIGUEZ

Defense Assistant
Colonel Wilfredo DIAZ NICOLAS

Administrative Assistant
Major Saúl SUAREZ

Military Attaché
Brigadier General Nelvi F. FERREIRA ACEVEDO

Naval Attaché
Rear Admiral Gerardo R. ESCALONA SERRANO

Air Attaché
Brigadier General Franklin ANGULO FERNANDEZ

Assistant Military Attaché
Lieutenant Colonel Henry J. GARCIA

Assistant Military Attaché
Lieutenant Colonel Eude DINATALE PAPA

Assistant Naval Attaché
Mr. Eduardo Antonio RUIZ

Military Attaché Office
2409 California Street, NW
Washington, DC 20008
Tel: (202) 234-3633/3634

Naval Attaché Office
2437 California Street, NW
Washington, DC 20008
Tel: (202) 265-7323

Air Attaché Office
2409 California Street, NW
Washington, DC 20008
Tel: (202) 234-9132

Defense Attaché Office
2437 California Street, NW
Washington, DC 20008
Tel: (202) 588-0384

US Embassies and Consulates in Hispanic Countries
Embajadas y consulados de EUA en los países hispanos

ARGENTINA

BUENOS AIRES (E)
International Mail: 4300 Colombia,
1425 Buenos Aires
APO Address: Unit 4334; APO AA 34034
Tel: [54] (1) 777-4533 and 777-4534
Fax: 777-0197; COM Fax 777-0673
Telex: 18156 AMÉMBAR
AMB: (Vacant)
AMB SEC: (Vacant)
CHG: Manuel Rocha
POL:Mark Sigler
ECO: Stephen Thompson
COM: Michael Liikala
SCI: Jeffrey T. Lutz
ADM: (Vacant)
RSO: Walter Huscilowitc
CON: Robert Raymer
PAO: Guy Burton
IRM: Ronnie Rontenot
EST: Philip Covington
DAO: Col. Robert Adams
MILGP: Col. Clark Lynn
AGR: Philip Shull
APHIS: Thomas Schissel
LAB: Thomas J. Morgan
FAA: Santiago García (res. in
Miami)
FAA/CASLO: Héctor Vela
IRS: Frederick Dulas (res. in
Mexico City)
DEA: Abel E. Reynoso

BOLIVIA

LA PAZ (E)
Ave. Arce No. 2780, P.O. Box 425
La Paz Bolivia; APO AA 34032
Tel: [591] (2) 430251
Fax: [591] (2) 433900
UNSAID Tel 786544
Fax 786654; Direct Lines
AMB: (591) (2) 432524
DCM: 431340; POST: 1 432540
DEA: 431481; CONS: 433758
CON Fax: 433854
USIS Tel: 432621
USAID DIR Tel: 786179
USAID EXEC OFF Tel 786399

AMB: Donna J. Hrinak
AMB SEC: Sonia D, Ramirez
DCM: George C. Lannon
POL/ECO: Hugh Neighbour
CON: Thomas H. Lloyd
ADM: Frederick B. Cook
RSO: (Vacant)
LBA: Kenneth R. Audroue

AID: Liliana Ayalde
AGR: Larry Fuell (res. in Lima)
COM: (Vacant)
DEA: Anthony Placido
PAO: Donald E. Terpstra
DAO: Col. Dennis Fowler, USAF
MILGP: Col. Dennis E. Keller, USA
NIMA: John Tomasovich
ICITAP: (Vacant)
PC: Meredith Smith
FAA: Santiago Garcia (res. in
Miami)
FAA/CASLO: Héctor Vella (res. in
Buenos Aires)
FAA/FSIDO: Tony Kijek (res. in
Miami)
NAS: J. Richard Baca
IRS: Frederick Dulas (res. in
Mexico City)

COCHABAMBA (CA)
Avenida Oquendo No 654, Torres Sofer, 6to piso,
Of. 601
Tel. [591](42) 56714;
DEA Address: Cruce Taquiña, Zona Linde
Tel [591](42) 88896, 98
CA: William Scarborough
DEA: John Emerson
AID: Richard Fisher
NAS: Francisco Alvarez
PC: Remigio Ancalle

SANTA CRUZ (CA)
313 Calle Guemes No. 6, Zona Equipetrol
Tel. [591] (3) 330725, 363842
Fax 325544
CA: Mary F. Telchi
DEA: James R. White
PC: Trevor Murray
NAS: Pedro T. Hernández

SUCRE
Av. Kilometro 7, Edificio No. 218, Of. 226
Tel.: [591] (06) 444411
PC: Eduardo Avila

BRAZIL

BRASILIA (E)
Avenida das Nacoes, Quadra 801, Lote 3, Brazilia,
DF Cep 70403-900 Brazil American Embassy
Brazilia, Unit 3500
APO AA 34030
Tel [55] (61) 321-7272
Fax 225-9136 (Stateside address)
ADM Fax 225-5857
COM Fax 225-3981
USIS Fax 321-2833, 322-0554
AID Fax 323-6875; FCS Fax 225-3981

NAS Fax 226-0171
SCI Fax 321-3615
POL Fax 223-0497
ECO Fax 224-9477
IVG No 921+0000+ext. Internet address is http://
www.embaixada-americana.org.br/

AMB: Anthony S. Harrington
AMB SEC: *(Vacant)*
DCM: Gerard M. Gallucci
POL: *(Vacant)*
ECO: Brian R. Stickney
SCI: Marc Nicholson
COM: Richard Lenaham
NIST: Ileana Martinez
CON: Gregory Frost
ADM: Jeffrey D. Levine
GSO: John Manuel
RSO: Christopuher J. Pauli
PAO: Gail Gulliksen
IRM: Alan Roecks
AID: Janice Weber
DEA: Patrick Healey
DAO: Col. Charles Rowcliffe, USA
MLO: Col. Donald Belche, USAF
AGR: Herbert "Finn" Rudd
BUREC: Peter Hradilek

RIO DE JANEIRO (CG)
Avenida President Wilson , 147 Castelo, Rio de
Janeiro-RJ 20030-020 Unit 3501, APO AA 34030
Tel: [55] (21) 292-7117
Fax: 220-0439
USIS Fax 262-1820
USIS Telex: 22831
Fax: 262-5131

CG: Cristobal R. Orozco
ECO/POL:Robert Taylor
COM: Judith Henderson
CON: Ronald Sinclair
ADM: Christhopher A. Lambert
RSO: Foon C. Chung
IRM: Simon Guerrero
DAO: Cdr. Craig J. Baranowski
MLO: Lcdr. Michael Rabang
AGR: Herbert "Finn" Rudd (res. in
Brasilia)
VOA: William Rodgers
LOC: Pamela Howard- Reguindin

SAO PAULO (CG)
Rua Padre Joao Manoel, 933, Sao Paulo 01411-
001; P.O. Box 2489, Unit 3502, APO AA
34030,Tel [55] (11) 881-6511, Fax 852-5154;
USIS BPAO Fax 852-1395; Press Fax 852-4438
CG: Carmen Martínez
ECO: Kenneth B. Davis
POL: Maria Sanchez-Carlo
CON: Rudolph Boone

COM: Richard Lenaham
ADM: Jesse I. Coronado
RSO: Jackson Booth
PAO: David Kurakane
LAB: Mark A. Mittlehauser
IRS: Frederick Dulas(res. in
Mexico City)
ATO: Mark Lower
IRM: Arthur Pollick
DEA: Jeffrey J. Fitzpatrick

RECIFE (C)
Rua Goncalves Maia, 163 , Boa Vlsta, Recife;
APO AA 34030 Tel: [55] (81) 421-2441
Emergency Tel: 421-5641 Fax: 231-1906
PO: Francisco J. Fernandez
CON: Duncan H. Walker

Commercial Office (Trade Center)
Rua Estados Unidos, 1812, 01427-002 Sao
Paulo, S.P. Tel [55] (11) 853-2811, Fax 853-
2744
COM: Richard Lenahan
Commercial and Agricultural offices are also
located at: Belo Horizonte (USIS and COM
Branch) Rua Fernandes Tourinho 147-14th Fl.,
302112-000, Belo Horizonte MG, Tel: [55]-(31)
281-7271, Fax: 281-6551

COM: Sean Kelly

BELEM (CA)
Rua Oswaldo Cruz 165 66, 017-090 Belem, Para,
Brazil
Tel 55-91223-0800/0413
Fax 091-223-0413, Telex 91-1092
CA: Cristine Serrao

FORTALEZA (CA)
Institute Brazil-Estados Unidos
Rua Nogueria Acioly, 891, Aldeota, Fortaleza,
Brazil
Tel/Fax: [55] (85) 221-1539
CA: Patricia C. Cavin

MANAUS (CA)
Rua Recife 1010, 67, 057, Amazonas, Brazil Tel:
[55] (92) 234-4546 Fax: (92) 234-4546
CA: James R. Fish

PORTO ALEGRE (CA)
Rio Riachuelo, 1257, 90010-271, Centro, Porto
Alegre, RS
CA: Debra T. Godoy

SALVADOR DA BAHIA (CA)
Av. Antonio Carlos Magalhaes S/N-Ed. Cidadella
Center 1, Sala 410,40
275-440 Salvador, Bahia, Brazil Tel: [55] 071-
358-9166 Telex: 712780
Fax: 071-351-0717

CA: Heather M. Marques

Information provided and updated by key officers of Foreign Service Posts.

CHILE

SANTIAGO (E)
Av. Andres Bello 2800, APO AA 34033
Tel [56] (2) 232-2600
Fax 330-3710
COM Fax: 330-3172
AID Fax: 638-0931
AGR Fax 56-2-330-3203
FBO fax 233-4108
CON 56-2-330-3710

AMB: John O'Leary
AMB SEC: Rosalie B. Kahn
DCM: James J. Carrgher
ECO/POL: Stephen G. Wesche
COM: John A. Harris
CON: Carl F. Troy
ADM: David F. Davison
RSO: John J. Root
PAO: Kathleen A. Brion
IRM: Patrick Meagher
DAO: Capt. Larry Pacentrilli, USN
MILGP: Col. Mark V. Mayer
IRS: Frederick Dulas (resident in Mexico City)
AGR: Richard J. Blabey
APHIS: Peter Fernández
LAB: Leonard A. Kusnitz
DEA: Victor Olivieri
LEGATT: Kevin Currier
PC: John McAward
FAA: Santiago Garcia (res. in Miami)

COLOMBIA

BOGOTA, (E)
Calle 22D-BIS, No. 47-51
Apartado Aereo 3831
APO AA 34038
Tel: [57] (1) 315-0811
Fax: [57] (1) 315-2197
CON Tel: 315-1566
COM Fax: [571] (315) 2171/2190
GSO Fax: [571] (315) 2207

AMB: Curtis WE. Kamman
AMB SEC: Sheila M. Jones
DCM: Barbara C. Moore
POL/ECO: Leslie A. Bassett
COM: Karka King
CON: Kenneth F. Sackett
ADM: Robert E. Davis
RSO: Seymour C. Dewitt
PAO: James H. Williams
IRM: Michael J. Kovick
AID: (Vacant)
DAO: Col. Leocadio Muniz, USA
USMILGP: Col. James C. Hiett, USAF
AGR: David G. Salmon
APHIS: John L. Shaw
FAA: Victor Tamariz (res. in Miami)
NAS: Luis G. Moreno
IRS: Luis O. Rivera
DEA: Leo Arreguin, Jr.
ATF: David O. Navarrete
CUS: Stephen J. Hayward
LEGATT: Joseph L. Rodríguez
USSS: Anthony M. Chapa

BARRANNQUILLA (CA)
Calle 77, No. 68-15
Tel: (95) 353-0970 or 0974
Fax: (95) 353-5216
CA: David S. Parrish

COSTA RICA

SAN JOSE (E)
Pavas, San Jose; APO AA 34020

Tel: (506) 220-3939
AMB 220-2303
DCM 220-2304
Afterhours Tel: 220-3127
Fax: 220-2305
COM Fax: 231-4783

AMB: Thomas J. Dodd
AMB SEC: Laura A. Bailey
DCM: Linda Jewell
POL/ECO: Perry E. Ball
COM: Frank Foster
CON: Janet M. Weber
ADM: Clark W. Allard
RSO: William J. Griffin
PAO: Gary McElhiney
IRM: Cinthia M. Ruby
DEA: Vance W. Stacy
FAA: Ruben Quiñones (resident in Miami)
ODR: Mark Wilkins
AGR: Charles Bertsch
APHIS Region V: Harold C. Hoffman
APHIS Region VI: Mark Knez
ENVIR HUB: Lawrence Gumbiner
IRS: Frederick Dulas (resident in Mexico City)

CUBA

HAVANA (USINT)
Swiss Embassy, Calzada between L y M Sts., Vedado, Havana
USINT Tel: (53) (7) 33-3551/9, 33-3543/5
Fax: 33-3700;
Refugee inquiries telephone numbers: 33-3546/7
Afterhours Marine Post: 1 33-3026,
USIS Direct Line: 33-3967
Fax: 33-3869
FBO Direct Line: 33-4096/97
Fax: 33-3975
INS Switchboard: 33-4511/33-3586
Fax: 33-4512

PO: Vikki Huddleston
DPO: John Boardman
POL/ECO: Jeffrey Delaurentis
CON: Patricia Murphy
ADM: John Hilliard
RSO: Michael French
PAO: Janet Edmunson
IRM: Paula Marx
FAA: Ruben Quiñones(res. in Miami)
FBO: James C. McQueen
INS (OIC): Silma Dimmel

DOMINICAN REPUBLIC

SANTO DOMINGO (E)
Corner of Calle Cesar Nicolas Penson and Calle Leopoldo Navarro
Unit 5500, APO AA 34041-5500
Tel: (809) 221-2171
Afterhours Tel: 221-8100
Fax: (809) 686-7437
CON Tel: 221-5511
Fax: 685-6959
AID Tel: 221-1100
Fax: 221-0444
INS Tel: 221-0113
Fax: 221-0110
PC Tel: 685-4102
Fax: 686-3241
IVG nos.: 848-0000 or 848+4+3-digits ext.:
Exec ext. 200, Fax: 686-4326
ADM ext. 255, Fax: 686-7166
FCS ext. 400, Fax 688-4838
USIS ext 486, Fax 541-1828
DEA ext. 381, Fax: 685-7507
DAO ext. 220, Fax: 687-5222
MAAG ext. 487, Fax: 682-3991
APHIS ext. 357, Fax: 686-0979
FAS ext. 344, Fax 685-4743

AMB: Charles Manatt
AMB SEC: (Vacant)
DCM: Linda E. Watt
DCM SEC: Dolores V. Appel
ECON/POL: Paul B. Larsen
COM: Robert L. Farris
CON: Edwin P. Cubbison
PAO: Merrie D. Blocker
ADM: Harry A. Blanchette
RSO: Gary Gibson
IRM: Jamie Esquivel
AID: Edward Kadunc
DEA: Efrain de Jesus
INS: Maria Aran
DAO: Ltc. George W. Murray, USMC
MAAG: Cdr. Larry McCabe, USN
TAT: Maria Leos
APHIS: Osvaldo Perez-Ramos
AGR: Kevin Smith
PC: Natalie S. Woodward
IRS: Frederick Dulas (res. in Mexico City)
FAA: Ruben Quiñones (res. in Miami)
NAS: Guido del Prado (res. in Miami)

PUERTO PLATA (CA)
Calle Beller 51, 2nd Fl. Off.#6
Tel. (809) 586-4204
Sousa Office Tel 571-3880

CA: William G. Kirkman

ECUADOR

QUITO (E)
Avenida 12 de Octubre y Patria; APO AA 34039
Tel: [593] (2) 562-890
Afterhours Tel: 561-749
Voice Mail: 561-624
Fax: 502-052
COM Fax: 504-550
direct-in-dialing: 644-6-0000 or office ext.

AMB: Gwen C. Clare
AMB SEC: Linda Hartsock
DCM: Larry Palmer
POL: W. Stuart Symmington IV
ECO: Michael Glover
COM: Robert Jones
CON: Joyce Deshazo
ADM: Earl Ferguson
RSO: Barry M. Moore
PAO: James Moore
IRM: Michael Cesena
NAS: Joel Cassman
AID: Hilda Arellano
DAO: Col. Phillip Stewart, USA
MILGP: Col. James Willey, USA
DEA: Salvador Rodríguez
PC: Marcy Kelley
INS: Charles Aycock
AGR: Lawrence D. Fuell (res. in Lima)
FAA: Victor Tamariz (resident in Miami)

GUAYAQUIL (CG)
9 de Octubre y Garcia Moreno
APO AA 34039
Tel: [593] (4) 323-570
After hours Tel: 321-152
Fax: 325-286
COM Fax: 324-558

CG: Timothy J. Dunn
CG SEC: Deanna Cotter
CON: Steve Hardesty
ADM: Keith Sanders
DEA: Víctor Cortéz
IRM: Bruce Chaplin
COM: Kaleb Belzer
INS: Robert Hlavac

EL SALVADOR

SAN SALVADOR (E)
Final Blvd. Santa Elena, Antiguo Cuscatlan
Unit 3116, APO AA 34023
Tel: (503) 278-4444
Fax: [503] 278-6011
USAID Tel: 298-1666
Fax: 298-0885
ECO/COM Fax: 298-2336
GSO Fax: 278-3347

AMB: Anne W. Patterson
AMB SEC: Carol L. Scannel
DCM: Mark M. Boulware
POL: Kevin M. Johnson
ECO/COM: Bruce Williamson
CON: William M. Barlett
ADM: Jorge Cintron
RSO: Kevin M. Barry
PAO: Marjorie Coffin
IRM: Richard J. Herkert
GSO: Rosina Schacknies
FMO: Thomas A. Lyman
PER: Marianne Kompa
DAO: Col. Richard Nazario, USA
AID/DIR: Kenneth C. Ellis
MILGP: Col. John L. Goetchius, Jr.
AGR: Suzanne Heinen (res. in Guatemala City)
APHIS/DIR: (Vacant)
PC: Michael L. Wise
DEA: Vincent J. Sparacino, Acting
DOJ: Robert Loosle
FAA: Ruben Quiñones (res. in Miami)
LAB: Edmund K. Sutow
IRS: Frederick Dulas (res. in Mexico City)
ICITAP: Louis Coarruviaz
LEGATT: Fernando M. Rivero
INS: Víctor W. Johnston

GUATEMALA

GUATEMALA CITY (E)
7-01 Avenida de la Reforma, Zone 10 APO AA 34024
Tel: [502] (2) 331-1541
Fax: 334-8477
AID Tel: 332-0202
Fax: 331-1511
CON: Fax: 331-0564
COM Fax: 331-7373
PC Tel: 334-8263
Embassy direct-in-dial/IVG: 8-799-0000
or 8-799-1+ ext.

AMB: Prudence Bushnell
AMB SEC: Linda Howard
DCM: William J. Brencick
POL: David Van Valkenburg
ECO: Brendan Hanniffy
COM: Daniel J. Thompson
CON: Peter Kaestner
ADM: Brian W. Wilson
RSO: Charlene Lamb
PAO: Mary Deane Conners
IRM: Thomas P. Phalen
AID: George Carner
DAO: Col. Mario Jimenez, USA
MILGP: Col. Joe Haning, USA
AGR: Suzanne Heinen
APHIS: Gordon Tween
NAS: Andrew W. Olytan
NIMA: James Hutchings
PC: Charles Reilly
ICITAP: Joseph Gannon
FAA: Ruben Quiñones (res. in Miami)
DEA: Pedro Velasco

INS: Jorge Eisermann
LAB: William Owen
IRS: Frederick Dulas(res. in Mexico City)
LEGATT: Fernando M. Rivero (res. in Miami)
CUS: Ed Mederos (res. in Miami)

HONDURAS

TEGUCIGALPA (E)
Avenida La Paz, Apartado Postal No. 3453; APO AA 34022
Tel: [504] 238-5114 or 236-9320
Afterhours Tel. 236-9325
Exec Off Tel: (504) 237-0696
Fax: (504) 236-9037
COM Fax: (504) 238-2888
USIS Fax: 236-9309
USAID Fax: 236-7776
CON Fax: 237-1792

AMB: Frank Almaguer
AMB SEC: Mary Navarro
DCM: Paul A. Trivelli
POL: Edward J. Michal
ECO/COM: David C. Wolfe
CON: Catherine M. Barry
COM: Daniel J. Thompson (resident in Guatemala City)
ADM: Samuel G. Durrett
RSO: John B. McKennan
PAO: Gregory M. Adams
IRM: Leon G. Galanos
AID: Elena Brineman
DAO: Col. David Kuhns, USAF
MILGP: Col. Mario Garza, USA
DEA: Thomas Berger
AGR: Suzanne Heinen (res. in Guatemala City)
APHIS: (Vacant)
INS: Joseph Banda, Jr.
FAA: Ruben Quiñones (res. in Miami)
PC: Stephen Miller
LAB: Robert L. Luaces
IRS: Frederick Dulas (res. in Mexico City)

MEXICO

MEXICO CITY (E)
Paseo de la Reforma 305, 06500
México D.F.; P.O. Box 3087
Laredo, TX 78044-3087
Tel: [52] (5) 209-9100
Fax: [52] (5) 208-3373 and 511-9980

AMB: Jeffrey Davidow
AMB SEC: Celestina Rentería
DCM: James M. Derham
POL: J. Christian Kennedy
ECO: William R. Brew
COM: Dale Slaght
CON: Thomas P. Furey
CG: Víctor A. Abeyta
ADM: James B. Lane
RSO: Kenneth E. Sykes
EST: S. Ahmed Meer
IRM: Wayne G. Adams
RAMC: Frederic C. Hassani
PAO: John Dickson
NAS: Gaye Maris
DAO: Col. Richard Downey
MLO: Col. Francisco Pedrozo
FBU: Bernardino G. González
SCI: Lawrence M. Kerr
AID: Paul White
EPA: Lawrence Sperling
AGR: Frank Lee
APHIS (reg.6): Scott D. Saxe

APHIS (reg.5): Elba Quintero
FAA: Ruben Quiñones (resident in Miami)
LAB: John Ritchie
INS: Hipólito Acosta
CUS: Pete González (Acting)
ATF: Keith Heinzerling
LEGATT: Edmundo L. Guevara
DEA: Michael G. Garland
IRS: Frederick Dulas
FIN: Steve Backes

USDA/AGR Trade Office (ATO)
Edif. Parque Virreyes, Monte Pelvoux #220
Esquina. Prado Sur,
11000 Mexico D.F.
P.O. Box 3087
Laredo, TX 78044-3087
Tel: [52] (5) 202-0434, 202-0168, and 202-0212 FAX: [52] (5) 202-0528
ATO: Chad R. Russell

US Export Development Office
Liverpool 31, 06600 México, D.F.
Tel: [52] (5) 591-0155
Fax: 566-1115
DIR/COM: John Kuehner

US Travel and Tourism Office
Plaza Comermex
M. Avila Camacho 1-402,
11560 Mexico, D.F.
Tel: [52] (5) 520-2101
Fax: [52] (5) 202-9231
DIR: Peter F. Bohen

CIUDAD JUAREZ (CG)
Chihuahua, Avenue López Mateos, 924 N
32000 Ciudad Juarez, Chihuahua
P.O. Box 10545
El Paso, TX 79995-0545 Tel: [52] (16) 113000
Fax: [52] (16) 169056
CG: Edward H. Vázquez
DPO: Philip Egger
RSO: Robert D. Barton
ADM: Jacqueline Holland
INS: Robert Ballow
DEA: Javier Jacquez

GUADALAJARA (CG)
JAL; Progreso 175
44100 Guadalajara, Jalisco, Mexico
Box 3088
Laredo, TX 78044-3088
Tel: [52] (3) 825-2998, 825-2700
Fax: 826-6549
CG: Edward H. Wilkinson
COM: Virginia Krivis
CON: William A. Muller
ADM: Carol J. Smetana
PAO: Judith L. Bryan
GSO: Daniel L. Foote
USDA/APHIS: Raymond Carbajal
LEGATT: Gregory Rodriguez
DEA: Pedro Pena

MONTERREY (CG)
N. L. Ave.
Constitución 411 Poniente
64000 Monterrey, N.L.
Box 3098
Laredo, TX 78044-3098
Tel: [52] (8) 345-2120
Fax: [52] (8) 342-0177
ADM: 343-7283
CG: Daniel A. Johnson
CG SEC: Patricia A. Rhoades
POL/ECO: Clark H. Crook Castan
COM: Janice Corbett
CON: (Vacant)

ADM: Nathan M. Bluhm
RSO: Gregory Houston
PAO: Stephen Holgate
INS: Arturo Nieto
CUS: Ventura Cerda
DEA: Jose A. Baeza
LEGATT: Salvador Escobedo

TIJUANA (CG)
B.C.N.; Tapachula 96
22420 Tijuana, Baja California Norte
P.O. Box 439039
San Diego, CA 92143-9039
Tel: [52] (66) 81-7400
Fax: [52] (66) 81-8016
CG: Nick Hahn
CON: Richard González
COM: Renato Davia
ADM: Susan L. Pazina
PAO: Clinton Wright
INS: Oscar E. Lujan
NIV: Lisa A. Gamble-Barker
DEA: Alexander G. Toth
CUS: Sonny Manzano
RSO: Joel Henderson

HERMOSILLO (C)
Sonora; Monterrey 141 Pre.
83260 Hermosillo, Sonora
P.O. Box 3598
Laredo, TX 78044-3598 (U.S. mailing address)
Calle Monterrey 141, Col. Centro, C.P. 8300,
Hermosillo, Sonora, Mexico (Mexican mailing address)
Tel: [52] (62) 172-375
Fax: 172-578
E-mail address is amconsul@rtn.uson.mx
PO: Ronald Kramer
CON: William E. Fitzgerald
ADM: Romulo A. Gallegos
IRM: Rudy R. Garcia
CUS: Terry Kirkpatrick
APHIS: Dale Rush
DEA: Harvey Goehring

MATAMOROS (C)
Tamps., Ave. Primera 2002
87330 Matamoros, Tamaulipas
Box 633
Brownsville, TX 78522-0633
Tel: [52] (88) 12-44-02
Fax: 12-21-71
PO: George B. Kopf
CON: Kelly S. Cecil
ADM: (Vacant)

MÉRIDA (C)
Yuc., Paseo Montejo 453
97000 Mérida, Yucatán
Box 3087
Laredo, TX 78044-3087
Tel: [52] (99) 25-5011
Fax: 2506219
PO: David R. Ramos
CON: Joseph Gallazzi
NIV: Anthony J. Kleiber
ADM: Kurt J. Hoyer
DEA: Jaime Camacho

NUEVO LAREDO (C)
Tamps; Calle Allende 3330, Col. Jardín
88260 Nuevo Laredo, Tamps.
Drawer 3089,
Laredo, TX 78044-3089
Tel: [52] (87) 14-0512
Fax: [52] (87) 14-7984 ext128
ATO Tel: [52] (87) 191-603
ATO Fax: [52] (87) 191-605
PO: Rufus Watkins

ADM: Juan Aguero
CON: Lana Chumley
AGR: Richard T. Drennan

NOGALES, SONORA (C)
Calle San José S/N, Nogales, Sonora
Nogales, AZ 85628
Tel: [52] (631) 34820
Fax: [52] (631) 34797
PO: Jane Gray
CON: Sean Murphy
ADM: David J. Savastuk

ACAPULCO (CA)
Hotel Acapulco Continental
Costera M. Aleman 121, Local # 14
Acapulco, Gro 39580
Tel: [52] (74) 81-1699
Fax: [52] (74) 84-0300
CA: Alexander Richards

CABO SAN LUCAS (CA)
Blvd. Marina y Pedregal Local No. 3
Zona Centro Cabo San Lucas, B.C.S.,
Tel: 114-3-35-66/3-34-47
Fax: 114-3-35-66
CA: Michael J. Houston

CANCÚN: (CA)
Plaza Caracol Dos, Segundo Nivel,
No 320-323, Blvd. Kukulkan, Cancún,
Q.R. 77500
Tel: [52] (98) 83-2450
Fax: [52] (98) 83-1373
CA: Lynette Belt

COZUMUL (CA)
Av. 35 Norte # 650, Entre 12 Bis y 14,
Cozumel, Q.R. 77500
Tel: [52] (987) 26152
Fax: [52] (987) 22339
CA: Anne R. Harris

MAZATLAN (CA)
Hotel Playa Mazatlan
Rodolfo T. Loaiza No. 202
Zona Dorada, 82100, Mazatlan, Sin
Tel: [52] (69) 16-5889
CA: Gerianne N. Gallardo

OAXACA (A)
Alcala #201 - Desp. 206 68000 Oaxaca
Apdo. Postal 54, Sec. "B";
Tel: [52] (951) 4-30-54
CA: Mark A. Leyes

PUERTO VALLARTA (CA)
Plaza Zaragoza 166, piso 2-18,
edif. Vallarta Plaza, Puerto Vallarta,
Jalisco, 48300
Tel: [52] (322) 2-0069
Fax: [52] (322) 2-0074
CA: Kelly A. Trainor

SAN LUIS POTOSI (CA)
Francisco de P. Moriel 103 Desp. 1, Esquina con
Venustiano Carranza
Tel: y Fax: [52] (481) 2-1528
CA: Carolyn Lazaro

SAN MIGUEL DE ALLENDE (CA)
Dr. Hernandez Macias 72,
Apdo. Postal 328; San Miguel de Allende,
Guanajato
Tel: [52] (415) 2-2357
Fax: [52] (415) 2-1588
CA: Philip J. Maher

NICARAGUA

MANAGUA (E)
Km. 4½ Carretera Sur.
APO AA 34021
Tel: [505] 266 2298/6010, 266-6012/13
Tel: [505] 266-6015/18, 266-6026/27, 266-6032/33
AMB Fax: 266-9074
ADM Fax: 266-3865
GSO Fax: 266-6046
CON Fax: 266-9943
ECO/COM Fax: 266-9056
USIS Fax: 266-3861
AGR Fax: 266-7006
AID Fax: 278-3828
DAO Fax: 266-8022
E-mail: usbusiness@amemb.org.ni
AMB: Oliver P. Garza
AMB SEC: Patricia A. Brania
DCM: Deborah A. McCarthy
POL: Casey H. Christensen
ECO/COM: Anthony J. Interlandi
ADM: Robert D. Goldberg
CON: Celio F. Sandate
RSO: Frederick A. Byron
IRM: Carig W. Spetch
PAO: Edward Loo
AID: Marilyn Zak
DAO:Ltc. Gerry G. Turnbow
PC: Howard T. Lyon
DEA: Joseph Petrauskas
AGR: Charles R. Bertsch (res. in San Jose)
APHIS: Dr. Alan Terrell
FAA: Celio Young (res. in Miami)
FAA: Ruben Quiñonez (resident in Miami)
IRS: Frederick Dulas (resident in Mexico City)

PANAMA

PANAMA CITY (E)
Apartado 6959, Panama 5
Rep. de Panama
Unit 0945, APO AA 34002
Tel: [507] 227-1377
Fax: [507] 227-1964
GSO Fax: 225-2720
PER Fax: 227-6850
AMB: Simon Ferro
AMB SEC: Yolanda Norvell
DCM: Frederick A. Becker
POL/ECO: W. Lewis Amselem
CON/GEN: Robert J. Blohm
ADM: Trevor A. Snellgrove
IRM: Terrence K. Williamson
RSO: Edward A. Lennon
PC: Janice Jorgensen
APHIS: John H. Wyss
ARS: (Vacant)
FAS: Charles R. Bertsch (res. in San Jose)
DEA: Jay Bergman
ABMC: Dannie Cooper
COM: Richard F. Benson
PAO:Joao M. Ecsodi
AID: Lawrence J. Klassen
CUS: Robert J. Benavente
NAS: Laura L. Livingston
ICITAP: (Vacant)
LEGATT:Gilbert C. Torrez
USCG: Cdr. James Parker
INS: John A. Mata

CRISTOBAL, COLON (CA)
Panama Agencias Bldg.,
Terminal and Pedro Prestan Sts.,
Cristobal, Colon Province; No residential or office mail delivery in Colon. Send all mail to: c/o American Embassy, Panama, Box E, APO Miami 34002
Tel: (507) 41-2440/2478
Fax: (507) 41-6039
CA: Frank X. Zeimetz

PARAGUAY

ASUNCION (E)
1776 Mariscal López Ave.
Casilla Postal 402
Unit 4711, APO AA 34036-0001
Tel: [595] (21) 213-715
FAX: [595] (21) 213-728
AMB: (Vacant)
AMB SEC: Ann Granatino
CHG: Stephen G. McFarland
POL: David Lindwall
ECO/COM: Richard Boly
CON: Julie L. Grant
ADM: Frank edahawsky
FMO: James H. Basso
RSO: William Vancio
IRM: Michael W. Meyers
AID: Wayne Tate
DAO: Ltc. William G. Graves, USA
DEA: Lewis R. Adams, Jr.
FBIS: Nancy Johnson
NIMA: John Tomasovichi
ODC: Col. Ahmed E. Labault, USA
PAO: James C. Dickmeyer
PC: John McCloskey
AGR: Philip Shull(res. in Buenos Aires)
FAA: Santiago García (res. in Miami)
IRS: Frederick Dulas (res.in Santiago)

PERU

LIMA (E)
Avenida Encalada, Cuadra 17
Monterrico, Lima
P.O. Box 1995, Lima 1
or American Embassy (Lima),
APO AA 34031-5000
Tel: [51] (1) 434-3000
Fax: 434-3037
Afterhours Tel: 434-3032
(RNX: 549-0000 or 549+four-digit ext.)
FAS Fax: 434-3043
APHIS Fax: 434-3043
FCS FAX: 434-3041
USIS Fax: 434-1299
DAO Fax: 434-0117
DEA Fax: 434-3054
MAAG Fax: 434-1199
NAMRID Fax: 561-2034
NIMA Fax: 476-3618
USAID address: Larrabure y Unanue 110, Lima 1
Tel: 433-3200
Fax: 433-7034
Internet address is last name and initials of recipient@limawpoa.us-state.gov.
AMB: John Hamilton
AMB SEC: María D. Guillory
DCM: Heather M. Hodges
NAS: Candis L. Cunningham
CON: Annette L. Veler
ADM: James G. Williard
PAO: Douglas M. Barnes
RSO:Gordon A. Sjue
POL: Arnold A. Chacon
ORA: Robert E. Gorelick
ECO: Krishna Urs
IRM: Richard L. Gunn
AID: Thomas Geiger
INS: Michael E. Wojticki
DAO: Col. Michael McCarthy, USAF
DEA: Randy K. Sales
MAAG: Col. Gilberto Pérez
NAMRID: Cdr. Truman W. Sharp, USN
NIMA: Eduardo Elinan
AGR: Lawrence D. Fuell
APHIS: Donald R. Wimmer
IRS: Frederick Dulas (res. in Santiago)
LEGATT: Kevin Currier (res. in Santiago)
FAA: Victor Tamariz (res. in Miami)

CUZCO (CA)
Avenida Tullumayo 125
Tel: [08] (4) 24-5102, 23-9451, 22-4112
Fax: 23-3541
CA: Olga Villagarcia

SPAIN

MADRID (E)
Serrano 75, 28006 Madrid
APO AE 09642
Tel: [34] (1) 91587-2200
FAX: 91587-2303
Inward dial (DID) numbers:
AMB [34] 91587-2205
DCM 91587-2205
POL 91587-2387
ECO 91587-2286
ADM 91587-2208
IPC 91587-2308
DAO 91587-2278
USIS 91587-2502
DEA 91587-2280
FAA 91587-2300
ODC 91549-3209
CON 91587-2236
BUD/FISC 91587-2211
PER 91587-3636
RSO 91587-3438
IPC duty phone 619-276-781
EMB duty phone 619-276-782
AMB: Edward L. Romero
AMB SEC: María de Lourdes Fernández
DCM: James D. Walsh
POL: Michael Butler
COM: Rafael Fermoselle
POL/MIL: Victor Bonilla
ECO: Stephen V. Noble
CON: Phillip French
ADM: Joseph Schreiber
RSO: Stanley J. Joseph
IRM: Nicodemo Romeo
PAO: Pamela Corey-Archer
AGR: Robert Wicks
LAB: Paul Siekert
EST/SCI: Marshall H. Carter -Tripp
DAO: Col. Bruce C. Balbin, USAF
DEA: Yvette Torres
ODC: Capt. Leroy E. Sheehan, USN
FAA: Tony Fazio (res. in Paris)
FAA/CASLO: Mike Galvan
FAA/CAAG: Miriam Santana
LEGATT: David Swhirmp
IRS: Frederick Pablo (res. in Paris)
NASA: Ingrid Desilvestre

DCMC: Ltc. John D. Swan
INS: Kent Johansson

BARCELONA (CG)
Reina Elisenda 23, 08034 Barcelona
PSC 61, Box 0005, APO AE 09642
Tel: [34] (93) 280-2227
Fax: (93) 205-5206
ADMIN Fax: (93) 205-7764
USIS Fax: (93) 205-5857
COM Fax: (93) 205-7705
CG: Douglas R. Smith
COM: Lewis Santamaría
CON/ADM: Marc J. Meznar
PAO: Deborah Galssman

LA CORUÑA (CA)
Canton Grande, 16-17, 8E, 15003
Tel: [34] 9891-21-32-33
Fax: [34] 981-22-2808
CA: Marcelino Fuentes-Ramos

LAS PALMAS (CA)
Frachy y Roica, 5-5, No. 13 35007
Tel: 34-928-271 259
Fax: 34-928-22-58-63
CA: Ana María Quintana-Figueroa

FUENGIROLA (MALAGA) (CA)
Centro Comercial "Las Rampas" Fase 2, Planta 1,
locales 12-G-7 y 12-G-8, Fuengirola, 29640 Malaga
Tel: 34-952-47-48-91
Fax: 34-952-46-51-89
CA: Robert G. Aaron

PALMA DE MALLORCA (CA)
Avenida Jamine 111, No. 26, Entresuelo 2-H-1 (97) 07012
Tel: 34-971-725051
Fax: 34-971-71-87-55
CA: Bartolomé Bestard

SEVILLE (CA)
Paseo de las Delicias, 7 Seville, 41012
Tel: 34-95-42 31885
Fax: 34-95-42 32040
CA: Jerry Lee Johnson

VALENCIA (CA)
CL de la paz, 6-5 Local 5, 46003 Valencia
Tel: 34-96-351-6973
Fax: 34-96-352-9565
CA: Mary A. Garrity

URUGUAY

MONTEVIDEO, (E)
Lauro Muller 1776
APO AA 34035
Tel: [598] (2) 203-6061
Fax: [598] (2) 408-7777
AMB: Christopher C. Ashby
AMB SEC: Irene C. Willig
DCM: Jonathan D. Farrar
PLEC: Paul T. Belmont
ECO/COM: Stephen K. Keat
COM: Michael Liikala (resident in Buenos Aires)
RSO: Dean L. De Villa
ADM:Michael St. Claire
CON: denise A. Boland
PAO: Peter M. Brennam
IRM: John C. Adams
ODC: Col. Randall L. James, USAF
AGR: Phil Shull (res. in Buenos Aires)
CUS: Roberto J. Fernandez
IRS: Frederick Dulas (res. in Santiago)
FAA/CASLO: Héctor Vela (res. in Buenos Aires)
FAA: Santiago García (res. in Rio de Janeiro)
PC: Peter A. Lara
LEGATT: Carlos H. Fernández
DEA: Abel E. Reynoso (resident in Buenos Aires)

CARACAS (E)

Calle F con Calle Suapure
Colinas de Valle Arriba
P.O. Box 62291, Caracas 1060-A
or APO AA 34037
Tel: [58] (2) 977-2011,
Telex: 35501AMEMB VE
Fax: 977-0843;
LEGATT Fax: 58-2-977-0364
AMB: John F. Maisto
AMB SEC: Ann Kirlian
DCM: Nancy Mason
POL: Thomas H. Ochiltree
ECO: Gary Maybarduk
COM: Louis Santamaría
CON: Marilyn F. Jackson
ADM: Robert Weisberg
RSO: Henry N. Jenkins
PAO: Philip Parkenson
IRM: John H. Varner, Jr.
GSO: Thomas F. Burke
CUS: Percival A. Jordan
DEA: Paul A. Herfing
DAO: Col. Gregory H. Landers, USAF
MILGP: Col. Michael B. Rhea, USA
PER: Eleanor Akahloun
AGR: Rodney McSherry
LAB: Bruce W. Friedman
FAA: Víctor Tamariz (res. in Miami)
FMO: Robert A. Wert
IRS: Frederick Dulas (res. in Mexico City)
NAS: Michael Corbin
LEGATT: Héctor Rodríguez

ABBREVIATIONS

ACDA-Arms Control and Disarmament
ACM-Assistant Chief of Mission
ADM-Adminstrative Section (USDA/FAS)
ADV-Adviser
AGR-Agricultural Section
AID-Agency for Int'l Devel.
ALT-Alternate
AMB-Ambassador
AMB SEC-Ambassador's Secretary
APHIS-Animal and Plant Health Inspection Service Officer
APO-Army Post Office
ARSO-Asst. Reg. Security Officer
ASG-Analytical Support Group
ATO-Agricultural Trade Office (USDA/FAS)
BCAO-Branch Cultural Affairs Officer (USIS)
Bg-Brigadier General
BIB-Board for International Broadcasting
BO-Branch Office (of Embassy)
BPAO-Branch Public Affairs Officer (USIS)
B.P.-Boite Postale
BUD-Budget
C-Consulate
CA-Consular Agency/Agent
CAO-Cultural Affairs Officer USIS)
Capt-Captain (USN)
DCD-Center for Disease Control
Cdr-Commander
CEO-Cultural Exchange Officer (USIS)

CG-Consul General, Consulate General
CG SEC-Consul General's Secretary
CHG-Chargé d'Affaires
CINCAFSOUTH-Commander-in-Chief Allied Forces Southern Europe
CINCEUR-Commander-in-Chief U.S. European Command
CINCUSAFE-Commander-in-Chief U.S. Air Forces Europe
CINCUSAREUR-Commander-in-Chief U.S. Army Europe
Col-Colonel
CM-Chief of Mission
COM-Commercial Section (FCS)
CON-Consul, Consular Section
COUNS-Counselor
C.P.-Caixa Postal
CPO-Communications Prog. Officer
CUS-Customs Service (Treasury)
DAC-Development Assistance Committee
DCM-Deputy Chief of Mission
DEA-Drug Enforcement Agency
DEP-Deputy
DEP DIR-Deputy Director
DIR-Director
DOE-Department of Energy
DPAO-Deputy Public Affairs Officer (USIS)
DPO-Deputy Principal Officer
DSA-Defense Supply Adviser
E-Embassy
ECO-Economic Section
ECO/COM -Economic/Commercial Section
EDO-Export Development Officer
ERDA-Energy Research and Development Admin.
EST-Environmental, Science, and Technology
EX-IM-Export-Import
FAA-Federal Aviation Administration
FAA/CASLO-Federal Aviation Administration Civil Aviation Security Liaison Officer
FAA/FSIDO-Federal Aviation Administration Flight Standards Int'l District Office
FIC/JSC-Finance Committee and Joint Support Committee
FIN-Financial Attaché (Treasury)
FODAG-Food and Agriculture Org.
FPO-Fleet Post Office
IAEA-Int'l Atomic Energy Agency
IAGS-Inter-American Geodetic Survey
ICAO-Int'l Civil Aviation Org.
IMO-Information Mgmt. Officer
IO-Information Officer (USIS)
IPO-Information Program Officer
IRM-Information Resources Mgmt.
ISM-Information Systems Mgr.
JUS/CIV-Dept. of Justice, Civil Div.
JUSMAG-Joint US Military Advisory Group

LAB-Labor Office
LO-Liaison Officer
Ltc-Lieutenant Colonel
LEGATT-Legal Attaché
M-Mission
Mg-Major General
MAAG-Military Assistance   Advisory Group
MILGP-Military Group
MSG-Marine Security Guard
MSC-Military Staff Committee
MIN-Minister
MLO-Military Liaison Officer
MNL-Minerals Officer
NARC-Narcotics
NATO-North Atlantic Treaty Org.
NAS-Narcotics Affairs Section
NCIS-Naval Criminal, U.S.
OAS-Org. of American States
ODA-Office of the Defense Attaché
ODC-Office of Defense Cooperation
OIC-Officer in Charge
OMC-Office of Military Cooperation
PAO-Public Affairs Officer (USIS)
PO-Principal Officer
PO SEC-Principal Officer's Secretary
POL-Political Section
POL/LAB-Political and Labor Section
POLAD-Political Adviser
POL/ECO-Political/Economic Section
RADM-Rear Admiral
RCON-Regional Consular Affairs Officer
REDSO-Regional Economic Dev. Services Office
REF-Refugee Coordinator
REP-Representative
RES-Resources
RHUDO-Regional Housing and Urban Dev. Office
ROCAP-Regional Officer for Central American Programs
RPSO-Regional Procurement and Support Office
RSO-Regional Security Officer
SAO-Security Assistance Office
SCI-Scientific Attaché
SEC DEL-Secretary of Delegation
SHAPE-Supreme Headquarters Allied Powers Europe
SLG-State and Local Government
STC-Security Trade Control
UNEP-United Nations Environmental Program
UNIDO-United Nations Industrial Development Organization
USA-US Army
USAF-US Air Force
USDA-US Department of Agriculture
USEU-US Mission to the European Union

USGS-US Geological Survey
USINT-US Interests Section
USIS-US Information Service
USLO-US Liaison Officer
USMC-US Marine Corps
USMTM-US Military Training Mission
USN-US Navy
USNATO-US Mission to the North Atlantic Treaty Organization
USOAS-US Mission to the Org. of American States
USOECD-US Mission to the Org. for Economic Cooperation and Development
USTTA-US Travel and Tourism Agent
USUN-US Mission to the United Nations
VC-Vice Consul
VOA-Voice of America

Hispanic Consulates in the US
Consulados hispanos en EUA

ARGENTINA

CALIFORNIA

Los Angeles – (CG)
5055 Wilshire Blvd., #210
Los Angeles, CA 90036
Tel: (323) 954-9155
Consul General
Mr. Luis María KRECKLER
Deputy Consul General
Mr. Raúl Ignacio GUASTAVINO
Deputy Consul
Mr. Roberto Héctor DIEZ
Deputy Consul
Mr. Leandro Federico FERNÁNDEZ SUÁREZ‹
Deputy Consul
Mr. Roberto Carlos DUPUY
Consular Agent
Mr. Juan Carlos TOCE
Consular Agent
Mrs. Viviana Judith AZERRAD DE VILLAVERDE
Consular Agent
Mrs. Claudia A. BONICALZI DE TABUYO

FLORIDA

Miami (CG)
800 Brickell Ave., Penthouse 1
Miami, FL 33131
Tel: (305) 373-7794
Deputy Consul General
Mr. Alejandro Héctor NIETO
Deputy Consul General
Mr. Guillrmo RODRIGUEZ
Deputy Consul General
Mr. Miguel E. REALMONTE
Deputy Consul
Mrs. Elena Leticia ROSSI MIKUSINSKI
Consular Agent
Mr. Juan Carlos DORGAMBIDE
Consular Agent
Mr. Juan José ÁLVAREZ
Consular Agent
Mr. Roberto Francisco ESPÓSITO

Tourism Office
2655 Le Jeune Rd., PH 1, #F
Coral Gables, FL 33134
Tel: (305) 442-1366
Consular Agent
Mr. Eduardo A. PIVA

GEORGIA

Atlanta (CG)
245 Peachtree Center Ave., #2101
Atlanta, GA 30303
Tel: (404) 880-0805
Consul General
Mr. Natalio Marcelo JAMER
Deputy Consul General
Mr. Edgardo Víctor GALOTTI

ILLINOIS

Chicago - (CG)
205 N. Michigan Ave., #4208/4209
Chicago, IL 60601-5968
Tel: (312) 819-2620
Fax: (312) 819-2626
Consul General
Mrs. Cristina VALLINA DE MARTÍNEZ
Deputy Consul
Mr. Maecelo PACE
Consul Agent
Mr. Jorge Luis MANGHI

NEW YORK

New York - (CG)
12 W. 56th St.
New York, NY 10019
Tel: (212) 603-0400
Deputy Consul General
Ms. Hebe Noemi PONGELLI
Deputy Consul General
Mr. Ciro L. CILIBERTO INFANTE
Deputy Consul
Mr. Javier Andrés GOLISZEWSKI
Deputy Consul
Mr. Mario Javier OYARZÁBAL
Deputy Consul
Mr. Carlos Alberto POFFO
Consular Agent
Ms. Ana María VACA
Consular Agent
Miss Beatriz Gregoria BUSTOS

TEXAS

Houston - (CG)
3050 Post Oak Blvd., #1625
Houston, TX 77056
Tel: (713) 871-8935
Consul General
Mr.Oracio WAMBA
Deputy Consul
Mr. Alejandro MERONIUC

BOLIVIA

ALABAMA

Mobile - (HC)
1301 Azalea Rd.
Mobile, AL 36693
Tel: (334) 660-5365
Honorary Consul
Mr. Thomas Joe PURVIS

ARIZONA

Phoenix - (HC)
The Castillo Company
2345 E. University Dr.
Phoenix, AZ 85034
Honorary Consul
Mr. Eduardo A. CASTILLO

CALIFORNIA

Los Angeles (CG)
483 S. Spring St., # 1212
Los Angeles, CA 90013
Tel: (213) 680-0190

San Francisco (CG)
870 Market St., # 575
San Francisco, CA 94102
Tel: (415) 495-5173
Consul General
Mr. Rolando GUMIEL GALARZA
Vice Consul
Mr. Carlos Mauricio RIVERO SÁNCHEZ

COLORADO

Aspen (HC)
21 Lemond Circle
Snowmass Village, CO 81615
Honoray Consul
Mr. James J. RAAF

DISTRICT OF COLUMBIA

Washington – (EMB)
3014 Massachusetts Ave. NW
Washington, DC 20008
Tel: (202) 483-4410
Fax: (202) 328-3712
Consul General
Ms. María Carolina TOLEDO CANEDO
Consular Agent
Mr. Fernando GRANDY CAVERO

Washington - (HC)
4339 Garfield St., NW
Washington, DC 20008
Tel: (202) 244-7648
Honorary Consul General
Mr. William R. JOYCE

FLORIDA

Miami – (CG)
700 Ingraham Bldg.
25 SE 2nd Ave., #545
Miami, FL 33131
Tel: (305) 670-0709
Consul General
Mr. Jaime PRADA VELASCO
Deputy Consul
Mr. Fernando Francisco LAZCANO DUNN
Vice Consul
Mr. Hugo Alfredo CUELLAR ALEXANDER

GEORGIA

Atlanta - (HCG)
1375 Peachtree St. NW, #180
Atlanta, GA 30309
Tel: (404) 522-0777
Honorary Consul General
Mr. S. George HANDELSMAN

ILLINOIS

Chicago - (HC)
1200 W. Superior
Melrose Park, IL 60160
Tel: (708) 343-1234
Honorary Consul
Mr. Jaime ESCOBAR

LOUISIANA

New Orleans – (HC)
643 Magazine St.
New Orleans, LA 70130
Tel: (504) 596-2720
Honorary Consul
Mr. David BALL

MASSACHUSETTS

Boston – (HCG)
85 Devonshire St., #1000
Boston, MA 02109

Information updated from *Foreign Consular Offices in the United States*.

Tel: (617) 742-1500
Honorary Consul General
Mr. Russell D. LEBLANG

MINNESOTA
Minneapolis - (HC)
20550 Hackamore Rd.
Hamel, MN 55340
Tel: (612) 478-9495
Honorary Consul
Mrs. Gloria STEINE

MISSOURI
St. Louis - (HC)
7710 Carondelet Ave., #404
St. Louis, MO 63105
Tel: (314) 725-9466
Honorary Consul
Mrs. Beatriz E. CALVIN

NEW YORK
New York – (CG)
211 E. 43rd St., #702
New York, NY 10017
Tel: (212) 687-0530
Consul General
Mr. Carlos Paul BRUCKNER BARBA
Deputy Consul
Mr. Alberto Gastón CANEDO ÁLVAREZ
Deputy Consul
Mr. Sixto Nelson FLEIG SAUCEDO
Vice Consul
Ms. Wilma F. BALLON ALVARADO

OHIO
Cincinnati - (HC)
5500 Mapleridge Dr.
Cincinnati, OH 45227
Tel: (513) 271-5381
Honorary Consul
Mr. David C. MITCHELL

PUERTO RICO
San Juan - (HC)
64 Washington St.
San Juan, PR 00907
Tel: (787) 757-3084
Honorary Consul
Mr. Hugh Alanson ANDREWS

TEXAS
Dallas - (HC)
611 Singleton
Dallas, TX 75212
Tel: (214) 571-6131
Honorary Consul
Ms. María URIOSTE

Houston - (HCG)
1880 Dairy Ashford, #691
Houston, TX 77077
Tel: (713) 497-4068
Honorary Consul General
Mr. Jorge GALATOIRE
Honorary Vice Consul
Mrs. Diana María GALINDO DE WALKER

WASHINGTON
Seattle - (HC)
5200 Southcenter Bldg., #5

Seattle, WA 98188
Tel: (206) 244-6696
Honorary Consul
Mr. René Ricardo ANTEZANA MONTANO

BRAZIL

ALABAMA
Birmingham – (HC)
1500 Resource Dr.
Birmingham, AL 35242
Tel: (205) 250-4731
Honorary Consul
Mr. Michael H. JOHNSON

ARIZONA
Phoenix – (HC)
7036 N. 69th Pl.,
Paradise Valley, AZ 85253
Tel: (602) 948-4402
Honorary Consul
Mr. K. Charles OELFKE

CALIFORNIA
Los Angeles – (CG)
8484 Wilshire Bl., #730/711/260
Beverly Hills, CA 90211
Tel: (213) 651-2664
Consul General
Mr. Jorio Salgado GAMA FILHO
Deputy Consul General
Mrs. Vera Lucia CAMPETTI
Deputy Consul
Mr. David SILVEIRA DA MOTA NETO
Deputy Consul
Ms. María De WINKLER
Deputy Consul
Mrs. María Ercilia MURAKAMI
Vice Consul
Mrs. Ana María AZEVEDO
Vice Consul
Mrs. Ananicia Martins GIMENEZ

San Diego (HC)
2380 Caminito Agrado
San Diego, CA 92107
Tel: (619) 224-1145
Honorary Consul
Mr. Nelson Da PEREIRA

San Francisco – (CG)
300 Montgomery #900
San Francisco, CA 94104
Tel: (415) 981-8170
Consul General
Mr. José Augusto ALVES
Deputy Consul
Ms. Carmen Lucía LOMONACO
Vice Consul
Ms Noemia WAINER

DISTRICT OF COLUMBIA
Washington – (EMB)
3006 Massachusetts Ave. NW
Washington, DC 20008
Tel: (202) 238-2700
Fax: (202) 238-2827
Consul
Ms. Wanja Campos NOBREGA
Vice Consul
Mrs. Elida De Souza MOORE

Vice Consul
Mr. Mauricio Souza LEITE

FLORIDA
Miami - (CG)
Penthouse 1, 2601 S. Bayshore Dr., #800
Miami, FL 33133
Tel: (305) 285-6200
Consul General
Mr. Luis Fernando BENEDINI
Deputy Consul General
Mr. Carlos Alfredo LAZARY TEIXEIRA
Deputy Consul General
Mr. José Mauro COUTO
Deputy Consul General
Mr. Augusto César DE VASCONSELLOS GONCALVES
Deputy Consul General
Ms. Regina Celia BITTENCOURT
Deputy Consul
Mr. Andre Luiz SANTOS
Deputy Consul
Mrs. Cynthia Altoe BUGANE
Deputy Consul
Mr. Osvaldo Dos PIZZA
Vice Consul
Mrs. Anamaria Nobrega FERNÁNDES
Vice Consul
Miss Marcia DOS SANTOS RIBEIRO
Vice Consul
Mr. Huberth Da NEIVA
Vice Consul
Mr. Euclides Santa OLIVEIRA
Vice Consul
Ms. María Emilia OLIVEIRA
Vice Consul
Mr. Bernardo FELLER

GEORGIA
Atlanta - (CG)
Cain Tower, 229 Peachtree St. NE, #2306
Atlanta, GA 30303
Tel: (404) 521-0061
Consul General
Mr. Mario Da ROITER
Vice Consul
Mr. Enoch De NASCIMENTO

Savannah - (HC)
107 Prosperity Dr.
Savannah, GA 31408
Tel: (912) 964-0711
Honorary Consul
Mr. James Robert MYRICK

HAWAII
Honolulu - (HC)
44-166 Nanamoana St.
Kaneohe, HI 96744
Honorary Consul
Mr. John E. POAST

ILLINOIS
Chicago - (CG)
401 N. Michigan Ave. 30th Floor
Chicago, IL 60611
Tel: (312) 464-0244
Fax: (312) 464-0299
Consul General
Mr. Alexandre ADDOR NETO
Deputy Consul
Mrs. Luiza María SANTIAGO
Vice Consul
Mr. Manuel C. MACHADO NETO

Vice Consul
Miss Marcia Gurgel VALENTE

LOUISIANA
Baton Rouge – (HC)
1465 Ted Dunham Ave.
Baton Rouge, LA 70802
Tel: (504) 336-4143
Honorary Consul
Mr. Joseph Simon BROWN

MASSACHUSETTS
Boston – (CG)
20 Park Plaza, The Statler Bldg., #810
Boston, MA 02116
Tel: (617) 542-4000
Fax: (617) 542-4318
Consul General
Mr. Mauricio Eduardo COSTA
Deputy Consul
Ms. Ana Claudia RODRIGUES
Deputy Consul
Ms. Marcia LOUREIRO
Vice Consul
Mr. Sergio Dourado MARTINS
Vice Consul
Mr. Israel Dos SANTOS
Vice Consul
Ms. Maria Josina RODRIGUES

Brazilian Air Force Office
20 Park Plaza, #810
Boston, MA 02148
Tel: (617) 542-4000

MISSISSIPPI
Jackson - (HC)
175 E. Capitol St., #700
Jackson, MI 39201
Tel: (601) 961-2600
Honorary Consul
Mr. James Kelly ALLGOOD

NEW YORK
New York – (CG)
1185 Avenue of Americas, 21st Floor
New York, NY 10036
Tel: (212) 916-3200
Consul General
Mr. Flavio Miragaia PERRI
Deputy Consul General
Mr. Paulo Cesar VASCONCELLOS
Deputy Consul
Mr. Silvio Meneses GARCÍA
Deputy Consul
Mr. Orlando Leite RIBEIRO
Deputy Consul
Mr. Rodrigo D'araujo GABSCH
Deputy Consul
Mr. Joao Carlos BELLOC
Vice Consul
Mr. Marcelo SALUM
Vice Consul
Mr. Darío Vasconcellos CAMPOS

Office of the Financial Counselor
600 5th Ave., 20th Floor
New York, NY 10020
Tel: (212) 489-7930
Deputy Consul
Mr. Pedro Gustavo WOLLNY
Deputy Consul
Mr. Guilherme Luiz LEITE RIBEIRO

PUERTO RICO

San Juan - (CG)
Banco de Ponce Bldg.
268 Muñoz Rivera Ave.
Hato Rey, PR 00918-2507

TENNESSEE

Memphis - (HC)
1256 N. McLean Blvd.
Memphis, TN 38108
Tel: (901) 272-6505
Honorary Consul
Mr. Edson Porto PEREDO

TEXAS

Houston – (CG)
1700 W. Loop S., #1450
Houston,TX 77027
Tel: (713) 961-3063
Consul General
Ms. María Lucía SANTOS POMPEU
BRASIL
Deputy Consul
Mr. Julio Víctor ESPIRITO SANTO
Vice Consul
Ms. Loretta María DA CRUZ
Vice Consul
Mr. Wilson Adelio DOMINGUES
Vice Consul
Mr. Helio de LOBO

VIRGINIA

Norfolk – (HC)
625 Chesopeian Trail
Virginia Beach, VA 23452
Honorary Consul
Mr. James Earnest THOMPSON

CHILE

CALIFORNIA

Los Angeles – (CG)
1900 Ave. of the Stars, #2450
Los Angeles, CA 90067
Tel: (310) 785-0113
Fax: (310) 785-0132
Consul General
Mr. Gonzalo MENDOZA NEGRI

San Diego – (HC)
550 West "C" St., #1820
San Diego, CA 92101-3509
Tel: (619) 232-6361
Fax: (619) 696-0991
Honorary Consul
Mr. George L. GILDRED

San Francisco – (CG)
870 Market St. #1062
San Francisco, CA 94102
Tel: (415) 982-7662
Fax: (415) 982-2384
Consul General
Mr. Alberto M. YOACHAM
SOFFIA
Honorary Consul
Mr. Fernando ALEGRÍA

Santa Clara - (HCA)

1376 Johnson St.
Santa Clara, CA 94025
Tel: (415) 688-3847
Fax: (415) 322-6403
Honorary Consular Agent
Mr. Carlos LOPEZ

DISTRICT OF COLUMBIA

Washington – (EMB)
1732 Massachusetts Ave. NW
Washington, DC 20036
Tel: (202) 785-1746
Fax: (202) 887-5579
Consul
Mr. Bernardo Jose DEL PICO RUBIO
Consul
Mr. José Miguel MENCHACA PINOCHET

FLORIDA

Miami – (CG)
800 Brickell Ave., #1230
Miami, FL 33131
Tel: (305) 371-3219
Fax: (305) 374-4270
Consul General
Mr. Carlos José DUCCI OSSA
Deputy Consul General
Mr. Pedro Alfredo GARCÍA
CASTELBLANCO
Consular Agent
Mr. Luis Amable MONTERO CORDOVA

Commercial Office
1101 Brickell Ave., #M-103
Miami, FL 33133
Tel: (305) 599-2224

GEORGIA

Atlanta -(HC)
2876 Sequoyah Dr., NW
Atlanta, GA 30327
Tel: (404) 355-7923
Honorary Consul
Mrs. Erika María MONCKEBERG

HAWAII

Honolulu – (HC)
1860 Ala Moana Blvd., #1900
Honolulu, HI 96815
Tel: (808) 949-2850
Honorary Consul
Ms. Keith E. ADAMSON

ILLINOIS

Chicago – (CG)
875 N. Michigan Ave., #3352
Chicago, IL 60611
Tel: (312) 654-8780
Fax: (312) 654-8948
Consul General
Mr. Alberto Antonio LABBE GALILEA
Consular Agent
Mr. Rodrigo Ignacio SALCEDO HANSEN

LOUISIANA

New Orleans – (HC)
World Trade Center
2 Canal St., 26th floor

P.O. Box 60046
New Orleans, LA 70130
Tel: (504) 528-3364
Fax: (504) 524-4156
Honorary Consul
Mr. Angel PELAYO CARRERAS

MASSACHUSETTS

Boston – (HC)
79 Milk St., #600
Boston, MA 02109-3986
Tel: (617) 426-1678
Fax: (617) 426-6925
Honorary Consul
Mr. Paul William GARBER
Honorary Consul
Mr. Philip C. GARBER

NEW YORK

New York – (CG)
866 United Nations Plaza, #302
New York, NY 10017
Tel: (212) 355-0612
Fax: (212) 688-5879
Consul General
Mr. Álvaro ZUNIGA BENAVIDES
Honorary Consul
Ms. Elba FUENTES
Consular Agent
Mr. Marcelo Mauricio SALAS REGINATO
Consular Agent
Mr. Wolfgang Andreas BAUER STAMPFLI
Consular Agent
Mr. Flavio Augusto CORTES ACEVEDO

PENNSYLVANIA

Philadelphia – (CG)
Public Ledger Bldg.
446 6th & Chestnut
Philadelphia, PA 19106
Tel: (215) 829-9520
Fax: (215) 829-0594
Consul General
Mrs. Lucía AVETIKIAN DE RENART

PUERTO RICO

San Juan - (CG)
American Airlines Bldg.
1509 Lopez Landron, #800
Santurce, PR 00911
Tel: (809) 725-6365
Fax: (809) 725-7295
Consul General
Mr. Antonio Alfonso MORAGA
FERGADIOTTI

SOUTH CAROLINA

Charleston - (HC)
948 Equestrian Dr.
Mount Pleasant, NC 29464
Tel: (803) 881-6224
Honorary Consul
Mr. Carlos SALINAS

TEXAS

Dallas – (HC)
3500 Oak Lawn Ave., #200
Dallas, TX 75219-4343

Tel: (214) 528-2731
Fax: (214) 522-7167
Honorary Consul
Ms. Dorothy J. REID

Houston – (CG)
1360 Post Oak Blvd., #1330
Houston, TX 77056
Tel: (713) 963-9066
Fax: (713) 961-3910
Consul General
Mr. Luis WINTER YGUALT
Consul
Mr. Francisco Javier TELLERIA RAMÍREZ

WASHINGTON

Olympia - (HC)
700 Sleater-Kinney Rd., SE #B-261
Olympia, WA 98503
Tel: (360) 754-8747
Honorary Consul
Mr. Jorge D. GILBERT

COLOMBIA

CALIFORNIA

Los Angeles – (CG)
8383 Wilshire Blvd., #420
Beverly Hills, CA 90211
Tel: (323) 653-9863
Consul General
Ms. Carmen Consuelo PEDRAZA
GALLARDO
Vice Consul
Mrs. Luz Amanda RESTREPO SABOGAL

San Francisco - (CG)
595 Market St., #2130
San Francisco, CA 94105
Tel: (415) 495-7195
Consul General
Ms. Fanny Margarita MONCAYO DUQUE
Consul
Mrs. Ana Victoria ROJAS GÓMEZ

DISTRICT OF COLUMBIA

Washington – (CG)
1875 Connecticut Ave. NW, #524
Washington, DC 20009
Tel: (202) 332-7476
Fax: (202) 332-7180
Consul
Mrs. Consuelo SÁNCHEZ-DURÁN

FLORIDA

Miami – (CG)
280 Aragón Ave.,
Coral Gables, FL 33134
Tel: (305) 448-5558
Consul General
Mrs. Carmenza JARAMILLO MAINCOURT
Consul
Mrs. Paulina María GÓMEZ BORDA
Vice Consul
Ms. María Beatriz UMANA SIERRA
Vice Consul
Mr. Manuel Enrique CAICEDO
MOSQUERA
Vice Consul

Mr. Assad José JATER PENA
Vice Consul
Ms. Beatriz Helena CALVO VILLEGAS

Trade Office
Brickell Bay Office Tower
1001 South Bay Shore Dr., #1904
Miami, FL 33131
Tel: (305) 374-3144
Deputy Consul General
Mrs. Ángela MONTOYA HOLGUÍN
Consul
Mr. Franz José SERRANO EVERS

GEORGIA
Atlanta – (C)
3379 Peachtree Rd., #555
Atlanta, GA 30326
Tel: (404) 237-1045
Consul
Mr. Cesar Felipe GONZALEZ HERNANDEZ
Vice Consul
Mr. Daniel AVILA CAMACHO

ILLINOIS
Chicago – (CG)
500 N. Michigan Ave., #2040
Chicago, IL 60611
Tel: (312) 923-1196
Fax: (312) 923-1197
Consul General
Mr. Jose Fernando GOMEZ MORA
Consul
Mr. María Mercedes PADRÓN DE OLIVEROS

LOUISIANA
New Orleans – (CG)
1844 World Trade Cntr.
2 Canal St.
New Orleans, LA 70130
Tel: (504) 525-5580
Consul General
Mrs. María Inés PANTOJA PONCE
Vice Consul
Mr. Fernando SALAMANCA ARCHILA

MASSACHUSETTS
Boston – (CG)
535 Boylston St., 11th Fl.
Boston, MA 02116
Tel: (617) 536-6222
Vice Consul
Mrs. Monica Cristina ACOUTURE PINEDO
Vice Consul
Mrs. Isabel PARDO URIBE

NEW YORK
New York – (CG)
10 E. 46th St.
New York, NY 10017
Tel: (212) 949-9898
Consul General
Mr. Mauricio SUÁREZ COPETE
Consul
Ms. Clemencia Inés LLORENTE DE GIL
Consul
Ms. Martha NOGUERA DE TURBAY
Consul
Mr. Federico MEJÍA MEJÍA
Consul

Mr. Rafael Hernando FORERO MENDOZA
Consul
Ms. María E. VILLA DE RESTREPO
Consul
Ms. Diana Yolima GARCÍA OROZCO
Consul
Mr. Jaime Alberto ACOSTA CARVAJAL
Consul
Ms. Yohama Malca WARTICOVSCHI MEKLER
Consul
Mr. Jose David NAME CARDOZO

Trade Office
277 Park Ave., 47th Floor
New York, NY 10172-4797
Tel: (212) 223-1120
Deputy Consul General
Ms. María Cecilia RUISECO GUTIERREZ

PUERTO RICO
San Juan - (CG)
Edificio Mercantil Plaza
Ponce de Leon Av., #814
Hato Rey, PR 00918
Tel: (809) 754-6885
Consul General
Ms. Ana Catalina DEL LLANO RESTREPO
Vice Consul
Mr. Rafael Guillermo ARISMENDY JIMENEZ

Trade Office
Banco Bilbao Vizcaya Plaza
1510 Esq. San Patricio
Caparra, PR 00968
Tel: (787) 273-1444
Fax: (787) 273-7006

TEXAS
Houston – (CG)
2990 Richmond Ave., #200
Houston, TX 77098
Tel: (713) 527-8919
Consul General
Mr. Roberto SERRANO ÁVILA
Consul
Mr. JOSE DAVID RUEDA VISBAL

COSTA RICA

CALIFORNIA
Los Angeles – (CG)
1605 W, Olimpic Blvd., #400
Los Angeles, CA 90015
Tel: (213) 380-7915
Fax: (213) 380-5639
Consul General
Mr. Carlos LONGAN KIEFFER
Consul
Ms. Lillian ELIZONDO

San Francisco – (CG)
P.O. Box 7643
Fremont, CA 94537
Tel: (510) 790-0785
Fax: (510) 792-5249
Honorary Consul
Mr. Manuel ESCOTO

COLORADO
Denver – (HCG)
3356 S. Xenia St.
Denver, CO 80231-4542
Tel: (303) 696-8211
Fax: (303) 696-1110
Honorary Consul
Mr. Tito CHAVERRI

DISTRICT OF COLUMBIA
Washington – (EMB)
2112 "S" St. NW
Washington, DC 20008
Tel: (202) 328-6628
Fa: (202) 265-4795
Consul General
Ms. Erika HARMS
Vice Consul
Ms. Carmen de CARVALHO
Vice Consul
Mr. Manuel NUNEZ

FLORIDA
Miami – (CG)
1101 Brickell Ave., #704-S
Miami, FL 33131
Tel: (305) 871-7485/87
Fax: (305) 871-0860
Consul General
Mr. Guillermo JIMÉNEZ
Consul
Mr. Rafael Eduardo ACOSTA CARBAJAL
Consul
Miss María de FERNANDEZ FONSECA
Consul
Miss Andrea FISHMAN FAINGEZICHT

Tampa – (CG)
2200 Barker Rd.
Clearwater, FL 33605
Tel: (813) 248-6741
Fax: (813) 248-6741
Consul
Mrs. Deidamia María MONGE URENA

GEORGIA
Atlanta – (CG)
1870 The Exchange, #100
Atlanta, GA 30339
Tel: (770) 951-7025
Fax: (770) 951-7073
Consul General
Mrs. Ana Virginia CASTRO JENKINS
Consul
Ms. Alejandra CHAVERRI ALVAREZ

ILLINOIS
Chicago – (CG)
185 N. Wabash Ave., #1123
Chicago, IL 60601
Tel: (312) 263-2772
Fax: (312) 263-5807
Consul General
Mr. Juan Bautista SALAS ARAYA

LOUISIANA
New Orleans – (CG)
World Trade Center
2 Canal St., #2334
New Orleans, LA 70130

Tel: (504) 581-6800
Fax: (504) 581-6850
Consul General
Mr. Gonzalo CALDERÓN AGUILAR
Vice Consul
Mr. Guillermo ROJAS MURILLO

MASSACHUSETTS
Boston - (HCG)
175 McClellan Hwy.
Boston, MA 02128
Tel: (617) 561-2444
Fax: (617) 561-2461
Honorary Consul General
Mr. Leonard FLORENCE

MINNESOTA
Minneapolis – (HC)
2424 Territorial Rd.
St Paul, MN 55114
Tel: (612) 481-3616
Fax: (612) 645-4684
Honorary Consul
Mr. Anthony L. ANDERSEN

NEW YORK
New York – (CG)
80 Wall St., #718-19
New York, NY 10005
Tel: (212) 509-3066
Fax: (212) 509-3068
Consul General
Mr. Otto Roberto VARGAS
Consul
Mr. Luis Gerardo RAMOS VÁSQUEZ
Vice Consul
Ms. Rebeca SIBAJA AQUILAR

PUERTO RICO
San Juan – (CG)
1510 Ponce de León,
Santurce, PR 00909
Tel: (787) 723-6227
Fax: (787) 723-6226
Consul General
Mr. Mario Alexander MONTERO CAMPOS

TEXAS
Dallas - (HC)
7777 Forrest La., #B-445
Dallas, TX 75230
Tel: (972) 566-7020
Fax: (972) 566-7943
Honorary Consul
Mr. Jaime Abraham DAVIDSON

Houston – (CG)
3000 Wilcrest Dr., #112
Houston, TX 77042
Tel: (713) 266-0484
Fax: (713) 266-1527
Consul General
Mr. Eduardo Augusto CORDERO SIBAJA
Consul
Mrs. María Gabriela BOLANOS CESPEDES

San Antonio – (CG)
6836 San Pedro, #116
San Antonio, TX 78216

Tel: (210) 824-8474
Fax: (210) 824-8489
Consul
Ms. Marta Cecilia ROJAS OROZCO

Phoenix - (HC)
1426 W. Key Largo Court
Gilbert, AZ 85233
Tel: (480) 632-0132
Fax: (480) 539-0590
Honorary Consul
Mr. Andrew Burke

DOMINICAN REPUBLIC

ALABAMA
Mobile – (C)
4009 Old Shell Rd., #E-16
Mobile, AL 36608
Consul
Ms. María Teresa DE DÍAZ

CALIFORNIA
Los Angeles - (CG)
548 S. Spring St., #309
Los Angeles, CA 90013

San Francisco – (CG)
870 Market St., #982
San Francisco, CA 94103
Tel: (415) 982-5144
Consul General
Mr. Manlio DORREGO JIMÉNEZ
Vice Consul
Mr. Amin RODRÍGUEZ TOUZERY

FLORIDA
Jacksonville – (C)
1914 Beach Way Rd. #6-0
Jacksonville, FL 32207
Tel: (904) 346-0909
Fax: (904) 0919
Consul
César Augusto MATEO
Vice Consul
Franklin CUEVAS

Miami – (CG)
1038 Brickell Ave.
Miami, FL 33131
Tel: (305) 358-3221
Vice Consul
Mr. Nelson Ahmed CHABEBE BÁEZ
Vice Consul
Mr. William DE LA ROSA LORENZO

Sarasota (HC)
2901 W. Tamiami Ci.
Sarasota, FL 33580
Honorary Consul
Mr. Don Ray SPIVEY

GEORGIA
Atlanta - (HC)
191 Peachtree St., #4600
Atlanta, GA 30303
Tel: (404) 572-4814
Honorary Consul
Mr. Horace Holden SIBLEY

ILLINOIS
Chicago – (CG)
451 N. Kilbourne Av.
Chicago, IL 60647
Tel: (773) 427-8863
Fax: (773) 283-0295

LOUISIANA
Lake Charles – (HC)
3566 Monroe St.
Lake Charles, LA 70605
Tel: (318) 477-4506
Honorary Consul
Mr. Glenn Armand BROUSSARD

New Orleans – (CG)
World Trade Center
2 Canal St., #1647
New Orleans, LA 70130
Tel: (504) 522-1843
Fax: (504) 522-1007
Consul General
Mr. Joaquín A. BALAGUER RICARDO

MARYLAND
Baltimore - (HC)
110 Hilton Ave.
Baltimore, MD 21228
Honorary Consul
Mrs. Wilvia Matilde MEDINA LEAL
Honorary Vice Consul
Mrs. Susana DEL DE MOYA

MASSACHUSETTS
Boston – (CG)
The Staler Building
20 Park Plaza, #601
Boston, MA 02116
Tel: (617) 482-8121
Fax: (617) 482-8133

MICHIGAN
Detroit – (C)
184 Middlesex,
Lathrup Village, 48076
Tel: (248) 559-0684
Honorary Vice Consul
Mr. Freddy RAFAEL SOSA

MINNESOTA
Minneapolis – (HCG)
One Financial Plaza
120 S. 6th St. #1910
Minneapolis, MN 55402
Tel: (612) 339-7566
Fax: (612) 339-9055
Honorary Consul General
Mr. Ralph S. PARKER

MISSOURI
St. Louis - (HC)
1173 Rico Dr.
St. Louis, MO 63126
Tel: (314) 454-0266
Honorary Consul
Mr. Fernando Emilio PEGUERO

NEW YORK
New York – (CG)
1501 Broadway Ave.,#410

New York, NY 10036
Tel: (212) 768-2480
Fax: (212) 768-2677
Consul General
Mr. Bienvenido De PÉREZ
Vice Consul
Ms. Delia J. FELIZ PENA
Vice Consul
Mr. Luis José POLANCO DE LOS SANTOS
Vice Consul
Mr. José Altagracia SANTANA
Vice Consul
Mr. Luis Armando HERNÁNDEZ RAMOS
Consular Agent
Mr. Luis Manuel PRINCE RODRÍGUEZ
Consular Agent
Ms. Milagros Altagracia CASTELLANOS DE VÁSQUEZ

PENNSYLVANIA
Philadelphia – (CG)
Lafayette Bldg. Assoc.
5th Fl. & Chestnut St., #422
Philadelphia, PA 19106
Tel: (215) 923-3006
Consul General
Mr. Wilson Amauris DÍAZ CUEVAS
Vice Consul
Mrs. Caperuza DE ALMONTE

PUERTO RICO
Mayaguez - (CG)
30 Calle McKinley, 2nd Floor
Box 3067
Mayaguez, PR 00708
Tel: (809) 833-0007

PONCE (C)
Marginal, Unit 303
Ponce, PR 00731
Tel: (809) 842-9004

SAN JUAN - (CG)
Avianca Bldg.
1612 Ponce de Leon Ave., #7, Santurce
San Juan, PR 00909
Tel: (809) 725-9550

TEXAS
Houston – (C)
3300 S. Gessner, #113
Houston, TX 77024
Tel: (713) 266-0165
Fax: (713) 780-1543

ECUADOR

CALIFORNIA
Los Angeles – (CG)
8484 Wilshire Blvd, #540,
Beverly Hills, California, CA 90211
Tel: (323) 658-5746
Fax; (323) 658-1934
Consul General de Primera
Mr. Jaime Humberto MOLINA RIVADENEIRA
Consul General
Fernando ARIAS BURNEO

Consular Agent
Mr. Cesar Vicente ALMEIDA REYES
Honorary Consul
Fernando SALCEDO HUERTA

San Francisco – (CG)
455 Market St., #980
San Francisco, CA 94105
Tel: (415) 957-5921
Fax: (415) 957-5923
Consul General de Primera
Mr. Fernando Iván FLORES MACÍAS
Consul de Primera
Enrique LASSO MENDOZA

DISTRICT OF COLUMBIA
Washington – (EMB)
2535 15th St., NW
Washington, DC 20009
Tel: (202) 234-7200
Fax: (202) 667-3482
First Secretary (Consular Affairs)
Silvia BERMEO MANCERO

FLORIDA
Miami – (CG)
B.I.V. Tower
1101 Brickell Ave., #M-102,
Miami, FL 33131
Tel: (305) 539-8214
Fax: (305) 539-8313
Consul de Primeral
Ms. Teresita De MENDENDEZ DE SUAREZ
Honorary Consul
Mr. Juan C. ISAIAS MAHUAD
Vice Consul
Mrs. María LORENA PÉREZ INTRIAGO DE FOCIL

Visa Office
Doral Exective Office
3785 NW 82nd Ave., #317
Miami, FL 33166
Tel: (305) 716-5252
Fax: (305) 716-9296
Consul
Mr. Emilio Gonzalo RUPERTI VÉLEZ

ILLINOIS
Chicago – (CG)
500 N. Michigan Ave., #1510
Chicago, IL 60611
Tel: (312) 329-0266
Fax: (312) 329-0359
Consul General
Mr. Fernando CHAVEZ DAVILA

LOUISIANA
New Orleans – (CG)
2 Canal St, #2338,
World Trade Center,.
New Orleans, LA 70130
Tel: (504) 523-3229
Fax: (504) 522-9675
Consul General
Mr. José CRUZ ESTRADA
Vice Consul
MRS. Marcela ESCUDERO de ESPINEL

MARYLAND

Baltimore – (HC)
2925 N. Charles St.
Baltimore, MD 21218
Tel: (301) 889-4422
Honorary Consul
Mr. Manuel L. JARAMILLO VÁSQUEZ

MASSACHUSETTS

Boston - (HC)
26 Wolcott Road Ext.,
Chesnut Hill, MA 02467
Tel: (617) 738-9465
Honorary Consul
Ms. Jaleh Joubine KHADEM

MICHIGAN

Detroit - (HC)
136 State St., Pontiac,
Detroit, MI 48341-1450
Tel: (313) 332-7356
Fax: (313) 332-7881
Honorary Consul
Mr. Héctor A. BUENO

NEVADA

Las Vegas – (HC)
5300 Paradise Rd.
Las Vegas, NV 89109
Tel: (702) 735-8193
Fax: (702) 332-7881
Honorary Consul
Mr. Pedro JARAMILLO CABEZAS

NEW JERSEY

Newark – (CG)
30 Montgomery St., #1020
Jersey City, NJ 07302
Tel: (201) 985-1300
Consul General
Dr. Benjamín VILLACÍS ESQUETINI
Consul
Mrs. Carolina Mariela ZAVALA CAPUTTI
Consular Agent
Mrs. Fabiola JARRÍN OLGUÍN
Consular Agent
Mr. José MONROY CAVIEDES

NEW YORK

New York – (CG)
800 2nd Ave., #600
New York, NY 10017
Tel: (212) 808-0170
Fax: (212) 808-0188
Consul General de Primera
Emb. Hernán HOLGUÍN RIOFRÍO
Deputy Consul General
Mr Gonzalo ANDRADE RIVERO
Deputy Consul General
Mr. Guillermo LARA CALDERÓN
Consular Agent
Ms. María De ARAUJO RIVADENEIRA
Consular Agent
Ms. Carmen Elizabeth NARANJO MANCERO
Consular Agent
Miss Gladys Cecilia JACOME ZAMBRANO

EL SALVADOR

ARIZONA

Phoenix – (HC)
4521 E. Charles Dr., Paradise Valley
P.O. Box 2979
Phoenix, AZ 85253
Tel: (602) 948-4899
Honorary Consul
Mr. Tracy R. THOMAS

CALIFORNIA

Los Angeles – (CG)
3450 Wilshire Blvd. #250
Los Angeles, CA 90010
Tel: (213) 383-8580
Consul General
Mr. Oscar Salvador BENAVIDES GUTIÉRREZ
Vice Consul
Mrs. Carmen Dolores PAREDES de MEJÍA

San Francisco – (CG)
870 Market St., #508
San Francisco, CA 94102
Tel: (415) 781-7924
Consul General
Mr. Carlos E. GONZALEZ

Santa Ana – (VC)
1212 N. Broadway Ave., #100
Santa Ana, CA 92701

DISTRICT OF COLUMBIA

Washington – (EMB)
2308 California St. NW
Washington, DC 20008
Tel: (202) 265-9671
Consul General
Mr. Walter Alfredo ANAYA ESCALANTE
Vice Consul
Ms. María Isabel ROSALES LAGUARDIA

FLORIDA

Miami – (CG)
300 Biscayne Blvd., #1020
Miami, FL 33131
Tel: (305) 371-8850
Consul General
Mr. Fernando Ernesto QUIÑONEZ MEZA
Honorary Consul
Mr. Raúl Jacinto VALDEZ FAULI
Vice Consul
Mrs. Ana María ÁIVAREZ de ESERSKI

ILLINOIS

Chicago – (CG)
104 S. Michigan Ave., #707
Chicago, IL 60603
Tel: (312) 332-1393
Fax: (312) 332-1393
Consul General
Mr. Alfredo ANGULO DELGADO

LOUISIANA

New Orleans – (CG)
1136 Int'l Trade Mart,
2 Canal St., #2310
New Orleans, LA 70130
Tel: (504) 522-4266

Consul General
Mr. Emilio R. GARCÍA PRIETO

MASSACHUSETT

Boston – (C)
222 3rd St. # 1221, Cambridge
Boston, MA 02139
Consul
Ms. Lorena SOL de POOL

MISSOURI

St. Louis – (HC)
7730 Forsyth, #150
St. Louis, MO 63105
Tel: (314) 862-0300
Honorary Consul
Mr. Michael Jay BOBROFF

NEW YORK

New York – (CG)
46 Park Ave.
New York, NY 10016
Tel: (212) 889-3608
Consul General
Ms. Marta Patricia MAZA DE PITTSFORD
Consul
Ms. Ana Vilma AVILA DE SOLER
Legal Assistance Office
13 N. Franklin St., Hempstead
New York, NY 11550

PENNSYLVANIA

Philadelphia – (HC)
119 Bleddyn Rd., Ardmore
Philadelphia, PA 19003
Tel: (215) 642-1354
Honorary Consul
Ms. Ana María KEENE

PUERTO RICO

Bayamon – (HCG)
Villa Caparra, Calle K-19
Bayamon, PR 00619
Honorary Consul General
Ms. María Teresa DE ESTEVEZ
Honorary Vice Consul
Mrs. Cecilia BERLINGERI

TEXAS

Dallas – (CG)
Oakbrook Plaza
1555 W.Mockingbird Ln., #216
Dallas, TX 75235
Consul General
Ms. Rosanna C. SALAVERRIA DE GUTIÉRREZ

Houston – (CG)
6420 Hillcroft St., #100
Houston, TX 77081
Tel: (713) 270-6239
Consul General
Ms. Astrid María SALAZAR DE ARIZ
Consul
Mr. Leocadio José CHACÓN CORADO
Vice Consul
Ms. Marlene Elizabeth ORANTES DE SALAZAR

EQUATORIAL GUINEA

FLORIDA

Miami (HCG)
5399 N.W. 36th St., 2nd Floor,
Miami, FL 33133,
Tel: (305) 871-2094
Honorary Consul General
Mr. Viktor JIMENO
Honorary Vice Consul
Mrs. Shirley Lim JIMENO

GUATEMALA

ALABAMA

Montgomery – (HC)
2023 Chestnut Street,.
Montgomery, AL 36106
Tel: (334) 269-2756
Honorary Consul
Mr. José Roberto ORTEGA-LÓPEZ

CALIFORNIA

Los Angeles – (CG)
1605 W. Olympic Blvd., #422
Los Angeles, CA 90015
Tel: (213) 365-9251
Consul
Mrs. Lissette ORDOÑEZ SAENZ
Honorary Consul
Mr. John L. LUMEN
Vice Consul
Ms. María E. FIGUEROA DE ALVARADO
Vice Consul
Mr. Germán Arnoldo CEREZO CASADO
Vice Consul
Ms. Lygia GUERRA GUZMÁN
Vice Consul
Ms. Zonia Patricia MEIGHAM JUÁREZ
Vice Consul
Mrs. Guadalupe VALENZUELA DE MURGA

San Diego – (HC)
10405 San Diego Mission Rd., #205
San Diego, CA 92108
Tel: (619) 282-8127
Honorary Consul
Mr. Eugene Herbert SAPPER

San Francisco – (CG)
870 Market St., #667
San Francisco, CA 94102
Tel: (415) 788-5651
Consul General
Ms. Nora Eugenia CIFUENTES PAIZ
Honorary Consul
Mr. Carlos Armando AFRE
Vice Consul
Mr. Francisco José ESCOBAR AGUIRRE

DISTRICT OF COLUMBIA

Washington – (EMB)
2220 R St. NW
Washington, DC 20008
Tel: (202) 745-4952
Fax: (202) 745-1908
Consul
Mr. Erwin Antonio BENTZEN-GRANADOS

FLORIDA

Ft Lauderdale – (HC)
2601 East Oakland Park Blvd,
Ft. Lauderdale, FL 33316
Tel: (954) 467-1700
Honorary Consul
Mr. John P. BAUER

Miami/Coral Gables – (CG)
1101 Brickwell Av, # 1003-S
Miami, FL 33131
Tel: (305) 679-9945
Consul General
Mr. Alejandro DE LEÓN
Honorary Consul
Mr. George L. COMBALUZIER
Vice Consul
Ms. Dunia Alicia MIRANDA MORALES

GEORGIA

Atlanta – (HC)
4772 E. Conway Dr., NW
Atlanta, GA 30327
Tel: (404) 255-7019
Honorary Consul
Ms. María Teresa FRASER

ILLINOIS

Chicago – (CG)
200 N. Michigan Ave., #610
Chicago, IL 60601
Tel: (312) 332-1587
Fax: (312) 322-4256
Consul General
Mr. Antulio CASTILLO BARAJAS
Vice Consul
Mr. Carlos FUENTES
Vice Consul
Raúl LÓPEZ ORELLANA

KANSAS

Leavenworth – (HC)
419 Delaware St.
Leavenworth, KS 66048
Tel: (913) 682-0342
Honorary Consul
Mr. Ralph E. DIX

LOUISIANA

Lafayette - (HC)
735 Rue Jefferson
Lafayette, LA 70501
Tel: (337) 291-5489
Honorary Consul
Mr. Enrique Leonardo HERRERA

New Orleans – (HC)
Plaza Tower
1001 Howard Ave., #2504
New Orleans, LA 70113
Tel: (504) 558-3777
Honorary Consul
Ms. Margarita Lourdes JEREZ

MINNESOTA

Minneapolis - (HC)
2105 1st Ave.
Minneapolis, MN 55404
Honorary Consul
Mr. Edgar Alex DAHINTEN

NEW YORK

New York – (CG)
57 Park Ave.
New York, NY 10016
Tel: (212) 679-4760
Consul General
Ms. Rosa María MÉRIDA de MORA
Consul
Ms. Maria Luz ENRIQUEZ de ZYRIEK
Vice Consul
Ms. Mara Elizabeth MEJÍA GARCÍA
Vice Consul
Mrs. Blanca Margarita SIMEONIDIS

PENNSYLVANIA

Philadelphia – (HC)
1245 Highland Ave., #301; Abington
Philadelphia, PA 19001
Tel: (215) 885-5551
Honorary Consul
Dr. Roberto RENDON MALDONADO

Pittsburgh – (HC)
709 Washington Dr.
Pittsburgh, PA 15229
Tel: (412) 366-7715
Honorary Consul
Ms. Margarita WINIKOFF

PUERTO RICO

San Juan – (HC)
Garden Hills, A-22 Serrania St.
Guaynabo, PR 00966
Tel: (809) 782-7409
Honorary Consul
Mr. Alberto M. PÉREZ NEGRONI

RHODE ISLAND

Providence – (HC)
11 Lancashire St.
Providence, RI 02908
Tel: (401) 751-8154
Honorary Consul
Mrs. Zoila R. GUERRA

TENNESSEE

Memphis – (HC)
Jefferson Plaza
147 Jefferson Ave., #900
Memphis, TN 38103
Tel: (901) 527-8466
Honorary Consul
Mr. George E. WHITWORTH

TEXAS

Houston – (CG)
31013 Fountainview, # 210,
Houston, TX 77057
Tel: (713) 953-9531
Consul General
Mr. José BARILLAS TRENNERT
Honorary Consul
Mr. Carlos Hugo MONSANTO
Honorary Consul
Mr. José Rafael ESPADA

HONDURAS

CALIFORNIA

Los Angeles – (CG)
3450 Wilshire Blvd., #230
Los Angeles, CA 90010
Tel: (213) 383-9244
Consul General
Miss Vivian Verónica PANTING GALO
Honorary Consul
Mr. George V. CHILINGAR
Vice Consul
Mrs. Tesla ALVARADO de COLLIER
Honorary Vice Agent
Ms. Susana de STEVENSON
Consular Agent
Ms. Aissa Alejandra ANTUNEZ PINEDA
Honorary Consular Agent
Mr. Oscar ARTILES PONCE

San Diego – (HC)
Union Bank Bldg.
525 B St., #2002
San Diego, CA 92101
Tel: (619) 533-4515
Honorary Consul
Ms. Ella Isabel FLORES-PARÍS

San Francisco – (CG)
Flood Bldg.
870 Market St., #449
San Francisco, CA 94102
Tel: (415) 392-0076
Consul General
Mr. Ramón Andrés TORRES PERDOMO
Consul
Mr. Farid Antonio CORTÉS RIVERA
Honorary Vice Consul
Mr. Henry LANGENBERG McINTYRE
Consular Agent
Mr. Farid Antonio CORTÉS RIVERA

FLORIDA

Jacksonville – (C)
1914 Beachway Rd., #3-0
Jacksonville, FL 33207
Tel: (904) 348-3550
Consul
Mr. Antonio J. VALLADARES

Miami-Coral Gables – (CG)
300 Sevilla Ave., #201
Coral Gables, FL 33134
Tel: (305) 447-8927
Consul General
Mrs. Míriam Bernarda YNESTROZA
Honorary Consul
Mr. Federico Alberto SMITH
Honorary Consul
Mr. Owen S. FREED
Vice Consul
Mr. Eunice PINEDA DE SUAZO
Consular Agent
Mr. José J. JALIL SALOMÓN
Consular Agent
Mr. Manuel VILLEDA-TOLEDO
Consular Agent
Mr. Augustín GONZÁLEZ
Consular Agent
Ms. María Gisela DE ZACAPA

Consular Agent
Ms. Virginia BUESO
Consular Agent
Capt. José Eduardo ESPINAL PAZ
Consular Agent
Mr. Jimmy Roberto KAFIE HANDAL
Consular Agent
Mrs. Emy ECHEVERRY LANZA
Consular Agent
Mr. Juan Carlos VÁSQUEZ ALVARADO
Consular Agent
Mr. David Enrique HOWELL MINEROS

ILLINOIS

Chicago – (CG)
2000 N. Racine Ave., #2110
Chicago, IL 60614
Tel: (773) 472-8726
Fax: (773) 472-8958
Consul General
José Erazmo MONTALVAN HERNÁNDEZ
Honorary Vice Consul
Ms. Maura Rosa ALCERRO PRUDOT
Consular Agent
Ms. Silvia Rina FLORES DE GONZÁLEZ
Consular Agent
Mrs. Erika Gabriela DÍAZ PÉREZ
Consular Agent
Miss Iris Xiomara MEZA VILLATORO

LOUISIANA

Baton Rouge - (HC)
11017 N. Oak Hills Parkway.
Baton Rouge, LA 70810
Honorary Consul
Ms. Vilma CABRERA CALHOUN

New Orleans – (CG)
World Trade Center
2 Canal St., #1641
New Orleans, LA 70130
Tel: (504) 522-3118
Consul General
Mr. Nicolás ATALA SIMÓN
Consular Agent
Miss Dylcia Marina CONTRERAS MAIER
Consular Agent
Mrs. María Dolores DÍAZ

NEW YORK

New York – (CG)
80 Wall St., #915
New York, NY 10005
Consul General
Mr. Octavio PINEDA ESPINOZA

PUERTO RICO

San Juan – (CG)
Mercantil Plaza Bldg.
Ponce de León Ave. #604
San Juan, PR 00918
Tel: (809) 764-2206
Consul General
Ms. Nuria Teresa SAN MARTÍN
RIBA de CORLETO
Consular Agent
Ms. Gina Elisabeth URCINA RASKOFF

TEXAS

Houston – (CG)
4151 S. W. Freeway, #700
Houston, TX 77027

Tel: (713) 622-4572
Consul General
Ms. Martha Irene PINEDA DE BUESO
Consular Agent
Mrs. María E. TORREZ DE GÓMEZ
Consular Agent
Mr. Eduardo Ernesto FAASCH PINEDA
Consular Agent
Ms. Sandra Yolanda VÁSQUEZ
VALLADARES
Consular Agent
Miss Karla Argentina ROMERO SUAZO
Consular Agent
Mr. Oscar CASTAÑEDA HERNÁNDEZ
Honorary Consular Agent
Ms. Mayra O. SIMÓN

MEXICO

ARIZONA
Douglas – (C)
1201 "F" Ave.
Douglas, AZ 85607
Tel: (520) 364-3107
Consul
Mr. Miguel ESCOBAR VALDÉS

Nogales – (CG)
571 N. Grand Ave.
Nogales, AZ 85621
Tel: (520) 287-2521
Consul
Mr. Roberto RODRÍGUEZ HERNÁNDEZ
Deputy Consul General
Mr. Gabriel GÓMEZ PADILLA
Vice Consul
Mr. Leonel ÁLVAREZ MORA

Phoenix – (CG)
1990 W. Camelback Rd., #110
Phoenix, AZ 85015
Tel: (602) 242-7398
Consul General
Ruben Alberto BELTRAN GUERRERO
Deputy Consul General
Mr. Miguel Ángel ISIDRO RODRÍGUEZ
Consul
Mr. Ricardo Francisco HERNÁNDEZ
LENCADA
Consul
Ms. Regino Nicolás RENTERÍA
GARCÍA

Tucson – (C)
553 S. Stone Ave.
Tucson, AZ 85701
Te: (520) 882-5595/96
Consul
Mr. Carlos A. TORRES GARCÍA

CALIFORNIA
Calexico – (C)
331-333 W. 2nd St.
Calexico, CA 92231
Tel: (760) 357-3863
Consul
Mrs. Rita María VARGAS TORREGROSA
Vice Consul
Mrs. Laura FERNÁNDEZ DE IVANKOVIC

Fresno – (C)
2409 Merced St..
Fresno, CA 93721

Tel: (559) 233-9770
Consul
Enrique Antonio ROMERO CUEVAS

Los Angeles – (CG)
2401 W. 6th St.
Los Angeles, CA 90057
Tel: (213) 351-6800/07
Consul General
Martha Irene LARA ALATORRE

Commercial Office
350 S. Figueroa St., 2nd Floor
Los Angeles, CA 90211
Vice Consul
Mr. Herminio HERNÁNDEZ RAMÍREZ

Tourism Office
1801 Century Park, #1080
Los Angeles, CA 90067
Tel: (310) 203-8328
Vice Consul
Mr. Jorge Antonio GAMBOA PATRÓN

Oxnard – (C)
210 E.4th St., #206-A
Oxnard, CA 93030
Tel: (805) 483-4684
Consul
Ms. Luz Elena Ines BUENO ZIRIÓN
Consul
Mrs. María de los Angeles MEDINA-
VINALES

Sacramento – (CG)
1010 8th St.
Sacramento, CA 95814
Tel: (916) 441-3287
Fax: (916) 441-3176
Consul General
Mr. José Luis SOBERANES REYES
San Bernardino – (C)
293 North "D" St.
San Bernardino, CA 92401
Tel: (909) 889-9836
Consul
Mr. Juan José SALGADO SAAVEDRA

San Diego – (CG)
1549 India St.
San Diego, CA 92101
Tel: (619) 231-8414
Consul General
Mr. Francisco Javier DÍAZ DE LEÓN

**Office of Agriculture & Forestry
Affairs**
12625 High Bluff Dr.
San Diego, CA 92130

Office of Mexican Fisheries
2550 Fifth Ave., 101
San Diego, CA 92101
Vice Consul
Mr. Santiago Ignacio GÓMEZ AGUILAR

San Francisco – (CG)
870 Market St., #528
San Francisco, CA 94102
Tel: (415) 782-9555
Consul General
Ms. Georgina Teresita LAGOS DONDE
Deputy Consul General
Mr. Arturo BALDERAS RODRÍGUEZ

Consul
Mr. Gilberto Javier AGUILAR CUEVAS
Consul
Mr. Héctor Edmundo VINDIOLA
ENRÍQUEZ

San Jose – (C)
540 N. First St.
San Jose, CA 95112
Tel: (408) 294-3414
Consul
Mr. Sergio Ernesto CASANUEVA
REGUART
Consul
Ms. Leticia DÍAZ INFANTE MÉNDEZ
Consul
Ms. Esther Adriana LARIOS ALZUA
Consul
Mr. Jeremías GUZMÁN BARRERA

Santa Ana – (C)
828 N. Broadway St.
Santa Ana, CA 92701
Tel: (714) 835-3069
Consul Titular
Miguel Ángel Isidro RODRÍGUEZ

COLORADO
Denver – (CG)
48 Steele St.
Denver, CO 80206
Tel: (303) 331-1110
Consul General
Mr. Carlos BARROS HORCASITAS
Deputy Consul General
Mr. Javier CHAGOYA ROMERO
Vice Consul
Mr. Lucrecia María BARRERA ROMERO

DISTRICT OF COLUMBIA
Washington - (EMB)
2827 16th St., NW
Washington, DC 20009
(202) 736-1000
Ministro Encargado Sec. Consular
Mr. Juan Carlos CUE VEGA

FLORIDA
Miami – (CG)
Miami Intl. Commerce Center
1200 NW 78th. Ave., #200
Miami, FL 33126
Tel: (305) 716-4977
Consul General
Mr. Manuel RODRIGUEZ ARRIAGA
Deputy Consul General
Mr. Juan Manuel CALDERÓN JAIMES
Consul
Ms. Sofía GARCÍA CEJA
Consul
Mr. Jesús CONTRERAS CANTU

Commercial Office
220 Alhambra Circle, #210
Coral Gables, FL 33134
Vice Consul
Samuel LARA SÁNCHEZ

Tourism Office
128 Aragon Ave.
Miami, FL 33156
Tel: (305) 443-9160

Vice Consul
Mr. Benito ECHEVERRÍA ZUNO

Orlando – (C)
100 W Washington St.
Orlando, FL 32801
Tel: (407) 422-0514
Consul
Mr. Martín TORRES GUTIÉRREZ-RUBIO
Vice Consul
Mrs. Hortensia GONZÁLEZ DE CASADO

GEORGIA
Atlanta – (CG)
2600 Apple Valley Rd.
Atlanta, GA 30319
Tel: (404) 266-2233
Consul General
Mr. Teodoro MAUS REISBAUM
Deputy Consul General
Mr. Hugo JUÁREZ CARRILLO
Consul
Mr. Bernardo MÉNDEZ LUGO
Consul
Ms. Carmen Dinorah MARTIN RAYO
SOLIS

Commercial Office
Cain Tower
229 Peachtree St. NE #907
Atlanta, GA 30303
Vice Consul
Ms. Concepción Virginia ARTEAGA SANZ

ILLINOIS
Chicago – (CG)
300 N. Michigan Ave., 2nd & 4th Floor
Chicago, IL 60601
Tel: (312) 855-1380
Consul General
Mr. Carlos Manuel SADA SOLANA

Mexican National Tourism Office
70 E. Lake St., #1413
Chicago, IL 60601
Tel: (312) 856-0316
Vice Consul
Mrs. Martha VARELA BARRAGAN

Commercial Office
Blvd. Towers North
225 N. Michigan Ave., #708
Chicago, IL 60601
Tel: (312) 856-0316
Consul
Mr. Miguel Angel LEAMAN RIVAS

LOUISIANA
New Orleans – (CG)
2 Canal St., #2240
New Orleans, LA 70130
Tel: (504) 522-3596
Consul General
Mr. Luis Arturo PUENTE ORTEGA
Deputy Consul General
Mr. Eduardo Jesús CERVERA CÁMARA
Consul
Ms. María C. ARGUDIN FURLONG
Consul
Mr. Víctor M. URIBE AVINA
Vice Consul
Ms. María Teresa CARPY VELÁZQUEZ

MASSACHUSETTS
Boston – (C)

20 Park Plaza, #506
Boston, MA 02116
Tel: (617) 426-4181
Consul General
Mr. Carlos RICO FERRAT

MICHIGAN
Detroit – (C)
The Penobscot Bldg.
645 Griswold Ave.#4372
Detroit, MI 48226
Tel: (313) 964-4515
Consul General
Mr. Eleazar Benjamin RUIZ Y AVILA
Consul
Ms. Alma Margarita CARVALHO SOTO
Deputy Consul
Mr. Miguel Angel REYES Y SOTO

Commercial Office
2000 Town Center, #1900
Southfield, MI 48075

MISSOURI
St. Louis – (C)
1015 Locust St., #922
St. Louis, MO 63101
Tel: (314) 436-3233
Consul
Mr. Luis Arturo PUENTE ORTEGA
Consul
Ms. Nohemi HERNÁNDEZ-CAMARGO
Consul
Mr. Fernando GONZÁLEZ SANTOYO
Consul
Mr. René Luis MORLET CASTRO
Deputy Consul
Ms. María PRIETO-ESPINOZA

NEBRASKA
Omaha - (HVC)
3552 Dodge St.
Omaha, NE 68131
(402) 595-1841
Consul General
José Luis CUEVAS HILDITCH

NEW MEXICO
Albuquerque – (C)
400 Gold Ave. SW, #100
Albuquerque, NM 87102
Tel: (505) 247-2147
Consul
Mr. Jaime PAZ Y PUENTE GUTIÉRREZ
Consul
Mr. José Antonio LARIOS PONCE
Deputy Consul
Mr. Pedro BLANCO PÉREZ

NEW YORK
New York – (CG)
27 E. 39th St.
New York, NY 10016
Tel: (212) 217-6400
Consul General
Mr. Salvador Beltran DEL RIO MADRID
Consul
Mrs. Mireya TERAN-MUNGUIA DE
TEUTLI
Consul
Mr. José Antonio LAGUNAS BORJA
Consul

Ms. Victoria FUENTES-MIRETTI
Consul
Ms. María Teresa ROSAS JASSO
Consul
Ms. Rosa Erika CHAIN MATOUK
Consul
Ms. Lucía LICEAGA ARTEAGA
Consul
Mr. Norberto SAÚL TERRAZAS ARREOLA
Deputy Consul
Mr. Joel A. HERNÁNDEZ GARCÍA

Commercial Office
150 E. 58th St., 17th Floor
New York, NY 10155
Vice Consul
Mr. Sergio HIDALGO MONROY PORTILLO

Tourism Office
405 Park Ave.
New York, NY 10022

Mexican Foreign Trade Institute
375 Park Ave., #1905
New York, NY 10152
Tel: (212) 826-2916

NORTH CAROLINA
Raleigh – (HC)
411 Fayettville St., #100
Raleigh, NC 27601
Tel: (919) 394-2198
Consul General
Ms. Carolina ZARAGOZA FLORES

OREGON
Portland – (C)
1234 SW Morrison St.
Portland, OR 97205
Tel: (503) 274-1450
Consul General
Ms. Alma Patricia SORIA AYUSO
Deputy Consul
Mr. José Luis ALVARADO GONZÁLEZ

PENNSYLVANIA
Philadelphia – (C)
Bourse Bldg.
111 S. Independence Mall East, #310
Philadelphia, PA 19106
Tel: (215) 922-3834
Consul
Mr. Juan Manuel LOMBERA LÓPEZ
COLLADA
Consul
Mrs. Elena URIBE CASTANEDA

PUERTO RICO
San Juan – (CG)
Edificio "IBM"
654 Avenida Muñoz Rivera, #1837
Hato Rey, PR 00918
Tel: (787) 764-8935
Consul General
Mr. Oliver Albert FARRES MARTINS
Deputy Consul
Mr. Héctor LERIN RUEDA
Vice Consul
Ms. María de GONZÁLEZ PÉREZ
FIGUEROA

TEXAS
Austin – (CG)

Little Field Bldg.
200 E. 6th St., #200
Austin, TX 78701
Consul Encargado
Vicente M. SANCHÉZ VENTURA
Deputy Consul General
Mr. Eusebio Augusto ROMERO ESQUIVEL
Consul
Mr. Jacob PRADO GONZÁLEZ

Brownsville – (C)
724 E. Elizabeth St.
Brownsville, TX 78520
Tel: (956) 542-4431
Consul
Ms. Berenice RENDÓN TALAVERA
Deputy Consul
Ms. Ana Laura PÉREZ SALAZAR
Vice Consul
Mr. Roberto Jorge HERNÁNDEZ LÓPEZ
Vice Consul
Mr. Juan Francisco DOMÍNGUEZ FABELA

Corpus Christi – (C)
800 N. Shoreline Blvd., #410
Corpus Christi, TX 78401
Tel: (361) 882-3375
Consul General
Mr. Sergio JACOBO PATIÑO

Dallas – (CG)
8855 N. Stemmons Frwy.
Dallas, TX 75247
Tel: (214) 252-9250
Consul General
Mr. Angel Luis ORTIZ MONASTERIO
CASTELLANOS
Consul
Ms. Ana M. FELDMAN DE MENDOZA
Consul
Ms. Julian ADEM DÍAZ DE LEÓN
Consul
Ms. Patricia Amalia BELMAR BUSTAMANTE
Consul
Mrs. Lorena LARIOS RODRÍGUEZ
Vice Consul
Mrs. Dolores Esther CABRERA de
PARKINSON
Vice Consul
Mr. Antonio CENDEJAS CONTRERAS

Office of The Commercial Counselor
2777 Stemmons Frwy., #1632
P.O. Box 40
Dallas, TX 52158
Vice Consul
Mr. Carlos José BELLO ROCH

Del Rio – (C)
South Park Plaza Bldg.,
2398, Spur 239
Del Rio, TX 78840
Tel: (830) 775-2352
Consul Titular
Mr. Roberto CANSECO MARTÍNEZ

Eagle Pass – (C)
140 N. Adams St.
Eagle Pass, TX 78852
Tel: (830) 773-9255
Consul
Mr. Jorge Ernesto ESPEJEL MONTES

El Paso – (CG)

910 E. San Antonio Ave.
El Paso, TX 79901
Tel: (915) 533-8555
Consul General
Mr. Miguel Antonio MEZA ESTRADA

Fort Worth – (HC)
108 N. Commerce St.
Fort Worth, TX 76102
Tel: (817) 870-2270
Honorary Consul
Mr. Jerry MURAD

Houston – (CG)
4507 San Jacinto St.
Houston, TX 77004
Tel: (713) 271-6800
Consul General
Mr. Rodolfo FIGUEROA ARAMONI
Deputy Consul General
Mr. José MENDOZA CAAMAÑO
Consul
Mr. Héctor José AGUILAR MEZA
Consul
Mrs. María Noemí HERNÁNDEZ TELLEZ
Consul
Mrs. Araceli GOROSTIZA OTERO
Consul
Mr. José Raúl ARCOS SANTAMARÍA
Consul
Mr. Juan Manuel SOLANA MORALES
Consul
Mr. Gilberto VELARDE MEIXUEIRO
Vice Consul
Mr. Carlos Humberto MACIN LEYVA
Vice Consul
Ms. Norma Edith AGUILAR ANDRADE
Vice Consul
MR. GERARDO GUERRERO GÓMEZ
Vice Consul
Mr. Ramiro NEPITA CHAVEZ

Tourism Office
2707 N. Loop, #450
Houston, TX 77008
Vice Consul
Mr. Leopoldo Octavio VIAL TORRES

Laredo - (CG)
1219 Matamoros St.
Laredo, TX 78040
Tel: (956) 723-6369
Consul
Mr. Daniel HERNÁNDEZ JOSEPH

McAllen – (C)
600 S. Broadway St.
McAllen, TX 78501
Tel: (956) 686-0243
Consul
Mr. Roberto RAMÍREZ VARGAS
Midland – (C)
511 W. Ohio St., #121
Midland, TX 79701
Tel: (915) 687-2334
Consul
Mrs. Lucinda Guadalupe GARZA
CÁRDENAS
Consul
Mrs. Juana María RUIZ MARTÍNEZ

San Antonio – (CG)
127 Navarro St.
San Antonio, TX 78205

Tel: (210) 227-9145
Consul General
Mr. Armando ORTIZ ROCHA

Mexican Cultural Institute
600 Hemisfair Plaza Wa.

San Antonio, TX 78205
Consul
Mr. Luis Felipe SANTANDER RODRÍGUEZ

Commercial Affairs Office
203 S. Saint Mary's St.

San Antonio, TX 78213

Office Of The Mexican Attorney General
Frost Bank Building

100 West Houston St., #1441

San Antonio, TX 78205
Consul
Mr. Carlos Cecilio LANDEROS HIJAR
Consul
Mr. Carlos DÍAZ DE LEÓN MARTÍNEZ
Consul
Mr. Carlos Ignacio LICONA SAENZ
Consul
Mr. Héctor Daniel DÁVALOS MARTÍNEZ
Vice Consul
Mr. Mario FUENTES ARIAS
Vice Consul
Mr. Rogelio Homero FLORES RENDON
Vice Consul
Mr. Lorenzo DE ANDA DE ANDA

UTAH

Salt Lake City – (C)
230 West 400 S, 2nd Floor

Salt Lake City, UT 84101

Tel: (801) 521-8502
Consul
Ms. Anacelia PÉREZ DE MEYER
Consul
Mr. Héctor Ignacio MENA LÓPEZ
Consul
Mrs. Juana María DELUERA CANCHOLA
Deputy Consul
Mr. Eduardo Héctor MOGUEL FLORES

VIRGINIA

Norfolk – (HC)
51 E. Virginia Beach Blvd.

Norfolk, VA 23502

Tel: (804) 461-4933
Honorary Consul
Mr. Roberto RODRÍGUEZ ITURRALDE

Richmond – (HC)
University Park Bldg.

2420 Pemberton Rd.

Richmond, VA 23233

Tel: (804) 747-9200
Honorary Consul
Mr. Walter W. REGIRER

WASHINGTON

Seattle – (C)
2132 Third Ave.

Seattle, WA 98121

Tel: (206) 448-3526
Consul General
Mr. Jorge MADRAZO CUELLAR
Deputy Consul
Mr. Juan Manuel PEREDA CHAGOYA
Vice Consul
Mr. Carlos HAMPE VELÁZQUEZ
Vice Consul
Mrs. María Del CASTAÑEDA DE YUDIN

WISCONSIN

Madison – (HC)
141 North Hancock St.

Madison, WI 53703

Tel: (608) 283-6000
Honorary Consul
Mr. Rudolph CARO HECHT

NICARAGUA

CALIFORNIA

Los Angeles – (CG)
3303 Wilshire Blvd., #410

Los Angeles, CA 90010

Tel: (213) 252-1170
Consul General
Mr. Silvio José MÉNDEZ NAVARRETE
Honorary Consul
Ms. Mina NELSON

San Francisco – (CG)
870 Market St., #1050

San Francisco, CA 94102

Tel: (415) 765-6821
Honorary Consul General
Dr. Maritza Socorro ROSALES GRANERA

DISTRICT OF COLUMBIA

Washington – (EMB)
1627 New Hampshire Ave. NW

Washington, DC 20009

Tel: (202) 939-6570
Consul General
Mr. Harold Fernando RIVAS REYES

FLORIDA

Miami – (CG)
8370 W. Flager St. #220

Miami, FL 33144

Tel: (305) 220-6900
Consul General
Ms. Lucía A. CARDENAL DE SALAZAR
Consular Agent
Ms. Hilda Eulalia SEQUEIRA CASTELLON

GEORGIA

Atlanta - (HC)
3161 Lemons Ridge Dr.

Atlanta, GA 30339

Tel: (770) 319-1673
Honorary Consul
Mr. Joseph Thomas RATCHFORD

LOUISIANA

New Orleans – (CG)
World Trade Center

2 Canal St., #1937

New Orleans, LA 70130

Tel: (504) 523-1507
Consul General
Ms. Mayra LACAYO GRIMALDI
Honorary Vice Consul
Mrs. Gertrudis Rebeca HASBUN

NEW YORK

New York – (CG)
820 2nd. Ave. #802

New York, NY 10017

Tel: (212) 344-4491
Honorary Consul
Ms. María R. URCUYO DE ZARRUK
Vice Consul
Ms. María Magdalena ZELEDON VALLE

PENNSYLVANIA

Philadelphia - (HC)
2nd& Girard, NE Corner

1201 North 2nd St.

Philadelphia, PA 19122-4501

Tel: (215) 627-9414

Fax: (215) 627-0734
Honorary Consul
Mr. Alejandro José GALLARD PRIO

Pittsburgh - (HC)
Miles, Inc. Building 4, Mobay Rd.

Pittsburgh, PA 15205
Honorary Consul
Mr. Richard L. WHITE

PUERTO RICO

San Juan - (HCG)
B1 Palma Sola Blvd., Guaynabo

San Juan, PR 00966
Honorary Consul
Mr. Jorge A. PICO BAUERMEISTER
Honorary Vice Consul
Ms. Bertha Carlota TEFEL TORRES

TEXAS

Houston – (CG)
6300 Hillcroft, #250

Houston, TX 77081

Tel: (713) 272-9628
Honorary Consul
Mr. José J. CORREA-REYES
Vice Consul
Mrs. María Mercedes REYES DE BECK

WISCONSIN

Milwaukee - (HC)
Hispanic Medical Center

3521 W. National Ave.

Milwaukee, WI 53215
Honorary Consul
Mr. Álvaro ALEMÁN

PANAMA

CALIFORNIA

Beverly Hills – (HC)
3137 W. Ball Rd., #104

Beverly Hills, CA 92804

Tel: (714) 547-6308
Honorary Consul

Mr. Fernando DALY AYARZA

San Diego – (HC)
2552 Chartsworth Blvd.

San Diego, CA 92106

Tel: (619) 225-8144
Honorary Consul
Mrs. Virna Cecilia LUQUE
Honorary Vice Consul
Mr. Adolfo GONZÁLEZ RUBIO BECKMANN

San Francisco – (CG)
The Flood Building

870 Market St., #551/553

San Francisco, CA 94102

Tel: (415) 391-4268

Fax: (415) 391-4269
Consul General
Mr. Oliver SERRANO

DISTRICT OF COLUMBIA

Washington – (EMB)
2862 McGill Terrace NW

Washington, DC 20008

Tel: (202) 483-1407
Consul General
Mr. Francisco MORALES
Consul
Ms. Mylene MARRONE RUIZ

FLORIDA

Miami – (CG)
2801 Ponce de León Blvd.,#1050,

Coral Gables, FL 33134

Tel: (305) 447-3700

Fax: (305) 447-4142
Consul General
Mr. Manuel COHEN
Consul
Mr. Yosef AVIAD
Consul
Mr. Franklin KARDONSKI
Honorary Consul
Mr. Sonny HOLTZMAN
Vice Consul
Ms. Irma FONSECA de TURCO

Trade Development Institute
1477 S. Miami Ave., 2nd Fl.

Miami, FL 33130

Tel: (305) 374-8823

Fax: (305) 374-7822
Consul General
Ms. Rosalinda PINILLA VALDES

Tampa – (CG)
Galleria Office Bldg.

4326 El Prado Blvd. #4

Tampa, FL 33629

Tel: (813) 251-0316

Fax: (813) 831-6685
Consul General
Mr. José B. ROBINSON HOOKER

GEORGIA

Atlanta – (CG)
Cain Tower - Peachtree Center

225 Peachtree St. NE, #503
Atlanta, GA 30303
Tel: (404) 522-4114
Consul General
Ms. Adriana ALEMAN KLERSZEN
Vice Consul
Ms. Connie CARDOZA de SHYNE

HAWAII
Honululu - (HCG)
P.O. BOX 75582
Honolulu, HI 96836
Tel: (808) 549-6883
Honorary Consul
Mr. Truman William BROPHY
ALTAMIRANDA

ILLINOIS
Chicago - (HC)
3930 N. Pine Grove Av., #903,
Chicago, IL 60610
Tel: (773) 933-7736
Honorary Consul
Ms. Lirella Jean SANDOVAL

LOUISIANA
Baton Rouge - (HCG)
12077 Old Hammond Hwy.
Baton Rouge, LA 70816
Tel: (504) 275-0796
Fax: (504) 272-3631
Honorary Consul General
Ms. Lizca BOMBET

New Orleans - (CG)
2424 World Trade Center
2 Canal St.
New Orleans, LA 70130
Tel: (504) 525-3458
Fax: (504) 524-8960
Consul General
Mr. Gabriel José BAZÁN KODAT

NEW YORK
New York - (CG)
1212 Ave. of The Americas, 6th Fl.
New York, NY 10036
Tel: (212) 840-2450
Fax: (212) 840-2469
Consul General
Ms. Rita GARCÍA de FROCHAUX
Vice Consul
Mrs. Angela Aurora GONZÁLEZ de
CARRERAS

Office of Maritime Safety
6 West 48th St., 10th Floor
New York, NY 10036
Tel: (212) 869-6440
Fax: (212) 575-2285
Consul
Mr. Christophe FROCHAUX

OHIO
Cleveland - (HC)
31300 Tuttle Dr.
Bay Village, OH 44140
Tel: (440) 835-8671

Honorary Consul
Mrs. Marie Antoinette FRASER

PENNSYLVANIA
Philadelphia - (CG)
124 Chestnut St.
Philadelphia, PA 19106
Tel: (215) 574-2994
Fax: (215) 625-4876
Consul General
Mrs. Georgia ATHANASOPULOS KONTU

PUERTO RICO
San Juan - (HC)
Marginal Kennedy Ave.
Esquina Calle Segarra
San Juan, PR 00922
Tel: (787) 792-1050
Honorary Consul
Mr. Jorge Francisco COLÓN NEVARES

TEXAS
Houston - (CG)
24 Greenway Plaza, #1307
Houston, TX 77046
Tel: (713) 622-4451
Fax: (713) 622-4468
Consul General
Ms. Miroslava Elizabeth VILAR
Honorary Consul
Mrs. Míriam R. SERA
Honorary Vice Consul
Mr. Camilo DÍAZ

PARAGUAY

CALIFORNIA
Los Angeles - (CG)
5115 Kester Av, # 1
Sherman Oaks, CA 90067
Tel: (818) 416-1588
Fax: (818) 907-1959
Consul General
Mr. Enrique INSFRAN MIRANDA

FLORIDA
Miami - (CG)
300 Biscayne Blvd. #907
Miami, FL 33131
Tel: (305) 374-9090
Consul General
Mr. Carlos WEISS LÓPEZ
Consular Agent
Mr. José Luis COSCIA LAGUARDIA
Consular Agent
Mrs. María Beatriz VASCONSELLOS
SÁNCHEZ

NEW YORK
New York - (CG)
675 Third Ave., #1604
New York, NY 10017
Consul General
Mr. Juan Alberto BAIARDI QUESNEL
Vice Consul
Mr. Fernando María FRONCIANI
CASSANELLO

PERU

CALIFORNIA
Los Angeles - (CG)
3460 Wilshire Blvd., #1005
Los Angeles, CA 90010
Tel: (213) 252-5910
Consul General
Mrs. Dora SALAZAR Vda. de WATKINS

San Francisco - (CG)
870 Market St. #1067
San Francisco, CA 94102
Tel: (415) 362-7136
Consul General
Mr. Jorge E. ROMÁN MOREY

COLORADO
Denver - (CG)
1001 S. Monaco Pkwy, # 210
Denver, CO 80224
Tel: (303) 355-8555
Consul General
Min. Carlos VELASCO MENDIOLA

DISTRICT OF COLUMBIA
Washington - (EMB)
1625 Massachusetts Ave. NW
Washington, DC 20036
Tel: (202) 462-1084
Fax: (202) 659-8124
Consul General
Min. Luis SANDOVAL DÁVILA

FLORIDA
Miami - (CG)
444 Brickell Ave., #M-135
Miami, FL 33131
Tel: (305) 374-8935
Consul General
Emb. Alfredo RAMOS SUERO
Deputy Consul
Ms. María Del BEDOYA GARCÍA
MONTERO
Consular Agent
Mr. Fernando Manuel ALBAREDA DEL
CASTILLO

Tampa - (HC)
2312 W. Waters Ave., #2
Tampa, CA 33604
Tel: (941) 923-7586
Honorary Consul
Mr. Julio Enrique VEGA GUANILO

GEORGIA
Atlanta - (HC)
4211 Erskine Rd., #C-2, Clarkston
Atlanta, GA 30021
Tel: (404) 299-8234
Honorary Consul
Mr. Thomas LEE SMITH

HAWAII
Honolulu - (HC)
225 Queen St. #18E
Honolulu, HI 96813
Tel: (808) 737-0223

Fax: (808) 535-7278
Honorary Consul
Mr. Luis Ricardo CORONADO

ILLINOIS
Chicago - (CG)
180 N. Michigan Ave., #1830
Chicago, IL 60601
Tel: (312) 853-6173
Consul General
Mr. Manuel BOZA HECK

LOUISIANA
New Orleans - (HC)
333 St. Charles Ave. #1705
New Orleans, LA 70130
Tel: (504) 861-7827
Honorary Consul
Mr. Raffaele G. BELTRAM DEBEUZ-
MILLONIG

MASSACHUSETTS
Boston - (HC)
223 Marlborough St.
Boston, MA 02116
Tel: (617) 267-8141
Consul General
Min. Mariano GARCÍA GODAS Mc BRIDE

MISSOURI
St. Louis - (HC)
1034 S. Brentwood Blvd., #520
St. Louis, MO 63117
Tel: (314) 726-6610
Honorary Consul
Mrs. Rosa Ana SCHWARZ

NEW JERSEY
Paterson - (CG)
Broadway Bank Bldg.
100 Hamilton Plaza, #1221
Paterson, NJ 07505
Tel: (973) 278-3324
Consul General
Min. Amalia MARIÁTEGUI SUCCAR

NEW YORK
New York - (CG)
215 Lexington Ave., 21st Floor
New York, NY 10016
Tel: (212) 481-7410
Fax: (212) 481-8606
Consul General
Mr. Julio VEGA ERAUSQUIN
Deputy Consul General
Mr. Gabriel Alejandro PACHECO CRESPO
Deputy Consul
Mr. Juan Guillermo WROBEL TABOADA

OKLAHOMA
Tulsa - (HC)
2430 E. 41 St.
Tulsa, OK 74105
Tel: (918) 245-5911
Honorary Consul
Dr. Luis Alberto REINOSO

PUERTO RICO
San Juan - (CG)
Home Mortgage Plaza

268 Avenida Ponce de León, #1009
San Juan, PR 00918
Tel: (809) 250-0391

TEXAS
Houston – (CG)
5177 Richmond Av., # 695
Houston, TX 77056
Tel: (713) 355- 9517
Consul General
Mr. Jorge Antonio SALAS REZKALAH
Honorary Consul
Mr. Bernardo TREISTMAN

San Antonio – (HC)
28055 Ruffian Dr.
San Antonio, TX 78006
Honorary Consul
Mrs. Carmela RUSSELL GILL

UTAH
Salt Lake City - (HC)
136 E. South Temple, #2200
Salt Lake City, UT 84111
Tel: (801) 328-4500
Honorary Consul
Mr. Juan A. MEJÍA

WASHINGTON
Seattle - (HC)
3717 N.E. 157th St., #100
Seattle, WA 98155
Honorary Consul
Mr. Miguel Angel VELÁSQUEZ GARCÍA

SPAIN

ALABAMA
Mobile - (HC)
250 N. Water St.
Mobile, AL 36602
Tel: (334) 441-7012
Honorary Consul
Dr. Robert John LAGER

ALASKA
Anchorage - (HVC)
14900 S. Windsor Circle
Anchorage, AK 99516
Tel: (907) 345-8645
Honorary Vice Consul
Mr. Roberto ALBACETE GONZÁLEZ

CALIFORNIA
Los Angeles – (CG)
5055 Wilshire Blvd. #960
Los Angeles, CA 90036
Tel: (213) 938-0158
Consul General
Mr. Herminio MORALES FERNÁNDEZ
Deputy Consul
Mr. Miguel LAHOZ

Spanish Commercial Office
Home Savings Tower
660 S. Figueroa St., #1050
Los Angeles, CA 90017
Tel: (213) 627-5284
Fax: (213) 627-0883

Consul
Mr. Alejandro NIETO GARCÍA
Consul
Mr. Genaro GONZÁLEZ PALACIOS

Spanish National Tourist Office
8383 Wilshire Bl., #960
Beverly Hills, CA 90211
Tel: (213) 658-7188
Consul
Mr. Ignacio DUCASSE GUTIÉRREZ

Spanish Education Office
6300 Wilshire Bl., #1740
Los Angeles, CA 90048
Tel: (213) 852-6997
Fax: (213) 852-0759
Consul:
Mr. Ignacio MORENO GOZALVEZ

San Diego - (HC)
Libros Hispanoamericanos
10922 Anja Way,Lakeside
San Diego, CA 92040-2717
Tel: (619) 448-7282
Honorary Consul
Mrs. María Ángeles OLSON

San Francisco – (CG)
1405 Sutter St.
San Francisco, CA 94123
Tel: (415) 922-2995
Consul General
Mr. Lorenzo GONZÁLEZ ALONSO

DISTRICT OF COLUMBIA
Washington – (EMB)
2375 Pennsylvania Ave. NW
Washington, DC 20037
Tel: (202) 728-2330
Fax: (202) 728-2302
Consul General
Mr. Rafael Adolfo JOVER DE MORA
FIGUEROA

FLORIDA
Miami - (CG)
Gables International Plaza
2655 Le Jeune Rd., #203
Coral Gables, FL 33134
Tel: (305) 446-5511
Consul General
Mr. Miguel Carlos DÍAZ PACHE
PUMAREDA
Deputy Consul General
Mr. Miguel Angel CARRASCO
RODRÍGUEZ

Commercial Office of Spain
Gables International Plaza
2655 Le Jeune Rd. #1065 & 1114
Coral Gables, FL 33134
Tel: (305) 446-4387
Consul
Mr. Joaquin DE LA HERRAN MENDIVIL
Deputy Consul
Mr. Emilio GUERRA RUFART

Spanish Tourist Office
1221 Brickell Ave., #1850
Coral Gobles, FL 33131
Tel: (305) 358-1992

Consul
Mr. José Manuel DE JUAN
GONZÁLEZ

Spanish Education Office
2655 Le Jeune Rd., #1008
Coral Gables, FL 33134
Tel: (305) 448-2146
Fax: (305) 445-0508
Consul
Mrs. Lucía María MORÁN
ALDARRAGA

Pensacola - (HVC)
100 Ingalls Dr.
Pensacola, FL 32506-5259
Tel: (904) 455-5360
Honorary Vice Consul
Ms. María Dolores DAVIS

GEORGIA
Atlanta – (HVC)
1010 Huntcliff, #2315
Atlanta, GA 30350
Tel: (404) 993-4883
Honorary Vice Consul
Mr. Ignacio Luis TABOADA

HAWAII
Honolulu – (HVC)
530 South King St., #202
Honolulu, HI 96813
Tel: (808) 523-4580
Fax: (808) 545-2024
Honorary Vice Consul
Mr. John Henry FÉLIX

IDAHO
Boise - (HVC)
277 N. 6th St., #200
Boise, ID 83702
Tel: (208) 388-1313
Honorary Vice Consul
Mr. Roy Lewis EIGUREN

ILLINOIS
Chicago – (CG)
180 N. Michigan Ave., #1500
Chicago, IL 60601
Tel: (312) 782-4588
Consul General
Mr. Rodrigo AGUIRRE DE CARCER
Consul
Mr. Guillermo DÍAZ PINTOS

National Spanish Tourist Office
Water Tower Place
845 N. Michigan Ave., #915-E
Chicago, IL 60611
(312) 642-1992
Vice Consul
Ms. Beatriz MARCO ARCE

Spanish Commercial Office
500 N. Michigan Ave., #1500
Michigan, IL 60611
Tel: (312) 644-1154
Consul
Mr. Pedro MORIYON DÍEZ
CANEDO
Consul
Miss Josefina BELTRÁN BELTRÁN

LOUISIANA
New Orleans – (CG)
2102 World Trade Center
2 Canal St.
New Orleans, LA 70130
Tel: (504) 525-4951
Consul General
Mr. José Gabriel NÚÑEZ IGLESIAS
MARTÍNEZ

MASSACHUSETTS
Boston – (CG)
545 Boylston St., #803
Boston, MA 02116
Tel: (617) 536-2506
Consul General
Mr. Ricardo PEDRO CONDE

MICHIGAN
Detroit - (HVC)
2890 Lakewoods Court, Orchard Lake
Detroit, MI 48324
Tel: (248) 683-9104
Honorary Vice Consul
Mr. Louis BETANZOS

MINNESOTA
Minneapolis (HVC)
824 Summit Av.
Minneapolis, MN 55403
Tel: (612) 377-4228
Honorary Vice Consul
Ms. Aurora Onia RIOS-REXACH

MISSOURI
Kansas City – (HVC)
1316 Avila Circle
Kansas City, MO 64114
Tel: (816) 942-2649
Fax: (816) 942-2649
Honorary Consul
Mr. Eugene Fancis GRAY

St. Louis - (HVC)
5715 Manchester Av.
St Louis, MO 63110
Honorary Vice Consul
Mr. José L. MOLINA

NEW JERSEY
Newark – (HC)
Rutgers University
249 University Ave.
Newark, MO 07102
Honorary Consul
Mr. Arturo LÓPEZ

NEW MEXICO
Santa Fe - (HC)
460 St. Michael's Dr., # 402
Santa Fe, NM 10155
Tel: (505) 988-4171
Vice Consul
Ms. Felice Gracia GONZÁLEZ

NEW YORK
New York – (CG)
150 E. 58th St., 30/31 Floor
New York, NY 10155

Tel: (212) 355-4080
Consul General
Mr. Emilio CASSINELLO AUBAN
Deputy Consul General
Mr. Joaquín BALSALOBRE OLIVA
Consul Para Asuntos Culturales
Mr. Juan SUNYE MENDIA

National Spanish Tourist Office
666 5th Ave., 35th Floor
New York, NY 10103
Tel: (212) 265-8822
Deputy Consul
Ms. Mónica SÁNCHEZ GONZÁLEZ
Consul
Mr. Álvaro Román RENEDO SENADO

Spanish Commercial Office
405 Lexington Ave., 44th Floor
New York, NY 10174
Tel: (212) 661-4959
Consul
Mr. Agustín María MAINAR ALFONSO
Consul
Ms. Ana María BRAVO GARCÍA
Consul
Mr. Manuel Luis VALLE MUÑOZ

Spanish Education Office
150 5th Ave. #918
New York, NY 10011
Consul
Mr. Angel DE GOYA CASTROVERDE

OHIO
Cincinnati - (HVC)
2605 Burnet Av.
Cincinnati, OH 45219
Tel: (513) 961-3737
Honorary Vice Consul
Mr. Sidney L. KAUFMAN

PENNSYLVANIA
Philadelphia - (HVC)
3410 Warden Dr.
Philadelphia, PA 19129
Honorary Vice Consul
Mr. Herminio MUÑIZ

PUERTO RICO
San Juan - (CG)
Edificio Mercantil Plaza, #1101,Hato Rey
San Juan, PR 00918
Tel: (787) 758-6090
Fax: (787) 763-0190
Consul General
Mr. Emilio BARCIA GARCÍA VILLAMIL
Consular Agent
Mr. Gabino IGLESIAS FERNÁNDEZ

Spanish Commercial Office
Capital Center Sur Building
239 Arterial Hostos Av., #705
San Juan, PR 00918
Tel: (787) 758 6345
Fax: (787) 758-6948
Consul
Mr. Enrique FONTANA LLOPIS

TEXAS
Corpus Christi - (HC)
7517 Yorkshire Blvd.
Corpus Chirsti, TX 78413

Tel: (512) 994-7517
Honorary Consul
Mr. Fernando Moral IGLESIAS

Dallas - (HC)
5499 Glen Lakes Dr., #209
Dallas, TX 75231
Tel: (214) 373-1200
Honorary Consul
Ms. Janet POLLMAN KAFKA

El Paso - (HC)
420 Golden Springs Dr.
El Paso, TX 79912
Tel: (915) 534-0677
Honorary Consul
Mr. Arthur Sheldon HALL

Houston - (CG)
1800 Bering Dr., #660
Houston, TX 77057
Tel: (713) 783-6200
Consul General
Mr. Jesús Julio LOPEZ JACOISTE

San Antonio - (HC)
8350 Delphian
San Antonio, TX 78148
Honorary Consul
Mrs. Isabel DE PEDRO MARÍN

WASHINGTON
Seattle - (HVC)
C/O Boeing Co., 8th & Park, N.,Renton
Seattle, WA 98055
Tel: (206) 237-9373
Honorary Vice Consul
Mr. Luis F. ESTEBAN BERNÁLDEZ

URUGUAY

CALIFORNIA
Los Angeles – (CG)
429 Santa Monica Blvd., #400
Santa Monica, CA 90401
Tel: (310) 394-5777
Consul General
Mr. Rodolfo INVERNIZZI

San Francisco – (HC)
41 Sutter St., #200
San Francisco, CA 94104
Tel: (415) 981-1115
Honorary Consul
Mr. Mark HAIDEN RITCHIE

FLORIDA
Miami – (CG)
1077 Ponce De Leon Blvd., Coral Gables
Miami, FL 33134
Tel: (305) 443-9764
Fax: (305) 443-7802
Consul General
Mr. Antonio Luis CAMPS VALGOI
Deputy Consul General
Min. Lucía TRUCILLO
Consul
Mr. Arturo Valentín VILLAREAL
RODRÍGUEZ

HAWAII
Honolulu – (HC)
1833 Kalakaua Ave., #710

Honolulu, HI 96815
Tel: (808) 947-2889
Honorary Consul
Mr. Luis Enrique ZANOTTA

ILLINOIS
Chicago – (HC)
875 N. Michigan Ave., #1422
Chicago, IL 60611
Tel: (312) 642-3430
Fax: (312) 642-3470
Consul General
Dr. Olga Graziella REYES DE PRIETO
Honorary Consul
Mr. Carlos Guillermo RIZOWY

LOUISIANA
New Orleans – (C)
2 Canal St. #2002
New Orleans, LA 70130
Tel: (504) 525-8354
Honorary Consul
Mr. Julio Emerson RÍOS PEÑA

MASSACHUSETTS
Boston – (HC)
Medical Building
67 Union St., Natick
Boston, MA 01760
Tel: (617) 650-7936
Honorary Consul
Mr. Raúl LAGUARDA

NEW YORK
New York – (CG)
747 3rd Ave. 21st Floor
New York, NY 10017
Tel: (212) 753-8581
Consul General
Mr. Juan José DI SEVO
Consul
Mr. Rolando VISCONTI

PUERTO RICO
San Juan - (HC)
Himalaya 254, Monterrey Urb.
San Juan, PR 00926
Honorary Consul
Ms. Josefina DE HILLYER
Honorary Vice Consul
Mr. Ariel ALONSO OROZ

WASHINGTON
Seattle – (HC)
Lane, Powell, Spears, Lubersky
420 Fifth Ave., #4100
Seattle, WA 99101
Tel: (804) 625-3658
Honorary Consul
Mr. Hartley PAUL

VENEZUELA

CALIFORNIA
San Francisco – (CG)
311 California St., # 620
San Francisco, CA 94104
Tel: (415) 955-1982
Consul General
Mr. Domingo LANOS ALDEREY

Consul
Mr. Gerardo COLL

FLORIDA
Miami – (CG)
1101 Brickell Ave., #901
Miami, FL 33131
Tel: (305) 577-4214
Consul General
Mr. Antonio HERNÁNDEZ BORGO
Consul
Ms. Nancy DA COSTA

ILLINOIS
Chicago – (CG)
20 N. Wacker Dr., #1925
Chicago, IL 60606
Tel: (312) 236-7122
Consul General
Ms. Bertha CAPELLA REVERON

LOUISIANA
New Orleans – (CG)
1908 World Trade Center,
2 Canal St.
New Orleans, LA 70130
Tel: (504) 522-3284
Consul General
Mr. Lola R. ANIYAR de CASTRO
Vice Consul
Ms. Carlos José RIVERO

MASSACHUSETTS
Boston – (CG)
545 Boylston St., 3rd Floor
Boston, MA 02115
Tel: (617) 266-9368
Consul General
Mr. Armando Rafael GONZÁLEZ
ANGARITA
Vice Consul
Mr. Freddy Gregorio HERRERA FUENTES

NEW YORK
New York – (CG)
7 E. 51st St.
New York, NY 10022
Tel: (212) 826-1680
Consul General
Mr. Pedro CONDE REGARDIZ

PUERTO RICO
San Juan – (CG)
Edificio Mercantil Plaza
Ponce de León Ave., #601, Hato Rey
San Juan, PR 00918
Tel: (787) 766-4250
Consul
Mrs. Andreina SAVELLI

TEXAS
Houston – (CG)
2925 Briarpark Dr., #900
Houston, TX 77042
Tel: (713) 974-0028
Consul General
Mrs. Csaba KATO
Vice Consul
Ms. Elizabeth Cecilia LEÓN LEÓN
Consul
Ms. Zulima Del ROJAS MAVARES

Hispanic Missions to the OAS
Misiones hispanas ante la OEA

The OAS (Organization of American States) was founded on April 30, 1948 in Bogotá, Colombia and has 35 member countries and 46 permanent observer countries.

La OEA (Organización de Estados Americanos) fue fundada el 30 de abril de 1948 en Bogotá, Colombia y la integran 35 países miembros y 46 países observadores permanentes.

ANTIGUA AND BARBUDA

3216 New Mexico Ave. NW
Washington, DC 20016
Tel: (202) 362-5122/5166/5211
Fax: (202) 362-5225
E-mail: EMBANTBAR@AOL.COM

Ambassador, Perm. Rep.:
Lionel Alexander Hurst;
Mrs. Ema-Mae Hurst

Minister Counselor, Alt. Rep.:
Deborah Mae Lovell

Minister Councelor, Alt. Rep.:
Starret D. Green

ARGENTINA

1816 Corcoran St. NW
Washington, DC 20009
Tel: (202) 387-4142/387-4146/387-4170
Fax: (202) 328-1591

Ambassador, Perm. Rep.:
Dr. Juan Jose Arcuri:
Mrs. Claudia Taboada de Arcuri

Counselor, Alt. Rep.:
Martín Gómez Bustillo;

First Secretary, Alt. Rep.:
Mauricio Alice

First Secretary, Alt. Rep.:
Federico Villegas Beltrán;
Mrs. María Eugenia Alvarado de Villegas
Beltrán

THE BAHAMAS

(Commonwealth of the Bahamas)
2220 Massachusetts Ave. NW
Washington, DC 20008
Tel: (202) 319-2660/to 67
Fax:(202) 319-2668
E-mail: BAHEMB@AOL.COM

Ambassador, Perm. Rep.:
Sir Joshua Sears

Minister Counselor, Alt. Rep.:
Sheila G. Carey

First Secretary:
Edda D. Dumont-Adolph
Mr. Ronald Adolph

First Secretary:
Rhoda M. Jackson

BARBADOS

2144 Wyoming Ave. NW
Washington, DC 20008
Tel: (202) 939-9200/01/02
Fax: (202) 332-7467
Telex: 64343 BARWASH
E-mail: BARBADOS@OAS.ORG

Ambassador, Perm. Rep.:
Michael Ian King

Counselor, Alt. Rep.:
David Bulbulia

First Secretary, Alt. Rep.:
Mr. Phillip St. Hill

First Secretary, Alt. Rep.:
Joyce Baurne

Attaché, Alt. Rep.:
Mrs. Rose Greaves

Attaché, Alt. Rep.:
Betty Callender

BELIZE

2535 Massachusetts Ave. NW
Washington, DC 20008
Tel: (202) 332-9636
Fax: (202) 332-6888

Ambassador, Perm. Rep.:
Lisa M. Shoman

Interim Representative:
Nestor Mendez

Counselor, Alt. Rep.:
Georgia Brown Williams

Attaché, Alt. Rep.:
Lauren L. Quiros

BOLIVIA

1819 H St. NW #410
Washington, DC 20006
Tel: (202) 785-0218/19/ 0224
Fax: (202) 296-0563
Telex: 248672 BOAS
E-mail: Delgalivia@erols.com

Ambassador, Perm. Rep.:
Marcelo Ostria Trigo

Minister Counselor, Alt. Rep.:
Mr. Alberto Quiroga
Mrs. Renata Ortiz

Counselor:
Guido Quevedo

Second Secretary, Alt. Rep.:
Yuri Monje

Second Secretary, Alt. Rep.:
Andrea Soruco

Second Secretary, Alt. Rep.:
Prudencio Raul Palsa

BRAZIL

2600 Virginia Ave. NW #412
Washington, DC, 20037
Tel: (202) 333-4224/25/26
Fax: (202) 333-6610

Ambassador, Perm. Rep.:
Valter Pecly Moreia

Minister Counselor, Alt. Rep.:
Cezar Augusto de Souza Lima Amaral

Mininster Counselor, Alt. Rep.:
Dante Coelho de Lima

Counselor, Alt. Rep.:
Roberto Coutinho

First Secretary, Alt. Rep.:
Clemente Baena Soares

First Secretary, Alt. Rep.:
Aldelmo Serafin Garcia, Jr.

First Secretary, Alt. Rep.:
Paulo Roberto Amora Alvarenga

Second Secretary, Alt. Rep.:
Lucia Reboucas Pires

CANADA

501 Pennsylvania Ave. NW
Washington, DC 20001
Tel: (202) 682-1768
Fax: (202) 682-7624
Telex: 89664

Ambassador, Perm. Rep.:
Peter M. Boehm;
Mrs. Catherine Dickson

Counselor, Alt. Rep.:
Renata I.Wielgos;

Counselor, Alt. Rep.:
Etinne Savoie

Counselor, Alt. Rep:
David Keithlin

First Secretary:
Ettienne Savoie

Second Secretary, Alt. Rep.:
Anne M. Lawson

Third Secretary:
Anne Tamara Lorre

Alternate Representative:
Basia Manitius

CHILE

2000 L St. NW #720
Washington, DC 20036
Tel: (202) 887-5475/76
Fax: (202) 775-0713
Telex: 247003 Emchi

Ambassador, Perm. Rep.:
Esteban Tomic Errazuriz

Counselor, Alt. Rep.:
Carlos Crohare

First Secretary, Alt. Rep.:
Miguel Angel Gonzalez

First Secretary, Alt. Rep.:
Frederick Heller

Adviser:
Monica Labarca

COLOMBIA

1609 22nd St. NW
Washington, DC 20008
Tel: (202) 332-8003/04
Fax: (202) 234-9781 Telex: 197395

Ambassador, Perm. Rep.:
Luis Alfredo Ramos Botero

Minister, Alt. Rep.:
Juan Jaime Casabianca Perdomo

Counselor, Alt. Rep.:
Aurelio Tobón Estrada

First Secretary, Alt. Rep.:
Camilo Rojas;

First Secretary, Alt. Rep.:
Ana María Villareal

Second Secretary, Alt. Rep.:
María Clara Faciolince

Second Secretary, Alt. Rep.:
Isaura Duarte

Second Secretary:
Augusto Posada Sanchez

COSTA RICA

2112 S St. NW
Washington, DC 20008
Tel: (202) 234-9280/1
Fax: (202) 986-2274
Telex: 3400-CREM

Ambassador, Perm. Rep.:
Hernán R. Castro Hernández

Ambassador Alt. Rep.:
Luis Guardia Mora

Minister Counselor, Alt. Rep.:
Rodrigo A. Sotela Alfaro
Mrs. Gabriela Sotela

Minister Counselor, Alt. Rep.:
Francisco J. Chacón

Minister Counselor:
Roxana Terán de la Cruz

Minister Counselor:
Marcela Matamoros

DOMINICA

(Commonwealth of Dominica)
3216 New Mexico Ave. NW
Washington, DC 20016
Tel: (202) 364-6781
Fax: (202) 364-9791

Ambassador, Perm. Rep.:
(Vacant)

Administrative Secretary:
Judith-Anne Rolle

DOMINICAN REPUBLIC

1715 22nd St. NW
Washington, DC 20008
(202) 332-9142/6280
Fax: (202) 265-8057
Telex: 440031 DOREMB

Ambassador, Perm. Rep.:
(Vacant)

Ambassador, Interim Rep.:
Ramón Quiñones

Counselor, Alt. Rep.:
Mayerlyn Cordero

Counselor:
Rhina Duran

ECUADOR

2535 15th St. NW
Washington, DC 20009
Tel: (202) 234-1494/1692
Fax: (202) 667-3482
Telex: 440129 EQUA-UI

Ambassador, Perm. Rep.:
Blasco Peñaherrera Padilla

Minister, Alt. Rep.:
Rafael Veintimilla

Counselor, Alt. Rep.:
Luis Felipe Valencia

Second Secretary, Alt. Rep.:
Andrés Montalvo

Military Attaché:
Cnel. Luis Paredes

Civil Attaché:
María Eugenia Romero

EL SALVADOR

1010 16th St. NW 4th Floor
Washington, DC 20036
Tel: (202) 467-0054/4290
Fax: (202) 467-4261
E-mail: ELSALVADOR-OEA@EROLS.COM

Ambassador, Perm. Rep.:
Margarita Escobar

Minister Counselor, Alt. Rep.:
Lic. Luis Menéndez Castro;
Mrs. Margarita Menéndez

Counselor, Alt. Rep.:
Eduardo A. Hernández González

Military Attaché:
Jorge Alfaro

GRENADA

1701 New Hampshire Ave. NW
Washington, DC 20009
Tel: (202) 265-2561
Fax: (202) 265-2468
Telex: 897029 GRENADA

Ambassador, Perm. Rep.:
Denis G. Antoine
Mrs. Marva M. Antoine

First Secretary:
Michaele Samuel

GUATEMALA

1507 22nd St. NW
Washington, DC 20036
Tel: (202) 833-4015/16/17
Fax: (202) 833-4011
E-mail: Guate95@AOL.COM

Ambassador, Perm. Rep.:
Ronalth Ochaeta Argueta

Minister Counselor, Alt. Rep.:
Alma Gladys Cordero

First Secretary, Alt. Rep.:
Carlos Chopen

Third Secretary, Alt. Rep.:
Héctor Rolando Palacios Lima;
Mrs. Sonía Hunn de Palacios

Attaché:
General Edgar Godoy

GUYANA

2490 Tracy Pl. NW
Washington, DC 20008
Tel: (202) 265-6900/01
Fax: (202) 232-1297
Telex: 64170 GUYAMB

Ambassador, Perm. Rep.:
Dr. Odeen Ishmael
Mrs. Evangeline Ishmael

First Secretary, Alt. Rep.:
Deborah Yaw

Second Secretary:
Donnette Critchlow

HAITI

2311 Massachusetts Ave., NW
Washington, DC 20008
Tel: (202) 332-4090/ 96
Fax: (202) 745-7215

Ambassador:
(Vacant)

Minister Counselor, Interim:
Jean Ricot Dormeus

Second Secretary, Alt. Rep.:
Pierre Daniel Laviolette

HONDURAS

5100 Wisconsin Ave. NW #403
Washington, DC 20016
Tel: (202) 362-9656/57
Fax: (202) 537-7170
Telex: 140193 HOOEA
E-mail: Honduras@OAS.ORG

Ambassador, Perm. Rep.:
Laura Elena Núñez Flores de Ponce

Minister Counselor:
Lic. Carlos Montoya Castro

Counselor:
Katyna Arqueta

Counselor, Alt. Rep.:
Lic .Maria Guadalupe Carias

Civil Attaché, Adviser:
Rosario Zapata-Laserna;

JAMAICA

1520 New Hampshire Ave. NW
Washington, DC 20036
Tel: (202) 452-0660
Fax: (202) 452-9395
Telex: 64352 EMJAMUW
E-mail: EMJAM@sisnet.net

Ambassador, Perm. Rep.:
Dr. Richard Bernal
Mrs. Margaret Bernal

Minister, Alt. Rep.:
Vilma Mc Nish

First Secretary:
Shorna-Kay Richards

First Secretary:
Rolande Pryce

MEXICO

2440 Massachusetts Ave. NW
Washington, DC 20008
Tel: (202) 332-3663/64/3984
Fax: (202) 332-9498
Telex: 248535 MIMX UR

Ambassador, Perm. Rep.:
Mr. Claude Heller

Minister, Alt. Rep.:
Juan Manuel Gómez Robledo

Minister, Alt. Rep.:
Maria de Lourdes Aranda

First Secretary, Alt. Rep.:
Julián Ventura

First Secretary, Alt. Rep.:
Juan José Gómez Camacho

Second Secretary, Alt. Rep.:
Edgar Cubero

Attaché, Adviser:
María Aguilera

NICARAGUA

1627 New Hampshire Ave. NW
Washington, DC 20009
Tel: (202) 332-1643/44
Fax: (202) 745-0710
Telex: 283051 EMBANIC-UR

Ambassador, Perm. Rep.:
Alvaro J. Sevilla Siero

Ambassador Alt. Rep.:
Victor M. Silva

Minister Counselor, Alt. Rep.:
Manuel Salvador Abaunza

Minister Counselor:
Bertha Arguello Roman

Counselor, Alt. Rep.:
Arturo Harding Tefel

PANAMA

2201 Wisconsin Ave. NW #240
Washington, DC 20007
Tel: (202) 965-4826/4819
Fax: (202) 965-4836

Ambassador, Perm. Rep.:
Juan Manuel Castulovich

Ambassador, Alt. Rep.:
Max José López Cornejo

Counselor, Alt. Rep.:
Cecilia Luz Vazquez

Counselor, Alt. Rep.:
Vladimir Franco

Legal Counselor, Alt. Rep.:
Nisla Lorena Aparicio Robles

Attaché:
Zaida Santamaría

PARAGUAY

2022 Connecticut Ave. NW
Washington, DC 20008
Tel: (202) 244-3003/483-6962
Fax: (202) 234-4508

Ambassador, Perm. Rep.:
Diego Abente Brun

Counselor:
Julio Cesar Arriola Ramirez

First Secretary:
Julio Duarte Van Humbeck

Second Secretary:
Alvaro Diaz de Vivar

Second Secretary:
Christian Maidana

PERÚ

2201 Wisconsin Ave. NW #220
Washington, DC 20007
Tel: (202) 232-2281
Fax: (202) 337-6866
Telex: 440151 PERUOEA

Ambassador, Perm. Rep.:
(Vacant)

Interim Rep.:
Antonio Garcia Revilla

Counselor, Alt. Rep.:
Maria Fátima Trigozo

First Secretary, Alt. Rep.:
Jorge Wurst

First Secretary, Alt. Rep.:
Carlos Chocano

Second Secretary, Alt. Rep.:
Eduardo Zeballos

ST. KITTS AND NEVIS

3216 New Mexico Ave. NW
Washington, DC 20016
Tel: (202) 686-2636
Fax: (202) 686-5740

Ambassador, Perm. Rep.:
Dr. Osbert W. Liburd

Minister Counselor, Alt. Rep.:
Kevin Isaac

Counselor, Alt. Rep.:
Jasmine E. Huggins

SAINT LUCIA

3216 New Mexico Ave., NW
Washington, DC 20016
Tel: (202) 364-6792
Fax: (202) 364-6723
Telex: 671148 LUCIA UW
E-mail: EOSAINTLU@AOL.COM

Ambassador, Perm. Rep.:
Sonia M. Johnny

Vice Counselor, Alt. Rep.:
Alba Becille

First Secretary, Alt. Rep.:
Martha Louis Auguste

First Secretary, Alt. Rep.:
Yasmine Venice Solitahe Odlum

Attaché:
Thais Mirroe

ST. VINCENT & GRENADINES

3216 New Mexico Ave. NW
Washington, DC 20016
Tel: (202) 364-6730
Fax: (202) 364-6736

Ambassador, Perm. Rep.:
Kingsley C. A. Layne;
Mrs. Cornelia M. Layne

Minister Counselor, Alt. Rep.:
Fitz Bramble

Counselor, Alt. Rep.:
Frank Clarke

SURINAME

4301 Connecticut Ave., NW #108
Washington, DC 20008
Tel: (202) 244-2501
Fax: (202) 244-5878
Telex: 6491089 AMBAS-UR

Ambassador:
(Vacant)

Interim Representative:
Natasha Halfhuid

Second Secretary:
Henry Mac Donald

Attaché:
Juliette Redman-Kasmin

TRINIDAD AND TOBAGO

1708 Massachusetts Ave. NW
Washington, DC 20036
Tel: (202) 467-6490
Fax: (202) 467-6490
E-mail: EMBTTGO@EROLS.COM

Ambassador, Perm. Rep.:
Michael A. Arneaud

Counselor:
Mackisack Adrian Logie

First Secretary.:
Jennifer Marchand

UNITED STATES

2201 CST NW, # 6494
Washington, DC 20521
Tel.: (202) 647-9430
Fax: (202) 649-0911

Ambassador, Perm. Rep.:
Luis J. Lauredo

Ambassador, Alt. Rep.:
Thomas Shannon

Counselor, Alt. Rep.:
Charlotte E. Roe

Counselor, Alt. Rep.:
Margarita Riva-Geoghegan
(202) 647-9913

Counsler, Alt. Rep.:
Joan E. Segerson
(202) 647-9914

URUGUAY

2801 New Mexico Ave. NW #1210
Washington, DC 20007
Tel: (202) 333-0588 / 0687
Fax: (202) 337-3758
Telex: 440221 URUOEA
URUOEA@EROLS.COM

Ambassador, Perm. Rep.:
Juan Enrique Fischer

Counselor, Alt. Rep.:
Dr. Eduardo Bouzout

Minister Counselor, Alt. Rep.:
Ricardo Varela

First Secretary, Alt. Rep.:
Susana Rosa

Military Attaché, Alt Rep.:
Carlos Alberto Giani

VENEZUELA

1099 30th St. NW 2nd Floor
Washington, DC 20007
Tel: (202) 342-5841/5837
Fax: (202) 625-5657
Telex: 248397 VOAS-UR
E-mail: missionvene@sisnet.net

Ambassador, Perm. Rep.:
Virginia M. Contreras Navarrete

Minister Counselor, Alt. Rep.:
Mahuampi Rodriguez de Orgiz

Counselor, Alt. Rep.:
Ilenia Medina

First Secretary, Alt Rep.:
Luis Niño

First Secretary, Alt. Rep.:
Marco Palavicini

Press Attaché:
Magaly Saavedra

Permanent Observers

ALGERIA, DEM. AND POP. OF

2118 Kalorama Road, N.W.
Washington, D.C.
Telephone: (202) 265-2800
Telefax: (202) 667-2174

His Excellency

Ambassador, Perm. Observer:
Ramtane Lamamra

ANGOLA, PEOPLE'S REPUBLIC OF

1615 M Street, N.W. Suite 900
Washington, D.C. 20036
Telephone: (202) 785-1156
Telefax: (202) 785-1258

His Excellency

Ambassador, Perm. Observer:
Antonio dos Santos França

AUSTRIA

3524 International Court, N.W.
Washington, D.C. 20008
Telephone: (202) 895-6700
Telefax: (202) 895-6750

His Excellency

Ambassador, Perm. Observer:
Peter Moser

BELGIUM

3330 Garfield Street, N.W.
Washington, D.C. 20008
Telephone: (202) 333-6900
Telefax: (202) 333-3079

His Excellency

Ambassador, Perm. Observer:
Alex Reyn

BOSNIA AND HERZEGOVINA

2109 E St., N.W.
Washington D.C. 20037
Telephone: (202) 337-1500
Telefax: (202) 337-1502

His Excellency

Ambassador, Perm. Observer:
Sven Alkalaj

BULGARIA

1621 22nd St., N.W
Washington D.C. 20008
Telephone: (202) 387-7669
Telefax: (202) 234-7973

His Excellency

Ambassador, Perm. Observer:
Philip Dimitrov

CROATIA

2343 Massachusetts Ave. N.W.
Washington D.C. 20008
Telephone: (202) 588-5899
Telefax: (202) 588-8937

His Excellency

Ambassador, Perm. Observer:
Miomir Zuzul

CYPRUS

2211 Street, N.W.
Washington, D.C. 20008
Telephone: (202) 462-5772
Telefax: (202) 483-6710

His Excellency

Ambassador, Perm. Observer
Erato Kozakou-Marcoullis

CZECH REPUBLIC

3900 Spring of Freedom St. N.W.
Washington D.C. 20008
Telephone: (202) 274-9100
Telefax: (202) 966-8540

His Excellency

Ambassador, Perm. Observer:
Alexandr Vondra

DENMARK

3200 Whitehaven St, NW
Washington, D.C. 20008
Telephone: (202) 797-5327
Telefax: (202) 328-1470

His Excellency

Ambassador, Perm. Observer:
Ulrik Federspiel

EGYPT

3521 International Court, N.W.
Washington, D.C. 20008
Telephone: (202) 895-5400
Telefax: (202) 244-4319-5131

His Excellency

Ambassador, Perm. Observer
Nabil Fahmy

EQUATORIAL GUINEA

1712 R Street N.W., Suite 410
Washington, D.C., 20006
Telephone: (202) 518-5700
Telefax: (202) 518-5252

His Excellency

Ambassador, Perm. Observer
Pastor Micha Ondo Bile

FINLAND

3301 Massachusetts Ave., N.W.
Washington, D.C. 20016
Telephone: (202) 363-2430
Telefax: (202) 298-6030

His Excellency

Ambassador, Perm. Observer:
Jaakko Laajava

FRANCE

4911 Loughboro Road, N.W.
Washington, D.C. 20016
Telephone: (202) 686-5061
Telefax: (202) 244-9328

His Excellency

Ambassador, Perm. Observer:
Sylvie Alvarez

GERMANY

4645 Reservoir Road, N.W.
Washington, D.C. 20007
Telephone: (202) 298-8140
Telefax: (202) 298-4391

His Excellency

Ambassador, Perm. Observer:
Juergen Chrobog

GHANA

3512 International Dr., N.W.
Washington, D.C. 20008
Telephone: (202) 686-4520
Telefax: (202) 686-4527

His Excellency

Ambassador, Perm. Observer:
Kobina Arthur Koomson

GREECE

2221 Massachusetts Ave., N.W.
Washington, D.C. 20008
Telephone: (202) 939-5800-1-2
Telefax: (202) 939-5824

His Excellency

Ambassador, Perm. Observer:
Alexander Philon

HOLY SEE

3339 Massachusetts Ave., N.W.
Washington, D.C. 20008-3687
Telephone: (202) 333-7121
Telefax: (202) 337-4036

His Excellency

Ambassador, Perm. Observer:
The Most Reverend Gabriel Montalvo

HUNGARY

3910 Shoemaker St., N.W.
Washington, D.C. 20008
Telephone: (202) 362-6730
Telefax: (202) 966-8135

His Excellency

Ambassador, Perm. Observer:
Géza Jeszensky

INDIA

2107 Massachusetts Ave., N.W.
Washington, D.C. 20008
Telephone: (202) 939-7000
Telefax: (202) 265-4351

His Excellency

Ambassador,

Perm. Observer:
Naresh Chandra

IRELAND

2234 Massachusetts Ave, N.W.
Washington, D.C. 20008
Telephone: (202) 462-3939
Telefax: (202) 232-5993

His Excellency

Ambassador, Perm. Observer:
Sean O'Huiginn

ISRAEL

3514 International Drive, N.W.
Washington, D.C. 20008
Telephone: (202) 364-5500
Telefax: (202) 364-5490

His Excellency

Ambassador, Perm. Observer:
David Ivry

ITALY

3000 Whitehaven St. N.W.
Washington, D.C. 20008
Telephone: (202) 612-4448
Telefax: (202) 518-2154

His Excellency

Ambassador, Perm. Observer:
Ferdinando Salleo

JAPAN

2520 Massachusetts Ave., N.W.
Washington, D.C. 20008
Telephone: (202) 238-6700
Telefax: (202) 265-9482

His Excellency

Ambassador, Perm. Observer:
Shunji Yanai

KAZAKHSTAN

3421 Massachusetts Ave., N.W., 20007
Telephone: (202) 333-4504/05/06/07
Telefax: (202) 333-4509

His Excellency

Ambassador, Perm. Observer
Bolat K. Nurgaliyev

KOREA

2450 Massachusetts Ave., N.W.
Washington, D.C. 20008
Telephone: (202) 939-5600
Telefax: (202) 797-0595

His Excellency

Ambassador, Perm. Observer:
Sung-Chul Yang

LATVIA

4325 17 St., N.W
Washington, D.C. 20011
Telephone: (202) 726-8213
Telefax: (202) 726-6785

His Excellency

Ambassador, Perm. Observer:
Ojars Eriks Kalnins

LEBANON

2560 28th Street, N.W.
Washington, D.C. 20008
Telephone: (202) 939-6300
Telefax: (202) 939-6324

His Excellency

Ambassador, Perm. Observer:
Farid Abboud

MOROCCO

1601 21st Street, N.W.
Washington, D.C. 20009
Telephone: (202) 462-7979
Telefax: (202) 265-0161

His Excellency

Ambassador, Perm. Observer:
Abdallah El Maaroufi

NETHERLANDS

4200 Linnean Ave., N.W.
Washington, D.C. 20016
Telephone: (202) 274-2604
Telefax: (202) 364-4213

His Excellency

Ambassador, Perm. Observer:
Joris M. Vos

NORWAY

2720 34th Street, N.W.
Washington, D.C. 20016
Telephone: (202) 333-6000
Telefax: (202) 337-0870

His Excellency

Ambassador, Perm. Observer:
Knut Vollebaek

PAKISTAN

2315 Massachusetts Ave., N.W.
Washington, D.C. 20008
Telephone: (202) 939-6200
Telefax: (202) 387-0484

His Excellency

Ambassador, Perm. Observer:
Riaz H. Khokhar

PHILIPPINES

1600 Massachusetts Ave., N.W.
Washington D.C. 20035
Telephone: (202) 467-9300
Fax: (202) 328-7614

His Excellency

Ambassador, Perm. Observer:
Ernesto M. Maceda

POLAND

2640 16th Street, N.W.
Washington, D.C. 20009
Telephones: (202) 234-3800-1/3822
Telefax: (202) 328-6271

Minister Deputy

Chief of Mission:
Piotr Ogrodzinski

PORTUGAL

2125 Kalorama Road, N.W.
Washington, D.C. 20008
Telephone: (202) 328-8610
Telefax: (202) 462-3726

His Excellency

Ambassador, Perm. Observer:
Antonio Augusto Jorge Mendes

ROMANIA

1607 23rd Street, N.W.
Washington, D.C. 20008
Telephones: (202) 332-4846, 4848, 232-3694
Telefax: (202) 232-4748

His Excellency

Ambassador, Perm. Observer:
Mircea Simion

RUSSIAN FEDERATION

2650 Wisconsin Ave., N.W.

Washington, D.C. 20007
Telephone: (202) 298-5755
Telefax: (202) 298-5735

His Excellency

Ambassador, Perm. Observer:
Yuri V. Ushakov

SAUDI ARABIA, KINGDOM OF

601 New Hampshire Ave. N.W.
Washington, D.C. 20037
Telephone: (202) 342-3800
Telefax: (202) 944-3113

His Excellency

Ambassador, Perm. Observer:
Ahmed A. Kattan

SPAIN

2915 Connecticut Ave., N.W. Suite 102
Washington, D.C. 20008
Telephones: (202) 265-8365-66/332-0315
Telefax: (202) 332-6889

His Excellency

Ambassador, Perm. Observer:
Eduardo Gutierrez

SRI LANKA

2148 Wyoming Ave., N.W.
Washington, D.C. 20008
Telephone: (202) 483-4025
Telefax: (202) 232-7181

His Excellency

Ambassador, Perm. Observer:
Warnasena Rasaputram

SWEDEN

1501 M. St., N.W.
Washington, D.C. 20005
Telephone: (202) 467-2600
Telefax: (202) 467-2699

His Excellency

Ambassador, Perm. Observer:
Jan Eliasson

SWITZERLAND

2900 Cathedral Ave., N.W.
Washington, D.C. 20008
Telephone: (202) 745-7900
Telefax: (202) 387-2564

His Excellency

Ambassador, Perm. Observer:
Alfred Defago

THAILAND

1024 Wisconsin Ave. N.W.
Washington, D.C. 20007
Telephone: (202) 944-3611
Telefax: (202) 944-3600

His Excellency

Ambassador, Perm. Observer:
Tej Bunnag

TUNISIA

1515 Massachusetts Ave. N.W.
Washington, D.C. 20005
Telephone: (202) 862-1850
Telefax: (202) 862-1858

His Excellency

Ambassador, Perm. Observer:
Noureddine Mejdoub

TURKEY

1714 Massachusetts Ave. N.W.
Washington, D.C. 20036
Telephone: (202) 659-8200
Telefax: (202) 659-0744

His Excellency

Ambassador, Perm. Observer:
Baki Iklin

UKRAINE

3350 M Street, N.W.
Washington D. C. 20007
Telephone: (202) 333-0606
Telefax: (202) 333-0817

His Excellency

Ambassador, Perm. Observer:
Kostyantyn Gryshchenko

UNITED KINGDOM,

GREAT BRITAIN AND

NORTHERN IRELAND

3100 Massachussetts Avenue, N.W.
Washington D.C. 20008
Telephone: (202) 588-6652
Telefax: (202) 588-7870

Director for the Americas

Foreign and Commonwealth Office:
Richard Wilkinson

YEMEN

2600 Virginia Avenue, N.W. Suite 705
Washington, D.C. 20037
Telephone: (202) 965-4760
Telefax: (202) 337-2017

His Excellency

Ambassador, Perm. Observer:
Abdulwahab Al-Hajjri

INTERNATIONAL ORGANIZATIONS

EUROPEAN UNION

2300 "M" Street, N.W.
Washington, D.C. 20037
Telephone: (202) 862-9500
Telefax: (202) 429-1766

His Excellency

Ambassador, Perm. Observer:
Guenter Burghardt

OFFICE OF PROTOCOL OAS

17th Street and Constitution Avenue, N.W.
Washington, DC 20006

Tel: (202) 458-3000
Fax: (202) 458-3722

Secretary General:
H. E. César Gaviria Trujillo

Chief of Staff of the Secretary General:
Dr. Fernando Jaramillo

Advisors to the Secretary General:
Mr. Jorge López
Mr. Manuel Metz
Mr. Peter Quilter
Mr. Camilo Granada
Mr. Eduardo Mendoza
Ms. Dolores Cullen
Mr. Michael Beaulieu
Mr. Felipe Robayo

Director Dept. of Legal Services:
Mr. William Berenson

Director, Office of Summit Follow Up:
Mr. Jaime Aparicio

Director of Office of External Relations:
Mr. Eduardo del Buey

Inspector General:
Mrs. Linda P. Fealing

Chief of Protocol:
Mrs. Ana Colomar O'Brien

Department of Public Information (in charge):
Mr. Eduardo del Buey

Director, Office of Cultural Affairs:
Ms. Sara Meneses

Director, Office of Science and Technology:
Mr. Sitoo Mukerji

Executive Secretary of the Inter-American Drug Abuse Control Commission (CICAD):
Mr. David Beall

Executive Secretary for Inter-American Commission on Human Rights (IACHR):
Amb. Jorge E. Taiana

Executive Secretary, Inter-American Tele-Communications Commission (CITEL):
Mr. Clovis Baptista Neto

Special Advisor on Trade Unit:
Mr. José Salazar Xirinachs

Director Unit for Environment and Sustainable Development:
Mr. Richard Meganck

Director for Intersectoral Unit for Tourism:
Dr. George Vincent

Executive Coordinator, Unit for the Promotion of Democracy:
Mrs. Elizabeth Spehar

Office of the Assistant Secretary General:
Amb. Luigi R. Einaudi

Chief of Staff of the Assistant Secretary General:
Mrs. Sandra Honoré Braithwaite

Advisors to the Assistant Secretary General:
Mr. Paul Spencer
Mr. Christopher Hernández
Ms. Juliana Magloire
Mrs. Cristina Tomassoni

Director, Secretariat of Conferences and Meetings:
Mr. Arturo Garzón

Executive Secretary for Inter-American Commission of Women (CIM):
Mrs. Carmen Lomellin

Director Art Museum of the Americas:
Mrs. Ana María Escallón

Director, Columbus Memorial Library:
Mrs. Virginia Newton

Assistant Secretary for Management:
Mr. James R. Harding

Director, Depertment of Human Resources Services:
Mr. Nelson Laporte

Director, Department of Management Analysis, Planning and Support Services:
Dr. Alfonso Munévar

Director, Department of Technology and Facilities Services:
Mr. Raúl Sanguinetti

Chief Office of Procurement Management Services:
Mr. Jay Rini

Assistant Secretary for Legal Affairs:
Dr. Enrique Lagos

Director, Dept. of International Law:
Mr. Jean M. Arrighi

Director, Dept. of Legal Cooperation and Information:
Mr. Jorge García González

Secretariat to the Administrative Tribunal:
Mr. Sergio Biondo

Director General, Inter-American Agency for Cooperation and Development:
Mr. Ronald Scheman

Chief of Staff:
Ms. Cece Mac Vaugh

Officer in Charge, Division of Cooperation in Development of Human Resources:
Mr. Santos Mahung

Officer in Charge, Division of Program and Project Management and Coordination:
Mr. Carlos Humud

Officer in Charge, Division of Budgetary and Administrative Matters:
Mr. Ofilio Pérez Balladares

Secretary-Treasurer, Office of Retirement and Pension Plan:
Mr. Eloy Mestre

Director of Publications and Technical Services:
Mr. Carlos Paldao

President, Staff Association:
Dr. Luis F. Jiménez

Hispanic Missions to the United Nations
Misiones hispanas ante la ONU

The UN (United Nations) is an entity which fights to maintain peace and provides humanitarian assistance throughout the world. It was founded on October 24, 1945 and is made up of 189 member states.

La ONU (Organización de las Naciones Unidas) es una entidad que lucha por el mantenimiento de la paz y la prestación de asistencia humanitaria a nivel universal. Fue fundada el 24 de octubre de 1945 y la integran 189 estados miembros.

ARGENTINA

One United Nations Plaza, 25th Floor
New York, NY 10017
Tel.: (212) 688-6300
Fax: (212) 980-8395
E-mail: argentina@un.int

Amb. E. and P., Perm. Repr.: Arnoldo Listre;
Isabel de Listre
Alt. Perm. Repr.: Luis Enrique Cappagli
Counselor: Ana María Moglia
Counselor: Osvaldo Narciso Mársico
Counselor: Ricardo Luis Bocalandro
Counselor: Gustavo Ainchil
First Secretary: Fabiana Loguzzo
Second Secretary: Horacio H. Fernández Palacio;
Mónica L. de Fernández Palacio
Second Secretary: Valeria María González Posse
Second Secretary: Mariano Simón Padrós
Second Secretary: Gabriela Martinic;
Mateo Estreme
Second Secretary: Alejandra Martha Ayuso;
Osvaldo R. Peroni
Third Secretary: Mateo Estreme;
Gabriela Martinic
Third Secretary: Guillermo Kendall
Military Attache: Col. Ricardo J. Etchegaray

BOLIVIA

211 East 43rd St., 8th Floor; #802
New York, NY 10017
Tel.: (212) 682-8132
Fax: (212) 687-4642
E-mail: bolnu@aol.com

Amb. E. and P., Perm. Repr.: Roberto Jordán-Pando;
Willma de Jordán-Pando
Amb., Alternate Perm. Repr.: Alberto Salamanca
Prado;
Victoria de Salamanca
Counselor: Martha Beatriz López de Mitre
Counselor: Liliana Limpias Chávez
Second Secretary: Jorge Osvaldo Rocha Aramburo
Second Secretary: Eduardo Gallardo Aparicio
Attaché: Giovana Calisaya
Attaché: Ruth Flores Pacheco
Attaché, Military Adviser: Lt. Col. Simón Rivera
Eterovic;
Ana Cristina de Rivera

BRAZIL

747 Third Avenue, 9th Floor
New York, NY 10017
Tel.: (212) 372-2600
Fax: (212) 371-5716
E-mail: braun@undp.org

Amb. E. and P., Perm. Repr.: Gelson Fonseca, Jr.
Amb. E. and P., Deputy Perm. Repr.: Luiz Tupy
Caldas de Moura
Minister P.: Enio Cordeiro;
Silvania B. Cordeiro
Counselor: Paulo Cordeiro de Andrade Pinto;
Vera L. R. Estrela de Andrade Pinto
Counselor: Marcela María Nicodemos;
Mario Augusto Matus Pavez
Counselor: Marcel Fortuna Biato
Counselor: Santiago Irazabal Mourao
First Secretary: Carlos Alberto Michaelsen den
Hartog;
Susana Regina Rapallo den Hartog
First Secretary: Barbara Briglia Tavora
Second Secretary: Antônio Ricardo Fernandes
Cavalcante
Second Secretary: Adriano Silva Pucci
Second Secretary: Leonardo Luis Gorgulho Nogueira
Fernandes;
Maria Alice Zilio Monteiro Fernandes
Second Secretary: Neil Giovanni Paiva Benevides
Third Secretary: Leonardo Lott Rodrigues
Military Adviser: General Benedito Onofre Bezerra
Leonel

CHILE

3 Dag Hammarskjöld Plaza
305 E. 47th St., 10th/11th Fl.
New York, NY 10017
Tel.: (212) 832-3323
Fax: (212) 832-8714
E-mail: chile@un.int

Amb. E. and P., Perm. Repr.: Juan Gabriel Valdés
Amb., Deputy Perm. Repr.: Cristián Maquieira;
Julie A. White
Counselor: Eduardo Gálvez;
Luisa de Gálvez
Counselor: Juan Eduardo Eguiguren;
Sana Istuany de Eguiguren
Counselor: Eduardo Tapia;
María del Pilar Muñoz de Tapia
Counselor: Waldemar Coutts
Counselor: Alejandra Quesada
First Secretary: Rodrigo Espinosa
Second Secretary: Loreto Leyton
Third Secretary: Álvaro Jara
Military Attache: Capt. Lorenzo de La Maza

COLOMBIA

140 East 57th St., 5th Floor
New York, NY 10022
Tel.: (212) 355-7776
Fax: (212) 371-2813
E-mail: colun@undp.org

Amb. E. and P., Perm. Repr.: Alfonso Valdivieso;
Martha Cecilia León de Valdivieso
Amb., Deputy Perm. Repr.: Andrés Franco;
María Eugenia Mujica de Franco
Minister P.: Fabio Ocaziones;
Lisette de Ocaziones
Minister Counselor: José Renato Salazar;
Nancy P. de Salazar
Counselor: Sofía Salgado de Gómez;
Rafael Gómez
Second Secretary: Mauricio Baquero;
Johanna de Baquero
Second Secretary: Mirza Cristina Gnecco
Second Secretary: Gustavo Paredes
Second Secretary: Aura Lucía Lloreda
Third Secretary: Leslie Andrea Guzmán

COSTA RICA

211 East 43rd St. #903
New York, NY 10017
Tel.: (212) 986-6373
Fax: (212) 986-6842
E-mail: missioncr@aol.com
E-mail: fobp@aol.com

Amb. E. and P., Perm. Repr.: Bernd Niehaus;
Gabriela Meinert de Niehaus
Amb., First Alternate Perm. Repr.: María Elena
Chassoul
Amb. Second Alternate Perm. Repr.: Nury Vargas
Minister Counselor: Elías Albert Assaf;
May de Assaf
Counselor: Carlos Fernándo Díaz Paniagua
Counselor: Carlos M. Lizano
Counselor: Zaida Aued
Counselor: Patricia Chaves
Third Secretary: Oriana Vargas de Mendiola;
Dionyssis Koutsoudimitropoulos
Attaché: Guillermo Seco
Attaché: Dina Dellale
Attaché: Frédéric Bijou
Attaché: Guadalupe Molina
Attaché: Jaime Gilinski;
Raquel Kardonski

CUBA

315 Lexington Ave. & 38th St.
New York, NY 10016
Tel.: (212) 689-7215/16/17
Fax: (212) 779-1697
E-mail: cuba@un.int

Amb. E. and P., Perm. Repr.: Bruno Rodríguez Parrilla;
Olga T. Pérez de Rodríguez
Amb. E. and P., Deputy Perm. Repr.: Rafael Dausá
Céspedes;
Mercedes de Armas de Dausá
Counselor: Mercedes de Armas García;
Rafael Dausá Céspedes
Counselor: Francisco González García;
Zulema Ramón de González
First Secretary: Mirtha María Hormilla Castro
First Secretary: Miguel Landeras Alvarez;
Carmen Gómez de Landeras
First Secretary: Ileana Bárbara Núñez Mordoche;
Luis Alberto Amorós Núñez
First Secretary: Soraya Elena Álvarez Núñez;
Eduardo Morales Monteagudo
First Secretary: Rodolfo Eliseo Benítez Versón;
Rebeca Y. Hernández de Benítez
First Secretary: Armando Tomás Amieva Dalboys
Second Secretary: Antonio Sánchez Núñez;
Haydeé López Rubio
Second Secretary: Carlos Augusto Suanes Feixas
Aidana Alonso de Suanes
Second Secretary: Julio César Oliva Perdueles;
Marisol Valdés de Oliva
Second Secretary: Dulce María Buergo Rodríguez;
Manlio Hernández Carboneli
Second Secretary: Gulliermo David Hernández
Martínez;
Carol Roy de Hernández
Second Secretary: Marco Antonio Gabriel Lluch
Second Secretary: Luis Alberto Amorós Núñez;
Ileana Bárbara Núñez de Amorós
Third Secretary: Olga T. Pérez Berra;
Bruno E. Rodríguez Parrilla
Third Secretary: Rafael Roberto Yaech Solís;
Niurka Chung de Yaech
Third Secretary: José Ignacio Borges Navia;
Ermis E. Valdés de Borges
Third Secretary: Manlio Hernández Carbonell;
Dulce María Buergo de Hernández
Third Secretary: Emilio Jiménez Taboas;
Vilma Henández Perello
Third Secretary: Orestes Ángel Hernández Hernández;
Lisette B. Pérez de Hernández
Third Secretary: Lisette B. Pérez Pérez;
Orestes Ángel Hernández Hernández
Third Secretary: Zaid Malluly Díaz Medina;
Miguel Moré Santana
Third Secretary: Miguel Moré Santana;
Zaid Malluly Díaz Medina de Moré
Third Secretary: Roberto Hernández de Alba Fuentes;
Tania Pérez de Hernández
Third Secretary: Rogelio Curbelo Cortón;
Ivette Colina de Curbelo
Attaché: Mario Gustavo García Hernández
Attaché: Floraida Santalo Lechuga
Attaché: Guillermo Francisco Trevejo Pérez
Attaché: Alejandro Rodolfo Guerra Seijo;
Olga Lidia Pérez de Guerra
Attaché: Rodolfo Matos Matos
Attaché: Amaury Hernández Chávez
Attaché: Jorge Sánchez Perojo
Attaché: Dioscorides Leyva Ramírez

Attaché: Alfredo González Gamboa
Attaché: Efrain Correa Rodríguez;
Magalys Montesinos Benavides
Attaché: Mario Vázquez Martínez
Attaché: José Raúl Rivero Capote
Attaché: Víctor Mons Sáez
Attaché: Eduardo Morales Monteagudo;
Soraya Elena Álvarez de Morales

DOMINICAN REPUBLIC

144 East 44th St. 4th Floor
New York, NY 10017
Tel: (212) 867-0833
Fax: (212) 986-9025
E-mail: undomrep@aol.com

Amb. E. and P., Perm. Repr.: Pedro Padilla Tonos
Amb., Alternate Perm. Repr.: Julia Tavares de Álvarez;
E. Álvarez
Amb., Alternate Perm. Repr.: Enriquillo A. del Rosario
Ceballos
Amb., Alternate Perm. Repr.: José Pimente
Amb., Alternate Perm. Repr.: Luis T. Graveley
Amb., Alternate Perm. Repr.: Ramón Osiris Blanco
Dornínguez
Amb., Alternate Perm. Repr.: Juan Ramón González
Amb., Alternate Perm. Repr.: Manuel E. Félix
Minister Counselor: Francisco Tovar Morillo;
Ruth Elizabeth Vargas de Tovar
Minister Counselor: María de Jesús Díaz Córdova
Minister Counselor: José Miguel Sosa Frías
Minister Counselor: Manuel Batista
Counselor: Olivio Fermín
Counselor: Eusebia Margarita Núñez Pichardo
Counselor: María P. Peña Jiménez
Counselor: Obdulia Guzmán
First Secretary: María Sanchez de la Cruz
First Secretary: Marlene A. Boves de Arroyo;
José L. Arroyo
First Secretary (Honorary): Margarita R. Guerra de
Sturla
Third Secretary: Federico Froilan Franco

ECUADOR

866 United Nations Plaza, #516
New York, NY 10017
Tel: (212) 935-1680/81
Fax: (212) 935-1835
E-mail: ecuador@un.int

Amb. E. and P., Perm. Repr.: Mario Alemán;
Ligia de Alemán
Amb., Deputy Perm. Repr.: Emilio Izquierdo;
Teresa de Izquierdo
Minister: Fernando Yépez Lasso;
Vivian Idrovo de Yépez
Counselor: Santiago Apunte;
María Eugenia de Apunte
Counselor: Marcelo Vázquez;
Suzanne de Vázquez
Second Secretary: Mónica Martínez;
Ricardo Salcedo
Second Secretary: Denys Toscano
Attaché (Civil): Maritza Piedrahita
Attaché: María Fernanda Zambrano de Díaz;
Alberto Díaz

EL SALVADOR

46 Park Ave.
New York, NY 10016
Tel.: (212) 679-1616/1617
Fax: (212) 725-7831
E-mail: esmun@earthlink.net
E-mail: gbeneke@missions.un.org

Amb. E. and P., Perm. Repr.: José Roberto Andino
Slazar;
Ana Victoria de Salazar
Amb., Deputy Perm. Repr.: Guillermo A. Meléndez-
Barahona;
Reina de Meléndez
Counselor, Alternate Perm. Repr.: Carlos E. García
González;
Inés E. Oviedo de García
First Secretary: Laura L. Cruz
Second Secretary: M. Aracely Jovel
Second Secretary: Beatriz E. Alfaro

EQUATORIAL GUINEA

57 Magnolia Ave.
Mount Vernon, N.Y. 10553
Tel: (212) 914-1882
Fax: (212) 914-6838

Amb. E. and P., Perm. Repr.: Teodoro Biyogo Nsue

GUATEMALA

57 Park Ave.
New York, NY 10016
Tel.: (212) 679-4760
Fax: (212) 685-8741
E-mail: guatemala@un.int

Amb. E. and P., Perm. Repr.: Gert Rosenthal;
Margit Uhlmann de Rosenthal
Minister P., Alternate Perm. Repr.: Luis Raúl Estévez-
López
Minister Counselor: Roberto Lavalle-Valdés;
Tomoko Lavalle
Minister Counselor: Luis Fernando Carranza-Cifuentes
Counselor: Silvia Cristina Corado-Cuevas
Second Secretary: María Rosa Noda-Núñez
Third Secretary: Mónica Bolaños Pérez
Attaché: Sonia Ovalle Trabanino

HONDURAS

866 United Nations Plaza, #417
New York, NY 10017
Tel.: (212) 752-3370/71
Fax: (212) 223-0498, 751-0403
E-mail: mihonduras@worldnet.att.net

Amb. E. and P., Perm. Repr.: Ángel Edmundo Orellana
Mercado
Rosa de Orellana
Amb., Deputy Perm. Repr.: José Antonio Gutiérrez
Navas;
Antonia A. Fons de Gutiérrez
Amb., Deputy Perm. Repr.: Noemí Espinoza Madrid
Counselor: Luis A. Discua Elvir;
Linda I. Cerrato de Discua
Counselor: Guadalupe Vega
Attaché: Edy Fajardo
Attaché: Juana Banegas Ramos
Attaché: Carlos Roberto Quesada López

MEXICO

Two United Nations Plaza, 28th Floor
New York, NY 10017
Telephone: (212) 752-0220
Fax: (212) 688-8862
E-mail: mexicoun@aol.com

Amb. E. and P., Perm. Repr.: Manuel Tello;
Rhonda M. de Tello
Amb., Deputy Perm. Repr.: Gustavo Albin;
Patricia R. de Albin
Minister (Political Affairs): Pablo Macedo
Minister (Disarmament): María Angélica Arce de Jeannet;
Frédéric-Yves Jeannet
Minister (Human Rights and Social Affairs): María Antonieta Monroy
Minister (Economic Affairs): Mauricio Escanero;
Xilunnasi de Escanero
Counselor: Luis Javier Campuzano
Second Secretary: Julián Juárez;
María Teresa Rosas de Juárez
Second Secretary (Adm. and Budgetary Affairs): Ernesto Herrera;
Deyanira Galindo de Herrera
Third Secretary (Political Affairs): María del Pilar Escobar;
Hugo Trejo
Third Secretary: Arturo Ponce Guardian;
Martha López de Ponce
Attaché: Yolanda Castro
Attaché: Salvador Victoria Hernández
Attaché: Carlos Alberto Osnaya;
Lorena de Osnaya
Attaché: María Teresa Zinser-Sierra
Attaché: María Luisa Ávalos
Attaché: Liliana Cerón Matchain

NICARAGUA

820 East Second Ave., 8th Floor
New York, NY 10017
Tel.: (212) 490-7997
Fax: (212) 286-0815
E-mail: nicaragua@un.int

Amb. E. and P., Perm. Repr.: Alfonso Ortega Urbina;
Norma Guerrero de Ortega
Amb., Alternate Perm. Repr.: Mario H. Castellón Duarte;
Esperanza Escorcia de Castellón
Amb., Alternate Perm. Repr.: José Antonio Flores Lovo
Counselor: Carlos A. Gómez;
Sandra I. de Gómez
Counselor: Félix R. Parrales
First Secretary: Luis Molina Cuadra
First Secretary: Mario Rodríguez Castillo
Second Secretary: Andrea Rosa Delgado Cantarero de Morales;
Wilfredo Morales

PANAMA

866 United Nations Plaza, #4030
New York, NY 10017
Tel.: (212) 421-5420/21/72; 759-1779
Fax: (212) 421-2694
E-mail: pan@missions.un.org

Amb. E. and P., Perm. Repr.: Ramón Morales;
Eleonora de Morales

Amb., Deputy Perm. Repr.: Brunilda Núñez de Baeza
José Manuel Baeza
Amb., Alternate Perm. Repr.: Mary Morgan-Moss
Michael Moss
Minister Counselor Alternate Perm. Repr.: Hernán Tejeira
Counselor: Elena Ng
Counselor: Judith María Cardoze
Attaché: María P. Sgro;
John J. Sgro
Attaché: Osvaldo Heilbron
Attaché: Angélica Jácome
Attaché: Odilio Villanero

PARAGUAY

211 East 43rd St., #400
New York, NY 10017
Tel.: (212) 687-3490/91
Fax: (212) 818-1282
E-mail: paraguay@un.int

Amb. E. and P., Perm. Repr.: Jorge Lara Castro
María Eugenia Escobar de Lara Castro
Counselor: Genaro Vicente Pappalardo;
Romina Araujo de Pappalardo
Counselor: Martha Moreno
First Secretary: Luis José González

PERU

820 Second Ave., #1600
New York, NY 10017
Tel.: (212) 687-3336
Fax: (212) 972-6975
E-mail: onuper@aol.com

Amb. E. and P., Perm. Repr.: Jorge Valdéz
Minister, Deputy Perm. Repr.: Manuel Picasso
Minister Counselor, Alternate Perm. Repr.: Marco Balares
Counselor: Raúl Balazar
Counselor: Alfredo Chuquihuara;
Liliana de Chuquihuara
First Secretary: Rubén Espinoza;
María Jenny Shu de Espinoza
First Secretary: Ezio Valfré
Second Secretary: Augusto Cabrera
Second Secretary: Paul Duclós
Third Secretary: Carmen-Rosa Arias
Counselor (Disarmament), Military Adviser: Lt. General Luis Salazar-Monroe

SPAIN

823 United Nations Plaza
345 East 46th Street, 9th Floor
New York, NY 10017
Tel.: (212) 661-1050
Fax: (212) 949-7247
E-mail: espun@undp.org

Amb. E. and P., Perm. Repr.: Inocencio F. Arias;
Ludmila Winogradov de Arias
Minister P., Deputy Perm. Repr.: Juan Luis Flores
Counselor, Military Adviser: José Pérez Aragón;
Manuela Iglesia de Pérez-Aragón
Counselor: Fransisco J. Rábena;
Blanca Camuñas de Rábena
Counselor (Information): Agustin Galán Machio;
Lucía de Juana de Galán
Counselor (Social Affairs): Aurelio Fernández;

María Dolores Admetila de Fernández
Counselor: Ana María Menéndez
Counselor: Julio Montesino;
Gabriela Torres de Montesino
Counselor: Francisco J. Aparicio Álvarez
Counselor: Manuel Gómez Acevo
Counselor: Carlos Morales
Counselor: Antonio J. Millán;
Rosa Ana Povedano de Millán
First Secretary: José Antonio de Ory
First Secretary: Silvia Josefina Cortés Martín
Attaché: José Fernando Santamarta;
Luisa Domínguez de Santamarta
Assistant Attaché: María Teresa Gómez;
Mohamad Habid

URUGUAY

747 Third Ave., 21st Floor
New York, NY 10017
Tel.: (212) 752-8240
Fax: (212) 593-0935
E-mail: uruguay@un.int

Amb. E. and P., Perm. Repr.: Felipe H. Paolillo
Amb., Deputy Perm. Repr.: Julio Benítez Sáenz;
María Inés de Benítez
Minister: Inés Rodríguez Fernández;
Minister Counselor: María Amalia Sereno;
José Terrenoire
Counselor: Alberto Guani
Counselor: Boris E. Svetogorsky Marino;
Mónica de Svetogorsky
Second Secretary: Santiago Wins
Attaché (Press): Jorge Reiner
Attache: Edison N. Wibmer
Military Attaché: Col. José Luis Viggiano

VENEZUELA

335 East 46th St.
New York, NY 10017
Tel.: (212) 557-2055
Fax: (212) 557-3528
E-mail: venun@undp.org

Amb. E. and P., Perm Repr.: Ignacio Arcaya
Counselor: Norman M. Monagas-Lesseur
Counselor: Martha Di Felice;
Vicenzo Mazziotti
First Secretary: María Emilia Pérez-Vera
First Secretary: Wilmer A. Méndez;
Yumaira Rodríguez de Méndez
First Secretary: Lydia Aponte de Zacklin;
Ralph Zacklin
Second Secretary: Luis Fernando Pérez-Segnini
Second Secretary: Rossanna Figuera
Third Secretary: Jesús Emiro Contreras
Third Secretary: Luisa Kislinger
Minister Counselor Military Adviser: B. Gen. Erasmo José Lara-Ortega;
Rosa de Lara
Minister Counselor Military Adviser: B. Gen. Gilberto Ferrer;
María R. de Ferrer
Second Secretary: Rossana Figuera
Third Secretary: Jesús Emiro Contreras
Third Secretary: Luisa Kislinger
Minister Counselor Military Adviser: B. Gen Erasmo José Lara-Ortega;
Rosa de Lara
Minister Counselor Military Adviser: B. Gen. Gilberto Ferrer;
María R. de Ferrer

The Hispanic-Lusitanian Countries of the World

Los países hispano-lusitanos en el mundo

Country	Area km²	Pop.	Life Exp. years	GDP Real Growth%	GDP Per Capita	Pop. Below Pov. Line%	Unemploy-ment Rate %	Electricity Consumption kwh	Exports	Imports
Afghanistan	652,000	25.8m	45	NA	800	NA	8	510m	80m⁽¹⁾	150m
Albania	28,748	3.4m	71	8	1,650	19.6	28	5.29b	242m	925m
Algeria	2,381,740	31.1m	69	3.9	4,700	23.0	30	19.8b	13.7b	9.3b
Andorra	468	66,824	83	NA	18,000	NA	0	NA	58m	1.077b
Angola	1,246,700	10.1m	38	4	1,030	NA	+50	1.754b	5b	3b
Antigua & B.	442	66,422	70	2.8	8,200	NA	7	84m	38m	330m
* **Argentina**	2,766,890	36.9m	75	-3	10,000	36	14	75.57b	23b	25b
Armenia	29,800	3.3m	66	5	2,900	45	20	5.361b	240m	782m
Australia	7,686,850	19.1m	79	4.3	22,200	NA	7.5	173.3b	58b	67b
Austria	83,858	8.1m	77	2	23,400	NA	4.4	51.8b	62.9b	69.9b
Azerbaijan	86,600	7.7m	62	7	1,770	60	20	15b	885m	1.6b
Bahamas, The	13,940	294,982	71	3	20,000	NA	9	1.2b	362m	1.7b
Bahrain	620	634,137	72	4	13,700	NA	15	1.09b	3.3b	3.5b
Bangladesh	144,000	129m	60	5.2	1,470	35.6	35.2	11.039b	5.1b	8.01b
Barbados	430	274,540	73	4.4	11,200	NA	12.0	625m	211.2m	1.01b
Belarus	207,600	10.3m	68	1.5	5,300	22	2.3	28.66b	6b	6.4b
Belgium	30,510	10.2m	77	1.8	23,900	4	9	74.5b	187b	172b
Belize	22,960	249,183	71	4	3,100	NA	14.3	163m	150m	320m
Benin	112,620	6.3m	50	5	1,300	33	NA	276m	396m	566m
Bhutan	47,000	2.0m	52	7	1,060	NA	NA	345m	111m	136m
* **Bolivia**	1,098,580	8.1m	64	2	3,000	70	11.4	2.4b	1.1b	1.6b
Bosnia and H.	51,129	3.8m	71	5	1,770	NA	37.5	2.0b	450m	2.95b
Botswana	600,370	1.5m	39	6.5	3,900	47	30	1.6b	2.36b	2.05b
* **Brazil**	8,511,965	173m	63	0.8	6,150	17.4	7.5	336b	46.9b	48.7b
Brunei	5,770	336,376	74	2.5	17,400	NA	4.9	2.3b	2.04b	1.38b
Bulgaria	110,910	7.7m	71	2.5	4,300	NA	15	35.4b	3.8b	5.3b
Burkina Faso	274,200	11.9m	47	5.5	1,100	NA	NA	209m	311m	572m
Burma	678,500	41.7m	55	4.6	1,200	23	7.1	4.0b	1.2b	2.5b
Burundi	27,830	6.0m	46	-1	730	36.2	NA	153m	56m	108m
Cambodia	181,040	12.2m	57	4	710	36	2.8	195m	821m	1.2b
Cameroon	475,440	15.4m	55	5.2	2,000	40	30	3.0b	2b	1.5b
Canada	9,976,140	31.2m	79	3.6	23,300	NA	7.6	484.5b	277b	259.3b
Cape Verde	4,033	401,343	69	5	1,500	NA	NA	37m	38m	225m
Cen. African Rep.	622,984	3.5m	44	5	1,700	NA	6	98m	195m	170m
Chad	1,284,000	8.4m	50	0.6	1,000	NA	NA	93m	288m	359m
* **Chile**	756,950	15.1m	76	-1	12,400	22	9	26.6b	15.6b	13.9b
China	9,596,960	1.2b	71	7	3,800	10	10	1.014t	194.9b	165.8b
* **Colombia**	1,138,910	39.6m	70	-5	6,200	17.7	20	41.963b	11.5b	10b

Argentina: has achieved control over inflation, which had been a serious problem at the beginning of the 1990s. In 1999 the rate was negative (-2%). On December 18, 2000, Argentina received $39.7 billion in financial support from the World Bank, of which $34.7 billion (87.4%) will be used to retire public debt. The remainder ($5 billion) will be used to finance assistance programs, such as health care reforms, improvements to low income housing, and employment programs, among other things.

Bolivia: 70% of Bolivia's population lives below the poverty line. In comparison, those nations with the most unfavorable statistics include Zambia (86%), Haiti (80%), and

Argentina: logró controlar la inflación, que fue un grave problema a principios de los '90, hasta llegar a un índice negativo en el año 1999 (-2%). El 12/18/00 Argentina logró un blindaje financiero proveniente del Banco Mundial, de 39.700 millones de dólares, de los cuales 34.700 millones (el 87,4%) serán destinados a pagar vencimientos de deuda pública. El resto ($ 5.000 millones), se utilizará para financiar programas de asistencia, como reformas en la salud, acceso a la vivienda en sectores de bajos ingresos y planes de empleo, entre otros aspectos.

Bolivia: el 70% de su población está por debajo de la línea de pobreza. En este aspecto los índices más desfavorables se dan en Zambia (86%), Haití (80%) y Liberia (80%). Mientras que

Continued on p. 176

Debt External	Tel. M.L.U.	Tel. Mobil	Radios	Television	Military Exp.	Inflation % (consumer)	Labor Force	Railways km	Country
5.5b	31,200	NA	167,000	100,000	NA	NA	8m	24.6	Afghanistan
820m	42,000	3,100	810,000	405,000	42m	0.5	1.6m	670	Albania
30b	1.1m	33,500	7.1m	3.1m	1.3b	4.2	9.1m	4,820	Algeria
NA	31,980	8,618	16,000	27,000	--	1.62	30,787	0	Andorra
10.5b	60,000	1,994	630,000	150,000	1.2b	270	5m	2,952	Angola
357m	20,000	NA	36,000	31,000	NA	1.6	30,000	77	Antigua & B.
149b	7.5m	1.8m	24.3m	7.95m	4.3b	-2	15m	38,326	**Argentina** *
862.7m	583,000	NA	850,000	825,000	75m	2.5	1.5m	825	Armenia
222b	92m	5.2m	25.5m	10.15m	6.9b	1.8	8.9m	33,819	Australia
31.7b	3.7m	2.3m	6.0m	4.25m	1.7b	0.5	3.7m	6,123	Austria
684m	640,000	6,000	175,000	170,000	121m	-6.8	2.9m	2,125	Azerbaijan
349m	77,000	2,400	215,000	67,000	20m	1.3	148,000	0	Bahamas, The
2b	141,000	130,000	338,000	275,000	318m	0.5	295,000	0	Bahrain
16.5b	470,000	41,000	6.15b	770,000	559m	9	56m	2,745	Bangladesh
550m	90,000	4,614	237,000	76,000	NA	1.7	136,000	0	Barbados
1.1b	2.5m	8,000	3.0m	2.5m	156m	295	4.3m	5,563	Belarus
28.3b	4.6m	664,000	8.0m	4.7m	2.8b	1	4.3m	3,437	Belgium
380m	29,600	1,237	133,000	41,000	15m	-0.9	71,000	0	Belize
1.6b	28,000	1,050	620,000	60,000	27m	3	NA	578	Benin
120m	5,000	NA	37,000	11,000	NA	9	NA	0	Bhutan
5.7b	368,874	7,229	5.25m	900,000	147m	2.1	2.5m	3,691	**Bolivia** *
4.1b	238,000	4,000	940,000	NA	NA	5	1.0m	1,021	Bosnia and H.
651m	78,000	NA	237,000	31,000	61m	7.7	235,000	971	Botswana
200b	19m	4m	71m	36.5m	13b	5	74m	27,882	**Brazil** *
0	68,000	57,000	319,408	196,000	343m	1.0	144,000	13	Brunei
10b	3.1m	300,000	4.51m	3.31m	379m	6.2	3.82m	4,294	Bulgaria
1.3b	30,000	0	370,000	100,000	66m	2.5	NA	622	Burkina Faso
5.9b	158,000	2,007	4.2m	260,000	39m	38	19.7m	3,991	Burma
1.2b	17,000	343	440,000	25,000	25m	26	1.9m	0	Burundi
829m	21,800	34,880	1.34m	94,000	85m	4.5	6m	603	Cambodia
11.5b	60,000	2,800	2.27m	450,000	155m	2.1	NA	1,104	Cameroon
253b	18.5m	3m	32.2m	21.5m	7.4b	1.7	15.9m	36,114	Canada
220m	22,000	0	73,000	2,000	4m	5	NA	0	Cape Verde
790m	8,000	79	283,000	18,000	29m	2.6	NA	0	Cen. African Rep.
1b	5,000	0	1.67m	10,000	39m	12	NA	0	Chad
39b	2.6m	197,300	5.18m	3.15m	2.5b	3.4	5.8m	6,782	**Chile** *
159b	110m	23.4m	417m	400m	12.6b	-1.3	700m	65,650	China
35b	5.4m	1.8m	21m	4.5m	3.4b	9.2	16.8m	3,380	**Colombia** *

Country	Area km²	Population	Life Exp. years	GDP Real Growth%	GDP Per Capita	Pop. Below Pov. Line%	Unemploy-ment Rate %	Electricity Consump-tion (kwh)	Exp.	Imp.
Comoros	2,170	578,400	60	0	725	NA	20	14m	9.3m	49.5m
Dem. Rep. Congo	2,345,410	52m	48	1	710	NA	NA	5.488b	530m	460m
Rep. congo	342,000	2.8m	47	5	1,530	NA	NA	588m	1.7b	770m
* Costa Rica	51,100	3.7m	75	7	7,100	NA	5.6	5.267b	6.4b	6.5b
Cote d'Ivoire	322,460	16m	45	5	1,600	NA	NA	3.1b	3.9b	2.6b
Croatia	56,538	4.2m	73	0	5,100	NA	20	12.949b	4.5b	8.4b
* Cuba	110,860	11m	76	6	1,700	NA	6	14.205b	1.4b	3.2b
Cyprus (Greek)	5,895	591,523	77	3	15,400	NA	3.3	2.488b	1.1b	3.5b
Cyprus (Turkish)	3,355	166,839	77	5.3	5,000	NA	6.4	NA	63.9m	374m
Czech Rep.	78,866	10.2m	75	-0.5	11,700	NA	9	54.733b	26.9b	29b
Denmark	43,094	5.3m	77	1.3	23,800	NA	5.7	33.037b	49.5b	43.9b
Djibouti	22,000	451,442	51	2	1,200	NA	45	165m	260m	440m
Dominica	754	71,540	73	2	3,400	NA	20	37m	60.8m	120.4m
* Dominican Rep.	48,730	8.4m	73	8.3	5,400	25	13.8	7.8b	5.1b	8.2b
* Ecuador	283,560	12.9m	71	-8	4,300	50	12	8.9b	4.1b	2.8b
Egypt	1,001,450	68.3m	63	5	3,000	NA	11.8	53.7b	4.6b	15.8b
* El Salvador	21,040	6.1m	70	2.2	3,100	48	7.7	4.17b	2.5b	4.15b
* Equatorial Guinea	28,051	474,214	54	15	2,000	NA	30	20m	555m	300m
Eritrea	121,320	4.1m	56	3	750	NA	NA	177.6m	52.9m	489m
Estonia	45,226	1.4m	70	-0.5	5,600	6.3	11.7	7.58b	2.5b	3.4b
Ethiopia	1,127,127	64.1m	45	0	560	NA	NA	1.2b	420m	1.25b
Fiji	18,270	832,494	68	7.8	7,300	NA	6	512m	393m	612m
Finland	337,030	5.1m	77	3.5	21,000	NA	10	79.2b	43b	30.7b
France	547,030	59.3m	79	2.7	23,300	NA	11	389b	304b	280b
Gabon	267,667	1.2m	50	1.7	6,500	NA	21	953m	2.4b	1.2b
Gambia, The	11,300	1.3m	53	4.2	1,030	NA	NA	70m	132m	201m
Georgia	69,700	5.0m	64	3.5	2,300	60	14.5	6.1b	330m	840m
Germany	357,021	82.7m	77	1.5	22,700	NA	10.5	488b	610b	587b
Ghana	238,540	19.5m	57	4.3	1,900	31	20	5.4b	1.7b	2.5b
Greece	131,940	10.6m	78	3	13,900	NA	9.9	42.18b	12.4b	27.7b
Grenada	340	89,018	65	5	3,700	NA	15	98m	26.8m	200m
* Guatemala	108,890	12.6m	66	3.5	3,900	75	7.5	2.914b	2.4b	4.5b
Guinea	245,857	7.4m	46	3.7	1,200	NA	NA	498m	695m	560m
Guinea-Bissau	36,120	1.2m	49	9.5	900	50	NA	37m	26.8m	22.9m
Guyana	214,970	697,286	64	1.8	2,500	NA	12	302m	574m	620m
Haiti	27,750	6.8m	49	2.4	1,340	80	70	677m	322m	762m
Holy See	0.44	880	-	-	-	-	-	NA	-	-
* Honduras	112,090	6.2m	70	-3	2,050	50	12	2.7b	1.6b	2.7b
Hungary	93,030	10.1m	71	4	7,800	25	10	33.3b	22.6b	25.1b
Iceland	103,000	276,365	79	4.5	23,500	NA	2.4	5.7b	1.9b	2.4b
India	3,287,590	1,014,003,817	62	5.5	1,800	35	NA	416b	36b	50b
Indonesia	1,919,440	224m	68	0	2,800	NA	17.5	68.011b	48b	24b
Iran	1,648	65.6m	70	1	5,300	53	25	88,638b	12.2b	13.8b
Iraq	437,072	22m	67	13	2,700	NA	NA	26.412b	12.7b	8.9b
Ireland	70,280	3.7m	77	8.4	20,300	10	5.5	18.415b	66b	44b
Israel	20,770	5.8m	79	2.1	18,300	NA	9.1	31.805b	23.5b	30.6b
Italy	301,230	57.6m	79	1.3	21,400	NA	11.5	266.705b	242.6b	206.9b
Jamaica	10,990	2.6m	75	-0.5	3,350	34	15.5	5.939b	1.4b	2.7b
Japan	377,835	126.5m	81	0.3	23,400	NA	4.7	926.263b	413b	306b
Jordan	89,213	4.9m	77	2	3,500	30	27.5	6.102b	1.8b	3.3b
Kazakhstan	2,717,300	16.7m	63	1.7	3,200	35	13.7	48.822b	5.2b	4.8b
Kenya	582,650	30.3m	48	1.5	1,600	42	50	4.078b	2.2b	3.3b
Kiribati	717	91,985	60	2.5	860	NA	2	7m	6m	37m
Korea, North	120,540	21.6m	71	1	1,000	NA	NA	29.737	680m	954m

Debt External	Tel. M.L.U.	Tel. Mobil	Radios	Television	Military Exp.	Inflation % (consumer)	Labor Force	Railways km	Country	
197m	5,000	0	90,000	1,000	NA	4	144,500	0	Comoros	
12.3b	36,000	10,000	18m	6.4m	250m	46	14.5m	5,138	Dem. Rep. Congo	
5b	21,000	NA	341,000	33,000	110m	4	NA	795	Rep. Congo	
3.9b	451,000	46,500	980,000	525,000	55m	10.8	1.377m	950	**Costa Rica**	*
16.8b	182,000	60,000	2.26m	900,000	94m	2.5	NA	660	Cote d'Ivoire	
8.1b	1.477m	187,000	1.51m	1.22m	950m	4.4	1.65m	2,296	Croatia	
11.2b	353,000	1,939	3.9m	2.64m	NA	0.3	4.5m	4,807	**Cuba**	*
1.27b	405,000	68,000	310,000	248,000	249m	2.3	298,400	0	Cyprus (Greek)	
NA	70,845	70,000	56,450	52,300	71m	66	80,200	0	Cyprus (Turkish)	
24.3b	3.7m	965,476	3.17m	3.42m	1.2b	2.5	5.2m	9,435	Czech Rep.	
44b	3.2m	1.3m	6.02m	3.121m	2.8b	2.5	2.8m	2,859	Denmark	
350m	8,000	NA	52,000	28,000	23m	0	282,000	100	Djibouti	
90m	18,000	NA	46,000	6,000	NA	1.1	25,000	0	Dominica	
3.7b	569,000	33,000	1.44m	770,000	180m	5.1	2.4m	757	**Dominican Rep.**	*
15.3b	748,000	49,776	4.15m	1.55m	720m	59.9	4.2m	812	**Ecuador**	*
30b	3.168m	380,000	20.5m	7.7m	3.28b	3.7	19m	4,955	Egypt	
3.3b	380,000	13,475	2.75m	600,000	105m	1.3	2.35m	602	**El Salvador**	*
290m	3,000	0	180,000	4,000	3.0m	6	NA	0	**Equatorial Guinea**	*
76m	23,578	0	345,000	1,000	196m	9	NA	317	Eritrea	
270m	476,078	246,000	1.0m	605,000	70m	3.7	785,500	1,018	Estonia	
10b	365,000	4,000	11.75m	320,000	138m	4	NA	681	Ethiopia	
213m	65,000	4,300	500,000	21,000	24m	0	235,000	597	Fiji	
30b	2.8m	2.1m	7.7m	3.2m	1.8b	1	2.5m	5,865	Finland	
117b	34.8m	11.0m	55.3m	34.8m	39.8b	0.5	25.4m	31,939	France	
4.6b	32,000	4,000	208,000	63,000	91m	2.9	600,000	649	Gabon	
430m	22,000	4,485	196,000	4,000	1m	2.5	400,000	0	Gambia, The	
1.8b	554,000	150	3.02m	2.57m	27m	19	3.08m	1,583	Georgia	
NA	46.5m	15.3m	77.8m	51.4m	32.8b	0.8	40.5m	40,826	Germany	
6b	200,000	30,000	4.4m	1.7m	53m	12.8	4m	953	Ghana	
41.9b	5.4m	328,500	5.02m	2.54m	4.04b	2.6	4.32m	2,548	Greece	
89.2m	23,000	400	57,000	33,000	NA	1.3	42,300	0	Grenada	
4.4b	342,000	29,999	835,000	640,000	124m	6.8	3.32m	884	**Guatemala**	*
3.15b	11,000	950	357,000	85,000	56m	4.5	2.4m	1,086	Guinea	
921m	13,120	NA	49,000	NA	8m	5.5	480,000	0	Guinea-Bissau	
1.4b	45,000	1,243	420,000	46,000	7m	5.5	245,492	187	Guyana	
1b	60,000	0	415,000	38,000	NA	9	3.6m	40	Haiti	
-	NA	NA	NA	NA	-	-	-	-	Holy See	
4.4b	190,200	0	2.45m	570,000	33m	14	2.3m	595	**Honduras**	*
27b	1.8m	1.2m	7.01m	4.42m	732m	10	4.2m	7.606	Hungary	
2.6b	162,310	65,746	260,000	98,000	0	1.9	131,000	0	Iceland	
98b	19m	2m	116m	63m	10.055b	6.7	NA	62,915	India	
140b	3.2m	1.2m	31.5m	13.7m	1b	2	88m	6,458	Indonesia	
21.9b	7m	265,000	17m	4.61m	5.787b	30	15.4m	5,600	Iran	
130b	675,000	NA	4.85m	1.75m	NA	135	4.4m	2,032	Iraq	
11b	1,642,541	941,775	2.55m	1.47m	732m	2.2	1.77m	1,947	Ireland	
18.7b	2.8m	2.5m	3.07m	1.69m	8.7b	1.3	2.3m	610	Israel	
45b	25m	17.7m	50.5m	30.3m	23.294b	1.7	23.193m	19,394	Italy	
3.8b	292,000	45,178	1.215m	460,000	30m	9.4	1.13m	370	Jamaica	
NA	60.3m	36.5m	120.5m	86.5m	42.9b	-0.8	67.76m	23,670	Japan	
8.4b	402,600	75,000	1.66m	500,000	608.9m	3	1.15m	677	Jordan	
7.9b	1.963m	4,600	6.47m	3.88m	322m	8.3	8.8m	14,400	Kazakhstan	
6.5b	290,000	6,000	3.07m	730,000	197m	6	9.2m	2,778	Kenya	
7.2	2,600	0	17,000	1,000	NA	2	7,870	0	Kiribati	
12b	1.1m	0	3.36m	1.2m	4.3b	NA	9.6m	5,000	Korea, North	

Country	Area km²	Population	Life Exp. years	GDP Real Growth%	GDP Per Capita	Pop. Below Pov. Line%	Unemploy- ment Rate %	Electricity Consump- tion (kwh)	Exp.	Imp.
Korea, South	98,480	47.4m	74	10	13,300	NA	6.3	205.77b	144b	116b
Kuwait	17,820	1,973,572	76	1.1	22,500	NA	1.8	25.105b	13.5b	8.1b
Kyrgyzstan	198,500	4,685,230	63	3.4	2,300	40	6	11.102b	515m	590m
Laos	236,800	5,497,459	53	5.2	1,300	46.1	5.7	514m	271m	497m
Latvia	64,589	2,404,926	68	0	4,200	NA	9.6	4.882b	1.9b	2.8b
Lebanon	10,400	3,578,036	71	1	4,500	28	18	9.629b	866m	5.7b
Lesotho	30,355	2,143,141	51	-10	2,240	49.2	+50	209m	235m	700m
Liberia	111,370	3,164,156	51	0.5	1,000	80	70	456m	39m	142m
Libya	1,759,540	5,115,450	75	2	7,900	NA	30	15.736b	6.6b	7b
Liechtenstein	160	32,207	79	NA	23,000	NA	1.8	NA	2.47b	917.3m
Lithuania	65,200	3,620,756	69	-3	4,800	NA	10	7.829b	3.3b	4.5b
Luxembourg	2,586	437,389	77	4.2	34,200	NA	2.7	5.856b	7.5b	9.6b
Macedonia	25,333	2,041,467	74	2.5	3,800	NA	35	6.198b	1.2b	1.56b
Madagascar	587,040	15,506,472	55	4.5	780	NA	NA	698m	600m	881m
Malawi	118,480	10,385,849	38	4.2	940	54	NA	857m	510m	512m
Malaysia	329,750	21,793,293	71	5	10,700	6.8	3	53.423b	83.5b	61.5b
Maldives	300	301,475	62	7	1,800	NA	NA	79m	98m	312m
Mali	1.24	10,685,948	47	5	820	NA	NA	288m	640m	650m
Malta	316	391,670	78	4	13,800	NA	5.5	1.507b	1.8b	2.7b
Marshall Islands	181.3	68,126	66	-5	1,670	NA	16	57m	28m	58m
Mauritania	1,030,700	2,667,859	51	3.7	1,910	57	23	141m	425m	444m
Mauritius	1,860	1,179,368	71	4	10,400	10.6	2	1.139b	1.7b	2.1b
* **Mexico**	1,972,550	100,349,766	71	3.7	8,500	27	2.5	164.767b	136.8b	142.1b
Micronesia	702	133,144	69	3	2,000	NA	27	NA	73m	168m
Moldova	33,843	4,430,654	64	-4.4	2,200	75	2	7.065b	470m	560m
Monaco	1.95	31,693	79	NA	27,000	NA	3.1	NA	NA	NA
Mongolia	1.565	2,650,952	67	3.5	2,320	40	4.5	2.816b	316.8m	472.4m
Morocco	446,550	30,122,350	69	0	3,600	13.1	19	12.363b	7.1b	9.5b
Mozambique	801,590	19,104,696	38	10	1,000	NA	NA	1.018b	300m	1.6b
Namibia	825,418	1,771,327	42	3	4,300	NA	35	1.81b	1.4b	1.5b
Nauru	21	11,845	61	NA	10,000	NA	0	28m	25.3m	21.1m
Nepal	140,800	24,702,119	58	3.4	1,100	42	NA	1.212b	485m	1.2b
Netherlands	41,532	15,892,237	78	3.4	23,100	NA	3.5	94.325b	169b	152b
New Zealand	268,680	3,819,762	78	3.1	17,400	NA	7	33.284b	12.2b	11.2b
* **Nicaragua**	129,494	4,812,569	69	6.3	2,650	50	10.5	2.52b	573m	1.5b
Niger	1.267	10,075,511	41	2	1,000	NA	NA	363m	269m	295m
Nigeria	923,768	123,337,822	52	2.7	970	34.1	28	13.717b	13.1b	10b
Norway	324,220	4,481,162	79	0.8	25,100	NA	2.9	111.001b	47.3b	38.6b
Oman	212,460	2,533,389	72	4	8,000	NA	NA	6.845b	7.2b	5.4b
Pakistan	803,940	141,553,389	61	3.1	2,000	34	7	55.114b	8.4b	9.8b
Palau	458	18,766	69	10	8,800	NA	7	200m	14.3m	72.4m
* **Panamá**	78,200	2,808,268	75	4.4	7,600	NA	13.1	4.329b	4.7b	6.4b
Papua New Guinea	462,840	4,926,984	63	3.6	2,500	NA	NA	1.618b	1.9b	1b
* **Paraguay**	406,750	5,585,828	74	-1	3,650	32	12	1.494b	3.1b	3.2b
* **Peru**	1,285,220	27,012,899	70	2.4	4,400	54	7.7	17.002b	5.9b	8.4b
Philippines	300,000	81,159,644	67	2.9	3,600	32	9.6	36.849b	34.8b	30.7b
Poland	312,685	38,646,023	73	3.8	7,200	23.8	11	121.938b	27.8b	40.8b
* **Portugal**	92,391	10,048,232	76	3.2	15,300	NA	4.6	36.18b	25b	34.9b
Qatar	11,437	744,483	72	1.5	17,000	NA	NA	6.245b	6.7b	4.2b
Romania	237,500	22,411,121	70	-4.8	3,900	21.5	11	49.552b	8.4b	9.6b
Russia	17,075,200	146,001,176	67	3.2	4,200	40	12.4	702.711b	75.4b	48.2b
Rwanda	26,338	7,229,129	39	5.3	720	51.2	NA	165m	70.8m	242m
St. Kitts and Nevis	261	38,819	71	1.6	6,000	NA	4.5	79m	42m	160m
Saint Lucia	620	156,260	72	2.9	4,300	NA	15	102m	75m	290m

Debt External	Tel. M.L.U.	Tel. Mobil	Radios	Television	Military Exp.	Inflation % (consumer)	Labor Force	Railways km	Country	
142b	23.1m	8.6m	47.5m	15.9m	9.9b	0.8	22m	6,240	Korea, South	
9.27b	411,600	150,000	1.175m	875,000	2.518b	2	1.3m	0	Kuwait	
1.1b	357,000	NA	520,000	210,000	12m	37	1.7m	370	Kyrgyzstan	
2.32b	20,000	1,600	730,000	52,000	77m	140	1.25m	0	Laos	
212m	748,000	175,348	1.76m	1.22m	60m	3.2	1.4m	2,412	Latvia	
8.8b	330,000	120,000	2.85m	1.18m	500m	4.5	1.3m	399	Lebanon	
675m	18,000	0	104,000	54,000	NA	8	689,000	2.6	Lesotho	
3b	5,000	0	790,000	70,000	1m	3	-	490	Liberia	
4b	318,000	NA	1.35m	730,000	NA	18	1.2m	-	Libya	
0	19,000	NA	21,000	12,000	-	0.5	22,891	18.5	Liechtenstein	
NA	1.048m	297,500	1.9m	1.7m	181m	0.3	1.8m	2,002	Lithuania	
NA	314,700	95,400	285,000	285,000	131m	1.1	236,400	274	Luxemburg	
1.7b	407,000	NA	410,000	510,000	77m	1	673,000	699	Macedonia	
4.1b	33,000	0	3.05m	325,000	29m	9.5	7m	883	Madagascar	
2.3b	34,000	382	2.6m	0	17m	45	3.5m	789	Malawi	
43.6b	4.4m	2.17m	9.1m	3.6m	1.211b	2.8	9.3m	1,801	Malaysia	
188m	21,000	300	35,000	10,000	NA	3	67,000	0	Maldives	
3.1b	17,000	0	570,000	45,000	49m	3	NA	729	Mali	
130m	171,000	15,650	255,000	280,000	201m	1.8	143,700	0	Malta	
125m	3,000	280	NA	NA	NA	5	NA	0	Marshall Island	
2.5b	9,000	0	360,000	62,000	41m	9.8	465,000	704	Mauritania	
1.9b	148,000	11,735	420,000	258,000	11m	6.8	514,000	0	Mauritius	
155.8b	9.6m	2.02m	31m	25.6m	4b	15	38.6m	31,048	**Mexico**	*
111m	8,000	NA	NA	NA	-	4	NA	0	Micronesia	
1.3b	566,000	14	3.22m	1.26m	6m	38	1.7m	1,328	Moldova	
NA	31,027	2,560	34,000	25,000	-	NA	30,540	1.7	Monaco	
715m	93,800	NA	360,000	118,000	20m	9.5	1.256m	1,928	Mongolia	
19.1b	1.391m	116,645	6.64m	3.1m	1.361b	1.9	11m	1,907	Morocco	
4.8b	60,000	NA	730,000	90,000	72m	4	NA	3,131	Mozambique	
159m	100,848	20,000	232,000	60,000	90m	8.5	500,000	2,382	Namibia	
33.3m	2,000	450	7,000	500	NA	-3.6	-	3.9	Nauru	
2.4b	236,816	NA	840,000	130,000	44m	11.8	10m	101	Nepal	
0	8.431m	1.016m	15.3m	8.1m	6.956b	2.2	7m	2,739	Netherlands	
53b	1.719m	588,000	3.75m	1.926m	883m	1.3	1.86m	3,913	New Zealand	
5.7b	140,000	4,400	1.24m	320,000	26m	12	1.7m	-	**Nicaragua**	*
1.3b	13,000	0	680,000	125,000	20m	4.8	70,000	0	Niger	
29b	405,000	10,000	23.5m	6.9m	236m	12.5	42.844m	3,557	Nigeria	
0	2,325,010	1,676,763	4.03m	2.03m	3.113b	2.8	2.7m	4,012	Norway	
4.8b	300,000	120,000	1.4m	1.6m	1.592b	-0.07	850,000	0	Oman	
32	2.861m	158,000	13.5m	3.1m	2.435b	6	38.6m	8,163	Pakistan	
100m	1,500	0	12,000	11,000	NA	NA	NA	0	Palau	
7b	325,300	0	815,000	510,000	132m	1.5	1.044m	355	**Panamá**	*
2.4b	44,000	0	410,000	42,000	42m	16.5	1.941m	0	Papua New Guinea	
2.7b	167,000	15,807	925,000	515,000	125m	5	1.7m	971	**Paraguay**	*
31b	1.509m	504,995	6.65m	3.06m	1.3b	5.5	7.6m	1,988	**Peru**	*
51.9b	1.9m	1.959m	11.5m	3.7m	995m	6.8	32m	492	Philippines	
44b	8.07m	1.58m	20.2m	13.05m	3.2b	8.4	15.3m	23,420	Poland	
13.1b	3.724m	887,216	3.02m	3.31m	2.458b	2.4	4.75m	2.850	**Portugal**	*
10b	146,980	18,469	256,000	230,000	816m	2	233,000	0	Qatar	
9b	3.84m	52,000	7.2m	5.25m	650m	44	9.6m	11,385	Romania	
166b	25.019m	645,000	61.5m	60.5m	NA	86	66m	150.000	Russia	
1.2b	15,000	NA	601,000	NA	92m	10	3.6m	0	Rwanda	
62m	14,000	0	28,000	10,000	NA	NA	18,172	58	St. Kitts and Nevis	
135m	31,000	1,000	111,000	32,000	5m	3.7	43,8000	0	Saint Lucia	

Country	Area km²	Population	Life Exp. years	GDP Real Growth%	GDP Per Capita	Pop. Below Pov. Line%	Unemploy-ment Rate %	Electricity Consump-tion (kwh)	Exp.	Imp.
St. Vincent & the G.	389	115,461	72	4	2,600	NA	22	60m	47.8m	180m
Samoa	2,860	179,466	69	1.8	2,100	NA	NA	60m	20.3m	96.6m
San Marino	60.5	26,937	81	NA	20,000	NA	3.6	NA	-	-
Sao Tome and Prin.	1,001	159,883	65	1.5	1,100	NA	50	14m	4.9m	19.5m
Saudi Arabia	1,960,582	22,023,506	68	1.6	9,000	NA	NA	102.423b	48b	28b
Senegal	196,190	9,987,494	62	5	1,650	NA	NA	1.116b	925m	1.2b
Serbia & Monten.	102,350	10,662,087	72	-20	1,800	NA	30	36.141b	1.5b	3.3b
Seychelles	455	79,326	70	1.8	7,500	NA	NA	116m	91m	403m
Sierra Leone	71,740	5,232,624	45	-10	500	68	NA	219m	41m	166m
Singapore	647.5	4,151,264	80	5.5	27,800	NA	3.2	24.725b	114b	111b
Slovakia	48,845	5,407,956	74	1.9	8,500	NA	20	23.3b	10.1b	11.2b
Slovenia	20,253	1,927,593	75	3.5	10,900	NA	7.1	10.661b	8.4b	9.7b
Solomon Islands	28,450	466,194	71	3.5	2,650	NA	NA	28m	142m	160m
Somalia	637,657	7,253,137	46	NA	600	NA	NA	246m	187m	327m
South Africa	1,219,912	43,421,021	51	0.6	6,900	NA	30	174.486b	28b	26b
Spain	504,782	39,996,671	79	3.6	17,300	NA	16	170.306b	112.3b	137.5b
Sri Lanka	65,610	19,238,575	72	3.7	2,600	22	9.5	5.12b	4.7b	5.3b
Sudan	2,505,810	35,079,814	57	3	940	NA	30	1.688b	580m	1.4b
Suriname	163,270	431,303	71	-1	3,400	NA	20	1.867b	406.1m	461.4m
Swaziland	17,363	1,083,289	40	3.1	4,200	NA	22	1,078b	825m	1.05b
Sweden	449,964	8,873,052	80	3.8	20,700	NA	5.5	135.098b	85.7b	67.9b
Switzerland	41,290	7,262,372	80	1.4	27,100	NA	2.8	50.8b	98.5b	99b
Syria	185,180	16,305,659	68	0	2,500	20	13.5	16.275b	3.3b	3.2b
Tajikistan	143,100	6,440,732	64	2	1,020	NA	5.7	12.561b	634m	770m
Tanzania	945,087	35,306,126	52	4	550	51.1	NA	1.625b	828m	1.44b
Thailand	514,000	61,230,864	69	4	6,400	12.5	4.5	80.293b	58.5b	45b
Togo	56,785	5,018,502	55	4	1,700	32	NA	434m	400m	450m
Tonga	748	102,321	68	-0.3	2,200	NA	11.8	33m	8m	69m
Trinidad & Tobago	5,128	1,175,523	68	5	8,500	21	14.2	4.43b	2.4b	3b
Tunisia	163,610	9,593,402	74	6	5,500	14.1	16.5	7.549b	5.8b	8.3b
Turkey	780,580	65,666,677	71	-5	6,200	NA	7.3	118.5b	26b	40b
Turkemenistan	488,100	4,518,268	61	9	1,800	NA	NA	5.45b	1.1b	1.25b
Tuvalu	26	10,838	66	8.7	800	NA	NA	3m	65,000	4.4m
Uganda	236,040	23,317,560	43	5.5	1,060	55	NA	622m	471m	1.1b
Ukraine	603,700	49,153,027	66	-0.4	2,200	50	4.3	144.011b	11.6b	11.8b
United Arab Em.	82,880	2,369,153	74	2.5	17,700	NA	NA	18.702b	34b	27.5b
United Kingdom	244,820	59,511,464	78	1.9	21,800	17	6	331.482b	271b	305.9b
United States	9,629,091	275,562,673	77	4.1	33,900	12.7	4.2	3.365t	663b	912b
Uruguay	176,220	3,334,074	75	-2.5	8,500	NA	12	6.526b	2.1b	3.4b
Uzbekistan	447,400	24,755,519	64	-1	2,500	NA	5	41.327b	2.9b	3.1b
Vanuatu	14,760	189,618	61	NA	1,300	NA	NA	30m	33.8m	76.2m
Venezuela	912,050	23,542,649	73	-7.2	8,000	67	18	64.463b	20.9b	11.8b
Vietnam	329,560	78,773,873	68	4.8	1,850	37	25	19.177b	11.5b	11.6b
Yemen	527,970	17,479,206	60	4	750	NA	30	2.083b	2b	2.3b
Zambia	752,614	9,582,418	37	1.5	880	86	25	6.419b	900m	1.15b
Zimbabwe	390,580	11,342,521	38	0	2,400	60	50	8.403b	2b	2b

Debt External	Tel. M.L.U.	Tel. Mobil	Radios	Television	Military Exp.	Inflation % (consumer)	Labor Force	Railways km	Country
83.6m	20,500	83	77,000	18,000	NA	2	67,000	0	St. Vincent & the G.
156m	8,000	1,200	178,000	11,000	NA	2.2	82,500	0	Samoa
NA	18,000	3,010	16,000	9,000	700,000	2	15,600	0	San Marino
274m	3,000	NA	38,000	23,000	1m	10.5	NA	0	Sao Tome and Prin.
28b	3.1m	1m	6.25	5.1m	18.1b	-1.2	7m	1,390	Saudi Arabia
3.4b	82,000	122	1.24m	361,000	68m	2	NA	906	Senegal
14.1b	2.017m	38,552	3.15m	2.75m	911m	42	1.6m	4,095	Serbia & Monten.
149m	17,844	2,249	42,000	11,000	13m	3	26,000	0	Seychelles
1.15b	17,000	NA	1.12m	53,000	46m	30	1.369m	84	Sierra Leone
NA	54.6m	1.02m	2.55m	1.33m	4.4b	0.4	1.932b	38.6	Singapore
10.6b	1.557m	641,000	3.12m	2.62m	332m	14	3.32m	3,660	Slovakia
4.9b	700,000	57,342	805,000	710,000	335m	6.3	857,400	1,201	Slovenia
135m	7,000	230	57,000	3,000	NA	10	26,842	0	Solomon Islands
2.6b	NA	NA	470,000	135,000	NA	NA	3.7m	0	Somalia
25.7b	5.075m	+2,000,000	13.75m	5.2m	2b	5.5	15m	21,431	South Africa
90b	17.336m	8.394m	13.1m	16.2m	6b	2.3	16.2m	13,950	**Spain** *
8.4b	494,509	228,604	3.85m	1.53m	719m	6	6.6m	1,463	Sri Lanka
24b	75,000	3,000	7.55m	2.38m	550m	20	11m	5,311	Sudan
175.6m	56,844	3,671	300,000	63,000	8.5m	170	100,000	166	Suriname
180m	20,000	0	155,000	21,000	23m	6	NA	297	Swaziland
66.5b	6.017m	3.835m	8.25m	4.6m	5b	0.4	4.3m	12,821	Sweden
NA	4.82m	810,170	7.1m	3.31m	3.1b	1	3.8m	4,492	Switzerland
22b	930,000	NA	4.15m	1.05m	900m	2.3	4.7m	2,750	Syria
1.3b	263,000	NA	1.291m	860,000	17m	22	1.9m	480	Tajikistan
7.7b	127,000	30,000	8.8m	103,000	21m	8.8	13.495m	3,569	Tanzania
80b	5.4m	2.3m	13.9m	15.2m	2.075b	2.4	32.6m	3,940	Thailand
1.3b	22,000	NA	940,000	73,000	27m	3	1.538m	525	Togo
62m	7,000	114	61,000	2,000	NA	3.2	36,665	0	Tonga
2.2b	209,000	5,615	680,000	425,000	83m	3.5	558,700	0	Trinidad & Tobago
12.1b	628,000	50,000	2.06m	920,000	356m	2.7	3m	2,168	Tunisia
104b	17.244m	3.2m	11.3m	20.9m	6.737b	65	23.8m	8,607	Turkey
2.1b	320,000	NA	1.22m	820,000	90m	30	2.34m	2,187	Turkemenistan
NA	400	0	4,000	NA	NA	3.9	NA	0	Tuvalu
3.1b	54,074	9,000	2.6m	315,000	95m	7	8.361m	1,241	Uganda
12.6b	9.45m	236,000	45.05m	18.05m	500m	20	22.8m	23,350	Ukraine
15.5b	915,223	1m	820,000	310,000	2.1b	4	1.38m	0	United Arab Em.
NA	29.41m	13m	84.5m	30.5m	36.8b	2.3	29.2m	16,878	United Kingdom
862b	178m	55.312m	575m	219m	276.7b	2.2	139.4m	240,000	United States
8b	622,000	40,000	1.97m	782,000	172m	4	1.38m	2,073	**Uruguay** *
3.2b	1.976m	26,000	10.2m	6.4m	200m	29	11.9m	3,380	Uzbekistan
48m	2,500	121	62,000	2,000	NA	3.9	NA	0	Vanuatu
32b	2.6m	2m	10.75m	4.1m	934m	20	9.9m	584	**Venezuela** *
7.3b	775,000	178,000	8.2m	3.57m	650m	4	38.2m	2,652	Vietnam
4.5b	188,000	8,250	1.05m	470,000	414m	10	NA	0	Yemen
6.7b	77,935	6,000	1.03m	277,000	76m	27.4	3.4m	2,164	Zambia
5b	212,000	70,000	1.14m	370,000	127m	59	5m	2,759	Zimbabwe

(*) Hispanic Countries

Abbreviations:

- **G.D.P.:** gross domestic product
- **Pop. Below. Pov. Line:** population below poverty line
- **Exp.:** exports
- **Imp.:** imports
- **Tel. M.L.U.:** telephones (main lines in use)
- **Military Exp.:** military expenditures

- **m:** millions
- **b:** billions (10^9)
- **t:** trillions (10^{12})
- **NA:** Not available
- **(1):** does not include opium
- **(2):** underemployment 70%

Liberia (80%). The nation with the lowest percentage of its population below the poverty line is Belgium (4%), while the Latin American nation with the lowest percentage of its population below the poverty line is Brazil (17.4%).

Brazil: the fifth largest country in the world (8,511,965 km2), following Russia, Canada, the United States, and China. Brazil is the Latin American nation with the highest level of military spending ($13 billion per year), or approximately $75 per person. Globally, the nation with the highest per capita military spending is the U.S. ($276 billion), with more than $1,000 per person.

Chile: spends $165 per person on defense, for the highest per capita military spending among Latin American nations. Chile's citizens have the highest average life expectancy (76 years) in Latin America. Worldwide, the highest average life expectancy is seen in Andorra (83 years) and Japan (81 years).

Colombia: one of the four Latin American nations (along with Chile, Ecuador, and Venezuela) with net exports higher than imports ($11.5 billion vs. $10 billion). Globally, this positive balance of trade occurs in only 46 nations out of 192.

Costa Rica: inhabitants of Costa Rica have an average life expectancy of 75 years, one of the highest in the world. Costa Rica has external debt in the amount of $3.9 billion, and exports $6.4 billion worth of goods per year.

Cuba: inhabitants of Cuba have the highest average life expectancy of all Latin American nations, equal to Chile (76 years). Despite the U.S. economic blockade, Cuba has achieved foreign investment, mainly from Spain and geared toward tourism. In the U.S., business interests in reopening commerce are on the rise.

Dominican Republic: a quarter of the population lives below the poverty line. Annual imports exceed exports by $3 billion. The Dominican Republic has a real annual growth rate of 8.3% of GDP, the highest among Latin American nations.

Ecuador: half of Ecuador's population lives below the poverty line. A positive aspect of Ecuador's economy is its positive balance of trade, with exports of $4.1 billion and imports of $2.8 billion. Annual military spending is $720 million, or $56 per Ecuadorian citizen.

El Salvador: has a long history of difficulties reflected in two statistics: High infant mortality-of each 1,000 births, almost 30 infants (29.2) die at birth. Poverty-48% of the population lives below the poverty line. On January 13, 2001, El Salvador suffered the worst natural disaster of its

el índice más favorable a nivel mundial es el de Bélgica (4%), entre los hispano-americanos el más favorable es el índice de Brasil (17,4%)

Brasil: tiene el quinto territorio más extenso del mundo, (8.511.965 km²) detrás de Rusia, Canadá, Estados Unidos y China. Es el país hispano-americano que más gasta en el aspecto militar (13.000 millones de dólares por año), que es equivalente a $75 por habitante.

En el mundo, el país que más gasta en este aspecto es Estados Unidos ($ 276.700 millones), o sea, más de $1.000 por habitante.

Chile: invierte anualmente $165 por cada habitante en el ámbito militar, siendo el país hispano-americano que, proporcionalmente, más gasta en ese aspecto.

Sus habitantes tienen la expectativa de vida más larga (76 años) entre los países hispano-americanos. Mundialmente, las espectativas más largas son las de Andorra (83 años) y Japón (81).

Colombia: es uno de los cuatro países de Hispano-América (junto con Chile, Ecuador y Venezuela) que exportan más de lo que importan (11.500 billones de dólares contra 10.000 millones). Esto sólo sucede mundialmente en 46 países, sobre un total de 192 países.

Costa Rica: sus habitantes gozan de una expectativa de vida de 75 años, una de las más altas entre todos los países del mundo. Tiene una deuda externa de 3.900 millones de dólares, y exporta 6.400 millones por año.

Cuba: sus habitantes tienen la expectativa de vida más larga de todos los países hispano- americanos, junto con Chile (76 años). A pesar del bloqueo económico de EUA ha logrado inversiones, preferentemente de España y aplicadas a la actividad turística. En EUA crece el sector empresarial que propicia la reanudación del comercio entre los dos países.

Dominican Republic: un cuarto de su población vive bajo la línea de pobreza. Cada año importa 3.000 millones de dólares más de los que exporta. Tiene un crecimiento real anual de su G.D.P. del 8,3%, el más alto entre todos los países hispano-americanos.

Ecuador: la mitad de su población vive bajo la línea de pobreza. Un aspecto positivo de su economía es que exporta más de lo que importa (exporta 4.100 millones de dólares e importa 2.800). Anualmente gasta $720 millones en el ámbito militar. Si se divide esta cifra por el número de habitantes resulta que invierte casi $56 por cada uno de ellos.

El Salvador: tiene una larga historia de dificultades que se documentan con dos cifras: de cada mil nacimientos, mueren al nacer casi treinta niños (29.2), y el 48 % de su población vive por debajo de la línea de pobreza. El día 13 de enero del

history: an earthquake that caused the death of more than 4,000 people and destroyed more than 8,000 dwellings and damaged more than 17,000 others.

Equatorial Guinea: has a real annual growth rate of 15% of GDP, the highest in the world. Its inhabitants have the lowest average life expectancy of any of the Hispanic nations (54 years); globally, lower life expectancies are observed in Zambia (37 years) and Angola (34 years).

Guatemala: 75% of the population lives below the poverty line. This is one of the highest percentages in the world, exceeded only by Haiti and Liberia (80%). Guatemala annually imports $2.1 billion more than it exports.

Honduras: annually spends $33 million for its military, the equivalent of $5 per citizen. In 1999, Hurricane Mitch desolated Honduras, killing more than 5,000 people. However, the country is recovering rapidly and has benefited through programs for "Highly Indebted Poor Countries."

Mexico: has the lowest unemployment rate among Latin American nations (2.5%). The highest unemployment rates globally are found in Haiti (70%), Angola (50%), Kenya (50%), Zimbabwe (50%), and Sao Tome & Principe (50%). Conditions in Kiribati deserve special notice, with an unemployment rate of only 2% and 70% of the population in a state of employment. Leaving aside those nations for whom such statistics are unavailable from the CIA, the lowest unemployment statistics globally are found in Andorra (0%), Nauru (0%), and Kuwait (1.8%).

Nicaragua: the Latin American nation with the lowest level of military spending ($26 million), the equivalent of $5 per capita. Internationally, the nation with the lowest annual military expenditure is The Gambia ($1 million), the equivalent of less than $1 per person. It is noteworthy that the inertia of material interests frequently creates unreasonable situations. Military spending does not constitute an investment in growing assets for the society, and can be justified only by motives of conflict. Moreover, it has been shown that when conflicts develop among nations, the U.S. usually intervenes and assumes the burden of resolution. Nevertheless, military investments continue to supplant the type of socio-economic investments that more effectively strengthen nations.

Panama: a unique nation. Panama has been the object of disputing forces with the goal of controlling the canal that joins the Pacific and Atlantic oceans. In 1977, President Jimmy Carter of the United States and General Omar Torrijo of Panama signed the treaty that effectively granted Panama dominion over the Canal Zone. Panama's history-including the construction of the Canal and stories of Panama's

2001 sufrió el peor desastre natural de su historia, un terremoto que causó la muerte de   más de 4.000 peronas y destruyó totalmente 8.000 viviendas, mientras que otras 17.000 resultaron dañadas en forma parcial.

Equatorial Guinea: tiene un crecimiento real anual de su G.D.P. del 15%, que es el más alto del mundo. Sus habitantes tienen la expectativa de vida más baja entre todos los países hispanos (54 años). A nivel mundial los registros más bajos se dan en Zambia (37 años) y Angola (38 años).

Guatemala: el 75% de su población vive bajo la línea de pobreza. Es uno de los índices más altos del mundo, sólo superado por los de Haití y Liberia (80%). Cada año importa 2.100 millones de dólares más de lo que exporta.

Honduras: gasta anualmente 33 millones de dólares en el ámbito militar, lo que equivale a $5 por cada habitante. En 1999 el huracán Mitch la desoló, matando a más de 5.000 personas. Pero está recuperándose con premura y ha sido beneficiada por el programa para "Highly Indebted Poor Countries".

Mexico: tiene el índice de desempleo más bajo entre todos los países hispano-americanos (2.5%). Los índices más desfavorables se dan en Haití (70%), Angola (50%), Kenia (50%), Zimbabwe (50%) y Sao Tomé and Principe (50%). Merece un párrafo aparte la situación de Kiribate, ya que si bien el índice de desempleo es sólo del 2%, tiene un 70% de su población activa en estado de subempleo. Todo esto , sin contar los países en que esta información no está disponible para los investigadores de la C.I.A. Mientras que los índices más favorables son los que se registran en Andorra (0%), Nauru (0%) y Kuwait (1,8%).

Nicaragua: es el país hispano-americano que menos gasta en el ámbito militar (26 millones de dólares), lo que equivale a poco más de $5 por habitante. Mientras que entre todos los países del mundo, el que menos gastos efectúa en este aspecto es Gambia ($1 millón) que equivale a menos de 1 dólar por habitante. Es curioso constatarlo pero la inercia de los intereses materiales crean con frecuencia, situaciones no razonables. Los gastos en armamentos no son redituables, y solo se justificarán con motivo de un conflicto. Pero se ha probado ya que producido el desacuerdo entre dos paises, interviene Estados Unidos y es él quién dirime la disensión. Mientras tanto, aquellas inversiones militares han restado aportes a las inversiones retributivas que son las que efectivamente fortalecen el país.

Panamá: un país singular. Ha sido asiento de fuertes disputas con motivo de contener en su territorio un canal que comunica, los océanos Pacífico y Atlántico. Recién en 1977 el Presidente Carter de Estados Unidos y el general Omar Torrijo firmaron en la ciudad de Washington los tratados que efectivizaron el dominio de Panamá sobre los territorios afectados por el Canal. La historia de su origen territorial, de la construcción

dead and imprisoned presidents-covers a relatively short period of time, but is of an intensity that almost unknown among other nations. The U.S. took jurisdiction over the Canal in 1903. Complete jurisdiction was rescinded in 1973 (Tack-Kissinger), and on the last day of 1999, the government of Panama assumed total responsibility for the operation and maintenance of the Canal. Panama has one of the highest per capita GDPs in Latin America, $7,600.

Paraguay: 32% of the population of Paraguay lives below the poverty level; unemployment lies at 12%. In 1991, the presidents and ministers of external relations of Argentina, Brazil, Uruguay, and Paraguay-meeting in the city of Asuncion-created a common market known as Mercosur. Although the market has become entangled in ongoing internal disputes and other obstacles, there is no doubt that the market will be consolidated over time.

Peru: 54% of Peru's population lives below the poverty line, and the poverty of the populace is reflected and finds its source in the corruption of the government. Moreover, the country's statistical trends do not reflect improvement, but rather a deepening of current problems. Peru has produced governors and intellectuals of the first caliber, but that is history. Peru spends an average of $48 per capita on the military annually.

Portugal: has the second highest per capita GDP among Hispanic-Iberian nations ($15,300); Spain has the highest. Portugal annually invests $2.45 billion in military spending, or $245 per capita.

Spain: the residents of Spain have the highest average life expectancy of any of the Hispanic nations, 79 years. It also has the highest per capita GDP among Hispanic nations ($17,300). Spain has a population density of 79 people per km².

Uruguay: with a territory of 176,220 km² and 3,334,074 inhabitants, Uruguay has a population density of 19 people per km².Uruguay's small territory is populated by citizens with a strong feeling for democracy. Following its origin as an area disputed by Brazil and Argentina, its final status as an independent nation is the most appropriate for its people. Uruguay spends $172 million annually on military spending. Per capita, the government invests less than $52 on the military per year.

Venezuela: presents a special case. Venezuela's exports exceed its imports, and it is rich in a globally desired natural resource. Nevertheless, Venezuela is the home of millions of poor. The oil companies operating in Venezuela have not benefited the populace. Currently, the president has used "strong arm" tactics and has agitated the population into

del Canal y de sus presidentes muertos y encarcelados, tiene un período temporal corto pero de una intensidad que no puede desconocerse. La jurisdicción estadounidense sobre el Canal se instituyo en 1903, derogandose en en 1974 (Tack-Kissinger). El último día del año 1999 el gobierno de Panamá, asumió la total responsabilidad por la administración, operación y manteniemiento del Canal. Tiene uno de los G.D.P. per capita más altos de Hispano-América ($7.600).

Paraguay: *Un 32% de su población se encuentra viviendo por debajo de la línea de pobreza, y tiene un índice de desempleo del 12%. En 1991 los presidentes y ministros de Relaciones Exteriores de Argentina, Brasil, Uruguay y Paraguay, reunidos en la ciudad de Asunción crean un mercado común conocido como el Mercosur. Desde entonces viene desenvolviendose con las disputas internas habituales en todos estos emprendimientos, pero no se duda que con el tiempo irá consolidándose.*

Perú: *un 54% de su población vive por debajo de la línea de pobreza. La pobreza de su población se expresa en la sucesiva corrupción de sus gobiernos. No logra salir de un cuadro de situación que por el contrario, tiende a profundizarse. Produjo gobernantes e intelectuales de primer nivel universal, pero todo eso ya es historia. Gasta anualmente $48 dólares por cada habitante en el ámbito militar.*

Portugal: *tiene el segundo G.D.P. per capita más alto entre todos los países hispano- lusitanos ($ 15.300); el más alto es el de España. Anualmente invierte 2.45 billones de dólares en el ámbito militar, el que dividido por el número de sus habitantes, resultan $245 por cada habitante.*

Spain: *sus habitantes tienen una expectativa de vida de 79 años (la más alta entre todos los países hispanos). Tiene el G.D.P. per capita más alto entre todos los países hispanos ($17.300) La densidad demográfica en este país es de 79 habitantes por Km².*

Uruguay: *su territorio es de 176.220 Km² y cuenta con 3.334.074 habitantes, de lo que resulta que tiene una densidad de 19 habitantes por cada Km². Es pequeño territorialmente pero su población tiene una definida vocación democrática. En sus origens fue disputada por Brasil y Argentina, pero su situacion final como país independiente ha resultado la más apropiada para su población. Gasta anualmente172 millones de dólares en el ámbito militar. Si se divide esa cifra por el número de habitantes, resulta que el gobierno invierte poco menos de $ 52 por cada uno de ellos.*

Venezuela: *este país es un caso notable. Exporta más de lo que importa, de un recurso altamente cotizado mundialmente. No obstante, alberga en su territorio millones de pobres. Las compañias petroleras que operan en su territorio, pareciera que no la han favorecido. En estos momentos, un presidente que se mueve con las caracteristicas de "hombre fuerte", ha logrado agitar una base poblacional dispuesta ha adherirse a*

accepting any situation except the current one . It is foreseeable that these tactics will lead to a situation little different from what existed before: violence and more violence that most affects the weakest members of society. Venezuela has a population of 23.5 million, 67% of which live below the poverty line-more than 15.7 million people. Venezuela annually exports $9 billion more than it imports.

In December 2000, the CIA, under the direction of the National Intelligence Council, published a summary report entitled *Global Trends 2015*. This report is based on the opinions of government institutions and experts.

Key issues that were considered in the projections included:

- Demographics
- Natural resources and the environment
- Science and technology
- The global economy and globalization
- National and international governing organizations
- Future conflicts
- The role of the United States.

It is clear that no single one of these issues will be a sole determinant of the world's future; each issue will have a different impact in the world's distinct regions, with some impacts compounding and complementing each other.

With respect to Latin America, the report states:

By the year 2015, Brazil and Mexico will each be more confident and capable as nations, and will be seeking leadership positions in the hemisphere. It is probable that the region will continue to be vulnerable to financial crises, motivated by external debt, as the majority of the region's economies depend on limited exportable natural resources.

The region's weakest nations, especially those in the Andean zone, are the most likely to deteriorate. It is projected that some of these nations may lose their democratic status because their governments have not been effectively responding to popular demands in the areas of crime-fighting, corruption, and narcotics trafficking.

Venezuela and Brazil will become the most important producers of petroleum by the year 2015, as their proven oil reserves are exceeded only by those of the Middle East.

Organizations such as Mercosur and the effective establishment of an American Free Trade Zone will generate employment and create a political context that will be sufficient for governments to enact substantial economic reforms, although some reforms may not be favored by minority groups.

cualquier propuesta que no sea la existente. *Las cosas, debemos preveer que terminarán como siempre: violencia y más violencia que caerá sobre los más débiles. Tiene una población de 23.500 millones de habitantes, y el 67% de esa gente vive por debajo de la línea de pobreza (más de 15.7 millones de personas). Cada año exporta 9.000 millones de dólares más de lo que importa.*

En diciembre del 2000, la CIA publicó un trabajo sobre las tendencias universales hacia el año 2015 (Global Trends 2015), bajo la dirección del National Intelligence Council. El mismo se realizó en base a las opiniones de instituciones y expertos no gubernamentales.

Los puntos claves que fueron tomados en cuenta para realizar dicha proyección son:

- *Demografía;*
- *Recursos naturales y Medio ambiente;*
- *Ciencia y Tecnología;*
- *La economía global y la Globalización;*
- *Gobiernos Nacionales e Internacionales;*
- *Conflictos futuros; y*
- *El rol de EE UU.*

Sobre estos puntos aclaran que ninguno de ellos va a ser determinante por sí sólo en el futuro mundial; que cada uno de ellos tendrá diferente impacto en las distintas regiones y que éstos no necesariamente se complementarán entre sí, por el contrario, en algunos casos se enfrentarán unos con otros.

Con respecto a América Latina manifiestan:

Para el año 2015 Brasil y México serán cada vez más confiables y capaces, y buscarán liderar los asuntos del hemisferio.

Pero también prevén que la región continuará siendo vulnerable a las crisis financieras, con motivo de la dependencia en la financiación externa, debido a que de la mayoría de esas economías dependen de limitados recursos exportables (materias primas).

Para los países más débiles de la zona, la proyección no es alentadora, especialmente los de la región andina, ya que prevén que irán desmejorando. Incluso insinúan que algunos de estos países perderán sus democracias por causa de no responder sus gobiernos en forma efectiva a las demandas populares que son: represión efectiva del crimen, la corrupción y el narcotráfico.

Venezuela y Brasil se convertirán en dos importantes productores de petróleo para el año 2015. Está comprobado que sus reservas sólo son superadas por las ubicadas en Medio Oriente.

The Latin American Internet market is positioned to grow, stimulating commerce and international investment, as well as creating new jobs and improved corporate efficiency. In this area, Argentina, Brazil and Mexico are expected to benefit the most.

Latin American demographics are projected to change significantly, assisting to decrease social tension and serving to create a base for economic growth. During the next fifteen years, the majority of Latin American nations will experience a decrease in the number of people seeking work, and this will help reduce unemployment and improve salaries.

However, not all countries prosper under this scenario: Bolivia, Ecuador, Guatemala, Honduras, Nicaragua, and Paraguay will continue to experience rapid increases in the number of unemployed.

Democratic institutions in Mexico, Argentina, Chile and Brazil appear to be positioned to continue their incremental consolidation. In other nations, crime, public corruption, the expansion of poverty, and the failure of governments to prevent a growing disparity in income levels will allow opportunities for dictatorship to arise.

Increasing crime rates will contribute to citizens' perception that they must take justice into their own hands, leading to an increase in extra-judicial actions on the part of the police, including assassinations.

By the year 2015, the gap between the wealthiest and the poorest nations will be even greater than today. Those nations that are incapable of modernizing their economies will for the most part experience very slow growth.

Political instability will continue to grow in Venezuela, Peru, and Ecuador due to continuing economic crises and profound popular cynicism about political institutions.

The future of Colombia rests on its ability to resolve the ongoing guerilla warfare within its boundaries.

The democratization of Cuba depends on how and when the government of Fidel Castro comes to an end.

Migration, legal and illegal, to the United States will be a major issue during the next fifteen years. El Salvador, Guatemala, Honduras and Nicaragua will be the principal sources of illegal immigrants.

Illegal immigration among Latin American nations will continue to increase substantially. Argentina and Venezuela already have millions of undocumented workers from neighboring countries within their borders.

Organizaciones como el Mercosur y la efectiva conclusión del Área de Libre Comercio de las Américas, generarán empleo y crearán el contexto político adecuado para que los gobiernos hagan reformas económicas sustanciales, aún en contra de los intereses de los grupos minoritarios.

El mercado latino americano de Internet está posicionado para crecer, estimulando el comercio y las inversiones internacionales y creando nuevos empleos y una mayor eficacia corporativa. En este campo los países que aparecen como los más beneficiados son Argentina, Brasil y México.

La demografía cambiará notablemente en América Latina, ayudando a disminuir la tensión social y servirá como base para el crecimiento económico. Durante los próximos quince años, la mayoría de los países de la región experimentarán un descenso sustancial en el número de personas en busca de empleo, lo que ayudará a reducir el desempleo y a mejorar los salarios.

Pero no todos los países gozarán de este fenómeno: Bolivia, Ecuador, Guatemala, Honduras, Nicaragua y Paraguay continuarán aumentando rápidamente el número de desempleados.

Las instituciones democráticas en México, Argentina, Chile y Brasil aparecen posicionadas para continuar incrementando su consolidación. En los otros países, el crimen, la corrupción pública, la expansión de la pobreza y el fracaso de los gobiernos en prevenir la creciente desigualdad de ingresos, generará oportunidades para los políticos autoritarios.

El crecimiento desmedido de los índices de crimen contribuirá a que los ciudadanos hagan justicia por mano propia y dará lugar a asesinatos extra judiciales por parte de la policía.

Para el año 2015 la brecha entre los países más prósperos y los más pobres será más amplia. Los países que sean incapaces de modernizar sus economías experimentarán, en el mejor de los casos, un lento crecimiento.

El cansancio ante las continuas crisis económicas y el profundo cinismo popular sobre las instituciones políticas, pueden llevar a la inestabilidad en Venezuela, Perú y Ecuador.

La resolución de la guerrilla es clave para los futuros proyectos de Colombia.

La democratización en Cuba depende de cómo y cuándo termine su gobierno Fidel Castro.

La migración, legal e ilegal, hacia los EE UU será cada vez mayor durante los próximos quince años. El Salvador, Guatemala, Honduras y Nicaragua serán las principales fuentes de la migración ilegítima.

La migración ilegal entre los países de América Latina crecerá en forma significativa. Argentina y Venezuela ya tienen millones de trabajadores indocumentados provinientes de países vecinos.

Educational Achievement of the Hispanic Population

Nivel académico de la población hispana

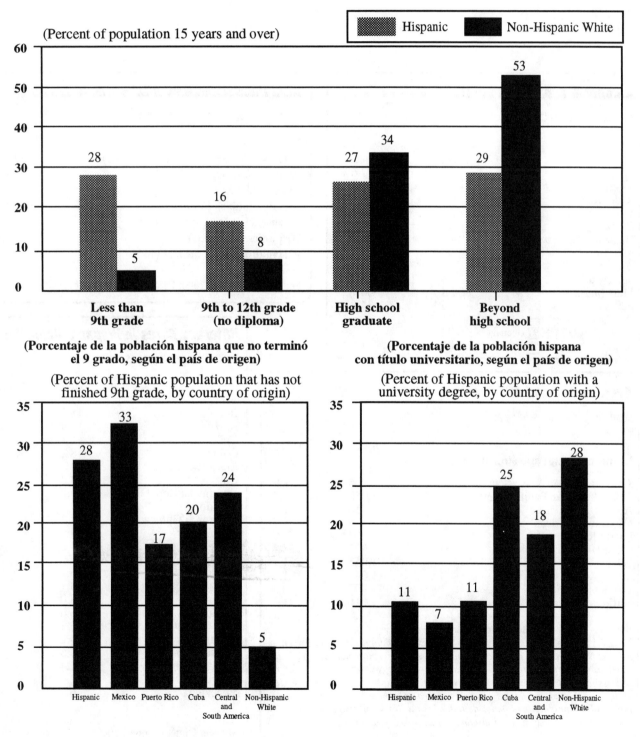

(Percent of population 15 years and over)

Legend: Hispanic, Non-Hispanic White

Less than 9th grade
9th to 12th grade (no diploma)
High school graduate
Beyond high school

(Porcentaje de la población hispana que no terminó el 9 grado, según el país de origen)

(Percent of Hispanic population that has not finished 9th grade, by country of origin)

Hispanic 28, Mexico 33, Puerto Rico 17, Cuba 20, Central and South America 24, Non-Hispanic White 5

(Porcentaje de la población hispana con título universitario, según el país de origen)

(Percent of Hispanic population with a university degree, by country of origin)

Hispanic 11, Mexico 7, Puerto Rico 11, Cuba 25, Central and South America 18, Non-Hispanic White 28

Source: U.S. Census Bureau (Press-Release/www/2000)

SAT/ACT. Alcohol and Tobacco. AIDS. Illiteracy

SAT/ACT. Alcohol y Tabaco. SIDA. Analfabetismo

Alcohol & Tobacco in the US

Alcohol y tabaco en EUA

	Alcohol*	Tobacco*
Total	51.7%	27.6%
Race (*raza*)		
White (*blanca*)"	53.3	27.4
Black (*afr.am.*)"	39.8	32.1
Hispanic (*hispana*)	45.4	26.2
"(*non-hispanic*)		
Sex (*sexo*)		
Male (*masc.*)	58.7	34.7†
Female (*fem.*)	45.1	34.9†

*1998 **1995 †1997 (teenagers)
Source: US Dept. of Health and Human Services

Average SAT and ACT Scores

Resultados promedios de SAT y ACT

	SAT	ACT
Ethnic group (grupo étnico)		
American Indian & Alaskan	965	18.9
Asian American Pacific Islander	1,058	21.7
African American	856	17.1
Mexican-American	909	NA
Puerto Rican	903	NA
Other Hispanic	927	18.9
White	1,055	21.7
Men	1,040	21.1
Women	997	20.9
National average	**1,016**	**21.0**

Source: The College Board, American College Testing
Nota: SAT (Scholastic Assessment Tests) es un examen administrado por Pricenton A.C. de New York City y evalúa habilidades verbales y matemáticas. ***ACT****, del American College Testing, es otro examen – de mayor uso al oeste del río Mississippi – administrado por este desde Iowa City, sobre cuatro temas: inglés, matemática, estudios sociales y ciencias naturales. Ambos tests son respondidos por similar cantidad de alumnos de todos los niveles y muestran similitudes en cuanto a sus diferencias de resultados, según sexo o grupo étnico.*

AIDS Deaths and New AIDS cases in the US

Muertes y nuevos casos de SIDA en EUA

Total New Cases (*Total casos nuevos*)	23,236
Whites (*blancos*)	6,629
Blacks (*afr. am.*)	7,681
Amerian Indians (*Indios am.*)	72
Asian-Pacific Islander (*Asiát.-Pacific.isl.*)	131
Hispanics (*hispanos*)	**3,212**
All children (*niños menores de 13 años*)	129

Source: Health, US, 2000; HIV/AIDS Report Vol II

Illiteracy Rates in Hispanic Countries

Analfabetismo en los países hispanos

	Men	Women
Argentina	3.1	3
Bolivia	15.2	19.6
Brazil	14.9	14.6
Chile	4.1	4.5
Colombia	8.2	8.2
Costa Rica	4.3	4.3
Cuba	3.2	3.4
Dominican Republic	17.2	19.8
Ecuador	9.0	11.1
Ecuatorial Guinea	21.3	22.8
El Salvador	18.3	23.8
Guatemala	23.8	38.7
Honduras	25.6	25.2
Mexico	6.7	10.6
Nicaragua	33.1	29.8
Panama	8.0	9.8
Paraguay	5.6	7.8
Peru	5.3	14.6
Portugal	5.2	10.0
Puerto Rico	6.5	6.1
Spain (España)	1.4	3.2
Uruguay	2.6	1.8
Venezuela	6.9	7.8
US	3.0	3.0

Source: United Nations, 2000

Education: Expectations

La educación: expectativas

SOME SCHOOLS SPELL OUT EXACTLY HOW TEACHERS MUST TEACH. AND THEIR SCORES ARE UP

PROS

- Scripts can raise test scores, studies show, especially among poor kids.
- They help new teachers and those asked to teach outside their speciality.
- They ensure that all kids will be exposed to the common skills tested on state exams.

CONS

- Teachers contend that the programs curb creativity and spontaneity in the classroom.
- Some experts say they teach only root facts without fostering true learning.
- The programs are so costly that some schools find it hard to keep them going.

ALGUNAS ESCUELAS ORDENAN EXACTAMENTE COMO LOS MAESTROS DEBEN ENSEÑAR. Y LAS NOTAS SUBEN

PROS

- El método puede elevar las notas de los exámenes, según los estudios efectuados, especialmente entre los niños pobres.
- Ayuda a la fundamentación de nuevos maestros y a quienes quieren enseñar en otra especialidad.
- Se asegura que todo los niños serán además, preparados para los test estatales comunes.

CONTRAS

- Los maestros manifiestan que el programa limita la creatividad y espontaneidad de las clases.
- Algunos expertos dicen que sólo se enseña por repetición, sin proponer verdades alternativas.
- El programa es tan costoso que muchas escuelas dudan llevarlo adelante.

DRAMATIC PROBABILITIES: Expected to Go to Prison (by Age, Gender, Race, and Hispanic Origin, in the US)

Probabilidades dramáticas: Expectativas de ir a prisión (por edad, sexo, raza u origen hispano, en USA)

Category (Categoría)	Age (Edad)			
	Birth (al nacer)	20	30	45
TOTAL	5.1%	4.5%	2.1%	0.6%
By gender (sexo)				
Male (masc.)	9.0	7.9	3.7	1.0
Female (fem.)	1.1	1.0	0.6	0.1
By race/hispanic (raza/hispano)				
White (non-hispanic)				
Male (masc.)	4.4	4.1	2.1	0.8
Female (fem.)	0.5	0.5	0.3	0.1
Black (non-hispanic)				
Male (masc.)	28.5	25.3	10.8	2.1
Female (fem.)	3.6	3.5	1.9	0.4
Hispanic				
Male (masc.)	16.0	14.8	8.6	3.0
Female (fem.)	1.5	1.5	0.9	0.2

Source: Bureau of Justice Statistics: Lifetime Likelihood.... (Press-Release/www/2000)

Federal Government Financial Aid for Students

Ayuda financiera del gobierno federal para estudiantes

RESIDENT STATUS

The U.S. Department of Education offers financial assistance in the form of grants, loans, and work-study. To be eligible, an applicant must be one of the following:

- U.S. Citizen
- U.S. National (includes natives of American Samoa or Swain's Island)
- U.S. Permanent Resident who has a I-51, I-551, or I-551C (Alien Registration Receipt Card)
- Legal immigrant in possession of an Arrival Departure Record (I-94) from the INS showing a series of specific designations approved by this office.

FINANCIAL NEED

The U.S Department of Education provides financial assistance to applicants who can prove financial need.' The exact amount of need is determined by a formula created by Congress. The amount determined to be the applicant's financial need is used by universities as well as other organizations offering financial aid programs. The formula is as follows:

Cost of Education

Expected Family Contribution

Financial Need

Cost of Education includes tuition, room and board, fees, books, supplies, transportation, child care, costs related to physical disabilities, and miscellaneous expenses. Family Contribution refers to the amount of money, determined by Congress, that the student's family is expected to contribute toward the cost of education. This information will be summed up for the student in the Student Aid Report (SAR), which should be received by the student approximately four weeks after the FAFSA application is received by the processor.

APPLICATION PROCESS

Only one form is needed to initialize application for federal programs. This form is called the Free Application for Student Aid (FAFSA). The application should be filled out very carefully, since a mistake might inadvertently disqualify the applicant. The completed application should be mailed as soon as possible after January 3 and must be received by the processor by May 1. For an application, the student should contact the financial aid office of his or her school.

TYPES OF FINANCIAL AID

Grants are known as "gift aid," because the money does not require repayment. Loans are long-term, low interest advances of money that students must repay following graduation, withdrawal from classes, or failure to maintain half-time status. Work-study lets the students work and earn money to help pay for school.

PELL GRANT

The Pell Grant is the largest federal grant program and is awarded to undergraduate students who have not yet completed a first degree. The maximum award is $2,400, and is based on financial need. Every applicant that qualifies for this grant will receive monies.

SUPPLEMENTAL EDUCATIONAL OPPORTUNITY GRANT (SEOG).

This grant is available to undergraduate students with exceptional financial need who are also Pell Grant recipients. Students may receive up to an additional $4,000 per year. This program is very similar to the Pell Grant program, the difference being that every applicant who does qualify for the SEOG does not necessarily receive assistance under this program.

PERKINS LOAN

This loan is available to both undergraduate and graduate students. The school is the lender and must be repaid nine months after the recipient graduates, leaves school, or drops below half-time enrollment. Undergraduate students may receive up to $3,000 per year, not to exceed $15,000. Graduate students or those working towards a professional degree may borrow up to $5,000 per year, not to exceed $30,000 (this includes monies borrowed as an undergraduate through this program).

STAFFORD LOAN

This loan is for students attending school at least half-time. This loan is low interest, and is made by a lender such as a bank, credit union, or savings and loan association. Repayment and interest begins either six months after the student graduates (subsidized), or immediately after the student graduates (unsubsidized-interest begins as soon as the loan is given). Depending on need and dependency status, the loans go as follows: $2,625-10,500 a year for first or second year undergraduates; $5,500-7,500 a year for those who have completed at least two years of the undergraduate curriculum; up to $18,500 a year for graduate students.

PARENTS LOANS FOR UNDERGRADUATES STUDENTS (PLUS) AND SUPPLEMENTAL LOANS FOR STUDENTS (SLS)

The PLUS loans enable parents to borrow money to help pay for their children's education. SLS loans are intended for student borrowers who are independent and at least 24 years old. Repayment and interest begins 60 days following the date of loan disbursement. PLUS and SLS lets parents or students borrow up to $4,000 per year, to a total of $20,000.

COLLEGE WORK-STUDY (CWS)

This program provides students who need financial aid with jobs on- or off-campus to help pay their educational expenses. The pay is at least current federal minimum wage, but also may be related to the type of position held and experience. Full-time students typically work 15- but no more than 20-hours a week

The U.S. government offers several different types of programs. For more information, call the Federal Student Aid Information Center

1-(800)-4 FED AID (433-3243) or write to the U.S. Department of Education for a complete guide to:

Federal Student Aid Information Center
P.O. Box 84
Washington, DC 20044-0084
www.ed.gov/offices/ope/

TIYM's Financial Aid
Ayudas financieras de TIYM

Since 1993, TIYM Publishing Co., Inc., publisher of the "ANUARIO HISPANO-HISPANIC YEARBOOK" has helped fund the Hispanic Division's summer fellowship program at the Library of Congress for recent graduates or current students. During the 2000 year, TIYM continued contributing funds for scholarships through the YEARBOOK presentations, held in Washington, DC, New York, Miami, Los Angeles, Puerto Rico, San Antonio and Albuquerque. A total of 19 "ANUARIO HISPANO-HISPANIC YEARBOOK" scholarships have been granted to different students, with a total sum of close to $50,000.

A N U A R I O

H I S P A N O

H I S P A N I C

Y E A R B O O K

ANUARIOHISPANO.COM

HISPANICYEARBOOK.COM

Richard Soto, from Puerto Rico, was the first recipient of the fellowship award, followed by Carmen Enciso, Camelia Picó, Luis Maldonado, Carlos Aguirre, Pablo Tagre, Abraham Smith, and Martha Irahefa.

Students at the University of Miami reception - 2000

Ricardo Romo, President of the University of Texas at San Antonio and Ruben Garcia, Assistant Executive Director of Adelante, presenting the second ANUARIO HISPANO-HISPANIC YEARBOOK scholarship at the University of Texas - 2000

1993 Ricardo Soto of Tulane University	1999 Antonio Sandoval of the University of California
1994 Carmen Enciso of the Univ. of California, Berkeley	1999 Christian Kelleher of the University of Texas in Austin
1995 Camelia Picó of the University of Johns Hopkins	2000 University of Puerto Rico
1995 Ana Maria Villamarin of the University of Johns Hopkins	2000 "The second endowment scholarship for Hispanic
1996 Pablo Tagre of the Univ. of California, Berkeley	students at the University of Miami"
1997 Martha Iraheta of the Catholic University	2000 Shannon K Ramirez of the University of Texas, San Antonio
1997 Carlos Aguirre of the Catholic University	2000 University of Albuquerque
1998 Luis Maldonado of Georgetown University	2000 The Hispanic Society of America
1999 Abraham Smith of Howard University	2000 University of California, Los Angeles (UCLA)
1999 "The first endowment scholarship for Hispanic students at the University of Miami"	2000 Jane Garrido of the University of Virginia

During the summer of 2000, the Hispanic Division of the Library of Congress hosted 12 interns. Pictured here are 11: Georgina Franco Forrester (Brazil), Celia Cibeiro (Brazil), Juan Carlos Román (Puerto Rico), Gemma Ivern (Spain), Nora Luaces (Argentina), Irisnéea Gomez de Lopes (Brasil), Melissa Guy (Washington State) Jane Garrido (Colombia), Carmen Menéndez (El Salvador), Gino de Luca (Colombia) and Damaris Raquel Martínez (El Salvador).

"Each of these had a successful career after their experience in learning to work in a large research library."
Dr. Georgette M. Dorn
Chief of the Hispanic Division
The Library of Congress

"....these scholarships mean so much to our University community, but more specifically, our Hispanic community. We truly appreciate your company's leadership in promoting excellence in education assisting Hispanic students to achieve their academic goals."
Steven Clark Director
University of Miami

"I am pleased to express my personal thanks to TIYM for its support of the $2,000 scholarship. Scholarships not only provide a financial motivation to attend school, but also send an important message to the recipient. That message is that individuals and businesses in the commmunity are there to help them realize their dreams."
Ricardo Romo
President, The University of Texas at San Antonio

Scholarsite.com Financial Aid

yudas financieras en Scholarsite.com

ow to Use this Guide

is section summarizes 42 sources of financial aid, including ιolarships, internships, fellowships and grants for a variety of ademic levels. These opportunities were selected for their focus on spanic students, and are part of TIYM's Scholar$ite database, ιich currently includes information on more than 600,000 ιolastic financial aid opportunities from more than 40,000 ιding sources. The Scholar$ite database is available on-line at vw.scholarsite.com.

The scholarship summaries included here provide information out the sponsoring organization, its address, the program name, d details of each opportunity.

Scholar$ite offers a $1,000 monthly Scholarship Giveaway!

---

ierican Association of Hispanic tified Public Accountants
rthern California Chapter Scholarship mmittee
). Box 26109
a Francisco, CA 94126

Scholarship
Contact: Laura Martinez
Tel: (415) 957-3100
Email: laura.e.martinez@us.pwcglobal.com
Eligible Inst.: US schools in Northern California
Deadline: October 25
Requirements: This scholarship is available to Hispanic students enrolled at accredited universities in Northern California. Applicants must be studying in the field of accounting and must be junior or senior undergraduates with a minimum GPA of 3.0.

Annual Awards: $1000

ιolarship Committee
) N. Main St. #406
a Antonio, TX 78205

Scholarship
Contact: Vivian Coto
Tel: (203) 255-7003
Email: aahcpa@netscape.net
Eligible Inst.: US schools
Deadline: September 15
Requirements: This scholarship is available to students of Hispanic descent who are enrolled in a graduate progam with an accounting emphasis or who are in the last year of a five-year accounting program and have a minimum GPA of 3.0. Financial need and community involvement are considered.

Annual Awards: Varies

American Institute for Studies Abroad
102 Greenwich Ave.
Greenwich, CT 06830

3   Beca para Minorías de AIFS
Contact: Ann Decker
Tel: (800) 727-2437
Eligible Inst.: US & Intl. schools
Requirements: This program provides opportunity for study in Austria, England, France, Germany, Italy, Mexico, or Spain.

Annual Awards: Varies

Amigos Scholarship Foundation, Inc.
c/o Partners for Community Development
901 Superior Ave.
Sheboygan, WI 53081

4   Scholarship
Tel: (414) 459-2780
Eligible Inst.: US schools
Resident of: Wisconsin
Requirements: This scholarship is available to Hispanic-American residents of Sheboygan County, Wisconsin planning to enter college or continue their education. Recipients must be willing to recruit other Hispanics to take part in this scholarship and must be willing to work as spokespersons for education to Hispanics.

Annual Awards: $1500

Association of Hispanic Affairs in Private Colleges and Universities
817 W. 34th St.
Los Angeles, CA 90089-2991

---

5   Scholarship
Tel: (213) 743-5374
Eligible Inst.: US schools
Requirements: This scholarship is available to students with financial need.

Annual Awards: Varies

AT&T
Management Employment Office
100 Southgate Parkway
Morristown, NJ 07960

6   Internship
Eligible Inst.: AT&T
Requirements: Internships are available to qualified applicants.

Annual Awards: Varies

Azusa Pacific University
Office of Multi-Ethnic Programs
P.O. Box 7000, 901 E. Alosta Ave.
Azusa, CA 91702-7000

7   TELACU Scholarship
Tel: (626) 815-6000 X3720 (800) TALK APU
Email: admissions@apu.edu
Eligible Inst.: Azusa Pacific University
Resident of: CA
Citizenship: US Residents
Deadline: April 1
Requirements: This scholarship is available to Hispanic/Latino undergraduate students. Applicants must be U.S. citizens and/or residents of Los Angeles County, with preference given to those who come from the following communities: East Los Angeles, Bell Gardens,

---

Commerce, Huntington Park, Montebello, Monterey Park, South Gate or the City of Los Angeles. Applicants must be incoming or returning students of Azusa Pacific University.

Annual Awards: $3000/yr

California State University, Fresno
Scholarship Office
Joyal Administration Bldg. #296
Fresno, CA 93740-8027

8 Cesar Chavez Scholars Program Scholarship
Tel: (559) 294-2200 (559) 278-2182
Eligible Inst.: California State University, Fresno
Requirements: This scholarship is available to Hispanic students who demonstrate merit, financial need and academic promise.

Annual Awards: Varies

California State University, Fullerton
Department of Sociology
Humanities, 730M
Fullerton, CA 92834

9 Cathy Torres Memorial Scholarship
Tel: (714) 278-2011
Eligible Inst.: California State University, Fullerton
Deadline: April 15
Requirements: This scholarship is available to Mexican American undergraduate continuing sociology majors. Applicants must demonstrate community involvement and a minimum GPA of 3.0 (3.2 in sociology).

Annual Awards: $500

Educational Opportunity Program Office
University Hall 230
Fullerton, CA 92834

10 American Golf, Tecate, Tlaquepaque, CSU Hispanic Scholarship
Tel: (714) 278-2011 (714) 278-2407
Fax: (714) 278-3772
Email: dharris@fullerton.edu
Eligible Inst.: California State University, Fullerton
Deadline: April 15
Requirements: This scholarship is available to students entering as first time freshmen or transfer students. Applicants must have a minimum GPA of 2.5, Consideration will be given to SAT scores, ACT scores, and school and community activities.

Annual Awards: Varies

School of Business Administration & Economics
Dean's Office, Langsdorf Hall 700
Fullerton, CA 92834

11 Francisco J. Valle Scholarship
Contact: Ray Murillo, Assistant Dean
Tel: (714) 278-2011

Eligible Inst.: California State University, Fullerton
Deadline: March 2
Requirements: This scholarship is available to Hispanic business students in good standing (minimum GPA of 2.0).

Annual Awards: $1000

12 La Puerta de Oportunidad Scholarship
Contact: Ray Murillo, Assistant Dean
Tel: (714) 278-2011
Eligible Inst.: California State University, Fullerton
Deadline: March 15
Requirements: This scholarship is available to Hispanic juniors or seniors with a minimum of two semesters remaining for their degree and a minimum cumulative GPA of 3.0. Consideration is given to financial need, personal commitment and sacrifice.

Annual Awards: Varies

School of Human Dev. & Community Service
HDCS Dean's Office, EC 324
Fullerton, CA 92834

13 Marilyn C. Brewer Scholarship
Tel: (714) 278-2011
Eligible Inst.: California State University, Fullerton
Resident of: CA
Citizenship: US Citizens, US Residents
Deadline: November 19
Requirements: This scholarship is available to new and returning Hispanic female CSUF students who have applied and are admissible or who have been accepted for the Multiple Subject Credential Program which requires graduate admission to the university, completion of two Pre-requisite courses, passing scores on CBEST and Praxis examinations. Applicants must be U.S. citizens and residents of Orange County.

Annual Awards: $1500

Concerned Media Professionals
c/o Tucson Daily Star
P.O. Box 26807
Tucson, AZ 85726

14 Tony Villegas Scholarship for Hispanics
Eligible Inst.: US schools in Arizona
Citizenship: US Residents
Deadline: March 31
Requirements: This scholarship is available to university or college juniors who are majoring in print or broadcast journalism. Applicants must be attending school in Arizona.

Annual Awards: Varies

Connecticut Association of Latin Americans in Higher Education, Inc
c/o Gateway Community - Technical College
60 Sargent Dr.
New Haven, CT 06511

15 Freshman Scholarship
Contact: Dr. Wilson Luna
Eligible Inst.: US schools
Resident of: CT
Citizenship: US Citizens, US Residents
Deadline: April 15
Requirements: This scholarship is available to h school seniors or students with a GED equi lent. Applicants must be involved with a committed to activities to promote Latinos their pursuit of education, must be accepted admission to an accredited institution of hig education, and must have a minimum GPA 3.0 for all completed school work. Applica must be U.S. citizens or permanent reside must have been residents of Connecticut for preceding 12 months, and must demonstrate nancial need. Applicants must be Latino.

Annual Awards: $500

16 Undergraduate Scholarship
Contact: Dr. Wilson Luna
Eligible Inst.: US schools
Resident of: CT
Citizenship: US Citizens, US Residents
Deadline: April 15
Requirements: This scholarship is available to h school seniors or students with a GED equi lent. Applicants must be involved with a committed to activities to promote Latinos their pursuit of education, must be accepted admission to an accredited institution of hig education, and must have a minimum GPA 3.0 for all completed school work. Applica must be U.S. citizens or permanent resider must have been residents of Connecticut for preceding 12 months, and must demonstrate nancial need. Applicants must be Latino.

Annual Awards: $500

Hispanic Council on International Relations
111 19th St. NW #1000
Washington, DC 20036

17 Fellowship
Contact: Lisa Bedolla, Program Administrato
Tel: (202) 776-1754
Eligible Inst.: US schools
Requirements: This fellowship is available to you Hispanic Americans. The program will introdu Hispanic Americans to foreign policy professie and issues, providing them with networking portunities necessary to pursue such a career.

Annual Awards: Varies

18 Internship
Contact: Lisa Bedolla, Program Administrato
Tel: (202) 776-1754
Eligible Inst.: US schools
Requirements: This internship is available young Hispanic Americans. The program w introduce Hispanic Americans to foreign poli professions and issues, providing them w

networking opportunities necessary to pursue such a career.

Annual Awards: Varies

spanic Scholarship Fund
D. Box 728
e Sansome St. #1000
n Francisco, CA 94104

College Retention/General Program
Tel: (877) 473-4636
Email: info@hsf.net
Eligible Inst.: US schools
Citizenship: US Citizens, US Residents
Deadline: October 15
Requirements: This program assists Latinos earning their bachelor's degrees at four-year institutions. Applicants must have completed 15 credits of college work, have a minimum GPA of 2.5, and be enrolled full-time at a college in the US or Puerto Rico. Applicants must be U.S. citizens or permanent residents of Hispanic background.

Annual Awards: $2000

Community College Transfer Program
Tel: (877) 473-4636
Email: info@hsf.net
Eligible Inst.: US schools
Citizenship: US Citizens, US Residents
Deadline: October 15
Requirements: This program assists Latinos making the transition from community colleges to four-year institutions. Scholarships are available for graduating or transferring community college students who have the potential to succeed at a four-year university.

Annual Awards: $600

High School Program
Tel: (877) 473-4636
Email: info@hsf.net
Eligible Inst.: US schools
Citizenship: US Citizens, US Residents
Deadline: October 15
Requirements: This program assists Latinos making the transition from high school to college. High school seniors are eligible for scholarships if they have a minimum GPA of 3.0 and have been accepted to a college program.

Annual Awards: Varies

Professional Program
Tel: (877) 473-4636
Email: info@hsf.net
Eligible Inst.: US schools
Citizenship: US Citizens, US Residents
Deadline: October 15
Requirements: This program assists Latinos in certain professional programs who will serve as future leaders for the Latino community. The program focuses on professions such as law, medicine, business, engineering, government, and the nonprofit sector.

Annual Awards: Varies

Indiana University Northwest
3400 Broadway
Gary, IN 46408

23 Andrew Fernandez Memorial Scholarship
Tel: (219) 980-6991 (800) 437-5409
Email: wlee@iunhawl.iun.indiana.edu
Eligible Inst.: Indiana University Northwest
Requirements: This scholarship is available to an outstanding student of Hispanic descent.

Annual Awards: $500

Knox College
Office of Admissions
Box K-148
Galesburg, IL 61401-4999

24 National Hispanic Scholarship
Tel: (800) 678-KNOX (309) 341-7100
Fax: (309) 341-7070
Email: admission@knox.edu
Eligible Inst.: Knox College
Deadline: February 15
Requirements: This scholarship is available to students who receive Finalist or Semifinalist status in the National Hispanic Scholarship program.

Annual Awards: $6000-$8000/yr

Latino Student Fund
P.O. Box 407
Washington, DC 20044-0407

25 Financial Aid
Tel: (202) 626-6639 Fax: (202) 626-6780
Eligible Inst.: US schools
Requirements: Scholarships are available to Latino families interested in parochial or magnet schools for their children in grades K-12.

Annual Awards: Varies

Montana State University–Billings
Financial Aid Office
McMullen Hall #103, 1500 North 30th St.
Billings, MT 59101-0298

26 Hearst Endowed Scholarhsip
Tel: (406) 657-2011 (800) 565-MSUB
Eligible Inst.: Montana State University Billings
Deadline: March 1
Requirements: This scholarship is available to students of Hispanic descent. Applicants must have a minimum GPA of 2.5, and must demonstrate community/extracurricular involvement.

Annual Awards: $350

27 Hispanic Scholarship
Tel: (406) 657-2011 (800) 565-MSUB
Eligible Inst.: Montana State University Billings
Deadline: March 1
Requirements: This scholarship is available to students of Hispanic descent with a minimum GPA

of 2.5. Applicants must demonstrate community and extracurricular involvement.

Annual Awards: $230

Mott Community College
Office Institutional Development
CM 1027, 1401 E. Court Street
Flint, MI 48503-2089

28 Joe Benavidez Scholarship
Tel: (810) 762-0144 (810) 762-8590
Fax: (810) 762-0257
Eligible Inst.: Mott Community College
Requirements: This scholarship is available to Hispanic students with a minimum GPA of 3.0 and financial need.

Annual Awards: Varies

National Hispanic Foundation for the Arts

29 Entertainment Industry Scholarship
Eligible Inst.: New York University, Columbia University, Yale University, University of California at Los Angeles, University of Southern California
Requirements: This scholarship is available to students who have been accepted or are enrolled as full-time graduate students at selected schools. Applicants must be pursuing degrees leading to careers in the entertainment arts and industry, including: acting, theater, radio and television, film, music, set design, costume design, lighting design, motion picture production, writing. Applicants may also be studying law or business with concentrations in entertainment-related fields. Applicants must be students in good standing with a minimum GPA of 3.0

Annual Awards: Varies

Northern Arizona University
Office of Student Financial Aid
P.O. Box 4108
Flagstaff, AZ 86011-4108

30 Bob Robles Memorial Scholarship Fund
Tel: (520) 523-4951 Fax: (520) 523-1551
Email: finaid@nau.edu
Eligible Inst.: Northern Arizona University
Deadline: March 1
Requirements: This scholarship is available to undergraduate Hispanic students with a minimum GPA of 2.5 and financial need.

Annual Awards: $390

32 Los Hacheros Hispanic Alumni Scholarship
Tel: (520) 523-4951 Fax: (520) 523-1551
Email: finaid@nau.edu
Eligible Inst.: Northern Arizona University
Deadline: March 1

Requirements: This scholarship is available to undergraduate students with a minimum 2.5 GPA and involvement in high school, college and/or community Hispanic activities or organizations. Preference is given to Hispanic students.

Annual Awards: $500

Northwest Missouri State University
Financial Assistance Office
800 University Dr.
Maryville, MO 64468

32 Greater Kansas City Hispanic Scholarship
Tel: (660) 562-1363 (816) 562-1562
Email: admissions@acad.nwmissouri.edu
Eligible Inst.: Northwest Missouri State University
Resident of: MO
Citizenship: US Citizens, US Residents
Deadline: March 9
Requirements: This scholarship is available to U.S. citizens or permanent residents who are of Hispanic descent. Applicants must be accepted or enrolled in a college or university and must be residents of the metropolitan Kansas City area (generally defined as Clay, Jackson, Johnson, and Wyandotte Counties).

Annual Awards: Varies

Oregon State Scholarship Commission
1500 Valley River Dr. #100
Eugene, OR 97401-2130

33 NIKE Hispanic Education Scholarship
Tel: (800) 452-8807 (541) 687-7400
Fax: (541) 687-7419
Eligible Inst.: US schools
Resident of: OR
Requirements: This scholarship is available to graduating high school seniors who are Hispanic Oregon residents.

Annual Awards: Varies

Pepperdine University
Office of Student Financial Assistance
24255 Pacific Coast Highway
Malibu, CA 90263

34 Hispanic Alumni Scholarship
Tel: (310) 456-4211 (310) 456-4000
Fax: (310) 456-4357
Eligible Inst.: Pepperdine University
Deadline: March 1
Requirements: This scholarship is available to qualified students.

Annual Awards: Varies

San Antonio College
Student Financial Services
1300 San Pedro Ave., Fletcher Admin. Center
San Antonio, TX 78212-4299

35 Allstate Foundation Scholarship
Tel: (210) 733-2150 Fax: (210) 733-2689
Eligible Inst.: San Antonio College
Deadline: May 1
Requirements: This scholarship is available to Hispanic nursing students with a minimum GPA of 2.0 and financial need. Applicants must have completed Level I by the time of the award.

Annual Awards: Varies

TELACU Education Foundation
Scholarship Program
5400 E. Olympic Blvd. #300
Los Angeles, CA 90022

36 Southern California Edison Scholarship
Contact: Veronica L. Soliz, Executive Director
Tel: (323) 721-1655 Fax: (323) 724-3372
Eligible Inst.: US schools
Resident of: CA
Citizenship: US Citizens, US Residents
Deadline: April 3
Requirements: This grant is available to graduating high school seniors who plan to pursue teaching careers. Applicants must attend school or live in an area served by Southern California Edison. Applicants must attend one of the following schools on a full-time basis: East Los Angeles College, Cal State campuses at Fullerton, Long Beach, Los Angeles and Northridge, Cal Poly Pomona, UC Irvine, UCLA, Azusa Pacific University, Loyola Marymount University, USC and Whittier College.

Annual Awards: $5,000

University of Akron
Office of Student Financial Aid
Akron, OH 44325-6211

37 National Hispanic Scholarship
Tel: (330) 972-7032 (800) 621-3874
Fax: (330) 972-7139
Email: admissions@uakron.edu
Eligible Inst.: University of Akron
Requirements: This scholarship is available to entering freshmen who are finalists in the National Hispanic Scholarship competition.

Annual Awards: Tuition+fees

University of Connecticut
Research Foundation, Rm. 117
Storrs, CT 06269

38 Rafael Cordero Graduate School Fellowship
Tel: (860) 486-3619 Fax: (860) 486-0945
Email: faid@uconnvm.uconn.edu
Eligible Inst.: University of Connecticut
Resident of: PR
Requirements: This fellowship is available to Puerto Ricans entering a Ph.D. program with regular graduate status. Candidates for this fellowship

may be recommended to the dean of the Graduate School by any graduate faculty member.

Annual Awards: Varies

University of Missouri-St. Louis
Student Financial Aid Office
8001 Natural Bridge
St. Louis, MO 63121

39 BECA Scholarship
Tel: (314) 516-5526
Email: sfinaid@umslvma.umsl.edu
Eligible Inst.: University of Missouri St. Louis
Deadline: March 31
Requirements: This scholarship is available graduate or undergraduate students at any level with a minimum cumulative GPA of 3.0. Preference is given to Hispanic and Latin students

Annual Awards: Varies

University of Southern California
Office of Admission and Financial Aid
University Park
Los Angeles, CA 90089-0911

40 National Hispanic Scholarship
Tel: (213) 740-1111
Eligible Inst.: University of Southern California
Deadline: December 10
Requirements: This scholarship is available to entering freshmen who have been designated National Hispanic Scholars and have selected USC as their first-choice college.

Annual Awards: Half Tuition

School of Public Administration
VonKleinSmid Center, 232
Los Angeles, CA 90089-0041

41 Paracelsus Fellowship
Contact: Kimberly C. Ellis, Coordinator, Graduate Recruitment and Admissions
Tel: (213) 740-6842 Fax: (213) 740-7573
Email: kellis@usc.edu
Eligible Inst.: University of Southern California
Requirements: This fellowship is awarded to Hispanic students in Health Administration.

Annual Awards: Varies

Washington University in St. Louis
Campus Box 1089, One Brookings Drive
St. Louis, MO 63130-4899

42 Scholarship for Hispanic Students
Contact: Peter R. Guzman, Coordinator of Hispanic Recruitment
Tel: (314) 935-7483 (800) 638-0700
Email: PeterGuzman@aismail.wustel.edu
Eligible Inst.: Washington University in St. Louis
Deadline: January 15
Requirements: This scholarship is available to incoming freshmen of Hispanic descent.

Annual Awards: Varies

National Association of Women Judges

815 Fifteenth Street, N.W. • Suite 601 • Washington, D.C. 20005

Striving for Justice in the American Legal System

The mission of the National Association of Women Judges (NAWJ) is to look out for disadvantaged groups who so often find themselves struggling for equal justice and access to the courts – groups such as the young, the elderly, minorities, the underprivileged and persons with disabilities. As NAWJ long has recognized, women in such groups face particular barriers to receiving fair treatment in our legal system.

NAWJ successfully focuses attention on social justice issues that affect women, children, families and other vulnerable groups. In particular, NAWJ currently is developing judicial education programs to ensure that Latinos and other immigrants receive equal justice in court.

For further information, please view NAWJ'S website at www.NAWJ.org or contact NAWJ at the address above, tel: 202-393-0222, fax: 202-393-0125, e-mail: NAWJ@prodigy.net.

CAREER &
BUSINESS OPPORTUNITIES
OPORTUNIDADES DE
EMPLEOS Y NEGOCIOS

TOP HISPANIC
COMPANIES
GRANDES EMPRESAS
HISPANAS

VOLUNTARY
HEALTH AGENCIES
AGENCIAS VOLUNTARIAS
DE SALUD

COMMERCIAL CONTACTS
IN LATIN AMERICA
LOS CONTACTOS
COMERCIALES EN AMERICA LATINA

ANUARIOHISPANO.COM
HISPANICYEARBOOK.COM

STUDENT
FINANCIAL AID
AYUDA FINANCIERA
PARA ESTUDIANTES

HISPANIC
PUBLICATIONS
PUBLICACIONES
HISPANAS

HISPANIC
ORGANIZATIONS & MEDIA
ORGANIZACIONES
HISPANAS Y MEDIOS

OPPORTUNITIES IN THE
U.S. DEPARTMENT OF DEFENSE
OPORTUNIDADES EN EL
DEPT. DE DEFENSA DE LOS EUA

2001

HAPCOA National Training Conference
Sacramento, California

Join us at the new

Sheraton Grand Hotel in Sacramento

August 21-24, 2001

Located in the heart of Downtown, the Sheraton
is walking distance to California's State Capitol
Building, Sacramento's historic Old Town, the
IMAX Theaters, shopping and more!

INFORMATION CONTACTS
www.hapcoa.com

Sponsorship and Exhibitor Information .... Frank Elizondo at NHR Consultants●(202) 484-8261

Conference Information .... Steve Campas at the Sacramento Police Dept.●(916) 264-5121

Jess Quintero at the HAPCOA National Office: .... Washington, DC●(301) 449-7967

**Hotel Reservations: Sheraton Hotels
(800) 325-3535
(Please state your attendance at the HAPCOA Conferene for special rates)**

Guaranteed Student Loan (GSL) Offices

Oficinas de préstamos garantizados para estudiantes (GSL)

Loans

UNITED STUDENT AID FUNDS
P.O. Box 6180
Indianapolis, IN 46206-6180
(317) 849-6510/ (800) 562-6872
Carl Dalstrom, Pres.

Loans and State Aid

ALABAMA STUDENT LOAN PROGRAM
Administered by KHEAA
100 N. Union Street, # 308
Montgomery, AL 36104
(334) 265-9720
Wayne Whitney, Program Coord.

Loans and State Aid

UNITED STUDENT AID FUNDS, INC. - ALASKA
P.O. Box 6180
Indianapolis, IN 46206-6180
(317) 849-6510
Carl Dalstrom, Pres.

Loans

UNITED STUDENT AID FUNDS, INC. - ARIZONA
25 South Arizona Place, #400
Chandler, AZ 85225
(480) 814-9988
John F. Crowe, Vice Pres.,
Arizona Program

Loans

STUDENT LOAN GUARANTEE FOUNDATION OF ARKANSAS
219 South Victory Street
Little Rock, AR 72201-1884
(501) 372-1491
Ronnie L. Nichoalds, Exec. Dir.

Loans and State Aid

CALIFORNIA STUDENT AID COMMISSION
P.O. Box 419026
Rancho Cordova, CA 95741
10834 International Drive
Rancho Cordova, CA 95670
(916) 526-8028

Loans

COLORADO STUDENT LOAN PROGRAM
One Denver Place, South Terrace
999 18th Street, # 425
Denver, CO 80202-2471
(303) 305-3000
Robert Fomer, Exec. Dir.

Loans

CONNECTICUT STUDENT LOAN FOUNDATION
P.O. Box 1009
Rocky Hill, CT 06067
525 Brook St.
Rocky Hill, CT 06067
(860) 257-4001
Mark W. Valenti, Pres.

Loans and State Aid

PENNSYLVANIA HIGHER EDUCATION ASSISTANCE AGENCY (DE)
1200 North Seventh Street
Harrisburg, PA 17102-1444
(717) 720-2850
Michael H. Hershock, Pres.

Loans

AMERICAN STUDENT ASSISTANCE (DC)
330 Stuart Street
Boston, MA 02116
(800) 999-9080
Paul C. Combe, Pres.

Loans

FLORIDA DEPARTMENT OF EDUCATION
Office of Student Financial Assistance
107 West Gaines Street, #70
Tallahassee, FL 32399
(850) 488-4095
Noah Powers, Dir.

Loans and State Aid

GEORGIA HIGHER EDUCATION ASSISTANCE CORPORATION
2082 E. Exchange Place, #200
Tucker, GA 30084
(770) 724-9132
E. Glenn Newsome, Exec. Dir.

Loans

UNITED STUDENT AID FUNDS, INC. - HAWAII
1314 South King Street, #861
Honolulu, HI 96814
(808) 593-2262
Lorraine M. Teniya, Exec. Dir.,
Hawaii Program

Loans

STUDENT LOAN FUND OF IDAHO, INC.
P.O. Box 730
Fruitland, ID 83619-0730
(208) 452-4058
Carrol Lee Lawhorn, Exec. Dir.
(New Loans - contact Northwest Education Loan Association in Washington)

Loans and State Aid

ILLINOIS STUDENT ASSISTANCE COMMISSION
1755 Lake Cook Road
Deerfield, IL 60015
(847) 948-8500
Larry E. Matejka, Exec. Dir.

500 W. Monroe, 3rd Fl.
Springfield, IL 62704
(217) 782-6767
Larry E. Matejka, Exec. Dir.

Loans and State Aid

UNITED STUDENT AID FUNDS, INC.
P.O. Box 6180
Indianapolis, IN 46206-6180
(317) 849-6510
Carl Dalstrom, Pres.

Loans and State Aid

IOWA COLLEGE STUDENT AID COMMISSION
200 10th Street, 4th Fl.
Des Moines, IA 50309-3609
(515) 281-4890
Gary W. Nichols, Exec. Dir.

Loans

UNITED STUDENT AID FUNDS, INC. - KANSAS
3 Townsite Plaza, #220
120 SE Sixth Street
Topeka, KS 66603
(913) 234-0072
Larry Viterna, Vice Pres., Kansas Program

Loans and State Aid

KENTUCKY HIGHER EDUCATION ASSISTANCE AUTHORITY
(KHEAA)
1050 U.S. 127 South, #102
Frankfort, KY 40601
(502) 696-7200
Londa Wolanin, Exec. Dir.

Loans and State Aid

OFFICE OF STUDENT FINANCIAL ASSISTANCE, LOUISIANA STUDENT FINANCIAL ASSISTANCE COMMISSION
P.O. Box #91202
Baton Rouge, LA 70821-9202
1885 Wooddale Blvd.
Baton Rouge, LA 70806
(225) 922-1012
Jack L. Guinn, Exec. Dir.

Loans and State Aid

FINANCE AUTHORITY OF MAINE
State House Station #199
P.O. Box 949
Augusta, ME 04332-0949
5 Community Drive
Augusta, ME 04330
(207) 623-3263
Charlie Spief, Dir.

Loans and State Aid

UNITED STUDENT AID FUNDS, INC. - MARYLAND
The RCM & D Building
555 Fairmount Avenue, # 310
Towson, MD 21286
(410) 337-0274
David Manning, Executive Director

Loans and State Aid

AMERICAN STUDENT ASSISTANCE
330 Stuart St.
Boston, MA 02116
(800) 999-9080
Paul C. Combe, Pres.

MICHIGAN

Loans

MICHIGAN HIGHER EDUCATION ASSISTANCE AUTHORITY
P.O. Box 30466
Lansing, MI 48909-7966
608 W. Allegan
Lansing, MI 48933
(517) 373-3399
H. Jack Nelson, Exec. Dir.

MINNESOTA

Loans and State Aid

NORTHSTAR GUARANTEE INC.
P.O. Box #64102
St. Paul, MN 55164-0102
444 Cedar Street, #1910
St. Paul, MN 55101
(952) 290-8780
Taige Thornton, Pres.

MISSISSIPPI

Loans

UNITED STUDENT AID FUNDS, INC. MISSISSIPPI
6508 Dogwood View Parkway, # A
Jackson, MS 39213
(601) 362-2770
Louanne Lanpston, Mktg. Dir.

MISSOURI

Loans and State Aid

MISSOURI COORDINATING BOARD FOR HIGHER EDUCATION
3515 Amazonas Drive
Jefferson City, MO 65109
(573) 751-2361
Lynn Hearnes, Dir.

MONTANA

Loans and State Aid

MONTANA GUARANTEED STUDENT LOAN PROGRAM
2500 East Broadway
Helena, MT 59620-3103
(406) 444-6594
Arlene J. Hannawalt, Interim Dir.

NEBRASKA

Loans

NEBRASKA STUDENT LOAN PROGRAM, INC. (NSLP)
P.O. Box 82507
Lincoln, NE 68501-2507
1300 "O" Street
Lincoln, NE 68508
(402) 475-8686
Nancy J. Wiederspan, Pres.

NEVADA

(Contact United Student Aid Funds, Inc. in Indiana)

NEW HAMPSHIRE

Loans

NEW HAMPSHIRE HIGHER EDUCATION ASSISTANCE FOUNDATION
P.O. Box 877
Concord, NH 03302
4 Barrell Court
Concord, NH 03301
(603) 225-6612
Rene Drouin, Pres.

NEW JERSEY

Loans and State Aid

NEW JERSEY HIGHER EDUCATION ASSISTANCE AUTHORITY
P.O. Box 540
4 Quakerbridge Plaza
Trenton, NJ 08625
(609) 588-7944
Scott Freedman, Exec. Dir.

NEW MEXICO

Loans

NEW MEXICO STUDENT LOAN GUARANTEE CORPORATION
P.O. Box 27020
Albuquerque, NM 87125
3900 Osuna, NE
Albuquerque, NM 87109
(505) 345-3371
Woody Farber, Pres.

NEW YORK

Loans and State Aid

NEW YORK STATE HIGHER EDUCATION SERVICES CORPORATION
99 Washington Avenue
Albany, NY 12255
(518) 474-5592
Peter J. Keitel, Pres.

NORTH CAROLINA

Loans

NORTH CAROLINA STATE EDUCATION ASSISTANCE AUTHORITY
P.O. Box 14103
Research Triangle Park, NC 27709
UNC RTP Bldg., 10 Alexander Dr.
Research Triangle Park, NC 27709
(919) 549-8614
Stephen Brooks , Exec. Dir.

NORTH DAKOTA

Loans

STUDENT LOANS OF NORTH DAKOTA
P.O. Box 5509
Bismarck, ND 58506-5509
715 E. Broadway
Bismarck, ND 58502
(701) 328-5791
Julie A. Kubisiak, Dir.

OHIO

Loans

OHIO STUDENT LOAN COMMISSION
P.O. Box 16610
Columbus, OH 43266-0610
309 South Fourth Street
Columbus, OH 43266-0610
(614) 292-2307
Glendon Forgey, Exec. Dir.

OKLAHOMA

Loans

OKLAHOMA STATE REGENTS FOR HIGHER EDUCATION - GSLP
P.O. Box 3000
Oklahoma City, OK 73101
999 N.W. Grand Boulevard #300
Oklahoma City, OK 73118
(405) 858-4340
Alice Strong Simmons, Dir.

OREGON

Loans and State Aid

STUDENT ASSISTANCE COMMISSION
Valley River Office Park
1500 Valley River Drive #100
Eugene, OR 97401
(541) 687-7400
Jeff Svejcar, Exec. Dir.

PENNSYLVANIA

Loans and State Aid

PENNSYLVANIA HIGHER EDUCATION ASSISTANCE AGENCY
1200 North Seventh Street
Harrisburg, PA 17102-1444
(717) 720-2850
Michael H. Hershock, Pres.

PUERTO RICO

Loans

P.R. COUNCIL ON HIGHER EDUCATION
P.O. Box 19900
Minillas Station
San Juan, PR 00910-1900
(787) 724-7100
Sandra Espada, Sec.

RHODE ISLAND

Loans and State Aid

RHODE ISLAND HIGHER EDUCATION ASSISTANCE AUTHORITY
560 Jefferson Blvd.
Warwick, RI 02886
(401) 736-1100
William H. Hurry, Jr., Exec. Dir.

SOUTH CAROLINA

Loans

SOUTH CAROLINA STUDENT LOAN CORPORATION
P.O. Box 21487
Columbia, SC 29221
Interstate Center
16 Berryhill Road #210
Columbia, SC 29210
(803) 772-9480
William M. Mackie, Jr., Exec. Dir.

SOUTH DAKOTA

Loans

EDUCATION ASSISTANCE CORPORATION
115 First Avenue, S.W.
Aberdeen, SD 57401
(605) 225-6423
Clark Wold, Exec. Dir.

TENNESSEE

Loans and State Aid

TENNESSEE STUDENT ASSISTANCE CORP.
Parkway Towers
404 James Robertson Parkway #1950
Nashville, TN 37243-0820
(615) 741-1346
Ron Gambill, Exec. Dir.

TEXAS

Loans

TEXAS GUARANTEED STUDENT LOAN CORPORATION
P.O. Box 201635
Austin, TX 78720
(512) 219-5700
Milton G. Wright, Pres.

UTAH

Loans

UTAH HIGHER EDUCATION ASSISTANCE AUTHORITY
P.O. Box 45202
Salt Lake City, UT 84145-0202
(801) 321-7200
Chalmers Gail Norris, Exec. Dir.

VERMONT

Loans and State Aid

VERMONT STUDENT ASSISTANCE CORPORATION
P.O. Box 2000
Winooski, VT 05404
Champlain Mill
1 Main Street
Winooski, VT 05404
(802) 655-9602
Donald R. Vickers, Exec. Dir.

VIRGINIA

Loans and State Aid

STATE COUNCIL OF HIGHER EDUCATION FOR VIRGINIA
James Monroe Bldg.
101 N. 14th St., 10th Fl.
Richmond, VA 23219
(804) 225-3146
Phyllis Palmiero, Dir.

WASHINGTON

Loans

NORTHWEST EDUCATION LOAN ASSOCIATION
811 First Avenue, 500 Colman Bldg.
Seattle, WA 98104
(206) 461-5300
Rob Ungaro, Pres.

WEST VIRGINIA

Loans

PENNSYLVANIA HIGHER EDUCATION ASSISTANCE AGENCY (WV)
1200 North Seventh Street
Harrisburg, PA 17102-1444
(717) 720-2000
Michael H. Hershock, Pres.

WISCONSIN

Loans

GREAT LAKES HIGHER EDUCATION GUARANTY CORPORATION
P.O. Box 7858
Madison, WI 53707
2401 International Lane
Madison, WI 53704
(608) 246-1800
Richard D. George, Pres.

WYOMING

Loans

UNITED STUDENT AID FUNDS, INC. - WYOMING
1912 Capitol Avenue, #320
Cheyenne, WY 82001
(307) 635-3259
Jim Lintzenich, Pres.

Entrance Examinations/Sample Letter
Exámenes de Ingreso/Carta Modelo

The following is a list of entrance examinations utilized by most universities and colleges in the United States. The exams are used to assess knowledge, skills, and understanding of information. For more detailed information and applications, either write or call the testing service listed.
La siguiente es una lista de exámenes de ingreso, utilizados por la mayoría de las universidades en los Estados Unidos. Estos exámenes evalúan conocimientos, habilidades y comprensión. Para conseguir mayor información y solicitudes de inscripción, diríjase por carta o por teléfono a los centros examinadores que siguen a continuación.

AT THE UNDERGRADUATE LEVEL
SCHOLASTIC APTITUDE TEST (SAT) AMERICAN COLLEGE TEST (ACT)
Purpose: to assess student's aptitude in both verbal and mathematical skills that are associated with success at the undergraduate university level.

> SAT
> College Board
> P.O. Box 6200
> Princeton, NJ 08541
> (609) 771-7588
>
> ACT
> P.O. Box 168
> Iowa City , IA 52243
> (319) 337-1270 or (319) 337-1281

TEST OF ENGLISH AS A FOREIGN LANGUAGE (TOEFL)
Purpose: to assess the English proficiency of international students.

> Educational Testing Service
> Rosedale Rd.
> Princeton, NJ 08541
> (609) 921-9000
> Iowa City, Iowa 52243
> (609) 736-7100 or (319) 337-1281

AT THE GRADUATE LEVEL
GRADUATE MANAGEMENT ADMISSIONS TEST (GMAT)
Purpose: to measure general verbal and mathematical skill development, that are associated with success in the graduate study of management.

> Educational Testing Service
> Rosedale Rd.
> Princeton, NJ 08541
> (609) 736-7330 or (609) 921-9000

GRADUATE RECORDS EXAMINATION (GRE)
Purpose: to evaluate the academic qualifications of applicants to graduate schools. Exams are offered for different subjects.

> Educational Testing Service
> Rosedale Rd.
> Princeton, NJ 08541
> (609) 736-7670 or (609) 921-9000

MEDICAL COLLEGE ADMISSIONS TEST (MCAT)
Purpose: to evaluate the mastery of basic concepts in biology, chemistry (general and organic), and physics; facility with scientific problem solving and critical thinking; and writing skills.

> Medical College Admission Testing
> P.O. Box 4056
> Iowa City, IA 52243
> (319) 337-1000 or (319) 337-1281

LAW SCHOOL ADMISSIONS TEST (LSAT)
Purpose: to measure skills that are considered essential for success in law school; such as reading and comprehension of complex texts, the ability to reason critically, and the analysis and evaluation of the reasoning and argument of others.

> Law Services
> P.O. Box 2000
> 661 Penn St.
> Newtown, PA 18940-0998
> (215) 968-1001

Sample Letter
Carta Modelo

This letter is an example of how the student should write to the admissions office of the college or university to request applications and financial aid information.
Esta carta muestra como se debe pedir a la oficina de admisión de la universidad, la solicitud correspondiente y la información sobre ayuda financiera.

Visit
www.scholarsite.com

SAMPLE LETTER

YOUR NAME
YOUR ADDRESS

Date

Director of Admissions
Name of School
Address of School

To whom it may concern:

My name is X and I am a student at XYZ High School (or University). I am interested in the College/University of ABC. Could you please send me an application for admission and any information you have on financial aid.

I would also like to request information on grants, scholarships, and loans in the field of XYZ, as I am considering a major in that field.

Thank you for your help.

Sincerely,

Your name

Hispanic Serving Institutions

Insituciones de Educación Superior para Hispanos

The following colleges and universities have been designated as Hispanic Serving Institutions, and are members of the Hispanic Association of Colleges and Universities (HACU). HACU's mission is: to promote the development of member colleges and universities; to improve access to and the quality of post-secondary educational opportunities for Hispanic students; and to meet the needs of business, industry and government through the development and sharing of resources, information and expertise.

ADAMS STATE COLLEGE
Adams State College
Alamosa, CO 81102
J. Thomas Gilmore, President
(719) 587-7011 Fax: (719) 587-7522
www.adams.edu/

ALAMO COMMUNITY COLLEGE DISTRICT
Northwest Vista
3535 N. Ellison Dr.
San Antonio, TX 78251
Jacqueline Claunch, President
(210) 348-2020 Fax: (210) 348-2024
www.accd.edu

Palo Alto College
1400 W. Villaret Blvd.
San Antonio, TX 78224
Enrique Selis, President
(210) 921-5000 Fax: (210) 921-5310
www.accd.edu

San Antonio College
1300 San Pedro
San Antonio, TX 78212
Vern Loland, President
(210) 733-2000 Fax: (210) 733-2579
www.accd.edu

ALLAN HANCOCK COLLEGE
800 S. College Dr.
Santa Maria, CA 93454
Ann Foxworthy, President
(805) 922-6966 Fax: (805) 922-3477
www.hancock.cc.ca.us

ANTELOPE VALLEY COLLEGE
3041 W. Ave. K
Lancaster, CA 93536
Patricia Sandoval, President
(661) 722-6305 Fax: (661) 722-6351
www.avc.edu

ARIZONA WESTERN COLLEGE
9500 S. Ave 8E
Yuma, AZ 85365
Don Schoenin, President
(520) 317-6000 Fax: (520) 344-7730
www.awc.cc.az.us

BAKERSFIELD COMMUNITY COLLEGE
1801 Panorama Dr.
Bakersfield, CA 93305
Sandra Serrano, President
(661) 395-4011 Fax: (661) 395-4500
www.bc.cc.ca.us

BARRY UNIVERSITY
11300 N.E. 2nd Ave.
Miami Shores, FL 33161
Sr. Jeanne O'Laughlin, President
(305) 899-3000 Fax: (305) 899-2971
www.barry.edu

BOROUGH OF MANHATTAN COMMUNITY COLLEGE
199 Chambers St.
New York, NY 10007
Antonio Pérez, President
(212) 346-8000 Fax: (212) 346-8110
Email: amiddleton@bmcc.cuny.edu
www.bmcc.cuny.edu

BRONX COMMUNITY COLLEGE
University Avenue and West 181 St.
Bronx, NY 10453
Carolyn Williams, President
(718) 289-5100 Fax: (718) 289-6352
Email: Loretta.Scott@bcc.cuny.edu
http://csf1.bcc.cuny.edu/

CALIFORNIA STATE UNIVERSITY
9001 Stockdale Hwy.
Bakersfield, CA 93311
Charles B. Reed, Chancellor
(661) 664-3036 Fax: (661) 664-3389
Email: web@csub.edu
www.csub.edu/

Dominguez Hills
1000 E. Victoria St.
Carson, CA 90747
James E. Lyons, Sr., President
(310) 243-3300 Fax: (310) 516-3609
Email: webmaster@csudh.edu
www.csudh.edu/

Fresno
5241 N. Maple Ave.
Fresno, CA 93740
John D. Welty, President
(559) 278-2191 Fax: (559) 278-4812
Email: webmaster@csufresno.edu
www.csufresno.edu

Fullerton
800 N. State College Blvd.
Fullerton, CA 92834
Dr. Milton Gordon, President
(714) 278-2300 Fax: (714) 278-7549
Email: dgordon@fullerton.edu@fullerton.edu
www.fullerton.edu

Los Angeles
5151 State University Dr.
Los Angeles, CA 90032
James M. Rosser, President
(323) 343-3000 Fax: (323) 343-3888
Email: sconroy@cslanet.calstatela.edu
www.calstatela.edu

Monterey Bay
100 Campus Center
Seaside, CA 93955
Peter Smith, President
(831) 582-3330 Fax: (831) 582-3087
Email: peter_smith@monterey.edu
www.monterey.edu

Northridge
18111 Nordhoff St.
Northridge, CA 91330
Jolene Koester, President
(818) 677-1200 Fax: (818) 677-3766
Email: jolene.koester@csun.edu
www.csun.edu

San Bernardino
5500 University Pkwy
San Bernardino, CA 92407
Dr. Albert Karnig, President
(909) 880-5000 Fax: (909) 880-7034
Email: akarnig@csusb.edu
www.csusb.edu

CARLOS ALBIZU UNIVERSITY
2173 NW 99th Ave.
Miami, FL 33172
Salvador Santiago-Negrón, President
(305) 593-1223 Fax: (305) 592-7930
ssantiago@prip.ccas.edu
www.mip.ccas.edu

CENTRAL ARIZONA COLLEGE
8470 N. Overfield Rd.
Coolidge, AZ 85228
Dr. John J. Klein, President
(520) 426-4444 Fax: (520) 426-4271
Email: paul_grillos@python.cac.cc.az.us
www.cac.cc.az.us

CERRITOS COLLEGE
11110 Alondra Blvd.
Norwalk, CA 90650
Dr. Morgan Lynn, President/CEO
(562) 860-2451 Fax: (562) 467-5068

Email: mrichardson@cerritos.edu
www.cerritos.edu

CHAFFEY COLLEGE
5885 Haven Ave.
Rancho Cucamonga, CA 91737
Jerry W. Young, President
(909) 987-1737 Fax: (909) 466-2875
Email: ypalos@chaffey.cc.ca.us
www.chaffey.cc.ca.us

THE CITY UNIVERSITY OF NEW YORK
Hostos Community College
500 Grand Concourse
Bronx, NY 10451
Dolores M. Fernández, President
(718) 518-4444 Fax: (718) 518-4256
Email: dfernandez@hostos.cuny.edu
www.hostos.cuny.edu

John Jay College of Criminal Justice
899 Tenth Ave.
New York, NY 10019
Gerald Lynch, President
(212) 237-8000 Fax: (212) 237-8777
Email: president@jjay.cuny.edu
www.jjay.cuny.edu

LaGuardia Community College
31-10 Thomson Avenue
Long Island City, NY 11101
Gail O. Mellow, President
(718) 482-7200 Fax: (718) 482-5112
Email: gmellow@lagcc.cuny.edu
www.lagcc.cuny.edu

Lehman College
250 Bedford Park Blvd. West
Bronx, NY 10468
Ricardo Fernández, President
(718) 960-8000 Fax: (718) 960-8712
Email: fori@lehman.cuny.edu
www.lehman.cuny.edu

COASTAL BEND COLLEGE
3800 Charco Rd.
Beeville, TX 78102
Dr. John Brockman, President
(361) 358-2838 Fax: (361) 354-2254
Email: martinez@bcc.cc.tx.us
www.cbc.cc.tx.us

THE COLLEGE OF AERONAUTICS
86-01 23rd Ave.
Flushing, NY 11369
John Fitzpatric, President
(800) PRO-AERO Fax: (718) 429-0256
Email: fitzpatric@aero.edu
www.aero.edu

THE COLLEGE OF SANTA FE
1600 St. Michael's Dr.
Santa Fe, NM 87505
Linda N. Hanson, President
(505) 473-6011 Fax: (505) 473-6125
Email: president@csf.edu
www.csf.edu

COLLEGE OF THE DESERT
Desert Community College District
43500 Monterey Ave.
Palm Desert, CA 92260
William R. Kroonen, President
(760) 346-8041 Fax: (760) 776-0136
Email: wkroonen@dccd.cc.ca.us
http://desert.cc.ca.us/

COLLEGE OF THE SEQUOIAS
915 S. Mooney Blvd.
Visalia, CA 93277
Kamiran S. Badrkhan, President
(559) 730-3700 Fax: (559) 737-4820
Email: obiWEBkanobi@giant.sequoias.cc.ca.us
http://zeus.sequoias.cc.ca.us/

COMMUNITY COLLEGE OF DENVER
P.O. Box 173363
Denver, CO 80217
George Delaney, Acting President
(303) 556-2411 Fax: (303) 556-3586
Email: cd_george@cccs.cccoes.edu
http://ccd.rightchoice.org/

DEL MAR COLLEGE
101 Baldwin Blvd.
Corpus Christi, TX 78404
Olga Gonzales, President
(361) 698-1200 Fax: (361) 698-1595
Email: colrel@delmar.edu
www.delmar.edu

EAST LOS ANGELES COLLEGE
1301 Avenida Cesar Chavez
Monterey Park, CA 91754
Ernest H. Moreno, President
(323) 265-8650 Fax: (323) 265-8688
Email: morenoeh@laccd.cc.ca.us
www.elac.cc.ca.us

EASTERN NEW MEXICO UNIVERSITY
Portales Campus
Portales, NM 88130
Everett L. Frost, President
(505) 562-1011 Fax: (505) 562-2118
Email: froste@email.enmu.edu
www.enmu.edu

Roswell Campus
P.O. Box 6000
Roswell, NM 88201
Travis Kirkland, Provost
(505) 624-7000 Fax: (505) 624-7144
Email: kirkland@lib.enmuros.cc.nm.us
www.roswell.enmu.edu

Ruidoso Instruction Center
709 Mechem Dr.
Ruidoso, NM 88345
Everet Frost, President
(505) 257-2120 Fax: (505) 257-9409
Email: kluthes@enmu.edu
www.ruidoso.enmu.edu

EL PASO COMMUNITY COLLEGE
P. O. Box 20500
El Paso, TX 79998
Ramón Domínguez, President
(915) 831-2000 Fax: (915) 831-2162
Email: ClaudiaG@epcc.edu
www.epcc.edu

ESTRELLA MOUNTAIN COMMUNITY COLLEGE
3000 N. Dysart Rd.
Avondale, AZ 85323
Homero López, President
(623) 935-8888 Fax: (623) 935-8008
Email: webmaster@emc.maricopa.edu
www.emc.maricopa.edu

FLORIDA INTERNATIONAL UNIVERSITY
11200 S.W. 8th St.
Miami, FL 33199
Modesto A. Maidique, President
(305) 348-2363 Fax: (305) 348-3648
Email: webmaster@fiu.edu
www.fiu.edu

FRESNO CITY COLLEGE
1101 E. University Ave.
Fresno, CA 93741
Dr. Daniel Larios, President
(559) 442-4600 Fax: (559) 485-3367
Email: ceo571@do1.scccd.cc.ca.us
www.fcc.cc.ca.us

FULLERTON COLLEGE
321 E. Chapman Ave.
Fullerton, CA 92832
Michael J. Viera, President
(714) 992-7000 Fax: (714) 526-6651
Email: webmaster@fullcoll.edu
www.fullcoll.edu

GLENDALE COMMUNITY COLLEGE
1500 North Verdugo Rd.
Glendale, CA 91208
John A. Davitt, President
(818) 240-1000 Fax: (818) 551-5255
Email: info@glendale.cc.ca.us
www.glendale.cc.ca.us

HARTNELL COMMUNITY COLLEGE
156 Homestead Ave.
Salinas, CA 93901
Edward J. Valeau, President
(831) 755-6711 Fax: (831) 759-6014
Email: Evaleau@hartnell.cc.ca.us
www.hartnell.cc.ca.us

HERITAGE COLLEGE
3240 Fort Rd.
Toppensih, WA 98948
Dr. Kathleen A. Ross, President
(509) 865-8500 Fax: (509) 865-4469
Email: webmaster@heritage.edu
www.heritage.edu

HOUSTON COMMUNITY COLLEGE
Central College
1300 Holman
Houston, Texas 77004
Jack E. Daniels, III, President
(713) 718-6000 Fax: (713) 718-6092
Email: daniels_j@hccs.cc.tx.us
www.hccs.cc.tx.us

HUDSON COUNTY COMMUNITY COLLEGE
162 Sip Avenue
Jersey City, NJ 07306
Robert F. Rosa, Dean
(201) 714-2127 Fax: (201) 714-2136
Email: rrosa@mail.hudson.cc.nj.us
www.hudson.cc.nj.us

THE INTER AMERICAN UNIVERSITY OF PUERTO RICO
Aguadilla Campus
P.O. Box 20000
Aguadilla, PR 00905
Manuel J. Fernós, President
(787) 891-0925 Fax: (787) 882-3020
Email: academia@interaguadilla.edu
www.interaguadilla.edu

Arecibo Campus
P.O. Box 4050
Arecibo, PR 00614-4050
Manuel J. Fernós, President
(787) 878-5475 Fax: (787) 880-1624
Email: Webmaster@arecibo.inter.edu
www.arecibo.inter.edu

Barranquitas Campus
P.O. Box 517
Barranquitas, PR 00794
Manuel J. Fernós, President
(787) 857-3600 Fax: (787) 857-2244
www.br.inter.edu

Bayamon Campus
Carr. 830 #500, Bo. Cerro Gordo
Bayamón, PR 00957
Manuel J. Fernós, President
(787) 279-1912 Fax: (787) 279-2205
Email: jcolon@bc.inter.edu
http://bc.inter.edu/index.html

Fajardo Campus
P.O. Box 70003
Fajardo, PR 00738-7003
Manuel J. Fernós, President
(787) 863-2390 Fax: (787) 860-3470
Email: webmaster@fajardo.inter.edu
http://fajardo.inter.edu

Guayama Campus
P.O. Box 10004
Guayama, PR 00785
Manuel J. Fernós, President
(787) 864-2222 Fax: (787) 864-8232
Email: briveras@inter.edu
http://guayama.inter.edu/

Metropolitano Campus
P.O. Box 191293
San Juan, PR 00919-1293
Manuel J. Fernós, President
(787) 250-1912
Email: jahumada@inter.edu
www.metro.inter.edu

Ponce Campus
104 Parque Industrial Turpo Rd. 1
Mercedita, PR 00715-1602

Manuel J. Fernós, President
(787) 284-1912 Fax: (787) 841-0103
Email: fldiaz@ponce.inter.edu
http://ponce.inter.edu/

San German Campus
P.O. Box 5100
San Germán, PR 00683
Manuel J. Fernós, President
(787) 264-1912 Fax: (787) 892-6350
Email: mgarcia@ponce.inter.edu
www.sg.inter.edu

LAREDO COMMUNITY COLLEGE
West End Washington St.
Laredo, TX 78040
Dr. Ramon H. Dovalina, President
(956) 722-0521 Fax: (956) 721-5493
Email: rdovalina@laredo.cc.tx.us
www.laredo.cc.tx.us

LONG BEACH CITY COLLEGE
4901 E. Carson St.
Long Beach, CA 90808
E. Jan Kehoe, President
(562) 938-4111 Fax: (562) 938-4858
Email: rschultz@lbcc.cc.ca.us
www.lbcc.cc.ca.us

LOS ANGELES CITY COLLEGE
855 N. Vermont Ave.
Los Angeles, CA 90029
Mary Spangler, President
(323) 953-4000 Fax: (323) 953-4536
Email: webmaster@email.lacc.cc.ca.us
www.lacc.cc.ca.us

LOS ANGELES COUNTY COLLEGE OF NURSING & ALLIED HEALTH
1237 N. Mission Rd.
Los Angeles, CA 90033
Michael Sue Cronin, President
(323) 226-4911 Fax: (323) 226-6343
Email: webmaster@dhs.co.la.ca.us
www.ladhs.org

LUNA VOCATIONAL TECHNICAL INSTITUTE
P.O. Box 1510
Hot Springs Blvd.
Las Vegas, NM 87701
Dr. Laurence Pino, President
(505) 454-2500 Fax: (505) 454-2588
Email: WebServices@lvti.cc.nm.us
http://lvti.cc.nm.us/

MACCORMAC COLLEGE
506 S. Wabash
Chicago, IL 60605
Dr. Edward Kies, President
(312) 922-1884 Fax: (312) 922-3196
Email: admissions@maccormac.edu
www.maccormac.edu

615 N. West Ave.
Elmhurst, IL 60126
Dr. Edward Kies, President
(630) 941-1200 Fax: (630) 941-0937
Email: admissions@maccormac.edu
www.maccormac.edu

MERCED COLLEGE
3600 M Street
Merced, CA 95348
Dr. Benjamin Duran, President
(209) 384 6000 Fax: (209) 384-6339
Email: webmaster@merced.cc.ca.us
www.merced.cc.ca.us

MERCY COLLEGE
555 Broadway
Dobbs Ferry, NY 10522
Lucie Lapovsky, President
(914) 693-4500 Fax: (914) 674-7382
www.mercynet.edu

MIAMI-DADE COMMUNITY COLLEGE
InterAmerican Campus
627 SW 27th Ave.
Miami, FL 33135
Jose A. Vicente, Campus President
(305) 237- 6045 Fax: (305) 237- 6095
Email: htomeu@mdcc.edu
www.mdcc.edu

Kendall Campus
11011 SW 104th St.
Miami, FL 33176
Richard Schinoff, President
(305) 237-2000 Fax: (305) 237-2964
Email: WebMaster@MDCC.Edu
www.mdcc.edu/kendall

Medical Center
950 NW 20th St.
Miami, FL 33127

Kathie S. Sigler, Campus President
(305) 237-4100 Fax: (305) 237-4339
Email: mednet@mdcc.edu
www.mdcc.edu/medical

North Campus
11380 NW 27 Avenue
Miami, FL 33167
Castell Vaughn Bryant, President
(305) 237-1000 Fax: (305) 237-8070
Email: cbryant@mdcc.edu
www.mdcc.edu

Wolfson Campus
3000 NE 2nd
Miami, FL 33137
Jon J. Alexiou, President
(305) 237-3131 Fax: (305) 237-3669
Email: aleon@mdcc.edu
www.mdcc.edu/wolfson/

MIDLAND COLLEGE
3600 N. Garfield
Midland, TX 79705
David E. Daniel, President
(915) 685-4500 Fax: (915) 685-6401
Email: ded@midland.cc.tx.us
www.midland.cc.tx.us

MOUNTAIN VIEW COLLEGE
4849 W. Illinois Ave.
Dallas, TX 75211
Monique Amerman, President
(214) 860-8600 Fax: (214) 860-8570
Email: MXA6110@dcccd.edu
www.mvc.dcccd.edu

MT. SAN ANTONIO COLLEGE
1100 N. Grand Ave.
Walnut, CA 91789
Bill Feddersen, President
(909) 594-5611 Fax: (909) 568-4068
Email: webmaster@mtsac.edu
www.mtsac.edu

NATIONAL HISPANIC UNIVERSITY
14271 Story Rd.
San Jose, CA 95127
Dr. Roberto Cruz, President
(408) 254-6900 Fax: (408) 254-1369
Email: university@nhu.edu
www.nhu.edu

NEW JERSEY CITY UNIVERSITY
2039 Kennedy Blvd.
Jersey City, NJ 07305
Dr. Carlos Hernández, President
(201) 200-2000 Fax: (201) 200-2044
Email: webmaster@mail.njcu.edu
www.njcu.edu

NEW MEXICO HIGHLANDS UNIVERSITY
P.O. Box 9000
Las Vegas, NM 87701
Selimo Rael, President
(505) 454-3439 Fax: (505) 454-3552
Email: webmaster@nmhu.edu
www.nmhu.edu

NEW MEXICO JUNIOR COLLEGE
5317 Lovington Hwy.
Hobbs, NM 88240
Steve McCleery, President
(505) 392-4510 Fax: (505) 392-2527
webmaster@nmjc.cc.nm.us
http://nmjc.cc.nm.us/

NEW MEXICO STATE UNIVERSITY
Las Cruces, NM 88003-8001
Dr. Jay Gogue, President
(505) 646-0111 Fax: (505) 646-6330
Email: admissions@nmsu.edu
www.nmsu.edu

Carlsbad Campus
1500 University Dr.
Carlsbad, NM 88220
Don Hanson, Acting Campus Executive Director
(505) 234-9200 Fax: (505) 885-4951
Email: webmaster@cavern.nmsu.edu
http://cavern.nmsu.edu/

Doña Ana Branch Community College
3400 S. Espina
Las Cruces, NM 88003
Jay Gogue, President
(505) 646-0111 Fax: (505) 646-6330
Email: admission@nmsu.edu
http://dabcc-www.nmsu.edu/

NEW YORK CITY TECHNICAL COLLEGE
300 Jay St.
Brooklyn, NY 11201
Fred Beaufait, President
(718) 260-5000 Fax: (718) 260-5504
Email: connect@citytech.cuny.edu
www.nyctc.cuny.edu

NORTHEASTERN ILLINOIS UNIVERSITY
5500 N. St. Louis Ave.
Chicago, IL 60625
Salme H. Steinberg, President
(773) 583-4050 Fax: (773) 442-4020
Email: webteam@neiu.edu
www.neiu.edu

NORTHERN NEW MEXICO COMMUNITY COLLEGE
Espanola Campus
921 Paseo de Onate
Espanola, NM 87532
Dr. Sigfredo Maestas, President
(505) 747-2100 Fax: (505) 747-2180
Email: priscilla@nnm.cc.nm.us
http://nnm.cc.nm.us/

OCCIDENTAL COLLEGE
1600 Campus Rd.
Los Angeles, CA 90041
Theodore R. Mitchell, President
(323) 259-2500 Fax: (323) 341-4875
Email: admission@oxy.edu
www.oxy.edu

OUR LADY OF THE LAKE UNIVERSITY
411 S.W. 24th St.
San Antonio, TX 78207
Sally Mahoney, President
(210) 434-6711 Fax: (210) 436-2314
Email: MAHOS@lake.ollusa.edu
www.ollusa.edu

PALO VERDE COLLEGE
811 West Chanslorway
Blythe, CA 92225
President Hoctois, President
(760) 922-6168 Fax: (760) 921-3608
Email: webmaster@paloverde.cc.ca.us
www.paloverde.cc.ca.us

PASADENA CITY COLLEGE
1570 E. Colorado Blvd.
Pasadena, CA 91106
James P. Kossler, President
(626) 585-7394
Email: jpkossler@paccd.cc.ca.us
www.paccd.cc.ca.us

PASSAIC COUNTY COMMUNITY COLLEGE
One College Boulevard
Paterson, NJ 07505
Steven M. Rose, President
(973) 684-6868 Fax: (973) 684-6778
Email: webmaster@pccc.cc.nj.us
www.pccc.cc.nj.us

PHOENIX COLLEGE
1202 W. Thomas Rd.
Phoenix, AZ 85013
Marie Pepicello, President
(602) 264-2492 Fax: (602) 285-7700
Email: marie.pepicello@pcmail.maricopa.edu
www.pc.maricopa.edu

PIMA COMMUNITY COLLEGE
4905 E. Broadway Blvd.
Tucson, AZ 85709
Dr. Robert Jenson, Chancellor
(520) 206-4500 Fax: (520) 206-4790
Email: PimaInfo@pimacc.pima.edu
www.pima.edu

POLYTECHNIC UNIV. OF PUERTO RICO
377 Ponce de Leon Ave.
Hato Rey, PR 00918
Ernesto Vazquez-Barquet, President
(787) 754-8000 Fax: (787) 763-8919
www.pupr.edu

PONTIFICIA UNIVERSIDAD CATÓLICA DE PUERTO RICO
2250 Avenida Las Américas, #584
Ponce, PR 00717-0777
José Alberto Morales, President
(787) 841-2000 Fax: (787) 651-2044
Email: admiones@pucpr.edu
www.pucpr.edu

PUEBLO COMMUNITY COLLEGE
900 W. Orman Ave.
Pueblo, CO 81004
Sandra Davis, President
(719) 549-3200 Fax: (719) 544-1179
Email: Sunny.Davis@pcc.cccoes.edu
www.pcc.cccoes.edu

RANCHO SANTIAGO COMMUNITY COLLEGE DISTRICT
Santa Ana Campus
1530 W. 17th St.
Santa Ana, CA 92706
Edward Hernandez, Chancellor
(714) 564-6000 Fax: (714) 564-6455

Email: Adm_Records@rsccd.org
www.rsccd.org
Santiago Canyon Campus
8045 E. Chapman Ave.
Orange, CA 92869
Edward Hernandez, Chancellor
(714) 564-4000 Fax: (714) 564-4379
Email: Adm_Records@rsccd.org
www.rsccd.org

RECINTO DE RIO PIEDRAS
UNIVERSITARIO DE MAYAGÜEZ
Mayagüez, PR 00681
(787) 832-4040
Email: webmaster@www.uprm.edu
www.uprm.edu

REEDLEY COLLEGE
995 N. Reed Ave.
Reedley, CA 93654
Thomas A. Crow, President
(559) 638-3641 Fax: (559) 638-5040
Email: Tom.Crow@do1.scccd.cc.ca.us
www.rc.cc.ca.us

RICHARD J. DALEY COLLEGE
7500 S. Pulaski Rd.
Chicago, IL 60652
Dr. Mark Warden, President
(773) 838-7500
Email: webmaster@ccc.edu
www.ccc.edu

RIO HONDO COLLEGE
3600 Workman Mill Rd.
Whittier, CA 90601
Jess Carreon, President
(562) 692-0921 Fax: (562) 699-7386
Email: trazor@rh.cc.ca.us
www.rh.cc.ca.us

RIVERSIDE COMMUNITY COLLEGE
Moreno Valley
16130 Lasselle St.
Moreno Valley, CA 92551
Grace Slocum, President
(909) 571-6100 Fax: (909) 571-6188
Email: webmstr@rccd.cc.ca.us
www.rccd.cc.ca.us

Norco Campus
2001 Third St.
Norco, CA 92860
Grace Slocum, President
(909) 372-7000 Fax: (909) 372-7050
Email: webmstr@rccd.cc.ca.us
www.rccd.cc.ca.us

Riverside City
4800 Magnolia Ave.
Riverside, CA 92506
Grace Slocum, President
(909) 222-8000 Fax: (909) 222-8036
Email: webmstr@rccd.cc.ca.us
www.rccd.cc.ca.us

SAN BERNARDINO COMMUNITY
COLLEGE DISTRICT
Crafton Hills College
11711 Sand Canyon Rd.
Yucaipa, CA 92399
Gloria Macías Harrison, President
(909) 794-2161 Fax: (909) 794-0423
Email: library@beep2.sbccd.cc.ca.us
http://chc.sbccd.cc.ca.us/

Human Resource Department
441 W. 8th St.
San Bernardino, CA 92401
(909) 884-2533
www.sbccd.cc.ca.us

San Bernardino Valley College
701 S. Mt. Vernon Ave.
San Bernardino, CA 92410
Sharon Caballero, President
(909) 888-6511 Fax: (909) 889-4988
Email: pbrubal@sbccd.cc.ca.us
http://sbvc.sbccd.cc.ca.us/

SAN DIEGO STATE UNIVERSITY
Imperial Valley
720 Heber Ave.
Calexico, CA 92231
Dr. Khosrow Fatemi, President
(760) 768-5520 Fax: (760) 768-5568
Email: phall2@mail.sdsu.edu
www.rohan.sdsu.edu

SANTA FE COMMUNITY COLLEGE
6401 Richards Ave.
Santa Fe, NM 87505-4887
Mike Mier, Ed.D, Chairman
(505) 428-1268 Fax: (505) 428-1468
Email: matthew@computer-tutor.org
www.santa-fe.cc.nm.us

SANTA MONICA COLLEGE
1900 Pico Blvd.
Santa Monica, CA 90405
Dr. Piedad Robertson, President
(310) 434-4000 Fax: (310) 434-3645
Email: admissions@smc.edu
www.smc.edu

SOUTH MOUNTAIN COMMUNITY
COLLEGE
7050 S. 24th St.
Phoenix, AZ 85040
John Córdova, President
(602) 243-8000 Fax: (602) 243-8329
Email: donna.barnes-molton@smcmail.maricopa.edu
www.smc.maricopa.edu

SOUTH TEXAS COMMUNITY
COLLEGE
P.O. Box 9701
McAllen, TX 78502
Dr. Shirley Reed, President
(956) 618-8311 Fax: (956) 618-8321
Email: itshelp@stcc.cc.tx.us
www.stcc.cc.tx.us

SOUTHWEST TEXAS JUNIOR COLLEGE
2401 Garner Field Rd.
Uvalde, TX 78801
Ismael Sosa, President
(830) 278-4401 Fax: (830) 591-7396
Email: ismael.sosa@swtjc.cc.tx.us
www.swtjc.cc.tx.us

SOUTHWESTERN COLLEGE
900 Otay Lakes Rd.
Chula Vista, CA 91910
Serafin Zasueta, President
(619) 421-6700 Fax: (619) 482-6489
Email: webmaster@swc.cc.ca.us
http://swc.cc.ca.us/

ST. EDWARD'S UNIVERSITY
3001 S. Congress Ave.
Austin, TX 78704
George E. Martin, President
(512) 448-8400 Fax: (512) 464-8877
Email: wendym@admin.stedwards.edu
www.stedwards.edu

ST. MARY'S UNIVERSITY
One Camino Santa Maria
San Antonio, TX 78228
Charles Cottrell, President
(210) 436-3011 Fax: (210) 431-6864
Email: admissions@stmarytx.edu
www.stmarytx.edu

ST. PHILIP'S COLLEGE
1801 Martin Luther King Dr.
San Antonio, TX 78203
Angie Stokes Runnels, President
(210) 531-3200 Fax: (210) 531-3278
Email: arunnels@accd.edu
www.accd.edu

ST. THOMAS UNIVERSITY
16400 N.W. 32nd Ave.
Miami, FL 33054
Rev. Monsignor Franklyn M. Casale, President
(305) 628-6546 Fax: (305) 628-6591
Email: restavil@stu.edu
www.stu.edu

SUL ROSS STATE UNIVERSITY
P.O. Box C-114
Alpine, TX 79832
Dr. Vlck Morgan, President
(915) 837-8011 Fax: (915) 837-8431
Email: rvmorgan@sulross.edu
www.sulross.edu

TEXAS A&M INTERNATIONAL
UNIVERSITY SYSTEM
Corpus Christi
6300 Ocean Drive
Corpus Christi, TX 78412
Robert R. Furgason, President
(361) 825-5700 Fax: (361) 825-5887
Email: andrus@falcon.tamucc.edu
www.tamucc.edu

Kingsville
700 University Blvd. MSC 114
Kingsville, TX 78363
Marc Cisneros, President
(361) 593.2111 Fax: (361) 593-2195
Email: webmaster@tamuk.edu
www.tamuk.edu

Texas A&M International University
5201 University Boulevard
Laredo, TX 78041
Dr. J. Charles Jennett, President
(956) 326-2001 Fax: (956) 326-2199
Email: enroll@tamiu.edu
www.tamiu.edu

TEXAS STATE TECHNICAL COLLEGE
1902 North Loop 499
Harlingen, TX 78550
J. Gilbert Leal, President
(956) 364-4000 Fax: (956) 364-5117
Email: gilbertleal@harlingen.tstc.edu
www.harlingen.tstc.edu

TRINIDAD STATE JUNIOR COLLEGE
600 Prospect St.
Trinidad, CO 81082
Harold Deselms, President
(719) 846-5625 Fax: (719) 846-5667
Email: Rick.Sciacca@tsjc.cccoes.edu
www.tsjc.cccoes.edu

UNIVERSIDAD DE PUERTO RICO
PO Box 364984
San Juan, PR 00936
Dr. Norman Maldonado, President
(787) 250-0000 Ext. 2001 Fax: (787) 759-6917
Email: N_MALDONADO@UPR1.UPR.CLU.EDU
http://www.upr.clu.edu/

Humacao
Estación Postal CUH, 100 Carr. 908
Humacao, PR 00791
(787) 850-0000
Email: web@cuhwww.upr.clu.edu
http://cuhwww.upr.clu.edu/

UNIV. DE PUERTO RICO EN CAYEY
Ave. Antonio R. Barceló
Cayey, PR 00736
Rafael Rivera Lehman, President
(787) 738-2161
Email: eocasio@go.com
www.cuc.upr.clu.edu

UNIVERSIDAD DEL TURABO
Sistema Universitario Ana G. Mendez
P.O. Box 3030, University Station
Gurabo, PR 00778-3030
Dennis Alicea Rodríguez, Ph.D., Dean
(787) 743-7979 Fax: (787) 743-7940
Email: webmaster@suagm.edu
www.suagm.edu/UT/default.htm

UNIVERSITY OF HOUSTON
Downtown Campus
One Main Street
Houston, TX 77002
Dr. Max Castillo, President
(713) 221-8000 Fax: (713) 221-8157
Email: uhdadmit@dt.uh.edu
www.dt.uh.edu

UNIVERSITY OF LA VERNE
1950 3rd St.
La Verne, CA 91750
Stephen Morgan, President
(909) 593-3511 Fax: (909) 593-0965
Email: morgans@ulv.edu
www.ulv.edu

UNIVERSITY OF MIAMI
Coral Gables, FL 33124
Edward T. Foote, President
(305) 284-2211 Fax: (305) 284-2507
Email: president@miami.edu
www.miami.edu

UNIVERSITY OF NEW MEXICO
Albuquerque, NM 87131
William Charles Gordon, President
(505) 277-0111 Fax: (505) 277-6686
Email: wgordon@unm.edu
www.unm.edu

Gallup Campus
200 College Rd.
Gallup, NM 87301
Robert Carlson, Ed.D., Executive Director
(505) 863-7500 Fax: (505) 863-7532
Email: pubrelations@gallup.unm.edu
www.gallup.unm.edu

Los Alamos Campus
4000 University Dr.
Los Alamos, NM 87544-1999
Carlos Ramírez, President
(505) 662-5919 Fax: (505) 662-0344
Email: webmaster@la.unm.edu
www.la.unm.edu

Valencia Campus
280 La Entrada
Los Lunas, NM 87031
Greg Candela, President
(505) 925-8500 Fax: (505) 925-8501
Email: gregcand@unm.edu
www.unm.edu/~unmvc

UNIVERSITY OF SOUTHERN
COLORADO
2200 Bonforte Blvd.
Pueblo, CO 81001
Tito Guerrero, III, President
(719) 549-2100   Fax: (719) 549-2419

Email: info@uscolo.edu
www.uscolo.edu

THE UNIVERSITY OF TEXAS
Brownsville and Texas Southmost
College
80 Fort Brown
Brownsville, TX 78520
Dr. Juliet V. García, President
(956) 544-8200 Fax: (956) 544-8832
Email: president@utb1.utb.edu
www.utb.edu

El Paso
500 West University Ave.
El Paso, TX 79968
Dr. Diana Natalicio, President
(915) 747-5000 Fax: (915) 747-5848
Email: www@utep.edu
www.utep.edu

Health Science Center at San Antonio
7703 Floyd Curl Dr.
San Antonio, TX 78229
Fransisco Cigarroa, President
(210) 567-7000 Fax: (210) 567-2685
Email: webadmin@uthscsa.edu
www.uthscsa.edu

Pan-American
1201 West University Dr.
Edinburg, TX 78539
Miguel Nevarez, President
(956) 381-2011 Fax: (956) 381-2212
Email: mn38f1@panam.edu
www.panam.edu

Permian Basin
4901 E. University
Odessa, TX 79762
Charles A. Sorber, President
(915) 552-2605 Fax: (915) 552-3605
Email: webmaster@utpb.edu
www.utpb.edu

San Antonio
6900 N. Loop 1604 W.
San Antonio, TX 78249
Ricardo Romo, President
(210) 458-4011 Fax: (210) 458-5959
Email: president@utsa.edu
www.utsa.edu

UNIVERSITY OF THE INCARNATE
WORD
4301 Broadway
San Antonio, TX 78209
Luis Agnese, Jr., President
(210) 829-6005 Fax: (210) 829-3921
Email: troyk@universe.uiwtx.edu
www.uiw.edu

VALENCIA COMMUNITY COLLEGE
Osceola
1800 Denn John Ln.
Kissimmee, FL 34744
Sanford C. Shugart, President
(407) 299-5000 Fax: (407) 932-0855
Email: sshugart@gwmail.valencia.cc.fl.us
http://valencia.cc.fl.us

THE VICTORIA COLLEGE
2200 E. Red River
Victoria, TX 77901
Dr. Jimmy Goodson, President
(361) 573-3291 Fax: (361) 572-3850
Email: george@vc.cc.tx.us
www.vc.cc.tx.us

WEST HILLS COLLEGE
300 Cherry Ln.
Coalinga, CA 93210
Frank Gornick, President
(559) 935-0801 Fax: (559) 935-2966
Email: forthdj@whccd.cc.ca.us
www.westhills.cc.ca.us

WESTERN NEW MEXICO UNIVERSITY
P.O. Box 680
Silver City, NM 88062
John Counts, President
(505) 538-6336 Fax: (505) 538-6155
Email: admstudnt@iron.wnmu.edu
www.wnmu.edu

WOODBURY UNIVERSITY
7500 Glenoaks Blvd.
Burbank, CA 91510
Dr.Kenneth Neilson, President
(818) 767-0888 Fax: (818) 767-7520
Email: aacel2@vaxb.woodbury.edu
www.woodburyu.edu

WRIGHT COLLEGE
North Campus
4300 N. Narragansett
Chicago, IL 60634
Charles Guengerich, President
(773) 777-7900 Fax: (773) 481-8053
Email: webmaster@ccc.edu
www.ccc.edu

Voluntary Health Agencies
Agencias voluntarias de salud

AMERICAN FOUNDATION FOR AIDS RESEARCH

120 Wall Street, Thirteenth Floor
New York, NY 10005
Tel: (212) 806-1600 or
(800) 39-AmFAR
Fax: (212) 806-1601
Web site: http://www.AmFAR.org
E-mail: donors@amfar.org

ALLIANCE FOR AGING RESEARCH

2021 K Street, NW, #305
Washington, DC 20006
Tel: (202) 293-2856 or
(800) 639-2421
Fax: (202) 785-8574
Web site: http://www.AgingResearch.org
E-mail: info@agingresearch.org

ALZHEIMER'S ASSOCIATION NATIONAL OFFICE

919 North Michigan Avenue, #1000
Chicago, Illinois 60611-1676
(800) 272-3900
(312) 335-8700
Fax: (312) 335-1110
Web site: http://www.Alz.org
E-mail: info@alz.org

AMC CANCER RESEARCH CENTER & FOUNDATION

1600 Pierce Street
Denver, CO 80214
Tel: (303) 233-6501 or
(800) 525-3777
Web site: http://www.AMC.org
E-mail: cicl.amc.org

AMERICAN CANCER SOCIETY

P. O. Box 6359
Glen Allen, Virginia 23058-6359
Tel: (804) 527-3700 or
(800) ACS-2345
Web site: http://www.cancer.org

AMERICAN DIABETES ASSOCIATION

1701 North Beauregard Street
Alexandria, VA 22311
Tel: (800) 342-2383
Web site: http://www.Diabetes.org
E-mail: customerservice@diabetes.org

AMERICAN HEART ASSOCIATION

7272 Greenville Avenue
Dallas, Texas 75231
Tel: (800) AHA-USA1
Web site: http://www.AmericanHeart.org

AMERICAN KIDNEY FUND

6110 Executive Boulevard, #1010
Rockville, MD 20852
Tel: (301) 881-3052 or
(800) 638-8299

Fax: (301) 881-0898 or
(301) 881-3311
Web site: http://www.akfinc.org
E-mail: www.helpline@akfinc.org

AMERICAN LUNG ASSOCIATION

1740 Broadway
New York, NY 10019
Tel: (212) 315-8700
Fax: (212) 265-5642
Web site: http://www.lungusa.org
E-mail: info@lungusa.org

AMERICAN PARKINSON DISEASE ASSOCIATION, INC.

1250 Hylan Boulevard, #4B
Staten Island, NY 10305-1946
Tel: (718) 981-8001 or
(800) 223-2732
Fax: (718) 981-4399
Web site: http://www.apdaparkinson.com
E-mail: info@apdaparkinson.com

AMERICAN TINNITUS ASSOCIATION

P.O. Box 5
Portland, OR 97207-0005
Tel: (503) 248-9985
Fax: (503) 248-0024
Web site: http://www.ata.org
E-mail: tinnitus@ata.org

ARTHRITIS FOUNDATION

1330 West Peachtree Street
Atlanta, Georgia 30309
Tel: (404) 872-7100 or
(800) 283-7800
Fax: (404) 872-0457
Web site: http://www.arthritis.org
E-mail: help@arthritis.org

CANCER RESEARCH INSTITUTE

681 Fifth Avenue
New York, NY 10022
Tel: (800) 99CANCER (992-2623)
Web site: http://www.cancerresearch.org
E-mail: info@cancerresearch.org

CHRISTOPHER REEVE PARALYSIS FOUNDATION

500 Morris Avenue
Springfield, NJ 07081
Tel: (973) 379-2690 or
(800) 225-0292
Fax: (973) 912-9433
Web site: http://www.apacure.org

CITY OF HOPE

1500 East Duarte Road
Duarte, California 91010
Tel: (626) 359-8111
Web site: http://www.cityofhope.org

COMMUNITY HEALTH CHARITIES

200 N Glebe Road, #801
Arlington, VA 22203
Tel: (703) 528-1007
Fax: (703) 528-1365
Web site: http://www.healthcharities.org
E-mail: info@healthcharities.org

CROHN'S & COLITIS FOUNDATION OF AMERICA, INC.

386 Park Avenue South, 17th Floor
New York, NY 10016-8804
Tel: (212) 685-3440 or
(800) 932-2423
Fax: (212) 779-4098
Web site: http://www.ccfa.org
E-mail: info@ccfa.org

CYSTIC FIBROSIS FOUNDATION

6931 Arlington Road
Bethesda, MD 20814
Tel: (301) 951-4422 or
(800) FIGHT-CF (344-4823)
Fax: (301) 951-6378
Web site: http://www.cff.org
E-mail: info@cff.org

DEAFNESS RESEARCH FOUNDATION

575 Fifth Avenue, 11th Floor
New York NY 10017
Tel: (212) 599-0027 or
(800) 535-3323 (535-DEAF)
Fax: (212) 599-0039
Web site: http://www.drf.org
E-mail: drf@drf.org

DIABETES RESEARCH INSTITUTE FOUNDATION

3440 Hollywood Boulevard, #100
Hollywood, FL 33021
Tel: (954) 964-4040
Fax: (954) 964-7036
Web site: http://www.drinet.org

D.E.B.R.A. OF AMERICA, INC.

(Dystrophic Epidermolysis Bullosa
Research Association)
40 Rector Street, #1403
New York, NY 10006
Tel: (212) 513-4090
Fax: (212) 513-4099
Web site: http://www.debra.org
E-mail: staff@debra.org
Executive Director: Jean P. Campbell

HUNTINGTON'S DISEASE SOCIETY OF AMERICA (HDSA)

158 West 29th Street, 7th Floor
New York, NY 10001-5300
Tel: (212) 242-1968 (ext. 10 for the
receptionist) or
(1-800) 345-HDSA
Fax: (212) 239-3430

Web site: http://www.hdsa.org
E-mail: hdsainfo@hdsa.org
Executive Director/CEO: Barbara T. Boyle
Email address: Bboyle@hdsa.org

JUVENILE DIABETES FOUNDATION INTERNATIONAL

120 Wall Street
New York, NY 10005
Tel: (212) 785-9500 or
800-JDF-CURE
Fax: (212) 785-9595
Web site: http://www.jdfcure.org
E-mail: info@jdfcure.org
Chairman: Robert Wood Johnson, IV

LEUKEMIA & LYMPHOMA SOCIETY

New York Chapter
475 Park Avenue South, 21st Fl.
New York, NY 10016
Tel: (212) 448-9206
Fax: (212) 448-9214
Web site: http://www.leukemia-lymphoma.org
E-mail: kozikm@nyc.leukemia-lymphoma.org
Executive Director: Mary Kozik

LITTLE CITY FOUNDATION

1760 West Algonquin Road
Palatine, IL 60067
Tel: (847) 358-5510
Fax: (847) 358-3291
Web site: http://www.littlecity.org
E-mail: people@little.city.org
Executive Director: Alen Dachman

LUPUS FOUNDATION OF AMERICA, INC.

1300 Piccard Drive, #200
Rockville, MD 20850-4303
Tel: 301-670-9292 or
(800) 558-0121
Web site: http://www.lupus.org
E-mail: LupusInfo@aol.com

MARCH OF DIMES BIRTH DEFECTS FOUNDATION

1275 Mamaroneck Avenue
White Plains, NY 10605
Tel: 888-MODIMES (663-4637)
Web site: http://www.modimes.org

MUSCULAR DYSTROPHY ASSOCIATION

3300 E. Sunrise Drive
Tucson, AZ 85718
Tel: (800) 572-1717
Web site: http://www.mdausa.org
E-mail: mda@mdausa.org

MYASTHENIA GRAVIS FOUNDATION OF AMERICA

5841 Cedar Lake Road, #204
Minneapolis, MN 55416
Tel: (952) 545-9438 or

(800) 541-5454
Fax: (952) 545-6073
Web site: http://www.myasthenia.org
E-mail: myasthenia@myasthenia.org

NATIONAL ALLIANCE FOR THE MENTALLY ILL (NAMI)
Colonial Place III
2107 Olson Boulevard, #300
Arlington, VA 22201-3042
Tel: (703)524-7600 or
(800) 950-NAMI (6264)
Fax: (703)524-9094
TDD: (703) 516-7227
Web site: http://www.nami.org
E-mail: webteam@www.nami.org

NATIONAL BRAIN TUMOR FOUNDATION
414 13th Street, #700
Oakland, CA 94612-2603
Tel: (510) 839-9777
Fax: (510) 839-9779
Patient Line: (800) 934-2873
Web site: http://www.braintumor.org
E-mail: nbtf@braintumor.org

NATIONAL COUNCIL ON ALCOHOLISM AND DRUG DEPENDENCE, INC
12 West 21 Street
New York, NY 10010
Tel: (212) 206-6770 or
(800) NCA-CALL
Fax: (212) 645-1690
Web site: http://www.ncadd.org
E-mail: national@ncadd.org

NATIONAL DOWN SYNDROME SOCIETY (NDSS)
666 Broadway
New York, NY 10012
Tel: (212) 460-9330 or
(800) 221-4602
Fax: (212) 979-2873
Web site: http://www.ndss.org
E-mail: info@ndss.org

NATIONAL EASTER SEAL SOCIETY
230 West Monroe Street, #1800
Chicago, IL 60606
Tel: (312) 726-6200 or
(800) 221-6827
TDD: (312) 726-4258
Fax: (312)-726-1494
Web site: http://www.easter-seals.org
E-mail: info@easter-seals.org.

NATIONAL HEMOPHILIA FOUNDATION
116 West 32nd Street, 11th Floor
New York, NY 10001
Tel: (212) 328-3700 or
(800) 42-HANDI
Fax: (212) 328-3777
Web site: http://www.hemophilia.org
E-mail: info@hemophilia.org

NATIONAL HOSPICE AND PALLIATIVE CARE ORGANIZATION
1700 Diagonal Road, #300
Alexandria, VA 22314
Tel: (703) 837-1500
Fax: (703) 525-5762
Web site: http://www.nhpco.org
E-mail: info@nhpco.org

NATIONAL INSTITUTE OF ART AND DISABILITIES
551 23rd Street
Richmond, CA 94804

Tel: (510) 620-0290
Fax: (510) 620-0326
Web site: http://www.niadart.org
E-mail: reddot@niadart.org
President: Elias Katz, Ph.D

NATIONAL KIDNEY FOUNDATION
30 East 33rd Street, #1100
New York, NY 10016
Tel: (212) 889-2210 or
(800) 622-9010
Fax: (212) 689-9261
Please direct all email inquiries to:
Web site: http://www.kidney.org
E-mail: info@kidney.org

NATIONAL MARFAN FOUNDATION
382 Main Street
Port Washington, NY 11050
Tel: (516) 883-8712 or
(800) 8-MARFAN
Fax: (516) 883-8040
Web site: http://www.marfan.org
E-Mail: staff@marfan.org

NATIONAL MENTAL HEALTH ASSOCIATION
1021 Prince Street
Alexandria, VA 22314-2971
Tel: (703) 684-7722 or
(800) 969-NMHA
TTY: (800) 433-5959
Fax: (703) 684-5968
Web site: http://www.nmha.org

NATIONAL MULTIPLE SCLEROSIS SOCIETY
733 Third Avenue
New York, NY 10017
Tel: (212) 986-3240 or
(800) Fight-MS (344-4867)
Web site: http://
www.nationalmssociety.org
E-mail: info@nmss.org

NATIONAL ORGANIZATION FOR RARE DISORDERS
P.O. Box 8923
New Fairfield, CT 06812-8923
Tel: (203) 746-6518 or
(800) 999-6673
Fax: (203) 746-6481
Web site: http://www.rarediseases.org
E-mail: orphan@rarediseases.org

NATIONAL PARKINSON FOUNDATION
Capital Chapter
7531 Leesburg Pike, #402
Falls Church, VA 22043-2120
(703) 356-2151
Web site: http://www.ccnpf.org
Chapter President: Larry Hossheimer

NATIONAL REYE'S SYNDROME FOUNDATION
P.O. Box 829
Bryan, OH 43506-0829
Tel: (419) 636-2679 or
(800) 233-7393
Fax: (419) 636-9897
Web site: http://www.bright.net/
~reyessyn
E-mail: reyessyn@mail.bright.net

NATIONAL SPINAL CORD INJURY ASSOCIATION
6701 Democracy Boulevard., #300
Bethesda, MD 20817
Tel: (301) 588-6959

Fax: (301) 588-9414
Web site: http://www.spinalcord.org

NATIONAL STROKE ASSOCIATION
9707 E. Easter Lane
Englewood, CO 80112
Tel: (303) 649-9299 or
(800)-STROKES (787-6537)
Fax: (303) 649-1328
Web site: http://www.stroke.org
E-mail: info@stroke.org

NATIONAL TUBEROUS SCLEROSIS ASSOCIATION
801 Roeder Road, #750
Silver Spring, MD 20910
Tel: (301) 562-9890 or
(800) 225-6872
Fax: (301) 562-9870
Web site: http://www.tsalliance.org
E-mail: ntsa@ntsa.org

PARKINSON'S DISEASE FOUNDATION, INC.
William Black Medical Building
Columbia-Presbyterian Medical Center
710 West 168th Street
New York, NY 10032-9982
Tel: (212) 923-4700 or
(800) 457-6676
Fax: (212) 923-4778
Web site: http://www.parkinsons-
foundation.org
E-mail: info@pdf.org
Chairman of the Board: William Black

PREVENT BLINDNESS AMERICA (NATIONAL SOCIETY TO PREVENT BLINDNESS)
500 E. Remington Road, #200
Schaumburg, IL 60173
Tel: (847) 843-2020 or
(800) 331-2020
Fax: (847) 843-8458
Web site: http://
www.preventblindness.org
E-mail: info@preventblindness.org

RESEARCH TO PREVENT BLINDNESS
645 Madison Avenue
New York, NY 10022-1010
Tel: (212) 752-4333 or
(800) 621-0026
Web site: http://www.rpbusa.org
E-mail: info@rpbusa.org

SICKLE CELL DISEASE ASSOCIATION OF AMERICA
200 Corporate Pointe, #495
Culver City, CA 90230-8727
Tel: (310) 216-6363 or
(800) 421-8453
(310) 215-3722 Fax
Web site: http://
www.sicklecelldisease.org
E-Mail: ascdaa@aol.com
Chairman of the Board: Vincent L.
Berkeley

SPINA BIFIDA ASSOCIATION OF AMERICA
4590 MacArthur Boulevard, NW, #250
Washington, DC 20007-4226
Tel: (202) 944-3285 or
(800) 621-3141
Fax: (202) 944-3295
Web site: http://www.sbaa.org
E-mail: sbaa@sbaa.org

ST. JUDE CHILDREN'S RESEARCH HOSPITAL
332 N. Lauderdale Street
Memphis, TN 38105
Tel: (901) 495-3300 or
(800) 822-6344
Web site: http://www.stjude.org
E-mail: info@stjude.org

SUDDEN INFANT DEATH SYNDROME ALLIANCE
1314 Bedford Avenue, #210
Baltimore, Maryland 21208
Tel: (410) 653-8226
(800) 221-7437
Fax: (410) 653-8709
Web site: http://www.sidsalliance.org
E-mail: sidshq@charm.net

THE AMYOTROPHIC LATERAL SCLEROSIS ASSOCIATION
27001 Agoura Road, #150
Calabasas Hills, CA 91301-5104
Tel: (800) 782-4747 or
(818) 880-9007
Web site: http://www.ALSA.org
E-mail: alsinfo@alsa-national.org

THE ARC OF THE UNITED STATES
1010 Wayne Avenue, #650
Silver Spring, MD 20910
Tel: (301) 565-3842
Fax: (301) 565-5342
Web site: http://TheArc.org
E-mail: info@thearc.org

THE COOLEY'S ANEMIA FOUNDATION, INC.
129-09 26th Avenue, #203
Flushing, NY 11354
Tel: (718) 321-CURE (2873) or
(800) 522-7222
Fax: (718) 321-3340
Web Site: http://www.thalassemia.org
E-mail: ncaf@aol.com

THE ENDOMETRIOSIS ASSOCIATION
8585 N. 76th Place
Milwaukee, WI 53223
Tel: (414) 355-2200 or
(800) 992-3636
Fax: (414) 355-6065
Web site: http://
www.endometriosisassn.org
E-mail: endo@endometriosisassn.org

THE NATIONAL ARTS AND DISABILITY CENTER
UCLA UAP
Los Angeles, CA 90095-6967
Tel: (310) 794-1141
Fax: (310) 794-1143
Web site: http://www.dcp.ucla.edu/nadc/
E-mail: oraynor@npih.mednet.ucla
Olivia Raynor, Program Director

UNITED CEREBRAL PALSY ASSOCIATIONS
1660 L Street, NW, #700
Washington, DC 20036
Tel: (202) 776-0406 or
(800) 872-5827
Fax: (202) 776-0414
Web site: http://www.ucpa.org
E-mail: ucpnatl@ucpa.org

Federal and State Offices of Minority Health
Oficinas federales y estatales de salud para las minorías

The Federal Office of Minority Health (OMH: www.omhrc.gov) was created by the U.S. Department of Health and Human Services (HHS) in 1985. The Office advises on public health issues affecting Hispanic Americans and other racial and ethnic groups. The mission of OMH is to improve the health of racial and ethnic populations through the development of effective health policies and programs that help to eliminate disparities in health. OMH works closely with sister agencies within HHS and their minority health representatives. State Offices of Minority Health have been established by the states to provide information and to develop effective health policies and programs for Hispanic Americans and other racial and ethnic populations.

La Oficina Federal para la Salud de las Minorias fue creada por el Departamento de Salud y Servicios Humanos de los Estados Unidos en el año 1985. La Oficina aconseja a los hispano-americanos y a otros grupos raciales y etnicos sobre los problemas de salud que lo afectan. La misión de OMH es mejorar la salud de los grupos raciales y etnicos de la población a través del desarrollo de políticas efectivas de salud y programas que ayuden a eliminar las disparidades en salud de la población.
OMH trabaja estrechamente con las agencias hermanas dentro de HHS y sus representantes de salud dentro de las minorías. Las oficinas estatales de salud para las minorías han sido establecidas por los estados para proveer información y un desarrollo efectivo a los programas y políticas de salud para los hispano-americanos y las otras poblaciones raciales y etnicas.

FEDERAL OFFICES

PHS REGION I MINORITY HEALTH PROGRAM CONSULTANT
(Connecticut, Massachusetts, Maine, New Hampshire, Rhode Island, Vermont)
John F. Kennedy Federal Bldg. #2126
Boston, MA 02203
(617) 565-1064 Fax: (617) 565-4265
Contact: Janet Lee Scott-Harris, Consultant

PHS REGION II MINORITY HEALTH PROGRAM CONSULTANT
(New Jersey, New York, Puerto Rico)
26 Federal Plaza #3835
New York, NY 10278
(212) 264-2127 Fax: (212) 264-1324
Contact: Claude Marie Colimon, Consultant
Email: ccolimon@os.dhhs.gov

PHS REGION III MINORITY HEALTH PROGRAM CONSULTANT
(Delaware, District of Columbia, Maryland, Pennsylvania, Virginia, West Virginia)
150 S. Independence Mall W. #436
Philadelphia, PA 19106-4618
(215) 861-4618 Fax: (215) 861-4639
Contact: Dorothy Kelly, Consultant
Email: dkelly@hrsa.gov

PHS REGION IV MINORITY HEALTH PROGRAM CONSULTANT
(Alabama, Florida, Georgia, Kentucky, Mississippi, North Carolina, South Carolina, Tennessee)
61 Forsyth St. SW #5B-59
Atlanta, GA 30303-8909
(404) 562-7888/7905 Fax: (404) 562-7899
Contact: Yvonne Johns, Consultant
Email: yjohns@osophs.dhhs.gov

PHS REGION V MINORITY HEALTH PROGRAM CONSULTANT
(Illinois, Indiana, Michigan, Minnesota, Ohio, Wisconsin)
233 N. Michigan Ave. #1300
Chicago, IL 60601-5519
(312) 353-1386 Fax: (312) 353-7800
Contact: Mildred Hunter, Consultant
Email: mhunter@hrsa.dhhs.gov

PHS REGION VI MINORITY HEALTH PROGRAM CONSULTANT
(Arkansas, Louisiana, New Mexico, Oklahoma, and Texas)
1301 Young St. #1124
Dallas, TX 75202
(214) 767-3523 Fax: (214) 767-3209
Contact: Epifanio Elizondo, Women's Health Coord./Acting Regional Minority Health Consultant

PHS REGION VII MINORITY HEALTH PROGRAM CONSULTANT
(Iowa, Kansas, Missouri, Nebraska)
601 E. 12th St. #210
Kansas City, MO 64106
(816) 426-3291 Fax: (816) 426-2178
Contact: William Mayfield, Consultant
Email: wmayfield@hrsa.dhhs.gov

PHS REGION VIII MINORITY HEALTH PROGRAM CONSULTANT
(Colorado, Montana, North Dakota, South Dakota, Utah, Wyoming)
1961 Stout St. #498
Denver, CO 80294-3538
(303) 844-7858 Fax: (303) 844-2019
Contact: Lorenzo Olivas, Consultant
Email: lolivas@hrsa.dhhs.gov

PHS REGION IX MINORITY HEALTH PROGRAM CONSULTANT
(Colorado, Montana, North Dakota, South Dakota, Utah, Wyoming)
United Nations Plaza #329
San Francisco, CA 94102
(415) 437-8124 Fax: (415) 437-8004
Contact: Christine Perez, RN, MN, FNP, Cons.
Email: cperez1@osophs.dhhs.gov

PHS REGION X MINORITY HEALTH PROGRAM CONSULTANT
(Arizona, California, Hawaii, Nevada, American Samoa, Guam)
2201 6th Ave. Mail Stop 20
Seattle, WA 98121
(206) 615-2475 Fax: (206) 615-2481
Contact: J. O'Neal Adams, Consultant
Email: nadams@hrsa.dhhs.gov

ALABAMA

ALABAMA DEPT. OF PUBLIC HEALTH
Division of Minority Health
Montgomery, AL 36130-3017
(334) 206-5396 Fax: (334) 206-5434
Contact: Gwendolyn Lipscomb, Director
Email: glipscomb@adph.state.al.us
Web: www.adph.state.al.us

ARKANSAS

ARKANSAS DEPARTMENT OF HEALTH
Office of Minority Health
4815 W. Markham St. Slot 55
Little Rock, AR 72205
(501) 661-2193 Fax: (501) 661-2414
Contact: Christine B. Patterson, Director
Email: cpattersn@mial.doh.state.ar.us
Web: http://health.state.ar.us

ARKANSAS MINORITY HEALTH COMMISSION
1123 S. University #250
Little Rock, AR 72204
(501) 686-2720 Fax: (501) 686-2722
Contact: Tommy L. Sproles, Director
Email: tommy.sproles@mail.state.ar.us
Web: http://health.state.ar.us

ARIZONA

ARIZONA DEPARTMENT OF HEALTH SERVICES
Center for Minority Health
1740 W. Adams St. #201
Phoenix, AZ 85007
(602) 542-2906 Fax: (602) 542-2722
Contact: Vanessa Hill, Acting Director
Email: vhill@hs.state.az.us
Web: www.state.az.us

CALIFORNIA

CALIFORNIA STATE DEPARTMENT OF HEALTH SERVICES
Office of Multicultural Health
714/744 P St.
Sacramento, CA 94234-7320
(916) 322-6851 Fax: (916) 327-6135
Contact: Greg Franklin, Chief
Email: gfrankli@dhs.ca.gov
Web: www.dhs.ca.gov/director/omh/index

CONNECTICUT

CONNECTICUT DEPARTMENT OF PUBLIC HEALTH
Bureau of Policy, Planning and Evaluation
410 Capitol Ave. MS 13PPE
Hartford, CT 06134-0308
(860) 509-7120 Fax: (860) 509-7160

DISTRICT OF COLUMBIA

D.C. DEPARTMENT OF HEALTH
825 N. Capitol St. NE #2100
Washington, DC 20002
(202) 442-9039 Fax: (202) 442-4833
Contact: Patricia K. Theiss, Public Health Advisor

DELAWARE

DELAWARE DIVISION OF PUBLIC HEALTH
Jesse Cooper Bldg.
Dover, DE 19903
(302) 739-4700 Fax: (302) 729-6659
Contact: Mawuna Gardesey, Min. Health Dir.
Email: mgardesey@state.de.us

FLORIDA

FLORIDA DEPARTMENT OF HEALTH
Equal Opportunity and Minority Health
4052 Bald Cypress Way, Bin #A00
Tallahassee, FL 32399-1701
(850) 245-4002 Fax: (850) 487-2168
Contact: Melvin L. Herring, Jr., Director
Email: melvin_herring@doh.state.fl.us
Web: www.doh.state.fl.us

GEORGIA

DEPARTMENT OF COMMUNITY HEALTH
Office of Minority Health
2 Peachtree St. NW #6.327
Atlanta, GA 30303-3186
(404) 657-6707 Fax: (404) 657-2769
Contact: Carol Snype Crawford, Exec. Dir.
Email: cscrawford@dhr.state.ga.us
Web: www.communityhealth.state.ga.us

HAWAII

STATE OF HAWAII DEPT. OF HEALTH
Kina'u Hale, Rm. 266, 1250 Punchbowl St.
Honolulu, HI 96801-3378
(808) 586-4616 Fax: (808) 586-4648
Contact: Gerald Ohta, Affirmative Action Officer

IOWA

IOWA DEPARTMENT OF PUBLIC HEALTH
Family and Community Health
321 E. 12th St. 5th Fl.
Des Moines, IA 50319-0075
(800) 383-3826/(515) 281-4904 Fax: (515) 242-6384
Contact: Janice Edmunds-Wells, Min. Health Liaison
Email: jwells@idph.state.ia.us
Web: www.state.ia.us

ILLINOIS

ILLINOIS DEPT. OF PUBLIC HEALTH
Center for Minority Health Services
100 W. Randolph #6-600
Chicago, IL 60601
(312) 814-5278 Fax: (312) 814-1583
Contact: Joann Chiakulas, Chief

INDIANA

INDIANA MINORITY HEALTH COALITION
3737 N. Meridian St.
Indianapolis, IN 46206
(317) 926-4011
Contact: Stephanie DeKemeper, Exec. Dir.

INDIANA STATE DEPT. OF HEALTH
Office of Minority Health
1330 W. Michigan St.
Indianapolis, IN 46206
(317) 233-7596 Fax: (317) 233-7001
Contact: Gloria Webster-French, Director
Email: gfrench@isdh.state.in.us
Web: www.state.in.us

KENTUCKY

DEPARTMENT OF PUBLIC HEALTH
Office of the Commissioner
275 E. Main St.
Frankfort, KY 40621
(502) 564-3970 Fax: (502) 564-6533
Contact: Sarah Wilding, RN, MPA, Chief Nurse
Email: swilding@mail.state.ky.us
Web: www.state.ky.us

LOUISIANA

LOUISIANA DEPT. OF HEALTH & HOSPITALS
Office of Minority Health
325 Loyola Ave. 5th Fl.
New Orleans, LA 70112
(504) 599-0749 Fax: (504) 599-0300
Contact: Claude J. Carbon, Dir. for Public Health
Email: ccarbo@dhhmail.dhh.state.la.us
Web: www.state.la.us

MASSACHUSETTS

DEPARTMENT OF PUBLIC HEALTH
POLICY AND PLANNING
Office of Minority Health
250 Washington St. 2nd Fl.
Boston, MA 02108
(617) 624-5278 Fax: (617) 624-5046
Contact: Brunilda Torres, Director
Email: brunilda.torrres@state.ma.us
Web: www.state.ma.us/dph/omh/omh2.htm

MARYLAND

MARYLAND DEPARTMENT OF HEALTH
AND MENTAL HYGIENE
Maryland Office of Minority Health
Herbert R. O'Conor Bldg. #516
Baltimore, MD 21201
(410) 767-6592 Fax: (410) 333-5958
Contact: Angela Brooks, Director
Email: abrooks@dmh.state.md.us
Web: www.dmh.state.md.us

MAINE

DEPARTMENT OF HUMAN SERVICES,
BUREAU OF HEALTH
Office of Rural Health and Primary Care
35 Anthony Ave. Station #11
Augusta, ME 04333-0011
(207) 624-5424 Fax: (207) 624-5431
Contact: Sophie Glidden, Director
Email: sophie.e.glidden@state.me.us

MICHIGAN

MICHIGAN DEPT. OF COMMUNITY HEALTH,
COMMUNITY PUBLIC HEALTH AGENCY
Office of Minority Health
3423 N. Martin Luther King, Jr. Blvd. Box 30195
Lansing, MI 48909
(517) 335-9287 Fax: (517) 335-9476
Contact: Cheryl Anderson-Small, Chief
Email: anderson-smallc@state.mi.us
Web: www.mdch.state.mi.us/pha/omh/index

MINNESOTA

MINNESOTA DEPARTMENT OF HEALTH
Office of Minority Health
85 E. Seventh St. #400
St. Paul, MN 55101
(621) 296-9799 Fax: (621) 215-5801
Contact: Lou Fuller, Director
Email: lou.fuller@health.state.mn.us
Web: www.state.mn.us

MISSOURI

MISSOURI OFFICE OF MINORITY HEALTH
912 Wildwood Dr.
Jefferson City, MO 65102-0570
(800) 877-3180/(573) 751-6064   Fax: (573) 522-1599
Contact: Ben Germany, Chief
Email: germab@mail.health.state.mo.us
Web: www.state.mo.us

MISSISSIPPI

MISSISSIPPI DEPARTMENT OF HEALTH
Office of Minority Health
240 Tower Dr.
Batesville, MS 38606
(662) 563-5603 Fax: (662) 563-6307
Contact: Lovetta A. Brown, MD, MPH, Acting Health Off.

MONTANA

MONTANA DEPT. OF PUBLIC HEALTH/
HUMAN SERVICES
Montana Prenatal Program
1400 Broadway #C314
Helena, MT 59620
(406) 444-2794 Fax: (406) 444-2606
Contact: Deborah Hendersen, Nurse Consultant
Email: dhendersen@state.mt.us
Web: www.state.mt.us

SPECIAL HEALTH SERVICES
FCHB-DPHHS
1400 Broadway
Helena, MT 59620
(406) 444-2794 Fax: (406) 444-2606
Contact: Sharon Wagner, Mgr.

NORTH CAROLINA

NORTH CAROLINA OFFICE OF MINORITY
HEALTH
1906 Mail Service Center
Raleigh, NC 27699-1906
(919) 715-0992 Fax: (919) 715-0997
Contact: Barbara Pullen-Smith, MPH, Exec. Dir.
Email: barbara.pullen-smith@ncmail.net
Web: www.communityhealth.dhhs.state.nc.us/minority

NEBRASKA

NEBRASKA DEPARTMENT OF HEALTH
Office of Minority Health
Lincoln, NE 68509-0152
(402) 471-0152 Fax: (402) 471-0383
Contact: Eva Serenil, Director

NEW HAMPSHIRE

NEW HAMPSHIRE DEPT. OF HEALTH
Office of Minority Health
129 Pleasant St.
Concord, NH 03301
(603) 271-8459 Fax: (603) 271-4727
Contact: William D. Walker, Director
Web: www.omhrc.gov/OMH

NEW JERSEY

NEW JERSEY DEPARTMENT OF HEALTH
AND SENIOR SERVICES
Office of Minority Health
Trenton, NJ 08625-0360
(609) 292-6962 Fax: (609) 292-8713
Contact: Linda Holmes, Exec. Dir.
Email: lh2@doh.state.nj.us
Web: www.state.nj.us/health/commiss/omh

NEW MEXICO

NEW MEXICO DEPARTMENT OF HEALTH
Public Health Division
53 Perdiz Canyon
Placitas, NM 87043
(505) 867-5340
Contact: Doris Fields, Spec. Projects Coordinator
Email: dorisf@doh.state.nm.us
Web: www.state.nm.us

NEVADA

NEVADA STATE HEALTH DIVISION
Primary Care Development Center
505 E. King St. #203
Carson City, NV 89807
(775) 684-4220 Fax: (775) 684-4046
Contact: Salli Vannucci Macaskill, RN, CPH, Prog. Mgr.
Email: svannuco@govmail.state.nv.us
Web: www.state.nv.us

NEW YORK

NEW YORK CITY DEPT. OF HEALTH
Office of Minority Health
253 Broadway #602
New York, NY 10007
(212) 676-2900
Contact: Victor Hunter, Director
Web: www.omhrc.gov/OMH

NEW YORK STATE DEPT. OF HEALTH
Office of Minority Health
Corning Tower Bldg. #1142
Albany, NY 12237-0092
(518) 474-2180 Fax: (518) 473-8389
Contact: Wilma Waithe, Director
Email: wew01@health.state.ny.us
Web: www.omhrc.gov/OMH

OHIO

OHIO COMMISSION ON MINORITY
HEALTH
Vern Riffe Center for Government and the
Performing Arts, 77 S. High St. 7th Fl.
Columbus, OH 43215
(614) 466-4000 Fax: (614) 752-9049
Contact: Cheryl Boyce, MS, Exec. Dir
Email: minhealth@ocmh.state.oh.us
Web: www.state.oh.us/mih

OREGON

OREGON DEPARTMENT OF HUMAN
SERVICES, HEALTH DIVISION
Office of Multicultural Health
800 NE Oregon St.
Portland, OR 97232
(503) 731-4601 Fax: (503) 731-4078
Contact: Vicki Nakashima
Email: vicki.nakashima@state.or.us
Web: www.ohd.hr.state.or.us/omh/welcome

PENNSYLVANIA

PENNSYLVANIA DEPARTMENT OF
HEALTH, BUREAU OF PREVENTIVE
HEALTH PROGRAMS
Division of Chronic Disease Intervention
Rm. 1011
Harrisburg, PA 17108-0090
(717) 787-6214 Fax: (717) 783-5498
Contact: Emilie M. Tierney, Director
Email: etierney@health.state.pa.us

PUERTO RICO

PUERTO RICO DEPARTMENT OF HEALTH
Consultant for Primary Care and
Coordinator Minority Health Issues
San Juan, PR 00936-8139
(787) 274-7735 Fax: (787) 759-6552
Contact: Nadia Gardana, Consultant/Coordinator

SAN JUAN DEPARTMENT OF HEALTH
Office of Preventive Services
San Juan, PR 00928
(787) 767-6525 Fax: (787) 764-5281
Contact: Diana de la Paz, MD, Director

RHODE ISLAND

RHODE ISLAND DEPARTMENT OF
HEALTH
Office of Minority Health
3 Capitol Hill #407
Providence, RI 02908-5097
(401) 222-5117 Fax: (401) 273-4350
Contact: Pheamo R. Witcher, Min. Health Coord.
Email: pheamo_witcher@health.state.ri.us
Web: www.health.state.ri.us

SOUTH CAROLINA

SOUTH CAROLINA DEPARTMENT OF
HEALTH AND ENVIRONMENTAL
CONTROL
Office of Minority Health
2600 Bull St.
Columbia, SC 29201
(803) 898-3808 Fax: (803) 898-3810
Contact: Gardenia B. Ruff, MSW, Director
Email: ruffgb@columb20.dhec.state.sc.us
Web: www.dhec.state.sc.us

TENNESSEE

TENNESSEE DEPARTMENT OF HEALTH
Office of Minority Health
Cordell Hull Bldg., 425 5th Ave. N.
Nashville, TN 37247
(615) 741-9443 Fax: (615) 253-1434
Contact: Robbie M. Jackman, MSSW, Exec. Dir.
Email: rjackman@mail.state.tn.us
Web: http://170.142.76.180/minorityhealth

TEXAS

TEXAS DEPARTMENT OF HEALTH
Office of Minority Health & Cultural
Competency
1100 W. 49th St.
Austin, TX 78756
(512) 458-7629 Fax: (512) 458-7713
Contact: Kevin Collins, Director
Email: kevin.collins@tdh.state.tx.us
Web: www.state.tx.us

UTAH

UTAH STATE DEPARTMENT OF HEALTH
Ethnic Health
288 N. 1460 W. 4th Fl.
Salt Lake City, UT 84114-2005
(801) 538-6965 Fax: (801) 536-0970
Contact: Khando Chazotsang, Ethnic Health Coord.
Email: kchazots@doh.state.ut.us
Web: www.ethnichealthutah.org

VIRGINIA

VIRGINIA OFFICE OF MINORITY HEALTH
1500 E. Main St. #214
Richmond, VA 23219
(804) 786-3561 Fax: (804) 786-4616
Contact: Henry C. Murdaugh, Acting Director
Email: hmurdaugh@vdh.state.va.us
Web: www.state.va.us

VIRGIN ISLANDS

VIRGIN ISLANDS DEPARTMENT OF
HEALTH
Office of Minority Health
48 Sugar Estate
St. Thoms, VI 00802
(340) 774-0117 Fax: (340) 777-4001
Contact: Phyllis L. Wallace, Ed.D, Dep. Comm.

VERMONT

VERMONT DEPARTMENT OF HEALTH
Office of Minority Health
108 Cherry St.
Burlington, VT 05402-0070
(802) 863-7273 Fax: (802) 651-3425
Contact: Corbett Sionainn, MSW, Pub. Health Spec.
Email: csionai@vdh.vt.state.us
Web: www.omhrc.gov/OMH

WASHINGTON

WASHINGTON STATE DEPARTMENT OF
HEALTH
Office of Minority Affairs
1112 Quince St.
Olympia, WA 98504-7890
(360) 236-4021 Fax: (360) 586-7424
Contact: Oscar Cerda, Director
Email: oec0303@doh.wa.gov
Web: www.state.wa.us

WISCONSIN

DEPARTMENT OF HEALTH AND FAMILY
SERVICES
Division of Public Health
1 W. Wilson St. #250
Madison, WI 53701-2659
(608) 267-3257 Fax: (608) 267-2832
Contact: Denise Carty, RN, Minority Health Officer

WEST VIRGINIA

WEST VIRGINIA BUREAU FOR PUBLIC HEALTH,
OFFICE OF RURAL HEALTH POLICY
Minority Health Program
350 Capitol St. #515
Charleston, WV 25301-3716
(304) 558-1327 Fax: (304) 558-1437
Contact: Savolia Spottswood, MS, Prog. Mgr.
Email: savolia@wvdhhr.org
Web: www.wvdhhr.org

WYOMING

WYOMING STATE DEPT. OF HEALTH
Community and Family Health Section
Hathaway Bldg. 4th Fl. Rm. 477
Cheyenne, WY 82002
(307) 777-5601 Fax: (307) 777-5215
Contact: Betty Sones, Minority Health Prog. Mgr.
Email: bsones@missc.state.wy.us
Web: www.state.wy.us

Anuario Hispano.com

Hispanic Yearbook.com

202

AnuarioHispano.**com**

Hispanic Adolescents
Los adolescentes hispanos

Pregnancy rates according to outcome of pregnancy among adolescents 15-19 years of age, by age, race, and Hispanic origin.
Promedio de preñez de acuerdo al resultado de preñez entre los adolescentes entre 15 y 19 años de edad, por edad, raza y origen hispano.

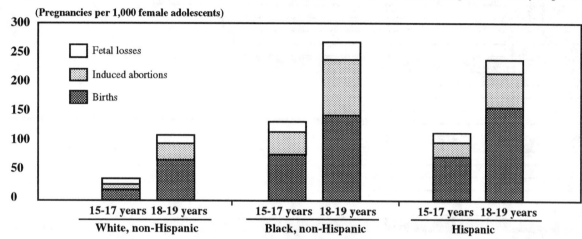

Birth rates among adolescents 13-19 years of age, by birth order, age, race, and Hispanic origin.
Promedio de nacimientos entre adolescentes de 13 a 19 años de edad, ordenados por nacimiento, edad, raza y origen hispano.

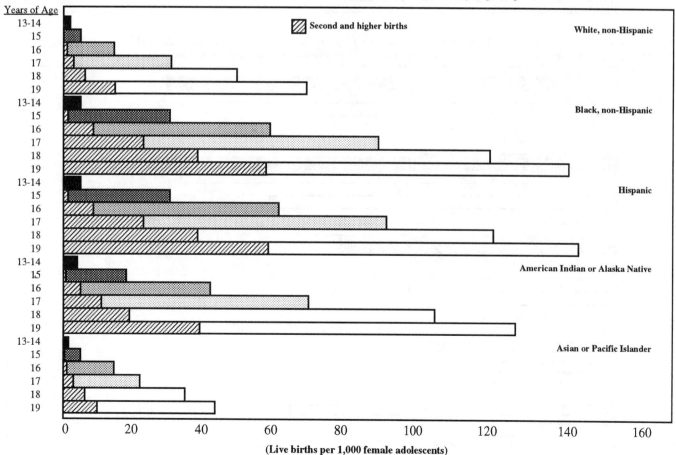

Source: U.S. Census Bureau (Health, US 2000)

Low-birthweight live births among adolescent mothers 13-19 years of age, by maternal age, race, and Hispanic origin.
Nacimientos con bajo peso al nacer entre madres adolescentes de 13 a 19 años de edad, por edad de la madre, raza y origen hispano.

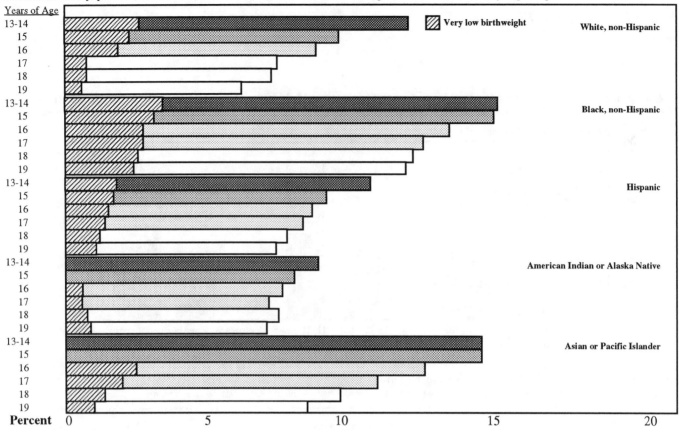

Infant mortality rates among infants of adolescent mothers 13-19 years of age, by maternal age, race, and Hispanic origin.
Promedio de mortalidad infantil entre hijos de madres adolescentes de 13 a 19 años de edad por edad de la madre, raza y origen hispano.

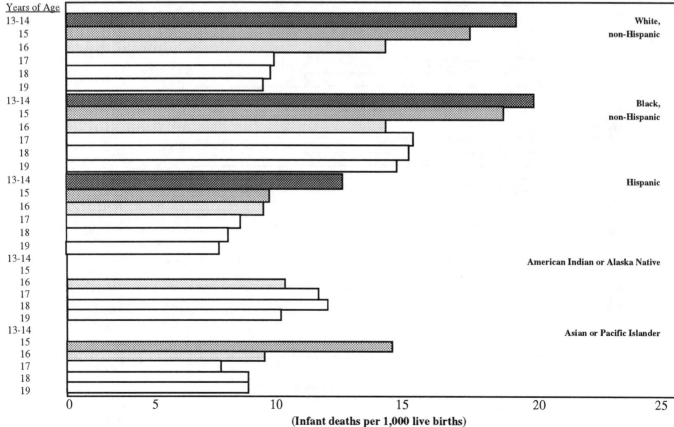

(Infant deaths per 1,000 live births)

Sexually transmitted disease rates reported for adolescents 10-19 years of age, by age, gender, race, and Hispanic origin.
Promedio de las enfermedades transmitidas sexualmente reportada por las adolescentes entre 10 y 19 años de edad por edad, sexo, raza y origen hispano.

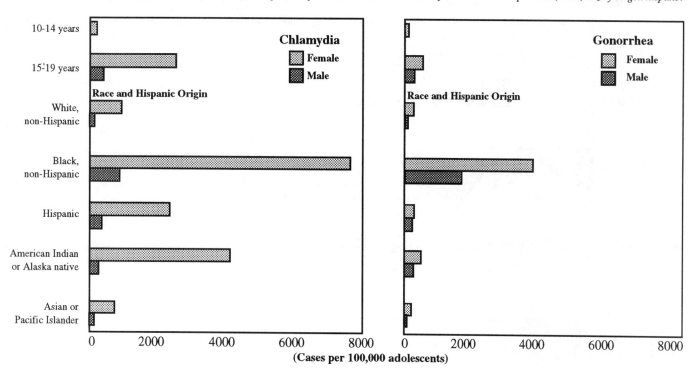

(Cases per 100,000 adolescents)

Acquired immunodeficiency syndrome (AIDS) rates reported for adolescents 11-19 years of age, by age, gender, race, and Hispanic origin.
Promedio del síndrome de inmune deficiencie (SIDA) reportado por adolescentes entre 11 y 19 anõs de edad por edad, sexo, raza y origen hispano.

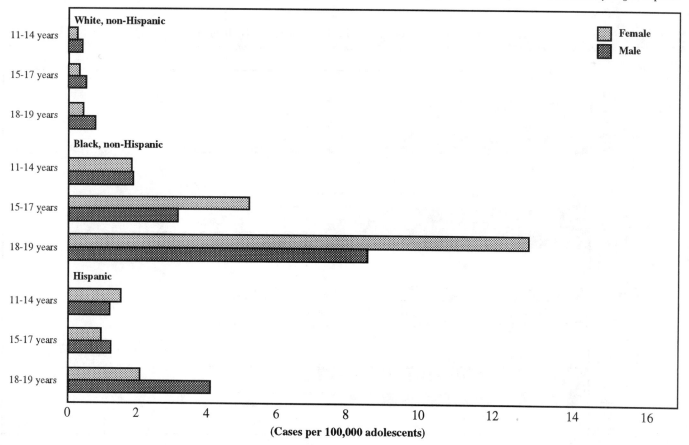

(Cases per 100,000 adolescents)

Current cigarette smoking among students in grades 9-12 by gender, grade level, race, and Hispanic origin.
Actual cantidad de estudiantes que fuman cigarrillos entre estudiantes de los grados de 9 a 12 por sexo, nivel de grado, raza y origen hispano.

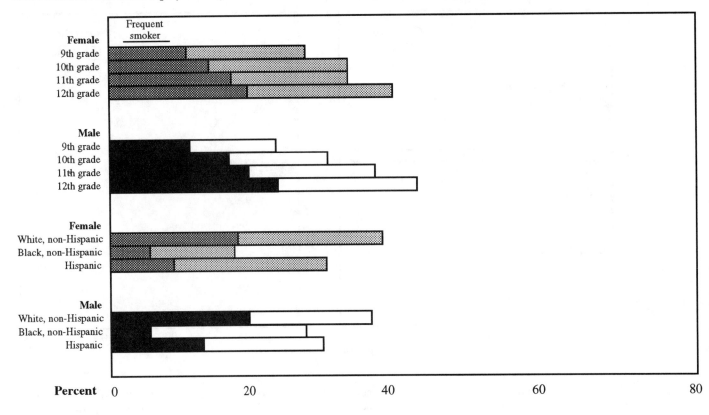

Current alcohol use among students in grades 9-12, by gender, grade level, race, and Hispanic origin.
Actual consumo de alcohol entre los estudiantes en los grados de 9 a 12 por sexo, nivel de grado, raza y origen hispano.

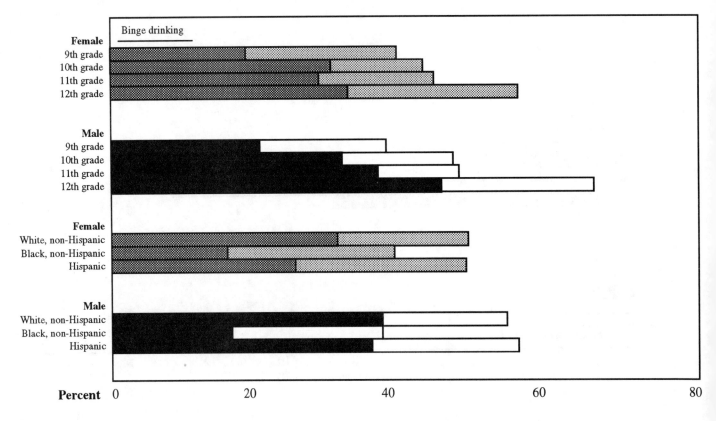

Lifetime marijuana use among students in grades 9-12, by gender, grade level, race, and Hispanic origin.
Periódo de vida en el que se consumió marihuana entre los estudiantes en los grados de 9 a 12, por sexo, nivel de estudios, raza y origen hispano.

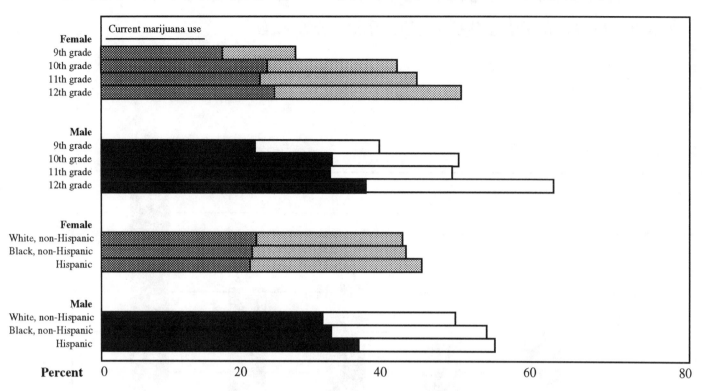

Lack of health care visit in the past 12 months among adolescents 10-19 years of age, by age, gender, health care coverage, race, and Hispanic origin
Ausencia de visitas para el cuidado de la salud en los últimos doce meses por adolescentes entre diez y diecinueve años de edad por edad, sexo, raza y origen hispano.

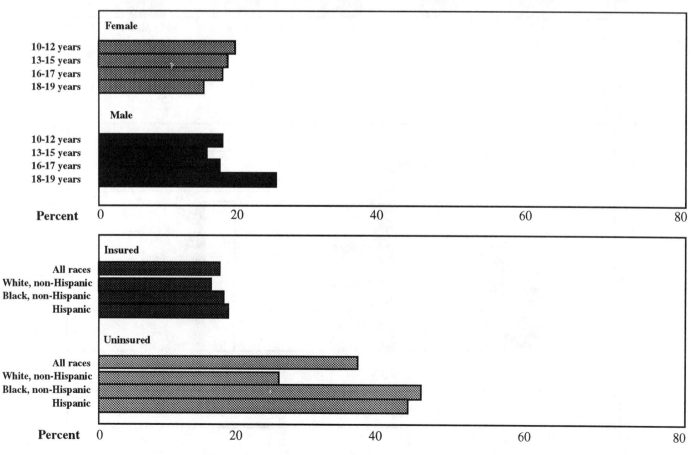

Persons Not Covered by Health Insurance in the US

Personas no cubiertas por seguro médico en EUA

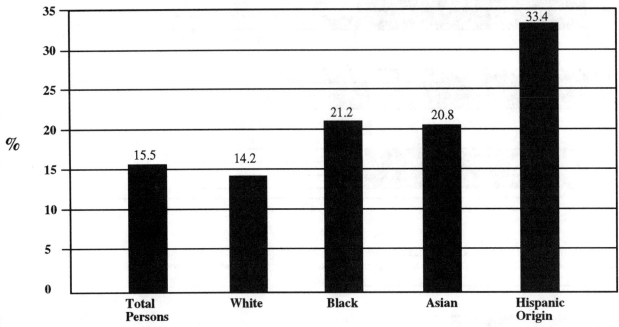

Source: Bureau of the Census (Press-Release/www/2000)

Health Care Visits in U.S.
(Visitas al médico)

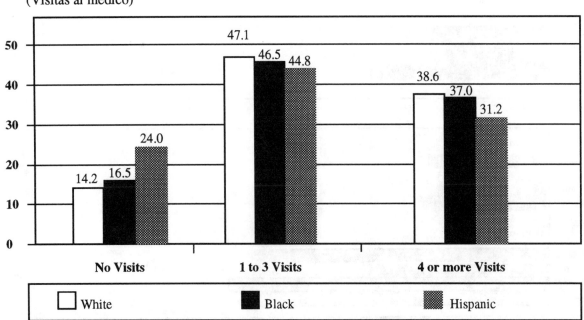

Source: National Health Interview Survey/www/2000

Hispanic Publications
Publicaciones hispanas

A

A COMMON VOICE
Southern Arizona AIDS Foundation
375 S. Euclid Ave.
Tucson, AZ 85719
Neal Liwanag, Admin. Asst.
(520) 628-7223 Fax: (520) 628-7222
Circ: 1,500

A DEMOGRAPHIC PROFILE OF CUBAN AMERICANS
Cuban American National Council, Inc.
1223 SW 4th St.
Miami, FL 33135
Guarioné M. Díaz, Pres.
(305) 642-3484 Fax: (305) 642-9122

AAMA ADELANTE
Association for the Advancement of Mexican Americans
204 Clifton St.
Houston, TX 77011
Gilbert Moreno, Exec. Dir.
(713) 926-4756 Fax: (713) 926-2672
Circ: 800

ABOARD, AEROPOSTAL
North-South Net, Inc.
100 Almeria Ave. #220
Coral Gables, FL 33134
Diana G. Bethel, Pub.
(305) 441-9744 Fax: (305) 441-9739

ABOARD, ECUATORIANA
North-South Net, Inc.
100 Almeria Ave. #220
Coral Gables, FL 33134
Diana G. Bethel, Pub.
(305) 441-9744 Fax: (305) 441-9739

ABOARD, LAB
North-South Net, Inc.
100 Almeria Ave. #220
Coral Gables, FL 33134
Diana G. Bethel, Pub.
(305) 441-9744 Fax: (305) 441-9739

ABOARD, LADECO
North-South Net, Inc.
100 Almeria Ave. #220
Coral Gables, FL 33134
Diana G. Bethel, Pub.
(305) 441-9744 Fax: (305) 441-9739

ABOARD, LAN-CHILE
North-South Net, Inc.
100 Almeria Ave. #220
Coral Gables, FL 33134
Diana G. Bethel, Pub.
(305) 441-9744 Fax: (305) 441-9739

ABOARD, PLUMA
North-South Net, Inc.
100 Almeria Ave. #220
Coral Gables, FL 33134
Diana G. Bethel, Pub.
(305) 441-9744 Fax: (305) 441-9739

ABOARD, TACA COSTA RICA
North-South Net, Inc.
100 Almeria Ave. #220
Coral Gables, FL 33134
Diana G. Bethel, Pub.
(305) 441-9744 Fax: (305) 441-9739

ABOARD, TACA EL SALVADOR
North-South Net, Inc.
100 Almeria Ave. #220
Coral Gables, FL 33134
Diana G. Bethel, Pub.
(305) 441-9744 Fax: (305) 441-9739

ABOARD, TACA GUATEMALA
North-South Net, Inc.
100 Almeria Ave. #220
Coral Gables, FL 33134
Diana G. Bethel, Pub.
(305) 441-9744 Fax: (305) 441-9739

ABOARD, TACA HONDURAS
North-South Net, Inc.
100 Almeria Ave. #220
Coral Gables, FL 33134
Diana G. Bethel, Pub.
(305) 441-9744 Fax: (305) 441-9739

ABOARD, TACA NICARAGUA
North-South Net, Inc.
100 Almeria Ave. #220
Coral Gables, FL 33134
Diana G. Bethel, Pub.
(305) 441-9744 Fax: (305) 441-9739

ABOARD, TACA PERÚ
North-South Net, Inc.
100 Almeria Ave. #220
Coral Gables, FL 33134
Diana G. Bethel, Pub.
(305) 441-9744 Fax: (305) 441-9739

THE ACADEMIC PERFORMANCE OF HISPANICS IN FLORIDA PUBLIC SCHOOLS
Cuban American National Council, Inc.
1223 SW 4th St.
Miami, FL 33135
Guarioné M. Díaz, Pres.
(305) 642-3484 Fax: (305) 642-9815

ACCIÓN AFIRMATIVA PARA PERSONAS CON IMPEDIMENTOS
President's Committee on Employment of People with Disabilities (PCEH)
1331 F St. NW #300
Washington, DC 20004-1107
Jill Greene, Publications
(202) 376-6200 Fax: (202) 376-6219

ACCIÓN VENTURES
Acción International
120 Beacon St.
Somerville, MA 02143-9853
Mandy Smith, Edtr.
(617) 492-4930 Fax: (617) 876-9509
Circ: 1,000

ACENTO HISPANO NEWS
The Merchandiser
P.O. Box 840
Lebanon, PA 17042
Moises Mañon Rossi, Edtr.
(717) 274-0491 Fax: (717) 273-0420
Circ: 36,000

ACENTO LATINO
Dickson Press, Inc.
119 West Elwood Ave.
Raeford, NC 28376
Violeta Taylor, Edtr.
(910) 875-2121 Fax: (910) 875-7256
Circ: 13,000

ACTUALIDAD NEWSPAPER
Actualidad
7356 Dinwiddie St.
Downey, CA 90241
Pedro M. Valdivieso, Edtr.
(562) 928-9424 Fax: (562) 927-9940
Circ: 25,000

ADELANTE!
National Puerto Rican Coalition, Inc.
1700 K St. NW #500
Washington, DC 20006
Kery Wilkie-Nufiez, Managing Edtr.
(202) 223-3915 Fax: (202) 429-2223
Circ: 12,500

AFFIRMATIVE ACTION REGISTER
Affirmative Action, Inc.
8356 Olive Blvd.
St. Louis, MO 63132
Joyce Green, Edtr.
(314) 991-1335 Fax: (314) 997 1788
Circ: 67,000

AGENDA DE DECORACIÓN
Casiano Communications
1700 Ave. Fernández Juncos
San Juan, PR 00909
Johan Maldonado, Edtr.
(787) 728-3000 Fax: (787) 728-1075
Circ: 40,000

AGENDA PARA LA NOVIA
Casiano Communications
1700 Ave. Fernández Juncos
San Juan, PR 00909
Johan Maldonado, Edtr.
(787) 728-3000 Fax: (787) 728-1075
Circ: 40,000

AGENDA PARA MAMÁ
Casiano Communications
1700 Ave. Fernández Juncos
San Juan, PR 00909
Johan Maldonado, Edtr.
(787) 728-3000 Fax: (787) 728-1075
Circ: 40,000

AGRICULTURA DE LAS AMÉRICAS
Keller International Publishing Corp.
150 Great Neck Rd.
Great Neck, NY 11021

Víctor Prieto, Edtr.
(516) 829-9210 Fax: (516) 829-3591
Published 6 issues/year
Circ: 39,692

AHA! HISPANIC ARTS NEWS
Association of Hispanic Arts, Inc. (AHA)
250 W 26th St., 4th Floor
New York, NY 10001
Alfredo Alvarez, Edtr.
(212) 727-7227 Fax: (212) 727-0549
Circ: 2,000

AHORA
Ahora Spanish-English Newspaper
P.O. Box 3582
Reno, NV 89509
Sheila Sepulveda, Pub.
(775) 323-6811 Fax: (775) 323-6995
Circ: 15,000

AHORA
Scholastic Magazine
P.O. Box 3710
Jefferson City, MO 65102-3710
David Goddy, Edtr.
(800) 724-6527 Fax: (573) 635-8937
Published 6 issues/year

AHORA NOW
Ahora Now
601 E San Ysidro Blvd. #180
San Ysidro, CA 92173
Bertha Alicia González, Edtr.
(619) 428-2277 Fax: (619) 428-0871
Circ: 20,000

AIDS CHICAGO
Chicago Dept. of Public Health
Epidemology/Aids Surveillance, 333 S State S., 2nd Floor
Chicago, IL 60604
Frank Oldham, Jr., Assistant Commissioner
(312) 747-9611 Fax: (312) 747-9663
Circ: 1,800

AIDS PREVENTION
Puerto Rican Association for Human Development, Inc.
100 1st St.
Perth Amboy, NJ 08861
Jose Angulo, Coordinator
(732) 442-1081 Fax: (908) 826-3082
Circ: 500

AIDSIDAINFO
The National Latina/o Lesbian, Gay, Bisexual & Transgender Organization
1612 K St. NW #500
Washington, DC 20006
(202) 466-8240 ext 109 Fax: (202) 466-8530
Circ: 3,000

AL DÍA
Al Día Newspaper, Inc.
211 N 13th St. #704
Philadelphia, PA 19107
Hernán Guaracao, Edtr./ Pub.

(215) 457-6999 Fax: (215) 457-6737
Circ: 14,000

AL DÍA, BILINGUAL DIRECTORY
Chicano Latino Affairs Council
555 Park St. #210
St. Paul, MN 55103
Gladys Zelaya, Off. Specialist
(651) 296-9587 Fax: (651) 297-1297
Circ: 900

**ALFI DIRECTORY OF MEMBERS
AND ASSOCIATE MEMBERS**
American League of Financial Institutions
900 19th St. NW #400
Washington, DC 20006
Dina Nicholson, Edtr.
(202) 628-5624 Fax: (202) 296-8716

ALIANZA METROPOLITAN NEWS
Alianza Metropolitan News
2849 Story Rd.
San Jose, CA 95127
George Villalobos , Pub.
(408) 272-9394 Fax: (408) 272-9395
Circ: 3,000

THE ALLIANCE
Hispanic Alliance for Career Enhancement
14 E Jackson Blvd. #1310
Chicago, IL 60604
Eva Serrano, Pres.
(312) 435-0498 Fax: (312) 435-1494
Circ: 10,000

ALMANAQUE MUNDIAL
Editorial Televisa
6355 NW 36th St.
Miami, FL 33166
(305) 871-6400 Fax: (305) 871-1520

ALPHA & OMEGA
P.O. Box 7400
Jersey City, NJ 07307
Nestor P. Hurtado, Pub.
(201) 915-0200 Fax: (201)915-1715
Circ: 10,000

ALTERNATIVE PRESS INDEX
Alternative Press Center
P.O. Box 33109
Baltimore, MD 21218
Debby Bors, Edtr.
(410) 243-2471 Fax: (410) 235-5325
Circ: 500

AMAT LATIN EVENTS CALENDAR
AMAT
2735 W 38th Ave.
Denver, CO 80211
Elisabeth Nietch, Edtr.
(303) 332-3184
Circ: 5,000

AMÉRICA ECONOMÍA
Dow Jones
800 Douglas Rd. #460
Coral Gables, FL 33134
Samuel Silva, Edtr.
(305) 444-7430 Fax: (305) 443-6237
Circ: 113,000

AMERICAN GI FORUM
American GI Forum
765 Story Rd.
San Jose, CA 95122
Abel Cota, Dir
(408) 288-9471 Fax: (408) 288-9473
Circ: 1,000

AMÉRICAS
Organization of American States
19th St. & Constitution Ave. NW #300
Washington, DC 20006
Organization of the American States
(202) 458-6218 Fax: (202) 458-6217
Circ: 68,000

THE AMERICAS REVIEW
Arte Público Press
University of Houston
4800 Calhoun
Houston, TX 77204-2090

Nicolás Kanellos, Dir.
(713) 743-2998 Fax: (800) 633-ARTE
Circ: 1,500

AMERICAS SOCIETY
Americas Society, Inc.
680 Park Ave.
New York, NY 10029
Alfred MacAdam, Edtr./Pub.
(212) 249-8950
Circ: 1,000

AMIGOS DE JESUS
Claretian Publications
205 West Monroe
Chicago, IL 60606
Carmen Aguinaco, Edtr.
(312) 236-7782 Fax: (312) 236-8207
Circ: 400

ANGELES MESA & TRIBUNE
Wave Community Newspapers, Inc.
2621 W 54th St.
Los Angeles, CA 90043
Pluria Marshall, Jr, Pres.
(323) 290-3000 Fax: (323) 291-0219

ANNUAL REPORT
*Alamo Area Council of Governments
(AACOG)*
8700 Tesoro Dr. #700
San Antonio, TX 78217
Laura Jane Stephens, Community Relations
Coord.
(210) 362-5200 Fax: (210) 225-5937

**ANNUAL REPORT & BIO
DIRECTORY**
National Urban Fellows, Inc.
59 John St. #310
New York, NY 10038
Luis Alvarez, Pres.
(212) 349-6200 Fax: (212) 349-7578
Circ: 3,000

ANNUAL REPORT OF IDB
Inter-American Development Bank
External Relations Office
1300 New York Ave. NW
Washington, DC 20577
IDB Bookstore
(202) 623-1154 Fax: (202) 623-3531

**ANNUAL REPORT OF THE
EXECUTIVE BOARD**
International Monetary Fund
Publication Services-700 19th St., NW #12-607
Washington, DC 20431
Dept. of Publications
(202) 623-7430 Fax: (202) 623-7201

ANTENNA
4809 Calle Alto
Camarillo, CA 93012
Sergio Cisneros, Edtr.
(805) 389-1680 Fax: (805) 389-1272
Circ: 10,000

**ANUARIO DE ESTADÍSTICAS DEL
TRABAJO**
International Labor Office
1828 L St., NW #600
Washington, DC 20036
Marjorie Crow, Marketing Assistant
(202) 653-7652 Fax: (202) 653-7687

**ANUARIO DE LA COMISIÓN DE
DERECHO INTERNACIONAL**
The United Nations
2 United Nations Pl. #DC2-853
New York, NY 10017
(212) 963-8302 Fax: (212) 963-3489

**ANUARIO DE LA COMISIÓN DE LAS
NACIONES UNIDAS**
The United Nations
2 United Nations Pl. #DC2-853
New York, NY 10017
(212) 963-8302 Fax: (212) 963-3489

**ANUARIO DE LAS NACIONES
UNIDAS SOBRE DESARME**
The United Nations
2 United Nations Pl. #DC2-853
New York, NY 10017
(212) 963-8302 Fax: (212) 963-3489

**ANUARIO ESTADÍSTICO DE
AMERICA LATINA Y EL CARIBE**
The United Nations
2 United Nations Pl. #DC2-853
New York, NY 10017
(212) 963-8302 Fax: (212) 963-3489

**ANUARIO HISPANO-HISPANIC
YEARBOOK**
TIYM Publishing Co., Inc.
6718 Whittier Ave., #130
McLean, VA 22101
Angela E. Zavala, Edtr.
(703) 734-1632 Fax: (703) 356-0787
Circ: 200,000

**ANUARIO JURÍDICO DE LAS
NACIONES UNIDAS**
The United Nations
2 United Nations Pl. #DC2-853
New York, NY 10017
(212) 963-8302 Fax: (212) 963-3489

AQUÍ LLEGÓ
*National Latino/a Lesbian & Gay
Organization*
1612 K St. NW #500
Washington, DC 20006
Matín Ornelas-Quintero, Exec. Dir.
(202) 466-8240 Fax: (202) 466-8530
Circ: 2,000

THE ARIZONA REPORT
*Mexican American Studies & Research
Center*
University of Arizona, Economics Bldg. #208
Tucson, AZ 85721-0023
Tom Gelsimon, Edtr.
(520) 621-7551 Fax: (520) 621-7966
Circ: 2,000

ARRIBA ART & BUSINESS NEWS
P.O. Box 12865
Austin, TX 78711
Romero Rodríguez, Pub.
(512) 479-6397
Circ: 8,500

ART DECO TROPICAL
Miami Beach Art Deco Publishing
221 Meridian Ave. #410
Miami Beach, FL 33139
Mirta Pestana, Edtr.
(305) 534-3884 Fax: (305) 674-3491
Circ: 5,000

ARTE AL DÍA
American Art Corporation
905 Brickell Bay Dr., Tower II #1021
Miami, FL 33131
Fermin Fevre, Edtr.
(305) 371-7106 Fax: (305) 371-7107
Circ: 25,000

ARTES GRÁFICAS
Carvajal International
901 Ponce de León Blvd. #901
Coral Gables, FL 33134
Juan Carlos Gayoso, Pub.
(305) 448-6875 Fax: (305) 448-9942
Circ: 3,000

ASC NEWSLETTER
American Spanish Co.
P.O. Box 119. Canal St. Station
New York, NY 10013
Anthony F. Gonzalez, Chairman & CEO
(201) 567-7417 Fax: (201) 816-9727

ASI SOMOS NEWSLETTER
*National Conference of Puerto Rican
Women, Inc. Long Island Chapter*
P.O. Box 357
Pt. Jefferson Station, NY 11776
Lynda Perdomo-Ayala, Pres.

(631) 476-4972 Fax: (631) 444-3218
Circ: 1,500

ASPIRA NEWS
Aspira Association, Inc. National Office
1444 & I St. NW #800
Washington, DC 20005
Johnny Villamil-Casanova, Exec. VP/Edtr.
(202) 835-3600 Fax: (202) 835-3613
Circ: 3,000

ATLAS PERSPECTIVE
*Association of Teachers of Latin American
Studies (ATLAS)*
P.O. Box 620754
Horace Harding Station
Flushing, NY 11362-0754
Daniel Mugan, Edtr.
(718) 428-1237 Fax: (718) 428-1237
Circ: 800

AUTOMOVIL PANAMERICANO
Editorial Televisa
6355 NW 36th St.
Miami, FL 33166
(305) 871-6400 Fax: (305) 871-1520
Circ: 37,944

AUTOMUNDO MAGAZINE
Automundo Productions, Inc.
2960 SW 8th St., 2nd Fl.
Miami, FL 33135
Jorge Koechlin, Pres.
(305) 541-4198 Fax: (305) 541-5138
Circ: 55,000

AVANCE HISPANO
Avance Hispano, Inc.
4230 Mission St.
San Francisco, CA 94112
Marco Tulio Meza, Edtr.
(415) 585-1080 Fax: (415) 585-1398

AZTECA NEWS
Azteca News
810 N Broadway
Santa Ana, CA 92701
Fernando Velo, Edtr.
(714) 972-9912 Fax: (714) 973-8117
Circ: 42,000

**AZTLAN. A JOURNAL OF CHICANO
STUDIES**
UCLA Chicano Studies Research Center
2307 Murphy Hall
Los Angeles, CA 90095-1544
Chon Moriega, Edtr.
(310) 825-2642 Fax: (310) 206-1784
Circ: 600

B

BAJO EL SOL
Freedom Press
2055 Arizona Ave.
Yuma, AZ 85364
Maria Chavoya, Edtr.
(520) 783-3333 Fax: (520) 539-6891
Circ: 21,000

**BANDA ORIENTAL
LATINOAMERICANA**
321 Rahway Ave.
Elizabeth, NJ 07202
Julia Moreira, Edtr./Pub.
(908) 965-0909 Fax: (908) 965-1724
Circ: 10,000

BASIC FACTS
Inter-American Development Bank
1300 New York Ave. NW
Washington, DC 20577
IDB Bookstore
(202) 623-1154 Fax: (202) 623-3531

THE BELL GARDENS SUN
Eastern Group Publications, Inc.
2500 S Atlantic Blvd., Bldg. A
Los Angeles, CA 90040
Dolores Sanchez, Edtr.
(323) 263-5743 Fax: (323) 263-9169
Circ: 10,000

BIENVENIDOS A MIAMI
Publishing Group
P.O. Box 630518
Miami, FL 33163
Clara Amsel, Edtr.
(305) 944-9444 Fax: (305) 949-0544
Circ: 16,000

BIENVENIDOS MAGAZINE
Coral Publications
403 Calle del Parque, Piso 11
San Juan, PR 00912-3709
Addie Romero, Edtr.
(787) 729-9060 Fax: (787) 729-9063
Circ: 187,000

BIENVENIDOS MAGAZINES
Welcome Publishing
1751 NE 162 St.
North Miami Beach, FL 33162
DeAnne C. Connolly, Office Manager
(305) 944¹9444
Circ: 16,000

BILINGUAL RESEARCH JOURNAL
National Association for Bilingual Education
1030 15th St. NW #470
Washington, DC 20005
Jose Gonzalez/ Alfredo Benavidez, Edtr.
(202) 898-1829 Fax: (202) 789-2866
Published 3 issues/year
Circ: 3,000

BILINGUAL SERVICES DIRECTORY
El Conquistador
1135 Sunbury Rd.
South Elgin, IL 60177
Laura Carrillo Barth, Edtr.
(847) 697-3533 Fax: (847) 697-3585
Circ: 10,000

BIOMEDICINA
Mundo Medico USA, Inc.
158 Danbury Rd., #8
Ridgefield, CT 06877
Sarah E. Gutierrez, Pub.
(203) 438-1056 Fax: (203) 438-1057

BOLETÍN ANOTA
Asociacion de Notarios de Puerto Rico
P.O. Box 363613
San Juan, PR 00936-3613
Lic. Julio L. Morales Roger, Exec. Dir.
(787) 758-2773 Fax: (787) 759-6703
Circ: 1,600

BOLETÍN DE ESTADÍSTICAS DEL TRABAJO
International Labor Office
1828 L St., NW #600
Washington, DC 20036
Marjorie Crow, Marketing Assistant
(202) 653-7652 Fax: (202) 653-7687

BOLETÍN DE PUERTO RICO
Boletín de Puerto Rico
P.O. Box 361716
San Juan, PR 00936-1716
Umberto García, Pres.
(787) 268-3733 Fax: (787) 268-3988
Circ: 1,000

BOLETÍN DEL CEPI
Círculo de Escritores y Poetas Iberoamericanos de Nueva York
P. O. Box 831 GPO
New York, NY 10116
Gerardo Piña, Pres.
(914) 354-6799
Circ: 150

BOLETÍN OFICIAL SERIE A
International Labor Office
1828 L St., NW #600
Washington, DC 20036
Marjorie Crow, Marketing Assistant
(202) 653-7652 Fax: (202) 653-7687

BOLETÍN OFICIAL SERIE B
International Labor Office
1828 L St., NW #600
Washington, DC 20036

Marjorie Crow, Marketing Assistant
(202) 653-7652 Fax: (202) 653-7687

THE BOOK OF LIST
Casiano Communications
1700 Ave. Fernández Juncos
San Juan, PR 00909
Diana Lozano, Edtr.
(787) 728-3000 Fax: (787) 728-1075
Circ: 35,000

BORDERLINES
Interhemispheric Resource Center
P.O. Box 2178
Silver City, NM 88062
George Kourous, Edtr.
(505) 388-0208 Fax: (505) 388-0619
Circ: 1,000

THE BOTTOM LINE
The National Society of Hispanic MBA's (NSHMBA)
8204 Elmbrook #235
Dallas, TX 75247-4067
Andrés Cordero, Edtr.
(877) 462-4622 Fax: (214) 267-1626

THE BRASILIANS
The Brasilians Press and Publications, Inc.
21 W 46th St. #203
New York, NY 10036
Edilberto Luciano Mendes, Edtr.
(212) 398-6464 Fax: (212) 382-3620
Circ: 45,000

BRAZZIL
P.O. Box 50536
Los Angeles, CA 90050
Rodney Mello, Edtr.
(323) 255-8062 Fax: (323) 257-3487
Circ: 12,000

BUENA VIDA MAGAZINE
Casiano Communications
1700 Ave. Fernández Juncos
San Juan, PR 00909
Annette Oliveras, Edtr.
(787) 728-3000 Fax: (787) 728-1075
Circ: 61,000

BUENHOGAR
Editorial Televisa
6355 NW 36th St.
Miami, FL 33166
Irene Carol, Edtr.
(305) 871-6400 Fax: (305) 871-1520
Circ: 31,083

BUSINESS REVIEW
Latin Business Association
5400 E Olympic Blvd. #130
Los Angeles, CA 90022
Veronica Sanchez, Edtr.
(323) 721-4000 Fax: (323) 722-5050
Circ: 1,000

C

CABLEGUÍA
International Media Reps.
4045 Bonita Rd. #209
Bonita, CA 91902
Patricia Ciccone, Principal
(619) 267-6010 Fax: (619) 267-5965
Circ: 37,000

CALIENTE MAGAZINE
Caliente Magazine
5725 Buford Hwy. #219
Doraville, GA 30340
Elmer Pineda, Edtr.
(770) 220-0055 Fax: (770) 220-2469

CAMACOL
Latin Chamber of Commerce of USA
1417 W Flagler St.
Miami, FL 33135
Luis Sabines, Pres.
(305) 642-3870 Fax: (305) 642-0653
Circ: 4,000

CAMINO, LUZ Y VIDA
P.O. Box 1189
Falls Church, VA 22041
Luis Oscar Torres, Edtr./Pres.
(703) 933-7216 Fax: (703) 933-7226
Circ: 15,000

CAMPESTRE
International Media Reps
4045 Bonita Rd. #209
San Diego, CA 91902
Demetrio Carrasco, Administrative Dir.
(619) 267-6010 Fax: (619) 267-5965
Circ: 12,000

CAMPUS POINTS
Spring Institute for International Studies
1610 Emerson St.
Denver, CO 80218
Myrna Ann Adkins, Pres.
(303) 863-0188 Fax: (303) 863-0178

CAPNEWS
Community Action Programs
2040 14th St.
Boulder, CO 80302
Janett Heimer, Dir.
(303) 441-3975 Fax: (303) 441-4550
Circ: 1,000

CAREER FOCUS
Communications Publishing Group, Inc.
3100 Broadway #660
Kansas City, MO 64111-2413
Georgia Lee Clark, Pub.
(816) 960-1988 Fax: (816) 960-1989
Circ: 250,000

CARIB NEWS
Carib News
15 W 39th St., 13th Floor
New York, NY 10018
Karl Rodney, Pub.
(212) 944-1991 Fax: (212) 944-2089
Circ: 67,000

CARIBBEAN BUSINESS-NEWSPAPER
Casiano Communications
1700 Ave. Fernández Juncos
San Juan, PR 00909
Francisco J. Cimadevilla, Esq., Edtr.
(787) 728-3000 Fax: (787) 728-1075
Circ: 44,500

CARIBBEAN BUSINESS-WHITE PAGES
Casiano Communications
1700 Ave. Fernández Juncos
San Juan, PR 00909
Diana Lozano, Edtr.
(787) 728-3000 Fax: (787) 728-1075
Circ: 35,000

CARIBBEAN TODAY
P.O. Box 6010
Miami, FL 33116-6010
Barbara Williams, Acct. Exec./Writer
(305) 238-2868 Fax: (305) 252-7843
Circ: 48,000

CARIBBEAN UPDATE
52 Maple Ave.
Maplewood, NJ 07040
Kal Wagenheim, Edtr./Pub.
(973) 762-1565 Fax: (973) 762-9585

CARIBBEAN YELLOW PAGES
Caribbean Publishing Co.
2655 Le Jeune Rd. #800
Coral Gables, FL 33134
Mark Ercolin, Edtr.
(305) 442-4205 Fax: (305) 442-8329
Circ: 50,000

CARISMA Y VIDA CRISTIANA
Strang Comunicaciones
600 Rinehart Rd.
Lake Mary, FL 32746
Tessie Güell, Edtr.
(407) 333-7117 Fax: (407) 333-7147
Circ: 30,000

CARRIZO SPRINGS JAVELIN
Carrizo Springs Javelin
604 N. 1st St.
Carrizo Springs, TX 78834
Annie García, Edtr.
(830) 876-2318 Fax: (830) 876-2620
Circ: 2,000

CARTA DE CUBA
Carta de Cuba, Inc.
P.O. Box 9352
San Juan, PR 00908-0352
(787) 759-8807 Fax: (787) 754-1139

CASA & ESTILO INTERNACIONAL
Linda International Publishing
12182 SW 128thSt.
Miami, FL 33186
José Alfonso Niño, Dir./Pub.
(305) 378-4466 Fax: (305) 378-9951
Circ: 55,000

THE CATHOLIC SUN
Catholic Diocese of Phoenix
P.O. Box 13549
Phoenix, AZ 85002-3549
Rob Difrancesco, Managing Edtr.
(602) 257-5565 Fax: (602) 258-6404
Circ: 106,000

THE CAULDRON
The Cauldron
3800 Montrose Blvd.
Houston, TX 77006
Erin McLain, Dir.
(713) 525-3579 Fax: (713) 525-2159
Circ: 1,800

CENTRO JOURNAL
Center for Puerto Rican Studies. Hunter College
695 Park Ave., 14th floor
New York, NY 10021
Mirian Jiménez Román, Edtr.
(212) 772-5689 Fax: (212) 650-3673
Circ: 1,000

CENTRO UNIDO EN ACCIÓN
Centro Unido de Detallistas de Puerto Rico
Apartado 190127
San Juan, PR 00919-0127
Emilio Torres Hernandez, Pres.
(787) 759-8405 Fax: (787) 754-7312
Circ: 45,000

CEPAL REVIEW
The United Nations
2 United Nations Pl. #DC2-853
New York, NY 10017
The United Nations, Edtr.
(212) 963-8302 Fax: (212) 963-3489

THE CHALLENGE OF EDUCATION
Cuban American National Council, Inc.
1223 SW 4th St.
Miami, FL 33135
Guarioné M. Díaz, Pres.
(305) 642-3484 Fax: (305) 642-9815

CHANCE EDUCATIONAL
Chance Bilingual Productions, Inc.
2426 Quenby St.
Houston, TX 77005
M.E. Oddo, Pres.
(713) 522-1273 Fax: (713) 524-8970
Circ: 35,000

CHCI NEWS
Congressional Hispanic Caucus Institute, Inc.
504 C St. NE
Washington, DC 20002
Juan Herrera, Edtr.
(202) 543-1771 Fax: (202) 543-2143

CHICAGO CATÓLICO
New World Publications
721 N LaSalle St.
Chicago, IL 60610
Maria del Carmen Macias, Edtr.
(312) 243-1300 Fax: (312) 243-1526
Circ: 12,000

CHICAGO DEPORTIVO
Chicago Deportivo
3748 S Cleveland Ave.
Brookfield, IL 60513
Julio Parrales, Edtr.
(708) 387-0380 Fax: (708) 485-4969
Circ: 30,000

CÍRCULO POÉTICO
Círculo de Cultura Panamericano
16 Malvern Pl.
Verona, NJ 07044-2554
Jose Corrales/René León, Co-Editors
(973) 239-3125 Fax: (973) 239-3125
Circ: 800

CÍRCULO: REVISTA DE CULTURA
Círculo de Cultura Panamericano
16 Malvern Pl.
Verona, NJ 07044-2554
Elio Alba-Buffill, Edtr.
(973) 239-3125 Fax: (201) 239-3125
Circ: 800

CITY TERRACE COMET
Eastern Group Publications, Inc.
2500 S Atlantic Blvd., Bldg. A
Los Angeles, CA 90040
Dolores Sanchez, Edtr.
(323) 263-5743 Fax: (323) 263-9169
Circ: 2,500

CLARÍN
10500 Rockville Pike #428
Rockville, MD 20852
Julio César Mosches, Edtr.
(301) 896-0049 Fax: (301) 896-0049
Circ: 10,000

CLASS! (DÍGANOS)
Class Publications
Univ. of Nevada, Las Vegas. Box 451025
Las Vegas, NV 89154-1025
Sari Aizley, Edtr.
(702) 895-1504 Fax: (702) 895-1505
Circ: 22,500

CLAVE
Latin American Folk Institute
3800A 34th St.
Mount Rainier, MD 20712
Luis Rumbaut, Edtr.
(301) 887-9331 Fax: (301) 887-0308

COLOMBIAN NEWSLETTER
Colombian American Association, Inc.
30 Vesey St. #506
New York, NY 10007
Peter S. Smith, Edtr.
(212) 233-7776 Fax: (212) 233-7779
Circ: 500

COMERCIO
Hispanic Chamber of Commerce, Inc.
930 W 7th Ave.
Denver, CO 80204
Sharon Vigel, C.E.O.
(303) 534-7783 Fax: (303) 595-8977

COMERCIO
Atlanta Hispanic Chamber of Commerce
1961 North Druid Hills Rd. #21-B
Atlanta, GA 30329
Sara J. Gonzalez, Pres.
(404) 929-9998 Fax: (404) 929-9908
Circ: 800

**COMERCIO Y PRODUCCIÓN.
REVISTA OFICIAL DE LA CÁMARA
DE COMERCIO DE PUERTO RICO**
Direct Marketing & Media Group
P.O. Box 9024182
San Juan, PR 00902-4182
Lillia Molina Ruiz, Pres.
(787) 268-1111 Fax: (787) 268-7044
Circ: 10,000

COMMERCE COMET
Eastern Group Publications, Inc.
2500 S Atlantic Blvd., Bldg. A
Los Angeles, CA 90040
Dolores Sanchez, Edtr.

(323) 263-5743 Fax: (323) 263-9169
Circ: 5,000

COMMODITY PRICE BULLETIN
The United Nations
2 United Nations Pl. #DC2-853
New York, NY 10017
(212) 963-8302 Fax: (212) 963-3489

COMMUNITY FOCUS/ENFOQUE
Bestinfo Communications, Inc.
3565 N 7th St., 3rd Floor
Philadelphia, PA 19140
Efrain Roche, Edtr.
(215) 227-0618/0628 Fax: (215) 227-0646
Circ: 23,500

**COMO PREPARAR LA
DECLARACIÓN DE IMPUESTO
FEDERAL, PUB. 579SP**
US Internal Revenue Service (IRS)
P. O. Box 85074
Distribution Center
Richmond, VA 23261-5074
(800) 829-3676

**COMUNICÁNDOSE CON LA
CÁMARA**
*Hispanic Chamber of Commerce of
Wisconsin*
816 W National Ave.
Milwaukee, WI 53204
María Monreal-Cameron, C.E.O.
(414) 643-6963 Fax: (414) 643-6994
Circ: 500

CONNECTION TO THE AMERICAS
Resource Center of the Americas
3019 Mennehaha Ave. S.
Minneapolis, MN 55406
Chip Mitchell, Edtr.
(612) 276-0788 Fax: (612) 276-0898
Published 10 issues/year
Circ: 1,600

CONNECTIONS
Catholic Youth Organization
305 Michigan Ave.
Detroit, MI 48226
Katheleen Burton, Dir. of Development
(313) 963-9768 Fax: (313) 963-7179

CONSCIENCE
Catholics for a Free Choice
1436 U St. NW #301
Washington, DC 20009-3997
Tegan Culler, Edtr.
(202) 986-6093 Fax: (202) 332-7995
Circ: 10,000

CONSTELACIÓN
The Arlington Dancing Company
4343 Lee Highway #505
Arlington, VA 22207
Simón R. Contreras, Edtr.
(703) 528-4094 Fax: (703) 358-6273
Circ: 600

CONSTRUCCION PAN-AMERICANA
International Construction Publishing
4913 SW 75th Ave.
Miami, FL 33155
Juan B. Escalante, Edtr.
(305) 668-4999 Fax: (305) 668-7774
Circ: 15,000

CONTACTO
1317 N San Fernando Blvd. #PMB-246
Burbank, CA 91504
Jesus Hernandez Cuellar, Edtr.
(818) 842-3308 Fax: (818) 557-6251
Circ: 25,000

CONTINENTAL
212 48th St.
Union City, NJ 07087
Mario Ciria, Edtr.
(201) 864-9505 Fax: (201) 864-9456
Circ: 38,000

COSMOPÓLITAN
Editorial Televisa
6355 NW 36th St.

Miami, FL 33166
Sara M. Castany, Edtr.
(305) 871-6400 Fax: (305) 871-1520
Circ: 52,630

COSTILLA COUNTY FREE PRESS
Costilla County Free Press
P.O. Box 306
San Luis, CO 81152
(719) 672-3764 Fax: (719) 671-3895
Circ: 250

**CRÉDITO POR INGRESO DEL
TRABAJO, PUB. 596SP**
US Internal Revenue Service (IRS)
P. O. Box 85074
Distribution Center
Richmond, VA 23261-5074
(800) 829-1040

CRISTINA LA REVISTA
Editorial Televisa
6355 NW 36th St.
Miami, FL 33166
Luz María Doria, Edtr.
(305) 871-6400 Fax: (305) 871-1520
Circ: 141,490

CUBA SURVEY
Cuban American National Foundation
1000 Thomas Jefferson St., NW, #505
Washington, DC 20007
José Cardenas, Dir./Edtr.
(202) 265-2822 Fax: (202) 338-0308
Circ: 5,000

CUBA UPDATE
Center for Cuban Studies
124 W 23rd St.
New York, NY 10011
Sandra Levinson, Edtr.
(212) 242-0559 Fax: (212) 242-1937
Circ: 1,000

**CUBAN AMERICAN NATIONAL
COUNCIL**
Cuban American National Council, Inc.
1223 SW 4th St.
Miami, FL 33135
Guarioné M. Díaz, Pres.
(305) 642-3484 Fax: (305) 642-9815
Circ: 10,000

**CUBAN AMERICAN NATIONAL
COUNCIL NEWSLETTER**
Cuban American National Council, Inc.
1223 SW 4th St.
Miami, FL 33135
Guarioné M. Díaz, Pres.
(305) 642-3484 Fax: (305) 642-9122

**THE CUBAN BALSEROS: VOYAGE
OF UNCERTAINTY**
Cuban American National Council, Inc.
1223 SW 4th St.
Miami, FL 33135
Guarioné M. Díaz, Pres.
(305) 642-3484 Fax: (305) 642-9815

**THE CUBANIZATION AND
HISPANIZATION OF METROPOLI-
TAN MIAMI**
Cuban American National Council, Inc.
1223 SW 4th St.
Miami, FL 33135
Guarioné M. Díaz, Pres.
(305) 642-3484 Fax: (305) 642-9815

CUIDA A TU HIJO
El Buen Vecino, Inc.
P.O. Box 3390
South Bend, IN 46619
Sara Haber, C.E.O.
(219) 287-8228 Fax: (219) 288-7505
Published 4 issues/year
Circ: 1,000

CULTURAL EXPLORING MAGAZINE
Sunsea Publishing
P.O. Box 920183
Norcross, GA 30010-0183
Barry Stepe, Edtr.

(770) 242-9815 Fax: (770) 242-9193
Circ: 8,000

D

DE NORTE A SUR
Norte a Sur
65-18 170th St.
Fresh Meadows, NY 11365-1950
Hebert Bonilla, Pub.
(718) 762-8833 Fax: (718) 353-8679
Circ: 30,000

DELHI NEWSLETTER
Delhi Center
542 E Central Ave.
Santa Ana, CA 92707
Margarita Chavez, Exec. Asst.
(714) 549-1317 Fax: (714) 549-5738

DENVER CATHOLIC REGISTER
Denver Catholic Diocese
1300 S Stevel St.
Denver, CO 80210
Peter Droege, Edtr.
(303) 722-4687 Fax: (303) 715-2045
Circ: 93,000

DENVER NOTICIERO
Hispanic Employees Program
1961 Stout St.
Denver, CO 80294
Rita Salomon, Chair.
(303) 844-4441 Fax: (303) 844-3674
Circ: 200

**DENVER VICTIMS SERVICE
CENTER**
Denver Victims Service Center
P. O. Box 18975
Denver, CO 80218
Kathy Fanning, Dir. Volunteer Services
(303) 860-0660 Fax: (303) 831-7282
Circ: 1,500

DEPORTE INTERNACIONAL
Editorial Televisa
6355 NW 36th St.
Miami, FL 33166
Eduardo Camarena, Edtr.
(305) 871-6400 Fax: (305) 871-1520
Circ: 39,800

DEPORTIMUNDO
845 N Eastern Ave.
Las Vegas, NV 89101
Eddie Escobedo, Jr., Pub.
(702) 649-8553 Fax: (702) 649-7429
Circ: 8,500

**DERECHOS DEL CONTRIBUYENTE,
PUB. 1SP**
US Internal Revenue Service (IRS)
P. O. Box 85074
Distribution Center
Richmond, VA 23261-5074
(800) 829-1040

**DESARROLLO MÁS ALLÁ DE LA
ECONOMÍA**
Inter-American Development Bank
External Relations Office
1300 New York Ave. NW
Washington, DC 20577
IDB Bookstore
(202) 623-1154 Fax: (202) 623-3531

DIÁLOGO
Univ. of Puerto Rico
P.O. Box 364984
San Juan, PR 00936-4984
Mariely Rivera Hernandez, Dir.
(787) 763-1370 Fax: (787) 250-8729
Circ: 40,000

DIÁLOGO MAGAZINE
*Center for Latino Research, DePaul
University*
2320 N Kenmore Ave., SAC 563
Chicago, IL 60614

Félix Masud-Piloto, Dir.
(773) 325-7316 Fax: (773) 325-7166
Published 2 issues/year
Circ: 5,000

DIALOGUE / DIÁLOGO
Inter-American Dialogue
1211 Connecticut Ave., NW, #510
Washington, DC 20036
Jenni Lukac, Publications Dir.
(202) 822-9002 Fax: (202) 822-9553
Published 3 issues/year

DIALOGUE ON DIVERSITY
Dialogue on Diversity, Inc.
1730 K St. NW #304
Washington, DC 20006
Maria Cristina C. Caballero, Pres.
(703) 631-0650 Fax: (703) 631-0617
Circ: 2,500

DIARIO DE JUAREZ
Editora Paso del Norte
6996 Industrial Ave. #A
El Paso, TX 79915
Osvaldo Rodríguez, Jr., Pres.
(915) 772-1043 Fax: (915) 722-1299
Circ: 80,000

DIARIO DE LA MUJER
P.O. Box 14-5393
Coral Gables, FL 33114-5393
Karmen González, Dir.
(305) 827-1537 Fax: (305) 827-2502
Circ: 25,000

DIARIO EL DÍA
Cuatro Comunicaciones
6120 Tarnef #100
Houston, TX 77074
Sergio R. Budini, Gen. Dir.
(713) 772-8900 Fax: (713) 772-8999
Circ: 25,000

DIARIO LAS AMÉRICAS
The Americas Publishing Co.
2900 NW 39th St.
Miami, FL 33142
Horacio Aguirre, Edtr.
(305) 633-3341 Fax: (305) 635-7668
Circ: 68,000

DIARIO METRO
Diario Metro, Inc.
Calle 4, H-10. Urb. Villa de La Marina
Carolina, PR 00979
Wilfredo Umpierre Hernández, Edtr./Pres.
(787) 791-7208 Fax: (787) 791-7304
Circ: 70,000

DIRECTORIO COMERCIAL
SBJ Publishing Co.
P.O. Box 16783
Seattle, WA 98116
Ramón Rodríguez, Pub.
(206) 297-8532 Fax: (206) 706-3082
Circ: 25,000

DIRECTORIO DE AGENCIAS PARTICIPANTES Y SERVICIOS
Fondos Unidos de Puerto Rico
P.O. Box 191914
San Juan, PR 00919-1914
María Elena Lampaya, Coord.
(787) 728-8500 Fax: (787) 728-7099

DIRECTORIO HISPANO
Directorio Hispano, Inc.
12005 NE 12th St. #26
Bellevue, WA 98005
Raúl Pérez-Calleja, Pres.
(425) 646-8846 Fax: (425) 646-8823
Circ: 22,000

DIRECTORIO HISPANO
Latino Publishing, Inc.
5665 Columbia Pike
Falls Church, VA 22041
Segundo Morillo, Pres.
(703) 671-4000 Fax: (703) 671-8886
Circ: 100,000

DIRECTORIO HISPANO DE LOUISIANA
Raices Inc.
P.O. Box 8399
New Orleans, LA 70182
Jose R. Cossio M., Edtr./Pres.
(504) 286-1700 Fax: (504) 286-1700
Circ: 15,000

DIRECTORIO PROFESIONAL HISPANO/ SPANISH-SPEAKING PROFESSIONALS IN EASTERN U.S.
Directorio Profesional Hispano
14205 Roosevelt Ave.
Flushing, NY 11354-6045
George E. Balbi, Edtr.
(718) 762-1432
Circ: 500

DIRECTORY OF HISPANIC ARTS
Association of Hispanic Arts, Inc. (AHA)
250 W 26th St., 4th Floor
New York, NY 10001
(212) 727-7227 Fax: (212) 727-0549
Circ: 2,750

DIRECTORY OF MINORITY ARTS AND ORGANIZATIONS
National Endowment for the Arts
Civil Rights Division
1100 Pennsylvania Ave. NW #219
Washington, DC 20506
Denise Peirson, Contact
(202) 682-5454 Fax: (202) 602-5553
Circ: 2,000

DIRECTORY OF MINORITY PUBLIC RELATIONS PROFESSIONALS
Public Relations Society of America
33 Irving Place, 3rd Floor
15th & 16th St.
New York, NY 10003
Barbara B. Hines, Edtr.
(212) 995-2230 Fax: (212) 995-5024

DIRECTORY OF PUERTO RICAN ORGANIZATIONS
National Puerto Rican Coalition, Inc.
1700 K St. NW #500
Washington, DC 20006
Manuel Mirabal, Edtr.
(202) 223-3915 Fax: (202) 429-2223
Circ: 1,000

DIRECTORY OF SPECIAL PROGRAMS FOR MINORITIES
Garrett Park Press, Inc.
P.O. Box 190 F
Garrett Park, MD 20896-0190
Willis L. Johnson, Edtr.
(301) 946-2553 Fax: (301) 949-3955
Circ: 500

DIRECTORY ON NATIONAL FELLOWSHIPS, INTERNSHIPS AND SCHOLARSHIPS FOR LATINO YOUTH
Congressional Hispanic Caucus Institute, Inc.
504 C St. NE
Washington, DC 20002
Carmen Joge, Edtr.
(202) 543-1771 Fax: (202) 543-2143

DISCOMUNDO
159 E 116th St.
New York, NY 10029
Julio Garcia, Assoc. Edtr.
(202) 722-2612 Fax: (202) 722-7666

DISIDENTE UNIVERSAL DE PUERTO RICO
Comisión Cubano de Derechos Humanos y Reconciliación Nacional
P.O. Box 360889
San Juan, PR 00936-0889
Angel W. Padilla Piña, Dir.
(787) 762-9853 Fax: (787) 762-3301
Circ: 10,000

DOS MUNDOS
902A Southwest Blvd.
Kansas City, MO 64108-2358
Clara Reyes, Pub.

(816) 221-4747 Fax: (816) 221-4894
Circ: 20,000

E

EAGLE PASS BUSINESS JOURNAL
P.O. Drawer 2160
438 N. Monroe St.
Eagle Pass, TX 78853
Ricardo E. Calderón, Pub.
(830) 757-2705 Fax: (830) 757-2703
Circ: 3,000

EAST L.A. BROOKLYN-BELVEDERE COMET
Eastern Group Publications, Inc.
2500 S Atlantic Blvd., Bldg. A
Los Angeles, CA 90040
Dolores Sanchez, Edtr.
(323) 263-5743 Fax: (323) 263-9169
Circ: 2,750

EAST LOS ANGELES CHAMBER OF COMMERCE NEWSLETTER
5401 E Whittier Blvd.
Los Angeles, CA 90022
Fanny Arroyo, Project Coord.
(323) 722-2005 Fax: (323) 722-2405
Circ: 600

EASTSIDE SUN
Eastern Group Publications, Inc.
2500 S Atlantic Blvd., Bldg. A
Commerce, CA 90040
Dolores Sanchez, Edtr.
(323) 263-5743 Fax: (323) 263-9169
Circ: 22,000

ECONOMIC IMPACT OF SPANISH-LANGUAGE PROFICIENCY IN METROPOLITAN MIAMI
Cuban American National Council, Inc.
1223 SW 4th St.
Miami, FL 33135
Guarioné M. Díaz, Pres.
(305) 642-3484 Fax: (305) 642-9815

ECOS BILINGUAL PUBLICITY
Ecos Bilingual Publicity
P.O. Box 10243
Winston-Salem, NC 27107
Deborah Ramírez, Vice Pres.
(336) 722-3267 Fax: (336) 727-9729
Circ: 10,000

ECUADOREAN NEWSLETTER
Ecuadorean American Association, Inc.
30 Vesey St. #506
New York, NY 10007
Peter S. Smith, Edtr.
(212) 233-7776 Fax: (212) 233-7779
Circ: 500

EDITORIAL PACE
Derus Media Service, Inc.
712 Vandustrial Dr.
Westmont, IL 60559
Matt McGaenn, Pres.
(630) 960-4690 Fax: (630) 960-4695
Circ: 10,000

EL ÁGUILA
Hispanic American Police Command Officers Association
12885 Research Blvd. #107
Austin, TX 78750
Ron Estrada, Edtr.
(787) 749-7610
Circ: 1,000

EL ANDAR
El Andar Media Corporation
P.O. Box 7745
Santa Cruz, CA 95061
Jorge Chino, Pub.
(831) 457-8353 Fax: (831) 457-8354
Circ: 50,000

EL ARGENTINO-MERCOSUR
P.O. Box 402039

Miami Beach, FL 33140
Alberto A. Micheli, Dir./Edtr.
(305) 532-6710 Fax: (305) 672-8511
Circ: 10,000

EL AVISADOR
A1 Ruiz & Son
1722 Junction Ave. #E
San Jose, CA 95112
Orlando Ruiz-Gessa, Edtr.
(408) 437-0909 Fax: (408) 437-1114
Circ: 40,000

EL AVISO
El Aviso de Ocasion, Inc
8101 Long Beach Blvd. #L
South Gate, CA 90280
José Ramiro Zepeda, Pres.
(323) 586-9199 Fax: (323) 589-9395
Circ: 100,000

EL BATÚ
Editorial Fundación
P.O. Box 1570
Bronx, NY 10459
Bomexi Iztaccihuatl, General Coordinator
(718) 328-9281

EL BOHEMIO NEWS
El Bohemio News, Inc.
4178 Mission St.
San Francisco, CA 94112
Fred Rosado, Edtr.
(415) 469-9579 Fax: (415) 469-9481
Circ: 45,000

EL BOLETÍN
The Greater Washington Ibero American Chamber of Commerce
1420 16th St. NW #102
Washington, DC 20036
Juan Albert, Pres.
(202) 728-0352 Fax: (202) 728-0355
Circ: 1,500

EL BORICUA
Boricua Publications
3109-C Voss Dr.
El Paso, TX 79936
Ivonne Figueroa, Edtr./Gen. Mgr.
(915) 595-1446 Fax: (915) 595-1409
Circ: 10,000

EL CAMARASUR
Cámara de Comercio de Ponce y Sur de Puerto Rico
Apartado 7455
Ponce, PR 00732
Bessie Nicole, Exec.Dir.
(787) 844-4400 Fax: (787) 844-4705
Circ: 2,500

EL CARDENAL
Image, Inc. San Louis Chapter
6651 Gravois #212
St. Louis, MO 63116
Liz Sanchez-Setser, Chapter Pres.
(314) 832-0790
Circ: 500

EL CENTINELA
Oregon Catholic Press
5536 NE Hassalo St.
Portland, OR 97213
Rocio Rios, Dir.
(503) 460-5406 Fax: (503) 282-3486
Circ: 10,000

EL CENTRO AMERICANO
CAYMEN
P.O. Box 3556
Van Nuys, CA 91407-3556
José Mariano Galvez, Pres.
(818) 997-1518 Fax: (818) 997-1518
Circ: 5,000

EL CHICANO
Inland Empire Community Newspaper
P.O. Box 6247
San Bernadino, CA 92412
Monica Mankin, Edtr.
(909) 381-9898 Fax: (909) 384-0406

EL CLARÍN
40 Broadway
Harvestraw, NY 10927
Rafael Espaillat, Edtr.
(914) 429-2949 Fax: (914) 429-6801

EL CLARÍN (WEEKLY SHOPPER)
Bcc-Bugle Communications Corp.
8900 SW 107th Ave. #306
Miami, FL 33176-1451
Jose Noboa, Pres.
(305) 270-3333 Fax: (305) 270-2272
Circ: 160,000

EL CLASIFICADO
1125 S Goodrich Blvd.
Los Angeles, CA 90022
Martha C. de la Torre, Edtr./Pub.
(323) 278-5310 Fax: (323) 278-5315
Circ: 110,000

EL COLOMBIANO NEWSPAPER
Latin Work Publishing
PMB 186
15751 Sheridan St.
Fort Lauderdale, FL 33331
Alfredo Mantilla, Edtr.
(954) 430-1090 Fax: (954) 438-4418
Circ: 35,000

EL COMPRADOR MEXICANO
Aegle Enterprises
501 S Escondido Blvd.
Escondido, CA 92025
Ruby Sandoval, Sales Mgr.
(760) 743-4450 Fax: (760) 743-3398
Circ: 5,000

EL CONQUISTADOR
El Conquistador
1135 Sunburry Rd.
South Elgin, IL 61077
Laura Carrillo Barth, Edtr.
(847) 697-3533 Fax: (847) 697-3585
Circ: 15,000

EL CONQUISTADOR LATINO JOURNAL
El Conquistador
64 E Downer Place
Aurora, IL 60505
Laura Barth, Edtr.
(630) 892-9691 Fax: (630) 892-9697
Circ: 15,000

EL CONQUISTADOR LATINO NEWS SOURCE
Conquistador Communications LLC
3220 W National Ave.
Milwaukee, WI 53215
Victor Huyke, Edtr.
(414) 383-1000 Fax: (414) 383-8885
Circ: 10,000

EL DEFENSOR CHIEFTAIN
World West, LLC
P.O. Box Q
Socorro, NM 87801
Julie Piotraschke, Edtr.
(505) 835-0520 Fax: (505) 835-1837
Circ: 3,800

EL DIA NEWSPAPER
El Día Publications
6013 W 26th St.
Cicero, IL 60804
Jorge A. Montes de Oca, Pub.
(708) 652-6397 Fax: (708) 652-6653
Circ: 30,000

EL DIARIO
El Diario Inc.
2553 NW 74th Ave.
Miami, FL 33122
Osvaldo Muñoz, Edtr.
(305) 593-6210 Fax: (305) 593-6213
Circ: 40,000

EL DIARIO -LA PRENSA
Latin Communications Group
345 Hudson St., 13th floor
New York, NY 10014
Gerson Borrero, Edtr.
(212) 807-4600 Fax: (212) 807-4705
Circ: 72,000

EL DIRECTORIO HISPANO-PÁGINAS AMARILLAS EN ESPAÑOL
P.O. Box 266604
Weston, FL 33326
Carmen Díaz Fabián, Edtr.
(954) 767-0643 Fax: (954) 767-9805
Circ: 50,000

EL ECONÓMICO
Los Angeles Newspaper Group
604 Pine Ave.
Long Beach, CA 90844
Bruno Arosa, Edtr.
(562) 499-1415 Fax: (562) 499-1484
Circ: 100,000

EL EDITOR NEWSPAPER
Amigo Publications
P.O. Box 11250
Lubbock, TX 79408
Bidal Agüero, Edtr.
(806) 763-3841 Fax: (806) 741-1110
Circ: 15,000

EL EDITOR PERMIAN BASIN
Chinati Tres Casas
1401 Rankin Hwy.
Midland, TX 79701
Manuel J. Orona, Edtr.
(915) 570-0405 Fax: (915) 580-5560
Circ: 14,840

EL ESPECIAL
3510 Bergenline Ave.
Union City, NJ 07087
Jose Sibaja, Edtr.
(201) 348-1959 Fax: (201) 348-3385
Circ: 76,000

EL ESPECIAL NEWSPAPER
El Especial, Inc.
175 Fontainbleau Blvd. #1F
Miami, FL 33172
José Sibaja, Edtr.
(305) 225-3742 Fax: (305) 223-6049
Circ: 35,000

EL ESTADIO
La Oferta
1376 N 4th St.
San Jose, CA 95112
Mary Andrade, Edtr.
(408) 436-7850 Fax: (408) 436-7861
Circ: 35,000

EL EXPRESO LATINOAMERICANO
El Expreso Publishing, Inc.
P.O.Box 2528
Perth Amboy, NJ 08862
Carlos Neira, Account Exec./Pub.
(732) 442-3344 Fax: (732) 442-3344
Circ: 60,000

EL EXTRA
Periódicos Hispanos de Texas
8012 Trade Village Place
Dallas, TX 75217
Emmy Silva, Pub.
(214) 309-0990 Fax: (214) 309-0204
Circ: 28,000

EL FINANCIERO
El Financiero International, Inc.
2300 S Broadway
Los Angeles, CA 90007
Martin Avila, Dir. of Sales & Marketing
(213) 747-7547 Fax: (213) 747-2489
Circ: 135,000

EL FUTURO NEWSLETTER
National Latino Children's Institute
1412 W 6th St.
Austin, TX 78703
Rebeca María Barrera, Pres.
(512) 472-9971 Fax: (512) 472-5845
Circ: 7,000

EL HERALDO CATÓLICO
Catholic Diocese of Sacramento
5890 Newman Ct.
Sacramento, CA 95819

Deacon Ricardo Olvera, Edtr.
(916) 452-3691 Fax: (916) 452-2945
Circ: 36,000

EL HERALDO COMMUNITY NEWS
El Heraldo de Broward, Inc.
1975 E Sunrise Blvd. #616
Ft. Lauderdale, FL 33304
Elaine Vázquez, Edtr.
(954) 527-0627 Fax: (954) 792-7402
Circ: 100,000

EL HERALDO DE BROWARD
El Heraldo de Broward, Inc.
1975 E Sunrise Blvd. #616
Ft. Lauderdale, FL 33304
Elaine Vázquez, Edtr.
(954) 527-0627 Fax: (954) 792-7402
Circ: 12,000

EL HERALDO DE BROWNSVILLE
Freedom Communications
1135 E Van Buren St.
Brownsville, TX 78520
Ramón Rodriguez, Edtr.
(956) 982-6625 Fax: (956) 542-0840
Circ: 6,500

EL HERALDO DE CHICAGO
El Heraldo
1325 W Grand Ave.
Chicago, IL 60622
Gonzalo Sánchez, Edtr.
(312) 455-0300 Fax: (312) 666-6397
Circ: 15,000

EL HERALDO HISPANO
El Heraldo Hispano
525 13th St. #806
Rome, GA 30165
Enrique Luna, Dir.
(706) 346-0756 Fax: (706) 346-0756
Circ: 10,000

EL HISPANIC NEWS
Padilla & Associates
2130 SW 5th Ave. #205
Portland, OR 97201
Clara Padilla-Andrews, Pub.
(503) 228-3139 Fax: (503) 228-3384
Circ: 20,000

EL HISPANO
Larenas Publishing Co, Inc.
1903 21st. St.
Sacramento, CA 95814
Bill Larenas, Edtr.
(916) 442-0267 Fax: (916) 442-2818
Circ: 20,000

EL HISPANO
Hispanos Unidos de Virginia, Inc.
6400-B Seven Corner Pl.
Falls Church, VA 22044
Jonny Simancas, Exec. Dir./Pres.
(703) 533-1760 Fax: (703) 533-9369
Circ: 25,000

EL HISPANO
López Publications, Inc.
8605 W Chester Pike
Upper Darby, PA 19082
Aaron López, Pub.
(610) 789-5512 Fax: (610) 789-5524
Circ: 38,000

EL HISPANO NEWS
El Hispano News
P.O. Box 986, 900 Park Ave. SW
Albuquerque, NM 87103
A.B. Collado, Edtr./Pub.
(505) 243-6161
Circ: 10,000

EL HISPANO NEWS
2102 Empire Central
Dallas, TX 72535
Marcos Nelson Suarez, Pub.
(214) 357-2186 Fax: (214) 357-2195
Circ: 35,000

EL HISPANO NEWS
Graph-ads Printing
1451 Grandville SW
Grand Rapids, MI 49509
Jaime Malone, Edtr.
(616) 452-1511 Fax: (616) 452-1542
Circ: 15,000

EL HOGAR CRISTIANO
Casa Bautista de Publicaciones
7000 Alabama St., P.O. Box 4255
El Paso, TX 79914
Ezequiel San Martin, Dir. of Production Division
(915) 566-9656
Circ: 33,000

EL IMPARCIAL
El Imparcial Publishing Co.
1502 E Brodway
Tuckson, AZ 85719
María Leon, Edtr.
(520) 792-2114 Fax: (520) 792-2189
Circ: 35,000

EL IMPARCIAL NEWSPAPER
Santelices Communications, Inc.
3615 W 26th St., 2nd Floor
Chicago, IL 60623
Alicia C. Santelices, Edtr./Pub.
(708) 484-1188 Fax: (708) 484-0202
Circ: 30,000

EL INFORMADOR
Grupo Cultura
P.O. Box 756
Duluth, GA 30096
Agustín Bossio, Dir.
(770) 623-6687 Fax: (770) 623-6687
Circ: 4,000

EL INFORMADOR DE DALTON
Thompson Newspapers Corporation
308 S Thornton Ave.
Dalton, GA 30720
Juan Varela, Dir.
(706) 272-7725 Fax: (706) 272-7713
Circ: 6,000

EL INFORMADOR HISPANO
Garcia Publications
P.O. Box 163661
Fort Worth, TX 76161
Hilda Manrique, Edtr.
(817) 626-8624 Fax: (817) 626-1855
Circ: 25,000

EL INFORME
Commission on Spanish-Speaking Affairs
741 N Cedar #102
Lansing, MI 48913
Olivares Mason, Edtr.
(517) 334-8626 Fax: (517) 334-8641
Circ: 1,500

EL INTÉRPRETE
United Methodist Communications
810 12th Ave. S
Nashville, TN 37203-4777
Martha Rovira de Raber, Edtr.
(615) 742-5101 Fax: (615) 742-5460
Circ: 6,000

EL LATINO
Latina & Associates, Inc.
1550 Broadway St. #U
Chula Vista, CA 91911
Fanny Miller, Edtr.
(619) 426-1491 Fax: (619) 426-3206
Circ: 60,500

EL LATINO SEMANAL
El Latino Semanal/Palm Beach Latino
4325 Georgia Ave.
West Palm Beach, FL 33405
Miguel Lavin/Jose R. Uzal, Edtr.
(561) 835-4913 Fax: (561) 655-5059
Circ: 36,000

EL MAÑANA
Editorial Argo
1 S Main Ave., Lower Level
Laredo, TX 78040-5935

Ramón Cantú-Deandar, Edtr.
(956) 712-1122 Fax: (956) 717-5091
Circ: 50,000

EL MAÑANA NEWS
El Mañana Daily
2700 S Harding
Chicago, IL 60623
Humberto Perales, Edtr.
(773) 521-9137 Fax: (773) 521-5351
Circ: 10,000

EL MENSAJERO
Cardenas Publications, Inc.
2760 Mission St.
San Francisco, CA 94110
Jose del Castillo, Edtr.
(415) 206-7230 Fax: (415) 206-7238
Circ: 60,000

EL MENSAJERO
Spanish Fiesta, Inc.
205 E Joppa Rd. #2502
Towson, MD 21286
Luis E. Queral, Dir./Edtr.
(410) 823-7948 Fax: (410) 823-7117
Circ: 10,000

EL MEXICALO
El Mexicalo
931 Niles St.
Bakersfield, CA 93305
Tony Manzano Jr., Edtr.
(661) 323-9334 Fax: (661) 323-6951
Circ: 15,000

EL MEXICANO
International Media Reps.
4045 Bonita Rd. #209
San Diego, CA 91902
Patricia Ciccone, Pres.
(619) 267-6010 Fax: (619) 267-5965
Circ: 150,000

EL MOMENTO CATÓLICO
Claretian Publications
205 West Monroe
Chicago, IL 60606
Carmen Aguinaco, Edtr.
(312) 236-7782 Fax: (312) 236-8207
Circ: 300,000

EL MUNDO
Alameda Publishing Co., Inc.
P.O. Box 1350
Oakland, CA 94612-1350
Mario Palacios, Edtr.
(510) 287-8200 Fax: (510) 763-9670

EL MUNDO
El Mundo
2116 E César Chavez St.
Austin, TX 78702
Roberto Angulo, Edtr.
(512) 476-8636 Fax: (512) 476-6402
Circ: 20,000

EL MUNDO
Caribe Communications
408 S Huntington Ave.
Boston, MA 02130-4814
Andres Rodriguez, Edtr./Pub.
(617) 522-5060 Fax: (617) 524-5886
Circ: 30,000

EL MUNDO
El Mundo
P.O. Box 2231
Wenatchee, WA 98807
Jim Tiffany, Edtr./Pub.
(509) 663-5737 Fax: (509) 663-6957
Circ: 15,000

EL MUNDO
El Mundo
760 N Eastern Ave.
Las Vegas, NV 89101
Eddie Escobedo, Jr., Pub.
(702) 649-8553 Fax: (702) 649-7429
Circ: 26,000

EL MUSEO DEL BARRIO
El Museo del Barrio
1230 5th Ave.
New York, NY 10029
Tania Saiz-Sousa, Public Relations
(212) 831-7272 Fax: (212) 831-7927
Published 3 issues/year
Circ: 10,000

EL NACIONAL
660 W 178th St. #1A
New York, NY 10033
Carlos Luciano, Edtr./Pub.
(212) 781- 1915 Fax: (212) 740-1299
Circ: 44,000

EL NACIONAL DE OKLAHOMA NEWS
Printing, Inc.
304 SW 25th St.
Oklahoma City, OK 73109
Randy King, Mgr.
(405) 632-4531 Fax: (405) 632-4533
Circ: 12,500

EL NORTE DE ATLANTA
239 Ezzard St., P.O. Box 263
Lawrenceville, GA 30046
Franco Vera, Gen. Mgr.
(770) 237-8868 Fax: (770) 237-8769
Circ: 10,000

EL NORTE NEWSPAPER OF AUSTIN
The Leading Hispanic Newspaper in Austin
P.O. Box 2781
Austin, TX 78768-2181
Gloria M. Aguilar, Edtr./Pub.
(512) 448-1023 Fax: (512) 448-9962
Circ: 20,000

EL NUEVO COQUI
258 Clifton Ave.
Newark, NJ 07104
Irvin Linares, Edtr.
(973) 481-3233 Fax: (973) 481-6807
Circ: 15,000

EL NUEVO DÍA
El Día, Inc.
P.O. Box 7512
San Juan, PR 00906
Luis Ferre, Edtr.
(787) 273-7600 Fax: (787) 641-3924
Circ: 198,500

EL NUEVO HERALD
The Miami Herald
One Herald Plaza
Miami, FL 33132-1693
Carlos M. Castañeda, Edtr./Dir.
(305) 376-3535 Fax: (305) 376-2207
Circ: 89,000

EL NUEVO HUDSON
El Jersey Journal
30 Journal Square
Jersey City, NJ 07306
Armando Bermúdez, Edtr.
(201) 217-2425 Fax: (201) 963-5854
Circ: 70,000

EL NUEVO PATRIA
El Nuevo Patria Publishing Co.
P. O. Box 2, Jose Martí Station
Miami, FL 33135-0002
Eladio José Armesto, Pub.
(305) 530-8787 Fax: (305) 577-8989
Circ: 28,000

EL OBSERVADOR
El Observador Publications, Inc.
P.O. Box 1990
San Jose, CA 95109
Hilbert Morales, Pub.
(408) 453-2944 Fax: (408) 453-2979
Circ: 33,000

EL ORIENTAL
Periodico El Oriental, Inc.
36 Ave. Cruz Ortiz Stella
Humacao, PR 00791
Vicente Pierantoni Pérez, Edtr.

(787) 852-1496 Fax: (787) 852-3405
Circ: 50,000

EL PASO TIMES
El Paso Times, Inc.
300 N Campbell St.
El Paso, TX 79901
Don Flores, Edtr.
(915) 456-6260 Fax: (915) 546-6415
Circ: 80,000

EL PERIODICO
Hispanic Pages, Inc.
340 E. Lake St. #207
Minneapolis, MN 55408
Beto Farias, Edtr.
(612) 728-1686 Fax: (612) 728-1690
Circ: 5,000

EL PERIÓDICO, USA
Newspapers and Directories, Inc.
1016 Ivy St.
McAllen, TX 78501
José Luis B. Garza C., Edtr.
(956) 631-5628 Fax: (956) 631-0832
Circ: 35,000

EL PLAYERO
Playeros, Inc.
P.O. Box 1508
Melbourne, FL 32902
Anselmo Baldonado, Edtr.
(321) 777-9225 Fax: (321) 777-1384

EL POLITÉCNICO
Universidad Politécnica de Puerto Rico
Apartado Postal 192017
San Juan, PR 00919-2017
Dr. Rafael López Valdés, Dir.
(787) 754-8000 x419 Fax: (787) 767-5343
Circ: 6,000

EL POPULAR
El Popular Spanish Newspaper
1206 California Ave. #A
Bakersfield, CA 93304
Raul R. Camacho, Sr., Edtr.
Fax: (661) 325-1351
Circ: 35,000

EL POPULAR
Laureti Publishing, Inc.
P.O. Box 190359
Miami Beach, FL 33119
Marco Laureti, CEO
(305) 673-5875 Fax: (305) 673-0507
Circ: 50,000

EL PREGONERO
145 Taylor St., NE.
P.O. Box 4464
Washington, DC 20017
Oscar Reyes, Edtr.
(202) 281-2440 Fax: (202) 281-2448
Circ: 30,000

EL PROGRESO HISPANO
El Progreso Hispano Newspaper
1101 Tayvola Rd. #105
Charlotte, NC 28217
José Herrera, Edtr.
(704) 529-6728/6624 Fax: (704) 525-2328

EL PUEBLO CATÓLICO
Archidiocesan Hispanic Office
1300 S Steele
Denver, CO 80210
Rosana Goñi, Dir.
(303) 715-3219 Fax: (303) 715-2045
Circ: 5,000

EL REPORTERO/THE REPORTER
2986 Mission St. #103
San Francisco, CA 94110
Marvin J. Ramírez, Pub.
(415) 648-3711 Fax: (415) 648-3721
Circ: 20,000

EL SEMANARIO
611 22nd St.
Denver, CO 80205
Toni C. Frésquez, Managing Edtr.
(303) 672-0800 Fax: (303) 298-8654

EL SOL
123 W. Alisle St.
Salinas, CA 93901
Silvia Medina, Edtr.
(831) 757-8118 Fax: (831) 757-1006
Circ: 15,000

EL SOL
El Buen Vecino, Inc.
P.O. Box 3390
South Bend, IN 46619
Sara Haber, C.E.O.
(219) 287-8228 Fax: (219) 288-7505
Published 4 issues/year
Circ: 1,000

EL SOL
El Sol
86-08 37th Ave.
Jackson Heights, NY 11372
Robert Rosado, Adv. Dir.
(718) 397-9071 Fax: (718) 397-9071
Circ: 25,000

EL SOL
El Sol
726 14th St. #A
Modesto, CA 95354
Eduardo Morales, Edtr.
(209) 522-7665 Fax: (209) 522-7741
Circ: 25,000

EL SOL
Scholastic Magazine
P.O. Box 3710
Jefferson City, MO 65102-3710
David Goddy, 6 issues/year
(800) 724-6527 Fax: (573) 635-8937

EL SOL DE JERUSALÉN
4615 Sur Park Ave.
Tucson, AZ 85714
Francisco Santa Cruz, Edtr.
(520) 294-3807 Fax: (520) 806-8411
Circ: 10,000

EL SOL DE SAN DIEGO
El Sol de San Diego
P.O. Box 13447
San Diego, CA 92170
Julie J. Rocha, Edtr./Pub.
(619) 233-8496 Fax: (619) 233-5017
Circ: 21,000

EL SOL DE TIJUANA
Mucho Media Marketing
589 Vance St.
Chula Vista, CA 91910
Kathleen Girard, Exec. Dir.
(619) 427-8291 Fax: (619) 427-8340

EL SOL LATINO
Grupo Bogotá
198 W Chew Ave.
Philadelphia, PA 19120
Ricardo Hurtado, Edtr.
(215) 424-1200 Fax: (215) 424-6064
Circ: 25,000

EL SOL LATINO
El Sol Latino
P. O. Box 126
Lubbock, TX 79408
Damiam P. Morales, Pub./Edtr.
(806) 741-1956 Fax: (806) 740-0045
Circ: 30,000

EL TEATRO NOTES
Teatro Campesino
P.O. Box 1240
San Juan Bautista, CA 95045
Anawak Valdez, Edtr.
(831) 623-2444 Fax: (831) 623-4127
Circ: 10,000

EL TECOLOTE
Acción Latina
2601 Mission St. #700
San Francisco, CA 94110
Juan González, Edtr.
(415) 648-1045 Fax: (415) 648-1046
Circ: 10,000

EL TEJANO HISPANIC COMMUNITY MAGAZINE
El Tejano
2505 Sarita St.
Corpus Christi, TX 78405
Adelita V. De La Paz, Edtr.
(361) 884-2238 Fax: (361) 888-7703
Circ: 35,000

EL TIEMPO
Laredo Morning Times
111 Esperanza Dr.
Laredo, TX 78041
Odie Arambula, Edtr.
(956)728-2500 Fax: (956)723-1227
Circ: 20,817

EL TIEMPO
Muntimedios Luna, Inc.
416 N Gleenwood Ave.
Dalton, GA 30721
Homero Luna Osejo, Dir.
(706) 278-6397 Fax: (706) 278-3636
Circ: 22,000

EL TIEMPO DE NUEVA YORK & NUEVA JERSEY
P. O. Box 1155
New York, NY 10116
José C. Cayón, Edtr./Pub.
(718) 507-0832 Fax: (718) 507-2105
Circ: 38,000

EL TIEMPO LATINO
Farragut Media Group
1916 Wilson Blvd. #204
Arlington, VA 22201
Armando C. Chapelli, Jr., Pub.
(703) 527-7860 Fax: (703) 527-0369
Circ: 27,500

EL TIEMPO LATINO/LATIN TIMES
United Media Publishing Group, Inc.
5808 W Pico Blvd. #1
Los Angeles, CA 90019
Chick Sponder, Edtr.
(323) 931-5736 Fax: (323) 931-7092
Circ: 100,000

EL TRABAJO EN EL MUNDO
International Labor Office
1828 L St., NW #600
Washington, DC 20036
Marjorie Crow, Marketing Assistant
(202) 653-7652 Fax: (202) 653-7687

EL UNIVERSAL
529 14th St. NW
Washington, DC 20045
Jose Carreño, Correspondent
(202) 662-7190 Fax: (202) 662-7189
Circ: 150,000

EL VENEZOLANO
Editorial Tricolor
1910 NW 97th Ave.
Miami, FL 33172
Oswaldo Muñoz, Edtr.
(305) 717-3266 Fax: (305) 717-6813
Circ: 20,000

EL VIERNES
The Miami Herald
One Herald Plaza
Miami, FL 33132-1693
Andres Reynaldo, Edtr.
(305) 376-3535 Fax: (305) 376-2207
Circ: 89,000

EL VISITANTE
Puerto Rican Catholic Conference
P.O. Box 41305. Minillas Sta.
San Juan, PR 00940-1305
Jose Ramón Ortiz Valladares, Dir.
(787) 728-3710 Fax: (787) 728-3656
Circ: 65,000

EL VISTAZO
La Oferta
1376 N 4th St.
San Jose, CA 95112
Mary Andrade, Edtr.

(408) 436-7850 Fax: (408) 436-7861
Circ: 35,000

EL VOCERO DE PUERTO RICO
Caribbean International News
P.O. Box 7515
San Juan, PR 00906-7515
Gaspar Roca, Edtr.
(787) 721-2300 Fax: (787) 725-0131
Circ: 220,000

EL VOCERO HISPANO
El Vocero Hispano
1438 Eastern SE
Grand Rapids, MI 49507
Andrés Abreu, Edtr.
(616) 246-6023 (616) 246-1116 Fax: (616) 246-1228
Circ: 20,000

EL VOLANTE
P.O. Box 1071
Lawrenceville, GA 30046
Mauricio Monreal, Edtr.
(770) 682-8012 Fax: (770) 560-5738
Circ: 6,000

ELECTRONIC BUYERS' NEWS—SMALL & DISADVANTAGED VENDOR DIRECTORY ISSUE
CMP Publications, Inc.
600 Community Dr.
Manhasset, NY 11030
Andrew MacLellan, Managing Edtr.
(516) 562-5000
Circ: 65,000

ELLE
Editorial Televisa
6355 NW 36th St.
Miami, FL 33166
Lucy Lara, Edtr.
(305) 871-6400 Fax: (305) 871-1520
Circ: 21,225

THE ELUSIVE DECADE OF HISPANICS
Cuban American National Council, Inc.
1223 SW 4th St.
Miami, FL 33135
Guarioné M. Díaz, Pres.
(305) 642-3484 Fax: (305) 642-9815

EMERGING MARKETS
Kaleidoscope Publishing
1888 Sherman St. #830
Denver, CO 80203
Linda Wilson, Pres.
(303) 860-7159 Fax: (303) 860-9156
Circ: 50,000

EN MARCHA!
National Conference of Catholic Bishops, Secretariat for Hispanic Affairs
3211 4th St. NE
Washington, DC 20017
Rosalva Castañeda, Edtr.
(202) 541-3150 Fax: (202) 722-8717
Circ: 7,500

ENCUENTRO
Asociacion para la Educ. Teológica Hispana
P.O.Box 520
Decatur, GA 30031
Evenezer Negron, Exec. Dir.
(404) 687-4560/4594 Fax: (404) 687-4660
Circ: 3,500

ENFOQUE
Center of U.S.-Mexican Studies
University of California, San Diego
9500 Gilman Drive, Dept. 0510
La Jolla, CA 92093-0510
Sandra del Castillo, Edtr.
(858) 534-4503 Fax: (858) 534-6447
Circ: 5,000

ENFOQUE METROPOLITANO
Metropolitan News
P.O. Box 650833
Miami, FL 33265
Silvio Mancha, Edtr.

(305) 223-8637 Fax: (305) 225-6719
Circ: 10,000

ENLACE/ CROSS CURRENTS
Washington Office on Latin America
1630 Connecticut Ave., NW, 2nd Floor
Washington, DC 20009
Rachel Neild, Edtr.
(202) 797-2171 Fax: (202) 797-2172
Circ: 1,000

ENTERTAINMENT
Entertainment Publications of Puerto Rico, Inc.
Bldg 11, Calle 1, Ground Fl.
Metro Office Park
Guaynabo, PR 00968
Tanya Rosario, Office Administrator
(787) 781-7272 Fax: (787) 781-5464
Circ: 20,000

EQ EDUCATIONAL QUARTERLY
Congressional Hispanic Caucus Institute, Inc.
504 C St. NE
Washington, DC 20002
Carmen Joge, Edtr.
(202) 543-1771 Fax: (202) 543-2143
Circ: 12,000

EQUAL OPPORTUNITY
Equal Opportunity Publications
1160 E Jerico Turnpike, #200
Huntington, NY 11743
John R. Miller, Pub.
(516) 421-9448 Fax: (516) 421-0359
Circ: 15,000

EQUITY & EXCELLENCE IN EDUCATION
Greenwood Publishing Group, Inc.
88 Post Rd., West
Westport, CT 06881
Gerry Katz, Edtr./Manager
(203) 226-3571 ext.3422 Fax: (203) 226-6009
Published 3 issues/year
Circ: 2,000

ERES
Editorial Televisa
6355 NW 36th St.
Miami, FL 33166
Maricel del Sol, Edtr.
(305) 871-6400 Fax: (305) 871-1520
Circ: 40,399

ESPAÑA Y PUERTO RICO
Cámara Oficial Española de Comercio
P.O.Box 9020894
San Juan, PR 00902
Iram Irizarri, Pres.
(787) 729-0099 Fax: (787) 729-0092
Circ: 1,000

ESPERANZA COMUNITARIA HISPANIC NEWSPAPER
1131 Butler St.
Reading, PA 19601
Moisés O. Manon-Rossi, Edtr.
(610) 371-0137 Fax: (610) 478-0851
Circ: 10,000

ESTADIO
Estadio, Inc.
6431 Norcross Tucker Rd.
Tucker, GA 30084
Will Ramirez, Dir.
(770) 414-1107 Fax: (770) 414-4115
Circ: 16,000

ESTYLO
Mandalay Publications, Inc.
3600 Wilshire Blvd. #1903
Los Angeles, CA 90010
Steven Roberts, Dir. of Circ.
(213) 383-6300 Fax: (213) 383-6499
Published 8 issues/year

ETHNIC BLOCK VOTING AND POLARIZATION IN MIAMI
Cuban American National Council, Inc.
1223 SW 4th St.
Miami, FL 33135
Guarioné M. Díaz, Pres.
(305) 642-3484 Fax: (305) 642-9815

ETHNIC GENEALOGY: A RESEARCH GUIDE
Greenwood Publishing Group
88 Post Rd. W
Westport, CT 06881
David Wilfinger, Product Coord.
(203) 226-3571 Fax: (203) 222-1502

ETHNIC SEGREGATION IN GREATER MIAMI: 1980-1990
Cuban American National Council, Inc.
1223 SW 4th St.
Miami, FL 33135
Guarioné M. Díaz, Pres.
(305) 642-3484 Fax: (305) 642-9815

EXCELSIOR DEL CONDADO DE ORANGE
117 W 4th St., Santa Ana
Anaheim, CA 92701
Miguel Jimenez, Edtr.
(714) 704-4347/978-1151 Fax: (714) 953-0345
Circ: 47,000

EXEGESIS
Universidad de Puerto Rico en Humacao
Estación Postal CUH, Humacao, Puerto Rico
Humacao, PR 00791-4300
Marcos Reyes-Davila, Dir.
(787) 850-9370 Fax: (787) 850-9371
Published 3 issues/year
Circ: 1,500

EXITO
Chicago Tribune
820 N Orleans Ave.
Chicago, IL 60610
Alejandro Escalona, Edtr.
(312) 654-3000 Fax: (312) 654-3027
Circ: 96,000

ÉXITO DEPORTIVO/EL INDEPENDIENTE
Spanish Sports Productions
11636 Spry St.
Norwalk, CA 90650
Rafael Ramirez, Pub.
(562) 929-3802 Fax: (562) 929-3842
Circ: 50,000

EXPERIMENTAL TREATMENT GUIDE
AIDS Treatment Data Network
611 Broadway #613
New York, NY 10012
Ken Fornataro/Richard Geffreys, Edtrs.
(212) 260-8868 Fax: (212) 260-8869

EXPORT MAGAZINE COMPRAR
Finocchiaro Enterprises
2921 Coral Way
Miami, FL 33145
Michael Finocchiaro, Edtr.
(305) 529-0142 Fax: (305) 529-9217
Circ: 50,000

EXTRA BILINGUAL NEWSPAPER
Tell-Cliff Corp.
3906 W North Ave.
Chicago, IL 60647
Carlos Hernandez, Edtr.
(773) 252-3534/6031 Fax: (773) 252-4073
Circ: 72,000

EXTRA MÁS NOTICIAS
Extra Más Noticias, Inc.
P.O. Box 2472
Norcross, GA 30091
José Galván, Edtr.
(770) 416-8692 Fax: (770) 242-6974
Circ: 7,500

EXTRA PUBLICATIONS
3906 W North Ave.
Chicago, IL 60647
Carlos Hernandez, Edtr.
(773) 252-3534 Fax: (773) 252-6031
Circ: 72,000

F

FACTS ABOUT CUBAN AMERICANS
Cuban American National Council, Inc.
1223 SW 4th St.
Miami, FL 33135
Guarioné M. Díaz, Pres.
(305) 642-3484 Fax: (305) 642-9815

FAMA MAGAZINE
Osmus Publishing Group Inc.
331 W 57th St. #282
New York, NY 10019
Al Vazquez, Edtr.
(212) 633-9975 Fax: (212) 633-9976
Published 6 issues/year
Circ: 120,000

FAMILIA SALUDABLE
Editorial Televisa
6355 NW 36th St.
Miami, FL 33166
(305) 871-6400 Fax: (305) 871-1520

FAMILY LEARNING CENTER
Family Learning Center
3164 34th St.
Boulder, CO 80301
Brenda Lyle, Exec. Dir.
(303) 442-8979 Fax: (303) 442-8979

FIELD MEMO
Migrant Legal Action Program
P.O. Box 53308
Washington, DC 20009
Roger Rosenthal, Edtr.
(202) 462-7744 Fax: (202) 462-7914
Circ: 400

FIESTA MAGAZINE
Arizona Mexican Chamber of Commerce
P.O.Box 626
Phoenix, AZ 85001
Hector Ledesma, Pres.
(602) 252-6448 Fax: (602) 230-1991
Circ: 5,000

FINANCE & DEVELOPMENT
International Monetary Fund
700 19th St. NW #12-607
Washington, DC 20431
Publications Services
(202) 623-7430 Fax: (202) 623-7201

FINANCIAL AID FOR HISPANIC AMERICANS
Reference Service Press
El Dorado Hills Business Park,
5000 Windplay Dr. #4
El Dorado Hills, CA 95762
Gail A. Schlachter
(916) 939-9620 Fax: (916) 939-9626

FINANCIAL AID FOR MINORITIES
Garrett Park Press, Inc.
P.O. Box 190F
Garrett Park, MD 20896
Robert Calver, Edtr.
(301) 946-2553 Fax: (301) 949-3955

FLEXO ESPAÑOL
Flexographic Technical Association
900 Marconi Ave.
Ronkonkoma, NY 11779
Gabriela I. Gilbride, Edtr.
(631) 737-6023 Ext.17 Fax: (631) 737-6813
Circ: 10,000

THE FLYER
Harte Hanks Corporation
11900 SW 128 St.
Miami, FL 33186
Carlos Guzmán, Pres.
(305) 232-4115 Fax: (305) 251-5141
Circ: 10,000

FOTO IMAGEN
7593 NW 8th St. #6
Miami, FL 33126
Aida Quimper, Edtr.
(305) 264-0900 Fax: (305) 264-9480

FREEDOM OF SPEECH IN MIAMI
Cuban American National Council, Inc.
1223 SW 4th St.
Miami, FL 33135
Guarioné M. Díaz, Pres.
(305) 642-3484 Fax: (305) 642-9815

FRONT LINES
Bureau for Legislative and Public Affairs
Ronald Reagan Building
Washington, DC 20523
Achsah Nesmith, Edtr.
(202) 712-4024 Fax: (202) 216-3035
Circ: 25,000

FRONTERA
Healy Newspaper
629 Third Ave. #J
Chula Vista, CA 91910
Javier Villegas, Editorial Dir.
(619) 422-5902 Fax: (619) 422-5942
Circ: 20,000

FRONTERA MAGAZINE
P.O. Box 26656
Los Angeles, CA 90026
Yvette Doss-Albornoz, Edtr.-in-Chief
(213) 975-9411 Fax: (323) 953-8915

FURIA MUSICAL
Editorial Televisa
6355 NW 36th St.
Miami, FL 33166
Blanca Martínez, Edtr.
(305) 871-6400 Fax: (305) 871-1520
Circ: 49503

G

GACETA IBEROAMERICANA
P.O. Box 4213
Gaithesburg, MD 20885
Raúl Miranda Rico, Dir./Edtr.
(301) 926-7848 Fax: (301) 926-7848
Circ: 10,000

GANAS NEWSLETTER
Greater Auraria Neighbors Affiliated for Service (GANAS)
1212 Mariposa St.
Denver, CO 80204
Patrick J. Vigil, Exec. Dir.
(303) 893-5114 Fax: (303) 573-8023
Circ: 500

THE GASTON INSTITUTE REPORT: NEWSLETTER OF THE MAURICIO GASTÓN INSTITUTE
Mauricio Gaston Institute for Latino Community Development
University of Massachusetts Boston
100 Morrisey Blvd.
Boston, MA 02125-3393
Leslie Bowen, Edtr.
(617) 287-5790 Fax: (617) 287-5788
Published 2 issues/year
Circ: 10,000

GEOMUNDO
Editorial Televisa
6355 NW 36th St.
Miami, FL 33166
Gabriel González, Edtr.
(305) 871-6400 Fax: (305) 871-1520
Circ: 13,412

GIRLS INCORPORATED OF METRO DENVER
3444 W Colfax Ave.
Denver, CO 80204
Rebecca Richardson, Exec. Dir.
(303) 893-4363 Fax: (303) 893-4363

GLOBAL ECONOMIC PROSPECT AND THE DEVELOPING COUNTRIES
The World Bank Bookstore (Infoshop)
701 18th St. NW
Washington, DC 20433
The World Bank, InfoShop

(800) 645-7247 Fax: (703) 661-1501

GLOBAL FAX
Agio Press, Inc.
315 W Ponce de Leon Ave. #1021
Decatur, GA 30030
Phillip Bolton, Edtr.
(404) 377-7710 Fax: (404) 377-7386
Circ: 10,000

GLOSARIO EN INGLÉS Y EN ESPAÑOL DE TÉRMINOS Y FRASES QUE SE USAN EN LAS PUBLICACIONES DEL SERVICIO DE RENTAS INTERNAS, PUB. 580SP
US Internal Revenue Service (IRS)
P. O. Box 85074
Distribution Center
Richmond, VA 23261-5074
(800) 829-1040

GO-GUÍA DE LA INDUSTRIA TURÍSTICA DE PR Y EL CARIBE
Go of Puerto Rico, Inc.
American Airlines Office Bldg. #900
1509 López Landrón St.
San Juan, PR 00911
Migdalia Medina, Edtr.
(787) 268-5220 Fax: (787) 725-5082
Circ: 15,000

GOL USA
6910 Woodside Ave., 2nd Floor
Woodside, NY 11377
Jorge Garcia, Edtr.
(718) 565-1818 Fax: (718) 565-0263
Circ: 22,500

GOVERNMENT FINANCE STATISTICS YEARBOOK
International Monetary Fund
Publication Services-700 19th St., NW #12-607
Washington, DC 20431
Dept. of Publications
(202) 623-7430 Fax: (202) 623-7201

GUÍA HISPANIC YELLOW PAGES
Cinco Estrellas International, Inc.
4724 W Lawrence Ave.
Chicago, IL 60630
Jordan Lichtenstain, Gen. Mgr.
(773) 725-4959 Fax: (773) 725-8075
Circ: 300,000

H

THE HACR CORPORATE OBSERVER
Hispanic Association for Corporate Responsiblity
1730 Rhode Island Ave. NW #1008
Washington, DC 20036
Fletcher Grundmann, Edtr.
(202) 835-9672 Fax: (202) 457-0455
Circ: 5,000

HARPER'S BAZAAR
Editorial Televisa
6355 NW 36th St.
Miami, FL 33166
Laura Laviada, Edtr.
(305) 871-6400 Fax: (305) 871-1520
Circ: 21,732

HDI
Hispanic Designers, Inc.
1101 30th St. NW. #500
Washington, DC 20007
Penny Harrison, Edtr./Pub.
(202)337-9636 Fax: (202) 337-9635

HEALTH WAVES
La Clínica de la Raza
1515 Fruitvale Ave.
Oakland, CA 94601
Rosa Villalobos, Edtr.
(510) 535-4000 Ext.4048 Fax: (510) 535-4197
Circ: 1,000

HERALD AMERICAN
Wave Community Newspapers, Inc.
2621 W 54th St.
Los Angeles, CA 90043
Pluria Marshall, Jr, Pres.
(323) 290-3000 Fax: (323) 291-0219

HISPANIA
AATSP
Dept. of Classical and Modern Languages
Texas Tech University
Lubbock, TX 79409-2071
Janet Perez, Edtr.
(806) 742-3145 Fax: (806) 742-3306
Published 4 issues/year
Circ: 15,000

HISPANIA NEWS
Con Fé Communications, Ltd.
2860 S Circle Dr. #2224
Colorado Springs, CO 80935-5116
Robert L. Armendariz, Edtr.
(719) 540-0220 Fax: (719) 540-0599
Circ: 10,000

THE HISPANIC AMERICAN HISTORICAL REVIEW
Duke University Press
P.O. Box 90660
Durham, NC 27708
David Bushnell, Edtr.
(919) 684-2173 Fax: (919) 688-3524
Circ: 1,000

HISPANIC AMERICAN VOLUNTARY ORGANIZATIONS
Greenwood Press, Inc.
Congressional Information Service, Inc.
88 Post Rd. W
Westport, CT 06881
Sylvia Alicia Gónzales, Edtr.
(203) 226-3571 Fax: (703) 222-1502

HISPANIC BUSINESS
Western Publications Association
425 Pine Ave.
Santa Barbara, CA 93117
Vaughn Hagerty, Managing Edtr.
(805) 964-4554 Fax: (805) 964-6139
Circ: 210,000

HISPANIC BUSINESS JOURNAL
Hispanic Chamber of Commerce of Silicon Valley
1376 N 4th. St.
San Jose, CA 95112
Alex C. Torres, Pres.
(408) 467-9890 Fax: (408) 467-9899
Circ: 5,000

HISPANIC CHAMBER NEWS
Hispanic Chamber of Commerce of Louisiana
P.O. Box 5985
Metairie, LA 70009
Norma Parrott, Edtr.
(504) 885-4262 Fax: (504) 887-5422
Circ: 250

HISPANIC COMMUNITY RESOURCE DIRECTORY
Washington State Commission on Hispanic Affairs
P.O. Box 40924
Olympia, WA 98504-0924
Esmeralda Cross, Exec. Assistant
(360) 753-3159 Fax: (360) 753-0199
Circ: 1,000

HISPANIC CULTURE REVIEW
George Mason University
Modern and Classical Languages, MSN 3E5
4400 University Dr.
Fairfax, VA 22030-4444
Hispanic Cultural Review
(703) 993-2904

HISPANIC ENTREPRENEURS RECRUITERS ORGANIZATION & SERVICES (HEROS)
HEROS
14927 James River Lane
Houston, TX 77084
Rosemary Acosta-Clark, Pres.
(281) 859-0564 Fax: (281) 859-2636
Circ: 2,000

HISPANIC HOTLINE
Hispanic Hotline
P. O. Box 163510
Sacramento, CA 95816
Tony Vásquez, Pres./Pub.
(916) 448-7594 Fax: (916) 989-4742
Circ: 8,000

HISPANIC IMPACT
Miami Today
P.O. Box 1368
Miami, FL 33101
Michael Lewis, Pub.
(305) 358-2663 Fax: (305) 358-4811

HISPANIC JOURNAL
Hispanic Journal, LLC
11029 Shady Trail #128
Dallas, TX 75229
Denise M. Nuño, Pres.
(214) 350-4774 Fax: (214) 358-0018
Circ: 35,000

HISPANIC LINK WEEKLY REPORT
Hispanic Link News Service, Inc.
1420 N St. NW #101
Washington, DC 20005
Charles Ericksen, Edtr.
(202) 234-0280 Fax: (202) 234-4090
Circ: 1,300

HISPANIC MAGAZINE
Hispanic Publishing Corporation
999 Ponce de Leon Blvd. #600
Coral Gables, FL 33134
Sam Verdeja, Pub.
(305) 442-2462 Fax: (305) 774-3578
Circ: 250,000

HISPANIC MARKET NEWS
Productive Media, Inc.
13014 N Dale Mabry Ave. #633
Tampa, FL 33618
Marc L. Vila, Pub.
(800) 766-4651 Fax: (813) 968-6852
Circ: 25,000

HISPANIC MEDIA & MARKETS
SRDS, Inc.
1700 Higgins Rd.
Des Plains, IL 60018
Debi Dunklebenger, Edtr.
(847) 375-5000 Fax: (847) 375-5002
Circ: 579

HISPANIC MEETINGS & TRAVEL MAGAZINE
International Association of Hispanic Meeting Professionals (IAHMP)
P.O. Box 58923
Houston, TX 77258
Ángela González Rowe, Edtr.
(281) 992-9639 Fax: (281) 992-2555

HISPANIC NETWORK MAGAZINE
Olive Tree Publishing, Inc.
22845 Savi Ranch Pkwy. #A
Yorba Linda, CA 92887
Roberto Alvarez, Managing Edtr.
(800) 433-9675 Fax: (909) 924-1139
Circ: 25,000

HISPANIC NETWORK MAGAZINE
Hispanic Network Magazine
5928 Broadway #305
San Antonio, TX 78209
Grace Abboud, Edtr.
(210) 828-2300 Fax: (909) 924-1139

THE HISPANIC NETWORK NEWSLETTER
Hispanic Business Association
420 S Euclid Ave. #115
Anaheim, CA 92802
Frank Rosales, Pres.& CEO
(714) 535-5899 Fax: (714) 778-3510
Circ: 1,500

HISPANIC NETWORK (NEWSLETTER)
Kern County Hispanic Chamber of Commerce
1401 19th St. #110
Bakersfield, CA 93301
Lou Gomez, Exec. Dir.
(661) 633-5495 Fax: (661) 633-5499
Circ: 650

HISPANIC NEWS
Spanish Chamber of Commerce of Long Island
131 E Riviera Dr.
Lindenhurst, NY 11757
Luis Van Den Essen, Pres.
(631) 226-7618
Circ: 1,000

HISPANIC NEWS OF FLORIDA
Magellan Media Corporation
300 S Orange Ave. #1500
Orlando, FL 32801
Phil Cobo, Pub.
(407) 895-0544 Fax: (407) 895-0543
Circ: 10,000

HISPANIC NEWS UPDATE
8531 Lamar Ave.
Overland Park, KS 66207
Rudy Padilla, Pub.
(913) 381-2272 Fax: (913) 341-1338

THE HISPANIC NURSE NEWSLETTER
National Association of Hispanic Nurses (NAHN)
1501 16th St. NW
Washington, DC 20036
Francesca Alcozer, Edtr.
(202) 387-2477 Fax: (202) 483-7183
Circ: 1,000

THE HISPANIC OUTLOOK IN HIGHER EDUCATION
The Hispanic Outlook in Higher Education
210 Route 4 E. #310
Paramus, NJ 07652
Susan Lopez, Managing Edtr.
(201) 587-8800 Fax: (201) 587-9105
Circ: 28,000

HISPANIC RESOURCE DIRECTORY
The Denali Press
P.O. Box 021535
Juneau, AK 99802-1535
Edward Schorr
(907) 586-6014 Fax: (907) 463-6780

HISPANIC SCHOLARSHIP DIRECTORY 2001
National Association of Hispanic Publications
941 National Press Bldg.
Washington, DC 20045
Zeke Montes, President
(202) 662-7250 Fax: (202) 662-7254
Published annually

HISPANIC TIMES MAGAZINE
Hispanic Times Enterprises
P.O. Box 579
Winchester, CA 92596
Gloria Davis, Edtr.-in-Chief
(909) 926-2119
Published 5 issues/year
Circ: 42,000

THE HISPANIC VOICE. LA VOZ HISPANA
National Organizations for the Advancement of Hispanics
2217 Princess Anne St. #205-1
Fredericksburg, VA 22401
David Martinez, Edtr.

(540) 372-3437 Fax: (540) 372-3437

HISPANIC YELLOW PAGES
Hispanic Yellow Pages, Inc.
5700 Memorial Hwy. #208
Tampa, FL 33615
Jeff Devin, Gen. Mgr.
(813) 886-4787 Fax: (813) 881-1515
Circ: 105,000

HISPANIC YELLOW PAGES
P.O. Box 2203
Hartford, CT 06145
Héctor Torres, Edtr./Pub.
(860) 560-8713
Circ: 130,000

HISPANIC YELLOW PAGES
Hispanic Yellow Pages, Inc.
5553 Rising Sun Ave.
Philadelphia, PA 19120
Arturo Suárez, Pres.
(215) 457-2101 Fax: (215) 329-6260
Circ: 25,000

HISPANIC YELLOW PAGES OF UTAH
Hispanic Media Services
P.O. Box 9434
Salt Lake City, UT 84109
Ana María Fereday, Vice President
(801) 274-8814 Fax: (801) 274-8815
Published 2 issues/year
Circ: 50,000

HISPANO DE TULSA
Zapata Multimedia
P.O. Box 52054
Tulsa, OK 74152
Margarita Treviño, Edtr.
(918) 622-8258 Fax: (918) 384-0096
Circ: 10,000

HISPANOS UNIDOS
411 W 9th Ave. #1
Escondido, CA 92025-5034
Jaime Castañeda, Edtr.
(619) 740-9561 Fax: (619) 737-3035
Circ: 21,000

HIV/AIDS: THE IMPACT ON HISPANICS
National Alliance for Hispanic Health
1501 16th St. NW
Washington, DC 20036
Odell Jackson, Pub.
(202) 387-5000 Fax: (202) 797-4353
Published once only, 6 months ago

HOGARAMA
2329 S. Purdue Ave.
Santa Monica, CA 90064-1727
Marcelino Mijares, Jr., Edtr.
(310) 914-3007 Fax: (310) 914-0607
Published 3 issues/year
Circ: 1,000,000

HOLA BERKS NEWS
Reading Eagle Company
345 Penn St.
P.O. Box 582
Reading, PA 19603-0582
Alfonso Peña, Edtr.
(610) 371-5038 Fax: (610) 371-5098
Circ: 15,000

HOLA BROOKLYN
Hola NY Publishing
29-28 41st Ave.
Long Island, NY 11101
H.M. Solano, Pres.
(718) 937-664 Fax: (718) 937-6641
Circ: 150,000

HOLA MAGAZINE
Spanish Publications, Inc.
6601 Tarnef St. #200
Houston, TX 77074
Raul Dueñas, Edtr.
(713) 774-4719 Fax: (713) 774-4666
Circ: 65,000

HOLA MANHATTAN
Hola NY Publishing
29-28 41st Ave.
Long Island, NY 11101
H.M. Solano, Pres.
(718) 937-6641 Fax: (718) 937-6641
Circ: 150,000

HOLA QUEENS
Hola NY Publishing
29-28 41st Ave.
Long Island, NY 11101
H.M. Solano, Pres.
(718) 937-6641 Fax: (718) 937-6641
Circ: 150,000

HORA DE CIERRE
Instituto de Prensa de la SIP
1801 SW 3rd Ave.
Miami, FL 33129
Oracio Ruiz, Edtr.
(305) 634-2465 Fax: (305) 635-2272
Published 6 issues/year
Circ: 10,000

THE HORIZONS
César Chávez Cultural Center
University of Northern Colorado
501 20th St.
Greeley, CO 80639
Diana Gonzalez, Ass. Edtr.
(970) 351-2424 Fax: (970) 351-2360
Published 6 issues/year
Circ: 900

HOY DÍA
Scholastic Magazine
P.O. Box 3710
Jefferson City, MO 65102-3710
David Goddy, Edtr.
(800) 724-6527 Fax: (573) 635-8937
Published 6 issues/year

HOY EN DELAWARE
Mundo Graphics
P.O. Box 593
Georgetown, DE 19947
José M. Somalo, Pub.
(888) 584-6933 Fax: (302) 947-9299
Circ: 7,000

HUMAN RIGHTS MONITOR
Cuban American National Foundation
1000 Thomas Jefferson St. NW #505
Washington, DC 20007
José Cardenas, Dir./Edtr.
(202) 265-2822 Fax: (202) 338-0308
Circ: 5,000

I

IBERO INQUIRER
Ibero American Action League, Inc.
817 E Main St.
Rochester, NY 14605
Eugenio Marlin, Edtr.
(716) 256-8900 Fax: (716) 256-0120

IDAHO UNIDO
Idaho Unido
556 S 6th Ave.
Pocatello, ID 83201
Farhana Hibbert, Dir.
(208) 234-7383
Circ: 10,000

THE IDB NEWSLETTER
Inter-American Development Bank
External Relations Office
1300 New York Ave. NW
Washington, DC 20577
(202) 623-1154 Fax: (202) 623-3531

IDB PROJECTS
Inter-American Development Bank
External Relations Office
1300 New York Ave. NW
Washington, DC 20577
(202) 623-1154 Fax: (202) 623-3531

IDB PUBLICATIONS CATALOG
Inter-American Development Bank
External Relations Office
1300 New York Ave. NW
Washington, DC 20577
(202) 623-1154 Fax: (202) 623-3531
Published 2 issues/year

IDEAS PARA SU HOGAR
Editorial Televisa
6355 NW 36th St.
Miami, FL 33166
Larisa Curies, Edtr.
(305) 871-6400 Fax: (305) 871-1520
Circ: 13,347

ILCA NEWSLETTER
Institute for Language and Cultures of the Americas
1411 K St. NW #500
Washington, DC 20005
Hernando Caicedo, Exec. Dir.
(202) 637-6065 Fax: (202) 639-7091

IMAGEN
Casiano Communications
1700 Ave Fernández Juncos
San Juan, PR 00909
Leonor Martin, Edtr.
(787) 728-3000 Fax: (787) 728-1075
Circ: 70,000

IMAGEN ARGENTINA
P.O. Box 5175. Meadowview Station
North Bergen, NJ 07047
Carlos Novotny, Dir./Edtr.
(201) 662-0347 Fax: (201) 662-1041
Circ: 22,000

IMAGEN PRENSA HISPANA
Imagen Prensa Hispana
11883 Plumpoint Dr.
Houston, TX 77099
Mariam Ramírez, Edtr.
(713) 787-5094 Fax: (713) 787-5097
Circ: 615,000

IMÁGENES OF LAS VEGAS
Ormo Enterprise
2112 Santa Clara Dr.
Las Vegas, NV 89104
Mónica Ortíz, Edtr.
(702) 796-1778 Fax: (702) 319-3571
Circ: 5,000

IMPACTO
Impacto
P.O. Box 544
Annandale, VA 22003
Julio C. Durán G., Edtr./Pub.
(703) 916-0238 Fax: (703) 914-5548
Circ: 15,000

IMPACTO, LATIN NEWS
853 Broadway #811
New York, NY 10003
Miguel Cruz, Edtr.
(212) 505-0288 Fax: (212) 674-6861
Circ: 60,000

IMPACTO NEWS MAGAZINE
Impacto Printing
5019 W Belmont Ave.
Chicago, IL 60641
Luis Reyes, Edtr.
(312) 202-9737 Fax: (312) 202-9737
Circ: 4,000

INDUSTRIA AVÍCOLA
Watt Publishing Co.
122 S Wesley Ave.
Mt. Morris, IL 61054
Christopher Wright, Edtr.
(815) 734-4171 Fax: (815) 734-4201
Circ: 1,874

INFORMACIÓN
Hispanic Committee of Virginia
5827 Columbia Pike #200
Falls Church, VA 22041
Jorge Figueredo, Exec. Dir.
(703) 671-5666 Fax: (703) 671-2325

Published 2 issues/year
Circ: 2,000

INFORMANDO A NUESTRA GENTE
Hispanic Business Networking
P. O. Box 617221
Orlando, FL 32861
J. R. Román, Edtr.
(407) 294-9038 Fax: (407) 578-5827
Circ: 5,000

INFORME ANUAL DE LA JUNTA EJECUTIVA
International Monetary Fund
700 19th St. NW #12-607
Washington, DC 20002
Publications Services
(202) 473-7430 Fax: (202) 623-7201

INFORME CUADRENIAL, LIDERAZGO EN SALUD PANAMERICANA
Pan American Health Organization (PAHO)
Programa de Publicaciones
525 23rd St. NW
Washington, DC 20037
Judith Navarro, Edtr.-in-Chief
(202) 974-3000 Fax: (202) 974-3663
Published every 4 years
Circ: 3,500

INFORME NEWSLETTER
Hispanic Chamber of Commerce
1250 6th Ave. #550
San Diego, CA 92101
Ron Valles, Edtr.
(619) 702-0790 Fax: (619) 696-3282
Circ: 2,000

INFORMES
Las Hermanas
6502 Balsam St.
Arvada, CO 80004
Paula Gonzalez, Edtr.
(303) 422-4970
Circ: 500

THE INLAND EMPIRE HISPANIC NEWS
Hispanic Communication and Development Corporation
1558 N Waterman Ave. #D
San Bernardino, CA 92404
Trini Gómez, Manager
(909) 381-6259 Fax: (909) 384-0419
Circ: 15,000

INSTITUTO CULTURAL MEXICANO
Instituto Cultural Mexicano
600 Hemisfair Plaza
San Antonio, TX 78205
Felipe Santander, Dir.
(210) 227-0123 Fax: (210) 223-1978
Circ: 3,500

INTER-AMERICAN REVIEW OF BIBLIOGRAPHY
Organization of American States
1889 F St. NW #200-A
Washington, DC 20006
Sara Meneses, Edtr.
(202) 458-3140 Fax: (202) 458-6115
Circ: 10,000

THE INTERAMERICAN MAGAZINE
Fundación InterAmericana de Desarrollo
4705 Eisenhower Ave.
Alexandria, VA 22304
Jorge Vallejos, Edtr.
(703) 461-7507 Fax: (703) 370-4017
Circ: 10,000

INTERNATIONAL FINANCIAL STATISTICS YEARBOOK
International Monetary Fund
Publication Services
700 19th St. NW #12-607
Washington, DC 20431
Dept. of Publications
(202) 623-7430 Fax: (202) 623-7201

THE INTERVIEWER MAGAZINE
902 Seco Rd., P.O. Box 7643

Eagle Pass, TX 78852
José Luis Perez Jr., Edtr.
(830) 757-0203 Fax: (830) 757-0220
Circ: 6,500

IRONBOUND VOICES
Ironbound Community Corp.
51 McWhorter St.
Newark, NJ 07105
Nancy Zak, Edtr./Pub.
(973) 589-3353 Fax: (973) 589-3637
Circ: 3,000

ISSUE BRIEFS
Cuban American National Foundation.
1000 Thomas Jefferson St. NW #505
Washington, DC 20007
José Cardenas, Dir./Edtr.
(202) 265-2822 Fax: (202) 338-0308
Circ: 5,000

J

THE JOURNAL NEWSPAPER
2720 Prosperity Ave.
Fairfax, VA 22034
(703) 846-8400

JOURNAL OF LATIN AMERICAN STUDIES
Cambridge Univ. Press
40 W 20th St.
New York, NY 10011
Professor James Dunkerley, Edtr.
(212) 924-3900 Fax: (212) 691-3239
Published 3 issues/year
Circ: 1,900

JUSTICIA
International Ladies' Garment Workers' Union
1710 Broadway
New York, NY 10019
Tony Lespier, Edtr.
(212) 265-7000 Fax: (212) 765-9541
Circ: 2,500

K

KANSAS CITY HISPANIC NEWS
Arce Communications
1911 Baltimore
Kansas City, MO 64108
José M. Arce, Operations Mgr./Pub.
(816) 472-5246 Fax: (816) 472-NEWS
Circ: 10,000

THE KINGDOM HERALD
P.O. Box 969
Powder Springs, GA 30127
Juan González, Dir.
(678) 945-5845 Fax: (678) 945-5846
Circ: 18,000

L

LA ACTUALIDAD (ECO DEL VALLE DELAWARE)
La Actualidad
4953 N 5th St.
Philadelphia, PA 19120
José A. Rivera, Edtr./Pub.
(215) 324-3838 Fax: (215) 457-4931
Circ: 20,000

LA BIBLIA EN LAS AMÉRICAS
Centro Reg. de Servicio para las Américas
1989 NW 88 Ct.
Miami, FL 33172
Melvin Rivera Velázquez, Edtr.
(305) 593-0009 Fax: (305) 593-5489

LA BOBINA
Miller Freeman, Inc.
P.O. Box 1986
Columbia, SC 29202
Lisa Rabon, Edtr.
(803) 771-7500 Fax: (803) 799-1461
Circ: 10,000

LA BUENA SUERTE
Información Publishing Co., Inc.
6065 Hillcroft #400-B
Houston, TX 77081
Emilio Sebastián Martínez, Edtr.
(713) 272-0100 Fax: (713) 272-0011
Circ: 5,000

LA CONEXIÓN
La Conexión, Inc.
722 N West St.
Raleigh, NC 27603
Mike Leary, Pub.
(919) 832-1225 Fax: (919) 856-0164
Circ: 25,000

LA COSECHA
Apostolado Hispano de la Diócesis Católica de Knoxville
119 Dameron Ave.
Knoxville, TN 37917
John "Jack" Kramer, Dir.
(865) 637-4769 Fax: (865) 971-3575
Circ: 1,800

LA CRÓNICA DE HOLLYWOOD
4913 Melrose Ave.
Los Angeles, CA 90029
Tracey Alexander, Edtr.
(323) 464-0515
Circ: 4,000

LA CRÓNICA DE LOS ANGELES
2413 S Vermont Ave.
Los Angeles, CA 90007
Rafael Zacarías, Edtr.
(323) 735-4050 Fax: (323) 734-8787
Circ: 3,500

LA DIMENSIÓN INTERNACIONAL DE LOS DERECHOS HUMANOS
Inter-American Development Bank
External Relations Office
1300 New York Ave. NW
Washington, DC 20577
IDB Bookstore
(202) 623-1154 Fax: (202) 623-3531

LA ERA DE AHORA
La Era de Ahora, Inc.
P.O. Box 6606
Santurce, PR 00914-6606
Helga M. Umpierre, Edtr.
(787) 723-1121 Fax: (787) 721-5376
Circ: 23,000

LA ESTRELLA DE ESPERANZA (STAR OF HOPE)
Rod & Staff Publishers, Inc
Highway 172
Crockett, KY 41413
Eugene G. Campbell, Edtr.
(606)522-4348 Fax: (606) 522-4896
Circ: 8,000

LA ESTRELLA DE NICARAGUA
15601 SW 109 Terrace St.
Miami, FL 33196
Nicolás López-Maltez, Edtr.
(305) 386-6491 Fax: (305) 386-7591
Circ: 35,000

LA ESTRELLA DE PUERTO RICO
La Estrella de Puerto Rico
P.O. Box 366298
San Juan, PR 00936-6298
Pete Curras, Edtr.
(787) 754-4440 Fax: (787) 754-4457
Circ: 123,250

LA EXPLOSIÓN
La Explosión Publication
P.O. Box 5744
Valdosta, GA 31603
Rita Palomba, Edtr.
(912) 245-0572 Fax: (912) 245-7791
Circ: 10,000

LA FAMILIA MAGAZINE
Hispanic Media Services
P.O. Box 9434
Salt Lake City, UT 84109

Ana María Fereday, Edtr.
(801) 274-8814 Fax: (801) 274-8815
Circ: 10,000

LA FÉ EN MARCHA
Ministerio Cristo Viene
P.O. Box 949
Camuy, PR 00627
Yiye Avila, Dir.
(787) 898-5120 Fax: (787) 820-4496

LA FUENTE
Dallas Morning News
508 Young St.
Dallas, TX 75202
Cindy Benavides, Dir.
(214) 997-7952 Fax: (214) 977-7967
Circ: 107,000

LA GACETA
La Gaceta Publishing, Inc.
3210 E 7th Ave.
Tampa, FL 33605
Roland Manteiga, Edtr./Pub.
(813) 248-3921 Fax: (813) 247-5357
Circ: 18,000

LA GAZETA
La Gazeta Publishing Inc.
3210 E 7th Ave.
Tampa, FL 33605
Patrick Manteiga, Edtr.
(813) 248-3921 Fax: (813) 247-5357
Circ: 18,000

LA GUIA
AIDS Treatment Data Network
611 Broadway #613
New York, NY 10012
Ken Fornataro/Richard Geffreys, Edtrs.
(212) 260-8868 Fax: (212) 260-8869

LA GUÍA FAMILIAR
Latin Publications, Inc.
P.O. Box 9190
Van Nuys, CA 91409
Diane Lerner, Edtr.
(818) 882-9200 Fax: (818) 882-2625
Circ: 211,000

LA HERENCIA DEL NORTE
P.O. Box 22576
Santa Fe, NM 87502
Ana Pacheco, Edtr.
(505) 474-2800 Fax: (505) 474-2828
Circ: 20,000

LA INFORMACIÓN
Información Publishing Co., Inc.
6065 Hillcroft #400-B
Houston, TX 77081
Lina Martinez, Edtr.
(713) 272-0100 Fax: (713) 272-0011
Circ: 10,000

LA LISTA LATINA HISPANIC DIRECTORY
La Lista Latina Hispanic Business Directory
2640 E 8th St.
Kansas City, MO 64124
William O. Lona, CEO
(816) 241-3347 Fax: (816) 241-2091
Circ: 25,000

LA NACIÓN
Washington Media Group
P.O. Box 21306
Washington, DC 20009
Jerry Pierce Santos, Edtr.
(202) 234-3898 Fax: (202) 462-3675
Circ: 22,500

LA NOTICIA
Eventos Premium
6101 Idlewild Rd. #328
Charlotte, NC 28212
Hilda Gurdián, Dir.
(704) 568-6966 Fax: (704) 568-8936

LA NUEVA ERA
Meister Publishing
37733 Euclid Ave.
Wiloughby, OH 44094-5992

Jim Moore, Edtr.
(440) 942-2000 Fax: (440) 942-0662
Published Every 6 Months

LA NUEVA PRENSA
La Nueva Prensa
P.O. Box 1333
Lafayette, CA 94549
Roberto Castellón, Dir.
(925) 210-1107 Fax: (925) 210-1108
Circ: 26,000

LA OFERTA REVIEW
La Oferta
1376 N 4th St.
San Jose, CA 95112
Mary Andrade, Edtr.
(408) 436-7850 Fax: (408) 436-7861
Circ: 45,000

LA OPINIÓN
411 W 5th St.
Los Angeles, CA 90013
Gerardo Lopez, Edtr.
(213) 896-2333 Fax: (213) 896-2080
Circ: 108,309

LA OPINIÓN
La Opinión Company, Inc.
P.O. Box 8340
402 College Ave.
Jacksonville, TX 75766
Judith B. Cantúa, Pres.
(903) 586-0827 Fax: (903) 586-7016
Circ: 10,000

LA OPINIÓN
La Opinión
2508 SE Ave.
Berwyn, IL 60402
Félix María Cáceres, Edtr./Pub.
(708) 795-1383 Fax: (708) 795-1383
Circ: 20,000

LA PERLA DEL SUR
La Perla del Sur
P.O. Box 8212
Ponce, PR 00732-8212
Juan J. Nogueras, Edtr./Pres.
(787) 842-5866 Fax: (787) 842-5823
Circ: 75,000

LA PRENSA
La Prensa
8033 Sunset Blvd. #704
Los Angeles, CA 90046
Carlos G. Groppa, Edtr.
(323) 654-6268
Circ: 25,000

LA PRENSA
La Prensa
111 Veterans Blvd. #1800
Metairie, LA 70005
Gina Cortez, Edtr.
(504) 830-7201 Fax: (504) 378-0000
Circ: 10,000

LA PRENSA
La Prensa Publications, Inc.
P.O.Box 6504
Austin, TX 78762
Cathy Vasques-Revilla, Pub.
(512) 478-3090 Fax: (512) 478-3137
Circ: 10,000

LA PRENSA CENTROAMERICANA
La Prensa Centroamericana
2961 W 12th Ave.
Hialeah, FL 33012
Filemón Orteaga, Edtr.
(305) 889-1287 Fax: (305) 889-1745
Circ: 5,000

LA PRENSA DE MINNESOTA
Hispanic Publishing Inc.
550 Concord St.
St. Paul, MN 55107
Mario Duarte, Edtr./Pub.
(651) 224-0404 Fax: (651) 224-0098
Circ: 14,500

LA PRENSA DE SAN ANTONIO
La Prensa de San Antonio
318 S Flores St.
San Antonio, TX 78204
Rolando Romero, Edtr.
(210) 242-7900 Fax: (210) 242-7901
Published 2 times a week
Circ: 172,000

LA PRENSA DE SAN DIEGO
La Prensa de San Diego
1950 5th St. #1, 2 & 3
San Diego, CA 92101-2309
Daniel L. Muñoz, Edtr.
(619) 231-2873 Fax: (619) 231-9180
Circ: 30,000

LA PRENSA GRAFICA
Prensa Gráfica News
P.O. Box 350-895
Miami, FL 33135
Dr. Raúl R. Oliva, Edtr.
(305) 649-6267 Fax: (305) 649-6300
Circ: 28,000

LA PRENSA NEWSPAPER
La Prensa Newspaper Corporation
685 S County Rd. 427
Longwood, FL 32750-6403
Manuel Toro, Edtr.
(407) 767-0070 Fax: (407) 767-5478
Circ: 30,000

LA PRENSA SPANISH NEWSPAPER
La Prensa Spanish Newspaper
P.O. Box 65661
Salt Lake City, UT 84165
Ingrid Quiroz, Edtr.
(801) 288-2352 Fax: (801) 281-1431
Circ: 8,000

LA PROMESA YEARBOOK
National Latino Children's Institute
1412 W 6th St.
Austin, TX 78703
Rebeca María Barrera, Pres.
(512) 472-9971 Fax: (512) 472-5845
Circ: 5,000

LA RAZA HABLA - MAGAZINE
P.O. Box 4188. NM State Univ
Las Cruces, NM 88003
David Gomez, Edtr./Pub.
(505) 646-4206
Circ: 5,000

LA RAZA LAW JOURNAL
La Raza
Simmon 585
UC Berkeley
Berkeley, CA 94720
Cristina Perez, Edtr.
(510) 642-9351
Circ: 500

LA RAZA NEWSPAPER
Rossi Publications, Inc.
3859 N Ashland Ave., 1st Fl.
Chicago, IL 60613
Luis H. Rossi, Pres.
(773) 525-6285 Fax: (773) 525-6449
Circ: 150,000

LA REVISTA
Universidad Politécnica de Puerto Rico
Apartado Postal 192017
San Juan, PR 00919-2017
Dr. Rafael López Valdés, Dir.
(787) 754-8000x419 Fax: (787) 767-5343
Circ: 6,000

LA REVISTA DE LA INDIERRA TAINA (TAINO AMERICAN INDIAN)
Taino Inter-Tribal Council Inc.
527 Mulberry St.
Millville, NJ 08332
Roy Cibabo McClellan, Edtr.
(856) 825-7776 Fax: (856) 825-7922
Circ: 3,000

LA SALUD HISPANA
La Salud Hiapana Inc.
225 Broadway #3009
New York, NY 10007
Dr. Rodrigo Cárdenas, Pub.

(212) 791-7177 Fax: (212) 791-7304
Circ: 65,000

LA SEMANA
La Semana
911 Massachusetts Ave.
Boston, MA 02118
Pedro Nicolas Cuenca, Edtr./Pub.
(617) 427-6212 Fax: (617) 427-6227
Circ: 15,000

LA SUBASTA
7120 Tarnef #110
Houston, TX 77074
Orlando Budini, Edtr.
(713) 777-1010 Fax: (713) 777-5896
Circ: 120,000

LA TRIBUNA HISPANA -USA
P.O.Box 186
Hempstead, NY 11550
Luis Aguilar, Edtr.
(516) 486-6457 Fax: (516) 292-3972
Circ: 30,000

LA VIDA NEWSPAPER
P.O. Box 751
Fort Worth, TX 76101
Ted Prewitt, Edtr.
(817) 543-2095 Fax: (817) 861-0195
Circ: 18,000

LA VOZ
948 Elizabeth Ave.
Elizabeth, NJ 07201
Virginia García, Edtr.
(908) 352-6654 Fax: (908) 352-9735
Circ: 38,000

LA VOZ
Palacios-Rios Communications
102 W Cuyler St.
Dalton, GA 30720
Francisco Palacios, Edtr.
(706) 272-0436 Fax: (706) 272-0442
Circ: 6,000

LA VOZ CATÓLICA
9401 Biscayne Blvd.
Miami, FL 33138-2970
Araceli M. Cantero, Exec. Dir.
(305) 762-1201 Fax: (305) 762-1223
Circ: 47,000

LA VOZ DE CHICAGO
Blue Island Printing
8626 S Houston Ave., 3rd Fl. #1
Chicago, IL 60617
Tomas Alvarez, Edtr.
(773) 221-9416 Fax: (773) 221-4798
Circ: 15,000

LA VOZ DE CUBA LIBRE
La Voz de Cuba Libre Educational Foundation
P.O. Box 741431
Los Angeles, CA 90004
José Fernandez, Dir.
(323) 572-1323 Fax: (323) 463-9363
Circ: 7,000

LA VOZ DE ESPERANZA
Esperanza Center
922 San Pedro
San Antonio, TX 78212
Graciela I. Sánchez, Dir.
(210) 228-0201 Fax: (210) 228-0000
Published 10 issues/year
Circ: 5,000

LA VOZ DE HOMESTEAD
Eduardo Rodriguez N.D.
P.O. Box901806
Homestead, Fl 33030
Eduardo Rodriguez, Edtr.
(305) 256-0319 Fax: (305) 251-3076
Circ: 17,000

LA VOZ DE HOUSTON
La Voz de Houston
6101 SW Freeway #127
Houston, TX 77057

Olga Ordóñez, Edtr.
(713) 664-4404 Fax: (713) 664-4414
Circ: 90,000

LA VOZ DE LA CALLE
The Voice Publishing Co., Inc.
4696 E 10th Ct.
Hialeah, FL 33013
Vicente P. Rodríguez, Dir./Edtr.
(305) 687-5555 Fax: (305) 681-0500
Circ: 25,000

LA VOZ DEL PUEBLO
La Voz del Pueblo
1282 Sugarwood Ln.
Norcross, GA 30093
Margarita Weichard, Edtr.
(770) 923-0345 Fax: (770) 806-9632
Circ: 20,000

LA VOZ ESTUDIANTIL
El Centro Hispanic Student Services
178 Student Center
Ft. Collins, CO 80523
Guadalupe Salazar, Dir.
(970) 491-5722 Fax: (970) 491-2534
Published 3 issues/year
Circ: 1,500

LA VOZ ETERNA
La Voz Eterna
6011 Lyons Ave.
Houston, TX 77020-4809
Harris Goodwin, Edtr.
(713) 674-7172
Circ: 17,000

LA VOZ HISPANA
La Voz Hispana
P.O. Box 10194
Amarillo, TX 79106
Glenda Grisham, Edtr./Pub.
(806) 372-4190 Fax: (806) 372-4349
Circ: 4,500

LA VOZ HISPANA
Casa Publications
159 E 116 St.
New York, NY 10029
Joaquin del Rio, Edtr.
(212) 348-8270 Fax: (212) 348-4469
Circ: 68,000

LA VOZ HISPANA DE CONNECTICUT
La Voz Hispana Newsprint, Inc.
35 Elm St.
New Haven, CT 06510
Abelardo King/Norma Rodriguez-Reyes, Edtr./Pres.
(203) 865-2272 Fax: (203) 787-4023
Circ: 15,000

LA VOZ LATINA
LCLAA
815 16th St. NW #310
Washington, DC 20006
Ana Polanco, Edtr.
(202) 347-4223 Fax: (703) 347 5095
Circ: 15,000

LA VOZ LATINA
La Voz Latina
1211 Park Ave. #104
San Jose, CA 95126
Raul León, Edtr.
(408) 297-1553 Fax: (408) 297-1428
Circ: 20,000

LA VOZ LATINA (BOLETIN INFORMATIVO)
La Voz Latina
P.O. Box 3195
Cumming, GA 30028
Julio Sánchez, Organizer
(678) 513-2859
Circ: 2,000

LA VOZ NEWS
Santa Fe Publishing Co., Inc.
2885 W 3rd Ave.
Denver, CO 80219
Wanda M. Padilla, Edtr./Pub.
(303) 936-8556 Fax: (303) 922-9632
Circ: 18,000

LAANC NEWSLETTER (BOLETÍN INFORMATIVO)
Latin American Association of North Carolina
P.O. Box 20863
Raleigh, NC 27619
Fernando Rodríguez, Pres.
(919) 932-1924 Fax: (919) 967-8637
Circ: 300

LABORATORIO Y ANÁLISIS
Keller International Publishing Corp.
150 Great Neck Rd.
Great Neck, NY 11021
Brian de Lucca, Edtr.
(516) 829-9210 Fax: (516) 829-3591
Published 6 issues/year
Circ: 25,000

THE LAEC NEWSLETTER
The Latin American Educational Center
2513 S Calhoun St.
Fort Wayne, IN 46807
Graciela Beecher, Edtr.
(219) 745-5421
Circ: 500

LAEDA
Latin American Economic Development Association
433 Market St. #202
Camden, NJ 08102
Alfonso Castillo, Dir.
(856) 338-1177 Fax: (856) 963-1835
Circ: 900

LAEF NEWSLETTER
Latin American Educational Foundation (LAEF)
930 W 7th Ave.
Denver, CO 80204
Larry Romero, Exec. Dir.
(303) 446-0541 Fax: (303) 446-0526
Circ: 2,000

LARASA DIRECTORY OF COLORADO'S LATINO ORGANIZATIONS
Latin American Research and Service Agency (LARASA)
309 W 1st Ave.
Denver, CO 80223
Lucia Lopez, Research Coord.
(303) 722-5150 Fax: (303) 722-5118
Circ: 500

LARASA UPDATES
Latin American Research and Service Agency (LARASA)
309 W 1st Ave.
Denver, CO 80223
Lucia Lopez, Research Coord.
(303) 722-5150 Fax: (303) 722-5118

LARASA/REPORTS
Latin American Research and Service Agency (LARASA)
309 W 1st Ave.
Denver, CO 80223
Lucia Lopez, Research Coord.
(303) 722-5150 Fax: (303) 722-5118

LAREDO MORNING TIMES, NOTICIAS EN ESPAÑOL
111 Esperanza Dr.
Laredo, TX 78041
Odie Arambula, Edtr.
(956) 728-2555 Fax: (956) 723-1227
Circ: 23,629

LAREDOS
Shoestring Productions, Inc.
1812 Houston St.
Laredo, TX 78040
Tom Moore, Edtr.
(956) 791-9950 Fax: (956) 791-4737
Circ: 10,000

LAS NOTICIAS DE FORT BEND
Las Noticias de Fort Bend
924 3rd St. #4
Rosenberg, TX 77471

Joe R. Morales, Edtr.
(281) 342-1622 Fax: (281) 342-1911
Circ: 10,000

LAS PÁGINAS AMARILLAS DE OKLAHOMA
Printing, Inc.
304 SW 25th St.
Oklahoma City, OK 73109
Rosa Quiroga King, Edtr./Pub.
(405) 632-4531 Fax: (405) 632-4533
Circ: 40,000

LAS PÁGINAS AMARILLAS EN ESPAÑOL-HOUSTON
Spanish Publications, Inc.
6601 Tarnef St. #200
Houston, TX 77074
Raul Dueñas, Edtr.
(713) 774-4719 Fax: (713) 774-4666
Circ: 100,000

LATIN AMERICA EVANGELIST
Latin America Mission
P.O. Box 52-7900
Miami, FL 33152
Susan Loobie, Edtr.
(305) 884-8400 Fax: (305) 885-8649
Published 3 issues/year
Circ: 30,000

LATIN AMERICA SUPPORT ORGANIZATION (LASO)
Denver Water Department/Latin America Support Organization (LASO)
1600 W 12th Ave.
Denver, CO 80254
Rose Delgado, Pres.
(303) 628-6346 Fax: (303) 628-6349
Circ: 300

LATIN AMERICAN LITERARY REVIEW
Latin American Literary Review Press
121 Edgewood Ave.
Pittsburg, PA 15218
Ivette Miller, Edtr.
(412) 371 9023 Fax: (412) 371 9025
Published 2 issues/year
Circ: 1,200

LATIN AMERICAN MUSIC REVIEW
University of Texas Press
P.O. Box 7819
Austin, TX 78703
Karen Crowther, Production Manager
(512) 471-4531 Fax: (512) 232-7178
Circ: 500

LATIN AMERICAN STUDIES ASSOCIATION—HANDBOOK & MEMBERSHIP DIRECTORY
Latin American Studies Association
William Pitt Union #946
University of Pittsburgh
Pittsburgh, PA 15260
Reid Reading, Pres.
(412) 648-7929 Fax: (412) 624-7145

LATIN AMERICAN STUDIES CENTER NEWSLETTER
Arizona State University
P.O. Box 872401
Tempe, AZ 85287-2401
Santa Young, Administrator Associate
(480) 965-5127 Fax: (480) 965-6679
Circ: 200

LATIN BEAT MAGAZINE
Latin Beat Magazine
15900 Crenshaw Blvd. #1-223
Gardena, CA 90249
Rudolph Mangual, Edtr./Pub.
(310) 516-6767 Fax: (310) 516-9916
Published 10 times a year
Circ: 50,000

LATIN CHAMBER NEWS
The Latin Chamber of Commerce of Nevada, Inc.
829 S 6th St. #3
P.O. Box 7500

Las Vegas, NV 89125
Otto Merida, Exec. Dir.
(702) 385-7367 Fax: (702) 385-2614
Circ: 3,000

LATIN HEAT
Latin Heat Entertainment
146 N San Fernando Blvd. #201
Burbank, CA 91502
Bal Hernandez, Edtr.
(818) 846-9259 Fax: (818) 846-9419
Circ: 10,000

LATIN STYLE
Latin Style Magazine
1542 Cassil Place
Hollywood, CA 90028
Walter Martínez, Edtr./ Pub.
(323) 462-4409 Fax: (323) 462-0842
Published 11 times a year
Circ: 120,000

LATIN TRADE
95 Merryrck Way #600
Coral Gables, FL 33134
Michael Zellner, Edtr.
(305) 358-8373 Fax: (305) 358-9166
Circ: 105,000

LATINA
Latina Publications, LLC
1500 Broadway #600
New York, NY 10036
Christy Haubegger , Pub.
(212) 642-0600 Fax: (212) 997-2553
Circ: 300,000

LATINA STYLE MAGAZINE
Latina Style
1730 Rhode Island NW #1207
Washington, DC 20036
Anna Maria Arias, Edtr./Pub.
(202) 955-7930 Fax: (202) 955-7934
Circ: 110,000

LATINFINANCE
Latin American Financial Publications, Inc.
2121 Ponce de Leon Blvd. #1020
Coral Gables, FL 33134
John Barham, Edtr.
(305) 448-6593 Fax: (305) 445-1895
Circ: 25,000

LATINO(A) RESEARCHREVIEW
Center for Latino, Latin American and Caribbean Studies (CELAC)
CELAC, SS-247, University at Albany, State University of New York
Albany, NY 12222
Dr. Edna Acosta-Belén, Edtr.
(518) 442-4590 Fax: (518) 442-4790
Circ: 1,000

LATINO BARRIO
The Latino Media Group
3024 W 25th St.
Cleveland, OH 44113
Randy Michael, CEO
(216) 344-0521 Fax: (216) 344-0511
Circ: 10,000

LATINO BASEBALL MAGAZINE
King Paniagua, L.L.C.
518 5th Ave., 5th Fl.
New York, NY 10036
Neil Perlich Porter, Edtr.-in-Chief
(212) 869-7007 Fax: (212) 869-7009
Circ: 60,000

LATINO BOXING MAGAZINE
King Paniagua, L.L.C.
518 5th Ave., 5th Fl.
New York, NY 10036
Neil Perlich Porter, Edtr.-in-Chief
(212) 869-7007 Fax: (212) 869-7009
Circ: 60,000

LATINO COUNCIL ON ALCOHOL AND TOBACCO NEWS
LCAT
1875 Connecticut Ave., NW, #732
Washington, DC 20009
Jeanette Noltenius, Exec. Dir.

(202) 265-8054 Fax: (202) 265-8056
Circ: 1,400

LATINO ELECTION HANDBOOK
National Association of Latino Elected and Appointed Officials (NALEO) Educational Fund
5800 S Eastern Ave. #365
Los Angeles, CA 90040
Rosalind Gold, Dir.of Policy, Research and Advocacy
(323) 720-1932 Fax: (323) 720-9519
Circ: 2,500

LATINO LEADERS
Ferraez Publications of America, Corp.
363 N. Sam Houston Pkwy #1100
Houston, TX 77060
Adam Garst, Edtr.
(888) 528-4532 Fax: (525) 651-5722
Circ: 100,000

LATINO POVERTY IN THE UNITED STATES
Cuban American National Council, Inc.
1223 SW 4th St.
Miami, FL 33135
Guarioné M. Díaz, Pres.
(305) 642-3484 Fax: (305) 642-9815

LATINO PRESS
Latino Press, Inc.
1494 Junction St.
Detroit, MI 48209
Elías M. Gutiérrez, Edtr.
(313) 841-9333 Fax: (313) 841-2950
Circ: 15,000

LATINO YELLOW PAGES/PÁGINAS AMARILLAS DEL LATINO
Latino News
85 Briarcliff Pt.
Rainbow City, AL 35906
Jairo Vargas, Pub.
(256) 442-8914 Fax: (256) 442-0372
Circ: 20,000

LATINO'S YELLOW PAGES
First Latino Yellow Pages, Inc.
450 W Broad St. #216
Falls Church, VA 22046
Silvia Velasco, Pres.
(703) 534-6050 Fax: (703) 534-6090
Circ: 100,000

THE LAWNDALE NEWS
The Lawndale News
5416 -18 W 25 St.
Cicero, IL 60804
Daniel Nardini, Edtr.
(708) 656-6400 Fax: (708) 656-2433
Published 2 times a week
Circ: 150,000

LAWYERS' COMMITTEE FOR CIVIL RIGHTS UNDER THE LAW— COMMITTEE REPORT
Lawyers' Committee for Civil Rights Under the Law
1401 New York Ave. #400
Washington, DC 20005
Peggy Cox, Edtr.
(202) 662-8600 Fax: (202) 783-0857
Circ: 1,000

LEARNING TO SUCCEED
League of United Latin American Citizens (LULAC)
720 N Main St. #455
Pueblo, CO 81003
Steve García, Dir.
(719) 542-9074 Fax: (719) 542-9075
Published 2 issues/year
Circ: 50

LECTURA Y VIDA
International Reading Association
800 Barksdale Rd./P.O. Box 8139
Newark, DE 19714-8139
María Elena Rodríguez, Edtr.
(302) 731-1600 Fax: (302) 731-1057
Circ: 1,500

LIBRE
Libre
904 SW 23rd Ave.
Miami, FL 33135
Demetrio Pérez, Pub.
(305) 643-4888 Fax: (305) 642-8402
Circ: 25,000

LIBROS EN VENTA
NISC
Apartado 41291
San Juan, PR 00940
Margaret Melcher, Edtr.
(787) 724-1352 Fax: (787) 724-2886

THE LINK
Kansas Advisory Committee on Hispanic Affairs
1430 SW Topeka Blvd.
Topeka, KS 66612-1853
Tina DeLaRosa, Exec. Dir.
(785) 296-3465 Fax: (785) 296-8118
Circ: 2,000

LINWOOD PRESS
Wave Community Newspapers, Inc.
2621 W 54th St.
Los Angeles, CA 90043
Pluria Marshall, Jr, Pres.
(323) 290-3000 Fax: (323) 291-0219

LION EN ESPAÑOL
Lions Clubs International
300 W 22nd St.
Oak Brook, IL 60523-8842
Fernando Fernández, Edtr.
(630) 571-5466 Fax: (630) 571-8890
Published 10 issues/year
Circ: 70,000

LITTLE VILLAGE BUSINESS DIRECTORY
Little Village Chamber of Commerce
3610 W 26th St., 2nd Floor
Chicago, IL 60623
Agustin Granja, Exec. Dir.
(773) 521-5387 Fax: (773) 521-5252
Circ: 10,000

LULAC NEWS
League of United Latin American Citizens
1133 20th St. NW #750
Washington, DC 22036
Scott Gunderson, Edtr.
(202) 833-6130 Fax: (202) 408-0064
Circ: 150,000

LUNA, SU FOLLETO HISPANO
Luna Advertising Services and Translations
P.O. Box 103
Hickory, NC 28603
José Luis y Josefina Mesa, Edtrs.
(828) 327-8045 Fax: (828) 327-9135
Circ: 5,000

LUSO-AMERICANO
88 Ferry St.
Newark, NJ 07105
Fernando Santor, Edtr.
(973) 589-4600 Fax: (973) 589-3848
Circ: 30,000

LUZ A LA FAMILIA
News Web
2425 W Division Ave.
Chicago, IL 60622
Andrea Castillo, Dir.
(773) 772-0954
Circ: 8,000

LUZ DE LA VIDA
Rod & Staff Publishers, Inc.
Highway 172
Crockett, KY 41413
Eugene G. Campbell, Edtr.
(606) 522-4348 Fax: (606) 522-4896
Circ: 8,000

M

MAAC NEWS
MAAC Project
22 W 35th St. #100
National City, CA 91950
Connie Hernández, Coord.
(619) 426-3595 Fax: (619) 474-5035
Circ: 3,000

MAGAZINE
Mexican American Grocers Association
405 N San Fernando Rd.
Los Angeles, CA 90031
Jerome Wilson Lloyd, Edtr.
(323) 227-1565 Fax: (323) 227-6935
Published 3 issues/year

MAJOR LEAGUE BASEBALL EN ESPAÑOL
Daily News
350 W 33rd St.
New York, NY 10001
Debbie Medina, Co-Publisher
(212) 210-1992
Circ: 465,000

MALDEF NEWSLETTER
Mexican American Legal Defense & Educational Fund (MALDEF)
634 S Spring St., 11th Floor
Los Angeles, CA 90014
David Damian, Edtr.
(213) 629-2512 Fax: (213) 629-3120

MANA NEWSLETTER
Mana A National Latina Organization
1725 K St. NW #501
Washington, DC 20006
Marieli Colo, Edtr.
(202) 833-0060 Fax: (202) 496-0588
Circ: 3,000

MANUFACTURA
Grupo Editorial Expansion
1018 W 9th Ave.
King of Prussia, PA 19406
Scott Sward, VP
(610) 337-5516 Fax: (610) 337—5520
Circ: 25,000

MARIE CLAIRE
Editorial Televisa
6355 NW 36th St.
Miami, FL 33166
Irene Carol, Edtr.
(305) 871-6400 Fax: (305) 871-1520
Circ: 150,000

THE MASRC WORKING PAPER SERIES
Mexican American Studies & Research Ctr. The University of Arizona
Economics Bldg., Room 208, P.O. Box 210023
Tucson, AZ 85721-0023
Tom Gelsinon, Publishing Coordinator
(520) 626-8103 Fax: (520) 621-7966

MBE- MINORITY BUSINESS ENTREPRENEUR
Minority Business Entrepreneur
3528 Torrance Blvd. #101
Torrance, CA 90503-4826
Angela Cranon, Edtr.
(310) 540-9398 Fax: (310) 792-8263
Circ: 50,000

MECÁNICA POPULAR
Editorial Televisa
6355 NW 36th St.
Miami, FL 33166
Gabriel González, Edtr.
(305) 871-6400 Fax: (305) 871-1520
Circ: 13,340

MEDICINA Y CULTURA
Mundo Medico USA, Inc.
158 Danbury Rd., #8
Ridgefield, CT 06877
Sarah E. Gutierrez, Pub.
(203) 438-1056 Fax: (203) 438-1057

MÉDICO DE FAMILIA
Interamerican College of Physicians & Surgeons (ICPS)
1712 I St. NW #200
Washington, DC 20006
Dr. René F. Rodríguez M.D., Edtr.
(202) 467-4756 Fax: (202) 467-4758
Circ: 65,000

MEDICO INTERAMERICANO
Interamerican College of Physicians and Surgeons
40 Galesi Drive
Wayne, NJ 07470
Javier Martinez, Edtr.
(973) 812-8098 Fax: (973) 812-9140
Circ: 39,160

MEDICS
Editorial Televisa
6355 NW 36th St.
Miami, FL 33166
(305) 871-6400 Fax: (305) 871-1520

MEMBER ORGANIZATIONS OF THE COUNCIL OF LATINO AGENCIES DIRECTORY
Council of Latino Agencies
2309 18th St. NW #2
Washington, DC 20009-1814
Teresa Doniger, Dir.of Member Services
(202) 328-9451 Fax: (202) 667-6135
Circ: 1,500

MEMBERSHIP DIRECTORY
Spain-US Chamber of Commerce in Florida
2655 Le Jeune Rd. #906
Coral Gables, FL 33134
Eulalia Mascort, Exec. Dir.
(305) 446-1992 Fax: (305) 529-2854
Circ: 1,000

MEMBERSHIP DIRECTORY
Hispanic Chamber of Commerce of Austin/ Travis County
823 Congress Ave. #1330
Austin, TX 78701
Eliza May, Pres.
(512) 476-7502 Fax: (512) 476-6417

MEMBERSHIP DIRECTORY OF UNITED STATES HISPANIC CHAMBER OF COMMERCE
United States Hispanic Chamber of Commerce
2175 K St., NW #100
Washington, DC 20037
George Herrera, Pres.
(202) 842-1212 Fax: (202) 842-3221

MEMBERSHIP RESOURCE DIRECTORY
Latino Chamber of Commerce of Pueblo, Inc.
215 S Victoria Ave.
Pueblo, CO 81003
Sandy Gutiérrez, Exec. Dir.
(719) 542-5513 Fax: (719) 542-4657
Circ: 1,000

MEN'S HEALTH EN ESPAÑOL
Editorial Televisa
Ave. Vasco De Quiroga #2000, Col. Santa Fe,
Delegacion Alvaro Obregon
Mexico D.F., Mexico 01210
(525) 261-2600 Fax: (525) 261-2732

MEN'S HEALTH EN ESPAÑOL
Editorial Televisa
6355 NW 36th St.
Miami, FL 33166
(305) 871-6400 Fax: (305) 871-1520
Circ: 30,900

MENSAJE
Latin American News and Book, Inc.
P.O. Box 2109
Elizabeth, NJ 07207
Jose Tenreiro-Napoles, Edtr.
(908) 355-8835 Fax: (908) 527-9160
Circ: 52,000

MEPS/USA: THE DIRECTORY OF PRECOLLEGE AND UNIVERSITY MINORITY ENGINEERING PROGRAMS
National Action Council for Minorities in Engineering
350 5th Ave. #2212
New York, NY 10118
Dundee Holt, VP, Public Information
(212) 279-2626 Fax: (212) 629-5178

MERCADO MAGAZINE
Mercado Magazine Inc.
1401 W Flagler St. #206
Miami, FL 33135
Juan Rigau, Edtr.
(305) 642-1445 Fax: (305) 642-1538
Circ: 40,000

MEXICAN AMERICAN COMMISSION NEWSLETTER
Mexican American Commission
P.O. Box 94965
Lincoln, NE 68509-4965
Cecilia Olivares Huerta, Dir.
(402) 471-2791 Fax: (402) 471-4381
Circ: 6,500

MEXICAN AMERICAN SUN
Eastern Group Publications, Inc.
2500 S Atlantic Blvd., Bldg. A
Los Angeles, CA 90040
Dolores Sanchez, Edtr.
(323) 263-5743 Fax: (323) 263-9169
Circ: 14,750

MEXICO BUSINESS MONTHLY
52 Maple Ave.
Maplewood, NJ 07040
Kal Wagenheim, Edtr./Pub.
(973) 762-1565 Fax: (201) 762-9585
Circ: 100

MEXICÓ EXPRESS
San Antonio Express News
P.O. Box 2171
San Antonio, TX 78297-2171
Beverly Purcella-Guerra, Edtr.
(210) 250-2552 Fax: (210) 250-2565
Published 6 issues/year
Circ: 50,000

MÉXICO LINDO
P.O. Box 1747
Gainesville, GA 30503
Dave Anderson, Edtr.
(770) 535-0455 Fax: (770) 535-1675
Circ: 1,300

MHAC NEWS
Midwest Hispanic AIDS Coalition
P.O. Box 470859
Chicago, IL 60647
Kathy Lins, Exec. Dir.
(773) 772-8195
Published 2 issues/year
Circ: 1,000

MI CASA RESOURCE CENTER FOR WOMEN
Mi Casa Resource Center for Women
571 Galapago St.
Denver, CO 80204
Carmen Carrillo, Exec. Dir.
(303) 573-1302 Fax: (303) 595-0422

MI GENTE
Mi Gente Publications
108 S. Hamilton St.
Saginaw, MI 48602
Larry J. Rodarte, Pub./ Edtr.-in-Chief
(517) 797-8060 Fax: (517) 797-8061
Circ: 40,000

MIAMI MENSUAL
Quantus Communications Group
104 Crandon Blvd. #424
Miami, FL 33149
Frank Soler, Edtr./Pub.
(305) 444-5678 Fax: (305) 361-9707
Published 10 issues/year
Circ: 30,000

MIAMI MOSAIC
Cuban American National Council, Inc.
1223 SW 4th St.
Miami, FL 33135
Guarioné M. Díaz, Pres.
(305) 642-3484 Fax: (305) 642-9815

MIAMI TODAY
Today Enterprises Inc.
710 Brickell Ave.
Miami, FL 33131
Michael Lewis, Edtr.
(305) 358-2663 Fax: (305) 358-4811
Circ: 33,000

MIGRANT EDUCATION NEWS
Migrant Legal Action Program
P.O. Box 53308
Washington, DC 20009
Roger Rosenthal, Edtr.
(202) 462-7744 Fax: (202) 462-7914
Circ: 1,000

MINERIA PAN-AMERICANA
International Construction Publishing
4913 SW 75th Ave.
Miami, FL 33155
Juan B. Escalante, Edtr.
(305) 668-4999 Fax: (305) 668-7774
Published 5 issues/year
Circ: 15,000

MINIONDAS
1742 S Main St.
Santa Ana, CA 92707
Carlos Lopez, Edtr./Pub.
(714) 547-0701 Fax: (714) 547-2404
Circ: 45,000

MINORITY BUSINESS NEWS USA
TexCorp Communications, Inc.
11333 N Central Expressway # 201
Dallas, TX 75243
Don Mckneely, Edtr./Pub.
(214) 369-3200 Fax: (214) 265-9393
Circ: 157,116

MINORITY BUSINESS INFORMA-TION RESOURCES DIRECTORY
Diversity Information Resources, Inc.
2105 Central Ave. NE
Minneapolis, MN 55418
Leslie Bonds, Exec. Dir.
(612) 781-6819 Fax: (612) 781-0109
Circ: 6,000

MINORITY STUDENT OPPORTUNI-TIES IN UNITED STATES MEDICAL SCHOOLS
Association of American Medical Colleges (AAMC)
2450 N St. NW
Washington, DC 20037
Laly May Johnson, Edtr.
(202) 828-0400 Fax: (202) 828-1125
Circ: 500

MONTEBELLO COMET
Eastern Group Publications, Inc.
2500 S Atlantic Blvd., Bldg. A
Los Angeles, CA 90040
Dolores Sanchez, Edtr.
(323) 263-5743 Fax: (323) 263-9169
Circ: 12,500

MONTEREY PARK COMET
Eastern Group Publications, Inc.
2500 S Atlantic Blvd., Bldg. A
Los Angeles, CA 90040
Dolores Sanchez, Edtr.
(323) 263-5743 Fax: (323) 263-9169
Circ: 6,000

MULTICULTURAL REVIEW
Greenwood Publishing Group, Inc.
P.O. Box 5007, 88 W Post Rd.
Westport, CT 06881-5007
Gerry Lynch Katz, Managing Edtr.
(203) 226-3571 Ext.422 Fax: (203) 222-6009

MUNDO ARTÍSTICO
Pressnet Corp.
P.O. Box 45-4111

Miami, FL 33245-4111
Luis Pardo, Pres.
(305) 262-6744 Fax: (305) 262-6744
Circ: 10,000

MUNDO HISPÁNICO
Mundo Hispánico
P.O. Box 13808
Atlanta, GA 30324-0808
Lino Domínguez, Dir.
(404) 881-0441 Fax: (404) 881-6085
Circ: 23,000

MUNDO HISPANO
Falcon Enterprise
9131 S Monroe St. #C
Sandy, UT 84070
Gladys González, Edtr.
(801) 569-3338 Fax: (801) 569-3335
Circ: 10,000

MUNDO LA
Latin Publications, Inc.
P.O. Box 9190
Van Nuys, CA 91409
Diane Lerner, Edtr.
(818) 781-2605 Fax: (818) 882-2625
Circ: 540,000

MUNDO LATINO MAGAZINE
P.O. Box 65766
Los Angeles, CA 90065-0766
César C. Cantú, Pub.
(323) 221-8044

N

NABE NEWS
National Association for Bilingual Education
1030 15th St. NW #470
Washington, DC 20005
Alicia Sosa, Edtr.
(202) 898-1829 Fax: (202) 789-2866
Published 8 issues/year
Circ: 4,500

NACLA REPORT ON THE AMERICAS
North American Congress on Latin America (NACLA)
475 Riverside Dr. #454
New York, NY 10115
Debbie Nathan, Edtr.
(212) 870-3146 Fax: (212) 870-3305
Circ: 9,000

NAHP PUBLISHING UNIVERSITY
National Assocation of Hispanic Publications
941 Nat'l Press Bldg.
Washington, DC 20045
Andres Tobar, Exec. Dir. & CEO
(202) 662-7250 Fax: (202) 662-7254
Circ: 2,000

NATIONAL LATINO COMMUNICA-TIONS CENTER NEWS
501 S Bixel St., 2nd Fl.
Los Angeles, CA 90017
Reba Vera, Edtr.
(323) 663-8294 Fax: (323) 663-5606
Circ: 500

NATIONAL ALLIANCE FOR HISPANIC HEALTH REPORTER
National Alliance for Hispanic Health
1501 16th St. NW
Washington, DC 20036
Adolph Falcon, Edtr.
(202) 797-4335 Fax: (202) 797-4353
Circ: 5,000

NATIONAL DIRECTORY OF HISPANIC ORGANIZATIONS
Congressional Hispanic Caucus Institute, Inc.
504 C St. NE
Washington, DC 20002
Juan Herrera, Edtr.
(202) 543-1771 Fax: (202) 543-2143
Circ: 20,000

NATIONAL DIRECTORY OF LATINO ELECTED OFFICIALS
National Association of Latino Elected Officials (NALEO) Educational Fund, Inc.
5800 S Eastern Ave. #365
Los Angeles, CA 90040
Rosalind Gold, Dir. of Policy, Research & Advocacy
(323) 720-1932 Fax: (323) 720-9519
Circ: 2,500

NATIONAL GEOGRAPHIC EN ESPAÑOL
Editorial Televisa
6355 NW 36th St.
Miami, FL 33166
(305) 871-6400 Fax: (305) 871-1520
Circ: 29,294

NATIONAL HISPANA LEADERSHIP INSTITUTE NEWSLETTER
National Hispanic Leadership Institute
1901 N Moore St. #206
Arlington, VA 22209
Marisa Rivera-Albert, Pres.
(703) 527-6007 Fax: (703) 527-6009
Published 2 issues/year
Circ: 2,000

THE NATIONAL HISPANIC REPORTER
NHR Consulting
P.O. Box 44082
Washington, DC 20026
Frank Elizondo, Edtr.
(202) 898-4153 Fax: (301) 258-1349
Circ: 20,000

NCBE PUBLICATIONS CATALOG
National Clearinghouse for Bilingual Education (NCBE)
2011 I St. NW #200
Washington, DC 20006
Patricia Anne DiCerbo, Research Assoc.
(202) 467-0867 (800) 321-NCBE
Fax: (202) 467-4283

NETWORK
Family Health International
P.O. Box 13950
Research Triangle Park, NC 27709
(919) 544-7040 Fax: (919) 544-7261

NETWORK
Council of Latino Agencies
2309 18th St. NW #2
Washington, DC 20009-1814
Teresa Doniger, Dir. of Member Services
(202) 328-9451 Fax: (202) 667-6135
Circ: 1,000

NETWORK NEWS
National Network for Immigrant & Refugee Rights
310 8th St. #307
Oakland, CA 94607
Cathi Tactaquin, Dir.
(510) 465-1984 Fax: (510) 465-1885
Circ: 5,000

NETWORKING
Telemundo Group, Inc.
1775 Broadway, 3rd Fl.
New York, NY 10019
(212) 492-5500 Fax: (212) 492-5629
Circ: 500

NEW HORIZONS
Hispanic Association of AT&T Employees (HISPA)
2535 E 40th Ave.
Denver, CO 80205
Shelly Durán, Ex Oficio Pres.
(303) 391-7404 Fax: (303) 294-6871
Circ: 500

THE NEWS
Wave Community Newspapers, Inc.
2621 W 54th St.
Los Angeles, CA 90043
Pluria Marshall, Jr., Pres.
(323) 290-3000 Fax: (323) 291-0219

NEWS HERALD & JOURNAL
Wave Community Newspapers, Inc.
2621 W 54th St.
Los Angeles, CA 90043
Pluria Marshall, Jr, Pres.
(323) 290-3000 Fax: (323) 291-0219

NEWSBITS
Ibero American Action League, Inc.
817 E Main St.
Rochester, NY 14605-2722
Eugenio Marlin, Edtr.
(716) 256-8900 Fax: 716) 256-0120

NEWSLETTER
*New England Council of Latin American
Studies, Inc. (NECLAS)*
Smith College, Seelye Hall #210
Northampton, MA 01063
Susan C. Bourque, Edtr.
(413) 585-3591 Fax: (413) 585-3593
Circ: 600

**NEYIA, LA REVISTA HISPANA DE
GEORGIA**
201 Concepts 21 Dr.
Norcross, GA 30092
Neyia Vargas, Dir.
(770) 582-1776 Fax: (770)582-1776
Circ: 10,000

NFHP
*National Federation of Hispanic
Publications*
853 Broadway #811
New York, NY 10003
Carlos Carrillo, Edtr./Pub.
(212) 505-0288 Fax: (212) 598-9414
Circ: 5,000

NHCC NEWS
National Hispanic Corporate Council
8201 Greensboro Dr. #300
McLean, VA 22102
Norma Khan, Prog. Manager
(703) 610-9016 Fax: (703) 610-9005
Circ: 600

**NHCOA NOTICIAS OF HISPANIC
ISSUES AND NEWS**
*National Hispanic Council on Aging
(NHCOA)*
2713 Ontario Rd., NW
Washington, DC 20024
Marta Sotomayor, Edtr.
(202) 265-1288 Fax: (202) 745-2522
Circ: 3,000

NICARAGUA MONITOR
Nicaragua Network Education Fund
1247 E St. SE
Washington, DC 20003
Morgan Guyton, Edtr.
(202) 544-9355 Fax: (202) 544-9359
Circ: 1,000

NORTHEAST SUN
Eastern Group Publications, Inc.
2500 S Atlantic Blvd., Bldg. A
Los Angeles, CA 90040
Dolores Sanchez, Edtr.
(323) 263-5743 Fax: (323) 263-9169
Circ: 24,3000

NOSOTRAS MAGAZÍN
Santelices Communications, Inc.
3615 W 26th St., 2nd Floor
Chicago, IL 60623
Alicia C. Santelices, Pub.
(708) 484-1188 Fax: (708) 484-0202
Circ: 30,000

NOTICAMARA
*Cámara de Comercio de Ponce y Sur de
Puerto Rico*
Apartado 7455
Ponce, PR 00732
Bessie Nicole, Exec.Dir.
(787) 844-4400 Fax: (787) 844-4705
Circ: 600

NOTICIA HISPANOAMERICANA
636 Seaman Ave.
Baldwin, NY 11510
Francisco Manrique, Edtr.
(516) 223-5678 Fax: (516) 377-6551
Circ: 40,000

NOTICIAS
*Hispanic Chamber of Commerce of Austin/
Travis County*
823 Congress Ave. # 1330
Austin, TX 78701
Eliza May, Exec. Dir
(512) 476-7502 Fax: (512) 476-6417
Circ: 1,000

NOTICIAS
National Association of Hispanic Journalists
1193 National Press Bldg.
Washington, DC 20045-2100
Joseph Torres, Communications Dir.
(202) 662-7145 Fax: (202) 662-7144
Circ: 1,200

NOTICIAS
Latino Chamber of Commerce of Pueblo, Inc.
215 S Victoria
Pueblo, CO 81003
Sandy Gutiérrez, Exec. Dir.
(719) 542-5513 Fax: (719) 542-4657
Circ: 700

NOTICIAS
Long Island Hispanic Chamber of Commerce
605 Albany Ave
Amityville, NY 11701
Luis Vazquez, Edtr.
(631) 841-0680 Fax: (631) 841-0370
Circ: 2,500

NOTICIAS DE CMAS
Center for Mexican American Studies
Mail Code F9200. University of Texas at Austin
Austin, TX 78712
Victor Guerra, Olga Mejia and Debra Támez, Edtrs.
(512) 471-4557 Fax: (512) 471-9639

NOTICIAS DEL MUNDO
Tiempos del Mundo
3842 9th St.
Long Island City, NY 11101
Manuel Alcantara, Edtr.
(718) 786-4343 Fax: (718) 786-7070
Circ: 32,162

NOTICIERO COLOMBIANO
108 Westfield Ave.
Elizabeth, NJ 07208
Nelson Franco, Edtr.
(908) 351-9390 Fax: (908) 351-9370
Circ: 40,000

NOTICUBA
Cuba Independiente y Democrática
10020 SW 37 Terrace
Miami, FL 33165
Angel De Fana, Edtr.
(305) 551-8484/0271 Fax: (305) 559-9365

NOVEDADES
Novedades News
121 S Zang Blvd.
Dallas, TX 75208
Marina Ruiz, Edtr.
(214) 943-2932 Fax: (214) 943-7352
Circ: 38,000

NOVEDADES
Lancer Productions, Inc.
1241 S Soto St. #213
Los Angeles, CA 90023
Víctor Benitez, Edtr.
(323) 881-6515 Fax: (323) 888-6524
Circ: 50,000

NOVEDADES
The National Law Center
2 E Congress St. #500
Tucson, AZ 85701
Mina Goldberg, Edtr.
(520) 622-1200 Fax: (520) 622-0957
Circ: 6,000

NUESTRA GENTE
2460 North Lake Ave. #126
Altadena, CA 91001-2442
Michelle Markman, Edtr.
(877) 441-7558

NUESTRA HERENCIA
*The Hispanic Genealogical Society of New
York*
P.O. Box 818, Murray Hill Station
New York, NY 10156-0602
Jorge Camuñas, Pres.
(212) 340-4659
Circ: 260

NUESTRA PARROQUIA
Claretian Publications
205 West Monroe
Chicago, IL 60606
Carmen Aguinaco, Edtr.
(312) 236-7782 Fax: (312) 236-8207
Circ: 1,500

NUESTRAS RAICES
Genealogical Society of Hispanic America
P. O. Box 9606
Denver, CO 80209-0606
Donie Nelson, Vice Pres.
(719) 564-0631 Fax: (719) 564-5913
Circ: 450

NUESTRO DIRECTORIO ANUARIO
Westtown Economic Development Corp.
2430 McVicker St.
Chicago, IL 60639
Antonio Irizarry, Edtr./Pub.
(773) 745-0420 Fax: (773) 745-6850
Circ: 25,000

NUESTRO MUNDO NEWSPAPER
3661 Davenport St.
Omaha, NE 68131
Benito Salazar, Pub./Edtr.
(402) 731-6210 Fax: (402) 731-6210
Circ: 7,500

**NUESTRO MUNDO-PEOPLE'S
WEEKLY WORLD**
Longview Publishing
235 W 23rd St.
New York, NY 10011
Tim Wheeler, Edtr.
(212) 924-2523 Fax: (212) 645-5436
Circ: 25,000

NUESTRO SEMANARIO
Ago Productions
P.O. Box 957298
Duluth, GA 30095
Winston García, Edtr.
(678) 584-1807 Fax: (678) 584-1808
Circ: 30,000

**NUEVA LUZ, A PHOTOGRAPHIC
JOURNAL**
32 E Kingsbridge Rd.
Bronx, NY 10468
Charles Biasiny Rivera, Edtr.
(718) 584-7718 Fax: (718) 584-7718
Published 3 issues/year
Circ: 5,000

NUEVA VIDA
The Resurrection Project
1818 S Paulina
Chicago, IL 60608
Raúl Raymundo, Exec. Dir.
(312) 666-1323 Fax: (312) 942-1123
Circ: 10,000

NUEVO MUNDO
San Jose Mercury News
750 Ridder Park Dr.
San Jose, CA 95190
Lorenzo Romero, Edtr.
(408) 920-5843 Fax: (408) 271-3732
Circ: 60,000

NUEVO SIGLO
Nuevo Siglo
7137 N Armenia Ave. #B
Tampa, FL 33604-5250
Neris Ramón Palacios, Edtr.
(813) 932-7181 Fax: (813) 932-8202

**OFFICIAL ETHNIC DESTINATION &
VISITORS GUIDE**
Aird & Associates
3838 Rayment Dr.
Las Vegas, NV 89121
Diana Aird, Edtr.
(702) 456-3838 Fax: (702) 456-4120
Published 3 issues/year
Circ: 100,000

OYE MAGAZINE
Oye Media
6380 Wilshire Blvd. #1113
Los Angeles, CA 90048
Cesar Recendez, Pub.
(323) 651-2064 Fax: (323) 651-2607
Circ: 50,000

P

PADF ANNUAL REPORT
*Pan American Development Foundation
(PADF)*
2600 16th St. NW, 4th Floor
Washington, DC 20009
Anita Winsor, Deputy Dir.
(202) 458-3969 Fax: (202) 458-6316
Circ: 2,000

PADRES DE SESAME STREET
1 Lincoln Pl.
New York, NY 10023
Daniel Santacruz, Edtr.
(212) 875-6981 Fax: (212) 875-6113
Published 4 issues/year
Circ: 400,000

PADRES E HIJOS
Editorial Televisa
6355 NW 36th St.
Miami, FL 33166
(305) 871-6400 Fax: (305) 871-1520

**PAGINAS AMARILLAS DE
COLORADO**
6795 E. Tennessee #355
Denver, CO 80224
Martha Rubí, Managing Partner
(303) 377-6664 Fax: (303) 377-6665
Circ: 60,000

**PÁGINAS AMARILLAS EN
ESPAÑOL**
Spanish Yellow Pages
13343 SE Stark St. #100
Portland, OR 97233
Victoria Lewis, Office Manager
(503) 257-2333 Fax: (503) 257-2333
Circ: 100,000

**PÁGINAS AMARILLAS HISPANAS,
LA SOLUCIÓN. DENVER**
Solid Future Publishing
200 S Sheridan Blvd. #110
Denver, CO 80226
Al McGregor, Manager
(303) 975-1142 Fax: (303) 975-1858
Circ: 60,000

**PÁGINAS AMARILLAS HISPANAS,
LA SOLUCIÓN. NORTE DE
COLORADO**
Solid Future Publishing
200 S Sheridan Blvd. #110
Denver, CO 80226
Al McGregor, Manager
(303) 975-1142 Fax: (303) 975-1858
Circ: 30,000

**PÁGINAS AMARILLAS HISPANAS,
LA SOLUCIÓN. NORTH EAST LA**
Solid Future Publishing
200 S Sheridan Blvd. #110
Denver, CO 80226
Al McGregor, Manager
(303) 975-1142 Fax: (303) 975-1858
Circ: 30,000

PÁGINAS AMARILLAS HISPANAS-HISPANIC YELLOW PAGES
Casablanca Publishing, Inc.
P. O. Box 191033
Atlanta, GA 31119
Zaida González, Edtr.
(404) 321-5211 Fax: (404) 321-6612
Circ: 60,000

PAMPAS NEWSLETTER
Pampas Broadcasting, Inc.
8370 Greensboro Dr. #1007
McLean, VA 22102
Ana Eliza, Edtr.
Circ: 30,000

PAN AMERICAN HEALTH ORGANI-ZATION (PAHO) CATALOG
Pan American Health Organization (PAHO)
Programa de Publicaciones
525 23rd St. NW
Washington, DC 20037
Judith Navarro, Edtr.-in-Chief
(202) 974-3000 Fax: (202) 974-3663
Circ: 8,000

PAPEL PERIÓDICO
Colegio Nacional de Periodistas de Cuba en el Exilio
900 SW 1st St.
Miami, FL 33130
Luis Felipe Marsans, Edtr.
(305) 324-6066 Fax: (305) 324-6066
Circ: 1,000

PARTICIPACIÓN DE LA MUJER EN LA ADOPCIÓN DE DECISIONES EN PRO DE LA PAZ: ESTUDIO MONOGRÁFICO SOBRE SUECIA
The United Nations
2 United Nations Pl. #DC2-853
New York, NY 10017
(212) 963-8302 Fax: (212) 963-3489
Published once

PARTNERS
Partners of the Americas
1424 K St. NW #700
Washington, DC 20005
Norman A. Brown, Pres.
(202) 628-3300 Fax: (202) 628-3306
Circ: 20,000

PARTNERS OF THE AMERICAS 1998 ANNUAL REPORT
Partners of the Americas
1424 K St. NW #700
Washington, DC 20005
Norman A. Brown, Pres.
(202) 628-3300 Fax: (202) 628-3306

PBS PARA LA FAMILIA
Familyeducation Company
20 Park Plaza #1420
Boston, MA 02116-9584
Cindy Bond, Dir. of Newsletter Publication
(617) 542-6500x1134 Fax: (617) 542-6564
Circ: 100,000

PC MAGAZINE
Editorial Televisa
6355 NW 36th St.
Miami, FL 33166
Moisés Cielak Eychenbaum, Edtr.
(305) 871-6400 Fax: (305) 871-1520
Circ: 135,000

PEOPLE - EN ESPAÑOL
Time, Inc.
1271 6th Ave.
New York, NY 10020
Angelo Figueroa/ Liza Quiroz, Edtr./Pub.
(212) 522-4988 Fax: (212) 467-4845
Circ: 250,000

PERIODICO COMERCIO Y PRODUCCIÓN
Cámara de Comercio de Puerto Rico
P.O. Box 9024033
San Juan, PR 00902-4033

Lic. Anibal Irizarry/Lourdes Aponte, Edtr.
(787) 721-6060 Fax: (787) 723-1891
Circ: 2,500

PERIODICO EL TODO
Periodico El Todo
5-S Calle 17 Flamboyan Gardens
Bayamón, PR 00959
Juan Soto, Jefe de Información
(787) 787-6011 Fax: (787) 740-0022
Circ: 75,000

PERIODICO LA CORDILLERA
Periodico La Cordillera
P.O. Box 690
Cidra, PR 00739
Maria del Rosario Pagan, Pres.
(787) 739-1854/3094 Fax: (787) 739-1854
Circ: 50,000

PERIODICOVISIÓN
Periodico Visión
Central Calle Post #178
Aptdo. 719
Mayaguez, PR 00681
Feizal Marrero, Pres.
(787) 834-6829 Fax: (787) 833-0722
Circ: 60,000

PERSPECTIVA MUNDIAL
408 Printing & Publishing Corp.
410 West St.
New York, NY 10014
M. Koppel, Edtr.
(212) 243-6392 Fax: (212) 924 6040
Circ: 2,000

PERSPECTIVES IN MEXICAN AMERICAN STUDIES
Mexican American Studies & Research Center, The University of Arizona
Economics Bldg. # 208, P.O. Box 210023
Tucson, AZ 85721-0023
Tom Gelsinon, Publishing Coordinator
(520) 626-8103 Fax: (520) 621-7966
Published every 18 Months

PERÚ PRESENTE
Cámara de Comercio Peruano-Californiana
444 W Ocuan Blvd. #500
Long Beach, CA 90802
Rosario Caparo, Chief Edtr.
(213) 386-7378 Fax: (562) 790-8763
Circ: 2,000

PETRÓLEO INTERNACIONAL
Keller International Publishing Corp.
150 Great Neck Rd.
Great Neck, NY 11021
Victor Prieto, Edtr.
(516) 829-9210 Fax: (516) 829-3591
Published 6 issues/year
Circ: 10,470

PLACES TO GO
Coral Publications
403 Calle del Parque, Piso 11
San Juan, PR 00912-3709
Addie Romero, Edtr.
(787) 729-9060 Fax: (787) 729-9063
Circ: 330,000

PLAZA
Plaza De La Raza
3540 N Mission Rd.
Los Angeles, CA 90031
María Jiménez Torres, Edtr.
(323) 223-2475 Fax: (323) 223-1804
Published every 10 Weeks
Circ: 5,000

POLICY BRIEF
Inter-American Dialogue
1211 Connecticut Ave. NW #510
Washington, DC 20036
Jenni Lukac, Publications Dir.
(202) 822-9002 Fax: (202) 822-9553

POSITIVE APPROACH
South Jersey AIDS Alliance
1301 Atlantic Ave.

Atlantic City, NJ 08401
(609) 348-2437

PREGONES AL DÍA
Teatro Pregones
700 Grand Concourse, 2nd Fl.
Bronx, NY 10451
Jorge B. Merced, Edtr.
(718)585-1202 Fax: (718) 585-1608

PRENSA HISPANA
Prensa Hispana
809 E Washington #209
Phoenix, AZ 85034
Manuel Garcia, Edtr.
(602) 256-2443 Fax: (602) 256-2644
Circ: 65,000

PRESENCIA PANAMEÑA E HISPANA NEWSPAPER
Morgan's Owne. Asociación de Panameños Residentes en NY
9845 57th Ave. #6F
Corona, NY 11368
Lic. Antonio Roberto Morgan, Edtr./Pub.
(718) 592-3002 Fax: (718) 592-3002
Circ: 20,000

THE PRESS
Wave Community Newspapers, Inc.
2621 W 54th St.
Los Angeles, CA 90043
Pluria Marshall, Jr, Pres.
(323) 290-3000 Fax: (323) 291-0219

PRODUCCÍON & DISTRIBUCIÓN
Izarra Publishing Group
13040 SW 120th St.
Miami, FL 33186
Andrea Nieto, Edtr.
(305) 256-6774 Fax: (305) 256-8487
Circ: 7,000

PRODUCTORES DE HORTALIZAS
Meister Publishing
37733 Euclid Ave.
Wiloughby, OH 44094-5992
Jim Moore, Edtr.
(440) 942-2000 Fax: (440) 942-0662
Circ: 10,000

PROGRESO, POBREZA Y EXCLUSIÓN
Inter-American Development Bank
External Relations Office
1300 New York Ave. NW
Washington, DC 20577
IDB Bookstore
(202) 623-1154 Fax: (202) 623-3531

THE PROGRESS
Archdiocese of Seattle
910 Marion St.
Seattle, WA 98104
Stephen Kent, Edtr.
(206) 382-4850 Fax: (206) 382-3487
Circ: 18,000

THE PROGRESS-POST ADVOCATE
Wave Community Newspapers, Inc.
2621 W 54th St.
Los Angeles, CA 90043
Pluria Marshall, Jr, Pres.
(323) 290-3000 Fax: (323) 291-0219

PROJECT EQUALITY—UPDATE
Project Equality
7132 Main St.
Kansas City, MO 64114
Bobbie Donato, Edtr.
(816) 361-9222 Fax: (816) 361-8997
Circ: 1,000

THE PROVIDENCE VISITOR EN ESPAÑOL
The Providence Visitor
184 Broad St.
Providence, RI 02903
Michael Brown, Edtr.
(401) 272-1010 Fax: (401) 421-8418
Circ: 2,000

PROYECTO
Latin Builders Association
782 NW Le Jeune Rd. #450
Miami, FL 33126
Jorge Abril, Edtr.
(305) 446-5989 Fax: (305) 446-0901
Circ: 1,000

PUBLICACIONES DE LAS NACIONES UNIDAS
The United Nations
2 United Nations Pl. #DC2-853
New York, NY 10017
The United Nations, Edtr.
(212) 963-8302 Fax: (212) 963-3489

PUBLICATIONS UPDATE
The World Bank Bookstore
701 18th St. NW
Washington, DC 20433
The World Bank, InfoShop
(800) 645-7247 Fax: (703) 661-1501

THE PUEBLO BUSINESS JOURNAL
Dolan Media
503 N Main St. #339
Pueblo, CO 81003
Laurie Budgar, Edtr.
(719) 542-3616 Fax: (719) 542-4506
Circ: 6,000

PUERTO RICO OFFICIAL INDUSTRIAL DIRECTORY
Direct Marketing & Media Group
P.O. Box 9024182
San Juan, PR 00902-4182
Lilia Molina Ruiz, Pres.
(787) 268-1111 Fax: (787) 268-7044
Circ: 5,000

PULSO
Universidad Internacional de la Florida
Biscayne Blvd. & NE 151 St. Building AC1-162
North Miami, FL 33181
John Virtue, Edtr.
(305) 919-5672 Fax: (305) 919-5498

Q

QUÉ ONDA!
Hispanic News & Entertainment
1415 N Loop W #950
Houston, TX 77008
Julio Esparza/Gabriel Esparza, Edtr.
(713) 880-1133 Fax: (713) 880-2322
Circ: 100,000

QUÉ PASA
Latino Communications, Inc.
1720 Vargrave St.
Winston-Salem, NC 27107
Jose Isasi, Pres.
(336) 784-9004 Fax: (336) 784-8337
Circ: 22,000

QUE PASA! HISPANIC MAGAZINE
Magellan Media Corporation
300 S Orange Ave. #1500
Orlando, FL 32801
Phil Cobo, Pub.
(407) 895-0544 Fax: (407) 895-0543
Circ: 20,000

QUE PASA NEWSLETTER
Utah Hispanic Chamber of Commerce
P.O. Box 1805
Salt Lake City, UT 84110
John Renteria, CEO
(801) 482-1218 Fax: (801) 354-8108
Circ: 100

¿QUÉ TAL?
Latin America Parents Association
P.O. Box 339-340
Brooklyn, NY 11234
Jonathan Woodbridge
(718) 236-8689
Published 3 issues/year
Circ: 2,000

QUE TAL
Scholastic Magazine
P.O. Box 3710
Jefferson City, MO 65102-3710
David Goddy, Edtr.
(800) 724-6527 Fax: (573) 635-8937
Published 6 issues/year

QUIPU
AIDS Project Rhode Island
232 W Exchange St.
Providence, RI 02903-1024
Miguel Rojas, Edtr.
(401) 831-5522 Fax: (401) 454-0299
Circ: 5,000

R

RAZATECA MAGAZINE
RazaTeca Publications
P.O. Box 611870
San Jose, CA 95161-1870
Circ: 10,000

REFORMA NEWSLETTER
*Natl. Assoc. to Promote Library &
Information Services to Latinos and The
Spanish Speaking*
P.O. Box 832
Anaheim, CA 92815-0832
Denice Adkins, Edtr.
(716) 645-2412 Fax: (716) 645-3775
Circ: 1,000

REPLICA
Replica Publishing
3017 NW 7th St.
Miami, FL 33125
Max Lesnik, Edtr.
(305) 643-5481 Fax: (305) 541-7410
Circ: 80,000

**REPORTERO INDUSTRIAL
MEXICANO**
Keller International Publishing Corp.
150 Great Neck Rd.
Great Neck, NY 11021
Brian de Lucca, Edtr.
(516) 829-9210 Fax: (516) 829-3591
Published 9 issues/year
Circ: 36,000

RESEÑA DE TRATAMIENTO
AIDS Treatment Data Network
611 Broadway #613
New York, NY 10012
Ken Fornataro/Richard Geffreys, Edtrs.
(212) 260-8868 Fax: (212) 260-8869

**RESIDENTIAL SEGREGATION BY
SOCIOECONOMIC CLASS IN
METROPOLITAN MIAMI**
Cuban American National Council, Inc.
1223 SW 4th St.
Miami, FL 33135
Guarioné M. Díaz, Pres.
(305) 642-3484 Fax: (305) 642-9815

RESUMEN NEWSPAPER
69-08 Roosevelt Ave.
Woodside, NY 11377-2934
Fernando F. Rojas, Edtr./Pub.
(718) 899-8603 Fax: (718) 899-7616
Circ: 25,000

**REVIEW: LATIN AMERICAN
LITERATURE & ARTS**
Americas Society, Inc.
680 Park Ave.
New York, NY 10021
Daniel Shapiro, Managing Edtr.
(212) 249-8950 Fax: (212) 249-5868
Published 2 issues/year
Circ: 5,000

**REVISIÓN DE LAS
DECLARACIONES DE IMPUESTOS,
DERECHO DE APELACIÓN Y
RECLAMACIONES DE
REEMBOLSOS, PUB. 556 SP**
US Internal Revenue Service (IRS)
P. O. Box 85074
Distribution Center
Richmond, VA 23261-5074
(800) 829-1040

**REVISTA AEREA
LATINOAMERICANA**
Strato Publishing Co.
310 E 44th St. #1601
New York, NY 10017
Elaine Asch, Edtr.
(212) 370-1740 Fax: (212) 949-6756
Published 8 issues/year
Circ: 13,000

REVISTA ANUAL DEL DIRECTOR
Pan American Health Organization (PAHO)
Programa de Publicaciones
525 23rd St. NW
Washington, DC 20037
Judith Navarro, Edtr.-in-Chief
(202) 974-3000 Fax: (202) 974-3663
Circ: 3,500

REVISTA IBEROAMERICANA
*Instituto Nacional de Literatura
Iberoamericana*
1312 Cathedral of Learning
University of Pittsburgh
Pittsburgh, PA 15260
Erika Braga, Adm.
(412) 624-5246 Fax: (412) 624-0829
Circ: 2,500

**REVISTA INTERNACIONAL DEL
TRABAJO**
International Labor Office
1828 L St., NW #600
Washington, DC 20036
Marjorie Crow, Marketing Assistant
(202) 653-7652 Fax: (202) 653-7687

REVISTA LUMBRE
Ediciones Dhearez, Inc.
P.O. Box 1495
Aguadilla, PR 00605
Dhennis Antonio Pérez, Edtr.
(787) 882-2457
Published 8 issues/year
Circ: 2,000

REVISTA MARYKNOLL
Maryknoll Fathers
P.O. Box 308
Maryknoll, NY 10545
Linda Unger, Edtr.
(914) 941-7590 Fax: (914) 946-0670
Published 11 issues/year
Circ: 80,000

**REVISTA PANAMERICANA DE LA
SALUD**
Pan American Health Organization (PAHO)
Programa de Publicaciones
525 23rd St. NW
Washington, DC 20037
Maria Luisa Clark, Edtr.-in-Chief
(202) 974-3000 Fax: (202) 974-3663
Circ: 11,000

REVOLUTIONARY WORKER
R.C.P. Publications
P.O. Box 3486 Merchandise Mart
Chicago, IL 60654
R.C.P. Publications, Edtr./Pub.
(773) 227-4066 Fax: (773) 227-4497

RUMORES
517 N Bristol St.
Santa Ana, CA 92703
Abel S. Torres, Edtr./ Pub.
(714) 547-8283 Fax: (714) 547-3674
Circ: 30,000

S

SACNAS NEWS
*Society for Advancement of Chicanos and
Native Americans in Service*
P.O. Box 8526
Santa Cruz, CA 95061-8526
Ronaldo Ramirez, Exec. Dir
(831) 459-0170 Fax: (831) 459-0194
Circ: 6,000

**SALALM DIRECTORY OF VENDORS
OF LATIN AMERICAN LIBRARY
MATERIALS**
*Seminar on the Acquisition of Latin
American Library Materials (SALALM)*
Widener 191, Harvard University
Cambridge, MA 02138
Nancy L. Hallock, Edtr.
(608) 262-3240
Published 6 issues/year
Circ: 500

SALUD COMUNAL
Asoc. de Salud Primaria de PR, Inc.
Edificio La Euskalduna,
Calle Navarro 56 Esq. Peñuelas
Hato Rey, PR 00918
Licenciada Sandra García, Dire. Ejecutiva
(787) 758-3411 Fax: (787) 758-1736
Circ: 700

**SALUDOS: A PUBLICATION FOR
HISPANIC-AMERICANS**
7210 Jordan Ave. PMB #D5
Canoga, CA 91303
Martin B. Cohen, Pub.
(818) 258-0041

SALUDOS HISPANOS
United Council of Spanish Speaking People
73-121 Fred Waring Dr. #100
Palm Desert, CA 92260
Rosemarie Garcia-Solomon, Pub.
(800) 371-4456 Fax: (760) 776-1214

THE SAN JUAN STAR
The San Juan Star
P.O. Box 364187
San Juan, PR 00936-4187
John Marino, Edtr.
(787) 782-4200 Fax: (787) 782-0310
Circ: 104,000

SANTA ROSA NEWS
Santa Rosa News
108 5th St., Drawer 505
Santa Rosa, NM 88435
Darrel Freeman, Pub.
(505) 472-5454 Fax: (505) 472-5453
Circ: 2,200

SE HABLA ESPAÑOL (SHE)
Hispanic Business Inc.
425 Pine Ave.
Santa Barbara, CA 93117
Tim Dougherty, Edtr.
(805) 964-4554 Fax: (805) 964-6139
Circ: 4,000

SED NEWS
Spanish Education Development Center
1840 Kalorama Rd. NW
Washington, DC 20009
José González, Edtr.
(202) 462-8848 Fax: (202) 462-6886
Circ: 1,000

**SELECCIONES DE READER'S
DIGEST**
Reader's Digest
Reader's Digest Road
Pleasantville, NY 10570
Audon Coria, Edtr.
(914) 238-1000 Fax: (914) 238-4559
Circ: 205,000

SELECTA MAGAZINE
Selecta Magazine, Inc.
1717 N. Bayshore Dr. #113
Miami, FL 33132
Michael Bulnes, Vice Pres.

(305) 579-0979 Fax: (305) 372-1811
Circ: 25,000

SEMANA NEWSPAPER
Spanish Publications, Inc.
6601 Tarnef St. #200
Houston, TX 77074
Raul Dueñas, Edtr.
(713) 774-4719 Fax: (713) 774-4666
Circ: 115,000

SENSACIONAL
275 Fountain Blue Blvd. #168
Miami, FL 33172
Martha Ramos, Edtr.
(305) 220-5023 Fax: (305) 220-5154
Circ: 30,000

SER NETWORK DIRECTORY
Ser-Jobs for Progress
100 Decker Dr. #200
Irving, TX 75062
Allison Parker, Edtr.
(972) 541-0616 Fax: (972) 650-0842

SIETE DIAS LATINO NEWSPAPER
Siete Dias, Inc.
12005 NE 12th St. #26
Bellevue, WA 98005
Raúl Pérez-Calleja, Owner
(425) 646-8846 Fax: (425) 646-8823
Circ: 7,000

SMALL BUSINESS JOURNAL
SBJ Publishing Co.
P.O. Box 16783
Seattle, WA 98116
Ramón Rodríguez, Edtr.
(206) 297-8532 Fax: (206) 706-3082
Circ: 7,000

SOCCER AMERICA
Soccer America Magazine
1235 10th St.
Berkeley, CA 94710
John Hooper, Marketing Edtr.
(510) 559-2218 Fax: (510) 528-5177
Circ: 40,000

SOLOAUTOS
Spanish Publications, Inc.
6601 Tarnef St. #200
Houston, TX 77074
Raul Dueñas, Edtr.
(713) 774-4719 Fax: (713) 774-4666
Circ: 36,000

**THE SOMOS AZTLAN
ENCYCLOPEDIA OF HISPANIC
AMERICANS**
Somos Aztlan Publications
6700 E 61st Pl.
Commerce City, CO 80022
Gary Archuleta, Pub.
(303) 288-3880

SOUTH TEXAS CATHOLIC
Diocese of Corpus Christi
620 Lipan St.
Corpus Christi, TX 78401361
Paula Estitia, Edtr.
(361) 882-6191 Fax: (361) 883-2556
Circ: 13,000

**SOUTHERN NEVADA HISPANIC
YELLOW PAGES**
Southern Nevada Hispanic Yellow Pages
1051 Northeastern
Las Vegas, NV 89101
Eddie Escobedo, Jr., Pub.
(702) 639-9080 Fax: (702) 639-9400
Published 2 issues/year
Circ: 25,000

SOUTHWEST TOPICS
Wave Community Newspapers, Inc.
2621 W 54th St.
Los Angeles, CA 90043
Pluria Marshall, Jr., Pres.
(323) 290-3000 Fax: (323) 291-0219

SOUTWEST WAVE
Wave Community Newspapers, Inc.
2621 W 54th St.
Los Angeles, CA 90043
Pluria Marshall, Jr, Pres.
(323) 290-3000 Fax: (323) 291-0219

THE SPANISH INSTITUTE ANNUAL REPORT
The Spanish Institute
684 Park Ave.
New York, NY 10021
(212) 628-0423 Fax: (212) 734-4177

SPANISH JOURNAL
Spanish Journal
152 W Wisconsin Ave. #613
Milwaukee, WI 53203
Robert Miranda, Edtr.
(414) 271-5683 Fax: (414) 271-5994
Circ: 20,000

THE SPECTRUM
Kansas Commission on Civil Rights
900 SW Jackson #851-S., Landon Off. Bldg.
Topeka, KS 66612
Mike Hollar, Asst. Dir.
(785) 296-3206 Fax: (785) 296-0589
Circ: 1,000

SUGAR Y AZUCAR
Ruspam Communications, Inc.
452 Hudson Terrace
Englewood Cliffs, NJ 07632
Richard B. Miller, Edtr.
(201) 871-9200 Fax: (201) 871-9639
Circ: 4,450

SUICIDE IN MIAMI AND CUBA
Cuban American National Council, Inc.
1223 SW 4th St.
Miami, FL 33135
Guarioné M. Díaz, Pres.
(305) 642-3484 Fax: (305) 642-9815

SUPER ONDA
Hispanic Business, Inc.
425 Pine Ave.
Santa Barbara, CA 93117
Vaughn Hagerty, Managing Edtr.
(805) 964-4554 Fax: (805) 964-6139
Circ: 110,000

SUPPORTING LATINO FAMILIES: LESSONS FROM EXEMPLARY PROGRAMS
Harvard Family Research Project
38 Concord Ave.
Cambridge, MA 02138-2357
Kathleen Crowley
(617) 495-9108 Fax: (617) 495-8594

SUS PÁGINAS AMARILLAS
Spanish Publishing
17-A Sparhowk St.
Brighton, MA 02135
Pedro Romero, Edtr.
(800) 572-1761 Fax: (617) 783-0806
Circ: 80,000

T.Q.S. NEWS
T.Q.S. Publications
P.O. Box 9275
Berkeley, CA 94709
Octavio Romano, Edtr.
(510) 655-8036 Fax: (510) 601-6938
Circ: 500

THE TABLET
The Tablet Publishing Company
653 Hicks St.
Brooklyn, NY 11231
Ed Wilkinson, Edtr.
(718) 858-3838 Fax: (717) 802-0021
Circ: 80,000

TACDC UPDATE
Texas Association of Community Development Corporations
700 Lavaca #120
Austin, TX 78701
Reymundo Ocañas, Exec. Dir.
(512) 457-8232 Fax: (512) 479-4090

TAHUANTINSUYO
18552 Clark St. #18
Tarzana, CA 91356
Mario Milton Mino, Edtr.
(818) 881-8722
Circ: 250,350

TALENT ROSTER OF OUTSTAND- ING MINORITY COMMUNITY COLLEGE GRADUATES
College Entrance Examination Board
45 Columbus Ave.
New York, NY 10023
(212) 713-8000

TAMACC TIMES
Texas Association of Mexican American Chambers of Commerce
823 Congress Ave. #1414
Austin, TX 78701
Erica I. Peña, Edtr.-in-Chief
(512) 708-8823 Fax: (512) 708-1808
Circ: 11,500

TANGO REPORTER
Tango Reporter
8033 Sunset Blvd. #704
Los Angeles, CA 90046
Carlos G. Groppa, Edtr.
(323) 654-6268
Circ: 10,000

THE TAOS NEWS/EL CREPÚSCULO
The Taos News
P.O. Box U
226 Albright St.
Taos, NM 87571
Inez Russell, Edtr.
(505) 758-5541 Fax: (505) 751-3026
Circ: 10,730

TEJANO JOURNAL
TexasTalent Musicians Association
1149 E Commerce #105
San Antonio, TX 78205
Robert Areano, Pres.
(210) 222-8862 Fax: (210) 222-1029
Circ: 5,000

TEJANO NOTES
TexasTalent Musicians Association
1149 E Commerce #105
San Antonio, TX 78205
Robert Areano, Pres.
(210) 222-8862 Fax: (210) 222-1029
Circ: 300

TELE GUÍA DE CHICAGO
Teleguía Publications, Inc.
3116 S Austin Blvd.
Cicero, IL 60804
Ezequiel "Zeke" Montes, Pub.
(708) 656-6666 Fax: (708) 656-6679
Circ: 26,000

TELE GUÍA DE COLORADO
Rojo Productions Inc.
6369 S. Windermere St.
Denver, CO 80211
Evelin Rojo, Mgr.
(303) 703-9584 Fax: (303) 433-5086
Circ: 10,000

TELE REVISTA
P.O. Box 145179
Coral Gables, FL 33134
Ana Pereiro, Edtr.
(305) 445-1755 Fax: (305) 445-3907
Circ: 75,000

TELEGUÍA
Lancer Productions, Inc.
1241 S Soto St. #213
Los Angeles, CA 90023
Víctor Benitez, Edtr.

(323) 881-6515 Fax: (323) 881-6524
Circ: 100,000

TELEGUIA USA
Lancer Productions
1241 S Soto St. #213
Los Angeles, CA 90023
Victor Benitez, Edtr.
(323) 881-6515 Fax: (323) 881-6524
Circ: 100,000

TEMAS
Temas Magazine, Inc.
300 W 55th St. #14-P
New York, NY 10019-5172
Lolita de la Vega, Edtr./Pub.
(212) 582-4750 Fax: (212) 541-7910
Circ: 114,000

TEXAS CATHOLIC
Diocese of Dallas
P.O. Box 190347
Dallas, TX 75219
Bronson Havard, Edtr.
(214) 528-8792 Fax: (214) 528-3411
Circ: 52,000

TEXAS COMMUNITY DEVELOPER
Texas Association of Community Development Corporations
700 Lavaca #120
Austin, TX 78701
Reymundo Ocañas, Exec. Dir.
(512) 457-8232 Fax: (512) 479-4090

TEXTILES PANAMERICANOS
Billian Publishing
2100 Powers Ferry Rd. #300
Atlanta, GA 30339
German Garcia, Edtr.
(770) 955-5656 Fax: (770) 952-0669
Circ: 17,000

TIEMPO
Record Journal
11 Crown St.
Meriden, CT 06450
Daniel Román, Prod. Supervisor
(203) 317-2335 Fax: (203) 235-4048
Circ: 20,000

TIEMPO LIBRE
Tiempo Libre
1111 W Bomanza Rd.
Las Vegas, NV 89125
Carlo Maffatt, Pub.
(702) 477-3845 Fax: (702) 251-0736

TIEMPOS DEL MUNDO
Tiempos del Mundo
3842 9th St.
Long Island City, NY 11101
David Ramirez, Edtr.
(718) 786-4343 Fax: (718) 786-7070
Circ: 30,000

TIEMPOS DEL MUNDO
Tiempos, USA Corp.
3600 New York Ave. NE
Washington, DC 20002
Jose Emilio Castellanos, Edtr.
(202) 636-8926 Fax: (202) 269-3206
Circ: 10,000

TIEMPOS LATINOS
Specialty Media Services ,Inc.
P.O. Box 1843
Tifton, GA 31793
Chuck Faaborg, Edtr.
(229) 388-8182 Fax: (229) 388-8189
Circ: 5,000

TODAY'S CATHOLIC
Achdiocesean Publishing Society, Inc.
2718 W Woodlawn Ave.
San Antonio, TX 78228
Martha Brinkmann, Edtr.
(210) 734-2620 Fax: (210) 734-2939
Circ: 26,500

TODAYS GROCER IN ESPAÑOL
Florida Grocer Publishing Co.
P.O. Box 430760

S Miami, FL 33243
Dennis M. Kane, Edtr.
(305) 441-1138 Fax: (305) 661-6720
Circ: 19,000

TORRE DE PAPEL
University of Iowa
111 Phillip Hall
Iowa City, IA 52242
Eduardo Guizar, Edtr.
(312) 886-3508 Fax: (319) 335-2990
Circ: 150

TOURISTS' ALTERNATIVES
Tourists' Alternatives
P.O. Box 11526
San Juan, PR 00922-1526
Maira Landa, Pres.
(787) 273-0478 Fax: (787) 273-1664
Circ: 250,000

TRASTORNO DE PÁNICO
National Institute of Mental Health (NIMH)/ Public Inquiries #15-C/05
6001 Executive Blvd. #8184MSC9663
Bethesda, MD 20892-9663
Information Resources
(301) 443-4513 Fax: (301) 443-4279

TREATMENT REVIEW
AIDS Treatment Data Network
611 Broadway #613
New York, NY 10012
Ken Fornataro/Richard Geffreys, Edtrs.
(212) 260-8868 Fax: (212) 260-8869

THE TRIBUNE
777 United Nations Plaza, 3rd Floor
New York, NY 10017
Anne S. Walker, Dir.
(212) 687-8633 Fax: (212) 661-2704
Circ: 12,000

TRIBUNE
Wave Community Newspapers, Inc.
2621 W 54th St.
Los Angeles, CA 90043
Pluria Marshall, Jr, Pres.
(323) 290-3000 Fax: (323) 291-0219

TRY US: NATIONAL MINORITY BUSINESS DIRECTORY
Diversity Information Resources, Inc.
2105 Central Ave., NE
Minneapolis, MN 55418
Leslie Bonds, Exec. Dir.
(612) 781-6819 Fax: (612) 781-0109
Circ: 6,000

TU
Editorial Televisa
6355 NW 36th St.
Miami, FL 33166
Nahir Acosta, Edtr.
(305) 871-6400 Ext. 283 Fax: (305) 871-1520
Circ: 18,932

TV Y NOVELAS
Editorial Televisa
6355 NW 36th St.
Miami, FL 33166
Dora Luz Vargas, Edtr.
(305) 871-6400 Fax: (305) 871-1520
Circ: 144994

U.N. CHRONICLE
The United Nations
2 United Nations Pl. #DC2-853
New York, NY 10017
(212) 963-8302 Fax: (212) 963-3489

UNIÓN HISPANA NEWSPAPER
Unión Hispana
825 N Broadway
Santa Ana, CA 92701
Juan G. García, Edtr.
(714) 541-6007 Fax: (714) 541-1603
Circ: 35,000

UNITED PUERTO RICAN NEWSLETTER
Puertorriqueños Unidos de Chicago, Inc.
2935 W 71st St.
Chicago, IL 60629
José Rivera/Elba Droz, Edtrs.
(773) 436-1159 Fax: (773) 436-6337

UPWORDS! NEWSLETTER
Houston Hispanic Chamber of Commerce
2900 Woodridge Dr. #312
Houston, TX 77087
Richard R Torres, Pres.
(713) 644-7070 Fax: (713) 644-7377

THE URBAN LATINO
3288 21st. St. #9
San Francisco, CA 94110
Gail Neira, Edtr./Pub.
(415) 821-4452 Fax: (415) 821-4452
Circ: 20,000

USAID DEVELOPMENT
U.S. Agency for International Development
M-01 1300 Pennsylvania Ave. NW
Washington, DC 20523
Betty Snead, Edtr.
(202) 712-4810 Fax: (202) 216-3524
Circ: 1,000

UTAH CATÓLICO
The Diocese of Salt Lake City
P.O. Box 2489
Salt Lake City, UT 84110
Bishop George Niederauer, Pub.
(801) 328-8641 Fax: (801) 537-1667
Circ: 13,800

UTOPÍAS
Cloudforest Initiatives
P.O. Box 40207
St. Paul, MN 55104
Teresa Ortiz, Dir.
(651) 592-4143
Circ: 2,000

V

VALOR: "EL REGALO DE LA VIDA"
Susannah Maria Gurule Foundation
2309 SW 1st Ave. #141
Portland, OR 97201
Clara Padilla Andrews, Dir.
(503) 228-0778 Fax: (503) 228-3384
Circ: 6,000

VANIDADES
Editorial Televisa
6355 NW 36th St.
Miami, FL 33166
Sarah B. Castany, Edtr.
(305) 871-6400 Fax: (305) 871-1520
Circ: 89,108

VEA NEW YORK
475 5th Ave., Penthouse
New York, NY 10017
Nuria Clark, Edtr./Pub.
(212) 545-7192 Fax: (212) 545-7305
Circ: 110,000

VEGA HISPANIC YELLOW PAGES
Vega & Associates
3040 Williams Dr., #404
Fairfax, VA 22301
Francisco Vega, Jr., Pres. & CEO
(703) 908-9600 Fax: (703) 908-9400
Circ: 160,000

20 DE MAYO SPANISH
20 de Mayo
1824 Sunset Blvd. #202
Los Angeles, CA 90026
Abel Pérez, Edtr./Pub.
(213) 483-8511 Fax: (213) 483-6474
Circ: 25,000

VENEZUELA NEWSLETTER
Venezuelan American Association, Inc.
30 Vesey St. #506
New York, NY 10007
Peter S. Smith, Edtr.

(212) 233-7776 Fax: (212) 233-7779
Circ: 500

VENEZUELA UP-TO-DATE
Embassy of Venezuela-Press Office
1099 30th St. NW
Washington, DC 20007
José Emilio Castellanos, Edtr.
(202) 342-2214 Fax: (212) 342-6820

VIAJERO VIP
7100 Vizcayne Blvd. #301
Miami, FL 33138
Ricardo Ceballos, Edtr.
(305) 758-9700
Circ: 10,100

VIDA
130 Palm Dr.
Oxnard, CA 93030
Carlos Olea/ Manuel M. Muñoz, Edtrs.
(805) 983-3401
Circ: 35,000

VIDA EN EL VALLE
The Fresno Bee
3425 N 1st St. #201
Fresno, CA 93726
John Esparza, Pub.
(559) 225-7753 Fax: (559) 225-4957
Circ: 37,000

VIDA MAGAZINE
Orbat Associates
3817-H, S George Mason Dr.
Falls Church, VA 22041
Carlos Orbezo, Edtr.
(703) 578-9884 Fax: (703) 578-9888
Circ: 10,000

VIDA NUEVA
3424 Wilshire Blvd., 6th Floor
Los Angeles, CA 90010
Víctor Alemán, Edtr.
(213) 637-7360 Fax: (213) 637-6360
Circ: 65,000

VIH/SIDA: BOLETÍN ESTADÍSTICO
Instituto del Sida de San Juan
P.O. Box 13964
Santurce, PR 00908
Mariselle Centeno, Edtr.
(787) 723-2424 x248 Fax: (787) 724-5104
Circ: 1,000

VISION
Roswell Hispano Chamber of Commerce
1426 N Maine
Roswell, NM 88201
Gailanne Teresa, Edtr.
(505) 624-0889 Fax: (505) 623-4096
Circ: 100

VISION
Mexican-American Cultural Center (MACC)
3115 West Ashby Pl.
San Antonio, TX 78228
María Elena Gonzalez, Pres.
(210) 732-2156   Fax: (210) 732-9072
Published 2 issues/year
Circ: 15,000

VISIONES
ALAS
1398 Valencia St.
San Francisco, CA 94110
Mercedes Sansores, Dir.
(415) 826-5090 Fax: (415) 826-1885

VISIONES
Corpus Christi Hispanic Chamber of Commerce
P.O. Box 5523
Corpus Christi, TX 78465
Manuel Ugues, Pres.
(361) 887-7408 Fax: (361) 888-9473

VISTA MAGAZINE
Hispanic Publishing
999 Ponce de León Blvd. #600
Coral Gables, FL 33134
Julia Bencomo Lobaco, Edtr.
(305) 442-2462 Fax: (305) 443-7650
Circ: 1,100,000

VISTAL DE VALLE
Bahia del Sol
1209 S 1st Ave.
Phoenix, AZ 85003
Carlos Galindo, Communications Coord.
(602) 258-6797 Fax: (620) 252-4964
Circ: 3,000

VIVA!
Albuquerque Hispanic Chamber of Commerce
202 Central Ave. SE #300
Albuquerque, NM 87102
Maria Elena Alvarez, Edtr.
(505) 842-9003 Fax: (505) 764-9664
Circ: 5,000

VIVA NEW YORK
King Paniagua, L.L.C.
518 5th Ave., 5th Fl.
New York, NY 10036
Neil Perlich Poter, Managing Edtr.
(212) 869-7007 Fax: (212) 869-7009
Circ: 465,000

VOCERO HISPANO NEWSPAPER
Vocero Hispano Newspaper, Inc.
17A West St.
Worcester, MA 01609-2306
Sergio Rivera, Jr., Edtr./Pres.
(508) 792-1942 Fax: (508) 792-1608
Circ: 12,500

VOCES UNIDAS
Southwest Community Resources
211 10th St., SW
Albuquerque, NM 87102
Matthew Lightfoot, Office Manager
(505) 247-8832 Fax: (505) 247-9972
Circ: 10,000

THE VOICE OF HISPANIC HIGHER EDUCATION
The Hispanic Association of Colleges & Universities (HACU)
8415 Datapoint Dr. #400
San Antonio, TX 78229
Deyanira R. Rossell, Exec. Dir. of Public Affairs
(210) 692-3805 Fax: (210) 692-0823
Circ: 5,500

THE VOICE OF LA PUENTE
La Puente Home Shelter
913 State Ave.
Alamosa, CO 81101
Lance Cheslock, Dir.
(719) 589-5909 Fax: (719) 587-0710
Circ: 3,000

W

WASHINGTON HISPANIC
1752 Columbia Rd. NW, 4th Fl.
Washington, DC 20009
Nelly Carrion, Edtr.
(202) 667-8881 Fax: (202) 667-8902
Circ: 25,000

WATCH ON WASHINGTON
Latin American Management Association
419 New Jersey Ave. SE
Washington, DC 20003
Massey Vllarreal, Pres.
(202) 546-3803 Fax: (202) 546-3807
Circ: 2,500

WEST NEBRASKA REGISTER
Hispanic Ministry Office- Diocese of Grand Island
214 W 5th St.
P.O. Box 651
North Plate, NE 69101
Mario Javier Delgado, Dir., Hispanic Ministry Office, Justice & Peace
(308) 532-2707 Fax: (308) 532-3574

WEST TEXAS HISPANIC NEWS
P.O. Box 24
Lubbock, TX 79408
Ernest Barton, Pub.
(806) 747-3467 Fax: (806) 747-3524
Circ: 4,000

WESTSIDE DRUG FREE YOUTH TEEN
Greater Auraria Neighbours Affiliated for Service (GANAS)
1212 Mariposa St.
Denver, CO 80204
Patrick J. Vigil, Exec. Dir.
(303) 893-5114 Fax: (303) 573-8023
Circ: 300

WHITE WING MESSENGER
White Wing Publishing House
P.O. Box 3000, Bible Place
Cleveland, TN 37320
Diana Garcia, Circ. Manager
(423) 559-5430 Fax: (423) 559-5444
Circ: 8,000

THE WHITTIER INDEPENDENT
Wave Community Newspapers, Inc.
2621 W 54th St.
Los Angeles, CA 90043
Pluria Marshall, Jr, Pres.
(323) 290-3000 Fax: (323) 291-0219

WINDOWS ON SOUTH AMERICA
South America Mission
5217 South Military Trail
Lake Worth, FL 33463-6099
Jeff Orcutt, Edtr.
(561) 965-1833 Fax: (561) 439-8950
Circ: 7,000

WORLD DEVELOPMENT INDICATORS
The World Bank Bookstore (Infoshop)
701 18th St. NW
Washington, DC 20433
The World Bank, InfoShop
(800) 645-7247 Fax: (703) 661-1501

WORLD DEVELOPMENT REPORT
The World Bank Bookstore
701 18th St. NW
Washington, DC 20433
The World Bank, InfoShop
(800) 645-7247 Fax: (703) 661-1501
Circ: 50,000

WYVERNWOOD CHRONICLE
Eastern Group Publications, Inc.
2500 S Atlantic Blvd., Bldg. A
Los Angeles, CA 90040
Dolores Sanchez, Edtr.
(323) 263-5743 Fax: (323) 263-9169
Circ: 2,700

Y

YSAC NEWSLETTER
York Spanish American Center
200 E Princess St.
York, PA 17403
Alex Ramos, Dir.
(717) 846-9434 Fax: (717) 843-5722
Circ: 100

Z

ZETA
Choice Editores
659 3rd Ave. #E
Chula Vista, CA 91910
Jesus Blanco Orlena, Co-Dir.
(619) 425-4848 Fax: (619) 426-4370
Circ: 60,000

ZIVA'S SPANISH DANCE ENSEMBLE'S NEWSLETTER
Ziva's Spanish Dance Ensemble
2505 Oakenshield Dr.
Potomac, MD 20854
Víctor Cohen, Business Manager
(301) 424-1355 Fax: (301) 251-4125
Published 2 issues/year
Circ: 500

ZOPILOTE MAGAZINE
El Quinto Sol
824 S. Mill Ave. #219
Tempe, AZ 85281
Marco A. Albarran, Pub.
(480)557-7195 Fax: (480)838-7264
Circ: 5,000

AnuarioHispano**.com**

Hispanic Organizations (by State)
Organizaciones hispanas (por Estado)

ALABAMA

ARCHDIOCESE OF MOBILE
Hispanic Pastoral Ministry
712 Dauphin Island Pkwy.
Mobile, AL 36606
(334) 478-3737 Fax: (334) 478-9990
Rev. Christopher J. Viscardi, SJ
Email: hispanic.ministry@zebra.net

DIOCESE OF BIRMINGHAM
Hispanic Affairs
P.O. Box 12047
Birmingham, AL 35202-2047
(205) 838-8308 Fax: (205) 836-1910
Brenda Bullock, Director for Hispanic Ministry
Email: bbullock@bhmdiocese.org

SOCIEDAD HONORARIA HISPANICA
Alabama Chapter/Alfred B. Thomas Chapter
Carroll High School, 101 Forest Ave.
Ozark, AL 36360
(334) 774-4915 Fax: (334) 774-1865
Christine Adams, Director

**SOUTH REGIONS MINORITY BUSINESS
COUNCIL, INC.**
NMSDC
3100 Cottage Hill, Suite 218
Mobile, AL 36608
(334) 471-6380 Fax: (334) 471-6385
Darlene M. Moore, Executive Director

ALASKA

ARCHDIOCESE OF ANCHORAGE
Hispanic Affairs
3900 Wisconsin St.
Anchorage, AK 99517
(907) 248-2000 Fax: (907) 245-1600
Sr. Mary Veronica Rivas, MCPD, Director for
Hispanic Ministry
Email: olq@alaskalife.org

DIOCESE OF FAIRBANKS
Hispanic Affairs
2890 N. Kobuk
Fairbanks, AK 99709
(907) 474-0753 Fax: (907) 474-8009
Rev.Normand Pepin, Hispanic Ministry
Coordinator

DIOCESE OF JUNEAU
Hispanic Ministry Office
419 6th St.
Juneau, AK 99801
(907) 586-2227 Fax: (907) 463-3237
Rev. Juan Gómez

**LEAGUE OF UNITED LATIN AMERICAN
CITIZENS (LULAC)**
Southwest Region-AK
125 Oakridge Cove
Maumelle, AK 72113
(501) 371-6809 or (501) 851-1876

Fax: (501) 371-4498
Robert Treviño, State Dir.
Email: rtrevino@littlerock.state.ar.us
orrptmpa@swbell.net

ARIZONA

**AMERICAN ASSOCIATION OF HISPANIC
CERTIFIED PUBLIC ACCOUNTANTS
(CPAS)**
Phoenix Chapter/ Price Waterhouse LLP
1850 N. Central Ave., #700
Phoenix, AZ 85004-4563
(602) 379-5500 Fax: (602) 379-5639
Ahna Marin, Chapter Representative
Email: ahna_marin@notes.pw.com
Web: www.aahcpa.org

AMERICAN BEGINNINGS
2215 S. 8th Ave.
Yuma, AZ 85366-4596
(520) 783-5794 Fax: (520) 783-2410
John Goldstein, Exec. Dir.
Email: www.American Beginnings.org

**ARIZONA HISPANIC CHAMBER OF
COMMERCE FOUNDATION (AHCC)**
Affiliate of NCLR
255 E. Osborn, #201
Phoenix, AZ 85012
(602) 279-1800 Fax: (602) 279-8900
Sergio Carlos, President
Email: ahcc@uswest.net
Web: www.azhispanic.chamber.org

**ARIZONA LATIN AMERICAN MEDICAL
ASSOCIATION**
909 N. 1st St.
Phoenix, AZ 85004
(602) 252-7139 Fax: (602) 495-9133
Adolfo Echeveste, Executive Director
Email: almaone@bigplanet.com

BORDER TRADE ALLIANCE
Two N. Central Ave, #2510
Phoenix, AZ 85004
(602) 262-8604 Fax: (602) 254-4088
Maria Luisa O'Connell, Executive Director
Email: mlo.bta@gpec.org
Web: www.thebta.org

CASA DE VIDA, INC.
1900 W. Speedway Blvd.
Tucson, AZ 85745-2215
(520) 792-0591
Joseph Parker, Supervisor

**CATHOLIC SOCIAL SERVICES OF
PHOENIX**
1825 W. Northern Ave.
Phoenix, AZ 85021
(602) 997-6105 Fax: (602) 870-3891
Maureen Webster, Executive Director

CENTER FOR LATIN AMERICAN STUDIES
Arizona State University
P.O. Box 872401
Tempe, AZ 85287-2401
(480) 965-5127 Fax: (480) 965-6679
Dr. Tod Swanson, Director
Email: santaann.young@asu.edu

CENTRO ADELANTE CAMPESINO
P.O. Box 1338
Surprise, AZ 85374
(602) 583-9830 Fax: (602) 583-3422
Lisa Miranda Lintz, Executive Director
Email: centro_campesino@yahoo.com

CENTRO CULTURAL MEXICANO
Phoenix Office
17 South 2nd Avenue, 4th floor
Phoenix, AZ 85003
(602) 271-4858 Fax: (602) 271-4883
Magda T. Rojas, Executive Director

CENTRO DE AMISTAD, INC.
Affiliate of NCLR
8202 S. Avenida del Yaqui
Guadalupe, AZ 85283
(480) 839-2926 Fax: (480) 839-9985
Santino Bernasconi, President & CEO
Email: sbcda-ceo@getnet.com

CHICANO RESEARCH COLLECTION
Arizona State University
P.O. Box 871006
Tempe, AZ 85287-1006
(480) 965-3145 Fax: (480) 965-9169
Christine Marin, Archivist

CHICANOS POR LA CAUSA, INC.
Arizona Migrant Head Start Program
1242 E. Washington St., #102
Phoenix, AZ 85034
(602) 265-7711 Fax: (602) 252-9534
Pete C. Garcia, Executive Director

National Headquarters / Affiliate of NCLR
1112 East Buckeye Rd.
Phoenix, AZ 85034
(602) 257-0700 Fax: (602) 256-2740
Pete C. García, President & CEO

**THE CHURCH OF JESUS CHRIST OF
LATTER DAY SAINTS**
Mesa Arizona Temple Visitors' Center
525 E. Main St.
Mesa, AZ 85204
(480) 964-7164 Fax: (480)964-7789
Elder Killpack, Director
Web: www.lds.org

**CLASS - CHICANO/LATINO LAW
STUDENT ASSOCIATION**
Arizona State University
College of Liberal Arts & Sciences
P.O. Box 871701
Tempe, AZ 85287-1701
(602) 965-6506 Fax: (602) 965-2110
Ed Delci, Advisor

DIOCESE OF PHOENIX
Hispanic Affairs
400 E. Monroe St.
Phoenix, AZ 85004-2376
(602) 257-0030 Fax: (602) 258-3425
Rev. Timothy Conlon, OSC, Vicar for Hispanic
Ministry

DIOCESE OF TUCSON
Regina Cleri Center
8800 E. 22nd St.
Tucson, AZ 85710-7399
(520) 886-5202 Fax: (520) 886-6481
Rubén Davalos

**EL CONCILIO - CHICANO/HISPANO
STUDENT COALITION**
Arizona State University
College of Liberal Arts & Sciences
P.O. Box 871701
Tempe, AZ 85287-1701
(480) 965-6506 Fax: (480) 965-2110
Ed Delci, Advisor

EL QUINTO SOL
824 S. Mill Ave. #219
Tempe, AZ 85281
(480) 557-7195 Fax: (480) 838-7264
Marco A. Albarrán, Publisher
Email: zopilote@inficad.com
Web: www.zopilote.com

**ESPIRITU COMMUNITY DEVELOPMENT
CORPORATION**
NFL YET Academy
4848 S. Second St.
Phoenix, AZ 85040
(602) 243-7188 Fax: (602) 243-7799
Armando Ruiz, Executive Director
Web: www.spiritucdc.org

FRIENDLY HOUSE, INC.
Academia del Pueblo, Youth Center
201 East Tarengo
Phoenix, AZ 85004
(602) 258-4353 Fax: (602) 258-1970
Salvador Pastrana, Director of Youth Services
Email: luis@friendlyhouse.org
Web: www.friendlyhouse.org

Adult Education Department
802 South First Ave.
Phoenix, AZ 85003
(602) 257-1870 Ext. 219 Fax: (602) 254-3135
Luis Enriquez, Director of Adult Education
Email: luis@friendlyhouse.org
Web: www.friendlyhouse.org

Immigr., Social Svc. & Counseling Dept.
723 South First Ave.
Phoenix, AZ 85003
(602) 257-1870 Fax: (602) 257-8278
Luis Ibarra, President & CEO
Email: luis@friendlyhouse.org
Web: www.friendlyhouse.org

GRAND CANYON MINORITY SUPPLIER DEVELOPMENT COUNCIL NMSDC
P.O. Box 1268
Phoenix, AZ 85001
(602) 495-9950 Fax: (502) 495-9943
Joseph A. Castillo, President

HISPANIC BUSINESS ALUMNI ASSOC.
Arizona State University
P.O. Box 871004
Tempe, AZ 85287-1004
(602) 965-2586 Fax: (602) 965-0225
Nancy Jordan, Associate Director

HISPANIC BUSINESS STUDENT ASSOC.
College of Liberal Arts and Sciences
P.O. Box 87170
Tempe, AZ 85287-2803
(602) 965-5407 Fax: (602) 965-2110

HISPANIC EDUCATION AWARENESS TEAM
Motorola Semiconductor Products Sector
2100 East Elliot Road, M/D: EL513
Tempe, AZ 85284
(602) 413-3828 Fax: (602) 413-5316
Casilda Llewellyn, Chair

HISPANIC NATIONAL BAR ASSOC. (HNBA)
400 North 7th St., Division 21
Phoenix, AZ 85006
(602) 261-8524 Fax: (602) 534-4479
Francisca Cota, Judicial Council Co-Liaison
Email: fcota@ci.phoenix.az.us
Web: www.hnba.com

Region XIV (AZ, NV)
1001 North Central Ave., #660
Phoenix, AZ 85004-1961
(602) 495-0000 Fax: (602) 253-7724
Francisco Gutierrez, Regional President
Email: FXGLaw@aol.com
Web: www.hnba.com

HISPANIC RESEARCH CENTER
Arizona State University
P.O. Box 872702
Tempe, AZ 85287-2702
(602) 965-3990 Fax: (602) 965-0315
Gary Keller, Director
Email: gary.keller@asu.edu

HISPANIC WOMEN'S CORPORATION
P.O. Box 20725
Phoenix, AZ 85036-0725
(602) 954-7995 or 1-888-388-4492
Fax: (602) 954-7563
Neli Moreno, Office Manager

HOUSING AMERICA CORPORATION
Affiliate of NCLR
P.O. Box 600
Somerton, AZ 85350
(520) 627-4221 Fax: (520) 627-4213
Agustín Tumbaga, Jr., Executive Director
Email: tum@cybertrails.com

HOUSING FOR MESA INC.
Affiliate of NCLR
P.O. Box 4457
Mesa, AZ 85211-4457
(602) 649-1335 Fax: (602) 649-1020
John R. Smith, President & CEO
Email: hfm@uswest.net

IMAGE DE PHOENIX (AZ)
National Image, Inc.
P.O. Box 149
Phoenix, AZ 85001-0149
(602) 940-8236
Robert D. Esquivel, President
Web: www.nationalimageinc.org

KAPPA DELTA CHI SORORITY
University of Arizona
Chicano/Hispano Resource Center Economics
Bldg. #217
P.O. Box 210023
Tucson, AZ 85721
(520) 621-5627
María Teresa Vélez, Director

LA FRONTERA-HOPE CENTER
260 S. Scott Ave.
Tucson, AZ 85701
(520) 884-8470 Fax: (520) 620-0434
Nancy Bradley, Director

LATIN AMERICAN CHURCH OF THE NAZARENE
191 S. California St.
Chandler, AZ 85224
(602) 963-4205
Ogdon Rico, Pastor

LEAGUE OF UNITED LATIN AMERICAN CITIZENS (LULAC)
Farwest Region-AZ
P.O. Box 2443
Tucson, AZ 85719
(520) 547-8398 (w) or (520) 903-2838
Fax: (520) 792-6388
Richard Fimbres, State Director
Web: www.lulac.org

National Executive Committee
2202 W. Anklam Rd.
Tucson, AZ 95709-0265
(520) 206-6790 (h) Fax: (520) 206-6693
Ana Valenzuela Estrada, National Vice-President for Women
Web: www.lulac.org

LOS DIABLOS ALUMNI ASSOCIATION
Arizona State University
P.O. Box 873702
Tempe, AZ 85287-3702
(480) 727-7914 Fax: (480) 965-0225
María Elena Cornado, President
Email: marilena@asu.edu
Web: www.losdiablos.zsundevils.com

LUZ SOCIAL SERVICES INC.
Tucson Office
345 E. Toole Ave., #101
Tucson, AZ 85701
(520) 882-6216 Fax: (520) 623-9291
Ricardo Jasso, Director
Web: www.luzsocialservices.org

MANA - A NATIONAL LATINA ORGANIZATION
Yuma Chapter
1326 W. 15th St.
Yuma, AZ 85364
(520) 329-8156 Fax: (520) 783-6360
Araceli Gaines, Chapter President
Email: hermana2@aol.com
Web: www.hermana.org

MARICOPA COUNTY DEPARTMENT OF PUBLIC HEALTH
HIV/AIDS Services
1825 E. Roosevelt
Phoenix, AZ 85006
(602) 506-1678

MEXICAN AMERICAN LEGAL DEFENSE AND EDUCATIONAL FUND (MALDEF)
Phoenix Program Office
202 E. McDowell Rd., #170
Phoenix, AZ 85004
(602) 307-5918 Fax: (602) 307-5928
Rudolph H. Pérez, Jr., Director
Email: maldefphx@aol.com
Web: www.maldef.org

MEXICAN AMERICAN STUDIES & RESEARCH CENTER
University of Arizona
Economics Bldg., #23, Room 208
P.O. Box 210023
Tucson, AZ 85721-0023
(520) 621-7551 Fax: (520) 621-7966
Adela de la Torre, Director
Email: masrc@u.arizona.edu

MEXICAYOTL ACADEMY
Affiliate of NCLR
412 N. Morley Ave.
Nogales, AZ 85621
(520) 287-6790 Fax: (520) 287-9131
David Bautista, Director
Email: divad56_99@hotmail.com

MOTHERS AGAINST GANGS
1401 E Thomas Rd.
Phoenix, AZ 85014
(602) 235-9823 Fax: (602) 235-9174
Therese Arvizu, Program Coordinator

MOVIMIENTO ESTUDIANTIL CHICANO DE AZTLAN (MECHA)
Arizona State University
College of Liberal Arts & Sciences
P.O. Box 871701
Tempe, AZ 85287-1701
(602) 965-6506 Fax: (602) 965-2110
Ed Delci, Advisor

Gateway Community College
108 N. 40th St.
Phoenix, AZ 85034
(602) 392-5171 Fax: (602) 392-5329
Sylvia Bejarano, Advisor

MULTI-CULTURAL AFFAIRS
Glendale Community College
6000 W. Olive Ave.
Glendale, AZ 85302
(623) 845-3565 Fax: (623) 845-3329
José Mendoza, Program Coordinator
Web: www.gc.maricopa.edu

NATIONAL ASSOC. FOR HISPANIC ELDERLY
Tucson Office/Project Ayuda
155 W. Helen St.
Tucson, AZ 85703-0746
(520) 623-0344 x3054 Fax: (520) 770-8514
Adela Zaccagnini, Project Coordinator

NATIONAL ASSOCIATION OF HISPANIC JOURNALISTS (NAHJ)
Region 7
1020 E. Mountain Vista
Phoenix, AZ 85048
(480) 460-7646 Fax: (480) 460-5456
Julie Amparano, Region Director
Email: Jamparanog@aol.com
Web: www.nahj.org

NATIONAL COUNCIL OF LA RAZA (NCLR)
Phoenix Office
111 W. Monroe, #1610
Phoenix, AZ 85003
(602) 252-7101 Fax: (602) 252-0315
Raul Yzaguirre, National President
Web: www.nclr.org

NATIONAL LATINO PEACE OFFICERS ASSOCIATION (NLPOA)
Arizona Chapter
P.O. Box 1551
Phoenix, AZ 85001
(602) 440-5601
Lou Espíndola, National President
Email: adam54@aol.com
Web: www.nlpoa.com

Tucson Chapter
P.O. Box 90180
Tucson, AZ 85742
(877) 657-6200
Daniel Lugo, Chapter President
Email: nlpoa@aol.com
Web: www.nlpoa.com

NOGALEZ SANTA CRUZ COUNTY CHAMBER OF COMMERCE
123 Kino Park
Nogalez, AZ 85621
(520) 287-3685 Fax: (520) 287-3688
Beth Daley, President
Email: beth@nogalezchamber.com
Web: www.nogalezchamber.com

NOSOTROS
440 N. Grande Ave.
Tucson, AZ 85745
(520) 623-3489 Fax: (520) 624-7999
Frank O. Romero, Director

OMEGA DELTA PHI FRATERNITY
University of Arizona
Chicano/Hispano Resource Center
Economics Bldg. #217
P.O. Box 210023
Tucson, AZ 85721
(520) 621-5627 or (520) 621-6773
María Teresa Vélez, Director

PORTABLE PRACTICAL EDUCATION PREPARATION, INC. (PPEP/MICRO)
Micro Program
802 E. 46th St.
Tucson, AZ 85713
(520) 622-3553 x39 Fax: (520) 622-1480
Frank Ballesteros, Director

PROJECT 1000
Arizona State University
c/o Graduate College - ASU
P.O. Box 871003
Tempe, AZ 85287-1003
(800) 327-4893 or (480) 965-3958
Fax: (480) 965-8309
Michael J. Sullivan, Director
Email: project1000@asu.edu
Web: http://mati.eas.asu.edu:8421/p1000

REFORMA
Arizona Chapter
University of Arizona Library
1510 E. University Blvd.
Tucson, AZ 85720-0055
(520) 621-7010 Fax: (520) 621-9733
Bob Diaz, Chapter President
Email: diazj@u.library.arizona.edu
Web: http://clnet.ucr.edu/library/reforma

REFORMA
Central Arizona Chapter
Ironwood Library
4333 E. Chandler Blvd.
Phoenix, AZ 85044
(602) 534-1900 Fax: (602) 261-8949
Lupita Barron-Rios, Chapter President
Email: lrios@lib.ci.phoenix.az.us
Web: http://clnet.ucr.edu/library/reforma

REGINA CLERI CENTER
8800 E. 22nd St.
Tucson, AZ 85710-7399
(520) 886-5202 Fax: (520) 886-6481
Rúben C. Dávalos, Jr.
Email: ruben@dplm.rtd.com

SER-JOBS FOR PROGRESS OF SOUTHERN ARIZONA, INC.
Affiliate of SER-Jobs for Progress
National, Inc.
40 W. 28th St.
Tucson, AZ 85713
(520) 624-8629 Fax: (520) 623-5754
Ernesto Urias, Executive Director
Web: www.sernational.org

SOCIETY OF HISPANIC PROFESSIONAL ENGINEERS (SHPE)
Arizona State University
College of Engineering and Applied Sciences
Office of Student Academic Services ECG-117
Tempe, AZ 85287-7006
(480) 965-3421 Fax: (480) 965-2267
Manuel Aroz, Advisor
Web: www.shpe.org

SOCIETY OF HISPANIC PROFESSIONAL ENGINEERS (SHPE)
Southern Arizona Professional Chapter
1400 E. Thomas Rd., #114B
Phoenix, AZ 85714
(520) 566-0942 Fax: (602) 264-0928
Elizabeth Macias, Chapter President
Email: h20bug520@aol.com
Web: http://members.aol.com/shpetucson/

University of Arizona/Minority Engineering Program
Engineering Room 200
P.O. Box 210020
Tucson, AZ 85721-0020
(520) 621-8103
Armando Valenzuela, Interim Dean
Email: avalenzua@uarizona.edu
Web: www.shpe.org

SOUTHERN ARIZONA AIDS FOUNDATION (SAAF)
Latina Leadership Project
375 S. Euclid Ave.
Tucson, AZ 85716
(520) 628-7223 Fax: (520) 628-7222
Velia Leyva, Program Coordinator
Email: info@saaf.org
Web: www.saaf.org

Salud es Poder, Latino Men's Health Project
375 S. Euclid Ave.
Tucson, AZ 85719
(520) 628-7223 Fax: (520) 628-7222
Ernie Perez, Program Manager
Email: salud@saaf.org
Web: www.saaf.org

TUCSON HISPANIC CHAMBER OF COMMERCE
823 E. Speedway Blvd.
Tucson, AZ 85702
(520) 620-0005 Fax: (602) 620-9685
Larry Lucero, President
Email: thcc@flash.net

VALLE DEL SOL, INC.
Affiliate of NCLR
1209 S. 1st Ave.
Phoenix, AZ 85003
(602) 258-6797 Fax: (602) 252-4964
Luz Sarmina-Gutierrez, Chief Executive Officer
Email: valle@primenet.com

VALLE DEL SOL, INC.
Hispanic Leadership Institute
1209 S. First Ave.
Phoenix, AZ 85003
(602) 258-6797 Fax: (602) 252-4964
Luz Sarmina-Gutierrez, Chief Executive Officer
Email: valle@primenet.com

ARKANSAS

ARKANSAS REG. MINORITY SUPPLIER DEVELOPMENT COUNCIL NMSDC
P.O. Box 2242
Little Rock, AR 72203
(501) 374-7026 Fax: (501) 371-0409
Charles King, Jr., Executive Director

DIOCESE OF LITTLE ROCK
Hispanic Ministry Office
P.O. Box 7417
2500 N. Tyler St.
Little Rock, AR 72217
(501) 664-0340 Fax: (501) 664-9075
Rev. Scott Friend

MOVIMIENTO ARTISTICO DEL RIO SALADO
206 E. Hermosa
Tempe, AR 85282
(602) 253-3541 Fax: (602) 253-3550
Web: www.mars-artspace.org

CALIFORNIA

ABOUT FACE DOMESTIC VIOLENCE INTERVENTION PROJECT
3400 W. 6th St. # 309
Los Angeles, CA 90020
(213) 384-7084 Fax: (213) 384-7653
Sandra G. Baca, Dir.

ACADEMIA DE ARTES YEPES
Salesian High School
960 South Soto St.
Los Angeles, CA 90023
(323) 261-7124 Fax: (323) 261-7600
Chris Rosales, Director

ACADEMY OF LATINO LEADERS IN ACTION (ALLA)
813 W. Whittier Blvd.,#202
Montebello, CA 90640
(323) 725-0640 Fax: (323) 725-7264
Marta Sámano, President
Email: alla@azteca.net

ACHIEVEMENT COUNCIL
3460 Wilshire Blvd. #420
Los Angeles, CA 90010
(213) 487-3194 Fax: (213) 487-0879
Phyllis J. Hart, Executive Director

ADAMS AND VERMONT COMMUNITY CENTER INC.
1732 W. 22nd St.
Los Angeles, CA 90007
(323) 737-2288 Fax: (323) 737-2288
Carlos L. Holguín, Director

ADELANTE
TRW Hispanic Network
One Space Park
S/1849
Redondo Beach, CA 90278
(310) 812-2269 Fax: (310) 814-8997
Karl M. Salinas, Senior Project Eng./Chair
Email: karl.salinas@trw.com

AHOME
9103 Tweedy Ln
Downey, CA 90240
(562) 806-4540
Xochitl Rodriguez, President

AID FOR BAJA CALIFORNIA
P.O. Box 4623
Anaheim, CA 92803-4623
(714) 774-5523 Fax: (562) 948-4405
Fernando Almanza, President

AIDS SERVICE CENTER
1030 S Aroyo Prkwy.
Pasadena, CA 91105
(626) 441-8495 Fax: (626) 799-6245
George Vargas, Public Benefit Specialist
Web: www.aidsservicecenter.org

ALANON
11627 E. Telegraph Rd. #110
Santa Fe Springs, CA 90670
(562) 948-2190 Fax: (562) 948-2122
Eunice Iraheta, Coord.

ALFONSO B. PEREZ SPECIAL EDUCATION CENTER
4540 Michigan Ave.
Los Angeles, CA 90022
(323) 269-0681 Fax: (323) 262-7781
Mr. Lawrence P. Birtja, Principal

ALISO-PICO MULTIPURPOSE CENTER
International Inst. of Los Angeles
1505 E 1st St.
Los Angeles, CA 90033
(323) 268-3231 Fax: (323) 268-3234
Luz Caballero, Program Director

ALL PEOPLES CHRISTIAN CENTER
822 E. 20th St.
Los Angeles, CA 90011
(213) 747-6357 Fax: (213) 747-0541
Saundra Bryant, Exec. Dir.
Email: Isaiah567@AOL.com

ALPHA 66
P.O. Box 6434
Torrance, CA 90504
(310) 324-8778 Fax: (562) 927-5622
Miguel Talleda, California Coordinator
Email: lvalpha66cal@earthlink.net
Web: www.alpha66.org

ALTAMED HEALTH SERVICES CORP.
Corporate Office / Affiliate of NCLR
500 Citadel Drive, #490
Los Angeles, CA 90040
(323) 725-8751 Fax: (323) 889-7399
Castulo de la Rocha, J.D., President & CEO
Email: altamed@crl.com

ALTAMED HIV SERVICES
5427 E. Whittier Blvd.
Los Angeles, CA 90022
(323) 869-1900 Fax: (323) 869-5362
Alvaro Ballesteros, Director

ALZHEIMER'S ASSOCIATION
Los Angeles Chapter
5900 Wilshire Blvd., #1710
Los Angeles, CA 90036
(213) 938-3370 Fax: (213) 938-1036
Michael Arthur, President

AMATEUR ATHLETIC FOUNDATION OF LOS ANGELES (AAFLA)
2141 West Adams Blvd.
Los Angeles, CA 90018
(323) 730-9630 Fax: (323) 730-9637
Anita L. DeFrantz, President
Email: library@mailgate.aafla.com
Web: www.aafla.com

AMERICA INDIGENA
1044 South Gage Ave.
Los Angeles, CA 90023
(323) 269-4431
Javier Quijas, Dir.

AMERICAN ASSOCIATION FOR HIGHER EDUCATION (AAHE)-HISPANIC CAUCUS
California State University, San Bernadino
5500 University Pkwy.
San Bernadino, CA 92407
(909) 880-5000 Fax: (909) 880-5000
Sherly Marie, Chairman
Web: www.AAHE.org

AMERICAN ASSOCIATION OF HISPANIC CERTIFIED PUBLIC ACCOUNTANTS (CPAS)
Los Angeles Chapter/Deloitte & Touche LLP
350 S. Grand Ave., #200
Los Angeles, CA 90071
(213) 996-6378 Fax: (213) 673-6949
Ramond Machado, Chapter Representative
Email: rmachado@dttus.com
Web: www.aahcpa-la.org

San Diego Chapter/Starguide Digital Networks, Inc
5754 Pacific Center Blvd.,#203
San Diego, CA 92121
(858) 452-4920 Fax: (858) 452-3095
Carmen Herrera, Chapter Representative
Email: Cherrera@starguidedigital.com
Web: www.aahcpa.org

San Francisco Chapter/ BoostWorks, Inc.
221 Main St., #770
San Francisco, CA 94105
(415) 546-9100 ext. 104 Fax: (415) 354-3324
Reynaldo E. Arellano, Chapter Representative
Email: rarellano@boostworks.com
Web: www.aahcpa.org

THE AMERICAN G.I. FORUM OF THE US
Greater San Diego Chapter
271 "I" St.
Chula Vista, CA 91910
(619) 422-6865 Fax: (619) 423-8367
Richard Resendez, Chairman

AMERICAN GI FORUM OF THE U.S.
11212 Archway Dr.
Whittier, CA 90604
(562) 941-2607 Fax: (562) 634-6986
Jake Alarid, Nat'l. Commander

AMERICAN SOCIETY OF ENGINEERS AND ARCHITECTS
1301 Avenida Cesear Chavez
East Los Angeles College
Monterey Park, CA 91754
(213) 265-8742 Fax: (213) 265-8622
Marcos Dominguez, Director

AMIGOS DE LAS AMERICAS
Stanford Uniersity Office of Student Activities
P.O. Box 7066
Stanford, CA 94309
(650) 497-7628
Kahwa Douoguih, Contact
Email: dduthoy@leland

AMITY INSTITUTE
10671 Roselle St., #101
San Diego, CA 92121-1525
(619) 455-6364 Fax: (619) 455-6597
Debra Hinman, Executive Director
Email: mail@amity.org
Web: www.amity.org

AMNESTY INTERNATIONAL
San Francisco Office
500 Sansome St., #615
San Francisco, CA 94111
(415) 291-9233 Fax: (415) 291-8722
Email: aiusasf@igc.apc.org

Western Region
9000 W. Washington Blvd., 2nd Fl.
Culver City, CA 90232
(310) 815-0450 Fax: (310) 815-0457
Bill Schulz, Executive Director
Email: aiusala@aiusa.org
Web: www.amnestyusa.org

ANAHEIM INDEPENDENCIA COMMUNITY CENTER, INC.
10841 Garza Ave.
Anaheim, CA 92804
(714) 826-9070 Fax: (714) 826-2732
Mike Boelna, Director

ANDALUCIA CLUB IN CALIFORNIA
1628 Fern St.
San Diego, CA 92102
(619) 234-7897 Fax: (619) 231-1942
Ms. Charo Monge, President

APPLE HISPANIC ASSOCIATION
1 Infinite Loop, Mailstop: 38-DM
Cupertino, CA 95014
(408) 974-2857
Oliver Krevet, President

ARBOR OF VENTURA
2675 N. Ventura Rd.
Port Hueneme, CA 93041
(805) 984-4388 Fax: (805) 984-8158
Melly Kelly, Director

ARCHDIOCESE OF LOS ANGELES
Hispanic Ministry Office
3424 Wilshire Blvd.
Los Angeles, CA 90010-2241
(213) 637-7280 Fax: (213) 637-6280
Luis D. Velásquez
Email: ldvelasquez@la-archdiocese.org

ARCHDIOCESE OF SAN FRANCISCO
Hispanic Affairs
713 S. Van Ness Ave.
San Francisco, CA 94110
(415) 824-1700 Fax: (415) 824-0844
Rev. José Rodríguez, Vicar for Hispanic Ministry

Hispanic Ministry Office
445 Church St.
San Francisco, CA 94114
(415) 565-3649 Fax: (415) 565-3668
Sr. Cecilia Rivas

ARGENTINE TANGO CLUB
University of California, Davis
Student Programs & Activities Ctr., Box #103
1 Shields Ave.
Davis, CA 95616-8706
(530) 752-2027 or (916) 448-8483
Fax: (530) 752-4951
Jose Higa, President
Email: jmhiga@ucdavis.edu
Web: www.ucdavis.edu

ARGENTINOS EN STANFORD
Office of Student Activities (Standford University)
Adelfa 404
Stanford, CA 94305
(650) 497-4944
Ezequiel Alvarez Saavedra, Contact
Email: paularaz@leland

ARRIBA JUNTOS
1850 Mission St.
San Francisco, CA 94103
(415) 863-9307 Fax: (415) 863-9314
Lorraine E. Vega, Chairman
Web: www.arribajuntos.org

ARTHRITIS FOUNDATION
Southern California Chapter
4311 Wilshire Blvd. #530
Los Angeles, CA 90010
(213) 954-5750 or (800) 954-2873
Fax: (213) 954-5790
Robert J. King, President
Email: www.arthritis.org

ARTIST OF LIFE THEATRICAL PRODUCTIONS
718 North Elm Drive
Beverly Hills, CA 90210
(310) 273-1319 Fax: (301) 273-1319
David, Cult. Arts Director

ASOCIACION CAMPESINA LAZARO CARDENAS (ACLC)
Affiliate of NCLR
42 N. Sutter St., #406
Stockton, CA 95202
(209) 466-6811 Fax: (209) 466-3465
Carol J. Ornelas, Executive Director
Email: cjornelas@aclc.org or sstone@aclc.org

ASOCIACION CULTURAL DE MICHOACANOS DE CALIFORNIA
18215 Burbank Blvd. #6
Tarzana, CA 91356-2500
(213) 627-8790 Fax: (818) 576-8619
Salvador Vasquez, President

ASOCIACION DE DAMAS GUATEMALTECAS
4003 Sunset Dr., #2
Los Angeles, CA 90027
(323) 663-4306 or (562) 942-1223
Magaly Mansilla, President

ASOCIACION DE INTELECTUALES HISPANOS
P.O. Box 65766
Los Angeles, CA 90065
(323) 221-6800
César C. Cantú, President

ASOCIACION DE PERIODISTAS DE LOS MEDIOS EN ESPAÑOL (APME)
7356 Dinwiddie St.
Downey, CA 90241
(562) 927-3423 or (562) 928-9424
Fax: (562) 927-9940
Pedro Valdivieso, President

ASOCIACION DE PROFESIONALES ARGENTINOS
8518 Orion Ave.
North Hills, CA 91343-8513
(818) 894-2239 Fax: (818) 894-2239
Mr. Mario Passo, President
Email: profarg@aol.com
Web: www.goctes.com

ASOCIACION ECUATORIANA
4530 S. Deland Ave.
Pico Rivera, CA 90660
(562) 692-6115
León Hi Fong, President

ASSISTANCE LEAGUE FAMILY SERVICES AGENCY
1360 North Saint Andrews Pl.
Hollywood, CA 90028
(323) 469-5893 Fax: (323) 469-5896
Damian Zavala, Executive Director

ASOCIACION DE PROFESIONISTAS MEXICANOS DE SILICON VALLEY, MEXPRO
P.O. Box 6484
Santa Clara, CA 95056-6484
Victor Arellano, President
Email: vma@ricochet.net
Web: www.mexpro.org

ASSOCIATED STUDENT BODY GOVT.
Los Angeles City College
855 N. Vermont Ave. CH117
Los Angeles, CA 90029
(323) 953-4054 Fax: (323) 953-4304
Jerry Rios, Vice President
Web: www.lacc-asbg.org

ASSOC. OF LATINA BUSINESS & EXECUTIVES
28626 Firestone Court
Rancho Palos Verdes, CA 90274
(310) 548-3374
Amanda Vallejo, President
Email: amanda@starone.com

ASSOC. OF MERCHANTS & COMMERCE
Bell Gardens
7214 Easten Ave. Ste B
Bell Gardens, CA 90201
(562) 806-2355 Fax: (562) 806-1585
Germán Encarnación, Jr., General Manager

ASSOCIATION OF SALVADOREANS IN LOS ANGELES/ASOCIACION DE SALVADOREÑOS EN L.A.
P.O. Box 79064
660 S. Bonnie Brae St.
Los Angeles, CA 90057
(213) 483-1244 Fax: (213) 483-9832
Carlos Ardon, Director
Email: asosal@pucbell.net
Web: www.asosal.com

AVANCE HUMAN SERVICES
1255 S. Atlantic Blvd.
Los Angeles, CA 90022
(323) 526-5819 Fax: (323) 526-5822
Alva Moreno, Executive Director

AYUDA AL NIÑO BOLIVIANO
9219 Trailhead Point
Riverside, CA 92509
(909) 681-6771 Fax: (909) 685-0814
Teresa Rivero Jackson, President
Email: Teresa@ayuda.org
Web: www.ayuda.org

BALLET FOLKLORICO DE STANFORD
Stanford University
Building 590-F, The Nitery
Stanford, CA 94305
(650) 723-2089
Annette Preciado, Contact
Email: folklorico@lists

BARRIO ASSISTANCE
Stanford University
El Centro Chicano
Building 590-F, Old Union
Stanford, CA 94305-3044
(650) 723-2089 Fax: (650) 725-6487
Chris Gonzalez Clarke, Assistant Director
Email: chris.clarke@stanford.edu
Web: www.stanford.edu/group/ba

BARRIO LOGAN COLLEGE INSTITUTE
1807 Main St.,
San Diego, CA 92113
(619) 232-4686 Fax: (919) 232-4689
Berenice J. Gil, Elementary School Coord.
Email: berenice@blci.org
Web: www.blci.org

BARRIO STATION
2175 Newton Ave.
San Diego, CA 92113
(619) 238-0314 Fax: (619) 238-0331
Rachel Ortiz, Executive Director

THE BARRIO SYMPHONY / LA SINFONICA DEL BARRIO
P.O. Box 26306
Los Angeles, CA 90026-0306
(323) 644-8864 Fax: (323) 662-5243
Peter A. Quesada, Music Director
Email: cndctvque@aol.com

BARRIO YOUTH ALTERNATIVES (BAYA)
University of California, Los Angeles
Community Programs Office
405 Hilgard Ave.,102 Men's Gym
Los Angeles, CA 90095-1454
(310) 825-5969 or (310) 206-3175
Michelle Eliot, Advisor

BARRIOS UNIDOS
313 Front Street
Santa Cruz, CA 95060
(831) 457-8208 Fax: (831) 457-0389
Nane Alejandrez, Exec. Dir.
Email: barrios@cruzio.com
Web: http://www.mercado.com/juventud/barrios/barrios.htm

BASIC ADULT SPANISH EDUCATION (BASE)
7009 Owensmouth Ave., Suite 101
Canoga Park, CA 91303
(818) 348-4771 Fax: (818) 883-5834
Virginia G. Rafelson, Exec. Dir.

BAY AREA NETWORK OF LATINAS
Chapter of MANA
601 Venice Ave., #E3-506
San Francisco, CA 94102
(415) 979-5894 Fax: (415) 647-5772
Belinda Gonzalez, President

BELVEDERE FOSTER PARENT ASSOC.
2358 Vancouver Ave.
Monterey Park, CA 91754
(323) 262-0545
Ms. Adela E. Márquez, President

BETHANIA COMMUNITY CENTER
7931 Seville Ave.
Huntington Park, CA 90255
(213) 589-2503 Fax: (213) 589-3145
Paul Maccias, President & Founder

BIENESTAR, LATINO AIDS PROJECT
1169 N. Vermont Avenue
Los Angeles, CA 90029
(323) 660-9680 Fax: (323) 660-6279
Oscar De La O, Exec. Dir.

BIENVENIDOS FOSTER FAMILY AGENCY
421 S. Glendora Ave.
West Covina, CA 91790
(626) 919-3579 Fax: (626) 919-2660
Lorraine Castro, Chief Executive Officer
Email: ffa@bienvenidos.org

BIG BROTHERS/BIG SISTERS
San Luis Obispo County
P.O. Box 12644
San Luis Obispo, CA 93406
(805) 781-3226 Fax: (805) 781-3029
JJ Lynch, Recruiting Coordinator
Email: bbbsoffice@slobigs.org
Web: www.slobigs.org

BILINGUAL & CITIZENSHIP CENTER
Los Angeles Southwest College
1600 W. Imperial Hwy.
Los Angeles, CA 90047
(323) 241-5281 Fax: (323) 241-5469
Linda Larson, Counselor

BILINGUAL FOUNDATION OF THE ARTS
National Headquarters
421 N. Ave. #19
Los Angeles, CA 90031
(323) 225-4044 Fax: (323) 225-1250
Carmen Zapata, President

BISHOP MORA SALESIAN HIGH SCHOOL ALUMNI ASSOCIATION
960 S. Soto St.
Los Angeles, CA 90023
(626) 334-6884 Fax: (626) 334-1179
Mr. Tom Gutiérrez, President

BLACK-LATINO AIDS PROJECT (BLAIDS)
University of California, Los Angeles
Community Programs Office
405 Hilgard Ave., 102 Men's Gym
Los Angeles, CA 90095-1454
(310) 825-5969 or (310) 825-0068
Fax: (310) 206-3175
Mauricio Vargas, Project Director
Email: blaids@ucla.edu

BOMBEROS OF NORTHERN CALIFORNIA
849 Tatra Ct.
San Jose, CA 95136
(408) 266-3898 Fax: (408) 266-6983
Oscar L. Guzmán, Secretary

BOWERS MUSEUM OF CULTURAL ART
2002 N. Main St.
Santa Ana, CA 92706
(714) 567-3600 Fax: (714) 567-3603
Peter Keller, Executive Director

BRAZILIAN STUDENT ASSOCIATION
Stanford Univ. Off. of Student Activities
1235 Jefferson Ave., #206
Redwood City, CA 94062
(415) 780-0525
Wanderley Liu, Contact
Email: BSA@lists

BUENA FE MEDIATION SERVICES
4716 Cesar Chavez Ave.
Los Angeles, CA 90022
(323) 260-2855 Fax: (323) 780-7986
Karen Ollen, Director

CALIFORNIA ASSOC. OF EDUCATION OFFICE PROFESSIONALS (CAEOP)
3013 N. Keystone St.
Burbank, CA 91504
(818) 848-1044 Fax: (818) 848-1044
Connie Maria Wilson, Cont.

CABRILLO ECONOMIC DEV. CORP.
Affiliate of NCLR
11011 Azahar St.
Saticoy, CA 93004
(805) 659-3791 Fax: (805) 659-3195
Rodney Fernández, Executive Director
Email: cabrillo@vcvista.net

CAFE DE CALIFORNIA, INC.
Affiliate of NCLR
748 Skylake Way
Sacramento, CA 95831
(916) 654-2452 Fax: (916) 441-7059
Paul Bocanegra, Statewide President

CALEXICO COMMUNITY ACTION COUNCIL
Affiliate of NCLR
2151 Rockwood Ave., #166
Calexico, CA 92231
(760) 357-6464 Fax: (760) 357-6614
Ruben Martínez, Executive Director
Email: ccac.ccac@usa.net

CALIFORNIA ASSOCIATION FOR BILINGUAL EDUCATION (CABE)
Affiliate of NCLR
660 S. Figueroa St., #1040
Los Angeles, CA 90017
(213) 532-3850 Fax: (213) 532-3860
Silvina Rubinstein, Executive Director
Email: silvina@bilingualeducation.org
Web: www.bilingualeducation.org

Region III
Orange Co. Dept. of Educ.
200 Kalmus Dr. Rm. B-1126
Costa Mesa, CA 92628
(714) 966-4395 or (310) 431-2049
Fax: (714) 545-8829
Estella Acosta, Reg. Rep.

CALIFORNIA CATHOLIC CONFERENCE DIVISION FOR HISPANIC AFFAIRS
1119 K St. 2nd Fl.
Sacramento, CA 95814-3904
(916) 443-4851 or (916) 313-4014
Fax: (916) 443-5629

CALIFORNIA CHICANO NEWS MEDIA ASSOCIATION (CCNMA)
Inland Chapter
P.O. Box 20562
Riverside, CA 92516-0562
(909) 737-1366 or (909) 640-8100
Fax: (909) 734-2518
Mark Acosta, Representative
Email: macosta@pe.com
Web: www.ccnma.org/iempccnma.htm

National Headquarters
3716 S. Hope St., #301
Los Angeles, CA 90007
(213) 237-7389 Fax: (213) 237-0755
Efrain Hernandez, Representative
Email: efrain.hernandez.jr@latimes.com
Web: www.ccnma.org

Sacramento Chapter
1710 Arden Way
Sacramento, CA 95815
(916) 614-1971 Fax: (916) 691-3068
Pablo Espinoza, Representative
Email: pespinoza@univision.net
Web: www.ccnma.org/sacraccnma.htm

San Diego Chapter
San Diego , CA
(619) 281-5940 Fax: (619) 281-1989
Elsa Sevilla, Representative
Email: samsevilla@yahoo.com
Web: http://www.sandiegoinsider.com/community/groups/ccnmasd/

San Jose Chapter
750 Ridder Park Dr.
San Jose, CA 95190
(408) 920-5021 Fax: (408) 884-2324
Sam Diaz, Representative
Email: sdiaz@sjmercury.com
Web: www.ccnma.org/sjccnma.htm

Tri-County Chapter
5250 Ralston St.
Ventura, CA 93003
(805) 645-1052 Fax: (805) 650-2950
Frank Moraga, Chapter President
Email: fmoraga@earthlink.net
Web: www.ccnma.org/triccnma.htm

CALIFORNIA COUNCIL FOR THE HUMANITIES
315 W. 9th St, #702
Los Angeles, CA 90015
(213) 623-5993 Fax: (213) 623-6833
Felicia Harmer Kelley, Program Officer
Email: fkelley@calhum.org
Web: www.calhum.org

CALIFORNIA DEMOCRATIC COUNCIL
NE Democratic Club
8124 West 3rd St., #207
Los Angeles, CA 90048
(213) 653-1091

CALIFORNIA HEALTHCARE FOUNDATION
476 Ninth Street
Oakland, CA 94607
(510) 238-1040 or (888) 430-2423
Fax: (510) 238-1388
Dr. Mark Smith, President/CEO
Web: www.chcf.org

CALIFORNIA HIGHWAY PATROL HISPANIC ADVISORY COMMITTEE
California Highway Patrol
c/o Ernie Garcia
411 N. Central Ave. #410
Glendale, CA 91203
(818) 240-8200 Fax: (818) 240-5962
Edward W. Gomez, Chief

CALIFORNIA HISPANIC CHAMBER OF COMMERCE
343 E. Main St., #701
Stockton, CA 95202
(209) 547-1337 Fax: (209) 946-0969
Andrew Ysiano, President
Email: lamkting@cwnet.com

CALIFORNIA HISPANIC COMMISSION ON ALCOHOL AND DRUG ABUSE
Administrative Office
2101 Capital Ave.
Sacramento, CA 95816
(916) 443-5473 Fax: (916) 443-1732
James Z. Hernandez, Executive Director
Email: chcada@jps.net

Garden Grove
9842 W. 13th St., #B
Garden Grove, CA 92844
(714) 531-4624 Fax: (714) 537-1189
Isabel Mellomi, Program Director

CALIFORNIA HISPANIC CULTURAL SOCIETY
10821 Petula Pl.
Cerritos, CA 90703
(562) 948-3250 Fax: (562) 984-4152
Nellie P. Walsborn, President

CALIFORNIA HUMAN DEV. CORP.
3315 Airway Dr.
Santa Rosa, CA 95403
(707) 523-1155 Fax: (707) 523-3776
George L. Ortíz, Executive Director
Email: chdc@fonic.net

CALIFORNIA LATIN AMERICAN MEDICAL ASSOCIATION (CLAMA)
13200 Crossroads Parkway N., #135
City of Industry, CA 91746
(562) 695-7387 Fax: (562) 695-8856
Juan Villagomez, Chairman
Web: www.phfe.org

CALIFORNIA MEXICAN AMERICAN CHAMBER OF COMMERCE (CAL MACC)
3526 E. Olympic Blvd.
Los Angeles, CA 90023
(323) 269-4092 Fax: (323) 269-4175
Frank C. Moreno, President
Email: mexamoreno@aol.com

CALIFORNIA MINI-CORP PROGRAM
California State University, Bakersfield
9001 Stockdale Hwy.
Bakersfield, CA 93311-1099
(661) 664-2429 Fax: (661) 664-2016
Alma Kumar, Director
Email: akumar@csubak.edu

CALIFORNIA MISSION STUDIES ASSOC.
P.O. Box 3357
Bakersfield, CA 93385
(213) 617-4143 or (626) 792-0333
Laurence K. Gould, Jr., President
Email: cmsa@lightspeed.net
Web: www.ca-missions.org

CALIFORNIA RURAL LEGAL ASSISTANCE
215 S. Coast Hwy.
Oceanside, CA 92054
(760) 966-0511 Fax: (760) 966-0291
Claudia E. Smith, Attorney/Director

CALIFORNIA TOMORROW
436, 14th St., #820
Oakland, CA 94612
(510) 496-0220 Fax: (510) 496-0225
Laurie Olsen, Executive Director
Email: info@californiatomorrow.org
Web: www.californiatomorrow.org

CAMARA DE COMERCIO EL SALVADOR - CALIFORNIA
1605 W. Olympic Blvd., #1009
Los Angeles, CA 90015
(213) 252-8471 Fax: (213) 252-0098
Edgardo Quintanilla, Esq., President
Email: elsalvadorca@camarasdecomercio.com

CAMARA DE COMERCIO NICARAGUENSE AMERICANA DE CALIFORNIA (CACONACA)
P.O. Box 92345
City of Industry, CA 91715-2345
(323) 953-9145 Fax: (323) 953-7991
Jorge Obregón, Jr., President
Email: nicaraguaca@camarasdecomercio.com
Web: www.camaradecomercio.com

CAMPESINOS UNIDOS, INC.
Affiliate of NCLR
P.O. Box 203
1005 C St.
Brawley, CA 92227
(760) 344-6300 Fax: (760) 344-0322
José M. López, Executive Director
Email: cuijml@brawleyonline.com

CARA A CARA, LATINO AIDS PROJECT
Hollywood Sunset Free Clinic
3324 Sunset Blvd.
Los Angeles, CA 90026
(213) 661-6752 Fax: (213) 660-1408
Teresa Dadua, Exec. Dir.

CARPINTERIA VALLEY HISTORICAL SOCIETY AND MUSEUM OF HISTORY
956 Maple Ave.
Carpinteria, CA 93013
(805) 684-3112 Fax: (805) 684-4721
David W. Griggs, Director

CASA BLANCA CHILD CARE CENTER
3020 Madison Street
Riverside, CA 92504
(909) 689-7891

CASA DE CATALANS
P.O. Box 91142
Los Angeles, CA 90009
(714) 557-5192 Fax: (714) 241-0185
Peter Balsells, President

CASA DE ESPERANZA
2112 South Gary, Suite C
Pomona, CA 91766
(909) 591-6773 or (909) 623-6131
Fax: (909) 591-4073
Patricia Recalde, Manager

CASA DE LA CULTURA COLOMBIANA
6002 Klump Ave.
North Hollywood, CA 91606
(818) 760-3158 Fax: (818) 760-3158
Dukardo Hinestrosa, Director

CASA DE LA CULTURA GUATEMALA
1138 Wilshire Blvd., #300
Los Angeles, CA 90017
(213) 250-9090 or (213) 250-3416
Fax: (213) 250-3705
Byron Vásquez, President

CASA ECUADOR
1322 Longwood Ave.
Los Angeles, CA 90019
(323) 934-2310
William Hidalgo, President

CASA FAMILIAR, INC.
Affiliate of NCLR
119 W. Hall Ave.
San Ysidro, CA 92173
(619) 428-1115 Fax: (619) 428-2802
Andrea Skorepa, Executive Director
Email: admin@casafamiliar.org

CASA MARAVILLA SENIOR CITIZENS NUTRITION CENTER
5721 Union Pacific Ave.
Los Angeles, CA 90022
(323) 728-0717 Fax: (323) 728-2604
Lupe Gloria, Project Director

CASA SANTA MARIA
7551 Orangetorpe Ave.
Buena Park, CA 90621
(714) 994-1404
Walter Warg, Manager

CASA YOUTH SHELTER
P.O. Box 216
10911 Reagan St.
Los Alamitos, CA 90720
(562) 594-6825 Fax: (562) 594-9185
Lucian Maulhard, President

CATHOLIC CHARITIES OF LOS ANGELES
Immigration And Refugee Div.
1530 W. 9th
Los Angeles, CA 90015-0095
(213) 251-3492 Fax: (213) 251-3444
Loc Naunguyen, Quality Assurance Director

CATHOLIC CHARITIES OF ORANGE CO.
1506 Brooke Hollow Dr., #112
Santa Ana, CA 92705
(714) 662-7500 or (714) 957-4613
Fax: (714) 662-1861
Christian Schlichct, Director

CATHOLIC CHARITIES OUTREACH
Community Services Program
3631 W. Warner
Santa Ana, CA 92703
(714) 668-1130 Fax: (714) 957-2523
Lupe Savastano, Director

CENTER FOR HUMAN RIGHTS AND CONSTITUTIONAL LAW
256 S. Occidental Blvd.
Los Angeles, CA 90057
(213) 388-8693 Fax: (213) 386-9484
Peter A. Schey, Exec. Dir.
Email: pschey@earthlink.net

CENTER FOR IBERIAN AND LATIN AMERICAN STUDIES
University of California, San Diego
9500 Gilman Dr.
La Jolla, CA 92093-0528
(858) 534-6050 Fax: (858) 534-7175
Peter H. Smith, Director
Email: latamst@ucsd.edu

CENTER FOR LATIN AMERICAN STUDIES
University of California, Berkeley
2334 Bowditch
Berkeley, CA 94720-2312
(510) 642-2088 Fax: (510) 642-3260
Harley Shaiken, Director

CENTER FOR STUDY OF BOOKS IN SPANISH FOR CHILDREN AND ADOLESCENTS
California State Univ., San Marcos
San Marcos, CA 92096-0001
(760) 750-4070 Fax: (760) 750-4073
Isabel Schon, Dir.
Email: ischon@mailhost1.csusm.edu
Web: www.csusm.edu/campus_centers/csb/

CENTER FOR THE STUDY OF LATINO HEALTH (CESLS)
UCLA School of Medine
924 Westwood Blvd., #730
Los Angeles, CA 90024
(310) 794-0663 Fax: (310) 794-2862
David E. Hayes-Bautista, Director
Web: www.med.ucla.edu/cesla

CENTER FOR TRAINING AND CAREERS, INC. (CTC)
Affiliate of NCLR
1600 Las Plumas Ave.
San Jose, CA 95133
(408) 251-3165 Fax: (408) 251-4978
Rose A. Amador, President & CEO
Email: ctc4u@aol.com

CENTER FOR U.S. - MEXICAN STUDIES
University of California, San Diego
9500 Gilman Dr., #0510
La Jolla, CA 92093-0510
(858) 534-4503 Fax: (858) 534-6447
Wayne A. Cornelius, Director
Email: usmex@weber.ucsd.edu
Web: www.usmex.ucsd.edu

CENTRAL CALIFORNIA HISPANIC CHAMBER OF COMMERCE (CCHCC)
National Headquarters
1900 Mariposa Mall, #105
Fresno, CA 93721
(559) 485-6640 Fax: (559) 485-3738
Gilbert Servin, President
Email: general@litespeed.net
Web: www.cchcc.com

CENTRAL CITY EAST BOYLE HEIGHTS LIONS CLUB
4249 Abbott Rd.
Lynwood, CA 90262
(323) 569-6149 Fax: (323) 569-6149
Terry Castañeda, President
Email: guapamusic@aol.com

CENTRAL-AMERICAN CHAMBER OF COMMERCE
Headquarters
3333 Wilshire Blvd., #612
Los Angeles, CA 90010
(213) 389-7193 Fax: (213) 389-5779
Hugo W. Mérida, Executive Director
Email: cca@usacatradexpo.com
Web: www.usacatradexpo.com

CENTRO CULTURAL DE LA MISION / MISSION CULTURAL LATINO ARTS CENTER
2868 Mission St.
San Francisco, CA 94110
(415) 821-1155 Fax: (415) 648-0933
Jennie Rodriguez, Director
Email: jennierodriguez@ejc.org
Web: www.latinoartcenter.cdsearch.com

CENTRO CULTURAL DE LA RAZA
Affiliate of NCLR
2125 Park Blvd.
San Diego, CA 92101-4792
(619) 235-6135 Fax: (619) 595-0034
Howard Hollman, Nancy Rodriguez, President of the Board, Administrative Manager

CENTRO CULTURAL MEXICANO
San Francisco Office
870 Market St., Suite 509
San Francisco, CA 94102
(415) 393-8003 or (415) 392-5564
Fax: (415) 393-8020
Lilia Aguilera, Executive Director
Email: ccmsf@aol.com
Web: http://members.aol.com/ccmsf/index.html

CENTRO CULTURAL NICARAGUENSE
529 South Alvarado
Los Angeles, CA 90057
(213) 413-3191 Fax: (213) 413-0083
Max Ocón, Coordinator

CENTRO CULTURAL PLACITA
P.O. Box 531734
Los Angeles, CA 90053-1734
(323) 343-0994
José Cohen, Executive Director

CENTRO DE ASISTENCIA SOCIAL GUATEMALTECO (CASGUA)
1138 Wilshire Blvd., #300
Los Angeles, CA 90017
(213) 250-3416 Fax: (213) 250-3705
Byron Vásquez, Exec. Dir.

CENTRO DE NIÑOS
379 S. Loma Drive
Los Angeles, CA 90017
(213) 484-1515 Fax: (213) 484-0880
Sandra Serrano Sewell, Executive Director

CENTRO HISPANO DE RECUPERACION DEL ALCOHOLISMO
5801 E. Beverly Blvd.
Los Angeles, CA 90221
(213) 780-0630 Fax: (213)722-4450
James Hernández, Exec. Dir.

CENTRO JUAN MONTALVO
5300 Santa Monica Blvd., #310
Los Angeles, CA 90029
(323) 463-2945
Ana Lucia Jaramillo, Director

CENTRO LATINO DE EDUCACION POPULAR
1709 West 8th St., #A
Los Angeles, CA 90017
(213) 483-7753 Fax: (213) 483-7973
Marcos Cajina, Director
Email: clubliteracy@earthlink.net

CENTRO LATINO DE SAN FRANCISCO
Affiliate of NCLR
1656 15th St.
San Francisco, CA 94103
(415) 861-8758 or (415) 861-8168
Fax: (415) 861-4028
Gloria Bonilla, Executive Director

CENTRO MARAVILLA SERVICE CENTER
4716 Cesar Chavez Ave.
Los Angeles, CA 90022
(323) 260-2805 Fax: (323) 780-7986
Karen Ollen, Director

CENTRO MEXICANO DE FRESNO
Fresno Office
830 Van Ness Ave., 2nd Floor
Fresno, CA 93721
(559) 445-2615 Fax: (559) 495-0535
Lurdes Chavez, Director
Email: imecal@worldnet.att.net

CENTRO SAN JOSE
204 Hampton Dr.
Venice, CA 90291
(310) 396-6468 Fax: (310) 392-8402
Judy Alexander, Asst. Dir.

CEPROMEX
4241 Jutland Dr., 100
San Diego, CA 92117
(619) 272-0974 Fax: (619) 272-8647
Miriam Cohen, Pres.

CESAR E. CHAVEZ FOUNDATION
P.O. Box 62, K
Keene, CA 93531
(661) 823-6230 Fax: (661) 823-6175
Lori de Leon, Administrator
Email: cecf@ufwmail.com

CHAMBER OF COMMERCE
San Luis Obispo Chapter
1039 Chorro St.
San Luis Obispo, CA 93401
(805) 781-2777 Fax: (805) 541-8416
Anja Schootnan, Dir. of Information Services
Email: slochamber@slochamber.org
Web: www.slochamber.org

CHARLES DREW MEDICAL SOCIETY
P. O. Box 83176
4477 W. 118th St.
Los Angeles, CA 90083
(213) 931-2247 Fax: (310) 676-0148
Dr. Wendy Green, Pres.

CHARO COMMUNITY DEV. CORP.
Branch Office
3951 E. Medford St.
Los Angeles, CA 90063-1698
(323) 268-1100 Fax: (323) 266-7910
Richard S. Amador, President & CEO
Web: www.charocorp.com

Main Office
4301 E. Valley Blvd.
Los Angeles, CA 90032
(323) 269-0751 Fax: (323) 266-4326
Richard S. Amador, President & CEO
Web: www.charocorp.com

CHARROS LOS AMIGOS DE LOS ANGELES
3047 Los Cerrillos Dr.
West Covina, CA 91791
(626) 915-7755 Fax: (626) 915-7756
Lauro J. Neri, Pres.

CHDP PROGRAM & CCS PROGRAM
Children's Medical Services
P.O. Box 1489
San Luis Obispo, CA 93406
(805) 781-5502 or (805) 781-5527
Fax: (805) 781-4492
Cesilia Marol, Contact

CHICANA SERVICE ACTION CENTER, INC.
Bilingual Shelter-Domestic Violence
P.O. Box 23366
Los Angeles, CA 90023
(323) 268-7564
Fax: (213) 430-0657 or (213) 430-0658
Alicia Reyes, Social Service Coordinator
Email: adrian.gutierrez@lacsac.com

Corporate and Administrative Offices
315 W. 9th St., #101
Los Angeles, CA 90015
(213) 629-5800
Fax: (213) 430-0657 or (213) 430-0658
Sophia Esparza, Executive Director
Email: adrian.gutierrez@lacsac.com

CSAC Volunteer Program
315 W. 9th St., #101
Los Angeles, CA 90015
(213) 629-5800
Fax: (213) 430-0657 or (213) 430-0658
José Claustro, Administrative Assistant
Email: adrian.gutierrez@lacsac.com

Downtown One-Stop Workforce Employment and Training
315 W. 9th St., #101
Los Angeles, CA 90015
(213) 629-5800
Fax: (213) 430-0657 or (213) 430-0658
José Claustro, Administrative Assistant
Email: adrian.gutierrez@lacsac.com

Free Spirit Shelter-Domestic Violence
P.O. Box 23366
Los Angeles, CA 90023
(323) 937-1312
Fax: (213) 430-0657 or (213) 430-0658
Alicia Reyes, Social Service Coordinator
Email: adrian.gutierrez@lacsac.com

Homeless Assistance Program and Transitional Housing
315 W. 9th St., #101
Los Angeles, CA 90015
(213) 629-5800
Fax: (213) 430-0657 or (213) 430-0658
Alicia Reyes, Social Service Coordinator
Email: adrian.gutierrez@lacsac.com

Mid-Cities Employment & Education Ctr.
7848 Pacific Blvd.
Huntington Park, CA 90255
(323) 588-9802 Fax: (323) 588-6177
Leticia Rivera, Intake Specialist
Email: adrian.gutierrez@lacsac.com

Pomona Employment & Education Ctr.
630 N. Park Ave.
Pomona, CA 91768
(909) 620-0383 Fax: (909) 629-3171
Sophia Esparza, Executive Director
Email: adrian.gutierrez@lacsac.com

Project Self-Sufficiency
315 W. 9th St., #101
Los Angeles, CA 90015
(213) 629-5800
Fax: (213) 430-0657 or (213) 430-0658
Sophia Esparza, Executive Director
Email: adrian.gutierrez@lacsac.com

Staples Arena Center
315 W. 9th St., #101
Los Angeles, CA 90015
(213) 629-5800
Fax: (213) 430-0657 or (213) 430-0658
Jose Claustro, Administrative Assistant
Email: adrian.gutierrez@lacsac.com

Youth Comprehensive Training Centers
315 W. 9th St., #101
Los Angeles, CA 90012
(213) 629-5800 or (800) 843-9675
Fax: (213) 430-0658
Jose Claustro, Administrative Assistant
Email: adrian.gutierrez@lacsac.com

CHICANA/LATINA RESEARCH CENTER
University of California, Davis
Social Sciences & Humanities, #122
1 Shields Ave.
Davis, CA 95616-8706
(530) 752-8882 Fax: (530) 754-8622
Adaliza Sosa-Riddell, Coordinator
Web: www.ucdavis.edu

CHICANO ALUMNI ASSOCIATION
Bakersfield College Student Affairs Office
1801 Panorama Dr.
Bakersfield, CA 93305
(805) 395-4532 Fax: (805) 395-4241
Rosa Garza, Advisor

CHICANO AND LATINO GRADUATE STUDENTS ASSOCIATION
Stanford University
El Centro Chicano, Building 590-F, Old Union
Stanford, CA 94305-3044
(650) 723-2089 Fax: (650) 725-6487
Chris Gonzalez Clarke, Assistant Director
Email: chris.clarke@stanford.edu
Web: www.stanford.edu/dept/elcentro/

CHICANO AND LATINO YOUTH LEADERSHIP PROJECT, INC.
P.O. Box 161566
2115 J Street, #210
Sacramento, CA 95816
(916) 446-1640 Fax: (916) 446-2899
Consuelo Zermeno, President
Web: www.clylp.org

CHICANO CULTURAL CENTER
Bakersfield College
801 Panorama Dr.
Bakersfield, CA 93305
(805) 395-4532 Fax: (805) 395-4241
Cornelio C. Rodriguez, Director

CHICANO FEDERATION OF SAN DIEGO COUNTY INC.
Affiliate of NCLR
610 22nd St.
San Diego, CA 92102
(619) 236-1228 Fax: (619) 236-8964
Raymond Uzeta, Executive Director

CHICANO INFORMATION MANAGEMENT CONSORTIUM OF CALIFORNIA
University of California, Santa Barbara
Davidson Library
Santa Barbara, CA 93106
(805) 893-8067 or (805) 893-2478
Fax: (805) 893-4676
Pat Dossan, Librarian
Email: dossan@library.ucsb.edu
Web: www.library.ucsb.edu/webstations/

CHICANO & LATINO ENGINEERS & SCIENTISTS SOCIETY (CALESS)
University of California, Davis
Student Programs & Activities Ctr., Box #132
1 Shields Ave.
Davis, CA 95616-8706
(530) 752-2027 or (530) 758-7218
Fax: (530) 752-4951
Haydee C. Trujillo, President
Email: hctrujillo@ucdavis.edu
Web: www.engr.ucdavis.edu/~caless/

CHICANO MEDICAL STUDENT ASSOCIATION (CMSA)
University of California, San Francisco
Associate Student's Office Box 0376
500 Parnasses Ave. #108 W MU Wet
San Francisco, CA 94143-0376
(415) 476-2010 Fax: (415) 476-7295
Erik Coenig, Advisor

University of California, Davis
Student Programs & Activities Ctr., Box #MED
1 Shields Ave.
Davis, CA 95616-8706
(530) 752-2027 or (530) 758-9538
Fax: (530) 752-4951
Rafael Rodriguez, President
Email: rrodriguez@ucdavis.edu
Web: www.ucdavis.edu

CHICANO RESOURCE CENTER
East Los Angeles Public Library
4801 E. Third St.
Los Angeles, CA 90022
(323) 263-5087 Fax: (323) 264-5465
Mrs. Doyle, Contact

CHICANO SERVICES
315 W. 9th St.
Los Angeles, CA 90015
(213) 253-5959 Fax: (213) 930-0657
Sofia Esparza, CEO

CHICANO STUDIES
Ethnic Studies Department
CSU-6000 J St.
Sacramento, CA 95819-6013
(916) 278-6645 Fax: (916) 278-5156
Sam Rios, Director
Email: sirios@csus.edu

CHICANO STUDIES DEPARTMENT (CSUF)
California State University
800 N. State College Blvd.
Fullerton, CA 92834
(714) 278-3731/2011 Fax: (714) 278-3306
Isaac Cárdenas, Chairman
Email: icardenas@fullerton.edu

CHICANO WRITERS & ARTISTS ASSOC.
California State University
Student Life & Development
CSU-5280 N. Jackson
Fresno, CA 93740-8023
(559) 278-4917
Ruben Sanchez, Advisor

CHICANO-LATINO EDUCATION COMMITTEE (UTLA)
3303 Wilshire Blvd., 10th floor
Los Angeles, CA 90010
(213) 368-6213 Fax: (213) 368-6256
Arturo Selva, Chair

CHICANO/A STUDIES RESEARCH CENTER
University of California, Los Angeles
2307 Murphy Hall
Los Angeles, CA 90095
(310) 825-2363 or (310) 825-2642
Fax: (310) 206-1784
Guillermo Hernandez, Director
Email: gmo@csrc.ucla.edu
Web: www.sscnet.ucla.edu/csrc

CHICANO/A/LATINO ART FORUM
Stanford Univ. Office of Student Activities
P.O. Box 17191
Stanford, CA 94305
(650) 497-2236
Pedro Toledo, Contact
Email: rwah@leland

CHICANO-LATINO ASSOCIATION OF STUDENT EDUCATORS
4969 North Bocker, #101
Fresno, CA 93726
(209) 292-8751
Juan G. Trujillo, Pres.

CHICANO/LATINO FACULTY ASSOCIATION
Dep. of Educational Research
5005 N. Maple Ave M/S 303
Fresno, CA 93740-8025
(209) 278-0318 Fax: (209) 278-0404
Robert Segura, President

CHICANO/LATINO STUDENT AFFAIRS CTR.
655 North Dartmouth Avenue
Claremont, CA 91711
(909) 621-8044 Fax: (909) 621-8981
María Aguiar Torres, Dean of Student Affairs
Email: Maria_Torres@cucmail.claremont.edu
Web: www.cuc.claremont.edu/chicano

CHICANO/LATINO STUDIES STUDENTS ASSOCIATION
California State University, Long Beach
1250 Bellflower Blvd.
Long Beach, CA 90815
(562) 985-4181

CHICANOS IN HEALTH EDUCATION
University of California of San Francisco
1220 20th Ave. #2
San Francisco, CA 94122
(415) 731-3113 Fax: (415) 476-7295
Tania Butkovic, President

CHICANOS IN LAW
California State University, Fresno
5150 N. Maple Ave., M/S JA62
Fresno, CA 93740-8026
(559) 278-5351 Fax: (559) 278-2323
Tony Garduque, Advisor
Email: tonyg@csufresno.edu
Web: www.csufresno.edu

CHICANOS - LATINOS IN HEALTH EDUCATION (CHE)
University of California, Davis
Student Programs & Activities Ctr., Box #261
1 Shields Ave.
Davis, CA 95616-8706
(530) 752-2027 or (530) 753-2584
Fax: (530) 752-4951
Michelle Dulude, President
Email: mzdulude@ucdavis.edu
Web: www.ucdavis.edu

CHICANO STUDIES DEPARTMENT (CSUF)

CHICANOS/LATINOS FOR COMMUNITY MEDICINE
California State University, Long Beach
1212 Bellflower Blvd.
Long Beach, CA 90815
(562) 985-4181
Martha Cordero, President

CHINATOWN SERVICES CENTER
767 N. Hill St. #400
Los Angeles, CA 90012-2381
(213) 253-0880 Fax: (213) 680-0787
Debbie Ching, Exec. Dir.

THE CHURCH OF JESUS CHRIST OF LATTER DAY SAINTS
Los Angeles CA Temple Visitors' Ctr.
10777 W. Santa Monica Blvd.
Los Angeles, CA 90025
(310) 474-1549 Fax: (310) 474-0651
Elder Derrick, Director
Web: www.lds.org

THE CHURCH OF JESUS CHRIST OF LATTER DAY SAINTS
Oakland CA Temple Visitors' Ctr.
4766 Lincoln Ave.
Oakland, CA 94602
(510) 531-1475 Fax: (510) 531-7625
Elder Kimball, Director
Web: www.lds.org

THE CHURCH OF JESUS CHRIST OF LATTER DAY SAINTS
San Diego Mormon Battalion Visitors' Ctr.
2510 Juan St.
San Diego, CA 92110
(619) 298-3317 Fax: (619) 298-5866
Elder Simmons, Director
Web: www.lds.org

CINE ACCION
346 9th St., 2nd Fl.
San Francisco, CA 94103
(415) 553-8135 Fax: (415) 553-8137
Lydia Johnson, Secretary
Email: coneaccion@aol.com
Web: www.cineaccion.com

CIRCULO DE AMIGOS DE LA VOZ LIBRE
3107 W. Beverly Blvd. #1
Los Angeles, CA 90057
(213) 388-4639 Fax: (213) 388-2053
Angel Prada, President

CIRCULO ESPAÑOL ORANGE CO.
821 Chicago Ave.
Placentia, CA 92670
(714) 893-2378 or (714) 891-2215
Cira Salinas, Pres.

CITY OF CARLSBAD HIRING CENTER
Carlsbad Satellite Office
5958 El Camino Real
Carlsbad, CA 92008
(760) 929-8121 Fax: (760) 929-8090
Pablo Jimenez, Manager

CLARE FDTN.-ADULT RECOVERY HOME
1871 9th St.
Santa Monica, CA 90404
(310) 314-6238 Fax: (310) 314-6257
Sandy Chapin, Dir.

CLCV EDUCATION FUND
10780 Santa Monica Blvd., #210
Los Angeles, CA 90025
(310) 441-4162 ext. 306 Fax: (310) 441-1685
Mr. Randy Jurado Ertll, New Voter Organizer
Email: rertll@ecovote.org
Web: www.ecovote.org

CLINICA COMUNITARIA MAYFIELD COMMUNITY CLINIC
Prog. Latino Contra el SIDA
270 Grant Ave.
Palo Alto, CA 94306
(650) 327-8717 Fax: (650) 323-6830
Raul Rojas, Latino AIDS Program

CLINICA DE LACTANCIA-HOSPITAL GENERAL
2180 Johnson Ave.
San Luis Obispo, CA 93401
(804) 541-2229
Olga Mireles, RNC, LCC

CLINICA MEDICA DEL PUEBLO
3106 W. Beverly Blvd.
Montebello, CA 90640
(213) 728-1274 Fax: (213) 720-9954
Saúl R. Ziperovich, President

CLINICA MONSEÑOR OSCAR A. ROMERO
1135 W. 6th St.
Los Angeles, CA 90017
(213) 482-6400 Fax: (213) 482-1124
Margie Martinez, Exec. Dir.

CLINICA PARA LAS AMERICAS (CPLA)
318 S. Alvarado St.
Los Angeles, CA 90057
(213) 484-8434 Fax: (213) 484-1814
Alice Heidy, Exec. Dir.

CLINICA TEPATI
1500 C St.
Sacramento, CA 95814
(530) 752-7028 Fax: (530) 752-2996
Jose Arevalo, Director

CLINICAS DE SALUD DEL PUEBLO INC.
Affiliate of NCLR
P.O. Box 1279
Brawley, CA 92227
(760) 344-6471 Fax: (760) 344-5840
Luis P. Lerma, Executive Director
Email: clinica@brawleyonline.com

CLUB AHUACATLENSE
5310 Buchannan St.
Los Angeles, CA 90042
(323) 256-7935
Mr. Marco Aguilar, President

CLUB AMBATO, ECUADOR
640 N. Hobart Blvd.
Los Angeles, CA 90004
(213) 665-4581
Efraín Albán, Pres.

CLUB AMISTAD
10121 La Cima Dr.
Whittier, CA 90603
(562) 696-3147
David Z. Sanchez, Pres.

CLUB BOHEMIA DE LOS ANGELES
P. O. Box 73A
Los Angeles, CA 90003
(213) 230-4868 Fax: (323) 778-0984
George De Aztlan, Pres.
Email: BOHEMIA2000@webtv.net

CLUB BUENA VOLUNTAD
Centro Maravilla
4716 Cesar Chavez Ave.
Los Angeles, CA 90022
(323) 260-2804 or (562) 904-0426
Anastasio Miranda, President

CLUB COJUMATLAN
2714 Humbert Ave.
South El Monte, CA 91733
(626) 575-0149
Mr. Juan Anaya

CLUB CULTURAL CUBANO
247 E. Pomona Blvd.
Monterey Park, CA 91755
(323) 721-2568 or (323) 725-9147
Osvaldo Batista, President

CLUB DE DAMAS ORQUIDEAS
COSTARRICENSES
6449 Triton Dr.
Pico Rivera, CA 90660
(562) 949-6868 Fax: (562) 949-6868
Nelly Orona, Fundadora

CLUB DEL PUEBLO HISPANO DE LINCOLN
HEIGHTS
2323 Workman St.
Los Angeles, CA 90031
(213) 225-9339
Samuel CastilloRoberto Miranda, Pres.

CLUB GUADALUPANO DE SAN BENEDITO
1022 W. Cleveland
Montebello, CA 90640
(213) 722-8402 Fax: (213) 721-5075
Stella Meléndez, Pres.

CLUB HERMANDAD NICARAGUENSE
AMERICANA
5712 Fountain Ave.
Los Angeles, CA 90028
(323) 467-4813 Fax: (232) 669-1029
Manuel Salazar, President

CLUB HISPANO DEL PUEBLO
2323 Workman St.
Los Angeles, CA 90031
(213) 225-9339 Fax: (213) 226-0994
Roberto Miranda, Pres.

CLUB PEGUEROS
1834 12th St.
Santa Mónica, CA 90404
(310) 450-1487 or (714) 968-6389
Fax: (310) 396-7875
Victoriano Gutierrez, Pres.

CLUB PUERTORRIQUEÑO DE PERSONAS
MAYORES
P.O. Box 65884
Los Angeles, CA 90065
(213) 257-1222
Margarita M. Rosales, Pres. & Founder

CLUB SAN JULIAN AYUDA
108 Rosalynn Dr.
Glendora, CA 91740
(626) 914-4818 Fax: (909) 620-7530
Max Hernández, Pres.

CLUB SOCIAL CULTURAL COLIMENSE
P.O. Box 2656
Redondo Beach, CA 90278
(310) 374-7270 Fax: (310) 374-3796
Armando Hernández, Pres.

CLUB SOCIAL FRESNILLO
11248 Barnwall St.
Norwalk, CA 90650
(562) 868-2863 Fax: (562) 868-2863
Manuel de la Crúz, Pres.

CLUB ZAPOPAN
3018 N. Charlotte
Rosemead, CA 91770
(626) 288-6671 x258 Fax: (626) 307-9218
Becky Castillo, Pres.

COACHELLA VALLEY MEXICAN-
AMERICAN CHAMBER
P.O. Box 1874
Fontana, CA 92202
(909) 829-1777 Fax: (619) 771-2301

COALICION ETNICA DEL SUR DE
CALIFORNIA
3175 S Hoober St., #442
Los Angeles, CA 90007
(213) 892-9204 Fax: (213) 680-4518
John W. Heath, Co-Chair

COALICION REVOLUCIONARIA
MEXICANA DE CALIFORNIA
2413 S. Vermont
Los Angeles, CA 90007-1661
(323) 734-8787 Fax: (323) 734-8787
Rafael Zacarías, President

COALITION AGAINST THE PRISON IN
EAST LOS ANGELES
5271 E Beverly Blvd.
Los Angeles, CA 90022
(323) 726-7734 Fax: (323) 721-9794
Frank Villalobos, Founder
Email: bpidesign@aol.com

COALITION FOR ECONOMIC SURVIVAL
1296 N Fairfax Ave.
Los Angeles, CA 90046
(323) 656-4410 Fax: (323) 656-4416
Larry Gross, Executive Director
Email: ces@loop.com

COALITION FOR HUMANE IMMIGRANT
RIGHTS OF LOS ANGELES (CHIRLA)
1521 Wilshire Blvd.
Los Angeles, CA 90017
(213) 353-1333 Fax: (213) 353-1344
Angelica Salas, Executive Director
Email: chirla@earthlink.net

COLECTIVA PARA NIÑOS
P.O. Box 77363
3817 S. San Pedro St.
Los Angeles, CA 90007
(213) 231-1367 Fax: (213) 231-6242
Jackie Kimbrough, Dir.

COLEGIO POPULAR
2839 Mariposa
Fresno, CA 93721
(559) 441-7131 or (800) 765-7131
Fax: (559) 441-7155
Tomás González, Executive Director
Email: admin@romerocenter.org

COLLEGE ASSISTANCE MIGRANT
PROGRAM OF STUDENTS
CSU Camp Office Bldg THH
River Front Center, #1, 6000 J St.
Sacramento, CA 95819-6108
(916) 278-7241 Fax: (916) 278-5193
Marco Sanchez
Email: msanchez@csus.edu

COLMENA HISPANA UNIVERSITARIA
Student Life & Development
CSU-5280 N. Jackson
Fresno, CA 93740-8023
(209) 278-7039 or (209) 278-4768
Raúl Moreno, Advisor

COLORADO RIVER COMMUNITY ACTION
COUNCIL, INC.
Affiliate of NCLR
P.O. Box 1274
721 E. Hopson Way
Blythe, CA 92226
(760) 922-7310 or (760) 922-2277
Fax: (760) 921-3022
Nicolás Rivera, Executive Director
Email: nicor@redrivernet.com

COMISION FEMENIL MEXICANA
NACIONAL (CFMN)
Affiliate of NCLR
303 South Loma Dr.
Los Angeles, CA 90017
(213) 483-2060 Fax: (213) 483-7848
Velma Sanchez, Contact

COMITE DE AMIGOS DE GUATEMALA
5533 1/2 W. Virginia Ave.
Hollywood, CA 90038
(213) 462-8593
Alberto Esmenjaud, Dir.

COMITE DE BENEFICENCIA MEXICANA
2900 Calle Pedro Infante
Los Angeles, CA 90063
(323) 264-1428 or (323) 264-1429
Fax: (323) 264-4962
Rubén Hoyos, Pres.

COMITE DE DAMAS PERUANAS DE L.A.
11508 Littchen St.
Norwalk, CA 90650
(310) 864-5671 Fax: (310) 929-0751
Teresa Snyder, Exec. Dir.

COMITE DE FESTEJOS DE LA
INDEPENDENCIA CENTROAMERICANA
529 S. Alvarado St.
Los Angeles, CA 90057
(213) 413-3191 Fax: (213) 413-0083
Luis Max Ocón, President
Email: oconjaen@aol.com

COMITE DE PADRES PRO DEFENSA DEL
ESTUDIANTE
3119 Faermount St.
Los Angeles, CA 90063
(323) 263-7915
Gabino Espinoza, President

COMITE GARDELIANO DE CALIFORNIA
4325 Bel-Air Dr.
La Cañada, CA 91011
(818) 790-0810 Fax: (818) 790-0810
Enrique Zayas, Pres./Fnder.

COMITE MEXICANO CIVICO PATRIOTICO
P.O. Box 60714
Los Angeles, CA 90051
(323) 268-4728 Fax: (323) 268-0941
Angel Morales, President

COMITE POR LA DEMOCRACIA Y EL
DESARROLLO EN EL SALVADOR (CODDES)
1636 W. 8th St. #103
Los Angeles, CA 90017
(213) 382-6343 Fax: (213) 382-2910
Isabel Beltrán, Pres.

COMMITTEE IN SOLIDARITY WITH THE
PEOPLE OF EL SALVADOR
P.O. Box 57337
Los Angeles, CA 90057
(323) 852-0721 or (323) 660-4587
Fax: (323) 913-1881
Don White, Coordinator

COMMUNITY COUNSELING SERVICES
1145 Wilshire Blvd., Suite 100
Los Angeles, CA 90017
(213) 481-1347 Fax: (213) 482-9466
Diana Aiello, Dir.

COMMUNITY FOOD BANK OF WEST
COVINA
P.O. Box 128
1501 West Del Norte
West Covina, CA 91793
(626) 814-2862
Elizabeth Geiger, Dir.

COMMUNITY IN ACTION (CEM)
Proyecto Pastoral at Dolores Mission
135 N. Mission Rd.
Los Angeles, CA 90033
(323) 881-0014 Fax: (323) 268-7228
Consuelo Valdez, Director
Email: info@proyectopastoral.org
Web: www.proyectopastoral.org

COMMUNITY MOTHERS CLUB
9255 Pioneer Blvd.
Santa Fe Springs, CA 90670
(562) 692-0261
Angelina Lopez, Pres.

COMMUNITY REHABILITATION
SERVICES, INC. (CRS)
4716 Cesar Chavez Ave.
Los Angeles, CA 90022
(213) 266-0453 Fax: (213) 266-7992
Al Rivera, Exec. Dir.

3325 Wilshire Blvd.
Los Angeles, CA 90010
(213) 427-9090 or (213) 427-0173
Fax: (213) 427-0172
Rene Bonilla, Administrator

COMMUNITY RESOURCES COUNCIL
(Placer County Concilio)
133 Church St.
Roseville, CA 95678
(916) 783-0481 Fax: (916) 783-4013
Yolanda Mindafel, Director
Email: pancrfb@foothill.net

COMMUNITY SERVICE OFFICE
Los Angeles Harbor College
1111 Figueroa Pl.
Wilmington, CA 90744
(310) 522-8380 Fax: (310) 549-3770
Carla Mussa-Muldoon, Director
Email: darian_costa@laccd.cc.ca.us

CONCERNED PARENTS OF THE
COMMUNITY
1515 W. 155th St.
Compton, CA 90220-2713
(310) 632-0139
Freddy G. Cortés, Chair/Founder

COUNCIL FOR THE SPANISH SPEAKING
Affiliate of NCLR
343 E. Main St., 2nd Floor
Stockton, CA 95202
(209) 547-2855 Fax: (209) 547-2870
Jose Rodriguez, Executive Director

COUNCIL OF MEXICAN-AMERICAN
ADMINISTRATORS OF THE LOS ANGELES
UNIFIED SCHOOL DISTRICT
Headquarters Ford Elementary
1112 S. Ford Blvd.
Los Angeles, CA 90022
(323) 268-8508 Fax: (323) 264-6953
Robert Venegas, President

Miles Avenue Elementary
6720 Miles Ave.
Huntington Park, CA 90255
(323) 588-8296 Fax: (323) 581-4567
José Velázquez, Principal

Wilmington Elementary
1700 Gulf Ave.
Wilmington, CA 90744
(310) 518-1120 Fax: (310) 549-5307
Ernest Tarango, Principal

COUNTY OF LOS ANGELES DEPARTMENT
OF CHILDREN AND FAMILY SERVICES
Adoption Division
695 South Vermont Ave.
Los Angeles, CA 90005
(213) 738-4577 or (213) 738-1502
Fax: (213) 383-1502
Amy Wong-Martinez, Supervising Soc. Worker
Email: jprusak@co.la.ca.us

CUADRATURA DEL CIRCULO POETICO
IBEROAMERICANO
P.O. Box 54
Santa Monica, CA 90406-0054
(310) 829-2694
Pedro Izquierdo-Tejido, President

CUBA INDEPENDIENTE Y DEMOCRATICA
P.O. Box 39462
Los Angeles, CA 90039
(805) 266-9324 Fax: (805) 266-9324
Mr. Evencio Blanco, Coordinator

CUBA-AMERICAN VOTERS NATIONAL UNITY COMMITTEE
4826 Oakwood Ave.
Los Angeles, CA 90004
(323) 463-9353 or (323) 463-9362
Fax: (323) 463-9363
Rafael Aguilar, President
Email: josefdez@aol.com

CUBAN-AMERICAN ALLIANCE EDUC. FUND
3161 Bridle Drive
Hayward, CA 94541
(510) 538-9694 Fax: (510) 538-9614
Delvis Fernandez Levy, Executive Director
Email: caaef@igc.org
Web: www.cubamer.org

CUBAN-AMERICAN TEACHERS ASSOCIATION (CATA)
12037 Peoria St.
Sun Valley, CA 91352
(818) 768-2669
Alberto C. del Calvo, Exec. Dir.

DAMAS DE LAS AMERICAS
8670 7th Street
Douney, CA 90241
(562) 861-7677 Fax: (213) 773-5152
Lupe Arce, Pres.

DAMAS PROTECTORAS DE LA NIÑEZ
P.O. Box 612
Valley View, CA 17963
(714) 968-0439 Fax: (570) 682-8063
Laura Jones

DANGERMAN EDUCATION FDTN. INC.
11684 Ventura Blvd. #368
Studio City, CA 91604
(818) 752-3952 Fax: (818) 752-3150
Roger Tinsley, President

DANZA ESPAÑOLA
Stanford Univ. Office of Student Activities
427 College Ave.
Palo Alto, CA 94306
(650) 723-3081
Deborah Henigson, Contact
Email: span-dance@lists

DANZA FLORICANTO/USA
4032 S. Overcrest Dr.
Whittier, CA 90601
(562) 695-3546 Fax: (562) 695-3546
Gema Sandoval, Executive Director

DARIN M. CAMARENA HEALTH CTR. INC.
Affiliate of NCLR
201 South B St.
Madera, CA 93638
(559) 675-5600 Fax: (559) 674-3870
Mary Murphy, Executive Director
Email: info@camarenahealth.org
Web: www.camarenahealth.org

DEAF & DISABLED TELECOMMUNICATIONS PROGRAM
California Relay Services
12901 Venice Blvd.
Los Angeles, CA 90066
(310) 398-9502 Fax: (310) 390-4906
Brenda Bailey, Outreach Specialist
Email: bbaileyla@ddtp.org
Web: www.ddtp.Qrg

California Relay Services
2647 International Blvd.
Oakland, CA 94601
(510) 261-2546 Fax: (510) 261-2741
Jewel Jauregui, Outreach Specialist
Email: jewelj@jps.net
Web: www.ddtp.org

DEL RIO VALDES COMMUNICATIONS
5349 W. El Segundo Blvd.
Belaire, CA 90250
(310) 797-1925 Fax: (310) 643-5866
Lourdes Del Rio, Owner

DELHI COMMUNITY CENTER
Affiliate of NCLR
542 E. Central Ave.
Santa Ana, CA 92707
(714) 549-1317 Fax: (714) 549-5738
Irene Martinez, Executive Director
Email: delhi1997@aol.com

DEPARTMENT OF HEALTH SERVICES
Central Health District
241 N. Figueroa St.
Los Angeles, CA 90012
(213) 240-8203 Fax: (213) 250-8763
Lupe Sánchez, Administrator

DIOCESAN HISPANIC MINISTRY COORD.
900 Lafayette St. #401
Santa Clara, CA 95050-0141
(408) 983-0141 Fax: (408) 983-0295
Lupita Vida, Hispanic Catechetical Director
Email: vida@dsj.org
Web: www.dsj.org

DIOCESE OF FRESNO
Hispanic Affairs
1550 N. Fresno St.
Fresno, CA 93703-3788
(559) 488-7475 Fax: (559) 493-2847
Zeferino González, Coord. for Hispanic Ministry
Email: aaranda@fwdioc.org

DIOCESE OF MONTEREY
Hispanic Affairs
P.O. Box 1684
Salinas, CA 93902-1684
(831) 424-4076 x25 Fax: (831) 424-5221
Sister. Patricia Murtagh, Dir. for Hispanic Ministry
Email: hispmin@dioceseofmonterey.org

DIOCESE OF MONTEREY HISPANIC OFFICE
22 Stone St.
Salinas, CA 93901-2643
(831) 424-4076 Fax: (831) 424-5221
Sister Patricia Murtagh, Director

DIOCESE OF OAKLAND
Hispanic Ministry Office
2900 Lakeshore Dr.
Oakland, CA 94610
(510) 267-8354 Fax: (510) 272-0738
Héctor Medina
Email: hmedina@oakdiocese.org

DIOCESE OF ORANGE
Juan Diego Center
2811 E. Villa Real Dr.
Orange, CA 92867-1999
(714) 282-3050 Fax: (714) 282-3029
Most Rev. Jaime Soto, Aux. Bishop of Orange

DIOCESE OF SACRAMENTO
Hispanic Affairs
2110 Broadway
Sacramento, CA 95818-2541
(916) 733-0177 Fax: (916) 733-0195
Deacon Germán A. Toro, Director for Hispanic Apostolate
Email: gtoro@diocese-sacramento.org

DIOCESE OF SAN BERNARDINO
Hispanic Affairs
1201 E. Highland Ave.
San Bernardino, CA 92404
(909) 475-5451 or (909) 475-5360
Fax: (909) 475-5379
Sr. Cecilia Calva, Director for Hispanic Ministry
Email: ccalva@sbdiocese.org

DIOCESE OF SAN DIEGO
Hispanic Affairs
3888 Paducah Dr.
San Diego, CA 92117
(619) 490-8249 Fax: (619) 490-8272
Enrique Méndez, Director for Hispanic Ministry
Email: emendez@diocese-sdiego.org

DIOCESE OF SAN JOSE
Hispanic Ministry Office
80 S. Market St.
San Jose, CA 95113
(408) 283-8100 Fax: (408) 283-8110
Rev. Luis Gerardo Menchaca

DIOCESE OF SANTA ROSA
St. John the Baptist Church
960 Caymus St.
Napa, CA 94559
(707) 226-9379 Fax: (707) 254-9262
Rev. Oscar Díaz, Director of Hispanic Ministry

DIOCESE OF STOCKTON
Hispanic Ministry Office
1125 N. Lincoln St.
Stockton, CA 95203
(209) 466-0636 Fax: (209) 463-5937
Digna Ramírez

DOLORES MISSION ALTERNATIVE SCHOOL (DMA)
Proyecto Pastoral at Dolores Mission
135 N. Mission Rd.
Los Angeles, CA 90033
(323) 264-9143 Fax: (213) 268-7228
Manuel Dominguez, Director
Web: www.proyectopastoral.org

DOLORES MISSION WOMEN'S COOPERATIVE CHILD CARE CTR. (DMWC)
Proyecto Pastoral at Dolores Mission
157 S. Gless St.
Los Angeles, CA 90033
(323) 881-0011 or (323) 881-0010
Fax: (323) 881-0770
Lupe Avila, Director
Email: dmwc@proyectopastoral.org or pndavids@earthlink.net
Web: www.proyectopastoral.org

DOMINGUEZ RANCHO ADOBE
18127 S. Alamenda St.
Compton, CA 90220
(310) 631-5981 Fax: (310) 631-3518
Robert Bishop, Father

EAST BAY SPANISH SPEAKING CITIZENS' FOUNDATION
Affiliate of NCLR
1470 Fruitvale Ave.
Oakland, CA 94601
(510) 261-7839 Fax: (510) 261-2968
José Arredondo, Executive Director
Email: EBSSCF@aol.com

EAST LOS ANGELES WOMEN CENTER
1255 South Atlantic Blvd.
Los Angeles, CA 90022
(323) 526-5819 or (800) 400-7432
Fax: (323) 526-5822
Alba Moreno, Director
Email: forraza@aol.com

EAST LOS ANGELES ALCOHOLISM COUNCIL
916 S. Atlantic Blvd.
Los Angeles, CA 90022
(323) 268-9344 Fax: (323) 268-9348
Carlos D. García, Executive Director

EAST LOS ANGELES CHAMBER OF COMMERCE
5401 E. Whittier Blvd.
Los Angeles, CA 90022
(323) 722-2005 Fax: (323) 722-2405
Fanny Arroyo, Project Coordinator

EAST LOS ANGELES COMMUNITY CENTER
4360 E. Dozier
Los Angeles, CA 90022
(213) 267-0012 Fax: (213) 267-1472
Alex Gomez, Exec. Dir.

THE EAST LOS ANGELES COMMUNITY UNION (TELACU)
5400 E. Olympic Blvd. #300
Los Angeles, CA 90022
(323) 721-1655 Fax: (323) 724-3372
David Lizarraga, President
Email: telacu@telacu.com
Web: www.telacu.com

EAST LOS ANGELES HOMEOWNERS ASSOCIATION
1435 N. Rollins Dr.
Los Angeles, CA 90063
(323) 269-2602 Fax: (323) 261-1753
Gloria Chávez, President

EAST LOS ANGELES MENTAL HEALTH SERVICES
Affiliate of NCLR
1436 Goodrich Blvd.
City of Commerce, CA 90022
(323) 725-1337 Fax: (323) 278-5344
Alfredo Larios, President & CEO

EAST LOS ANGELES NEIGHBORHOOD SERVICE CENTER
133 N. Sunol Dr.
Los Angeles, CA 90063
(323) 260-2801 Fax: (323) 266-6457
Richard Murillo, Director

EAST LOS ANGELES OCCUPATIONAL CENTER
2100 Marengo St.
Los Angeles, CA 90033
(213) 223-1283 Fax: (213) 223-6365
Bob Bieggar, Principal
Web: www.lausd.k12.ca.us/dace/elaoc

EAST LOS ANGELES ROTARY CLUB
2600 W. Beverly Blvd.
Montebello, CA 90640
(213) 721-5306 Fax: (213) 721-2802
Carolyn Rienhart, Pres.
Email: warner@pacificnet.net

EAST LOS ANGELES SERVICES CENTER
1231 S. Gerhart Ave.
Los Angeles, CA 90022-4522
(323) 887-3970 Fax: (323) 728-7615
Jose Gutierrez, Manager

EAST LOS ANGELES SKILLS CENTER
3921 Selig Pl.
Los Angeles, CA 90031
(213) 227.0018 Fax: (213) 222-2351
Norma Chavez-Orr, Teacher Advisor
Email: info@lausd.k12.us.elasc
Web: http://www.lausd.k12.ca.us/lausd/offices/dace/East_Los_Angeles_SC/

EASTMONT COMMUNITY CENTER
Affiliate of NCLR
701 S Hoefner Ave.
Los Angeles, CA 90022
(323) 726-7998 Fax: (323) 726-9237
Manny Martínez, Executive Director
Email: eastmont@compuserv.com

EASTSIDE BOYS AND GIRLS CLUB
324 North McDonnell Ave.
Los Angeles, CA 90022
(323) 263-4955 Fax: (323) 263-6814
Mark Chavez, Exec. Dir.
Email: elabgc@aol.com

EDUCATIONAL OPPORTUNITY PROGRAMS AND SERVICES
Palo Verde College
811 W. Chanslorway
Blythe, CA 92225
(760) 921-5339 Fax: (760) 922-0230
Patricia Kester, Director

Rancho Santiago College
EOPS-1530 W.17th St.
Santa Ana, CA 92706
(714) 564-6232 Fax: (714) 564-6239
Susana Sandoval, Director
Email: csandoval@cc.rancho.cc.ca.us

EDUCATIONAL SERVICE CENTERS
Mt. San Antonio College
1100 N. Grand Ave.
Walnut, CA 91789
(909) 594-5611x4845
Margie High, Director

EL CAMINO MENTAL HEALTH CTR.
11721-A E. Telegraph Rd.
Santa Fe Springs, CA 90670
(562) 949-8455 Fax: (562) 949-4807
Bill Fujihara, Dir.

EL CENTRO CHICANO
Stanford University
Building 590-F, Old Union
Stanford, CA 94305-3044
(650) 723-2089 Fax: (650) 725-6487
Dr. Frances Morales, Assistant Dean/Director
Email: fmorales@stanford.edu
Web: www.stanford.edu/dept/elcentro/main.html

University of Southern California
817 W. 34th St. #300
Los Angeles, CA 90089-2991
(213) 740-1480 Fax: (213) 745-6721
Abel Amaya, Director
Web: www.usc.edu

EL CENTRO DE AMISTAD
7024 Deering Ave.
Canoga Park, CA 91303
(818) 347-8565 Fax: (818) 347-0506
Angel Perez, Exec. Dir.

EL CENTRO SUBSTANCE ABUSE TREATMENT CENTER
1972 Cesar Chavez Ave.
Los Angeles, CA 90033
(323) 265-9228 Fax: (323) 265-7166
Raul Astrada, Dir.

EL CENTRO/SER-JOBS FOR PROGRESS, INC.
Affiliate of SER-Jobs for Progress National, Inc.
770 Main St.
El Centro, CA 92243
(760) 352-8514 Fax: (760) 352-5790
Rubén García, Executive Director
Web: www.sernational.org

EL CONCILIO DEL CONDADO DE VENTURA
400 South "B" Street
Oxnard, CA 93030
(805) 486-9777 Fax: (805) 486-9881
Francisco Dominguez, Executive Director
Email: elconcilio@aol.com

EL CONCILIO OF SAN MATEO COUNTY
1419 Burlingame Ave., #N
Burlingame, CA 94010
(650) 373-1080 Fax: (650) 373-1090
Ostencia Lopez, President

EL FUERTE SINALOA
1910 West Verdugo Ave.
Burbank, CA 91506
(818) 845-0353 Fax: (818) 845-0353
Ms. Chiquita Reyna, President

EL MARIACHI CARDENAL DE STANFORD
Stanford Univ. Office of Student Activities
P.O. Box 14721
Stanford, CA 94309
(650) 497-1788
Carlos Santana, Contact
Email: sprout@leland
Web: www.stanford.edu/group/mariachi/

EL MONTE COMPREHENSIVE HEALTH CTR.
10953 Ramona Blvd.
El Monte, CA 91731
(626) 579-8302 Fax: (626) 448-6210
Andrés Martinez, CEO

EL MONTE YOUTH DEVELOPMENT CTR.
3800 Penn Mar
El Monte, CA 91732
(626) 350-4029 Fax: (626) 350-4038
Laura Quijada, Prog. Mngr.

**EL MONTE/SOUTH EL MONTE CHAMBER
OF COMMERCE**
P.O. Box 5866
El Monte, CA 91734-1866
(626) 443-0180 Fax: (818) 443-0463
Karin Crehan, Executive Director
Email: chamber@ksb8.com
Web: www.emsem.org

EL PROYECTO DEL BARRIO, INC.
Affiliate of NCLR
8902 Woodman Ave.
Arleta, CA 91331
(818) 830-7133 Fax: (818) 830-7280
Corinne Sánchez, President & CEO

**EL PUEBLO DE LOS ANGELES HISTORIC
MONUMENT**
Administrative Offices
125 Paseo de la Plaza
Los Angeles, CA 90012
(213) 485-6855 Fax: (213) 485-8238
Kenneth Cothran, Acting Director

EL RESCATE
1340 S. Bonnie Brae
Los Angeles, CA 90006
(213) 387-3284 Fax: (213) 387-9189
Lesbia Henao, Director

EL SANTO NIÑO COMMUNITY CENTER
601 E. 23rd St.
Los Angeles, CA 90011
(213) 748-5246 Fax: (213) 748-9006
Fiona Gibson, Director

EL SERENO RECREATION CENTER
4721 Klamath St.
Los Angeles, CA 90032
(323) 225-3517
Ramon Bernal, Director

EL TEATRO CAMPESINO
National Headquarters
P.O. Box 1240
San Juan Bautista, CA 95045
(831) 623-2444 Fax: (831) 623-4127
Luis Valdéz, Artistic Director
Email: teatro@hollinet.com
Web: www.elteatro.com

EL TEATRO DE LA TIERRA
414 N. Park
Fresno, CA 93701
(559) 237-3016
Agustin Lira, Director
Email: almas2@earthlink.net
Web: www.home.earthlink.net/~almas2/

**ESCUELA ARGENTINA DE LOS ANGELES -
LEALA**
P.O. Box 5322
Whittier, CA 90607
(310) 946-3076 Fax: (310) 946-3076
Elba D. Bonini, Dir.

ESCUELA DE LA RAZA UNIDA
Affiliate of NCLR
P.O. Box 910 , 137 N. Broadway
Blythe, CA 92226
(760) 922-2582 Fax: (760) 921-3261
Rigoberto Garnica, Executive Director
Email: jeru72@aol.com

**ESPERANZA COMMUNITY HOUSING
CORPORATION**
2337 S Figueroa St.
Los Angeles, CA 90007
(213) 748-7285 Fax: (213) 748-9630
Sister Diane Donoghue, Executive Director
Email: diane@esperanzachc.org
Web: www.esperanzachc.org

**EVALUATION DISSEMINATION &
ASSESSMENT CENTER (EDAC-LA)**
California State University, Los Angeles
5300 Paseo Rancho Castilla, Box 2-019
Los Angeles, CA 90032
(323) 343-4870 Fax: (323) 343-4338
Charles Leyba, Director

FAMILIA
Stanford Univ. Office of Student Activities
Bldg. 560-F, The Nitery
Stanford, CA 94305
(650) 497-7427
Brenda Chavez, Contact
Email: sarvai@leland
Web: www.stanford.edu/group/familia

FAMILIA CENTER
Affiliate of NCLR
711 E. Cliff Dr.
Santa Cruz, CA 95060
(831) 423-5747 Fax: (831) 423-5922
Yolanda Henry Goda, Executive Director

FAMILY HEALTH CARE ANAHEIM CLINIC
University of California, Irvine
300 Carl Karcher Way
Anaheim, CA 92801
(714) 774-9804 or (714) 774-2782
Fax: (714) 535-5407
Lora Mansilla, Administrator

FAMILY HEALTH CENTER OF ALVISO
P.O. Box 1240
1621 Gold St.
Alviso, CA 95002
(408) 262-7944 Fax: (408) 935-3984
Juan Posada, Medical Dir.

FAMILY SERVICE OF LONG BEACH
Administrative Office
1041 Pine Ave.
Long Beach, CA 90813
(562) 436-9893
Don L. Westerland, Executive Director

FEDERACION DE CLUBES ZACATECANOS
1332 N. Miller Ave.
Los Angeles, CA 90063
(323) 262-1360 Fax: (323) 262-1462
Mr. Rafael Barajas, President
Web: www.zacatecanos.com

**FEDERATION OF EMPLOYED LATIN
AMERICAN DESCENDANTS (FELAD)**
Affiliate of NCLR
420 Virginia St.
Vallejo, CA 94590-6018
(707) 644-4470 Fax: (707) 644-5228
Alberto Rocha, President

FEEDBACK FOUNDATION, INC.
1200 N. Knollwood Cir.
Anaheim, CA 92801
(714) 220-0224 Fax: (714) 220-1374
Shirley Cohen, Executive Director

FIESTA EDUCATIVA
3839 Selig Place
Los Angeles, CA 90031
(323) 221-6696 Fax: (323) 221-6699
Irene Martinez, Executive Director
Email: fiestaed@aol.com

FIRST FUNDAMENTAL BIBLE CHURCH
2301 Findlay Ave.
Monterey Park, CA 91754
(323) 728-3897 Fax: (323) 728-0257
Alex D. Montoya, Pastor
Email: info@ffbc.net
Web: www.ffbc.net

**FORMER STUDENTS & PROFESSORS OF
THE JOSE MARTI INSTITUTE IN LA HABANA**
4778 North Peck Rd.
El Monte, CA 91732
(626) 350-3917 Fax: (626) 350-5259
Dr. Roberto Román, President

**FOUNDATION CENTER FOR
PHENOMENOLOGICAL RESEARCH, INC.**
Affiliate of NCLR
414 12th St.
Sacramento, CA 95814
(916) 447-2087 Fax: (916) 447-2098
Marta Bustamante, President
Email: foundcen@aol.com

FDTN. FOR EAST LOS ANGELES COLLEGE
East Los Angeles College
1301 César Chavez Ave.
Monterey Park, CA 91754
(323) 265-8650x8610 Fax: (323) 260-8197
Selina Chi, Executive Director & Dean of
Recourse Development
Email: selinas_schi@laccd.cc.ca.us
Web: www.laccd.edu

**FOUNDATION FOR THE CHILDREN OF
THE CALIFORNIAS**
P.O. Box 84178
San Diego, CA 92138
(858) 279-0591 Fax: (858) 279-0593
Pamela Torlone, Director
Web: www.fnc.org.mx

FRANCISCO MARTINEZ DANCE THEATRE
6723 Matilija Ave.
Van Nuys, CA 91405-4818
(818) 988-2192 Fax: (818) 988-2192
David Allen Jones, Exec. Dir.
Email: smdt@ slash.net
Web: www.flash.net/tildaday/smdt

FRESNO ART MUSEUM
2233 N. 1st St.
Fresno, CA 93703
(559) 441-4220 Fax: (559) 441-4227
Marie LaFollette, Development Director
Email: fam@qnis.net

**FRESNO COUNTY COMMISSION ON
ALCOHOLISM FOR THE SPANISH
SPEAKING**
1444 Fulton St.
Fresno, CA 93721
(209) 268-6475 Fax: (209) 268-6967
Domingo Zapata, Director

FRESNO/SER-JOBS FOR PROGRESS, INC.
Affiliate of SER-Jobs for Progress
National, Inc.
407 S. Clozis Ave., #109
Fresno, CA 93721
(559) 452-0881 Fax: (559) 452-8038
Rebecca Mendibles, Executive Director
Web: www.sernational.org

FRESQUEZ & ASSOCIATES
405 14th St., #208
Oakland, CA 94612
(925) 274-9360 Fax: (925) 274-1875
Ernesto Fresquez, Principal
Email: efresquez@aol.com
Web: www.fresquez.com

FRIENDS OF CLINICA TEPATI
University of California, Davis
Student Programs & Activities Ctr., Box #MED
1 Shields Ave.
Davis, CA 95616-8706
(530) 752-2027 or (530) 750-0504
Fax: (530) 752-4951
Patty Garcia, President
Email: spac@ucdavis.edu
Web: www.ucdavis.edu

FUTURE LEADERS OF AMERICA INC. (FLA)
National Headquarters
1110 Camelia St.
Oxnard, CA 93030
(805) 485-5237 Fax: (805) 485-5237
Gilbert G. Cuevas, President
Email: flacorp@aol.com

GALERIA DE LA RAZA
2857 24th St.
San Francisco, CA 94110
(415) 826-8009 Fax: (415) 826-5128
Carolina Ponce de Leon, Director

THE GARY CENTER
341 Hillcrest St.
La Habra, CA 90631
(562) 691-3263 Fax: (562)690-5063
Martha Lester, Executive Director

**GENEALOGICAL SOCIETY OF HISPANIC
AMERICA**
P.O. Box 2472
Santa Fe Springs, CA 90670
(310) 204-6808
Donie Nelson, Acting President

GIRL SCOUT COUNCIL OF ORANGE CO.
1620 Adams Ave.
Costa Mesa, CA 92626
(714) 979-7900 or (714) 850-1299
Fax: (714) 850-1299
Mona Ware, Executive Director
Web: www.girlscouts.org

**GLENDALE HISPANIC BUSINESS &
PROFESSIONAL ASSOCIATION**
P.O. Box 3172
Glendale, CA 91221-0172
(818) 613-4810
Raúl Flamenco, President
Email: novamed@compuserve.com

GLOBAL EDUCATION PARTNERSHIP
310 8th St. #303
Oakland, CA 94607
(510) 834-7255 Fax: (510) 834-7256
Email: info@globaledpartnership.org
Web: www.globaledscholarship.org

GOLDEN STATE MINORITY FOUNDATION
333 S. Beaudry Ave. #216-C
Los Angeles, CA 90017
(213) 482-6300 Fax: (213) 482-6305
Ivan Houston, President
Email: gsmf@earthlink.net
Web: www.gsmf.org

**GREATER CORONA NORCO HISPANIC
CHAMBER OF COMMERCE**
1353 W. 6th St.
Corona, CA 91720
(909) 737-9440 Fax: (909) 737-5668
Tom Ruiz, President

**GREATER EAST LOS ANGELES SENIOR
CITIZENS ORGANIZATION (GELASCO)**
133 N. Sunol Dr.
Los Angeles, CA 90063
(323) 260-2801 Fax: (323) 266-6457
Richard Murillo, Coordinator

**THE GREATER MERCED COUNTY MULTI-
CULTURAL CHAMBER**
P.O. Box 2286
Merced, CA 95340
(209) 725-8182 Fax: (209) 725-8192

**GREATER RIVERSIDE HISPANIC CHAMBER
OF COMMERCE**
P.O. Box 56022
Riverside, CA 92517
(909) 328-1385 Fax: (909) 788-8772

GRUPO JUVENIL FUERZA NUEVA
407 S. Chicago St.
Los Angeles, CA 90033
(323) 268-7432 Fax: (323) 268-8076
Father Jim Nieblas, Pastor

GUADALUPE CYCS CENTER
21600 Hart St.
Canoga Park, CA 91303
(818) 340-2050
Moeed Khan, Dir.

GUADALUPE HOMELESS PROJECT (GHP)
Proyecto Pastoral at Dolores Mission
171 S. Gless St.
Los Angeles, CA 90033
(323) 881-0032 Fax: (323) 268-7228
Arturo Lopez, Director
Email: info@proyectopastoral.org
Web: www.proyectopastoral.org

**GUATEMALA-CALIFORNIA CHAMBER OF
COMMERCE**
P.O. Box 57429
Los Angeles, CA 90057
(213) 385-5955 Fax: (213) 389-5775
Hugo Alexander Gonzales, President
Email: Guatemalaca@camarasdecomercio.com
Web: www.usacaexpo.com

GUATEMALAN EDUCATION ACTION PROJECT
8124 W. 3rd St. #105
Los Angeles, CA 90048
(213) 782-0953 Fax: (213) 782-0954
Stevan Garth Sovensen, Coord.

GUATEMALAN TRADE CENTER
1138 Wilshire Blvd. #300
Los Angeles, CA 90017
(213) 250-3416 Fax: (213) 250-3705
Byron Vásquez, Trade Commissioner
Email: guatexpo98@aol.com

HACEMOS
National Headquarters
2600 Camino Ramon #1E200E
San Ramon, CA 94583
(925) 824-8961 Fax: (925) 866-1585
Manuel, President

HEALTHY START
Centro De Bienestar Para La Gente
1511 19th St., P.O. 367
Oceano, CA 93445
(805) 781-5389 or (805) 473-4242
Ray Segura, Director

HEBER PUBLIC UTILITY DISTRICT
Affiliate of NCLR
P.O. Box H
Heber, CA 92249
(760) 353-0323 Fax: (760) 353-9951
Manuel Castañeda, General Manager
Email: mcastaneda@icoe.k12.ca.us

HERMANDAD DEL SEÑOR DE LOS MILAGROS DEL VALLE DE SAN FERNANDO
Saint Elizabeth Church
6635 Tobias Ave.
Van Nuys, CA 91405
(818) 779-1756 Fax: (818) 785-4492
Marta Rivera, Pres.

HERMANDAD MEXICANA NACIONAL
Affiliate of NCLR
523 W. 6th St., #542
Los Angeles, CA 90014
(213) 244-9581 Fax: (213) 244-9588
Angelina Corona, Executive Director

HERMANOS DE LUNA Y SOL
Center for AIDS Prevention Studies, UCSF
74 New Montgomery, #600
San Francisco, CA 94105
(415) 597-9100 Fax: (415) 597-9125
Dr. Rafael M. Diaz, Contact
Web: www.caps.ucsf.edu

HERMANOS MACEHVAL
University of California, Davis
Student Programs & Activities Ctr., Box #271
1 Shields Ave.
Davis, CA 95616
(530) 752-2027 or (530) 759-9702
Fax: (530) 752-4951
Oscar Brambila, President
Email: obrambila@ucdavis.edu
Web: www.ucdavis.edu

HESED CHRISTIAN MINISTRIES
Agape Homes
15445 Old Morro Rd.
Atascadero, CA 93422
(805) 462-9325
Danny R. Andrews, Child Care Worker
Email: www.agape.cncoffice.com

HIGH DESERT HISPANIC CHAMBER OF COMMERCE
14455 Park Ave. #A, P.O. Box 2157
Victorville, CA 92393
(760) 241-6661 Fax: (760) 951-0556
James Coronado, President
Email: hdhcc_1@netzero.net
Web: www.hdhcc.com/

HIGHLAND PARK CHAMBER OF COMMERCE
P.O. Box 42949
Los Angeles, CA 90050-0949
(323) 256-0920
Laura Mora, President

HISPANAS ORGANIZED FOR POLITICAL EQUALITY (HOPE)
634 S. Spring St., #920
Los Angeles, CA 90014
(213) 622-0888 Fax: (213) 622-0007
Martha Diaz Askenazy, Pres.
Email: latinas@latinas.org

Web: www.latinas.org

HISPANIC ADVISORY COUNCIL TO THE LOS ANGELES POLICE COMMISSION
841 Coffman Dr.
Montebello, CA 90640-2405
(909) 923-9694 Fax: (626) 450-6262
Al Robles, Chair

HISPANIC AGENTS & BROKERS ASSOC.
8534 B Long Beach Blvd.
S. Gate, CA 90280
(213) 587-6326 Fax: (213) 587-2082
Javier F. Rodríguez, Pres.

HISPANIC AMERICAN ALLERGY AND IMMUNOLOGY ASSOCIATION
4644 Lincoln Blvd., #4644
Marina del Rey, CA 90292
(310) 823-6766 Fax: (310) 823-6966
Email: email@haama.org
Web: www.haama.org

HISPANIC BUSINESS ASSOCIATION INTERNATIONAL (HBA)
420 South Euclid Ave., #115
Anaheim, CA 92802
(714) 535-5899 Fax: (714) 788-3510
Mr. Frank Rosales, President
Email: frank@hispanic.org
Web: www.hispanicbusiness.org

HISPANIC BUSINESS STUDENT ASSOCIATION (HBSA)
Stanford Univ. Office of Student Activities
Grad. School of Business
350 Memorial Way
Stanford, CA 94309
(650) 328-4492
María D. Olide, Contact
Email: manjarrez_eli@gsb.stanford.edu

California State University
Craig School of Business
Fresno, CA 93740-8001
(559) 278-2194/5036/0333 Fax: (559) 278-4911
Rafael Solis, Advisor

California State University, Fresno
University Student Union, #306
5280 N. Jackson Ave., M/S SU36
Fresno, CA 93740-8023
(559) 278-2741
Rito Meza, President
Email: mtn03@csufresno.edu
Web: www.hbsa.net

HISPANIC CHAMBER OF COMMERCE CONTRA COSTA COUNTY
P.O. Box 23964
Pleasant Hill, CA 94523
(925) 335-5125 or (925) 427-5260
Fax: (925) 228-5515
Javier Aguero, Member
Email: info@h5c.org

HISPANIC CHAMBER OF COMMERCE MONTEREY COUNTY
5 E. Gabilon St., #214
Salinas, CA 93901
(831) 757-1251 Fax: (831) 757-1607
Blanca Zarazua, President & CEO
Email: hccmc@redshift.com

HISPANIC CHAMBER OF COMMERCE OF ALAMEDA COUNTY
1840 Embarcadero St., #101
Oakland, CA 94606
(510) 536-4477 Fax: (510) 536-4320
Pete Uribes, President
Email: hcca@pacbell.net

HISPANIC CHAMBER OF COMMERCE OF MARIN COUNTY
P.O. Box 4423
San Rafael, CA 94913
(415) 721-9686 or (415) 898-0644
Fax: (415) 331-2223
Raul Lara, President

HISPANIC CHAMBER OF COMMERCE OF ORANGE COUNTY
2323 N. Broadway St., #305
Santa Ana, CA 92706
(714) 953-4289 Fax: (714) 953-0273
Ruben Alvarez, Executive Director
Web: www.hcoc.org

HISPANIC CHAMBER OF COMMERCE OF SONOMA COUNTY
P.O. Box 11392
Santa Rosa, CA 95406
(707) 526-7744 Fax: (707) 526-5049

Estela Sterner, Executive Director

HISPANIC CHAMBER OF COMMERCE OF STANISLAUS COUNTY
400 12th St., #2
Modesto, CA 95354
(209) 575-2597 Fax: (209) 575- 4371
Geraldo Ramos, President
Email: slackykey@hispaniccommerce.org
Web: www.hispaniccommerce.org

HISPANIC CHAMBER OF COMMERCE OF THE CITY AND COUNTY OF MERCED
1640 N. St., #2240
Merced, CA 95340
(209) 384-9537 Fax: (209) 783-5051
Liz Chavez, Executive Director
Email: admin@adelantemerced.org
Web: www.adelantemerced.org

HISPANIC CHAMBER OF COMMERCE SAN MATEO COUNTY
c/o Centro de Libertad
650 Main St., #200
Redwood City, CA 94062
(650)371-4133 Fax: (650) 599-9821
Ostencia Lopez, President

HISPANIC CHAMBER OF COMMERCE SANTA CLARA COUNTY
1376 N. 4th St.
San Jose, CA 95112
(408) 467-9890 Fax: (408) 467-9899
Alex C. Torres, President & CEO
Email: info@hispanicchamberonline.com
Web: www.hispanicchamberonline.com

HISPANIC CHAMBER OF VENTURA COUNTY
P.O.Box 426
Oxnard, CA 93032
(805) 486-0266 Fax: (805) 385-3341
Mary Ellison, Director

HISPANIC CLUSTER GROUP
291 S. La Cienaga Blvd., #308
Beverly Hills, CA 90211
(310) 652-6449 Fax: (310) 652-5462
Richard Cervantes, Pres.

HISPANIC COALITION OF MONTEBELLO
P.O. Box 3171
Montebello, CA 90640
(562) 464-3707 Fax: (562) 464-3709
Ms. María C. Halpern, President

HISPANIC COMMUNITY FOUNDATION
National Headquarters
50 California St., Suite 300
San Francisco, CA 94111
(415) 981-8421 Fax: (415) 981-8421
Richard Santos Navarro, President
Email: info@hispanicfoundation.org
Web: www.hispanicfoundation.org

HISPANIC CONTRACTORS ASSOCIATION
420 Euclid Ave.
Anaheim, CA 92802
(714) 491-0900 Fax: (714) 778-3510
Mr. Frank Rosales, President
Email: frank@hispanic.org
Web: www.hispanicbusiness.org

HISPANIC EDUCATION FOUNDATION
Granada Village Ctr.
P.O. Box 33257
Granada Hills, CA 91394-0028
(818) 360-1475 Fax: (818) 360-0788
José G. Castillo, Pres.
Email: josecast@aol.com

HISPANIC EDUCATION MEDIA GROUP INC.
P.O. Box 221
Sausalito, CA 94966
(415) 331-8560 or (415) 332-2731
Fax: (415) 331-2636
Email: PublicRelations@hemg.org
Web: www.hemg.org

HISPANIC EMPLOYEES ASSOCIATION OF PG&E
Pacific Gas and Electric Co.
PO Box 770000
Mail Code B9A, Rm. 959
San Francisco, CA 94177
(415) 973-3633 Fax: (415) 973-7131
Maria Uribe Padrones, Corporate Liaison

HISPANIC EMPLOYMENT PROGRAM
Veterans Affairs Medical Center
5901 E. 7th St.
Long Beach, CA 90822
(562) 494-2611x4209 Fax: (562) 494-5531

Rafael Rivera-Cotto, Prog. Manager

HISPANIC ENGINEER NATIONAL ACHIEVEMENT AWARDS CONF. (HENAAC)
242 West Hammel Street
Monterey Park, CA 91754
(323) 727-9673 Fax: (323) 727-9384
Loretta Rosas, Executive Director
Web: www.henaac.org

HISPANIC FESTIVITIES COMMITTEE, LOS ANGELES CO.
USC Medical Center
1200 N. State St., 1112 K
Los Angeles, CA 90033
(323) 226-6899 Fax: (323) 226-2608
Adelaida de la Cerda, Public Relations
Email: adlacerda@lacusc.com

HISPANIC FOSTER PARENTS ASSOCIATION
712 Rio del Sol
Montebello, CA 90640
(213) 722-4900
Frank Gallegos, Pres.

HISPANIC LAW ENFORCEMENT ADMINISTRATORS (HLEA)
Hollenbeck Division
2111 E. 1st. Street
Los Angeles, CA 90033
(213) 485-2941 Fax: (323) 264-8167
Paul Pesqueira, Pres.

HISPANIC LEADERS COALITION OF CALIFORNIA
219 N. Segovia Ave.
San Gabriel, CA 91775-2945
(626) 570-0502 Fax: (626) 570-1208
Ralph Roy Ramírez, Pres.

HISPANIC NATIONAL BAR ASSOC. (HNBA)
550 West C St., #1880
San Diego, CA 92101
(619) 615-6672 Fax: (619) 615-6673
Roberta Sistos, Secretary
Email: rsistos@bwslaw.com
Web: www.hnba.com

Region XVII (Northern CA, HI)
280 S. 1st St., #371
San Jose, CA 95113
(408) 535-5065 Fax: (408) 535-5066
Carlos Singh, Regional President
Email: Carlos.Singh@usdoj.gov
Web: www.hnba.com

Region XVIII (Southern CA)
1875 Century Park East, #500
Los Angeles, CA 90049
(310) 556-8861 Fax: (310) 553-2165
Lester Aponte, Regional President
Email: laponte@ebglaw.com
Web: www.hnba.com

HISPANIC NETWORK (HI-NET)
1147 E. Broadway #138
Glendale, CA 91205
(818) 956-0555 Fax: (818) 956-8001
Carlos Rodríguez, President
Email: hinet@eralatina.com
Web: www.eralatina.com

HISPANIC NETWORK (HISNET)
P.O. Box 92426
Los Angeles, CA 90009
(310) 334-2089 Fax: (310) 973-0675
Jaime Sanchez, Pres.
Email: gmonteros@earthlink.net

HISPANIC OUTREACH TASKFORCE (HOT)
12102 Washington Blvd.
Whittier, CA 90606
(562) 945-5096 Fax: (562) 698-6238
Pete Gomez, Pres.

HISPANIC PUBLIC RELATIONS ASSOC.
National Headquarters
735 S. Figueroa St., #818
Los Angeles, CA 90017-2571
(213) 239-6555 ext. 204 Fax: (213) 239-6550
Charles Sifuentes, President

HISPANIC SCHOLARSHIP FUND (HSF)
National Headquarters
1 Sansome St., #1000
San Francisco, CA 94104
(415) 445-9930 Fax: (415) 445-9942
Sara Martínez Tucker, President
Email: info@hsf.net
Web: www.hsf.net

HISPANIC STUDENT BUSINESS ASSOCIATION (HSBA)
California State University, Long Beach
Student Life & Development
1250 Bellflower Blvd. USU 206
Long Beach, CA 90840
(562) 985-4181 or (562) 667-9847 (H)
Fax: (562) 985-5683
Eugene A. Santos, President

HISPANIC STUDENTS FELLOWSHIPS
Biola Universtly
13800 Biola Ave.
La Mirada, CA 90639
(562) 903-4874 Fax: (562) 906-4567
Cesar Gallardo, President
Web: www.biola.edu

HISPANIC TRADITIONS & HERITAGE COUNCIL.
3509 1/2 W. Beverly Blvd.
Montebello, CA 90640
(323) 728-9991 Fax: (323) 725-0939
Mary George, President
Email: hucla@aol.com

HISPANIC URBAN LEAGUE
1201 E. 1st. St.
Los Angeles, CA 90033
(323) 264-4494 Fax: (323) 621-0937
Rosie Rosales, Director

HISPANIC WOMEN'S COUNCIL OF CALIFORNIA
Affiliate to NCLR
3509 W. Beverly Blvd.
Montebello, CA 90640-1540
(323) 728-9991 Fax: (323) 725-0939
Isela Carbajal-Edwards, President

HISPANICS FOR L.A. OPERA
135 North Grand Ave.
Los Angeles, CA 90012
(213) 368-9600 Fax: (213) 972-3007
Mr. Gilbert Moret, Chair
Email: rmarquez@laopera.com
Web: www.laopera.org

HISPANICS FOR LIFE & HUMAN RIGHTS
P.O. Box 9086
Torrance, CA 90501
(310) 320-9640 or (310) 863-8483
Steve Barbosa, Pres.

HISPANICS IN ACTION
St. Domenics Church
2002 Merton Ave.
Los Angeles, CA 90041
(213) 254-2519 Fax: (213) 255-3067
Humberto Salas, Pres.

HISPANO-AMERICAN CLUB
El Monte Sr. Ctr.
3120 N. Tyler Ave.
El Monte, CA 91731
(626) 580-2210 Fax: (626) 444-5056
Susan Villalobos, Pres.
Email: MLast@juno.com

HOLLENBECK CULTURAL CENTER
Department of Recreation and Parks
415 South St. Louis St.
Los Angeles, CA 90033
(213) 261-0113 Fax: (818) 547-1150
Monica Resendez, Dir.

HOMELESS OUTREACH PROGRAM
333 South Central Ave.
Los Angeles, CA 90013
(213) 621-2800 Fax: (213) 621-4119
Mike Neely, Dir.

HOSPITALS AND SERVICE EMPLOYEES UNION
Local 399
1247 West 7th St.
Los Angeles, CA 90017
(213) 680-9567 Fax: (213) 680-4702
David Bullock, President

HOTEL EMPLOYEES, RESTAURANT EMPLOYEES
Local 11, AFL-CIO
321 S. Bixel St.
Los Angeles, CA 90017
(213) 481-8530 Fax: (213) 481-0352
María Elena Durazo, Pres.

Local 814
525 Colorado Ave.
Santa Monica, CA 90401
(310) 451-9701 Fax: (310) 451-4385
Tom Walsh, President

HOUSE OF PRAYER LUTHERAN CHURCH
795 N. Rose
Escondido, CA 92027
(760) 738-8940
Roberto López, Director

HUMAN RELATIONS COMMISSION CITY OF LOS ANGELES
200 N. Main St, City Hall East, Room 700
Los Angeles, CA 90012
(213) 485-4495 Fax: (213) 485-4390
Joe Hicks, Exec. Dir.

HUNTINGTON PARK CHAMBER OF COMMERCE
6330 Pacific Blvd. #208
Huntington Park, CA 90255
(213) 585-1155 Fax: (213) 585-2176
Ray Reyna, Pres.

IBERIA: SPANISH ASSOCIATION AT STANFORD
Stanford Univ. Office of Student Activities
Escondido Village 42D
Stanford, CA 94305
(650) 497-7490
Pablo Molinero-Fernández, Contact
Email: manel@leland

IMAGE DE HAYWARD
National Image, Inc.
27273 S. Sleepyhollow #102
Hayward, CA 94542
(510) 783-5059
Sonya Valderrama, President
Web: www.nationimageinc.org

IMAGE DE SAN DIEGO
Nation Image, Inc.
P.O. Box 17273
San Diego, CA 92177-7273
(619) 545-5646 or (619) 656-2856 (H)
(619) 979-7542 (Pager)
Marlow Martínez, President
Email: Martinez_M@A1.nadepni.navy.mil
Web: www.nationalimageinc.org

IMAGEN FOUNDATION
18034 Ventura Blvd., PMB 261
Encino, CA 91316
(323) 644-7965 Fax: (323) 644-2797
Ms. Helen Hernández, Chair
Email: info@imagen.org
Web: www.imagen.org

IMANI UNIDOS AIDS PROJECT
1713 West 108th St.
Los Angeles, CA 90047
(323) 754-8453 Fax: (323) 754-1506
Rev. Velma Miller, Administrative Council

IMPACTO
Proyecto Pastoral at Dolores Mission
1836 E. 1st St.
Los Angeles, CA 90033
(323) 269-7552 Fax: (323) 269-8554
Francisco Chavez, Director
Web: www.proyectopastoral.org

INDIOS DE JUAREZ BASEBALL CLUB
608 N. Duff Ave.
La Puente, CA 91744
(626) 918-6927
José Ramiro Pérez, Coach

INLAND EMPIRE HISPANIC CHAMBER OF COMMERCE
255 North D St., #217
San Bernardino, CA 92401
(909) 888-2188 Fax: (909) 888-1151
Linda Boswell, President
Email: ie_chamber@eee.org
Web: www.iehcc.org

INLEKECH CULTURAL ARTS CENTER
632 W. Guava St.
Oxnard, CA 93033
(805) 486-7468 Fax: (805) 486-7468
Javier M. Gomez, Director

INNER CITY ARTS
720 Kohler St.
Los Angeles, CA 90021
(213) 627-9621 Fax: (213) 627-6469
Cynthia Harnisch, Executive Director
Email: cynthia@inner-cityarts.com
Web: www.inner-cityarts.com

INSTITUTE OF THE AMERICAS
University of California, San Diego
10111 N. Torrey Pines Rd.
La Jolla, CA 92037
(619) 453-5560 Fax: (619) 453-2165
Paul H. Boeker, President
Web: www.iamericas.org

INSTITUTO FAMILIAR DE LA RAZA
Administrative Office
2837 Mission Street
San Francisco, CA 94110
(415) 647-4141 Fax: (415) 647-3662
Concepcion Salcedo, Director

Latino AIDS Services
2639 24th St.
San Francisco, CA 94110
(415) 647-5450 Fax: (415) 647-0740
Gerardo Ramos, Director

INSTITUTO LABORAL DE LA RAZA
2947 16th St.
San Francisco, CA 94103
(415) 431-7522 Fax: (415) 431-4846
Sarah M.Shaker, Director
Email: llaboral@aol.com

INSTITUTO LITERARIO Y CULTURAL HISPANICO
8452 Furman Ave.
Westminster, CA 92683
(714) 892-8285 Fax: (714) 892-8285
Juana A. Arancibia, Pres.
Email: enchja@aol.com

INTER-AMERICAN CLUB
15009 Hamblin St.
Van Nuys, CA 91411
(818) 765-0469 Fax: (818) 765-3931
Angel M. Suarez, Pres.

INTERCOMMUNITY CHILD GUIDANCE CTR.
8106 Broadway Ave.
Whittier, CA 90606
(562) 692-0383 Fax: (562) 692-0380
Charlene Dimas Peinado, Director
Email: icgc@cernet. com

INTERNATIONAL CHAMBER OF COMMERCE OF SAN YSIDRO
522 E. San Ysidro Blvd.
San Ysidro, CA 92173
(619) 428-9530 Fax: (619) 428-9467
Alberto R. García, President

INTERNATIONAL INSTITUTION OF L. A.
435 S. Boyle Ave.
Los Angeles, CA 90033
(213) 264-6217 or (213) 264-6210
Fax: (213) 264-4623
Stephen Boss, Exec. Dir.

INTERNATIONAL RESCUE COMMITTEE, INC.
1801 W. 17th St.
Santa Ana, CA 92706
(714) 741-6146 or (714) 547-5683
Fax: (714) 547-8738
Cindy Janson, Chair.

4535 30th St., #110
San Diego, CA 92116
(619) 641-7510 Fax: (619) 641-7520
Cindy Janson, Chair.

INTERNATIONAL STUDENTS ASSOCIATION
Santa Barbara City College
721 Cliff Dr.
Santa Barbara, CA 93109
(805) 965-0581 ext 2296 Fax: (805) 965-7221
Gail Reynolds, Advisor

JALISCO CLUBS FEDERATION
11100 Valley Blvd. # 202
El Monte, CA 91734
(626) 448-6261 Fax: (626) 448-7219
Lorena Vargas, President

JET PROPULSION LABORATORY (JPL) - AMIGOS UNIDOS
4800 Oak Grove Dr., M.S: 169-315
Pasadena, CA 91109
(818) 354-3211 Fax: (818) 393-4802
Ruth Monárrez, Software Engineer
Email: ruth.monarrez@jpl.nasa.gov

JOBS FOR A FUTURE (JFF)
Proyecto Pastoral at Dolores Mission
1848 E. 1st St.
Los Angeles, CA 90033
(323) 526-1254 Fax: (323) 526-1257
Fr. Greg Boyle, S.J., Director
Email: info@proyectopastoral.org

Web: www.proyectopastoral.org

JOBS FOR PROGRESS, INC./SER EAST L.A.
Affiliate of SER-Jobs for Progress National, Inc.
5161 E. Pomona Blvd., #106
Los Angeles, CA 90022
(323) 881-0588 Fax: (323) 881-0575
Salvador F. Rivera, Executive Officer
Web: www.sernational.org

JOBS FOR PROGRESS, INC./SER-SOUTH BAY
Affiliate of SER-Jobs for Progress National, Inc.
15342 S. Hawthorne Blvd., #301
Lawndale, CA 90260
(310) 263-2650 Fax: (310) 263-2663
Rick D. Sánchez, Executive Director
Email: seracademy@earthlink.net
Web: www.serjobswest.org

JOVENES, INC.
300 W. Cesar Chavez Ave.
Los Angeles, CA 90026
(213) 346-0123 Fax: (213) 346-0120
Richard Estrada, Exec. Dir.

JUNTA PATRIOTICA CUBANA REGIONAL DE CALIFORNIA
710 S. Verdugo Rd.
Glendale, CA 91205
(818) 240-3474 or (909) 595-2088
Ruz Aparicio, President

JUVENTUD FRANCISCANA
218 E. 12th St.
Los Angeles, CA 90015
(213) 748-5394 Fax: (213) 748-4793
Father Pedro Oumana, Dir.

KAISER FAMILY FOUNDATION
2400 Sand Hill Rd.
Menlo Park, CA 94025
(650) 854-9400 Fax: (650) 854-4800
Drew E. Altman, Ph.D., President
Web: www.kff.org

KAISER PERMANENTE LATINO ASSOCIATION (KPLA)
6600 Bruceville Rd.
Sacramento, CA 95823
(916) 688-6334 Fax: (916) 688-6098
Susana Korn, Pres.

KEDREN HEADSTART
710 East 111th Place
Los Angeles, CA 90059
(323) 299-9742 Fax: (323) 777-6208
Carlos Fuentes, Administrative Assistant

KERN COUNTY HISPANIC CHAMBER OF COMMERCE
1401 19th St., #110
Bakersfield, CA 93301
(661) 633-5495 Fax: (661) 633-5499
Lou Gomez, President
Email: staff3@lightspeed.net
Web: www.kchcc.org

LA CASA DE LA RAZA
601 E. Montesido
Santa Barbara, CA 93103
(805) 965-8581 Fax: (805) 965-6451
Grace Florez, Director

LA CLINICA DE LA RAZA
Affiliate of NCLR
1515 Fruitvale Ave.
Oakland, CA 94601
(510) 535-4000 Fax: (510) 535-4189
Jane García, Executive Director
Email: mtorres@laclinica.org
Web: www.laclinica.org

LA CLINICA DE LA RAZA
Clinica Alta Vista
3022 International Blvd.
Oakland, CA 94601
(510) 535-4230 Fax: (510) 535-4019
Tina Simmons, Site Manager
Web: www.laclinica.org

LA CLINICA DE LA RAZA
San Antonio Neighborhood Health Ctr.
1030 International Blvd.
Oakland, CA 94606
(510) 238-5400 Fax: (510) 238-5437
Philipa Barron, Site Manager
Web: www.laclinica.org

LA CLINICA DEL PUEBLO
1547 N. Avalon Blvd.
Wilmington, CA 90744
(310) 830-0100 Fax: (310) 830-0187
Gina Aquino, Exec. Dir.

LA FAMILIA COUNSELING SERVICE
Affiliate of NCLR
26081 Mocine Ave.
Hayward, CA 94544
(510) 881-5921 Fax: (510) 881-5925
Héctor Méndez, Executive Director
Email: lfamilia@ix.netcom.com

LA RAZA CENTRO LEGAL
474 Calle Valencia, #295
San Francisco, CA 94103
(415) 575-3500 Fax: (415) 255-7593
Victor Marquez, Executive Director

LA RAZA FACULTY ASSOCIATION OF THE CALIFORNIA COMMUNITY COLLEGES
5209 E. Hamilton
Fresno, CA 93727
(559) 251-2486
Venancio Ganoa, President

LA RAZA GRADUATE STUDENT ASSOCIATION
University of California, Los Angeles
Cesar E. Chavez Center
405 Hilgard Ave. 7349 Bunch Hall
Los Angeles, CA 90095-1559
(310) 206-7695 Fax: (310) 825-2449
Eli Hernandez, Advisor

LA RAZA INFORMATION CENTER, INC.
474 Valencia Street, Suite 100
San Francisco, CA 94103
(415) 863-0764 Fax: (415) 863-1690
Melba Maldonado, Exec. Dir.
Email: la-raza@pacbell.com

LA RAZA JOURNAL
University of California, Berkeley
Student Activities & Services
102 Sproul Hall
Berkeley, CA 94720
(510) 642-9351 or (510) 649-0400
Ernest Ceverio
Email: ernic@uclink4.berkeley.edu

LA RAZA STUDENT ASSOCIATION
California State U.-203, Long Beach
1212 Bellflower Blvd.
Long Beach, CA 19815
(562) 985-5223 or (562) 985-4181
Salvador Madrigal, President

LA RAZA TRANSLATING SERVICES
474 Valencia St., #100
San Francisco, CA 94103
(415) 863-1503 Fax: (415) 863-1690
Silvia Ramírez, Director

LA RAZA UNIDA PARTY
P.O. Box 13
San Fernando, CA 91340
(818) 365-6534 or (818) 361-5994
Genaro Ayala, Dir.

LABOR COUNCIL FOR LATIN AMERICAN ADVANCEMENT (LCLAA)
Los Angeles Chapter
P.O. Box 31198
2130 West 9th St.
Los Angeles, CA 90006
(213) 630-2112 Fax: (213) 427-9056
Armando Olivos, Chapt. Pres.

LAKEWOOD PAN AMERICAN FESTIVAL
Recreation & Community Services
Department, Lakewood City Hall
5050 N. Clark Ave.
Lakewood, CA 90712
(562) 866-9771 x 2408
Fax: (562) 866-0505
Lisa Litzenger, Cont.

LAMBDA THETA NU SORORITY, INC.
University of California, Davis
Student Programs & Activities Ctr., Box #432
1 Shields Ave.
Davis, CA 95616-8706
(530) 752-2027 or (530) 750-3976
Fax: (530) 752-4951
Analilia Gurrola, President
Email: amgurrola@ucdavis.edu
Web: www.ucdavis.edu

LAMP/LAMPARA
627 S. San Julian St.

Los Angeles, CA 90014
(213) 488-0031 or (213) 488-9559
Fax: (213) 488-4934
Mollie Lowre, ED

LAS FAMILIAS
307 E. 7th St.
Los Angeles, CA 90014
(213) 614-1745 Fax: (213) 614-2046
Alice Calaghan, Director

LATIN AMERICAN CENTER
University of California, Los Angeles
10343 Bunche Hall
405 Hilgard Ave.
Los Angeles, CA 90095-1447
(310) 825-4571 Fax: (310) 206-6859
Carlos Alberto Torres, Director

LATIN AMERICAN CHILDREN FDTN.
1709 N. Buena Vista St.
Burbank, CA 91505
(818) 842-9441 Fax: (818) 842-1349
Hugo Héctor Rodríguez, Treasurer

LATIN AMERICAN CIVIC ASSOCIATION
340 Parkside Dr.
San Fernando, CA 91340
(818) 361-8641 Fax: (818) 361-1546
Irene Tovar, Secretary to the Director
Email: laca@gte.net

1248 Kewen St.
San Fernando, CA 91340
(818) 361-8641 Fax: (818) 361-1546
Irene Tovar, Secretary to the Director
Email: laca@gte.net

LATIN AMERICAN DENTAL ASSOC. (LADA)
528 S. Amalia Avenue
Los Angeles, CA 90022
(323) 262-2727 Fax: (323) 263-8707
Ramiro F. Sanchez, President

LATIN AMERICAN MUSICIANS UNION
2765 Willow Pl.
South Gate, CA 90280
(323) 564-2016
María Graciela, President

LATIN AMERICAN NATIONAL SENIOR CITIZENS ASSOCIATION
1241 Valencia
San Francisco, CA 94110
(415) 282-6337
Luis Manuel Blandino, President

LATIN AMERICAN PROFESSIONAL WOMEN'S ASSOCIATION (LAPWA)
Affiliate of NCLR
P.O.Box 31532
Los Angeles, CA 90031
(213) 227-9060 or (562) 803-1400
Fax: (213) 227-8698 or (562) 803-1211
Rose Provencio-Meza, President

LATIN AMERICAN STUDENT ASSOC. (LASA)
501Westwood Plaza
312F Kerckhoff Hall
Los Angeles, CA 90024
(310) 206-2631
Sandra Escalante, President
Email: lasa@ucla.edu

Stanford Univ. Office of Student Activities
P.O. Box 13618
Stanford, CA 94305
(650) 497-3951
Paola Marusich, Contact
Email: fichtner@leland

LATIN AMERICAN STUDENT ORG.
College of San Mateo
1700 W. Hillsdale Blvd.
San Mateo, CA 94402
(650) 574-6332 or (415) 574-6248
Martha Gutierrez/Tania Beliz, Director

LATIN AMERICAN STUDIES
California State University, Fullerton
800 N. State College Blvd.
Fullerton, CA 92834
(714) 278-2594 Fax: (714) 278-5898
Robert Voeks, Coordinator
Email: rvoeks@fullerton.edu
Web: http://hss.fullerton.edu

LATIN AMERICAN STUDIES CENTER
California State University, Los Angeles
5151 State University Dr.
Los Angeles, CA 90032
(323) 343-2180 Fax: (323) 343-5485
Margarie Bray, Coordinator

LATIN BUSINESS ASSOCIATION (LBA)
5400 E. Olympic Blvd., #130
Los Angeles, CA 90022-5113
(323) 721-4000 Fax: (323) 722-5050
Richard Verches, President
Web: www.lbausa.com

LATINA & ASSOCIATION, INC.
P.O. Box 550
San Diego, CA 92112
(619) 426-1491 Fax: (619) 426-3206
Fanny Miller, Pres.

LATINA LAWYERS COMMITTEE OF THE MEXICAN AMERICAN BAR ASSOCIATION
Los Angeles Chapter.
312 N. Spring St. #1503
Los Angeles, CA 90012
(213) 894-4298 Fax: (213) 894-0081
Teresa Sánchez-Gordon, Chair.

LATINA LEADERSHIP NETWORK
Gavilan College
5055 Santa Teresa Blvd.
Gilroy, CA 95020
(408) 848-4740 or (408) 848-4790
Fax: (408) 848-4801
Gloria Luna, Advisor
Email: gluna@mad1.gavilan.cc.ca.us

LATINA LEADERSHIP NETWORK OF THE CALIFORNIA COMMUNITY COLLEGES BUTTE COLLEGE
3536 Butte Campus Dr.
Oroville, CA 95965
(530) 895-2289 or (530) 895-2547
Fax: (530) 895-2345
Marge Rivas, President
Email: rivasma@butte.cc.ca.us
Web: www.butte.cc.ca.us

LATINAS RECOVERY HOME
Centro Hispano de Recuperacion del Alcoholismo
327 N. St. Louis
Los Angeles, CA 90033
(626) 444-6374 Fax: (626) 444-8602
Irene Soto Simmons, Project Director

LATINIC SOCIETAS UNITAS
UC Riverside, Chicano Students Program
229 Costo Hall
Riverside, CA 92521
(909) 787-3821 Fax: (909) 787-2189
Alfredo Figueroa, Director
Email: alfredo.figueroa@ucr.edu

LATINO BUSINESS STUDENT ASSOC.
UC Riverside
Chicano Student Program
229 Costo Hall
Riverside, CA 92521
(909) 787-3821 Fax: (909) 787-2189
Alfredo Figueroa, Director
Email: alfredo.figueroa@ucr.edu

LATINO BUSINESS STUDENT ASSOC.
Loyola Marymount University Student Life
7900 Loyola Blvd.
Los Angeles, CA 90045
(310) 338-5808 or (310) 338-2877
Fax: (310) 338-1805
Marshal Sauceda, Advisor
Web: www.lmu.org

Cal State Polytechnic University, Pomona
3801 W. Temple Ave.
Pomona, CA 91768
(909) 869-3367 or (909) 869-4672
Art Covarrubias, Advisor

LATINO CHAMBER OF COMMERCE OF COMPTON
208 N. Long Beach Blvd.
Compton, CA 90221
(310) 639-4455 Fax: (310) 639-4455
Pedro Pallan, President

LATINO CHAMBER OF COMMERCE OF POMONA VALLEY
142 East 3rd St.
Pomona, CA 91766
(909) 469-0702 Fax: (909) 469-0604
Manuel Castillejos, President
Email: camlat@gte.net

LATINO CHAMBER OF COMMERCE OF SANTA CRUZ COUNTY
P.O. Box 1436
Watsonville, CA 95077
(831) 728-2881 Fax: (831) 728-1627
Luis De La Cruz, Executive Director

LATINO COALITION FOR A HEALTHY CALIFORNIA
1535 Mission St.
San Francisco, CA 94103
(415) 431-7430 Fax: (415) 431-1048
Lia Margolis, Executive Director
Email: info@lchc.org
Web: www.lchc.org

LATINO ENTERTAINMENT MEDIA INSTITUTE (LEMI)
146 N. San Fernando Blvd., #201
Burbank, CA 91502
(818) 846-1394 Fax: (818) 846-9419
Bel Hernández, President

LATINO FACULTY, STAFF AND STUDENT ASSOCIATION,CAL POLY POMONA
Office of Financial Aid, California State Polytechnic University, Pomona
Pomona, CA 91768
(909) 869-3715 or (909) 869-3700
Fax: (909) 869-4757
Roseanna Ruiz, President
Email: RRuiz@CSUPOMONA.edu

LATINO FAMILY ALCOHOL AND DRUG ABUSE CENTER
5801 East Beverly Blvd.
Los Angeles, CA 90022
(323) 722-4529 Fax: (323) 722-4450
Isabel Lanzana, Director

LATINO FAMILY INSTITUTE
9920 La Cienaga Boulevard #806
Inglewood, CA 90301
(800) 294-9161 Fax: (310) 348-7310
Maria Quintanilla, Prog. Coord.

LATINO FAMILY PRESERVATION PROJECT
2501 Davidson Dr.
Monterey Park, CA 91754
(323) 260-3120 Fax: (323) 264-2675
Robert Lafarge, Prog. Dir.

LATINO FORUM
Pamona Valley Center for Community Development
1155 W. Grand
Pomona, CA 91766
(909) 629-4649 Fax: (909) 620-1599
Irma Medrano, Director

LATINO HEALTH ACCESS
1717 N. Broadway
Santa Ana, CA 92706-2605
(714) 542-7792 Fax: (714) 542-4853
America Bracho, President & CEO
Web: www.latinohealthaccess.org

THE LATINO HERITAGE MONTH ORGANIZING COMMITTEE
10850 Wilshire Blvd., #350
Los Angeles, CA 90024
(800) 756-1900 or (310) 234-6954
Fax: (310) 446-7092
Rutely Conde, Director of Public Relations
Email: festival_la@earthlink.com
Web: www.festival-la.com

LATINO ISSUES FORUM
785 Market St., 3rd Fl.
San Francisco, CA 94103
(415) 284-7220 Fax: (415) 284-7210
Guillermo Rodriguez, Jr., Executive Director
Email: LIFcentral@lif.org
Web: http://latino.sscnet.ucla.edu/community/lif/

National Headquarters
785 Market St., 3rd Floor
San Francisco, CA 94103
(415) 284-7220 Fax: (415) 284-7210
Viola Gonzales, Director
Email: lifcentral@lif.org
Web: www.lif.org

LATINO JEWISH BUSINESS ROUNDTABLE
10495 Santa Monica Blvd.
Los Angeles, CA 90025
(310) 446-8000 Fax: (310) 470-8712
Loren Stephens, Director of Development
Email: los-angeles@adl.org
Web: www.adl.org

LATINO PARENTS ASSOCIATION (LPA)
USC El Centro Chicano
817 W. 34th St., 3rd Floor
Los Angeles, CA 90089-2991
(213) 740-1480 Fax: (213) 745-6721
Martin Veras, President

LATINO PRINT NETWORK
National Association of Hispanic Publications
3445 Catalina Drive
Carsbad, CA 92008-2856
(760) 434-7474 Fax: (760) 434-7476
Kirk Whisler, Sales Coordinator
Email: kirk@whisler.com
Web: www.nahp.org

LATINO RECOVERY HOME
California Hispanic Commission on Alcohol and Drug Abuse, Inc.
2436 Wabash Ave.
Los Angeles, CA 90033
(323) 780-8756 Fax: (616) 813-0928
Christina, Assistant Director

LATINO RESOURCE ORGANIZATION
610 California Ave.
Venice, CA 90291
(310) 578-6069 Fax: (310) 578-0490
Forrest Freed, Acting Executive Director

LATINO SOCIAL WORK NETWORK OF CALIFORNIA
P.O. Box 31256
Los Angeles, CA 90031-0256
(818) 784-3815 Fax: (323)229-6699
Dolores Rodríguez, Contact

LATINO STUDENT CENTER
Santa Monica College
1900 Pico Blvd.
Santa Monica, CA 90405
(310) 450-5150x9452 Fax: (310) 399-1730
Oscar Galindo, Coord.

LATINO STUDENT HEALTH SERVICES
University of California, Los Angeles
Community Programs Office
405 Hilgard Ave., 102 Men's Gym
Los Angeles, CA 90095-1454
(310) 825-5969 or (310) 825-0068
Fax: (310) 206-3175
Michelle Eliot, Advisor

LATINO STUDENTS ASSOCIATION
Citrus Community College
1000 West Foothill Blvd.
Glendora, CA 91741
(626)914-8610 Fax: (626) 335-3159
Patricia C. Barney, Chair
Web: www.citrus.cc.ca.us/search.htm

LATINO/A COLLEGE LEADERSHIP INSTITUTE (LCLI)
1055 Wilshire Blvd. # 1615
Los Angeles, CA 90017
(213) 250-8787 Fax: (213) 250-8799
Daniel Loera, Inst. Coord.

LATINO/LATINA UNITY COALITION
610 22nd St.
San Diego, CA 92102
(619) 236-7005 Fax: (619) 236-8964
Luis Natividad, President

LATINOS IN ENGLISH
3911 Roderick Rd.
Los Angeles, CA 90065
(213) 256-6603 Fax: (818) 845-1773
Rose Sánchez, Dir.
Email: angels817@juno

LATINOS IN SCIENCE
Chicano Student Programs
UC Riverside
229 Costo Hall
Riverside, CA 92521
(909) 787-3821 Fax: (909) 787-2189
Alfredo Figueroa, Director
Email: alfredo.figueroa@ucr.edu

LAWYER REFERRAL & INFORMATION SERVICE
P. O. Box 55020
Los Angeles, CA 90055-2020
(213) 896-6443 or (213) 243-1525
Fax: (213) 896-6500
Patricia Holt, Dir.
Email: lris@lacba.org

LEAGUE OF UNITED LATIN AMERICAN CITIZENS (LULAC)
Anaheim Chapter
2736 Hempstead St.
Anaheim, CA 92806
(714) 630-1678
Rose Jurado, Chapter President
Web: www.lulac.org

National Executive Committee
17439 Bellflower Blvd.
Bellflower, CA 90706
(562) 867-4910 or (562) 936-3424
Pager: (562) 630-4206
Fax: (562) 634-4826
José R. Pacheco, V.P. for Farwest
Web: www.lulac.org

Orange County Chapter
2845 W. Ball Rd., #7
Anaheim, CA 92804
(714) 761-7928
Celia Ortega, Chapter President
Web: www.lulac.org

Orange County District #1
11591 Candy Lane
Garden Grove, CA 92840
(714) 636-7576 Fax: (714) 636-7770
Benny Diaz, District Director
Web: www.lulac.org

LEGAL AID FOUNDATION OF L.A.
Administrative Office
1102 South Crenshaw Blvd.
Los Angeles, CA 90019
(323) 964-7950 or (800) 399-4LAW
Fax: (323) 801-7945
Bruce Iwasaki, Executive Director

LEGAL SERVICES PROGRAM
Eastern Valley Branch
201 E. Mission Boulevard
Pomona, CA 91766
(909) 623-6357
Lauralea T. Saddick, Exec. Dir.

Western Valley Branch
81 North Mentor Avenue
Pasadena, CA 91106
(626) 795-3233
Lauralea T. Saddick

LEGAL SERVICES PROGRAM FOR PASADENA AND SAN GABRIEL-POMONA VALLEY
Admission Office
243 E. Mission Blvd.
Pomona, CA 91766
(909) 620-5547 Fax: (909) 865-1794
Lauralea Saddick, Executive Director
Email: lauralea@earthlink.net

LIBERTY FOR CUBAN POLITICAL PRISONERS
P.O. Box 638
2932 East Florence Avenue
Huntington Park, CA 90255
(213) 277-7990 Fax: (213) 277-7999
René Crúz, Dir.

LICEO INTERNACIONAL DE CULTURA
5456 Barton Ave.
Hollywood, CA 90038-3204
(213) 464-2419
Ela Lee, Pres.

LIDERAZGO DEL PUEBLO
1055 Wilshire Blvd., # 1615
Los Angeles, CA 90017
(213) 250-8787 Fax: (213) 250-8799
Daniel Loera, Inst. Coord.

LIGA DE ASISTENCIA CUBANA
1824 Sunset Blvd., #202
Los Angeles, CA 90026
(213) 483-4890 Fax: (213) 483-6474
Abel Pérez, President

LINCOLN HEIGHTS CHAMBER OF COMMERCE
2716 N. Broadway, #210
Los Angeles, CA 90031
(323) 221-6571 Fax: (323) 222-1030
Ron Boltz, Treasurer

LINCOLN HEIGHTS OPTIMIST CLUB
2722 N. Broadway
Los Angeles, CA 90031
(213) 625-6989 Fax: (213) 626-6439
Eiko Moriyama, Pres.

LINCOLN HEIGHTS RECREATION CENTER
2303 Workman St.
Los Angeles, CA 90031
(323) 225-2838
James J. Campbell, Director

LOAVES AND FISHES III
Santa Rosa Community Ctr.
511 Kalisher St.
San Fernando, CA 91340

(818) 365-3194 Fax: (818) 365-4645
Gabriel Hernandez, Coord.

LOLA MONTES FOUNDATION FOR DANCES OF SPAIN AND THE AMERICAS
1529 N. Commonwealth Ave.
Los Angeles, CA 90027-5513
(323) 664-3288 Fax: (323) 663-7742
Lola Montes, Director

LONG BEACH FAIR HOUSING FOUNDATION
200 Pine Ave. #240
Long Beach, CA 90807
(562) 901-0608 Fax: (562)901-0814
Barbara Mowery, Executive Director

LOS AMIGOS DEL PUEBLO
P.O. Box 1595
Beverly Hills, CA 90213-1595
(310) 271-4386 Fax: (310) 271-4571
Lauro Neri, Pres.

LOS ANGELES BAPTIST CITY MISSION SOCIEDAD
605 W. Olympic Blvd. #700
Los Angeles, CA 90015
(213) 955-9948 Fax: (213) 955-4940
Samuel Chetti, Exec. Minister

LOS ANGELES BOYS AND GIRLS CLUB
2635 Pasadena Ave.
Los Angeles, CA 90031
(213) 221-9111 Fax: (213) 223-9846
Robert Dyer, Exec. Dir.

LOS ANGELES COUNTY BAR ASSOC. DISPUTE RESOLUTION SERVICES, INC.
P.O. Box 55020
617 S. Olive Street, Suite 610
Los Angeles, CA 90014
(213) 896-6533 Fax: (213) 613-1299
Deborah Thomas, Exec. Dir.
Email: drs@lacba.org

LOS ANGELES COUNTY BILINGUAL DIRECTORS ASSOCIATION
Office of the Superintendent of Schools
Los Angeles Office of Education
9300 E. Imperial Hwy., Room 299
Downey, CA 90242-2890
(562) 922-6320 Fax: (562) 922-6699
Norma Acuña, Co-Chair
Email: austin-norma@lacoe.ew

LOS ANGELES COUNTY HISPANIC MANAGERS ASSOCIATION (LACHMA)
P.O. Box 92462
City of Industry, CA 91715
(323) 890-7945 Fax: (323) 890-7818
Angie Medina, President
Email: anmedina@dhs.co.la.ca.us

LOS ANGELES MISSION
303 E. 5th St.
Los Angeles, CA 90013
(213) 629-1227 Fax: (213) 430-0567
Eric Soley, Pres.

LOS ANGELES MOTHERS AGAINST DRUNK DRIVING (LA MADD)
P.O. Box 451217
Westchester, CA 90045
(818) 325-0235 or (310) 215-2905
Fax: (310) 215-2908
Tina Pasco, Exec. Dir.
Email: MADDLACA@PACBELL.NET
Web: www.maddlosangeles.org

LOS ANGELES MUSIC AND ART SCHOOL
3630 E. 3rd St.
Los Angeles, CA 90063
(213) 262-7734 or (213) 261-3289
Fax: (213) 262-2805
Isella Sotelo, Dir.

LOS ANGELES NEIGHBORHOOD DEVELOPMENT CORP. (LANDCORP)
Afiliated to NCLR
1 West Hellman, Suite 10
Alhambra, CA 91803
(626) 572-2690 Fax: (626) 572-6695
Claude Martinez, Exec. Dir.

LOS ANGELES TEAM MENTORING, INC.
600 Wilshire Blvd., #620
Los Angeles, CA 90017
(213) 489-5667 Fax: (213) 489-3744

Barbara Lehrner, Executive Director
Email: TeamWorkLA@aol.com
Web: http://clnet.ucr.edu/community/intercambios/latm/

LOS ANGELES TIMES SUMMER CAMP FUND
Times Mirror Square, 2nd Floor
Los Angeles, CA 90053
(213) 237-5763 Fax: (213) 237-4609
Raul Bustillas, Executive Director

LOS ANGELES WOMEN'S FOUNDATION
6030 Wilshire Blvd., #303
Los Angeles, CA 90036
(323) 938-9828 Fax: (323) 938-0129
Bernice Bratter, President
Web: www.lawf.org

LOS ANGELES YOUTH NETWORK
1550 Gower St.
Los Angeles, CA 90028
(323) 957-7364 Fax: (323) 957-7369
Kissiah Young, Program Coordinator
Email: contactus@layn.org
Web: www.layn.org

LOS BOMBEROS
P.O. Box 532743
Los Angeles, CA 90053-2743
(213) 485-5979 Fax: (213) 847-5458
Martin Garza, Pres.

LOS CALIFORNIANOS
P.O. Box 1693
San Leandro, CA 94577-0169
(510) 276-5429 or (510) 638-3496
Beatrice C. Turner, Treasurer

LOS DANZANTES DE AZTLAN
California State University
Department of Chicano/Latin American Studies
5340 N. Campus Drive, M/S 97
Fresno, CA 93740-0097
(209) 278-2836 or (209) 278-3991
Fax: (209) 278-6468
Victor Torres, Advisor

LOS HERMANOS DE STANFORD
Stanford Univ. Office of Student Activities
P.O. Box 16260
Stanford, CA 94309
(650) 497-2411
José Ferrel, Contact
Email: angarcia@leland
Web: www.stanford.edu/group/hermanos

LOS INGENIEROS
UC Santa Barbara
College of Engineering
Santa Barbara, CA 93106
(805) 893-4026 Fax: (805) 893-4697
Raymond Norton, Advisor

LOS LUPEÑOS DE SAN JOSE
P.O. Box 997
San Jose, CA 95108
(408) 292-0443 Fax: (408) 292-0470
Richard Aldeg, Executive Director
Email: loslupenos@aol.com
Web: www.loslupenos.org

LOS NIÑOS
287 G. St.
Chula Vista, CA 91910
(619) 426-9110 Fax: (619) 426-6664
William Bramley, Chair of Board
Email: losninos@electriciti.com
Web: www.electriciti.com/~losninos

LOS POBLADORES 200
1122 West Cruzes St.
Willmington, CA 90744-1904
(310) 326-9556
Robert E. Smith, Pres.

LULAC STATE COUNCIL & DISTRICT OFFICES
Placentia
5340 Circulo Nuevo
Yorba Linda, CA 926810
(714) 777-6810
Cory A. Aguirre, President
Web: www.lulac.org

LULAC-NATIONAL EDUCATIONAL SERVICES CENTER, INC. (LNESC)
360 E. Holt Ave.

Pomona, CA 91767
(909) 623-0588 Fax: (909) 620-5488
María Vanegas, Director
Email: lnesclapo@aol.com
Web: www.lulac.org

2390 Mission St., #304
San Francisco, CA 94110
(415) 206-1155 Fax: (415) 206-1156
Angel Max Guerrero, Director
Web: www.lulac.org

M.E.N.T.E.
Education Opportunity Program, Chicano
Component
UC Santa Barbara Bldg #434
Santa Barbara, CA 93106
(805) 893-4484

**MADERA HISPANIC CHAMBER OF
COMMERCE**
123 North D St., #F
Madera, CA 93638
(559) 674-8821 Fax: (559) 674-9084
Marge Esquibel, President

**MADRES DEL ESTE DE LOS ANGELES
SANTA ISABEL**
924 South Mott Street
Los Angeles, CA 90023
(213) 269-9898 Fax: (213) 269-2446
Juana B. Gutiérrez, President
Email: melasi@earthlink.net
Web: http://clnet.ucr.edu/community/
intercambios/melasi/

MAHAR HOUSE CYCS
1115 Mahar Ave.
Wilmington, CA 90744
(310) 834-7265 Fax: (310) 834-8813
Shirley Alencio, Dir.

MANA - A NATIONAL LATINA ORG.
Bay Area Chapter
601 Van Ness Ave., #E-3-506
San Francisco, CA 94102
(415) 979-5894 Fax: (415) 647-5772
Linda Gonzales, Chapter President
Email: hermana2@aol.com
Web: www.hermana.org

Greater California Chapter
1130 Menlo Dr.
Davis, CA 95616
(530) 756-5416
Charlotte Apodaca-Lucero, Chapter President
Email: hermana2@aol.com
Web: www.hermana.org

Imperial Valley Chapter
P.O.Box 73
El Centro, CA 92244
(760) 312-9800 Fax: (760) 312-9838
Debbie Trujillo, Chapter President
Email: hermana2@aol.com
Web: www.hermana.org

Orange County Chapter
P.O. Box 4081
Santa Ana, CA 92702-4081
(714) 563-6262
Nelly Caudillo Keniski, Chapter President
Email: hermana2@aol.com
Web: www.hermana.org

Salinas Chapter
2014 Santa Rita St.
Salinas, CA 93906
(831) 443-7221 Fax: (831) 443-7228
Luz Elena Romero, Chapter President
Email: hermana2@aol.com
Web: www.hermana.org

San Diego Chapter
P.O. Box 3159
San Diego, CA 92103
(619) 441-1524 Fax: (619) 469-3257
Olivia Puentes Reynolds, Chapter President
Email: hermana2@aol.com
Web: www.hermana.org

Sonoma County Chapter
P.O. Box 2845
Santa Rosa, CA 95405
(707) 525-8577 Fax: (707) 525-8582
Irma Pérez-Cordova, Chapter President
Email: hermana2@aol.com
Web: www.hermana.org

**MANNY MOTA INTERNATIONAL
FOUNDATION**
2222 Foot Hill Blvd.,#103
La Canada, CA 91011
(818) 957-0384 Fax: (818) 957-0354
Perry Goldstain, President
Email: ccmota@aol.com
Web: www.mannymotafoundation.org

MANOS DE ESPERANZA
14530 Hamlin St.
Van Nuys, CA 91405
(818) 901-4854 Fax: (818) 908-4995
Alda Fenster, Executive Director

MAR VISTA FAMILY CENTER
5070 Slauson Ave.
Culver City, CA 90230
(310) 390-9607 Fax: (310) 390-4888
Lucía Díaz, Dir.
Email: marvistain@aol.com

MARAVILLA FOUNDATION
5729 E. Union Pacific
Commerce, CA 90022
(213) 721-4162 Fax: (213) 721-0356
Alex Sotomayor, CEO

**MARGARET CRUZ LATINA BREAST
CANCER FOUNDATION**
7 Joost Ave., #101
San Fransisco, CA 94131
(415) 239-4802 or (415) 585-1163
Fax: (415) 586-7453
Olivia Fe, Executive Director
Email: MCLBCF@aol.com
Web: www.mclatinabcf.org

MARIACHI U.S.A. FOUNDATION
11684 Ventura Blvd. #6710
Studio City, CA 91604
(213) 848-7717 Fax: (213) 656-4017
Rodri Rodriguez, Prod.
Email: www.mariachiusa.com

**MCDONALD'S HISPANIC OPERATORS
ASSOCIATION (MHOA)**
P.O. Box 884
Murrieta, CA 92564
(909) 698-1245 Fax: (909) 698-0427
Mr. Ernie Sandoval, Chairman
Web: www.mcdonalds.com

MECHA (MOVIMIENTO ESTUDIANTIL)
333 N. Glassell St.
Orange, CA 92866
(714) 997-6761 Fax: (714) 744-7021
Paul Apodaca, Advisor

**METROPOLITAN AREA ADVISORY
COMMITTEE (MAAC PROJECT)**
Affiliate of NCLR
22 W. 35th Street
National City, CA 91950
(619) 426-3595 Fax: (619) 426-2173
Roger Cazares, President & CEO
Email: roger@pacbell.net
Web: www.innercitynet.org

METROPOLITAN SKILLS CENTER
2801 W. 6th St.
Los Angeles, CA 90010
(213) 386-7269 Fax: (213) 252-9435
Elaine James, Principal

**METROPOLITAN WATER DISTRICT OF
SOUTHERN CALIFORNIA-HISPANIC
EMPLOYEES ASSOCIATION (MWDSC-HEA)**
P.O. Box 54153 Terminal Annex
Los Angeles, CA 90054
(213) 217-7631 Fax: (213) 217-6002
Benjamin Ocasio, Pres.
Email: bocasio@mwd.dst.ca.us

MEXICA MOVEMENT
P.O. Box 5088
Huntington Park, CA 90255-9088
(323) 981-0352
Email: mixcoatl@mexica-movement.org
Web: www.mexica-movement.org

MEXICAN AMERICAN ALUMNI ASSOC.
California State University Los Angeles
Student Union Bldg., Room 203
Los Angeles, CA 90089-4890
(213) 740-4735 Fax: (213) 740-7250
Raul Vargas, Exec. Dir.

**MEXICAN AMERICAN BOWLING
ORGANIZATION (MAMBO)**
8309 Honeyconb Way
Sacramento, CA 95828
(888) 682-8362
Kanji Montalvo
Email: info@mambo.org
Web: www.mambo.org

**MEXICAN AMERICAN BUSINESS AND
PROFESSIONAL ASSOCIATION**
San Diego Data Processing
1200 3rd Ave., Suite 1400
San Diego, CA 92101
(619) 533-5921 Fax: (619) 533-5993
Roger Talamantez, Pres.

**MEXICAN AMERICAN CHAMBER OF
COMMERCE**
343 E. Main St., #700
Stockton, CA 952302
(209) 943-6117 Fax: (209) 943-0114
Dora Martinez, President

**MEXICAN AMERICAN CHAMBER OF
COMMERCE & INDUSTRY**
P.O. Box 65766
Los Angeles, CA 90065
(323) 221-6800
César C. Cantú, President

**MEXICAN AMERICAN EDUCATION
COMMISSION (LAUSD)**
450 North Grand Ave. Rm. H-138
Los Angeles, CA 90012
John Fernandez, Dir.
Email: mrf@ucla.edu

**MEXICAN AMERICAN GROCERS
ASSOCIATION & FOUNDATION (MAGA)**
National Headquarters
405 N. San Fernando Rd.
Los Angeles, CA 90031
(323) 227-1565 Fax: (323) 227-6935
Steven A. Soto, President & CEO
Web: www.maga.org

**MEXICAN AMERICAN HEALTH AND
EDUCATIONAL SERVICES CENTER**
9844 Bryson Ave.
South Gate, CA 90280
(213) 569-5151 or (213) 715-4809
Fax: (213) 569-5151
María M. Vargas, Exec. Dir.

**MEXICAN AMERICAN LEGAL DEFENSE
AND EDUCATIONAL FUND (MALDEF)**
National Headquarters
634 S. Spring St., 11th Floor
Los Angeles, CA 90014
(213) 629-2512 Fax: (213) 629-0266
Antonia Hernández, President/General Counsel
Email: maldefla@aol.com
Web: www.maldef.org

Sacramento Satellite Office
926 J St., #408
Sacramento, CA 95814
(916) 443-7531 Fax: (916) 443-1541
Elizabeth Guillen, Legislative Counsel
Email: maldef@tomatoweb.com
Web: www.maldef.org

San Francisco Regional Office
660 Market St., #206
San Francisco, CA 94104
(415) 248-5803 Fax: (415) 248-5816
Maria Blanco, Regional Counsel
Email: mblanco@maldef.org
Web: www.maldef.org

**MEXICAN AMERICAN OPPORTUNITY
FOUNDATION (MAOF)**
401 N. Garfield Ave.
Montebello, CA 90640
(323) 890-9616 Fax: (323) 890-9632
Dionicio Morales, President/Founder

**MEXICAN AMERICAN POLITICAL
ASSOCIATION (MAPA)**
(559) 846-8869 Fax: (559) 846-8116
Gloria Torres, National and State Pres.
Web: www.mapa.org

MEXICAN CULTURAL INSTITUTE
125 Paseo de la Plaza, #300
Los Angeles, CA 90012
(213) 624-3660 Fax: (213) 624-9387
Leticia Quezada, Executive Director
Email: mexcultinst@earthlink.net

MEXICAN GRADUATE STUDENT ASSOC.
University of California, Davis
Student Programs & Activities Ctr., Box #202
1 Shields Ave.
Davis, CA 95616-8706
(530) 752-2027 or (530) 758-2043
Fax: (530) 752-4951
Chad Leidy, President
Email: ccleidy@ucdavis.edu
Web: www.ucdavis.edu

MEXICAN HERITAGE CORP. OF SAN JOSE
Affiliate of NCLR
P.O. Box 4, San Jose, CA 95103
476 Park Ave., #106
San Jose, CA 95110
(408) 292-5197 Fax: (408) 292-9401
Pete Carrillo, President
Web: www.mhcviva.org

MEXICAN HERITAGE CULTURAL BOARD
P.O. Box 65766
Los Angeles, CA 90065
(323) 221-6800
Cesar C. Cantú, Chairman

MEXICAN MOTHER OF THE YEAR ASSOC.
La Placita Church
216 Casa Grande Ave.
Montebello, CA 90640-2733
(323) 722-4275 Fax: (323) 629-1951
Carmen M. Sandoval, Pro Treasurer

MEXICAN MUSEUM
National Headquarters
Fort Mason Center Bldg., D
San Francisco, CA 94123
(415) 202-9700 Fax: (415) 441-7683
Lorraine García Nacata, Executive Director

MEXICAN STUDENT ASSOCIATION
Stanford Univ. Office of Student Activities
Escondido Village, Barnes 6H
Stanford, CA 94305
(650) 497-2082
Lucrecia Santibanez, Contact
Email: landeros@leland

MEXICAN-AMERICAN BAR ASSOCIATION
3500 W. Beverly Blvd.
Montebello, CA 90640
(323) 724-4249 Fax: (323) 725-0350
Arnoldo Casillas, President
Web: www.maba4u.org

**MEXICAN-AMERICAN CORRECTIONAL
ASSOCIATION**
15605 Newton St.
Hacienda Heights, CA 91745
(323) 727-1258 or (818) 961-0744
Fred Martel, Pres.

**MEXICAN-AMERICAN SENIOR CITIZENS
SOCIAL CLUB OF PICO RIVERA**
4632 Orange St.
Pico Rivera, CA 90660
(562) 948-4844 or (562)696-8849
Rubén López, Pres.

MINI-CORPS
Stanislaus University
801 W. Montevista
Turlock, CA 95382
(209) 667-3259 Fax: (209) 667-3333
Fernando Peña, Coord.

MINORITY AIDS PROJECT
5149 W. Jefferson Blvd.
Los Angeles, CA 90016
(323) 936-4949 Fax: (323) 936-4973
Barbara J. Draden, Director of Client Services
Email: map5149@aol.com

MINORITY APARTMENT OWNERS ASSOC.
11215 S. Western Ave.
Los Angeles, CA 90047
(323) 754-2818 Fax: (323) 754-0540
Ruth Haylas, Executive Director

**MINORITY BUSINESS DEVELOPMENT
AGENCY (MBDA)**
San Francisco Office/U.S. Department
of Commerce
221 Main St., #1280
San Francico, CA 94105
(415) 744-3001 Fax: (415) 744-3061
Melda Cabrera, Regional Director
Email: MCabrera@mbda.gov
Web: www.mbda.gov

MINORITY PRE-LAW COALITION
University of California, Berkeley
316 Eshelman Hall
Berkeley, CA 94720
(510) 643-9656
Cabrina Cau, Director
Email: cabrina@uclinky.berkeley.edu

MISIONEROS COMBONIANOS
Casa Comboni
525 N. Pasadena Ave.
Azusa, CA 91702
(626) 812-0818 or (626) 334-3531
Fax: (626) 969-8681
José Luis Cuevas, Director
Email: pepe44@earthlink.net or
casacomb@aol.com

MISS LATIN WORLD BEAUTY PAGEANT
P.O. Box 65766
Los Angeles, CA 90065
(323) 221-6800
César C. Cantú, President

MISSION SAN CARLOS BORROMEO DEL RIO CARMELO
3080 Rio Rd.
Carmel, CA 93923
(831) 624-3600 Fax: (831) 624-0658
Richard J. Menn, Director & Curator

MISSION SAN JUAN BAUTISTA MUSEUM
Administrative Office
P.O. Box 400
San Juan Bautista, CA 95045
(831) 623-2127 Fax: (831) 623-2433
Father Edward Fitz-Henry, Director

MISSION SAN LUIS REY MUSEUM
Administrative Office
4050 Mission Ave.
San Luis Rey, CA 92057-6402
(760) 757-3651 Fax: (760) 757-4613
Mary C. Whelan, Director & Curator
Email: mary@sanluisrey.org
Web: www.sanluisrey.org

MONTEBELLO FAMILY YMCA
2000 W. Beverly Blvd.
Montebello, CA 90640
(213) 887-YMCA Fax: (213) 722-5354
Joe Naylor, Exec. Dir.

MORENO VALLEY HISPANIC CHAMBER OF COMMERCE
24895 Sunny Mead Blvd., #333
Moreno Valley, CA 92553
(909) 685-8185 Fax: (909) 697-0995
Anita Franco, President
Email: aspirevents@yahoo.com

MOTHERS OF EAST LOS ANGELES (MELA)
3354 East. Olympic Blvd.
Los Angeles, CA 90023
(562) 806-2104 (h) or (323) 266-8832 (w)
Fax: (323) 266-8832
Marylu Travis, President

P.O. Box 23151
3324 Opal St.
Los Angeles, CA 90023
(323) 726-7734 or (323) 268-1143
Fax: (323) 721-9794
Terry Griffin, Secretary

Santa Isabel (MELA-SI)
924 South Mott St.
Los Angeles, CA 90023
(323) 269-9898 Fax: (323) 269-2446
Ms. Juana Gutiérrez, President
Email: mothermelasi@earthlink.net

MOVIMIENTO ESTUDIANTIL CHICANO DE AZTLAN (MECHA)
Bakersfield College
Student Affairs Office
1801 Panorama Dr.
Bakersfield, CA 93305
(805) 395-4532 Fax: (805) 395-4241
Rosa Garza, Advisor

California State University, Bakersfield
STAAR
9001 Stockdale Highway
Bakersfield, CA 93311-1099
(805) 664-2281 Fax: (805) 664-2215
Ray Cuesta, Advisor
Email: rcuesta@csubak.edu

California State University Hayward
c/o Associated Students
Student Academic Services, University Union #314
Hayward, CA 94542
(510) 885-3657
Ramon Camacho, President

California State University, Los Angeles
5154 State University Dr.
Los Angeles, CA 90032
(323) 343-5047 Fax: (323) 343-5101
Enrique Ochoa, Advisor
Email: mecha@calstatela.edu
Web: www.calstatela.edu

California State University, San Marcos
Office of Student Activities
Craven Hall, #416
San Marcos, CA 92096
(760) 750-4970 or (760) 744-4806
Carmen Lopez, President

Loyola Marymount University
Student Life
7900 Loyola Blvd.
Los Angeles, CA 90045-8465
(310) 338-2877 or (310) 338-2700
Roberto Flores, Advisor

Palomar College
1140 W. Mission Rd.
San Marcos, CA 92069
(760) 744-1150 x2594 Fax: (760) 744-8251
John Valdez, Director

San Diego City College
1313 12th Ave.
San Diego, CA 92101
(619) 230-2498 or (619) 230-2634
John Anderson, Acting President

San Joaquin Delta Community College
5151 Pacific Ave.
Stockton, CA 95207
(209) 954-5100 or (209) 954-5151
Fax: (209) 954-5600
Anthony Sedillo, EOPS Counselor

University of California, Davis
Student Programs & Activities Ctr., Box #177
1 Shields Ave.
Davis, CA 95616-8706
(530) 752-2027 or (530) 297-5321
Fax: (530) 752-4951
Isela C. Gracian, President
Email: icgracia@ucdavis.edu
Web: www.ucdavis.edu

University of California, Los Angeles
407 Kerckhoff Hall, 308 Westwood Plaza
Los Angeles, CA 90024
(323) 343-5047

University of California, Riverside
229 Costo Hall
Riverside, CA 92521
(909) 787-3821 Fax: (909) 787-2189
Alfredo Figueroa, Director
Email: alfredo.figueroa@ucr.edu

MOVIMIENTO FAMILIAR CRISTIANO U.S.A. (MFC/USA)
3570 Thompson Place
Hayward, CA 94541
(510) 728-1319 or (510) 727-1361 (h)
Margarita y Mario Gavidia, President

MUJERES UNIDAS
Chicano Student Programs
UC Riverside
229 Costo Hall
Riverside, CA 92521
(909) 787-3821 Fax: (909) 787-2189
Alfredo Figueroa, Director

MULTI-ETHNIC STUDENT ALLIANCE (MESA)
Azusa Pacific University
901 E. Alosta Ave.
Azusa, CA 91702
(626) 815-6000 ext. 3513 Fax: (626) 815-3800
Grace Gutierrez, Co. Leader
Email: jalew@apu.edu
Web: www.apu.edu

MULTICULTURAL AREA HEALTH EDUCATION CENTER (MAHEC)
Affiliate of NCLR
5051 E. Third St.
Los Angeles, CA 90022
(323) 780-7640 Fax: (323) 780-7646
Luis Mata, President & CEO
Email: mahec@msn.com

MULTICULTURAL COLLABORATIVE - COLABORACION MULTICULTURAL
315 W 9th St., #315
Los Angeles, CA 90015
(213) 624-7992 Fax: (213) 624-7924
Bonghwan Kim, Director

MULTICULTURAL EDUCATION TRAINING & ADVOCACY (META)
785 Market Street, #420
San Francisco, CA 94103
(415) 546-6382 Fax: (415) 546-6363
Peter Roos, Co-Director

MULTICULTURAL INSTITUTE FOR LEADERSHIP (MIL)
620 Newport Center Drive, 11th Floor
Newport Beach, CA 92660
(949) 721-6644 Fax: (949) 653-9855
Lucia de Garcia, President
Email: elaninter@worldnet.att.net

MUNDO LATINO PRODUCTIONS
P.O. Box 65766
Los Angeles, CA 90065-0766
(213) 221-6800
Cesar C. Cantú, President

MUSEUM OF LATIN AMERICAN ART
628 Alamitos Ave
Long Beach, CA 90802
(562) 437-1689 Fax: (562) 437-7043
Susan Golden, Director
Email: info@molaa.com
Web: www.molaa.com

NATIONAL ASSOCIATION FOR HISPANIC ELDERLY
Los Angeles Office/Project Ayuda
1452 W. Temple St., #100
Los Angeles, CA 90026
(213) 202-5900 Fax: (213) 202-5905
Ramona Soto, Project Coordinator
Email: lapaemploy@aol.com

National Headquarters/Project Ayuda
234 E. Colorado Blvd., #300
Pasadena, CA 91101
(626) 564-1988 Fax: (626) 564-2659
Carmela G. Lacayo, President
Email: anppm@aol.com

San Diego Office/Project Ayuda
22 W. 35th St., #127
National City, CA 91950
(619) 425-3734 Fax: (619) 425-6563
Lillian Urbanski, Project Coordinator
Email: nahesd@aol.com

NATIONAL ASSOCIATION OF HISPANIC REAL ESTATE PROFESSIONALS
1650 Hotel Circle North., #215-A
San Diego, CA 92108
(800) 964-5373 Fax: (619) 209-4773
Ruben R. Garcia, President & COO
Email: info@nahrep.org
Web: www.nahrep.org

NATIONAL ASSOCIATION OF IMMIGRATION CONSULTANTS
National Headquarters
3807 Wilshire Blvd., #925
Los Angeles, CA 90010
(213) 386-4649 Fax: (213) 386-3593
Arturo Aguirre, President

NATIONAL ASSOC. OF LATINO ELECTED & APPOINTED OFFICIALS (NALEO)
Los Angeles Chapter
5800 SE Ave. #365
Los Angeles, CA 90040
(323) 720-1932 Fax: (323) 720-9519
Arturo Vargas, Executive Director
Email: avnaleo@neleo.org
Web: www.naleo.org

NATIONAL ASSOCIATION OF MINORITIES IN CABLE (NAMIC)
Southern California Chapter
P.O. Box 3066
Cerritos, CA 90703-3066
(562) 404-6208 Fax: (602) 404-4848
Clayton Banks, Pres.
Email: namicassociation@prodigy.com

NATIONAL COALITION OF BARRIOS UNIDOS
Salinas Chapter
683 Fremont St.
Salinas, CA 93905
(831) 751-9054 Fax: (831) 751-9011
Email: Info@barriosunidos.org
Web: www.barriosunidos.salinas.com

NATIONAL CONFERENCE FOR COMMUNITY AND JUSTICE
1055 Wilshire Blvd., #1615
Los Angeles, CA 90017
(213) 250-8787 Fax: (213) 250-8799
Fran Fpears, Executive Director

NATIONAL COUNCIL OF LA RAZA (NCLR)
Los Angeles Office
523 W. 6th St., #301
Los Angeles, CA 90014
(213) 489-3428 Fax: (213) 489-1167
Magdalena Duran, Director
Web: www.nclr.org

NATIONAL COUNCIL ON ALCOHOLISM AND DRUG DEPENDENCY
181 North Hudson Ave.
Pasadena, CA 91101
(626) 795-9127 Fax: (626) 795-0979
Larry Patino, Latino Outreach Worker

NATIONAL HISPANIC ACADEMY OF MEDIA, ARTS & SCIENCES
4457 Oak St.
Pico Rivera, CA 90660
(310) 712-5739
Herik Venegas, Exec. Dir.
Email: nhamas@hotmail.com

NATIONAL HISPANIC EMPLOYEE ASSOC.
San Jose State University
One Washington Square
San Jose, CA 95192-0046
(408) 924-2262 or (408) 283-6223
Fax: (408) 924-2284
Gustavo de la Torre, President
Web: www.nhea.org

THE NATIONAL HISPANIC LEADERSHIP AGENDA (NHLA)
5800 S. Eastern Ave., # 365
Los Angeles, CA 90040
(323) 720-1932 Fax: (323) 720-9519
Arturo Vargas, Chairman
Email: avnaleo@aol.com

NATIONAL HISPANIC MEDIA COALITION
5400 E. Olympic Blvd., #250
Los Angeles, CA 90022-5142
(323) 722-4191 Fax: (323) 722-1554
Esther Renteria, Pres.

National Headquarters
3550 Wilshire Blvd. #670
Los Angeles, CA 90010
(213) 746-6988
Alex Nogales, National Chairman
Email: www.nhmc.com

NATIONAL HISPANIC UNIVERSITY
14271 Story Rd.
San Jose, CA 95127
(408) 254-6900 Fax: (408) 254-1369
B. Roberto Crúz, President & CEO
Email: university@nhu.edu
Web: www.nhu.edu

NATIONAL IMMIGRATION LAW CENTER
Legal Aid Foundation
1102 South Crenshaw Blvd. #101
Los Angeles, CA 90019
(213) 938-6452 Fax: (213) 964-7940
Susan Drake, Dir.
Email: drake@nilc.org

NATIONAL LATINA HEALTH ORGANIZATION/ORGANIZACION NACIONAL DE LA MUJER LATINA
P.O. Box 7567
Oakland, CA 94601
(510) 534-1362 Fax: (510) 534-1364
Luz Alvarez Martinez, Executive Director
Email: latinahealth@aol.com

NATIONAL LATINO ARTS, EDUCATION, AND MEDIA INSTITUTE
1114 Stratford Ave.
S. Pasadena, CA 91030
(323) 890-7140
Paula Crisostomo, Exec. Dir.

NATIONAL LATINO COMMUNICATIONS CENTER (NLCC)
National Headquarters
3171 Los Feliz Blvd., #200
Los Angeles, CA 90039
(323) 663-8294/5606 Fax: (323) 663-5606
Bea O. Stotzer, Board of Directors
Email: emedia@nlcc.com
Web: www.nlcc.com

NATIONAL LATINO PEACE OFFICERS ASSOC. Alameda Chapter
P.O. Box 17083
Oakland, CA 94601
(877) 657-6200
Stevan Fajando, Chapter President
Email: lpoa@usa.net
Web: www.nlpoa.com

California State Chapter
P.O. Box 4244
Diamond Bar, CA 91765
(877) 657-6200
Jose Miramontes, State President
Email: castlpoa@pacbell.net
Web: www.nlpoa.com

Central Coast Chapter
P.O. Box 13606
San Luis Obispo, CA 93406
(877) 657-6200
Adrian Garcia, Chapter President
Email: nlpoa@aol.com
Web: www.nlpoa.com

Coachella Valley Chapter
80352 Corte El Dorado
Indio, CA 92201
(877) 657-6200
Luis Bautista, Chapter President
Email: lpoa1@juno.com
Web: www.nlpoa.com

East Los Angeles Chapter
6136 E. Whittier Blvd., #B
Los Angeles, CA 90022
(877) 657-6200
Gilbert O. Parra, Chapter President
Email: gop@relaypoint.com
Web: www.nlpoa.com

Kern Metro Chapter
816 Minter Ave.
Shafter, CA 93263
(877) 657-6200
Lou Flores, Chapter President
Email: lpoacvp@jps.net
Web: www.nlpoa.com

Kings/Fresno Chapter
24405 6th Ave.
Corcoran, CA 93212
(877) 657-6200
Jess Martinez, Chapter President
Email: sammyr@lightspeed.net
Web: www.nlpoa.com

Modesto Chapter
429 13th St.
Modesto, CA 95354
(877) 657-6200
Jose Vasquez, Chapter President
Email: modestolpoa@yahoo.com
Web: www.nlpoa.com

National Office
133 Southwest Blvd., #B
Rohnert Park, CA 94928
(877) 657-6200
Adrian Garcia, National President
Email: nlpoa@aol.com
Web: www.nlpoa.com

North San Diego Chapter
P.O. Box 605
San Marcos, CA 92079
(877) 657-6200
Adrian Garcia, National President
Email: nlpoa@aol.com
Web: www.nlpoa.com

Orange County Chapter
P.O. Box 6773
Fullerton, CA 92834
(877) 657-6200
Tom Barcelo, Chapter President
Email: nlpoa@aol.com
Web: www.nlpoa.com

Sacramento Chapter
P.O. Box 1135
Sacramento, CA 95812
(877) 657-6200
Adrian Garcia, National President
Email: nlpoa@aol.com
Web: www.nlpoa.com

San Bernardino/Riverside
1040 S. Mt. Vernon Ave., #G164
Colton, CA 92324
(877) 657-6200
Teresa Franco, Chapter President
Email: nlpoa@aol.com
Web: www.nlpoa!com

San Diego County Chapter
P.O. Box 122708
San Diego, CA 92112
(877) 657-6200
David A. Ardilla, Chapter President
Email: 925mary@worldnet.att.net
Web: www.nlpoa.com

San Diego Metro Chapter
P.O. Box 128025
San Diego, CA 92112
(877) 657-6200
Manuel Rodriguez, Chapter President
Email: nlpoa@aol.com
Web: www.nlpoa.com

San Francisco Chapter
P.O. Box 410692
San Francisco, CA 94141
(877) 657-6200
Adrian Garcia, National President
Email: nlpoa@aol.com
Web: www.nlpoa.com

San Gabriel Valley Chapter
P.O. Box 4411
Montebello, CA 90640
(877) 657-6200
Henry Aguilar, Chapter President
Email: fvsainz@aol.com
Web: www.nlpoa.com

San Joaquin Chapter
P.O. Box 2142
Stockton, CA 95201
(877) 657-6200
Chuck Arellano, Chapter President
Email: socheese@aol.com
Web: www.nlpoa.com

Santa Clara Chapter
P.O. Box 2145
San Jose, CA 95109
(877) 657-6200
Raul Martinez, Chapter President
Email: nlpoa@aol.com
Web: www.nlpoa.com

Santa Cruz Chapter
P.O. Box 2188
Freedom, CA 95019
(877) 657-6200
Adrian Garcia, National President
Email: nlpoa@aol.com
Web: www.nlpoa.com

Tulare Chapter
P.O. Box 3835
Visalia, CA 93278
(877) 657-6200
Ramón Alanis, Chapter President
Email: nlpoa@aol.com
Web: www.nlpoa.com

NATIONAL MINORITY ORGAN TISSUE TRANSPLANT EDUCATION PROGRAM (MOTTEP) OF LA
National Kidney Fdtn. of Southern CA
5777 W. Century Blvd., #1450
Los Angeles, CA 90045
(800) 747-5527 or (310) 641-8152
Fax: (310) 641-5246
Luis R. Cabrales, Local Program Coordinator
Email: lrcabrales@kidneysocal.org
Web: www.kidneysocal.org

NATIONAL NETWORK FOR IMMIGRANT & REFUGEE RIGHTS (NNIRR)
310 Eighth St., #307
Oakland, CA 94607
(510) 465-1984 Fax: (510) 465-1885
Cathi Tactaquin, Director
Email: nnirr@nnirr.org

NATIONAL RESOURCE CENTER ON MINORITY AGING POPULATIONS
San Diego State University
Center on Aging
5500 Campanile Dr.
San Diego, CA 92182-4124
(619) 594-6765 Fax: (619) 594-2811
Dr. E. Percil Stanford, Director
Web: www.rohan.sdsu.edu/dept/chhs

NATIVIDAD MEDICAL CENTER
1441 Constitution Blvd.
Salinas, CA 93906
(831) 755-4111 Fax: (831) 769-8632
Laura Solorio, Chief of Internal Medicine
Web: www.natividad.com

NEIGHBORHOOD HOUSING SERVICES OF ORANGE COUNTY, INC. (NHSOC)
Affiliate of NCLR
198 W. Lincoln Ave. 2nd Fl.
Anaheim, CA 92805
(714) 547-7143 Fax: (714) 490-1263/2
Stella Trujillo, Community Outreach Coord.
Email: nhsockmutter@yahoo.com

350 S. Hillcrest St.
La Habra, CA 90631
(562) 694-2051 Fax: (562) 694-2052
Glenn Hayes, Executive Director

NEIGHBORHOOD MUSIC SCHOOL ASSOC.
Boyle Heights
358 S Boyle Ave.
Los Angeles, CA 90033
(323) 268-0762 Fax: (323) 269-2992
Terry Castaneda, President
Email: guapamusic@aol.com

NEIGHBORHOOD YOUTH ASSOCIATION
Las Doradas Children Center
17552 Camino de Yatasto
Pacific Palisades, CA 90272
(310) 454-7620 Fax: (310) 459-6643
Marge Lundstrum, President

NEW ECONOMICS FOR WOMEN
Affiliate of NCLR
303 South Loma Dr.
Los Angeles, CA 90017
(213) 483-2060 Fax: (213) 483-7848
Beatriz Stotzer, President
Email: email4new@aol.com

NIÑOS LATINOS UNIDOS
10016 Pioneer Blvd., #123
Sante Fe Springs, CA 90670
(562) 801-5454 Fax: (562) 942-8955
Fahir Milian, President & CEO
Email: Info@nlu.org
Web: www.nlu.org

NIPOMO COMMUNITY MEDICAL CENTER
150 Tejas Pl.
Nipomo, CA 93444
(805) 929-3211 Fax: (805) 929-6359
Dr. Zigelman, Director

NORTHERN CALIFORNIA SUPPLIER DEVELOPMENT COUNCIL
NMSDC
1999 Harrison St.
Oakland, CA 94612
(510) 587-0636
Carida Pickens, Executive Director
Email: cpickens@ncsdc.org
Web: www.ncsdc.org

NOSOTROS
650 N Bronson Av., #102
Hollywood, CA 90004
(323) 465-8110 Fax: (323) 465-8540
Jerry G. Velasco, President
Email: info@nosotros.org
Web: www.nosotros.org

NUESTRA COSA
Chicano Student Programs
UC Riverside
229 Costo Hall
Riverside, CA 92521
(909) 787-3821 Fax: (909) 787-2189
Alfredo Figueroa, Director
Email: alfredo.figueroa@ucr.edu

NUEVO AMANECER LATINO CHILDREN'S SERVICES
5400 Pomona Blvd.
Los Angeles, CA 90022
(323) 720-9951
Jorge Alberto Acosta, President/CEO

OFFICE OF MULTI-ETHNIC PROGRAMS
Azusa Pacific University
901 East Alosta Ave.
Azusa, CA 91702
(626) 969-3434 ext. 3720 Fax: (626) 815-3800
Jonathan Lew, Director
Email: jalew@apu.edu
Web: www.apu.edu

OLVERA STREET MERCHANTS ASSOC.
W-17 Olvera St.
Los Angeles, CA 90012
(213) 628-4349 or (213) 687-4344
Fax: (213) 687-0800
Vivien Bonzo, Pres.

ONE STOP - IMMIGRATION AND EDUCATION CENTER
3600 Whitter Blvd.
Los Angeles, CA 90023
(323) 268-8472 Fax: (323) 268-2231
Mario Villa, Executive Director
Email: OSIEC@aol.com

ORANGE COUNTY/SER-JOBS FOR PROGRESS, INC.
Affiliate of SER-Jobs for Progress National, Inc.
1243 E. Warner Ave.
Santa Ana, CA 92705
(714) 556-8741 Fax: (714) 556-0640
Ronald W. Puente, Executive Director
Web: www.sernational.org

ORTHOPEDIC HOSPITAL INTERNATIONAL CHILDREN'S PROGRAM
2400 South Flower St.
Los Angeles, CA 90007
(213) 742-1339 Fax: (213) 742-1078
María Aguilar, Coordinator

OSCAR ROMERO PEACE AND JUSTICE CENTER
2839 Mariposa
Fresno, CA 93721
(559) 441-7131 or (800) 765-7131
Fax: (559) 441-7155
Tomás González, Executive Director
Email: admin@romerocenter.org

PACOIMA SKILLS CENTER
13545 Van Nuys Blvd.
Pacoima, CA 91331
(818) 896-9558 Fax: (818) 899-7087
Al Topalian, Asst. Principal

PACTO LATINO AIDS ORGANIZATION
P.O. Box 86793
San Diego, CA 92138
(619) 563-3901 Fax: (619) 563-3902
Cesar Enriquez, Director
Email: apacto97@aol.com

PAJARO VALLEY CHAMBER OF COMMERCE
444 Main St.
Watsonville, CA 95077
(831) 724-3900 Fax: (831) 728-5300
Bob Dwyer, President & CEO
Email: commerce@pvchamber.com
Web: www.pvchamber.com

PAN AMERICAN CLUB OF LOS ANGELES
5232 Atlantic Blvd.
Los Angeles, CA 90022
(323) 261-2574 Fax: (323) 724-6823
Henry Estrada, Cont.

PAN AMERICAN SOCIETY OF CALIFORNIA, THE
600 Montgomery St., #350
San Francisco, CA 94111-2701
(415) 788-4764 Fax: (415) 788-4764

PANAMANIAN CULTURAL ARTS CENTER
P.O. Box 207
Canoga Park, CA 91305
(818) 410-1236
Victor Grimaldo, Director
Email: miembros@vivapanama.org
Web: www.vivapanama.org/artcenter-en.html

PARA LOS NIÑOS
845 E. 6th St.
Los Angeles, CA 90021
(213) 623-8446 Fax: (213) 623-8716
Miki Jordan, Executive Director

PARENT INSTITUTE FOR QUALITY EDUCATION
Affiliate of NCLR
4010 Morena Blvd., #200
San Diego, CA 92117
(619) 483-4499 Fax: (619) 483-4646
Patricia Mayer, Director

PARENTS FOR UNITY
1820 S. Catalina St.
Los Angeles, CA 90006
(323) 734-9353 Fax: (323) 735-8105
Mr. Gabriel Medel, Executive Director

PARENTS INVOLVED IN COMMUNITY ACTION (PICA)
4555 East 3rd St. #14
Los Angeles, CA 90022
(213) 269-7541 Fax: (323) 269-1066
Ruby Aguilar, Executive Director

PASOS DE VIDA
3450 Broad St.
San Luis Obispo, CA 93401
(805) 481-2505 Fax: (805) 481-2377
Gina Pinto, Director
Web: www.lifestepsfoundation.org

PATRONATO JOSE MARTI, INC.
8160 Barson St.
Douney, CA 90242
(213) 588-1408 Fax: (213) 587-2061
Dra. Norma Montero, Pres.

PEÑA CULTURAL "EL ATENEO"
10977 Santa Monica Blvd.
Los Angeles, CA 90025
(323) 772-6474
Bernard Hamel, President

PERRIS VALLEY HISPANIC CHAMBER OF
COMMERCE
424 South D St.
Perris, CA 92570
(909) 940-4442 Fax: (909) 940-4442
Cecilia Larios, President

PERUVIAN CHAMBER OF COMMERCE OF
CALIFORNIA
444 West Ocean Blvd., #800
Long Beach, CA 90802
(652) 624-2836 Fax: (562) 790-8763
Rosario Caparó, President
Web: www.perucam.org

PERUVIAN CHAMBER OF COMMERCE OF
SAN DIEGO-USA
P.O. Box 17690
San Diego, CA 92177-7690
(619) 898-9955 Fax: (619) 422-1176
Roberto Arca Patiño, Presidente
Web: www.perucam.org

PLAZA DE LA RAZA SCHOOL OF THE
PERFORMING AND THE VISUAL ARTS
Cultural Enrichment Program
3540 N. Mission Rd.
Los Angeles, CA 90031
(323) 222-2786 Fax: (213) 223-1804
María Jiménez Tarres, School Coordinator
Email: admin@plazaraza.org

PLAZA FAMILY SUPPORT CENTER
4018 City Terrace Dr.
Los Angeles, CA 90063
(323) 268-1041 Fax: (323) 268-2578
Gloria Ornelas, Dir.
Email: pcc@surfnet.com

POMONA VALLEY YOUTH EMPLOYMENT
SERVICES
568 E. Foothill Blvd.
Pomona, CA 91767-1220
(909) 621-5077 Fax: (909) 626-0068
John Owsley, Director

POMONA-INLAND VALLEY COUNCIL OF
CHURCHES
1753 N. Park Ave.
Pomona, CA 91768
(909) 622-3806 Fax: (909) 622-0484
Joyce M. Ewen, Executive Director

PREGNANCY COUSELING CLINIC
10211 Sepulveda Blvd.
Mission Hills, CA 91345
(818) 895-2500 Fax: (818) 895-2921
Gail Hamilton, Dir.

PRESBYTERIAN HISPANIC CHURCH
112 E. Beach St.
Watsonville, CA 95076-4704
(831) 728-8653
Martha Countar, Pastor

PROFESSIONAL HISPANICS IN ENERGY
20505 Yorba Linda Blvd., #324
Yorba Linda, CA 92886-7109
(714) 777-7729 Fax: (714) 777-7728
Cynthia Verdugo-Peralta, Pres.
Email: vpcnrg@aol.com
Web: www.phie.org

PROFESSIONAL MUSICIANS, LOCAL 47,
AFM
817 N. Vine St.
Hollywood, CA 90038-3779
(323) 993-3159 or (323) 462-2161
Fax: (323) 461-3090
Alfredo Rubalcada, Coordinator
Web: www.afm.org

PROJECT MOTIVATION
Stanford University
El Centro Chicano
Building 590-F, Old Union
Stanford, CA 94305-3044
(650) 723-2089 Fax: (650) 725-6487
Chris Gonzalez Clarke, Assistant Director
Email: chris.clarke@stanford.edu
Web: www.stanford.edu/group/promo

PROTECCION LEGAL FEMENINA
5300 E. Beverly Blvd., #D
Los Angeles, CA 90022-2187
(323) 721-9882 Fax: (323) 721-7731
Carmen de Arce, Director

PROYECTO CONTRA SIDA POR VIDA
2973 16th St.
Mission Viejo, CA 94103
(415) 864-7278 Fax: (415) 575-1645
Operator, Contact

PROYECTO PASTORAL AT DOLORES
MISSION
Headquarters
135 N. Mission Rd.
Los Angeles, CA 90033-3307
(323) 881-0018 Fax: (323) 268-7228
Olivia Montes, Executive Director
Email: info@proyectopastoral.org
Web: www.proyectopastoral.org

PUBLIC HEALTH FOUNDATION
ENTERPRISES, INC. (PHFE)
13200 Crossroads Pkwy. N., #135
City of Industry, CA 91746
(562) 699-7320 or (800) 201-7320
Fax: (562) 692-6950
Charles A. Norris, President & CEO
Email: mailbox@phfe.org
Web: www.phfe.org

PUEBLO CENTER
1157 Lemoyne St.
Los Angeles, CA 90026
(213) 483-6335 Fax: (213) 483-5523
Sandra Figueroa, Executive Director

PUENTE LEARNING CENTER
People United to Enrich the
Neighborhood Through Education
(PUENTE)
501 South Boyle Ave.
Los Angeles, CA 90033
(323) 780-8900 Fax: (323) 780-0359
Sister Jennie Lechtenberg, Executive Director

PUENTE PROJECT
University of California
Office of the President
300 Lakeside Dr., 7th Floor
Oakland, CA 94612-3550
(510) 987-9619 Fax: (510) 834-0737
Yanira Guzman, Mentor
Email: yanira.guzman@ucop.edu
Web: www.puente.net

RAINBOW/PUSH COALITION
Los Angeles Bureau
12021 Wilshire Blvd.
Los Angeles, CA 90025
(310) 889-1111 Fax: (310) 471-1453
Tracy Rice, Los Angeles Bureau Chief
Web: www.rainbowpush.org

RANCHO LOS AMIGOS MEDICAL CENTER
7601 East Imperial Highway
Downey, CA 90242
(562) 401-7022 Fax: (562) 803-0056
Consuelo Diaz, CEO
Web: www.rancho.org

RAZA ARTISTAS DEL PUEBLO
University of California, Los Angeles
Community Programs Office
405 Hilgard Ave. #102 Men's Gym
Los Angeles, CA 90095-1454
(310) 825-5969 Fax: (310) 206-3175
Isidro Rodriguez, Program Advisor

RAZA RECRUITMENT AND RETENTION
CENTER
University of California, Berkeley
500 Eshelman Hall
Berkeley, CA 94720
(510) 642-1322
Alexis Parra, Director
Email: alx_e@uclinky4.berkeley.edu

REFORMA
California State University, Los Angeles
301 S. Granada Ave.
Alhambra, CA 91801
(323) 343-2019
Romelia Salinas, Chapter President
Email: rsalina@calstatela.edu
Web: http://clnet.ucr.edu/library/reforma

LIBROS, San Diego Chapter
San Diego Public Library
3795 Fairmount Ave.
San Diego, CA 92105
(619) 641-6100 Fax: (619) 640-8902
Ramiro Gonzalez, Chapter President
Email: r4g@library.sannet.gov
Web: http://clnet.ucr.edu/library/reforma

Northern California Chapter
Glen Park Branch Library
653 Chenery St.
San Francisco, CA 94131
(415) 337-4740
Mark Hall, Chapter President
Email: markh@sfpl.lib.ca.us
Web: http://clnet.ucr.edu/library/bplg

Orange County Chapter
Fullerton Public Library
353 E. Commonwealth Ave.
Fullerton, CA 92632
(714) 738-6383 Fax: (714) 447-3280
Al Milo, Chapter President
Email: alm@ci.fullerton.ca.us
Web: http://clnet.ucr.edu/library/reforma

REFUGIO DE CRISTO
8050 Lloyd Ave.
North Hollywood, CA 91605
(818) 909-0005 Fax: (818) 785-7309
Hugo Fraga, Vice Pres.

REGIS HOUSE
11346 Iowa Ave.
West Los Angeles, CA 90025
(310) 477-8168 Fax: (310) 479-6146
Sister Jennifer Goeta, Dir.

REPUBLICAN NATIONAL HISPANIC
ASSEMBLY OF CALIFORNIA (RNHA)
1903 W. Magnolia Blvd.
Burbank, CA 91506
(818) 841-5210 Fax: (818) 841-6668
John McGraw, Chairman
Web: www.rnha.org

RURAL COMMUNITY ASSISTANCE
CORPORATION (RCAC)
Associate-affiliate of NCLR
3120 Freeboard Dr., #201
West Sacramento, CA 95691
(916) 447-2854 Fax: (916) 447-2878
William French, Executive Director
Email: mail@rcac.org
Web: www.rcac.org

SACRAMENTO HISPANIC CHAMBER OF
COMMERCE
930 Alhambra Blvd., #100
Sacramento, CA 95816
(916) 554-7420 Fax: (916) 554-7429
Joseph Martel, President
Web: www.sachcc.org

SAINT FRANCIS CENTER
1835 S. Hope St
Los Angeles, CA 90015
(213) 747-5347 Fax: (213) 765-8915
Edward Delgado, Executive Director
Email: stfrasisi@aol.com

SALESIAN BOYS AND GIRLS CLUB OF LOS
ANGELES
3218 Wabash Ave.
Los Angeles, CA 90063
(213) 263-7519 Fax: (213) 263-8558
William Schofer, Exec. Dir.

SALSA & MERENGUE CLUB
University of California, Davis
Student Programs & Activities Ctr., Box #238
1 Shields Ave.
Davis, CA 95616-8706
(530) 752-2027 or (530) 297-7268
Fax: (530) 752-4951
Elnaz Nazmi, President
Email: enazmi@ucdavis.edu
Web: www.ucdavis.edu

SALUD PARA LA GENTE
Proyecto Alarma Sida
204 E. Beach St.
Watsonville, CA 95076
(408) 728-8250 Fax: (408) 728-8266
Archavio Viveras, Executive Director

SALUDOS HISPANOS
73-121 Fred Waring Dr., #100
Palm Desert, CA 92260
(760) 776-1206 or (800) 371-4456
Fax: (760) 776-1214
Maureen Harring, Editor
Email: maureen@saludos.com
Web: www.saludos.com

SALVADORAN-AMERICAN LEADERSHIP
AND EDUCATIONAL FUND (SALEF)
1605 West Olympic Blvd., 1040
Los Angeles, CA 90015
(213) 480-1052 Fax: (213) 487-2530
Mr. Carlos H. Hernández-Vaquerano, Exec. Dir.
Email: salef1@aol.com

SALVATION ARMY DAY CARE CENTER
836 Stanford Ave.
Los Angeles, CA 90021
(213) 623-9022 Fax: (213) 623-9093
Sara Varela, Dir.
Web: www.angecila.com

SAN ANTONIO MENTAL HEALTH CENTER
6450 Garfield Ave.
Bell Gardens, CA 90201
(562) 806-4921 Fax: (562) 928-9826
Lupe Tovar, Senior Typist Clerk

SAN BENITO COUNTY HISPANIC
CHAMBER OF COMMERCE
P.O. Box 2131
Hollister, CA 95024
(831) 638-1163 Fax: (831) 636-0882
Ignacio Velazques, President

SAN DIEGO COUNTY HISPANIC
CHAMBER OF COMMERCE
1250 6th Ave., #550
San Diego, CA 92101
(619) 702-0790 Fax: (619) 696-3282
Manny Aguilar, President
Email: sdchcc@sdchcc.com
Web: www.sdchcc.com

SAN DIEGO LA RAZA LAWYERS
ASSOCIATION
P.O. Box 8234
Chula Vista, CA 91912
(619) 425-9500 Fax: (619) 425-3602
Alvin Gomez, President

SAN DIEGO/SER-JOBS FOR PROGRESS, INC.
Affiliate of SER-Jobs for Progress
National, Inc.
3355 Mission Ave., #123
Oceanside, CA 92054
(760) 754-6500 Fax: (760) 967-6357
George López, President & CEO
Web: www.sernational.org

SAN FERNANDO CHAMBER OF
COMMERCE
519 South Brand Blvd.
San Fernando, CA 91340
(818) 361-1184 Fax: (818) 898-1986
Patti Friedman, President

SAN FERNANDO VALLEY INTERFAITH
COUNCIL (VIC)
10824 Topanga Canyon Blvd. #7
Chatsworth, CA 91311
(818) 718-6460 ext 3011 Fax: (818) 718-0734
Barry Smedberg, Exec. Dir.

SAN FRANCISCO HISPANIC CHAMBER OF
COMMERCE
600 Haight St.
San Francisco, CA 94117
(415) 864-4795 Fax: (415) 864-4796
Joe Dominguez, President
Email: sfacc@aol.com

SAN GABRIEL VALLEY HISPANIC
CHAMBER OF COMMERCE
P.O. Box 517
Baldwin Park, CA 91706
(626) 813-9947 Fax: (626) 813-9226
Marina Montenegro
Email: info@sgvhcc.org
Web: www.sgvhcc.org

SAN JOSE PUBLIC LIBRARY
Biblioteca Latinoamericana
921 S First St.
San Jose, CA 95110
(408) 294-1237
Email: bla.sjpl@ci.sj.ca.us

SAN JUAN MACIAS ORIENTATION
IMMIGRANT CENTER
13672 Van Nuys Blvd.
Pacoima, CA 91331
(818) 896-1156 Fax: (818) 896-1157
Mike S. Garcia, Exec. Dir.

SAN MARTIN SOCIETY OF SAN
FERNANDO VALLEY
8518 Orion Ave.
North Hills, CA 91343
(818) 894-2239 .Fax: (818) 894-2239
Mr. Mario Passo, President
Email: yapeyu@aol.com

SANMARTINECOS UNIDOS
7724 Ramish
Bell Gardens, CA 90201
(562) 806-1677
Miguel Enrique Tepez, Pres.

SANTA BARBARA HISTORICAL MUSEUM
136 E. De la Guerra St.
Santa Barbara, CA 93101
(805) 966-1601 Fax: (805) 966-1603
George Anderjack, Director

SANTA FE SPRINGS NEIGHBORHOOD
MULTIPURPOSE CENTER
9255 Pioneer Blvd.
Santa Fe Springs, CA 90670
(562) 692-0261 Fax: (562) 695-8620
Ana Price, Dir.
Email: social_services@santafesprings.org

SANTA PAULA CHAMBER OF COMMERCE
P.O. Box 1
Santa Paula, CA 93061
(805) 525-5561 Fax: (805) 525-8950
Anne Davis, President

SCIENCE CAREERS OPPORTUNITY
PROGRAM (SCOP)
School of Natural Sciences
California State University Fresno
2555 East San Ramon Avenue #68
Fresno, CA 93740-8034
(209) 278-4748 Fax: (209) 278-7804
Francisco Piñeda, Director
Email: francisc@csufresno.edu

SELF HELP GRAPHICS AND ART, INC.
3802 Cesar E. Chavez Ave.
Los Angeles, CA 90063
(323) 881-6444 Fax: (323 881-6447
Tomás Benitez, Director
Email: http://www.slfhelpgraphics.com

SHARE FOUNDATION - BUILDING A NEW
EL SALVADOR
National Headquarters
995 Market St., #1400
San Francisco, CA 94103
(415) 882-1530 Fax: (415) 882-1540
Jose Artiga, Executive Director
Email: share@igc.org

SIGMA DELTA PI - NATIONAL SPANISH
HONORARY SOCIETY
UCLA Dept. of Spanish and Portuguese
P.O. Box 951532
5310 Rolfe Hall
Los Angeles, CA 90095
(310) 825-1036 Fax: (310) 206-4757
John Skirius, Advisor
Email: jskirius@humnet.ucla.edu

Mount St. Mary's College Department of
Modern Languages
12001 Chalon Rd.
Los Angeles, CA 90049
(310) 954-4270
Michele Fine, Chair of the Department of
Modern Languages
Email: mfine@msmc.la.edu
Web: www.msmc.la.edu

SOCIEDAD GUADALUPANA DE TODOS
LOS SANTOS
All Saints Catholic Church
3431 Portola Ave.
Los Angeles, CA 90032
(323) 223-1101 Fax: (323) 223-9592
Elvia Najar, President

SOCIEDAD PRO NIÑOS SALVADOREÑOS
850 North Hobart Blvd.
Los Angeles, CA 90029
(213) 665-6937 Fax: (213) 664-0754
Concepción Alvarez, Pres.

SOCIEDAD PROGRESISTA MEXICANA
P.O. Box 7082
Riverside, CA 92513
(909) 689-3054
Arnoldo Zoto, State Pres.

SOCIETY FOR THE ADVANCEMENT OF
CHICANOS AND NATIVE AMERICANS IN
SCIENCE (SACNAS)
P.O. Box 8526
Santa Cruz, CA 95061
(831) 459-0170 Fax: (831) 459-0194
Ronaldo Ramirez, Executive Director
Email: info@sacnas.org
Web: www.sacnas.org

SOCIETY OF HISPANIC HISTORICAL AND
ANCESTRAL RESEARCH (SHHAR)
P.O. Box 490
Midway City, CA 92655-0490
(714) 894-8161 Fax: (714) 898-7063
Mimi Lozano, President
Email: mimilozano@aol.com
Web: www.somosprimos.com

SOCIETY OF HISPANIC PROFESSIONAL
ENGINEERS (SHPE)
800 N. State College Blvd.
Fullerton, CA 92834
(714) 278-3879 Fax: (714) 278-4171
Carla Padia, President
Email: officers@shpe.ecs.fullerton.edu
Web: http://shpe.ecs.fullerton.edu/contents.html

California Institute of Technology
Minority Students Affairs Office
P.O. Box 204-85
Pasadena, CA 91125
(626) 395-6208 Fax: (626) 683-1392
Sue Borrego, Advisor
Email: sueb@caltech.edu
Web: www.shpe.org

California State University, Chico
O'Connell 114
Chico, CA 95929-0100
(530) 898-4017 Fax: (530) 898-6093
Paul Villegas, Advisor
Web: www.csuchico.edu/ltc

California State University, Fresno
2220 E. San Ramon, MS 94
Fresno, CA 93740-8028
(559) 278-2976 Fax: (559) 278-4517
Hernán Maldonado, Advisor
Email: hernanm@csufresno.edu

California State University, Sacramento
Student Activities Box 172, 6000 J St.
Sacramento, CA 95819
(916) 278-5957 Fax: (916) 278-7086
Madeline Fish, Advisor
Web: www.gaia.ecs.csus.edu/~clacse

Fresno Professional Chapter
P.O. Box 4887
Fresno, CA 93744
(559) 445-6898 Fax: (559) 445-6377
Marco A. Sanchez, President
Email: marco_sanchez@dot.ca.gov
Web: www.shpe.org

Greater Los Angeles Professional Chapter
P.O. Box 226722
Los Angeles, CA 90022
(323) 255-0077 Fax: (323) 255-0040
Hector A. Castillo, President
Email: hacastillo@earthlink.net
Web: www.shpe-losangeles.org

Loyola Marymount University
c/o Math Department
7900 Loyola Blvd.
Los Angeles, CA 90045
(310) 338-5113 or (310) 338-2877
Fax: (310) 338-5976
Herbert Medina, Advisor
Email: hmedina@lmumail.lmu.edu

National Headquarters, Affiliate of NCLR
5400 E. Olympic Blvd., #210
Los Angeles, CA 90022
(323) 725-3970 or (323) 278-4835
Fax: (323) 725-0316
Leticia Araceli Vidal, Executive Director
Email: shpenational@shpe.org
Web: www.shpe.org

Orange County Professional Chapter
P.O. Box 44
Irvine, CA 92650
(949) 368-7444 Fax: (949) 368-5360
Fred Alcocer, Chapter President
Email: alcocef@songs.sce.com
Web: www.shpe.org

Sacramento City College
MESA Center/Student Activities
3835 Freeport Blvd.
Sacramento, CA 95822
(916) 558-2490 Fax: (916) 558-2650
Guemu Johnson, Advisor
Email: johnsom@scc.losrio.cc.ca.us

San Diego Professional Chapter
P.O. Box 910131
San Diego, CA 92191
(858) 826-4953 Fax: (858) 826-7877
David Trevino, Chapter President
Email: david.g.trevino@cpmx.saic.com
Web: http://reg2.shpe.org/sdshpe/

San Jose Professional Chapter
645 Wool Creek Rd.
San Jose, CA 95112
(650) 852-5428 Fax: (916) 237-4488
Alvaro Sanchez, Chapter President
Email: alvaroiii@hotmail.com
Web: www.shpe.sgi.com

University of California, Davis
1050 Engineering Unit II
1 Shields Ave.
Davis, CA 95616-8706
(530) 752-3390 Fax: (530) 752-8058
Irma Nevarez, Co-President
Email: ienevarez@ucdavis.edu
Web: www.engr.ucdavis.edu/~caless/

Ventura County Professional Chapter
P.O. Box 2397
Camarillo, CA 93011
(805) 989-9257 or (805) 488-4838 (h)
Fax: (805) 989-9259
Jesse M. Zapata, Co-President
Email: zapataji@mugu.navy.mil
Web: www.geocities.com/CapeCanaveral/Hangar/4141

SOCIETY OF LATINO ENGINEERS AND
SCIENTISTS
University of California, Los Angeles
P.O. Box 6722
Los Angeles, CA 90022
(323) 255-8950 Fax: (323) 255-0046
Hector Castillo, President

SOCIETY OF MEXICAN AMERICAN
ENGINEERS AND SCIENTISTS (MAES)
California State University, Long Beach
Student Life and Development
1250 Bellflower Blvd.
Long Beach, CA 90840
(562) 985-5140 or (213) 581-1016 (H)
Fax: (562) 985-5683
William Fernandez, President
Web: www.maes-natl.org

SOLANO/NAPA COUNTY HISPANIC
CHAMBER OF COMMERCE
P.O. Box 2723
Fairfield, CA 94553
(707) 643-5037 Fax: (707) 557-9844
Carlos Solorzano, Public Relations
Email: hccsolnapa@aol.com

SOLES
San Jose State University
1 Washington Square #366
San Jose, CA 95192-0181
(408) 924-3830
Horacio Alfaro, Advisor

SOMOS FAMILIA, PLAZA FAMILY
PRESERVATION NETWORK
4127 César Chavez Ave.
Los Angeles, CA 90063
(323) 261-0414 Fax: (323) 261-9178
Dr. Evelyn Márquez, Program Director

SOUTH GATE CHAMBER OF COMMERCE
3350 Tweedy Blvd.
South Gate, CA 90280
(323) 567-1203 Fax: (213) 567-1204
Ted Chandler, Executive Director
Web: www.southgatechamber.org

SOUTHERN CALIFORNIA ECUMENICAL
COUNCIL
54 North Oakland Ave.
Pasadena, CA 91101-2086
(626) 578-6371 Fax: (626) 578-6358
Rev. Albert G. Cohen, Executive Director

SOUTHERN CALIFORNIA REGIONAL
PURCHASING COUNCIL
NMSDC
3325 Wilshire Boulevard, Suite 804
Los Angeles, CA 90010
(213) 380-7114 Fax: (213) 380-8026
Hollis Smith, President

SOUTHERN CALIFORNIA-ARGENTINA
PARTNERS OF THE AMERICAS
CSU Los Angeles, International Prog. &
Services
5151 State University Dr.
Los Angeles, CA 90032
(323) 343-3170 Fax: (323) 343-3039
Michael D. Fels, President
Email: mfels@calstatela.edu

SOUTHWEST LOS ANGELES CHAMBER OF
COMMERCE
1732 W. 22nd St.
Los Angeles, CA 90007
(323) 737-2288 Fax: (323) 737-2288
Carlos L. Holguín, Director

SOUTHWEST MINORITY ECONOMIC
DEVELOPMENT ASSOCIATION
1601 W. 2nd St.
Santa Ana, CA 92703
(714) 547-4073 or (714) 543-8933
Fax: (714) 543-8933
John Collins, Pres.

SOUTHWEST VOTER REGISTRATION
EDUCATION PROJECT (SVREP)
California Office
2914 N. Main St., 2nd Floor
Los Angeles, CA 90031
(323) 343-9299 Fax: (323) 343-9100
Antonio González, President
Email: SVRP@aol.com

SPANISH CLUB
Santa Barbara City College
720 Cliff Dr.
Santa Barbara, CA 93109
(805) 965-0581 ext 2262 Fax: (805) 965-7221

SPANISH CULTURAL RESOURCE CENTER
University of Southern California
Waite Phillips Hall B-29
3470 Trousdale Pkwy.
Los Angeles, CA 90089-0031
(213) 740-5896 Fax: (213) 740-7985
Margarita Ravera, Dir.
Email: ravera@caroli.usc.edu
web: http://www-bcf.usc.edu/~ravera

SPANISH SPEAKING SENIOR CENTER
Affiliate to Chicano Fed. of San Diego
Co., Inc.
3751Boston Ave.
San Diego, CA 92113
(619) 263-7785 Fax: (619) 263-7786
Peggy de la Peña, Manager

SPANISH SPEAKING STUDENTS FOR
PROGRESSIVE ACTION
University of California, Davis
Student Programs & Activities Ctr., Box #148
1 Shields Ave.
Davis, CA 95616-8706
(530) 752-2027 or (530) 757-2966
Fax: (530) 752-4951
Clementina Acosta, President
Email: cacosta@ucdavis.edu
Web: www.ucdavis.edu

SPANISH SPEAKING UNITY COUNCIL,
THE
1900 Fruitvale Ave., #2A
Oakland, CA 94601
(510) 535-6900 Fax: (510) 534-7771
Arabella Martinez, CEO
Email: talderete@unitycouncil.org
Web: www.unitycouncil.org

SPANISH STUDENT ASSOCIATION
Student Life and Development
California State University, Long Beach
1212 Bellflower Ave.
Long Beach, CA 90815
(562) 985-4181

STANFORD CHICANO/LATINO ALUMNI ASSOCIATION OF SOUTHERN CALIFORNIA
National. Stanford Chicano/Latino Alumni Club
P.O. Box 86204 Terminal Annex
Los Angeles, CA 90086-0204
(213) 847-1596 Fax: (213) 847-2203
Mario Vásquez, Membership Chair
Email: mvazquez@cao.ci.la.ca.us
Web: www.mrluna.com/stanford/alumni.html

STANFORD LATINO BUSINESS ASSOC.
Stanford Univ. Office of Student Activities
P.O. Box 16260
Stanford, CA 94305
(650) 723-0927
Erika Ornelas, Contact
Email: jjam@leland

STANFORD LATINO LAW STUDENT ASSOCIATION (SLLSA)
Stanford University
El Centro Chicano
Building 590-F, Old Union
Stanford, CA 94305-3044
(650) 723-2089 Fax: (650) 725-6487
Chris Gonzalez Clarke, Assistant Director
Email: chris.clarke@stanford.edu
Web: www.stanford.edu/dept/elcentro/

STANFORD LITERACY IMPROVEMENT PROJECT
Stanford University
El Centro Chicano
Building 590-F, Old Union
Stanford, CA 94305-3044
(650) 723-2089 Fax: (650) 725-6487
Chris Gonzalez Clarke, Assistant Director
Email: chris.clarke@stanford.edu
Web: www.stanford.edu/dept/elcentro/

STANFORD RAZA MEDICAL ASSOCIATION (SRMA)
Stanford University
Office of Students Affairs
M105, School of Medicine
Stanford, CA 94309
(650) 561-9517
Yolanda Agredano, Director

STANFORD SOCIETY OF CHICANO/ LATINO ENGINEERS & SCIENTISTS
Stanford Univ. Office of Student Activities
P.O. Box 2342
Stanford, CA 94309
(650) 497-0575
Christopher Hernández, Contact
Email: sscles@lists

STANFORD SPANISH ASSOCIATION
Stanford Univ. Office of Student Activities
Escondido Village 42 D
Stanford, CA 94305
(650) 497-7490
Pablo Molinero-Fernández, Contact
Email: manel@leland

STANFORD UNIVERSITY MINORITY MEDICAL ALLIANCE (SUMMA)
Stanford Univ. Office of Student Activities
Off. of Student Affairs, M-105
Stanford Medical School
Stanford, CA 94305
Stacey Anderson, Contact
Email: rachstel@leland

STOCKTON MEXICAN-AMERICAN CHAMBER OF COMMERCE
343 E. Main St., #800
Stockton, CA 95202
(209) 943-6117 Fax: (209) 943-0114

STUDENT ADVOCACY FOR BILINGUAL EDUCATION
Loyola Marymount University
7900 Loyola Blvd.
Los Angeles, CA 90045-8425
(310) 338-2863 Fax: (310) 338-1976
Magaly Lavadenz, Education Department
Email: mlavade@lmumail.lmu.edu

SYNOD OF SOUTHERN CALIFORNIA & HAWAII, PRESBYTERIAN CHURCH (USA)
Hispanic Commission
1501 Wilshire Blvd.
Los Angeles, CA 90017
(213) 483-3840 Fax: (213) 483-4275
Rev. Ernesto Hernandez, Pres. of Hispanic Community

TEATRO QUINTO SOL
Chicano Student Program
UC Riverside, 229 Costo Hall
Riverside, CA 92521
(909) 787-3821 Fax: (909) 787-2189
Alfredo Figueroa, Director
Email: alfredo.figueroa@ucr.edu

TEATRO UNIVERSITARIO EN ESPAÑOL
Dept. of Modern Languages, CSU L. A.
5151 State University Dr.
Los Angeles, CA 90032
(323) 343-4230 or (323) 343-4241
Fax: (323) 343-4234
Dr. Felipe Díaz Jimeno, Director
Email: fdiaz@calstatela.edu

TEEN LEADERSHIP CHALLENGE (TLC)
Proyecto Pastoral at Dolores Mission
1826 E. 1st St.
Los Angeles, CA 90033
(323) 881-0024 Fax: (323) 881-0035
Martiza Alvarez, Director
Email: info@proyectopastoral.org
Web: www.proyectopastoral.org

TOMAS RIVERA POLICY INSTITUTE (TRPI)
Pitzer College, Scott Hall
1050 N. Mills Ave.
Claremont, CA 91711-6101
(909) 621-8897 Fax: (909) 621-8898
Harry Pachón, President
Email: info@trpi.org
Web: www.trpi.org

TOURIST OFFICE OF SPAIN
8383 Wilshire Blvd., #956
Beverly Hills, CA 90211
(323) 658-7188 Fax: (323) 658-1061
Ignacio Ducasse, Director
Email: losangeles@tourspain.es
Web: www.okspain.org

TRABAJADORES DE LA RAZA, INC.
P.O. Box 251
Alhambra, CA 91802
(323) 226-5253 Fax: (323) 226-4341
Olga Sarabia, Contact
Email: osarabia@hsc.usc.edu

TRAINING OF THE CENTRAL COAST COUNTIES
Center for Employment
701 Vine St.
San Jose, CA 95110
(408) 287-7924 Fax: (408) 294-7849
Russel Tershy, Executive Director

UC LINGUISTIC MINORITY RESEARCH INSTITUTE
Graduate School of Education
University of California, Santa Barbara
Building-528, Room 4722
Santa Barbara, CA 93106
(805) 893-2250 Fax: (805) 893-5477
Prof. Russell Rumberger, Dir.
Email: lmri@lmrinet.ucsb.edu

UCR BALLET FOLKLORICO
Chicano Student Program
UC Riverside
229 Costo Hall
Riverside, CA 92521
(909) 787-3821 Fax: (909) 787-2189
Alfredo Figueroa, Director
Email: alfredo.figueroa@ucr.edu

UNIDAD ESPAÑOLA DE CALIFORNIA "LA PEÑA"
150 N. Willow Ave.
City of Industry, CA 91746
(626) 961-9800 Fax: (626) 961-8530
José Mazaira, Pres.

UNIDAS
Stanford University Office of Student Activities
Bldg. 590-F The Nitery
Stanford, CA 94305
(650) 497-2608
Vanessa Delgado, Contact
Email: unidas@lists

UNIDOS
9842 W. 13th St.
Garden Grove, CA 92644
(714) 531-4624 Fax: (714) 531-1189
Alfonso Villalobos, Director

UNIFICATION OF DISABLED LATIN AMERICANS (UDLA)
3727 West 6th St. #511
Los Angeles, CA 90020
(213) 388-8352 Fax: (213) 388-3802
Rubén B. Hernández, Fndr & Pres.

UNION ESPAÑOLA DE CALIFORNIA, INC.
2850 Alemany Blvd.
San Francisco, CA 94112
(415) 587-5115
Manuel Hume, President

UNION ESTUDIANTIL DE LA RAZA
Chicano Student Program
UC Riverside, 229 Costo Hall
Riverside, CA 92521
(909) 787-3821 Fax: (909) 787-2189
Alfredo Figueroa, Director, Chicano Student Programs
Email: alfredo.figueroa@ucr.edu

UNITED FARM WORKERS OF AMERICA (UFW)
P.O. Box 62
Keene, CA 93531
(661) 822-5571 ext105 Fax: (661) 822-6103
Arturo S. Rodriguez, President
Email: pubaction@ufwmail.com
Web: www.ufw.org

c/o AFL-CIO Region VI
3325 Wilshire Blvd. #1208
Los Angeles, CA 90010
(213) 387-1974 Fax: (213) 387-3525
Irving Hershenbaum, Vicepresident
Web: www.ufw.org

Los Angeles Public Action Office
2130 West 9th St.
Los Angeles, CA 90006
(213) 381-5611 Ext. #17 Fax: (213) 383-0772
Roman Pinal, Manager
Email: ufwla@lightspeed.net

UNITED LATINO FUND
315 W. 9th St., #709
Los Angeles, CA 90015
(213) 236-2929 Fax: (213) 236-2930
Anthony Espinoza, Pres.& Gen. Mgr.

UNITED NEIGHBORHOOD ORGANIZATION (UNO)
4800 East Olympic Blvd.
Los Angeles, CA 90022
(213) 266-0577 Fax: (213) 266-7246

UNITED STATES EQUAL OPPORTUNITY COMMISSION
Los Angeles District Office
255 E.Temple 4th Floor
Los Angeles, CA 90012
(213) 894-1000 Fax: (213) 894-1118
Thelma Taylor, District Director

UNITED STATES-MEXICO CHAMBER OF COMMERCE (USMCOC)
Pacific Chapter
444 S. Flower St., 9th Floor
Los Angeles, CA 90071
(213) 623-7725 Fax: (213) 623-0032
James Charles Clark, Executive Director
Email: usmcoc@aol.com

UNITED STATES-MEXICO SISTER CITIES ASSOCIATION, INC.
3133 S. Hacienda Blvd.
Hacienda Heights, CA 91745-6304
(626) 961-6556 Fax: (626) 961-8994
Donald D. Goertz, President
Email: classiccruise@earthlink.net
Web: http://home.earthlink.net/~tohancuff/

UNITED WAY HISPANIC BUSINESS INITIATIVE
United Way of Greater Los Angeles
523 W. 6th Street
Los Angeles, CA 90014
(213) 630-2161 Fax: (213) 630-2369
Helen Torres, Manager
Email: htorres@unitedwayla.org

USC GOOD BEGINNINGS FAMILY OPPORTUNITY CENTER
1839 S. Hoover St.
Los Angeles, CA 90006
(213) 747-6254 Fax: (213) 747-4572
Ms. Mary Helen Barajas, Asst. Project Director

VARIETY BOYS AND GIRLS CLUB
2530 Cincinnati St.
East Los Angeles, CA 90033
(323) 269-3177 Fax: (323)269-3268
Mr. Pérez, Exec. Dir.

VICTORY OUTREACH
454 Coberta Ave.
La Puente, CA 91746
(626) 961-4910 Fax: (626) 961-7710
Pastor Sonny Arguinzoni, Exec. Dir.

VILLA DE NIÑOS
9999 Feron Blvd., Suite B
Rancho Gucamanga, CA 91730
(909) 484-1903 Fax: (909) 481-0051
Lucia Torres, Supervisor

VISION UNIDA
P.O. Box 15856
San Luis Obispo, CA 93406-5856
(804) 545-6650
Gil Apodaca, President

WALSBORN PRODUCTIONS/605 CITIZENSHIP PROJECT
10016 Pioneer Blvd., Ste. 107
Santa Fe Springs, CA 90670
(562) 948-3250 or (562) 801-1069
Fax: (562) 948-4152
Nelly Paredes-Walsborn, Pres./Dir.

WATTS CENTURY LATINO ORGANIZATION
Affiliate of NCLR
10360 Wilmington Ave.
Los Angeles, CA 90002
(323) 564-9140 Fax: (323) 564-2737
Arturo Ybarra, President

WHITTIER BOULEVARD MERCHANTS ASSOCIATION (WBMA)
4726 Whittier Blvd.
Los Angeles, CA 90022
(323) 261-2591 Fax: (323) 261-9098
Ray Abboud, President

WILLIAM C. VELASQUEZ INSTITUTE
California Office
2914 N. Main St., 1st Floor
Los Angeles, CA 90031
(323) 222-2217 Fax: (323) 222-2011
Antonio González, President

WILLIAM GRANT COMMUNITY ARTS CENTER
2520 W. View St.
Los Angeles, CA 90016
(323) 734-1164 Fax: (213) 485-1614
James Burks, Director

WOMEN AND FAMILY CRISIS CENTER
630 N. Park Ave.
Pomona, CA 91767
(213) 253-5959 or (909) 623-9751
Fax: (909) 629-3171
Sophia Esparza, Executive Director

WOMEN'S CENTER & ADULT REENTRY CALIFORNIA STATE UNIVERSITY
P.O. Box 6830, 800 N. State College Blvd.
Fullerton, CA 92834
(714) 278-3928 Fax: (714) 278-5134
Barbara McDowell, Director

YOLO COUNTY HISPANIC CHAMBER OF COMMERCE
117 W. Main St., # 15
Woodland, CA 95695
(530) 666-5335 Fax: (530) 752-9250
Lidia Salsiedo, President

YOUNG LATINO LEADERS
South San Mateo County
2600 Middle Field Rd.
Redwood City, CA 94063
(650) 780-7522 Fax: (650) 362-1360
Paul Vega, Director

YOUTH OPPORTUNITIES FOUNDATION
8820 Sepulveda Blvd. #208
Los Angeles, CA 90045
(310) 670-7664 Fax: (310) 670-5238
Mr. Félix Castro, Executive Director

YOUTH OPPORTUNITIES UNLIMITED (YOU)
8419 S. Vermont Ave.
Los Angeles, CA 90044
(323) 789-4977 Fax: (323) 789-4975
James L. Watson, Director
Email: youinc@pacbell.net
Web: www.youinc.homestead.com

ZONA SECA, INC.
26 W. Figueroa Street
Santa Barbara, CA 93101
(805) 963-8961 Fax: (805) 963-8964
Mr. Frank Banales, Executive Director
Email: administration@zonaseca.com
Web: www.zonaseca.com

COLORADO

AMERICAN GI FORUM OF COLORADO
P.O. Box 11590
Denver, CO 80211
(303) 458-1700 Fax: (303) 458-1634
James Maestas, Executive Director
Email: amgiforum@uswest.net

AMERICAN GI FORUM OF THE U.S.
National Headquarters
2870 N. Speer Blvd. #220
Denver, CO 80211-0440
(303) 458-1700 Fax: (303) 458-1634
Greg Archuleta, Executive Director
Email: amgiforum@uswest.net

AMERICAN JEWISH COMMITTEE
Latino Jewish Dialogue
300 S Dahlia St., #201
Denver, CO 80222
(303) 320-1742 Fax: (303) 320-1742
Anita Fricklas, Director
Email: fricklasa_ajc@compuserve.com

AMIGOS DE LA COMUNIDAD
309 W. 1st Ave.
Denver, CO 80223
(303) 722-5150 Fax: (303) 722-5118

AMISTAD
Lockheed Martin Astronautics
P.O. Box 179
Mail Stop: DC 0092
Denver, CO 80201
(303) 977-4332 Fax: (303) 971-2201
Carol Romero, Pres.

ARCHDIOCESAN HISPANIC OFFICE
3600 Zuni St.
Denver, CO 80223
(303) 433-9013

ARCHDIOCESE OF DENVER
Hispanic Affairs
1300 S. Steele St.
Denver, CO 80210-2599
(303) 715-3235 or (303) 433-9013
Fax: (303) 715-2042
Mar Muñoz, Director for Hispanic Ministry
Email: marmunoz@archden.org

Hispanic Ministry Office
1300 S. Steele St.
Denver, CO 80210-2599
(303) 715-3206 Fax: (303) 715-2042
Rev. Raymond Jones, Vicar

**ASSOCIATION OF HISPANIC
ADMINISTRATORS (AHA)**
Denver Public Schools/Beach Court
Elementary School
4950 Beach Court
Denver, CO 80221
(303) 455-3607
Kay Close, Principal

AZTLAN RECREATION CENTER
4435 Navajo St.
Denver, CO 80211
(303) 458-4899 Fax: (303) 458-4887
Rosmary Ornalez, Recreation Director

BROTHERS REDEVELOPMENT, INC. (BRI)
Affiliate of NCLR
2250 Eaton St., Suite B
Garden Level, CO 80214
(303) 202-6340 Fax: (303) 274-1314
José Girón, Executive Director
Email: bri@orci.com

**BUENO CENTER FOR MULTICULTURAL
EDUCATION**
University of Colorado at Boulder
Educ. Bldg. #247, Campus Box 249
Boulder, CO 80309
(303) 492-5416 Fax: (303) 492-2883
Leonard Baca, Director
Email: Buenoctr@colorado.edu
Web: www.colorado.edu

**BUENO HIGH SCHOOL EQUIVALENCY
PROGRAM**
University of Colorado at Boulder
Education Bldg., Campus Box 249
Boulder, CO 80309
(303) 492-5419 Fax: (303) 492-2883

CATCHER'S MITT
Adams City High School
4625 E. 68th Ave.
Commerce City, CO 80022
(303) 853-7733 Fax: (303) 853-7868

CENTRO CULTURAL MEXICANO
Denver Office
48 Steel St.
Denver, CO 80206
(303) 331-1870 Fax: (303) 331-0169
Marcela De Lamar, Executive Director
Email: culture@terapath.com

CENTRO DE LAS FAMILIAS
75 Meade St.
Denver, CO
(303) 934-2963

CENTRO HISPANIC STUDENT SERVICES
Colorado State University
178 Lory Student Center
Fort Collins, CO 80523
(970) 491-5722 Fax: (970) 491-2534
Guadalupe Salazar, Director
Email: rsalas@lamar.coloatate.edu
Web: www.colostate.edu/orgs/ElCentro

CESAR CHAVEZ CULTURAL CENTER
University of Northern Colorado
1410 20th St.
Greeley, CO 80639
(970) 351-2424 Fax: (970) 351-2360
Silvana Carlos, Director
Email: cchavez@bentley.unco.edu

**CHELTENHAM RAZALOGIA PARENT
EMPOWERMENT PROGRAM**
1480 Julian St.
Denver, CO 80204
(303) 764-7573 Fax: (303) 825-3826

**CHICANO HUMANITIES AND ARTS
COUNCIL**
P.O.Box 2512
Denver, CO 80204
(303) 571-0440 or (303) 213-1962
Fax: (303) 221-3268
Crystal O'Brien, Chairperson
Email: CHAC2515@aol.com
Web: www.chacweb.org/

CINCO DE MAYO FESTIVAL
1029 Santa Fe Dr.
Denver, CO 80204
(303) 534-8342 Fax: (303) 534-7418
Pauline Madrid Johnson, Director
Web: www.newsed.org

**COLORADO ASSOCIATION FOR
BILINGUAL EDUCATION (CABE)**
930 McKinley Ave.
Fort Lupton, CO 80621
(303) 492-5416 Fax: (303) 592-7090
John C. Rocha, Pres.
Email: Buenoctr@colorado.edu

**COLORADO DEMOCRATIC PARTY LATINO
INITIATIVE**
5200 E Colfax Ave.
Denver, CO 80203
(303) 830-8989 Fax: (303) 830-2743
Email: info@coloradodems.org
Web: www.coloradodems.org

**COLORADO HISPANIC MEDIA
ASSOCIATION (CHMA)**
940 Logan St.
Denver, CO 80203
(303) 892-0109
Judy Montero, Pres.

**COLORADO INSTITUTE FOR HISPANIC
EDUCATION**
1445 Market St. #280
Denver, CO
(303) 620-4436

COLORADO LEGAL SERVICES, INC.
Fort Morgan Office
209 State St.
Fort Morgan, CO 80701
(970) 867-3096 Fax: (970) 867-0625
Jacquelyn Higinbotham, Managing Attorney
Email: jackyj@twol.com

COLORADO LEGAL SERVICES, INC.
Grand Junction Office
101 S. 3rd St. #301
Grand Junction, CO 81501
(970) 243-7940 Fax: (970) 243-7941
Colin Wilson, Manager

Greeley Office
1020 9th St. #300
Greeley, CO 80631-1122
(970) 353-7554 Fax: (970) 353-7557
Mario Rivera, Managing Attorney

La Junta Office
P. O. Box 1026
309 Santa Fe
La Junta, CO 81050
(719) 384-5438 Fax: (719) 384-8676
Robert Hunt, Mannaging Attorney

COLORADO MIGRANT HEALTH PROG.
P. O. Box 870
405 N. 12th Street
Rocky Ford, CO 81067
(719) 254-6481 Fax: (719) 254-5112
Mitt Garcia, Cont.

P. O. Box G, 721 Peach Ave.
Palisade, CO 81526
(970) 464-5862 Fax: (970) 464-7352
Evangline Mondargon, Area Coordinator

P.O. Box 507, 308 Main, #102
Olathe, CO 81425
(970) 323-0538 or (970) 323-0531
Fax: (970) 323-0534
Mary Jane Place, Health Services Coordinator
Email: MaryJane@online.com

La Clinica Campesina Rural Health Clinic
1345 Plaza Court N.
Lafayette, CO 80026
(303) 665-9310 Fax: (303) 665-4459
Teresa Collins, Contact

PCHC/Avondale Clinic
P.O. Box 159, 328 Avondale Blvd.
Avondale, CO 81022
(719) 947-3344 Fax: (719) 947-3346
Maria Fox, Cont.

Pueblo Community Health Center (PCHC)
110 East Route
Pueblo, CO 81004
(719) 543-8711 Fax: (719) 543-0171
Maria Fox, Case Manager

Valley-Wide Health Services
P. O. Box 459
186 N. Hurt Street
Center, CO 81125
(719) 754-2778 Fax: (719) 754-2166
Antonia Romero, Mgr. & Migrant Health Coord.
Email: romeroan@vwhs.org

**COLORADO RURAL HOUSING
DEVELOPMENT CORPORATION (CRHDC)**
Affiliate of NCLR
3621 W 73rd Ave., #C
Westminster, CO 80030
(303) 428-1448 Fax: (303) 428-1989
Alfred Gold, Executive Director

COLORADO RURAL LEGAL SERVICES, INC.
Alamosa Office
906 1/2 Main St.
Alamosa, CO 81101
(719) 589-4993 Fax: (719) 589-4995

Durango Office, Legal Aid Office
1474 Main Ave. #108
Durango, CO 81301-5140
(970) 247-0266 Fax: (970) 385-7378

Fort Collins Office
424 Pine St.
Fort Collins, CO 80524-2434
(970) 493-2891 Fax: (970) 493-3758
David Bye, Contact

Migrant Division
1905 Sherman St. #810
Denver, CO 80203
(303) 893-6468 Fax: (303) 825-5532
Mario Rivera, Exec. Dir.

**COLORADO'S FINEST ALTERNATIVE HIGH
SCHOOL**
2323 W. Baker Ave
Englewood, CO 80110
(303) 934-5786 Fax: (303) 934-9183
Cher Tufly, Principal
Email: cher_tufly@ceo.cudenver.edu
Web: www.cfahs.org

COMMUNITY COLLEGE OF DENVER (CCD)
P.O. Box 173363, Campus Box 250
Denver, CO 80217
(303) 556-2600
Byron McClenney, President
Web: www.ccd.rightchoice.org

CONGRESS OF HISPANIC EDUCATORS
7412 E Bates Dr.
Denver, CO 80231
(303) 751-4284 Fax: (303) 750-4918
Esther Romero

COORS HISPANIC EMPLOYEE NETWORK
PO Box 1454
Golden, CO 80401
(303) 277-5577 Fax: (303) 277-5337
Linda Reffel, Pres.

CULTURE THROUGH TEXTILES
2333 Eudora St.
Denver, CO 80207
(303) 377-0187

CUMBRES PROGRAM
University of Northern Colorado
President's Office, Carter Hall
Greeley, CO 80639
(970) 356-7754 Fax: (970) 351-8045

**DEL NORTE NEIGHBORHOOD
DEVELOPMENT**
2926 Zuni St., #202
Denver, CO 80211
(303) 477-4774 Fax: (303) 433-0924
Marvin Kelly, Executive Director

DENVER CIVIC THEATER
721 Santa Fe Drive
Denver, CO 80204
(303) 595-3800 Fax: (303) 265-9366
Brantly Dunaway, Executive Artistic Director
Email: artistic@denvercivic.com
Web: www.denvercivic.com

DENVER EDUCATION NETWORK (DEN)
Community College of Denver
P.O. Box 173363, Campus Box 250
Denver, CO 80217
(303) 556-3786 Fax: (303) 556-3586

**DENVER HISPANIC CHAMBER OF
COMMERCE, INC.**
930 W. 7th Ave.
Denver, CO 80204
(303) 534-7783 or (303) 595-8977
Fax: (303) 595-8977
Sharon J. Vigil, President
Email: sharonvigil.uswest.net
Web: www.dhcc.com

DENVER WATER DEPARTMENT
Latin American Support Organization
1600 W 12th Ave.
Denver, CO 80254
(303) 628-6346 Fax: (303) 628-6349
Patricia Gonzales, Contact
Web: www.water.denver.co.gov

DEPARTMENT OF ETHNIC STUDIES
University of Colorado at Boulder
Campus Box 339, Ketchum 30
Boulder, CO 80309-0339
(303) 492-8852 Fax: (303) 492-7799
Evelyn Hu DeHart, Chair
Email: ethinic.studies@colorado.edu

DIOCESE OF COLORADO SPRINGS
Catholic Community Services
29 W. Kiowa St.
Colorado Springs, CO 80903-1498
(719) 636-2345 x168 Fax: (719) 636-1216
Sr. Peggy Malone, RSM

DIOCESE OF PUEBLO
Hispanic Affairs
1001 Grand Ave.
Pueblo, CO 81003-2948
(719) 544-9861 Fax: (719) 544-1220
Sr. Andrea Vásquez, OSB, Dir. of Pastoral
Outreach
Email: savasquez@usa.net

EL CENTRO SU TEATRO
4725 High St.
Denver, CO 80216
(303) 296-0219 Fax: (303) 296-4614
Anthony García, Executive Director
Email: centro@suteatro.org
Web: suteatro.org

EL COMITE DE LONGMONT
455 Kimbart St.
Longmont, CO 80501
(303) 651-6125 Fax: (303) 702-0314
Emma Peña McCleave, President

ESCUELA TLATELOLCO CENTRO DE ESTUDIOS
2949 N. Federal Blvd.
Denver, CO 80211
(303) 964-8993 Fax: (303) 964-9795
Nita Gonzales, President & CEO
Email: tlafelolco@uswest.net

FAMILY LEARNING CENTER
3164 34th St
Boulder, CO 80301
(303) 442-8979 Fax: (303) 442-0901
Brenda Lyle, Director
Email: flcboulder_2000@yahoo.com
Web: www.flcboulder.org

FARMWORKER HEALTH SERVICES OF COLORADO
4300 Cherry Creek Dr. South
Denver, CO 80246
(303) 692-2430 Fax: (303) 782-5576
Rubén Melgoza, Health Serv. Coordinator

Colorado Dept. of Public Health & Environment
4300 Cherry Creek Dr. S.
Denver, CO 80246-1530
(303) 692-2430 Fax: (303) 782-5576
Susan Jager, Program Dir.

GENEALOGICAL SOCIETY OF HISPANIC AMERICA
P. O. Box 9606
Denver, CO 80209-0606
(303) 771-7427
Wilfred Martínez, President

Trinidad Chapter
811 Linden Ave.
Trinidad, CO 81081
(310) 204-6808
Donie Nelson, Acting President

P.O. Box 9606
Denver, CO 80209-0606
(310) 204-6808
Donie Nelson, Acting President

Pueblo Chapter
P.O. Box 3027
Pueblo, CO 81004
(310) 204-6808
Donie Nelson, Acting President

GREATER AURARIA NEIGHBORS AFFILIATED FOR SERVICES, (GANAS)
1212 Mariposa St.
Denver, CO 80204
(303) 893-5114 Fax: (303) 573-8023
Patrick Vigil, Executive Director

HISPANIC ADVISORY COALITION OF EMPLOYEES RESOURCES (HACER)
c/o Norwest Bank, Denver
1740 Broadway
Denver, CO 80274
(303) 863-5907 Fax: (303) 863-6066
Rudy Sánchez, Cont.

HISPANIC ADVISORY COUNCIL AWARDS PROGRAM
Brighton School District
630 S. 8th Ave.
Brighton, CO 80601
(303) 655-2900 Fax: (303) 655-2870

HISPANIC ANNUAL SALUTE (HAS)
P. O. Box 4720
Denver, CO 80204-4720
(303) 538-4959
Luis Valdez, Chair. of the Board.

HISPANIC BUSINESS STUDENT ASSOCIATION (HBSA)
Colorado State University
El Centro, 178 Lory Student Center
Fort Collins, CO 80523-8033
(970) 491-5722 Fax: (970) 491-2534
Guadalupe Salazar, Director of El Centro

HISPANIC CHAMBER OF COMMERCE OF COLORADO SPRINGS
25 N. Wahsatch Ave., #201
Colorado Springs, CO 80903
(719) 635-5001 Fax: (719) 635-6311
Robert Armendariz, President
Email: cshcc@netzero.com

HISPANIC CONTRACTORS OF COLORADO
2789 W. Alameda
Denver, CO
(303) 727-9450

HISPANIC CULTURAL CENTER
University of Northern Colorado
1410 20th St.
Greeley, CO 80639
(970) 351-2424 Fax: (970) 351-2363
Vicky Leal, Dir.

HISPANIC EDUCATION ADVISORY COUNCIL
900 Grant St., #400
Denver, CO 80203
(303) 764-3577 Fax: (303) 764-3841
Flor Amaro, Representative

HISPANIC EDUCATION FOUNDATION
P. O. Box 2102
Longmont, CO 80502
(303) 651-8445
Gay Hempton, President

HISPANIC EDUCATIONAL ADVISORY COUNCIL (HEAC)
Denver Public Schools
900 Grant St.
Denver, CO 80203
(303) 405-8270 Fax: (303) 764-3958
Joseph Gonzalez, Coord.

HISPANIC EMPLOYEES PROGRAM (HEP)
Colorado Council of Hispanic Employees
Program Manager
6760 E. Irvington Pl., P.O. Box 3402
Golden, CO 80401
(303) 275-1289 Fax: (303) 275-1838
Vince Ortega, Chair.

HISPANIC ENTREPRENEURSHIP TRAINING PROGRAM (HETP)
P. O. Box 173363, Campus Box #900
Denver, CO 80217-3363
(303) 556-2487 Fax: (303) 556-6319
Peter Battaglia, Dir.
Email: PeterB@cccs.cccoes.edu

HISPANIC FACULTY STAFF ASSOCIATION
c/o Metropolitan State College, Box 23
P. O. Box 173362
Denver, CO 80217-3362
(303) 556-3908 Fax: (303) 556-4685
Yolanda Erickson, Vice President
Email: ERICKSEY@MSCD.EDU
Web: www.mscd.edu

HISPANIC HEALTH COALITION OF COLORADO
309 W. 1St. Ave.
Denver, CO 80223
(303) 722-5150 Fax: (303) 722-5118
Bárbara Sánchez Martín, Dir.of Health Program
Email: larasa@larasa.org
Web: www.larasa.org

HISPANIC LEAGUE
660 Sherman St.
Denver, CO

HISPANIC NATIONAL BAR ASSOCIATION REGION XIII (CO, KS, NE, WY)
4535 West Lakeridge Road
Denver, CO 80219
(303) 936-1722
Dolores S. Atencio, Regional President
Email: dsatencio@hotmail.com
Web: www.hnba.com

HISPANIC UNITED GROUPS (HUG)
900 Grant St.
Denver, CO 80203
(303) 764-3577 Fax: (303) 764-3958
Joseph González, Coord.

HISPANIC WOMEN'S CAUCUS
P.O. Box 12496
Denver, CO
(303) 393-0770

HISPANIC-AMERICAN DOCTORS OF COLORADO
1717 York st.
Denver, CO
(303) 329-0511

HISPANICS OF COLORADO, INC. (HOC)
1029 Santa Fe Dr.
Denver, CO 80204
(303) 534-8342 Fax: (303) 534-7418
Verónica Barela, Pres.

HOPE VI FAMILY LEARNING CENTER
1450 W. 46th Ave.
Denver, CO
(303) 298-0300

IMAGE
National Image, Inc.
2964 W.119th Avenue
Westminster, CO 80234
(303) 466-8569 (H) or (303) 861-5515 x3549
Ramón Montoya, Regional Director
Web: www.nationalimageinc.org

IMAGE DE AMERICAN MILITARY VETERANS (I AM VET)
National Image, Inc.
8732 Snowbird Way
Parker, CO 80134
(303) 617-0923 (H)
Vincent L. Lucero, Commander
Web: www.nationalimageinc.org

IMAGE DE BOULDER
National Image, Inc.
325 Broadway, MC52
Boulder, CO 80303
(303) 497-6465
Albert Romero, President
Web: www.nationalimageinc.org

IMAGE DE COLORADO, DEPARTMENT OF CORRECTIONS
Colorado Dept. Corrections Chap.
427 Nathrop
Pueblo West, CO 81007
(719) 547-3021
Angel Medina, President

IMAGE DE STATE OF COLORADO
National Image, Inc.
2719 W. 32nd Avenue
Denver, CO 80211
(303) 480-0582(H) or (303) 672-5437 x 1387 (W)
Norbert Montano, President
Web: www.nationalimageinc.org

INROADS/DENVER
P. O. Box 13439
Denver, CO 80201-3439
(303) 607-0385 Fax: (303) 292-4561
Hollis Booker, Managing Dir.

LA ALMA RECREATION CENTER
1325 W. 11th Avenue
Denver, CO 80204
(303) 534-9282 Fax: (303) 572-4660
David Rodríguez, Recreation Director
Web: www.denvergov.org

LA CASA QUICK NEWTON FAMILY HEALTH CENTER
4545 Navaho St.
NW Denver, CO 80211
(303) 436-8700 Fax: (303) 436-8609
Sharon Salazar, Manager

LA FAMILIA RECREATION CENTER
65 S Elati St.
Denver, CO 80223
(303) 698-4995 Fax: (303) 698-5512
Sid Schuck, Recreation Director

LA FRATERNIDAD HISPANA DE COLORADO
2127 Larimer St.
Denver, CO 80205
(303) 295-1990
Frank Ponce

LA LEY
P. O. Box 4838
Denver, CO 80204
(720) 865-9177
Frank Mondragón, Pres.

LA MARIPOSA HEALTH CLINIC
1020 W. 11th Ave.
Denver, CO 80204
(303) 572-4782 Fax: (303) 572-4786
Tina Quitana, Practice Manger

LA XICANA
Metropolitan State College of Denver
Campus Box 41
P.O. Box 173362
Denver, CO 80217-3362
(303) 556-3124 or (303) 403-4936
Fax: (303) 556-3178
Maria Rodriguez, President

LAMBDA THETA NU
Metropolitan State College of Denver
P.O. Box 173362, Campus Box 41
Denver, CO 80217-3362
(303) 556-3124 or (303) 937-1576
Fax: (303) 556-3178
Cynthia Saenz, Pres.

Colorado State University
El Centro, 178 Lory Student Center
Fort Collins, CO 80523-8033
(970) 491-5722 Fax: (970) 491-2534
Guadalupe Salazar, Director of El Centro

LATIN AMERICAN EDUC. FDTN. (LAEF)
National Headquarters
930 W. 7th Ave.
Denver, CO 80204
(303) 446-0541 Fax: (303) 446-0526
Michael Barela, President
Email: laef@uswest.net
Web: www.laef.org

LATIN AMERICAN RESEARCH & SERVICE AGENCY (LARASA)
Affilate of NCLR, National Headquarters
309 W. 1St. Ave.
Denver, CO 80223-1509
(303) 722-5150 Fax: (303) 722-5118
Rufina Hernández, Executive Director
Email: larasa@larasa.org
Web: www.larasa.org

Amigos de la Comunidad
309 W. 1St. Ave.
Denver, CO 80223
(303) 722-5150 Fax: (303) 722-5118
Stacy Czerniak, Program Director
Email: sczerniak@larasa.org
Web: larasa@larasa.org

Strenthening Latino Families
309 W. 1St. Ave.
Denver, CO 80223
(303) 722-5150 Fax: (303) 722-5118
Rufina Hernández, Executive Director
Email: larasa@larasa.org
Web: www.larasa.org

LATIN AMERICAN STUDENT ORGANIZATION (LASO)
Colorado State University
El Centro
178 Lory Student Center
Fort Collins, CO 80523-8033
(970) 491-5722 Fax: (970) 491-2534
Guadalupe Salazar, Director of El Centro
Email: cwis57@yuma.acns.colostate.edu

Denver Water Department
1600 W. 12th Ave.
Denver, CO 80254
(303) 628-6057 or (303) 628-6318
Fax: (303) 628-6349
Donaldo Márquez, Training Specialist

THE LATINO BOOK COLLECTION
2700 West Barberry Place
Denver, CO 80204
(303) 698-9866 or (303) 446-0860
Adrianna Abarca, Dir.

LATINO CHAMBER OF COMMERCE OF PUEBLO
215 S. Victoria Ave.
Pueblo, CO 81003
(719) 542-5513 Fax: (719) 542-4657
Sandy Gutiérrez, Executive Director

LATINO INITIATIVE
Colorado Democratic Party
770 Grant St. #200
Denver, CO 80203
(303) 830-8989 Fax: (303) 830-2743
Margaret Atencio, Official Manager

LOS HERMANOS UNIDOS
1590 W. Fillmore St.
Colorado Springs, CO 80904
(719) 520-2574 Fax: (719) 520-2526

LOS VETERANOS PROFILES OF COURAGE, INC.
Veterans
P.O. Box 29332
Thornton, CO 80229
(303) 280-8061
Stephen Urioste, Founder
Email: losveteranos@profilesofcourage.com

**LULAC-NATIONAL EDUCATIONAL
SERVICES CENTER, INC. (LNESC)**
720 N. Main St., #455
Pueblo, CO 81003
(719) 542-9074 Fax: (719) 543-7287
Steve García, Director
Web: www.lulac.org

**LULAC-NATIONAL EDUCATIONAL
SERVICES CENTER, INC. (LNESC)**
829 N. Circle Dr., #101
Colorado Springs, CO 80909
(719) 637-0037 Fax: (719) 637-0038
Steve García, Director
Web: www.lulac.org

**LULAC-NATIONAL EDUCATIONAL
SERVICES CENTER, INC. (LNESC)**
1111 Osage St. Bldg., D
Denver, CO 80204
(303) 892-8455 Fax: (303) 620-9112
Eddie Duarte, Counselor
Web: www.lulac.org

MANA DE DENVER
1591 W. Alamedia
Denver, CO 80210
(303) 777-6525
Steve or Joe, President

MENTAL HEALTH CORP. OF DENVER
Centro de las Familias
75 Meade St.
Denver, CO 80022
(303) 504-1900 Fax: (303) 935-0294
Silvia Puicon, Support Staff
Web: www.mhcd.org

**MEXICAN AMERICAN STATE
LEGISLATORS**
Policy Institute
709 Sherman St.
Denver, CO
(303) 860-8935

MEXICAN CULTURAL CENTER
48 Steele Street
Denver, CO 80206
(303) 331-0169 Fax: (303) 331-0169
Carlos Barros, President
Email: informacion@consulmex/denver/.com

**MI CASA RESOURCE CENTER FOR
WOMEN, INC.**
Affiliate of NCLR
571 Galapago St.
Denver, CO 80204-5032
(303) 573-1302 Fax: (303) 595-0422
Carmen Carrillo, Executive Director
Email: info@micasadenver.org
Web: www.micasadenver.org

**MINORITY EDUCATION COALITION OF
COLORADO (MECC)**
1300 Broadway, 2nd Floor
Denver, CO 80203
(303) 866-2723 Fax: (303) 860-9750
Dwayne Nuzom, Exec. Dir.
Email: www.state.co.us

**MORRISON ROAD BUSINESS
ASSOCIATION OF DENVER**
4450 Morrison Rd.
Denver, CO 80204
(303) 936-4302
Debbie Nedrano, Executive Director
Email: denu@msn.com

**MOVIMIENTO ESTUDIANTIL CHICANO
DE AZTLAN (MECHA)**
Otero Junior College
La Junta, CO 81050
(719) 556-2595

P. O. Box 173362, Campus Box 41
Denver, CO 80217-3362
(303) 936-5632 or (303) 556-3124
Fax: (303) 556-3178
Jason del Grasso, President
Email: dlrosso@artifacts.nu

Metropolitan State College of Denver
P. O. Box 173362
Student Activities., Campus Box 39
900 Aurarie Parkway Suite 346
Denver, CO 80217-3362
(303) 556-8073 Fax: (303) 556-8087
Beatriz Salazar, President

MUSEO DE LAS AMERICAS
861 Santa Fe Dr.
Denver, CO 80204
(303) 571-4401 Fax: (303) 607-9761
José Aguayo, Exec. Director

**NATIONAL ASSOCIATION FOR CHICANA/
CHICANO STUDIES (NACCS)**
Metropolitan State College of Denver
PO Box 173362
Campus Box 41
Denver, CO 80217-3362
(303) 556-3124 Fax: (303) 556-3178
Dr.Torres, Chairman
Email: EMOERAGM@MSCD.EDU

**NATIONAL COALITION AGAINST
DOMESTIC VIOLENCE**
P.O. Box 18749
Denver, CO 80218
(303) 839-1852
Rita Smith, Executive Director

National Headquarters
P.O. Box 18749
Denver, CO 80218
(303) 839-1852 Fax: (303) 831-9251
Rita Smith, Executive Director
Web: www.ncadv.org

**NATIONAL EMPLOYMENT LAW
INSTITUTE**
1601 Emerson St.
Denver, CO 80218
(303) 861-5600 Fax: (303) 861-5665
John Fisher, Director
Web: www.neli.org

**NATIONAL HISPANA LEADERSHIP
INSTITUTE**
500 E. 8th Ave.
Denver, CO
(303) 861-2888

**NATIONAL HISPANIC EMPLOYEE
ASSOCIATION**
c/o Coors Brewing Co.
4030 (INH 440)
Golden, CO 80401-0030
(303) 277-5525/279-6565 Fax: (303) 277-2746
Paul Mendieta, Director
Email: paul@coors.com

NATIONAL IMAGE, INC.
Image de Denver
P. O. Box 1206
Denver, CO 80201-1206
(303) 986-4770 (H) or (303) 556-4569 (W)
Fax: (303) 556-4941
Tony Montoya, Chapter President
Email: montoyat@mscd.edu
Web: www.nationalimageinc.org

National Headquarters
930 W. 7th Ave., #139
Denver, CO 80204-4417
(303) 534-6534 Fax: (303) 534-0796
Alberto S. Rocha, National President
Email: ealvarado@uswest.net
Web: www.nationalimageinc.org

**NEWSED COMMUNITY DEVEDLOPMENT
CORPORATION**
Affiliate of NCLR
1029 Santa Fe Dr.
Denver, CO 80204
(303) 534-8342 Fax: (303) 534-7418
Verónica Barela, Executive Director

NORTHEAST DENVER HOUSING
1735 Gaylord St.
Denver, CO 80206
(303) 377-3334 Fax: (303) 377-3327
Getabecha Mekonnen, Executive Director
Email: gmekonnen@nedenverhousing.org
Web: http://www.nedenverhousing.org

**NORTHWEST COALITION 4 BETTER
SCHOOLS**
P.O. Box 11264
Denver, CO 80200
(303) 964-2850 Fax: (303) 964-2850

PARENT AND CHILD TOGETHER (PACT)
Holyoke Elementary School
326 E. Kellogg St.
Holyoke, CO 80734
(970) 854-3411 Fax: (970) 854-2703

PLAN DE SALUD DEL VALLE
1115 2nd St.
Fort Lupton, CO 80621
(303) 892-0004 Fax: (303) 892-1511
Jerry Brasher, Executive Director
Email: pfaulkner@saludclinic.org

PROJECT SALUTE
University of Denver
2450 S. Vine
Denver, CO 80208
(303) 871-2477 Fax: (303) 871-4456

REACH OUT AND READ
Westside Family Health Center
1100 Federal Blvd.
Denver, CO 80204
(303) 436-4407 Fax: (303) 436-4409

REFORMA
Colorado Chapter
Auraria Library, 1100 Lawrence St.
Denver, CO 80204
(303) 556-4999 Fax: (303) 556-2178
Judith Valdez, Chapter President
Email: jvaldez@carbon.cudenver.edu
Web: http://carbon.cudenver.edu/public/library/
reforma

RICARDO FALCON COMMUNITY CENTER
City Center
29 North Main St., #108
Brighton, CO 80601
(303) 659-5736
Betty Roybal, Director

**ROCKY MOUNTAIN/SER-JOBS FOR
PROGRESS, INC.**
Affiliate of SER-Jobs for Progress
National, Inc.
3555 Pecos St.
Denver, CO 80211
(800) 748-2074 or (303) 480-9394
Fax: (303) 480-9214
Charles P. Tafoya, Executive Director
Email: rtymtser@aol.com
Web: www.sernational.org

1016 West Ave. #5
Alamosa, CO 81101
(719) 589-5821 Fax: (719) 589-0344
Pete Gómez, Senior Field Representative
Email: pgomez@ccufc.net
Web: www.sernational.org

1931 E. Bridge
Brighton, CO 80601
(303) 659-5128 Fax: (303) 659-2940
Lourdes Villa, Senior Field Representative
Email: lvilla@co.adams.co.us
Web: www.sernational.org

215 Raton
La Junta, CO 81050
(719) 384-5463 Fax: (719) 384-8317
León Ortega, Senior Field Representative
Web: www.sernational.org

103 E. Elm St.
Lamar, CO 81052
(719) 336-9010 Fax: (719) 336-2259
Ernest Cienfuegos-Baca, Senior Field
Representative
Web: www.sernational.org

801 Chestnut Ave.
Rocky Ford, CO 81067
(719) 254-7666 Fax: (719) 254-3877
León Ortega, Senior Field Representative
Web: www.sernational.org

309 N. Commercial
Trinidad, CO 81082
(719) 846-4438 Fax: (719) 846-4778
Judy Gallegos, Senior Field Representative
Web: www.sernational.org

528 Main St.
Walsenburg, CO 81089
(719) 738-3004 Fax: (719) 738-3616
Mary Anderson, Senior Field Representative
Email: manderson@cwfc.net
Web: www.sernational.org

2079 Sherman Ave.
Monte Vista, CO 81144
(719) 852-5171 Fax: (719) 852-3817
Pete Gómez, Senior Field Representative
Email: pgomez@ccufc.net
Web: www.sernational.org

201 N Weber
Colorado Springs, CO 80903
(719) 578-5444 Fax: (719) 578-9752
Lynn Dyatt, Senior Field Representative
Email: rmser6587@uswest.net
Web: www.sernational.org

3555 Pecos St. 2nd Floor
Denver, CO 80211
(303) 480-9214 Fax: (303) 480-9214
Charles Tafoya, Executive Director
Web: www.sernational.org

P.O. Box 1010
Alamosa, CO 81101
(719) 589-5821 Fax: (719) 589-0344
Pete Gómez, Senior Field Representative
Email: pgomez@ccufc.net
Web: www.sernational.org

SANTA FE DRIVE REDEV. CORP.
1029 Santa Fe Dr.
Denver, CO 80204
(303) 534-8342 Fax: (303) 534-7418
Virginia Martínez, Exec. Dir.
Email: martinez@orci.com

SERVICIOS DE LA RAZA, INC.
Affiliate of NCLR
4055 Tejon St.
Denver, CO 80211
(303) 458-5851 Fax: (303) 455-1332
José R. Mondragón, Executive Director

SIGMA GAMMA RHO
Metropolitan State College of Denver
P.O. Box 173362
Campus Box 41
Denver, CO 80217-3362
(303) 361-9491 or (303)556-3124
Fax: (303) 556-3178
Teresa Harper, President

SIGMA LAMBDA BETA FRATERNITY
P.O. Box 173362, Campus Box 41
Denver, CO 80217-3362
(303) 274-7897 or (303)556-3178
Fax: (303) 556-3178
Darren Parks, President

**SIGMA LAMBDA BETA INTERNATIONAL
FRATERNITY**
Colorado State University
El Centro, 178 Lory Student Center
Fort Collins, CO 80523-8033
(970) 491-5722 Fax: (970) 491-2534
Guadalupe Salazar, Director of El Centro

SMEDLEY FAMILY RESOURCE SCHOOL
4250 Shoshone
Denver, CO 80237
(303) 433-3321 Fax: (303) 764-7899

SNAPSHOT ASSESSMENT SYSTEM
P.O. Box 628
Greeley, CO 80014
(970) 396-9283

**SOCIETY OF HISPANIC HUMAN
RESOURCE PROFESSIONALS (SHHRP)**
1380 Lawrence #610 Box B, P.O. Box 173361
Denver, CO 80217-3361
(303) 556-6212 Fax: (303) 556-4596
LeRoy Romero, President
Email: romerol@ahec.edu

**SOCIETY OF HISPANIC PROFESSIONAL
ENGINEERS (SHPE)**
Colorado State University
A102 Engineering
Fort Collins, CO 80523
(970) 491-6603 Fax: (970) 491-3429
Dawn Campbell, President
Web: www.shpe.org

**SOCIETY OF SPANISH AND SPANISH-
AMERICAN STUDIES**
University of Colorado, Boulder
Department of Spanish Portuguese
McKenna Language Bldg., CB 278
Boulder, CO 80309-0278
(303) 492-7308 Fax: (303) 492-3699
Luis T. González del Valle, Director
Email: sssas@spot.colorado.edu

**SOMOS: SERVICE ORIENTED MEMBERS
OFFERING SUPPORT**
US West Inc.
PO Box 1918
Denver, CO 80201-1918
(303) 707-6393 Fax: (303) 707-9330
Senida G. Rael, President

STRENGTHENING LATINO FAMILIES
Latin American Research and Service Agency
309 W. 1st Ave.
Denver, CO 80223
(303) 722-5150 Fax: (303) 722-5118

TRINIDAD HISTORY MUSEUM
300 E. Main
Trinidad, CO 81082
(719) 846-7217
Paula Manini, Director

TU CASA
P. O. Box 473
Alamosa, CO 81101
(719) 589-4729 Fax: (719) 589-1465
Lynn johnson, Executive Director
Email: tucasa@phone.net

TWILIGHTERS ANCIANO ASSOC., INC.
4154 Osage St.
Denver, CO 80211
(303) 433-6963 Fax: (303) 433-6963
Theresa Ortíz, President

UNITED MEXICAN-AMERICAN STUDENTS
University of Colorado-Boulder
Campus Box 207, UMC 182
Boulder, CO 80309
(303) 492-6571
Aracely Arscon, President

UNITED STATES-MEXICO CHAMBER OF COMMERCE
Rocky Mountain Chapter
720 Kipling, #119
Lakewood, CO 80215
(303) 237-7080 Fax: (303) 237-5568
Gil Cisneros, Executive Director
Email: gcil@ix.netcom.com
Web: www.usmcoc.com

YOUTH AT WORK-YEAR ONE
1111 Osage #210A
Denver, CO 80204
(303) 892-8485

CONNECTICUT

AETNA HISPANIC NETWORK
Aetna Inc.
151 Farmington Ave.
Hartford, CT 06156
(860) 273-2464 Fax: (860) 273-7232
Teodoro Mercado-Pérez

AIDS PROJECT HARTFORD
110 Batholomew Ave.
Hartford, CT 06106
(860) 951-4833 Fax: (860) 951-4779
Sandy D'Amato, Office Manager
Web: www.aidsprojecthartford.org

AMERICAN ASSOCIATION OF HISPANICS CERTIFIED PUBLIC ACCOUNTANTS (CPAS)
New York Chapter/ Rosario & Co.
64 Hunter Rd.
Fairfield, CT 06430
(203) 254-2704 Fax: (203) 259-2872
Robert F. Rosario, Chapter Representative
Email: rfr@luca.com
Web: www.aahcpa.org

ARCHDIOCESE OF HARTFORD
Hispanic Affairs
467 Bloomfield Ave.
Bloomfield, CT 06002
(860) 243-0940 Fax: (860) 286-2797
Rev. Rafael López, Dir. for Hispanic Ministry

ASPIRA OF CONNECTICUT, INC.
1600 State St.
Bridgeport, CT 06605
(203) 335-5762 Fax: (203) 366-5803
Alma Maya, Executive Director
Email: amaya1600@aol.com
Web: www.aspira.org/connecticut.html

ASSOCIATION OF LATINO AMERICAN STUDENTS
Housatonic Community College
900 Lafayette Blvd.
Bridgeport, CT 06604
(203) 332-5017 Fax: (203) 332-5123
Hernán Yepes, Advisor

BRIDGE ACADEMY
Affiliate of NCLR
510 Barnum Ave., P.O. Box 2267
Bridgeport, CT 06608
(203) 336-9999 Fax: (203) 336-9852
Felipe Reinoso, Executive Director
Email: bridgeacademy@yahoo.com

BRIDGEPORT COMMUNITY HEALTH CENTER., INC.
471 Barnum Ave.
Bridgeport, CT 06608
(203) 333-6864 Fax: (203) 332-0376
Ludwig Spineloi, Director

CASA BORICUA DE MERIDEN, INC.
204 Colony St.
Meriden, CT 06451
(203) 235-1125 Fax: (203) 686-0832
Magali Kupfer, Director

CASA OTOÑAL, INC.
135 Sylvan Ave.
New Haven, CT 06519
(203) 773-1847 Fax: (203) 773-3045
Patricia McCann, Executive Director

CATHOLIC CHARITIES MIGRATION & REFUGEE SERVICES
125 Market St.
Hartford, CT 06103
(860) 548-0059 Fax: (860) 549-8697
Sister Dorothy, Director

CENTER FOR LATIN AMERICAN AND CARIBBEAN STUDIES
University of Connecticut
843 Bolton Rd.
Storrs, CT 06269-1161
(860) 486-4964 Fax: (860) 486-2963
Elizabeth Mahan, Director

CENTRO DE LA COMUNIDAD
109 Blinman St.
New London, CT 06320
(860) 442-4463 Fax: (860) 443-4391
William García, Executive Director

CENTRO DE SAN JOSÉ
290 Grand Ave.
New Haven, CT 06513
(203) 562-3135
Peter Noble, Executive Director

CHEMICAL ABUSE SERVICES AGENCY
690 Artic St.
Bridgeport, CT 06608
(203) 339-4112 Fax: (203) 339-4115
Asher Delerme, Executive Director
Email: casa690@aol.com

COMMUNITY ACTION FOR GREAT MIDDLETOWN
51 Green St.
Middletown, CT 06457
(860) 344-8334 Fax: (860) 346-6813
Patricia Dicks-Cotte, Supervisor

CONNECTICUT ASSOCIATION FOR UNITED SPANISH ACTION (CAUSA)
204 Colony Street
Meriden, CT 06450
(860) 442-4463
Víctor Malendez
Web: www.causa.org

CONNECTICUT PUERTO RICAN FORUM, INC.
95 Park St., 2nd, Floor
Hartford, CT 06120
(860) 247-3227 Fax: (860) 549-5761
Frank Pérez, Executive Director

CROSSROADS, INC.
54 E. Ramsdell St.
New Haven, CT 06515
(203) 387-0094 Fax: (203) 387-2610
Miguel Laguna, Executive Director

DESPIERTA BORICUA
Yale College Dean's Office
P.O. Box 208241
New Haven, CT 06520-8241
(203) 432-2906 Fax: (203) 432-7369
Edgar Letriz-Nuñez, Dean
Email: edgar.letriz-nunez@yale.edu

DIOCESE OF BRIDGEPORT
St. Peter Rectory
695 Colorado Ave.
Bridgeport, CT 06605
(203) 366-5611 Fax: (203) 335-1924
Rev. Msgr. Aniceto Villamide, Vicar for Hispanic Ministry

DIOCESE OF NORWICH
Hispanic Affairs
61 Club Rd.
Windham, CT 06280
(860) 456-3349 Fax: (860) 423-4157
Sr. Mary Jude Lazarus, SCMC, Director for Hispanic Ministry
Email: aposthispano@juno.com

GE HISPANIC FORUM
3135 Easton Tpke.
Fairfield, CT 06431
(203) 373-2194 Fax: (203) 373-2342
Ricardo Artigas, Chairman

GUAKIA, INC.
335 Wethersfield Ave.
Hartford, CT 06114
(860) 296-9141 Fax: (860) 296-1424
Ana Lozada, Program Director

HARTFORD ACTION PLAN, INC.
30 Arbor St.
Hartford, CT 06120
(860) 236-9357 Fax: (860) 232-8321
Jack Cullin, Program Director

HARTFORD AREAS RALLY TOGETHER 227 LAWRENCE ST.
Hartford, CT 06106
(860) 525-3449 Fax: (860) 525-7759
Ann Prett, Director

HARTFORD DISPENSARY
12-14 Weston St.
Hartford, CT 06120
(860) 527-5100 Fax: (860) 280-1080
Gerald Garret, Administration Director

HARTFORD SEMINARY
77 Sherman St.
Hartford, CT 06105
(860) 509-9500 Fax: (860) 509-9509
Barbara Brown Zikmund, President
Web: www.hartsem.edu

HISPANIC CENTER OF GREATER DANBURY, INC.
87 West St.
Danbury, CT 06810
(203) 798-2855 Fax: (203) 798-6337
María Cinta Lowe, Director
Email: hispaniccenter@aol.com

HISPANIC CULTURAL SOCIETY, INC.
87 West St.
Danbury, CT 06810
(203) 798-2855 Fax: (203) 798-6337
Marlene Ríos, President
Email: hispaniccenter@aol.com

HISPANIC HEALTH COUNCIL (HHC)
Affiliate of NCLR
175 Main St.
Hartford, CT 06106
(860) 527-0856 Fax: (860) 724-0437
Rolando Martínez, Executive Director
Web: www.hispanichealth.com

HISPANIC NATIONAL BAR ASSOCIATION (HNBA)
280 Trumbull St.
Hartford, CT 06103
(860) 275-8247 Fax: (860) 275-8299
Rafael Santiago, President
Email: RSantiago@rc.com
Web: www.hnba.com

HISPANIC SERVICES PROGRAM GOODWILL INDUSTRIES, INC.
165 Ocean Terrice
Bridgeport, CT 06605
(203) 368-6511 Fax: (203) 335-9326
Carmen Williams, Director

HISPANOS UNIDOS CONTRA SIDA-AIDS, INC.
116 Sherman Ave., 1st Floor
New Haven, CT 06511
(203) 781-0226 Fax: (203) 781-0229
Luz González, Executive Director
Email: hunidos@yahoo.com

HOGAR CREA INTERNATIONAL OF CONNECTICUT, INC.
18 New Park Ave.
Hartford, CT 06106
(860) 232-7353 Fax: (860) 223-4733
Edwin Rivera Pacheco, Director

HUMAN RESOURCES AGENCY OF NEW BRITAIN, INC.
180 Clinton St.
New Britain, CT 06053
(860) 225-8601 Fax: (860) 224-4843
Òlga Egipciaco, Deputy Director

HUMANIDAD, INC.
Affiliate of NCLR
1800 Silas Deane Hwy., #159

Rocky Hill, CT 06067
(860) 563-6103 Fax: (860) 721-7215
Lillian Cruz, Executive Director

INSTITUTE FOR LIFE COPING SKILLS INC.
141 Franklin Street
Stanford, CT 06901
(203) 353-0752 Fax: (203) 353-0699
Lydia Brown, Executive Director
Email: lycabrown@aol.com
Web: www.tc.columbia.edu/~ilcs

INSTITUTE FOR THE HISPANIC FAMILY
80 Jefferson St.
Hartford, CT 06106
(860) 527-1124 Fax: (860) 724-2539
Galo Rodríguez, Director

INTERNATIONAL EXECUTIVE SERVICE CORPS
333 Ludlow St.
Stanford, CT 06902-2005
(203) 967-6000 Fax: (203) 324-2531
Hobart Gardner, President

JUNTA FOR PROGRESSIVE ACTION, INC.
169 Grand Ave.
New Haven, CT 06513
(203) 787-0191 Fax: (203) 787-4934
Frank Taylor, Executive Director

THE KENNEDY CENTER, INC.
184 Garden St.
Bridgeport, CT 06605
(203) 576-0211 Fax: (203) 332-4545
Martin D. Schwartz, Director

LA CASA BIENVENIDA SENIOR CENTER
135 E. Liberty St.
Waterbury, CT 06706
(203) 754-5684
Emperatriz Ochoa, Project Director

LA CASA DE PUERTO RICO
48 Main St.
Hartford, CT 06106
(860) 522-7296 Fax: (860) 246-6070
Carmen M. Rodríguez, Executive Director

LAMBDA THETA ALPHA, LATINA SORORITY
University of Connecticut
2110 Hill Side Rd. Box U-3008GK
Storrs, CT 06269-3008
(860) 486-5173 Fax: (860) 486-4484
Judith Preston, Advisor

LATINO COMMUNITY SERVICES PROGRAM, UNITED SERVICES, INC.
132 Mansfield Ave.
Willimantic, CT 06226
(860) 456-2261 Fax: (860) 450-1357
Ron Miller, Manager

LATINO YOUTH DEVELOPMENT, INC.
154 Minor St.
New Haven, CT 06519
(203) 776-3649 Fax: (203) 777-7620
Juan Candelario, Executive Director

LATINOS CONTRA SIDA (LCS)
331 Wethersfield Ave.
Hartford, CT 06114
(860) 296-6400 Fax: (860) 947-3130
Zahira Medina, Director

LEAGUE OF UNITED LATIN AMERICAN CITIZENS (LULAC)
375 James St.
New Haven, CT 06513
(203) 777-7501 Fax: (203) 773-9320
Abel Padro, Director
Web: www.lulac.org

MINISTERIO NUEVA VISION INTERNACIONAL
New Vision International Ministries
P.O. Box 2724
New Britain, CT 06051
(860) 826-8968 or (860) 655-8933
Fax: (860) 826-8968
Rev. Sal Acevedo, President

MOVIMIENTO ESTUDIANTIL CHICANO DE AZTLAN (MECHA)
295 Crown St.
New Haven, CT 06511
(203) 432-2931 Fax: (203) 432-7369
Mary Lee Hsu, Dean
Email: rafaeltrujillo@yale.edu

NATIONAL ASSOCIATION OF LATINO FRATERNAL ORGANIZATIONS, INC.
P.O. Box 322
Falls Village, CT 06031-0322
(860) 435-2880
Aimee R. Thorne-Thomsen, Chair, Board. of
Director
Email: chair@nalfo.org
Web: www.nalfo.org

NATIONAL LATINO PEACE OFFICERS ASSOCIATION (NLPOA)
Connecticut State Chapter
79 West Field St.
West Haven, CT 06516
(877) 657-6200
Adrián García, National President
Email: nlpoa@aol.com
Web: www.nlpoa.org

NATIONAL SOCIETY OF HISPANIC MBAS
Hartford Chapter
P.O. Box 231712
Hartford, CT 06123-1712
(214) 267-1622 (National Office)
Fax: (214) 267-1626 (National Office)
Raquel Santiago Martínez, Chapter President
Email: hartford@nshmba.org
Web: www.nshmba.org

NEW HAVEN ADULT AND CONTINUING EDUCATION
580 Ella Grasso Blvd.
New Haven, CT 06519
(203) 946-5884 Fax: (203) 946-6384
James Boger, Director

NEW HAVEN-LEON SISTER CITY PROJECT
608 Whitney Ave.
New Haven, CT 06511
(203) 562-1607 Fax: (203) 624-1683
Patricia Nielsen, Administrative Director
Email: newhavenleon@igc.apc.org
Web: www.igc.org

PUERTO RICAN / LATIN AMERICAN CULTURAL CENTER
University of Connecticut
267 Glenbrook Rd. U-3188
Storrs, CT 06269-3188
(860) 486-2204 Fax: (860) 486-4642
Isnoel Ríos, Director
Email: prcadm01@uconnvm.uconn.edu

PUERTO RICAN ORGANIZATION PROGRAM (PROP), INC.
744 Main St., 2nd Floor
Willimantic, CT 06226
(860) 423-8476 Fax: (860) 423-8478
Juan Vélez, Executive Director

PUERTO RICO FEDERAL AFFAIRS ADMINISTRATION
Connecticut Regional Office
100 Pearl St. 12th Floor
Hartford, CT 06103
(860) 522-2434 Fax: (860) 522-2579
Virgilio Cruz, Director
Web: www.prsaa.com

RAÚL JULIÁ ENDING HUNGER FUND
37 Emerald Land
Stamford, CT 06903
Email: info@rauljulia.com

REFORMA
Connecticut Chapter
The Ferguson Library, 1 Public Library Plaza
Stamford, CT 06904
(203) 964-1000 Fax: (203) 425-9789
José Ruiz-Alvarez, State Coordinator
Email: jruiz@fergusonlibrary.org
Web: www.fergusonlibrary.org

SAN JUAN CENTER, INC.
1293 Main St.
Hartford, CT 06103
(860) 522-2205 Fax: (860) 808-0088
George Cruz, Executive Director

SAN JUAN TUTORIAL PROGRAM
26 Ely St.
Hartford, CT 06103
(860) 247-7166 Fax: (860) 522-3432
Leslie Torres Rodríguez, Acting Executive
Director

SOCIETY OF HISPANIC PROFESSIONAL ENGINEERS (SHPE)
Connecticut-Harford Professional Chapter
1028 Blvd., #235
West Harford, CT 06119
(860) 557-2407
Albert Avancena, Chapter President
Email: avanceaj@pweb.com
Web: www.shpect.com

SPANISH ACTION COUNCIL, INC.
1663 S. Main St.
Waterbury, CT 06706
(203) 756-2220 Fax: (203) 756-4958
Migdalia Rosario, President

SPANISH AMERICAN CULTURAL ORGANIZATION
Centro de la Comunidad, Inc.
109 Blinman St.
New London, CT 06320
(860) 442-4463 Fax: (860) 443-4391
Víctor Menéndez, Director

SPANISH AMERICAN DEVELOPMENT AGENCY, INC. (SADA)
1317 State St.
Bridgeport, CT 06605
(203) 333-5193 Fax: (203) 333-7970
Ramón Larracuente, Executive Director

Spanish Senior Center
1057 E. Main St.
Bridgeport, CT 06608
(203) 333-9332
Miguel Cardozo, Program Director

SPANISH AMERICAN MERCHANTS ASSOCIATION OF CONNECTICUT (SAMA)
Connecticut
95 Park St., 3rd, Floor
Hartford, CT 06106
(860) 278-5825 Fax: (860) 278-1726
Julio Mendoza, Executive Director

SPANISH COMMUNITY OF WALLINGFORD
P.O. Box 6092
37 Hall Ave.
Wallingford, CT 06492
(203) 265-5866 Fax: (203) 294-2256
Blanca Santana, Executive Director
Email: scow@snet.net

SPANISH SPEAKING CENTER
83 Cherry St.
Waterbury, CT 06702
(203) 574-5156
Juan Blackald, Director

SPANISH SPEAKING CENTER OF NEW BRITAIN, INC.
118 Main St.
New Britain, CT 06050
(860) 224-2651 Fax: (860) 225-1713
Mary Sanders, Executive Director

THE STATE OF CONNECTICUT LATINO AND PUERTO RICAN AFFAIRS COMMISSION
18-20 Trinity St.
Hartford, CT 06106
(860) 240-8330 Fax: (860) 240-0315
Fernando Betancourt, Executive Director
Email: LPRAC@po.state.ct.us
Web: www.cga.state.ct.us/lprac

TAINO HOUSING AND DEVELOPMENT CORPORATION
490 Ann St.
Hartford, CT 06103
(860) 525-2799 Fax: (860) 727-9494
Joseph Pérez, Executive Director

TEEN FATHERS PROGRAM/YMCA
A Branch of Central Connecticut Coast Young Men's Christian Association
651 State St.
Bridgeport, CT 06604
(203) 334-5551
Manuel Cardona, Director

UNITED HISPANIC ACTION OF NORWALK
P.O. BOX 628
Norwalk, CT 06856-0628
(203) 866-5369
Jose A. Bermudez, Treasure
Email: lyiyibz4@aol.com
Web: http://norwalk.ct.us/uhan

URBAN LEAGUE
P.O. Box 320590
Hartford, CT 06132
(860) 527-0147 Fax: (860) 249-1563
James E. Willinghanm Senior., Director

DELMARVA RURAL MINISTRIES, INC.
Affiliate of NCLR / Agency of United Way
26 Wyoming Ave.
Dover, DE 19904
(302) 678-2000 Fax: (302) 678-0545
Debra Singletary, Chief Executive Officer
Email: drmino@erols.com

DIOCESAN HISPANIC MINISTRY
1010 W. 4th St.
Wilmington, DE 19805
(302) 655-6596 Fax: (302) 655-7694
Rev. Lawrence Hayes, Pastor

DIOCESE OF WILMINGTON
St. Paul Parish
1010 W. 4th St.
Wilmington, DE 19805
(302) 655-6596 Fax: (302) 655-7684
Bro. Christopher Posch, OFM, Director for
Hispanic Ministry

DUPONT HISPANICS NETWORK
Barley Mill Plaza Bldg. 24
Wilmington, DE 19880-0024
(302) 892-0915 Fax: (302) 892-0777
Richard Otero, Business Director

GOVERNOR'S COUNCIL ON HISPANIC AFFAIRS
Carvel State Office Bldg.
820 N. French St., 4th Floor
Wilmington, DE 19801
(302) 994-9441 Fax: (302) 995-5624
Dr. Jaime Rivera, Chair.

HISPANIC NATIONAL BAR ASSOCIATION REGION IV (DE, PA)
1007 Market St., D-4022-2
Wilmington, DE 19898
(302) 774-5325 Fax: (302) 774-5454
Ramona Romero, Regional President
Email: Ramona.E.Romero@usa.dupont.com
Web: www.hnba.com

LATIN AMERICAN COMMUNITY CENTER
403 N. Van Buren St.
Wilmington, DE 19805
(302) 655-7338 Fax: (302) 655-7334
María Matos, Executive Director

OFICINA DE LA FAMILIA Y DE LOS NIÑOS, INC.
301 N. Harrison St.
Wilmington, DE 19805
(302) 655-6486 Fax: (302) 655-9815
María Christina Navaro, Program Manager

TELAMON CORPORATION
Colonial Gardens Head Start Center 4
1000 Hayes Dr.
Dover, DE 19904
(302) 741-2490 or (302)741-2798
Fax: (302) 741-2499
Rose Cypress, Director
Web: www.telamon.org

Harrington Head Start Center 6
112 East St.
Harrington, DE 19952
(302) 398-9196 or (302) 398-9198
Fax: (302) 398-9252
Juanita Parker, Director
Web: www.telamon.org

Primeros Pasitos Center 10
137 A N. Layton St.
Georgetown, DE 19947
(302) 856-4542 Fax: (302) 856-4901
Charlotte Thompson , Education/Disabilities
Specialist
Web: www.telamon.org

Primeros Pasos Center 11
410 S. Bedford St.
Georgetown, DE 19947
(302) 855-9140 Fax: (302) 855-9178
Pilar Ramírez, Director
Web: www.telamon.org

Smyrna Head Start Center 5
101 South Locust St.
Smyrna, DE 19977
(302) 653-3703 Fax: (302) 653-3862
Margaret Sommer, Director
Web: www.telamon.org

State Head Start Office 1
514 N. DuPont Hwy.
Dover, DE 19901

(302) 736-3281 or (302) 736-3298
Fax: (302) 736-3785
Constance Pogue, State Head Start Director
Email: cpogue@bellatlantic.net
Web: www.telamon.org

State Office 7
504 N. Dupont Hwy.
Dover, DE 19901
(302) 734-1903 or (302) 734-1904
Fax: (302) 734-0382
Karen Webster, State Director
Email: tcmdjtpa@onp.wdsc.org
Web: www.telamon.org

White Oak Head Start Center 2
195 Willis Rd.
Dover, DE 19901
(302) 736-5933 or (302) 736-5934
Fax: (302) 736-5932
Paula Haggard, Director
Web: www.telamon.org

ACCION INTERNATIONAL
Washington Office
733 15th St., NW 7th Floor
Washington, DC 20005
(202) 393-5113 Fax: (202) 393-5115
María Otero, President & CEO
Email: info@accion.org
Web: www.accion.org

ADAMS ELEMENTARY SCHOOL
19th & California St., NW
Washington, DC 20009
(202) 673-7311 Fax: (202) 673-6500
Andrew Topts, Principal

ADAMS MILL ABSTINANCE CENTER
1808 Adams Mill Rd., NW
Washington, DC 20009
(202) 673-6618 Fax: (202) 673-2037
Steven Wright, Clinic Manager

ADAMS MORGAN COMMUNITY HEALTH CENTER
2250 Champlain St. NW
Washington, DC 20009
(202) 673-7702 or (202) 724-4370
Fax: (202) 673-2266
Kevin Denise, Chief Mgr.

ADAMS MORGAN HEALTH CENTER
2200 11th St., NW
Washington, DC 20009
(202) 745-5531 Fax: (202) 745-5516
Luis Galarza, Supervisor

ALMA BOLIVIANA
1510 31st St., NW
Washington, DC 20007
(202) 338-2522 Fax: (202) 337-4102
María de Martini, President

AMAZING LIFE GAMES PRE-SCHOOL
1844 Mintwood Pl., NW
Washington, DC 20009
(202) 265-0114
Pickett Craddock, Director

AMERICAN ASSOCIATION FOR HIGHER EDUCATION (AAHE)-HISPANIC CAUCUS
1 Dupont Circle NW, #360
Washington, DC 20036-1110
(202) 293-6440 Fax: (202) 293-0073
Margaret Miller, President
Web: www.AAHE.org

AMERICAN CENTER FOR INTERNATIONAL LABOR SOLIDARITY
1925 K St., NW, #300
Washington, DC 20006
(202) 659-6300 Fax: (202) 778-6344
Bruce Jay, Coordinator for the Americans
Email: Bjay@acils.org

AMERICAN COUNCIL OF EDUCATION
Office of Minorities in Higher Education
1 DuPont Circle, #800
Washington, DC 20036
(202) 939-9395 Fax: (202) 785-2990
William Harvey, Director
Web: www.acenet.edu

AMERICAN PUBLIC WELFARE ASSOC.
810 1st St., NE, #500
Washington, DC 20002-4267
(202) 682-0100 Fax: (202) 289-6555
Linda Wols, Executive Director
Email: www.apwa.org

THE AMERICAS FOUNDATION
1115 Massachusetts Ave., NW
Washington, DC 20005
(202) 371-9696 Fax: (202) 371-9668
Víctor Pinzón, President
Email: vicpinzon@aol.com
Web: www.theamericas.org

AMNESTY INTERNATIONAL
Mid-Atlantic Region
600 Pennsylvania Ave., SE 5th Floor
Washington, DC 20003
(202) 544-0200 Fax: (202) 546-7142
Steven Rackard, Dir.
Email: aiusamaro@igc.apc.org

ANDROMEDA - CENTRO HISPANO DE SALUD MENTAL
1400 Decatur St., NW
Washington, DC 20011
(202) 291-4707 Fax: (202) 723-4560
Dr. Ricardo Galbis, Executive Director, M.D.

ARCHDIOCESE FOR THE MILITARY SERVICES, USA
Hispanic Affairs
415 Michigan Ave. #300
Washington, DC 20017-0469
(202) 269-9100 x17 Fax: (202) 269-9022
Most Rev. Joseph J. Madera, MSPS, DD, Aux.
Bishop of the Archdiocese of the MS

ARCHDIOCESE OF WASHINGTON
Hispanic Affairs
P.O. Box 29260
5001 Eastern Ave.
Washington, DC 20017
(301) 853-4566 Fax: (301) 853-7671
Rev. Francisco González, Vicar for Hispanic Ministry

ART MUSEUM OF THE AMERICAS
Affiliate of Org. of American States
1889 F St. NW
Washington, DC 20006
(202) 458-6016 Fax: (202) 458-6021
Ana María Escallón, Director
Web: www.oas.org

ASOCIACIÓN COSTA RICA, INC.
P.O. Box 53331
Washington, DC 20009
(202) 623-3825
X. Díaz, President
Email: asociacion_costarica@hotmail.com

ASOCIACIÓN DE AYUDA SALVADOREÑA
1754 Columbia Rd., NW
Washington, DC 20009
(202) 367-4848
Stephany Shaw, President

ASOCIACIÓN DE DAMAS PARAGUAYAS
3545 16th St. NW
Washington, DC 20010
(202) 387-0654 Fax: (202) 387-0654
Rosita Becker, President

ASOCIACIÓN PARA LA CONSERVACIÓN DEL PATRIMONIO CULTURAL DE LAS AMÉRICAS (APOYO)
P.O. Box 76932
Washington, DC 20013
(202) 707-1026 or (202) 707-1120
Fax: (202) 707-3434
Amparo R. de Torres, Director
Email: ator@loc.gov

ASPIRA ASSOCIATION, INC.
National Headquarters
1444 I St. NW, #800
Washington, DC 20005
(202) 835-3600 ext.160 Fax: (202) 835-3613
Ronald Blackburn-Moreno, President
Email: aspira@aspira.org
Web: www.aspira.org

ASSOCIATION OF AMERICAN CHAMBERS OF COMMERCE IN LATIN AMERICA
1615 H St. NW
Washington, DC 20062-2000
(202) 463-5485 Fax: (202) 463-3126
John Murphy, Director
Web: www.aacla.org

AYUDA, INC.
National Headquarters Affiliate of NCLR
1736 Columbia Rd. NW
Washington, DC 20009
(202) 387-4848 or (202) 387-2870

Fax: (202) 387-0324
Yvonne Martínez Vega, Executive Director
Email: immayuda@erols.com
Web: www.incacorp.com/ayuda

BANQUETE DEL MILLÓN Y DEL AMOR, INC.
101 Q Street, NE
Washington, DC 20002
(202) 269-0599 Fax: (202) 832-8115
Marco A. Hechavarría, Chairman

BARBARA CHAMBERS CHILDREN'S CENTERS
1470 Irving St. NW
Washington, DC 20010
(202) 387-6755 Fax: (202) 319-9066
Francisca Ventura-Torres, Executive Director

BARNEY SENIOR CENTER
1737 Columbia Rd., NW
Washington, DC 20009
(202) 939-9025 Fax: (202) 939-9041
Ron McLean, Director

BELL MULTICULTURAL HIGH SCHOOL MCIP SER
3145 Hiatt Pl. NW
Washington, DC 20010
(202) 673-3551 Fax: (202) 673-7581
María Tukeva, Principal

BRAZILIAN AMERICAN CULTURAL INSTITUTE
4103 Connecticut Ave., NW
Washington, DC 20008
(202) 362-8334 Fax: (202) 362-8337
José Neistein, Director
Email: baci-us@worldnet.att.net

BRAZILIAN BAPTIST CHURCH
5671 Western Ave., NW
Washington, DC 22191
(202) 537-7280 Fax: (202) 537-9106
Rev. Carlos Mendes, Pastor
Email: ibbrasil@hotmail.com
Web: www.ibbwdc.com

BREAD FOR THE CITY
1525 7th St., NW
Washington, DC 20001
(202) 332-0440 Fax: (202) 745-1081
George Jones, Director
Email: bread@org.com

BUSINESS AND PROFESSIONAL WOMEN'S FOUNDATION
Sally Butler Memorial Fund for Latina Research
2012 Massachusetts Ave., NW
Washington, DC 20036
(202) 293-1200 Fax: (202) 861-0298
Gale Shaffer, Executive Vice President
Web: www.bps.usa.org

CALVARY MULTICULTURAL LEARNING CENTER
Affiliate of NCLR
1420 Columbia Rd. NW
Washington, DC 20009
(202) 332-4200 Fax: (202) 745-2562
Beatriz Otero, Executive Director
Email: cbmlc@erols.com

CARIBBEAN/LATIN AMERICAN ACTION
1818 N. St., NW, #500
Washington, DC 20036
(202) 466-7464 Fax: (202) 822-0075
Peter B. Johnson, Executive Director
Email: Info@claa.org.
Web: www.claa.org

CARLOS ROSARIO INTERNATIONAL CAREER CENTER
3101 16th Street NW
Washington, DC
(202) 234-6522

711 8th Street NW
Washington, DC
(202) 347-3872

c/o Lincoln Middle School
16th & Irving Street, NW Room 115
Washington, DC 20016
(202) 234-6522 Fax: (202) 234-6563
Sonia Gutiérrez, Executive Director
Email: rosariointernational@juno.com

CASA DEL PUEBLO
National Headquarters
1459 Columbia Rd., NW
Washington, DC 20009
(202) 332-1082 Fax: (202) 667-7783

María José Recino, Program Director
Email: cdelpueblo@aol.com

CATHEDRAL OF ST. MATTHEWS
1725 Rhode Island Ave. NW
Washington, DC 20036
(202) 347-3215 Fax: (202) 347-7184
Rev. Msgr. Ronald Jameson, Pastor
Email: cathstmatt@aol.com
Web: www.stmatthewscathedral.org

CATHOLIC CHARITIES
1438 Rhode Island Ave., NE
Washington, DC 20018
(202) 526-4100 Fax: (202) 526-1829
Ed Orzechowski, President

CATHOLIC CHARITIES IMMIGRATION SERVICES
1221 Massachusetts Ave., NW
Washington, DC 20005
(202) 628-6861 or (202) 628-4263
Fax: (202) 737-3421
Nancy Shestack, Director

CATHOLICS FOR A FREE CHOICE
1436 U St., NW, #301
Washington, DC 20009-3997
(202) 986-6093 Fax: (202) 332-7995
Francis Kisling, Director

CENTER FOR APPLIED LINGUISTICS
4646 40th St. NW
Washington, DC 20016
(202) 362-0700 Fax: (202) 362-3740
Donna Christian, Director
Web: www.cla.org

CENTER FOR IMMIGRATION STUDIES
1522 K St., NW, #820
Washington, DC 20005-1202
(202) 466-8185 Fax: (202) 466-8076
Mark Krikorian, Director
Email: center@cis.org
Web: www.cis.org

CENTER FOR THE ADVANCEMENT OF HISPANICS IN SCIENCE & ENGINEERING EDUCATION (CAHSEE)
George Washington University
707 22nd St., NW, #105
Washington, DC 20052
(202) 994-6529 Fax: (202) 994-2459
Charles E. Vela, Executive Director
Email: cahsee@seas.gwu.edu
Web: www.cahsee.org

CENTRAL AMERICAN RESOURCE CENTER
Affiliate of NCLR
1459 Columbia Rd., NW.
Washington, DC 20009
(202) 328-8399 Fax: (202) 328-0023
Saúl Solórzano, Executive Director
Email: carecendc@aol.com

CENTRO DE ARTE
1470 Irving Street, NW
Washington, DC 20009
(202) 588-5143
Lilo González, Executive Director

CENTRO ESPAÑOL DE WASHINGTON DC
P.O. Box 9485
Washington, DC 20016
(301) 983-1408 or (301) 217-9684
Fax: (301) 983-6847
Irene Bascuñana, President

CHANGE, INC.
1413 Park Rd. NW
Washington, DC 20010
(202) 387-3725 Fax: (202) 387-3729
Grace Rolling, Executive Director

CHILDREN'S DEFENSE FUND
25 E St., NW
Washington, DC 20001
(202) 628-8787 Fax: (202) 662-3510
Marian W. Edelman, President & Founder
Email: www.cdsinfo@childrensdefense.org
Web: www.childrensdefense.org

CHURCHES CENTER FOR THEOLOGY & PUBLIC POLICY
4500 Massachusetts Ave. N.W.
Washington, DC 20016
(202) 885-8648 Fax: (202) 885-8605
James A.Nash, Exec. Dir.

CITIWIDE COMPUTER TRAINING CENTER
3636 16th Street, NW, Suite AS-1
Washington, DC 20010
(202) 667-3719 Fax: (202) 336-5797
Anthony Chuukwu, Executive Director

COALITION FOR THE HOMELESS
1234 Massachusetts Ave. NW Rm. C-1015
Washington, DC 20005
(202) 347-8870 Fax: (202) 347-7279
Michael Ferrell, Executive Director

COLUMBIA ROAD HEALTH SERVICES
1660 Columbia Rd., NW
Washington, DC 20009
(202) 328-3717 Fax: (202) 588-8101
Allen Goetcheus, Pres.

COMMISSION ON LATINO COMMUNITY DEVELOPMENT
District of Columbia Govt.
2000 14th St., NW, 2nd Floor
Washington, DC 20009
(202) 541-5929 Fax: (202) 673-4557
Tomás Vialet

COMMONWEALTH OF PUERTO RICO
1100 17th St. NW #800
Washington, DC 20036
(202) 778-0710 Fax: (202) 632-1288
Alfonso Aguilar, Director

COMMUNITY HEALTH CARE, INC.
3020 14th St. NW
Washington, DC 20009
(202) 745-4300 Fax: (202) 265-9834
Benson Keane, Executive Director

CONFERENCE OF MINORITY PUBLIC ADMINISTRATORS
1120 G St. NW, # 700
Washington, DC 20005
(202) 393-7878 Fax: (202) 638-4952
Mary Hamilton, Executive Director
Web: www.aspanet.org

CONGRESSIONAL HISPANIC CAUCUS
National Headquarters
2465 Rayburn Bldg.
Washington, DC 20515
(202) 225-4065 Fax: (202) 225-1655
Laura Campos, Executive Assistant
Web: www.house.gov/roybal-allard/CHC.htm

CONGRESSIONAL HISPANIC CAUCUS INSTITUTE, INC. (CHCI)
504 C St. NE
Washington, DC 20002
(202) 543-1771 Fax: (202) 546-2143
Ingrid Durán, Executive Director
Email: chci@chci.org
Web: www.chci.org

CONGRESSIONAL HISPANIC STAFF ASSOCIATION (CHSA)
214 Cannon HOB
Washington, DC 20515
(202) 225-3035 Fax: (202) 225-5866
Dean Aguillen, President/Legislative Assistant

COUNCIL OF LATINO AGENCIES (CLA)
2835 16th St. NW
Washington, DC 20009
(202) 328-9451 Fax: (202) 667-6135
Arnold Ramos, Executive Director
Email: mrodriguez@consejo.org
Web: www.consejo.org

COUNCIL OF LATINO AGENCIES (CLA)
Affiliate of NCLR
2437 15th St., NW, 2nd Floor
Washington, DC 20009
(202) 328-9451 Fax: (202) 667-6135
Arnoldo Ramos, Executive Director
Email: consejo@cais.com
Web: www.consejo.org

COUNCIL ON HEMISPHERIC AFFAIRS
1444 I Street., NW #211
Washington, DC 20005
(202) 393-3322 Fax: (202) 216-9193
Laurence Birns, Director

CUBAN-AMERICAN ALLIANCE EDUCATION FUND
614 Maryland Ave. NE, #2
Washington, DC 20002
(202) 543-6780 Fax: (202) 543-6434
Delvis Fernandez Levy, Executive Director
Email: caaef@igc.or
Web: www.cubamer.org

CUBAN-AMERICAN NATIONAL FOUNDATION.
Washington Office
1000 Thomas Jefferson St. NW. #505
Washington, DC 20007
(202) 265-2822 Fax: (202) 338-0308
José Cardenas, Director
Email: canfdc@aol.com
Web: www.canfnet.org

THE DC CENTER FOR INDEPENDENT LIVING, INC.
1400 Florida Ave. N.E., #3
Washington, DC 20002
(202) 388-0033 Fax: (202) 398-3018
María Barragán, Hispanic Coordination

DC IMAGE, INC.
National Image, Inc.
P.O. Box 76417
801 Floral Place, NW
Washington, DC 20013
Pedro de Jesús, President
Web: www.nationalimageinc.org

DEMOCRATIC NATIONAL COMMITTEE HISPANIC CAUCUS
National Headquarters
430 S. Capitol St., SE
Washington, DC 20003
(202) 863-8000 Fax: (202) 863-8174
Lina García, Deputy Press Secretary
Email: garcia@dnc.democrats.org
Web: www.democrats.org

DIALOGUE ON DIVERSITY
1730 K. Street, N.W., #304
Washington, DC 20006
(703) 631-0650 Fax: (703) 631-0617
Cristina C. Caballero, President
Email: Dialog.Div@internetMCL.com
Web: www.Dialogueondiversity.org

DISTRICT OF COLUMBIA OFFICE ON AGING
441 4th. Street NW #900
Washington, DC
(202) 724-5622 or (202) 724-5626
Fax: (202) 724-4979

E. MAZIQUE PARENT/CHILD RESOURCE CENTER
1719 13th St. NW 3rd Floor
Washington, DC 20009
(202) 462-3375 or (202) 939-6105
Fax: (202) 939-8696
Leslie Johnson, Director
Email: ecmpcco31@aol.com

ECUMENICAL PROGRAM ON CENTRAL AMERICA AND THE CARIBBEAN (EPICA)
1470 Irving St. NW, #2nd Floor
Washington, DC 20010
(202) 332-0292 Fax: (202) 332-1184
Ann Butwell, Coordinator
Email: epica@igc.apc.orgwww:center1.com/epica.html

EDUCATIONAL ORGANIZATION FOR UNITED LATIN AMERICANS, INC. (EOFULA)
Spanish Senior Center.
1844 Columbia Rd.
Washington, DC 20009
(202) 483-5800 Fax: (202) 588-5806
Ana María Neris, Executive Director

EDUCATIONAL VIDEO IN SPANISH (EVS)
3039 Fourth Street, N.E.
Washington, DC 20017
(202) 635-2606 Fax: (202) 635-2603
Arturo Salcedo Martínez, Executive Director

EL HOGAR DE LA FAMILIA
3309 16th St. NW
Washington, DC 20010
(202) 265-0149 Fax: (202) 483-0650
Patricia Patterson, Executive Director

ENCUENTROS
El Centro Latinoamericano de la Juventud
3043 calle 15, NW
Washington, DC 20009
(202) 667-6545 Fax: (202) 667-9535
Carlos Vera, Director

EOFULA SPANISH SENIOR CENTER
1844 Columbia Rd., NW
Washington, DC 20009
(202) 483-5800 Fax: (202) 558-5806
Ana María Neris, Executive Director

ESPACIO CULTURAL SALVADOREÑO
C/O Consulado general de El Salvador
1724 20th St., NW
Washington, DC 20009
(202) 256-6542 Fax: (202) 331-4036
Mario Cader-Frech, Director of Art
Email: culturasal@aol.com

FAMILY & CHILD SERVICES OF WASHINGTON DC, INC.
929 L St. NW
Washington, DC 20001-4394
(202) 289-1510 Fax: (202) 371-0863
Rhoda Veney, Director

FAMILY PLACE, INC.
Mount Pleasant Center.
3309 16th St., NW
Washington, DC 20010
(202) 265-0149 Fax: (202) 483-0650
Camille Fountain, Executive Director

FARMWORKER HEALTH SERVICES
1234 Massachusetts Ave. NW., C1017
Washington, DC 20005
(202) 347-7377 Fax: (202) 347-6385
Sarah Etkin, Operation Adm.
Email: fwhealth@aol.com
Web: www.farmworkerhealth.org

FONDO DEL SOL VISUAL ART AND MEDIA CENTER
2112 R St., NW
Washington, DC 20008
(202) 483-2777
Marc Zuver, Adm. Director

FOUNDATION FOR INTERNATIONAL COMMUNITY ASSISTANCE (FINCA)
1101 14th St., NW
Washington, DC 20005
(202) 682-1510
Monique LeNoir, Community Coordinator
Email: mlenoir@villagebanking.org

FOUNDATION FOR THE ADVANCEMENT OF HISPANIC AMERICAN, INC. (FAHA)
National Headquarters
P.O. Box 66012
Washington, DC 20035
(703) 866-1578 Fax: (703) 256-6700
Dr. Pedro De Mesones, President

FUNDACIÓN SOLIDARIDAD MEXICANO-AMERICANA, A.C.
1111 19th St. NW #1000
Washington, DC 20036
(202) 785-1670 Fax: (202) 785-0851
Concepción Romero, Director
Web: www.nclr.gov

GAP
3636 16th St. NW
Washington, DC 20010
(202) 462-3636 Fax: (202) 462-5942
Mónica Guyot, Director
Email: mguyot@eudoramail.com

GIRL SCOUT COUNCIL OF THE NATION'S CAPITAL
Linguistic Outreach Program
2233 Wisconsin Ave. NW #410
Washington, DC 20007
(202) 337-4300 x 261 Fax: (202) 625-1775
Maribel Ruiz, Coordinator

GREATER AMERICA BUSINESS COALITION
Ronald Reagan Building & International Trade Center
1300 Pennsylvania Ave., #270
Washington, DC 20004-3021
(202) 312-1644 Fax: (202) 312-1646
Albert Zapanta, Chairman
Email: panamerica@msn.com

GREATER WASHINGTON IBERO-AMERICAN CHAMBER OF COMMERCE
1420 16th St. NW, #102
Washington, DC 20036
(202) 728-0352 Fax: (202) 728-0355
Juan Albert, Executive Vice President
Email: gwiacc@aol.com
Web: http://hometown.aol.com/gwiacc

THE GREEN DOOR
1623 16th St. NW
Washington, DC 20009
(202) 462-4092 Fax: (202) 462-7562
Judith Johnson, Director
Email: admin@aol.com

GRUPO DE ARTISTAS LATINOAMERICANOS (GALA) THEATRE
P.O. Box 43209
Washington, DC 20010
(202) 234-7174 Fax: (202) 332-1247
Hugo Medrano, Director
Email: galadc@aol.comwww.incacorp.com/gala.

GUATEMALA HUMAN RIGHTS COMMISSION-USA
3321 12th St. NE
Washington, DC 20017-4008
(202) 529-6599 Fax: (202) 526-4611
Sister Alice Zackman, Director

H.D. COOKE SCHOOL
2525 17th St. NW
Washington, DC 20009
(202) 673-7294 Fax: (202) 673-6980
Dr. Emma Bonner, Principal

HEALTH STREET - COMMUNITY ADOLESCENT PROGRAM
Upper Cardozo Health Center
3020 14th St., NW
Washington, DC 20009
(202) 518-6442/745-4300 Fax: (202) 462-6128
Vincent Keane, Executive Director

HERMANOS Y HERMANAS MAYORES-BIG BROTHERS BIG SISTERS OF THE NATIONAL CAPITAL AREA
Latino Program
666 11th St., NW
Washington, DC 20001
(202) 783-5585 Fax: (202) 783-5169
Jorge Bustios, Director
Email: Jbustios@bbbsnca.org
Web: www.bbbsnca.org

HIGHER ACHIEVEMENT PROGRAM (HAP)
19 I St. NW 4th Floor Bldg. 49
Washington, DC 20001
(202) 842-5116 Fax: (202) 842-5123
Robert D. Williams, Executive Director

HISPANIC AMERICAN POLICE COMMAND OFFICERS ASSOCIATION (HAPCOA)
Ronald Reagan Bldg., International Trade Center
1300 Pennsylvania Ave., NW, #270
Washington, DC 20004-3021
(301) 449-7967 Fax: (301) 449-7077
Jess Quintero, Executive Director
Email: ECG1mundo@aol.com

HISPANIC ASSOCIATION OF COLLEGES & UNIVERSITIES (HACU)
HNIP Office
Legislative Affairs Office
One Dupont Circle NW, #605
Washington, DC 20036
(202) 833-8361 Fax: (202) 833-8367
Deyanira R. Rossell, Exec. Dir. Public Affairs
Email: dcgovrel@erols.com
Web: www.hacu.net

Washington DC Office
1367 Connecticut Ave. NW, 2nd Floor
Washington, DC 20036
(202) 261-5080 or (202) 833-8362
Fax: (202) 496-9177
William Gil, Executive Director
Web: www.hacu.org

HISPANIC ASSOCIATION ON CORPORATE RESPONSIBILITY (HACR)
National Headquarters
1730 Rhode Island Ave., NW, #1008
Washington, DC 20036
(202) 835-9672 Fax: (202) 457-0455
Anna Escobedo Cabral, President & CEO
Email: HACR@aol.com
Web: www.hacr.org

THE HISPANIC BAR ASSOCIATION OF THE DISTRICT OF COLUMBIA (HBA-DC)
P.O. Box 1011
Washington, DC 20013-1011
(202) 624-2904 Fax: (202) 225-4977
Ignacio Moreno, President
Email: info@hbadc.org
Web: www.hbadc.org

HISPANIC COALITION FOR PUERTO RICAN SELF-DETERMINATION
1133 20th St. NW, Suite 750
Washington, DC 22036
(202) 408-0060 or (202) 543-4720
Fax: (202) 408-0064
Brent A. Wilkes, National Executive Director

HISPANIC COLLEGE FUND
One Thomas Circle, NW, #375
Washington, DC 20005
(202) 296-5400 Fax: (202) 296-3774
Adam Chavarria, National Director
Email: Hispanic.Fund@cwixmail.com
Web: www.Hispanicfund.org

HISPANIC COUNCIL ON INTERNATIONAL RELATIONS (HCIR)
National Headquarters
1111 19th St. NW, #1000
Washington, DC 20036
(202) 776-1754 Fax: (202) 776-1790
Roxana Jordan, President
Email: rcjordon@hcir.org
Web: www.hcir.org

HISPANIC DESIGNERS, INC. (HDI)
1101 30th St. NW, #500
Washington, DC 20007
(202) 337-9636 Fax: (202) 337-9635
Penny Harrison, President
Email: hispdesign@aol.com
Web: www.hispanicdesigners.org

HISPANIC ELECTED LOCAL OFFICIALS CAUCUS
National Headquarters
1301 Pennsylvania Ave. NW #550
Washington, DC 20004
(202) 626-3169 Fax: (202) 626-3043
Mary Gordon, Manager-Constituency Services

HISPANIC EMPLOYMENT PROGRAM
National HEP Council, Washington DC
400 L St. SW, Mail Stop: S/32
Washington, DC 20595
Harry Salinas, President
Email: hepm@aol.com
Web: www.hepm.org

HISPANIC HERITAGE AWARDS FOUNDATION.
2600 Virginia Ave., #406
Washington, DC 20037
(202) 861-9797 Fax: (202) 861-9799
Susan Santana, Director
Web: www.hispanicawards.org

THE HISPANIC LINK JOURNALISM FOUNDATION FELLOWSHIP
1420 N St. NW
Washington, DC 20005
(202) 238-0705 Fax: (202) 238-0706
Héctor Ericksen-Mendoza, Executive Director
Email: zapotec@aol.com

HISPANIC NATIONAL BAR ASSOCIATION
Region V (DC, MD, VA, WV)
901 15th St. NW, #70
Washington, DC 20005
(202) 371-6275 Fax: (202) 371-6279
Juan Carlos Iturregui, Regional President
Email: jciturregui@verner.com
Web: www.hnba.com

HISPANIC ORGANIZATION OF PROFESSIONAL AND EXECUTIVES (HOPE)
1700 17th St., NW, #405
Washington, DC 20009
(202) 234-2351 Fax: (202) 234-5468
Guillermo Lescano, Vice President

HISPANIC POLICY DEVELOPMENT PROJECT (HPDP)
Washington Office
5039 Connecticut Ave. NW, #1
Washington, DC 20036
(202) 822-8414
Georgianna Mcguire, Vice President
Email: siobhan96@aol.com

HISPANIC SERVICE CENTER, INC.
1805 Belmont Rd. NW Suite 205
Washington, DC 20009
(202) 234-3435 Fax: (202) 328-6218
Marta E. Bustos, Manager
Email: mbutos@erols.com

THE HISPANIC SERVING HEALTH PROFESSIONS SCHOOLS
1411 K St. NW, #200
Washington, DC 20005
(202) 783-5262 Fax: (202) 628-5898
Elena Ríos, M.D., Executive Director
Email: HisHps@aol.com
Web: WWW.HsHps.com

HISPANIC SUPPORT GROUP
3900 Wisconsin Ave.
Washington, DC 20016
(202) 752-7587 Fax: (202) 752-6845
Judy M. Majors, Chair

**HOSPITALITY SALES & MARKETING
ASSOCIATION INTERNATIONAL**
1300 L St. NW #1020
Washington, DC 20005
(202) 789-0089 Fax: (202) 789-1725
Robert Gilbert, Executive Vice President and
CEO

HOUSE OF COLOMBIA
1111 Good Hope Rd., SE
Washington, DC 20020
(202) 889-5050 Fax: (202) 610-4497
Alberto Gómez, President
Email: www.casadecolombia.org

HOUSING COUNSELING SERVICES, INC
2430 Ontario Rd. NW
Washington, DC 20009
(202) 667-7006 Fax: (202) 462-5305
Carmelita Edwards, Director

IMMIGRATION SERVICES
Catholic Charities Immigration Services
1221 Massachusetts Ave. NW
Washington, DC 20005
(202) 628-6861 Fax: (202) 737-3421
Nancy Shistack, Director

**INSTITUTE FOR LANGUAGES & CULTURES
OF THE AMERICAS (ILCA)**
1411 K St., NW
Washington, DC 20005
(202) 637-7065 Fax: (202) 637-7091
Hernando Caicedo, Executive Director

**INSTITUTE FOR PUERTO RICAN ARTS &
CULTURE**
413 8th St., NE
Washington, DC 20002
(202) 544-3692 Fax: (202) 544-1395
Cristóbal Caban, Director

INSTITUTO CULTURAL MEXICANO
Washington Office
2829 16th St., NW
Washington, DC 20009
(202) 728-1628 or (202) 728-1629
Fax: (202) 462-7241
Dr. Alvaro Rodríguez Tirado, Director
Email: altirado@erols.com

INSTITUTO DE LIDERAZGO LATINO
Affiliate of NCLR
2309 18th St. NW, Suite 2
Washington, DC 20009
(202) 328-9451 Fax: (202) 667-6135
Jessica Alvarez, Coordinator

INTER-AMERICAN BAR ASSOCIATION
1211 Connecticut Ave., NW #202
Washington, DC 20036-2201
(202) 393-1217 Fax: (202) 393-1241
Luis Serrand, Secretary General
Email: iaba@iaba.org
Web: www.erols.com/iaba/

INTER-AMERICAN CHILDREN'S INSTITUTE
Affiliate of Org. of American States
U.S. Department of Education
330 C St., #5000
Washington, DC 20037
(202) 205-5557 Fax: (202) 205-5381
Norma Cantu, United States Delegate
Email: Norma_v_cantu@ed.gov
Web: www.oas.org

**INTER-AMERICAN COLLEGE OF
PHYSICIANS AND SURGEONS (ICPS)**
1712 I Street, NW, #200
Washington, DC 20006
(202) 467-4756 Fax: (202) 467-4758
Dr. René F. Rodríguez, President
Email: icpsdc@erols.com
Web: www.icps.org

**INTER-AMERICAN COMMISSION OF
WOMEN (CIM)**
Affiliate of Org. of American States
1889 F St. #880
Washington, DC 20006
(202) 458-6084 Fax: (202) 458-6094
Carmen Lomellin, Executive Secretary
Email: clomellin@oas.org
Web: www.oas.org

**INTER-AMERICAN DEFENSE BOARD AND
COLLEGE**
Affiliate of Org. of American States
2600 16th St. NW & Euclid Ave.
Washington, DC 20441-0002
(202) 939-7490 or (202) 939-7491
Fax: (202) 939-6620
Major General Carl H. Freeman, Chairman
Email: brownj@jid.org
Web: www.oas.org

**INTER-AMERICAN DEVELOPMENT BANK
YOUTH DEVELOPMENT & OUTREACH
PROGRAM**
IDB Youth Network
Stop #B0570, 1300 New York Ave. NW
Washington, DC 20057
Fax: (202) 623-1402
Email: bjuventud@iadb.org
Web: www.iadb.org/EXR/mandates/youth/
index.htm

THE INTER-AMERICAN DIALOGUE
1211 Connecticut Ave., NW #510
Washington, DC 20036
(202) 822-9002 Fax: (202) 822-9553
Peter Hakim, Director
Email: iad@iadialog.org
Web: www.thedialogue.org

JOHN QUINCY ADAMS COMM. SCHOOL
2020 19th St. NW
Washington, DC 20009
(202) 673-7311 Fax: (202) 673-5000
Andrew Totts, Principal

JUBILEE HOUSING, INC.
1750 Columbia Rd. NW
Washington, DC 20009
(202) 332-4020 Fax: (202) 332-4983
William Branner, President

JUBILEE JOBS
2712 Ontario Rd. NW
Washington, DC 20009
(202) 667-8970 Fax: (202) 667-8833
Terry Flood, Director

KAISER FAMILY FOUNDATION
Washington Office
1450 G Street NW, #250
Washington, DC 20005
(202) 347-5270 Fax: (202) 347-5274
Michael Sinclair, Senior Vice President
Web: www.kff.org

KALORAMA RECREATION CENTER
DC Department of Recreation
1875 Columbia Rd.
Washington, DC 20009
(202) 673-7606
Earl Johnson, Facility Manager

LA CASA
Drug and Medical Treatment Program
1436 Irving St., NW
Washington, DC 20010
(202) 673-3592 Fax: (202) 462-5669
Velarie Lassiter, Director

LA CLÍNICA DEL PUEBLO
Affiliate of NCLR
1470 Irving St., NW, 2nd Floor
Washington, DC 20010
(202) 462-4788 or (202) 667-1909
Fax: (202) 667-3706
Dr. Juan Romagoza, Executive Director

**LABOR COUNCIL FOR LATIN AMERICAN
ADVANCEMENT (LCLAA)**
National Headquarters
815 16th St., NW, #310
Washington, DC 20006
(202) 347-4223 Fax: (202) 347-5095
Oscar Sánchez, Director
Email: Natlclaa@aol.com
Web: www.lclaa.org

**LAS AMÉRICAS AVENUE DEVELOPMENT
CORPORATION.**
2329 Champlin St.
Washington, DC 20009
(202) 265-9561 Fax: (202) 265-7971
Hernando Caicedo, Director
Email: victorhecter1@aol.com

2025 I St. NW #1019
Washington, DC 20006
(202) 265-9561 Fax: (202) 265-7971

V. Héctor Rodríguez, Executive Director

LATIN AMERICAN LAW STUDENT ASSOC.
Catholic University of America
210 Leahy Hall
Washington, DC 20064
(202) 319-5398
Harold McDougall, Professor

LATIN AMERICAN MANAGEMENT ASSOC.
National Headquarters
419 New Jersey Ave., SE
Washington, DC 20003
(202) 546-3803 Fax: (202) 546-3807
Carlos González, Program Director
Email: lamadc@earthlink.net
Web: www.ourworld.compuserve.com/
homepages/LAMANational

LATIN AMERICAN YOUTH CENTER (LAYC)
Affiliate of NCLR
1419 Columbia Rd., NW
Washington, DC 20009
(202) 319-2225 Fax: (202) 462-5696
Lori M. Kaplan, Executive Director
Email: info@mail.layc-dc.org
Web: www.layc-dc.org

**LATINO ASSOCIATION DRUG
ENFORCEMENT AGENTS (LEDEA)**
1405 Eye St. NW
Washington, DC 20537
(202) 307-1000 Fax: (207) 307-7965
Donnie Marshel, Administrator
Web: www.dea.gov

LATINO CIVIL RIGHTS CENTER
Affiliate of NCLR
2701 Ontario Rd., NW, 2nd Floor
Washington, DC 20009
(202) 332-1053 Fax: (202) 483-7460
Mario Acosta, Executive Director
Email: latinotask@aol.com

**LATINO COUNCIL ON ALCOHOL AND
TOBACCO**
1875 Connecticut Ave. NW #732
Washington, DC 20009
(202) 265-8054/8055 Fax: (202) 265-8056
Jeannette Noltenius, Executive Director
Email: lcat@erols.com
Web: www.lcat.org

**LATINO ECONOMIC DEVELOPMENT
CORPORATION (LEDC)**
Affiliate of NCLR
2316 18th Street, NW
Washington, DC 20009-1815
(202) 588-5102 Fax: (202) 588-5204
Celina Treviño Rosales, Executive Director
Email: ledcsfs@aol.com

LATINO STUDENT FUND
P.O. Box 5403
Washington, DC 20016
(202) 338-3327 Fax: (202) 337-1700
Marisa Ramírez de Arellano, Executive Director
Email: lsf@diploma.com
Web: www.incacorp.com/lsf

**LEADERSHIP CONFERENCE ON CIVIL
RIGHTS**
1629 K St. NW #1010
Washington, DC 20006
(202) 466-3311 Fax: (202) 466-3435
Wade Henderson, Executive Director

**LEAGUE OF UNITED LATIN AMERICAN
CITIZENS (LULAC)**
2000 L St. NW #610
Washington, DC 20036
(703) 833-6130 Fax: (202) 835-9685
Richard Roybal, Executive Director
Email: lulacdc@aol.com
Web: www.lulac.org

Law Office
1730 Rhode Island, NW, #1208
Washington, DC 20036
(202) 835-1555 Fax: (202) 835-1569
Eduardo Peña, President
Email: edpenalaw@aol.com
Web: www.lulac.org

LIFE SKILLS CENTER
3166 Mt. Pleasant St., NW
Washington, DC 20010
(202) 234-9351 Fax: (202) 234-3057
José García, Executive Director

**"LLEGO" THE NATIONAL LATINA/O
LESBIAN, GAY, BISEXUAL AND**

TRANSGENDER ORGANIZATION
1612 K St., NW, #500
Washington, DC 20006
(202) 466-8240 Fax: (202) 466-8530
Martin Orneles, Executive Director
Email: aquilgvt@llego.org
Web: www.LLEGO.org

LUTHERAN SOCIAL SERVICES
4406 Georgia Ave. NW
Washington, DC 20011
(202) 723-3000 Fax: (202) 723-3303
Mark Cooper, Director

**MANA - A NATIONAL LATINA
ORGANIZATION**
National Headquarters
1725 K St. NW #501
Washington, DC 20006
(202) 833-0060 Fax: (202) 496-0588
Alma Morales Riojas, President & CEO
Email: hermana2@aol.com
Web: www.hermana.org

MARIE REED SCHOOL
2200 Champlain St.
Washington, DC 20009
(202) 673-7308 Fax: (202) 673-3410
John Sparrow, Principal

MARTHA'S TABLE
2114 14th St.
Washington, DC 20009
(202) 328-6608 Fax: (202) 387-0011
Veronica Parke, Director

**MARY'S CENTER FOR MATERNAL AND
CHILD CARE**
Affiliate of NCLR
2333 Ontario Road, NW
Washington, DC 20009
(202) 483-8196 Fax: (202) 797-2628
María Gómez, Executive Director
Email: info@maryscenter.org
Web: www.maryscenter.org

MARY'S HOUSE
4303 13th St. NE
Washington, DC 20017
(202) 635-0534 Fax: (202) 529-5793
Sharon Murphy, Director

MAYOR'S OFFICE ON LATINO AFFAIRS
2000 14th St. NW 2nd. Floor
Washington, DC 20009
(202) 671-2825 Fax: (202) 673-4557
Rosario Gutiérrez, Executive Director

**MEXICAN AMERICAN LEGAL DEFENSE
AND EDUCATIONAL FUND (MALDEF)**
Washington, D.C. Regional Office
1717 K St., NW, #311
Washington, DC 20036
(202) 293-2828 Fax: (202) 293-2849
Marisa J. Demeo, Regional Counsel
Email: mjdemeo@aol.com
Web: www.maldef.org

**THE MEXICAN AND AMERICAN
SOLIDARITY FOUNDATION**
1111 19th St., NW #1000
Washington, DC 20036
(202) 776-1707 Fax: (202) 776-1792
Raúl Izaguirre, President/CEO
Email: Estevan@nclr.org

MI CASA, INC.
1769 Lanier Place, N.W.
Washington, DC 20009
(202) 232-1375 Fax: (202) 232-7649
Fernando Lemos, Executive Director

MIGRANT LEGAL ACTION PROGRAM
P.O. Box 53308
Washington, DC 20009
(202) 462-7744 Fax: (202) 462-7914
Roger Rosenthal, President & Executive
Director
Web: www.mlap.org

**MINORITY BUSINESS DEVELOPMENT
AGENCY (MBDA)**
Headquarters/U.S. Dept. of Commerce
14th & Constitution Ave. NW, #5055
Washington, DC 20230
(202) 842-5061 or (202) 482-6022
Fax: (202) 501-4698
Raúl Quiros, Senior Business Specialist
Email: RQuiros@mbda.gov
Web: www.mbda.gov

MT. PLEASANT HIGHER ACHIEVEMENT PROG.
19 Eye Street, NW
Washington, DC 20001
(202) 842-5116 Fax: (202) 842-5123
Carolina Lugo, Center Director

MY SISTER'S PLACE
P.O. Box 29596
Washington, DC 20017
(202) 529-5991 Fax: (202) 529-5984
July Blum, Executive Director

NAFSA - ASSOCIATION OF INTERNATIONAL EDUCATORS
National Headquarters
1307 New York, #800 NW
Washington, DC 20005
(202) 737-3699 Fax: (202) 737-3657
Marlene Johnson, Executive Director
Email: marlenej@nafsa.org
Web: www.nafsa.org

NATIONAL ALLIANCE FOR HISPANIC HEALTH
National Headquarters
1501 16th St., NW
Washington, DC 20036-1401
(202) 387-5000 Fax: (202) 797-4353
Jane Delgado, President & CEO
Email: alliance@hispanichealth.org
Web: www.hispanichealth.orh

NATIONAL ALLIANCE OF SPANISH SPEAKING PEOPLE FOR EQUALITY
National Headquarters
P.O. Box 2385
Washington, DC 20013
(202) 234-8198
Dr. Miguel Sandoval, President

NATIONAL ASSOCIATION FOR BILINGUAL EDUCATION (NABE)
National Headquarters, Affiliate of NCLR
1030 15th St., NW. #470
Washington, DC 20005
(202) 898-1829 Fax: (202) 789-2866
Delia Pompa, Executive Director
Email: c_riddick@nabe.org or nabe@nabe.org
Web: www.nabe.org

NATIONAL ASSOCIATION FOR HISPANIC ELDERLY
Washington D.C. Office/Project Ayuda
1015 18th St., NW, #401
Washingtonn, DC 20036-5214
(202) 293-9329 Fax: (202) 466-9028
Julia Neidecker-Gonzales, Project Coordinator
Email: oscarjul@capaccess.org

NATIONAL ASSOCIATION OF HISPANIC JOURNALISTS (NAHJ)
National Headquarters
1193 National Press Bldg., 529 14th St., NW
Washington, DC 20045-2100
(202) 662-7145 or (888) 346-NAHJ
Fax: (202) 662-7144
Cecilia Alvear, President
Email: nahj@nahj.org
Web: www.nahj.org

National Headquarters
1501 16th St., NW
Washington, DC 20036
(202) 387-2477 Fax: (202) 483-7183
Mary Lou de Leon Siantz, President
Email: info@nahnhq.org
Web: http://www.nahnhq.org

NATIONAL ASSOCIATION OF HISPANIC PUBLICATIONS (NAHP)
National Headquarters
652 National Press Bldg. NW
Washington, DC 20045
(202) 662-7250 Fax: (202) 662-7254
Andrés Tobar, Executive Director
Email: atobar@nahp.org
Web: www.nahp.org

NATIONAL ASSOCIATION OF INVESTMENT COMPANIES
733 15th St. NW #700
Washington, DC 20005
(202) 289-4336 Fax: (202) 289-4329
Bettyelynn Smith, President

NATIONAL ASSOCIATION OF LATINO ELECTED & APPOINTED OFFICIALS
Washington Office
311 Massachusetts Ave. NE

Washington, DC 20002
(202) 546-2536 or 1 800 446 2536
Fax: (202) 546-4121
Larry González, Director
Email: lgonzalez@naleo.org
Web: www.naleo.org

NATIONAL ASSOCIATION OF MINORITY CONTRACTORS (NAMC)
National Headquarters
666 11th St., NW, #520
Washington, DC 20001
(202) 347-8259 Fax: (202) 628-1876
Samual A. Carradine, Executive Director

NATIONAL ASSOCIATION OF NEIGHBORHOODS (NAN)
National Headquarters
1651 Fuller St. NW
Washington, DC 20009
(202) 332-7766 Fax: (202) 332-3314
Ricardo Berd, Executive President

NATIONAL ASSOCIATION OF SOCIAL WORKERS (NASW)
750 1st St., NE, #700
Washington, DC 20002
(202) 336-8200 Fax: (202) 336-8310
Josephine Nieves, Executive Director
Web: www.socialworkers.org

NATIONAL CATHOLIC CONFERENCE FOR INTERRACIAL JUSTICE
National Headquarters
1200 Varnum St., NE
Washington, DC 20017
(202) 529-6480 Fax: (202) 526-1262
Joseph M. Conrad, Executive Director

NATIONAL CLEARINGHOUSE FOR BILINGUAL EDUCATION
The George Washington University
2121 K St., NW, #260
Washington, DC 20037
(202) 467-0867 or (800) 321-NCBE
Fax: (202) 467-4283
Minerva Gorena, Director
Email: askncbe@gwu.edu
Web: www.ncbe.gwu.edu

NATIONAL COMMUNITY FOR LATINO LEADERSHIP, INC. (NCLL)
1701 K St., NW, #301
Washington, DC 20006
(202) 721-8290 Fax: (202) 721-8296
Alfred Ramírez, President
Email: aramirez@latinoleadership.org
Web: www.latinoleadership.org

NATIONAL CONFERENCE OF PUERTO RICAN WOMEN (NACOPRW)
National Headquarters
5 Thomas Circle NW
Washington, DC 20005
(202) 387-4716 or (202) 778-0726 (w)
Fax: (301) 217-0192
Vanny Marreo, National President
Web: WWW.nacoprw.org

NATIONAL COUNCIL FOR COMMUNITY & EDUCATION PARTNERSHIPS
1400 20th St., NW, Dupont Circle, #116
Washington, DC 20036
(202) 530-1135 FAX: (202) 530-0809
Hector Garza, President
Web: www.edpartnerships.org

NATIONAL COUNCIL OF HISPANIC WOMEN
1300 Crystal Drive, #1610
Arlington, VA 22202
(310) 746-1541x3477 FAX: (310) 746-1541x3477
Litizia Ramirez Erickson, National Secretary
Email: nchwomen@hotmail.com
Web: www.go.to/nchw

NATIONAL COUNCIL OF LA RAZA (NCLR)
National Headquarters
1111 19th St., NW, #1000
Washington, DC 20036
(202) 785-1670 or (800) 311-NCLR
Fax: (202) 776-1792
Raul Yzaguirre, President & CEO
Web: www.nclr.org

NATIONAL EDUCATION ASSOCIATION (NEA)
1201 16th St. NW
Washington, DC 20036-3290
(202) 822-7642 Fax: (202) 822-7619

Nadine Burnside, HR Manager
Email: www. nea.org/jobs

NATIONAL EMPLOYMENT LAW INSTITUTE
Headquarters, East Coast
1200 G St. NW #800
Washington, DC 20005
(202) 434-8742 Fax: (202) 434-8707
Lenard Biermenn, Director
Web: www.neli.org

NATIONAL FAIR HOUSING ALLIANCE
1212 New York Ave., NW, #525
Washington, DC 20005
(202) 898-1661 Fax: (202) 371-9744
Shanna Smith, Director
Email: nfha@erols.com

NATIONAL FOUNDATION FOR WOMEN BUSINESS OWNERS (NFWBO)
National Headquarters
1411 K St. NW #1350
Washington, DC 20005
(202) 638-3060
Sharon Hadary, Executive Director
Email: nfwbo.worldnet.att.net
Web: www.nfwbo.org

NATIONAL GAY & LESBIAN TASK FORCE
1700 Kalorama Rd. NW #101
Washington, DC 20009-2624
(202) 332-6483 Fax: (202) 332-0207
Elizabeth Toledo, Executive Director
Email: ngltf@ngltf.org
Web: www.ngltf.org

NATIONAL HISPANIC CAUCUS OF STATE LEGISLATORS (NHCSL)
National Headquarters
444 North Capitol St., NW #404
Washington, DC 20001
(202) 434-8070 Fax: (202) 434-8072
Senator Efraín González, Jr., President
Email: nhcsl@sso.org

NATIONAL HISPANIC COUNCIL ON AGING (NHCOA)
National Headquarters
2713 Ontario Rd. NW
Washington, DC 20009
(202) 265-1288 Fax: (202) 745-2522
Marta Sotomayor, President & CEO
Email: nhcoa@worldnet.att.net
Web: www.nhcoa.org

NATIONAL HISPANIC FOUNDATION. FOR THE ARTS
Water Front Center
1010 Wisconsin Ave. NW #210
Washington, DC 20007
(202) 293-8330 Fax: (202) 965-5252
Felix Sánchez, President
Email: fsanchez@hispanicarts.org
Web: www.hispanicarts.org

NATIONAL HISPANIC HOUSING COUNCIL
National Headquarters
318 4th St., NE
Washington, DC 20002
(202) 543-8580 or (888) 543-8580 Fax: (202) 543-3750
Ruth Pagani, Executive Director
Email: nhhcenter@erols.org

NATIONAL HISPANIC MEDICAL ASSOCIATION
1700 17th St., NW, #405
Washington, DC 20009
(202) 265-4297 Fax: (202) 234-5468
Dr. René Rodríguez, President
Web: http://home.earthlink.net/~nhma

NATIONAL HISPANIC RELIGIOUS PARTNERSHIP FOR COMMUNITY HEALTH
5 Thomas Circle NW, 4th floor
Washington, DC 20005
(202) 265-3338 Fax: (202) 265-3339

NATIONAL INFORMATION CENTER. FOR CHILDREN AND YOUTH WITH DISABILITIES (NICHCY)
National Headquarters
P.O. Box 1492
Washington, DC 20013-1492
(202) 884-8200 or (800) 695-0285
Fax: (202) 884-8441
Susan Ripley, Director
Email: nichcy@aed.org
Web: www.nichcy.org

NATIONAL LATINA HEALTH NETWORK
National Office
1000 Thomas Jefferson St. #309
Washington, DC 20007
(202) 965-9633 Fax: (202) 965-9637
Jeanette Beltran, National Director of Special Programs
Email: j-beltran@erols.com

NATIONAL LATINA INSTITUTE FOR REPRODUCTIVE HEALTH (NLIRH)
1200 New York Ave., NW, #206
Washington, DC 20005
(202) 326-8970 Fax: (202) 371-8112
Arcelly Panameño, Executive Director
Email: nlirh@igc.apc.org
Web: www.nlirh.org

NATIONAL LEAGUE OF CITIES/HISPANIC LOCAL OFFICIALS CAUCUS
National Headquarters
1301 Pennsylvania Ave. NW #550
Washington, DC 20004
(202) 626-3160 Fax: (202) 626-3103
Nelly Gutierrez, Administrative Assistant

NATIONAL MINORITY AIDS COUNCIL
National Headquarters
1931 13th St., NW
Washington, DC 20009-4432
(202) 483-6622 Fax: (202) 483-1135
Paul Kawata, Executive Director
Email: nmac@nmac.org
Web: www.nmac.org

NATIONAL MINORITY ORGAN TISSUE TRANSPLANT EDUCATION PROGRAM
Ambulatory Care Center
2041 Georgia Ave. NW, #3100
Washington, DC 20060
(202) 865-4888 or (800) 393-2839
Fax: (202) 865-4880
Elba R. Sanchez, National Latina Coordinator
Web: www.mottep.org

NATIONAL MULTICULTURAL INSTITUTE
National Headquarters
3000 Connecticut Ave. NW, #438
Washington, DC 20008-2556
(202) 483-0700 Fax: (202) 483-5233
Elizabeth P. Salett, President
Email: nmci@nmci.org
Web: www.nmci.org

NATIONAL PUERTO RICAN COALITION, INC.
National Headquarters
1700 K St. NW #500
Washington, DC 20006
(202) 223-3915 Fax: (202) 429-2223
Manuel Mirabal, President & CEO
Email: nprcinc@nprcinc.org
Web: www.bateylink.org

NATIONAL WOMEN'S POLITICAL CAUCUS (NWPC) HISPANIC CAUCUS
National Headquarters
1630 Connecticut Ave. NW #201
Washington, DC 20009
(202) 785-1100 Fax: (202) 785-3605
Anita Pérez Ferguson, President
Email: pereznwpc@aol.com
Web: www.nwpc.org

NEIGHBORS' CONSEJO
1624 Lamont St. NW
Washington, DC 20010
(202) 234-6855 Fax: (202) 234-4863
Najiya Shana'-Salvador, Executive Director

NETWORK IN SOLIDARITY WITH THE PEOPLE OF GUATEMALA (NISGUA)
1830 Connecticut Ave. NW
Washington, DC 20009-1817
(202) 223-6474 or (202) 518-7638
Fax: (202) 223-8221
Lael Parish, Director
Email: nisgua@igc.apc.org

NETWORK OF EDUCATORS ON THE AMERICAS (NECA)
P.O. Box 73038
Washington, DC 20056
(202) 238-2379 Fax: (202) 238-2378
Deborah Menkart, Director

NICARAGUA NETWORK
1247 E. St. SE
Washington, DC 20003

(202) 544-9355 Fax: (202) 544-9359
Lisa Zimmerman, Coordinator

OFFICE OF HISPANIC AFFAIRS
Howard University
2041 Georgia Avenue, NW
Washington, DC 20060
(202) 865-5284 Fax: (202) 865-3245
Patricia Moran, Director

OFFICE OF THE RESIDENT COMMISSIONER FROM PUERTO RICO
U.S. HOUSE of REPRESENTATIVES
2443 Rayburn Building
Washington, DC 20515
(202) 225-2615 Fax: (202) 225-2154
Carlos Romero Barceló, Res. Commisioner

ORGANIZATION OF AMERICAN STATES
17th St. & Constitution Ave., NW #20
Washington, DC 20006
(202) 458-3000 Fax: (202) 458-3967
César Gaviria-Trujillo, Secretary General
Web: www.oas.org

OYSTER SCHOOL
29th & Calvert St. NW
Washington, DC 20008
(202) 673-7277 Fax: (202) 673-3419
Paquita Holand, Principal

PAN-AMERICAN DEVELOPMENT FOUNDATION (PADF)
Affiliate of Organization of American States
2600 16th St., NW, 4th Floor
Washington, DC 20009
(202) 458-3969 Fax: (202) 458-6316
Anita Winsor, Deputy Executive Director

PAN-AMERICAN HEALTH ORGANIZATION
Affiliate of Org. of American States
525 23rd St., NW
Washington, DC 20037
(202) 974-3000 Fax: (202) 974-3663
George Alleyne, Director
Web: www.paho.org

PANAMERICAN SYMPHONY ORCHESTRA
Trinity College
125 Michigan Ave. NE
Washington, DC 20017-1094
(202) 884-9000 or (202) 884-9008
Fax: (202) 884-9229
Sergio A. Buslje, Artistic Director & Conductor

PARALYZED VETERANS OF AMERICA
801 18th St. NW
Washington, DC 20006
(202) 872-1300 Fax: (202) 416-7643
Gordon H. Mansfield, Executive Director

PARTNERS OF THE AMERICAS
1424 K St. NW #700
Washington, DC 20005
(202) 628-3300 Fax: (202) 628-3306
Kate Rastery, Acting President

PARTNERS OF THE AMERICAS
1424 K Street NW #700
Washington, DC 20005
(202) 628-3300 Fax: (202) 628-3306
Norman A. Brown, Director
Email: info@partners.poa.com
Web: www.partners.net

PHARMACEUTICAL MANUFACTURERS ASSOCIATION
1100 15th St. NW
Washington, DC 20005
(202) 835-3400 Fax: (202) 785-4834
Alan Homer, President
Web: www.phrma.org

PLANNED PARENTHOOD
1108 16th St. NW
Washington, DC 20036
(202) 347-8500 Fax: (202) 783-1007
Rocío González, Contact

PROGRAMA DE ENLACE COMUNITARIO
Girl Scout Council of the Nation's Capital
4301 Connecticut Ave. NW
Washington, DC 20008
(202) 237-1670 x 361 or (800) 523-7898
Fax: (202) 274-2162
Maribel Ruiz, Linguistic Outreach Specialist
Email: info@gscnc.org or mruiz@gscnc.org
Web: www.gscnc.org

PROYECTO AMISTAD/AMERICAN UNIVERSITY
Dept. of Language and Foreign Studies
4400 Massachusetts
Washington, DC 20016-8045
(202) 885-2381 Fax: (202) 885-1076
Prof. Clemencia Alvarez, Director
Email: lfs@american.edu

PUBLIC ALLIES
1015 18th St. NW #200
Washington, DC 20036
(202) 822-1180 Fax: (202) 822-1199
Jay Kim, Executive Director
Web: www.publicallies.org

PUERTO RICO FEDERAL AFFAIRS ADMIN.
National Headquarters
1100 17th St. NW #800
Washington, DC 20036
(202) 778-0710 Fax: (202) 778-0721
Alfonso Aguilar Sartorie, Executive Director
Web: www.prfaa.com

QUALITY EDUCATION FOR MINORITIES NETWORK
1818 N St., NW, #350
Washington, DC 20036
(202) 659-1818 Fax: (202) 659-5408
Sherly McBay, President
Email: qemnetwork@qem.org
Web: http://qemnetwork.qem.org

RAINBOW/PUSH COALITION
District of Columbia Chapter
1612 Buchanan St., NW
Washington, DC 20011
(202) 882-3127 Fax: (202) 726-2355
Jerry A. Moore, President
Web: www.rainbowpush.org

Washington, DC Bureau
1002 Wisconsin Ave., NW
Washington, DC 20007
(202) 333-5270 Fax: (202) 728-1192
Dr. Karin Stanford, Executive Director
Web: www.rainbowpush.org

RAPE CRISIS CENTER OF D.C.
P. O. Box 34125
Washington, DC 20043
(202) 232-0789 or (202) 333-7273 Hotline
Fax: (202) 387-3812
Julia López, Hispanic Coordinator
Email: dcrcc@erols.com
Web: www.dcrr.org

REGIONAL ADDICTION PREVENTION, INC.
1949 4thSt. NE
Washington, DC 20002
(202) 462-7500 Fax: (202) 462-7507
Ron Clark, Executive Director

REPUBLICAN NATIONAL COMMITTEE
National Headquarters
310 1st St., SE
Washington, DC 20003
(202) 863-8500 Fax: (202) 863-8820
Jim Nicholson, Chairman

REPUBLICAN NATIONAL HISPANIC ASSEMBLY (RNHA)
National Headquarters
600 Pennsylvania Ave. SE #300
Washington, DC 20003
(202) 544-6700 or (877) 544-6701
Fax: (202) 544-6869
Tomas Bilbao, Executive Director
Email: info@rnha.org
Web: www.rnha.org

THE ROSEMOUNT CENTER
2000 Rosemount Ave. NW
Washington, DC 20010
(202) 265-9885 Fax: (202) 265-2636
Dr. Roderlyn Greene, Executive Director
Carmen Peirera, Office Manager

SACRED HEART COMMUNITY CENTER
3211 Line Street, NW
Washington, DC 20010-3354
(202) 234-8000 Fax: (202) 234-9159
Sisiter Delfina García, Coordinator

SALOMÓN ZELAYA REHABILITATION CENTER
1345 Newton Street, NW
Washington, DC 20010
(202) 745-7719
Pablo M. Sánchez, Executive Director

SANZ SCHOOL, INC
Main Location
1720 I St. NW
Washington, DC 20036
(202) 872-4700 Fax: (202) 872-9009

SARAH'S CIRCLE
2551 17 th. St. NW #103
Washington, DC 20009
(202) 332-1400 Fax: (202) 667-9529
Ruth Sachs, Director

SCHOOL INTERNATIONAL SERVICE
American University
4400 Massachusetts Ave. NW
Washington, DC 20016-8071
(202) 885-1600 Fax: (202) 885-2494
Louis Goodman, Dean

SECRETARIAT FOR HISPANIC AFFAIRS NATIONAL CONFERENCE OF CATHOLIC BISHOPS
National Headquarters
3211 4th St. NE
Washington, DC 20017
(202) 541-3150 Fax: (202) 722-8717
Most Reverend Gerald Barnes, Chairman
Web: www.nccb_uscc.org

SHARE FOUNDATION - BUILDING A NEW EL SALVADOR
D.C. Office
P.O. Box 16, Cardinal Station
Washington, DC 200064
(202) 319-5540 Fax: (202) 319-5541
Jean Stokan, Policy Director
Email: share@igc.org

SHRINE OF THE SACRED HEART
3211 Pine St.
Washington, DC 20010
(202) 234-8000 Fax: (202) 234-9159
Fransico Javier Russo, Pastor
Email: russos@prodigy.com

SISTER CITIES INTERNATIONAL
1300 Pennsylvania Ave., NW, #250
Washington, DC 20004-3002
(202) 312-1200 Fax: (202) 312-1201
Edmund Benner, Executive Director
Web: www.sister-cities.org

SOCIETY OF MEXICAN AMERICAN ENGINEERS AND SCIENTISTS (MAES)
Nation's Capital Area Chapter
1305 Delafield Place, Nw
Washington, DC 20011
(202) 723-3173 Fax: (703) 318-9799
Ignacio Rojas, Regional Vice President
Email: irojas@doubled.com

SPANISH CATHOLIC CENTER - CENTRO CATOLICO HISPANO
Headquarters/Medical and Dental Clinic
1618 Monroe St., NW
Washington, DC 20010
(202) 939-2400/2426/2402/2404
Fax: (202) 234-7323
Rev. Mark J. Poletunow, Executive Director
Email: sccdc@erols.com
Web: www.centrocatolicohispano.org

SPANISH CLUB
Catholic University of America
208 McMahon Hall
Washington, DC 20064
(202) 319-5240 Fax: (202) 319-6077
Dr. Zentri, Director
Web: www.cua.edu

SPANISH EDUCATIONAL DEVELOPMENT (SED) CENTER.
Affiliate of NCLR
1848 Kalorama Rd. NW
Washington, DC 20009
(202) 462-8848 Fax: (202) 462-6886
Martha Egas, Executive Director
Email: sedcen@erols.com
Web: www.sedcen.com

SPANISH SENIOR CENTER (EOFULA)
1832 Calvert St.
Washington, DC 20009
(202) 483-5800 Fax: (202) 588-5806
Ana María Neris, Director

ST. DOMINIC
630 & "E" Street, SW
Washington, DC 20024
(202) 554-7863 Fax: (202) 554-0231
Rev. Robert L. Walker, Pastor
Email: stdom@pipeline.com

ST. GABRIEL
26 Grant Circle, NW
Washington, DC 20011
(202) 726-9092 or (202) 291-5365
Fax: (202) 291-0334
Rev. Vidal A. Rivas Lima, Associate Pastor

ST. THOMAS THE APOSTLE
2665 Woodley Rd. NW
Washington, DC 20008
(202) 234-1488 Fax: (202) 234-1480
Rev. Mark Brennan, Pastor

STAFF ASSOCIATION OF THE INTER-AMERICAN DEVELOPMENT BANK
1300 New York Ave. NW
Washington, DC 20577
(202) 623-3330 Fax: (202) 623-2154
Jose Santaballa, President
Email: meryh@iadb.org
Web: www.iadb.org

TEATRO DE LA LUNA
4411 Kansas Ave. NW
Washington, DC 20011
(202) 882-6227 Fax: (202) 291-2357
Mario Marcel, Executive Director
Email: teatrodelaluna@hotmail.com
Web: www.teatrodelaluna.org

UNITED STATES CATHOLIC CONFERENCE/HISPANIC AFFAIRS
National Headquarters
3211 4th St., NE
Washington, DC 20017
(202) 541-3000 or (202) 541-3150
Fax: (202) 722-8717
Ronaldo Crúz, National Director Hispanic Affairs

UNITED STATES HISPANIC CHAMBER OF COMMERCE (USHCC)
National Headquarters
2175 K St., NW, #100
Washington, DC 20037
(202) 842-1212 Fax: (202) 842-3221
George Herrera, President & CEO
Email: info@ushcc.com
Web: www.ushcc.com

UNITED STATES-MEXICO CHAMBER OF COMMERCE
1300 Pennsylvania Ave., NW, #270
Washington, DC 20004-3021
(202) 371-8680 Fax: (202) 371-8686
Albert Zapata, President & CEO
Email: news-hq@usmcoc.org
Web: www.usmcoc.org

UNITED STATES-PANAMA BUSINESS COUNCIL (USPA)
1726 M St. NW Suite 704
Washington, DC 20036
(202) 728-0773 Fax: (202) 728-0768
Amb. Juan B. Sosa
Email: Panamerica@msn.com

VILLAGE DAY CARE CENTER
2900 14th St. NW
Washington, DC 20009
(202) 234-5114/3855 Fax: (202) 234-1252
Stephanie Tindal, Director

THE WASHINGTON FREE CLINIC
P. O. Box 43202
Washington, DC 20010
(202) 667-1106 Fax: (202) 328-2652
Sharon Zilewski, Director
Email: szilewski@wfclinic.org

WASHINGTON HEARING & SPEECH SOCIETY
United Way Agency
5255 Loughboro Rd. NW
Washington, DC 20016
(202) 244-4420 Fax: (202) 537-0585
Diane McCarthy, Director

WASHINGTON OFFICE ON LATIN AMERICA (WOLA)
1630 Connecticut Avenue, NW, #200
Washington, DC 20009
(202) 797-2171 Fax: (202) 797-2172
George Vickers, Executive Director
Email: wola@wola.org
Web: www.wola.org

WHITE HOUSE OFFICE OF PUBLIC LIAISON
National Headquarters/Hispanic
Outreach
Old Executive Office Bldg.
1700 Pennsylvania Ave. #122
Washington, DC 20502
(202) 456-2930 Fax: (202) 456-6218
Maritza Rivera, Assistant Director
Web: www.whitehouse.gov

WHITMAN WALKER CLINIC
Office of Latino Services
1407 S St. NW
Washington, DC 20009
(202) 939-7863 Fax: (202) 319-7012
Larry Villegas, Director

FLORIDA

ACTION COMMUNITY CENTER, INC.
970 SW First St. #304
Miami, FL 33130
(305) 545-9298 Fax: (305) 545-0203
María P. Albo, Program Director

ALPHA 66
Plaza de la Cubanidad, 1714 W. Flagler St.
Miami, FL 33135
(305) 541-5433 Fax: (305) 541-2252
Andrés Nazario Sargén, Secretary General
Email: pedroa@shadow.net
Web: www.alpha66.org

**AMERICAN CANCER SOCIETY HISPANIC
OUTREACH SUBCOMMITTEE**
3407 N.W. 9th. Ave. #100
Ft. Lauderdale, FL 33309
(954) 564-0880 Fax: (954) 5618072
Ellen Graves, Director
Email: egraves@cancer.org
Web: www.cancer.org

**ANCIENT SPANISH MONASTERY OF ST.
BERNARD DE CLAIRVAUX**
16711 W. Dixie Hwy.
North Miami Beach, FL 33160
(305) 945-1462 Fax: (305) 945-6986
Vivian Jones, Office Administrator
Email: Monastery@earthlink.net
Web: www.spanishmonastery.com

ARCHDIOCESE OF MIAMI
Hispanic Ministry Office
9401 Biscayne Blvd.
Miami Shores, FL 33138
(305) 762-1091 Fax: (305) 762-1138
Most Rev. Gilberto Fernández
Email: bpfernan@mail.miamiarch.org

ARGENTINA ARTS ORGANIZATION
7752 Forestay Dr.
Lake Worth, FL 33467
(561) 966-7640 Fax: (561) 967-8567
Carlos Fiore, President

**ARGENTINE-FLORIDA CHAMBER OF
COMMERCE**
2666 Brickell Ave., 3rd Floor
Miami, FL 33129
(305) 858-1516 Fax: (305) 858-3767
Edgardo De Fortuna, President
Email: aascc@aol.com
Web: www.argentinaflorida.com

**ASOCIACIÓN ARGENTINA DE FLORIDA
CENTRAL**
P.O. Box 1149
Goldenrod, FL 32733-1149
(407) 344-0270 Fax: (407) 344-1750
Haydee Gibson, President
Email: gotan@aol.com

**ASOCIACIÓN ARGENTINA DE LA BAHÍA
DE TAMPA**
324 S. Hide Park Ave.
Tampa, FL 33606
(813) 251-8601 or (813) 251-5913
Fax: (813) 254-1109
Osvaldo Laino, Chairman

ASOCIACIÓN DOMINICANA USA
P.O. Box 1715
Coral Gables, FL 33134
(305) 444-6864 Fax: (305) 447-1622
Nelcida Hanley de Chakoff, Executive Director
Email: nelcida@bellsouth.net

ASOCIACIÓN MUJERES ARGENTINA
710 NE 29 Street
Miami, FL 33137
(305) 573-2005 Fax: (305) 573-0282

Margot Rivero, President

ASPIRA OF FLORIDA, INC.
3650 N. Miami Ave.
Miami, FL 33137
(305) 576-1512 Fax: (305) 576-0810
Raúl Martínez, President
Email: aspirafl@aol.com
Web: www.aspira.org/florida.html

AYUDA: LATIN YOUTH
Happy Kids
2217 Norman Dr.
Miami Beach, FL 33141
(305) 864-2273 Fax: (305) 864-1020
Diana Susi, Exec. Dir.
Email: ayudainc@aol.com

THE BARBACHANO FOUNDATION
480 W. 83rd St.
Miami Lakes, FL 33014
(800) 327-2254 Fax: (305) 362-6200
Lavanda De Gregory, Office Manager

**BILINGUAL PRIVATE SCHOOLS
ASSOCIATION (BIPRISA)**
National Headquarters
904 S.W. 23rd Ave.
Miami, FL 33135
(305) 643-4888 Fax: (305) 642-8402
Demetrio Pérez, Jr., President

**BRAZILIAN-AMERCAN CHAMBER OF
COMMERCE OF FLORIDA**
1101 Brickel Ave. #1102
Miami, FL 33131
(305) 579-9030 Fax: (305) 579-9756
Flávio Carvalho, President
Email: baccf@brazilchamber.org

**CÁMARA DE COMERCIO PERUANO-
AMERICANA EN MIAMI**
444 Brickell Avenue, Suite 311
Miami, FL 33131
(305) 375-0885 Fax: (305) 375-0884
Jorge Prugue, President
Email: PeruUsa@netrus.net
Web: www.perucam.org

CASA ALIANZA
Covenant House Latin America - SJO 1039
P.O. Box 025216
Miami, FL 33102-5216
(506) 253-5439 Fax: (506) 224-5689
Bruce Harris, Regional Director
Email: info@casa-alianza.org
Web: www.casa-alianza.org

CASA DE PUERTO RICO
6908 C Easter St.
Winter Park, FL 32792
(407) 679-8842
Magím López, President

CENTER FOR LATIN AMERICAN STUDIES
University of Florida
P.O. Box 115530
319 Grinter Hall
Gainesville, FL 32611
(352) 392-0375 Fax: (352) 392-7682
Dr. Charles Wood, Director
Email: cwood@latam.ufl.edu
Web: www.latam.ufl.edu

**CENTRO CAMPESINO-FARMWORKER
CENTER, INC.**
Affiliate of NCLR
P.O. Box 343449
35801 SW 186th Ave.
Florida City, FL 33034
(305) 245-7738 Fax: (305) 247-2619
Steven Mainster, Executive Director

**CENTRO CULTURAL ESPAÑOL DE
COOPERACIÓN IBEROAMERICANA
(CCECI)**
800 Douglas Rd. # 170
Coral Gables, FL 33134
(305) 448-9677 Fax: (305) 448-9676
Email: info@cceci-miami.com
Web: www.cceci-miami.com

CENTRO CULTURAL MEXICANO
Miami Office
1200 NW 78 Ave., #200
Miami, FL 33126
(305) 716-0095 or (305) 716-4977
Fax: (305) 593-2758
Teresa Villareal, Executive Director

CENTRO EDUCACIONAL BILINGUE
1040 SW 27th Ave.
Miami, FL 33135
(305) 649-4600 Fax: (305) 649-1049
Diana González, Contact

**CHILE-UNITED STATES CHAMBER OF
COMMERCE**
The Biltmore Executive Off. Ctr. #210
1200 Anastasia Ave.
Coral Gables, FL 33134
(305) 447-0908 Fax: (305) 447-1644
Lita Haiger, President

**CÍRCULO CUBANO DE TAMPA/
CUBAN CLUB**
P.O. Box 5625
Tampa, FL 33675
(813) 248-2954
Paul Dosal, President

CLUB IBÉRICO ESPAÑOL
P.O. Box 261841
Tampa, FL 33685
(813)884-4832
Rafael Sánchez, Director

**COALITION OF FLORIDA FARMWORKER
ORGANIZATIONS, INC. (COFFO)**
National Headquarters Affiliate of NCLR
P.O. Box 900368, Homestead, FL 33090
305 S. Flager Ave.
Homestead, FL 33030
(305) 246-0357 Fax: (305) 246-2445
Arturo López, Executive Director

**Immigration and Literacy / New Paths
Substance Abuse Center**
21 S. Krome Ave.
Homestead, FL 33030
(305) 247-4779 Fax: (305) 242-0701
Dr. Oscar D. Pozo, Outreach
CoordinatorSubstance Abuse Center Project
Coordinator

**COALITION OF HISPANIC AMERICAN
WOMEN**
P.O. Box 144982
Coral Gables, FL 33114-4982
(305) 445-0507 Fax: (305) 995-2047
Evette Morgan, President

COALITION OF IMMOKALEE WORKERS
P.O. Box 603
Immokalee, FL 34143
(941) 657-8311 Fax: (941) 657-8311
Lucas Benitec, Assistance Director
Email: coaimmwkr@aol.com
Web: www.geocities.com/coaimmwkr

COCONUT GROVE PLAYHOUSE
3500 Main Hwy.
Coconut Grove, FL 33133
(305) 442-2662 Fax: (305) 444-6437
K. William Kerlin, Director of Operations
Web: www.cgplayhouse.com

**COLEGIO NACIONAL DE ABOGADOS DE
CUBA EN EXILIO**
3383 NW 7th St., # 204
Miami, FL 33125
(305) 541-0763
Luis Rodríguez Cepero, President

COLLEGE HISPANIC COUNCIL
Miami-Dade Community College
NorthCampus; School of Business
11380 Northwest 27th Avenue
Miami, FL 33167-3418
(305) 237-2673 Fax: (305) 237-1620
María Mari, President

**COLOMBIAN AMERICAN CHAMBER OF
COMMERCE OF GREATER MIAMI**
2355 S. Salzedo St., #209
Coral Gables, FL 33134
(305) 446-2542 Fax: (305) 448-5028
Ernesto Cordovez, President

**COLOMBIAN AMERICAN SERVICE
ASSOCIATION (CASA)**
3138 Coral Way
Miami, FL 33145
(305) 448-2272 Fax: (305) 448-0178
Juan Carlos Zapata, Chairman
Email: info@casa-usa.org
Web: www.casa-usa.org

COLOMBIAN STUDENTS ASSOCIATION
University Center
1306 Stanford Dr. #209
Coral Gables, FL 33124

(305) 284-6399 or (305) 860-6769
Fax: (305) 284-5987
Mónica Gluksted, Director

**COLOMBIAN-AMERICAN COALITION OF
FLORIDA**
12205 S.W. 71 Court
Pinecrest, FL 33156-5449
(305) 665-7278 Fax: (305) 661-2577
Carlos A. Cabrera, President
Email: CACabrera@aol.com

**CONSEJO DEMÓCRATA COLOMBO-
AMERICANO**
12205 SW 71 Court
Miami, FL 33156-5449
(305) 665-7278 Fax: (305) 661-2577
Carlos A. Cabrera, President
Email: CACabrera@aol.com

**CONFERENCE ON LATIN AMERICA
HISTORY**
University of South Florida
4202 E. Fowler Ave., SOEC-107
Tampa, FL 33620
(813) 974-8132 Fax: (813) 974-6828
Paul Dosal, Executive Secretary
Email: clah@chuma.cas.usf.edu

CUBA FREE PRESS, INC.
Proyecto Cuba Prensa Libre
P.O. Box 652035
Miami, FL 33265-2035
(305) 270-8779 Fax: (305) 595-1883
Juan A. Granados, President
Email: mailbox@cubafreepress.org
Web: www.cubafreepress.org

CUBAN AMERICAN CPA ASSOC., INC.
P.O. Box 442061
Miami, FL 33144
(305) 220-3771 Fax: (305) 220-2373
Manuel García, President
Web: www.cacpa.org

CUBAN AMERICAN FOUNDATION
3155 N. W. 77 Ave.
Miami, FL 33122
(305) 477-1202 Fax: (305) 592-7889
José F. Hernández, President

CUBAN AMERICAN NATIONAL COUNCIL
National Headquarters
1223 SW 4th St.
Miami, FL 33135
(305) 642-3484 Fax: (305) 642-7463
Guarioné M. Díaz, President
Email: info@cnc.org
Web: www.cnc.org

**CUBAN HEBREW CONGREGATION OF
MIAMI**
1700 Michigan Ave.
Miami, FL 33139
(305) 534-7213 Fax: (305) 534-5143
Pincho Papir, President

CUBAN MEDICAL ASSOCIATION IN EXILE
P. O. Box 141016
Coral Gables, FL 33114-1016
(305) 445-1429 Fax: (305) 445-9310
Dr. Enrique Huertas, President

CUBAN RESEARCH INSTITUTE
Florida International University
DM 363 University Park
Miami, FL 33199
(305) 348-1991 Fax: (305) 348-3593
Lisandro Pérez, Director
Email: perezl@fiu.edu
Web: www.lacc.fiu.edu/cri

**CUBAN-AMERICAN NATIONAL
FOUNDATION**
National Headquarters
1312 SW 27th Ave.
Miami, FL 33145
(305) 592-7768 Fax: (305) 592-7889
Francisco Hernández, President
Email: canfnet@icanect.net
Web: www.canfnet.org

CUBANET NEWS, INC.
145 Madeira Ave., #207
Coral Gables, FL 33134
José Alberto Hernández, M.D., President
Email: cubanet@cubanet.org
Web: www.cubanet.org

DADE COUNTY HISPANIC AFFAIRS ADVISORY BOARD
111 N.W. First St.
Miami, FL 33128
(305) 375-2104 Fax: (305) 375-5715
María Lazo, Director

DE HOSTOS SENIOR CENTER
2902 NW 2nd Ave.
Miami, FL 33127
(305) 573-6220 Fax: (305) 573-2193
Esther Couvierter, Executive Director
Web: dehostos@juno.com

DIOCESAN HISPANIC MINISTRY COORDINATOR
9401 Biscayne Blvd.
Miami Shores, FL 33138
(305) 757-6241 Fax: (305) 754-1797
Agustín Román, Bishop
Email: bproman@miamiarch.org
Web: www.miamiarch.org

134 E. Church St.
Jacksonville, FL 32202
(904) 353-3243 Fax: (904) 353-0630
Alba Orosco, Coordinator
Email: hispanicministry@juno.com

DIOCESE OF ORLANDO
Hispanic Affairs
P.O. Box 1800
421 E. Robinson
Orlando, FL 32802
(407) 246-4930 Fax: (407) 246-4932
Rev. Robert Markunas, Dir.for Hispanic Ministry
Email: shunis@aol.com

DIOCESE OF PALM BEACH
Hispanic Affairs
P.O. Box 109650
9995 N. Military Trail
Palm Beach, FL 33410-9650
(561) 775-9544 Fax: (561) 775-9556
Sr. Regina Tutzo, Director for Hispanic Ministry
Email: claretian.sr.delray@worldnet.att.net

DIOCESE OF PENSACOLA-TALLAHASSEE
Hispanic Affairs
P.O. Box 17329
Pensacola, FL 32522
(850) 432-1515 x25 Fax: (850) 436-6424
Sr. María Lauren Donohue, MSBT, Director for Hispanic Ministry
Email: laurenmsbt@juno.com

DIOCESE OF ST. AUGUSTINE
Hispanic Affairs
134 E. Church St.
Jacksonville, FL 32202-3130
(904) 353-3243 Fax: (904) 353-0630
Alba M. Orozco, Coord. for Hispanic Ministry
Email: Hispanicministry2@juno.com

DIOCESE OF ST. PETERSBURG
Hispanic Affairs
P.O. Box 40200
6363 Ninth Ave. N.
St. Petersburg, FL 33743
(727) 344-1611 Fax: (727) 345-2143
Msgr. Frank M. Monch, Vicar for Hispanic Ministry

DIOCESE OF ST. PETERSBURG
Hispanic Affairs
6363 Ninth Ave. N.
St. Petersburg, FL 33743
(727) 344-1611 x435 Fax: (727) 345-2143
Deacon John A. Sierra

DIOCESE OF VENICE
Hispanic Affairs
506 26th St. W.
Palmeto, FL 34221-5425
(941) 729-3891 Fax: (941) 721-9402
Rev. Nicanor Lobato, Director, Spanish Speaking Apostolate
Email: llarrea@dioceseoftyler.org

DIRECTORIO LIBERAL COLOMBIANO DE LA FLORIDA, INC.
12205 SW, 71 Ct.
Miami, FL 33156-5449
(305) 665-7278 Fax: (305) 661-2577
Carlos A. Cabrera, Registered Agent
Email: CACabrera@aol.com

DIRECTORIO REVOLUCIONARIO DEMOCRÁTICO CUBANO
P.O. Box 110235
Hialeah, FL 33011

(305) 264-2917
Javier de Céspedes, President
Email: drdc5@directorio.org
Web: www.directorio.org

EVERGLADES COMMUNITY ASSOCIATION (ECA)
Affiliate of NCLR
P.O. Box 343529
Homestead, FL 33034-0529
(305) 242-2142 Fax: (305) 242-2143
Steven C. Kirk, Executive Director

FAMILY COUNSELING SERVICES OF GREATER MIAMI
10651 N Kendall Dr., #100
Miami, FL 33176
(305) 271-9800 Fax: (305) 270-3330
Phil Klees, Director
Web: www.familycounseling.org

FARMWORKER ASSOCIATION OF FLORIDA
8155 Park Ave.
Apopka, FL 33703
(407) 886-5151

FEDERATION OF CUBAN STUDENTS
University of Miami
P.O. Box 249116, Whiten Univ. Ctr. #209
Coral Gables, FL 33124-6923
(305) 284-6290 or (305) 498-1732
Daniel Fernández, President

FLORIDA REGIONAL MINORITY PURCHASING COUNCIL
600 N.W. 79th Avenue, Suite 136
Miami, FL 33166
(305) 260-9901 Fax: (305) 260-9902
Wendell Paige, President

FLORIDA SER-JOBS FOR PROGRESS, INC.
Affiliate of SER-Jobs for Progress
National, Inc.
42 NW 27th Ave., #421
Miami, FL 33125
(305) 649-7500 Fax: (305) 644-2100
José L. Cela, President
Email: jlcela@sernational.org
Web: www.sernational.org/florida

GOVERNMENT OF PUERTO RICO OFFICE
Orlando Regional Office
400 S. Orange Ave. 9th Floor
Orlando, FL 32802
(407) 423-4422 Fax: (407) 423-0330
Donna Bisihnano, Director

GREATER MIAMI CHAMBER OF COMMERCE
Hispanic Business Group
1601 Biscayne Blvd.
Miami, FL 33132
(305) 577-5471 Fax: (305) 579-8605
Virginia Del Pino, Senior Manager
Web: www.greatermiami.com

GULF COAST LATIN CHAMBER OF COMMERCE
8051 N. Pamiamitrail, #37
Sarasota, FL 34243
(941) 358-7065 Fax: (941) 358-7584
Gladis Vargas, Administrative Assistant
Email: golatcom@aol.com

HERMANOS AL RESCATE / BROTHERS TO THE RESCUE
P.O. Box 430846
Miami, Fl 33243-0846
(305) 477-1868 Fax: (305) 663-9510
Email: Brothers@hermanos.com
Web: www.hermanos.org

HIALEAH HISPANIC CHAMBER OF COMMERCE
4410 W. 16th Ave., #62
Hialeah, FL 33012
(305) 557-5060 Fax: (305) 556-7333
Vicente P. Rodríguez, President
Email: thevoicepub@mindspring.com

HIALEAH LATIN CHAMBER OF COMMERCE & INDUSTRIES
1840 W. 49th St., #700
Hialeah, FL 32012
(305) 828-9898 Fax: (305) 828-9777
Daniel Hernández, President
Email: infor@hialeahchamber.com
Web: www.hialeahchamber.com

HISPANIC AMERICAN ALLIANCE / ALIANZA HISPANO AMERICANA
Affiliate of NCLR
731 N. Lime Ave.

Sarasota, FL 34237
(941) 366-1130 Fax: (941) 365-0733
Yolanda Beltrán Halstead, Executive Director

HISPANIC AMERICAN BUSINESS ASSOCIATION
P.O. Box 17091
Jacksonville, FL 32211-8906
(904) 725-9444 Fax: (904) 241-9728
Sergio Arnaiz, President
Email: sfarnaiz@juno.com

HISPANIC BUSINESS INITIATIVE FUND OF GREATER ORLANDO, INC. (HBIF)
319 N. Magnolia Ave.
Orlando, FL 32805
(407) 428-5872 Fax: (407) 428-5873
José L. Fernández, Jr., President
Email: generalinfo@hbiforl.org

HISPANIC CHAMBER OF COMMERCE OF CENTRAL FLORIDA
319 N. Magnolia Ave.
Orlando, FL 32801
(407) 428-5870 Fax: (407) 428-5871
Victoria Pinzón, Assisant to Director
Email: vpinzon1@bellsouth.net
Web: www.hispanicchamber.net

HISPANIC CHAMBER OF COMMERCE OF PALM BEACH COUNTY, INC.
P.O. Box 15788
West Palm Beach, FL 33416-5788
(561) 832-1986 Fax: (561) 366-9689
Sylvia Hansen, Administrator
Email: hccofpbc@bellsouth.net

HISPANIC COALITION, INC.
Affiliate of NCLR
5659 W. Flager St.
Miami, FL 33134
(305) 262-0060 or
Fax: (305) 262-0518
Rosa E. Kasse, President & CEO

HISPANIC ENGINEERING SOCIETY
University of Florida
345 Weil Hall
Gainesville, FL 32611
(352) 392-1033 or (352) 335-8583
F. Najafi, Faculty Advisor

HISPANIC HERITAGE COUNCIL, INC.
4011 W. Flagler St. #204
Miami, FL 33134
(305) 541-5023 Fax: (305) 541-5176
Eloy Vázquez, Executive Director
Email: info@hispanicfestival.com
Web: www.hispanicfestival.com

HISPANIC HERITAGE FESTIVAL
4011 W. Flagler St. #204
Miami, FL 33134
(305) 541-5023 Fax: (305) 541-5176
Eloy Vázquez, Director
Web: www.hispanicfestival.org

HISPANIC NATIONAL BAR ASSOCIATION
P.O. Box 231
Orlando, FL 32803-0231
(407) 843-7860 Fax: (407) 843-6610
Albert Tellechea, General Counsel
Email: ATellechea@akerman.com
Web: www.hnba.com

Region III (AL, FL, GA, MS, NC, SC)
Pérez, Goran & Rodríguez
1320 S. Dixie Hwy. #1000
Coral Gables, FL 33146
(305) 667-9878 Fax: (305) 667-9657
Javier Rodríguez, Regional President

Region VIII (FL)
200 South Biscayne Blvd., 47th Floor
Miami, FL 33131
(305) 373-5400 Fax: (305) 374-4796
Robert Fernández, Regional President
Email: Fernandez@colson.com
Web: www.hnba.com

HISPANIC STUDENT ASSOCIATION
University of Florida
P.O. Box 118505
300-39 J. Wayne Reitz Union
Gainesville, FL 32611
(352) 392-1665 ext. 326 Fax: (352) 392-8072
José González, President
Web: http://grove.ufl.edu/~hsauf

HISPANIC STUDENT BUSINESS ASSOCIATION, "LA CASITA"
University of Florida
1504 W. University Ave.
Gainesville, FL 32603

(352) 392-3781 Fax: (352) 846-3005
Dr. Naranjo, Finance Professor

HISPANIC UNITY OF FLORIDA
The United Way of Florida
5840 Johnson Street
Hollywood, FL 33021
(954) 964-8884 Fax: (954) 964-8646
Dennis Adams, Director

HISPANOS DANDO ESPERANZA HISPANICS GIVING HOPE
Marrow Donor Program
10100 9th St., N.
St. Petersburg, FL 33716
(727) 568-2115 or (727) 529-4499
Fax: (727) 568-2175
Iván D. Mangual, Recruitment Specialist
Web: www.fbsblood.org

IMAGE DE PENSACOLA, NORTHWEST FLORIDA
Pensacola Chapter - Northwest Florida
P.O. Box 12162
Pensacola, FL 32507-2162
(850) 456-0962 Fax: (850) 452-3367
Theresa Montez, President
Web: www.nationalimageinc.org

THE INSTITUTE OF HISPANIC-LATINO CULTURES "LA CASITA"
University of Florida
1504 West University Avenue
Gainesville, FL 32603
(352) 846-0405 Fax: (352) 846-3005
Inés Ruiz-Houston, Assistant Director
Web: www.ufsa.ufl.edu/lacasita

INTER-AMERICAN BUSINESSMEN ASSOC.
250 Catalonia Ave., #402
Coral Gables, FL 33134
(305) 442-8038 Fax: (305) 442-8039
José L. Guillén, President

INTER-AMERICAN PRESS ASSOCIATION
2911 NW 39th St.
Miami, FL 33142
(305) 634-2465 Fax: (305) 635-2272
Julio Muñoz, Executive Director
Email: info@sipiapa.org
Web: www.sipiapa.org

KIDCO CHILD CARE
Miami Satellite Office
3630 NE 1st St.
Miami, FL 33137
(305) 576-6990 Fax: (305) 576-5321
Nilsa M. Velázquez, Executive Director
Email: kidco@kidco-childcare.org
Web: www.kidco-childcare.org

LA PLAYA PROMOTIONS, INC.
P.O Box 524183
Miami, FL 33152
(305) 477-0577 or (305) 532-5274
Fax: (305) 532-8606
Astur Morsella, Director

LA PRENSA
685 South County Rd., #427
Longwood, FL 32750
(407) 767-0070 Fax: (407) 767-5478
Manuel A. Toro, Executive Director
Email: laprensa@earthlink.net

LATIN AMERICAN AND CARIBBEAN CENTER.
Florida International University
University Park, Bldg., DM 353
Miami, FL 33199
(305) 348-2894 Fax: (305) 348-3593
Eduardo Gamarra, Director
Email: lacc@fiu.edu

LATIN AMERICAN CHAMBER OF COMMERCE OF LOWER KEY WEST
P.O. Box 629
Key West, FL 33041
(305) 294-6156
Arturo Espínola Arnau, President

LATIN AMERICAN STUDENTS ASSOCIATION
Council of International Students
1306 Stanford Dr. #216
Coral Gables, FL 33124-6923
(305) 221-3678
Manuel García, President

LATIN BUILDERS ASSOCIATION
782 NW Le Jeune Rd. #450
Miami, FL 33126

(305) 446-5989 Fax: (305) 446-0901
William J. Delgado, President
Email: lba@bellsouth.net

LATIN CHAMBER OF COMMERCE OF BROWARD COUNTY
6363 Tast St., #205
Hollywood, FL 33024
(954) 983-6552 Fax: (954) 983-2628
Laura Corry, President
Email: lbabrwd@bellsouth.net

LATIN CHAMBER OF COMMERCE OF UNITED STATES (CAMACOL)
National Headquarters
1417 W. Flagler St.
Miami, FL 33135
(305) 642-3870 Fax: (305) 642-0653
Luis Sabines, President
Email: info@camacol.org
Web: www.camacol.org

LEAGUE AGAINST AIDS
3050 Biscayne Blvd. #509
Miami, FL 33137
(305) 576-1000 Fax: (305) 576-4097
Dr. Manuel M. Vega, Executive Director

LEAGUE AGAINST CANCER LIGA CONTRA EL CÁNCER
2180 SW 12th Ave.
Miami, FL 33129
(305) 856-4914 Fax: (305) 856-8172
María Callava, General Coordinator
Email: mariacallava@ligacontraelcancer.org
Web: www.ligacontraelcancer.org

LULAC-NATIONAL EDUCATIONAL SERVICES CENTER, INC. (LNESC)
946 SW, 82nd Ave.
Miami, FL 33144
(305) 261-5341 Fax: (305) 267-5200
Dulce Díaz Vega, Director
Email: lnesc@aol.com
Web: www.lulac.org

MEXICAN AMERICAN COUNCIL, INC.
Affiliate of NCLR
P. O. Box 343546
Florida City, FL 33034-0546
(305) 248-1650 or (305) 245-5865
Fax: (305) 248-7115
María C. Garza, President

MIAMI BEACH LATIN CHAMBER OF COMMERCE
235 Lincoln Rd., #216
Miami Beach, FL 33139
(305) 674-8857 or (305) 674-1231
Fax: (305) 674-9052
Manny Warszavski, President
Email: mblcc@bellsouth.net
Web: www.miamibeach.org

MIAMI CAPITAL DEVELOPMENT
300 Biscayne Blvd. Way #614
Miami, FL 33131
(305) 358-1025 Fax: (305) 530-3593
Juan del Cerro, Executive Director

MIAMI/SER-IBM BUSINESS INSTITUTE
42 NW 27th Ave. #421
Miami, FL 33125
(305) 649-7500 Fax: (305) 644-2100
Madeline Weisman, Director of Education
Email: ilcela@sernational.org
Web: www.sernational.org/florida

MINORITY BUSINESS DEVELOPMENT AGENCY (MBDA)
Miami Office/U.S. Dept. of Commerce
51 SW 1st. Ave. #1314
Miami, FL 33130
(305) 536-5054 Fax: (305) 530-7068
Dolores Figueras, Secretary
Email: DFigueras@mbda.gov
Web: www.mbda.gov

MOVEMENT FOR AN INDEPENDENT AND DEMOCRATIC CUBA
10020 SW 37th Terrace
Miami, FL 33165
(305) 551-8484 Fax: (305) 599-9365
Cmdr. Huber Matos, Secretary General
Email: elcid@gate.net
Web: www.elcid.org

MUNICIPIO DE SANTIAGO DE CUBA EN EXILIO
845 SW 14th Ave.
Miami, FL 33135
(305) 858-6739

Antonio González Bustos, President

MUNICIPIOS DE CUBA EN EL EXILIO
4610 NW 7th St.
Miami, FL 33126
(305) 447-8866 Fax: (305) 442-4206
Benito González, President

MUSEUM OF ARTS AND SCIENCES
1040 Museum Blvd.
Daytona Beach, FL 32114
(904) 255-0285 Fax: (904) 255-5040
Gary Russell Libby, Director
Web: www.moas.org

MUSEUM OF FLORIDA HISTORY
500 S. Bronough St.
Tallahassee, FL 32399-0250
(850) 488-1484 Fax: (850) 921-2503
Susan Ollsen, Director
Web: http://dhr.dos.state.fl.us/museum

NATIONAL ASSOCIATION FOR HISPANIC ELDERLY
Miami Office/Project Ayuda
1150 SW First St., #113
Miami, FL 33130
(305) 545-7270 Fax: (305) 545-9234
María Miyares, Project Coordinator

Tampa Office/Project Ayuda
2700 N. MacDill Ave. #101
Tampa, FL 33607
(813) 870-3172 Fax: (813) 876-0019
Carolyn Deese, Project Coordinator
Email: nahetpal@aol.com

NATIONAL ASSOCIATION OF CUBAN AMERICAN EDUCATORS (NACAE)
National Headquarters
7930 NW 36th St. #23 Suite 418
Miami, FL 33166
(305) 593-2555 Fax: (305) 471-7616
Gastón Fernández de la Torriente, Executive Director

NATIONAL ASSOCIATION OF HISPANIC JOURNALISTS (NAHJ)
Region 4
200 E. Las Olas Blvd.
Fort Lauderdale, FL 33301
(954) 356-4538 Fax: (954) 356-4559
Michele Salcedo, Region Director
Email: mselcedo@sun-sentinel.com
Web: www.nahj.org

NATIONAL ASSOCIATION OF HISPANIC PUBLIC ADMINISTRATORS (NAHPA)
P.O. Box 42171
Coral Gables, FL 33114-2171
(305) 828-8999 Fax: (305) 220-1746
Mario García, President
Email: nahpa@nahpa.com
Web: www.nahpa.com

NATIONAL FEDERATION OF HISPANIC OWNED NEWSPAPERS
685 S. County Rd., #427
Longwood, FL 32750
(407) 767-0070 Fax: (407) 767-5478
Manuel A. Toro, Executive Director

NATIONAL HISPANIC CORPORATE ACHIEVERS
445 Douglas Ave.
Altamonte Springs, FL 32714
(407) 682-2883 Fax: (407) 831-3807
Daniel Ramos, Chairman
Email: info@hispanicachievers.org
Web: www.hispanicachievers.com

NATIONAL LATINO PEACE OFFICERS ASSOCIATION (NLPOA)
Florida Chapter
P.O. Box 171882
Hialeah, FL 33017
(877) 657-6200
Adrián García, Chapter President
Email: nlpoa@aol.com
Web: www.nlpoa.com

NATIONAL MINORITY SUPPLIER DEVELOPMENT COUNCIL OF FLORIDA
7200 Lake Ellenor Dr., #242
Orlando, FL 32809
(407) 859-3901 Fax: (407) 857-8547
Malik Ali, Executive Director
Email: nmsdc@aol.com
Web: www.nmsdcfl.com

NATIONAL SOCIETY OF HISPANIC MBAS
Orlando Chapter
300 S. Orange Ave., #1500

Orlando, FL 32801
(407) 895-0544 Fax: (407) 895-0543
Phil Cabo-Estrella, Chapter President
Email: orlando@nshmba.org
Web: www.nshmba.org

NEW THEATER, INC.
65 Almaria Ave.
Coral Gables, FL 33134
(305) 443-5909 Fax: (305) 443-1642
Eilene Suarez, Managing Director

NICARAGUAN AMERICAN CHAMBER OF COMMERCE
P.O. Box 527723
Miami, FL 33152
(305) 599-2737 Fax: (305) 271-1620
Ana Arguello, President
Email: nacoc@netzero.net
Web: www.nacc-miami.com

OLDEST HOUSE AND THE MUSEUM OF FLORIDA'S ARMY
271 Charlotte St.
St. Augustine, FL 32084
(904) 824-2872 Fax: (904) 824-2569
Taryn Rodríguez-Boette, Director
Email: sahs@aug.com
Web: www.oldcity.com/oldhouse/

PUERTO RICAN STUDENTS ASSOCIATION
Florida International University
Student Activities GC 340, UP
Miami, FL 33199
(305) 348-3215 Fax: (305) 348-3823
Dr.Luis Martínez Pérez, Advisor
Email: PRSA@hotmail.com

PUERTO RICO CHAMBER OF COMMERCE
Gulf Coast of Florida
222 E. Bullard Pkwy.
Temple Terrace, FL 33617
(813) 985-3175 Fax: (813) 988-6188
José Ramos, Administrator

PUERTO RICO CHAMBER OF COMMERCE OF FLORIDA, ORLANDO
P. O. Box 520443
Longwood, FL 32750-0443
(407) 831-2926 Fax: (407) 767-5478
Manuel A. Toro, President

REDLANDS CHRISTIAN MIGRANT ASSOC.
Affiliate of NCLR
402 W. Main St.
Immokalee, FL 34142
(941) 658-3572 Fax: (941) 658-3571
Barbara Mainster, Executive Director
Email: barbara@rcma.org

REFORMA
University of South Florida
Tampa Campus Library, 4202 E. Fowler Ave., LIB 122
Tampa, FL 33620-5400
(813) 974-3901 Fax: (813) 974-9875
Carol Ann Borchert, Chapter President
Email: borchert@lib.usf.edu
Web: www.lib.usf.edu/~borchert/reforma.html

ROSA VALDEZ CENTER
1802 N. Albany Ave.
Tampa, FL 33607
(813) 253-3853 Fax: (813) 259-9581
Lisa Lockhart, Manager

RYDER HISPANIC NETWORK (RHN)
3600 NW 82nd Avenue
Miami, FL 33166
(305) 500-3013 Fax: (305) 500-5481
Odalys Ismail, President

SIGMA LAMBDA GAMMA SORORITY INC. IOTA
Alpha Chapter
982 W. Brevard St. Box C17
Tallahassee, FL 32304
(850) 224-8342
Melissa Jannet Alvarez, Assistant
Email: candela12ia@yahoo.com
Web: www.kcnet.com/~taina/Gammas

SOCIEDAD ARGENTINA DE AUTORES Y COMPOSITORES (SADAIC)
825 Brickell Bay Dr. Suite 1751
Miami, FL 33131
(305) 381-9326 Fax: (305) 358-2502
Hernán Beillard, General Manager
Email: sadaicmia@aol.com
Web: www.sadaicmia.com

SOCIEDAD CUBANA DE ORLANDO, INC.
5088 Hoffner Avenue
Orlando, FL 32812
(407)856-4105 Fax: (407) 856-4111
Pedro Carral, President

SOCIETY OF HISPANIC PROFESSIONAL ENGINEERS (SHPE)
Central Florida Professional Chapter
P.O. Box 340
Orlando, FL 32802-0340
(407) 909-9500 Fax: (407) 909-0500
Grace Pierce, Chapter President
Email: ppiercel@ix.netcom.com
Web: www.shpe.org

Tampa International Professional Chapter
8201 Almond Place
Tampa, FL 33615
(813) 882-9615 Fax: (813) 882-9615
Máximo Pérez, Chapter President
Web: www.shpe.org

University of Central Florida
P.O. Box 162450
Orlando, FL 32816-2450
(407) 823-5027 or (407) 823-2786
Fax: (407) 823-5835
Avelino J. González, Faculty Advisor
Web: www.shpe.org

SOUTH AMERICAN MISSION
5217 S. Military Trail
Lake Worth, FL 33463-6099
(561) 965-1833 Fax: (561) 439-8950
William Ogden, Executive Director
Email: williamogden@samlink.org
Web: www.samlink.org

SOUTH BEACH HISPANIC CHAMBER OF COMMERCE OF GREATER MIAMI
1111 Lincoln Rd., #810
Miami Beach, FL 33139
(305) 534-1903 Fax: (305) 534-8960
Liliam López, President

SOUTH FLORIDA PUERTO RICAN CHAMBER OF COMMERCE
1801 Coral Way #214
Miami, FL 33145
(305) 857-9985 Fax: (305) 857-9285
Luis De Rosa, President

SOUTHEAST PASTORAL INSTITUTE
7700 SW 56th St.
Miami, FL 33155
(305) 279-2333 Fax: (305) 279-0925
Rev. Mario Vizcaino, Director
Email: sepimiami@aol.com

SOUTHWEST FLORIDA HISPANIC CHAMBER OF COMMERCE
10051 McGregor Blvd., #201
Ft. Myers, FL 33919
(941) 489-1441 Fax: (941) 418-1475
Tulio G. Suárez, President

SOUTHWEST SOCIAL SERVICES, INC.
25 Tamiami Blvd.
Miami, FL 33144
(305) 261-6202 Fax: (305) 266-8110
Ángela Vázquez, Executive Director

SPAIN-U.S. CHAMBER OF COMMERCE
2655 Le Jeune Rd., #906
Coral Gables, FL 33134
(305) 446-1992 Fax: (305) 529-2854
José M. Marquina, President
Email: spainusa@aol.com
Web: http://www.spainuscc.org

SPANISH AMERICAN LEAGUE AGAINST DISCRIMINATION (SALAD)
900 SW First St. #201
Miami, FL 33130
(305) 326-8585 Fax: (305) 324-4482
Osvaldo Soto, Chairman

SPANISH EVANGELICAL PUBLISHERS ASSOCIATION
434 Seawane Circle
Auburndale, FL 33823
(941) 669-9616 Fax: (941) 669-9616
Harold Kregel, Executive Director

THE SPANISH QUARTER MUSEUM
P.O. Box 210
St. Augustine, FL 32085
(904) 825-6830
Lisa Calvert, Museum Manager
Web: www.ci.st/augustine.fl.us

ST. SIMON'S EPISCOPAL CHURCH
10950 SW 34 St.
Miami, FL 33165
(305) 221-4753
Rev. Carlos Sandoval, M.D., Rector
Email: info@stsimons.org
Web: www.stsimons.org

TAMPA BAY CHAMBER OF COMMERCE
P.O. Box 15722
Tampa, FL 33814
(813) 414-9411 Fax: (813) 414-0811
Tiki Clark, Progam Coordinator
Email: spatiki@aol.com

TEATRO MARTI
420 SW 8th Ave.
Miami, FL 33130
(305) 545-7866 Fax: (305) 545-7361
Ernesto Capote, Director

TOURIST OFFICE OF SPAIN
1221 Brickell Ave. #1850
Miami, FL 33131
(305) 358-1992 Fax: (305) 358-8223
Manuel Butler, Director
Email: oetny@tourspain.es
Web: www.okspain.org

**UNION IBEROAMERICANA DE
MUNICIPALISTAS (UIM)**
National Headquarters
6822 SW. 34th Ct.
Miramar, FL 33023
(954) 987-5969 Fax: (954) 964-2698
Lilly Guzmán, Chair
Email: lily@heral.info.net

**UNITED CORRECTIONS OFFICERS
FEDERATION, INC.**
P.O. Box 164853
Miami, FL 33116-4853
(305) 270-4844 Fax: (305) 274-2757
Mr. Edgar Nieves, President

**UNITED STATES-MEXICO CHAMBER OF
COMMERCE**
Inter-American Chapter
701 Brickell Ave., 16th Floor
Miami, FL 33131
(305) 379-6090 Fax: (305) 379-6422
Elba Hentschel, Executive Director
Email: usmcoc@bellsouth.net
Web: www.usmcoc.org

YOUTH CO-OP
Main Office
801 NW, 37th Ave., #212
Miami, FL 33125
(305)643-6730ext.121
Fax:(305)643-1908
María Rodríguez, Executive Director

GEORGIA

AID ATLANTA
1438 W. Peachtree St. NW #100
Atlanta, GA 30309-2955
(404) 872-0600 Fax: (404) 885-6799
María Rivas, Hispanic Coordinator
Web: www.aidatlanta.org

ALFA CENTRO HISPANO
Doraville Center
3609 Shallowford Rd., B-501
Doraville, GA 30340
(770) 455-4416 or (770) 455-4328
Fax: (770) 457-8446
Luz Cediel, Executive Director

ALFA CENTRO HISPANO
Forest Park Center
4584 Jonesboro Rd., #A
Forest Park, GA 30297
(404) 608-8459 Fax: (404) 608-8458
Luz Cediel, Executive Director

Smyrna Center
675 Windy Hill Rd., #101
Smyrna, GA 30080
(770) 333-9603 Fax: (770) 333-0953
Luz Cediel, Executive Director

AMNESTY INTERNATIONAL
Southern Region
131 Ponce De Leon Ave., NE, #220
Atlanta, GA 30308
(404) 876-5661 Fax: (404) 876-2276
Email: aisouth@igc.apc.org

ARCHDIOCESE OF ATLANTA
Hispanic Affairs
680 W. Peachtree St. NW
Atlanta, GA 3038-1984
(404) 888-7839 Fax: (404) 978-2778
Gonzalo Saldaña, Director for Hisp. Apostolate
Email: gsaldana@archatl.com

ASOCIACIÓN LATINAMERICANA EN COBB
48 Henderson St.,
Marietta, GA 30064
(770) 420-6556
Web: www.latinamericanassoc.org

ATLANTA CUBAN CLUB
5797 New Peachtree Rd.
Doraville, GA 30340
(770) 451-3477
Raúl P. Delgado, President

**ATLANTA HISPANIC CHAMBER OF
COMMERCE**
1961 N. Druid Hills Rd., NE, #201B
Atlanta, GA 30329
(404) 929-9998 Fax: (404) 929-9908
Sara J. González, President
Email: info@ahcc-atl.org
Web: www.accessatlanta.com/business/groups/
ahcc

**BRAZILIAN AMERICAN CHAMBER OF
COMMERCE - GEORGIA, ATLANTA**
World Trade Center, Atlanta
303 Peachtree St., NE. ,#100 Lower Lobby
Atlanta, GA 30308
(404) 880-1551 Fax: (404) 880-1555
W. Taylor Boone, Jr., President
Email: info@bacc-ga.com

CENTRO CULTURAL MEXICANO
Atlanta Office
2600 Apple Valley Rd.
Atlanta, GA 30305
(404) 264-1240 Fax: (404) 264-1929
Pilar Aceves, Executive Director
Email: mca@iainc.net
Web: www.enespanol.com/atlanta/
mexican.center/

CLUB ARGENTINO DE ATLANTA
1076 Greenbriar Circle
Decatur, GA 30033
(404) 296-1363 Fax: (404) 296-1363
Susana Macri Brady, Coordinator
Email: susanamb@aol.com

DIOCESE OF SAVANNAH
Hispanic Ministry Office
201 Telfair Ave.
McRae, GA 31055
(912) 374-4031 Fax: (912) 374-4454
Rev. Michael Smith
Email: mhsmcrae@juno.com

ENRICHMENT SERVICES PROGRAM, INC.
DHR-DCA-Head Start
P.O. Box 788
900 Linwood Blvd.
Columbus, GA 31902
(706) 649-1606/1608 Fax: (706) 649-1603
Justíno López, Jr., Comm. Services Director

**GEORGIA MINORITY SUPPLIER
DEVELOPMENT COUNCIL**
100 Edgewood Avenue N.E., Suite 1610
Atlanta, GA 30303
(404) 589-4925 Fax: (404) 589-4929
Edward G. Dawson, Executive Director

GRUPO JÓVENES DE ATLANTA
110 Maple St.
Gainesville, GA 30501
(770) 297-8537
Carlos Santoya

HERMANDAD DE SAN MARTÍN DE PORRES
6087-B Buford Hwy,
Norcross, GA 30071
(770) 409-9710
Roddy Padilla, Director
Email: rpadilla@gsu.edu

HISPANIC NATIONAL BAR ASSOCIATION
Region VII (AL, GA, MS)
124 Church St.
Decatur, GA 30030
(404) 377-7600 Fax: (404) 377-8700
Antonio Del Campo, Regional President
Email: jad@nixdelcampo.com
Web: www.hnba.com

HISPANIC STUDENT ASSOCIATION
University of Georgia
404 Memorial Hall
Athens, GA 30602
(706) 542-5773 Fax: (706) 542-8478
Leslie Bates, Director

IMAGE
National Image, Inc.
1955 Indian Trail Road #603
Norcross, GA 30071
(770) 441-1401 (H) or (404) 679-1903 (W)
Fax: (404) 679-1819
Mario L. Artesiano, Regional Director
Email: imageregionIV@yahoo.com
Web: www.nationalimageinc.org

LATIN AMERICAN ASSOCIATION
2665 Buford Hwy.
Atlanta, GA 30324
(404) 638-1800 Fax: (404) 638-1806
Maritza Keen, Director

**LATIN AMERICAN AWARENESS
ORGANIZATION**
Emory Univ. Off. of Multicultural Prog.
1495 Clifton Rd. #348
Atlanta, GA 30322
(404) 727-6754 Fax: (404) 727-2059
Steven Chen, Program Coordinator

**LEAGUE OF UNITED LATIN AMERICAN
CITIZENS (LULAC)**
Southeast Region-GA
4322 Alison Jane Drive
Kennesaw, GA 30144-1710
(770) 924-3440 Fax: (770) 638-1806
Frank Stratton, State Director

**METRO-ATLANTA CHAMBER OF
COMMERCE**
235 International Blvd., NW
Atlanta, GA 30303
(404) 586-8524 Fax: (404) 586-8427
Sam Williams, President
Web: www.metroatlantachamber.com

**MEXICAN AMERICAN LEGAL DEFENSE
AND EDUCATIONAL FUND (MALDEF)**
Atlanta Census Regional Office
3355 Lenox Rd., #750
Atlanta, GA 30326
(404) 504-7020 Fax: (404) 504-7021
Jacqueline Rosier, Regional Census Director
Web: www.maldef.org

NATIONAL IMAGE, INC.
Image de Greater Atlanta
P. O. Box 1512
Atlanta, GA 30301-1512
(404) 266-1956 Fax: (404) 266-1956
Sylvia Sánchez, President
Web: www.nationalimageinc.org

RAINBOW/PUSH COALITION
Columbus Chapter
P.O. Box 6921
Columbus, GA 31917
(706) 687-0022
Dr. William B. Howell, President/CEO
Web: www.rainbowpush.org

**SOCIETY OF HISPANIC PROFESSIONAL
ENGINEERS (SHPE)**
Georgia Tech
681 Cherry St.
Atlanta, GA 30032-0600
(404) 894-3959 Fax: (404) 894-1608
Kivanc Ozseden, President
Web: www.shpe.org

SPANISH SPEAKING ORGANIZATION
Georgia Tech
Service Bldg. #123 - ISSP Office
Atlanta, GA 30332-0284
(404) 894-7475 Fax: (404) 894-9862
María Lewis, Coordinator
Email: maria.lewis@intprog.gatech.edu

TELAMON CORPORATION
Georgia Office 10/Housing Office
P.O. Box 413, 3351 W. Hwy 84
Blackshear, GA 31516
(912) 449-3016 or (912) 449-3017
Fax: (912) 449-4579
Catriona Campbell, Office Manager
Email: ccampbell@telamon.org
Web: www.telamon.org

Georgia Office 12/Kiddie Kastle III
P.O. Box 469, 133 Serena Dr.
Norman Park, GA 31771
(912) 769-3627 or (912) 769-3628
Fax: (912) 769-3182
Sara Van Der Wansen, Director
Web: www.telamon.org

Georgia Office 3
112 E. Johnson St.
Dublin, GA 31021
(912) 275-0127 Fax: (912) 275-7545
Barbara Mosley, Regional Manager
Web: www.telamon.org

Georgia Office 4
P.O. Box 966
Douglas, GA 31534
(912) 384-8856 or (912) 384-8858
Fax: (912) 384-8929
Myrtice Moore, Regional Manager
Web: www.telamon.org

Georgia Office 5
120 E. Liberty Ave.
Lyons, GA 30436
(912) 526-3094 or (912) 526-3095
Fax: (912) 526-5906
Elmira Reynolds, Regional Manager
Email: ereynolds@telamon.org
Web: www.telamon.org

Georgia Office 6
P.O. Box 645
Statesboro, GA 30458
(912) 764-6169 Fax: (912) 489-6516
Elsie Tretheway, Regional Manager
Web: www.telamon.org

Georgia Office 7
200 E. Mary St.
Valdosta, GA 31601
(912) 244-4920 or (912) 244-4921
Fax: (912) 244-0907
Carmen Wilkinson, Regional Manager
Email: cwilkinson@telamon.org
Web: www.telamon.org

Georgia Office 8/Kiddie Kastle II
P.O. Box 815
Glennville, GA 30427
(912) 654-2182 Fax: (912) 654-2190
Billie Fuller, Director
Web: www.telamon.org

Georgia Office 9/Kiddie Kastle I
684 N. Washington St.
Lyons, GA 30436
(912) 526-9556 Fax: (912) 526-3424
Paulette Burnside, Director
Email: coremhskk1@cybersouth.com
Web: www.telamon.org

Georgia State Office
2720 Sheraton Dr., #140, Bldg. D
Macon, GA 31204
(912) 750-7134 Fax: (912) 750-7375
Herbert Williams, State Director
Email: hwilliams@telamon.org
Web: www.telamon.org

HAWAII

**THE CHURCH OF JESUS CHRIST OF
LATTER DAY SAINTS**
Laie Hawaii Temple Visitors' Center
55-600 Naniloa Loop
Laie, Oahu, HI 96762
(808) 293-9297 Fax: (808) 293-8592
Elder Hilton, Director
Web: www.lds.org

DIOCESE OF HONOLULU
Hispanic Affairs
1184 Bishop St.
Honolulu, HI 96813
(808) 533-1791 Fax: (808) 521-8428
Sr. Grace Dorothy Lim, MMJCL, Hispanic Ministry
Coordinator

**HAWAII HISPANIC CHAMBER OF
COMMERCE**
P.O. Box 23563
Honolulu, HI 96823
(808) 545-4344 Fax: (808) 944-0887
Joe Pérez, President

IMAGE DE HAWAII
National Image, Inc.
4224 Waialae Avenue, Suite 5125
Honolulu, HI 96816

(808) 951-0573 Fax: (808) 946-6205
Rod Todorovich, President
Web: www.nationalimageinc.org

MAUI ECONOMIC OPPORTUNITY, INC.
Proyecto Hispanic Link / Affiliate of NCLR
P.O. Box2122
Kahului, HI 96733
(808) 871-5940 or (808) 877-0626
Fax: (808) 871-5206
Cesar Flores, Project Coordinator

PUERTO RICAN HERITAGE SOCIETY OF HAWAII
5180 Nohu St.
Honolulu, HI 96821
(808) 373-2394
Blase Camacho Souza, President

UNITED PUERTO RICAN ASSOCIATION OF HAWAII, INC.
1249 N. School St.
Honolulu, HI 96817
(808) 847-2751
Norma Carr, President

IDAHO

CATHOLIC MIGRANT FARMWORKER NETWORK
Boise, ID
(208) 384-1778

THE CHURCH OF JESUS CHRIST OF LATTER DAY SAINTS
Idaho Falls Idaho Temple Visitors' Center
1000 Memorial Dr.
Idaho Falls, ID 83402
(208) 523-4504 Fax: (208) 552-1699
Elder Fergueson, Director
Web: www.lds.org

DIOCESAN HISPANIC MINISTRY
303 Federal Way
Boise, ID 83705
(208) 342-1311 Fax: (208) 342-0224
John Hitchman
Email: jhitchman@rcdb.org

DIOCESE OF BOISE
Ethnic Ministries Office
303 Federal Way
Boise, ID 83705-5925
(208) 342-1311 Fax: (208) 342-0224
John W. Hitchman, Director

IDAHO COMMISSION ON HISPANIC AFFAIRS
5460 W Franklin Rd. #B
Boise, ID 83705
(208) 334-3776 Fax: (208) 334-3778
Don Pena, Administrator
Email: jsaldana@icha.state.id.us/
Web: www.2.state.id.us/icha

IDAHO MIGRANT COUNCIL, INC.
Affiliate of NCLR
317 Happy Day Blvd., #400
Caldwell, ID 83605-8115
(208) 454-1652 Fax: (208) 459-0448
Humberto Fuentes, Executive Director
Email: betof@micron.net

IMAGE DE IDAHO
First Security Bank
Airport Plz. Bldg., 3295 Elder St. #420
Boise, ID 83705
(208) 393-4189   Fax: (208) 393-4767
Silvia F. Rojas, President
Email: srojas@fscnet.org
Web: www.nationimageinc.org

IMAGE DE IDAHO DEL SUDESTE
Pocatello, Idaho Branch
P.O. Box 1341
Pocatello, ID 83204
(208) 232-1549 Fax: (208) 232-1549
Andy Guerra, Secretary
Email: andres@dcdi.net

IMAGE STATE OF IDAHO
Idaho Chap.
P.O. Box 519
Boise, ID 83701
(208) 345-0960 Fax: (208) 345-3235
Natalie Camacho Mendoza, State President
Web: www.nationimageinc.org

MINORITY STUDENT SERVICES
Office of Mulitcultural affairs UCC 228
University of Idaho, P.O. Box 442431
Moscow, ID 83844-2431

(208) 885-6757 Fax: (208) 885-9494
Dona Walker, Director
Email: donaw@uidaho.edu
Web: uidaho.edu

NATIONAL ASSOCIATION FOR THE ADVANCEMENT OF COLORED PEOPLE
Pocatello Branch
3964 McDougall
Pocatello, ID 83204-2030
(208) 232-1549 Fax: (208) 232-1549
Andy Guerra, Complaint Investigator
Email: andres@dcdi.net

SOCIETY OF HISPANIC PROFESSIONAL ENGINEERS (SHPE)
Boise Professional Chapter
P.O. Box 11311 Chinden Blvd. M/S SHPE
Boise, ID 83714
(208) 368-4961 Fax: (208) 368-2514
Ulises Lozano, Chapter President
Email: shpe-boise@shpe.org
Web: http://reg3.shpe.org/boise-pro/index.htm

VALLEY FAMILY HEALTH CARE
Payette ID
1441 N.E. 10th Ave.
Payette, ID 83660
(208) 642-9376 Fax: (208) 642-9598
Hugh Phillips, Executive Director
Email: vfhc@primenet.com

ILLINOIS

ADAS MCKINLEY COMMUNITY SERVICES, INC.
Central Office - National Headquarters
725 S. Wells St., #1-A
Chicago, IL 60607
(312) 554-0600 Fax: (312) 554-0293
George Jones, Jr., Executive Director

ADVOCATE HEALTH CARE
2025 Windsor Dr.
Oak Brook, IL 60523-1586
(800) 3 ADVOCATE or (630) 990-5606
Daniel Parker, Vice Pres., Public Relations
Email: dan.parker@advocatehealth.com
Web: www.advocatehealth.com

ALBANY PARK COMMUNITY CENTER
3403 W. Lawrence Ave. #300
Chicago, IL 60625
(773) 583-5111 Fax: (773) 583-5062
Email: info@albanyparkcommunitycenter.org
Web: www.albanyparkcommunitycenter.org

ALDO CASTILLO GALLERY
233 W. Huron Ave.
Chicago, IL 60610
(312) 337-2536 Fax: (312) 337-3627
Email: Info@ArtAldo.com
Web: www.artaldo.com

ALIVIO MEDICAL CENTER
Affiliate of NCLR
2355 S. Western Ave.
Chicago, IL 60608
(773) 650-1224 Fax: (773) 650-1226
Carmen Velásquez, Executive Director
Email: aliviocv@aol.com

ALPHA PSI LAMBDA, INC.
Univ. of Illinois, Chicago, Zeta Chapter
UIC Campus Programs, M/C 118
750 S. Halstead, #300 CCC
Chicago, IL 60607
(312) 413-5070
Louie Amaya, President
Web: http://alpha-psi-lambda.org/zeta/

ALPHA SIGMA OMEGA LATINA SORORITY, INC.
Eastern Illinois University
University Union 316, 600 Lincoln Ave.
Charleston, IL 61920
Doris A. Maldonado-Fernández, National President
Email: epsilon_aso@hotmail.com
Web: www.geocities.com/alphasigomega

AMERICAN FRIENDS SERVICE
Committee-Proyecto Urayoan
59 E Van Buren. #1400
Chicago, IL 60605
(312) 427-2533 Fax: (312) 427-4171
Michael Macano, Regional Director
Email: mikemcl384@aol.com

Web: www.afsc.org

AMERICAN GI FORUM OF ILLINOIS
Veterans Of All Wars
1401 South Stewart
Lombard, IL 60148
(630) 953-8717 Fax: (630) 953-1326
Al Galvan, IL State Public Relations

AMERICAN GI FORUM OF THE U.S.
2022 N. Tripp
Chicago, IL 60639
(773) 235-5074
Virginia E. Fuentes, Treasurer-Women

AMERICAN SPANISH INSTITUTE (ASI)
2619 W Armitage Ave.
Chicago, IL 60647-4208
(773) 278-5130 Fax: (773) 278-1380
Rebecca Crúz, Executive Director
Email: asi_homecare@ameritech.net

AMERITECH HISPANIC ADVISORY PANEL
Ameritech Hdqtrs.
PO Box 54-4115
Chicago, IL 60654-0115
(312) 727-4800
Esther Zurita, President

AMNESTY INTERNATIONAL
Midwest Region
53 W. Jackson, #1162
Chicago, IL 60604
(312) 427-2060 Fax: (312) 427-2589
Nancy G. Bothne, Director
Email: aiusmwro@igc.apc.org

ANIXTER CENTER
CALOR
3220 W Armitage Ave.
Chicago, IL 60647
(773) 235-3161 Fax: (773) 772-0484
Omar López, Director
Email: sferst@anixter.org
Web: www.anixter.org

ARCHDIOCESE OF CHICAGO
Hispanic Affairs
155 E. Superior St.
Chicago, IL 60611
(312) 751-8301 or (312) 751-8308
Fax: (312) 751-5207
Rev. Ezequiel Sánchez, Dir. for Hispanic Ministry

Kolbe House, Catholic Prison Ministry at Assumption Church
2434 S. California
Chicago, IL 60608
(773) 247-0070 Fax: (773) 247-0569
Rev. Charles G. Huber, Dir. of Voluntary Services
Email: KHjailmin@aol.com

ASOCIACIÓN MÉDICA CUBANA DE CHICAGO
990 N. Lake Shore Dr., Suite 26B
Chicago, IL 60611-1379
(312) 266-9546
Aldo Pedroso, Delegate

ASPIRA OF ILLINOIS, INC.
2435 N. Western Ave.
Chicago, IL 60647
(773) 252-0970 Fax: (773) 252-0994
José Rodríguez, Executive Director
Web: www.aspira.org/illinois.html

ASSOCIATION HOUSE OF CHICAGO
Affiliate of NCLR
2150 W. North Ave.
Chicago, IL 60647
(773) 276-0084 Fax: (773) 276-7395
Harriet Sadauskas, Executive Director

ASSOCIATION HOUSE OF CHICAGO
Headquarters / Affiliate of NCLR
1116 N. Kedzie Ave.
Chicago, IL 60651
(773) 772-7170 Fax: (773) 384-0560
Harriet Sadauskas, Executive Director

ASSOCIATION OF HISPANIC STATE EMPLOYEES
P.O. Box 641526
Chicago, IL 60664-1526
(312) 814-8942
Peter Viña, President

ASSURANCE CORPORATION
The College of Office Technology
1520 W Division St.
Chicago, IL 60622

(773) 278-0042 Fax: (773) 278-0143
Kathleen Murphy, Director
Email: cot89@hotmail.com

AURORA HISPANIC CHAMBER OF COMMERCE
P.O. Box 7111
Aurora, IL 60507
(630) 851-2422 Fax: (630) 686-2161
Wilfredo Alicea, President
Web: www.ahcc-il.com

BACK OF THE YARD NEIGHBOORHOOD COUNCIL
1751 W. 47th St., 2nd Floor
Chicago, IL 60609-3889
(773) 523-4416 Fax: (773) 254-3525
Patrick J. Salmon, President & CEO

BARRETO BOYS CLUB
2713 W. Crystal
Chicago, IL 60622
(773) 235-0870 Fax: (773) 235-8244
Mariano Acevedo, Director

BICKERDIKE REDEVELOPMENT CORP.
2550 W North Ave.
Chicago, IL 60647
(773) 278-5669 Fax: (773) 278-5673
Joey Aruguete, Director
Email: brcadm@wwa.com

BOLIVIAN-AMERICAN MEDICAL ASSOCIATION
111 W. Superior St., Suite 309
Melrose Park, IL 60160
(708) 343-0420 Fax: (708) 343-4290
Dr. Jaime Escobar, President

BOYS AND GIRLS CLUBS OF CHICAGO
Corporate Headquarters
820 N. Orleans #235
Chicago, IL 60610
(312) 627-2700 Fax: (312) 258-0005
Email: webmaster@bgcc.org
Web: www.bgcc.org

BROADER URBAN INVOLVEMENT LEADERSHIP DEVELOPMENT (BUILD)
1223 N Milwaukee, 2nd Floor
Chicago, IL 60622
(773) 227-2880 Fax: (773) 227-3012
Freddy Calixto, Director
Email: build@chicagonet.net
Web: www.buildchicago.org

CASA AZTLAN
1831 S. Racine St.
Chicago, IL 60608
(312) 666-5508 Fax: (312) 666-7829
Carlos Aranjo, Executive Director

CASA CENTRAL
Headquarters/ Daycare Center
1343 N. California Ave.
Chicago, IL 60622
(773) 645-2300 Fax: (773) 645-2475
Ann R. Alvarez, President & CEO
Email: inforequest@casacentral.org
Web: www.casacentral.org

Nursing Home
1401 N. California Ave.
Chicago, IL 60622
(773) 782-8700 Fax: (773) 276-0465
Ann R. Alvarez, Executive Director
Email: inforequest@casacentral.org
Web: www.casacentral.org

CASA HISPANA
Northwestern University
1859 Sheridon Rd.
Evanston, IL 60208
(847) 467-2156 Fax: (847) 491-8128
Martin Mueller, Chairman

CASA LATINA CULTURAL CENTER
Western Illinois University
900 W. Adams St.
Macomb, IL 61455
(309) 298-3379 Fax: (309) 298-2567
Nazareth Hattwick, Director
Email: C-Latina@wlu.edu

CATHOLIC CHARITIES OF THE ARCHDIOCESE OF CHICAGO, THE
126 N. Des Plaines St. 1st Floor
Chicago, IL 60661
(312) 427-7078 or (312) 655-7860
Fax: (312) 427-3130

J. Zeferio Ochoa, Executive Director

CENTER FOR LATIN AMERICAN AND CARIBBEAN STUDIES
University of Illinois, Urbana-Champaign
910 S. 5th St., #201
Champaign, IL 61820
(217) 333-3182 Fax: (217) 244-7333
Cynthia Radding, Director
Web: www.uiuc.edu/unit/lat

CENTER FOR LATIN AMERICAN STUDIES
University of Chicago
5848 S. University Ave., K308
Chicago, IL 60637
(773) 702-8420 Fax: (773) 702-1755
Thomas Cummins, Director
Email: clas@uchicago.edu

CENTER FOR LATINO & LATIN AMERICAN STUDIES
Northern Illinois University
Center for Latino & Latin American Studies
Dekalb, IL 60115-2854
(815) 753-1650 Fax: (815) 753-1531
Prof. Michael Gonzales, Director
Email: gonzales@niu.edu

CENTER FOR LATINO RESEARCH (CLR)
De Paul University
2320 N. Kenmore Ave., SAC 563
Chicago, IL 60614
(773) 325-7316 or (773) 325-7317
Fax: (773) 325-7304
Dr. Félix Masud Piloto, Director
Email: fmasud-p@wppost.depaul.edu
Web: www.depaul.edu

CENTER FOR MULTICULTURAL PROGRAMS
Minority Program
HUB 113, 3241 S. Federal St.
Chicago, IL 60616
(312) 567-5250 or (800) 448-2329
Fax: (312) 567-5114
Genaro Balcazar, Director

CENTER FOR NEIGHBORHOOD TECHNOLOGY
2125 W. North Ave.
Chicago, IL 60647
(773) 278-4800 Fax: (773) 278-3840
Scott Bernstein, President
Email: info@cng.org
Web: www.cng.org

CENTRAL STATES SER-JOBS FOR PROGRESS, INC.
Affiliate of SER-Jobs for Progress National, Inc.
1116 N. Kedzie, 4th Floor
Chicago, IL 60651
(773) 227-3377 Fax: (773) 292-6055
Rose Mary Bombela, Director
Email: rbombela@sernational.org
Web: www.sernational.org

CENTRO CRISTO REY
315 N. Root St.
Aurora, IL 60505
(630) 851-1890 Fax: (630) 851-3625
Derta Amanzo, Area Coordinator

CENTRO DE INFORMACION Y PROGRESO
62 Fountain Sq. Plaza
Elgin, IL 60120
(847) 695-9050 Fax: (847) 931-7991
Audry Reed, Director

CENTRO LATINO UNIVERSIDAD POPULAR
1510 N Rockwell
Chicago, IL 60622
(773) 772-0836 Fax: (773) 772-0837
Olivia Flores Godinez, Director
Email: upopular@prodigy.net

CENTRO NUESTRO/YOUTH CENTER
3208 W North Ave.
Chicago, IL 60647
(773) 489-3157 Fax: (773) 489-3417
Sarah Raphert, Executive Director

CENTRO PARA DESARROLLO COMUNITARIO Y LIDERATO
4720 W. Deversey
Chicago, IL 60639
(773) 286-9590 Fax: (773) 286-9592
Raphael Morales, Director
Email: rafa_centro@yahoo.com

CENTRO SIN FRONTERAS AND UNITED METHODIST CHURCH
1205 N. Milwaukee
Chicago, IL 60622
(773) 772-8383 Fax: (773) 772-9173
Ema Lozano

CERMAK ROAD CHAMBER OF COMMERCE & INDUSTRY
3042 W. Cermak Rd.
Chicago, IL 60623
(773) 762-6565 Fax: (773) 762-6837
Greg Salgado, President

CHICAGO ABUSED WOMEN COALITION
P.O. Box 477916
Chicago, IL 60647-7916
(773) 278-4566 or (773) 489-9081
Email: cawcadmin@mindspring.com
Web: www.cawc.org

CHICAGO AVENUE BUSINESS ASSOC.
755 N. Ashland Ave.
Chicago, IL 60622
(312) 733-4002 Fax: (312) 733-4068
Phil Friedman, President

CHICAGO BOYS & GIRLS CLUB
General Wood Unit
2950 W 25th St.
Chicago, IL 60623
(773) 247-0700 Fax: (773) 927-4599
Victor Ceballos, Director

Little Villa Unit
2801 S. Ridgeway
Chicago, IL 60623
(773) 277-1800 Fax: (773) 277-4777
Roberto Cepeda, Dir.

Logan Square Unit
3228 W Palmer St.
Chicago, IL 60647
(773) 342-8800 Fax: (773) 342-3898
John Stephan, Dir.
Email: logansquare@bgcc.org

CHICAGO COMMONS ASSOCIATION
915 N Wolcott Ave.
Chicago, IL 60622
(773) 342-5330 Fax: (773) 342-4532
Franz Seever, Executive Director

CHICAGO LAKESHORE HOSPITAL
4840 N. Marine Dr.
Chicago, IL 60640
(773) 878-9700 Fax: (773) 907-4607
Web: www.chicagolakeshorehospital.com

CHICAGO LATINO CINEMA
600 S Michigan Ave.
Chicago, IL 60605
(312) 663-1600 Fax: (312) 360-0629
José Vargas, Executive Director
Web: www.colum.edu

CHICAGO LEGAL CLINIC
2938 E. 91st. St.
Chicago, IL 60617
(773) 731-1762 Fax: (773) 731-4264
Edward Grossman, Exec. Dir.

CHICAGO MINORITY BUSINESS DEVELOPMENT COUNCIL
11 South LaSalle Street, Suite 850
Chicago, IL 60603
(312) 263-0105 Fax: (312) 263-0280
Maye Foster-Thompson, Executive Director

CHICANO HISPANIC HEALTH COALITION
Chicago Department of Public Health,
DePaul Center
333 S. State St. #2144
Chicago, IL 60604
(312) 747-8820 Fax: (312) 747-9694
Esther Sciammarella, MS, Director
Email: sciammarella_esther@cdph.org

CHILD ABUSE UNIT FOR STUDIES, EDUCATION, AND SERVICES
1009 W. Wellington Ave.
Chicago, IL 60657
(773) 248-5500 Fax: (773) 248-5688
Richard LaBrie, MA, Exec. Dir.

CHILDSERV
1845 N. Kidzie Ave.
Chicago, IL 60647
(773) 772-8305
Aurelia Rosa, Dir.

CITIZEN INFORMATION SERVICES
322 S. Michigan #1232
Chicago, IL 60604
(312) 939-4636 Fax: (312) 939-5348
Lauren Collette, Exec. Dir.

CLARENTIAN MEDICAL CENTER
9119 S. Exchange
Chicago, IL 60617
(312) 768-5000 Fax: (312) 785-9661
Ramona López, Exec. Dir.

COMMUNITY T.V. NETWORK
2035 W. Wabansia
Chicago, IL 60647
(773) 278-8500 Fax: (773) 278-8635
Denise Zaccardi, Dir.
Email: ctvn@msn.com

CONFEDERATION OF LATIN AMERICAN STUDIES
University of Illinois, Chicago
UIC Campus Programs, M/C 118
750 S. Halsted, #300 CCC
Chicago, IL 60607
(312) 355-0579
Erendira G. Morales, President
Web: www.uic.edu

CORDI-MARIAN CENTER
1100 S. May
Chicago, IL 60607
(312) 666-3787 Fax: (312) 666-3562
Marie Ramírez, Dir.

COSMOPOLITAN CHAMBER OF COMMERCE
1326 S. Michigan Ave., #100
Chicago, IL 60605
(312) 786-0212 Fax: (312) 786-9079
Consuelo Pope, President

COUNSELING CENTER OF LAKEVIEW
3225 N. Sheffield
Chicago, IL 60657
(773) 549-5886 Fax: (773) 549-3265
Norman Groetzinger, Exec. Dir.

CUBAN AMERICAN CHAMBER OF COMMERCE OF ILLINOIS
3330 N. Ashland Ave.
Chicago, IL 60657
(773) 248-2400 Fax: (773) 248-6437
José García, President

CUBAN-AMERICAN NATIONAL FOUNDATION
Chicago Chapter
P.O. Box 3
2635 Washington Blvd., 2nd Floor
Bellwood, IL 60104
(708) 544-4491 Fax: (708) 544-4493
Iván H. Fernández, Area Director
Email: ferbelbio@aol.com

DAVID GOMEZ & ASSOCIATES, INC.
20 N. Clark, # 2900
Chicago, IL 60602
(312) 346-5525 Fax: (312) 346-1438
David Gomez, President & CEO
Web: www.dgai.com

DIOCESAN HISPANIC MINISTRY COORDINATOR
P.O. Box 1979
Chicago, IL 60690
(312) 751-8301 Fax: (312) 751-5207
Annaceli Leon, Secretary
Web: www.archdiocese-chgo.org

DIOCESE OF BELLEVILLE
Hispanic Affairs
P.O. Box 237
Cobden, IL 62920
(618) 893-2276
Rev. Federico Higuera, Dir. for Hispanic Ministry

DIOCESE OF CHICAGO (EPISCOPAL)
65 E. Huron St.
Chicago, IL 60611
(312) 751-4214 Fax: (312) 787-4534
Sue Cromer, Youth Ministries Coord.
Email: scromer@epischicago.org

DIOCESE OF JOLIET
Hispanic Affairs
402 S. Independence Blvd.
Romeoville, IL 60446

(815) 834-4038 Fax: (815) 838-8129
Sr. Judy Callahan, BVM, Dir. for Hispanic Ministry
Email: sjcallahan@dioceseofjoliet.org

DIOCESE OF PEORIA
Hispanic Ministry Office
1010 Jefferson St.
Mendota, IL 61342
Rev. Brian Rejsek

DIOCESE OF ROCKFORD
Centro Sembrador
921 W. State St.
Rockford, IL 61102-2808
(815) 962-8142 Fax: (815) 968-2808
Edgard Beltran, Director

DIOCESE OF ROCKFORD
Hispanic Affairs
921 W. State St.
Rockford, IL 61102-2808
(815) 962-8042 Fax: (815) 968-2808
Very Rev. William Schuessler, Vicar for Hispanic Ministry

DIOCESE OF SPRINGFIELD IN ILLINOIS
Office for Social Concerns
P.O. Box 3187
1615 W. Washington St.
Springfield, IL 62708-3187
(217) 698-8500 x130 Fax: (217) 698-9581
Sr. Jane Boos, SSND
Email: sjboos@dio.org

DIRECTIVA GENERAL DE GRUPOS JUVENILES
Equipo Coordinador
5512 Hyd Park Blvd.
Chicago, IL 60637
(773) 667-8920 Fax: (773) 667-6414
Lorenzo Diez Maezo, Supervisor

DIVISION STREET BUSINESS DEVELOPMENT ASSOCIATION
2548 W. Division St.
Chicago, IL 60622
(773) 278-1818 Fax: (773) 278-1811
Roberto Maldonado, Coord.

EASTER SEAL SOCIETY
2345 W. North Ave.
Chicago, IL 60647
(773) 276-4000 Fax: (773) 276-5653
Deir Cutletfed, Dir.

EIGHTEENTH STREET DEVELOPMENT CORP.
Affiliate of NCLR
1843 S. Carpenter St.
Chicago, IL 60608
(312) 733-2287 Fax: (312) 733-8242
Maria Munoz, Interim Executive Director
Email: esdc1839@aol.com

EL CENTRO DE LA CAUSA
731 W. 17th St.
Chicago, IL 60616
(312) 243-8508 Fax: (312) 243-8414
Felipe Ayala, Director

EL HOGAR DEL NIÑO
Affiliate of NCLR
2325 S. California Ave.
Chicago, IL 60608
(773) 523-1629 Fax: (773) 523-8230
Jane Garza Mancillas, Executive Director

EL RINCON COMMUNITY PROJECT
1874 N. Milwaukee Ave.
Chicago, IL 60647
(773) 276-0200 Fax: (773) 276-4226
Rafael Ríos, Exec. Dir.

EL VALOR CORPORATION
1850 W. 21st St.
Chicago, IL 60608
(312) 666-4511 Fax: (312) 666-6677
Vince Alloco, Exec. Director

THE ELEANOR ASSOCIATION
1550 N. Dearborn Pkwy.
Chicago, IL 60610
(773) 664-8245 Fax: (312) 664-8062
Susan Unwohl, Contact

ELGIN HISPANIC NETWORK
P.O. Box 1554
Elgin, IL 60121
(847) 931-6019 Fax: (708) 810-9412
Gilbert Feliciano, President

Email: ehn@i.am
Web: ehn.i.am

ENGLISH AS A SECOND LANGUAGE ACADEMIC PROGRAM
MacCormac College
506 S. Wabash Ave.
Chicago, IL 60605
(312) 922-1884 Fax: (312) 922-3196
Edgar Santa Cruz, Director
Email: esantacruz@maccormac.edu
Web: www.maccormac.edu

ENSEMBLE ESPAÑOL
5500 N. St. Louis Ave.
Chicago, IL 60625
(773) 583-4050 Fax: (773) 794-6243
Libby Komaiko Fleming, Dir.

ERIE FAMILY HEALTH CENTER
1701 W. Superior Ave.
Chicago, IL 60622
(312) 666-3488 Fax: (312) 666-5867
Rupert Evans, Exec. Dir.

ERIE NEIGHBORHOOD HOUSE
1347 W. Erie St.
Chicago, IL 60622
(312) 666-3430 Fax: (312) 666-3955
Esther Nieves, Exec. Dir.

ESPERANZA COMMUNITY SERVICES SCHOOL
520 N. Marshfield
Chicago, IL 60622
(312) 243-6097 Fax: (312) 243-2076
Barbara Fields, Executive Director

FAMILY Y RESCUE
9204 S. Commercial #401
Chicago, IL 60617
(773) 375-1918 Fax: (773) 734-1245
Joyce M. Cowan, Exec. Dir.

FUERZA UNIDA
Northwestern University
1936 Sheridon Rd.
Evanston, IL 60208
(847) 491-2350 Fax: (847) 491-4337
Andy Daniels, Coordinator of Student Affairs

GADS HILL CENTER
1919 W. Cullerton
Chicago, IL 60608-2697
(312) 226-0963 Fax: (312) 226-2248
Barbara Castellano, Exec. Dir.

GIRL SCOUTS OF CHICAGO
222 S. Riverside Plaza #2120
Chicago, IL 60606
(312) 416-2500 Fax: (312) 416-2932
Email: jsomogyi@girlscouts-chicago.org
Web: www.girlscouts-chicago.org

GRACIELA KENIG & ASSOCIATES, CAREER DEVELOPMENT SPECIALISTS FOR HISPANICS
4334 Ivy Dr., #100
Glenview, IL 60025-1085
(847) 699-1817 Fax: (847) 699-1864
Graciela Kenig, President & Founder
Email: kenigassoc@cs.com
Web: www.careersforlatinos.com

HEALTH ORIENTED LATINO ASSOCIATION (HOLA)
University of Illinois, Chicago
UIC Campus Programs, M/C 118
750 S. Halsted, #515
Chicago, IL 60607
(312) 355-0548
Cristina Terrazas, President
Email: c_terrazas@hotmail.com
Web: www2.uic.edu/stud_orgs/cultures/hola/

HEALTHCARE ALTERNATIVE SYSTEMS
(Systema Alternative de Salud)
2755 W. Armitage
Chicago, IL 60647
(773) 252-3100 Fax: (773) 252-8945
Marto Gacome, Exec. Dir.

HEARTLAND ALLIANCE FOR HUMAN NEEDS & HUMAN RIGHTS
208 S. La Salle St. #1818
Chicago, IL 60604
(312) 660-1300 Fax: (312) 660-1500
Email: moreinfo@heartland-alliance.org
Web: www.heartland-alliance.org

HERMANDAD HISPANA
4618A Patrick Henry Circle
Belleville, IL 62225

(618) 229-8219 or (618) 229-8264
Fax: (618) 229-0110
Daniel Davila, Chairman
Email: ddavila223@aol.com

HISPANIC ALLIANCE FOR CAREER ENHANCEMENT (HACE)
14 E. Jackson Blvd., #1310
Chicago, IL 60604
(312) 435-0498 Fax: (312) 435-1494
José Gómez, Executive Director
Email: haceorg@enteract.com
Web: www.hace-usa.org

HISPANIC AMERICAN CONSTRUCTION INDUSTRY ASSOCIATION
641 W. Lake St.
Chicago, IL 60661
(312) 258-9621 Fax: (312) 258-9628
Rafael Hernandez, Executive Director
Email: hacia@msn.com
Web: www.hacia.org

HISPANIC AMERICAN LABOR COUNCIL
2538 S. Christian Ave.
Chicago, IL 60623
(773) 762-4726
Augus Sallas, Pres.

HISPANIC ASSOCIATION FOR CULTURAL EXPRESSION & RECOGNITION (H.A.C.E.R.)
5706 S.University Ave.
Chicago, IL 60637
(773) 702-8787 Fax: (773) 702-7718
Web: http://home.uchicago.edu/orgs/hispanic-association/

HISPANIC CENTER OF EXCELLENCE
UIAC Hispanic Center of Excellence
1819 West Polk M/C 786
Chicago, IL 60612
(312) 996-6491 Fax: (312) 996-9006
Jorge Girotti, Director

HISPANIC DENTAL ASSOCIATION (HDA)
188 West Randolph St., #1811
Chicago, IL 60601
(312) 577-4013 or (800) 852-7921
Fax: (312)577-0052
Sandy Reed, Executive Director
Email: hdassoc@aol.com
Web: www.hdassoc.org

HISPANIC HERITAGE CLUB
Morton College, 3801 S. Central Ave.
Cicero, IL 60804
(708) 656-8000 ext 352 Fax: (708) 656-3297
Jose Gallo, Advisor

HISPANIC HOUSING DEVELOPMENT CORPORATION
205 E. Wacker Pl. #2300
Chicago, IL 60606
(312) 443-1360 Fax: (312) 443-1058
Hipolito P. Roldán, Pres.

HISPANIC ILLINOIS STATE LAW ENFORCEMENT ASSOCIATION (HISLEA)
P.O. Box 470086
Chicago, IL 60647
(773) 881-4179
Peter Garza, President
Email: info@HISLEA.org
Web: www.hislea.org

HISPANIC LAW STUDENTS ASSOCIATION
565 West Adams St.
Chicago, IL 60661-3691
(312) 906-5000 or (312) 906-5147
Fax: (312) 906-5280
Francelyn Perez, President
Email: fperez@kentlaw.edu

HISPANIC NATIONAL BAR ASSOCIATION
120 S. State St., 7th Fl
Chicago, IL 60603
(312) 424-0800 x 116 Fax: (312) 424-0700
Angel G. Gomez , President-elect
Email: agomez@juritas.com
Web: www.hnba.com

HISPANIC SOCIAL SERVICE AGENCY
3859 W. 26th St.
Chicago, IL 60623
(773) 277-7330 Fax: (773) 277-7340
Cristina Quintana, Prog. Coord.

HISPANIC WOMEN'S PROJECT
1 E. Jackson Blvd. #9100
Chicago, IL 60604-2287
(312) 362-8315 Fax: (312) 362-5749
Maria Elena Motina, Coord.

HISPANO ALCOHOLIC SERVICES
North Side Branch
2755 W. Armitage Ave.
Chicago, IL 60647
(773) 252-3100 Fax: (773) 252-8945
Marco Gacome, Exec. Dir.

South Side Branch
4534 South West
Chicago, IL 60609
(773) 254-5141 Fax: (773) 254-5753
Arturo Valdéz, Dir.

HISPANOCARE, INC.
836 Wellington Avve.
Chicago, IL 60657
(773) 296-7157 Fax: (773) 327-8208
Omaida Hernandez, Admin. Asst.
Email: Omaida_Hernandez@immc.org

HOUSE OF THE GOOD SHEPHERD
P.O.Box 13453
1114 W. Grace
Chicago, IL 60613
(773) 935-3434 Fax: (773) 935-3523
Sister Kathleen Moore, Dir.

HOWARD AREA COMMUNITY CENTER
7648 N. Paulina St.
Chicago, IL 60626
(773) 262-6622 Fax: (773) 262-6645
Ida Galván, Dir. of Social Service

HUMAN RESOURCE DEVELOPMENT INSTITUTE
2207 W. 18th St.
Chicago, IL 60608
(312) 226-6989 Fax: (312) 243-3820
Lois Himpten, Dir.

ILLINOIS HISPANIC HUMAN SERVICES ASSOCIATION
P. O. Box 641526
2635 W. 23rd Street
Chicago, IL 60608
(773) 523-1155 Fax: (773) 523-1188
Joseph M. Martens, Agency Coord.

ILLINOIS MIGRANT COUNCIL
Affiliate of NCLR
28 E. Jackson Blvd., #1600
Chicago, IL 60604
(312) 663-1522 Fax: (312) 663-1994
Eloy Salazar, Executive Director

IMAGE DE CENTRAL ILLINOIS CHAPTER
Central Illinois Chapt.
1021 S. Grand Ave., West
Springfield, IL 62704
(217) 726-8576
Ana Cecilia Velasco, President
Web: www.nationalimageinc.org

IMAGE, INC.
Central Illinois Chapter
P.O. Box 1082
Collinsville, IL 62234
(618) 256-7546 (W) or (314) 832-0790
Liz Sánchez-Setser, Reg. Dir. & Chapt. Pres.t
Email: sanchez@medgrop.safb.mil
Web: www.nationalimageinc.org

IN ROADS CHICAGO, INC.
117 W. Harrison #700
Chicago, IL 60605
(312) 663-9892 Fax: (312) 663-9882
Harold Abraham, Dir.

INFANT WELFARE SOCIETY OF CHICAGO
1931 N. Halsted
Chicago, IL 60614
(312) 751-2800 Fax: (312) 751-8804
Francis Genther, Exec. Director

INSTITUTE FOR LATINO PROGRESS
2570 S. Blue Island
Chicago, IL 60608
(312) 890-0055 Fax: (312) 890-1537
María Teresa Ayala, Exec. Dir.

INSTITUTO MEXICANO DE CULTURA Y EDUCACION DE CHICAGO
Chicago Office
702 N. Wells St.
Chicago, IL 60610
(312) 255-1556 Fax: (312) 255-9294
Flavia Moylan, Director

JANE ADDAMS CENTER
Sheridan Day Care
3212 N. Broadway
Chicago, IL 60657
(773) 549-1631 Fax: (773) 549-3049
Nanet Crespo-Ramirez, Dir.

JORGE PRIETO FAMILY HEALTH CENTER
2424 S. Pulaski
Chicago, IL 60623
(773) 521-0750 Fax: (773) 762-1758
Andrea Muñoz, Exec. Dir.

JOSPHINUM HIGH SCHOOL
1501 N. Oakley Blvd.
Chicago, IL 60622
(773) 276-1261 Fax: (773) 292-3963
Donna Collins, Principal

JUAN ANTONIO CORRETJER
Puerto Rican Cultural Ctr.
1671 N. Claremont
Chicago, IL 60647
(773) 342-8023 Fax: (773) 342-6609
José E. López, Exec. Director

KRAFT FOODS HISPANIC EMPLOYEE COUNCIL
Philip Morris/Kraft Foods
801 Waukegan Rd.
Glenview, IL 60025
(847) 646-3731 Fax: (847) 646-3864
Celso Bejarano, President

LA CASA CULTURAL LATINA
1203 W. Nevada
Urbana, IL 61801
(217) 333-4950 Fax: (217) 244-4513
Giraldo Rosales, Director
Email: lacasa@uius.edu

LA CASA STUDENT ORGANIZATION
University of Illinois, Urbana-Champaign
1203 W. Nevada St.
Urbana, IL 61801
(217) 333-4950 Fax: (217) 244-4513
Giraldo Rosales, Director
Email: lacasa@uic.edu

LA LECHE LEAGUE INTERNATIONAL
1400 North Meacham Rd.
Schaumburg, IL 60168
(847) 519-7730 Fax: (847) 519-0035
Paulina Smith, Executive Director
Web: www.lalecheleague.org

LA PROGRESIVA PRE-SCHOOL
2609 N. Kimball
Chicago, IL 60647
(773) 342-6690 Fax: (773) 235-8885
Norma Reyes, Dir.

LA VOZ LATINA
814 North Court Street
Rockford, IL 61103
(815) 965-5784 Fax: (815) 965-5935
Marco Lenis, Pres.

LAKEVIEW SHELTER, INC.
835 W. Addison
Chicago, IL 60613
(773) 327-1389
William A. Teeple, Resource/Vol. Coord.
Email: Lakeview@mail.anet-chi.com

LAS AMERICAS SENIOR APARTMENTS
1611 S. Racine
Chicago, IL 60608
(312) 666-9205 Fax: (312) 899-1300

LATIN AMERICAN CENTER
126 N. Displayarce
Chicago, IL 60661
(312) 427-7078 Fax: (312) 427-3130
Zeferino Ochoa, Exec. Dir.

LATIN AMERICAN CHAMBER OF COMMERCE
3512 Fullerton Ave.
Chicago, IL 60647
(773) 252-5211 Fax: (773) 252-7065
Lorenzo Padron, Chairman
Email: mbdclacc@ix.netcom.com
Web: www.lacc1.com

LATIN AMERICAN POLICE ASSOCIATION
Chicago
P.O. Box 4551
Chicago, IL 60680-4551
(773) 927-5058 Fax: (312) 666-2981
Salvador A. Martinez, President

LATIN AMERICAN STUDENT ORG. (LAOS)
Olive-Harvey College
10001 South Woodlawn Ave.
Chicago, IL 60628
(773) 291-6361 or (773) 291-6100
Irene Toscano, President

Eastern Illinois University
Student Union
600 Lincoln Ave.
Charleston, IL 61920
(217) 581-2219 Fax: (217) 581-6764
Kary Brito, Advisor

LATIN AMERICAN STUDENTS IN ARCHITECTURE
University of Illinois, Chicago
1200 W. Harrison, Mail Code #220
Chicago, IL 60607
(312) 996-3356 Fax: (312) 413-2903
Jose Perales, President
Email: jperales@uic.edu

LATIN AMERICAN STUDIES PROGRAM
University of Illinois, Chicago
P.O. Box 4348
Chicago, IL 60608
(312) 996-2445 Fax: (312) 996-1796
Dr. Baird, Director
Email: llopez@uic.edu

LATIN UNITED COMMUNITY HOUSING ASSOCIATION (LUCHA)
2750 W. North Ave. #210
Chicago, IL 60647
(773) 276-5338 Fax: (773) 276-5358
Juan Rivera, Exec. Dir.

LATINO ASSOCIATION OF BUSINESS STUDENTS
University of Illinois, Chicago
UIC Campus Programs, M/C118
750 S. Halsted St., #516 CCC
Chicago, IL 60607-3525
(312) 355-0501
Anthony D. Esteban, President
Email: labs@uic.edu
Web: www.labs.uic.edu

LATINO ASSOCIATION OF HISPANIC FIREFIGHTERS
Fatindo Firefighters Association
P.O. Box 388281
Chicago, IL 60638
(773) 229-0926 Fax: (773) 229-0933
Charles Vazquez, President
Email: HOSES1@aol.com
Web: //www.nahf.org

LATINO COMMITTEE ON THE MEDIA (LCOM)
2011 W. Pershing Rd.
Chicago, IL 60609
(773) 247-0707 Fax: (773) 247-3924
Teresa Martínez, Chair.

LATINO COUNSELING SERVICES
3225 N. Sheffield Ave.
Chicago, IL 60657
(773) 549-5886 Fax: (773) 549-3265
Norman Groeteinger, Dir.

LATINO CULTURAL CENTER
University of Illinois, Chicago
803 S. Morgan
Chicago, IL 60607
(312) 996-3095 Fax: (312) 996-9092
Rodrigo Carramina, Director

LATINO INITIATIVES FOR THE NEXT CENTURY (LINC)
401 N. Michigan Ave., #2900
Chicago, IL 60611
(877) 510-5462 Fax: (312) 321-0736
Rudy J. Mulder, Chairman & Founder
Email: rmulder@linc-usa.org
Web: www.linc-usa.org

LATINO INTERVENTION CENTER
2608 W. Peterson Ave.
Chicago, IL 60659
(773) 465-2233 Fax: (773) 465-7693
María E. Pujalsd, Dir.

LATINO LAW STUDENT ASSOCIATION
DePaul University
25 E. Jackson Blvd.
Chicago, IL 60604
(312) 362-6110
Homero Tristan, President
Email: htristan@shrike.depaul.edu
Web: www.depaul.edu/~llsa/

LATINO TREATMENT CENTER
2608 West Peterson
Chicago, IL 60618
(773) 465-1161 Fax: (773) 465-1693
María Eugenia Pujals, Prog. Dir.

LATINO VOTE USA
La Casa Cultural Latina
Univ of Illinois, 1203 W. Nevada
Urbana, IL 61801
(217) 333-4950 Fax: (217) 244-4513
Geraldo Rosales, Dir.

LATINO YOUTH, INC.
Affiliate of NCLR
2200 S. Marshall Blvd.
Chicago, IL 60623
(773) 277-0400 Fax: (773) 277-0401
Carmen Avilar, Executive Director
Email: Emont15709@aol.com

LAWYERS' COMMITTEE FOR BETTER HOUSING
220 S. State St. #1700
Chicago, IL 60604
(312) 347-7600 Fax: (312) 347-7604
Email: lcbh@enteract.com

LITTLE MEXICO
115 W. Wolf Rd.
Whilad, IL 60090
(847) 419-8904
Teresa María Martínez, Dir.

LITTLE VIILAGE CHAMBER OF COMMERCE
3610 W. 26th St., 2nd Floor
Chicago, IL 60623
(773) 521-5387 Fax: (773) 521-5252
Agustin Granja, President
Web: http://www.lavillitachaver.com/

LOGAN SQUARE NEIGHBORHOOD ASSOCIATION
3321 W. Wrightwood
Chicago, IL 60647
(773) 384-4370 Fax: (773) 384-0624
Nancy Ardema, Dir.
Email: pinvino@one.org

LOGAN SQUARE YMCA
3600 W. Fullerton
Chicago, IL 60647
(773) 235-5150 Fax: (773) 235-4489
Maria Nodel, Dir.

LULAC-NATIONAL EDUCATIONAL SERVICES CENTER, INC. (LNESC)
4355 W. 26th St., #3
Chicago, IL 60623
(773) 277-2513 Fax: (773) 521-0217
Gabriel Hernández, Director
Web: www.lulac.org

MANOS, LA CASA CULTURAL LATIN
El Centro para los Trabajadores
1011 South Wright Street
Champagne, IL 61820
(217) 328-6420
Sandy Poole, Pres.

MARSHALL SQUARE BOYS & GIRLS CLUB
2628 W. Cermak Rd.
Chicago, IL 60608
(773) 247-7557 Fax: (773) 247-7815
Gil Aguia, Dir.

MCKINLEY FAMILY SERVICES
2938 E. 91st St.
Chicago, IL 60617
(773) 768-5452 Fax: (773) 768-5522
Gregory Terry, Dir.

MCKINLEY NEIGHBORHOOD HOUSE
8458 S. Mackinaw
Chicago, IL 60617
(773) 731-8187 Fax: (773) 731-8130
Gregory Terry, Dir.

MCKINLEY TRUMBULL PARK COMMUNITY CENTER
10530 S. Oglesby Ave.
Chicago, IL 60617
(773) 375- 7022 Fax: (773) 375-5528
Greggory Terry, Dir.

METROPOLITAN FAMILY SERVICES
14 E. Jackson Blvd.
Chicago, IL 60604
(312) 986-4000
Email: webadmin@metrofamily.org
Web: www.metrofamily.org

MEXICAN AMERICAN CHAMBER OF COMMERCE OF ILLINOIS, INC.
122 S. Michigan Ave.,#1449
Chicago, IL 60603
(312) 554-0844 Fax: (312) 554-0848
Juan Ochoa, President & CEO
Email: macc@maccbusiness.com

MEXICAN AMERICAN LEGAL DEFENSE AND EDUCATIONAL FUND (MALDEF)
Chicago Regional Office
188 W. Randolph St., #1405
Chicago, IL 60601
(312) 782-1422 Fax: (312) 782-1428
Patricia Mendoza, Regional Counsel
Email: pmendoza@aol.com
Web: www.maldef.org

MEXICAN CIVIC COMMITTEE
3934 W. 26th St.
Chicago, IL 60623
(773) 521-2700 Fax: (773) 521-7908
Anita Villareal, Dir.

MEXICAN COMMUNITY COMMITTEE
Affiliate of NCLR
2939 E. 91st St.
Chicago, IL 60617
(773) 978-6441 or (773) 978-0123
Fax: (773) 978-2376
Henry Martínez, Director

9101 S. Exchange Ave.
Chicago, IL 60617
(773) 978-6441 Fax: (773) 978-2376
Henry Martinez, Director

MEXICAN FINE ARTS CENTER MUSEUM
1852 W. 19th St.
Chicago, IL 60608
(312) 738-1503 Fax: (312) 738-9740
Carlos Tortolero, Director
Email: dmurga@mfacmchicago.org
Web: www.mfacmchicago.org

MEXICAN FOLKLORIC DANCE COMPANY OF CHICAGO
3842 S. Archer Ave.
Chicago, IL 60632
(773) 247-1522 Fax: (773) 247-1502
Henry A. Roa, Executive Director

MEXICAN HONORARY COMMISSION OF ALTON, THE
1411 Spaulding Dr.
Alton, IL 62002
(618) 465-3224
Jose Morales, President
Email: vato1411@aol.com

MIDWEST ASSOCIATION OF HISPANIC ACCOUNTANTS
University of Illinois, Chicago
UIC Campus Programs, M/C 118
750 S. Halsted, #312H
Chicago, IL 60607
(312) 355-0571
Blanca Rodríguez, President
Email: brodri1@uic.edu
Web: www2.uic.edu/stud_orgs/prof/maha

MIDWEST HISPANIC AIDS COALITION
P.O. Box 470859
Chicago, IL 60647
(773) 772-8195
Marianela Chaumeil, Resource Center Coordinator
Email: mhac@techinter.com

MINORITY BUSINESS DEVELOPMENT AGENCY (MBDA)
Chicago Office/U.S. Dept. of Commerce
55 E. Monroe St., #1406
Chicago, IL 60603-5792
(312) 353-0182 Fax: (312) 353-0191
David Vega, Regional Director
Email: DVega@mbda.gov
Web: www.mbda.gov

MINORITY ECONOMIC RESOURCES CORPORATION- EDUCATION AND TRAINING SERVICES
2570 E. Devon Ave.
Des Plaines, IL 60018
(847) 297-4705 Fax: (847) 297-5343
Michero B. Washington, President

MOVIMIENTO ARTISTICO CHICANO, INC.
P.O. Box 2890
Chicago, IL 60690
(773) 935-6188
Carlos Cumpián, Dir.

MUJERES LATINAS EN ACCION
Affiliate of NCLR
1823 W. 17th St.
Chicago, IL 60608
(312) 226-1544 Fax: (312) 226-2720
Norma Seledon Tellez, Director

NAMI OF GREATER CHICAGO
The Alliance for the Mentally Ill of Greater Chicago
1536 W. Chicago Ave.
Chicago, IL 60622
(312) 563-0445 Fax: (312) 563-0467
Suzanne M. Andriukaitis, MA, LACSW, Exec. Dir.

NATIONAL ASSOCIATION FOR HISPANIC ELDERLY
Chicago Office/Project Ayuda
1325 W. Howard St., #204
Evanston, IL 60202
(847) 475-9913 Fax: (847) 475-9942
Judy Matthews, Project Coordinator

NATIONAL CENTER FOR LATINOS WITH DISABILITIES, INC.
Affiliate of NCLR
1915-17 South Blue Island Ave.
Chicago, IL 60608
(312) 666-3393 Fax: (312) 666-1787
Maria Elena Rodriguez- Sullivan, Executive Director

NATIONAL COUNCIL OF LA RAZA (NCLR)
Chicago Office
203 N. Wabash Ave., #918
Chicago, IL 60601
(312) 269-9250 or (312) 819-0746
Fax: (312) 269-9260
Maria Ayala, Director
Web: www.nclr.org

NEIGHBORHOOD HOUSING SERVICES
West Humboltdt Division
3601 W. Chicago Ave.
Chicago, IL 60651
(773) 533-5570 Fax: (773) 227-1926
Jeannett Jackson, Director
Web: www.nw.org

NEIGHBORHOOD HOUSING SERVICES OF CHICAGO
747 N. May St.
Chicago, IL 60622
(312) 738-2227 Fax: (312) 738-2491
Bruce Gottschall, Executive Director
Email: nhschgo@wwa.com

NORTH PARK COLLEGE
3225 W. Foster Ave.
Chicago, IL 60625
(773) 583-2700 Fax: (773) 244-4953
David G. Horner, Pres.

NORTH-PULASKI CHAMBER OF COMMERCE
4054 W. North Ave.
Chicago, IL 60639
(773) 384-6403 Fax: (773) 384-3850
William Anderson, President

OFFICE OF THE CHICAGO COMMISSION OF HUMAN RELATIONS
510 N. Reshtigo Court
Chicago, IL 60611
(312) 744-9391 or (312) 744-4111
Fax: (312) 744-1081
Catherine Hartrick, Dir.

ONWARD NEIGHBORHOOD HOUSE
600 N. Leavitt St.
Chicago, IL 60612
(312) 666-6726 Fax: (312) 666-6735
Jeff Fenwick

ORGANIZATION OF LATIN AMERICAN STUDENTS
Chicago State University
Office of Hispanic Programs, IUC 106
9501 S. King Dr.
Chicago, IL 60628
(773) 995-2526 Fax: (773) 995-2969
Abraham de Leon, Pres.
Email: http://www.geocities.com/collegepark/4803

Elgin Community College/Affiliate of NCLR
1700 Spartan Dr.
Elgin, IL 60123
(847) 888-7998/697-1000 Fax: (847) 608-5458

Jane Barbosa, Multicultural Admissions Coord.

OUR LADY OF GUADALUPE
9050 S. Berley Ave.
Chicago, IL 60617
(773) 768-0999 Fax: (773) 768-0529
Robert McNamara, Principal

PEOPLES MUSIC SCHOOL
931 W. Eastwood Ave.
Chicago, IL 60640
(773) 784-7032 Fax: (773) 784-7134
Rita Simo, Dir.

PILSEN NEIGHBORS COMMUNITY COUNCIL
2026 S. Blue Island Ave.
Chicago, IL 60608
(312) 666-2663 Fax: (312) 666-4661
Juan Soto, Exec. Dir.

PILSEN RESURRECTION DEVELOPMENT CORPORATION
1818 S. Paulina St.
Chicago, IL 60608
(312) 666-1323 Fax: (312) 942-1123
Raúl I. Raymundo, Exec. Dir.

PILSEN YMCA
1608 W. 21st Place
Chicago, IL 60608
(312) 738-0282 Fax: (312) 738-1915
Hildy Santos, Exec. Dir.

PILSEN-LITTLE VILLAGE
Community Mental Health Center
2635 W. 23rd St.
Chicago, IL 60608
(773) 927-1228 Fax: (773) 927-0237
Albert Vázquez, Exec. Dir.
Web: www.urbanvista.com/plvcmhc/plvcmhc.html

Community Mental Health Center
1858 W. Cermak Rd.
Chicago, IL 60608
(312) 226-1120
Katherine Ortiz, Dir.

Community Mental Health Center
CILA Program
4115 W. 26th St.
Chicago, IL 60623
(773) 762-5300 Fax: (773) 762-7362
Nora Navarro, Dir.

Community Mental Health Center-Hands of Life Against AIDS Program (HOLA)
2007 S. Blue Island Ave.
Chicago, IL 60608
(312) 226-5864 Fax: (312) 226-7367
Albert Vasquez, Dir.
Email: nolaa@uss.net

POR UN BARRIO MEJOR
3444 W. 26th St.
Chicago, IL 60623
(312) 521-2157
Carlos Heredia, Dir.

PROYECTO ASISTENCIA SOCIAL
c/o Counseling Center of Lakeview
3225 N. Sheffield
Chicago, IL 60657
(773) 549-5886 Fax: (773) 549-3265
Betty Shibata, Dir.

PUERTO RICAN CHAMBER OF COMMERCE OF ILLINOIS
2436 W. Division St.
Chicago, IL 60622
(773) 486-1331 Fax: (773) 486-1340
Angela Chanchez, Executive Director
Email: tatobien@aol.com

PUERTO RICAN CULTURAL CENTER
1671 N. Claremont
Chicago, IL 60647
(773) 342-8023 Fax: (773) 342-6609
Jose Lopez, Executive Director

PUERTO RICAN PARADE COMMITTEE OF CHICAGO
1237 N. California
Chicago, IL 60622
(773) 292-1414 Fax: (773) 292-1860
Efrain Malave, Pres.

PUERTO RICAN PARADE OF CHICAGO
1237 N. California
Chicago, IL 60622

(773) 292-1414 Fax: (773) 292-1860
Rubén Rosado, Pres.

PUERTO RICAN STUDENT ASSOCIATION
University of Illinois, Chicago
UIC Campus Programs, M/C 118
750 S. Halsted, #516
Chicago, IL 60607
(312) 355-0501
Adriana Feliciano, President
Web: www2.uic.edu/stud_orgs/cultures/prsa

PUERTO RICO FEDERAL AFFAIRS ADMINISTRATION
Chicago Regional Office
30 N. La Salle St., #2330
Chicago, IL 60602
(312) 372-9377 Fax: (312) 664-9882
Rey Rubio, Director

PUERTORRIQUEÑOS UNIDOS DE CHICAGO, INC. (UNITED PUERTO RICANS OF CHICAGO)
2935 W. 71st St.
Chicago, IL 60629
(773) 436-1159
Paulina Carballo, President

RAFAEL CINTRON-ORTIZ LATINO CULTURAL CENTER
University of Illinois, Chicago
803 S. Morgan St., Lecture Center B-2
Chicago, IL 60607-7028
(312) 996-3095 Fax: (312) 996-9092
Rodrigo Carramiñana, Director
Email: rodrigoc@uic.edu
Web: www.uic.edu

RAINBOW HOUSE/ARCO IRIS
P.O. Box 29019
Chicago, IL 60629
(773) 521-5501 Fax: (773) 521-4866
Deirdre Cutliffe, Exec. Dir.
Email: rainbowhouse@iqc.org

RAINBOW/PUSH COALITION
National Office
930 E. 50th St.
Chicago, IL 60615
(773) 373-3366 Fax: (773) 373-3571
Axel Adams, Deputy Director
Web: www.rainbowpush.org

RUIS BELVIS CULTURAL CENTER
1632 N. Milwaukee Ave.
Chicago, IL 60647
(773) 235-3988
America Sorentini, Executive Director

SAINT PIUS SENIOR CITIZEN CENTER
1919 S. Ashland Ave.
Chicago, IL 60608
(312) 226-6161 Fax: (312) 226-6119
Father Chuck Tham, Pastor

SEGUNDO RUIZ BELVIS CULTURAL CENTER
1632 N Milwaukee
Chicago, IL 60647
(773) 235-3988 Fax: (773) 235-8080
Web: www.ruizbelvis.org

SER-JOBS FOR PROGRESS, INC. OF LAKE COUNTY, ILLINOIS
Affiliate of SER-Jobs for Progress National, Inc.
117 N. Genesee St.
Waukegan, IL 60085
(847) 336-1004 Fax: (847) 336-1050
Dawn Erickson, Executive Director
Web: www.sernational.org

SERVICIO JEAN
1817 S. Loomis
Chicago, IL 60608
(312) 435-4550 Fax: (312) 421-0923
Hector Hernandez, Supervisor
Web: www.heartland/alliance.org

SIGMA LAMBDA BETA FRATERNITY
DePaul University, Lincoln Park
2311 N. Clifton Ave., #200
Chicago, IL 60614
(773) 325-7361 Fax: (773) 325-7359
Isaac M. Carter, Advisor
Email: slb@condor.depaul.edu
Web: www.depaul.edu/

Illinois State Univ.-Gamma Chapter
209 N. Sail Street, Apt. #1
Bloomington, IL 61761
(309) 454-3757 or (309) 438-2111

Luis Dies, Pres.

Western Illinois Univ.-Beta Chapter
P.O. Box 6053
Macomb, IL 61455
(309) 298-3204
Kimberly Branch, Advisor

SIGMA LAMBDA BETA, INTERNATIONAL
University of Illinois, Chicago
UIC Campus Programs, M/C 118
750 S. Halstead, #300 CCC
Chicago, IL 60607
(312) 413-5070
Manuel Rangel, President
Web: www.uic.edu

SOCIAL & EDUCATIONAL SERVICES (SES)
5244 N. Lakewood St.
Chicago, IL 60640
(773) 878-6035 Fax: (773) 878-6037
Elida Scalfi, Exec. Dir.

SOCIETY OF HISPANIC PROFESSIONAL ENGINEERS (SHPE)
1221 W. 142nd St.
E. Chicago, IN 46312
(219) 391-8357 Fax: (219) 391-8401

Midwest Regional Chicago Prof. Chapter
P.O. Box 2230
Chicago, IL 60690-2330
(630) 713-1172 Fax: (630) 713-1640
Jaime Viteri, President
Email: jviteri@lucent.com
Web: www.enteract.com/~shpe/

University of Illinois, Chicago
Campus Programs (M/C 118), #306CCC
750 S. Halsted
Chicago, IL 60607
(312) 355-0880 Fax: (312) 413-7577
Jason Perez, President
Email: jperez9@uic.edu
Web: http://SHPE.stuorg.uic.edu

University of Illinois, Urbana-Champaign
105 S. Goodwin Ave., #315
Urbana, IL 61801
(217) 333-3558 Fax: (217) 244-4974
Dean Paul Parker, Advisor

SOUTHWEST COMMUNITY CONGRESS
2832 W. 63rd St.
Chicago, IL 60629
(773) 436-6150 Fax: (773) 436-7135
Alfred Rodgers, Pres.
Email: scc10@juno.com

SPANISH ACTION COMMITTEE OF CHICAGO
2450-52 W. Division St.
Chicago, IL 60622
(773) 292-1052 Fax: (773) 292-1073
Leoncio Vásquez, Dir.

THE SPANISH CENTER OF JOLIET
309 N. Eastern Ave.
Joliet, IL 60432
(815) 727-3683 Fax: (815) 727-9459
Lois Nelson, Exec. Dir.

SPANISH COALITION FOR HOUSING
4035 W. North Ave.
Chicago, IL 60639
(773) 342-7575 Fax: (773) 342-8528
Ofelia Navarro, Exec. Dir.

SPANISH COALITION FOR JOBS, INC.
National Headquarters
2011 W. Pershing Rd.
Chicago, IL 60609
(773) 247-0707 Fax: (773) 247-3924
Kathleen S. Petefish, Executive Director

SPANISH COALITION FOR JOBS PLACEMENT OFFICE
1737 W. 18th St.
Chicago, IL 60608
(312) 243-3032 Fax: (312) 243-9109
Judith Nicholson, Office Manager

SPANISH INFORMATION SERVICES
The Chicago Public Library
400 S. State St. 10th Fl. South
Chicago, IL 60605
(312) 747-4790 Fax: (312) 747-4745
Lia Londoño, Director

SPANISH & PORTUGUESE TRANSLATORS ASSOCIATION
79 W. Monroe Ave.#1310

Chicago, IL 60603
(312) 236-3366 Fax: (312) 236-3370
Félix Stungevicius, Dir.

SPANISH-AMERICAN LANGUAGE NEWSPAPER AGENCY
55 E. Jackson Blvd. #1820
Chicago, IL 60604
(312) 368-4840

SPECIAL OPPORTUNITIES TO LEARN
4014 W. Chicago Ave.
Chicago, IL 60651
(773) 252-3320 Fax: (773) 252-3323
Kathy Englsman, Dir.

SSI COALITION
205 W. Monroe 3rd Fl.
Chicago, IL 60606-503
(312) 223-9600 or (800) 427-0766 TTY
Fax: (312) 223-9518
Email: ssic@ssic.org
Web: www.ssic.org

TOURIST OFFICE OF SPAIN
845 N. Michigan Ave.
Chicago, IL 60611
(312) 642-1992 Fax: (312) 642-9817
Beatriz Marco, Director
Email: chicago@tourspain.es
Web: www.okspain.org

TRINA DAVILA CENTER
Department of Human Services
3636 W. Armitage, First Fl.
Chicago, IL 60622
(312) 744-2014 Fax: (312) 744-6235

U.S. HISPANIC LEADERSHIP INSTITUTE
431 S. Dearborn St., #1203
Chicago, IL 60605
(312) 427-8683 Fax: (312) 427-5183
Juan Andrade Jr., President
Email: ushli@aol.com
Web: www.ushli.com

UNION FOR PUERTO RICAN STUDENTS
Northeastern Illinois University
5500 North St. Louis Ave.
Chicago, IL 60625
(773) 583-4050 x3805
Michael Rodriguez, President

UNITED STATES-MEXICO CHAMBER OF COMMERCE
Mid-America Chapter
150 N. Michigan Ave., #2910
Chicago, IL 60601
(312) 236-8745 Fax: (312) 781-5925
Leroy Allala, Director

UNITED WAY OF CHICAGO
560 W. Lake
Chicago, IL 60661
(312) 580-2800
Williams Ketchum, Pres.

VALOR CORPORATION
1850 W. 21st St.
Chicago, IL 60608
(312) 666-4511 or (312) 492-5936
Fax: (312) 666-6677
Vincent Allocco, Executive Director
Email: vallocco@elvalor.org
Web: www.elvalor.org

VIVA FAMILY CENTER
2516 W. Division St.
Chicago, IL 60622
(773) 252-6277 Fax: (773) 252-6866
Petra Porres, Exec. Director
Email: areyes@viv.chasi.org

VOICE OF THE PEOPLE IN UPTOWN, INC.
1456 W. Montrose Ave.
Chicago, IL 60613
(773) 769-2442
Deanne Mann

WEST TOWN CONCERNED CITIZENS COALITION
3524 W. Armitage Ave.
Chicago, IL 60647
(773) 235-2144 Fax: (773) 235-2159
Tito Vargas, Exec. Dir.
Email: westown@ameritech.com

WEST TOWN NEIGHBORHOOD HEALTH CENTER
2418 W. Division St.
Chicago, IL 60622
(312) 744-0943 Fax: (312) 744-5516
Georgina Rivera, Dir.

WICKER PARK CHAMBER OF COMMERCE
1608 N. Milwaukee Ave., #204-205
Chicago, IL 60622
(773) 384-2672 Fax: (773) 384-7525
Kara Salgado, Director
Web: www.wickerpark.org

Y.M.C.A.
Metropolitan Chicago
801 N. Dearborn
Chicago, IL 60610
(312) 932-1200 Fax: (312) 932-1318
Tino Montella, Pres.

Y.M.C.A. -SOUTH CHICAGO
South Chicago
3039 E. 91st. St.
Chicago, IL 60617
(773) 721-9100 Fax: (773) 721-9330
Annete Teriquez, Dir.

YOUTH GUIDANCE
53 W. Jackson Blvd. #950
Chicago, IL 60604
(312) 435-3900 Fax: (312) 435-3917
Nancy Johnstone, Dir.

YOUTH OUTREACH SERVICES
6417 W. Irving Park Rd.
Chicago, IL 60634
(773) 777-7112 Fax: (773) 777-7611
Email: info@yos.org
Web: www.yos.org

YOUTH SERVICE PROJECT, INC.
3942 W. North Ave.
Chicago, IL 60647
(773) 772-6270 Fax: (312) 772-8755
Mary Scott, Director

INDIANA

ALSE CLEMENTE CENTER, INC.
3616 Elm St.
E. Chicago, IN 46312
(219) 391-8486 Fax: (219) 391-8394
Gloria Balerini, President

BRAZILIAN ASSOCIATION (BAIU)
Indiana University
La Casa/ Latino Cultural Center
715 E. 7th St.
Bloomington, IN 47401
(812) 855-0174
Marlene Andrade Martins, Coordinator
Email: baiu@indiana.edu
Web: www.indiana.edu/~baiu/

CENTER FOR LATIN AMERICAN AND CARIBBEAN STUDIES
Indiana University, Bloomington
1125 E. Atwater
Bloomington, IN 47405
(812) 855-9097 Fax: (812) 855-5345
Jeff Gould, Director

DELTA PHI MU
1001 Stewart Center, Box 631
West Lafayette, IN 47906
Email: dphi@expert.cc.purdue.edu
Web: http://www.latinogreeks.com/greeks/dphimu.htm

DIOCESAN HISPANIC MINISTRY
317 N. New Jersey St.
Indianapolis, IN 46204
(317) 637-3983 Fax: (317) 637-0111
Rev. Michael O'Mara, Pastor

DIOCESAN HISPANIC MINISTRY COORDINATOR
908 Clay St.
Jasper, IN 47546
(812) 634-7206 Fax: (812) 634-7809
Rev. Eugene Heerdink, Pastor

DIOCESAN HISPANIC MINISTRY COORD.
114 W. Monroe St.
Goshen, IN 46526
(219) 533-3385 Fax: (219) 533-1814
Jodi Magallanes, Hispanic Coordinator
Email: juan@bnin.net

DIOCESE OF EVANSVILLE
Hispanic Affairs
908 Clay St.
Jasper, IN 47546
(812) 634-7206 Fax: (812) 634-7809
Rev. Gene Heerdink, Hisp. Ministry Coord.
Email: gheerdink@evansville-diocese.org

DIOCESE OF FORT WAYNE-SOUTH BEND
Hispanic Affairs
125 N. Harrison
Warsaw, IN 48580
(219) 267-5842 Fax: (219) 268-1030
Rev. Paul Beuter, Coord. for Hispanic Ministry

DIOCESE OF GARY
Hispanic Affairs
1709 E. 138 St.
East Chicago, IN 46312
(219) 397-2125 or (219) 397-6179
Fax: (219) 397-2168
Angel Torres, Director for Hispanic Ministry
Email: acthchile@aol.com

DIOCESE OF INDIANAPOLIS
Hispanic Affairs
P.O. Box 1410
317 N. New Jersey St.
Indianapolis, IN 46204
(317) 637-3983 Fax: (317) 236-1406
Rev. Kenneth Taylor

DIOCESE OF LAFAYETTE IN INDIANA
Hispanic Affairs
401 W. Buckingham Dr.
Marion, IN 46952
(765) 662-6078
Deacon Domingo Castillo, Coord. for Hispanic Min.

EL BUEN VECINO, INC.
P.O. Box 3390, 404 South Walnut St., 2nd Floor
South Bend, IN 46619
(219) 287-8228
Sara Haber, Founder and CEO

GREATER FT. WAYNE HISPANIC CHAMBER OF COMMERCE
826 Ewing St.
Ft. Wayne, IN 46802
(219) 422-6697 Fax: (219) 493-4585
Al Rodriguez, President

HISPANIC CENTER-EL CENTRO HISPANO
Community Centers of Indianapolis, Inc.
617 East North St.
Indianapolis, IN 46204
(317) 636-6551 Fax: (317) 686-6500
Arturo Bustamante, Director

HISPANIC CENTER/EL CENTRO HISPANO
Hisp. AIDS Prevention Prog. In Indiana
617 E. North St.
Indianapolis, IN 46204
(317) 636-6551 Fax: (317) 686-6500
Arturo Bustamante, Director

HISPANIC EDUCATION CENTER
580 E Stevens St.
Indianapolis, IN 46203
(317) 634-5022 Fax: (317) 634-0442
Marikay Duffy, Exec. Dir.
Email: hec_indy@yahoo.com

INDIANA HISPANIC CHAMBER OF COMMERCE
342 N. Senate Ave.
Indianapolis, IN 46204
(317) 655-7068 Fax: (317) 879-1441
Ed Colon, President

INDIANA REGIONAL MINORITY SUPPLIER DEVELOPMENT COUNCIL
NMSDC
1100 West 42nd Street, Suite 200
Indianapolis, IN 46208
(317) 823-2110 Fax: (317) 923-2204
Donald E. Jones, Executive Director

INTER-UNIVERSITY PROGRAM FOR LATINO RESEARCH
University of Notre Dame
P.O. Box 764
Notre Dame, IN 46556
(219) 631-9781 Fax: (219) 631-3522
Hilberto Gilverto, Executive Director
Web: ww.ND.edu/~iuplr

LACASA OF NW INDIANA, INC.
LATIN AMERICAN COMMUNITY ALLIANCE FOR SUPPORT ASSISTANCE
837 W. 45th Ave.
Gary, IN 46408
(219) 884-0095/(219) 980-0991 Fax: (219) 884-0384
June M. Long, Director
Email: lacasa@surfnetinc.com

LATIN AMERICAN MUSIC CENTER
Indiana University, Bloomington
School of Music
Bloomington, IN 47405
(812) 855-2991 Fax: (812) 855-2991
Dr. Carmen Tellez, Director
Email: lamc@indiana.edu
Web: www.music.indiana.edu/som/lamc

LATINO CULTURAL CENTER / LA CASA
Indiana University, Bloomington
715 E. 7th St.
Bloomington, IN 47405
(812) 855-0174
Monica G. Gonzales, Program Assistant

LATINOS UNIDOS
Indiana University, Bloomington
La Casa
715 E. 7th St.
Bloomington, IN 47405
(812) 855-0174
Monica G. Gonzales, Program Assistant

NATIONAL CONSORTIUM FOR GRADUATE DEGREES FOR MINORITIES IN ENGINEERING AND SCIENCE, INC. (GEM)
The GEM Center - National Headquarters
P.O. Box 537
Notre Dame, IN 46556
(219) 631-7771 Fax: (219) 287-1486
E. George Simms, Executive Director

NATIONAL LEAGUE OF CUBAN AMERICAN COMMUNITY-BASED CENTERS
Educational Opportunities Center
2513 S. Calhoun St.
Fort Wayne, IN 46807
(219) 745-5421 Fax: (219) 744-1363
Graciela Beecher, Director

PUERTO RICAN STUDENT ASSOCIATION
Indiana University, Bloomington
La Casa, 715 E. 7th St.
Bloomington, IN 47405
(812) 855-0174
Monica G. Gonzales, Program Assistant

SIGMA LAMBDA BETA FRATERNITY
Indiana University, Bloomington
La Casa, 715 E. 7th St.
Bloomington, IN 47405
(812) 855-0174
Monica G. Gonzales, Program Assistant

SOCIETY OF HISPANIC PROFESSIONAL ENGINEERS (SHPE)
Purdue University Calumet
2233 171th St.
Hammond, IN 46323-2094
(219) 989-2369 Fax: (219)989-3260
Ismael Muhammad Nieves, President
Web: www.shpe.org

TELAMON CORPORATION
Indiana Office 11/Transition Resources
3303 Plaza Dr., #3
New Albany, IN 47150
(812) 941-1617 Fax: (812) 941-1618
Bob Young, Regional Manager
Web: www.telamon.org

Indiana Office 12/Transition Resources
36 W. 5th St., #3
Peru, IN 46970
(765) 472-3562 Fax: (765) 473-7361
Kathleen Brooks, Office Manager
Web: www.telamon.org

Indiana Office 13/Transition Resources
100 W. 9th St., #102
Rochester, IN 46975
(219) 223-8542 Fax: (219) 223-6172
Lorna Stroschein, Office Manager
Web: www.telamon.org

Indiana Office 2/Transition Resources
P.O. Box 307
Kokomo, IN 46903-0307
(765) 457-5201 Fax: (765) 457-5202
Eva Mejia, Regional Manager
Web: www.telamon.org

Indiana Office 3/Transition Resources
620 Green Rd.
Madison, IN 47250
(812) 273-5451 Fax: (812) 273-1881
Bob Young, Regional Manager
Web: www.telamon.org

Indiana Office 4/Transition Resources
850 N. Miller Ave.

Marion, IN 46952
(765) 664-7275 Fax: (765) 664-7260
Miguel De Mott, Office Manager
Email: mdemott@transitionresources.org
Web: www.telamon.org

Indiana Office 5/Transition Resources
2015 W. Western Ave., #410
South Bend, IN 46619
(219) 237-9407 Fax: (219) 237-9408
Norma Cruz, Regional Manager
Web: www.telamon.org

Indiana Office 7/Transition Resources
1805 Smith St.
Logansport, IN 46947
(219) 722-6652 Fax: (219) 753-8653
Terri Simons, Office Manager
Web: www.telamon.org

Indiana Office 8/Transition Resources
80 W. Canal St.
Wabash, IN 46992
(219) 563-8421 Fax: (219) 563-8424
Carolyn Biltz, Office Manager
Web: www.telamon.org

Indiana State Office/Transition Resources
2511 E. 46th St., #J2
Indianapolis, IN 46205
(317) 547-1924 Fax: (317) 547-6594
Diane Swift, State Director
Web: www.telamon.org

IOWA

ARCHDIOCESE OF DUBUQUE
Hispanic Ministries-Catholic Charities
P.O. Box 1309, 1229 Mt. Loretta
Dubuque, IA 52002
(319) 556-2580 Fax: (319) 556-5464
Rev. James L. Yeast, LMSW
Email: dbqcccd@arch.put.k12.ia.us

Hispanic Ministry Office, St. Bridget Church
P.O. Box 369, 135 W. Williams
Postville, IA 52162
(319) 864-3138 Fax: (319) 864-3138
Rev. Lloyd Paul Ouderkirk
Email: dbqchm@netins.net

CASA LATINA
1121 Pierce St.
Sioux City, IA 51105
(712) 252-4259
Christy Nicolsen, Director
Email: lacasalatina@excite.com

CHICANO HISPANIC ASSOCIATION FOR LEGAL EDUCATION
Iowa Memorial Union, University of Iowa
382 Boyd Law Bldg. 145 Imu
Iowa City, IA 52242
(319) 335-3059 Fax: (319) 353-2245
Carlos Serrato, Director

COMMISSION ON LATINO AFFAIRS DEPARTMENT OF HUMAN RIGHTS
National Headquarters
Lucas State Office Bldg., 1st Floor
Des Moines, IA 50319
(515) 281-4070 Fax: (515) 242-6119
Sylvia Tijerina, Director
Email: stijeri@max.state.ia.us

DIOCESAN HISPANIC MINISTRY COORDINATOR
516 Filmar St.
Davenport, IA 52802
(319) 322-3383 Fax: (319) 322-3383
Rev. Rudolph Juarez, Pastor

P.O. Box 479
Dubuque, IA 52004
(319) 556-2580 Fax: (319) 556-5464
Ilene Govern, Contact

12 W. Linn St.
Marshalltown, IA 50158
(641) 753-7815 Fax: (641) 752-6277
Christin Feagan, Director of Hispanic Ministry

DIOCESE OF DAVENPORT
Hispanic Affairs
2706 N. Gaines St.
Davenport, IA 52804
(319) 324-1911 Fax: (319) 324-5842
Fr. Rudolph Juarez, Vicar for Hispanic Ministry

Hispanic Affairs
519 Fillmore St.
Davenport, IA 52802

(319) 322-1450 Fax: (319) 324-5842
Sr. Charlotte Seubert, Coord. for Hispanic
Ministry

DIOCESE OF DES MOINES
Hispanic Affairs
1271 E. 9th St.
Des Moines, IA 50316
(515) 266-6695 Fax: (515) 266-9803
Rev. Kevin Cameron, Dir. of Hispanic Affairs
Email: kevincameron@cwix.com

DIOCESE OF SIOUX CITY
Office of Minorities and Human Dev.
P.O. Box 3379
1821 Jackson St.
Sioux City, IA 51102
(712) 255-1637 Fax: (712) 233-7598
Rev. Randy Guerdet, Co-Director

**HISPANIC AMERICAN CLUB OF MASON
CITY**
1313 Meadow Brook Dr.
Mason City, IA 50401
(515) 424-4282 Fax: (515) 424-4282
Nick Aguilera, Pres.

HISPANIC AMERICAN STUDENT COUNCIL
Minority Student Affairs
2224 Student Service Bldg.#280
Ames, IA 50011-2224
(515) 294-6338 Fax: (515) 294-6397
Susana Rundquest, Program Assistant
Email: omsa@iastate.edu

LA CASA LATINA, INC.
Affiliate to NCLR
206 6th St., 715 Douglas St.
Sioux City, IA 51101
(712) 252-4259 Fax: (712) 252-5655
Christy Nicotaisen, Director

LAS GUADALUPANAS
Sacred Heart Church
3425 Ave. Q
Ft. Madison, IA 52627
(319) 372-4408
Aurelia Martínez, Vice President

LATINO STUDENT UNION
Iowa Memorial Union
Room #46 S.A.C.
Iowa City, IA 52242
(319) 335-3059 Fax: (319) 353-2245
Carlos Serrato, Director

**LEAGUE OF UNITED LATIN AMERICAN
CITIZENS (LULAC)**
1809 Hillside St.
West Des Moines, IA 50265
(515) 225-6865 Fax: (515) 261-7270
Ila R. Plasencia, Past National Vice President
Web: www.lulac.org

Council #304
P.O. Box 542
Ft. Madison, IA 52627
(319) 372-3287 or (319) 372-1722 (H)
Sheila Garcia, Pres.

LOS AMIGOS CLUB
P. O. Box 5674
Cedar Rapids, IA 52406-5674
(319) 364-1339
Pat Arenas, Secretary

LOS CURANDEROS
The University of Iowa, 126 CAMB
Iowa City, IA 52242
(319) 335-3059 Fax: (319) 353-2245
Carlos Serrato, Advisor

**MEXICAN AMERICAN YOUNG ACHIEVERS
SOCIETY**
Iowa State University
301 Beardshear
Ames, IA 50011
(515) 294-6338
Susana Rundquest, Advisor

MEXICAN FIESTA COMMITTEE, THE
1231 32nd St.
Ft. Madison, IA 52627
(319) 372-9537
Arturo Prado, President

**MIDWEST EDUCATIONAL RESOURCE
DEVELOPMENT FUND, INC.**
Affiliate of NCLR
1240 E. 12th St.
Des Moines, IA 50316
(515) 261-7270 (w) or (515) 225-6865 (h)
Fax: (515) 262-4036
R. Plasencia, President

PROTEUS, INC.
P. O. Box 10385, 175 NW 57th Pl.
Des Moines, IA 50306
(515) 244-5694 Fax: (515) 244-4166
Terry Meek, Executive Director

**QUAD CITIES MEXICAN AMERICAN
ORGANIZATION, INC.**
COL Ballroom
P.O. Box 2557
Davenport, IA 52809
(319) 386-5174 or (319) 322-4431
Fax: (319) 322-1448
Michael Cervantes, Operations Mngr.

SACRED HEART CATHOLIC CHURCH
221 S. Jackson
Eagle Grove, IA 50533
(515) 448-4765 Fax: (515) 448-4765
Todd Flowerday, Pastoral Associate
Email: dbq070@netins.net
Web: www.netins.net/showcase/sacredheart/

SIGMA LAMBDA GAMMA
University of Iowa
#145 Iowa Memorial Union
Iowa City, IA 52242
(319) 335-3059 Fax: (319) 353-2245
Mary Peterson, Director

**SOCIETY OF HISPANIC PROFESSIONAL
ENGINEERS (SHPE)**
Iowa State University
403B Marston Hall
Ames, IA 50011
(515) 294-6385
Ivan Maldonado, Advisor
Email: maldonad@iastate.edu
Web: www.shpe.org

SPANISH CLUB
Iowa State University
300 Pearson Hall
Ames, IA 50011
(515) 294-9015 Fax: (515) 294-9914
Elas Lorenzo, Faculty Adivsor
Email: elorenzo@iastate.edu
Web: www.webspawner.com/users/
spanishclub/

YWCA
425 Lafayette
Waterloo, IA 50703
(319) 234-7589 Fax: 319234-3462
Pam Hays, Exec. Director

KANSAS

AMERICAM GI FORUM OF THE U.S.
539 SE Dupont Rd.
Tecumseh, KS 66542
(785) 379-5690 (h) or (785) 350-3111 (w)
Louis Serrano, Sgt. at Arms

1000 N. Cheyenne
Ulysses, KS 67880
(316) 356-4070 (h) or (316) 356-4079 (w)
Fax: (316) 356-1195
José Olivas, National Treasurer

**ARCHDIOCESE OF KANSAS CITY IN
KANSAS**
Casa Juan Diego
229 S. 8th St.
Kansas City, KS 66101
(913) 342-1276 Fax: (913) 281-1256
Rev. Ramón Gaitán, OAR

Hispanic Affairs
12615 Parallel Pkwy.
Kansas City, KS 66109
(913) 721-1570 x148 Fax: (913) 721-1577
Peter Jaramillo, Director for Hispanic Ministry
Email: p.m.jaramillo@worldnet.att.net

**CATHOLIC CHARITIES-SOCIAL SERVICES,
INC.**
Refugee Resettlement
437 N. Topeka
Wichita, KS 67202
(316) 264-8344 Fax: (316) 267-4222
Bill Gress, Program Director

CATHOLIC SOCIAL SERVICE, INC.
Migration and Refugee Services
437 N Topeka
Wichita, KS 67202
(316) 264-0197 Fax: (316) 264-4442
David Osio, Program Director
Email: doco@wkscatholiccharities.org
Web: www.wkscatholiccharities.org

**CENTER FOR INTERCULTURAL
COMMUNICATIONS, INC.**
1333 S. 27th St.
Kansas City, KS 66106
(913) 677-0100 Fax: (913) 362-8250
Gene T. Chávez, Co-Director

CENTER OF LATIN AMERICAN STUDIES
University of Kansas
107 Lippincott Hall
Lawrence, KS 66045
(785) 864-4213 Fax: (785) 864-3000
Elizabeth Kuznesof, Director
Email: latamst@ukans.edu

**DEPARTMENT OF COMMERCE AND
HOUSING**
**Office of Women and Minority-Owned
Business**
700 SW Harrison, #1300
Topeka, KS 66603-3712
(785) 296-3481 Fax: (785) 296-3490
Rhonda Egans, Director
Web: www.kansascommerce.com

DIOCESAN HISPANIC MINISTRY
1333 S. 27th St.
Kansas City, KS 66106
(913) 677-0100 Fax: (913) 362-8250
Lisa Castro, Supervisor

DIOCESE OF DODGE CITY
Hispanic Ministry Office
P.O. Box 137, 910 Central Ave.
Dodge City, KS 67801-0137
(316) 223-3442
Rev. Ted Skalsky

DIOCESE OF SALINA
Hispanic Affairs
P.O. Box 980, 103 N. Ninth St.
Salina, KS 67402
(913) 827-8746
, Hispanic Ministry Coordinator

DIOCESE OF WICHITA
Hispanic Affairs
437 N. Topeka
Wichita, KS 67202
(316) 269-5851 Fax: (316) 269-5852
Irma S. Nolla, Hispanic Ministry Director

EDUCATIONAL TALENT SEARCH
Gateway Tower II, #1019
Kansas City, KS 66101
(913) 342-9823
Fax: (913) 371-8558
Ngondi Kamatoka, Director

**EL CENTRO DE SERVICIOS PARA
HISPANOS**
216 NE, Branner
Topeka, KS 66616
(785) 232-8207 Fax: (785) 232-8834
Manuel Pérez, Administrator

EL CENTRO, INC.
Affiliate of NCLR
1333 S. 27th St.
Kansas City, KS 66106
(913) 677-0100 Fax: (913) 362-8250
Richard A. Ruiz, Executive Director

GARDEN CITY SER
**Affiliate of SER-Jobs for Progress
National, Inc.**
304 N. Main, #201
Garden City, KS 67846
(316) 275-2181
Grace Suárez, Executive Director
Web: www.sernational.org

GUADALUPE CLINIC
940 S. St. Francis
Wichita, KS 67211
(316) 264-8974 Fax: (316) 262-4938
Marlene Dreiling, Director

HARVEST AMERICA CORPORATION
P.O. Box 752, 212 East 17th Street
Goodland, KS 67635-0752
(785) 899-3878 Fax: (785) 899-6651
Susana Rodríguez, Area Director
Email: hamerica@goodland.ixks.com

118 1/2 Grant Ave.
Garden City, KS 67845-5421
(316) 275-1619 Fax: (316) 275-1762
Lidia Acosta, Assistant Area Director

P. O. Box 770
211 North 4th Street

Leoti, KS 67816-0770
(316) 375-2548 Fax: (316) 375-2410
Susana Rodríguez, Area Director

1201 First Street, Space B
Dodge City, KS 67801-3919
(316) 225-7022
Martha Archuleta, Area Director

c/o Job Service
807 South Kansas Ave.
Liberal, KS 67901-4193
(316) 624-1864
Lidia Acosta, Assistant Area Director

National Headquarters
14th & Metropolitan St.
Kansas City, KS 66103
(913) 342-2121 Fax: (913) 342-2861
Michelle Olson, Director of Program Operations
Email: molson@harvestamerica.org

**HISPANIC AMERICAN LEADERSHIP
ORGANIZATION**
Garden City Community College
801 Campus Dr.
Garden City, KS 67846
(316) 272-0303
Monte Soza, President

HISPANIC AMERICAN LEADERSHIP ORG.
Kansas State University
224 Anderson Hall
Manhattan, KS 66506
(785) 532-6436 Fax: (785) 532-6337
Melissa Validez, President

Wichita State University
1845 N. Fairmount
Wichita, KS 67260-0066
(316)978-3022
Delia García, President
Email: delia@latino.com
Web: www.twsu.edu/~halo/

**KANSAS ADVISORY COMMITTEE ON
HISPANIC AFFAIRS (KACHA)**
National Headquarters Affiliate of NCLR
1430 SW Topeka Blvd.
Topeka, KS 66612-1853
(785) 296-3465 Fax: (785) 296-8118
Tina De La Rosa, Executive Director
Email: tdelarosa@hr.state.ks.us

LA FAMILIA COMMUNITY CENTER
841 W. 21st St.
Wichita, KS 67203
(316) 267-1700 Fax: (316) 267-7112
Jacqueline Arenado, Director

**LULAC-NATIONAL EDUCATIONAL
SERVICES CENTER, INC. (LNESC)**
801 Campus Dr.
Garden City, KS 67846
(316) 276-9621 Fax: (316) 276-9630
Lydia González, Area Director
Web: www.lulac.org

**MANA - A NATIONAL LATINA
ORGANIZATION**
Topeka Chapter
3317 SE, Peck Rd.
Topeka, KS 66605
(785) 861-2730 Fax: (785) 861-2906
Patti Valdivia, Chapter President
Email: hermana2@aol.com
Web: www.hermana.org

MEXICAN-AMERICAN MINISTRIES
311 N. Grant
Liberal, KS 67901
(316) 624-6865 Fax: (316) 624-4723
Donna Sánchez, Community Developer/
Organizer
Email: ummam@midusa.net

**NATIONAL ASSOCIATION FOR HISPANIC
ELDERLY**
Kansas City Office/Project Ayuda
1333 S. 27th St., #220
Kansas City, KS 66106
(913) 722-1155 Fax: (913) 722-6646
Terri K. Bookless, Project Coordinator
Email: tbookless@aol.com

**NATIONAL LATINO PEACE OFFICERS
ASSOCIATION (NLPOA)**
Greater Kansas City Chapter
320 S. Kansas Ave., #100
Topeka, KS 66603
(877) 657-6200 or (913) 573-6019
Gregory Conchola, Sr., Chapter President
Email: gconchola@aol.com
Web: www.nlpoa.com

REFORMA
Heartland Chapter
P.O. Box 2933
Shawnee Mission, KS 66201
(913) 722-7400 or (913) 261-2345
Fax: (913) 722-7402
Jean Hatfield, Chapter President
Email: hatfield@jcl.lib.ks.us
Web: www.skyways.org/orgs/reforma/
hearthom.html

SER-CORPORATION OF KANSAS, INC.
Affiliate of SER-Jobs for Progress
National, Inc.
709 E. 21st St.
Wichita, KS 67214
(316) 264-5372 Fax: (316) 264-0194
Richard López, Executive Director
Web: www.sernational.org

**SOCIETY OF HISPANIC PROFESSIONAL
ENGINEERS (SHPE)**
University of Kansas
4010 Learned Hall
Lawrence, KS 66045
(785) 864-3620
Florence Boldridge, Dir. of Diversity Programs
Web: www.shpe.org

SPANISH SPEAKING OFFICE
1333 South 27th Street
Kansas City, KS 66106
(913) 384-8904
José Carrillo, Contact

UNITED METHODIST WESTERN KANSAS
Mexican-American Ministries
P. O. Box 766, 224 N. Taylor
Garden City, KS 67846-0766
(316) 275-1766 Fax: (316) 275-4729
Penny Schwab, Executive Director

**UNITED METHODIST WESTERN KANSAS
MEXICAN-AMERICAN MINISTRIES**
Dodge City Care Center
708 Ave. H
Dodge City, KS 67801
(316) 225-0625 Fax: (316) 225-2422
Martha Mendoza, Director

**UNITED METHODIST WESTERN KANSAS
MEXICAN-AMERICAN MINISTRIES**
Garden City Care Center
224 N. Taylor
Garden City, KS 67846
(316) 275-5634 Fax: (316) 275-4729
Delores Esquivel, Director

Liberal Care Center
311 N. Grant
Liberal, KS 67901
(316) 624-6865 Fax: (316) 624-4723
Donna Sánchez Jennings, Director

Ulysses/Johnson/Santanta Care Centers
321 W Grant
Ulysses, KS 67880
(316) 275-1766 Fax: (316) 624-4723
José Olivas, Director

KENTUCKY

ARCHDIOCESE OF LOUISVILLE
Office of Multicultural Ministry
1200 S. Shelby St.
Louisville, KY 40203
(502) 636-0296 x218 Fax: (502) 636-2379
Adam Ruiz
Email: aruiz@archlou.org

**DIOCESAN HISPANIC MINISTRY
COORDINATOR**
P.O. Box 12350
Louisville, KY 40201
(502) 585-3291 Fax: (502) 585-2466
Annette Turner, Hispanic Coordinator
Web: www.archlou.org

DIOCESE OF COVINGTON
Hispanic Affairs
P.O. Box 18548
947 Donaldson Rd.
Erlanger, KY 41018-0548
(606) 283-6337 or (888) 889-2155
Fax: (606) 283-6334
Luis Fernando Poppe, Dir. for Hispanic Ministry
Email: fpoppe@dioofcovky.org

DIOCESE OF LEXINGTON
Hispanic Affairs
1310 W. Main St.
Lexington, KY 40508-2040

(859) 253-1933 x308 Fax: (859) 254-6284
Sr. Sandra Delgado, OP, Dir. for Hisp. Ministry
Email: sdelgado@cdlex.org

DIOCESE OF OWENSBORO
Hispanic Affairs
600 Locust St.
Owensboro, KY 42301
(270) 764-1983 Fax: (270) 683-6883
Rev. Stan Puryear, Dir. for Hispanic Ministry
Email: puryear502@aol.com

**KENTUCKIANA MINORITY SUPPLIER
DEVELOPMENT COUNCIL**
NMSDC
600 West Main Street, 2nd Floor
Louisville, KY 40202
(502) 625-0135 Fax: (502) 625-0082
Michael A. Bateman, President

**LOUISVILLE MINORITY BUSINESS
DEVELOPMENT CENTER**
609 W. Maine St. 3rd Floor
Louisville, KY 40202
(502) 589-6232 Fax: (502) 589-3228
Brenda Bankstone, Exec. Director
Email: louisvillembdc@attglobal.net

**NATIONAL ASSOCIATION OF HISPANIC
AND LATINO STUDIES (NAHLS)**
Morehead State University
212 Rader Hall
Morehead, KY 40351-1689
(606) 783-2650 Fax: (606) 783-5046
Lemuel Berry, Jr., Ph.D., Executive Director
Email: l.berry@msuacad.morehead/st.edu

LOUISIANA

ARCHDIOCESE OF NEW ORLEANS
Apostolado Hispano
P.O. Box 19104, 3368 Esplanade Ave.
New Orleans, LA 70119
(504) 486-1983 or (504) 482-5883
Fax: (504) 486-3985
Martín Gutiérrez, Director of Hispanic Ministry
Email: mgutier740@aol.com

**ASOCIACIÓN DE ABOGADOS HISPANOS
DE LOUISIANA**
2 Canal Street, #2305
New Orleans, LA 70130
(504) 488-3726 or (504) 523-6496
Fax: (504) 525-2846
Cesar Bulgors, President

**ASOCIACIÓN DE DAMAS VOLUNTARIAS
DE COLOMBIA**
4712 Richland
Metairie, LA 70002
(504) 455-5339
María Consuelo Hursel, President

BRAZILIAN ASSOCIATION
Louisiana State University
Chemistry Department, Box C-13
Baton Rouge, LA 70894
(504) 388-2141 or (504) 388-5160
Dr. Power, Advisor
Email: power@unix1.sncc.lsu.edu

COLOMBIAN STUDENT ASSOCIATION
Louisiana State University
Office for Student Organization Services
332-A LSU Union
Baton Rouge, LA 70894
(504) 388-4207 or (504) 388-5160
Luz Barona, Advisor
Email: csa@unix1.sncc.lsu.edu

DIOCESE OF ALEXANDRIA
Hispanic Affairs
2618 Vanderburg Dr.
Alexandria, LA 71303
(318) 445-2401 Fax: (318) 448-6121
Rev. Pedro Sierra, Dir. for Hispanic Ministry
Email: info@diocesealex.org

DIOCESE OF BATON ROUGE
Hispanic Affairs
5850 Florida Blvd.
Baton Rouge, LA 70806-4247
(225) 927-8700 Fax: (225) 927-8787
Rev. Rafael Juantorena, Dir. for Hisp. Ministry
Email: apostolado2@juno.com

DIOCESE OF HOUMA-THIBODAUX
Hispanic Affairs
P.O. Box 966
721 Canal Blvd.
Thibodaux, LA 70302
(504) 446-1387 or (504) 446-1388
Fax: (504) 446-6571

Rev. John L. Ruiz, Hisp. Ministry Coordinator
Email: frjohn@mobiletel.com

DIOCESE OF LAFAYETTE IN LOUISIANA
Hispanic Affairs
1408 Carmel Ave.
Lafayette, LA 70501
(337) 261-5542 Fax: (337) 261-5635
Rev. Arturo Lozano, Dir. for Hispanic Ministry

DIOCESE OF LAKE CHARLES
Hispanic Affairs
4029 Ave. G
Lake Charles, LA 70615
(318) 439-7439 Fax: (318) 439-7413
Rev. Edward Lavine, Vicar for Hispanic Ministry

DIOCESE OF LAKE CHARLES
Hispanic Affairs
P.O. Box 146
Kinder, LA 70648
(337) 738-5612 Fax: (337) 738-2728
Rev. Carlos A. GarcEia Cardona, Director for
Hispanic Ministry
Email: carlospeto@hotmail.com

DIOCESE OF SHREVEPORT
Hispanic Affairs
939 Jordan St.
Shreveport, LA 71101-4391
(318) 221-5296
Rev. Rigoberto Betancurt Cortez, Chaplain for
Hispanic Ministry

DIOCESE OF SHREVEPORT
Hispanic Affairs
3500 Fairfield Ave.
Shreveport, LA 71104
(318) 868-4441 or (318) 219-7288
Fax: (318) 868-4605
Elisa C. Milazzo, Coord. for Hispanic Ministry
Email: emilazzo@dioshpt.org

GUATEMALAN STUDENT ASSOCIATION
Louisiana State University
Office for Student Organization Services
332-A LSU Union
Baton Rouge, LA 70894
(504) 388-5942 or (504) 388-5160
William Davidson, Advisor
Email: wvdavid@lsuvm.sncc.lsu.edu

**GULF SOUTH MINORITY SUPPLIER
DEVELOPMENT COUNCIL**
NMSDC
935 Gravier Street, Suite 2023
New Orleans, LA 70112
(504) 523-7110 or (504) 592-6645
Patrice A. Williams-Smith, Executive Director

**HISPANIC AMERICAN MEDICAL
ASSOCIATION OF LOUISIANA**
3321 Florida Ave.
Kenner, LA 70065
(504) 465-0800 Fax: (504) 461-8516
Raúl Rodríguez, President

HONDURAN STUDENT ASSOCIATION
Louisiana State University
Office for Student Organization Services
332-A LSU Union
Baton Rouge, LA 70894
(504) 388-5942 or (504) 388-5160
William Davidson, Advisor
Email: wvdavid@lsuvm.sncc.lsu.edu

**JEFFERSON PARISH HUMAN SERVICES
AUTHORITY**
3101 W. Napoleon Ave., #226
Metairie, LA 70001
(504) 846-6902 Fax: (504) 838-5591
María Zuñiga-Arzu, HIV/AIDS Prevention
Counselor

**LA ALIANZA DEL DERECHO / HISPANIC
LAW STUDENT ASSOCIATION**
Tulane University
Office of Multicultural Affairs
223 University Center
New Orleans, LA 70118
(504) 865-5181 Fax: (504) 862-8795
Carolyn Barber-Pierre, Advisor

**LATIN AMERICAN MEDICAL STUDENT
ASSOCIATION (LAMSA)**
Tulane University
Office of Multicultural Affairs
223 University Center
New Orleans, LA 70118
(504) 865-5181 Fax: (504) 862-8795
Carolyn Barber-Pierre, Advisor

LATIN AND AMERICAN STUDENT

ASSOCIATION (LASA)
Tulane University
Office of Multicultural Affairs
223 University Center
New Orleans, LA 70118
(504) 865-5181 Fax: (504) 862-8795
Carolyn Barber-Pierre, Advisor

LATINOS UNIDOS
4215 S. Carrollton Ave.
New Orleans, LA 70119
(504) 486-1771 Fax: (504) 483-7992
Roberto C. Prieto, President

**LOUISIANA HISPANIC CHAMBER OF
COMMERCE**
P.O. Box 5985
Metairie, LA 70009-5985
(504) 885-4262
Max Moreno, President

MEXICAN STUDENT ASSOCIATION
Louisiana State University
Office of Student Organizations Services
332-A LSU Union
Baton Rouge, LA 70894
(504) 388-8633 or (504) 388-5160
José L. Montiel, Advisor
Email: JMonta@lsu.edu

MEXICAN STUDENTS AT TULANE
Tulane University
Office of Multicultural Affairs
223 University Center
New Orleans, LA 70118
(504) 865-5181 Fax: (504) 862-8795
Carolyn Barber-Pierre, Advisor

**NATIONAL ASSOCIATION FOR HISPANIC
ELDERLY**
New Orleans Office/Project Ayuda
4321 Magnolia St.
New Orleans, LA 70115
(504) 899-2707 Fax: (504) 891-8226
Alfredo Sánchez, Project Coordinator

**NATIONAL ASSOCIATION OF HISPANIC
INVESTMENT BANKERS AND ADVISORS**
National Headquarters
4037 Tulane Ave., #100
New Orleans, LA 70119
(504) 482-4116 Fax: (504) 488-8354
Miguel Uria, Chairman
Email: nahiba@aol.com

**ROGER THAYER STONE CENTER FOR
LATIN AMERICAN STUDIES**
Tulane University
100 Jones Hall
New Orleans, LA 70118
(504) 865-5164 Fax: (504) 865-6719
Dr. Thomas Reese, Director
Web: www.tulane.edu/~clas

SOCIEDAD ESPAÑOLA DE LOUISIANA
200 Industrial Ave.
New Orleans, LA 70121
(504) 831-2961 Fax: (504) 838-8969
Eduardo Guevara, Member

**SOCIETY OF HISPANIC PROFESSIONAL
ENGINEERS (SHPE)**
Louisiana State University
Dept. of Electrical & Computer Engineering
#102 EE Bldg.
Baton Rouge, LA 70803-5901
(225) 388-5537 Fax: (504) 388-5200
Jorge L. Aravena, Coordinator

**SPANISH AMERICAN BUSINESS
ASSOCIATION (SABA)**
801 N. Broad St.
New Orleans, LA 70119
(504) 482-9142
Félix Figueroa, President

UNIDAD HISPANOAMERICANA
3600 Airline Hwy.
Metairie, LA 70001
(504) 834-2020 Fax: (504) 834-2029
Oscar Rivas, President

VENEZUELAN STUDENT ASSOCIATION
Louisiana State University
Office for Student Organization Services
332-A LSU Union
Baton Rouge, LA 70894
(504) 388-8633 or (504) 388-5160
José L. Montiel, Advisor
Email: wvdavid@lsuvm.sncc.lsu.edu

MAINE

DIOCESAN HISPANIC MINISTRY COORDINATOR
510 Ocean Ave.
Portland, ME 04104
(207) 773-6471 Fax: (207) 773-0182
Rev. Arthur Pare, SJ, Pastor
Web: www.dioceseportlandmaine.org

DIOCESAN HISPANIC MINISTRY COORDINATOR
Sacred Heart/St. Dominic Parish
80 Sherman St.
Portland, ME 04101
(207) 772-6182 Fax: (207) 772-9615
Rev. Fred Morse, Pastor
Email: shsdp@ime.net
Web: www.dioceseportlandmaine.org

DIOCESE OF PORTLAND IN MAINE
Hispanic Affairs
Cathedral 307 Congress St.
Portland, ME 04101
(412) 456-3000
Rev. Vincent McCann, Hisp. Min. Coordinator

MARYLAND

ALICE HAMILTON OCCUPATIONAL HEALTH CENTER
1310 Apple Ave.
Silver Spring, MD 20910
(301) 565-4590 Fax: (301) 565-4596
Brian Christopher, Executive Director

AMERICAN GI FORUM OF THE U.S.
6801 Coolridge Road
Camp Springs, MD 20748
(301) 449-7967 or (301) 449-4277
Fax: (301) 449-7077
Jess Quintero, National Secretary
Web: www.incacorp.com/agif

AMERICAN PERUVIAN CHAMBER OF COMMERCE
P.O. Box 443
Rockville, MD 20848
(301) 881-6668 Fax: (301)-230-5808
Rolando Ore, President
Email: washdc@peruchamber.com
Web: www. peruchamber.com

27507 Mt. Radnor Drive
Damascus, MD 20872
(703) 524-1606 or (703) 525-2674
Alfonso Bartra, President
Email: inca@tcon.com
Web: www.perucam.org

AMIGOS DE LA CULTURA HISPANO-AMERICANA (ACHA)
705 Camellia Rd.
Salisbury, MD 21804
(410) 749-2115 or (410) 667-4308
Mayra Elassal, President

AMIGOS EN ACCION
114 W. Montgomery Ave.
Rockville, MD 20850
(301) 309-8775 Fax: (301) 762-2939
Mónica Barberis-Young, Director
Email: fia@communityministrymc.org

APOSTOLADO HISPANO/SPANISH APOSTOLATE
430 S. Broadway St., 3rd Floor
Baltimore, MD 21231
(410) 522-2668 or (410) 522-2669
Fax: (410) 675-1451
Sister Mary Neil Corcoran, Executive Director
Email: mcorcora@catholiccharities-md.org

ARCHDIOCESE OF BALTIMORE
Hispanic Ministry Office
320 Cathedral St.
Baltimore, MD 21201
(410) 547-5363 Fax: (410) 727-5432
María Johnson, Director for Hispanic Ministry
Email: mtpjohnson@archbalt.org

ASOCIACIÓN DE DAMAS BOLIVIANAS DE MD, DC Y VA
18725 Shremor Dr.
Deerwood, MD 20855
(301) 977-6708
Yolanda Heintze, President

ASOCIACIÓN DE MÉDICOS DE BOLIVIA
212 Swancreek Road
Fort Washington, MD 20744
(301) 843-8843 Fax: (301) 681-7864
Dr. Carlos Celis, President

ASOCIACIÓN MEXICANA DE MARYLAND, INC.
P. O. Box 43403
Baltimore, MD 21236
(410) 931-1640 Fax:(410) 937-7640
Petra P. Piñeyro, President

ASSISI HOUSE OF ST. PATRICK'S
P.O. Box 6076
Baltimore, MD 21231
(410) 276-5809
Jeanne Vélez, Coordinator

BALTIMORE ACTION FOR JUSTICE IN THE AMERICAS (BAJA)
Central America Solidarity Committee
1443 Gorsuch Ave.
Baltimore, MD 21218
(410) 467-9388 Fax: (410) 235-5325
Jodie Zisow, Co-Coordinator
Email: baltimoreaction@erols.com

BALTIMORE CITY HEALTH DEPARTMENT
Aids Outreach/Health Educator
210 Guilford Ave.
Baltimore, MD 21202
(410) 396-1927
Richard Kelly, Program Manager

BALTIMORE COUNTY HISPANIC ADVISORY COMMITTEE
4000 Washington Ave., #124
Towson, MD 21204
(410) 887-5557 Fax: (410) 769-8914
Miguel E. Albán, Chairman
Web: www.co.ba.md.us

BALTIMORE SISTER CITIES
250 City Hall
Baltimore, MD 21202
(410) 545-3185 Fax: (410) 396-1632
Marjorie Shaxted, Prog. Coord.
Email: mayor@baltimorecity.gov
Web: www.baltimorecity.gov

BALTIMORE-CADIZ SISTER CITY COMMITTEE
8402 Kellogg Court
Lutherville, MD 21093
(410) 321-1751 Fax: (410) 396-1632
Lilian Laszlo, Vice Chair

BILINGUAL CHRISTIAN CHURCH
417 S. Eaton Street
Baltimore, MD 21224
(410) 675-7256 Fax: (410) 558-2933
Ángel Núñez, Contact
Email: spanishch@aol.com

CASA DE MARYLAND INC.
Affiliate of NCLR
310 Tulip Ave.
Takoma Park, MD 20912
(301) 270-0442 Fax: (301) 270-8659
Gustavo Torres, Executive Director
Email: casamd@clark.net

Langley Park Office
734 University Blvd. East
Silver Spring, MD 20903
(301) 431-4177 Fax: (301) 431-4179
E. Ricardo Campos, Executive Director

CATHOLIC CHARITIES IMMIGRATION SERVICES
11160 Veris Mill Rd., #700
Wheaton, MD 20902
(301) 942-1856 Fax: (301) 434-5982
Betty Shaw Smith, Center Admis

CENTRO CRISTIANO VIDA NUEVA
Instituto de Música Hispano
8508 Adelphi Rd.
Adelphi, MD 20783
(301) 422-2029 Fax: (703) 929-0026
Rev. Carlos Santiago, Pastor
Email: vidanueva2000@netzero.net
Web: www.ccvn.turincon.com

CENTRO DE APOYO A LA FAMILIA
8908 Riggs Rd.
Adelphi, MD 20783
(301) 431-6210 Fax: (301) 431-6212
Janet Klenkle, Director

CENTRO DE LA COMUNIDAD, INC.
Affiliate of NCLR
321 Eastern Ave.
Baltimore, MD 21224
(410) 675-8906 Fax: (410) 675-3146
Carmen L. Nieves, Executive Director
Email: centro@us.net
Web: www.centrodelacomunidad.org

CHRIST THE KING
2300 East-West Highway
Silver Spring, MD 20910
(301) 589-8616 Fax: (301) 587-1929
Rev. Luis Antonio Marroquín, Pastor

CHURCH OF JESUS CHRIST OF LATTER DAY SAINTS, THE
Washington DC Visitor Center
9900 Stoneybrook Dr.
Kensington, MD 20895
(301) 587-0144 Fax: (301) 588-5685
Elder Salsbury, Director
Email: dcstake@washingtonlds.org
Web: www.washingtonlds.org

CÍRCULO CUBANO DE MARYLAND
12303 Tilbury Ln.
Bowie, MD 20715
(301) 262-9480
Miguel Boluda, President

CLUB AMIGOS DEL NIÑO COLOMBIANO
2901 Boston St., #218
Baltimore, MD 21224
(410) 563-4967 Fax: (410) 563-4222
Bertha Albornoz, President

CLUB DE PUERTO RICO OF MARYLAND
9004 Hamor Rd.
Randallstown, MD 21133
(410) 922-9533 or (410) 786-7628
Jesús Manuel Miranda, President

DIOCESAN HISPANIC MINISTRY COORD.
320 Cathedral St.
Baltimore, MD 21201
(410) 547-5423 Fax: (410) 727-5432
Gordon Bennett, Bishop
Email: mtpjohnson@archbalt.org
Web: www.archbalt.org

DIVISION OF REHABILITATION SERVICES
1515 W. Mt. Royal Ave.
Baltimore, MD 21217
(410) 333-6130 Fax: (410) 333-3134
Millie Gray, Counselor

EDUCATION BASED LATINO OUTREACH
1001 S. Potomac St.
Baltimore, MD 21224
(410) 563-3160 Fax: (410) 426-2046
Juanita Díaz, Executive Director
Web: www.eblo.orgorg

ESCUELA ARGENTINA
P.O.Box 59937
Rockville, MD 20859-9937
(301) 299-4616
Ilda Valeiras, President
Email: babbok@tidalwave.net

EVENGELICAL MISIONARY CHURCH
10508 Calumet Dr.
Silver Spring, MD 20901-4608
(301) 681-1006 Fax: (301) 681-1021
José Manzano, Pastor
Email: verenice220@cs.com

FEDERATION OF HISPANIC ORGANIZATIONS OF THE BALTIMORE METROPOLITAN AREA, INC.
P. O. Box 25915
317 S. Broadway
Baltimore, MD 21231
(410) 992-5512 or (410) 727-7365
Fax: (410) 992-5641
Carmen L. Nieves, President
Email: chf@erols.com

FIRST BAPTIST CHURCH OF LAUREL
811 5th St.
Laurel, MD 20707-5195
(301) 725-1688 or (301) 725-3064
Rev. Segundo Mir, Pastor

FIRST BAPTIST CHURCH OF MARYLAND
8503 Riggs Rd.
Hyattsville, MD 20783-2133
(301) 216-1453
Rev. Moises Naves, Pastor

FOREIGN BORN INFORMATION AND REFERRAL NETWORK (FIRN)
5999 Harpers Farm Rd., Suite E-200
Columbia, MD 21044
(410) 992-1923 Fax: (410) 730-0113
Gary Hughes, Executive Director
Email: firn@ipo.net

GOVERNOR'S COMMISSION ON HISPANIC AFFAIRS
Maryland Chapter
311 W. Saratoga St., #279

Baltimore, MD 21201
(410) 767-7857 Fax: (410) 333-3980
Luis Ortega, Executive Director
Web: www.dhr.state.md

GRACEWORKS, INC.
8415 Bellona Ln., #214
Towlson, MD 21204
(410) 828-1881 Fax: (410) 828-1832
Margarita I. Gurri, President
Email: graceworks@graceworks4kids.com
Web: www.graceworks4kids.com

GRUPO FOLKLÓRICO DE PANAMÁ
1613 Billman Ln.
Silver Spring, MD 20902
(301) 933-6764 or (301) 933-2085
Fax: (202) 806-5786
Norma Small Warren, Director
Email: nsmall-warren@howard.edu

GRUPO FOLKLORICO LATINOAMERICANO
105 Aspinwood Way., #E
Baltimore, MD 21237
(410) 682-5670 Fax: (410) 955-7587
Vanessa Ortiz, Coordinator
Email: vortiz@jhsph.edu
Web: www.folkloric.20m.com

HERMANOS Y HERMANAS MAYORES-BIG BROTHERS BIG SISTERS OF THE NATIONAL CAPITAL AREA
Administrative Office
10210 Greenbelt Rd., #900
Lanham, MD 20706
(301) 794-9170 ext. 15 Fax: (301) 794-9180
Jorge Bustios, Coordinator
Email: bbbsnca@aol.com
Web: htttp://www.bbbsnca.org

HISPANIC ADVISORY COMMITTEE
Office of County Executive
14741 Governor Oden Bowie Dr., 5th Floor
Upper Marlboro, MD 20772
(301) 292-9734 Fax: (301) 952-3339
Bill Stagg, Chairman of Hispanic Advisory Committee

HISPANIC ALLIANCE OF MONTGOMERY COUNTY
4874 Chevy Chase Blvd.
Chevy Chase, MD 20815
(301) 657-3542 Fax: (301) 657-3543
Fernando Cruz-Villalba, President
Email: vlacruz@erols.com

HISPANIC RESOURCE CENTER
1701 Sanford Dr.
Accokeek, MD 20607
(301) 292-9734 Fax: (301) 292-9734
William Stagg, Director

HISPANIC UNITED OF MARYLAND
422 N. Stonestreet Ave.
Rockville, MD 20850
(301) 315-2245 Fax: (301) 315-2682
Galo A. Correa, Sr., President

HISPANICS IN HISTORY CULTURAL ORG., INC.
9659 Basket Ring Rd., #2
Columbia, MD 21045
(410) 964-9594 Fax: (410) 884-3749
Hector L. Díaz, President
Email: hldiaz@erols.com

IGLESIA LUTERANA "CRISTO SEÑOR DE LA VIDA"/ CENTRO HISPANO LUTERANO
Affiliate of Lutheran Church Missouri Synod
3799 East-West Highway
Hyattsville, MD 20782
(301) 277-4729 Fax: (301) 699-0071
Rev. Aurelio Magarino, Contact

LATIN AMERICAN FOLK INSTITUTE
3800A 34th St.
Mount Rainier, MD 20712
(301) 887-9331 Fax: (301) 887-0308
Carlos Giménez, Director
Email: info@lafi.org
Web: www.lafi.org

LATIN AMERICAN PAPER MONEY SOCIETY (LANSA)
3304 Milford Mill Rd.
Baltimore, MD 21244
(410) 655-3109
Arthur C. Matz, President

LOS PEÑEROS ESPAÑOLES
4707 Ebenezer Rd.
Baltimore, MD 21236
(410) 256-2797
Soriano Santomé, Director

MARYLAND HISPANIC BAR ASSOCIATION (MHBA)
Whiteford Taylor and Preston LLP
Seven St.Paul St.
Baltimore, MD 21202-1626
(410) 347-8700 Fax: (410) 347-9478
Carmina Pérez-Fowler, President
Email: president@hispanicbar.com
Web: www.hispanicbar.com

MARYLAND HISPANIC CHAMBER OF COMMERCE
Martin State Airport
701 Wilson Point Rd., Box 15
Baltimore, MD 21220
(410) 391-3007 Fax: (410) 391-2072
Héctor Viñas, President

MARYLAND STATE ARTS COUNCIL
175 W Ostend St. #E
Baltimore, MD 21230
(410) 767-6555 Fax: (410) 333-1062
James Backas, Executive Director
Email: jbackas@mdbusiness.state.md.us
Web: www.msac.org

MAYOR'S OFFICE OF THE HISPANIC AFFAIRS /ENLACE DEL ALCALDE CON LA COMUNIDAD HISPANA
100 N. Holliday St., #221
Baltimore, MD 21202
(410) 396-4847 or (410) 396-9378
Fax: (410) 396-9568
Dr. Sonia Fierro-Luperini, Mayor Liaison for Hispanic Affairs

MCIL RESOURCES FOR INDEPENDENT LIVING
5807 Harford Rd.
Baltimore, MD 21214
(410) 444-1400 Fax: (410) 444-0825
Camilo Quintero, Liaison
Email: mcil@clark.net

MINISTERIO HISPANO DE BALTIMORE
1630 Bank St.
Baltimore, MD 21231
(410) 276-1660 Fax: (410) 276-1660
Fidel Compres, Pastor

MISSION HELPERS OF THE SACRED HEART
1001 W. Joppa Rd.
Baltimore, MD 21204
(410) 823-8585 Fax: (410) 825-6355
Sister Judeth Waldt, Director
Email: csbmhsh@aol.com

MONTGOMERY COUNTY DEPARTMENT OF PUBLIC LIBRARIES
Cultural Minorities Services
99 Maryland Ave.
Rockville, MD 20850
(240) 777-0026 Fax: (240) 777-0064
Yuli Estler, Library Associate
Email: estley@mont.lib.md.us
Web: www.montgomerylibrary.org

MOTHER SETON
19951 Father Hurley Blvd.
Germantown, MD 20874
(301) 924-3838 Fax: (301) 428-4951
Rev. Robert Gessetto, Priest
Web: www.adw.org

MULTICULTURAL PROGRAM - MONTGOMERY COUNTY
Department of Health & Human Services
8818 Georgia Ave. 2nd Floor
Silver Spring, MD 20910
(240) 777-1323 Fax: (240) 777-3226
Viviana Azar, Family Therapist
Email: viviana.azar@co.mo.ma.us

THE NATIONAL CLEARINGHOUSE FOR ALCOHOL AND DRUG INFORMATION
P.O. Box 2345
Rockville, MD 20847
(800) 729-6686 or (877) 767-8432
Fax: (301) 468-6433
Email: info@health.org
Web: www.health.org

NATIONAL CONFERENCE OF PUERTO RICAN WOMEN (NACOPRW)
Maryland Chapter
1438 Longhill Dr.
Rockville, MD 20854
(301) 217-9039 Fax: (703) 683-7846
Vanny Marreo, National President

NATIONAL COUNCIL FOR THE TRADITIONAL ARTS (NCTA)
National Headquarters
1320 Fenwick Ln. #200
Silver Spring, MD 20910
(301) 565-0654
Joseph Wilson, Executive Director

NATIONAL LEADERSHIP INSTITUTE (NLI)
P.O. Box 8755
Silver Spring, MD 20907-8755
(301) 562-8618 or (800) 411-0814
Fax: (301) 562-8633
Stephenie Colston, Project Director
Email: info@nli4cbos.org
Web: www.nli4cbos.org

NIÑOS UNIDOS DE MONTGOMERY COUNTY
644 Lakeworth Drive
Gaithersburg, MD 20878
(301) 947-4300 Fax: (301) 519-1968
Elizabeth Jaramillo, President
Email: ninosunidos@aol.com

OFICINA INTERGRUPAL HISPANA DEL ESTADO DE MARYLAND
7930 Georgia Ave. #103
Silver Spring, MD
(301) 587-6191

ORGANIZACIÓN LATINA ESTUDIANTIL
Johns Hopkins University
Office of Student Activities
3505 N. Charles St.
Baltimore, MD 21218-2686
(410) 516-5435 Fax: (410) 516-4703
Ralph Johnson, Prog. Coord.
Email: rjohnson@jhu.edu
Web: www.jhu.edu

OUR LADY OF LOURDES
7500 Pearl St.
Bethesda, MD 20814
(301) 654-1287 Fax: (301) 986-8716
Rev. Mario Dorsonville, Pastor
Email: ololserra@yahoo.com

OUR LADY OF SORROWS
1006 Larch Ave.
Takoma Park, MD 20912
(301) 891-3500 Fax: (301) 891-1523
Rev. James J. Suntum, Pastor
Email: oloschurch@aol.com
Web: www.angelfire.com/md2/olos

PANAMANIAN ASSOCIATION OF METROPOLITAN WASHINGTON DC
3036 Schubert Dr.
Silver Spring, MD 20904
(301) 890-9113
Al Lovell, Coordinator

PENTACOSTAL HISPANIC CHURCH
303 S. Broadway Street
Baltimore, MD 21231
(410) 563-2410
Ariel Santos, Pastor

PUERTO RICAN-AMERICAN RESEARCH INSTITUTE
P.O. Box 2274
Gaithersburg, MD 20879
(301) 216-1380
Ernest Acosta, Chairman
Email: ernest.acosta@mix.cpcug.org

RESTORATION "ELIM" EVANGELICAL CHURCH INTERNATIONAL
8725 Flower Ave.
Silver Spring, MD 20901-4035
(301) 589-8606 Fax: (301) 589-8851
Neri Espana, Pastor
Email: restauracionelim@aol.com
Web: www.geocities.com/restauracionelim

SANZ SCHOOL, INC.
1310 Apple Ave.
Silver Spring, MD 20910
(301) 608-2300 Fax: (301) 608-0802

SHARE DC-METRO
5170 Lawrence Pl. #4
Hyattsville, MD 20781
(301) 864-3118 Fax: (301) 864-5370
German R. Rodriguez, Hispanic Outreach Coordinator

SPANISH CATHOLIC CENTER - CENTRO CATÓLICO HISPANO
Gaithersburg Branch/Computer Training
117 N. Frederick Ave.
Gaithersburg, MD 20877

(301) 417-9113 or (301) 434-3339(computers)
Fax: (301) 417-9895 or (301) 434-5160(clinic)
Celia Rivas, LLM, Coordinator
Email: sccdc@erols.com
Web: www.centrocatolicohispano.org

Langley Park Branch/Clinic
1015 University Blvd. E.
Silver Spring, MD 20903
(301) 431-3773 or (301) 434-3999(clinic)
Fax: (301) 431-0886 or (301) 434-5160(clinic)
Sister Carmen Banegas, Coordinator
Email: sccdc@erols.com
Web: www.centrocatolicohispano.org

Wheaton Clinic
2424 Reedie Drive
Silver Spring, MD 20903
(301) 929-0207 Fax: (301) 929-0594
Sister Helene Hicks, IHM, RN, Coordinator
Email: sccdc@erols.com
Web: www.centrocatolicohispano.org

SPANISH FIESTA, INC.
205 E. Joppa Rd., #2502
Towson, MD 21286
(410) 823-7948 Fax: (410) 823-7117
Dr. Luis E. Queral, Director
Email: lqueral@prodigy.net

SPANISH SPEAKING COMMUNITY OF MARYLAND, INC.
Hyattsville Office
7411 Riggs Rd., #210
Hyattsville, MD 20783
(301) 434-5055 Fax: (301) 445-0822
Emilio P. Rivas, Director

Silver Spring Office
8519 Piney Branch Rd.
Silver Spring, MD 20901
(301) 587-7217 Fax: (301) 589-1397
Emilio P. Rivas, Director

ST. BARTHOLOMEW
7212 Blacklock Rd.
Bethesda, MD 20817
(301) 229-7933 Fax: (301) 229-7998
Rev. Luis Salcedo, Pastor

ST. BERNARD
5700 St. Bernard's Dr.
Riverdale, MD 20737
(301) 277-1000 Fax: (301) 277-3464
Rev. John McKay, Pastor

ST. BERNARDINE OF SIENA
2400 Brooks Dr.
Suitland, MD 20746-1144
(301) 736-0707 Fax: (301) 736-2984
Rev. Arnold De Porter, Pastor

ST. CAMILLUS
1600 St. Camillus Dr.
Silver Spring, MD 20903
(301) 434-8400 Fax: (301) 434-8041
Rev. Michael Tyson, Pastor

ST. CATHERINE LABOURE
11801 Claridge Rd.
Wheaton, MD 20902
(301) 946-1020 Fax: (301) 946-5064
Rev. José Mauricio Henríquez, Pastor

ST. JAMES
3628 Rhode Island Ave.
Mt. Rainier, MD 20712
(301) 927-0567 Fax: (301) 927-5289
Rev. Agustín Mateo Ayala, Pastor

ST. JOHN THE EVANGELIST
8910 Old Branch Ave.
Clinton, MD 20753-2527
(301) 868-1070 Fax: (301) 868-7915
Rev. Richard Scott, Associate Pastor

ST. JOSEPH MEDICAL CENTER AUXILIARY
7601 Ausler Dr.
Towson, MD 21204
(410) 337-1000 or (410) 337-1700
Ms. Lourdes Morales, President

ST. MARK'S
7501 Adelphi Rd.
Hyattsville, MD 20783
(301) 422-8300 Fax: (301) 422-2313
Rev. Jeff Defayette, Associate Pastor

ST. MARTIN OF TOUR
201 S. Frederick Ave.
Gaithersburg, MD 20877
(301) 840-1830 or (301) 990-9196
Fax: (301) 990-7538
Rev. William Ryan, Pastor
Email: stmartin@kreative.net

ST. MICHAEL THE ARCHANGEL
824 Pershing Dr.
Silver Spring, MD 20910
(301) 589-1155 Fax: (301) 589-3470
Rev. Vincent Rigdon, Pastor
Email: stmichael@dsd.dil.com

ST. PETER, OLNEY
2900 Sandy Spring Rd.
Olney, MD 20832
(301) 924-3774 Fax: (301) 774-5259
Thomas M. Kalita, Pastor

ST. PETER'S PARISH
3320 St. Peter Dr.
Waldorf, MD 20601
(301) 843-8916 Fax: (301) 843-3163
Rev. Msgr. Henry Otero, Pastor
Email: stpeter@olg.com

ST. RAPHAEL
1590 Kimblewick Rd.
Rockville, MD 20854-6198
(301) 762-2143 or (301) 424-4966
Fax: (301) 762-0719
Rev. John Dakes, Pastor

TEEN CHALLENGE
6900 Central Ave.
Capitol Heights, MD 20743
(301) 350-6373 Fax: (301) 350-4217
Manuel Baerga, Director

TELAMON CORPORATION
Maryland State Office
237 Florida Ave.
Salisbury, MD 21801
(410) 546-4604 or (410) 546-4605
Fax: (410) 546-0566
Karen Webster, State Director
Email: tcmdjtpa@onp.wdsc.org
Web: www.telamon.org

TOWSON UNIVERSITY
Office of Diversity
8000 York Road
Towson, MD 21252
(410) 830-2051 Fax: (410) 830-3763
Dr. Camille Clay, Assistant Vice President
Email: cclay@towson.edu
Web: www.towson.edu

UNIDOS POR EL PERÚ
13604 Middlevalle Lane
Silver Spring, MD 20906
(301) 460-0317 or (301) 329-4544
Orlando Flores, President

UNITED COLOMBIAN-AMERICAN ASSOCIATION, (UCAA)
8819 Thomas Lea Terrace
Montgomery Village, MD 20886-4346
(301) 519-1110 or (703) 812-4798
Fax: (301) 519-2292
Carlos Soles, President
Email: comiteandino@egroups.com
Web: www.u-c-a-a.org

UNITED WAY OF CENTRAL MARYLAND
First Call For Help
P.O. Box 1576
100 South Charles St., 5th Floor
Baltimore, MD 21201
(410) 685-0525 or (800) 492-0618
Fax: (410) 895-1556
Saundra Bound, Director
Email: info@uwcm.org
Web: www.uwcm.org

VOCES VS. VIOLENCIA (VVV)
(301) 424-0656 ext 145
Jessica Twedt

ZIVA'S SPANISH DANCE ENSEMBLE
2505 Oakenshield Dr.
Potomac, MD 20854
(301) 424-1355 or (202) 679-5966
Fax: (301) 251-4125
Victor Cohen, Business Mngr.
Email: spanish_dance@hotmail.com
Web: http://members.tripod.com/~spanishdance

MASSACHUSETTS

A BETTER CHANCE
419 Boylston St.
Boston, MA 02116
(617) 421-0950 Fax: (617) 421-0965
Judith B. Griffin, President
Web: www.abetterchance.org

ACCIÓN INTERNATIONAL
National Headquarters
120 Beacon St.
Somerville, MA 02143
(617) 492-4930 Fax: (617) 876-9509
María Otero, President & CEO
Email: info@accion.org
Web: http://www.accion.org

ALIANZA
Wellesley College
106 Central
Wellesley, MA 02181
(781) 283-2489 Fax: (781) 283-3674
Irma Tryon, Advisor
Email: iTryon@wellesley.edu

AMNESTY INTERNATIONAL
Regional Office
58 Day Street, David Square
Somerville, MA 02114
(617) 623-0202 Fax: (617) 623-2005
Joshua Rubenstean, Exec. Director
Email: aiusanero@igc.apc.org

ARCHDIOCESE OF BOSTON
Hispanic Apostolate Office
2121 Commonwealth Ave.
Boston, MA 02135
(617) 746-5816 Fax: (617) 783-5642
Rev. James E. Gaudreau, Director
Email: reverendjamesgaudreau@rcab.org

ASOCIACIÓN SAN MARTIN DE PORRES, INC.
155 Crescent St.
Brockton, MA 02301
(508) 584-2241 Fax: (508) 583-6339
Jorge Lovatón, Board President

BLESSED SACRAMENT, DIOCESAN HISPANIC MINISTRY
35 Harry St.
Springfield, MA 01107
(413) 736-8208 Fax: (413) 731-0962
Rev. Juan García, Director

BOSTON YMCA LATIN AMERICAN PROGRAM
316 Huntington Ave.
Boston, MA 02115
(617) 536-7800 Fax: (617) 536-3240
Ionela Istrati, Director
Web: www.ymcaboston.org

CASA DEL SOL
Affiliate of NCLR
419 Shawmut Ave.
Boston, MA 02118
(617) 266-3040
Carmelo Iglesias, Executive Director

CASA ESPERANZA
291 Eustis St.
Roxbury, MA 02119
(617) 445-7411 Fax: (617) 541-0844
Rick Quiroga, Director

CASA LATINA, INC.
National Headquarters
141B Damon Rd.
North Hampton, MA 01060
(413) 586-1569 Fax: (413) 586-1597
Lillian Torres, Coordinator
Email: Casa1@map.com

CASA MYRNA VÁZQUEZ, INC.
P.O. Box 180019
Boston, MA 02118
(617) 521-0100 Fax: (617) 521-0105
Sheila Moore, Executive Director
Email: smoore@casamyrna.org
Web: www.casamyrna.org

CENTRO DE LA FAMILIA SAN ANDRÉS
171 Amory St.
Jamaica Plain, MA 02130
(617) 522-1535
Luis Enrique Benavides, Pastor

CENTRO LAS AMÉRICAS
11 Sycamore St.
Worcester, MA 01608
(508) 798-1900 x222 Fax: (508) 798-1908
Teresita Orosko, Executive Director

CENTRO PANAMERICANO
101 Amesbury St.
Lawrence, MA 01841
(978) 794-1025 Fax: (978) 687-1381
Dona Rivera, Executive Director

CENTRO PRESENTE, INC.
Affiliate of NCLR
54 Essex St.
Cambridge, MA 02139
(617) 497-9080 ext.11 Fax: (617) 497-7247
María Elena Letona, Director
Email: cpresente@igc.org

CHICANO CAUCUS OF AMHERST
Office of the Dean of Students
Amherst College - Box 152
Amherst, MA 01002-5000
(413) 542-2000
Antonio Martinez, Director

COALITION FOR A BETTER ACRE, INC.
450 Marrimack St.
Lowell, MA 01854
(978) 452-7523 Fax: (978) 452-4923
Frank Carbalho, Director

COMMONWEALTH OF MASSACHUSETTS
Executive Department
State House, Suite 360
Boston, MA 02133
(617) 727-3600 Fax: (617) 727-9725
Argio Paul Cellucci, Governor

CONCILIO HISPANO DE CAMBRIDGE, INC.
Affiliate of NCLR
105 Windsor St., 3rd Floor
Cambridge, MA 02139
(617) 661-9406 Fax: (617) 661-8008
Sylvia Saavedra-Keber, Executive Director
Email: concilio@shore.net

COUNCIL OF HISPANIC EMPLOYMENT PROGRAM MANAGERS
10 Causeway St. #501
Boston, MA 02222-1063
(617) 565-6390 Fax: (617) 565-6472
Louis Meyi, CR/EEO, Chair.
Email: louis.meyi@fns.usda.gov
Web: www.sns.usda.gov/fns/menu/civilrights/

DAVID ROCKEFELLER CENTER FOR LATIN AMERICAN STUDIES
Harvard University
61 Kirkland St.
Cambridge, MA 02138
(617) 495-3366 Fax: (617) 496-2802
John Coatsworth, Director
Web: www.fas.harvard.edu/~drclas

DEPARTMENT OF HUMAN SERVICES
Office of Cultural Affairs
133 William St, #219
New Bedford, MA 02740
(508) 979-1516 Fax: (508) 991-6148
Adonis Ferreira, Coordinator

DIOCESE OF FALL RIVER
Hispanic Affairs
P.O. Box 40605
New Bedford, MA 02744-0006
(508) 969-8703 Fax: (508) 992-2208
Rev. Paul E. Canuel, Dir. for Hispanic Ministry
Email: pecanuel@aol.com

DIOCESE OF SPRINGFIELD
Holy Family Parish
235 Eastern Ave.
Springfield, MA 01109
(413) 732-1422
Rev. Paul Manship, Dir. for Hispanic Ministry
Email: p.emanshhip@att.net

DIOCESE OF WORCESTER
Hispanic Ministry Office
St. Peter's Church, 929 Main St.
Worcester, MA 01610
(508) 752-4674 Fax: (508) 767-1511
Rev. José Andrés Rodríguez, Vicar
Email: krmomsen@yahoo.com

EL CENTRO DEL CARDENAL
76 UNION PARK ST.
Boston, MA 02118
(617) 542-9292 Fax: (617) 542-6912
Ruth Rubacalva, Executive Director

GANDARA HEALTH CENTER
333 E. Columbus Ave.
Springfield, MA 01105-12515
(413) 736-8329 Fax: (413) 746-4270
Henry East-Trou, Executive Director

GAY & LESBIAN LATINO ORGANIZATION
Graper Valley Health Center
19 Tacoma St.
Worcester, MA 01613
(508) 854-3260 Fax: (508) 854-3265
Leo Negrón, Representative

GREATER LAWRENCE COMMUNITY ACTION COUNCIL, SPANISH COMMUNITY PROGRAMS
350 Essex St.
Lawrence, MA 01840
(978) 681-4901 or (978) 681-4905
Fax: (978) 681-4949
Isabel Meléndez, Director
Web: www.glcac.org

HARVARD PILGRIM HEALTH CARE MAINTENANCE ORGANIZATION
1200 Crown Colony
Quincy, MA 02169
1(800) 421-3590 Multi-lingual Services

HIGHER EDUCATION
Youth Programs Department
100 Boylston Street, LL1
Boston, MA 02116
(617) 542-3900 Fax:(617) 574-5048
Arturo Iriarte
Educational Awareness Specialist

HISPANIC AMERICAN CHAMBER OF COMMERCE
67 Broad St.
Boston, MA 02109
(617) 261-4222 Fax: (617) 261-6333
Geraldo Villacres, Executive Director
Email: haccatbos@compuserv.com
Web: www.hacc.com

HISPANIC AMERICAN LAW STUDENTS ASSOCIATION
c/o Student Activities Office
Boston University
775 Commonwealth Ave.
George Sherman Union, 4th Floor
Boston, MA 02215
(617) 353-3635 Fax: (617) 353-5257

HISPANIC CHAMBER OF COMMERCE
P.O. Box 16542
Worcester, MA 01601
(508) 853-3309 Fax: (508) 798-1908
Octavio Sánchez, Vice President

HISPANIC NATIONAL BAR ASSOCIATION
55 Village Brook Ln., Apt. #8
Natick, MA 01760
(508) 655-4603
Víctor J. Medina, Law Student Division Pres.
Email: victorjmedina@hotmail.com
Web: www.hnba.com

Region I (CT, ME, MA, NH, RI, VT)
53 State St.
Boston, MA 02115
(617) 248-5000 Fax: (617) 248-4000
Tracey Hubbard-Rentas, Regional President
Email: tmh@choate.com
Web: www.hnba.com

HISPANIC OFFICE OF PLANNING AND EVALUATION, INC. (HOPE)
Affiliate of NCLR
165 Brookside Ave., Extension
Jamaica Plain, MA 02130
(617) 524-8888 Fax: (617) 524-4939
José Durán, Executive Director
Email: HOPENAME@aol.com

HISPANO NETWORK
430 N. Canal St.
Lawrence, MA 01840
(978) 683-9505 Fax: (978) 683-1026
Kay Frishman, Co-Chairman

IGLESIA DE CRISTO
Ministerios Cosecha
2150 Boston Providence Hwy.
Walpole, MA 02081
(508) 660-2644 Fax: (508) 660-2907
Sergio Pérez, Pastor

INQUILINOS BORICUAS EN ACCIÓN, INC.
405 Shawmut Ave.
Boston, MA 02118
(617) 927-1707 Fax: (617) 536-5816
David Cortiella, Executive Director
Email: iba@aol.com

INSTITUTE FOR ECONOMIC
Boston University
264 Bay State Rd.
Boston, MA 02215
(617) 353-4454 Fax: (617) 353-4143
Dilip Mookherjee, Director
Email: ied@bu.edu

LA ALIANZA HISPANA, INC.
Affiliate of SER-Jobs for Progress National, Inc.
409 Dudley St.
Roxbury, MA 02119
(617) 427-7175 Fax: (617) 442-2259
Carlos Martínez, Executive Director
Email: info@Laalianza.org
Web: www.Laalianza.org

LA CAUSA
Amherst College
P.O. Box 1836
Amherst, MA 01002-5000
Email: lacausa@unix.amherst.edu
Web: http://www.amherst.edu/~lacausa/menu.html

LA UNIÓN CHICANA POR AZTLAN
Massachusetts Institute of Technology
77 Massachusetts Ave. 3-107
Cambridge, MA 02139
(617) 258-5515 Fax: (617) 253-9899
Joe Jasso, Assistant Director of Admissions
Email: Lucha-request@mit.edu
Web: http://web.mit.edu/lucha/www/

LATIN AMERICAN SCHOLARSHIP PROGRAM OF AMERICAN UNIVERSITIES
25 Mt. Auburn St.
Cambridge, MA 02138
(617) 495-5255 Fax: (617) 495-8990
Ned Strong, Executive Director
Web: www.laspau.harvard.edu

LATINO HEALTH INSTITUTE
95 Berkeley St.
Boston, MA 02116
(617) 350-6900 Fax: (617) 350-6901
Nicolás Carballeira, Director
Email: EXEC@LHI.ORG
Web: www.lhi.org

LATINO STUDENT CAUCUS
Harvard University
John F. Kennedy School of Government
79 John F. Kennedy St.
Cambridge, MA 02138
(617) 495-1155 Fax: (617) 496-1165
Joseph Nye, Dean
Web: http://ksgwww.harvard.edu

LATINOS UNIDOS
c/o Student Affairs Office
Boston University
775 Commonwealth Ave.
George Sherman Union, 4th Floor
Boston, MA 02215
(617) 353-3635 Fax: (617) 353-5257
Jennifer Vásquez, President
Email: latinosunidos@bu.edu

LEAGUE OF UNITED LATIN AMERICAN CITIZENS (LULAC)
National Executive Committee
91 Annafran Street
Rosalindale, MA 02131
(617) 635-2505 or (617) 327-6760 (h)
Fax: (617) 323-4181
Regla González, National. VP for NE
Email: regla@lulac.com www.LULAC.com

Northeast Region-MA
1096 N. Shore Road, #3
Revere, MA 02157
(617) 989-2206 or (617) 323-4181 (h)
Sara Barrientos, State Dir.

MAURICIO GASTÓN INSTITUTE
University of Massachusetts
100 Morrisey Boulevard
Boston, MA 02125-3393
(617) 287-5790 Fax: (617) 287-5788
Andrés Torres, Director
Email: Latino_2@umbsky.cc.umb.edu

MERRIMACK VALLEY CHAMBER OF COMMERCE
264 Essex St.
Lawrence, MA 01840
(978) 686-0900 Fax: (978) 794-9953
Joseph Bevilacqua, President & CEO
Email: thechamber@merrimackvalleychamber.com

MEZCLA
Wellesley College
106 Central
Wellesley, MA 02181
(781) 283-2489 Fax: (781) 283-3674
Irma Tryon, Advisor

MIT ASSOCIATION OF PUERTO RICAN STUDENTS
Office of Minority Education
77 Massachusetts Ave. Room 7-145
Cambridge, MA 02139
Bárbara Jiménez, President
Email: apr-request@mit.edu

MULTICULTURAL EDUCATION TRAINING & ADVOCACY (META)
240A Elm St., #22
Somerville, MA 02144
(617) 628-2226 Fax: (617) 628-0322
Roger Rice, Co-Director

MUSICAMADOR
199 Pemberton Street
Cambridge, MA 02140
(617) 492-1515 Fax: (617) 492-1515
Rosi Amador, Director

NATIONAL ASSOCIATION OF HISPANIC NURSES (NAHN)
Massachusetts Chapter
350 Warren Wright Street
Belchertown, MA 01007
(413) 545-5084 or (413) 733-1132 (w)
(413) 253-0422 (h) Fax: (413) 577-1200
Migdalia V. Rivera Goba, RN

NATIONAL COALITION OF ADVOCATES FOR STUDENTS, VIVIREMOS HIV EDUCATIONAL PROJECT
National Headquarters
100 Boylston St. #737
Boston, MA 02116
(617) 357-8507 Fax: (617) 357-9549
Joan First, Executive Director
Web: www.ncas1.org

NETWORK FOR LATINO PROFESSIONALS
P.O. Box 6019
Boston, MA 02209
(617) 247-1818 Fax: (617) 265-1513
Betty Figara, Director

NEW ENGLAND COUNCIL OF LATIN AMERICAN STUDIES, INC.
c/o Project on Women and Social Change
Smith College, Seelye Hall, Suite 210
Northampton, MA 01063
(413) 585-3591 Fax: (413) 585-3593
Kathleen E. Gauger, Adm. Asst.
Email: KGAUGER@SOPHIA.SMITH.EDU
Web: www.SMITH.EDU/~K.GAUGER

NEW ENGLAND FARM WORKERS COUNCIL (NEFWC)
Affiliate of Corporation for Public Management
1628-1640 Main St.
Springfield, MA 01103
(413) 781-2145 Fax: (413) 781-5928
Heriberto Flores, Executive Director
Email: eanefwc@aol.com

NEW ENGLAND MINORITY PURCHASING COUNCIL
4 Copley Pl., #125
Boston, MA 02116
(617) 578-8900 Fax: (617) 578-8902
Mary Collier, Executive Director
Web: webmaster:www.nempc.org

NEW NORTH CITIZENS COUNCIL, INC./ EL INSTITUTO DE LA FAMILIA, INC.
2383 Main St.
Springfield, MA 01107
(413) 746-4885 Fax: (413) 737-2321
Bárbara Rivera, Director
Email: nncc@rcn.com

NEW WORLD THEATRE
P.O. Box 31810
Amherst, MA 01003
(413) 545-1972 Fax: (413) 545-4414
Dennis Conway, Director
Web: www.newworldtheater.org

NUESTRA COMUNIDAD DEVELOPMENT CORP.
391 Dudley St.
Roxbury, MA 02119
(617) 427-3599 Fax: (617) 989-1216
Evelyn Freedman, Executive Director
Email: NUESTRA@EARTHLINK.NET

NUESTRA SEÑORA DE GUADALUPE
P.O. Box 40605
73 Division St.
New Bedford, MA 02744
(508) 996-5862 Fax: (508) 992-2208
Padre Pablo Canuel, Contact
Email: PECANUEL@AOL.COM

NUEVA ESPERANZA INC.
401 Main St.
Holyoke, MA 01040
(413) 533-9442 Fax: (413) 533-2661
Carlos Vega, Director

Email: nueva@javanet.Com
Web: www.incommn.org/nueva/

PUERTO RICAN CULTURAL CENTER, INC.
38 School St.
Springfield, MA 01105
(413) 737-7450 Fax: (413) 737-1305
Juan Gerena, Director

RAZA
Harvard-Radcliffe College
4 University Hall
Cambridge, MA 02138
(617) 495-1581 Fax: (617) 496-0256
Aurelio Ramirez, Advisor
Email: Raza@hcs.harvard.edu
Web: hcs.harvard.edu/~raza/

ROCA, INC.
101 Park St.
Chelsea, MA 02150
(617) 889-5210 Fax: (617) 889-2645
Molí Baldwin, Executive Director

SELECTED EXECUTIVES, INC.
76 Winn St.
Woburn, MA 01801
(781) 933-1500 Fax: (781) 933-4145
Lee Sanboin, Director

SOCIEDAD LATINA, INC.
1530 Tremont St.
Roxbury, MA 02120
(617) 442-4299 Fax: (617) 442-4087
Alex Oliver, Executive Director
Email: SOSLATINA@AOL.COM

SOCIETY OF HISPANIC PROFESSIONAL ENGINEERS (SHPE)
Greater Boston Professional Chapter
34 Forest St., MS 4-09
North Attleboro, MA 02703
(508) 236-1624 or (508) 695-2487 (h)
Fax: (508) 236-3825
Irene Lam, Chapter President
Email: ilam@ti.com
Web: www.shpeboston.org

SOCIETY OF HISPANIC PROFESSIONAL ENGINEERS (SHPE)
Massachusetts Institute of Technology
77 Massachusetts Ave. #7-145
Cambridge, MA 02139
(617) 253-5010 or (617) 253-1332
Fax: (617) 253-9899
Leo Osgood, Jr., Dean of the Off. of Min. Ed.
Email: SHPE-REQUEST@MIT.EDU
Web: www.shpe.org

SOL Y CANTO (FLOR DE CAÑA)
199 Pemberton St.
Cambridge, MA 02140
(617) 492-1515 Fax: (617) 492-1515
Rosi Amador, Manager
Email: SolCanto@Concentrec.net
Web: WWW.musicamador.com

SOUTHEASTERN MASSACHUSETTS/SER-JOBS FOR PROGRESS, INC.
Affiliate of SER-Jobs for Progress National, Inc.
164 Bedford St.
Fall River, MA 02720
(508) 676-1916 Fax: (508) 676-2330
M. Paula Raposa, Executive Director
Web: www.sernational.org

SPANISH AMERICAN CENTER, INC.
16 Cross St.
Leominster, MA 01453
(978) 534-3145 Fax: (978) 534-5146
Nery Latima, Director

SPANISH AMERICAN UNION, INC.
2335 Main St.
Springfield, MA 01107
(413) 734-7381 Fax: (913) 734-8293
Mareia Morales Loebl, Executive Director
Email: donazia@hotmail.com

ST. JOHNS CHURCH/ DIOCESAN HISPANIC MINISTRY
44 Temple St.
Worcester, MA 01604
(508) 756-7165 Fax: (508) 754-5153
Rev. Joseph Mahony, Director

SUMAJ CHASQUIS
201 Forest St.
Arlington, MA 02174
(781) 474-1224 or (781) 643-0316
Fax: (781) 474-1261 or (781) 232-6782
Juan Carlos Ferrufino, Director

Email: YAMASS@EOL.COM

WESTERN MASSACHUSETTS HISPANIC CHAMBER OF COMMERCE
167 Chestnut St.
Holyoke, MA 01040
(413) 533-7032 Fax: (413) 533-7423
Daniel Torres, President
Email: info@wmhispanicchamber.com
Web: wmhispanicchamber.com

WOBURN COUNCIL OF SOCIAL CONCERN, INC. - HISPANIC PROGRAM
19 Campbell St.
Woburn, MA 01801
(781) 935-6495 Fax: (781) 935-1923
José A. Santiago, Director
Web: www.socialconcern.com

WOMEN'S SHELTER/COMPAÑERAS
P.O. Box 1099
Holyoke, MA 01041-1099
(413) 538-9717 Fax: (413) 538-9411
Caren Cavanaugh, Director
Email: womensshelter@org

MICHIGAN

ADRIAN COLLEGE
Admissions Office
110 S. Madison St.
Adrian, MI 49221
(517) 265-5161 Fax: (517) 264-3331
Dr. Ronaldo Elardo, Chair of Language Dept.

ALCONA HEALTH CENTER
P.O. Box 279
177 N. Barlow Rd.
Lincoln, MI 48742
(517) 736-8157 Fax: (517) 736-8380
Christine Baumgardner, Administrator

ALIANZA
University of Michigan
Multi-Ethnic Student Affairs
2202 Michigan Union
Ann Arbor, MI 48109-1349
(734) 763-9044 Fax: (734) 647-4133
Diana N. Derige, President
Email: alianza.net@umich.edu or ronnysan@umich.edu

ALLEGAN COUNTY FAMILY INDEPENDENCE AGENCY
2233 33rd St.
Allegan, MI 49010
(616) 673-7777 or (616) 673-7700
Fax: (616) 673-7705
Susan Bailey Carmen, Director

ALMA COLLEGE
Office of Admissions
614 West Superior St.
Alma, MI 48801
(517) 463-7111 or (800) 292-9078
Fax: (517) 463-7277
Mark Nazario, Minority Director

ALMA LATINA
University of Michigan
Multi-Ethnic Student Affairs
2202 Michigan Union
Ann Arbor, MI 48109-1349
(734) 763-9044 Fax: (734) 647-4133
Alice Robinson, President
Email: alma.latina@umich.edu or alicer@umich.edu

ALPENA MIGRANT RESOURCE COUNCIL
Alpena County Family Independence
711 W. Chisholm
Alpena, MI 49707
(517) 354-7200 Fax: (517) 534-7242
Robert Roberge, Acting Director

AMERICAN G.I. FORUM
604 Oak St.
Saginaw, MI 48605
(517) 754-2131
Joe A. Contreras, Director

22059 Cherry Lawn Drive
Brownstown, MI 48134
(734) 692-3991 (h) or (248) 3454-7206
Jessica Crespo, National Queen

ARCHDIOCESE OF DETROIT
Hispanic Affairs
305 Michigan Ave.
Detroit, MI 48226-2605
(313) 237-5761 Fax: (313) 237-5869
Raúl Feliciano, Director for Hispanic Ministry

ARENAC COUNTY, MIGRANT PROGRAM
P.O. Box 130
3709 Deep River Rd.
Standish, MI 48658
(517) 846-4551 Fax: (517) 846-4365
Dave Smith, Gral. Program Superv.

AZTECA ATHLETIC CLUB
195 W. Montcalm
Pontiac, MI 48058
(248) 332-6514
Ruben Flores, Director

BENCY COUNTY FAMILY INDEPENDENT AGENCY
Government Center
P.O. Box 114
448 Court Plaza
Beulah, MI 49617
(616) 882-4443 Fax: (616) 882-9078
Mary Marois, Director

BILINGUAL/MIGRANT CAREER DEV. CTR.
North Middle School
910 N. Walnut St.
Saginaw, MI 48602
(517) 759-3672 Fax: (517) 759-3676
José Garza, Assistant Principal/Supervisor

BONIFACE COMMUNITY ACTION CENTER
5886 W. Fort St.
Detroit, MI 48209
(313) 843-0402 Fax: (313) 843-2426
Anita Kanakaris, Prog. Director

CAM-TRE INNOVATIONS, INC.
18800 West 10 Mile Road, #204
Southfield, MI 48075
(248) 552-8690 Fax: (248) 552-8783
Carmen C. Thurman, President
Email: camtre@gatecom.com

CAPITAL AREA COMMUNITY SERVICES
101 E. Willow St.
Lansing, MI 48906
(517) 482-6281 or (517) 393-7077
Fax: (517) 482-7747
Ivan W. Love, Jr., Director

CASA DE UNIDAD
1920 Scotten
Detroit, MI 48209
(313) 843-9598
Marta Lagos, Director

CASA MARÍA FAMILY SERVICE CENTER
1500 Trumbull Ave.
Detroit, MI 48216
(313) 962-4230 or (313) 962-4231
Fax: (313) 962-4251
Carla Spight, Executive Director

CENTRO LATINO
339 E. 16th St., 201
Holland, MI 49423
(616) 396-3391 Fax: (616) 396-1103
Imelda Martínez, Executive Director

CHICANO & BORICUA STUDIES CENTER
Wayne State University
656 W. Kirby, #3326
Detroit, MI 48202
(313) 577-4378 Fax: (313) 993-4073
José Cuello, Director

CHICANO LATINO YOUTH CLUB
1619 Broadway
Bay City, MI 48708
(517) 894-0661 Fax: (517) 894-0771
María Cepeda, Pastoral Administrator

COMMUNITY ACTION AGENCY
400 W. South St.
Adrian, MI 49221
(517) 263-7861 Fax: (517) 263-6531
Chris Rojo, Community Information Specialist

Lincoln School
154 W. Clark
Jackson, MI 49203
(517) 788-6010 Fax: (517) 788-5998
Willie Coast Baldwin, Family Service Mngr.

CORRECTIONAL ASSESSMENT & TREATMENT SERVICES
630 N. Cedar St.
Mason, MI 48854
(517) 676-2431 x254 Fax: (517) 676-8280
Judish Kaith, Director

CRISTO REY CHURCH
201 W. Miller Rd.
Lansing, MI 48910
(517) 394-4639 Fax: (517) 394-8090
Rev. Federico Thelen, Pastor

CRISTO REY COMMUNITY CENTER
1717 N. Hight St.
Lansing, MI 48906
(517) 372-4700 Fax: (517) 372-8499
Tony Benavides, Executive Director

CUBAN AMERICAN STUDENT ASSOCIATION
University of Michigan
Multi-Ethnic Student Affairs
2202 Michigan Union
Ann Arbor, MI 48109-1349
(734) 763-9044 Fax: (734) 647-4133
Delia Cabrera Fernández, President
Email: fcabrera @umich.edu

DELTA TAU LAMBDA SORORITY, INC.
University of Michigan
Multi-Ethnic Student Affairs
2202 Michigan Union
Ann Arbor, MI 48109-1349
(734) 763-9044 Fax: (734) 647-4133
Alejandra Montes, President
Email: delta.tau.lambda@umich.edu or nncc@umich.edu

DETROIT INSTITUTE OF ARTS
Latin American Advisory Board
5200 Woodward Ave.
Detroit, MI 48202
(313) 833-7975 Fax: (313) 833-7355
Nancy Jones, Director of Education
Web: www.dia.org

DIOCESE OF GAYLORD
CFCS-Catholic Charities
611 North St.
Gaylord, MI 49735
(517) 732-5147 Fax: (517) 705-3589
Mike Steffel, Director

Hispanic Affairs
720 Second St.
Traverse St., MI 49684
(231) 946-1205 Fax: (231) 946-0567
Angel Torres, Coordinator for Hispanic Ministry
Email: silviacortesl@hotmail.com

DIOCESE OF GRAND RAPIDS
Hispanic Affairs
660 Burton St. SE
Grand Rapids, MI 49507
(616) 243-0491 x557 Fax: (616) 243-1442
Luis L. Beteta, Director for Hispanic Ministry
Email: lbeteta@dioceseofgrandrapids.org

DIOCESE OF KALAMAZOO
Hispanic Affairs
215 N. Westnedge
Kalamazoo, MI 49007-3760
(616) 349-8714 Fax: (616) 349-6440
Fanny Tabares, Director for Hispanic Ministry
Email: ftabares@dioceseofkalamazoo.org
Web: www.dioceseofkalamazoo.org

DIOCESE OF LANSING
Hispanic Affairs
300 W. Ottawa St.
Lansing, MI 48933
(517) 342-2498 Fax: (517) 342-2468
Serapio Hernández, Dir. for Hispanic Ministry
Email: sherna@dioceseoflansing.org

DIOCESE OF MARQUETTE
Hispanic Affairs
P.O. Box 550
444 S. Fourth St.
Marquette, MI 49855
(906) 2225-1141 Fax: (906) 225-0437

DIOCESE OF SAGINAW
Hispanic Affairs
405 Hayes St.
Saginaw, MI 48602
(517) 755-4478 Fax: (517) 755-5223
María Cepeda, Vicar for Hispanic Ministry
Email: andrea@dioceseofsaginaw.org

EL CENTRO "LA FAMILIA"
Oakland County Comm.Mental Health
35 W. Huron, #200
Pontiac, MI 48342
(248) 858-5320 Fax: (248) 858-1604
Dr. Sonya Acosta, Supervisor

EMPLOYEE ASSISTANCE/SUBSTANCE ABUSE SERVICES
405 Mill Road Professional Building

Adrian, MI 49221
(517) 263-2625 Fax: (517) 263-7369
Vicki Hall, Site Director

FAMILY INDEPENDENCE AGENCY
National Headquarters
429 Montague St.
Caro, MI 48723
(517) 673-9100 Fax: (517) 673-9209
Thomas Dillon MSW, Director

FAMILY MEDICAL CENTER
8765 Lewis Ave.
Temperance, MI 48182
(313) 847-3802 Fax: (313) 847-3418
Catherine Lamb, Exec. Director

FANTASÍA 2000 BALLET OF MARÍA VALDEZ
531 Ash St.
Lansing, MI 48906
(517) 372-3023 Fax: (517) 372-3023
Margarita Valdez, Director
Email: valdezm1@pilotmsu.edu

FARMWORKER LEGAL SERVICES
668 Three Mile Rd.
Walker, MI 49544
(616) 785-8666 Fax: (616) 785-8840
Janice Morgan, Attorney Mngr.

FARRAGUT AGENCY CENTER
301 N. Farragut St., #201
Bay City, MI 48708
(517) 892-6605
Eudora Ortega, Director

GOOD SAMARITAN MINISTRIES
513 E. A Street, Suite 25
Holland, MI 49423
(616) 392-7159 Fax: (616) 392-5889
Janet De Young, Dir.

GRAND TRAVERSE COUNTY FAMILY INDEPENDENT AGENCY
P. O. Box 1250
920 Hastings St.
Traverse City, MI 49685-1250
(616) 929-0141 or (616) 941-3900
Fax: (616) 941-0037
Bob Porter, Acting Dir.

GRATIOT COUNTY FAMILY INDEPENDENT AGENCY
P. O. Box 250
Ithaca, MI 48847
(517) 875-5181 Fax: (517) 875-2811
Dona Ogrady, Director

GREATER LANSING HISPANIC CHAMBER OF COMMERCE
515 N. Larch
Lansing, MI 48912
(517) 484-1007 Fax: (517) 485-8119
Gonzalo Ríos, President
Email: line@voyager.net

HEALTH DELIVERY, INC.
Administrative Offices
3605 Davenport
Saginaw, MI 48602-3310
(517) 792-8751 Fax: (517) 792-2570
Dave Gámez, President

HISPANIC AIDE PROGRAM
Michigan State University
338 Student Services
East Lansing, MI 48824-1113
(517) 353-7745 Fax: (517) 432-1495
Luis Alonzo García, Chicano/Latino Student Affairs Coordinator

HISPANIC AMERICAN COUNCIL, INC.
Affiliate of NCLR
1627 W. Main St.
Kalamazoo, MI 49006-3154
(616) 385-6279 Fax: (616) 385-2803
Armando Romero, Board President

HISPANIC AND LATIN BUSINESS STUDENTS' ASSOCIATION
University of Michigan
Multi-Ethnic Student Affairs
2202 Michigan Union
Ann Arbor, MI 48109-1349
(734) 763-9044 Fax: (734) 647-4133
Sylvia K. Paas, President
Email: spaas@umich.edu

HISPANIC BUSINESS ALLIANCE
4128 W. Bernor, #101
Detroit, MI 48209
(313) 963-4700 Fax: (313) 963-8379
Andre Arvelaez, Director

HISPANIC CENTER
1537 S. Washington
Saginaw, MI 48601
(517) 753-5806 Fax: (517) 753-5106
Dolores Gómez, Center Manager.

HISPANIC CENTER OF WESTERN MICHIGAN, INC.
Affiliate of NCLR
730 Grandville Ave.
Grand Rapids, MI 49503-4920
(616) 742-0200 Fax: (616) 742-0205
Nick Garza, Executive Director
Email: hcwm@iserv.net
Web: www.iserv.net/~hcwm/

HISPANIC INTERNAL REVENUE EMPLOYEES (HIRE)
Detroit Chapter
985 Michigan Ave., 2nd Floor
Detroit, MI 48226
(313) 234-1205 Fax: (313) 234-1293
Barbara R. Parra-Vasquez, Vice-Chair

HISPANIC JOURNALISM PROGRAM
Michigan State University
School of Journalism
305 Communication Arts
East Lansing, MI 48824-1212
(517) 353-6430 Fax: (517) 335-7710
Raye Grill, Coordinator

HISPANIC SERVICE CENTER
P. O. Box 284
Imlay City, MI 48444
(810) 724-3665 Fax: (810) 924-7731
Santiago Vásquez, Director
Email: hscenter.org@worldnet.att.net

HISPANIC YOUTH LEADERSHIP DEVELOPMENT PROGRAM, PROYECTO ESPERANZA
Affiliate of Catholic Youth Organization
305 Michigan Ave., 9th Floor
Detroit, MI 48226
(313) 963-7177 Fax: (313) 963-7179
Frederick Feliciano, Coordinator

HURON COUNTY FAMILY INDEPENDENT AGENCY
1911 Sand Beach Rd.
Bad Axe, MI 48413
(517) 269-9201 Fax: (517) 269-9875
David Hollandback, AP Superv.

IDA PUBLIC SCHOOLS
Migrant/Bilingual Education Programs
3145 Prairie St.
Ida, MI 48140
(734) 269-3485 Fax: (734) 269-2294
Mr. Wenman, Dir. of Lang. Dept.

IMAGE DE MICHIGAN
National Image, Inc.
8051 Clippert
Taylor, MI 48180
(313) 226-6075 Fax: (313) 226-4769
Conrad S. Valle, Jr, Regional Director & Chapter President
Email: conrad.valle@sba.gov
Web: www.nationalimageinc.org

INGHAM COUNTY FAMILY INDEPENDENT AGENCY
P. O. Box 30088
5303 S. Cedar St.
Lansing, MI 48909
(517) 887-9400 Fax: (517) 887-9500
Janet Stope, Director

INTERCARE COMMUNITY HEALTH NETWORK
697 Weld Street
Benton Harbor, MI 49024
(616) 927-5400 or (616) 927-5300
Fax: (616) 927-5493
Jody Elliott, Manager.

6270 W. Main Street
Eau Claire, MI 49111
(616) 461-6927 or (616) 461-6927
Fax: (616) 461-3068
Zully Westraite, Manager.

Administration
P. O. Box 130
308 Charles St.
Bangor, MI 49013
(616) 427-7967 Fax: (616) 427-8779
Zully Westraite, Manager.

Migrant & Rural Community Health Association
285 James St., James Center
Holland, MI 49424
(616) 399-0200 Fax: (616) 399-5055
Ena Gunnick, Director

INTERFAITH COUNCIL OF PEACE
730 Tappan St.
Ann Arbor, MI 48104
(313) 663-1870 Fax: (313) 663-9458
Tobi Hanna-Davies, Director

INTERNATIONAL INSTITUTE
111 E. Kirby
Detroit, MI 48202
(313) 871-8600 Fax: (313) 817-1651
Rosemary Bannon, Director

IONIA COUNTY FAMILY INDEPENDENT AGENCY
920 E. Lincoln
Ionia, MI 48846
(616) 527-5200 or (616) 527-5274
Fax: (616) 527-1849/5298
Phaul Lorson, Interim Director

JOHNSON DAY CARE CENTER
615 S. Dalrymple St.
Albion, MI 49224
(517) 629-9550
Mary L. Lueken, Director

JULIÁN SAMORA RESEARCH INSTITUTE
Michigan State University
112 Paolucci Bldg.
East Lansing, MI 48824-1110
(517) 432-1317 Fax: (517) 432-2221
Refugio Rochin, Director
Web: www.jsri.msu.edu

JUNCTION HEALTH CENTER
4771 Michigan Ave.
Detroit, MI 48210
(313) 897-2600 Fax: (313) 897-2424
Pam Hipsher, Director

LA SALUD PUBLIC HEALTH STUDENT ORGANIZATION
University of Michigan
Multi-Ethnic Student Affairs
2202 Michigan Union
Ann Arbor, MI 48109-1349
(734) 763-9044 Fax: (734) 647-4133
Dana Cruz Santana, President
Email: la.salud@umich.edu or ydiaz@umich.edu

LA VOZ MEXICANA
University of Michigan
Multi-Ethnic Student Affairs
2202 Michigan Union
Ann Arbor, MI 48109-1349
(734) 763-9044 Fax: (734) 647-4133
Richard Nunn, President
Email: lavoz@umich.edu

LABOR NOTES
7435 Michigan Ave.
Detroit, MI 48210
(313) 842-6262 Fax: (313) 842-0227
Kim Moody, Director
Email: labornotes@igc.apc.ort

LAMBDA THETA PHI, FRATERNIDAD LATINA, INC.
University of Michigan
Multi-Ethnic Student Affairs
2202 Michigan Union
Ann Arbor, MI 48109-1349
(734) 763-9044 Fax: (734) 647-4133
Diego M. Bernal, President
Email: lambda.theta.phi@umich.edu

LATIN AMERICAN AND NATIVE AMERICAN MEDICAL ASSOCIATION
University of Michigan
Multi-Ethnic Student Affairs
2202 Michigan Union
Ann Arbor, MI 48109-1349
(734) 763-9044 Fax: (734) 647-4133
Pablo Pazmino, President
Email: lanamamed@umich.edu

LATIN AMERICAN FAMILY SERVICES
Child & Family Services of Western Michigan, Inc.
412 Century Ln.
Holland, MI 49423

(616) 396-2301 Fax: (616) 396-8070
Frederick Groen, Executive Director
Email: jrios@cfswm.org
Web: www.cfswm.org

LATIN AMERICAN SERVICES
Sheldon Complex
121 Franklin St., SE
Grand Rapids, MI 49507
(616) 336-4018 Fax: (616) 336-4012
Zoraida Sánchez, Director
Email: sanchezz@nwd.org

LATIN AMERICAN STUDIES CENTER
Michigan State University
Center for International Programs, #206
East Lansing, MI 48824
(517) 353-1690 Fax: (517) 432-7471
Dr. Scott Whiteford, Director
Web: www.isp.msu.edu/clacs/

LATIN AMERICANS FOR SOCIAL AND ECONOMIC DEVELOPMENT, INC.
4138 W. Vernor
Detroit, MI 48209
(313) 554-2025 Fax: (313) 554-2242
Eva Garza-Dewealsche, Executive Director

Senior Citizens Center, Affiliate of NCLR
7150 W. Vernor
Detroit, MI 48209
(313) 841-8840 Fax: (313) 841-2884
María Garcia, Director

LATIN COUNTS
5427 W. Vernor
Detroit, MI 48209
(313) 554-4480 Fax: (313) 554-4480
Sal Prado, Director

LATINO ADVOCATE OFFICE
Western Michigan University
A-211 Ellsworth
Office of Minority Student Services
Kalamazoo, MI 49008
(616) 387-3329 or (616) 387-4420
Fax: (616) 387-3390
Mike Ramírez, Coordinator

LATINO STUDENT ASSOCIATION
Eastern Michigan University
001-L Mckenny Union, Mail Box 10
Ypsilanti, MI 48197
(734) 487-1470 or (734) 482-2680 (h)
Fax: (734) 487-0940
Cinthya Rodríguez, President

LATINO/A LAW STUDENT ASSOCIATION
University of Michigan
Multi-Ethnic Student Affairs
2202 Michigan Union
Ann Arbor, MI 48109-1349
(734) 763-9044 Fax: (734) 647-4133
Tom I. Romero, II, President
Email: llsa@umich.edu or romeroii@umich.edu

LEAGUE OF UNITED LATIN AMERICAN CITIZENS (LULAC)
Midwest Region-MI
2435 South Outer Drive
Saginaw, MI 48601
(517) 753-3412 x119 or (517) 755-1748
Fax: (517) 753-3417
Ramiro González, State Director
Email: ramirog@juno.com

LEELANAU COUNTY FAMILY INDEPENDENCE AGENCY
7322 E. Ducklake Rd.
Lake Leelanau, MI 49653
(616) 256-6100 Fax: (616) 256-2312
Debbie Johnson, Mgr.

LENAWEE COUNTY FAMILY INDEPENDENCE AGENCY
1040 S. Winter St., #3013
Adrian, MI 49221
(517) 264-6300 or (517) 264-6320
Fax: (517) 264-6357
Bob Hamilton, Secretary

LVA CAPITOL AREA LITERACY COALITION
1028 E. Saginaw
Lansing, MI 48906
(517) 485-4949 Fax: (517) 485-1924
Neil Hagarty, Asst. Director
Email: lvacalc@pilot.msu.edu

MANA - A NATIONAL LATINA ORGANIZATION
Michigan Chapter
7752 W. Vernor, #103

Detroit, MI 48209
(313) 554-2400 Fax: (313) 554-2442
Angela Reyes, Chapter President
Email: hermana2@aol.com
Web: www.hermana.org

MANISTEE COUNTY FAMILY INDEPENDENCE AGENCY
1672 U.S. 31 South
Manistee, MI 49660
(616) 723-8375 Fax: (616) 398-2106
Mary Adamski, Office Manager.

MARIACHI AMERICA
1433 Campbell
Detroit, MI 48209
(313) 849-1914
Manuel Zaragoza, Director

MEXICAN INDUSTRIES IN MICHIGAN
Dearborn Office
13500 Rotunda Dr.
Dearborn, MI 48120
(313) 581-0077 Fax: (313) 581-6440
Tom Libby, Plant Manager.

MEXICAN INDUSTRIES IN MICHIGAN
Detroit Office
1801 Howard St.
Detroit, MI 48216
(313) 963-6114 Fax: (313) 963-3019
Marcy McTharlin, Dir. President

MICHIGAN COMMISSION ON SPANISH SPEAKING AFFAIRS
National Headquarters
State of MI Dept. of Civil Rights/Affiliate of NCLR
741 N. Cedar, #102
Lansing, MI 48913
(517) 334-8626 Fax: (517) 334-8641
Marylou Olivarez Mason, Executive Director
Email: masonm@state.mi.us

MICHIGAN EDUCATION ASSOCIATION
Bilingual/Migrant Education Program
P. O. Box 2573
East Lansing, MI 48826
(517) 332-6551 x6665 Fax: (517) 336-4013
Janille Jackson, Director
Email: jjackson@mea.org
Web: www.mea.org

MICHIGAN EDUCATIONAL OPPORTUNITY FUND, INC.
Affiliate of NCLR
P.O. Box 19152
Lansing, MI 48901
(517) 334-8626 Fax: (517) 482-2006
Marylou Olivarez Mason, Board Chair Person
Email: masonm@state.mi.us

MICHIGAN HISPANIC CHAMBER OF COMMERCE
24445 Northwestern Hwy., #206
Southfield, MI 48075
(248) 208-9915 Fax: (248) 208-9936
Yolanda Gómez Stupka, President & CEO
Email: mhccchairman@ameritech.net
Web: www.MHCC.org

MICHIGAN LEAGUE FOR HUMAN SERVICES
300 N. Washington Sq. #401
Lansing, MI 48933
(517) 487-5436 Fax: (517) 371-4546
Ana Marston, Pres./CEO
Email: http://pilot.msu.edu/~/mLhs

MICHIGAN MINORITY BUSINESS DEVELOPMENT COUNCIL
3011 W. Grand Blvd., #230
Detroit, MI 48202
(313) 873-3200 Fax: (313) 873-4783
Thomas Ferrebee, Certification Director
Email: mmbdc@mmbdc.org
Web: www.mmbdc.org

MICHIGAN PRIMARY CARE ASSOCIATION
2369 Woodlake Dr. #280
Okemos, MI 48864
(517) 381-8000 Fax: (517) 381-8008
Kim Sibilski, Executive Director
Email: ksibilsk@michpca.org
Web: www.michpca.org

MICHIGAN TEEN CHALLENGE OF SAGINAW, INC.
P.O. Box 1020, 503 N. Jefferson Ave.
Saginaw, MI 48606
(517) 753-1103
Rev. John Taylor, Contact

MIGRANT AIDS EDUCATION INITIATIVE
American Red Cross/Ottawa Co. Chapter
270 James St.
Holland, MI 49424
(616) 396-6545 Fax: (616) 396-3921
Julie Hulst, Director

MIGRANT HEALTH PROMOTION - PROMOVIENDO VIDAS SALUDABLES
National Headquarters
224 W. Michigan Ave.
Saline, MI 48176
(734) 944-0244 Fax: (734) 944-1405
Kim Kratz, Executive Director
Email: migranthealth@voyager.net

MOVIEMIENTO ESTUDIANTIL CHICANO/ A DE AZTLAN (MECHA)
University of Michigan
Multi-Ethnic Student Affairs
2202 Michigan Union
Ann Arbor, MI 48109-1349
(734) 763-9044 Fax: (734) 647-4133
Manuel Munguia, President
Email: mecha-um@umich.edu or mmunguia@umich.edu

MULTI-ETHNIC STUDENT AFFAIRS
University of Michigan
2202 Michigan Union
Ann Arbor, MI 48108-1349
(734) 763-9044 Fax: (734) 647-4133
Katalina Berdy, Latino Coordinator

MUSEO INDIGENISTA
4000 W. Vernor
Detroit, MI 48209
(313) 841-5470 or (313) 554-1619
Lucile Cruz Gajec, Director

MUSKEGON-OCEANA COMMUNITY ACTION AGAINST POVERTY
1706 Clinton, #003
Muskegon, MI 49442
(616) 725-9436 Fax: (616) 722-1959
Maxine Lenear, Director

NATIONAL ASSOCIATION FOR HISPANIC ELDERLY
Detroit Office/Project Ayuda
220 Bagley, #222
Detroit, MI 48226
(313) 965-6117 Fax: (313) 965-6312
Lydia Hryzodub, Project Coordinator

NEIGHBORHOOD LEGAL SERVICE
3400 Cadillac Towers
Detroit, MI 48226
(313) 962-0466 Fax: (313) 962-6374
Linda Bernard, Dir. & CEO
Email: LDBernard@WCNLS.ORG

NEW DETROIT, INC.
Affiliate of NCLR
3011 W. Grand Blvd., #1200
Detroit, MI 48202-3013
(313) 664-2000 Fax: (313) 664-2071
Horacio Vargas, Director
Web: www.newdetroit.org

NORTHWEST MICHIGAN HEALTH SERVICES, INC.
Affiliate of NCLR
10767 Traverse Hwy., #B
Traverse City, MI 49684
(231) 947-1112 Fax: (231) 947-7739
Bill Reimer, Executive Director
Email: wehintvc@aol.com

NORTHWEST MICHIGAN MIGRANT RESOURCE COUNCIL
c/o M.E.S.C.
P. O. Box 159
1909 North Mitchell
Cadillac, MI 49601
(616) 775-3408 Fax: (616) 775-1584
Jerry Bear, St. Manager.

OCEANA COUNTY FAMILY INDEPENDECE AGENCY
P. O. Box 70, 535 Russell Rd.
Hart, MI 49420
(616) 873-7251 or (616) 873-7230
Fax: (616) 873-7152
Belvet Sabagi, Act. Director

OFFICE OF MULTICULTURAL AFFAIRS
Madonna University
36600 Schoolcraft Rd.
Livonia, MI 48066

(734) 432-5541 Fax: (734) 432-5393
Osvaldo Rivera, Director
Email: rivera@smtp.munrt.edu

PERUVIAN AMERICAN MEDICAL SOCIETY
National Headquarters
Administrative Office
6488 Tamerlane Dr.
West Bloomfield, MI 48322
(248) 851-2709 Fax: (248) 851-2044
Ana May Salgado, Administrator

PHILADELPHIA HOUSE
218 Washington St.
Monroe, MI 48161
(313) 242-4266
Leo Hamilton, Director

PUERTO RICAN ASSOCIATION
University of Michigan
Multi-Ethnic Student Affairs
2202 Michigan Union
Ann Arbor, MI 48109-1349
(734) 763-9044 Fax: (734) 647-4133
Juan Pablo Gaztambide, President
Email: jgaztamb@umich.edu

PUERTORRICAN SOLIDARITY ORG.
University of Michigan
Multi-Ethnic Student Affairs
2202 Michigan Union
Ann Arbor, MI 48109-1349
(734) 763-9044 Fax: (734) 647-4133
Katherine T. Tossas-Rodríguez, President
Email: prso@umich.edu or ktossas@umich.edu

PULLMAN HEALTH CENTER
5498 109th Ave.
Pullman, MI 49450
(616) 236-5021 Fax: (616) 236-5411
Linda Siskel, Interim Director

REGION II COMMUNITY ACTION AGENCY
P. O. Drawer 1107
Jackson, MI 49204
(517) 784-4800 Fax: (517) 784-5188
Marsha Kruecher, Executive Director
Email: tpheart@dmci.com
Web: www.caajlh.org

SAINT JOHN'S CATHOLIC CHURCH
879 Finley Dr.
Albion, MI 49224
(517) 629-4532
Father Gordon Greene, Contact

SAINT JOSEPH CATHOLIC CHURCH
61 N. 23rd St.
Battle Creek, MI 49015
(616) 962-0165 Fax: (616) 962-5937
James O'Leavy, Contact

SAINT JOSEPH CHURCH
924 E. 2nd St.
Monroe, MI 48161
(313) 241-9590 Fax: (313) 241-5296
Rev. William Fischer, Cont.

SER-METRO-DETROIT JOBS FOR PROGRESS, INC.
Affiliate of SER-Jobs for Progress National, Inc.
9301 Michigan Ave.
Detroit, MI 48210
(313) 846-2240 Fax: (313) 846-2247
Ignacio Salazar, Director
Email: isalazar@detroitnwa.org
Web: www.sernational.org

SIGMA LAMBDA BETA FRATERNITY, INC.
University of Michigan
Multi-Ethnic Student Affairs
2202 Michigan Union
Ann Arbor, MI 48109-1349
(734) 763-9044 Fax: (734) 647-4133
Efrain Martínez, President
Email: chamucos@umich.edu or aurelio@umich.edu

SOCIETY OF HISPANIC PROFESSIONAL ENGINEERS (SHPE)
Detroit Professional Chapter
P.O. Box 1728
Dearborn, MI 48121
(313) 248-6022 Fax: (313) 337-1201
Mario Campos, Vice President External Relations
Email: mcampos1@ford.com
Web: www.shpe-detroit.org

University of Michigan
Multi-Ethnic Student Affairs
2202 Michigan Union
Ann Arbor, MI 48109-1349
(734) 763-9044 Fax: (734) 647-4133
Ilka Vázquez, President
Email: shpe@umich.edu or
jrgarcia@engin.umich.edu

SOUTHWEST COUNSELING &
DEVELOPMENT SERVICES
1700 Waterman
Detroit, MI 48209
(313) 841-8905 Fax: (313) 841-3756
Graciela Vellalobos, Director

SOUTHWEST DETROIT COMMUNITY
MENTAL HEALTH SERVICES
1700 Waterman
Detroit, MI 48209
(313) 841-8905 Fax: (313) 841-4470
John Van Camp, President

SPANISH SPEAKING INFORMATION
CENTER (SSIC)
Affiliate of NCLR
202 E. Boulevard Dr., #320
Flint, MI 48503
(810) 239-4417 Fax: (810) 239-4419
Lily Tamez-Kehoe, Executive Director
Email: centro4417@aol.com

SPARTA HEALTH CENTER
475 South State St.
Sparta, MI 49345
(616) 887-8831 Fax: (616) 875-5989
Sarah Gold, Exec. Director

ST. FRANCIS XAVIER CHURCH
4250 W Jefferson
Ecorse, MI 48229
(313) 383-8514 Fax: (313) 383-7508
Víctor Román, Priest

ST. GABRIEL CHURCH
8118 W Vernor
Detroit, MI 48209
(313) 841-0753 Fax: (313) 841-0916
Charles Farrar, Pastor

STATE BAR ASSOCIATION
Latin American Bar Activities Section
25050 W. Outer Dr., #201
Lincoln Park, MI 48146
(313) 389-4955 Fax: (313) 389-4955
David Merchan, Attorney

TELAMON CORPORATION
Michigan Migrant Head Start
38 Applewood Dr., NW
Sparta, MI 49345
(616) 887-0180 Fax: (616) 887-1098
Carol Whyte, Regional Coordinator
Web: www.telamon.org

Michigan Office 17
10767 Traverse Hwy., #A
Traverse City, MI 49684
(231) 941-5300 Fax: (231) 941-0924
Dagoberto Garza, Regional Manager
Web: www.telamon.org

Michigan Office 2
1040 S. Winter St., #1014
Adrian, MI 49221
(517) 263-6825 Fax: (517) 263-6914
Paula Lozano, Regional Manager
Web: www.telamon.org

Michigan Office 20
3310 Coloma Rd.
Benton Harbor, MI 49022
(616) 849-2909 Fax: (616) 849-0734
Jacquelyn Polaskey, Regional Manager
Web: www.telamon.org

Michigan Office 3
710 Chicago, #310
Holland, MI 49423
(616) 396-5160 Fax: (616) 396-6992
Rubén Santellán, Regional Manager
Email: rsantellan@novagate.net
Web: www.telamon.org

TELAMON CORPORATION
Michigan Office 4
232 E. Michigan Ave.
Paw Paw, MI 49079
(616) 655-9916 Fax: (616) 655-9507
Molly Swabash, Regional Manager
Web: www.telamon.org

Michigan Office 5
38 Applewood Dr., NW
Sparta, MI 49345
(616) 887-0180 Fax: (616) 887-1098
Dante Villareal, Regional Manager
Email: vdante@compuserv.com
Web: www.telamon.org

Michigan Office 6
820 Washington Ave.
Bay City, MI 48708
(517) 894-8941 Fax: (517) 894-8944
Jose M. Costilla, Regional Manager
Email: jcostilla@compuserve.com
Web: www.telamon.org

Michigan State Office
6250 W. Michigan Ave., #C
Lansing, MI 48917
(517) 323-7002 Fax: (517) 323-9840
Sam R. García, State Director
Web: www.telamon.org

TRI-CITY/SER-JOBS FOR PROGRESS, INC.
Affiliate of SER-Jobs for Progress
National, Inc.
604 Oak St.
Saginaw, MI 48602
(517) 753-3412 Fax: (517) 753-3410
Ramiro López, Executive Director
Web: www.sernational.org

TUSCOLA COUNTY FAMILY
INDEPENDENCE AGENCY
1365 Cleaver Rd.
Caro, MI 48723
(517) 673-9100 Fax: (517) 795-9209
Thomas Dillon, Director

UNITED STATES-MEXICO CHAMBER OF
COMMERCE
Great Lakes Chapter/Michigan
21170 Bridge Street
Southfield, MI 48034
(248) 827-1127 Fax: (248) 827-1138

VAN BUREN COUNTY FAMILY
INDEPENDENCE AGENCY
P. O. Box 7, C.R. 681
Hartford, MI 49057
(616) 621-2800 or (616) 621-2883
Fax: (616) 621-2962 or (616) 621-2840
Mark Del Mariani, Director

MINNESOTA

BLACK, INDIAN, HISPANIC, AND ASIAN
WOMEN IN ACTION
122 W. Franklin Ave., #306
Minneapolis, MN 55404
(612) 870-1193 Fax: (612) 870-0855
Alice O. Lynch, Executive Director
Email: BIHA@worldnet.att.net

CADA HOUSE
P.O. Box 466
Mankato, MN 56002
(507) 625-7233 Fax: (507) 625-9431
Judy Anderson, Coordinator
Email: cada@ic.mankato.mn.us

CATHOLIC CHARITIES
Rural Outreach
105 NW Third St.
Montgomery, MN 56069
(507) 364-7321 Fax: (507) 364-7322
Bob Kell, Program Developer
Email: ccrop@frontiernet.net

CENTRO DE CRISIS
203 W Clark St.
Albert Lea, MN 56007
(507) 373-2223 Fax: (507) 377-5505
Rose Homestead, Assistant Supervisor

CHICANO & LATIN AMERICAN STUDENT
ASSOCIATION (CLASA)
Mankato State University
P.O. Box 8400, Stu Union Room 22
Office of Multicultural Affairs MSU 65
Mankato, MN 56001-8400
(507) 389-6300 Fax: (507) 389-6209
Raquel Pena, Cult. Div. Asst. for Latin Affairs
Email: raquelapena@hotmail.com

CHICANO LATINO AFFAIRS COUNCIL
Affiliate of NCLR
555 Park St., #210
St. Paul, MN 55103
(651) 296-9587/9541 Fax: (651) 297-1297
Ytmar Santiago, Executive Director
Email: clac.desk@state.mn.us
Web: www.clac.state.mn.us

CHICANO-LATINO YOUTH LEADERSHIP
INSTITUTE
Region Nine Development Commission
P.O. Box 3367, 410 Jackson Street
Mankato, MN 56001
(507) 387-5643 or (507) 389-8889
Fax: (507) 387-7105
Verónica Alba, Community Prevention Planner
Email: valba@rndc.mankato.mn.us
Web: www.rndc.org

CHICANOS LATINOS UNIDOS EN SERVICIO
Affiliate of NCLR
220 S. Robert St. #103
St. Paul, MN 55107
(651) 292-0117 Fax: (651) 292-0347
Jesse Bethke, Director
Web: www.clues.org

CLOUDFOREST INITIATIVES
P.O. Box 40207
St. Paul, MN 55104
(651) 592-4143
Shelley Sherman, US Coordinator

DIOCESE OF CROOKSTON
Hispanic Ministry Officce
P.O. Box 610
1200 Memorial Dr.
Crookston, MN 56716
(218) 281-4533 Fax: (218) 281-3328
Sr. Leona Ulewicz, CDP
Email: lulewicz@crookston.org

DIOCESE OF DULUTH
Hispanic Affairs
2830 E. 4th St.
Duluth, MN 55812
(218) 724-9111 Fax: (218) 724-1056
, Hispanic Ministry Coordinator

DIOCESE OF NEW ULM
1400 N. 6th St.
New Ulm, MN 56073
(507) 359-2966 Fax: (507) 354-3667
Rev. Anthony J. Stubeda, Dir. for Hisp.Ministry
Email: padretony@hotmail.com

DIOCESE OF ST. CLOUD
Hispanic Affairs
116 8th Ave. SE
Little Falls, MN 56345
(320) 632-2981 Fax: (320) 632-6313
Sr. Adela Gross, OSF, Coordinator for
Multicultural Ministry
Email: agross@fslf.org

DIOCESE OF ST. PAUL & MINNEAPOLIS
Hispanic Affairs
840 E. 6th St.
St. Paul, MN 55106
(651) 793-9791 Fax: (651) 776-2759
Anne Attea, Coordinator for Hispanic Ministry
Email: hispanicministry@archspm.org

DIOCESE OF WINONA
Catholic Charities
P.O. Box 379
111 Market St.
Winona, MN 55897
(507) 454-2270 Fax: (507) 457-3027
Kelly Momsen, Director for Hispanic Ministry
Email: krmomsen@yahoo.com

HISPANIC NATIONAL BAR ASSOCIATION
Region XI (IA, MN, MO, ND, SD)
162 College Ave., #3
St. Paul, MN 55102
(651) 221-4855 Fax: (651) 244-5362
Manuel Guerrero, Regional President
Email: guerr002@tc.umn.edu
Web: www.hnba.com

HISPANIC PRE-COLLEGE PROJECT
University of St. Thomas
CHC217, 2115 Summit Ave.
St. Paul, MN 55105-1096
(651) 962-6340 Fax: (651) 962-6353
Ramona A. De Rosales, Director
Email: raderosales@stthomas.edu
Web: www.stthomas.edu/hpcp

HISPANOS EN MINNESOTA
HIV/AIDS Prevention Program
155 S Wabasha St., #128
St. Paul, MN 55107
(651) 227-0831 Fax: (651) 227-0834
Jerry Guevara, Executive Director

HONEYWELL HISPANIC NETWORK (HHN)
PO Box 524
Minneapolis, MN 55440-0524

(612) 951-0054 Fax: (612) 951-0433
Sarah Hernandez, Chair

JOB SERVICE SECURITY
Department of Economic Security
12 Civic Center Plaza, #1600A
Mankato, MN 56001
(507) 389-6723 Fax: (507) 389-2708
Janie Sandoval, Migrant Labor Representative
Email: janie.sandoval@state.mn.us
Web: www.mnworks.org

LA OPORTUNIDAD, INC.
1821 University Ave. W. N494
St. Paul, MN 55104-2801
(612) 646-6115 Fax: (612) 646-7564
Miguel Ramos, Director

LA RAZA STUDENT CULTURAL CENTER
University of Minnesota
720 Washington Ave SE, #8
Minneapolis, MN 55414
(612) 625-2995 Fax: (612) 627-7680
Michelle Lopez, Intercultural Representative
Email: laraza@umn.edu
Web: www.laraza.umn.edu

LATIN AMERICAN-MEXICAN
ASSOCIATION FOR NETWORKING AND
OPPORTUNITY (LA-MANO)
P.O. Box 3373
12 Civic Center Plaza, #1370
Mankato, MN 56002-3373
(507) 344-8361 Fax: (507) 344-8590
Victoria Salas, Director
Email: lamano@gotocrystal.net

LIFE-WORK PLANNING CENTER
201 N Broad, #100
Mankato, MN 56001
(507) 345-1577 Fax: (507) 345-1469
Susan Bruss, Director
Web: www.lwpc.org

MIGRANT HEALTH SERVICE, INC.
810 4th Ave. S
Moorhead, MN 56560
(218) 236-6502 Fax: (218) 236-6507
Joan Altanbernd, Director

MIGRANT LEGAL SERVICES-SOUTHERN
MN Regional Legal Services
46 E 4th St., #700
St. Paul, MN 55101
(651) 291-2837 or (800) 652-9733
Fax: (651) 228-9450
Jennifer Stohl, Director
Email: jennifer.stohl@smrls.org

MINNESOTA DEPT. OF HUMAN RIGHTS
190 E. 5th St.
St. Paul, MN 55101
(612) 296-5663 Fax: (612) 296-9064
Vicky Olivo, Coordinator

MINNESOTA HISPANIC EDUC. PROG.
Affiliate of NCLR
1821 University Ave., W, #S308
St. Paul, MN 55104
(651) 917-1913 Fax: (651) 917-1914
Mario Vargas, Executive Director
Email: mhep@uswest.net

MUJERES UNIDAS
55 8th S
St. James, MN 56081
(507) 375-5770 Fax: (507) 375-5049
Melinda López, Outreach Advocate

MULTICULTURAL INSTITUTE OF THE
ACADEMIC HEALTH CENTER
University of Minnesota
1-125 Moos Twr. #515 Delaware St. SE
Minneapolis, MN 55455
(612) 624-9400 Fax: (612) 624-2191
Jaki Cottingham-Vierdt, Director

NEIGHBORHOOD HOUSE ASSOCIATION
179 E Robie St.
St. Paul, MN 55107
(651) 227-9291 Fax: (651) 227-8734
Dan Hoxworph, Director
Email: dhoxworph@nighb.org

NEIGHBORHOOD JUSTICE CENTER
500 Laurel Ave.
St. Paul, MN 55102
(651) 222-4703 Fax: (651) 222-0931
Joey Bartscher, Director
Email: info@njcinc.org
Web: www.njcinc.org

OUR LADY OF GUADALUPE CATHOLIC CHURCH
401 Concord St.
St. Paul, MN 55107
(612) 228-0506
Hugo Montero, Pastor

PROGRAM FOR CULTURAL COOPERATION SPAIN-USA
University of Minnesota
Global Campus 230 Heller Hall 271,19th Ave. S
Minneapolis, MN 55455
(612) 625-9888 Fax: (612) 626-8009
Holly Zimmerman, Coordinator
Email: zime001@umn.edu
Web: www.umabroad.umn.edu/pub/pcc/
pcc.html

RIVERVIEW ECONOMIC DEVELOPMENT ASSOC.
176 Concord St.
St. Paul, MN 55107
(651) 222-6347 Fax: (651) 222-8398
Julie Eigenseld, Executive Director
Email: wsreda@aol.com

SOCIETY OF HISPANIC PROFESSIONAL ENGINEERS (SHPE)
Minneapolis/St. Paul Professional Chapter
P.O. Box 28098
Woodbury, MN 55128
(651) 736-7576
Elda García Bloemendal, President
Email: etgarcia@mmm.com
Web: www.shpe.org

Minnesota State University, Mankato
P.O. Box 8400
Office of Multicultural Affairs - MS 65
Mankato, MN 56002-8400
(507) 389-6300 Fax: (507) 389-6209
Michael T. Flagin, Vice-Pres. of Cult. Diversity
Web: www.mankato.msus.edu/~shpe/
homepage/welcome.html

SOUTHERN MINNESOTA LEGAL SERVICES
12 Civic Center Plaza, #3000
Mankato, MN 56002
(507) 387-5588 Fax: (507) 387-2321
Rosa Mooney, Paralegal
Email: mankato@smrls.org

SPANISH CLUB
University of St. Thomas
CHC217, 2115 Summit Ave.
St. Paul, MN 55105-1096
(651) 962-5000 Fax: (651) 962-6353
Ramona A. De Rosales, Director
Web: www.stthomas.edu/reaction

SPANISH INTEREST NETWORK (S.P.I.N.)
IDS Tower 10
Minneapolis, MN 55440
(612) 671-4045 Fax: (612) 671-4916
Gloria Vallejo, Co-Chair

MISSISSIPPI

DIOCESE OF BILOXI
St. Thomas the Apostle
720 E. Beach Blvd.
Long Beach, MS 39560
(601) 863-1610
Rev. Louis Lohan, Director

DIOCESE OF JACKSON
Hispanic Affairs
P.O. Box 2248
237 E. Amite St.
Jackson, MS 39225-2248
(601) 949-6931 Fax: (601) 960-8455
Bro. Ted Dausch, Director for Hispanic Ministry
Email: ted.dausch@jacksondiocese.org

MISSOURI

ACCIÓN SOCIAL COMUNITARIA
3646 Fairview Ave.
St. Louis, MO 63116-4747
(314) 664-5565 Fax: (314) 772-8009
William Chignoli, Exec. Director
Email: LaClinica@aschl.org
Web: www.aschl.org

AMICOL
4728 Westminster Pl.
St. Louis, MO 63108

(314) 367-2206 Fax: (314) 367-2326
Jaime Ramírez
Email: amicol@prodigy.net

AMISTAD HISPANOHABLANTE
3957 Geraldine, #A
St. Ann, MO 63074
(314) 427-4390
Tomas Diaz, President
Email: mukai@zach.wustl.edu

ARGENTINE SOCIETY OF ST.LOUIS
P.O. Box 6063
Chesterfield, MO 63006-6063
(636) 230-5044 Fax: (636) 230-5044
Ciprinao Casado, President
Email: ctraboulsi@aol.com

ATLA-ARTS & TREASURES FROM LATIN AMERICA
1820 Market Street, #107
St. Louis, MO 63103
(314) 436-1666 Fax: (314) 436-1666
Susan Hamilton, President
Email: atla@artslatin.org
Web: www.artslatin.org

AYUDA SERVICIOS LATINOS
8837 Lucerne Court
St. Louis, MO 63136
Sally M. Moreno, President

AZTECA DE GREATER KANSAS CITY
P.O. Box 3277
Kansa City, MO 64171
(816) 931-8869
Kenneth Atrchuleta, President
Email: ajoropeza@aol.com

CABOT WESTSIDE CLINIC (CWL)
1810 Summit St.
Kansas City, MO 64108
(816) 471-0900 Fax: (816) 471-3150
Ken Siderly, Executive Director
Email: johnv@cabot.org
Web: www.cabot.org

CAMP FIRE BOYS AND GIRLS
4601 Madison Ave.
Kansas City, MO 64112-1278
(816) 756-1950 Fax: (816) 756-0258
Email: info@campfire.org
Web: www.campfire.org

THE CHURCH OF JESUS CHRIST OF LATTER DAY SAINTS
Independence Visitors' Center
937 W. Walnut St.
Independence, MO 64051
(816) 836-3466 Fax: (816) 252-6256
Elder Barlow, Director
Web: www.lds.org

DIOCESE OF JEFFERSON CITY
Hispanic Ministry Office
P.O. Box 220
373 W. Jackson
Marshall, MO 65340
(660) 886-3112 Fax: (660) 886-6606
Sr. Ellen Orf, CPPS
Email: selen@cdsinet.net

DIOCESE OF KANSAS CITY-ST. JOSEPH
Hispanic Affairs
P.O. Box 419037
Kansas City, MO 64141-6037
(816) 756-1850 Fax: (816) 756-0878
Bro. Dale Mooney, FSC, Coord. for Hisp. Min.
Email: dalejuan@juno.com

DIOCESE OF SPRINGFIELD-CAPE GIRARDEAU
Hispanic Affairs
601 S. Jefferson Ave.
Springfield, MO 65806-3143
(417) 866-0841 Fax: (417) 866-1140
Sr. Sandra Straub, CSJ, Hisp. Ministry Director
Email: sstraub@diocspfdcape.org

DIOCESE OF ST. LOUIS
Hispanic Affairs
5418 Louisiana St.
St. Louis, MO 63111
(314) 351-7009 Fax: (314) 351-3372
Juan Escarfuller, Director for Hispanic Ministry
Email: lapastoral@yahoo.com

DON BOSCO COMMUNITY CENTER, INC.
531 Garfield St.
Kansas City, MO 64124
(816) 691-2900 Fax: (816) 691-2958
Bob Magee, Director of Administration
Web: www.donbosco.org

FOLKLORIC GROUP COLOMBIA
1443 Meadowside Dr.
St.Louis, MO 63146
(314) 569-2119 Fax: (314) 569-2119
Nelly Patiño, Director
Email: folkloricol@yahoo.com

GRUPO ATLÁNTICO FROM COLOMBIA
1111 Dunston Dr.
St.Louis, MO 63146
(314) 362-8425 or (314) 227-7983
Carmen S. Dence, Director
Email: dence@mir.wustl.edu

GUADALUPE CENTER, INC.
Affiliate of NCLR
1015 César E.Chávez Ave.
Kansas City, MO 64108
(816) 472-4770 Fax: (816) 472-4773
Cristóbal Medina, Executive Director
Email: gcivolunteer@juno.com
Web: www.latinoweb.com/guadinc/

Alta Vista Education Center
1722 Holly
Kansas City, MO 64108
(816) 471-2582 Fax: (816) 471-2139
Cristóbal Medina, Executive Director
Email: gcivolunteer@juno.com
Web: www.latinoweb.com/guadinc/

Casa Feliz Senior Center
2600 Belleview
Kansas City, MO 64108
(816) 531-6911
Cristóbal Medina, Executive Director
Email: gcivolunteer@juno.com
Web: www.latinoweb.com/guadinc/

Our Lady of Guadalupe Elem. School
2310 Madison
Kansas City, MO 64108
(816) 221-2539
Cristóbal Medina, Executive Director
Email: gcivolunteer@juno.com
Web: www.latinoweb.com/guadinc/

Plaza de Niños Pre-School
2541 Belleview
Kansas City, MO 64108
(816) 472-5108 Fax: (816) 472-1735
Cristóbal Medina, Executive Director
Email: gcivolunteer@juno.com
Web: www.latinoweb.com/guadinc/

Sacred Heart Youth Center
814 W. 26th St.
Kansas City, MO 64108
(816) 221-5226 Fax: (816) 221-5347
Cristóbal Medina, Executive Director
Email: gcivolunteer@juno.com
Web: www.latinoweb.com/guadinc/

Salud Center, Health & Social Services
2641 Belleview
Kansas City, MO 64108
(816) 561-6885 Fax: (816) 561-7009
Cristóbal Medina, Executive Director
Email: gcivolunteer@juno.com
Web: www.latinoweb.com/guadinc/

HISPANIC ARTS COUNCIL OF ST. LOUIS
#3 The Prado
St. Louis, MO 63124
(314) 863-0570 or (314) 991-1750
Fax: (314) 726-3494
Rosa Schwarz, President
Email: mvbraxs@artsci.wustl.edu

HISPANIC CHAMBER OF COMMERCE OF GREATER KANSAS CITY
1125 Grand Ave., #1803
Kansas City, MO 64106
(816) 472-6767 Fax: (816) 472-1252
Joaquín Serrano, Executive Director
Email: KCHCC@latino-net.org
Web: www.latino-net.org/kchcc

HISPANIC CHAMBER OF COMMERCE OF METROPOLITAN ST. LOUIS
P.O. Box 78386
St. Louis, MO 63178
(314) 621-1991
Guillermo Rodríguez, Chair of the Board
Email: info@hccstl.com
Web: www.hccstl.com

HISPANIC CONTRACTORS OF AMERICA, INC. (HCA)
1224 East 9th St
Kansas City, MO 64106
(816) 421-3626 or (816) 474-8105
Fax: (816) 221-6760

Jerry B. Adriano, Management Consultant
Email: kchace@earthlink.net

HISPANIC CULTURAL DANCERS
2484 Pontchartrain Dr.
Florissant, MO 63033
(314) 837-5746 Fax: (314) 837-4143
Elisa Hillberg, Director
Email: ehillberg@aol.com

HISPANIC ECONOMIC DEV. CORP.
Affiliate of NCLR
1427 West 9th St., #201
Kansas City, MO 64101
(816) 221-3442 Fax: (816) 221-6458
Nick Scielvo, President
Email: hedc@latino-net.org
Web: www.latino-net/hedc

HISPANIC LEADERS OF GREATER ST. LOUIS
1221 Locust St.
St. Louis, MO 63103
(314) 621- 5237 Fax: (314) 621-5237
Tony Ramírez, Chairman

IMAGE DE GREATER KANSAS CITY
National Image, Inc.
P. O. Box 8457
Kansas City, MO 64114
(913) 596-2972 (H) or (913) 551-6980 (W)
(888) 532-6947 (Pager)
Stella Alejos, President, Acting Treasurer
Email: Salejos@swbell.net
Web: www.nationalimageinc.org

IMAGE, INC.
St. Louis Chapter
6651 Gravois Ave., #212
St. Louis, MO 63116-1125
(314) 832-0790
Liz Sánchez-Setser, President

IONIA MONTCALM DISTRICT FAMILY INDEPENDENCE AGENCY
Montcalm County
609 N State, P.O. Box 278
Stanton, MO 48888-0278
(517) 831-8400 Fax: (517) 831-8496

LA CLÍNICA
3346 Fairview Ave.
St. Loius, MO 63116
(314) 664-5565
William Chignolli, Director

LEAGUE OF UNITED LATIN AMERICAN CITIZENS (LULAC)
Midwest Region-MO
1025 Claytonia Terr
St. Louis, MO 63117
(314) 919-9403 or (314) 646-1476 (h)
Fax: (314) 919-8907
Homer Flores, State Director
Email: hflores@spectrumhealth.com

LULAC-NATIONAL EDUCATIONAL SERVICES CENTER, INC. (LNESC)
3515 Broadway, #201
Kansas City, MO 64111
(816) 561-0227 Fax: (816) 561-8319
Yvonne Vásquez-Rangel, Director
Web: www.lulac.org

MANA - A NATIONAL LATINA ORG.
Kansas City Chapter
4929 Holly
Kansas City, MO 64112
(816) 421-7577 Fax: (816) 756-5181
Rita Botello, Chapter President
Email: hermana2@aol.com
Web: www.hermana.org

MATTIE RHODES COUNSELING & ART CTR.
Affiliate of NCLR
1740 Jefferson St.
Kansas City, MO 64108
(816) 471-2536 Fax: (816) 471-2521
Mary Lou Jaramillo, Executive Director
Email: mattie@coop.crn.com

MEXICAN CULTURAL INSTITUTE OF MID-AMERICA
1015 Locust St. #922
St. Louis, MO 63101
(314) 436-3233 or (314) 436-2695
Ernesto Gutierrez, President

MINORITY ENGINEERING PROGRAM
University of Missouri, Rolla
1870 Miner Circle., #212 E.R.L
Rolla, MO 65409-0150
(573) 341-4213 Fax: (573) 341-4890
Floyd Harris, Director, Minority Engineering Prog.
Web: www.umr.edu/

NATIONAL LATINO PEACE OFFICERS ASSOC.
Kansas City, MO Chapter
P.O. Box 15078
Kansas City, MO 64106
(877) 657-6200
Adrián García, National President
Email: nlpoa@aol.com
Web: www.nlpoa.com

NOSOTROS
George Warren Brown of Social Work
Campus Box 1196 One Brookings
St. Louis, MO 63130-4899
(314) 935-6676 Fax: (314) 725-6676
Hugo Perales, Co-Leader
Email: hgp1@gwbmail.wustl.edu

PANAMANIAN SOCIETY OF ST. LOUIS
P.O. Box 22
St. Ann, MO 63074
(314) 428-0523
Janice Sheffer, President
Email: sheffer90@hotmail.com

PERUVIAN SOCIETY OF ST. LOUIS
2147 Cedarroyal Dr.
St. Louis, MO 63131
(314) 991-1750
Mr. Leopoldo Gonzales, President

PUERTO RICAN SOCIETY OF ST. LOUIS
P.O. Box 6351
Chesterfield, MO 63006
(314) 426-2000 Fax: (314) 426-2164
Nancy Vega-Smith, President
Email: jvs221@hotmail.com

RURAL MISSOURI, INC.
1014 Northeast Dr.
Jefferson City, MO 65109
(573) 635-0136 Fax: (573) 635-5636
Ken Lueckenotte, Executive Director
Email: info@rmiinc.org
Web: www.rmiinc.org

SOCIEDAD HISPANOAMERICANA DE ST. LOUIS
26 Praise Ct.
Fenton, MO 63026
(314) 427-4390
Dinorah Bommarito, President
Email: mukai@zach.wustl.edu

SOCIEDAD MEXICANA BENITO JUÁREZ
8937 Lucerne Ct.
St. Louis, MO 63136
(314) 869-4292
Sally Moreno, President

SPANISH SOCIETY OF ST. LOUIS
7107 Michigan
St. Louis, MO 63111
(314) 351-2232
Joe Carretero, Club Interpreter
Email: ircarr1@aol.com

ST. LOUIS CULTURAL FLAMENCO SOCIETY
Dance Co.
P.O. Box 21818
St. Louis, MO 63109
(314) 781-1537 Fax: (314) 781-6263
Marisel Salascruz, Artistic Director
Email: marisel@wanlab.com

UNION PACIFIC LATINO EMPLOYEE NETWORK (UPLEN)
210 N. 13th St. #600
St. Louis, MO 63103
(800) 925-6396 x 69576 Fax: (314) 992-2993
Tony Navarrete, President
Email: tnavarrete@notes.up.com

WARA BOLIVIAN FOLKLORIC DANCES
59 Forun Ctr.
Chesterfield, MO 63017
(314) 878-3033
Frida Mena, Director
Email: waradancers@yahoo.com

WESTSIDE HOUSING ORGANIZATION
Affiliate of NCLR
919 W. 24th St.
Kansas City, MO 64108
(816) 421-8048 Fax: (816) 421-8131
Gerald Shechter, Executive Director

MONTANA

DIOCESE OF GREAT FALLS-BILLINGS
Hispanic Affairs Office
P.O. Box 1399, 121 23rd St.
Great Falls, MT 59403

Paul Kaiser

DIOCESE OF HELENA
Hispanic Affairs
P.O. Box 1729
515 N. Ewing St.
Helena, MT 59624-1729
(406) 442-5820 Fax: (406) 442-5191

MONTANA MIGRANT & SEASONAL FARM WORKER COUNCIL
3318 3rd Ave N #100
Billings, MT 59101
(406) 248-3149 Fax: (406) 245-6636
María Stephen, Executive Director
Email: mmcmt@wtp.net

RURAL EMPLOYMENT OPPORTUNITIES
Billings Office
1739 Grand Ave., Room A
Billings, MT 59102
(406) 256-1140 Fax: (406) 256-8411
Lois Brandt, Dist. Supervisor
Email: reo@mcm.net
Web: www.montana.net/~reo/

RURAL EMPLOYMENT OPPORTUNITIES
National Headquarters
P.O. Box 831
Helena, MT 59624
(406) 442-7850 Fax: (406) 442-7855
Sharon Leiderman, Executive Director
Web: www.mt.net

NEBRASKA

ARCHDIOCESE OF OMAHA
Hispanic Affairs
3216 N. 60th St.
Omaha, NE 68104
(402) 558-3134 Fax: (402) 551-3050
Sr. Angela Erevia, Director for Hispanic Ministry
Email: mcdp@omahahmo.creighton.edu

ARCHDIOCESE OF OMAHA
Juan Diego Center
5211 S. 31st St.
Omaha, NE 68107
(402) 731-5413 Fax: (402) 731-5865
Ana Barrios
Email: AnaB@ccomaha.org

CHICANO AWARENESS CENTER
Affiliate of NCLR
4821 S. 24th St.
Omaha, NE 68107-2704
(402) 733-2720 Fax: (402) 733-6720
Gina Ponce-Guidoni, Executive Director

DIOCESE OF GRAND ISLAND
Hispanic Ministry Office
P.O. Box 996
311 W. 17th St.
Grand Island, NE 68802
(308) 382-6565 Fax: (308) 382-6569
Email: hmo@ns.nque.com

DIOCESE OF LINCOLN
Hispanic Affairs
3128 S St.
Lincoln, NE 68503-3237
(402) 435-3559
Rev. Julias Turdy, Hisp. Ministry Coordinator
Email: jt11835@navix.net

HISPANIC COMMUNITY CENTER - CENTRO DE LA COMUNIDAD HISPANA
Affiliate of NCLR
2300 O St.
Lincoln, NE 68510
(402) 474-3950 Fax: (402) 474-3842
Joel Gajardo Ph.D., Executive Director

HISPANIC MINISTRY
Catholic Archdiocese of Omaha
3216 N 60th St.
Omaha, NE 68104
(402) 558-3134 Fax: 4025513050
Sister Angela Ervia, Director
Email: mcdp@omahahom.creighton.edu

LA RAZA - JOB TRAINING INC.
4911 S. 25th St., #10
Omaha, NE 68107
(402) 734-1321 Fax: (402) 734-1293
Enrique Brodsky, Executive Director

MEXICAN AMERICAN COMMISSION
National Headquarters
P.O. Box 94965
State Capitol Bulding
Lincoln, NE 68509-4965

(402) 471-2791 Fax: (402) 471-4381
Cecilia Olivarez Huerta, Executive Director
Email: mac1000@vmhost.cdp.state.ne.us

MEXICAN FIESTA, INC.
1221 E. E St.
North Platte, NE 69101
(308) 532-4156
Mary Martínez, Chair

MEXICAN LADIES ASSOCIATION
3216 Rodeo Rd.
North Platte, NE 69101
(308) 534-2494
Peggy Nila Mata, President

NAF MULTICULTURAL HUMAN DEV. CORP.
North Platte Regional Office/NCLR Affiliate
P. O. Box 2131, North Platte, NE 69103-2131
414 E. 4th St.
North Platte, NE 69101
(308) 534-4532 or (308) 534-4539
Fax: (308) 534-9451
Melinda Magdaleno, Regional Director

Administrative Office Affiliate of NCLR
P.O. Box 1459, North Platte, NE 69103-1459
416 E. 4th St.
North Platte, NE 69101
(308) 534-2630 Fax: (308) 534-9451
Ella Ochoa, Executive Director
Email: eochoa@nafmhdc.org

Grand Island Regional Office
312 N. Elm St., #101
Grand Island, NE 68801
(308) 382-3956 Fax: (308) 382-3956
Rosa Barrios, Case Manager

Lexington Regional Office
P. O. Box 616
1308 N. Adams
Lexington, NE 68850-0616
(308) 324-4266 Fax: (308) 324-3267
Norma Mendoza, Case Manager

Lincoln Regional Office
941 O St., #818
Lincoln, NE 68508
(402) 434-2821 Fax: (402) 435-4803
Federico Torres, Regional Director
Email: na83007@navix.net

Omaha Regional Office
4826 S. 24th
Omaha, NE 68107
(402) 933-6002 Fax: (402) 933-6003
Ivonne González, Case Manager

Scottsbluff Regional Office
P. O. Box 552
3305 N. 10th St.
Gering, NE 69341-0552
(308) 632-5831 Fax: (308) 632-3771
Vira Robinson, Case Manager

South Sioux City Regional Office
2509 Dakota Ave.
South Sioux City, NE 68876
(402) 494-6576 Fax: (402) 494-2784
Turmalina Delgadillo, Case Manager

NATIONAL LATINO PEACE OFFICERS ASSOCIATION (NLPOA)
Nebraska Chapter
P.O. Box 7164
Omaha, NE 68107
(877) 657-6200
Mark Martínez, State President
Email: nlpoa@aol.com
Web: www.nlpoa.com

OFFICE OF HISPANIC MINISTRIES
P.O. Box 651, 214 W. 5th St.
North Platte, NE 69103
(308) 532-2707 Fax: (308) 532-3574
Mario Delgado, Director
Email: hmo@nf.netquest.com

SER-JOBS FOR PROGRESS, INC.
Omaha Chapter
4911 S. 25th St., #10
Omaha, NE 68107
(402) 734-1321 Fax: (402) 734-1293
Enrique Bardoska, Director
Email: jobtraining@larazaomaha.org
Web: www.larazaomaha.org

WESTERN NEBRASKA COMMUNITY COLLEGE
1601 E. 27th St.
Scottsbluff, NE 69361
(308) 635-3606 Fax: (308) 635-6100

John Harms, President
Web: www.wncc.net

NEVADA

CHILEAN CLUB OF LAS VEGAS
4650 E. Paterson
Las Vegas, NV 89104
(702) 431-7922
Paulina Tilley, Director

COMITÉ PATRIÓTICO MEXICANO
845 N. Eastern Ave.
Las Vegas, NV 89101
(702) 649-8553

DIOCESE OF LAS VEGAS
Hispanic Ministry Office
P.O. Box 18316
Las Vegas, NV 89114
(702) 735-3500 Fax: (702) 735-8941
Rev. Robert Stoeckig
Email: stoeckig@dioceseoflasvegas.org

DIOCESE OF RENO
Hispanic Affairs
290 S. Arlington Ave.
Reno, NV 89504-1211
(775) 329-9274 x426 Fax: (775) 384-8619
José Domingo Ojeda, Dir. for Hispanic Ministry
Email: jdojeda@pyramid.net

EL MUNDO
845 N. Eastern Ave.
Las Vegas, NV 89101
(702) 649-8553 Fax: (702) 649-7429
Eddy Escobedo, President
Email: elmundo@wizard.com

HISPANIC CHAMBER OF COMMERCE OF NORTHERN NEVADA
P.O. Box 7458
Reno, NV 89510
(775) 324-1452 Fax: (775) 784-4337
Ramón González, President

LATIN CHAMBER OF COMMERCE OF NEVADA
P.O. Box 7500
Las Vegas, NV 89125-7500
(702) 385-7367 Fax: (702) 385-2614

LEAGUE OF UNITED LATIN AMERICAN CITIZENS (LULAC)
Farwest Region-NV
895 Capitol Hill
Reno, NV 89502
(702) 329-7021 Fax: (702) 329-7021
John Castro, State Director
Web: www.lulac.org

NATIONAL LATINO PEACE OFFICERS ASSOCIATION (NLPOA)
Clark County Chapter
P.O. Box 15322
Las Vegas, NV 89114
(877) 657-6200
Adrian Garcia, National President
Email: nvlpoa@aol.com
Web: www.nlpoa.com

Nevada State Chapter
P.O. Box 16012
Las Vegas, NV 89101
(877) 657-6200
Eloy Abeyta, Chapter Vice President
Email: mrmenudo@netnevada.net
Web: www.nlpoa.com

Washoe County Chapter
P.O. Box 7789
Reno, NV 89510-7789
(775) 575-4816
Mercy Nagel, Chapter President
Email: nlpoa@aol.com
Web: www.nlpoa.com

NEVADA ASSOCIATION OF LATIN AMERICANS, INC. (NALA)
National Headquarters
323 N. Maryland Pkwy.
Las Vegas, NV 89101-3130
(702) 382-6252 Fax: (702) 383-7021
Zullie Franco, President & CEO

NEVADA HISPANIC SERVICES, INC. (NHS)
National Headquarters
3905 Neil Rd.
Reno, NV 89502

(775) 826-1818 Fax: (775) 826-1819
Jesse Gutierrez, President

REFORMA
Nevada Chapter
Washoe County Library
P.O. Box 2151
Reno, NV 89505
(775) 327-8300 or (775) 785-4009
Fax: (775) 327-8390
Sally Kinsey, Chapter President
Email: skinsey@mail.co.washoe.nv.us
Web: http://clnet.ucr.edu/library/reforma

SOCIEDAD CULTURAL HISPANA, INC.
2065 Wagon Wheel Ave.
Las Vegas, NV 89119
(702) 736-3881
Fidel Torea, President

NEW HAMPSHIRE

DIOCESE OF MANCHESTER
Spanish Speaking Apostolate
231 Merrimack St.
Manchester, NH 03103-5295
(603) 625-4603 Fax: (603) 626-1517
Sr. María Luz Cervantes, MSC

Spanish Speaking Apostolate
41 Chandler St.
Nashua, NH 03060
(603) 881-8065
Sr. Nancy Braceland, CSJ

LATIN AMERICAN CENTER, AIDS/SIDA INFORMATION REFERRAL
521 Maple St.
Manchester, NH 03104
(603) 669-5661 or (603) 668-8010
Nick Lorang, Director

LATIN AMERICAN CENTER OF MANCHESTER
521 Maple St.
Manchester, NH 03104
(603) 669-5661 Fax: (603) 669-5265
Carol Birch, Director
Email: micentro@juno.com

SOCIETY OF HISPANIC PROFESSIONAL ENGINEERS (SHPE)
Lawrence Professional Chapter
103 Spit Brook Rd., #C-6
Nashua, NH 03062
(603) 884-3390 (w) or (603) 897-1322 (h)
Fax: (603) 884-5191
Carlos Arévalo, Chapter President
Email: carlos.arevalo@compaq.com
Web: www.shpe.org

NEW JERSEY

AMERICAN SPANISH COMMITTEE
P.O. Box 42
Leonia, NJ 07605-0042
(201) 567-7417 Fax: (201) 816-9727
Anthony F. González, Chairman

ARCHDIOCESE OF NEWARK
Hispanic Affairs
P.O. Box 9500
171 Clifton Ave.
Newark, NJ 07104-9500
(973) 497-4337 or (973) 497-4335
Fax: (973) 497-4317
Maricela Quintana, Director for Hisp.Ministry
Email: quintanama@rcan.org

ASPIRA OF NEW JERSEY, INC.
390 Broad St., 3rd Floor
Newark, NJ 07104
(973) 484-7554 Fax: (973) 484-0184
William Colón, Executive Director
Email: wcapsira@bellatlantic.net
Web: www.aspira.org/NewJersey.html

ASSOCIATION FOR HISPANIC HANDICAPPED OF NEW JERSEY
24 DeGrasse Street
Paterson, NJ 07505
(973) 742-7500 Fax: (973) 523-1150
Rosita Kardshian, Director

ASSOC. OF LATIN AMERICAN STUDENTS
1000 Morris Ave., Kean College IRC
Union, NJ 07083
(908) 527-2797 Fax: (908) 527-0320
María Pérez, Assistant Director

ASSOC. OF PUERTO RICANS IN SCIENCE
University of Medicine and Dentistry of NJ
150 Bergen St. #C-437
Newark, NJ 07103-2400
(973) 972-3665 Fax: (973) 972-2230
Dr. Muñoz, Director

ATAHUALPA YUPANQUI
7404 Bergenline Ave.
North Bergen, NJ 07047
(201) 869-1885 Fax: (201) 869-4282
Joseph O. Paladino, President

BERGEN COUNTY COMMUNITY ACTION PROGRAM, INC.
241 Moore St.
Hackensack, NJ 07601
(201) 342-5189 Fax: (201) 342-9339
Robert F. Halsch, Director

BERGEN COUNTY HISPANIC-AMERICAN CHAMBER OF COMMERCE
740 Route 17 N.
Paramus, NJ 07652
(201) 498-9180 Fax: (201) 612-8631
Miriam López, President
Email: bchaco@aol.com

CÁMARA DE COMERCIO LATINA DE ELIZABETH
603 Elizabeth Ave., 1st Floor
Elizabeth, NJ 07206
(908) 289-0677 Fax: (908) 355-0677
Manuel Perez Quebas, President

CÁMARA MEXICANA DEL PEQUEÑO Y MEDIANO COMERCIANTE
9-15 Porete Ave.
North Arlington, NJ 07031
(201) 997-0002 Fax: (201) 997-7767
Jaime Lucero, President

CAMDEN COUNTY OFFICE OF HISPANIC AFFAIRS AND COMMUNITY DEV.
Court House 306
520 Market St., 3rd Floor
Camden, NJ 08102-1375
(856) 225-5312 Fax: (856) 225-5591
Israel Nieves, Director
Email: hispanic@co.camden.nj.us
Web: www.co.camden.nj.us

CASA PUERTO RICO ACTION COMMITTEE, INC.
511 Grape St.
Vineland, NJ 08360
(609) 692-2331 Fax: (609) 794-5183
Noemi Santiago, Director

CENTER FOR HISPANIC POLICY, RESEARCH & DEVELOPMENT
National Headquarters
P.O. Box 800
101 S. Broad St.
Trenton, NJ 08625-0800
(609) 984-3223 Fax: (609) 984-0821
Angie Armand, Director

CENTER FOR NON-PROFIT CORPORATIONS
1501 Livingston Ave.
North Brunswick, NJ 08902
(732) 227-0800 Fax: (732) 227-0087
Linda M. Czipo, Executive Director
Email: center@njnonprofits.org
Web: http://www.njnonprofits.org

CENTRO COMUNAL BORINCANO
832 South 4th St.
Camden, NJ 08103
(856) 5410179
Sonia Plaza, Director
Email: elcentro1211@aol.com

COMITÉ DE APOYO A LOS TRABAJADORES AGRÍCOLAS (CATA)
P.O. Box 510
4 S. Delsea Dr.
Glassboro, NJ 08028
(609) 881-2507 Fax: (609) 881-2027
Nelson Carrasquillo, Director

CURA, INC.
729 E. Landis Ave.
Vineland, NJ 08360
(609) 696-7335 Fax: (609) 696-7334
John Lusiano, Director

DIOCESE OF CAMDEN
Hispanic Affairs
410 S. 8th St.
Vinelan, NJ 08360

(609) 692-8992 Fax: (609) 338-0793
Msgr. Víctor S. Muro, Director for Hispanic Apostolate

DIOCESE OF METUCHEN
Hispanic Affairs
625 Florida Grove Rd.
Perth Amboy, NJ 08861
(732) 826-2771
Rev. Msgr. Glenn J. Comandini, Director for Hispanic Ministry

DIOCESE OF PATERSON
Hispanic Affairs
777 Valley Rd.
Clifton, NJ 07013
(973) 777-8818 x239 Fax: (973) 473-3353
Rev. Terrence Moran, CSSR, Dir. for Hisp. Min.
Email: tmoran@patersondiocese.org

DIOCESE OF TRENTON
St. Mary's Cathedral
151 N. Warren St.
Trenton, NJ 08608
(609) 396-8447
Rev. Manuel Fernández, Vicar for Hisp. Min.

EL PRIMER PASO, LTD
73 Richards Ave.
Dover, NJ 07801
(973) 361-0880 Fax: (973) 361-8033
Jean Seavey, Director

FOCUS- HISPANIC CENSOR FOR COMMUNITY DEVELOPMENT
441-443 Broad St.
Newark, NJ 07102
(973) 624-2528 Fax: (973) 624-6450
Loyza Rivera, Public Relations Director

FOCUS NEWARK, INC.
441-443 Broad St.
Newark, NJ 07102
(973) 624-2528 Fax: (973) 624-6450
Costo Maldonado, President
Email: Focus441@aol.com

FOREIGN LANGUAGE EDUCATORS OF NEW JERSEY
1600 Martine Ave.
Scotch Plains, NJ 07076
(908) 889-1600 Fax: (908) 889-7867
Bruce E. Zehnle, Vice-Pres.
Email: BZehnle@unioncatholic.org

HISPANIC AFFAIRS OFFICE
Rutgers University
Armitage Hall
311 N. 5th St., 2nd Floor
Camden, NJ 08102
(609) 225-1766 Fax: (609) 225-6049
Mike Greenup, Director

HISPANIC AFFAIRS & RESOURCES CENTER OF MONMOUTH CO.
913 Cewall Ave.
Ashbury Park, NJ 07712
(732) 774-3282 Fax: (732) 502-8955
Carlos Hernández, Director
Email: harc@monmouth.com

HISPANIC CENTER OF EXCELLENCE
University of Medicine and Dentistry of NJ
185 S. Orange Ave., MSB A-550
Newark, NJ 07103
(973) 975-3762 Fax: (973) 972-3768
Dr. María Soto Greene, Director
Email: HCOE@UMDNJ.EDU

HISPANIC CULTURE CLUB
Saint Peter's College
2641 Kennedy Blvd.
Jersey City, NJ 07306
(201) 915-9250 Fax: (201)915-9209
Rolando Manna, Professor

HISPANIC EMPLOYMENT PROGRAM (HEP)
Atlantic City International Airport , FAA (Act-223)
Atlantic City, NJ 08405
(609) 485-7072 Fax: (609) 485-8050
Christ Medina
Email: christ_Medina@admini.tc.faa.gov

HISPANIC FAMILY CENTER, INC.
2700 Westfield Ave.
Camden, NJ 08105
(609) 365-7393 Fax: (609) 356-1862
Elsa Candelario, Coordinator

HISPANIC FAMILY CENTER OF SOUTHERN NEW JERSEY, INC.
35 Church St.

Camden, NJ 08105
(856) 541-6985 Fax: (856) 963-2663
Elsa Candelario, Director
Email: hscfnj@aol.com

2700 Westfield Ave.
Camden, NJ 08105
(856) 365-7393 Fax: (856) 3651862
Elsa Candelario, Director
Email: hscfnj@aol.com

HISPANIC IMAGES PROJECT
Rutgers Univ., Newark Campus
AFC, 175 University Ave., Conklin Hall
Newark, NJ 07102-1814
(973) 353-1675 Fax: (973) 353-5700
Miriam Cruz, MSW, EOF Counselor Special Programs / Hispanic Images Project Coordinator
Web: www.andromeda.rutgers.edu/afc/

HISPANIC INFORMATION CENTER OF PASSAIC, INC.
186 Gregory Ave.
Passaic, NJ 07055
(973) 779-0260 or (973) 779-7022
Fax: (973) 779-0453
Lorenzo Hernández, Director

HISPANIC INSTITUTE FOR RESEARCH AND DEVELOPMENT OF BERGEN COUNTY
17 Arcadian Ave.
Paramus, NJ 07652
(201) 368-1414 Fax: (201) 368-8985
Mr. Dennis González, Executive Director

HISPANIC MULTI-PURPOSE SERVICE CENTER
911 E. 23rd St.
Paterson, NJ 07513
(973) 357-1006 or (973) 684-3320
Fax: (973) 684-7442
Ms. María Magda O'Keese, Director
Email: hmpsc@webspan.net

HISPANIC NATIONAL BAR ASSOCIATION
PO Box 387, 30 Montgomery St.
Jersey City, NJ 07303-0387
(201) 309-0002 Fax: (201) 309-1208
Lourdes I. Santiago, Vice President
Membership & Regions
Email: lourdessantiago@mindspring.com
Web: www.hnba.com

Region III (NJ)
432 Broad Ave.
Ridgefield, NJ 07657
(201) 313-9889 Fax: (201) 313-1425
Ramón de la Cruz, Regional President
Email: abogado@bellatlantic.net
Web: www.hnba.com

HISPANIC STATE PARADE OF NEW JERSEY, INC.
2911 Summit Ave.
Union City, NJ 07087
(201) 854-8419 Fax: (201) 867-1009
William Hernández, Pres.
Email: pgranda@aol.com

HISPANIC WOMEN'S RESOURCE CENTER
533, 35th St.
Union City, NJ 07087
(201) 866-3208 Fax: (201) 866-5854
Marta San Martín, Director
Web: www.ccsnewark.org/hwrs.htm

HUDSON COUNTY HISPANIC CHAMBER OF COMMERCE
600 Madison St.
West New York, NJ 07093
(201) 662-0052 Fax: (201) 662-8485
Hilda Sosa, President

INTER-AMERICAN SAFETY COUNCIL
80 E Commerce Way
Totowa, NJ 07512-1154
(973) 237-1766 Fax: (973) 237-1755
Glen F. Mickey, President
Email: info@cias-iasc.org

INTERNATIONAL RESCUE COMMITTEE, INC.
144 Elmora Ave., #202
Elizabeth, NJ 07202
(908) 282-0881 Fax: (908) 289-8108
Clifford Raimes, Executive Director
Email: GWElizabeth@interestcom.org

LA CASA DE DON PEDRO, INC.
Community Improvement Center
317 Roseville Ave.
Newark, NJ 07104
(973) 485-0701 Fax: (973) 485-7555

Norma Gutiérrez, Director
Email: lc.donpedro@aol.com
Web: www.lacasa-tlc.org

Executive Office/Day Care Center
75 Park Ave.
Newark, NJ 07104
(973) 482-8312 or (973) 485-0850
Fax: (973) 482-1883
Raymond Ocasio, Executive Director
Email: lc.donpedro@aol.com
Web: www.lacasa-tlc.org

Hispanic Women Resource Center
86 Broadway
Newark, NJ 07104
(973) 481-6639 Fax: (973) 497-0540
Wendy Melandez, Director
Email: lc.donpedro@aol.com
Web: www.lacasa-tlc.org

**LAMBDA SIGMA UPSILON LATINO
FRATERNITY, INC.**
National Headquarters
P.O. Box 11526
New Brunswick, NJ 08903
(732) 937-6524
John A. Santana, Pres.

**LATIN AMERICAN CHAMBER OF
COMMERCE OF CENTRAL JERSEY**
120 W. 7th St., #217
Plainfield, NJ 07060
(908) 754-7250 Fax: (908) 754-5580
Nelly Dixon, President
Email: CJCC@EROLS.COM

**LATIN AMERICAN ECONOMIC
DEVELOPMENT ASSOCIATION, INC.**
Affiliate of NCLR
433 Market St., #202
Camden, NJ 08102
(609) 338-1177 Fax: (609) 963-1835
Nenilsa Lebrom, Executive Director
Email: laeda@aol.com

LATIN AMERICAN STUDENT ORG.
Montclair State University
Student Center Annex 100
Upper Montclair, NJ 07043
(973) 655-4440 or (973) 655-4000
Fax: (973) 655-7433
Orlando Ruiz, President

LATINO COMMUNITY LAND TRUST
206 E. Hanover St.
Trenton, NJ 08608
(609) 695-1401 Fax: (609) 695-0710
David Baldes, Director

**LEAGUE OF UNITED LATIN AMERICAN
CITIZENS (LULAC)**
Northeast Region-NJ
14 Clark St.
Patterson, NJ 07505
(201) 278-4800 or (201) 633-8220 (h)
Fax: (201) 278-6560
Peggy Anastos, State Dir.

**MEADOWLANDS REGIONAL CHAMBER
OF COMMERCE**
201 Route 17 North
Rutherford, NJ 07070
(201) 939-0707 Fax: (201) 939-0522
Richard Fritzky, President

**MERCER COUNTY HISPANIC
ASSOCIATION (MECHA)**
P.O. Box 1331
2000 E. State St., 2nd Fl., Fleet Bank Bldg.
Trenton, NJ 08607
(609) 392-2446 Fax: (609) 695-7618
Francis Blanco, Executive Director

**MORRIS COUNTY HISPANIC CHAMBER
OF COMMERCE**
211 South St.
Morristown, NJ 07960
(973) 267-8990 Ext. 222   Fax: (973) 984-3360
Esperanza Porras-Field, President

**MOVIMIENTO ESTUDIANTIL CHICANO
DE AZTLAN (MECHA)**
P.O. Box 1331
Trenton, NJ 08607
(609) 392-2446 Fax: (609) 695-7618
Francis Blanco, Director

MULTI-LINGUAL CENTER
Catholic Family and Community Service
24 Degrasse St.

Patterson, NJ 07505
(973) 742-7500 Fax: (201) 523-1150
Rose Kardashian, Director
Email: socmin@hji.com

**NATIONAL ASSOCIATION OF CUBAN-
AMERICAN WOMEN OF THE U.S.A**
National Headquarters
308 38th St.
Union City, NJ 07087
(201) 864-4879 Fax: (201) 223-0035
Ziomara Sánchez, National President

**NATIONAL BORICUA-LATINO HEALTH
ORGANIZATION**
UMDNJ-RWJMS
675 Hoes Ln.
Piscataway, NJ 08854
(732) 235-4684 Fax: (908) 235-5078
Luz M. Ortiz, Program Administrator

**NATIONAL WOMEN'S POLITICAL
CAUCUS (NWPC) HISPANIC CAUCUS**
New Jersey Chapter
P.O. Box 1546
Highland Park, NJ 08904-1546
(732) 985-3967 Fax: (732) 393-0295
Carmen Delia Díaz, Regional Representative
Email: diaz@rci.rutgers.edu

**NORTH HUDSON COMMUNITY ACTION -
HEAD START PROGRAM**
535 41st St.
Union City, NJ 07087
(201) 617-0901 Fax: (201) 601-0137
Alicia Cejas, Activities Coordinator

NUESTROS NIÑOS DAY CARE CENTER, INC.
301 Garden St.
Hoboken, NJ 07030
(201) 656-8317 Fax: (201) 656-3797
Linda Lorence, Director

P.R. COMMUNITY DAY CARE CENTER
331 Hamilton Ave.
Trenton, NJ 08609
(609) 392-8787 or (609) 392-8786
Fax: (609) 392-7905
Ana I. Berdecia, Dir.

**PACO-GRASS ROOTS INITIATIVE
PROGRAM**
180 4th St.
Jersey City, NJ 07302
(201) 798-1446 Fax: (201) 798-0363
Jesús González, Project Coord.

**PARENTS AND CHILDREN TOGETHER
ORGANIZED FOR FAMILY LEARNING**
P.O. Box 114
Allentown, NJ 08501
(609) 259-7177
José Oliva, Director

PERTH AMBOY CHAMBER OF COMMERCE
214 Smith St.
Perth Amboy, NJ 08861
(732) 442-7400 Fax: (732) 442-7450
Leona Biagini, Executive Director

**PLAINFIELD BILINGUAL DAY CARE
CENTER.**
225 W. 2nd. St.
Plainfield, NJ 07060
(908) 753-3124 Fax: (908) 753-3540
Ms. Eva-Rosa-Amirault, Dir.

PRAB DAY CARE CENTER
P.O. Box 240
New Brunswick, NJ 08903
(732) 828-4572 Fax: (732) 828-4546
Lise Dubios, Director

**PUERTO RICAN ACTION BOARD/JUNTA
DE ACCIÓN PUERTORRIQUEÑA, INC.**
P.O. Box 240
22 Joyce Kilmer Ave., 2nd Floor
New Brunswick, NJ 08903-0240
(732) 828-4510 Fax: (732) 828-4546
Guillermo Beytagh Maldonado, Executive
Director
Email: prabinc@aol.com

**PUERTO RICAN ACTION COMMITTEE OF
SALEM COUNTY**
P.O. Box 444
114 E. Main St.
Penns Grove, NJ 08069
(856) 299-5800 Fax: (856) 299-3276
David Rodríguez, Executive Director

**PUERTO RICAN ASSOCIATION FOR
COMMUNITY ORGANIZATION (PACO)**
390-392 Manila Ave.
Jersey City, NJ 07302
(201) 963-8282 Fax: (201) 653-5229
Eliu Rivera, Executive Director

**PUERTO RICAN CONGRESS OF NEW
JERSEY, INC.**
515 S. Broad St.
Trenton, NJ 08611
(609) 989-8888 Fax: (609) 989-8883
Lydia Valencia, Executive Director
Web: www.prcongress.org

14 S. Clifton Ave.
Lakewood, NJ 08701
(732) 905-7217 Fax: (732) 905-7969
Lydia Valencia, Executive Director
Web: www.prcongress.org

PUERTO RICAN CUATRO PROJECT
31 Central Avenue
East Brunswick, NJ 08816
(732) 238-3087
Juan Sotomayor, Events Director
Email: J.Sotomayor@prodigy.net

PUERTO RICAN FAMILY INSTITUTE, INC.
New Jersey Clinic
40 Journal Square, #302
Jersey City, NJ 07306
(201) 610-1446 Fax: (201) 610-9426
Olga Víctor, Director
Web: www.prfi.org

PUERTO RICAN INSTITUTE
400 S. Orange Ave.
South Orange, NJ 07079
(973) 761-9422 Fax: (201) 761-9788
Frank Morales, Director
Web: www.fhu.edu/depts/tri/

**PUERTO RICAN ORGANIZATION FOR
COMMUNITY EDUCATION AND
ECONOMIC DEVELOPMENT , INC.**
815 Elizabeth Ave.
Elizabeth, NJ 07201
(908) 351-7727 Fax: (908) 353-5185
Heriberto Sánchez Soto, Executive Director
Email: proceez@aol.com

PUERTO RICAN UNITY FOR PROGRESS, INC.
**Affiliate of SER-Jobs for Progress
National, Inc.**
427 Broadway St.
Camden, NJ 08103
(856) 541-1418 Fax: (856) 541-1476
Carmen D. Pores, Executive Director
Email: prupcm@aol.com
Web: www.sernational.org

**PUERTO RICO FEDERAL AFFAIRS
ADMINISTRATION**
Trenton Regional Office
744 Broad St.
Nork, NJ 07102-3802
(973) 824-6030
John Santana, Director
Web: www.prfaa.com

**PUERTORRIQUEÑOS ASOCIADOS FOR
COMMUNITY ORGANIZATION, INC.**
392 Manila Ave.
Jersey City, NJ 07302
(201) 963-8282 Fax: (201) 653-5229
Elio Rivera, Director

REFORMA
New Jersey Chapter
Vineland Public Library, 1058 E. Landis Ave.
Vineland, NJ 08360
(856) 794-4244 ext. 4729 Fax: (856) 691-0366
Jeanne Garrison, State Coordinator
Email: jgarrison@vineland.lib.nj.us
Web: www.vineland.lib.nj.us

RURAL OPPORTUNITIES, INC.
New Jersey Division
510-12 E. Landis Ave.
Vineland, NJ 08360
(609) 696-1000 Fax: (609) 696-4892
John Schmidt, Exec. Director

**S.A.S.C.A. CENTRO HISPANO DE
SERVICIOS SOCIALES/SPANISH
AMERICAN SOCIAL CULTURAL
ASSOCIATION**
P.O. Box 2248
Levitt Parkway& Charleston Rd.
Willingboro, NJ 08046
(609)835-1111 Fax: (609)835-4366
Jose Ramos, Executive Director

SOCIEDAD CULTURAL BORINCANA, INC.
181 Market St., #2
Patterson, NJ 07505
(973) 278-9545 Fax: (973) 742-2710
José A. Villalongo, Sr., President
Email: scboriken@aol.com

SOCIEDAD HONORARIA HISPANA
Union Catholic Regional H.S.
1600 Martine Ave.
Scotch Plains, NJ 07076
(908) 889-1600 Fax: (908) 889-7867
Bruce E. Zehnle, NE Zone Director
Email: bzehnle@unioncatholic.org
Web: www.unioncatholic.org

SPANISH MERCANTILE FEDERATION
4113 Palisade Ave.
Union City, NJ 07087
(201) 865-1570 Fax: (201) 865-1570
Manuel Fernandez, Director

SPANISH SPEAKING PEOPLE
P.O. Box 61, 303 Summer St.
Landisville, NJ 08326
(609) 697-2967
Lydia Muñoz, Director
Email: spancomctr@aol.com

**SPANISH SPEAKING PEOPLES'
COMMUNITY CENTER**
Eastern Division
3900 Ventnor Ave.
Atlantic City, NJ 08401
(609) 345-1249 Fax: (609) 345-8533
Lydia Muñoz, Director

ST. COLUMBIA NEIGHBORHOOD CLUB
25 Pennsylvania Ave.
Newark, NJ 07114
(973) 624-4222 Fax: (973) 624-2932
Luz C. Emiliano, Executive Director

**STATEWIDE HISPANIC CHAMBER OF
COMMERCE OF NEW JERSEY**
150 Warren St., #110
Jersey City, NJ 07302
(201) 451-9512 Fax: (201) 451-9547
Daniel H. Jara, President & CEO
Email: shccnj@worldnet.att.net
Web: www.shccnj.org

TO SAVE LATIN AMERICA, INC.
3510 Bergenline Ave.
Union City, NJ 07087
(201) 867-3380 Fax: (201) 348-3385
Antonio Ibarría, Chairman

NEW MEXICO

**ALBUQUERQUE HISPANO CHAMBER OF
COMMERCE**
Affiliate of NCLR
202 Central SE, #300
Albuquerque, NM 87102
(505) 842-9003 Fax: (505) 764-9664
Herald Gonzales, President
Web: www.ahcnm.org

**AMERICAN ASSOCIATION OF HISPANIC
CERTIFIED PUBLIC ACCOUNTANTS (CPAS)**
Albuquerque Chapter
Office of Internal Audit
One Civic Plaza, P.O. Box 1293
Albuquerque, NM 87103
(505) 768-3156 Fax: (505) 768-3158
Phyllis J. Griego, Chapter Representative
Email: pjgriego@cabq.gov
Web: www.aahcpa.org

AMERICAN GI FORUM OF ALBUQUERQUE
3301 Mountain Rd., NW
Albuquerque, NM 87104
(505) 247-4910 Fax: (505) 247-2993
Juan Jose Peña, Local Commander

ARCHDIOCESE OF SANTA FE
Hispanic Affairs
4000 St. Joseph Pl. NW
Albuquerque, NM 87120
(505) 831-8152 Fax: (505) 831-8345
Rev. Luis Gerardo Menchaca, Dir. of Hisp. Min.

BILINGUAL EDUCATION STUDENT ORG.
Eastern New Mexico University
Bilingual Education Department
Station #25
Portales, NM 88130
(505) 562-2995 Fax: (505) 562-2523
Dr. Julia R. Emslie, Director
Email: emsliej@enmu.edu

**BORDER EPIDEMIOLOGY &
ENVIRONMENTAL HEALTH CENTER**
New Mexico State University / New
Mexico Department of Health
P.O. Box 30001, 4200 Research Dr.
Las Cruces, NM 88003-8001
(505) 646-7966 Fax: (505) 646-8131
Hugo Vilchis, Director
Email: bec@nmsu.edu
Web: http://www.nmsu.edu–bec/welcome.htm

CAPOEIRA CLUB OF UNM
University of New MexicoDivision of
Student Affairs
Student Union 105, Box 98
Albuquerque, NM 87131
(505) 255-4055
Betsy Kiddy, Vice President

**CARLSBAD HISPANO CHAMBER OF
COMMERCE**
P.O. Box 3262
Carlsbad, NM 88220
(505) 887-6127
Manny Sosa, President

CENTER FOR LATIN AMERICAN STUDIES
New Mexico State University
1200 University Ave. Box: 3LAS
Las Cruces, NM 88003
(505) 646-2842 Fax: (505) 646-2842
José García, Director
Web: www.nmsu.edu/~clas

CLÍNICA DE FAMILIA
1100 S Main #A
Las Cruces, NM 88005
(505) 526-1105 Fax: (505) 524-4266
Frank Crespin, Medical Director
Web: www.lcdsnm.org

COMMUNITY ACTION AGENCY
P.O. Drawer 130
Las Cruces, NM 88004
(505) 523-1639 Fax: (505) 523-7543
William Strauss, Director
Email: strousew@zianet.com

CONEXIONES
Northern New Mexico Community
College
1002 N. Onate
Española, NM 87532
(505) 747-2200
Hilario Romero, Director

DIOCESE OF GALLUP
Hispanic Affairs
217 E. Wilson Ave.
Gallup, NM 87301
(505) 722-5511 Fax: (505) 863-0075
Magda L. Garcia, HNSG, Hispanic Ministry
Coordinator
Email: sistersquadalupesj@juno.com

DIOCESE OF LAS CRUCES
Hispanic Affairs
1280 Med Park
Las Cruces, NM 88005
(505) 523-7577 Fax: (505) 524-3874
Rev. Robert Power, Vicar for Hispanic Ministry

DIOCESE OF LAS CRUCES
Hispanic Affairs
1280 Med Park
Las Cruces, NM 88005
(505) 523-7577
Carlos Corral, Director for Hispanic Ministry

EL CENTRO DE LA RAZA
1153 Mesa Vista Hall
Albuquerque, NM 87131
(505) 277-5020 or (505) 277-5182
Fax: (505) 277-5182
Verónica Méndez Cruz, Director

**EL RANCHO DE LAS GOLONDRINAS
MUSEUM**
334 Los Pinos Rd.
Santa Fe, NM 87505
(505) 471-2261 Fax: (505) 471-5623
George B. Paloheimo, Director

GENEALOGY CLUB OF ALBUQUERQUE
P.O. Box 25512
Albuquerque, NM 87125-0511
Email: info@abqgen.swnet.com
Web: www.abqgen.swnet.com

GERÓNIMO SPRINGS MUSEUM
211 Main St.
Truth or Consequences, NM 87901
(505) 894-6600 Fax: (505) 894-1968
Ann Welborn, Director

GUADALUPE HISTORIC FOUNDATION
Santuario de Guadalupe
100 Guadalupe St.
Santa Fe, NM 87501
(505) 988-2027
Emilio I. Ortiz, Executive Director

**HANDS ACROSS CULTURES
CORPORATION (HACC)**
Affiliate of NCLR / National Headquarters
P.O. Box 2215
Española, NM 87532
(505) 747-1889 Fax: (505) 747-1623
Harry Montoya, President & CEO
Email: hmontoya@aol.com

**HISPANIC ADVISORY COUNCIL OF
CLOVIS COMMUNITY COLLEGE**
417 Schepps Blvd.
Clovis, NM 88101
(505) 769-4015 or (505) 769-4933
Fax: (505) 769-4190
Erich Polack, Faculty Advisor
Email: cervantezv@clovis.cc.nm.us
Web: www.clovis.cc.nm.us

**HISPANIC BUSINESS STUDENT
ASSOCIATION (HBSA)**
New Mexico State Univ. Chicano Programs
Box 30001, MSC 4118
Las Cruces, NM 88003
(505) 646-4206 or (505) 382-0109 (h)
Fax: (505) 646-1962
Luz Franke, President
Email: lfranke@nmsu.edu

HISPANIC CULTURE FOUNDATION
P.O. Box 7279
Albuquerque, NM 87194-7279
(505) 766-9858 Fax: (505) 766-9665
Mary Peña-Noskin, President
Web: www.hcfoundation.org

HISPANIC EDUCATION FOUNDATION
3301 Mountain Rd., NW
Albuquerque, NM 87104
(505) 243-7551 Fax: (505) 247-2993
Isabelle Ogaz Tellez, Founder & Board Member
Web: www.incacorp.com/hef

HISPANIC EDUCATORS ASSOCIATION
New Mexico State University
P.O. Box 30001, MSC 4188
Las Cruces, NM 88003
(505) 646-4206 Fax: (505) 646-1962
Lina Benavidez, President
Email: hea@nmsu.edu
Web: www.nmsu.edu/~hea

HISPANIC ENGINEERING & SCIENCE ORG.
The University of New MexicoDivision of
Student Affairs
Engineering Annex 101 B
Albuquerque, NM 87131
(505) 277-6610
Chris Maestas, President

**HISPANIC GENEALOGICAL RESEARCH
CENTER OF NEW MEXICO**
P.O. Box 51088
Albuquerque, NM 87181
(505) 836-5438
Ronaldo Miera, President
Email: hgrc@hgrc-nm.org
Web: www.hgrc-nm.org

HISPANIC HONOR SOCIETY, THE
UNM Division of Student Affairs
Student Un. 105 Box 111, Mesa Vista Hall, #1153
Albuquerque, NM 87131
(505) 757-2213
Jacqueline Tapia, President
Email: jackt@unm.edu

HISPANIC NATIONAL BAR ASSOCIATION
9847 Sita Rd., NW
Albuquerque, NM 87114
(505) 841-7311 Fax: (505) 841-7317
Geraldine Rivera, Judicial Council Co-Liaison
Web: www.hnba.com

Executive Committee
Crider, Bingham & Hurst
3908 Carlisle NE
Albuquerque, NM 87107
(505) 881-4545 Fax: (505) 889-0988
Ms. Lillian G. Apodaca, Regional President
Email: cbhnm@aol.com
Web: cbhlawyers.com

Region XV (NM, UT)
1526 Vassar NE
Albuquerque, NM 87106
(505) 266-4154
Alan Varela, Regional President
Email: amvarela@uswest.net
Web: www.hnba.com

**HISPANIC ROUND TABLE OF NEW
MEXICO**
P.O. Box 27217
Albuquerque, NM 87125-2717
(505) 242-8085 Fax: (505) 764-8527
Juan Larranaga, Webmaster
Email: info@hrtnm.org
Web: http://www.hrtnm.org

HISPANIC STUDENTS CLUB
1600 St. Michaels Dr.
Santa Fe, NM 87501
(505) 473-6217
Paul Kippert, Assistant Dean

**HISPANO CHAMBER OF COMMERCE DE
LAS CRUCES**
P. O. Box 1964
Las Cruces, NM 88004
(505) 523-2681 Fax: (505) 523-4639
Elie López, Executive Director

**HOME EDUCATION LIVELIHOOD
PROGRAM, INC. (HELP)**
Affiliate of NCLR
5101 Copper NE
Albuquerque, NM 87108
(505) 265-3717 Fax: (505) 265-5412
Ernesto " Gene " Ortega, Executive Director

HOURGLASS PRISON ART MUSEUM
305 Lagunitas SW
Albuquerque, NM 87105
(505) 877-7318 or (505) 831-8067
Rudy Padilla, Director / Collector

INSTITUTE FOR SPANISH ARTS
P.O. Box 8418
Santa Fe, NM 87504-8418
(505) 983-8477 Fax: (505) 983-1395
María Cecilia Benitez, Director
Email: flamenco@mariabenitez.com

INTERHEMISPHERIC RESOURCE CENTER
Albuquerque Office
P.O. Box 4506
Albuquerque, NM 87196-4506
(505) 842-8288 Fax: (505) 246-1601
Tom Barry, Director
Email: irc@irc-online.org
Web: www.zianet.com/irc1/mission.html

Silver City Office
P.O. Box 2178
Silver City, NM 88062-2178
(505) 388-0208 Fax: (505) 388-0619
Deborah Preusch, Director
Email: irc@irc-online.org
Web: www.zianet.com/irc1/mission.html

**INTERNATIONAL TRADE COUNCIL OF
NEW MEXICO**
2935 Louisiana NE, #D
Albuquerque, NM 87110
(505) 768-0482 or (505) 298-3368
Fax: (505) 298-2370
Mery Alonso, President
Email: itcnmalb@netscape.net
Web: www.fita.org/itcnm

**LA COMPAÑIA DE TEATRO DE
ALBUQUERQUE**
P.O. Box 884
Albuquerque, NM 87103-0884
(505) 242-7929
Ramón A. Flores, Artistic Director

LAMBA THETA PHI
UNM Division of Student Affairs
Student Activities, 105, Box 99
Albuquerque, NM 87131
(505) 822-8328
Steve Aguilar, Vice President

LAS CRUCES/SER-JOBS FOR PROGRESS, INC.
Affiliate of SER-Jobs for Progress Nat'l, Inc.
575 S. Alameda, #B7
Las Cruces, NM 88001
(505) 524-1946 Fax: (505) 524-1946
Carrie García, Executive Director
Web: www.sernational.org

LATIN AMERICAN AND IBERIAN INST.
University of New Mexico
801 Yale NE
Albuquerque, NM 87131

(505) 277-2961 Fax: (505) 277-5989
Gilber W. Merkx, Director
Email: laiinfo@unm.edu
Web: www.unm.edu/~laiinfo

LOS REYES DE ALBUQUERQUE FDTN.
1205 Lester Dr., NE
Albuquerque, NM 87112
(505) 299-3055
Roberto Martínez, Director

**LULAC-NATIONAL EDUCATIONAL
SERVICE CENTER, INC. (LNESC)**
500 2nd St. NW, #500
Albuquerque, NM 87102
(505) 243-3787 Fax: (505) 243-7850
Frances A. Gandara, Director
Web: www.lulac.org

**MANA - A NATIONAL LATINA
ORGANIZATION**
Alburquerque Chapter
5707 Morgan Ln., NW
Albuquerque, NM 87102
(505) 262-1200 Fax: (505) 262-1119
Evangeline Trujillo, Chapter President
Email: hermana2@aol.com
Web: www.hermana.org

Santa Fe Chapter
P.O. Box 9236
Santa Fe, NM 87504
(505) 471-6599 Fax: (505) 471-6292
Geri Jaramillo, Chapter President
Email: hermana2@aol.com
Web: www.hermana.org

MARTÍNEZ HACIENDA
Kit Carson Historic Museums
P.O. Drawer CCC
Taos, NM 87571
(505) 758-1000 Fax: (505) 758-0330
Skip Miller, Co-Director

**MECHA (MOVIMIENTO ESTUDIANTIL
CHICANO DE AZTLAN)**
New Mexico State University
P.O. Box 30001
4118 MSC
Las Cruces, NM 88003
(505) 646-2631 Fax: (505) 646-1962
Hortencia Kayser, Advisor
Email: mechadenmsu@yahoo.com

UNM Division of Student Affairs
Student Union 105, Box 4
Albuquerque, NM 87131
(505) 277-5020
Adriann Barboa, Coordinator

**MEXICAN AMERICAN LAW STUDENT
ASSOCIATION**
UNM Division of Student Affairs
1117 Stanford, Law School
Albuquerque, NM 87131
(505) 277-6420
Israel Torres, President

**MEXICAN AMERICAN LEGAL DEFENSE
AND EDUCATIONAL FUND (MALDEF)**
Albuquerque Program Office
1606 Central Ave., SE, #201
Albuquerque, NM 87106
(505) 843-8888 Fax: (505) 246-9164
Nieves Torres, Director
Web: www.maldef.org

**MEXICANO/CHICANO CHAMBER OF
COMMERCE**
P.O. Box 248
Bayard, NM 88023
(505) 537-7534 Fax: (505) 538-5598
Juan Castañon, President

MILLICENT ROGERS MUSEUM
P.O. Box A
Taos, NM 87571
(505) 758-2462 Fax: (505) 758-5751
Dr. Patrick T. Houlihan, Executive Director
Email: mrm@newmex.com
Web: http://taosmuseums.org

MINORITY ENGINEERING PROGRAM
University of New Mexico
Engineering Annex #211
Albuquerque, NM 87131
(505) 277-8795 Fax: (505) 277-5476
Maurice Thompson, Interim
Email: mepdept@urim.edu
Web: www.unm.edu/~mepdept/

MUSEUM OF INTERNATIONAL FOLK ART
P.O. Box 2087
Santa Fe, NM 87504-2087
(505) 827-6350 Fax: (505) 827-6349
Charlene Cerny, Director
Web: www.moifa.org

**NATIONAL INSTITUTE FOR
PROFESSIONAL DEVELOPMENT INC.**
Project Uplift
P.O. Box 30246
Albuquerque, NM 87110
(505) 265-4464 Fax: (505) 256-0870
Henry J. Casso, President
Email: proguplift@aol.com

**NATIONAL LATINO PEACE OFFICERS
ASSOCIATION (NLPOA)**
New Mexico Chapter
P. O. Box 1773
Albuquerque, NM 87103
(877) 657-6200
Adrián García, National President
Email: nlpoa@aol.com
Web: www.nlpoa.com

**NEIGHBORHOOD HOUSING SERVICES OF
SANTA FE, INC.**
Affiliate of NCLR
1570 Pacheco St., #A-1
Santa Fe, NM 87505
(505) 983-6214 Fax: (505) 983-4655
Michael Loftin, Executive Director
Email: nhsofsf@ix.netcom.com

**NEW MEXICO ALLIANCE FOR HISPANIC
EDUCATION**
P.O. Box 25806
Albuquerque, NM 87125-5806
(505) 342-3504 Fax: (505) 345-5351
Erma Sterling, Director
Email: nmnhsf@nmalliance.org
Web: www.nmalliance.org

**NEW MEXICO HISPANIC CULTURAL
CENTER**
600 Central, SW, #201
Albuquerque, NM 87102
(505) 246-2261 Fax: (505) 246-2613
Eugene Matta, Director
Web: www.museums.state.nm.us

**NEW MEXICO HISPANO CHAMBER OF
COMMERCE DEL NORTE**
943 Don Cubero Ave.
Santa Fe, NM 87501
(505) 982-3094 Fax: (505) 982-3094
Andrés Romero, President

**NEW MEXICO MATHEMATICS,
ENGINEERING, SCIENCE ACHIEVEMENT,
INC. (MESA)**
Affiliate of NCLR
2808 Central SE, #122
Albuquerque, NM 87106
(505) 262-1200 Fax: (505) 262-1119
Evangeline Sandoval Trujillo, Executive Director
Email: ES@NMMESA.NMT.EDU
Web: http://nmmesa.nmt.edu

PETROGLYPH NATIONAL MONUMENT
National Headquarters
6001 Unser Boulevard NW
Albuquerque, NM 87120
(505) 899-0205 Fax: (505) 899-0207
Judith Córdoba, Superintendent
Email: www.nps.gov

**RATON COLFAX COUNTY HISPANO
CHAMBER OF COMMERCE**
P.O. Box 1041
Raton, NM 87740
(505) 445-8242 Fax: (505) 445-8242
Arturo Cruz, President

RAZA EN ACCIÓN
UNM Division of Student Affairs
Student Union 105, Box 51
Albuquerque, NM 87131
(505) 277-5020
Rosa I. Cervantes, President
Email: isela@unm.edu

RAZA GRADUATE STUDENT ASSOC.
UNM Division of Student Affairs
1153 Mesa Vista, El Centro de la Raza
Albuquerque, NM 87131
(505) 277-5503
Eric-Christopher García, President

REFORMA
New Mexico Chapter
New Mexico State University Library
P.O. Box 30006, Dept. 3475
Las Cruces, NM 88003-8006
(505) 646-1508 Fax: (505) 646-6940
Gwen Gregory, Chapter President
Email: ggregory@lib.nmsu.edu
Web: http://lib.nmsu.edu/reforma/

RESOURCE CENTER FOR RAZA PLANNING
UNM Division of Student Affairs
School of Architecture and Planning
Albuquerque, NM 87131
(505) 266-7339 or TDD (505) 277-7871
Jen Glew, President
Email: sac@unm.eduhttp://www.edu/~sac

RIO GRANDE CENTER
Affiliate of NCLR
P.O. Box 310
Embudo, NM 87531
(505) 579-4251 Fax: (505) 579-4016
Frances Rodarte, Executive Director

**ROSWELL HISPANIC CHAMBER OF
COMMERCE**
426 N. Main St.
Roswell, NM 88201
(505) 624-0889 Fax: (505) 624-0538
Ray Baca, Executive Director
Email: rhccvic@lookingglass.net
Web: roswellhcc.com

**SER OF ALBUQUERQUE JOBS FOR
PROGRESS, INC.**
Affiliate of SER-Jobs for Progress
National, Inc.
2118 Central Ave., SE, #33
Albuquerque, NM 87106
(505) 268-4500 Fax: (505) 268-4499
Pete Salazar, Executive Director
Email: serdee@qwest.net
Web: www.sernational.org

SER, SANTA FE JOBS FOR PROGRESS, INC.
Affiliate of SER-Jobs for Progress
National, Inc.
2516 Cerillos Rd.
Santa Fe, NM 87501
(505) 473-0428 Fax: (505) 438-4813
Alex A. Martínez, Executive Director
Web: www.sernational.org

SIETE DEL NORTE
Affiliate of NCLR
P.O. Box 400
Embudo, NM 87531
(505) 579-4217 Fax: (505) 579-4206
Amos A. Atencio, President

**SOCIETY OF HISPANIC PROFESSIONAL
ENGINEERS (SHPE)**
New Mexico State University
Chicano Programs
P.O. Box 30001, MS 4188
Las Cruces, NM 88003
(505) 646-4206 Fax: (505) 646-1962
Dr. Laura Gutiérrez Spencer, Director
Email: lgutzspc@nmsu.edu

SOUTH BROADWAY CULTURAL CENTER
1025 Broadway SE
Albuquerque, NM 87102
(505) 848-1320 Fax: (505) 848-1329
Linda Ulibarri, Manager
Email: lulibarri@cabq.gov
Web: www.cabq.gov

SOUTHERN NEW MEXICO LEGAL SERVICES
300 N. Downtown Mall
Las Cruces, NM 88001
(505) 526-4451 Fax: (505) 541-4840
Ismael Alvarez, Executive Director

**SOUTHWEST HISPANIC RESEARCH
INSTITUTE / CHICANO STUDIES**
University of New Mexico
1829 Sigma Chi Rd., NE
Albuquerque, NM 87131
(505) 277-2965 Fax: (505) 277-3343
Mr. Felipe Gonzales, Director
Email: gonzales@unm.edu

**SPANISH AND PORTUGUESE GRADUATE
STUDENT ASSOCIATION**
University of New Mexico
Department of Spanish & Portuguese
Ortega Hall, Room 235
Albuquerque, NM 87131-1146
(505) 277-5907 Fax: (505) 277-3885
Jon Tolman, Chair
Email: tolman@unm.edu

SPANISH CLUB
Eastern New Mexico University
Station #34
Portales, NM 88130
(505) 562-2451 Fax: (505) 562-2251
Sylvia Turrubiales, Student Advisor

SPANISH CLUB
Eastern New Mexico University, Roswell
P.O. Box 6000
Roswell, NM 88202-6000
(505) 624-7223 Fax: (505) 624-9119
Louis Brady, Sponsor
Email: bradyl@lib.enmuros.cc.nm.us

SPANISH COLONIAL ARTS SOCIETY, INC.
P.O. Box 5378
Santa Fe, NM 87502-5378
(505) 983-4038 Fax: (505) 982-4585
Bud Redding, Executive Director
Web: www.spanishcolonial.org

SPANISH COLONIAL RESEARCH CENTER
University of New Mexico
Zimmerman Library, #214
Albuquerque, NM 87131
(505) 766-8743 Fax: (505) 346-2879
Joseph P. Seanchez, Director

**STUDENT ORGANIZATION FOR LATIN
AMERICAN STUDIES (SOLAS)**
UNM Division of Student Affairs
LAI, 801 Yale NE
Albuquerque, NM 87131
(505) 277-6847
Lindsay E. Jones, President

YOUTH DEVELOPMENT, INC. (YDI)
Affiliate of NCLR
6301 Central NW
Albuquerque, NM 87105
(505) 831-6038 Fax: (505) 352-3400
Chris Baca, President & CEO

NEW YORK

116TH ST. BLOCK ASSOCIATION, INC.
23 E. 115 St., 3rd Floor
New York, NY 10029
(212) 860-4100 Fax: (212) 860-4100
Dr. Aurea Rodríguez, Director

52 PEOPLE FOR PROGRESS
855 E. 233rd St., #11B
Bronx, NY 10466
(718) 324-9328
Al Quiñones, President

ACCIÓN INTERNATIONAL
New York Affiliate
235 Havemeyer St., 2nd Floor
Brooklyn, NY 11211
(718) 599-5170 Fax: (718) 387-9686
Terri Lubwig, Director
Email: info@accion.org
Web: www.accion.org

ACTION PRESBYTERIAN HISPANA
161 S. 3rd St.
Brooklyn, NY 11211
(718) 388-0700
Daniele Rivera, Pastor

ADELANTE OF SUFFOLK COUNTY, INC.
10 Third Ave.
Brentwood, NY 11717
(516) 434-3481 Fax: (516) 434-3496
Miriam M.E. García, Executive Director
Email: adelanteSC@world.att.net

**ADMINISTRACIÓN DE ASUNTOS
FEDERALES DE PUERTO RICO**
475 Park Avenue South., 7th Floor
New York, NY 10016
(212) 252-7300 Fax: (212) 252-7323
Carlos A. Linera, Director

ADULT BASIC TRAINING
329 E. 149th. St., 2nd Floor
Bronx, NY 10451
(718) 665-6969 Fax: (718) 292-3113
Philip Morrow, President

ADULT OUT PATIENT SERVICES
781 E. 142nd St.
Bronx, NY 10454
(718) 993-1400 Fax: (718) 993-0647
O' Conner, Director

AESTHETIC REALISM FOUNDATION
141 Greene St.
New York, NY 10012
(212) 777-4490 Fax: (212) 777-4426

Margot Carpenter, Executive Director
Web: www.AestheticRealism.org

**AFRICANA & LATINO GREEK LETTERED
COUNCIL**
Cornell University
434 Rockefeller Hall
Ithaca, NY 14853
(607) 255-3197 Fax: (607) 255-2433
Susie Nelson, Advisor
Email: mfd1@cornell.edu
Web: http://latino.lsp.cornell.edu

AGUADILLA DAY CARE CENTER
656 Willoughby Ave.
Brooklyn, NY 11206
(718) 443-2900 Fax: (718) 443-2905
Eva Martin, Director

**AGUSTIN PUCHO OLIVENCIA
COMMUNITY CENTER**
261 Swan St.
Buffalo, NY 14204
(716) 852-1648
Carlos Olivencia, President

AIDS COMMUNITY RESOURCES, INC.
627 W. Genesee St.
Syracuse, NY 13204
(315) 475-2430 Fax: (315) 472-6515
Michael Crinnin, Executive Director

AIDS ROCHESTER, INC.
1350 University Ave.
Rochester, NY 14607
(716) 442-2220 Fax: (716) 442-5049
Paula Silvestrone, Executive Director
Email: nfo@AIDSRochester.org
Web: www.aidsrochester.org

844 North Clinton Ave.
Rochester, NY 14605
(716) 454-5556
Paula Silvestrone, Executive Director
Email: info@AIDSRochester.org
Web: www.AIDSRochster.org

605 West Washington St.
Geneva, NY 14456
(315) 781-6303 or (800) 422-0282
Paula Silvestrone, Executive Director
Email: info@AIDSRochester.org
Web: www.AIDSRochster.org

122 Liberty St.
Bath, NY 14810
(607) 776-9166 or (800) 954-2437
Paula Silvestrone, Executive Director
Email: info@AIDSRochester.org
Web: www.AIDSRochster.org

**ALCOHOL & DRUG DEPENDENCY
SERVICES, INC.**
291 Elm St.
Buffalo, NY 14203
(716) 854-2977 Fax: (716) 854-1223
Richard J. Gallager, Executive Director

ALIANZA DOMINICANA, INC.
Affiliate of NCLR
2340 Amsterdam Ave.
New York, NY 10033
(212) 928-4992 Fax: (212) 543-0029
Moisés Pérez, Executive Director

Family Center / Affiliate of NCLR
715 W. 179th St.
New York, NY 10033
(212) 795-4226 Fax: (212) 795-4285
Moisés Pérez, Executive Director

Headquarters / Affiliate of NCLR
2410 Amsterdam Ave. 4th Floor
New York, NY 10033
(212) 740-1967 Fax: (212) 740-1960
Moisés Pérez, Executive Director

La Plaza Beacon School /Affiliate of NCLR
518 W. 182th St.
New York, NY 10033
(212) 928-4992 Fax: (212) 795-8590
Moisés Pérez, Executive Director

ALIANZA LATINA
Pace University
Civic Center Campus
41 Park Row, 8th Floor
New York, NY 10038
(212) 346-1918 or (212) 346-1590
Fax: (212) 346-1916
Sandra Evelisse Rivera, Alumni Advisor

ALMA SOLANA BALLET
45 Alto Ave.
Port Chester, NY 10573
(914) 939-2409
John Mecca, Director

ALPHA RHO LAMBDA SORORITY, INC
Alianza de Raíces Latinas
365 W. 25th St. Apt. 2-J
New York, NY 10001
(212) 929-6126 Fax: (212) 367-7182
Maribel A. Lara, President
Email: sp96apple@aol.com
Web: http://www.eecs.tufts.edu/~wvargas/anim.html

ALPHA SIGMA OMEGA LATINA SORORITY, INC.
1963 Edison 1st. Floor
Bronx, NY 10461
Doris A. Maldonado-Fernández, National President
Email: unica_aso@hotmail.com
Web: www.geocities.com/athens/forum/6517/index.html

AMERICAN COUNCIL ON INTERNATIONAL PERSONNEL
515 Madison Ave. 6th Floor
New York, NY 10022
(212) 688-2437 Fax: (212) 593-4697
Arnold E. Eagle, President
Email: arnold@acip.com
Web: www.acip.com

AMERICAN RED CROSS MINORITY OUTREACH
HIV/AIDS Services
786 Delaware Ave.
Buffalo, NY 14209
(716) 886-7500 Fax: (716) 878-2345
Nancy Blafchak, Director
Web: www.redcross.org/ny/buffalo

AMERICAN SPANISH DANCE THEATER
Andrea Del Conte Danze España
144 E. 24th St., #4A
New York, NY 10010-3730
(212) 674-6725 Fax: (212) 674-6725
Andrea del Conte, Artistic/Executive Director
Email: adelconte@aol.com
Web: www.delconte-danza.com

AMERICAS SOCIETY ART GALLERY
680 Park Ave.
New York, NY 10021
(212) 249-8950 Fax: (212) 249-5868
Elizabeth Stein, Director
Web: www.america-society.org

AMERICAS SOCIETY, INC.
680 Park Ave.
New York, NY 10021
(212) 249-8950 Fax: (212) 517-6247
Thomas E. McNamara, President
Email: webmaster@americas-society.org
Web: www.americas-society.org

AMIGOS DE LA ZARZUELA
241 W. 97th St., #4M
New York, NY 10025
(212) 222-2655 Fax: (212) 666-7614
Antonio Pérez-Outeiral, President

AMISTAD CHILD DAY CARE CENTER
110-15 164 Pl.
Jamaica, NY 11433
(718) 526-5911
Eddie P. Smith, Executive Director

THE ANDREW GLOVER YOUTH PROGRAM
100 Center St. #1541
New York, NY 10013
(212) 349-6381 Fax: (212) 349-6388
Ángel Rodríguez, Executive Director
Email: gloveryouth@aol.com

ANNABELLA GONZÁLEZ DANCE THEATER
4 E. 89th St., P-C
New York, NY 10128
(212) 722-4128
Annabella González, Director

ANTHONY L. JORDAN HEALTH CORP.
82 Holland St.
Rochester, NY 14605
(716) 423-5800 Fax: (716) 423-0739
Marshall J. Spurlock, President

AQUINAS HOUSING CORPORATION
1912 Crotona Parkway
Bronx, NY 10460

(718) 842-6440 Fax: (718) 542-4223
Megan Shannon, Executive Director
Email: AquinesHOB@aol.com

ARCHDIOCESE OF NEW YORK
Hispanic Affairs
1011 First Ave.
New York, NY 10022
(212) 371-1000 x2982 Fax: (212) 319-8265
Rev. Josu Iriondo, Vicar for Hispanic Ministry

ARGENTINE AMERICAN CHAMBER OF COMMERCE, INC.
630 5th Ave., 25th Floor, #2518
New York, NY 10111
(212) 698-2238 Fax: (212) 698-2239
Carlos E. Alfaro, President

ARGENTINE AMERICAN MEDICAL SOCIETY
333 Broadway, #4
Amityville, NY 11701
(631) 226-2814
Luis A. Palma, President

ARMS ACRES, INC.
75 Seminary Hill Rd.
Carmel, NY 10512
(845) 225-3400 Fax: (845) 225-5660
Patrice Wallace-Moore, Executive Dircetor
Web: www.armsacres.com

ARMS ACRES, INC.
1841 Broadway., #300
New York, NY 10023
(212) 399-6902 Fax: (212) 399-6906
Joseph Pais, Executive Director
Web: www.armsacres.com

80-02 Kew Gardens Rd.
Kew Gardens, NY 11415
(718) 520-1513 Fax: (718) 520-6460
Dan Clune, Executive Director
Web: www.armsacres.com

ASOCIACIÓN HISPANA DE SAN MIGUEL
136-76 41st Ave.
Flushing, NY 11355
(718) 961-0295 Fax: (718) 961-1403
Víctor Muñoz, President

ASOCIACIONES DOMINICANAS, INC.
510 West 145th St
New York, NY 10031
(212) 690-3290 Fax: (212) 690-3295
Sukhwant Walia, Executive Director

ASPIRA OF NEW YORK, INC.
470 7th Ave., 3rd Floor
New York, NY 10018
(212) 564-6880 Fax: (212) 564-7152
Héctor Gesualdo, Executive Director
Web: www.aspira.org/NewYork.html

ASSOCIATION FOR DRUG ABUSE PREVENTION AND TREATMENT, INC.
2230 1st Ave.
New York, NY 10029
(212) 289-1957 Fax: (212) 876-8269
Divine Piyor, Executive Director

ASSOCIATION FOR PUERTO RICAN-HISPANIC CULTURE, INC.
National Headquarters
83 Park Terrace West
New York, NY 10034
(212) 942-2338 Fax: (718) 367-0780
Peter Bloch, President

ASSOCIATION OF COLOMBIAN PROFESSIONALS
P.O. Box 720037
Jackson Heights, NY 11371
(718) 848-4737
Luz Leguizamo, President

ASSOCIATION OF HISPANIC ARTS (AHA)
National Headquarters
250 W. 26th St., 4th Floor
New York, NY 10001
(212) 727-7227 x13 Fax: (212) 727-0549
Sandra Pérez, Executive Director
Email: aha96@aol.com
Web: www.latinoarts.org

ASSOCIATION OF HISPANICS ORGANIZED TO RAISE AWARENES (AHORA)
American Express Co.
World Financial Center
200 Vesey St., 31st Floor
New York, NY 10285
(212) 640-1941 Fax: (212) 619-8610

Lourdes Sierra, Director
Email: lourdes.sierra@aexp.com

ASSOCIATION OF LATINO SPEAKERS
85 4th Ave., #JJ
New York, NY 10003
(212) 353-9114 or (212) 866-0125
Fax: (212) 353-9114
Alberto O. Cappas, President
Web: www.donpedrocookies.com/mission1.htm

ASSOCIATION OF SPANISH SPEAKING AMERICAN BAPTIST CHURCHES OF THE NEW YORK METROPOLITAN AREA
475 Riverside Dr., #432
New York, NY 10115
(212) 870-3195 Fax: 8703228
Hilda Río, President

ASTOR HEAD START EARLY CHILDHOOD PROGRAM
95 Catherine St.
Beacon, NY 12508
(914) 831-1791 Fax: (914) 831-4325
Trudy Hoffmann, Executive Director

ATA CARNET
United States Council for International Business
1212 Avenue of the Americas
New York, NY 10036-1689
(212) 354-4480 Fax: (212) 944-0012
Cynthia Duncan, Marketing Manager

AUDUBON PARTNERSHIP FOR ECONOMIC DEVELOPMENT
Affiliate of NCLR
5000 Broadway, #A
New York, NY 10034
(212) 544-2470 Fax: (212) 544-0248
Walther Delgado, Executive Director
Email: apedldc@datatone.com

AVON HISPANIC NETWORK
1345 6th Ave., 27th Floor
New York, NY 10105
(212) 282-5610 Fax: (212) 282-6086
Anna María Vitek, President

BADEN STREET SETTLEMENT, INC.
485 N. Clinton Ave.
Rochester, NY 14605
(716) 325-4910 Fax: (716) 546-3777
Ron Thomas, Executive Director

BALLET HISPÁNICO OF NEW YORK
167 W. 89th St.
New York, NY 10024
(212) 362-6710 Fax: (212) 362-7809
Verdery Roosevelt, Executive Director
Web: www.ballethispanico.org

BANANA KELLY, INC.
863 Prospect Ave.
Bronx, NY 10459
(718) 328-1064 Fax: (718) 991-3242
Yolanda Rivera, Chairman

BANK STREET COLLEGE OF EDUCATION
Bilingual Education Program
610 W. 112th St.
New York, NY 10025
(212) 875-4468 Fax: (212) 875-4753
Olga Romero, Chairperson
Email: olgar@bnkst.edu
Web: www.bnkst.edu

BETANCES EARLY CHILDHOOD DEVELOPMENT CENTER
528 E. 146th St.
Bronx, NY 10455
(718) 665-1100
Miriam Kende, Director

BETANCES HEALTH UNIT INC.
280 Henry St.
New York, NY 10002
(212) 227-8401 Fax: (212) 227-8842
Paul Ramos, Executive Director

BETANCES SENIOR CITIZENS CENTER
401 St. Anns Ave.
Bronx, NY 10454
(718) 292-4922
Ester Sanchez, Director

THE BILINGUAL SCHOOL, PUBLIC SCHOOL 25
811 E. 149th St.
Bronx, NY 10455
(718) 292-2995 Fax: (718) 292-2947
Miriam Diaz, Executive Director

BILINGUAL STUDIES PROGRAM
Kingsboro Community College
2001 Oriental Blvd.
Brooklyn, NY 11235
(718) 368-5576 Fax: (718) 368-4906
Diego Colón, Director

BLACK AND LATINO STUDENT ALLIANCE
Schenectady County Community College
78 Washington Ave.
Student Activities Rm. 222
Schenectady, NY 12305
(518) 381-1200
Xavier M. Mc Daniels, Sr., President

BLACK AND PUERTO RICAN COALITION OF CONSTRUCTION WORKERS
874 Freeman St.
Bronx, NY 10459
(718) 842-5140
Stephen B., Director

BORINQUEN HEALTH CENTER
2253 3rd Ave., #3rd Floor
New York, NY 10035
(212) 289-6650
Elli Sánchez, Director

BORINQUEN PLAZA SENIOR CITIZENS CENTER
80 Seigal St.
Brooklyn, NY 11206
(718) 782-6334
Mary Rivera, Program Director

BOY'S HARBOR, INC.
1 E. 104th St.
New York, NY 10029
(212) 427-2244 Fax: (212) 427-2311
Dr. Robert North, Executive Director

BRAZILIAN AMERICAN CHAMBER OF COMMERCE
509 Madison Ave. #304
New York, NY 10022
(212) 751-4691 Fax: (212) 751-7692
Gabriel R. Safdie, President
Email: info@brazilcham.com
Web: www.brazilcham.com

BRAZILIAN AMERICAN CULTURAL CENTER
16 W. 46th St., 2nd Floor
New York, NY 10036
(212) 730-0515 Fax: (212) 869-2685
Wendy Smith, Executive Director

BRONX AIDS SERVICES, INC.
1 Fordham Plaza, #903
Bronx, NY 10458
(718) 295-5605 Fax: (718) 733-3429
Sarageon Avery, Executive Director

THE BRONX CHAMBER OF COMMERCE
1111 Calhoun Ave.
Bronx, NY 10465
(718) 829-4111 Fax: (718) 829-5156
John Collazzi, President
Email: chamber@chamberbronx.com
Web: www.bronxchamber.com

BRONX CHILDREN CENTER COMMUNITY PROGRAM
4215 3rd Ave.
Bronx, NY 10457
(718) 299-2304
Allison Upton, Director

BRONX COUNCIL ON THE ARTS, INC.
Corner Morris Park
1738 Hone Ave.
Bronx, NY 10461
(718) 931-9500 Fax: (718) 409-6445
Bill Aguado, Executive Director

BRONX DEVELOPMENTAL SERVICES
1200 Waters Pl.
Bronx, NY 10461
(718) 430-0845 Fax: (718) 430-0382
Dr. Hugh Tarpley, Executive Director

BRONX MUSEUM OF THE ARTS
1040 Grand Concourse 165th St.
Bronx, NY 10456-3999
(718) 681-6000
Jane Delgado, Director

BRONX ORGANIZATION FOR THE LEARNING DISABLED (BOLD)
1180 Rev. James Polite Ave.
Bronx, NY 10459
(718) 589-7379 Fax: (718) 589-2052
M. Egan, Director

BRONX OVERALL ECONOMIC
DEVELOPMENT CORPORATION, INC.,
THE
198 E. 161th St., '#201
Bronx, NY 10451
(718) 590-3948 Fax: (718) 590-3499
José L. Ithier, President
Email: info@boedc.org
Web: www.boedc.com

C.A.S.E.S.
346 Broadway
New York, NY 10013
(212) 732-0076 Fax: (212) 553-6508
Joel Copperman, Executive Director

CABS NURSING HOME CO., INC.
270 Nostrand Ave.
Brooklyn, NY 11205-4991
(718) 638-0500 Fax: (718) 857-3200
David Wieder, Executive Vice-President

CÁMARA DE COMERCIO SALVADOREÑA
80 Clinton St.
Hempstead, NY 11550
(516) 481-8030 Fax: (516) 481-9693
Juan Mijango, President
Web: www.camarasalusa.org

CAPOEIRA FOUNDATION/DANCE BRASIL
104 Franklin St.
New York, NY 10013
(212) 382-0555 Fax: (212) 925-0369
Jelon Vieira, Artistic Director

CARIBBEAN AMERICAN CENTER OF NEW
YORK
195 Cadman Plaza W 1st Floor
Brooklyn, NY 11201
(718) 625-1515 Fax: (718) 625-0717
Jean Alexander, Executive Director
Email: jeanpalexander@hotmail.com
Web: caribbeancenter.org

CARIBBEAN CULTURAL CENTER
408 W. 58th St.
New York, NY 10019
(212) 307-7420 Fax: (212) 315-1086
Marta Vega, Executive Director
Email: info@caribectr.org
Web: www.caribectr.org

CARIBBEAN-AMERICAN CHAMBER OF
COMMERCE & INDUSTRY
Bldg., #5, Brooklyn Navy Yard
Brooklyn, NY 11205
(718) 834-4544 Fax: (718) 834-9774
Roy A. Hastick, Sr., President
Email: rahascick@msn

CARLOTA SANTANA SPANISH DANCE CO.
154 Christopher St., #3D
New York, NY 10014
(212) 229-9754
Carlota Santana, Executive Director

CARVER COMMUNITY CENTER
55 E. 102nd St. ,
New York, NY 10029
(212) 289-2708 Fax: (212) 360-1947
María E. Rivera, Director

CARVER COMMUNITY COUNSELING
SERVICES
949 State St.
Schenectady, NY 12307
(518) 382-7838 Fax: (518) 382-1641
Guido Iovinella, Program Director

CASA BORICUA SENIOR CITIZEN'S
CENTER
910 E. 172nd St.
Bronx, NY 10460
(718) 542-0222
Wilma Castro, Director

CASA DEL SOL
P.O. Box 493, 674 E. 136 St.
Bronx, NY 10454
(718) 292-6443
Rafaél Bueno, Director

CASITA MARÍA, INC.
928 Simpson St.
Bronx, NY 10459
(718) 589-2230
Cristina Toosie, Executive Director

CATHOLIC CHARITIES OF MONTGOMERY
COUNTY
1 Kimball St.
Amsterdam, NY 12010
(518) 842-4202 Fax: (518) 842-4245
Digna Betancourt Swingle, Executive Director

CATHOLIC FAMILY CENTER
La Lucha Program
218 Clifford Ave.
Rochester, NY 14621
(716) 232-2050 Fax: (716) 232-3352
Jacquelin Martin Turner, Program Manager

CATHOLIC FAMILY CENTER RESTART
55 Troup St.
Rochester, NY 14608
(716) 546-3046 Fax: (716) 546-2607
Carl Hatch, Director

CENTER FOR CUBAN STUDIES
124 W. 23rd St.
New York, NY 10011
(212) 242-0559
Sandra Levinson, President
Web: www.cubanartspace.net

CENTER FOR FAMILY LIFE EMPLOYMENT
SERVICES
269 37th St.
Brooklyn, NY 11232
(718) 788-8302 Fax: (718) 788-9277
María Ferreira, Coordinator

CENTER FOR FAMILY LIFE IN SUNSET
PARK
345 43rd St.
Brooklyn, NY 11232
(718) 788-3500 Fax: (718) 788-2275
Sister Mary Paul, Project Director

THE CENTER FOR HISPANIC MENTAL
HEALTH RESEARCH
Fordham University
Graduate School of Social Services
113 W. 60th St., #704
New York, NY 10023
(212) 636-7083 Fax: (212) 636-7079
Dr. Luis H. Zayas, Director
Email: CHMHR@Mary.Fordham.edu

CENTER FOR LATIN AMERICAN AND
CARIBBEAN STUDIES
New York University
53 Washington Square South, #4W
New York, NY 10012
(212) 998-8686 Fax: (212) 995-4163
Andrés Velasco, Director

CENTER FOR MIGRATION STUDIES
209 Flagg Pl.
Staten Island, NY 10304-1148
(718) 351-8800 Fax: (718) 667-4598
Dr. Lydio F. Tomasi, Executive Director
Email: cmslft@aol.com

CENTER FOR PUERTO RICAN STUDIES
Hunter College of CUNY
695 Park Ave.
New York, NY 10021
(212) 772-5686 Fax: (212) 650-3673
Gabriel Haslip-Viera, Director
Web: www.centerpr.org

CENTRAL AMERICAN LEGAL ASSISTANCE,
INC.
240 Hooper St.
Brooklyn, NY 11211
(718) 486-6800 Fax: (718) 486-5281
Anne Pilsbury, Director

CENTRO CARISMÁTICO CATÓLICO
HISPANO
826 E. 166th St.
Bronx, NY 10459
(718) 378-1734
Josu Iriondo, Executive Director

CENTRO CÍVICO CHILENO - EEUU
305 Seventh Ave., 11th Floor
New York, NY 10001
(212) 714-8209 Fax: (212) 633-0645
Mario E. Tapia, President
Email: tapcentro@erols.com
Web: www.chilelindo.com

CENTRO CÍVICO CULTURAL
AGUADILLANO, INC.
656 Willoughby Ave.
Brooklyn, NY 11206
(718) 443-2900 Fax: (718) 443-2900
Eva Martin, Director

CENTRO CÍVICO HISPANOAMERICANO,
INC.
20 Rensselaer St. #3B
Albany, NY 12202
(518) 465-1138 Fax: (518) 465-1138
Cecilia Sanz, Director

CENTRO CÍVICO OF AMSTERDAM, INC.
143-145 E. Main St.
Amsterdam, NY 12010
(518) 842-3762 Fax: (518) 842-9139
Ladan Alomar, Executive Director
Email: civico@telenet.net

CENTRO CULTURAL BALLET QUISQUEYA,
INC.
P.O. Box 500
2153 Amsterdam Ave. # 11
New York, NY 10032
(212) 795-0107 Fax: (212) 795-0107
Normandía Maldonado, Executive Director

CENTRO CULTURAL MEXICANO
New York Office
27 E. 39th St.
New York, NY 10016
(212) 217-6421 Fax: (212) 217-6425
Erika Vilfort, Contact
Email: mexcult@quicklink.com

CENTRO CULTURAL "VAMOS A LA PEÑA
DEL BRONX"
226 E. 144th St. 3rd Floor
Bronx, NY 10451
(718) 402-9411
Nieves Ayress & Víctor Toro, Founders

CENTRO DE ESTUDIOS
PUERTORRIQUEÑOS
Hunter College, CUNY
695 Park Ave.
New York, NY 10021
(212) 772-5688 Fax: (212) 650-3673
Juan Flores, Director

CENTRO MÉDICO DOMINICANO DE
DIAGNÓSTICO Y TRATAMIENTO
629 W. 185th St.
New York, NY 10033
(212) 928-3900 Fax: (212) 781-2190
Jacquelin Almonte, Administration

CENTRO SOCIAL LA ESPERANZA
21 Audubon Ave.
New York, NY 10032
(212) 928-5810
James Malley, Executive Director

CHARAS/ EL BOHIO COMMUNITY
CULTURAL CENTER
605 E. 9th St.
New York, NY 10009
(212) 533-6835 Fax: (212) 505-8008
Carlos " Chino " García, Director
Email: charas@erols.com

CHARAS, INC.
605 E. 9th St.
New York, NY 10009
(212) 982-0627 or (212) 533-6835
Fax: (212) 505-8008
Carlos García, Executive Director

CHI UPSILON SIGMA
Grand Chapter Board
99 Park Avenue, #278A
New York, NY 10016
(212) 969-0793 Fax: (212) 867-7904
Glenda Gracia-Rivera, President
Email: gcb@justbecus.org
Web: www.justbecus.org

CHILDREN AND ADOLESCENT SERVICES,
INC.
781 E. 142nd St., 2nd Floor
Bronx, NY 10454
(718) 993-1400 Fax: (718) 993-0647
Julio Ortega, Director

CHILDREN'S ART & SCIENCE
WORKSHOPS
300 Fort Washington Ave., #1H
New York, NY 10032
(212) 923-7766 Fax: (212) 795-5901
Yocasta Morales, Executive Director
Email: casworg@aol.com

CHRISTIAN COMMUNITY IN ACTION, INC.
910 E. 172nd St., 4th Floor
Bronx, NY 10460
(718) 542-5900
Rubén Díaz, Executive Director

THE CHURCH OF JESUS CHRIST OF
LATTER DAY SAINTS
Hill Cumorah Visitors' Center
603 Route 21 S.
Palmyra, NY 14522
(315) 597-5851 Fax: (315) 597-0165
Elder Hess, Director
Web: www.lds.org

CHURCH WORLD SERVICE IMMIGRATION
AND REFUGEE PROGRAM
475 Riverside Dr., #656
New York, NY 10115
(212) 870-3153 Fax: (212) 870-2132
William Sage, Director
Web: www.churchworldservice.org

CÍRCULO DE ESCRITORES Y POETAS
IBEROAMERICANOS DE NUEVA YORK
(C.E.P.I.)
G.P.O. Station P.O. Box 831
New York, NY 10116
(914) 354-6799
Gerardo Piña, President

CÍRCULO DE LA HISPANIDAD, INC.
62 West Park Ave.
Long Beach, NY 11561
(516) 889-3869 Fax: (516) 889-4572
Gil Bernardino, Executive Director
Email: circulo@aol.com

CITIZENS ADVICE BUREAU, INC.
178 Bennet Ave.
New York, NY 10040
(212) 923-2599 Fax: (212) 923-4329
Abigal Ochado, Project Director

CITIZENS ADVICE BUREAU, INC.
2054 Morris Ave.
Bronx, NY 10453
(718) 731-0720 Fax: (718) 365-0697
Carolyn Mc Laughlin, Executive Director

CITY OF WHITE PLAINS SERVICE OFFICE
65 Mitchell Pl.
White Plains, NY 10601
(914) 422-1255 Fax: (914) 422-1295
Martha Guarini, Assiatant Officer

CLAREMONT NEIGHBORHOOD CENTER
489 E 169th St.
Bronx, NY 10456
(718) 588-1000 Fax: (718) 681-0736
Rachel Spivey, Executive Director

CLEMENTE SOTO VÉLEZ CULTURAL &
EDUCATIONAL CENTER
107 Suffolk St., #130
New York, NY 10002
(212) 260-4080 Fax: (212) 353-3707
Orlando Plaza, Executive Director
Email: info@csvcenter.org

CLÍNICA CENTRAL DE DIAGNÓSTICO Y
TRATAMIENTO SERVICIOS MÉDICOS
HISPANOS
82-09 Roosevelt Ave., 2nd Floor
Jackson Heights, NY 11372
(718) 507-8000
Amanda Martínez, Executive Director

COALITION FOR HISPANIC FAMILY
SERVICES
315 Wyckoff Ave., 4th Floor
Brooklyn, NY 11237
(718) 497-6090 Fax: (718) 497-9495
Denise Rosario, Executive Director
Email: Info@chfs.bizland.com
Web: http://chfs.bizland.com

CODELA
P.O. Box 442
New York, NY 10009
(212) 260-1147
Héctor Quintana, President

THE COLOMBIAN-AMERICAN
ASSOCIATION, INC.
30 Vesey St., #506
New York, NY 10007
(212) 233-7776 Fax: (212) 233-7779
Bert Ruiz, President
Email: anden@nyct.net
Web: www.colombianamerica.org

COLONY-SOUTH BROOKLYN HOUSES
297 Dean St.
Brooklyn, NY 11217
(718) 625-3810 Fax: (718) 875-8719
Balaguru Cacarla, Executive Director

COMITÉ NOVIEMBRE
c/o Inst. for Puerto Rican/Hispanic Elderly
105 E. 22nd Street, # 615
New York, NY 10010
(212) 677-4181 Fax: (212) 777-5106
Teresa Santiago, Chair
Email: iprhe@aol.com

COMMITTEE FOR HISPANIC CHILDREN AND FAMILIES, INC.
Affiliate of NCLR
140 W. 22nd St., #301
New York, NY 10011
(212) 206-1090 Fax: (212) 206-8093
Elba Montalvo, Director
Email: chcfinc@aol.com

COMMONWEALTH OF PUERTO RICO
Dept. of Puerto Rican Community Affairs
3 Park Ave., 33rd Floor
New York, NY 10016
(212) 252-7300
Carlos Linera, Director
Web: www.prfaa-govpr.org

COMMUNITY ACTION ORGANIZATION
70 Harvard Pl.
Buffalo, NY 14209
(716) 881-5150 Fax: (716) 881-2927
Julián B. Dargan, Executive Director

COMMUNITY ACTION ORG./DART
1237 Main St.
Buffalo, NY 14209
(716) 884-9101 Fax: (716) 884-7703
James Covial, Program Administrator

COMMUNITY ASSOCIATE DEVELOPMENT CORPORATION
544-60 Park Ave.
Brooklyn, NY 11205
(718) 852-8600 Fax: (718) 797-1148
Félix Milán, President

COMMUNITY ASSOCIATION OF PROGRESSIVE DOMINICANS
Affiliate of NCLR
3940 Broadway, 2nd Floor
New York, NY 10032
(212) 781-5500 or (212) 740-3866
Fax: (212) 740-1543
Víctor Morisete, Executive Director
Email: acdp@datatone.com

COMMUNITY HEALTH CARE NETWORK BRONX CENTER
975 W Chester Ave.
Bronx, NY 10459
(718) 991-9250 Fax: (718) 991-3829
Freddy Molano, Executive Director

COMMUNITY SUPPORT SYSTEM PROG.
1241 Lafayette Ave.
Bronx, NY 10454
(718) 378-6500 Fax: (718) 842-3846
Liduvina Martínez, Director

COMPREHENSIVE COMMUNITY DEVELOPMENT CORPORATION (CCDC)
731 White Plains Rd.
Bronx, NY 10473
(718) 589-8771 or (718) 589-2232
Pedro Espada, President

CONCERNED CITIZEN OF QUEENS, INC.
40-18 Junction Blvd. 2nd Floor
Entrance 40th Rd.
Corona, NY 11368
(718) 478-1600 Fax: (718) 478-4318
Rafael Grasso, Executive Director
Web: ccq4028@aol.com

CONCERNED CITIZENS ASSOCIATION
2191 Creston Ave., #1
Bronx, NY 10453
(718) 220-2819
Rubén Pérez, Chairman

CONCILIO PUERTO RICO DAY CARE CENTER
180 Suffolk St.
New York, NY 10002
(212) 674-6730
Beatriz Ladiana, Executive Director

CONIFER FOR COUNSELING
1150 University Ave., #7
Rochester, NY 14607
(716) 442-8422 Fax: (716) 442-8494
Bárbara Pacitti, Executive Director

CONSUMER ACTION PROGRAM OF BEDFORD STUYVESANT
7 Debevoise St.
Brooklyn, NY 11206
(718) 388-1601 Fax: (718) 388-4143
Adolfo Alayon, President

CONTINUING DAY TREATMENT PROGRAM
781 E 142nd St., 3rd Floor
Bronx, NY 10454
(718) 993-1400 Fax: (718) 993-0647
Nancy Faunt, Director

COOPER SQUARE COMMITTEE, INC
61 E. 4th St.
New York, NY 10003
(212) 228-8210 Fax: (212) 473-4537
Steven Herrick, Director
Email: coopersqre@msn.com
Web: www.coopersquare.org

COORDINATING AGENCY FOR SPANISH AMERICANS (CASA)
239 Fulton Ave.
Hempstead, NY 11550
(516) 572-0750 Fax: (516) 572-0756
Luis Vázquez, Executive Director

COUNCIL OF BROOKLYN ORGANIZATIONS, INC.
278 Broadway
Brooklyn, NY 11211
Led Litvintchock, Director
(718) 782-2832

COUNCIL OF THE AMERICAS
Affiliate of Americas Society, Inc.
680 Park Ave.
New York, NY 10021
(212) 249-8950 Fax: (212) 517-6247
Thomas E. McNamara, President
Email: webmaster@americas-society.org
Web: www.counciloftheamericas.org

CUBAN AMERICAN STUDENT ASSOC.
Cornell University
434 Rockefeller
Ithaca, NY 14853
(607) 255-3197 Fax: (607) 255-2433
Patty Alvarez, Advisor
Email: mfd1@cornell.edu
Web: http://latino.lsp.cornell.edu

CUBAN-AMERICAN ASSOCIATES
142-05 Roosevelt Ave., #324
Flushing, NY 11354
(718) 762-1432
Jorge Valvi, Director

CUNY DOMINICAN STUDIES INSTITUTE
City College of New York
138th St. and Convent Ave.
New York, NY 10031-9198
(212) 650-7496 Fax: (212) 650-7489
Sarah Aponte, Librarian
Email: dsi@phantom.cct.ccny.cuny.edu

DANCE THEATER WORKSHOP
219 W. 19th St.
New York, NY 10011
(212) 691-6500 Fax: (212) 633-1974
Besie Schonberg, Chairperson
Email: dtw@dtw.org
Web: www.dtw.org

DAVIDSON COMMUNITY CENTER
2038 Davidson Ave.
Bronx, NY 10453
(718) 731-6360
Angel Caballero, Executive Director

DAWNIN VILLAGE DAY CARE CENTER
2090 First Ave.
New York, NY 10029
(212) 369-5313
Mary Loughman, Director

DEPARTMENT OF BLACK AND PUERTO RICAN STUDIES
Hunter College, CUNY
1711W Bld Room
New York, NY 10021
(212) 772-5035 or (212) 772-5144
Fax: (212) 650-3596
Joyce Toney, Chairperson
Email: jtoney@shiva.hunter.cuny.edu

DEPARTMENT OF PUERTO RICAN AND LATINO STUDIES
Brooklyn College
2900 Bedford Ave.
Brooklyn, NY 11210-2889
(718) 951-5563 or (718) 951-5561
Fax: (718) 951-4183
Hector Carrasquillo, Director
Email: vsankorr@brooklyn.cuny.edu

DEPARTMENT OF PUERTO RICAN STUDIES
John Jay College of Criminal Justice
1552 N Hall
New York, NY 10019
(212) 237-8749 Fax: (212) 237-8742
José Luis Morin, Director

DIOCESE OF ALBANY
Family Life Office
40 N. Main Ave.
Albany, NY 12203
(518) 453-6677 Fax: (518) 453-6793
Mrs. Marta Arenas-Fenn
Email: martha.arenasfenn@rcda.org

Hispanic Affairs
901 Stanley St.
Schenectady, NY 12207
(518) 346-0261 Fax: (518) 393-9265
Michael Hogan, Director of Hispanic Apostalate

DIOCESE OF BROOKLYN
Hispanic Affairs
7200 Douglaston Pkwy.
Douglaston, NY 11362
(718) 229-8001 x741 Fax: (718) 229-2658
Deacon Jorge Arturo González, Director for Hispanic Ministry
Email: Hispminbklyn@worldnet.att.net

DIOCESE OF BUFFALO
Hispanic Affairs
795 Main St.
Buffalo, NY 14203
(716) 847-2217 Fax: (716) 847-2206
Msgr. David M. Gallivan, Dir. for Hisp. Apostolate
Email: dgallivan@buffalodiocese.org

DIOCESE OF OGDENSBURG
Hispanic Affairs
P.O. Box 369
622 Washington St.
Ogdensburg, NY 13669
(315) 393-2920 Fax: (315) 393-0981
Rev. George F. Maroun, Hisp. Ministry Director
Email: mission@northweb.com

DIOCESE OF ROCHESTER
Hispanic Affairs
1150 Buffalo Rd.
Rochester, NY 14624
(716) 328-3210 or (716) 328-3328 x336
Fax: (716) 328-3149
Gabriela Jaramillo, Dir. of the Span. Apostolate
Email: jaramillo@dor.org

DIOCESE OF ROCKVILLE CENTRE
Hispanic Affairs
50 N. Park Ave.
Rockville Centre, NY 11570
(516) 678-5800 x618 Fax: (516) 678-1786
Sr. Margaret Mayce, OP, Dir. for Hisp. Ministry

Our Lady of Loreto Church
104 Greenwich St.
Hempstead, NY 11550-5692
(516) 489-3675
Rev. Pablo M. Rodríguez, Vicar for Span. Speaking

DIOCESE OF SYRACUSE
Hispanic Affairs
1515 Midland Ave.
Syracuse, NY 13205
(315) 422-9390 Fax: (315) 422-9390
Rev. Robert D. Chryst, Dir. for Span. Apostolate

DOMINICAN STUDENT ASSOCIATION
Cornell University
434 Rockefeller Hall
Ithaca, NY 14853
(607) 255-3197 Fax: (607) 255-2433
Héctor Vélez, Advisor
Email: mfd1@cornell.edu
Web: http://latino.lsp.cornell.edu

DOMINICAN STUDENTS ASSOCIATION
Cuny Herbert H. Lehman College
250 Bedford Park Blvd . West
Bronx, NY 10468
(718) 960-8535
Rafael Martínez, Director

DOMINICAN WOMEN'S DEV. CENTER
359 Fort Washington Ave., #1-G
New York, NY 10033
(212) 740-1929 Fax: (212) 740-8352
Rosita M. Romero, Executive Director

DOMINICAN-AMERICAN CHAMBER OF COMMERCE
825 Third Ave., 11th Floor, #122
New York, NY 10022
(212) 709-0218 Fax: (212) 269-2383
Rafael A. Ginebra, President

DR. MARTIN LUTHER KING, JR. HEALTH CTR.
3674 Third Ave.
Bronx, NY 10456
(718) 681-3400 ext.3023 Fax: (718) 942-6165
Patricia Thomps, Administrator

DR. RICHARD GREEN DAY CARE CENTER
450 Castle Hill Ave.
Bronx, NY 10473
(718) 904-1689 Fax: (718) 904-1833
Milagros del Marrero, Director

EAST HARLEM BLOCK NURSERY, INC.
94 E. 111th St.
New York, NY 10029
(212) 722-6350 Fax: (212) 722-5283
Dianne Morales, Director
Email: ehbs@aol.com

EAST HARLEM COLLEGE & CAREER COUNSELING PROGRAM
1 E. 104th St.
New York, NY 10029
(212) 348-9200
Paula J. Martin, Executive Director
Email: hceunderscorestaf@aol.com

EAST HARLEM COUNCIL FOR COMMUNITY IMPROVEMENT, INC.
413 E. 120th St.
New York, NY 10035
(212) 410-7707
Raúl Rodríguez, Executive Director

EAST HARLEM COUNCIL FOR HUMAN SERVICES, INC.
Head Start Program
440-446 E. 116th St.
New York, NY 10035
(212) 427-9010 Fax: (212) 996-1738
Brenda López, Acting Director

2253 Third Ave., 3rd Floor
New York, NY 10035
(212) 289-6650 Fax: (212) 360-6149
Elizabeth Sánchez, Executive Director

EAST HARLEM EMPLOYMENT SERVICES
1820 Lexington
New York, NY 10035
(212) 360-1100 Fax: (212) 360-5634
Robert Carmona, President

EAST HARLEM REDEVELOPMENT PILOT BLOCK PROJECT, INC.
2253 3rd Ave.
New York, NY 10035
(212) 369-3755
Emilio Ho, Chairman

EAST SIDE HOUSE SETTLEMENT
337 Alexander Ave.
Bronx, NY 10454
(718) 665-5250 Fax: (718) 585-1433
John A. Sánchez, Director
Web: www.eastsidehouse.org

EASTCHESTER COMMUNITY ACTION PROGRAM
W.E.S.T.C.O.P
142-144 Main St.
Tuckahoe, NY 10707
(914) 337-7768 Fax: (914) 337-2751
Vivian T. Yancy, Director

EASTERN FARMWORKERS ASSOCIATION
58 Beaver Dam Rd.
Bellport, NY 11713
(631) 286-8004
Tom Kessler, Director

ECUADOREAN AMERICAN ASSOC., INC.
30 Vesey St., #506
New York, NY 10007-2914
(212) 732-4333 Fax: (212) 723-0660
Montserrat Hernández, Director
Email: andean@nyct.net

EDENWALD-GUN HILL NEIGHBORHOOD CENTER, INC.
1150 E. 229th St.
Bronx, NY 10466
(718) 652-2232 Fax: (718) 652-2501
Kenneth Mercer, Executive Director

EDWIN GOULD SERVICES FOR CHILDREN OF UNITED FAMILIES OF EAST HARLEM
1968 2nd Ave.
New York, NY 10029
(212) 876-0367
Paula Martin, Director

EL BARRIO CHAMBER OF COMMERCE
1665 Lexington Ave.
New York, NY 10029
(212) 860-2455 Fax: (212) 876-5079
Luis Malave, President

EL BARRIO'S OPERATION FIGHT BACK, INC.
413 E. 120th St., #403
New York, NY 10035
(212) 410-7900 Fax: (212) 410-7997
Gustavo Rosado, Executive Director

EL COMIENZO ALCOHOL PROGRAM
951 Niagara St.
Buffalo, NY 14213
(716) 883-5344 Fax: (716) 885-0643
Ventura Colón, Director

EL MUSEO DEL BARRIO
1230 5th Ave.
New York, NY 10029
(212) 831-7272 Fax: (212) 831-7927
Susana Torruella Leval, Executive Director
Email: elmuseo@aol.com

EL PUENTE
Arts and Cultural Council for Youth
211 S. 4th St.
Brooklyn, NY 11211
(718) 387-0404
Luis Garden Acosta, Director

EL REGRESO INC.
North Brooklyn Communities of
Williamsburg-Bushwick-Greenpoint
189-191 South 2nd St.
Brooklyn, NY 11211
(718) 384-6400 Fax: (718) 384-0540
Carlos Pagan, Executive Director
Email: ElRegreso@aol.com

ELMCOR SENIOR CENTER
98-19 Astoria Blvd.
East Elmhurst, NY 11369
(718) 457-9757 Fax: (718) 898-4600
Ann Henderson, Director

ELMCOR YOUTH ADULT ACTIVITIES, INC.
107-20 Northern Blvd.
Corona, NY 11368
(718) 651-0096 Fax: (718) 533-1357
Linda Booth, Clinical Supervisor

EN FOCO, INC.
32 E. Kingsbridge Rd.
Bronx, NY 10468
(718) 584-7718 Fax: (718) 584-7718
Charles Biasiny Rivera, Executive Director
Email: info@enfoco.org
Web: www.enfoco.org

ERIC CLEARING HOUSE ON URBAN EDUCATION
Inst. for Urban and Minority Education
P.O. Box 40 Teacher's College,
Columbia University
New York, NY 10027
(212) 678-3433 Fax: (212) 678-4012
Erwin Flaxman, Director
Email: eric-que@columbia.edu
Web: http://eric-web.tc.columbia.edu

ERIE REGIONAL HOUSING DEVELOPMENT CORPORATION
104 Maryland Ave.
Buffalo, NY 14201
(716) 845-0485 Fax: (716) 845-0486
Douglas Ruffin, Executive Director

ESCUELA ARGENTINA EN NUEVA YORK
6813 Nansen St.
Forest Hills, NY 11375
(718) 268-3235 Fax: (718) 268-3144
Martha Liboreiro, Contact

ESCUELA HISPANA MONTESSORI
18 Ave. D
New York, NY 10009
(212) 982-6650
Diomedes Rosario, Executive Director

ESLABÓN CULTURAL HISPANO AMERICANO, INC. (ECHA)
P.O. Box 82
New York, NY 10032
(212) 923-8033
Conchita Ruiz, President

ESPERANZA DAY TREATMENT CENTER
21 Audubon Ave.
New York, NY 10032
(212) 928-5810 Fax: (212) 740-2053
Jim Malley, Director

ESPERANZA: LATINO YOUTH MENTORING PROGRAM
Cornell University
434 Rockefeller Hall
Ithaca, NY 14853-1601
(607) 255-3197 Fax: (607) 255-2433
Lenardo Vargas-Méndez, Advisor
Email: mfd1@cornell.edu
Web: http://latino.lsp.cornell.edu

EVERYWOMAN OPPORTUNITY CTR., INC.
Dunkirk Branch
10825 Bennett Rd.
Dunkirk, NY 14048
(716) 366-7020 Fax: (716) 366-1925
Susan Reilly, Executive Director
Email: ewocbuf@everywoman.org
Web: www.everywoman.org

Headquarters
237 Main St. #330
Buffalo, NY 14203
(716) 847-1120 Fax: (716) 847-1550
Myrna F. Young, Executive Director
Email: ewocbuf@everywoman.org
Web: www.everywoman.org

Niagara Falls Branch
800 Main St. #3D
Niagara Falls, NY 14301
(716) 282-8472 Fax: (716) 282-4868
Linda Randolph, Center Director
Web: www.everywoman.org

Olean Branch
132 N. Union St. #107
Olean, NY 14760
(716) 373-4013 Fax: (716) 373-7668
Mary Snodgrass, Center Director
Email: ewocol@everywoman.org
Web: www.everywoman.org

Tonawanda Branch
2440 Sheridan Dr. 2nd Floor
Tonawanda, NY 147150
(716) 837-2260 Fax: (716) 837-0124
Sandra Velasco, Center Director
Email: ewocol@everywoman.org
Web: www.everywoman.org

FAMILY COUNSELING SERVICE OF THE FINGER LAKES, INC.
671 S Exchange St.
Geneva, NY 14456
(315) 789-2613 Fax: (315) 789-2524
Bonnie Deier, Executive Director

FAMILY OF ELLENVILLE
14 Church St.
Ellenville, NY 12428
(845) 647-2443 Fax: (845) 647-2460
Lisa Cavanaugh, Program Director
Email: foe430@warwick.net
Web: www.familyofwoodstockinc.org

FAMILY OF NEW PALTZ
51 North Chestnut St.
New Paltz, NY 12561
(914) 255-8801 Fax: (914) 255-3498
Kathy Cartagena, Executive Director
Email: familynp@juno.com
Web: www.familyofwoodstockinc.org

FARMWORKER LEGAL SERVICE OF NEW YORK, INC.
80 St. Paul St.
Rochester, NY 14604
(716) 325-3050 Fax: (716) 325-7614
James F. Schmidt, Executive Director
Email: jschmidt@wnylc.com

FARMWORKERS COMMUNITY CENTER
P. O. Box 607
Goshen, NY 10924
(845) 651-4272 Fax: (845) 651-4351
Stash Grajewski, Director
Email: dhealamo@warwick.net

FEDERATION EMPLOYMENT & GUIDANCE SERVICE
315 Hudson St.
New York, NY 10013
(212) 366-8401
Alfred Miller, Exec. Vice Pres./CEO

FEDERATION OF PUERTO RICAN ORGANIZATIONS, INC.
2 Van Sinderen Ave.
Brooklyn, NY 11207
(718) 345-9500 Fax: (718) 498-1779
Víctor Medina, President & CEO

FIFTH AVENUE COMMUNITIE, INC.
141 5th Ave.
Brooklyn, NY 11217
(718) 857-2990 Fax: (718) 857-4322
Brad Lander, Executive Director
Email: fac@fifthave.org
Web: www.fifthave.org

FIRST SATURDAY IN OCTOBER, INC. (FSIO)
198 E. 161 St., #201
Bronx, NY 10451
(718) 590-2502 Fax: (718) 590-3499
Julie Reyes, President
Email: fsio@excite.com

FOREST HILLS COMMUNITY HOUSE
108-25 62nd Dr.
Forest Hills, NY 11375
(718) 592-5757 Fax: (718) 592-5757
O. Lewis Harris, Executive Director

FOTOGRÁFICA
484 W. 43rd St., #22T
New York, NY 10036
(212) 244-5182
Perla de León, Director

FOUNDLING HOSPITAL
542 W 153rd St.
New York, NY 10031
(212) 862-3427 Fax: (212) 491-9563
Jeannette Acosta, Administrative Supervisor

FUERZA LATINA
State University of New York, Albany
Campus Center 116
1400 Washington Ave.
Albany, NY 12222
(518) 442-5679 Fax: (518) 442-5622
Christian Santiago, President

GALA-INC. GRUPO DE ARTISTAS LATINO AMERICANOS, INC.
21 W. 112th St., #9-J
New York, NY 10026
(212) 369-3401
Pedro Villarini, President

GLENN E. HINES BOYS AND GIRLS CLUB
285 Liberty St.
Newburgh, NY 12550
(914) 561-4936 Fax: (914) 561-5288
Nelson McCallester, Executive Director

GODDARD-RIVERSIDE COMMUNITY CTR.
593 Columbus Ave.
New York, NY 10024
(212) 873-6600 Fax: (212) 595-6498
Stephan Russo, Executive Director
Email: response@goddard.org
Web: http://www.goddard.org

GOVERMENT OF PUERTO RICO INDUSTRIAL DEVELOPMENT, CO.
666 5th Ave., 15th Floor
New York, NY 10103
(212) 245-1200 Fax: (212) 581-2667
Carol Roman Esqurie, Director
Web: www.pridco.com

GRAND COUNCIL OF HISPANIC SOCITIES IN PUBLIC
P.O. Box 636
Stuyvesant St.
New York, NY 10009
(212) 615-6625 Fax: (718) 488-6466
Debra Martínez, Contact

GRAND STREET SETTLEMENT
80 Pitt St.
New York, NY 10002
(212) 677-4246 Fax: (212) 979-8677
Margarita Rosa, Executive Director

GRAND STREET SETTLEMENT
Grand Coalition of Seniors
80 Pitt St.
New York, NY 10002
(212) 674-1740 Fax: (212) 979-8677
Luz Lavin, Director

GROSVENOR NEIGHBORHOOD HOUSE
176 W 105th St.
New York, NY 10025
(212) 749-8500 Fax: (212) 749-4060
William Rivera, Executive Director
Email: GNH105@aol.com

Web: www.grosvenorhouse.org/

GUACARA CENTER FOR THE ADVANCEMENT OF DOMINICAN ARTS AND CULTURE
60 W. 106th St., 1C
New York, NY 10025
(212) 316-4011
Arelis Ayala, Executive Director

HAMILTON-MADISON HOUSE
50 Madison St.
New York, NY 10038
(212) 349-3724 Fax: (212) 791-7540
Frank T. Modica, Executive Director
Email: frank@hmh100.com
Web: www.hmh100.com

HARBOR PERFORMING ARTS CENTER
1 E. 104th St., #573
New York, NY 10029
(212) 427-2244 Ext.572 Fax: (212) 427-3969
Ramón Rodríguez, Director

HARTLEY HOUSE
413 W. 46th St.
New York, NY 10036
(212) 246-9872
Mary Follet, Executive Director

HARVESTRAW ECUMENICAL PROJECT/ DAY CARE CENTER
34 First St.
Haverstraw, NY 10927
(914) 429-5263 Fax: (914) 429-0507
Daysi Rivera, Director

THE HEALTH ASSOCIATION
One Mount Hope Ave.
Rochester, NY 14620
(716) 423-9490 Fax: (716) 423-1908
Susan L. Costa, Executive Director
Email: information@TheHealthAssociation.org
Web: www.thehealthassociation.org

HEALTH INDUSTRY RESOURCES ENTERPRISES, INC. (HIRE)
989 Avenue of the Americas
New York, NY 10018
(212) 219-1618 Fax: (212) 219-2087
Alfred Arango, Executive Director

HEMPSTEAD HISPANIC CIVIC ASSOC.
232-236 Main St.
Hempstead, NY 11550
(516) 292-0007 or (516) 292-0032
Fax: (516) 292-0026
Agnes M. Rodríguez, Executive Director

HENRY STREET SETTLEMENT
265 Henry St.
New York, NY 10002
(212) 766-9200 Fax: (212) 791-5710
Daniel Kronenfeld, Executive Director

HERGO SERVICE CENTER, INC.
82-19 Roosevelt Ave., 2nd Floor
Jackson Heights, NY 11372
(718) 507-4646 Fax: (718) 779-6361
Efraín Hernández, Executive Director

HERMANDAD DE SIGMA IOTA ALPHA, INC.
P.O. Box 237 Prince St., Station
New York, NY 10012
(201) 356-1316 x1076 Fax: (877) 810-8165
Dora María Abreu, Founder
Email: shorty@hermandad-sia.orgsia_web@hotmail.com
Web: www.hermandad-sia.org

HERMANDAD DOMINICANA
935 Bruckner Blvd.
Bronx, NY 10459
(718) 842-2779
Héctor Ramos, President

HERMANOS FRATERNOS DE LOIZA ALDEA, INC.
1702 Lexinton Ave.
New York, NY 10029
(212) 410-4220
Blanca Irizarry, Executive Director

HISPANIC AFFAIRS OFFICE
1011 First Ave., #1902
New York, NY 10022
(212) 371-1000 Fax: (212) 319-8265
Josu Iriondo, Director

HISPANIC AIDS FORUM
184 Fifth Ave. 7th Floor
New York, NY 10010
(212) 741-9797 Fax: (212) 741-0010
Heriberto Sánchez Soto, Executive Director
Email: nyc2@hafnyc.org
Web: www.hafnyc.org

HISPANIC AMERICAN CAREER EDUC. RESOURCES, INC. (HACER) - HISPANIC WOMEN'S CTR.
Day Care Center
31 East 32nd St.
New York, NY 10016
(212) 779-8064 Fax: (212) 779-8067
Dr. Norma Stanton, President & CEO

HISPANIC ASSOCIATION FOR PROFESSIONAL ADVANCEMENT (HAPA)
c/o XEROX
100 Clinton Ave. S.
Rochester, NY 14644
(716) 423-1377 Fax: (716) 423-8307
Esteban Ramírez, President
Email: paulreyes@soxerox.com
Web: www.hapa.org

HISPANIC AUXILIARY POLICE ASSOC.
P.O. Box 380
New York, NY 10040
(718) 320-5357
Dolores Roque, President

HISPANIC BROTHERHOOD OF ROCKVILLE CENTER, INC.
143 N Park Ave.
Rockville Center, NY 11570
(516) 766-6610 Fax: (516) 776-60405
Margarita Grasing, Executive Director

HISPANIC COUNSELING CENTER, INC.
175 Fulton Ave., #500
Hempstead, NY 11550
(516) 538-2613 Fax: (516) 538-2515
Gladys Serrano, Executive Director
Email: hispaniccc@aol.com
Web: hispaniccounseling.com

HISPANIC COURT OFFICERS SOCIETY OF THE STATE OF NY, INC.
National Headquarters
Bronx Supreme Court
215 E. 151St.
Bronx, NY 10451
(718) 590-3709 Fax: (718) 590-8914
Frank Arce, President

HISPANIC FEDERATION
130 William St., 9th Floor
New York, NY 10038
(212) 233-8955 Fax: (212) 233-8996
Lorraine Cortés Vázquez, President & CEO
Email: hispfedny@aol.com
Web: www.hispanicfederation.org

HISPANIC FEDERATION OF NYC
Bronx Office
2530 Grand Concourse
Bronx, NY 10458
(718) 562-6224 Fax: (718) 562-6225
Lorraine Cortés Vázquez, President
Web: www.hispanicfederation.org

THE HISPANIC GENEALOGICAL SOCIETY OF NEW YORK, INC.
Murray Hill Station, P.O. Box 818
New York, NY 10056-0206
(212) 340-4659
Jorge Camuñas Muñiz, President
Email: raices@hispanicgenealogy.com
Web: www.hispanicgenealogy.com

HISPANIC INFORMATION AND TELECOMMUNICATIONS NETWORK
449 Broadway, 3rd Floor
New York, NY 10013
(212) 966-5660 Fax: (212) 966-5725
José Luis Rodríguez, President
Web: www.hitn.org

HISPANIC INST. OF COLUMBIA UNIVERSITY
612 W. 116th St.
New York, NY 10027
(212) 854-4187 Fax: (212) 854-5322
Elzbieta Szokca, President

HISPANIC LABOR COMMITTEE-JOBS DEVELOPMENT PROGRAM
1950 3rd Ave.
New York, NY 10029
(212) 996-9222 Fax: (212) 423-9421
María C. Serrano, Executive Director

HISPANIC NATIONAL BAR ASSOCIATION
Region II (NY)
76-03 Roosevelt Ave.
New York, NY 11372
(718) 478-4868 Fax: (718) 478-8540

Salvador Cheda, Regional President
Email: scheda@aol.com
Web: www.hnba.com

HISPANIC NATIONAL LAW ENFORCEMENT ASSOCIATION
New York Chapter
P. O. Box 3524
Church St. Station
New York, NY 10008
(212) 726-1460
Héctor Hernández, President
Email: HNLEANYCHP@AOL.COM

HISPANIC ORGANIZATION OF LATIN ACTORS (HOLA)
107 Suffolk St., 3rd Floor
New York, NY 10002
(212) 253-1015 Fax: (212) 253-9651
Manny Alfaro, Director
Email: holagram@aol.com
Web: www.hellohola.org

HISPANIC OUTREACH SERVICES
Administrative Office
40 N. Main Ave.
Albany, NY 12203
(518) 453-6655 Fax: (518) 453-6792
Anne Tranelli, Executive Director

Albany Outreach Office
29 Walter Street
Albany, NY 12204
(518) 463-1217 Fax: (518) 453-1218
Gladys Cruz, Director

Schenectady Outreach Office
801 Stanley St.
Schenectady, NY 12307
(518) 382-2004 Fax: (518) 382-2696
Nilda Giraldi, Site Coordinator

Troy Outreach Services
c/o Sunnyside Center
9th St. & Ingalls Ave.
Troy, NY 12180
(518) 273-7869 Fax: (518) 273-6089
Meredeth Menzies, Director

HISPANIC POLICY DEV. PROJECT (HPDP)
National Headquarters
36 E. 22nd St., 9th Floor
New York, NY 10010
(212) 529-9323 Fax: (212) 477-5395
Siobhan Oppenheimer Nicolau, President
Email: siobhan96@aol.com

HISPANIC PUBLIC RELATIONS ASSOC. OF GREATER NEW YORK, INC. (HPRA/GNY)
Burson-Marsteller, 230 Park Ave., S.
New York, NY 10003-1566
(212) 781-6728 Fax: (212) 781-6761
Juan Ulloa, President
Web: www.hpragny.org

HISPANIC SERVICES SOCIETY
231 Troutman St.
Brooklyn, NY 11237
(718) 821-5161 Fax: (718) 821-5970
Carmen Gonzales, Director

THE HISPANIC SOCIETY
SUNY Fredonia
Student Association Office, G107 - William Ctr.
Fredonia, NY 14063
(716) 673-3149

THE HISPANIC SOCIETY OF AMERICA
613 W 155th St.
New York, NY 10032
(212) 926-2234 Fax: (212) 690-0743
Vicente Criado, Marketing Coordinator
Email: info@hispanicsociety.org
Web: www.hispanicsociety.org

HISPANIC SUPPORT ORGANIZATION
P.O. Box 2924
New York, NY 10008-2924
(212) 395-4462 Fax: (212) 395-5287
Al Torres, President

HISPANICS UNITED OF BUFFALO (HUB)
Network of Western New York
254 Virginia St.
Buffalo, NY 14201
(716) 856-7110 Fax: (716) 856-9617
Israel González, Executive Director
Web: www.hispanicunited.org

HOLY CROSS ASISTENCIA SOCIAL
600 Soundview Ave.
Bronx, NY 10473
(718) 893-5550 Fax: (718) 378-3655
Aubrey McNeil, Pastor

HOSTOS CTR. FOR THE ARTS & CULTURE
Hostos Community College
450 Grand Concourse Ave.
Bronx, NY 10451
(718) 518-6700 Fax: (718) 518-6690
Wallace I. Edgecombe, Director

HOSTOS COUNSELING WOMEN'S SVCS.
Savoy Bldg., 120 E. 149th St., 1st Floor, #102E
Bronx, NY 10451
(718) 518-4311 Fax: (718) 518-4252
Ivette Rodrigues, Assistant Executive Director

HUDSON GUILD
441 W. 26th St.
New York, NY 10001
(212) 760-9804 Fax: (212) 268-9983
Janice Mc Guire, Executive Director

HUNTS POINT MULTI-SERVICE CENTER
Drug Abuse Center
785 Westchester Ave.
Bronx, NY 10455
(718) 589-5500 Fax: (718) 589-8096
Cahrles La Port, Program Administrator

HUNTS POINT MULTI-SERVICE CENTER
Family Day Care
754 51st St.
Bronx, NY 10455
(718) 993-3004 Fax: (718) 993-3005
Sandra Stone, Director

Health Clinic
754 E. 151st St.
Bronx, NY 10455
(718) 402-2800 Fax: (718) 665 -9782
Bansmy Busher, Director

IBERO-AMERICAN ACTION LEAGUE, INC.
Affiliate of United Way
817 E. Main St.
Rochester, NY 14605
(716) 256-8900 Fax: (716) 256-0120
Julio Vázquez, President & CEO

IGLESIA EVANGÉLICA ESPAÑOLA
800 E 156th St.
Bronx, NY 10455
(718) 993-1260 Fax: (718) 993-8378
Miguel Díaz, Pastor

IMAGE OF US CUSTOMS SERVICE (AIU)
National Image, Inc.
6 World Trade Center, Room 555
New York City, NY 10048
(212) 637-4789 Fax: (212) 637-4880
Rosa E. Rivera, Region Director & Chap. Pres.
Web: www.nationalimageinc.org

INSTITUTE FOR THE PUERTO RICAN/ HISPANIC ELDERLY
105 E. 22nd St., #615
New York, NY 10010
(212) 677-4181 Fax: (212) 777-5106
Suleika Cabrera Drinane, Executive Director

INSTITUTE OF LATIN AMERICAN & IBERIAN STUDIES
Columbia University
Mailcode 3339, 420 W. 118th St.
New York, NY 10027
(212) 854-4643 Fax: (212) 854-4607
Prof. Douglas Chalmers, Director

INSTITUTO CERVANTES
122 E. 42nd St., #807
New York, NY 10168
(212) 689-4232 Fax: (212) 545-8837
María Lozano, Director
Email: ny@cervantes.org
Web: www.cervantes.org

INTAR (HISPANIC-AMERICAN ARTS CTR.)
P.O. Box 756
New York, NY 10036
(212) 695-6134 Fax: (212) 268-0102
Max Ferra, Artistic Director

INTER-AMERICAN COLLEGE OF PHYSICIANS & SURGEONS
New York Office
915 Broadway, #1105
New York, NY 10010-7108
(212) 777-3642 Fax: (212) 505-7984
James P. Tierney, Chief Operating Officer

INTERNATIONAL CENTER FOR LAW & DEVELOPMENT
777 United Nations Plaza, #7E
New York, NY 10017
(212) 687-0036 Fax: (212) 370-9844
Dr. Clarence Díaz, President

INTERNATIONAL INSTITUTE OF BUFFALO, NEW YORK
864 Delaware Ave.
Buffalo, NY 14209
(716) 883-1900 Fax: (716) 883-9529
Hinke T. Boot, Director
Email: boot@iibuff.org
Web: www.iibuff.org

INTERNATIONAL WOMEN'S TRIBUNE CENTER, INC. (IWTC)
777 United Nations Plaz., 3rd Floor
New York, NY 10017
(212) 687-8633 Fax: (212) 661-2704
Anne S. Walker, Director

INTERRACIAL COUNCIL FOR BUSINESS OPPORTUNITY
51 Madison Ave., #2212
New York, NY 10010
(800) 252-4226 Fax: (212) 779-4365
Lorraine Kelsey, Executive Director

INWOOD COMMUNITY SERVICE
651 Academy St., 3rd Floor
New York, NY 10034
(212) 942-0043 Fax: (212) 567-9476
Charly Corliss, Program Director

JOHN THE BAPTIST COMMUNITY ACTION CENTER
14 Stuyvesant Ave.
Brooklyn, NY 11221
(718) 443-5551 Fax: (718) 443-5551
Molly Golden, Executive Director

JOINT NEIGHBORHOOD PROJECT
532 E. 2nd St.
Jamestown, NY 14701
(716) 664-7101 Fax: (716) 664-7103
Carmen Lydell, Director

KINGSBRIDGE HEIGHTS COMMUNITY CENTER
3101 Kingsbridge Terrace
Bronx, NY 10463
(718) 884-0700 Fax: (718) 884-0858
Charles Shayne, Executive Director

KIPS BAY BOYS AND GIRLS CLUB
1930 Randall Ave.
Bronx, NY 10473
(718) 893-8254 Fax: (718) 589-9214
Harold Maldonado, Director

LA ASOCIACIÓN BENÉFICA CULTURAL PADRE BILLINI
25-28 89th St.
Jackson Heights, NY 11370
(718) 651-8427 Fax: (718) 651-5572
Ana López, Executive Director
Email: fba4000@hotmail.com

LA ASOCIACIÓN LATINA
Cornell University
434 Rockefeller Hall
Ithaca, NY 14853-1601
(607) 255-3197 Fax: (607) 255-2433
Jonathan White, Advisor
Email: mfd1@cornell.edu
Web: http://latino.lsp.cornell.edu

LA ASOCIACIÓN NUESTRA SEÑORA DE LUJÁN
1064 Madison Ave.
New York, NY 10028
(212) 288-3217 Fax: (212) 288-3217
Roberto Aparicio, President

LA CASA HERENCIA CULTURAL PUERTORRIQUEÑA, INC.
1230 5th Ave. #458
New York, NY 10029
(212) 722-2600 Fax: (212) 722-3033
Otilio Díaz, Executive Director
Web: www.webcom.com/lacasa

LA ESCUELITA
773 Prospect Ave.
Bronx, NY 10455
(718) 991-7100 Fax: (718) 991-7643
Lorraine Montenegro, Executive Director
Web: ubpexec@aol.com

LA FUERZA UNIDA DE GLEN COVE, INC.
14 Glen St. #307
Glen Cove, NY 11542
(516) 759-0788 Fax: (516) 759-3465
Pascual Blanco, Executive Director
Email: lafuerzaunida@aol.com

LA GUARDIA MEMORIAL HOUSE
307 E 116th St.
New York, NY 10029
(212) 534-7800 Fax: (212) 534-6068
Luis Zuchman, Executive Director

LA LUCHA
Cornell University
434 Rockefeller Hall
Ithaca, NY 14853-1601
(607) 255-3197 Fax: (607) 255-2433
Helena Viramontes, Advisor
Email: mfd1@cornell.edu
Web: http://latino.lsp.cornell.edu

LA ORG. DE LATINAS UNIVERSITARIAS
Cornell University
434 Rockefeller Hall
Ithaca, NY 14853-1601
(607) 255-3197 Fax: (607) 255-2433
Pedro Caban, Director
Email: mfd1@cornell.edu
Web: http://latino.lsp.cornell.edu

LA PUERTA ABIERTA
2864 W. 21st St.
Brooklyn, NY 11224
(718) 373-1100 Fax: (718) 449-0538
Jayne Doyle, Director

LA SALUD HISPANA, INC.
225 Broadway, #3009
New York, NY 10007
(212) 791-7177/568-9001 Fax: (212) 791-7304
Dr. Rodrigo Cárdenas, CEO
Email: editor@lasaludhispana.com
Web: http://www.lasaludhispana.com

LA UNIDAD LATINA/LAMBDA UPSILON LAMBDA FRATERNITY, INC.
Cornell University
722 University Ave.
Ithaca, NY 14853-1601
(607) 255-3197 Fax: (607) 255-2433
Héctor Vélez, Advisor
Email: mfd1@cornell.edu
Web: http://latino.lsp.cornell.edu

LA VOZ BORIKEN
Cornell University
434 Rockefeller Hall
Ithaca, NY 14853
(607) 255-3197 Fax: (607) 255-2433
Ken Glover, Advisor
Email: mfd1@cornell.edu
Web: http://latino.lsp.cornell.edu

LADIES COMMITTEE PUERTO RICAN CULTURAL, INC.
24 Van Sinderen Ave.
Brooklyn, NY 11207
(718) 345-4775 Fax: (718) 485-0086
Alicia Ponce de León, Executive Director

LAMBDA ALPHA UPSILON
National Headquarters
29 John Street, #181
New York, NY 10038
Email: info@latinogreeks.com
Web: http://www.latinogreeks.com/greeks/lau.htm

LAMBDA PHI CHI SORORITY
Univ. at Albany, State Univ. of New York
Campus Center 332
Albany, NY 12222
(518) 442-5297
Director of Student Activities

LAMBDA PI CHI
Latinas Promoviendo Comunidad
Grand Central Station
New York, NY 10163
Email: ssm19@hotmail.com/
jeanette.rodriguez@pfizer.com
Web: http://www.latinogreeks.com/greeks/lpchi.htm

LAMBDA THETA PHI, FRATERNIDAD LATINA, INC.
Cornell University
434 Rockefeller Hall
Ithaca, NY 14853-1601
(607) 255-3197 Fax: (607) 255-2433
David De Jesús Cruz, Advisor
Email: mfd1@cornell.edu
Web: http://latino.lsp.cornell.edu

LAMBDA UPSILON LAMBDA FRATERNITY
Univ. at Albany, State Univ. of New York
Campus Center 332
Albany, NY 12222
(518) 442-5297
Director of Student Activities

LAMBERT HOUSE COMMUNITY
Development Department
1005 E 179th St.
Bronx, NY 10460
(718) 542-9377 Fax: (718) 542-7441
Rosmary Ordinar, Director

LATIN AMERICA PARENTS ASSOCIATION
P.O. Box 339-340
Brooklyn, NY 11234
(718) 236-8689
Joan Giurdanella & Christian Smeets, Co-Presidents
Email: joet@highcaliber.com
Web: www.lapa.com

LATIN AMERICAN AND HISPANIC CARIBBEAN STUDIES
City College of New York
138th St. and Convent Ave., 6th Floor, #108
New York, NY 10031
(212) 650-6763 or (212) 650-6764
Fax: (212) 650-6799
Iris López, Chairperson
Web: www.cuny.ccny.edu

LATIN AMERICAN INTEGRATION CENTER, INC.
Affiliate of NCLR
49-06 Skillman Ave.
Woodside Queens, NY 11377
(718) 565-8500 Fax: (718) 565-0646
Saramaría Archila, Executive Director

LATIN AMERICAN LAW STUDENTS ASSOC.
Columbia University
Law School
435 W. 116th St., #108
New York, NY 10027
(212) 854-6044
Tina Villanueva, Director

LATIN AMERICAN SOCIETY
180 Remsen St.
St. Francis College
Brooklyn, NY 11201
(718) 522-2300 ext 325
Enildo García, Director

LATIN AMERICAN STUDENT ASSOC.
Mercy College
555 Broadway
Dobbs Ferry, NY 10522
(914) 674-7236 Fax: (914) 693-9455

LATIN AMERICAN STUDENT ORG.
State University of New York, Stony Brook
Student Activities Center #202
Stony Brook, NY 11794-2800
(516) 632-6460 Fax: (516) 632-6834

LATIN AMERICAN STUDIES PROGRAM
Cornell University
190 Uris Hall
Ithaca, NY 14853
(607) 255-3345 Fax: (607) 255-0469
Debra Castillo, Director
Email: mjd9@cornell.edu

LATIN AMERICAN THEATER ENSEMBLE
P. O. Box 18, Radio City Station
New York, NY 10101
(212) 394-3262 Fax: (212) 394-3262
Margarita Toirac, Executive Producer

LATIN AMERICAN THEATER EXPERIMENT & ASSOCIATED, INC.
107 Suffolk St., 2nd Floor
New York, NY 10002
(212) 529-1948 Fax: (212) 529-7362
Nelson Landrieu, Executive Director
Email: latea@sprintmail.com

LATIN AMERICAN WOMEN'S NETWORK
P.O. Box 229 Washington Heights
New York, NY 10033
(212) 927-2800 Fax: (212) 527-8548
Trisilla Ramos, Executive Director

THE LATINA RIGHTS INITIATIVE
Affiliate of PRLDEF
99 Hudson St., #1400
New York, NY 10013
(212) 219-3360 Fax: (212) 431-4276
Juan A. Figueroa, President & General Counsel
Email: info@prldef.org
Web: www.igc.org/IPR/

LATINO COMMISSION ON AIDS
80 Fifth Ave. #150
New York, NY 10011-8002
(212) 675-3288 Fax: (212) 675-3466
Dennis de León, President
Email: ddeleon@latina.as.org

LATINO CULTURE CENTER
SUNY New Paltz Student Affairs
75 South Manheim Blvd. SUB 428
New Paltz, NY 12561
(914) 257-3070
Jill Polos, President
Email: jp_superba@yahoo.com
Web: www.newpaltz.edu/sa

LATINO GERONTOLOGICAL CENTER
305 7th Ave. 11th Floor
New York, NY 10001
212-633-0435 Fax: 212-633-0645
Mario E. Tapia, President
Email: info@gerolatino.org
Web: www.gerolatino.org

LATINO GREEK COUNCIL
University at Albany, SUNY
Campus Center 332
Albany, NY 12222
(518) 442-5297
Director of Student Activities

LATINO HERITAGE MONTH
Columbia University Student Government
521 W 114th St. Room 201
New York, NY 10027
(212) 854-3611

LATINO LABOR & EDUCATION COALITION
Cornell University
434 Rockefeller Hall
Ithaca, NY 14853
(607) 255-3197 Fax: (607) 255-2433
Pedro Caban, Director
Email: mfd1@cornell.edu
Web: http://latino.lsp.cornell.edu

LATINO MALE AND FEMALE INITIATIVE
Borough of Manhattan Comm. College
199 Chambers St.
New York, NY 10007
(212) 346-8148 or (212) 346-8131
Fax: (212) 346-8134
Prof. Pedro Pérez, Counselor/Lecturer
Email: prof_perez99@hotmail.com

LATINO RELIGIOUS LEADERSHIP PROJ.
80 Fifth Ave. #1501
New York, NY 10011-8002
(212) 675-3288 Fax: (212) 675-3466
Guillermo Chacón, Director
Email: gchacon@latino.aids.org

LATINO STUDIES PROGRAM
Cornell Universiy
434 Rockefeller Hall
Ithaca, NY 14853-1601
(607) 255-3197 Fax: (607) 255-2433
Pedro Caban, Director
Email: mfd1@cornell.edu
Web: http://latino.lsp.cornell.edu

LEAGUE OF UNITED LATIN AMERICAN CITIZENS (LULAC)
Northeast Region-NY
85 Livingston Street
Brooklyn, NY 11201
(212) 475-0222 (w) or (718) 834-0106 (h)
Fax: (212) 475-1972
Julie Aguilera, State Director

THE LEARNING DISABILITIES ASSOCIATION OF NEW YORK
27 W. 20th St. #303
New York, NY 10011
(212) 645-6730 Fax: (212) 924-8896
Doris Rodríguez, Hispanic Outreach Coordinator

LENOX HILL NEIGHBORHOOD ASSOCIATION, INC.
331 E 70th St.
New York, NY 10021
(212) 744-5022 Fax: (212) 744-5150
Nancy Wackstein, Executive Director
Email: admin@lenoxhill.org
Web: lenoxhill.org

LEWIS STREET CENTER/PROJECT FIND
57 Central Park
Rochester, NY 14605
(716) 327-7225/7200 Fax: (716) 546-3230
Chris Carry, Project Director

LIGA DE ACCIÓN HISPANA
700 Oswego St.
Syracuse, NY 13204
(315) 475-6153 Fax: (315) 474-5767
Fanny Villarreal, Director

LINCOLN SQUARE NEIGHBORHOOD CENTER, INC.
250 W. 65th St.
New York, NY 10023
(212) 874-0860 Fax: (212) 799-6574
Stephanie Pinder, Executive Director

LINCOLN WIC PROGRAM
234 E. 149th St.
Bronx, NY 10451
(718) 579-5398 Fax: (718) 579-4604
Lorena Drago, Exectutive Director

LITERACY VOLUNTEERS OF AMERICA-WESTCHESTER COUNTY AFFILATE, INC.
85 Executive Blvd.
Elmsford, NY 10523
(914) 592-2656 Fax: (914) 592-1456
Patricia P. Rajala, Executive Director
Email: wchester@aol.com

LITTLE SHEPHERDS DAY CARE CENTER
2260 Andrews Ave.
Bronx, NY 10468
(718) 295-2740 Fax: (718) 364-6706
Birnice Flashner, Executive Director

LOISAIDA, INC.
710 E. 9th St., 4th Floor
New York, NY 10009
(212) 353-0272 Fax: (212) 473-5462
Esther García Cartagena, Executive Director

LONG ISLAND ASSOCIATION FOR AIDS CARE, INC. (LIAAC)
P. O. Box 2859
Huntington Station, NY 11746-0685
(516) 385-2437 Fax: (516) 385-2496
Gail Barouh, Executive Director/C.E.O.
Web: www.liaac.org

LONG ISLAND HISPANIC CHAMBER OF COMMERCE
605 Albany Ave.
Amityville, NY 11741
(516) 572-0750 Fax: (516) 572-0756
Luis Pasquez, President

LOS PLENEROS DE LA 21
1680 Lexington Ave., #209
New York, NY 10029-4603
(212) 427-5221
Juan Gutiérrez, Director

LOWER EAST SIDE FAMILY UNION COOPERATION
27 Ave. B
New York, NY 10009
(212) 677-6140 Fax: (212) 529-3244
Darryl Chisoln, Executive Director

LOWER WEST SIDE COUNSELING SERVICE, INC.
490 Niagara St.
Buffalo, NY 14201
(716) 856-2000 Fax: (761) 853-1305
Dawn Ferguson, Program Director
Web: www.lake.-shore.org.

LOWER WESTSIDE HOUSEHOLD SERVICES COOPERATION
250 W. 57th St., #1511
New York, NY 10107-0814
(212) 307-7107
Lucía Pons, Executive Director

MAMARONECK OPPORTUNITY CENTER
134 Center Ave.
Mamaroneck, NY 10543
(914) 698-7140 Fax: (914) 698-6964
Beverly Brewer Villa, Area Director

MANHATTAN VALLEY GOLDEN AGE
Senior Citizen Center
135 W. 106th St.
New York, NY 10025
(212) 749-7015 Fax: (212) 749-8611
Anna Nary Cox, Director

MANHATTAN VALLEY MANAGEMENT CORPORATION
73 W. 108th St.
New York, NY 10025
(212) 678-4410 Fax: (212) 666-4770
José Valerio, Executive Director
Email: jvale7253@aol.com

MARBLE HILL NEIGHBORHOOD IMPROVEMENT COOPERATION, INC.
135 Terrace View Ave.
New York, NY 10463
(718) 562-8866 Fax: (716) 562-8920
Michael Pichardo, Director

METROPOLITAN CENTER FOR MENTAL HEALTH
Hispanic Family Services
130 W. 97th St.
New York, NY 10025
(212) 864-7000 Fax: (212) 932-2103
Francine Ruskin, EDD-Director

MICA CONTINUING TREATMENT PROG.
1241 Lafayette Ave.
Bronx, NY 10474
(718) 378-6500 Fax: (718) 842-3846
Harry Megenes, Assistance Director

MID-BRONX YOUTH SKILLS
489 St. Paul's Pl.
Bronx, NY 10456
(718) 590-0655 Fax: (718) 681-2411
Sandra Atwell, Executive Director

MILLBROOK SENIOR CITIZENS CENTER
201 St. Anns Ave.
Bronx, NY 10454
(718) 401-4901
Rey Colón, Assistant Director

MIND BUILDERS CREATIVE ARTS CENTER
3415 Olinville Ave.
Bronx, NY 10467
(718) 652-6256 Fax: (718) 652-7324
Dr. Major Thomas, Assistent Director

MINORITY BAR ASSOCIATION
P.O. Box 211, Niagara Sq. Station
Buffalo, NY 14201
(716) 852-6781
John Elmore, President

MINORITY BUSINESS DEV. AGENCY (MBDA)
New York Office/U.S. Dept. of Commerce
26 Federal Plaza, #3720
New York, NY 10278
(212) 264-3483/3262 Fax: (212) 264-0725
Ralph J. Perez, Business Dev. Specialist
Email: RPerez@mbda.gov
Web: www.mbda.gov

MIRIAM DE SOYZA LEARNING CENTER
1180 Rev. James Polite Ave.
Bronx, NY 10459
(718) 378-1370 Fax: (718) 378-1975
Theodora de Soyza, Director

MOBILIZATION FOR YOUTH HEALTH SERVICES, INC.
199 Ave. B
New York, NY 10009
(212) 254-1456 Fax: (212) 505-8437
Willie Zayerz, Director

THE MOMENTUM AIDS PROJECT, INC.
155 W. 23rd St., 11th Floor
New York, NY 10011
(212) 691-8100 Fax: (212) 691-2960
John Bryan, Executive Director

MOTT HAVEN CHAMBER OF COMMERCE, INC.
622 E. 138th St.
Bronx, NY 10454
(718) 665-2055 Fax: (718) 402-9062
Raúl Ortiz, President

MOVIMIENTO ESTUDIANTIL CHICANO DE AZTLAN (MECHA)
Cornell University
434 Rockefeller Hall
Ithaca, NY 14853
(607) 255-3197 Fax: (607) 255-2433
Eloy Rodríguez, Advisor
Email: mfd1@cornell.edu
Web: http://lation.lsp.cornell.edu

MUSIC AGAINST DRUGS, INC.
250 Broadway
Brooklyn, NY 11211
(718) 384-3299 or (718) 218-7640
Fax: (718) 384-3193
Alma Billegas, Director

N.Y. ASSOC. FOR NEW AMERICANS, INC.
Executive Office
17 Battery Pl.

New York, NY 10004-1102
(212) 425-2900 Fax: (212) 344-1621
Mark Handleman, Director
Web: www.nyana.org

N.Y. FOUNDATION HOME ATTENDENT PROGRAMS FOR SENIOR CITIZENS, INC.
11 Park Pl., #1416
New York, NY 10007
(212) 962-7559 Fax: (212) 227-2952
Linda R. Hoffman, Executive Director

NASSAU/SUFFOLK LAW SERVICES COMMITTEE, INC.
1757-50 Veterans Memorial Hwy., #5
Islandia, NY 11722
(631) 232-2400 or (516) 232-2400
Fax: (631) 232-2489
Jeffrey Segel, Executive Director
Email: nslsl@earthlink.net
Web: www.freespeach.org/nslawservices/

NATIONAL ACTION COUNCIL FOR MINORITIES IN ENGINEERING (NACME)
350 5th Ave., #2212
New York, NY 10118
(212) 279-2626 Fax: (212) 629-5178
Dr. George Campbell Jr., President
Web: www.nacme.org

NATIONAL ASSOCIATION OF HISPANIC JOURNALISTS (NAHJ)
Region 2
16 Court St., 5th Floor, #503
Brooklyn, NY 11241
(718) 875-4455 Fax: (718) 875-7795
Carolina González, Region Director
Email: cgonzam@hotmail.com
Web: www.nahj.org

NATIONAL ASSOCIATION OF LATINO ELECTED & APPOINTED OFFICIALS
New York Chapter
853 Broadway, #1920
New York, NY 10003
(212) 777-8335
Enrique Ortiz, Director
Email: NALEO@aol.com
Web: www.naleo.org

THE NATIONAL ASSOC. OF LATINO FRATERNAL ORGANIZATIONS, INC.
320 Quimby Rd.
Rochester, NY 14623
(716) 424-1824
Mónica L. Miranda, Vice Chair, Bd. of Directors
Email: vicechair@nalfo.org
Web: www.nalfo.org

NATIONAL ASSOCIATION OF PUERTO RICAN/HISPANIC SOCIAL WORKERS
P. O. Box 651
Brentwood, NY 11717
(631) 864-1536 or (631) 471-6967
Fax: (516) 864-1536
Eva L. Padilla, President
Web: http://www.naprhsw.bizland.com/

NATIONAL CONFERENCE OF PUERTO RICAN WOMEN, INC.
Long Island Chapter
P.O. Box 357
Pt. Jefferson Station, NY 11776
(613) 476-4972 Fax: (631) 444-3218
Lynda Perdomo-Ayala, President
Email: lynda@pharm.sunysb.edu
Web: htttp://nacoprw.org

NATIONAL CONGRESS FOR PUERTO RICAN RIGHTS
National Headquarters
105 E. 22nd St., #901
New York, NY 10010
(212) 614-5355 Fax: (212) 260-2861
Richie Pérez, National Coordinator
Email: rperez@boricuanet

NATIONAL CONGRESS OF PUERTO RICAN VETERANS, INC.
669 Base St.
Bronx, NY 10304
(718) 822-8077
P.A. Carrero, National Chairman

NATIONAL FEDERATION OF HISPANIC OWNED NEWSPAPERS (NFHON)
National Headquarters
853 Broadway #811

New York, NY 10003
(212) 420-0009 Fax: (212) 674-6861
Carlos Carrillo, President
Web: http://idp.natl~impacto

NATIONAL LABOR COMMITTEE IN SUPPORT OF WORKER & HUMAN RIGHTS
National Headquarters
275 7th Ave
New York, NY 10001
(212) 242-3002 Fax: (212) 242-3821
Charles Kernaghan, Excutive Director
Email: nlc@nlc.org
Web: www.nlcnet.org

NATIONAL LATINAS CAUCUS (NLC)
National Headquarters
61 Broadway, 12th Floor
New York, NY 10006
(212) 510-0903 or (212) 510-0900
Yolanda Sánchez, President

NATIONAL LATINO PEACE OFFICERS ASSOCIATION (NLPOA)
New York State Chapter
P.O. Box 237
Bronx, NY 10475
(877) 657-6200
Minerva Osorio, Chapter President
Email: nlpoa@aol.com
Web: www.nlpoa.com

NATIONAL MEDICAL FELLOWSHIPS, INC.
110 W. 32nd St., 8th Floor
New York, NY 10001
(212) 714-0933 Fax: (212) 239-9718
Vivian Manning Fox, President

NATIONAL MIGRANT EDUCATION HOTLINE
State University of New York, Oneonta
Bugbee Hall-304
Oneonta, NY 13820
(607) 432-0781 Fax: (607) 432-7102
Bob Levy, Director

NATIONAL MINORITY SUPPLIER DEVELOPMENT COUNCIL, INC. (NMSDC)
National Headquarters
104 6th Ave., 2nd Floor
New York, NY 10018
(212) 944-2430 Fax: (212) 719-9611
Harriet Michel, National President
Web: www.nmsdcus.org

NATIONAL PUERTO RICAN FORUM, INC.
Bronx Office
1910 Webster Ave., 3rd Floor
Bronx, NY 10457
(718) 716-1300 Fax: (718) 716-3767
Kofi A. Boateng, Executive Director

NATIONAL PUERTO RICAN FORUM, INC.
National Headquarters
31 E. 32nd St., 4th Floor
New York, NY 10016
(212) 685-2311 Fax: (212) 685-2349(212) 689-5034
Kofi A. Boateng, Executive Director
Email: kofib@nprf.org
Web: www.nprf.org

NATIONAL SOCIETY OF HISPANIC MBAS
New York Chapter
P.O. Box 3328
New York, NY 10017
(212) 439-8054 or (214) 267-1622 (Nat'l Office)
Fax: (214) 267-1626 (Nat'l Office)
Graciela Flores, Chapter President
Email: newyork@nshmba.org
Web: www.nshmba.org

NATIONAL SUPERMARKETS ASSOC., INC.
17-20 Whitestone Expressway, #302
Whitestone, NY 11357
(708) 747-2860 Fax: (718) 741-2859
William Rodríguez, President

NATIONAL URBAN FELLOWS, INC.
National Headquarters
59 John St., #310
New York, NY 10038
(212) 349-6200 Fax: (212) 349-7478
Luis Alvarez, President
Web: www.nuf.org

NEIGHBORHOOD ASSOCIATION FOR INTERCULTURAL AFFAIRS
1055 Grand Concours, #1
Bronx, NY 10452

(718) 538-4830 Fax: (718) 537-3195
Eduardo Lagurre, Director
Email: naica981@cs.com

NEIGHBORHOOD ASSOCIATION FOR PUERTO RICAN AFFAIRS (NAPRA)
1997 Bathgate Ave.
Bronx, NY 10457
(718) 583-3220 Fax: (718) 731-4096
Carmen Bermúdez, Executive Director

NEIGHBORHOOD YOUTH FAMILY SVCS.
601 E. Tremond Ave., 2nd Floor
Bronx, NY 10457
(718) 294-0499 Fax: (718) 294-2189
Lizette H. Tait, Executive Director

NERVE, INC.
18 E. 116th St.
New York, NY 10029
(212) 427-0555 Fax: (212) 427-0875
Roberto Anazagasti, General Manager

NEW YORK CITY MISSION SOCIETY
105 E 22nd St. 6th Floor
New York, NY 10010
(212) 674-3500 Fax: (212) 979-5764
Stephanie Palmer, Executive Director
Email: nycmissionsock@mindspring.com

NEW YORK CITY TECHNICAL COLLEGE
300 Jay St.
Brooklyn, NY 11201
(718) 260-5000 Fax: (718) 260-5198
Dr. Fred Wbeaufait, President

NEW YORK COUNCIL ON ADOPTABLE CHILDREN
666 Broadway, #820
New York, NY 10012
(212) 475-0222 Fax: (212) 475-1972
Ernesto Loperena, Executive Director
Web: www.coac.org

NEW YORK HISPANIC AND AFRO-AMERICAN POLITICAL PARTY
131 E. Riviera Dr.
Lindenhurst, NY 11757
(631) 226-7618
Louis Van Den Essen, President

NEW YORK STATE ASSOCIATION FOR BILINGUAL EDUCATION
350 Martha Ave.
Delport, NY 11713
(516) 286-6551 Fax: (516) 286-6556
María E. Valverde, Membership Chair

NEW YORK STATE BLACK AND PUERTO RICAN AND HISPANIC LEGISLATIVE CAUCUS, INC.
Legislative Office Building., #4424
Albany, NY 12248
(518) 455-5345 Fax: (518) 455-4535
Keith Wright, Chairman
Email: bpcaucus@assembly.state.ny.us

NEW YORK STATE FEDERATION OF HISPANIC CHAMBERS OF COMMERCE
2710 Broadway, 2nd Floor
New York, NY 10025
(212) 222-8300 Fax: (212) 222-8412
Alfred Placeres, President

NEW YORK TECHNICAL ASSISTANCE CTR.
Hunter College of CUNY
695 Park Ave., #924 W
New York, NY 10021
(212) 772-4764
José Vázquez, Coordinator

NONTRADITIONAL EMPLOYMENT FOR WOMEN (NEW)
243 W 20th St.
New York, NY 10011
(212) 627-6252 Fax: (212) 255-8021
Martha Baker, Executive Director
Email: new@new-nyc.org
Web: www.new-nyc.org

NORTH AMERICAN CONGRESS ON LATIN AMERICA (NACLA)
475 Riverside Dr., #454
New York, NY 10115
(212) 870-3146 Fax: (212) 870-3305
Fred Rosen, Executive Director
Email: nacla@nacla.org
Web: www.nacla.org

NORTH BROOKLYN YMCA
570 Jamaica Ave.
Brooklyn, NY 11208
(718) 277-1600 Fax: (718) 277-2081
Sid Rivero, Executive Director

NORTH EAST PASTORAL CENTER
1011 First Ave. #1233
New York, NY 10022
(212) 751-7045 Fax: (212) 753-5321
Mario Paredes
Email: nhcc1011@aol.com

NORTH/SOUTH CONSONANCE, INC.
P. O. Box 698 - Cathedral Station
New York, NY 10025-0698
(212) 663-7566
Max Lifchitz, Director
Email: ns.concerts@att.net
Web: www.nsmusic.com

NORTHEAST HISPANIC CATHOLIC CTR.
Episcopal Regions I,II,III & IV
1011 First Ave.
New York, NY 10022-4134
(212) 751-7045 Fax: (212) 753-5321
Mario J. Paredes, Executive Director
Email: nhcc1011@aol.com

NORTHERN MANHATTAN COALITION
FOR IMMIGRANTS RIGHTS
2 Bennett Ave., 2nd Floor
New York, NY 10033
(212) 781-0355 or (212) 781-0648
Fax: (212) 781-0943
Michael Maestquita, Executive Director

NORTHERN MANHATTAN
IMPROVEMENT CO.
76 Wadsworth Ave., 1st Floor
New York, NY 10033
(212) 822-8300 Fax: (212) 740-9646
Bárbara Lowry, Executive Director
Email: info@nmic.org
Web: www.nmic.org

NUESTROS NIÑO - DAY CARE CENTER
384 S. 4th St.
Brooklyn, NY 11211
(718) 963-1555 Fax: (718) 963-0240
Mirian L. Cruz, Director

NUEVO EL BARRIO PARA LA
REHABILITACIÓN DE LA VIVIENDA Y
ECONOMIA
18 E. 116th St.
New York, NY 10029
(212) 427-0555 Fax: (212) 427-0875
Roberto Anazagasti, Manager

NUYORICAN POETS CAFE
P.O. Box 20794
236 E. 3rd St.
New York, NY 10009
(212) 505-8183 Fax: (212) 475-6541
Miguel Algarín, Director
Web: www.nuyorican.org

OFFICE OF BILINGUAL EDUCATION AND
FOREIGN LANGUAGES
731 City Hall
Buffalo, NY 14202
(716) 851-3705 Fax: (716) 851-3882
David E. Báez, Director

OFFICE OF HISPANIC AMERICAN AFFAIRS
State University of New York, System
Systems Administration
Suny Plaza
Albany, NY 12246
(518) 443-5891 Fax: (518) 443-5223
Dr. Manuel Salvador Alguero, Director

OFFICE OF THE SPANISH APOSTOLATE
Diocese of Rochester
1150 Buffalo Rd.
Rochester, NY 14624
(716) 328-3210 Fax: (716) 328-4142
Rev. Jesús Flores, Interim Director
Email: flores@dor.org
Web: www.dor.org

OLLANTAY CENTER FOR THE ARTS, INC.
P.O. Box 720636
Jackson Heights, NY 11372-0636
(718) 565-6499 Fax: (718) 446-7806
Pedro R. Monge Rafuls, Executive Director

OMEGA PHI BETA SORORITY
University at Albany, SUNY
Campus Center 332
Albany, NY 12222
(518) 442-5297
Director of Student Activities

OPPORTUNITIES FOR A BETTER TOMORROW
783 4th Ave.
Brooklyn, NY 11232
(718) 369-0303 Fax: (718) 369-1598
Sister Mary Franciscus, Executive Director
Email: sistermaryob@erols.com

ORGANIZATION OF LATIN AMERICAN
STUDENTS
Pace University
Office of Student Life
41 Park Row, 8th Floor
New York, NY 10038
(212) 346-1590 Fax: (212) 346-1916
Greg Brown, Director

PAMELA C. TORRES DAY CARE CTR., INC.
161 Saint Anns Ave.
Bronx, NY 10454
(718) 585-2540 Fax: (718) 585-2421
Nilza Cruz, Director
Email: nilzan@aol.com

PARK SLOPE FAMILY DAY CARE
333 14th St.
Brooklyn, NY 11215
(718) 788-7803 Fax: (718) 788-0631
Lucía B. Ferraz, Director

PEQUEÑOS SOULS DAY CARE CENTER
114-34 E. 122nd St.
New York, NY 10035
(212) 427-7644 Fax: (212) 427-7645
Esther L. Smith, Director

PHI IOTA ALPHA FRATERNITY
c/o SUNY New Paltz
College Activities Off. SUB #209
New Paltz, NY 12561
(914) 257-4845
José Herrera, Pres.

University at Albany, SUNY
Campus Center 332
Albany, NY 12222
(518) 442-5297
Director of Student Activities

PHI THETA CHI SORORITY, INC.
Cornell University
434 Rockefeller Hall
Ithaca, NY 14853-1601
(607) 255-3197 Fax: (607) 255-2433
María Cristina García, Advisor
Email: mfd1@cornell.edu
Web: http://latino.lsp.cornell.edu

PHIPPS WEST FARMS BEACON
West Farms
1970 West Farms Rd.
Bronx, NY 10460
(718) 991-6331 Fax: (718) 991-6653
Alice J. Jenkins, Director

PHOENIX HOUSES
Long Island
153 Eastmain St.
Smithtown, NY 11787-9021
(631) 979-7300 Fax: (631) 979-6890
Matt Cassidy, Executive Director

PODER LATINO
Alfred University
Powell Campus Center
Alfred, NY 14802
(607) 871-2669
Miriam Valero, Treasurer

PORT WASHINGTON
Community Action Council, Inc.
382 Main St.
Port Washington, NY 11050
(516) 883-3201 Fax: (516) 883-2467
Mario Martínez, Director

PORTCHESTER CARVER CENTER
400 Westchester Ave.
Port Chester, NY 10573
(914) 939-4469 Fax: (914) 939-3761
Jill Beltran, Executive Director

PREGONES TOURING PUERTO RICAN
THEATER COLLECTION, INC.
700 Grand Concourse, 2nd Floor
Bronx, NY 10451
(718) 585-1202 Fax: (718) 585-1608
Rosalba Rolón, Executive Director
Email: pregones@aol.com
Web: www.pregones.org

PRLDEF INSTITUTE FOR PUERTO RICAN
POLICY
Affiliate of PRLDEF
99 Hudson St., 14th Floor
New York, NY 10013
(212) 219-3360 Fax: (212) 431-4276
Angelo Falcón, Director
Email: prpolicy@aol.com
Web: www.igc.org/IPR/

PROGRESS, INC.
120 Wall St., #2301
New York, NY 10005
(212) 480-0202 Fax: (212) 480-9734
Juan D. Martínez, Executive Director
Email: progressinc@earthlink.net

PROJECT TRABAJO-NYS DEPT. OF LABOR
Community Service Center Division
247 W. 54th St., 6th Floor
New York, NY 10019
(212) 621-0880 or (800) 848-4949
Fax: (212) 621-0882
Yolanda de los Reyes, Coordinator

PROMESA
1776 Clay Avenue
Bronx, NY 10457-7239
(718) 299-1100 Fax: (718) 716-7822
Rubén Medina, Chief Executive Director
Email: info@promesa.org
Web: www.promesa.org

PRONTO OF LONG ISLAND, INC.
128 Pineaire Dr.
Bay Shore, NY 11706
(631) 231-8290 Fax: (631) 231-8390
Nilda Alvarez, Coordinator

PROYECTO AMÉRICA
69 Reeve Pl.
Brooklyn, NY 11218
(718) 437-4878 Fax (718) 437-4878
Blanca Monroig, Director
Email: bmonroig@prodigy.net

PUEBLO EN MARCHA
c/o St. Plus
401 E 145th St.
Bronx, NY 10454
(718) 665-7375
Máximino Rivera, Executive Director

PUEBLO (POLITICALLY UNITED
EMPOWERING BARRIOS LATINOS
ORGANIZATION)
66 Moore St.
Brooklyn, NY 11211
(718) 599-5900
Héctor Quiñones, President

PUERTO RICAN ASSOCIATION FOR
COMMUNITY AFFAIRS (PRACA)
National Headquarters
61 Broadway, 12th Floor
New York, NY 10006
(212) 510-0900 or (212) 510-0903
Yolanda Sánchez, Executive Director

PUERTO RICAN EDUCATIONAL &
CULTURAL CENTER
24 Van Sinderen Ave.
Brooklyn, NY 11207
(718) 345-4775 Fax: (718) 485-0086
Alicia Ponce de León, Executive Director

PUERTO RICAN EDUCATORS
ASSOCIATION (PREA)
P. O. Box 826
Bronx, NY 10462
(212) 860-5887 or (212) 828-3552
Fax: (212) 828-3587
Alejandrina Hendrick, President
Email: wrknmom50@aol.com

PUERTO RICAN FAMILY INSTITUTE, INC.
Adolescent Day Treatment Program
145 W. 15th St.
New York, NY 10011
(212) 229-6960 Fax: (212) 414-7825
Yolanda Winn, Program Coordinator
Web: www.prfi.org

Adult Supportive Care Management
145 W. 15th St.
New York, NY 10011
(212) 229-6970 Fax: (212) 414-7827
David Ortiz, Program Director
Web: www.prfi.org

Bronx Child Placement Prevention
Program
384 E. 149th St., #622

Bronx, NY 10455
(718) 665-0005 Fax: (718) 665-1282
Luis A. Rivera, Program Director
Web: www.prfi.org

Bronx HIV Care Network
384 E. 149th St., #622
Bronx, NY 10455
(718) 665-7900 Fax: (718) 665-1282
Barbara Hart, Program Director
Web: www.prfi.org

Bronx Mental Health Clinic
4123 Third Ave.
Bronx, NY 10457
(718) 299-3045 Fax: (718) 716-2604
Lourdes Sánchez, Program Director

Brooklyn Head Start Program
185 Marcy Ave., Lower level
Brooklyn, NY 11211
(718) 388-8060 Fax: (718) 388-6373
Carmen Fontanez, Program Coordinator
Web: www.prfi.org

Brooklyn HIV Care Network
217 Havemeyer St., 4th Floor
Brooklyn, NY 11211
(718) 486-7937 Fax: (718) 486-7939
Michelle Ocasio, Program Coordinator
Web: www.prfi.org

Brooklyn Mental Health Clinic
217 Havemeyer St., 4th Floor
Brooklyn, NY 11211
(718) 963-4430 Fax: (718) 963-0814
Abigail Juárez-Karic, Program Director
Web: www.prfi.org

Child Placement Prevention Program,
Bushwick
845 Broadway, 2nd Floor
Brooklyn, NY 11206
(718) 387-5200 Fax: (718) 387-5250
Esther M. Huertas, Program Director
Web: www.prfi.org

Children's Intensive Care Mgmt. Prog.
175 Remsen St., 11th Floor
Brooklyn, NY 11201
(718) 596-1320 Fax: (718) 596-1250
Eva Morales, Program Director
Web: www.prfi.org

Home Based Crisis Intervention Program
217 Havemeyer St., 4th Floor
Brooklyn, NY 11211
(718) 388-8934 ext. 497 Fax: (718) 963-0814
Oscar Arroyo, Program Director
Web: www.prfi.org

Intermediate Care Facility #1
3050 Laconia Ave.
Bronx, NY 10469
(718) 231-6532 Fax: (718) 405-2044
Angelina Rivera, Residence Manager
Web: www.prfi.org

Intermediate Care Facility #2
1668 Grand Ave.
Bronx, NY 10453
(718) 731-8434 Fax: (718) 731-8442
Carmen López, Residence Manager
Web: www.prfi.org

Intermediate Care Facility #3
194 W. 180th St.
Bronx, NY 10467
(718) 716-6175 Fax: (718) 716-6071
Leslie Berly, Residence Manager
Web: www.prfi.org

Main Office
145 W. 15th St.
New York, NY 10011
(212) 924-6320/6330 Fax: (212) 691-5635
María Elena Jirone, Executive Director
Web: www.prfi.org

Manhattan Child Placement Prevention
Prog.
145 W. 15th St.
New York, NY 10011
(212) 229-6920 Fax: (212) 414-7834
Gloria Otoya, Program Director
Web: www.prfi.org

Manhattan Mental Health Services
145 W. 15th St.
New York, NY 10011
(212) 229-6905 Fax: (212) 924-4404
Mary J. García, Program Director
Web: www.prfi.org

New Arrivals Program
145 W. 15th St.
New York, NY 10011
(212) 229-6910 Fax: (212) 414-7833
Daisy Vázquez, Program Director
Web: www.prfi.org

Partial Hospitalization Program
217 Havemeyer St., 3rd Floor
Brooklyn, NY 11211
(718) 963-1655 Fax: (718) 963-1776
Zivia Bairey, Program Coordinator
Web: www.prfi.org

Placement Prevention Program for Juveniles on Probation
145 W. 15th St.
New York, NY 10011
(212) 229-6930 Fax: (212) 414-7831
Sonia Acobo Morales, Program Director
Web: www.prfi.org

Queens Mental Health Clinic
97-45 Queens Blvd., #503
Rego Park, NY 11374
(718) 275-0983 Fax: (718) 275-7973
Arina Sylva, Program Director
Web: www.prfi.org

PUERTO RICAN HISPANIC GENEALOGICAL SOCIETY, INC.
P.O. Box 260118
Bellerose, NY 11426-0118
(516) 834-2511 Fax: (718) 464-3866
Miguel J. Hernández, President
Email: prhgs@yahoo.com
Web: www.rootsweb.com/~prhgs

PUERTO RICAN HOME ATTENDANT SERVICE, INC.
564 Southern Blvd.
Bronx, NY 10455
(718) 292-8770 Fax: (718) 585-2114
Juan Hernández, Assistant Director

PUERTO RICAN/LATINO BUSINESS DEVELOPMENT CENTER
Empire State Development Corporation
633 Third Ave., 32nd Floor
New York, NY 10017
(212) 803-3238 Fax: (212) 803-3223
Nicolas Torrens, Director
Email: ntorrens@empire.state.ny.us

PUERTO RICAN LEGAL DEFENSE AND EDUCATION FUND (PRLDEF)
National Headquarters
99 Hudson St., 14th Floor
New York, NY 10013-2815
(212) 219-3360 or (800) 328-2322
Fax: (212) 431-4276
Juan A. Figueroa, President & General Counsel
Email: info@prldef.org
Web: www.igc.org/IPR/

PUERTO RICAN ORGANIZATION FOR GROWTH, RESEARCH, EDUCATION AND SELF-SUFFICIENCY, INC. (PROGRESS)
120 Well St., 23rd Floor
New York, NY 10005
(212) 480-0202 Fax: (212) 982-2534
Juan Martínez, Executive Director
Email: progressinc@earthlink.net

PUERTO RICAN STUDENT ASSOCIATION
Cornell University
434 Rockefeller Hall
Ithaca, NY 14853-1601
(607) 255-3197 Fax: (607) 255-2433
Pedro Caban, Advisor
Email: mfd1@cornell.edu
Web: http://latino.lsp.cornell.edu

PUERTO RICAN TRAVELING THEATER COMPANY INC.
141 W. 94th St.
New York, NY 10025
(212) 354-1293
Miriam Colón Valle, Executive Artistic Director

PUERTO RICAN WORKSHOP, INC. (TALLER BORICUA)
1685 Lexington Ave.
New York, NY 10029
(212) 831-4333 Fax: (212) 831-6274
Fernando Salicrup, Director

PUERTO RICAN YOUTH DEVELOPMENT AND RESOURCE CENTER (PRYD)
997 N. Clinton Ave.
Rochester, NY 14621
(716) 325-3570 Fax: (716) 325-3767
Nancy Padilla, Executive Director
Email: pryd@frontiernet.net

PUERTO RICANS FOR INVOLVEMENT, DEVELOPMENT AND ENLIGHTENMENT (P.R.I.D.E.)
Baruch College
17 Lexington Ave., Box F1512
New York, NY 10010
(212) 802-6770 Fax: (212) 802-6581

PUERTO RICO FEDERAL AFFAIRS ADMINISTRATION
New York City Regional Office
475 Park Ave. S 7th Fl.
New York, NY 10016
(212) 252-7300 Fax: (212) 252-7323
Carlos Linera, Director
Web: www.prfaa.com

PUERTO RICO TOURISM COMPANY
666 5th Ave.
New York, NY 10103
(212) 586-6262 Fax: (212) 586-1212
Narciso Moreno, Director of Operations
Web: www.prtourism.com

RAINBOW/PUSH COALITION
Wall Street Project
Empire State Bldg.
350 Fifth Ave., #2723
New York, NY 10118
(212) 425-7874 Fax: (212) 968-1412
Chichi Williams, Executive Director
Web: www.rainbowpush.org

REFORMA
New York Chapter
41-17 Main St., 3rd Floor
Flushing, NY 11355
(718) 661-1230/990-6243 Fax: (718) 661-1291
Alexandra Sánchez, State Coordinator
Email: asanchez@queenslibrary.org
Web: http://clnet.ucr.edu/library/reforma

RIDGEWOOD BUSHWICK SENIOR CITIZENS COUNCIL, INC.
280 Wyckoff Ave.
Brooklyn, NY 11237
(718) 821-0254 Fax: (718) 821-2664
Christina Fisher, Executive Director

ROBERTO CLEMENTE CENTER
540 E. 13th St., Between Ave A & B
New York, NY 10009
(212) 387-7400 Fax: (212) 387-7432
Jaime Inclan, Director

ROCHESTER EDUCATIONAL OPPORTUNITY CENTER
305 Andrews St.
Rochester, NY 14604
(716) 232-2730 Fax: (716) 546-7824
Dr. Melva Brown, Executive Director
Web: www.brockport.edu/~reoc/reoc.htm

ROCHESTER HISPANIC BUSINESS ASSOCIATION
P.O. Box 20284
Rochester, NY 14602
(716) 424-3460 Fax: (716) 424-1908
Valerio Kusimnsky, Chairman

ROCHESTER MINORITY BUSINESS DEVELOPMENT CENTER
350 North St.
Rochester, NY 14605
(716) 232-6120 Fax: (716) 546-8689
Daryl E. Greene, Director

ROCHESTER REHAB CENTER, INC.
1000 Elmwood Ave.
Rochester, NY 14620
(716) 271-2520 Fax: (716) 271-1198
George Gieselman, President

ROOTS OF BRAZIL
c/o Lezly Dance School
416 Bergen St., #1
Brooklyn, NY 11217
(718) 622-1561 or (212) 603-9663
Ligia Barreto, Artistic Director

RURAL OPPORTUNITIES, INC.
Affiliate of NCLR
400 East Ave.
Rochester, NY 14607
(716) 546-7180 Fax: (716) 340-3337
Stuart J. Mitchell, President
Email: RO13LIB@worldlink.org

RYAN NENA COMMUNITY HEALTH CTR.
279 E. 3rd St.
New York, NY 10009
(212) 477-8500 Fax: (212) 473-4900
Kathy Gruben, Project Director

SABOR LATINO DANCE ENSEMBLE
Cornell University
434 Rockefeller Hall
Ithaca, NY 14853-1601
(607) 255-3197 Fax: (607) 255-2433
Hector Velez, Advisor
Email: mfd1@cornell.edu
Web: http://lation.lsp.cornell.edu

SAINT MARTIN DE PORRES GUILD
141 E. 65th St.
New York, NY 10021
(212) 744-2410 Fax: (212) 737-3875
Father Reymond Halligan, Reverend

SCHOOL SETTLEMENT ASSOCIATION, INC.
120 Jackson St.
Brooklyn, NY 11211
(718) 389-1810 Fax: (718) 383-7739
Rick Vescovi, Director

SCHOOL SITE MENTAL HEALTH PROGRAM, INC.
781 E. 142nd St.
Bronx, NY 10451
(718) 993-1400 Fax: (718) 993-0647
Julio Ortega, Director

SCIENCE ORGANIZATION OF LATINOS
Cornell University
434 Rockefeller Hall
Ithaca, NY 14853-1601
(607) 255-3197 Fax: (607) 255-2433
Eloy Rodríguez, Advisor
Email: mfd1@cornell.edu
Web: http://latino.lsp.cornell.edu

SEGUNDO RUIZ BELVIS DIAGNOSTICS & TREATMENT CENTER
545 East 142nd St.
Bronx, NY 10454
(718) 579-1702 Fax: (718) 579-9024
Barbra Rosser, Executive Director

SEÑORITAS LATINAS UNIDAS/SIGMA LAMBDA UPSILON SORORITY, INC.
Cornell University
434 Rockefeller Hall
Ithaca, NY 14853
(607) 255-3197 Fax: (607) 255-2433
Helena Viramontes, Advisor
Email: mfd1@cornell.edu
Web: http://latino.lsp.cornell.edu

SER OF WESTCHESTER, INC.
Affiliate of SER-Jobs for Progress National, Inc.
171 E. Post Rd., #201
White Plains, NY 10601
(914) 681-0996 Fax: (914) 681-1978
Ilse Vélez, Executive Director
Email: admin@serwestchester.org
Web: www.serwestchester.org

SHARE, SELF-HELP FOR WOMEN WITH BREAST OR OVARIAN CANCER
Latina SHARE
1501 Broadway, #1720
New York, NY 10036
(212) 719-0364 or (212) 719-4454
Fax: (212) 869-3431
Ivis Sampayo, Director
Email: isampayo@sharecancersupport.org
Web: www.sharecancersupport.org

SHIRLEY CHISHOLM DAY CARE CENTER
333 14th St.
Brooklyn, NY 11215
(718) 499-7154 Fax: (718) 832-3880
Philip David, Director

SIGMA IOTA ALPHA SORORITY
State University of New York, Albany
Campus Center 332
Albany, NY 12222
(518) 442-5297
Director of Student Activities

SIGMA LAMBDA BETA FRATERNITY INC.
SUNY at Stony Brook
Student Activities Center, #219
Stony Brook, NY 11794-2800
(516) 216-4325
Gregory Rodríguez, President
Email: morro5@excite.com

SIGMA LAMBDA GAMMA SORORITY
SUNY at Stony Brook
Student Activities Center # 219
Stony Brook, NY 11794 -2800
(516) 632-9392

Cheryl Chambers, Director
Email: cherylchambers@suny.org

SIGMA LAMBDA UPSILON
State University of New York, Albany
Campus Center 332
Albany, NY 12222
(518) 442-5297
Director of Student Activities

SINERGIA, INC.
15 W. 65th. St., 6th Floor
New York, NY 10023
(212) 496-1300 Fax: (212) 496-5608
Emilio Bermiss, Executive Director

SOCIEDAD GENERAL DE AUTORES Y EDITORES (SGAE)
240 E. 47th St., #12-B
New York, NY 10017
(212) 752-7230 Fax: (212) 754-4378
Emilio García, Executive Director
Email: egarcia@sgae.org
Web: www.sgae.es

SOCIEDAD PUERTORRIQUEÑA DE QUEENS, INC.
P. O. Box 6282
Long Island City, NY 11106
(718) 204-9035
Betsy Dávila, President

SOCIETY OF HISPANIC PROFESSIONAL ENGINEERS (SHPE)
Cornell University Student Chapter
Engineering Minority Programs Office
167 Olin Hall
Ithaca, NY 14853-1601
(607) 255-3197 Fax: (607) 255-2433
Ferdinand Rodríguez, Advisor
Email: mfd1@cornell.edu
Web: http://latino.lsp.cornell.edu

New York City Professional Chapter
270 7th St.
Brooklyn, NY 11215
(212) 386-0746 Fax: (212) 584-6456
Eladio Martin, Chapter President
Email: eladiomartin98@yahoo.com
Web: www.shpe.com/nyc

Rochester New York Professional Chapter
P.O. Box 15668
Rochester, NY 14615
(716) 422-8098 or (716) 461-3820 (h)
Fax: (716) 265-5384
Lucy Pérez, Chapter President
Email: lucy.perez@usa.xerox.com
Web: http://shperoc.speedhost.com

SOCIETY OF SPANISH ENGINEERS, PLANNERS & ARCHITECTS, INC. (SSEPA)
308 Pleasant Ave.
New York, NY 10035
(212) 410-4931 Fax: (212) 410-3721
Raymond Plume, Board Member

SOCIETY OF WOMEN ENGINEERS
120 Wall Street., 11th Floor
New York, NY 10005-3902
(212) 509-9577 Fax: (212) 509-0224
Jane Ryan, Executive Director & CEO
Web: www.swe.org

SOUTH BRONX ACTION GROUP
384 E. 149th St., #220
Bronx, NY 10455
(718) 993-5869 Fax: (718) 993-7904
Carmen Allende, Director
Email: sbheinc@aol.com

SOUTH BRONX COMMUNITY ACTION THEATRE
Affiliate to SER
345 Brook Ave.
Bronx, NY 10454
(718) 292-5050 Fax: (718) 665-6355
Frederick Daris, Exec. Dir.

SOUTH BRONX COMMUNITY CORPORATION
455 E. 155th St.
Bronx, NY 10454
(718) 585-5234 Fax: (718) 401-0154
Belinda de Jesús, Executive Director

SOUTH BRONX MENTAL HEALTH
COUNCIL, INC.
781 E. 142nd St.
Bronx, NY 10454
(718) 993-1400 x301 Fax: (718) 993-0647
Dr. Humberto L. Martínez, Director

SOUTH BRONX MENTAL HEALTH
COUNCIL, INC.
952 Anderson Ave.
Bronx, NY 10452
(718) 588-4770 Fax: (718) 588-2518
Dennis Reardon, Director

Alcoholism Out Patient Clinic
1241 Lafayette Ave.
Bronx, NY 10474
(718) 378-6500 Fax: (718) 842-3846
Albert Negrón, Program Director

Bronx III Intensive Supportive Apartment
Program
932 Kelly St.
Bronx, NY 10459
(718) 542-0880 Fax: (718) 993-0647
David Carrion, Director

SOUTH BRONX NEIGHBORHOOD
ORIENTATION CENTER
630 Southern Blvd.
Bronx, NY 10455
(718) 993-1150 Fax: (718) 737-3875
Caroline Vélez, Director

SOUTH BRONX SENIOR
TRANSPORTATION NETWORK
910 E 172nd St.
Bronx, NY 10460
(718) 589-4295 Fax: (718) 589-0751
Ralf Madera, Director

SOUTHERN TIER AIDS PROGRAM, INC.
122 Baldwin St.
Johnson City, NY 13790
(607) 798-1706 Fax: (607) 798-1977
Tina Barber, Assistance Director

SOUTHSIDE COMMUNITY MISSION, INC.
280 Marcy Ave.
Brooklyn, NY 11211
(718) 388-3784 Fax: (718) 384-3739
John Mulhurn, Supervisor

SOUTHSIDE COMMUNITY MISSION, INC.
Annex
250 Hooper St.
Brooklyn, NY 11211
(718) 387-3803
Kathryn Walsh, Program Coordinator

SOUTHSIDE UNITED HOUSE
DEVELOPMENT FUND CORPORATION
(LOS SURES), INC.
213 S. 4th St.
Brooklyn, NY 11211
(718) 387-2418 Fax: (718) 387-4683
David Pagan, Executive Director

SOUTHVIEW HEALTH CENTER, INC.
731 White Plains Rd.
Bronx, NY 10473
(718) 589-2232 Fax: (718) 378-2880
Pedro Espada, President

SPAIN-UNITED STATES CHAMBER OF
COMMERCE
Northeast Region
350 5th Ave., #2029
New York, NY 10118
(212) 967-2170 Fax: (212) 564-1415
Ana Diaz, Executive Director
Email: info@spainuscc.org
Web: www.spainuscc.org

SPANISH ACTION COALITION
821 N. Clinton Ave.
Rochester, NY 14621
(716) 232-4050 Fax: (716) 232-2271
Mario Escalante, Director

SPANISH CHAMBER OF COMMERCE OF
LONG ISLAND
131 E. Riviera Dr.
Lindenhurst, NY 11757
(631) 226-7618
Louis Van Den Essen, President

SPANISH COMMUNITY PROGRESS
FOUNDATION, INC.
204 Hawthorne Ave.
Yonkers, NY 10705
(914) 969-5400 Fax: (914) 969-5890
Wilda Mejias, Director

THE SPANISH INSTITUTE
684 Park Ave.
New York, NY 10021
(212) 628-0420 Fax: (212) 734-4177
Inmaculada de Habsburgo, President and CEO
Email: spanishinst@cdiusa.com
Web: www.cdiusa.com/spanishInstitute

SPANISH SPEAKING AGENCY COUNCIL
RAICES, INC.
30 Third Ave. #617
Brooklyn, NY 11217
(718) 643-0232 Fax: (718) 643-8257
Edwin Méndez Santiago, Executive Director

SPANISH THEATER REPERTORY CO., LTD
138 E. 27th St.
New York, NY 10016
(212) 889-2850 Fax: (212) 686-3732
Gilberto Zaldiva, Executive Producer
Email: repertorio@mindspring.com
Web: www.repertorio.org

SPANUSA, EXECUTIVE RECRUITERS OF
SPANISH-SPEAKING PROFESSIONALS
135 Beach Ave.
Mamaroneck, NY 10543
(914) 381-5555 Fax: (914) 381-0811
Manuel Boado, President
Email: spanusa@aol.com
Web: www.spanusa.net

SPONSORS FOR EDUCATIONAL
OPPORTUNITY
23 Gramercy Park South
New York, NY 10003
(212) 979-2040 Fax: (212) 674-0870
Michael Whittingham, Vice-President
Web: www.sea-ny.org

STAGG STREET CENTER FOR CHILDREN
77-83 Stagg St.
Brooklyn, NY 11206
(718) 388-1395 Fax: (718) 599-6053
Cecilie Newton, Education Director

SUFFOLK COUNTY REPUBLICAN
NATIONAL HISPANIC ASSEMBLY
P.O. Box 1481
Smithtown, NY 11787
(631) 382-3972
Sylvia A. Díaz, President
Web: www.rnha.org

SULLIVAN COUNTY COUNCIL ON
ALCOHOL/DRUG ABUSE, INC.
17 Hamilton Ave.
Monticello, NY 12701
(914) 794-8080 Fax: (845) 794-8343
Veronica Uss, Executive Director

SUNSET PARK REDEVELOPMENT
COMMITTEE
5101 4th Ave.
Brooklyn, NY 11220
(718) 492-8580 Fax: (718) 439-0961
Nelson Ramos, Director

SUNSET PARK SENIOR CITIZEN CTR., INC
4520 4th Ave.
Brooklyn, NY 11220
(718) 492-9370 Fax: (718) 492-5042
María Cardona, Director

SYRACUSE EMPLOYMENT & TRAINING
AGENCY
677 S. Salina St., #200 Cab House Commons
Syracuse, NY 13202
(315) 473-8250 Fax: (315) 472-9492
John Williams, Director
Email: jwilliams@cnyworks.com
Web: www.cnyworks.com

TAHUANTISUYO
P.O. Box 2340
Astoria, NY 11102
(718) 728-1793
Guillermo Guerrero, President
Email: tawawan@aol.com

TEATRO MODERNO PUERTORRIQUENO, INC.
181 E. 111th St.
New York, NY 10029
(212) 289-2633 Fax: (212) 289-2633
Edwin Marcial, Executive Director

TEATROTALLER
Cornell University
434 Rockefeller Hall
Ithaca, NY 14853-1601
(607) 255-3197 Fax: (607) 255-2433
Debra Castillo, Advisor
Email: mfd1@cornell.edu
Web: http://latino.lsp.cornell.edu

THALIA SPANISH THEATER
P.O. Box 4368, 41-17 Greenpoint Ave.
Sunnyside, NY 11104
(718) 729-3880
Silvia Brito, Executive Artistic Director

THIRD STREET MUSIC SCHOOL
SETTLEMENT
235 E 11th St.
New York, NY 10003
(212) 777-3240 Fax: (212) 477-1808
Bárbara E Field, Executive Director

TOURIST OFFICE OF SPAIN
666 5th Ave. 35th Fl.
New York, NY 10103
(212) 265-8822 Fax: (212) 265-8864
Albaro Remedo, Director
Email: oetny@tourspain.es
Web: www.okspain.org

TREMONT CROTONA DAY CARE CENTER
1600 Crotona Park E.
Bronx, NY 10460
(718) 378-5600 Fax: (718) 569-1766
Patrick Rodríguez, Executive Director

ULSTER COUNTY COMMUNITY ACTION
COMMITTEE, INC.
15 Church St.
Highland, NY 12528
(914) 691-8722
Regena Daunicht, Executive Director

UNION DE ENTIDADES ARGENTINAS
P.O. Box 1020
9453 Corona Ave.
Elmhurst, NY 11373
(718) 762-7323

UNITAS THERAPEUTIC COMMUNITY, INC.
940 Garrison Ave.
Bronx, NY 10474
(718) 589-0551 Fax: (718) 328-4265
Anne Grosso, Executive Director

UNITED BRONX PARENT DAY CARE
CENTER NO. 1
888 Westchester Ave.
Bronx, NY 10459
(718) 378-5000 Fax: (718) 378-2395
Laly Woodards, Director

UNITED BRONX PARENTS, INC.
773 Prospect Ave.
Bronx, NY 10455
(718) 991-7100 Fax: (718) 991-7643
Lorena Montenegro, Executive Director
Web: www.unitedbronxparentsinc.org

UNITED BRONX PARENTS MRS. A PLACE, INC.
966 Prospect Ave.
Bronx, NY 10459
(718) 991-7188 or (718) 617-6060
Fax: (718) 589-2986
Lorena Montenegro, Executive Director

UNITED COMMUNITY OF
WILLIAMSBURG DAY CARE CENTER
152 Manhattan Ave.
Brooklyn, NY 11206
(718) 388-4298 or (718) 388-4299
Fax: (718) 388-5590
Anna Butler, Executive Director

UNITED PUERTO RICAN ORGANIZATION
OF SUNSET PARK
5417 4th Ave.
Brooklyn, NY 11220
(718) 492-9307 Fax: (718) 492-9030
Elizabeth C. Yeampierre, Director

U.S. LATINA/O GRADUATE STUDENT
COALITION
Cornell University
250 Goldwin Smith Hall
Ithaca, NY 14853-1601
(607) 255-3197 Fax: (607) 255-2433
Annete Portillo, Co-Chair
Email: mfd1@cornell.edu
Web: http://latino.lsp.cornell.edu

UNITED STATES POSTAL SERVICE
Hispanic Program-New York Metro Area
142-02 20th Ave., # 318
Flushing, NY 11351-0600
(718) 321-5806 Fax: (718) 321-7149
Guillermina C. Colón (Gigi), Prog. Spec.

UNITED STATES-MEXICO CHAMBER OF
COMMERCE
Northeast Chapter
335 Madison Ave., 4th Floor
New York, NY 10017
(212) 949-0601 Fax: (212) 949-0603
Jorge Suárez-Vélez, President
Email: usmcoc@erols.com
Web: www.usmcoc.org

URBAN HEALTH PLAN, INC.
1070 Southern Blvd.
Bronx, NY 10459
(718) 991-4833 Fax: (718) 589-4793
Paloma Hernández, President & CEO
Email: cu9376@aol.com

VENEZUELAN-AMERICAN ASSOCIATION
OF U.S., INC.
National Headquarters
30 Vesiy St., #506
New York, NY 10038
(212) 233-7776 Fax: (212) 233-7779
Alfredo González, President
Web: www.venezuelanamerican.org

VICTIM SERVICES
336 Fort Washington Ave., #1G
New York, NY 10033
(212) 740-7446
Alida Camacho, Director

VIDA FAMILY SERVICES, INC.
127 E 105th St.
New York, NY 10029
(212) 289-1004 Fax: (212) 427-3433
Sheela Harrington, CEO

VOLUNTEER LAWYERS FOR THE ARTS
1 E. 53rd St., 6th Floor
New York, NY 10022
(212) 319-2910
Amy Schwartzman, Executive Director

WALL STREET CHAPTER OF IMAGE
National Image, Inc.
P. O. Box 3
New York, NY 10163
(718) 234-3863
Linda Salavaria, Pres.

WASHINGTON HEIGHTS CHILD CARE
610-614 W. 175th St.
New York, NY 10033
(212) 781-6910 or (212) 781-2472
Fax: (212) 781-2472
Nettie Hill, Executive Director

WESTCHESTER HISPANIC CHAMBER OF
COMMERCE
171 E. Post Rd., #201
White Plains, NY 10601
(914) 328-7181 Fax: (914) 681-1978
Felix Sánchez, President

WESTCHESTER HISPANIC COALITION
46 Waller Ave.
White Plains, NY 10605
(914) 948-8466 Fax: (914) 948-0311
Graciela Heymann, Executive Director
Email: whc10601@aol.com

WESTERN NEW YORK HISPANICS &
FRIENDS CIVIC ASSOCIATION
429 W. Delavan Ave.
Buffalo, NY 14213
(716) 885-6533 Fax: (716) 859-1409
Andrés García, President
Email: garcia@worldnet.att.net

WILDCAT SERVICE CORPORATION
17 Battery Pl., 1st Floor
New York, NY 10004
(212) 209-6000 or (212) 209-6001
Amelia V. Betanzos, President & CEO
Email: villamanol@wildcatatwork.org
Web: www.wildcat-at-work.org

WOMEN'S COMMUNITY HEALTH CLINIC
975 Westchester Ave.
Bronx, NY 10454
(718) 991-9250 Fax: (718) 991-3829
Dr. Freddie Molano, Center Director

WOMEN'S MEDICAL CENTER, INC.
2115 Chili Ave.
Rochester, NY 14624
(716) 247-0640 or (716) 275-8061
Fax: (716) 247-0755
Constantino Fernández, Director
Email: constantino-
fernandez@urme.rochester.edu

WOMEN'S PRISON ASSOCIATION
110 2nd Ave.
New York, NY 10003
(212) 674-1163 Fax: (212) 677-1981
Ann Jacobs, Executive Director

NORTH CAROLINA

ALIANZA
P.O. Box 1531
Pittsboro, NC 27312
(919) 542-6644 ext.12 Fax: (919) 542 0902
Florence Siman, Coordinator
Email: latinoprogram_ccn@juno.com

THE BUSINESS DEVELOPMENT GROUP
Raleigh/Durham/Charlotte Minority
Business Development Center
200 N. College St., Suite 2040
Charlotte, NC 28202
(704) 372-9412 Fax: (704) 372-9417
Srideep Patnaik, Dir.
Email: charlottembdc@ibm.net

CAROLINA HISPANIC ASSOCIATION
University of North Carolina, Chapel Hill
Box 25 FPG Student Union, Campus Box 5210
Chapel Hill, NC 27514
(919) 962-5299 Fax: (919) 962-7236
Chris Agosto, President

CASA INTERNACIONAL
322 Hawthorne Ln.
Charlotte, NC 28204
(704) 333-8099 Fax: (704) 334-2423
José Hernández París, Executive Director
Web: www.ihclt.org

CATHOLIC HISPANIC MINISTRIES
715 Nazareth St.
Raleigh, NC 27606-2187
(919) 821-9764 Fax: (919) 821-9705
Teresa Aldahondo, Coordinator

CATHOLIC SOCIAL MINISTRIES
Cape Fear Regional Office
4006 Princess Place Dr.
Wilmington, NC 28405
(910) 251-8130 Fax: (910) 251-8491
Diane Pisczek, Director
Email: csrhaf@raldisc.org

CATHOLIC SOCIAL SERVICES
1123 South Church St.
Charlotte, NC 28203-4003
(704) 370-3228 Fax: (704) 370-3377
Elizabeth Thurbee, Exec. Director
Web: www.cssnc.org

50 Orange St.
Asheville, NC 28801
(828) 255-0146 or (828) 255-0146
Fax: (828) 253-7339
Jerry Tudela, Director
Email: latino@cssnc.org
Web: www.cssnc.org

CENTRO HISPANO
201 W Main St., #100
Durham, NC 27701
(919) 687-4635 Fax: (919) 687-0401
Iván Parra, Director
Email: elcentrohispano@mindspring.com
Web: www.centrohispano.org

CENTRO HISPANO/LATINO
222 Rowan St.
Fayetteville, NC 28301
(910) 486-1146 or (910) 822-2812
Fax: (910) 321-1495
Flora Santor, Director of the Board
Email: hlcenter@mindspring.com
Web: www.centrohispano.net/page49.html

COALICION LATINOAMERICANA/LATIN AMERICAN COALITION
322 Hawthorne Ln.
Charlotte, NC 28204
(704) 333-5447 Fax: (704) 333-2290
Teresa Vásquez McCullough, President
Email: latinamc@bellsouth.net

DIAMANTE, INC.
8004 Chadbourne Court
Raleigh, NC 27613
(919) 875-0551 or (919) 676-6628
Lizette Cruz-Watko, Executive Director

DIOCESE OF CHARLOTTE
Hispanic Affairs
2117 Shenandoah Ave.
Charlotte, NC 28205-6021

(704) 335-1281
Rev. Vincent Finnerty, CM, Dir. for Hispanic Ministry

DIOCESE OF CHARLOTTE
Hispanic Affairs
97 Haywood St.
Asheville, NC 28801
(828) 252-8826 Fax: (828) 252-8683
Sr. Mary Kay McDonald, MSBT, Hispanic Ministry
Email: mkaymsbt@juno.com

DIOCESE OF RALEIGH
Hispanic Affairs
715 Nazareth St.
Raleigh, NC 27606-2187
(919) 821-9738 Fax: (919) 821-9705
Rev. Roberto Keenan, Vicar/Dir. for Hispanic Ministry
Email: keenan@raldioc.org

EL PUEBLO, INC.
118 S Pearson St.
Raleigh, NC 27601
(919) 835-1525 Fax: (919) 835-1526
Andrea Bazán-Manson, Executive Director
Email: elpueblo@elpueblo.org
Web: www.elpueblo.org

EL VÍNCULO HISPANO
105 E. 2nd St.
Siler City, NC 27344
(919) 742-1448 Fax: (919) 742-1451
Ilana Dubester, Director
Email: hispaliason@chatham.net

FARMWORKER PROJECT
105 E. Main St., P.O. Box 352
Benson, NC 27504
(919) 894-7406 Fax: (919) 894-7406
Guadalupe Martínez, Administrator
Email: pdeta@aol. com

HELPING HANDS CENTER
107 E 2nd St.
Siler City, NC 27344
(919) 742-6100 Fax: (919) 742-9221
Rosa Sutton, Director

HISPANIC CHAMBER OF COMMERCE OF NORTH CAROLINA (HCCNC)
P.O. Box 14308
Research Triangle Park, NC 27709
(919) 806-2209 Fax: (919) 484-8575
Sandra Herrera-Rock, Executive Director
Web: www.ncneighbors.com/976

HISPANIC NATIONAL BAR ASSOCIATION
Region VI (NC, SC)
719 Sandridge Rd.
Charlotte, NC 28210
(704) 523-1113 Fax: (704) 523-2627
Georgia Jacquez Lewis, Regional President
Email: Madreabogada@aol.com
Web: www.hnba.com

HISPANIC TASK FORCE OF LEE CO.
P.O. Box 123, 711 Cathage St.
Sanford, NC 27330
(919) 775-5447 Fax: (919) 777-5295
Lucy Hurley, Executive Director

INTERNATIONAL HOUSE
322 Hawthorne Ln.
Charlotte, NC 28204
(704) 333-8099 Fax: (704) 334-2423
Linda Holland, Director
Email: ashea@international.charlotte.org

LA UNIDAD LATINA/LAMBDA UPSILON LAMBDA FRATERNITY, INC.
Rho Chapter, Duke University
Office of University Life
101-3 Bryan Center, Box 90834
Durham, NC 27708
(619) 684-4741 Fax: (619) 684-8395
Christopher Brandt, President
Web: www.duke.edu/web/lul

LATIN AMERICAN RESOURCE CENTER
P.O. Box 31871
Raleigh, NC 27622-1871
(919) 839-7200 Fax: (919) 839-7201
Aura Maas, Director
Web: www.thlarc.org

LATINAS PROMOVIENDO COMUNIDAD/ LAMBDA PI CHI SORORITY, INC.
Kappa Chapter, Duke University
Office of University Life
101-3 Bryan Center, Box 90834
Durham, NC 27708
(619) 684-4741 Fax: (919) 684-8395

Jeannette Rodríguez, National Exec. Dir.
Web: www.duke.edu/web/lpc/home.html

LATINO STUDENT ASSOCIATION
Duke University, School of Law
P.O. Box 90360
Durham, NC 27708
(919) 613-7007 Fax: (919) 613-7231
Sonia Macias, President
Email: sonia_macias@law.duke.edu
Web: www.law.duke.edu/student/act/latino.html

MI CASA SU CASA CENTRO DE RECURSOS
1460 & 1062 Columbia Rd.
Charlotte, NC 28205
(704) 536-9845 Fax: (704) 536-9876
Christina La Paz, Front Desk Director
Email: micasa@dasia.net

MI GENTE, ASOCIACIÓN DE ESTUDIANTES LATINOS
Duke University
Office of University Life
101-3 Bryan Center, Box 90834
Durham, NC 27708
(919) 684-4741 Fax: (919) 684-8395
Milagros Hill, Co-President
Email: dukemigente@hotmail.com
Web: www.duke.edu/web/migente

NORTH CAROLINA SOCIETY OF HISPANIC PROFESSIONALS (NCSHP)
109 Conner Dr., #2200
Chapel Hill, NC 27514
(919) 932-1924 Fax: (919) 967-8637
Dr. Fernando Rodríguez, President
Email: mailbox@TheNCSHP.org
Web: www.TheNCSHP.org

OFFICE OF CITIZENS SERVICES
2012 Mail Service Center
Raleigh, NC 27699-2012
(919) 733-4261 or (800) 662-7030
Fax: (919) 715-3604
Leslie J. Mann, Director

RALEIGH/ DURHAM/ MINORITY BUSINESS DEVELOPMENT CENTER
205 Fayetteville St. Mall
Raleigh, NC 27601
(919) 833-6122 Fax: (919) 821-3572
Ned Harris, Executive
Web: www.denncorp.com

ST. JULIA CATHOLIC CHURCH
1002 West 3rd., St.
Siler City, NC 27344-0526
(919) 742-5584 Fax: (919) 742-5584
Daniel Quakenbush, Pastor

TELAMON CORPORATION
Angier Migrant Head Start Center 19
143 Fish Dr.
Angier, NC 27501
(919) 639-3319 Fax: (919) 639-3145
Rosa María Matthews, Director
Web: www.telamon.org

Hendersonville Head Start Center 13
2 Sugar Hill Dr.
Hendersonville, NC 28792
(828) 696-3407 or (828) 697-8266
Fax: (828) 697-9132
Shawn Wolff, Director
Web: www.telamon.org

North Carolina 12
P.O. Box 7074, 703 W. Nash St., #C
Wilson, NC 27893
(252) 291-1203 or (252) 291-9003
Fax: (252) 291-7165
Faye Lucas, Regional Manager
Email: flucas@fimflex.com
Web: www.telamon.org

North Carolina 2
P.O. Box 37, 216 North St.
Ahoskie, NC 27910
(252) 332-4381 Fax: (252) 332-3260
Brenda Chamblee, Regional Manager
Web: www.telamon.org

North Carolina Housing Office 14
P.O. Box 54
Goldsboro, NC 27533-0054
(919) 734-2378 Fax: (919) 734-6878
Donna Sharp, Project Developer
Web: www.telamon.org

North Carolina Office 11
P.O. Box 1626
Whiteville, NC 28472

(910) 642-8229 or (910) 642-7516
Fax: (910) 642-8555
Sonya Hall, Regional Manager
Web: www.telamon.org

North Carolina Office 18
P.O. Box 129
Prospect Hill, NC 27314
(336) 562-5737 Fax: (336) 562-5739
Denise Pierce, Director
Web: www.telamon.org

North Carolina Office 21
32 Stonegate Trail
Leicester, NC 28748
(828) 683-6822 Fax: (828) 683-6823
Mary Bradford, Regional Coordinator
Web: www.telamon.org

North Carolina Office 22
5300 Foxfire Rd.
Fayetteville, NC 28303
(910) 826-1185 Fax: (910) 826-1027
Karina Fonseca, Regional Coordinator
Web: www.telamon.org

North Carolina Office 3
P.O. Box 1668
Clinton, NC 28328
(910) 592-1919 or (910) 592-2161
Fax: (910) 592-5282
Michael Dunn, Regional Manager
Web: www.telamon.org

North Carolina Office 4
20 Hannah Grace Way
Hendersonville, NC 28792
(828) 692-0593 Fax: (828) 692-0282
Jairo Mercado-Estay, Regional Manager
Web: www.telamon.org

North Carolina Office 6
302 E. Church St.
Benson, NC 27504
(919) 207-5813 or (919) 207-1491
Fax: (919) 207-1914
Enrique Torres, Regional Manager
Email: etorres@interstar.net
Web: www.telamon.org

North Carolina Office 7
220 Wintergreen Dr., #F
Lumberton, NC 28358
(910) 671-0504 Fax: (910) 671-0190
Margie Atkinson, Regional Manager
Email: 2nikki@interstar.net
Web: www.telamon.org

North Carolina Office 9
801 E. Broad St.
Rockingham, NC 28379
(910) 997-5541 Fax: (910) 997-5610
Elaine Gibson, Regional Manager
Web: www.telamon.org

North Carolina State Office
4917 Waters Edge Dr., #220
Raleigh, NC 27606
(919) 851-6141 Fax: (919) 851-2605
Thom Myers, State Director
Web: www.telamon.org

St. Martin Migrant Head Start Center 17
3201 Easy St.
Dunn, NC 28334
(910) 567-5510 Fax: (910) 567-5519
Josephine Lorenzo, Director
Web: www.telamon.org

Telamon Corporate Office
P.O. Box 33315, 3937 Western Blvd.
Raleigh, NC 27636-3315
(919) 851-7611 Fax: (919) 851-1139
Richard A. Joanis, Executive Director
Web: www.telamon.org

Yanceyville Migrant Head Start Center 20
P.O. Box 819
Yanceyville, NC 27379
(336) 694-7096 Fax: (336) 694-7259
Linda Fuller, Director
Web: www.telamon.org

UNITED WAY OF CENTRAL CAROLINAS, INC.
301 South Brevard St.
Charlotte, NC 28202
(704) 377-1100 Fax: (704) 342-4482
Gloria King, Director
Web: www.uwcentralcarolinas.org

WILIMINGTON HISPANIC CHAMBER OF COMMERCE
1514B Cameron Ct.
Wilmington, NC 28401
(910) 392-3040 Fax: (910) 313-0587
Fernando Trulin, President

NORTH DAKOTA

DIOCESE OF BISMARCK
Hispanic Ministry Office
P.O. Box 1575
Bismarck, ND 58502-1575
(701) 223-1347 Fax: (701) 223-3693
Joanne Graham, OSB

DIOCESE OF FARGO
Hispanic Affairs
P.O. Box 1750, 1310 Broadway
Fargo, ND 58107
(701) 256-4636 Fax: (701) 235-0296
Rev. James Geoffrey, Coord. for Hispanic
Ministry

MIGRANT LEGAL SERVICES
North Dakota Office
118 Broadway, #305
Fargo, ND 58102
(701) 232-8872 Fax: (701) 232-8366
Charles Vaala, Supervisor

OHIO

**ADVOCATES FOR BASIC LEGAL
EQUALITY, INC. (ABLE)**
740 Spitzer Bldg., 520 Madison Ave.
Toledo, OH 43604
(800) 837-0814 Fax: (419) 259-2880
Joe Tafelski, Executive Director

**AKRON PUBLIC SCHOOLS/FOREIGN
LANGUAGES**
Division of Curriculum & Instruction
65 Steiner Ave.
Akron, OH 44301-1392
(330) 761-1661 Fax: (330) 761-3114
Michael Hauber, Coordinator
Web: www.akronschools.com

ALMA DE MEXICO
4603 Willow Ave.
Lorain, OH 44055
(440) 277-4676
Consuela Villa, Teacher

ALPHA PSI LAMBDA, INC.
Ohio State University
Office of Student Activities
218 Ohio Union, 1739 N. High St.
Columbus, OH 43210-1392
(614) 292-8763 or (614) 299-2532
Fax: (614) 292-6061
Damián Ayala, President
Web: http://alpha-psi-lambda.org

ARCHDIOCESE OF CINCINNATI
Hispanic Ministries Office
2900 W. Galbraith Rd.
Cincinnati, OH 45239
(513) 521-8440 Fax: (513) 521-7221
Rev. William J. Jansen, MCCJ
Email: wjanmccj@fuse.net

ARCHDIOCESE OF CINCINNATI
Hispanic Ministry Office St. Charles
115 W. Seymour Ave.
Cincinnati, OH 45216
(513) 761-1588 Fax: (513) 761-9538
Rev. Joseph Nelson
Email: joenels@juno.com

**CATHOLIC CHARITY SERVICES OF
CUYAHOGA COUNTY**
Affiliate of NCLR
2012 West 25th St., #507
Cleveland, OH 44113
(216) 631-3499 Fax: (216) 696-2088
Bamonita Rodríguez Johnson, Director
Email: hisctr25@mail.cle.dioc.org

CATHOLIC SOCIAL SERVICES
7800 Detroit Ave.
Cleveland, OH 44102
(216) 631-3499 or (216) 696-6525
Fax: (216) 631-3654
David Mordarsky, Director

**CENTRAL OHIO HISPANIC CHAMBER OF
COMMERCE**
92 N. Woods Blvd.
Columbus, OH 43235
(614) 431-1500 Fax: (614) 431-3885
John Pérez, President

CINCINNATI LATIN ARTS SOCIETY
8052 Surrey Brook Pl.

West Chester, OH 45069
(513) 777-1603
Karol Marchevsky, Director
Email: kmarchevsky@cinci.rr.com

**CITY OF DAYTON - BUREAU OF
CULTURAL AFFAIRS**
216 N. Main St.
Dayton, OH 45402
(937) 223-2489 Fax: (937) 223-0795
Pamela Harrington, Artist Curator

CLEVELAND STATE UNIVERSITY
Office of Minority Affairs & Community
Relations
1860 East 22nd Street, Rt. 1227
Cleveland, OH 44114-4435
(216) 523-7421 or (216) 687-9394
Fax: (216) 687-5442
Lisa R. Elliott, Communications Coordinator
Email: lr.elliott@popmail.csuohio.edu

**COALITION FOR HISPANIC ISSUES AND
PROGRESS (CHIP)**
P.O. Box 614
Lorain, OH 44052
(440) 934-5909
Frank Jacinto, President

COAR PEACE MISSION
4395 Rocky River Dr.
Cleveland, OH 44135
(216) 252-5572 Fax: (216) 252-5573
Melissa Acierno, Contact

**COLUMBUS MINORITY CONTRACTORS
AND BUSINESS ASSISTANCE PROGRAM**
1000 Eastmain St.
Columbus, OH 43205
(614) 252-8005 Fax: (614) 258-9661
Frank Watson, President

**COMMISSION ON CATHOLIC
COMMUNITY ACTION**
Affiliate of NCLR
1027 Superior Ave. NE #140
Cleveland, OH 44114-2565
(216) 696-6525 Ext. 4050 Fax: (216) 696-3923
Leonard Calabrese, Executive Director

CSU HISPANIC AWARENESS COMMITTEE
Minority Affairs
1860 E. 22nd. St. Rhodes Tower Room 1227
Cleveland, OH 44115
(216) 687-9394 Fax: (216) 687-5442
Maritza L. Pérez, Multicultural Prog. Coord.
Email: m.lperrea@csuohio.edu
Web: www.csuohio.edu

CUBAN ASSOCIATION OF DAYTON, INC.
1846 Quail Hollow Rd.
Dayton, OH 45459
(937) 434-3523 Fax: (937) 434-3683
Olga Maristany Basham, Vice President
Email: obasham@aol.com

DIOCESE OF CLEVELAND
Hispanic Ministry Office
1031 Superior Ave.
Cleveland, OH 44114
(216) 696-6525 x2530 Fax: (216) 696-6243
Sr. Alicia Alvarado, OP
Email: aalvarado@dioceseofcleveland.org

DIOCESE OF COLUMBUS
Hispanic Ministry Office
256 E. Rich St.
Columbus, OH 43215-5223
(614) 469-9178
Ms. Aida Barroso

DIOCESE OF STEUBENVILLE
Hispanic Ministry Office
P.O. Box 969
422 Washington St.
Steubenville, OH 43952-5969
(740) 282-3631 Fax: (740) 282-3327
Linda A. Nichols, Contact
Email: lnichols@diosteub.org

DIOCESE OF TOLEDO
Hispanic Affairs
P.O. Box 985
1933 Spielbusch
Toledo, OH 43697-0985
(419) 244-6711 x 294 Fax: (419) 244-4791
Elena Caballero, Director for Hispanic Ministry
Email: ecaballero@toledodiocese.org

DIOCESE OF TOLEDO
Ministerial Leadership Formation
1933 Spielbusch
Toledo, OH 43697-0985

(419) 244-6711 Fax: (419) 244-4791
Alfredo Díaz
Email: adiaz@toledodiocese.org

DIOCESE OF YOUNGSTOWN
Hispanic Ministry Office
144 W. Wood St.
Youngstown, OH 44503
(216) 744-8451 Fax: (216) 744-2848

EL BARRIO
2001 W. 65th St.
Cleveland, OH 44102
(216) 281-0109 Fax: (216) 281-6465
Nelson Bardecio, Director

EL CENTRO DE SERVICIOS SOCIALES, INC.
Affiliate of NCLR
1888 E. 31st St.
Lorain, OH 44055
(440) 277-8235 Fax: (440) 277-9236
Crystell Ivonne Llado, Executive Director

EL CENTRO DE SERVICIOS SOCIALES, INC.
Youth Center
1910 E. 28th St.
Lorain, OH 44055
(440) 277-4711 Fax: (440) 277-9236
Crystell Ivonne Llado, Executive Director

ESPERANZA, INC.
4115 Bridge Ave. #107
Cleveland, OH 44113
(216) 651-7178 Fax: (216) 651-7183
Joanne Bailis, Interim Director

**FARM LABOR RESEARCH PROJECT - FARM
LABOR ORGANIZING COMMITTEE**
Affiliate of NCLR
1221 Broadway St.
Toledo, OH 43609-2007
(419) 243-3456 Fax: (419) 243-5655
Baldemar Velásquez, Director
Email: info@floc.com
Web: www.floc.com

**GOLDEN ACRES MIGRANT MINISTRANT
CENTER**
8365 State Rd., #202
Tipp City, OH 45371-9471
(937) 667-5145 or (937) 879-5072
Fax: (937) 879-5072
Philip Morones, President
Email: pmorones@gte.net

**GREATER DAYTON HISPANIC CHAMBER
OF COMMERCE**
1045 E. Centerville Station Rd.
Centerville, OH 45459
(937) 433-0252 Fax: (937) 433-5032
Alexander Luque, President

**HISPANIC ASSOCIATION OF LUCENT
TECHNOLOGIES EMLOYEES INC. (HISPA)**
PO Box 30141
Gahama, OH 43230
(614) 337-8138 Fax: (614) 337-0824
Hoverth A. Serrate, Pres.

HISPANIC BUSINESS ASSOC. OF OHIO
4115 Bridge Ave., #206
Cleveland, OH 44113
(216) 281-4422 Fax: (216) 281-4222
Ángel Guzmán, CEO
Email: hbahcco@aol.com

HISPANIC BUSINESS STUDENT ASSOC.
Ohio State Univ. Hispanic Student Svcs.
1739 N. Hight St., #311
Columbus, OH 43210
(614) 292-8763 or (614) 291-6459 (h)
Fax: (614) 292-2061
Evangelina Cantu, President
Email: cantu.7@osu.edu

**HISPANIC CHAMBER OF COMMERCE OF
GREATER CINCINNATI**
P.O. Box 2593
Cincinnati, OH 45201
(513) 929-2723 Fax: (513) 622-0133
Roberto P. Peraza, Chair.
Email: president@hispaniccccgc.com
Web: www.hispaniccccgc.com

HISPANIC COUNCIL OF UAW MEMBERS
1725 W. 42nd St.
Lorain, OH 44053
(440) 960-0481
Arsenio Rodríguez

**HISPANIC FUND-COMMUNITY
FOUNDATION OF GREATER LORAIN
COUNTY**
1865 North Ridge Rd., E., #A
Lorain, OH 44055
(440) 277-0142 Fax: (440) 277-6955
Frank Jacinto, Chairman
Web: www.cfglc.org

HISPANIC GRADUATE STUDENT ORG.
Ohio State University
Office of Student Services
218 Ohio Union, 1739 N. High St.
Columbus, OH 43210-1392
(614) 292-8763 Fax: (614) 292-6061
Zachary Shivanek, President

HISPANIC LAW STUDENTS ORGANIZATION
Ohio State University College of Law
1659 North High St.
Columbus, OH 43210
(614) 292-7750
Kathryn Northern, Director

HISPANIC NATIONAL BAR ASSOCIATION
935 W. Market St.
Akron, OH 44313
(330) 869-8700 Fax: (330) 869-4040
Duard Bradshaw, Vice President – Programs &
Committees
Email: Bradshaw@bkb-akron.com
Web: www.hnba.com

Region X (KY, OH, TN)
2795 Vandemark Rd.
Litchfield, OH 44253
(330) 722-4936 Fax: (330) 722-4936
Lillian Ortiz, Regional President
Email: lortiz@bright.net
Web: www.hnba.com

HISPANIC SENIOR CENTER
7800 Detroit Ave.
Cleveland, OH 44102
(216) 631-3599 Fax: (216) 631-3654
Ted Feliciano, Dir.

**HISPANIC URBAN MINORITY
ALCOHOLISM AND DRUG ABUSE
OUTREACH PROGRAM (HUMADAOP)**
Affiliate of NCLR
3305 W. 25th St.
Cleveland, OH 44109
(216) 459-1222 Fax: (216) 459-2696
Mr. Miguel Prieto, Executive Director
Email: humadaop@aol.com

**IGLESIA UNIDA DE CRISTO BUENAS
NUEVAS**
4401 Clark Avenue
Cleveland, OH 44102
(216) 961-9798
Edward Rivera-Santiago, Reverendo
Web: netministries.org/see/churches

IMAGE OF NW OHIO (TOLEDO)
National Image, Inc.
4022 Peak
Toledo, OH 43612
(419) 478-7350
Luciana Vargas, President
Web: www.nationalimageinc.org

**INTERNATIONAL FAMILY RESOURCE
CENTER**
Travelers Aid International of Greater
Cincinnati
707 Race St. #300
Cincinnati, OH 45202
(513) 721-7660 Fax: (513) 287-7604
Ernest J. Barbeau, Executive Director
Email: ifrc@fuse.net
Web: www.servingfamilies.com

LA ALIANZA IBEROAMERICANA
Case Western Reserve University
10900 Euclid Ave. Calvin Smith #105
Cleveland, OH 44106-7062
(216) 368-5230 Fax: (216) 368-8826
Judith Olson-Fallon, Educational Support
Services

**LA UNIÓN DE ESTUDIANTES LATINOS/
LATINO STUDENT UNION**
Bowling Green State Univ.
Student Service, #460
Bowling Green, OH 43403
(419) 372-8325 Fax: (419) 372-8322
Jesse Sandovao, President
Web: www.bgsu.edu/studentlife/organizations/
lsu/main.html

LATINS UNITED/LATINOS UNIDOS
706 South St. Clair Street
Toledo, OH 43602
(419) 255-5746
Joe Carmona, President

LORAIN COUNTY URBAN LEAGUE
401 Broad St., #205
Elyria, OH 44035
(440) 323-3364 Fax: (440) 323-5299
Wanda Dudak, Administrative Asst.
Email: wdudak@lcul.org

LORAIN URBAN MINORITY ALCOHOLISM AND DRUG ABUSE OUTREACH PROGRAM
Affiliate of NCLR
2314 Kelly Pl.
Lorain, OH 44052
(440) 246-4616 Fax: (440) 246-1997
Evelyn Claudio Vansant, Director

LOS LATINOS AND FRIENDS
Cleveland State University Student Life
1983 E. 24th St.
Cleveland, OH 44115
(216) 687-2000 or (216) 687-2262
Fax: (216) 687-5442
Maritza Pérez, Advisor
Email: m.l.perez@csuohio.edu

LOS UNIDOS
Lorain County Community College
1005 N. Abbe Rd.
Elyria, OH 44035
(440) 366-4036 Fax: (440) 365-6519
Elizabeth Escandon, President
Email: escandon00@hotmail.com

MEXICAN AMERICAN CITIZENS CLUB
2938 Randall St.
Lorain, OH 44052
(440) 934-5909
Pauleen García, President

MEXICAN MUTUAL SOCIETY
Covain-Ohio
1820 E 28th St.
Lorain, OH 44055
(440) 277-7375 Fax: (440) 322-6089
Joel Aredondo, President

MEXICO CLUB OF GREATER DAYTON
8365 State Route 202
Tipp City, OH 45371
(937) 667-5145 Fax: (937) 669-9996
Philip Morones, President
Email: pmorones@gte.net

NATIONAL ASSOCIATION OF HISPANIC JOURNALISTS (NAHJ)
Region 6
1801 Superior Ave.
Cleveland, OH 44114
(216) 999-4987 Fax: (216) 999-6366
Rosa María Santana, Region Director
Email: rsantana@plaind.com
Web: www.nahj.org

NATIONAL LATINO PEACE OFFICERS ASSOCIATION (NLPOA)
Ohio Chapter
P.O. Box 352442
Toledo, OH 43635
(877) 657-6200
Rolando I. Belmares, Chapter President
Email: nlpoaohio@hotmail.com
Web: www.nlpoa.com

THE NORD CENTER
6140 South Broadway
Lorain, OH 44053-3891
(440) 233-7232 Fax: (440) 233-5552
Dr. Rubén Ocasio, Director
Email: rocasio@nordcenter
Web: www.norcare.org

NORTHWESTERN OHIO COMMUNITY ACTION COMMISSION
1933 E. 2nd St.
Defiance, OH 43512
(419) 784-2150 Fax: (419) 782-5648
Deborah A. Gerken, Executive Director

OHIO COMMISSION ON HISPANIC/ LATINO AFFAIRS
77 S. High St., 18th Floor
Columbus, OH 43266-0323

(614) 466-8333 Fax: (614) 995-0896
Jeremy Marks, Liaison Officer
Email: jmarks_ochla@yahoo.com
Web: www.state.oh.us/spa/

OHIO COMMISSION ON SPANISH SPEAKING AFFAIRS
National Headquarters
77 S.High St., #18 Floor
Columbus, OH 43215
(614) 466-8333 Fax: (614) 644-8112
Nestor Colón, Chairman

OHIO HISPANIC COALITION
1966 Morser Rd.
Columbus, OH 43229
(614) 840-9934 Fax: (614) 840-9935
Julia Arbini-Carbonell, President
Email: ohio@juno.com

OHIO HISPANIC DEMOCRATIC ORG.
271 E. State St.
Columbus, OH 43215
(614) 221-6563 Fax: (614) 221-0721
Bill Demora, Political Director
Email: bdemora@ohiodems.org
Web: www.ohiodems.org

ORGANIZACIÓN CÍVICA Y CULTURAL HISPANA AMERICANA (OCCHA)
Affiliate of NCLR
10 South Fruit St.
Youngstown, OH 44506
(330) 744-1808 Fax: (330) 744-1953
Mary Isa Garayua, Executive Director
Email: occha01@sceinet.com

ORGANIZACIÓN DE LAS DAMAS LATINAS, INC.
2950 E. Main St.
Columbus, OH 43209
(614) 231-4744 Fax: (614) 231-6842
Cecilia Román Gerling, President
Email: cromangerling@webtv.net

QUEEN OF APOSTLES SCHOOL
235 Courtland Ave.
Toledo, OH 43609
(419) 241-7829 Fax: (419) 241-4180
Brenda Haynes, Principal

QUEST INTERNATIONAL
1984 Coffman Rd.
Newark, OH 43055-0566
(800) 446-2700 Fax: (740) 522-6580
Leslie Chastiain, Program Representative
Email: lesliec@quest.edu
Web: www.quest.edu

SOCIETY OF HISPANIC PROFESSIONAL ENGINEERS (SHPE)
Columbus Professional Chapter
1653 Bennigan Dr.
Hilliard, OH 43026-8160
(937) 645-6279 Fax: (937) 645-6157
Richard Velázquez, President
Email: richard@velazquez.org
Web: www.shpe.org

Northeast Ohio Professional Chapter
P.O. Box 81812
Cleveland, OH 44181-0812
(216) 433-3559
Adavelle Narváez, Chapter President
Web: www.shpe.org

SOUTH LORAIN COMMUNITY DEVELOPMENT CORPORATION
P.O. Box 1351
Lorain, OH 44055
(440) 277-6142 Fax: (440) 277-7097
Rebecca Jones, Director
Email: rjslcdc@kelnet.com

SPANISH AMERICAN COMMITTEE FOR A BETTER COMMUNITY
Day Care Center
2357 Tremont Ave.
Cleveland, OH 44113
(216) 696-8275 Fax: (216) 623-3723
Emely Delgado-Colón, Executive Director
Email: sac4407@stratos.net
Web: www.spanamericancommittee.org

Main Office
4407 Lorain Ave.
Cleveland, OH 44113
(216) 961-2100 Fax: (216) 961-3305
Emely Delgado-Colón, Executive Director
Email: sac4407@stratos.net
Web: www.spanamericancommittee.org

ST. BERNARD HISPANIC COMMUNITY
St. Bernard Parish
44 University Ave.
Akron, OH 44308-1609
(330) 253-5364 Fax: (330) 253-6949
Sister Catherine, Parish Minister
Email: stbernardchurch@aol.com

TOGETHER, ORGANIZED, DILIGENTLY, OFFERING SOLIDARITY
Ohio State University
1800 Cannon Dr., 5th Floor
Columbus, OH 43210
(614) 292-8889
Shannon González, Director

UNITED STATES-MEXICO CHAMBER OF COMMERCE
Great Lakes Chapter/Ohio
200 Tower City Center ,50 Public Square
Cleveland, OH 44113-2291
(216) 621-3300 or (216) 592-2446
Fax: (216) 687-6788
Laura Kraus, Representative

VICE CONSULATE OF SPAIN FOR OHIO
2605 Burnet Ave.
Cincinnati, OH 45219
(513) 961-3737 Fax: (513) 221-1097
Sidney Louis Kaufman, Vice-Consul

WOMEN'S CENTER OF GREATER CLEVELAND
6209 Storer Ave.
Cleveland, OH 44102
(216) 651-1450 Fax: (216) 651-4351
Mary Jane Chichester, Executive Dir.
Email: mpower@womensctr.org
Web: www.wormensctr.org

OKLAHOMA

AMERICAN GI FORUM OF THE U.S.
1016 Chalmers
Altus, OK 73521-2826
(580) 482-0515
Cecilia Rodrigues, Nat'l. Vice Chairwoman

712 E. Pecan
Altus, OK 73521
(580) 477-0311 (h)
Ana Maria Ortiz, Nat'l Youth Chair

1016 Chalmers
Altus, OK 73521-2826
(580) 482-0515
Perfecto Rodrigues, National Vice-Commander

ARCHDIOCESE OF OKLAHOMA CITY
Hispanic Affairs
P.O. Box 32180
Oklahoma City, OK 73123
(405) 728-3561 Fax: (405) 721-5210
Sr. Elsa Galdeano, Director for Hispanic Ministry

ASSOCIATION OF AMERICAN INDIAN PHYSICIANS
1225 Sovereign Row # 103
Oklahoma City, OK 73108
(405) 946-7072 Fax: (405) 946-7651
Margaret Knight, Director
Email: aaip@ionet.net

COALITION OF LATIN AMERICAN (HUMAN & CIVIL) RIGHTS ADVOCATES
3015 NW 31st St.
Oklahoma City, OK 73112
(405) 943-8684
Iris Santos Rivera, Coordinator

DIOCESE OF TULSA
Hispanic Affairs
1541 E. Newton Pl.
Tulsa, OK 74106
(918) 584-2424 Fax: (918) 584-2421
Rev. Patricio Brankin, Dir. for Hispanic Ministry

GREATER TULSA HISPANIC CHAMBER OF COMMERCE
10802 E. 31st St., #A
Tulsa, OK 74147
(918) 664-5326 Fax: (918) 384-0096
Robert Tobías, President & CEO
Email: hispanicchamber@aol.com
Web: www.tulsahispanicchamber.com

HISPANIC AMERICAN FOUNDATION
Oklahoma Chapter
P.O. Box 472114

Tulsa, OK 74147
(918) 461-1162 Fax: (918) 250-1189
Sebastián Lantos, Executive Director
Email: haftulsa@worldnet.att.net
Web: www.webtek.com/hispanicamerican

HISPANIC STUDENT ASSOCIATION
Oklahoma State University, 060 Student Union
Stillwater, OK 74078
(405) 744-6482
Howard Shipp, Coordinator

LATINO COMMUNITY DEV. AGENCY
420 SW 10th St.
Oklahoma City, OK 73109-5610
(405) 236-0701 Fax: (405) 236-0773
Patricia B. Fennell, Executive Director
Email: latinoag@juno.com

LEAGUE OF UNITED LATIN AMERICAN CITIZENS (LULAC)
Southwest Region-OK
2524 Southwest, 125th St.
Oklahoma City, OK 73170
(405) 736-2036 or (405) 692-1618 (h)
Fax: (405) 692-7793
Antonio Borrego, Jr., State Dir.
Web: www.lulac.org

OKLAHOMA RURAL OPPORTUNITIES DEVELOPMENT CORPORATION (ORO)
Affiliate of NCLR
5929 N. May Ave., #204
Oklahoma City, OK 73112
(405) 840-7077 Fax: (405) 848-7871
José Angel Gómez, Executive Director

SER OKLAHOMA, INC.
Affiliate of SER-Jobs for Progress National, Inc.
10802 E. 31st St., #A
Tulsa, OK 74147
(918) 664-5326 Fax: (918) 384-0096
Julián Rodríguez, Chairman
Email: seroklahoma@aol.com
Web: www.sernational.org

OREGON

ARCHDIOCESE OF PORTLAND IN OREGON
Hispanic Ministry Office
2838 E. Burnside St.
Portland, OR 97214
(503) 233-8325 Fax: (503) 234-2545
Raúl Velázquez, Director
Email: rvelazquez@archdpdx.org

CENTRO CULTURAL CESAR CHAVEZ
Oregon State Univ. Campus
1969 A St.
Corvalis, OR 97331
(541) 737-3790 Fax: (541) 737-7504
Cessa Heard Johnson, Executive Director
Email: ccc@mu.orst.edu

CENTRO HISPANO OF SOUTHERN OREGON
Affiliate of NCLR
229 W. Main St., #3
Medford, OR 97501
(541) 772-7760 Fax: (541) 772-7611
María Aranda, President
Email: chso@mindspring.com

CENTRO LATINOAMERICANO
944 West 5th St.
Eugene, OR 97402
(541) 687-2667 Fax: (541) 687-7841
Carmen Bauer, Executive Director
Email: centrola@efn.org

DIOCESE OF BAKER
Hispanic Ministry Office
P.O. Box 5999
Bend, OR 97708
(541) 388-4004 Fax: (541) 385-8879

DIOCESE OF PORTLAND IN OREGON
Hispanic Affairs
P.O. Box 644, N. 10th and Adair St.
Cornelius, OR 97113
(503) 359-0304 Fax: (503) 992-8634
Rev. Mark Cach, Vicar for Hispanic Ministry
Email: mcach@archgdpdx.org

FOREST GROVE CITY LIBRARY
2114 Pacific Ave.
Forest Grove, OR 97116
(503) 359-3247 Fax: (503) 359-3201
Colleen Winters, Director

HISPANIC METROPOLITAN CHAMBER OF OREGON
2402 NE, Oregon St.
Portland, OR 97232-2329
(503) 222-0280 Fax: (503) 292-0709
Gale Castillo, President
Email: hmcc@uswest.net
Web: www.hmccoregon.com

IMAGE DE WASHINGTON COUNTY
Nation Image, Inc.
1720 Sequoia Court
Forest Grove, OR 97116
(503) 359-8134 x277 (W) Fax: (503) 359-2560
Kathy Rodríguez, State Pres./Chapter Pres.
Email: Krod@teleport.com

LATIN AMERICAN TRADE COUNCIL OF OREGON (LATCO)
P. O. Box 9
Lake Oswego, OR 97034
(503) 292-0107 Fax: (503) 292-2919
Jene Borstael, Representative
Email: info@latco.org
Web: http://www.latco.org/

MANA - A NATIONAL LATINA ORGANIZATION
Oregon Chapter
3009 NE, 70th St.
Portland, OR 97213
(503) 248-3999 ext. 28814
Linda Castillo, Chapter President
Email: hermana2@aol.com
Web: www.hermana.org

NATIONAL IMAGE, INC.
Image State of Oregon
1720 Sequoia Crt.
Forest Grove, OR 97116
(503) 359-8134 Ext. 277 (W)
Fax: (503) 359-2560
Kathy Rodríguez, Chapter President
Email: Krod@teleport.com
Web: www.nationalimageinc.org

NIKE HISPANIC NETWORK
Nike Inc.
One Bowerman Dr.
Beaverton, OR 97005
(503) 671-6453 Fax: (503) 671-6306
Vance Muñoz, Chair

NORTH WEST REGIONAL OFFICE
2838 E. Burnside St.
Portland, OR 97214-1895
(503) 233-8338 Fax: (503) 234-2545
Tadeo Saenz
Email: tsaenz@archdpdx.org

OREGON COMMISSION ON HISPANIC AFFAIRS
Public Service Building - 255 Capitol St. NE
Salem, OR 97310
(503) 378-2422 ext.415 Fax: (503) 378-5511
Christopher Santiago Williams, Exec. Dir.
Email: hispanic.affairs@gte.net
Web: www.blworld.net\ocoha

OREGON COUNCIL FOR HISPANIC ADVANCEMENT (OCHA)
108 NW 9th Ave., #201
Portland, OR 97209
(503) 228-4131 or (503) 248-5936
Fax: (503) 228-0710
Carlos Vega-Cortés, Information & Referral Spec.
Email: info@ocha-nw.org
Web: www.ocha-nw.org

OREGON HUMAN DEVELOPMENT CORP.
Hillsboro Ayuda
448 S. 1st St., #100
Hillsboro, OR 97123-3905
(503) 640-5223 Fax: (503) 844-6585
Carmen García, Director

Hillsboro-Region 10
1049 SW Baseline-E500
Hillsboro, OR 97123-3858
(503) 640-5496 Fax: (503) 640-9416
Guadalupe Flores, Counselor

Hispanic Access Center
1715 E. Burnside
Portland, OR 97214-1531
(503) 236-9670 Fax: (503) 236-9671
Oscar Sweeten López, Director

Klamath Falls-Region 30
829 Klamath Ave.
Klamath Falls, OR 97601-6162
(541) 883-7186 Fax: (541) 883-7187
Norman Fitzgerald, Office Manager

National Headquarters
Central Administration
9620 SW, Barbur Blvd., #110
Portland, OR 97219-6000
(503) 245-2600 Fax: (503) 245-9602
Ron Hauge, Executive Director

Ontario-Region 60
2880 SW, 4th Ave., #8
Ontario, OR 97914-1874
(541) 881-1491 Fax: (541) 881-1491
Laura Solis, ETC
Email: ohdcont@cmc.net
Woodburn-Region 20
476 N. 2nd St.
Woodburn, OR 97071-3938
(503) 982-5100 Fax: (503) 982-4837
Frances Alvarado, Emp. Training Counselor

Youth Center
233 SE, Washington St.
Hillsboro, OR 97123-3905
(503) 640-6442 Fax: (503) 640-0215
José Estrada, Youth Director

PINEROS Y CAMPESINOS UNIDOS DEL NORESTE PCUN (NORTHWEST TREEPLANTERS AND FARMWORKERS UNITED)
300 Young St.
Woodburn, OR 97071
(503) 982-0243 Fax: (503) 982-1031
Ramon Ramires, President
Email: farmworkerunion@pcun.org
Web: www.pcun.org

ROGUE VALLEY HISPANIC CHAMBER OF COMMERCE
1133 S. Riverside Ave., #7
Medford, OR 97501
(541) 779-7669 Fax: (541) 779-7669

SALUD MEDICAL CENTER
P.O. Box 66
Woodburn, OR 97071
(503) 982-2000 Fax: (503) 981-5839
Barbara Owens, Director

VALLEY HEALTH CARE, MIGRANT HEALTH CLINIC, NYSSA OFFICE
17 S 3rd. St.
Nyssa, OR 97913
(541) 372-5738 Fax: (541) 372-5732
Hugh Philips, Manager

THE WOODBURN PUBLIC LIBRARY
280 Garfield St.
Woodburn, OR 97071
(503) 982-5252 Fax: (503) 982-2808
Linda Sprauer, Director
Email: woodburn@ccrls.org
Web: www.ccrls.org/woodburn/

YAKIMA VALLEY FARMWORKERS CLINIC
595 NW 11th St.
Hermiston, OR 97838
(541) 567-1717 Fax: (541) 567-9662
Jim Galagher, Administrator

PENNSYLVANIA

ACADEMIA TIMOTEO (TIMOTHY ACADEMY)
2637 N. 4th St.
Philadelphia, PA 19133
(215) 423-0416
William Elliott, Head Master

AMERICAN CANCER SOCIETY
1626 Locus St.
Philadelphia, PA 19103
(215) 985-5400 Fax: (215) 871-5796
Rosa Ortiz, Program Specialist Special Population

AMPARO DE LA NIÑEZ INC.
P.O. Box 18338
111 E. Luray St.
Philadelphia, PA 19120
(215) 324-2919 Fax: (215) 324-4350
Felipe Castro, Executive Director

ARCHDIOCESE OF PHILADELPHIA
Hispanic Affairs
222 N. 17th St. 8th Fl.
Philadelphia, PA 19103-1299
(215) 587-3786 Fax: (215) 587-3561
Anna C. Vega, Director for Hispanic Ministry

ASOCIACIÓN CÍVICA Y CULTURAL DOMINICANA DE READING Y EL CONDADO DE BERKS / BERKS CIVIC & CULTURAL DOMINICAN ASSOC., INC.
P.O. Box 8632

1131 Butler St.
Reading, PA 19601
(610) 371-0137 Fax: (610) 478-0851
Moises O. Mañón-Rossi, President

ASOCIACIÓN DE MÚSICOS LATINOAMERICANOS (AMLA)
2726 N. 6th St.
Philadelphia, PA 19133
(215) 634-4150 Fax: (215) 223-3294
Jesse Bermúdez, Executive Director

ASOCIACIÓN DE PUERTORRIQUEÑOS EN MARCHA (APM)
National Headquarters
2147 N. 6th St.
Philadelphia, PA 19122
(215) 235-6788 Fax: (215) 232-9450
Jesús M. Sierra, Executive Director

ASPIRA OF PENNSYLVANIA, INC.
2726 N. 6th St.
Philadelphia, PA 19133
(215) 739-7488 Fax: (215) 739-7464
María Quiñones, Executive Director
Web: www.aspira.org/pennsylvania.html

BORINQUEN CREDIT UNION
629 W. Erie Ave.
Philadelphia, PA 19140
(215) 228-4180
Cynthia Cruz, Director

CARIBBEAN AND LATIN AMERICAN ASSOCIATION
University of Pittsburgh
4E04 Forbes Quad
Pittsburgh, PA 15260
(412) 648-7395
John Frechione, Director

CASA DEL CARMEN
4400 N. Reese St.
Philadelphia, PA 19140
(215) 329-5660 Fax: (215) 329-6722
Giovanni Morante, Director

CASA GUADALUPE CENTER
143 Linden St.
Allentown, PA 18102
(610) 435-9902 Fax: (610) 435-6792
Gloria T. Marshall, Executive Director

CATHOLIC CHARITIES
1431 Walnut St.
Lebanon, PA 17042
(717) 273-8514
Kurt Reider, Director

CATHOLIC CHARITIES/IMMIGRATION AND REFUGEE SERVICES
900 N. 17th St.
Harrisburg, PA 17103
(717) 232-0568
Norman Lederer, Program Director

CENTRO AMANECER
1102 Rising Sun Ave.
Philadelphia, PA 19140
(215) 223-0578
Allen Willis, Director

CENTRO DE SERVICIOS PARA HISPANOS
J.F.K. Community Mental Health
2742 N. 5th St.
Philadelphia, PA 19133
(215) 427-3400 Fax: (215) 427-3420

CENTRO PEDRO CLAVER
3565 N. 7th St.
Philadelphia, PA 19140
(215) 227-7111 Fax: (215) 227-7111
Roger Zepernick, Executive Director
Email: centro@libertynet.org
Web: www.libertynet.org/~centro/

CHOICE, INC.
1233 Locust St., 3rd Floor
Philadelphia, PA 19107
(215) 985-3355 Fax: (215) 985-2838
Trina Johnston, Executive Director
Email: info@choice-phila.org
Web: www.choice-phila.org

CHRISTIAN CHURCHES UNITED / LA CASA DE AMISTAD MINISTRY (CCU)
Affiliate of NCLR
P.O. Box 60750, Harrisburg, PA, 17106-0750
413 S. 19th Street
Harrisburg, PA 17104
(717) 236-3279 or (717) 230-9550
Fax: (717) 230-9554
Jacqueline Rucker, Executive Director

COMMUNITY LEGAL SERVICES
1424 Chestnut Street
Philadelphia, PA 19102
(215) 981-3700

CONCILIO DE VIVIENDA JUSTA MONTGOMERY COUNTY
PO Box 578
Glendside, PA 19038
(215) 576-7711 Fax: (215) 576-1509
Rene Langley, Director

CONGRESO DE LATINOS UNIDOS, INC.
719 W. Girard Ave.
Philadelphia, PA 19123
(215) 763-8870 Fax: (215) 763-7023
Wanda Mial, Executive Director

CONSORTIUM FOR LATINO HEALTH
121 S. Broad Street 20th Floor
Philadelphia, PA 19107
(215) 735-9695 Fax: (215) 790-1267
Luis Bonilla, Director

COUNCIL OF SPANISH SPEAKING ORGANIZATIONS, INC.
705-09 N. Franklin St.
Philadelphia, PA 19123
(215) 627-3100 Fax: (215) 627-7440
Roberto Santiago, Executive Director
Email: concilio@libertynet.org
Web: www.libertynet.org/concilio

COUNCIL OF SPANISH SPEAKING ORGANIZATIONS OF LEHIGH VALLEY, INC.
520 E. 4th St.
Bethlehem, PA 18015
(610) 868-7800 Fax: (610) 868-4096
Sis-Obed Torres Cordero, Executive Director
Email: cssolb@aol.com

COUNCIL OF SPANISH SPEAKING ORGANIZATIONS OF LEHIGH VALLEY, INC.
Latino AIDS Outreach Program
128 W. 4th St.
Bethlehem, PA 18015
(610) 861-6845 Fax: (610) 861-2947
Sandra Pedrosa, Regional Coordinator

CROSS ROADS COMMUNITY CENTER
2916-18 N 6th Street
Philadelphia, PA 19133
(215) 223-7897

DANZANTE
200 Crescent Dr.
Harrisburg, PA 17104
(717) 232-2615
Camille Erice, Executive Director

DELAWARE VALLEY COMMUNITY HEALTH, INC.
1412 Fairmont Ave.
Philadelphia, PA 19130
(215) 235-9600 Fax: (215) 232-4093
Scott Mc Neal, Medical Director

DELAWARE VALLEY HISPANIC CHAMBER OF COMMERCE
Rd-2 Box 263
425 6th Ave., #701
Olyphant, PA 15219
(412) 201-9140
Nelson Malave, Chairman

DIOCESE OF ALLENTOWN
Office of Hispanic Affairs
900 S. Woodward St.
Allentown, PA 18103-4179
(610) 289-4900 Fax: (610) 289-7917
Rev. George R. Winne, Director for Hispanic Ministry

DIOCESE OF ERIE
Hispanic Affairs
1237 W. 21 St.
Erie, PA 16502
(814) 459-0543
Rev. Jorge Villegas, Director for Hispanic Ministry

DIOCESE OF GREENSBURG
Hispanic Affairs
723 E. Pittsburgh St.
Greensburg, PA 15601
(724) 837-0901 Fax: (724) 837-0857

DIOCESE OF HARRISBURG
Hispanic Affairs
119 S. Prince St.
Harrisburg, PA 17603
(717) 392-258 Fax: (717) 394-6549

Rev. Bernard Pistone, Vicar for Hispanic Apostolate

DIOCESE OF PITTSBURGH
Hispanic Ministry Office
111 Blvd. of the Allies
Pittsburgh, PA 15222
(412) 456-3000

DIOCESE OF SCRANTON
Hispanic Affairs
300 Wyoming Ave.
Scranton, PA 18503
(570) 207-2213 Fax: (570) 207-5596
Martin Kearney, Director of Hispanic Ministry
Email: opm@epix.net

ESPERANZA HEALTH CENTER
1331 E. Wyoming Ave., Lower Level
Philadelphia, PA 19124
(215) 831-1100 Fax: (215) 631-0500
Bryan Hollinger, Medical Executive
Web: http://doctor.medscape.com/esperanza

FRIENDS NEIGHBORHOOD GUILD
704 W. Gerald St.
Philadelphia, PA 19123
(215) 923-1544
Phillip Fazah, Director

GAY AND LESBIAN LATINO AIDS EDUCATION INITIATIVE (GALAEI)
1233 Locust St. 3rd Floor
Philadelphia, PA 19107
(215) 985-3382 Fax: (215) 985-3388
David Acosta, Director
Web: www.critpath.org/galaei

GOVERNOR'S ADVISORY COMMISSION ON LATINO AFFAIRS
Department of Community Affairs
544 Forum Bldg.
Harrisburg, PA 17120
(717) 783-3877 or (800) 233-1407
Fax: (717) 705-0791
Dr. Maritza Robert, Executive Director
Email: mrobert@doc.state.pa.us

GREATER ERIE COMMUNITY ACTION COMMITTEE
18 W. 9th St.
Erie, PA 16501
(814) 459-4581 Fax: (814) 456-0161
Benjamin Wiley, Chief Executive Officer
Web: www.gecac.org

GREATER PHILADELPHIA HEALTH ACTION
Southeast Health Center
930 Washington Avenue
Philadelphia, PA 19147
(215) 339-5100 Fax: (215) 271-6835
Verónica López, Medical Case Manager
Web: www.gpha.org

HISPANIC AMERICAN CORRECTIONAL OFFICES ASSOCIATION
519-21 W. Erie Avenue
Philadelphia, PA 19140
(215) 226-5493

HISPANIC AMERICAN COUNCIL OF ERIE
554 E. 10th St.
Erie, PA 16503
(814) 455-0212 Fax: (814) 453-2363
Erika Freeman, Executive Director

HISPANIC AMERICAN ORGANIZATION, INC.
Affiliate of SER-Jobs for Progress, Inc.
136 S. 4th St.
Allentown, PA 18102
(610) 435-5334 Fax: (610) 435-2131
Lupe Piarce, Executive Director

Los Niños Learning Center
136 S. 4th St.
Allentown, PA 18102
(610) 435-3968 Fax: (610) 435-2131
Deemarie Mantille, Director

Los Niños Learning Center
511-513 Linden St.
Allentown, PA 18102
(610) 435-0355 Fax: (610) 435-2131
Deemarie Mantille, Director

HISPANIC ASSOCIATION OF CONTRACTORS & ENTERPRISES, INC.
167 W. Alligheny Ave.
Philadelphia, PA 19140
(215) 426-8025 Fax: (215) 426-9122
Guillermo Salas, President

Email: gsalas@hacecdc.org
Web: www.hacecdc.org

HISPANIC CENTER OF READING AND BERKS COUNTY, INC.
501 Washinton St., Lower Level
Reading, PA 19603
(610) 376-3748 Fax: (610) 372-2619
Jonathan Encarnacion, Executive Director
Email: centrohispano@usa.net

HISPANIC NATIONAL BAR ASSOCIATION
1515 Arch St., 17th Fl. – One Parkway
Philadelphia, PA 19102-1595
(215) 683-5003 Fax: (215) 683-5068
Kenneth I. Trujillo, Convention Co-Chair
Email: Kenneth.i.trujillo@phila.gov
Web: www.hnba.com

HISPANIC NATIONAL BAR ASSOCIATION
525 Delancey St.
Philadelphia, PA 19106
(215) 925-7711 Fax: (215) 925-7337
Laura Luna Trujillo, Convention Co-Chair
Email: LLTrujillo@aol.com
Web: www.hnba.com

HISPANIC OUTREACH PROGRAM
1012 Brock Dr.
Lebanon, PA 17046
(717) 273-8901 Fax: (717) 273-8942
Michael Barrett, Supervisor

HOGAR CREA DE PHILADELPHIA
2018 E. Cumberland Street
Philadelphia, PA 19125
(215) 739-1479 Fax: (215) 739-1558
David Bulgos, Director

HOGAR CREA, LANCASTER
26 Green St.
Lancaster, PA 17602
(717) 397-8633
Ceasar Gerena, Director

HOLY INFANCY
312 E. 4th St.
Bethlehem, PA 18015
(610) 866-1121 Fax: (610) 866-7094
Robert Biszek, Pastor

HOUSE OF COUNSELING AND INTEGRAL HEALTH, INC.
213 W. Allegheny Avenue
Philadelphia, PA 19133
(215) 634-3259 Fax: (215) 634-1234
Birma Montes, Executive Director

IGLESIA SINAI-ASAMBLEAS DE DIOS
2806-18 N. 5th Street
Philadelphia, PA 19133
(215) 229-1656
Rev.Sergio Martínez, President

IMAGE
National Image, Inc.
6391 Oxford Avenue PMB 128
Philadelphia, PA 19111
Rubén A. Filomeno, Regional Director
Email: rfilomeno@dscp/dia.mil
Web: www.nationalimageinc.org

IMAGE DE BUCKS COUNTY
National Image, Inc.
209 Westbury Drive
Warminster, PA 18974
(215) 674-4216
Ada Tuleja, Chap. Pres.
Web: www.nationalimageinc.org

IMAGE OF PENNSYLVANIA
National Image, Inc.
731 W. Rockland St.
Philadelphia, PA 19120
(215) 967-2356 Fax: (215) 967-2356
Víctor M. Vidal, State President
Web: www.nationalimageinc.org

IMAGE OF PHILADELPHIA
National Image, Inc.
6289 Kindred Street
Philadelphia, PA 19149
(215) 737-5738
Carlos Deno, President
Web: www.nationalimageinc.org

INCARNATION OF OUR LORD
5105 N. 5th St.
Philadelphia, PA 19120
(215) 329-2320 Fax: (215) 329-6149
Father John Halloran, Priest
Email: incarnation2000@hotmail.com

INSTITUTO INTERNACIONAL DE LITERATURA IBEROAMERICANA
University of Pittsburgh
1312 Cathedral of Learning
Pittsburgh, PA 15260
(412) 624-3359 Fax: (412) 624-0829
Mabel Morafia, Director
Email: iiili@pitt.edu
Web: www.pitt.edu/~iiili

KOINONIA CHRISTIAN MINISTRIES
The Spanish Health Ministry
205 E. State St.
Kennett Square, PA 19348
(610) 444-1972 Fax: (610) 444-8815
Dona J. Sensemig RN, Director

LATIN AMERICAN CULTURAL UNION
P.O. Box 19403
Pittsburgh, PA 15213
(412) 361-7633 Fax: (412) 396-5884
Brent Rondon, President
Email: lacus@geocities.com
Web: http://lacu.ctb.net

LATIN AMERICAN STUDENT ASSOC.
Penn State University
135A Boucke Building
University Park, PA 16802
(814) 865-6348 or (814) 238-5826
Juan Nino, Director

LATIN AMERICAN STUDIES ASSOCIATION
University of Pittsburgh
William Pitt Union, #946
Pittsburgh, PA 15260
(412) 648-7929 Fax: (412) 624-7145
Franklin Knight, President
Email: lasa+@pitt.edu

LATINA MOBILE PROJECT
2753 N. 5th Street
Philadelphia, PA 19133
(215) 739-8600 or (215) 972-0700
Fax: (215) 739-8604
JoAnne Fischer, Executive Director
Web: www.momobile.org

LATINO AMERICAN ALLIANCE OF NORTH EASTERN OF PENNSYLVANIA
East Stroudsburg University
1657 Hillside Dr.
Stroudsburg, PA 18560
(570) 422-3433 Fax: (717) 422-3918
Fernando Perez, CEO-SSS

LATINO CAUCUS
Pennsylvania State University
020 HUB / Robeson Center
University Park, PA 16802
(814) 865-3776 Fax: (814) 863-3820
Jennifer Hernández, President
Email: jxh315@psu.edu

LATINO CELEBRATION
Millersville University
Lyle Hall, P.O. Box 1002
Millersville, PA 17551
(717) 872-3258 Fax: (717)871-2632
Aída Ceara, Developmental Studies

LATINO HEALTH LITERACY PROJECT
311 S. Juniper Street Suite 308
Philadelphia, PA 19107-5803
(215) 546-4872 Fax: (215) 545-1345
Aracelli Rosales, Director

LATINO INSTITUTE FOR BEHAVIORAL HEALTH
Affiliate of Nueva Esperanza
855 E. Hunting Park Ave., 2nd Floor
Philadelphia, PA 19124
(215) 288-1907 Fax: (215) 288-4337
Ms. Fior Veras, Executive Director

LATINO LEADERSHIP ALLIANCE OF BUCKS COUNTY
227-229 Mill Street
Balstol, PA 19007
(215) 788-4452 Fax: (215) 788-4623
Gladys Mendieta, Executive Director

LEAGUE OF UNITED LATIN AMERICAN CITIZENS (LULAC)
Northeast Region-NJ
109 Oriole Drive
Swedesboro, PA 08085
(302) 791-4500 or (609) 467-4158
Fax: (302) 791-4511
Lew Muñoz, State Director

LEHIGH COUNTY CHAMBER OF COMMERCE
462 Walnut St.
Allentown, PA 18102-5497
(610) 437-9661 Fax: (610) 437-4907
T. Anthony Iannelli, President
Email: Lehighcc@fast.net
Web: www.lehighcountychamber.org

LIGHTHOUSE
152 W. Leahigh Ave.
Philadelphia, PA 19133
(215) 425-7800
Millie Mendez, Director

THE LITERACY COUNCIL OF LANCASTER-LEBANON
1 Cumberland St.
Lebanon, PA 17042
(717) 274-3461
Cathy Roth, Coordinator

LUDLOW SOCIAL SERVICE CENTER
1437 N. 7th St.
Philadelphia, PA 19122
(215) 232-1615 Fax: (215) 232-9519
Marvin Lewis, Director

LULAC-NATIONAL EDUCATIONAL SERVICES CENTER, INC. (LNESC)
119 E. Lehigh Ave.
Philadelphia, PA 19125
(215) 423-4811 Fax: (215) 423-4819
Colleen Davis, Director
Email: lnesc@liberty.org
Web: www.lulac.org

MANPOWER
1891 Santa Barbara Dr., #108
Lancaster, PA 17601
(717) 581-0700 Fax: (717) 581-3420
Lorraine McGill, Director
Email: loorraine.mcgill@na.manpower.com
Web: www.manpower.com

MARÍA DE LOS SANTOS CLINIC
452 W. Allgheny Ave.
Philadelphia, PA 19133
(215) 291-2500
Brenda Robles, Director

MAYOR'S COMMISSION ON PUERTO RICAN/LATINO AFFAIRS
City Hall, #143
Philadelphia, PA 19107
(215) 686-7598 Fax: (215) 686-2170
Manny Ortiz, Deputy Mayor
Email: Mac@phila.gov

MINORITY ARTS RESOURCE COUNCIL
1421 W. Girard Ave.
Philadelphia, PA 19130
(215) 236-2688 Fax: (215) 236-4255
Curtis E. Brown, Executive Director

MT. PLEASANT HISPANIC AMERICAN CTR.
301 S. 13th St.
Harrisburg, PA 17104
(717) 232-7691 Fax: (717) 233-7227
Lourdes Tanon, Director

NATIONAL ASSOCIATION FOR HISPANIC ELDERLY
Philadelphia Office/Project Ayuda
3150 N. Mascher St., #100
Philadelphia, PA 19133
(215) 426-1212 Fax: (215) 426-6313
Gladys M. Llevat, Project Coordinator

NATIONAL COALITION BUILDING INST.
1835 K St. NW, #715
Washington, PA 20006
(202) 785-9400 Fax: (202) 785-3385
Guillermo López, Jr., Latino Constituency Leader
Email: ncbilatins@aol.com

NATIONAL CONGRESS FOR PUERTO RICAN RIGHTS
Philadelphia Chapter
160 Lippincott St.
Philadelphia, PA 19133
(215) 425-6150
Priscilla Curet, Executive Director

NORRIS SQUARE CIVIC ASSOCIATION
149 W. Susquehanna Ave.
Philadelphia, PA 19122
(215) 426-8723 Fax: (215) 426-5822
Patricia De Carlo, Director

NORRIS SQUARE SENIOR CITIZEN CTR.
2121-37 N. Howard St.
Philadelphia, PA 19122
(215) 423-7241 Fax: (215) 634-7751
Carmen Contable, Director

**NORTH EAST COMMUNITY MENTAL
HEALTH CENTER**
2927 N. 5th St., 2nd Floor
Philadelphia, PA 19133
(215) 291-4357 Fax: (215) 426-6610
Melchor Martínez, President

NUEVA ESPERANZA, INC.
Affiliate of NCLR
4261 N.5th. St.
Philadelphia, PA 19140
(215) 324-0746 Fax: (215) 324-2542
Luis Cortés, Executive Director

**PENNSYLVANIA STATEWIDE LATINO
COALITION (PSLC)**
P.O. Box 7425
680 Topaz Drive
Lancaster, PA 17604-7425
(717) 431-2100 Fax: (717) 431-1824
Lilian Escobar-Haskins, Coordinator
Email: syntonic@epix.netwww2.epix.net/
~escobar/stateconf.html
Web: www2.epix.net/escobar/stateconf.html

PENSYLVANIA RURAL OPPORTUNITIES
1500 N 2nd St., #11
Harrisburg, PA 17102
(717) 234-6616 or (800) 692-7450
Fax: (717) 234-6692
Kay Washington, Director
Email: klaracu372@aol.com
Web: www.ruralinc.org

**PHILADELPHIA HISPANIC CHAMBER OF
COMMERCE (CCHP)**
2749 N. 5th St.
Philadelphia, PA 19133
(215) 425-PHCC Fax: (215) 425-3602
Judy Delgado, President
Email: phcc@@snip.net

PRIMERA IGLESIA CRISTIANA HISPANA
P. O. Box 467
Harrisburg, PA 17108-0467
(717) 233-1588 Fax: (717) 233-6828
Emilio Martínez, Pastor

PUERTO RICAN LATIN ASSOCIATION
804 Franklin St.
Reading, PA 19602
(610) 582-8728 Fax: (610) 582-8728
Eli Velásquez, President

**PUERTO RICO FEDERAL AFFAIRS
ADMINSTRATION**
2 Penn Center, #450, 15th & JFK Blvd.
Philadelphia, PA 19102
(215) 851-9930 or (215) 851-9931
Diana Roca, Regional Director

RAÍCES CULTURALES LATINOAMERICANAS
P.O. Box 80
Morton, PA 19070
(610) 328-6504 Fax: (610) 328-6504
Michael Esposito, President
Email: raicescult@aol.com

RAINBOW CHILD INTERNATIONAL (RCI)
P.O. Box 1180
Bryn Mawr, PA 19010
(610) 520-9937
Sandy Taylor, Founder & Director
Email: rainbow@pond.com
Web: www.rainbowchild.com

SACA DEVELOPMENT CORPORATION
Affiliate of NCLR
545 Pershing Ave.
Lancaster, PA 17602
(717) 293-4150 or (717) 397-6267
Fax: (717) 295-7762
José López, Program Director

SACRED HEART OF JESUS
336 N 4th St.
Allentown, PA 18102
(610) 434-5171 Fax: (610) 434-2441
Joseph R. Sobiesiak, Pastor

SALVATION ARMY
P.O. Box 60973
Philadelphia, PA 19133
(215) 739-2366 Fax: (215) 739-8509

**SIERVAS MISIONERAS DE LA SANTÍSIMA
TRINIDAD**
3501 Solly Ave.
Philadelphia, PA 19136
(215) 335-7550 Fax: (215) 335-7559
Bárbara DeMoranville, General Custodian

**SOCIETY OF HISPANIC PROFESSIONAL
ENGINEERS (SHPE)**
Carnegie Mellon University
5000 Forbes Ave., #125
Pittsburgh, PA 15213-3890
(412) 268-2150 Fax: (412) 268-1527
Pierre Ponce, President
Web: www.shpe.org

**Greater Philadelphia Professional
Chapter**
P.O. Box 1497
Philadelphia, PA 19105
(215) 652-4109 or (609) 877-1520 (h)
Fax: (609) 877-2738
Gregg Quiñones, Chapter President
Email: gregg_quinones@merck.com
Web: www.shpe-gpc.org/

SOUTH EAST HEALTH CENTER
930 Washington Ave.
Philadelphia, PA 19147
(215) 339-5100
Verónica López, Medical Case Manager

**SOUTHCENTRAL EMPLOYMENT
COOPERATION, (SEC)**
100 N. Cameron St. Rm 1st. Floor
Harrisburg, PA 17101-2428
(717) 236-7931 Fax: (717) 236-9016
Richard Kopecky, Executive Director

**SPANISH AMERICAN CIVIC
ASSOCIATION, INC.**
545 Pershing Ave.
Lancaster, PA 17602
(717) 397-6267 Fax: (717) 295-7762
Carlos Graupera, Director
Email: cegraupera@aol.com

ST. BONIFACE
174 W. Diamond St.
Philadelphia, PA 19122
(215) 739-6376 Fax: (215) 739-5102
Father McGillicuddy, Pastor

ST. FRANCIS OF ASSISI CHURCH
1439 Market St.
Harrisburg, PA 17103
(717) 232-1003 Fax: (717) 232-4436
Daniel Mitzel, Pastor

ST. JOHN BOSCO CHURCH
235 E. County Line Rd.
Hatboro, PA 19040
(215) 672-7280
Charles H. Hagan, Pastor
Web: www.stjohnbosco.org

ST. MARK
1025 Radcliffe St.
Bristol, PA 19007
(215) 788-2319 Fax: (215) 785-4121
Father Francis Lewis, Pastor

ST. PETER THE APOSTLE CHURCH
1019 N. 5th St.
Philadelphia, PA 19123
(215) 627-2386 Fax: (215) 627-3296
Father Joseph Tizio, Pastor
Web: www.stjohnneumann.org

ST. VERONICA'S RECTORY
533 W. Tioga St.
Philadelphia, PA 19140
(215) 225-5677 Fax: (215) 228-0381
Father Eduardo Coll, Pastor

TALLER PUERTORRIQUEÑO
2721 N. 5th St.
Philadelphia, PA 19133
(215) 426-3311 Fax: (215) 426-5682
Carmen Febo, Executive Director
Email: tallerprpuertorico@libertynet.org

YORK SPANISH AMERICAN CENTER
200 E. Princess St.
York, PA 17403
(717) 846-9434 Fax: (717) 843-5722
Alex Ramos, Director
Email: spanishcenter@yahoo.com

A.D.F.A.N., INC.
Aquamarina #54 Villa Blanca
Caguas, PR 00725
(787) 258-9690
Lizaide R. Rodrigues, Director

ABA (AMERICAN BAR ASSOCIATION)
Pontificia Universidad Católica de Puerto Rico
2250 Avenida Las Américas, #625
Ponce, PR 00717-0777
(787) 841-2000 ext. 324
Coral González, Vice Pres. of Student Affairs
Web: www.pucpr.edu

ACADEMIA DAILEN
Colinas Montas, San José #1
Utuado, PR 00641
(787) 894-1083
Daisy Rodríguez, Director

ACADEMIA INFANTIL AURIMAR
HC-02-Box 13413
San German, PR 00683
(787) 892-1901
Marianela Rosado, Director

ACADEMIA PENTECOSTAL BETHEL
P.O. Box 602
Mayaguez, PR 00681
(787) 832-3570 Fax: (787) 832-4542
María González, Director

ALBERGUE LA PROVIDENCIA, INC.
P.O. Box 10142
Ponce, PR 00731
(787) 841-2119 or (787) 844-8074
Fax: (787) 840-6642
Padre Francisco Garcia, Director
Email: fupr@coqui.net

ALPHA BETA CHI
Pontificia Universidad Católica de Puerto Rico
2250 Avenida Las Américas, #625
Ponce, PR 00717-0777
(787) 841-2000 ext. 324
Coral González, Vice Pre. of Student Affairs
Web: www.pucpr.edu

ALPHA CHI
Pontificia Universidad Católica de Puerto Rico
2250 Avenida Las Américas, #625
Ponce, PR 00717-0777
(787) 841-2000 ext. 324
Coral González, Vice Pres. of Student Affairs
Web: www.pucpr.edu

ALPHA OMEGA ALPHA
Univ. of Puerto Rico, Ciencias Médicas
P.O. Box 365067
San Juan, PR 00936-5067
(787) 758-2525
María E. Cora-Block, Dean
Web: www.upr.clu.edu

ALPHA OMICRON SIGMA
Pontificia Universidad Católica de Puerto Rico
2250 Avenida Las Américas, #625
Ponce, PR 00717-0777
(787) 841-2000 ext. 324
Coral González, Vice Pres. of Student Affairs
Web: www.pucpr.edu

**AMERICAN MEDICAL STUDENT
ASSOCIATION**
Universidad de Puerto Rico, Cayey
Avenida R. Barcelo
Cayey, PR 00736
(787) 738-5016 or (787) 738-2161x2062
Fax: (787) 263-0676
Rosa L. Aponte, Decana de Estudiantes
Web: www.upr.clu.edu

**AMERICAN STUDENT DENTAL
ASSOCIATION**
Univ. of Puerto Rico, Ciencias Médicas
P.O. Box 365067
San Juan, PR 00936-5067
(787) 758-2525
María E. Cora-Block, Dean
Web: www.upr.clu.edu

ANTILLAS MILITARY ACADEMY
P.O. Box 1919
Trujillo Alto, PR 00977
(787) 761-1710 Fax: (787) 761-1710
Nerién Bermúdez, Director

**APOYO EMPRESARIAL PENÍNSULA DE
CANTERA, INC.**
Affiliate of Fondos Unidos de Puerto Rico
P.O. Box 7187
San Juan, PR 00916-7187
(787) 268-3138 Fax: (787) 728-7658
Sr. Jorge Torres, Director

ASAMBLEA FAMILIAR VIRGILIO DÁVILA
Affiliate of Fondos Unidos de Puerto Rico
Residencial Virgilio Davila
Edificio 4 Apto. 29
Bayamón, PR 00961
(787) 269-0325 Fax: (787) 269-0325
Sister Ana M. Adrover, Director

ASOCIACIÓN ADVENTISTA DEL ESTE
P.O. Box 29027
65 Infantería Station
San Juan, PR 00929
(787) 758-8282 Fax: (787) 759-6819
Abdiel Acosta, President

ASOCIACIÓN ALZHEIMER, INC.
P.O. Box 362026
San Juan, PR 00936-2026
(787) 727-4151 Fax: (787) 727-4890
María Elena Rodrigues, President
Email: alzheimerpr@alzheimerpr.org
Web: www.alzheimerpr.org

**ASOCIACIÓN AMERICANA DEL CÁNCER
DIVISIÓN DE PUERTO RICO., INC.**
Caguas
P.O. Box 1368
Caguas, PR 00726
(787) 744-4336 Fax: (787) 744-4336
Dadba Pacheco, Director

**ASOCIACIÓN CHOFERES
METROPOLITANOS DE PUERTO RICO, INC.**
Padre capuchin 1085, Calle José Padin #191
Rio Piedras, PR 00918
(787) 758-8305
José Díaz, Executive Director

ASOCIACIÓN DE ABANDERADAS
Inter American Univ. of Puerto Rico, Ponce
104 Parque Industrial Turpó, Rd. 1
Mercedita, PR 00715-1602
(787) 284-1912 x2092 or (787) 841-0110
Fax: (787) 841-0103
Dilia Rodríguez, Director
Email: drodrigu@ponce.inter.edu
Web: http://ponce.inter.edu/nhp/contents/
OrganizacionesEstudiantiles.html

**ASOCIACIÓN DE AGENCIAS
PUBLICITARIAS DE PUERTO RICO, INC.**
P.O. Box 195239
San Juan, PR 00919-5239
(787) 764-9906 Fax: (787) 764-6956
Rachelle Whitten, Executive Director
Email: aap@caribe.net

**ASOCIACIÓN DE ALCALDES DE PUERTO
RICO, INC.**
P.O. Box 906-6565
San Juan, PR 00906-6565
(787) 724-1939 Fax: (787) 721-8333
Ángel M. Castillo Rodrigues, Executive Director

**ASOCIACIÓN DE ANTIGUOS ALUMNOS
COLEGIO SAN. IGNACIO DE LOYOLA**
Calle Sauco 1940
Urb. Sta. María
San Juan, PR 00927
(787) 767-0022 Fax: (787) 767-0022
Andrés Richner, President

ASOCIACIÓN DE ARTES PLÁSTICAS
Pontificia Universidad Católica de Puerto Rico
2250 Avenida Las Américas, #625
Ponce, PR 00717-0777
(787) 841-2000 ext. 324
Coral González, Vice Pres. of Student Affairs
Email: asoc.ArtesPlasticas@pucpr.edu
Web: www.pucpr.edu

**ASOCIACIÓN DE BANCOS DE PUERTO
RICO**
208 Ave. Ponce de Leon
San Juan, PR 00918-1002
(787) 753-8630 Fax: (787) 754-6077
Arturo Carrión, Executive Director

**ASOCIACIÓN DE CENTROS DE SALUD
PRIMARIA DE PUERTO RICO**
Affiliate of NCLR
Villa Nevárez Prof. Center, #406
San Juan, PR 00927
(787) 758-3411 Fax: (787) 758-1736
Ms. Sandra V. García, Executive Director
Email: acsppr@coqui.net

ASOCIACIÓN DE COMERCIANTES DE MATERIALES DE CONSTRUCCIÓN, INC.
P.O. Box 4889
San Juan, PR 00902-4889
(787) 721-4872/4520 Fax: (787) 721-7359
Rafael Feliciano Ferrer, Director

ASOCIACIÓN DE COMERCIANTES DE UTADO
P.O. Box 1388
Utado, PR 00641
(787) 894-2610 Fax: (787) 894-2610
Wilfredo Orama, President

ASOCIACIÓN DE COMUNICACIONES
Pontificia Universidad Católica de Puerto Rico
2250 Avenida Las Américas, #625
Ponce, PR 00717-0777
(787) 841-2000 ext. 324
Coral González, Vice Pres. of Student Affairs
Email: asoc.comunicaciones@pucpr.edu
Web: www.pucpr.edu

ASOCIACIÓN DE CONTRATISTAS GENERALES DE AMÉRICA
Calle Perseo 501, #211
San Juan, PR 00920
(787) 781-2200 Fax: (787) 782-3480
Jorge Berlingeri, Executive Director
Web: www.agcconstruct.com

ASOCIACIÓN DE CRIADORES DE CABALLOS PURA SANGRE DE CARRERA DE PUERTO RICO, INC.
Edificio Centro de Seguro
#312 Ave. Ponce de León, #701
San Juan, PR 00907
(787) 725-8715 Fax: (787) 725-8606
Orlando Gutiérrez, Executive Director

ASOCIACIÓN DE DETALLISTAS DE GASOLINA DE PUERTO RICO, INC.
P.O. Box 193652
San Juan, PR 00919
(787) 726-0961 or (787) 726-0876
Fax: (787) 268-3035
Miguel Rivera, President

ASOCIACIÓN DE DUEÑOS DE MUEBLERIAS DE PUERTO RICO, INC.
P.O. Box 360814
San Juan, PR 00936-0814
(787) 754-1645 Fax: (787) 751-1471
John Lugo, President

ASOCIACIÓN DE ENFERMERÍA VISITANTE GREGORIA AUFANT, INC.
Av. E. Roosevelt 114
Hato Rey, PR 00918
(787) 759-7036 Fax: (787) 753-4399
Carmen Martino, Director

ASOCIACIÓN DE ENFERMERÍA VISITANTE GREGORIA AUFANT, INC.
Av. Campo Rico 784, Urbanización Country Club
Rio Piedras, PR 00924
(787) 762-7666 Fax: (787) 762-7715
Carmen Martino, Director

ASOCIACIÓN DE ENFERMERÍA VISITANTE GREGORIA AUFANT, INC.
3ra. Sección-Urbanización Lomas Verdes
Policia Carlos Andaluz X-48
Bayamón, PR 00956
(787) 780-4010 or (787) 780-4294
Fax: (787) 787-5787
Carmen Santana, Supervisora

ASOCIACIÓN DE ESPECIALISTAS EN BELLEZA DE PUERTO RICO INC.
P.O. Box 8517
Santurce, PR 00910-0517
(787) 727-6813 Fax: (787) 727-2440
Juanita Rosa, President
Web: www.aeppr.org

ASOCIACIÓN DE ESPINA BÍFIDA E HIDROCEFALÍA
Affiliate of Fondos Unidos de Puerto Rico
P.O. Box 8262
Bayamón, PR 00960-8032
(787) 740-0033/6695 Fax: (787) 787-1377
Sra. Nereida Díaz, Director

ASOC. DE ESTUDIANTES CATÓLICOS
Univ. of Puerto Rico, Ciencas Medicas
School of Pharmacy, P.O. Box 365067
San Juan, PR 00936
(787) 758-2525
María E. Cora-Block, Dean
Web: www.upr.clu.edu

ASOCIACIÓN DE ESTUDIANTES DE ADMINISTRACIÓN PÚBLICA
Pontificia Universidad Católica de Puerto Rico
2250 Avenida Las Américas, #625
Ponce, PR 00717-0777
(787) 841-2000 ext. 324
Coral González, Vice Pres. of Student Affairs
Email: asoc.AdminPublica@pucpr.edu

ASOCIACIÓN DE ESTUDIANTES DE CONTABILIDAD
Pontificia Universidad Católica de Puerto Rico
2250 Avenida Las Américas, #625
Ponce, PR 00717-0777
(787) 841-2000 ext. 324
Coral González, Vice Pres. of Student Affairs
Email: asoc.est.contabilidad@pucpr.edu

Inter American University of Puerto Rico, Ponce
104 Parque Industrial Turpó, Rd. 1
Mercedita, PR 00715-1602
(787) 284-1912 x2092 or (787) 841-0110
Fax: (787) 841-0103
Dilia Rodríguez, Director
Email: drodrigu@ponce.inter.edu
Web: http://ponce.inter.edu/nhp/contents/OrganizacionesEstudiantiles.html

ASOCIACIÓN DE ESTUDIANTES DE CRIMINOLOGÍA
Pontificia Universidad Católica de Puerto Rico
2250 Avenida Las Américas, #625
Ponce, PR 00717-0777
(787) 841-2000 ext. 324
Coral González, Vice Pres. of Student Affairs
Email: asoc.est.Criminologia@pucpr.edu
Web: www.pucpr.edu

ASOCIACIÓN DE ESTUDIANTES DE ECOLOGÍA
Inter American Univ. of Puerto Rico, Ponce
P.O. Box 7186
Ponce, PR 00732-7186
(787) 844-8181 x2354 Fax: (787) 899-1796
Migdalia Alvarez, Catedrática Asociada
Email: biomar@cogui.net

ASOCIACIÓN DE ESTUDIANTES DE ECONOMÍA DOMÉSTICA
Pontificia Universidad Católica de Puerto Rico
2250 Avenida Las Américas, #625
Ponce, PR 00717-0777
(787) 841-2000 ext. 324
Coral González, Vice Pres. of Student Affairs
Web: www.pucpr.edu

ASOCIACIÓN DE ESTUDIANTES DE EDUCACIÓN FÍSICA
Pontificia Universidad Católica de Puerto Rico
2250 Avenida Las Américas, #625
Ponce, PR 00717-0777
(787) 841-2000 ext. 324
Coral González, Vice Pres. of Student Affairs
Web: www.pucpr.edu

ASOCIACIÓN DE ESTUDIANTES DE GERONTOLOGÍA
Pontificia Universidad Católica de Puerto Rico
2250 Avenida Las Américas, #625
Ponce, PR 00717-0777
(787) 841-2000 ext. 324
Coral González, Vice Pres. of Student Affairs
Email: asoc.est.gerontologia@pucpr.edu
Web: www.pucpr.edu

ASOCIACIÓN DE ESTUDIANTES DE HISTORIA
Pontificia Universidad Católica de Puerto Rico
2250 Avenida Las Américas, #625
Ponce, PR 00717-0777
(787) 841-2000 ext. 324
Coral González, Vice Pres. of Student Affairs
Email: asoc.est.historia@pucpr.edu
Web: www.pucpr.edu

ASOCIACIÓN DE ESTUDIANTES DE MBA
Pontificia Universidad Católica de Puerto Rico
2250 Avenida Las Américas, #625
Ponce, PR 00717-0777
(787) 841-2000 ext. 324
Coral González, Vice Pres. of Student Affairs
Email: asoc.est.MBA@pucpr.edu
Web: www.pucpr.edu

ASOCIACIÓN DE ESTUDIANTES DE PSICOLOGÍA
Pontificia Universidad Católica de Puerto Rico
2250 Avenida Las Américas, #625
Ponce, PR 00717-0777
(787) 841-2000 ext. 324
Coral González, Vice Pres. of Student Affairs
Email: aep@pucpr.edu
Web: www.pucpr.edu

ASOCIACIÓN DE ESTUDIANTES DE SISTEMAS DE INFORMACIÓN (ADESI)
Inter American Univ. of Puerto Rico, Ponce
104 Parque Industrial Turpó, Rd. 1
Mercedita, PR 00715-1602
(787) 284-1912 x2092 or (787) 841-0110
Fax: (787) 841-0103
Dilia Rodríguez, Director
Email: drodrigu@ponce.inter.edu
Web: http://ponce.inter.edu/nhp/contents/OrganizacionesEstudiantiles.html

ASOCIACIÓN DE ESTUDIANTES PROGRAMA MCNAIR
Pontificia Universidad Católica de Puerto Rico
2250 Avenida Las Américas, #625
Ponce, PR 00717-0777
(787) 841-2000 ext. 324
Coral González, Vice Pres. of Student Affairs
Email: asoc.Est.McNair@pucpr.edu
Web: www.pucpr.edu

ASOCIACIÓN DE EXALUMNOS
University of Puerto Rico, Humacao
Estación Postal CUH, 100 car., 908
Humacao, PR 00791-4300
(787) 852-4638
Margarita Vives, President
Email: me_morales@cuhad.upr.clu.edu
Web: www.upr.clu.edu

ASOCIACIÓN DE FOMENTO EDUCATIVO, INC.
Calle A 48
Guaynabo, PR 00966
(787) 781-5170 Fax: (787) 775-0478
Tomás Villanueva, Secretary of Organization

ASOCIACIÓN DE FRAILES CAPUCHINOS, INC.
P.O. Box 21350
Rio Piedras, PR 00928-1350
(787) 764-3090 Fax: (787) 764-4070
Jorge Macias, President
Email: pochi@coqui.net
Web: loscopuchinos.com

ASOCIACIÓN DE FUTUROS ADMINISTRADORES DE OFICINA
Pontificia Universidad Católica de Puerto Rico
2250 Avenida Las Américas, #625
Ponce, PR 00717-0777
(787) 841-2000 ext. 324
Coral González, Vice Pres. of Student Affairs
Email: afao@pucpr.edu
Web: www.pucpr.edu

ASOCIACIÓN DE HOSPITALES DE PUERTO RICO, INC.
Villanevares Professional Bldg. #101
San Juan, PR 00927
(787) 764-0290/0987 Fax: (787) 753-9748
Sr. Juan Rivera, Executive Vice President
Email: asohospr@coqui.net
Web: asociacionehosppr.org

ASOCIACIÓN DE INDUSTRIALES DE PUERTO RICO
P.O. Box 195477
San Juan, PR 00919-5477
(787) 759-9445 Fax: (787) 756-7670
Miguel Nazario, President
Email: PRMA@i-lan.com
Web: www.i-lan.com

ASOCIACIÓN DE JUSTICIA CRIMINAL
Inter American Univ. of Puerto Rico, Ponce
104 Parque Industrial Turpó, Rd. 1
Mercedita, PR 00715-1602
(787) 284-1912 x2092 Fax: (787) 841-0103
Dilia Rodríguez, Director
Email: drodrigu@ponce.inter.edu
Web: http://ponce.inter.edu/nhp/contents/OrganizacionesEstudiantiles.html

ASOC. DE LA DISTROFIA MUSCULAR, INC.
Capitulo de Puerto Rico
Ave. Ponce de Leon 431 Edif. Nacional Plaza, #705
Hato-Rei, PR 0091

(787) 751-4088 Fax: (787) 250-4414
José Roberto Acarón, Director
Email: puertoricodistric@mdausa.org

ASOCIACIÓN DE LÍDERES ESTUDIANTILES CON LIMITACIONES FÍSICAS
Pontificia Universidad Católica de Puerto Rico
2250 Avenida Las Américas, #625
Ponce, PR 00717-0777
(787) 841-2000 ext. 324
Coral González, Vice Pres. of Student Affairs
Email: ALLF@pucpr.edu
Web: www.pucpr.edu

ASOC. DE MAESTROS DE PUERTO RICO
Apartado 191088
San Juan, PR 00919-1088
(787) 765-3995 Fax: (787) 754-8874
José E. Vélez Torres, President

ASOCIACIÓN DE MERCADEO, INDUSTRIA Y DISTRIBUCIÓN DE ALIMENTOS (MIDA)
F. D. Roosevelt 1510, #902-A
Guaynabo, PR 00968
(787) 792-7575 Fax: (787) 792-8085
Johnny Luna, President

ASOCIACIÓN DE NIÑOS Y ADULTOS CON RETARDACIÓN MENTAL, INC. (ANARM)
Apartado 361904
San Juan, PR 00936-1904
(787) 764-5970
Karen Vásquez, Executive Director

ASOC. DE NOTARIOS DE PUERTO RICO
P.O. Box 363613
San Juan, PR 00936-3613
(787) 758-2773 Fax: (787) 759-6703
Licenciado Juan C. Salichas-Bou, President
Email: asociacion@notariospr.org
Web: www.anota.org

ASOC. DE PERSONAS IMPEDIDAS, INC.
Affiliate of Fondos Unidos de Puerto Rico
P.O. Box 1358
San German, PR 00683
(787) 892-5363 Fax: (787) 892-6246
Sra. Wanda Feliu, Director

ASOCIACIÓN DE PSICOLOGÍA DE PUERTO RICO
Apartado 363435
San Juan, PR 00936-3435
(787) 751-7100 Fax: (787) 758-6467
Dr. Carlos V. Sosa, President
Email: appr@coqui.net
Web: www.asppr.org

ASOCIACIÓN DE REALTORS DE PUERTO RICO, INC.
P.O. Box 8998
San Juan, PR 00910-0998
(787) 725-1325 Fax: (787) 725-1363
Adelia Visente, Executive Director
Email: prealtor@carriben.net
Web: www.prealtor.com

ASOCIACIÓN DE URÓLOGOS PUERTO RICO
MSC 256 138 Winston Churchill
San Juan, PR 00926-6023
(787) 753-8630 Fax: (787) 754-6077
Edwin Maeso González, President

ASOCIACIÓN DUEÑOS DE TAXI DE CAROLINA, INC.
P.O. Box 953
Carolina, PR 00986
(787) 762-6066
Israel Mendez Mendez, President

ASOCIACIÓN ESTUDIANTES DE ENFERMERÍA
Universidad del Sagrado Corazón
Programa de Enfermería
P.O. Box 12383
San Juan, PR 00914-0383
(787) 728-1515 ext. 2427, 2430
Keina Alcantra Vicente, Member
Email: aee@sagrado.edu
Web: www.sagrado.edu

ASOCIACIÓN ESTUDIANTES DE FINANZAS
Pontificia Universidad Católica de Puerto Rico
2250 Avenida Las Américas, #625
Ponce, PR 00717-0777
(787) 841-2000 ext. 324
Coral González, Vice Pres. of Student Affairs
Email: asoc.est.finanzas@pucpr.edu
Web: www.pucpr.edu

ASOCIACIÓN ESTUDIANTIL DE CIENCIAS SECRETARIALES Y SISTEMAS DE OFICINA
Inter American Univ. of Puerto Rico, Ponce
104 Parque Industrial Turpó, Rd. 1
Mercedita, PR 00715-1602
(787) 284-1912 x2092 Fax: (787) 841-0103
Dilia Rodríguez, Director
Email: drodrigu@ponce.inter.edu
Web: http://ponce.inter.edu/nhp/contents/OrganizacionesEstudiantiles.html

ASOCIACIÓN ESTUDIANTIL DE TECNOLOGÍA Y COMPUTADORAS
Inter American Univ. of Puerto Rico, Ponce
104 Parque Industrial Turpó, Rd. 1
Mercedita, PR 00715-1602
(787) 284-1912 x2092 Fax: (787) 841-0103
Dilia Rodríguez, Director
Email: drodrigu@ponce.inter.edu
Web: http://ponce.inter.edu/nhp/contents/OrganizacionesEstudiantiles.html

ASOCIACIÓN FUTURAS SECRETARIAS PROFESIONALES
Pontificia Universidad Católica de Puerto Rico
2250 Avenida Las Américas, #625
Ponce, PR 00717-0777
(787) 841-2000 ext. 324
Coral González, Vice Pres. of Student Affairs
Email: afsp@pucpr.edu
Web: www.pucpr.edu

ASOCIACIÓN FUTUROS PROFESIONALES DE LA EDUCACIÓN
Pontificia Universidad Católica de Puerto Rico
2250 Avenida Las Américas, #625
Ponce, PR 00717-0777
(787) 841-2000 ext. 324
Coral González, Vice Pres. Student Affairs
Email: AFPE@pucpr.edu
Web: www.pucpr.edu

ASOCIACIÓN INTER-AMERICANA DE HOMBRES DE EMPRESA
Capitulo del Oeste de Puerto Rico
Apartado 342
Mayagüez, PR 00681
(787) 831-4210 Fax: (787) 831-357
Angel del Toro, President

ASOCIACIÓN MAYAGUENZA DE PERSONAS CON IMPEDIMENTOS
Affiliate of Fondos Unidos de Puerto Rico
P.O. Box 745
Mayaguez, PR 00681-0681
(787) 832-7460 Fax: (787) 832-7460
Sra. Esther Caro, Director

ASOCIACIÓN MÉDICA DE PUERTO RICO, INC.
P.O. Box 9387
San Juan, PR 00908-9387
(787) 721-6969 Fax: (787) 722-1191
Rafael Alicea, Executive Director
Web: www.hom.coqui.net/asocmed

ASOCIACIÓN MIEMBROS DE LA POLICÍA
RR3 Box 3724
Rio Piedras, PR 00928
(787) 720-1313 Fax: (787) 720-1327
Sr. José Taboada de Jesús, President

ASOCIACIÓN PADRES PRO BIENESTAR NIÑOS IMPEDIDOS, INC.
P.O. Box 21301
San Juan, PR 00928-1301
(787) 763-4665 or (787) 981-8492
Fax: (787) 765-0345
Carmen Selles, Exective Director

ASOCIACIÓN PRO, CIUDADANO IMPEDIDO DE SABANA GRANDE
Affiliate of Fondos Unidos de Puerto Rico
P.O. Box 360
Sábana Grande, PR 00637
(787) 873-2060EXT. 213 Fax: (787) 873-2590
Nora Valentín Alvino, Director

ASOCIACIÓN PRO JUVENTUD Y COMUNIDAD DEL BARRIO PALMAS
Affiliate of Fondos Unidos de Puerto Rico
Barrio Palmas, 257 Cucharilla
Cataño, PR 00962
(787) 788-5105 Fax: (787) 788-6269
Sra. Gloria Maldonado, Director

ASOCIACIÓN PRO-DEPORTES Y RECREACIÓN DE LEVITTOWN, INC.
Affiliate of Fondos Unidos de Puerto Rico
P.O. Box 50890
Levittown, PR 00950

(787) 795-1103 Fax: (787) 261-2120
Sr. Rafael Vasallo, President

ASOCIACIÓN PRO-VIDA DE PUERTO RICO, INC.
#235 ZMS - Plaza Rio Hondo
Bayamón, PR 00961-3100
(787) 261-6793
Carlos Sánchez, President

ASOCIACIÓN PRODUCTOS DE PUERTO RICO
P.O. Box 363631
San Juan, PR 00936-3631
(787) 753-8484 Fax: (787) 753-0855
Fransisco Martínez, President
Web: www.hechoenpr.com

ASOCIACIÓN PUERTORRIQUEÑA DE DIABETES
P.O. Box 190842
San Juan, PR 00919-0842
(787) 281-0617 or (787) 756-5835
Fax: (787) 281-7175
Elba Blanes, Executive Director

ASOCIACIÓN PUERTORRIQUEÑA DE PARKINSON
Affiliate of Fondos Unidos de Puerto Rico
P.O. Box 66
Carolina, PR 00986
(787) 762-1140 or (787) 276-5000
Fax: (7870 757-6635
Sra. Iris Glenys Sánchez, Director

ASOCIACIÓN PUERTORRIQUENA DEL CORAZÓN / PUERTO RICO HEART ASSOC.
Affiliate of Fondos Unidos de Puerto Rico
P.O. Box 191752
San Juan, PR 00919-1752
(787) 751-6595 Fax: (787) 250-0281
Juan Rivera, Executive Director
Email: rivera@heart.org
Web: www.heart.org

ASPIRA OF PUERTO RICO, INC.
65 Infantry Station, P.O. Box 29132
Rio Piedras, PR 00929
(787) 641-1985 Fax: (787) 257-2725
Hilda Maldonado, Executive Director
Web: www.aspira.org/PuertoRico.html

ASSIST
P.O. Box 32
San Juan, PR 00902
(787) 721-2160 Fax: (787) 721-6976
Belén Pietri, Chair
Andrés Richner, President

ASSOCIATION OF BIOMEDICAL SCIENCES
University of Puerto Rico, Ciencias Médicas
School of Medicine
P.O. Box 365067
San Juan, PR 00936
(787) 758-2525
María E. Cora-Block, Dean
Web: www.upr.clu.edu

ATENEO PUERTORRIQUEÑO
P.O. Box 902-1180
San Juan, PR 00902-1180
(787) 722-4839 Fax: (787) 725-3873
Eduardo Morales Coll, President
Email: ateneopr@caribe.net

BAMBI
HC-03,Box 11215-Bo. Puente
Camuy, PR 00627
(787) 898-5974
Silvia Quiñones, Director

BANCO DE ALIMENTOS DE PUERTO RICO
Affiliate of Fondos Unidos de Puerto Rico
P.O. Box 2989
Bayamón, PR 00960-2989
(787) 740-3663 Fax: (787) 786-8810
Sra. Angela Menchaca, Executive Director

BEBE AMOR
Calle Gautier Benitez 78, Esq. Forastieri
Caguas, PR 00725
(787) 743-1232
Milagros Carrasquillo, Director

BETA SIGMA KAPPA SOCIETY
Inter American University of Puerto Rico
School of Optometry
P.O. Box 191049

San Juan, PR 00919-1049
(787) 765-1915 Fax: (787) 767-3920
José Colón, Director
Email: jcolon@inter.edu
Web: www.optonet.inter.edu

BETTER BUSINESS BUREAU OF PUERTO RICO
P.O. Box 363488
San Juan, PR 00936-3488
(787) 756-5400 Fax: (787) 721-6976
Lydia S. López-Vicente, Executive Director

BIG BROTHERS BIG SISTERS OF PUERTO RICO, INC.
Affiliate of Fondos Unidos de Puerto Rico
Call Box 7886, Suite 496
Guaynabo, PR 00970-7886
(787) 783-4444 Fax: (787) 783-6822
Olga Meléndez, Director

BILL'S KITCHEN
Affiliate of Fondos Unidos de Puerto Rico
OSS Box 38, P.O. Box 70292
San Juan, PR 00936-8292
(787) 268-6525 Fax: (787) 268-6585
Sra. Sandra Torres, Executive Director

BOY SCOUTS OF AMERICA
Affiliate of Fondos Unidos de Puerto Rico
P.O. Box 70181
San Juan, PR 00936
(787) 790-0323 Fax: (787) 790-0357
Kenneth C. D'Apice, Director

BOYS & GIRLS CLUB DE MAYAGUEZ
Affiliate of Boys & Girls Club de P.R.
P.O. Box 363929
San Juan, PR 00936
(787) 831-6119 Fax: (787) 831-8346
Sr. José A. Campos, Director

BOYS & GIRLS CLUB DE PUERTO RICO
Affiliate of Fondos Unidos de Puerto Rico
P.O. Box 363929
San Juan, PR 00936-3929
(787)282-0125 Fax: (787) 7282-8142
Sr. José A. Campos, Director
Email: bgcdpr@prtc.net

BUSINESS HONOR SOCIETY
Pontificia Universidad Católica de Puerto Rico
2250 Avenida Las Américas, #625
Ponce, PR 00717-0777
(787) 841-2000 ext. 324
Coral González, Vice President of Student Affairs
Email: BusinessHS@pucpr.edu
Web: www.pucpr.edu

C.C.D. CARMEN ORTIZ ORTIZ
P.O. Box 198
Ave. Muñoz Marin #4
Hormigueros, PR 00660
(787) 849-7136
Carmen Ortiz Ortiz, Director

C.C.D.N. PARCELAS MAMEY
Centro Comunal Sabana
286 Ramón Pellot
Moca, PR 00676
(787) 877-6088
Carmen Méndez, Director

C.C.D. OROCOVIS
Km 27 Hm. 4-Carr., #155
Orocovis, PR 00720
(787) 867-3460 Fax: (787) 867-3460
Adaelva Menéndez, Director

C.C.D. PEQUEÑINES RYDER
P.O. Box 859
Ave. Font Martelo, #317
Humacao, PR 00792
(787) 852-0588
Maira Ortiz, Director

C.C.D. ZENAIDA TIRADO SANTIAGO
Calle Pablo Casals, #119
Mayagüez, PR 00680
(787) 833-0702
Zenaida Tirado Santiago, Director

CABALLEROS DE COLÓN
P.O. Box 70181
Carolina, PR 00986
(787) 725-0485
Pablo Collazo, Administrator

CÁMARA DE COMERCIANTES MAYORISTAS DE PUERTO RICO
P.O. Box 195337

San Juan, PR 00919-5337
(787) 754-6262 Fax: (787) 754-2620
Alvin Báez, Executive Director

CÁMARA DE COMERCIO DE PONCE Y SUR DE PUERTO RICO
P.O. Box 7455
Ponce, PR 00732
(787) 844-4400 Fax: (787) 844-4705
Bessie Nicole, Executive Director

CÁMARA DE COMERCIO DEL OESTE DE PUERTO RICO
P.O. Box 9, Mayaguez, PR, 00681
Merrill Lynch Plaza, 9th Floor, #905
Mayaguez, PR 00680
(787) 832-3749 Fax: (787) 832-3250
CPA Elisamuel Rivera, President
Email: ccopr@coqui.net

CÁMARA OFICIAL ESPAÑOLA DE COMERCIO
P.O. Box 9020894
San Juan, PR 00902-0894
(787) 729-0099 Fax: (787) 729-0092
Hiram Irisarri, President

CAPÍTULO DE FUTUROS TRABAJADORES SOCIALES
Pontificia Universidad Católica de Puerto Rico
2250 Avenida Las Américas, #625
Ponce, PR 00717-0777
(787) 841-2000 ext. 324
Coral González, Vice Pres. of Student Affairs
Email: FTS@pucpr.edu
Web: www.pucpr.edu

CAPÍTULO ESTUDIANTIL DE MICROBIOLOGÍA
Universidad del Sagrado Corazón
Departamento de Ciencias Naturales
P.O. Box 12383
San Juan, PR 00914-0383
(787) 728-1515
Mayra Rolón, Advisor
Email: mrolon@sagrado.edu
Web: www.sagrado.edu

CARIBE GIRL SCOUTS COUNCIL
500 Elisa Colberg
San Juan, PR 00907
(787) 721-5771 Fax: (787) 721-6291
Isabel Daleccio-Miranda, Board Pres.

CASA BETSAN
Affiliate of Fondos Unidos de Puerto Rico
P.O. Box 154
Angeles, PR 00611
(787) 894-7959 Fax: (787) 894-7959
Sra. Milagros Martínez, Director

CASA DE LA BONDAD
Affiliate of Fondos Unidos de Puerto Rico
MSC - 406, P.O. Box 890
Humacao, PR 00792-0890
(787) 852-7265 Fax: (787) 852-2087
Sra. Marta A. Mercado, Director

CASA DE NIÑOS MANUEL FERNÁNDEZ JUNCOS
Affiliate of Fondos Unidos de Puerto Rico
P.O. Box 9020163
San Juan, PR 00902-0163
(787) 724-2904 Fax: (787) 724-0980
Padre Luis Gerardo Fernández, Director

CASA DE TODOS
Affiliate of Fondos Unidos de Puerto Rico
HC 1 Box 6128
Juncos, PR 00777-9710
(787) 734-5511 Fax: (787) 734-4565
Sor María Rosa Portuondo, Director

CASA FAMILIAR LA NUEVA ESCUELA
Bo. Juan Domingo
55 Calle Robles (Interior)
Guaynabo, PR 00966
(787) 792-3550 Fax: (787) 792-3550
Jackeline Lugo, Director

CASA LA PROVIDENCIA
Affiliate of Fondos Unidos de Puerto Rico
P.O. Box 9020614
San Juan, PR 00902-0614
(787) 725-5358 Fax: (787) 725-0058
Sor Aída Iris Cruz, Director

CASA PENSAMIENTO MUJER DEL CENTRO
Affiliate of Fondos Unidos de Puerto Rico
P.O. Box 2002
Aibonito, PR 00705

(787) 735-3200 Fax: (787) 735-3200
Sra. Carmen Hilda Rosario, Director

CASA PROTEGIDA JULIA DE BURGOS
Affiliate of Fondos Unidos de Puerto Rico
P.O. Box 362433
San Juan, PR 00936-2433
(787) 723-3500 Fax: (787) 725-8580
Sra. Evangelista Colón, Director

CASITA DE PEPITA
Luis Almansa #730 Esq. Bernard Boil
San Juan, PR 00926
(787) 755-0629
Josefa Moreno García, Director

CENTRO A.P.A.C.E.D.O.
Affiliate of Fondos Unidos de Puerto Rico
P.O. Box 20197
Rio Piedras, PR 00928
(787) 754-3287 Fax: (787) 754-3287
Sra. Milagros Ortiz, Director

CENTRO ALBA MONTESSORI
Calle 13 Q-1-Cupey Gardens
Rio Piedras, PR 00927
(787) 760-2186
Mercedes Narvaez, Director

**CENTRO COMUNIDAD PARA
ENVEJECIENTES PERLA DEL SUR**
Calle P. Montaner-Urb. Per.del Sur
Ponce, PR 00731
(787) 843-0436
Lidia Echeverría R., Director.

CENTRO COMUNITARIO CORRALES
P.O. Box 600603
Buzon 121 A, Bo. Corrales
Aguadilla, PR 00603
(787) 891-3763
Wanda Infante, Director

CENTRO COMUNITARIO LUCERITO
P.O. Box 600603, Buzon 121 Aguadilla
Aguadilla, PR 00603
(787) 891-1415
Wanda Infante, Director

CENTRO CUIDADO NIÑOS
Carr. 779 Km. 5 HO, Barrio Palomas
Comerío, PR 00782
(787) 875-0061
Ginnie Cruz, Director

**CENTRO CULTURAL Y DE SERVICIOS DE
CANTERA**
Affiliate of Fondos Unidos de Puerto Rico
Bo. Obrero Station
P.O. Box 7152
Santurce, PR 00916
(787) 728-0566 Fax: (787) 727-8533
Hna. Isabel Pérez Calderón, Director

**CENTRO DE ACTIVIDADES MÚLTIPLES
JUAN DE LOS OLIVOS, INC.**
Affiliate of Fondos Unidos de Puerto Rico
P.O. Box 1613
Vega Alta, PR 00692
(787) 883-2370 Fax: (787) 883-2370
Orlando García Allende, Director

**CENTRO DE ACTIVIDADES MÚLTIPLES
SANTA LUISA**
Affiliate of Fondos Unidos de Puerto Rico
RR6 BOX 9492
San Juan, PR 00926
(787) 720-2764 Fax: (787) 731-7795
Sor Catalina Sánchez, Director

**CENTRO DE ADIESTRAMIENTO Y
SERVICIOS COMUNITARIOS EPI, INC.**
Affiliate of Fondos Unidos de Puerto Rico
P.O. Box 1918
Guayama, PR 00785
(787) 864-4225 Fax: (787) 864-4225
Sra. Myrna Pomales, Director

CENTRO DE ADOLESCENTES
Affiliate of Fondos Unidos de Puerto Rico
Apartado 856
Gurabo, PR 00778
(787) 737-3434 Fax: (787) 737-3481
Sra. Glenda A. Torres, Director

**CENTRO DE AYUDA A NIÑOS CON
IMPEDIMENTOS, INC. (CANII)**
Affiliate of Fondos Unidos de Puerto Rico
133 Calle Dr. Gonzalez

Isabela, PR 00662
(787) 872-5565 Fax: (787) 872-4665
Sonia M. Ramos Velásquez, Director

CENTRO DE AYUDA SOCIAL
Affiliate of Fondos Unidos de Puerto Rico
Bo. Obrero Station
P.O. Box 7093
San Juan, PR 00916-7093
(787) 781-3965 or (787) 781-9334
Fax: (787) 781-2333
Rev. Aurea Martínez Villar, Director

**CENTRO DE CUIDADO DIURNO
AURISTELA SÁNCHEZ**
P.O. Box 795
Ave., Luis Muñoz Rivera #2
Yabucoa, PR 00767
(787) 893-2168
Carmen Villegas, Director

**CENTRO DE CUIDADO DIURNO
MUNICIPAL HOCONUCO BAJO**
Carr. 119 Km. 4.1
San German, PR 00683
(787) 892-7150 Fax: (787) 892-1114
María Delgado Acosta, Director

**CENTRO DE CUIDADO DIURNO SANTA
MAGDALENA SOFÍA**
Apartado 7152
San Juan, PR 00916-7152
(787) 728-0566 Fax: (787) 727-8533
Isabel P. Calderón, Director

**CENTRO DE CUIDADO Y DESARROLLO
ALIDA MARTÍNEZ**
Calle Marginal F 3 A-Mayagüez
Mayagüez, PR 00680
(787) 834-8023 Fax: (787) 834-8023
Alida Martínez, Director

**CENTRO DE CUIDADO Y DESARROLLO
AMÉRICA CAPO 5**
Calle Roosevelt #29
Ponce, PR 00731
(787) 844-2045
María Lugo, Director

**CENTRO DE CUIDADO Y DESARROLLO
CANA, INC.**
Calle 402 Bloque 133, #10
Carolina, PR 00984
(787) 769-3015
Carmen Lugo Martínez, Director

**CENTRO DE CUIDADO Y DESARROLLO
CEMADI**
P.O. Box 21494
San Juan, PR 00931-1494
(787) 720-4070
Elizabeth Concepción, Director

**CENTRO DE CUIDADO Y DESARROLLO
DEL NIÑO MR. COLÓN**
Urbana La Planicie-Calle 3 E-17
Cayey, PR 00736
(787) 263-3619
Mitza Colón Torres, Director

**CENTRO DE CUIDADO Y DESARROLLO
DUMBO**
Calle Carrau#31-Bo. Sabalos
Mayagüez, PR 00680
(787) 833-6106
Zaida Rodríguez Ríos, Director

**CENTRO DE CUIDADO Y DESARROLLO
ESPERANZA GARCIA VALENTIN**
Urb. Brisas de Añasco-Calle 6 E 24
Añasco, PR 00610
(787) 826-2723
Esperanza G. Valentín, Director

**CENTRO DE CUIDADO Y DESARROLLO
INFANTILANDIA**
Zambeses, #142
Rio Piedras, PR 00926
(787) 763-1814
Dominga C. González, Director

**CENTRO DE CUIDADO Y DESARROLLO
ISABELA**
Carr. PR 113-Km. 1.7-Ave. N. Estrada
Isabela, PR 00662
(787) 872-2895
Vivian Quiñonez, Director

**CENTRO DE CUIDADO Y DESARROLLO
JANDYGIL**
Calle F. Garcia #211
Fajardo, PR 00738
(787) 863-0186
Belén Maldonado Figueroa, Director

**CENTRO DE CUIDADO Y DESARROLLO
LOS QUERUBINES**
Calle 10 #1024-Villa Nevarez
Rio Piedras, PR 00927
(787) 751-5465
Sara Ríos, Director

**CENTRO DE CUIDADO Y DESARROLLO
MAMI-PUCHA**
Calle 7 F#1-Alta Vista
Ponce, PR 00731
(787) 843-6879
Aurea Luz Lebrón, Director

**CENTRO DE CUIDADO Y DESARROLLO
MARGARITA MELÉNDEZ**
Urbana Vives-Calle 4, #292
Guayama, PR 00784
(787) 864-6125
Meléndez de Jesús, Director

**CENTRO DE CUIDADO Y DESARROLLO
MATERNAL NORMA**
Calle Valencia #77-Bo. Cristy
Mayagüez, PR 00680
(787) 834-2271
Norma Vargas Ortiz, Director

**CENTRO DE CUIDADO Y DESARROLLO MI
SEGUNDO HOGAR**
Ave. Hostos #404
Hato Rey, PR 00918
(787) 754-7682 Fax: (787) 765-6960
Pura Ramírez, Director

**CENTRO DE CUIDADO Y DESARROLLO
MUNDO DE JUGUETE**
Calle 12 Q-12-Urb. Borinquen
Cabo Rojo, PR 00623
(787) 851-3691
Marlene Ramirez, Director

**CENTRO DE CUIDADO Y DESARROLLO
NURSERY AMERICA**
Las Palomas 151-Santurce
San Juan, PR 00911
(787) 727-5126
Noris Nuñez Borges, Administrator

**CENTRO DE CUIDADO Y DESARROLLO
PARAÍSO INFANTIL**
Cañada 1157-Puerto Nuevo
Río Piedras, PR 00920
(787) 781-4223
María Rullán, Adminstrator

**CENTRO DE CUIDADO Y DESARROLLO
PARCELAS MAMEY**
Calle Ramón Pellot #286
Moca, PR 00676
(787) 877-6088
Carmen Méndez M., Director

**CENTRO DE CUIDADO Y DESARROLLO
PIOLÍN**
Calle Lucheti 31
Villalba, PR 00766
(787) 847-2627
Roberto Torres F., Administrator

**CENTRO DE CUIDADO Y DESARROLLO
ROSAMAR**
Ave. Central Blvd-Esq. Ave. 24-3º ext.
Carolina, PR 00985
(787) 257-4350
Rosa de Jesús de Cora, Director

**CENTRO DE CUIDADO Y DESARROLLO
ROSI**
Calle 2-D-7 - Urb. Santa Juana II
Caguas, PR 00725
(787) 746-5986
Rosa Cintrón, Director

**CENTRO DE CUIDADO Y DESARROLLO
TITI RAQUEL**
P.O. Box 3
Urb. Bello Horizonte-Calle 7 D-6
Guayama, PR 00784
(787) 864-4281
Raquel Enchautegui, Director

**CENTRO DE DESARROLLO EDUCACIONAL
DEL NIÑO (CDEN)**
Ave. Periferal A1#2-Cdad. Universidad
Trujillo Alto, PR 00976
(787) 761-4207

Keila Guzmán, Director

CENTRO DE DESARROLLO INFANTIL
Colegio Univ.Cayey-Av. R. Barcelo
Cayey, PR 00736
(787) 263-5651
Evelyn Collazo, Director

CENTRO DE DESARROLLO SENDEC
HC-03-Box 27101
Lajas, PR 00667-9629
(787) 899-4380
Nelly Vega Rodríguez, Director

CENTRO DE ENVEJECIENTES CLUB DE ORO
Affiliate of Fondos Unidos de Puerto Rico
P.O. Box 9176
Caguas, PR 00726
(787) 743-3359 or (787) 745-0282
Fax: (787) 743-3359
Sra. Aída I. Miranda Marín, Director

**CENTRO DE ENVEJECIENTES CORAZONES
UNIDOS**
Proyecto Hope
P.O. Box 1452
Orocovis, PR 00720
(787) 867-2240
Cándido Alvarado, Director

**CENTRO DE ENVEJECIENTES DAVID
CHAPEL BETANCES**
Calle 1 #16
Anasco, PR 00610
(787) 826-3383
Diana Sánchez Q., Director

CENTRO DE ENVEJECIENTES DE HATILLO
Section Acueducto-Box 8
Hatillo, PR 00659
(787) 898-6879
Reynaldo Morales, Director

CENTRO DE ENVEJECIENTES DE TOA ALTA
Apartado 82-Barrio Galateo
Toa Alta, PR 00954
(787) 870-3808 Fax: (787) 870-6883
Aída Rivera Pérez, Director

CENTRO DE ENVEJECIENTES EDAD DE ORO
Calle S. Iglesias Pantin, #51
San Lorenzo, PR 00754
(787) 736-8374
Carmen Rita Pujoles, Director

**CENTRO DE ENVEJECIENTES HOGAR PAZ
DE CRISTO**
Affiliate of Fondos Unidos de Puerto Rico
Llanos del Sur
Calle Los Claveles 47-747
Coto Laurel, PR 00780
(787) 848-2135 Fax: (787) 840-3450
Melba Cintrón, Director

**CENTRO DE ENVEJECIENTES JULIO PÉREZ
IRIZARRY, INC.**
P.O. Box 566
Hormigueros, PR 00660
(787) 849-2626 Fax: (787) 849-1251
Lilliam M. Torres, Director

**CENTRO DE ENVEJECIENTES JUVENTUD
DE AYER**
Calle Julián Sanchez, #160
Arecibo, PR 00612
(787) 879-1909
Elías R. Tavares Correa, Director

**CENTRO DE ENVEJECIENTES MANUEL
ACEVEDO ROSARIO**
Apart. 633-Bo. Puente Peña
Camuy, PR 00627
(787) 898-2190
Sara Avilés, Director

**CENTRO DE ENVEJECIENTES MARIBEL
GARCÍA**
Carr. 829, Km. 1.7, Bo. Buena Vista
Bayamón, PR 00957
(787) 730-3936
Maribel García, Directora

CENTRO DE ENVEJECIENTES MAUNABO
P.O. Box 8, Barrio Emajaguas
Maunabo, PR 00707
(787) 861-0808
Jenny Torres, Director

**CENTRO DE ENVEJECIENTES REMANSO
DE PAZ**
10 Calle Quiñonez - Municipio de Manati
Manati, PR 00674
(787) 854-4100
Carmén M. Lugo, Director

CENTRO DE ENVEJECIENTES-LUZ N. RUIZ
HC-03 Box 14303-Caguanas
Utuado, PR 00641
(787) 894-7463
Luz N. Ruiz, Director

CENTRO DE ENVEJECIMIENTO DE TRUJILLO ALTO
Carr. 175-Km. 11.7
Trujillo, PR 00976
(787) 761-2309
Milagros Soto, Director

CENTRO DE ENVEJECIMIENTO HOPE
Calle Unión Final 76
Santurce, PR 00915
(787) 726-1850
Rafael Rey Rivera, Director

CENTRO DE ENVEJECIMIENTO LOS APRINES
Calle Ca. Lebrim #449
Vieques, PR 00765
(787) 741-2262 Fax: (787) 741-2262
Lorna G. Ortiz Ventura, Director

CENTRO DE FORTALECIMIENTO E.S.C.A.P.E.
Affiliate of Fondos Unidos de Puerto Rico
P.O. Box 2598
Guaynabo, PR 00970-2598
(787) 287-6161 Fax: (787) 287-6110
Sra. Emma González, Director

CENTRO DE INFORMACIÓN Y REFERIDO ESTEBAN F. BIRD
Affiliate of Fondos Unidos de Puerto Rico
P.O. Box 191914
San Juan, PR 00919-1914
(787) 268-5353 or (877) 72AYUDA
Fax: (787) 728-7099
Sra. Judith Matos, Director

CENTRO DE ORIENTACIÓN MUJER Y FAMILIA
Affiliate of Fondos Unidos de Puerto Rico
Altos Oficina 3
Calle Nuñez Romeu 51
Cayey, PR 00763
(787) 263-2115 Fax: (787) 263-2114
Sra. Inés León, Director

CENTRO DE PROMOCIÓN ESCOLAR
Affiliate of Fondos Unidos de Puerto Rico
165 Professional Bldg.
122 Calle José Celso Barbosa
Las Piedras, PR 00771
(787) 733-4661 Fax: (787) 733-4661
Sor Carmen Carmona, Director

CENTRO DE SERVICIOS A LA JUVENTUD
Affiliate of Fondos Unidos de Puerto Rico
Coto Station, P.O. Box 9368
Arecibo, PR 00613
(787) 878-6776 Fax: (787) 878-6890
Srta. Nilda Torres Martínez, Director

CENTRO DE SERVICIOS FERRÁN
Affiliate of Fondos Unidos de Puerto Rico
Bda. Ferrán, A58 Calle Final
Ponce, PR 00731
(787) 840-2621 Fax: (787) 840-2621
Sor María Rosa Rivera, Director

CENTRO DE VOLUNTARIOS DE FONDOS UNIDOS
Affiliate of Fondos Unidos de Puerto Rico
P.O. Box 191914
San Juan, PR 00919-1914
(787) 728-8500 Ext. 220 Fax: (787) 728-7099
Sra. Carmen L. Rodríguez, Director

CENTRO EDUCATIVO JOAQUINA DE VEDRUNA
Affiliate of Fondos Unidos de Puerto Rico
2017 Carretera 177
Guaynabo, PR 00969-5120
(787) 789-4627 Fax: (787) 789-4627
Hna. Virgenmina Rivera, Director

CENTRO ESPERANZA
Affiliate of Fondos Unidos de Puerto Rico
P.O. Box 482
Loiza, PR 00772
(787) 876-1545 Fax: (787) 876-1545
Sor Carmen G. Alayón, Director

CENTRO ESPIBI
Affiliate of Fondos Unidos de Puerto Rico
P.O. Box 216
Mayaguez, PR 00681-0216
(787) 834-7991 Fax: (787) 834-5451
Sra. Olga López, Director

CENTRO GERIÁTRICO CARITATIVO "LA MILAGROSA, INC."
P.O. Box 2247
Mayagües, PR 00681-2247
(787) 834-0688 Fax: (787) 834-0688
Yovania Bacó, Director

CENTRO GERIÁTRICO EL REMANSO
Affiliate of Fondos Unidos de Puerto Rico
RR11 Box 4103
Bayamón, PR 00956
(787) 797-5083 Fax: (787) 797-5083
Sister Zayda González, Director

CENTRO GERIÁTRICO SAN RAFAEL
Calle Cervantes, #50
Arecibo, PR 00612
(787) 878-3813
Carmen M. Rodríguez, Director

CENTRO GERIÁTRICO "VIRGILIO RAMOS CASELLAS"
P.O. Box 3052
Manati, PR 00674
(787) 854-1253
Segundo Llanos Saez, Director

CENTRO INFANTIL NORMARIS
P.O. Box 1128
Cabo Rojo, PR 00623
(787) 851-6656
Ada I. Ramos, Director

CENTRO INFANTIL PINOCHO
Turabo Gardens-C.Milo Borges Z 4-1
Caguas, PR 00725
(787) 746-5899
Hilda Báez, Director

CENTRO MARGARITA, INC.
Affiliate of Fondos Unidos de Puerto Rico
P.O. Box 1638
Cidra, PR 00739
(787) 739-6030 or (787) 739-6050
Fax: (787) 739-0808
Sra. Janet Febo Méndez, Director

CENTRO MI ESCUELITA INFANTIL
Cierabayamon Calle 37 Bl. 40
Bayamón, PR 00957
(787) 787-8322 Fax: (787) 787-8322
Carmen Boyef, President

CENTRO NUEVOS HORIZONTES, INC.
Affiliate of Fondos Unidos de Puerto Rico
Urb. Alturas de Flamboyan
Calle 23 N 16
Bayamón, PR 00959
(787) 269-1577 or (787) 780-3782
Fax: (787) 269-1577
Sra. Hilda Rosa Kairuz, Director

CENTRO PARA NIÑOS EL NUEVO HOGAR
Affiliate of Fondos Unidos de Puerto Rico
P.O. Box 212
Adjuntas, PR 00601
(787) 829-8835 Fax: (787) 829-5032
Gabriel Mass, Director

CENTRO PARA PERSONAS DE MAYOR EDAD
Calle F. Mariano Quiñones #17-Box 356
Sabana Grande, PR 00637
(787) 873-2060
Lilian Torres Ayala, Director

CENTRO PRE-ESCOLAR KIDDY
Angueises 1772-Venus Gardens
San Juan, PR 00926
(787) 761-2167 Fax: (787) 761-2167
Raquel Torres, Director

CENTRO PRE-ESCOLAR TITI LYDIA
P.O. Box 1312
Cayey, PR 00736
(787) 263-3162
Lydia M. Rodríguez, Director

CENTRO PRECIOSOS MOMENTOS
Calle Ponce de Leon #58
Arecibo, PR 00612
(787) 878-9285 Fax: (787) 878-9285
Cibelle Arce, Director

CENTRO PRESCHOOLER MONTALVO
Mariano Quiñones 23
Coamo, PR 00769
(787) 825-2287
Irma Montalvo, Director

CENTRO PROVIDENCIA PARA PERSONAS DE MAYOR EDAD
Affiliate of Fondos Unidos de Puerto Rico
P.O. Box 514
Loiza, PR 00772
(787) 876-3595 Fax: (787) 876-8303
Cruz M. Torres de Jesús, Director

CENTRO RAMÓN FRADE PARA PERSONAS DE MAYOR EDAD
Affiliate of Fondos Unidos de Puerto Rico
Res. Benigno Fernández García
Buzón 105
Cayey, PR 00736
(787) 738-3864 Fax: (787) 738-3864
Sra. Lydia Oquendo, Director

CENTRO RENACER, INC.
Affiliate of Fondos Unidos de Puerto Rico
P.O. Box 3772
Guaynabo, PR 00970-3772
(787) 720-0235 Fax: (787) 731-8747
Rev. Félix Cabrera, Director

CENTRO RIVERA RIVERA
Alta Vista C-2 A-1
Ponce, PR 00731
(787) 840-5082
Guillermina Rivera, Director.

CENTRO SAN FRANCISCO
Affiliate of Fondos Unidos de Puerto Rico
P.O. Box 10479
Ponce, PR 00731
(787) 844-2434 Fax: (787) 842-2776
Sister Anita Moseley, Director

CENTRO SAN VICENTE DE PAUL - AYUDA AL DEAMBULANTE
Affiliate of Fondos Unidos de Puerto Rico
Apartado 25073
Río Piedras, PR 00925
(787) 764-0466 Fax: (787) 765-6278
Sor María Pérez Verdes, Director

CENTRO SISTER ISOLINA FERRE - ABC
Affiliate of Fondos Unidos de Puerto Rico
P.O. Box 30213
Ponce, PR 00734-0213
(787) 843-1910 Fax: (787) 844-7665
Rosita M. Bauzá, Executive Director

CENTRO SISTER ISOLINA FERRE - SUBIENDO PELDAÑOS
RR 1 Box 6786
Guayama, PR 00784-9608
(787) 842-0000 or (787) 843-1910
Fax: (787) 840-5020
Sra. Marta Almodóvar, Director

CENTRO UNIDO DE DETALLISTAS DE PUERTO RICO
P.O. Box 190127
San Juan, PR 00919-0127
(787) 759-8405 Fax: (787) 754-7312
Emilio Torres Hernández, President
Email: cud@centrounido.org
Web: www.centrounido.org

CHAMBER OF COMMERCE OF PUERTO RICO / CÁMARA DE COMERCIO DE PUERTO RICO
P.O. Box 9024-033
San Juan, PR 00902-4033
(787) 721-6060 Fax: (787) 723-1891
Luis Torres, President
Email: camarapr@coqui.net
Web: http://camarapr.coqui.net

CHRISTIAN COMMUNITY CENTER
Affiliate of Fondos Unidos de Puerto Rico
65 de Infantería
P.O. Box 300024
Rio Piedras, PR 00929
(787) 789-8758 Fax: (787) 789-8758
Rev. Juan A. Figueroa, Director

CINDERELLA NURSERY DAY CARE
Calle Coqui #720
Mayagüez, PR 00680
(787) 834-3770 Fax: (787) 834-3770
Luz González, Director

CÍRCULO DE ESTUDIANTES EMBAJADORES DEL PRESIDENTE
Inter American Univ. of Puerto Rico, Ponce
104 Parque Industrial Turpó, Rd. 1
Mercedita, PR 00715-1602
(787) 284-1912 x2092 Fax: (787) 841-0103
Dilia Rodríguez, Director
Email: drodrigu@ponce.inter.edu
Web: http://ponce.inter.edu/nhp/contents/

CÍRCULO DE PRE-MÉDICO
Pontificia Universidad Católica de Puerto Rico
2250 Avenida Las Américas, #625
Ponce, PR 00717-0777
(787) 841-2000 ext. 324
Coral González, Vice Pres. of Student Affairs
Email: Circulo.Premedico@pucpr.edu
Web: www.pucpr.edu

CÍRCULO LITERARIO RENÉ MÁRQUEZ
Pontificia Universidad Católica de Puerto Rico
2250 Avenida Las Américas, #625
Ponce, PR 00717-0777
(787) 841-2000 ext. 324
Coral González, Vice Pres. of Student Affairs
Email: Cir.Lit.ReneMarquez@pucpr.edu
Web: www.pucpr.edu

CLUB CÍVICO DE DAMAS
P.O. Box 10185
San Juan, PR 00908
(787) 751-1471 or (787) 751-9264
Fax: (787) 751-9264
Wanda Lee Navajas, President

CLUB DE BIOLOGÍA
Pontificia Universidad Católica de Puerto Rico
2250 Avenida Las Américas, #625
Ponce, PR 00717-0777
(787) 841-2000 ext. 324
Coral González, Vice Pres. of Student Affairs
Email: Club.Biologia@pucpr.edu
Web: www.pucpr.edu

CLUB DE ENFERMERÍA
Pontificia Universidad Católica de Puerto Rico
2250 Avenida Las Américas, #625
Ponce, PR 00717-0777
(787) 841-2000 ext. 324
Coral González, Vice Pres. of Student Affairs
Email: Club.Enfermeras@pucpr.edu
Web: www.pucpr.edu

CLUB DE FILOSOFÍA
Pontificia Universidad Católica de Puerto Rico
2250 Avenida Las Américas, #625
Ponce, PR 00717-0777
(787) 841-2000 ext. 324
Coral González, Vice Pres. of Student Affairs
Email: Club.Filosofia@pucpr.edu
Web: www.pucpr.edu

CLUB DE INGLÉS
Pontificia Universidad Católica de Puerto Rico
2250 Avenida Las Américas, #625
Ponce, PR 00717-0777
(787) 841-2000 ext. 324
Coral González, Vice Pres. of Student Affairs
Email: Club.Ingles@pucpr.edu
Web: www.pucpr.edu

CLUB DE LOS DEPARTAMENTOS DE FÍSICA Y MATEMÁTICAS
Pontificia Universidad Católica de Puerto Rico
2250 Avenida Las Américas, #625
Ponce, PR 00717-0777
(787) 841-2000 ext. 324
Coral González, Vice Pres. of Student Affairs
Email: Club.Fisica.Mat@pucpr.edu
Web: www.pucpr.edu

CLUB DE QUÍMICA
Pontificia Universidad Católica de Puerto Rico
2250 Avenida Las Américas, #625
Ponce, PR 00717-0777
(787) 841-2000 ext. 324
Coral González, Vice Pres. of Student Affairs
Email: Club.Quimica@pucpr.edu
Web: www.pucpr.edu

CLUB PIONERO
Pontificia Universidad Católica de Puerto Rico
2250 Avenida Las Américas, #625
Ponce, PR 00717-0777
(787) 841-2000 ext. 324
Coral González, Vice Pres. of Student Affairs
Web: www.pucpr.edu

COLEGIO AMARILLEEN
Calle Naranjo AK-14 Valle Arriba Height
Carolina, PR 00982
(787) 769-4284
Nilsa Peña, Director

COLEGIO EDUCACIÓN ESPECIAL Y REHABILITACIÓN INTEGRAL (CODERI)
Affiliate of Fondos Unidos
Urb. El Cerezal, 1628 Calle Guadiana
Rio Piedras, PR 00926
(787) 765-0259 or (787) 765-6147
Fax: (787) 764-8135
Sr. José del Valle, Director

COLEGIO EVA RIVERA
Ave. Eduardo Conde 1871
Santurce, PR 00912
(787) 728-1882
Nilca Camacho, Director

COLEGIO MARÍA REINA
Calle 18-Buzon 7-Imbery
Barceloneta, PR 00617
(787) 846-6887
María E. Reina Roger, Director

COLEGIO MIRANG
Ave. Campo Rico GQ-2-Country Club
Carolina, PR 00982
(787) 769-8338 Fax: (787) 769-8338
Elva Coto de Santana, Director

COLUMBIA COLLEGE
Centro de Yauco
P.O. Box 3062
Yauco, PR 00698
(787) 856-0845 or (787) 856-0945
Fax: (787) 267-2335
Carmen L. Martínez, Director

COMERCIANTES DE PLAZA LAS AMÉRICAS, INC.
P.O. Box 363268
San Juan, PR 00936-3268
(787) 767-1558 Fax: (787) 250-6062
Franklin Domensh, Coordinator

COMISIÓN DEL CENTENARIO
P.O. Box 9024198
San Juan, PR 00902-4198
(787) 722-1998 Fax: (787) 722-1989
Zulma R. Rosario Vega, Esq., Executive Director
Email: pruscent@t1d.net
Web: www://PUERTORICOUSA100.ORG

COMITÉ JUVENIL PRO-SER
Pontificia Universidad Católica de Puerto Rico
2250 Avenida Las Américas, #625
Ponce, PR 00717-0777
(787) 841-2000 ext. 324
Coral González, Vice Pres. of Student Affairs
Email: ComiteJuvenilProSer@pucpr.edu
Web: www.pucpr.edu

COMITÉ PRO RESCATE DEL BUEN AMBIENTE DE GUAYANILLA
P.O. Box 82
Guayanilla, PR 00656
(787) 835-2341 Fax: (787) 835-2232
Efrain A Emanualli, President

COMMUNITY LEARNING CENTER
Duarte 20-Floral Park
Hato Rey, PR 00917
(787) 758-6990 Fax: (787) 753-8786
Rosana Soto, Director

COMUNICADORES Y PERIODISTAS INDEPENDIENTES DE PUERTO RICO (O.C.P.I.)
P.O. Box 6251, Loiza Station
Santurce, PR 00914
(787) 765-4483 or (787) 752-4709
Fax: (787) 723-2982
Gilberto Ramos, President

COMUNIDAD PARA ENVEJECIENTES
P.O. Box 868
Rincón, PR 00677
(787) 823-4000
Silvette Rosario, Director

COMUNIDAD PUNTO CUBANO, INC.
Apartado 1597
Hormigueros, PR 00600
(787) 849-2624
Ligsia E. Hernández, President

CONCIENCIA JURÍDICA
Pontificia Universidad Católica de Puerto Rico
2250 Avenida Las Américas, #625
Ponce, PR 00717-0777
(787) 841-2000 ext. 324
Coral González, Vice President of Student Affairs
Web: www.pucpr.edu

CONCILIO DE LA COMUNIDAD
Affiliate of Fondos Unidos de Puerto Rico
Res. Luis Llorens Torres
Edificio 66 Apt. #1252
San Juan, PR 00913
(787) 727-4468 Fax: (787) 727-4468
Sra. Violeta Figueroa, Director

CONCILIO IGLESIA PENTECOSTAL DE JESUCRISTO INC.
P.O. Box 1658
Yauco, PR 00698
(787) 856-1200 Fax: (787) 856-6060
Rev. Santiago Gonzalez, President

CONDADO ASSOCIATION
1351 Calle Lucchetti
San Juan, PR 00907
Nelson Biaggi, President

CONSEJO RENAL DE PUERTO RICO
Affiliate of Fondos Unidos de Puerto Rico
Centro Comercial Repto. Metropolitano
Oficina 208-C
Rio Piedras, PR 00921
(787) 764-8689 Fax: (787) 250-0360
Sr. Alfredo Paredes, Director

CONSERVATION TRUST OF PUERTO RICO
P.O. Box 9023554
San Juan, PR 00902-3554
(787) 722-5834 Fax: (787) 722-5872
Francisco J. Blanco, Executive Director

CONSERVATORY OF MUSIC OF PUERTO RICO
350 Calle Rafael Lamar Esq. F.D. Roosevelt
San Juan, PR 00918
(787) 751-0160 Fax: (787) 758-8268
María del Carmen Gil, Chancellor
Email: mcgil@cmpr.prstar.net

CORPORACIÓN PARA EL DESARROLLO ECONÓMICO Y SOCIAL DE SAN SEBASTIÁN
Affiliate of Fondos Unidos de Puerto Rico
P.O. Box 845
San Sebastián, PR 00685
(787) 896-3645 Fax: (787) 896-3645
Zoraida Rosa Méndez, Executive Director

CRAYOLITAS CENTRO PRE-ESCOLAR
Jardines de Ponce H-16
Ponce, PR 00731
(787) 840-3595
Teresa Irizarri, Director

CRISPIN COUNTRY HOME CARE
Calle 4 #258-Saint Just
Carolina, PR 00978
(787) 768-0730
Tomasa C. de Alvarez, Director

CRUZ ROJA AMERICANA
Capítulo de Puerto Rico
P.O. Box 9021067
San Juan, PR 0090-1067
(787) 758-8150 Fax: (787) 758-6086
Coronel Pedro Negrón, Executive Director

CUERPO DE VOLUNTARIOS DEL DEPARTAMENTO DE TRABAJO SOCIAL
Pontificia Universidad Católica de Puerto Rico
2250 Avenida Las Américas, #625
Ponce, PR 00717-0777
(787) 841-2000 ext. 324
Coral González, Vice Pres. of Student Affairs
Email: CuerpoVoluntarioDTS@pucpr.edu
Web: www.pucpr.edu

CUERPO VOLUNTARIO DE SERVICIOS MEDICOS DE EMERGENCIA, INC.
Affiliate of Fondos Unidos de Puerto Rico
P.O. Box 1290
Hatillo, PR 00659
(787) 262-1686 Fax: (787) 262-1686
Sr. Angel L. Crespo, Director
Email: cusme911@coqui.net
Web: www.cusme.com

DENTISTRY STUDENTS INTERNATIONAL ASSOCIATION
Univ. of Puerto Rico, Ciencias Medicas
School of Dentistry
P.O. Box 365067
San Juan, PR 00936
(787) 758-2525
María E. Cora-Block, Dean
Web: www.upr.clu.edu

DENTON NURSERY
HC-03, Box 19654
Arecibo, PR 00612
(787) 878-3081
Carmen J. Denton, Director

DEPARTAMENTO DE EDUCACIÓN
Instituto Tecnológico de Puerto Rico

Recinto de Ponce
P.O. Box 7284
Ponce, PR 00732
(787) 843-1305 or (787) 843-0935
Fax: (787) 841-0689
Prof. Leovigildo López, Director

DONATIVOS EN ESPECIE / GIFT IN KIND
Affiliate of Fondos Unidos de Puerto Rico
P.O. Box 191914
San Juan, PR 00919-1914
(787) 728-8500 Ext. 262 Fax: (787) 728-7099
Ivonne M. Bernard, Coordinator

ECONOMIC DEVELOPMENT BANK FOR PUERTO RICO
PO Box 2134
San Juan, PR 00922-2134
(787) 793-7422 Fax: (787) 793-7504
Agnes B. Suárez, President

ECOS (ESTUDIANTES COORDINADORES EN ORIENTACIÓN Y SERVICIO)
Pontificia Universidad Católica de Puerto Rico
2250 Avenida Las Américas, #625
Ponce, PR 00717-0777
(787) 841-2000 ext. 324
Coral González, Vice Pres. of Student Affairs
Email: ECOS@pucpr.edu
Web: www.pucpr.edu

EL CENTRO DE AYUDA Y TERAPIA AL NIÑO CON IMPEDIMENTO (AYANI)
#5 Calle Isaura
Moca, PR 00676
(787) 877-4213 Fax: (787) 877-4213
Hector Colon, Director

EL CENTRO EDÉN
Calle Eider 968-Urb. Country Club
Rio Piedras, PR 00982
(787) 757-5110
Isabel Figueroa, Director

EL HOGAR DEL NIÑO
Affiliate of Fondos Unidos de Puerto Rico
P.O. Box 20667
San Juan, PR 00928-0667
(787) 761-2805 or (787) 761-2820
Fax: (787) 283-1345
Hna. María Goretti Vásquez, Director

EL PAÍS DE LAS MARAVILLAS
Calle Mayagüez B-25
Caguas, PR 00725
(787) 746-0243
Victoria Reyes, Director

EL VERDE HOME CARE
Carr. 186-Km. 25.3 - Urb. Villa Calzada #19
Rio Grande, PR 00745
(787) 888-7811
Brunilda Aponte, Director

EMMANUEL CENTRO EDUCATIVO
Calle Palmer, #90
Canóvanas, PR 00729
(787) 876-5146
Awilda Rodríguez, Director

ENVIRONMENTAL HEALTH STUDENTS ASSOCIATION
University of Puerto Rico, Ciencias Médicas
Biosocial Sciences and Graduate School of Public Health, P.O. Box 365067
San Juan, PR 00936
(787) 758-2525
María E. Cora-Block, Dean
Web: www.upr.clu.edu

ESCUELA DE ARTES PLÁSTICAS DE PUERTO RICO
P.O. Box 9021112
San Juan, PR 00902-1112
(787) 725-8120 Fax: (787) 725-8111
Marimar Benítez, Rectora
Email: eap@coqui.net

ESCUELA DE MEDICINA SAN JUAN BAUTISTA
P.O. Box 71365
San Juan, PR 00936-8465
(787) 743-3038/4696 Fax: (787) 746-3093
Sr. Juan Chaves Abreu, President

ESCUELA PARQUE INFANTIL
Calle José Marti #665-Miramar
Santurce, PR 00907
(787) 725-1763
Rosa María Dones, Director

ESPELEOLÓGICA UNIVERSITARIA DEL SUR
University of Puerto Rico, Ponce
Departamento de Biología
Apartado 7186
Ponce, PR 00732-7186
(787) 844-8181 Fax: (787) 844-9231
Sandra Moyá Guzmán, President
Web: www.upr.edu

ESPERANZA PARA LA VEJEZ (HOPE)
Affiliate of Fondos Unidos de Puerto Rico
P.O. Box 366049
San Juan, PR 00936-6049
(787) 783-7953 or (787) 783-8748
Fax: (787) 781-5120
Sra. Concepción Silva, Director

ESQUILIN-MANGUAL CUIDADO DE NIÑOS
Calle 2B y 2-Urb. Bairoa
Caguas, PR 00725
(787) 744-8792
Carmen R. Magoal, Director

ESTANCIA CORAZÓN, INC.
P.O. Box 3309-Marina Station-Carretera #2Centro Medico de Mayagüez
Casa de Salud- 4to. Piso
Mayagüez, PR 00681
(787) 831-5095 Fax: (787) 265-2850
Ivonne Santiago Nieves, Executive Director
Email: ecorazon@coqui.net

ESTUDIANTES UNIVERSITARIOS PRO-ESTADIDAD
Universidad de Puerto Rico
P.O. Box 439
Patillas, PR 00723
(787) 850-0000 or (787) 850-9328
Iris y Cintrón Báez, President

ETA GAMMA DELTA
Pontificia Universidad Católica de Puerto Rico
2250 Avenida Las Américas, #625
Ponce, PR 00717-0777
(787) 841-2000 ext. 324
Coral González, Vice Pres. of Student Affairs
Web: www.pucpr.edu

ETA PHI ZETA
Pontificia Universidad Católica de Puerto Rico
2250 Avenida Las Américas, #625
Ponce, PR 00717-0777
(787) 841-2000 ext. 324
Coral González, Vice Pres. of Student Affairs
Web: www.pucpr.edu

EVA'S NURSING HOME
Buckingham S-6 - Villa del Rey 1ra. Seccion
Caguas, PR 00725
(787) 743-3308
Eva Ortiz Fuentes, Director

EXITO A LOS SEIS / SUCCESS BY SIX
Affiliate of Fondos Unidos de Puerto Rico
P.O. Box 191914
San Juan, PR 00919-1914
(787) 728-8500 Ext. 224 Fax: (787) 728-7099
Lucinda Colón, Coordinator

FAMILY MEDICINE INTEREST GROUP
University of Puerto Rico, Ciencias Medicas
School of Medicine
P.O. Box 365067
San Juan, PR 00936-5067
(787) 758-2525
María E. Cora-Block, Dean
Web: www.upr.clu.edu

FEDERACIÓN DE ASOCIACIONES PECUARIAS DE PUERTO RICO, INC.
P.O. Box 2635, Malecón Zona Portuario
Mayagüez, PR 00681
(787) 834-9191 Fax: (787) 833-1055
David A. Giménez, President
Email: pecuaria@coqui.net

FEDERACIÓN DE TIRO DE PERSONAS CON IMPEDIMENTOS
P.O. Box 41309
San Juan, PR 00907
(787) 725-2333 or (800) 981-4125
Fax: (787) 721-2455
David Cruz-Vélez, President
Email: oppi@oppi.prstar.net
Web: www.oppi.prstar.net

FEDERACIÓN INTERNATIONAL DE ATLETISMO AFICIONADO
(North American, Central American &Caribbean)
Apartado 11040
San Juan, PR 00910-2140
(787) 724-0782 Fax: (787) 721-5236
Amadeo I. D. Francis, Area Representative
Email: nacac@isla.net

FEDERACIÓN PUERTORRIQUENA DE BOXEO AFICIONADO, INC.
P.O. Box 9065964 - Puerta de Tierra Station
San Juan, PR 00906-5964
(787) 721-5575 Fax: (787) 721-4252
José-Luis Uvellón, President

FEDERACIÓN PUERTORRIQUENA DE CICLISMO
P.O Box 194674
San Juan, PR 00919-4674
(787) 721-8755 Fax: (787) 723-0140
Héctor Ramos, President

FEDERACIÓN PUERTORRIQUENA DE VOLEIBOLL
P.O. Box 363711
San Juan, PR 00936-3711
(787) 282-7524 or (787) 282-7525
Fax: (787) 282-7526
Mongui, Director
Web: http://home.coqui.net/voleiboll

FIDEICOMISO DE CONSERVACIÓN DE PR.
P.O. Box 9023554
San Juan, PR 00902-3554
(787) 722-5834
Francisco Javier Blanco, Director

FIDEICOMISO DE CONSERVACIÓN E HISTORIA DE VIEQUES
138 Flamboyan
Vieques, PR 00765
(787) 741-8850 Fax: (787) 741-8850
Rubén Reyes, President

FONDITA DE JESÚS
Affiliate of Fondos Unidos de Puerto Rico
P.O. Box 19384
San Juan, PR 00910-1384
(787) 724-4051 Fax: (787) 722-0992
Sra. Olga Ruiz, Director

FOUNDATION FOR COMMUNITY DEVELOPMENT OF P.R., INC. (FUNDESCO)
P.O. Box 6300
Caguas, PR 00726-6300
(787) 258-5162 Fax: (787) 743-7658
Norberto Menéndez, Executive Director

FRATERNIDAD PRE-LEGAL PHI ALPHA DELTA
Pontificia Universidad Católica de Puerto Rico
2250 Avenida Las Américas, #625
Ponce, PR 00717-0777
(787) 841-2000 ext. 324
Coral González, Vice Pres. of Student Affairs
Email: PhiAlphaDelta@pucpr.edu
Web: www.pucpr.edu

FUNDACIÓN ABRIENDO PUERTAS, INC.
P.O. Box 9066315
San Juan, PR 00906-6315
(787) 723-6915 Fax: (787) 723-6915
Padre Tomás Travers, Director
Email: tjtrower@coqui.net

FUNDACIÓN ACCIÓN SOCIAL REFUGIO ETERNO
Affiliate of Fondos Unidos de Puerto Rico
P.O. Box 8388
Bayamón, PR 00960
(787) 799-8811 Fax: (787) 279-8407
Sra. Ruth Cuevas, Director

FUNDACIÓN D.A.R.
Affiliate of Fondos Unidos de Puerto Rico
P.O. Box 360648
San Juan, PR 00936-0648
(787) 751-9379 Fax: (787) 753-6841
Sra. Marilyn Torres, Director

FUNDACIÓN DR. GARCÍA RINALDI
Affiliate of Fondos Unidos de Puerto Rico
P.O. Box 8816
San Juan, PR 00910-0816
(787) 725-4065 Fax: (787) 725-4319
Sra. Teresita Ibarra, Director

FUNDACIÓN HOGAR NIÑITO JESÚS
Affiliate of Fondos Unidos de Puerto Rico
P.O. Box 192503
San Juan, PR 00919-2503
(787) 748-5682 Fax: (787) 748-5630
Sra. Ana Gloria Arias, Director

FUNDACIÓN MODESTO GOTAY
Apartado #665 Barrio Las Cuevas
Trujillo Alto, PR 00977-0665
(787) 761-6244 Fax: (787) 761-6376
Aída Torres de Nevares, Director

FUND. PUERTO RICO EN EL SIGLO 21, INC.
989 Madrid Street, Santa Rita
San Juan, PR 00925
(787) 764-0074; (787) 722-2121 ext. 357
(787) 721-5841 or (787) 763-7106
Mr. José Eduardo Rey, Coordinator

FUNDACIÓN PUERTORRIQUEÑA DE CONSERVACIÓN
278-B Ave. Jesús T Pinero
San Juan, PR 00927
(787) 763-9875 Fax: (787) 772-4645
Esther M. Rojas, Executive Director
Email: fconserv@tld.net
Web: www.tld.net/users/fconserv

FUNDACIÓN PUERTORRIQUEÑA DE SÍNDROME DOWN
Affiliate of Fondos Unidos de Puerto Rico
P.O. Box 195273
San Juan, PR 00919-5273
(787) 268-3696 Fax: (787) 728-5700
Prof. Carmen L. Aviles, Director

FUNDACIÓN SIDA DE PUERTO RICO
P.O Box 364842
San Juan, PR 00936-4842
(787) 782-9600 Fax: (787) 782-1411
José Toro Alfonso, Director

GRUPO HUELLAS
Pontificia Universidad Católica de Puerto Rico
2250 Avenida Las Américas, #625
Ponce, PR 00717-0777
(787) 841-2000 ext. 324
Coral González, Vice Pres. of Student Affairs
Email: Grupo.Huellas@pucpr.edu
Web: www.pucpr.edu

GUARDERIA EL REGAZO
Urb. San Tomas E-15-Playa Ponce
Ponce, PR 00731
(787) 843-1910 x255
Milagros Ramos, Coordinator

HERALDOS DE CRISTO
Pontificia Universidad Católica de Puerto Rico
2250 Avenida Las Américas, #625
Ponce, PR 00717-0777
(787) 841-2000 ext. 324
Coral González, Vice Pres. of Student Affairs
Email: Heraldos.de.Cristo@pucpr.edu
Web: www.pucpr.edu

HERMANDAD UNIVERSITARIA CRISTIANA
Inter American Univ. of Puerto Rico, Ponce
104 Parque Industrial Turpó, Rd. 1
Mercedita, PR 00715-1602
(787) 284-1912 x2092 Fax: (787) 841-0103
Dilia Rodríguez, Director
Email: drodrigu@ponce.inter.edu
Web: http://ponce.inter.edu/nhp/contents/

HILDMONT COLLEGE
P.O. Box 21148
Rio Piedras, PR 00928
(787) 755-3638
Hilda Montalvo, Director

HISPANIC NATIONAL BAR ASSOCIATION
270 Munoz Rivera Ave.
Hato Rey, PR 00918
(787) 250-5638 Fax: (787) 759-9225
Richard Graffam, Treasurer
Email: rgraffam@mcvpr.com
Web: www.hnba.com

HISPANIC NATIONAL BAR ASSOCIATION
Avenida Franklin D. Roosevelt, #355
Hato Rey, PR 00918-2138
(787) 763-1144 Fax: (787) 753-6874
Alice Velázquez, Immediate Past President
Email: Alvelazq@preda.com
Web: www.hnba.com

Region XIX (PR, USVI)
827 Marti St., Apt. 402 Miramar
San Juan, PR 00907
(787) 772-3177 Fax: (787) 759-3123

Andres Lopez, Regional President
Email: lopez@post.harvard.edu
Web: www.hnba.com

HOGAR ALBERGUE NIÑOS MALTRATADOS PORTAL DE AMOR
Affiliate of Fondos Unidos de Puerto Rico
P.O. Box 1375
San Germán, PR 00753
(787) 892-3515 Fax: (787) 892-3515
Sra. Liduvina Montalvo, Director

HOGAR ALBERGUE PARA NIÑOS JESÚS DE NAZARET, INC.
Affiliate of Fondos Unidos de Puerto Rico
Apartado 1147
Mayagüez, PR 00681
(787) 831-6161 Fax: (787) 831-6161
Sra. Margarita Mari Lamourt, Director

HOGAR CARIÑO I
Luis Pardo 1016
Río Piedras, PR 00924
(787) 757-5119 Fax: (787) 752-2339
María Inés Caballero, Director

HOGAR CARMELITANO
Calle J. Bengochea 1326
Río Piedras, PR 00924
(787) 769-3110
Maribel Mejía, Director

HOGAR CARMEN PIMENTEL
Calle Alejo Cruzado #1037
Río Piedras, PR 00924
(787) 752-7788
Carmen Pimentel, Director

HOGAR CASA MARGARITA
Carr. 742-KM. 3.2-Apdo. 371414
Cayey, PR 00737
(787) 738-8035
María M. Colón Larrauri, Director

HOGAR CREA, DISTRITO DE CAYEY
P.O. Box 3361
Cayey, PR 00736
(787) 738-7268 Fax: (787) 263-7467
Enrique Luna Acosta, Director

HOGAR CRISTIANO
Calle 1 #1083 - Villa Nevares
Río Piedras, PR 00928
(787) 763-9712
Ramonita Núñez, President

HOGAR CRISTO ES LA ROCA
Affiliate of Fondos Unidos de Puerto Rico
Apartado 3281
Manatí, PR 00674
(787) 854-6706 Fax: (787) 854-6706
Sra. Ana Rodríguez, Director

HOGAR CUNA SAN CRISTÓBAL
Affiliate of Fondos Unidos de Puerto Rico
Private Mail Boxes 428
HC 1 Box 29030
Caguas, PR 00725-8900
(787) 747-9488 Fax: (787) 747-9488
Sra. Elidia González, Director

HOGAR DE ANCIANOS BETZAIDA
Bo. Ceiba Baja-HC-02- Box 8976
Aguadilla, PR 00603
(787) 882-9004
Carmela Arce, Director

HOGAR DE ANCIANOS EL EDÉN
Km.1 Barrio Sonadora - Ramal 792
Aguas Buenas, PR 00703
(787) 732-8520
Valentina Rivera, Director

HOGAR DE ANCIANOS KANORA
Bo. Maleza Alta-Box 240
San Antonio, PR 00690
(787) 890-3518
Dra. Nora Mirán, Director

HOGAR DE ANCIANOS LA ANTIGUA MURALLA
Carr. 795-Km2.2HC-05-Box 59563
Caguas, PR 00725
(787) 747-0348
Juana Román, Director

HOGAR DE ANCIANOS NUESTA SRA. DEL ROSARIO
Calle Bonanza, #5-Villa Esperanza
Cagua, PR 00725
(787) 746-1290
Luz M. Martinez, Director

HOGAR DE ANCIANOS REMANZO DE LA VEJEZ
Calle Hospital, #13
Lares, PR 00669
(787) 897-2400
José Villegas, Director

HOGAR DE ANCIANOS RESIDENCIAL GLADYS
Calle 12 ABK-2
Humacao, PR 00791
(787) 850-7615 Fax: (787) 850-7615
Gladys Rivera, Director

HOGAR DE ANCIANOS SAN VICENTE DE PAUL
Affiliate of Fondos Unidos de Puerto Rico
P.O. Box 4196
Vega Baja, PR 00694
(787) 855-0487 Fax: (787) 855-0487
Gilma Osorio, Director

HOGAR DE AYUDA EL REFUGIO
Affiliate of Fondos Unidos de Puerto Rico
Amelia Contract Station
P.O. Box 3118
Cataño, PR 00963-3118
(787) 792-1117 Fax: (787) 782-7858
María Ramos Andino, Director

HOGAR DE ENVEJECIENTES "IRMA FE POL MÉNDEZ, INC."
Calle P. Albizú Campos #52
Lares, PR 00669
(787) 897-6090
Sor Rosario, Director

HOGAR DE GRUPO SALEM, INC.
P.O. Box 2270
Arecibo, PR 00613
(787) 878-2272
Evelín Toledo, Director

HOGAR DEL CARMEN
C. Los Angeles #1025 - Urb. del Carmen
Río Piedras, PR 00924
(787) 758-6982
Santa Morales, Director

HOGAR DEL NIÑO EL AVE MARÍA
Affiliate of Fondos Unidos de Puerto Rico
BMS 239, P.O. Box 607061
Bayamón, PR 00960-7061
(787) 279-3003 Fax: (787) 799-1977
Padre Pedro Gorena, Director

HOGAR DIOS ES NUESTRO REFUGIO
Affiliate of Fondos Unidos de Puerto Rico
P.M.B. 642 HC-01, Box 29030
Caguas, PR 00725
(787) 731-0756 Fax: (787) 731-0756
Sr. Alfredo L. Roca, Director

HOGAR EL PARAÍSO DE ISRAEL
Carr. 175 Km. 13.3 - Sector Variante
Trujillo Alto, PR 00926
(787) 760-9418
Hernández I. Reyes, Director

HOGAR EMANUEL, INC.
HC-01-Box 3452
Las Marias, PR 00670
(787) 827-4837 Fax: (787) 827-4837
Lydia Olabarría, Director

HOGAR ESCUELA SOR MARÍA RAFAELA
Affiliate of Fondos Unidos de Puerto Rico
P.O. Box 3024
Bayamón, PR 00960
(787) 785-9517 Fax: (787) 785-9586
Sor Nélida Gonzales Medina, Director

HOGAR FORJADORES DE ESPERANZA
Affiliate of Fondos Unidos de Puerto Rico
Bayamón Gardens Station
P.O. Box 4181
Bayamón, PR 00958
(787) 730-0200 Fax: (787) 730-0909
Sra. Damaris Robles, Director

HOGAR FUENTE DE SILOE
Carr. 795, Km. 3.9
Caguas, PR 00725
(787) 747-8867
Edwin Bonilla, Director

HOGAR GUADALUPE
Carr. 785-Km. 5.8, HC02 Box 34190
Caguas, PR 00726-9420
(787) 747-8726
Cecilio Cabrera, Director

HOGAR INFANTIL JESÚS NAZARENO
Affiliate of Fondos Unidos de Puerto Rico
P.O. Box 1671
Isabela, PR 00662
(787) 872-0015, Ext. Fax: (787) 872-0015
Hna. Lourdes Mercado, Director

HOGAR INSTITUCIÓN LA BUENA FÉ
Apdo. HC-646, Box 6289
Trujillo Alto, PR 00976
(787) 760-5439
Jesús Márquez, Director

HOGAR JUANITA
Calle 10, #280, Ext. S. Agustin
Río Piedras, PR 00926
(787) 765-6423 Fax: (787) 765-6423
Zenaida García Dones, Director

HOGAR KATHY
Calle 36 #465
Río Piedras, PR 00924
(787) 764-5749
Yolanda Torres, Director

HOGAR LA POSADA DEL ÁNGEL
Calle 6 #69-Saint Just
Carolina, PR 00976
(787) 762-4593
Vicky Torres, Director

HOGAR LOMA LINDA
HC-01-Box 5226
Guaynabo, PR 00971
(787) 731-2741 Fax: (787) 793-0673
María del Pilar Nevares, Director

HOGAR MADRE Y REINA
Calle Polar #792-Venus Gardens
Río Piedras, PR 00926
(787) 755-8518
Manuela Alvarado, Director

HOGAR MARÍA TERESA
C. Volturno A-12
Río Piedras, PR 00924
(787) 761-3783
María Teresa Martínez, Director

HOGAR MERCCI RECCI
Calle 54 SE #1284
Río Piedras, PR 00921
(787) 781-9109
Mercedes Torres, Director

HOGAR NUESTRA SEÑORA FÁTIMA
Affiliate of Fondos Unidos de Puerto Rico
Bayamón Garden Station
P.O. Box 4228
Bayamón, PR 00958
(787) 787-2580 Fax: (787) 787-2580
Hna. Ligia M. Latorre, Director

HOGAR NUEVA MUJER SANTA MARÍA DE LA MERCED
Affiliate of Fondos Unidos de Puerto Rico
P.O. Box 927
Cayey, PR 00737
(787) 263-6473 Fax: (787) 263-9305
Sra. Rosael Jaiman, Director

HOGAR NUEVA VIDA
P.O. Box 449
Gurabo, PR 00778
(787) 737-2442
José A. Pereira, Executive Director

HOGAR PARA ENVEJECIENTES MARÍA LUISA
Calle 30 SO - 1425
Río Piedras, PR 00921
(787) 781-2571
Patricia Angulo, President

HOGAR PARA ENVEJECIENTES VILLA FONTANA
Via 68-19-Villa Fontana
Carolina, PR 00976
(787) 769-1524
Rebecca Lara, Director

HOGAR POSADA LA VICTORIA
Affiliate of Fondos Unidos de Puerto Rico
Santa Rosa Unit
P.O. Box 6789
Bayamón, PR 00960
(787) 870-3474 Fax: (787) 870-5314
Sra. Gladys C. Vázquez, Director

HOGAR REMANSO DE MONTANA
Carr. 836 Km. 2.7 #640
Guaynabo, PR 00971
(787) 731-2150 Fax: (787) 731-2150
Angelina Villegas, Director

HOGAR REMEMBRANZA
Carr. 806 Km 0.3
Toa Alta, PR 00953
(787) 870-3227
Carmen E. Rivera, Director

HOGAR RESURRECCIÓN, INC.
Affiliate of Fondos Unidos de Puerto Rico
P.O. Box 8608
Caguas, PR 00726
(787) 747-1393 Fax: (787) 747-1319
Sra. Nancy Martínez, Director

HOGAR RETIRO LAS MARÍAS
Calle Mayagüez 18
Hato Rey, PR 00919
(787) 758-4368 Fax: (787) 758-4368
María Núñez, Director

HOGAR RIDER
Hospital Rider Memorial
Call Box 859
Humacao, PR 00792
(787) 852-0768 or (787) 852-0266
Fax: (787) 852-0314
Lydia Abreu, Director

HOGAR RUTH, INC.
Affiliate of Fondos Unidos de Puerto Rico
Box 538
Vega Alta, PR 00692
(787) 883-1884 or (787) 792-6596
Fax: (787) 883-1884
Sra. Ileana Aymat, Director

HOGAR SAMARITANO
#75 Calle 7 - Apartado 346
Cidra, PR 00739
(787) 739-6821
Luz Pérez, Director

HOGAR SAN GERARDO, INC.
Señorial Mail Station #250
Rio Piedras, PR 00926
(787) 761-8383 Fax: (787) 748-2065
José Baez, Director.

HOGAR SAN JERÓNIMO, INC.
HC-02-Box 11215
Carr. 101 Km. 2.4
San German, PR 00683
(787) 892-6834
Evelyn Irizarri Martínez, Director.

HOGAR SAN JOSÉ DE LA MONTAÑA
Affiliate of Fondos Unidos de Puerto Rico
P.O. Box 11164
San Juan, PR 00922-1164
(787) 783-3856 Fax: (787) 781-8835
Madre Elvira Cárdenas, Director

HOGAR SANTA ELENA
Urbana Sta. Elena C-11 G-8
Guayanilla, PR 00656
(787) 835-4273
Carmen Segarra, Director

HOGAR SANTA TERESA DE JORNET
Carr. 176, Km. 3.8-Apart. 21012
Río Piedras, PR 00928
(787) 761-5805 Fax: (787) 755-5575
Carmen Vasques, Director

HOGAR SANTÍSIMA TRINIDAD
Affiliate of Fondos Unidos de Puerto Rico
BMS 326, P.O. Box 607061
Bayamón, PR 00960-7061
(787) 799-6208 or (787) 799-6120
Fax: (787) 799-6208
Padre Pedro Gorena, Executive Director

HOGAR SANTOS-ECHEVARRÍA
Apartado 642
Ceiba, PR 00735
(787) 885-3609
Miriam Echevarría, Director

HOGAR SEGUNDA RODRÍGUEZ
Calle 26, #327, Villa Nevarez
Río Piedras, PR 00927
(787) 763-9748
Segunda Rodríguez, Directora

HOGAR SINAI
Calle Davila, #16-La Milagrosa
Bayamón, PR 00956
(787) 798-5202
Héctor Guzmán, Director

HOGAR SUSTITUTO EL MODELO
Calle Aleli #69-Bzn 1868 - Barrio Duque
Naguabo, PR 00718
(787) 874-3867
Victoria Germán, Director

HOGAR SUSTITUTO EL PARAÍSO
P.O. Box 2716
Mayagüez, PR 00681
(787) 265-4055
Francisco Pichardo, Director

HOGAR SUSTITUTO JUAN ROSADO MORALES
P.O. Box 1606
Cayey, PR 00737
(787) 738-6829
Carmen Olga Rivera, Director

HOGAR SUSTITUTO MANZANO-ROSA
Bo. Sabana Seca, #116
Manati, PR 00674
(787) 854-6569
María Milagros Rosa, Director

HOGAR SUSTITUTO PISCIS
Calle Yucaey #98
Río Grande, PR 00745
(787) 887-1141
Salustiana Viñales, Director

HOGAR SUSTITUTO RODRIGUEZ ORTIZ
P.O. Box 1314
Carolina, PR 00986
(787) 750-6219 Fax: (787) 750-6219
Evelyn Rodríguez, Director

HOGARES RAFAELA YBARRA
Affiliate of Fondos Unidos de Puerto Rico
Embalse San José
432 Calle Torrelaguna
Río Piedras, PR 00923
(787) 763-1204 Fax: (787) 763-6266
Hna. Julia José Brecord, Director

HOGARES TERESA TODA
Affiliate of Fondos Unidos de Puerto Rico
P.O. Box 868
Canóvanas, PR 00729
(787) 886-2060 Fax: (787) 886-2060
Hna. Inés Peña, Director

HOPE WORLD WIDE PUERTO RICO, INC.
Affiliate of Fondos Unidos de Puerto Rico
Doctor's Medical Center
800 Ave., Hipódromo, #201
San Juan, PR 00909
(787) 721-3872 Fax: (787) 721-3872
Dr. William Torruellas, Director

HUERTO DE LA ESPERANZA
Centro Solar, #8-Apdo. 869
Aguas Buenas, PR 00703
(787) 732-3052
Sandra Navarro, Director

IMAGE DE RÍO PIEDRAS
National Image, Inc.
1967 Calle Salvia (Urb. San Ramón)
Guaynabo, PR 00657
(787) 789-5285 (H) Fax: (787) 720-6590
Jorge Chiriboga, President
Web: www.nationalimageinc.org

IMAGE DE SAN JUAN
National Image, Inc.
1967 Calle Salvia (Urb. San Ramón)
Guaynabo, PR 00657
(787) 789-5285 (H) Fax: (787) 720-6590
Jorge Chiriboga, President
Web: www.nationalimageinc.org

INICIATIVA COMUNITARIA DE INVESTIGACIÓN (ICI)
Affiliate of Fondos Unidos de Puerto Rico
P.O. Box 366535
San Juan, PR 00936-6535
(787) 250-8629 or (787) 250-6817
Fax: (787) 753-4454
Dr. José Vargas Vidot, Director

INSTITUTO DE CIENCIAS DE LA CONDUCTA
Pontificia Universidad Católica de Puerto Rico
2250 Avenida Las Américas, #625
Ponce, PR 00717-0777
(787) 841-2000 ext. 324
Coral González, Vice Pres. of Student Affairs
Email: ICC@pucpr.edu
Web: www.pucpr.edu

INSTITUTO DE FORMACIÓN SANTA ANA
Affiliate of Fondos Unidos de Puerto Rico
P.O. Box 554
Adjuntas, PR 00601-0554
(787) 829-2504 Fax: (787) 829-2504
Hna. María Gregoria Reillo, Director

INSTITUTO DE LA FAMILIA PUERTORRIQUEÑA
Aff. of Puerto Rican Family Institute, Inc.
312 Ave. De Diego, #403
Santurce, PR 00909
(787) 723-0373 Fax: (787) 721-6638
Carlos M. Zapata González, Director
Web: www.prfi.org

INSTITUTO DE ORIENTACIÓN Y TERAPIA FAMILIAR
Affiliate of Fondos Unidos de Puerto Rico
P.O. Box 861
Caguas, PR 00726
(787) 746-5756 Fax: (787) 746-3080
Rosa Luz Ramírez, Director

INSTITUTO DEL HOGAR CELIA Y HARRIS BUNKER
Affiliate of Fondos Unidos de Puerto Rico
P.O. Box 20155
Río Piedras, PR 00928-0155
(787) 765-7895 or (787) 765-7874
Fax: (787) 767-4904
Sra. Miriam M. Matos, Director

INSTITUTO ESPECIAL PARA EL DESARROLLO INTEGRAL DEL INDIVIDUO, FAMILIA Y COMUNIDAD
Affiliate of Fondos Unidos de Puerto Rico
P.O. Box 1241
Yauco, PR 00698
(787) 856-1573 Fax: (787) 856-4192
Sor María A. de Jesús, Director

P.O. Box 1370
Guánica, PR 00653
(787) 856-4256 or (787) 821-0546
Fax: (787) 856-4192
Sor María de la Monserrate Velásquez, Director

P.O. Box 846
Maricao, PR 00606
(787) 838-4002 or (787) 838-2272
Fax: (787) 838-0142
Sor María M. Mangual, Director

INSTITUTO PRE-VOCACIONAL E INDUSTRIAL DE PUERTO RICO
Affiliate of Fondos Unidos de Puerto Rico
P.O. Box 1800
Arecibo, PR 00613
(787) 879-3300 Fax: (787) 879-3834
Nilsa López, Director

INSTITUTO PSICOPEDAGÓGICO DE PUERTO RICO
Affiliate of Fondos Unidos de Puerto Rico
P.O. Box 363744
San Juan, PR 00936-3744
(787) 783-5431 or (787) 783-6378
Fax: (787) 792-3610
Carmen Vizcarrondo, Director

INTERNATIONAL JUNIOR COLLEGE
P.O. Box 8245
Av. Ponce de León 1612
Fernández Juncos Station
San Juan, PR 00910-8425
(787) 725-8718 Fax: (787) 724-0281
Sr. Carlos Montano Bosque, Pres.

JANE STERN DORADO COMMUNITY LIBRARY
Affiliate of Fondos Unidos de Puerto Rico
P.O. Box 609
Dorado, PR 00646
(787) 796-3675 Fax: (787) 796-1227
Sra. Tere V. Arroyo, Director

JARDÍN DE ENVEJECIENTES DE LUQUILLO
Calle Fernández Garcia #56 Apart. 1343
Luquillo, PR 00773
(787) 889-3490
Aída I. Carrasquillo, Director

JARDÍN DE LA ESPERANZA
Carr. 775 Km. 0.7-Barrio. Piñas
Comerio, PR 00782
(787) 875-2625
Wilma Rivera, Director

JARDÍN INFANTIL
Urb. La Mela Calle 5, Casa 5
Isabela, PR 00662
(787) 872-1187
Ortencia Cortez, Director

JARDÍN INFANTIL BAN BAN
#326 - P.O. Box 79999
Mayagüez, PR 00680
(787) 833-3512 Fax: (787) 265-4475
Alice Sallejo de Sulzona, Director

JARDÍN INFANTIL EL ENCANTO
Ave. Emiliano Pool 497 #23
San Juan, PR 00926
(787) 789-2157
Obed Encarnación Díaz, Director

JARDÍN INFANTIL ISA, INC.
Bo. Santana, Buzon 168
Arecibo, PR 00612
(787) 881-0230
Isamaris Colón, Director

JARDÍN INFANTIL RELIGIOSAS TEATINA
P.O. Box 969
Mayagüez, PR 00681
(787) 832-9504
Sor María Ruíz, Executive Director

JESÚS DE SANTA MARÍA
Carr. 785-HC-02-Box 34127
Caguas, PR 00725
(787) 747-7546
Gloria E. Hernández, Director

JÓVENES DE AYER
Carr. 941-Km. 4.9-Box 3092
Gurabo, PR 00778
(787) 737-7296
Hilda Rodríguez, Director

JUAN DOMINGO EN ACCIÓN
Affiliate of Fondos Unidos de Puerto Rico
Bo. Juan Domingo
55 (Interior) Calle Robles
Guaynabo, PR 00966
(787) 783-4034 Fax: (787) 783-4034
Sra. Natividad Montalvo, Director

JUVENTUD SCHOENSTATTIANA UNIVERSITARIA
Pontificia Universidad Católica de Puerto Rico
2250 Avenida Las Américas, #625
Ponce, PR 00717-0777
(787) 841-2000 ext. 324
Coral González, Vice Pres. of Student Affairs
Web: www.pucpr.edu

LA NUEVA AURORA
Bo. Mameyal - Apartado 588
Dorado, PR 00646
(787) 796-2469
Dora Martínez Torres, Director

LA VOZ DEL EVANGELIO, INC.
P.O. Box 9066214
San Juan, PR 00906-6214
(787) 728-3066 or (787) 726-7287
Fax: (787) 728-8568
Ricardo López Serrano, Director-Editor
Email: www.PRChristianlLinks.org/Lavoz

LAMBDA THETA ALPHA
Pontificia Universidad Católica de Puerto Rico
2250 Avenida Las Américas, #625
Ponce, PR 00717-0777
(787) 841-2000 ext. 324
Coral González, Vice Pres. of Student Affairs
Web: www.pucpr.edu

LEAGUE OF UNITED LATIN AMERICAN CITIZENS (LULAC)
National Executive Committee
Camara de Representantes, El Capitolio
San Juan, PR 00901
(787) 724-0209 or (787) 798-5499
(787) 381-4043 (cell) Fax: (787) 723-7007
Carlos López Nieves, Nat'l. VP for SE
Web: www.lulac.org

Southeast Region-PR
HC 02, Box 47862
Vega Baja, PR 00693
(787) 754-4347 or (787) 754-8235 (h)
(787) 383-4284 cell Fax: (787) 754-1275
Elsie Valdes, State Dir.

LICEO INFANTIL NIEVES
Parque Asturias 5X 19-Via. Fontana Park
Carolina, PR 00983
(787) 762-3367 Fax: (787) 276-1716
Elizabeth Nieves, Director

LIGA DE COOPERATIVAS DE PUERTO RICO
P.O. Box 360707
San Juan, PR 00936-0707
(787) 764-2727 Fax: (787) 250-6093
Gregorio Vasquez, Director
Email: ligacoop@caribe.net

LIGA DE ESTUDIANTES DE ARTE DE SAN JUAN
Apartado 9066221
San Juan, PR 00906-6221
(787) 722-4468 Fax: (787) 722-4468
Elsa Costas, Director

LYDIA'S HOME CARE
715 Carr. 349
Mayagüez, PR 00680
(787) 833-7882 Fax: (787) 831-5446
Lydia Casilla, Director

MADRE DE LA EUCARISTÍA
HCI Buzon Robles, Box 11715
San Sebastian, PR 00685
(787) 896-0648
Estebania Tirado, Director

MADRES SOLTERAS SANTA MARÍA EUFRACIA
Calle Andres García, #10
Arecibo, PR 00612
(787) 878-5166 Fax: (787) 880-2632
Francisca Tores Calbo, Director

MAKE-A-WISH FOUNDATION
Affiliate of Fondos Unidos de Puerto Rico
San Jorge Children's Hospital
Calle San Jorge 252, Oficina 306
San Juan, PR 00907
(787) 728-7987 Fax: (787) 727-5595
Sr. Brent Huffman, Director

MARRERO-ORTIZ
P.O. Box #231
Villalba, PR 00766
(787) 867-5332
Luz Ortiz Alvarado, Director

McCONNELL VALDÉS
270 Munoz Rivera Ave.
San Juan, PR 00918
(787) 759-9292 Fax: (787) 759-8282
Antonio Escudero Viera, Managing Partner
Email: aev@mcvpr.com
Web: www.mcvpr.com

MENTAL HEALTH AND ANTI-ADDICTION SERVICES ADMINISTRATION
Puerto Rico Chapter
P.O. Box 21414
San Juan, PR 00928-1414
(787) 764-3795 or (787) 764-3670
Fax: (787) 765-5895
Dr. José A. Acevedo Martínez, Administrator

MI PRIMERA ENSEÑANZA
P.O. Box 886
Las Piedras, PR 00771
(787) 733-3939
Norma Cruz, Director

MI SEGUNDO HOGAR
P.O. Box 357, Bo. Honduras, El Portón A-17
Barranquitas, PR 00794
(787) 857-0875
Margarita Nuñezmorels, Director

MINISTERIO DE AYUDA AL NECESITADO "CASA MISERICORDIA"
Affiliate of Fondos Unidos de Puerto Rico
P.O. Box 765
Gurabo, PR 00778
(787) 737-0271 Fax: (787) 737-0271
Sra. Vilma Escalante, Director

MISIÓN RESCATE
Affiliate of Fondos Unidos de Puerto Rico
Mayagüez Station, P.O. Box 6125
Mayagüez, PR 00681
(787) 831-4015 Fax: (787) 832-6080
Sr. Gabriel R. Cintrón, Director

Centro de Arecibo
Bo. Juncos, Sector Hato Arriba, Carr. 651 Km. 2.7
Arecibo, PR 00612
(787) 879-3625 Fax: (787) 832-6080
Sr. Gabriel R. Cintrón, Director

Centro de Sabana Grande
Bo. Rayo Guara
Carr. 328 Km. 5.7 Interior
Sabana Grande, PR 00637
(787) 873-0126 Fax: (787) 832-6080
Sr. Gabriel R. Cintrón, Director

MISIONALES PONTIFICIAS
Asociación de la Santa Infancia
P.O. Box 191882
San Juan, PR 00919-1882
(787) 754-0995 Fax: (787) 754-0749
Bárbara I. Molina, Delegada Nacional
Email: impr@hotmail.com

San Pedro Opostol
P.O. Box 191882
San Juan, PR 00919-1882
(787) 754-0995 or (787) 754-0747
Fax: (787) 754-0749
Esteban Rivera, Director

MU ALPHA PHI
Pontificia Universidad Católica de Puerto Rico
2250 Avenida Las Américas, #625
Ponce, PR 00717-0777
(787) 841-2000 ext. 324
Coral González, Vice Pres. of Student Affairs
Web: www.pucpr.edu

MUNDO DE AMOR
HC-02, Box 6537
Morovis, PR 00687
(787) 862-2822
Melba Ginez Santiago, Director

MUNDO DE LOS NIÑOS
P.O. Box 6173
Caguas, PR 00726
(787) 739-5824
Minova Carro, Director

MUÑOZ NURSERY SCHOOL
Ave. De Diego 224-San Francisco
San Juan, PR 00927-
(787) 764-6419 Fax: (787) 767-6550
Rosa Luisa Muñoz, Director

NATIONAL ASSOCIATION FOR HISPANIC ELDERLY
Puerto Rico Office/Project Ayuda
Condominio Cobian Plaza
Ponce de León 1607, #212, Parada 24
Santurce, PR 00909
(787) 721-4505 Fax: (787) 721-3160
Lourdes M. Torres-Ruiz, Project Coordinator

NATIONAL ASSOCIATION OF SOCIAL WORKERS
Puerto Rico Chapter
P.O. Box 192051
San Juan, PR 00919-2051
(787) 758-3588 Fax: (787) 281-8433
Antonio S. Rodríguez, Executive Director

NATIONAL COLLEGE OF BUSINESS AND TECHNOLOGY
Recinto de Bayamón
P.O. Box 2036
Edificio Ramos Carr. Núm. 2
Bayamón, PR 00960
(787) 780-5134 or (787) 780-5348
Fax: (787) 740-7360
Sr. Jesús Siverio Orta, President

NATIONAL COUNCIL OF LA RAZA (NCLR)
Puerto Rico Office
1528 Calle Bori, #C, Urb. Belisa
San Juan, PR 00927
(787) 212-4454 Fax: (787) 772-9263
Raúl Yzaguirre, National President
Web: www.nclr.org

NATIONAL OPTOMETRIC STUDENT ASSOCIATION
Inter American University of Puerto Rico
School of Optometry
P.O. Box 191049
San Juan, PR 00919-1049
(787) 765-1915 Fax: (787) 767-3920
José Colón, Director
Email: jcolon@inter.edu
Web: www.optonet.inter.edu

NATIONAL STUDENTS SPEECH LANGUAGE HEARING ASSOCIATION
University of Puerto Rico, Ciencias Medicas
College of Health Allied Professions
P.O. Box 365067
San Juan, PR 00936-5067
(787) 758-2525
María E. Cora-Block, Dean
Web: www.upr.clu.edu

NILDA SANTIAGO CHILD CARE
Calle C-3, Rep. San Juan
Arecibo, PR 00612
(787) 879-3256
Nilda Santiago, Director

NUESTRA SEÑORA DE LA PROVIDENCIA
Hermanitas de Ancianos Desamparados
Ave. Ponce de León Pda.
#5 Puerta de Tierra #5279
San Juan, PR 00906-6571
(787) 722-1331
Angela Estévez, Director

NUEVA ESCUELA MONTESSORI
Mariana Bracetti W., #16
Río Piedras, PR 00925
(787) 763-2561
Aída Doble, Director

NURSERY SAGRADO CORAZÓN
Calle Clemson 328 y Howard University Gardens
Río Piedras, PR 00927
(787) 763-1080
Evelyn Cardona Morales, Director

NURSING STUDENTS ASSOCIATION
University of Puerto Rico, Ciencias Medicas
School of Nursing
P.O. Box 365067
San Juan, PR 00936-5067
(787) 758-2525
María E. Cora-Block, Dean
Web: www.upr.clu.edu

OFICINA DE PROMOCIÓN Y DESARROLLO HUMANO
Affiliate of Fondos Unidos de Puerto Rico
Apartado 353
Arecibo, PR 00613
(787) 817-6951 Fax: (787) 817-7597
Hna. Roberta Grzelak, Director

OLD SAN JUAN MERCHANTS ASSOCIATION
P.O. Box 1110
San Juan, PR 00902
(787) 725-4050 or (787) 725-5042
Fax: (787) 724-8717
José Luis López Muñoz, President

OMICRON KAPPA UPSILON SOCIETY
University of Puerto Rico, Ciencias Médicas
P.O. Box 365067
San Juan, PR 00936-5067
(787) 758-2525
María E. Cora-Block, Dean
Web: www.upr.clu.edu

ORGANIZACIÓN BRAZOS ABIERTOS
Pontificia Universidad Católica de Puerto Rico
2250 Avenida Las Américas, #625
Ponce, PR 00717-0777
(787) 841-2000 ext. 324
Coral González, Vice Pres. of Student Affairs
Email: org.Brazos.Abiertos@pucpr.edu
Web: www.pucpr.edu

ORGANIZACIÓN DE ESTUDIANTES EXTRANJEROS
Pontificia Universidad Católica de Puerto Rico
2250 Avenida Las Américas, #625
Ponce, PR 00717-0777
(787) 841-2000 ext. 324
Coral González, Vice Pres. of Student Affairs
Email: Org.Est.Extranjeros@pucpr.edu
Web: www.pucpr.edu

ORGANIZACIÓN DE LÍDERES DE LA PAZ
Pontificia Universidad Católica de Puerto Rico
2250 Avenida Las Américas, #625
Ponce, PR 00717-0777
(787) 841-2000 ext. 324
Coral González, Vice Pres. of Student Affairs
Email: Org.Lideres.Paz@pucpr.edu
Web: www.pucpr.edu

ORGANIZACIÓN PRO-DERECHOS A LA MUJER
Pontificia Universidad Católica de Puerto Rico
2250 Avenida Las Américas, #625
Ponce, PR 00717-0777
(787) 841-2000 ext. 324
Coral González, Vice Pres. of Student Affairs
Web: www.pucpr.edu

ORGANIZACIÓN OF STUDENT REPRESENTATIVES (OSR)
University of Puerto Rico, Ciencias Medicas
School of Medicine, P.O. Box 365067
San Juan, PR 00936-5067
(787) 758-2525
Maria E. Cora-Block, Dean
Web: www.upr.clu.edu

ORIENTACION VOCACIONAL PARA JOVENES EMBARAZADAS N.S.C.
Matienzo Cintron #20-Urb. Floral Park
San Juan, PR 00917
(787) 250-6323
Sor Irene Cuervo, Director

PARA EL FOMENTO DEL DESARROLLO DEL PENSAMIENTO, INC.
Apartado 706 Ave., W. Churchil 138
El Señorial Mail Station
San Juan, PR 00926-603
(787) 274-1948 Fax: (787) 274-1948
Sonia Flores, President

PASCUAL-GARCÍA
Jardines del Caribe C-21 N114
Ponce, PR 00731
(787) 844-9126
Alejandro Pascual, Director

PEQUEÑÍN
Calle 23 ZZ-13, Urb. Mariolga
Caguas, PR 00725
(787) 746-1054
Gloria Guzmán, Director

PERSONAS DE EDAD AVANZADA LAS MONJAS
Calle Santiago Iglesias esq. Uruguay
Hato Rey, PR 00917
(787) 754-7844
Marlene Yadina, Director

PHI ALPHA THETA
Pontificia Universidad Católica de Puerto Rico
2250 Avenida Las Américas, #625
Ponce, PR 00717-0777
(787) 841-2000 ext. 324
Coral González, Vice Pres. of Student Affairs
Web: www.pucpr.edu

PHI EPSILON CHI
Pontificia Universidad Católica de Puerto Rico
2250 Avenida Las Américas, #625
Ponce, PR 00717-0777
(787) 841-2000 ext. 324
Coral González, Vice Pres. of Student Affairs
Web: www.pucpr.edu

PHI ETA MU
Pontificia Universidad Católica de Puerto Rico
2250 Avenida Las Américas, #625
Ponce, PR 00717-0777
(787) 841-2000 ext. 324
Coral González, Vice Pres. of Student Affairs
Web: www.pucpr.edu

PHI LAMBDA SIGMA
University of Puerto Rico, Ciencias Medicas
School of Pharmacy, P.O. Box 365067
San Juan, PR 00936
(787) 758-2525
María E. Cora-Block, Dean
Web: www.upr.clu.edu

PHI SIGMA ALPHA
Pontificia Universidad Católica de Puerto Rico
2250 Avenida Las Américas, #582
Ponce, PR 00731
(787) 841-2000 ext. 324, 227, 229, 230
Rafael J. Hernández, Representative
Email: gammafsa@yahoo.com
Web: www.pucpr.eduwww.geocities.com/gammafsa

PHI ZETA CHI
Pontificia Universidad Católica de Puerto Rico
2250 Avenida Las Américas, #625
Ponce, PR 00717-0777
(787) 841-2000 ext. 324
Coral González, Vice Pres. of Student Affairs
Web: www.pucpr.edu

PLAYEROS EN ACCIÓN
P.O. Box 4266
Carolina, PR 00984
(787) 268-0932 Fax: (787) 268-0932
María V. Corraliza, Director

PONCE JUNIOR COLLEGE
Calle Salud 23
Ponce, PR 00731
(787) 844-7940 Fax: (787) 259-2938
Sr. Fernando Torres Velazquez, President

POSADA DE AMOR, INC.
P.O Box 1552, Bo. Guajataca
Quebradillas, PR 00678
(787) 895-5519 Fax: (787) 895-4481
Carmen Lydia Vives, Director

PROGRAMA DE APOYO Y ENLACE COMUNITARIO, INC.
Affiliate of Fondos Unidos de Puerto Rico
P.O. Box 991, Suite 629
Aguada, PR 00602
(787) 252-3439 Fax: (787) 252-3439
Sra. María A. Hernández, Director

PROGRAMA DE EDUCACION COMUNAL DE ENTREGA Y SERVICIOS (PECES)
Affiliate of Fondos Unidos de Puerto Rico
Punta Santiago, P.O. Box 647

Humacao, PR 00741-0647
(787) 852-5888 Fax: (787) 852-9348
Hna. Nancy Madden, Director

PROGRAMA DEL ADOLESCENTE DE NARANJITO
Affiliate of Fondos Unidos de Puerto Rico
P.O. Box 891
Naranjito, PR 00719
(787) 869-4283
Sra. Lilia M. Rivera Morales, Director

PROGRAMA MANOS QUE AYUDAN - CENTROS SOR ISOLINA FERRE INC.
Affiliate of Fondos Unidos de Puerto Rico
Parcela Amalia Marín; C/ Ballena (final playa)
Ponce, PR 00734-0213
(787) 843-1910 x236-237 Fax: (787) 844-7665
Guillermo Tejas, Director

PROGRAMA SERVICIOS DE ENVEJECIMIENTO CENTRO DIAMANTINO
Carr. 860-K. 1.1
Carolina, PR 00986
(787) 757-0606
José Cordero, Director

PROYECTO CHILD CARE
Municipio San Sebastián
P.O. Box 1603
Bo. Guatemala, Carr. 125, Km 17.8
San Sebastián, PR 00685
(787) 896-6825 Fax: (787) 896-6825
Enid Giménez, Director

PUERTO RICAN CONGRESS
San Juan Branch
P.O. Box 190278
San Juan, PR 000919-0278
(787) 727-5657 Fax: (787) 274-1554
Carmen Miranda, Director
Web: www.prcongress.org

PUERTO RICAN CUATRO PROJECT
Proyecto del Cuatro/Puerto Rico Office
P.O. Box 36
Humacao, PR 00792
(787) 893-8874 (H) or (787) 852-0010
Myrna Pérez, Coordinator
Email: cuatro.2k@east-net.com

PUERTO RICO BANKS ASSOCIATION
209 Ave. Muñoz Rivera #1014
San Juan, PR 00918-1002
(787) 753-8630 Fax: (787) 754-6022
Arturo L. Carrión, Executive Vice President

PUERTO RICO COMMUNITY FDTN.
P.O. Box 70362
San Juan, PR 00936-8362
(787) 721-1037 Fax: (787) 721-1673
Dr. Ethel Ríos de Betancourt, Director

PUERTO RICO CORPORATE LIAISON GROUP
Cond. Venus Plaza B202
Urban Pinero
Hato Rey, PR 00917
(787) 723-0077 ext. 3064
María M. Marchago, President

PUERTO RICO HEAD START PROGRAM
Affiliate of SER-Jobs for Progress National, Inc.
P.O. Box 364583
San Juan, PR 00936-4583
(787) 763-4085 Fax: (787) 771-4602
Aída L. Torres de Nevares, Executive Director
Web: www.sernational.org

PUERTO RICO HOTEL & TOURISM ASSOCIATION
Miramar Plaza
954 Avenida Ponce de León , #702
San Juan, PR 00907
(787) 725-2901 Fax: (787) 725-2913
Erin Benítez, Executive Vice Presidente

PUERTO RICO LUPUS SUPPORT GROUP
P.O. Box 50817
Levittown, PR 00950
(787) 795-3942 or (787) 798-1053
Fax: (630) 982-6537
Sallie Valcárcel, President
Email: prlupus@usa.net

PUERTO RICO MANUFACTURERS ASSOCIATION
P.O. Box 195477
San Juan, PR 00919-5477

(787) 759-9445 Fax: (787) 756-7670
William Riefkohl, Executive Vice President

PUERTO RICO MEDICAL ASSOCIATION
University of Puerto Rico, Ciencias Medicas
Student Chapter, P.O. Box 365067
San Juan, PR 00936
(787) 758-2525
María E. Cora-Block, Dean
Web: www.upr.clu.edu

PUERTO RICO OPTOMETRIC STUDENT ASSOCIATION
Inter American University of Puerto Rico
School of Optometry, P.O. Box 191049
San Juan, PR 00919-1049
(787) 765-1915 Fax: (787) 767-3920
José Colón, Director
Email: jcolon@inter.edu
Web: www.optonet.inter.edu

QUERUBÍN PRESCHOOLER MONTESSORI
Baldorioty A-13-Urb. Colimar
Guaynabo, PR 00969
(787) 789-2418
Teresa Ramírez, Director

RAINBOW DAY CARE CENTER
Calle M.J., Cabrero 66 Bajos
San Sebastián, PR 00685
(787) 896-6464 Fax: (787) 896-6464
Carmen Martínez, Director

RAMÍREZ COLLEGE OF BUSINESS AND TECHNOLOGY
P.O. Box 195460
San Juan, PR 00919-5460
(787) 763-3120 Fax: (787) 763-7038
Rogena Kyles, President

RAMONITA FUENTES CHILD CARE
Calle 50 AR-10, Rexville
Bayamón, PR 00957
(787) 797-0121
Ramonita Fuentes, Director

REFORMA
Puerto Rico Chapter
P.O. Box 22897
Calle Robles 54
San Juan, PR 00925-3060
(787) 764-0000 or (787) 722-4753
Fax: (787) 725-0261
Josefina Gómez-Hillyer, Chapter President
Web: http://clnet.ucr.edu/library/reforma

REMANSO DE LA VEJEZ
Calle Hospital, #13
Lares, PR 00669
(787) 897-2400
José Villegas, Director

REPUBLICAN NATIONAL HISPANIC ASSEMBLY (RNHA)
Puerto Rican Chapter
P.O. Box 11457 Fernandez Juncos Station
Urb. Villa Avila
Humacao A-45 St.
Guaynabo, PR 00657
(787) 289-0030 Fax: (787) 289-0037
Freddy Valentín, Advisor

RHO CHI SOCIETY
University of Puerto Rico, Ciencias Medicas
School of Pharmacy, P.O. Box 365067
San Juan, PR 00936
(787) 758-2525
María E. Cora-Block, Dean
Web: www.upr.clu.edu

RHO OMICRON RHO
Pontificia Universidad Católica de Puerto Rico
2250 Avenida Las Américas, #625
Ponce, PR 00717-0777
(787) 841-2000 ext. 324
Coral González, Vice Pres. of Student Affairs
Web: www.pucpr.edu

RHO SIGMA GAMMA
Pontificia Universidad Católica de Puerto Rico
2250 Avenida Las Américas, #625
Ponce, PR 00717-0777
(787) 841-2000 ext. 324
Coral González, Vice Pres. of Student Affairs
Web: www.pucpr.edu

RIÓS LÓPEZ CHILD CARE
Bo. Terranova, Raval, #477, P.O. Box 434
Quebradillas, PR 00678
(787) 895-7048
Margarita López, Director

SALCAP
P.O. Box 2070
Vega Alta, PR 00692-2070
(787) 883-3984 Fax: (809) 883-3984
Milton Picón, President
Email: morality@prtc.net

SALES & MARKETING EXECUTIVES
PO Box 364025
San Juan, PR 00936-4025
(787) 764-8595 Fax: (787) 751-8313
Waleska Olivencia, Executive Vice President

SALÓN DE LA FAMA DEL DEPORTE RÍO PEDRENSE
P.O. Box 191184
San Juan, PR 00919-1184
(787) 792-7372 or (787) 765-9470
Fax: (787) 765-9470
Dr. Víctor Díaz Bonnet, President

SEMINARIO EVANGÉLICO DE PUERTO RICO
Av. Ponce de León 776
San Juan, PR 00925
(787) 751-6483 x242 Fax: (787) 751-0847
Dr. Samuel Pagan Rosa, President

SER TRAVEL AND TOURISM ACADEMY
Affiliate of SER-Jobs for Progress National, Inc.
Carretera #2, Esquina #167, #202
Bayamón, PR 00961
(787) 269-5454 or (787) 269-2330
Fax: (787) 269-5499
Wanda Martino, Executive Director
Web: www.sernational.org

SER-JOBS FOR PROGRESS, INC. OF PUERTO RICO
Affiliate of SER-Jobs for Progress National, Inc.
Ave. Roberto Clemente, Bloque 27, #11
Carolina, PR 00986
(787) 276-2300 Fax: (787) 276-2370
Gladys Osoto, Executive Director
Web: www.sernational.org

SERVICIOS SOCIALES CATÓLICOS DE MAYAGUEZ
Affiliate of Fondos Unidos de Puerto Rico
P.O. Box 2272
Mayagüez, PR 00681
(787) 833-3627 Fax: (787) 265-7060
Sister Silvia Arias, Director

SERVICIOS SOCIALES CATÓLICOS DE SAN JUAN
Affiliate of Fondos Unidos de Puerto Rico
Fernández Juncos Station
P.O. Box 8812
San Juan, PR 00910
(787) 727-7373 Fax: (787) 727-7938
Sor Clotilde Arce, Director

SERVICIOS SOCIALES EPISCOPALES
Affiliate of Fondos Unidos
P.O. Box 775
Saint Just Sta., PR 00978-0775
(787) 755-0055 Fax: (787) 283-0640
Rev. Efrain Ayala, Director

SHALOM
Colegio Cristiano El Rohi
P. O. Box 3158, Carr. #2 Km. 123.7
Aguadilla, PR 00605
(787) 891-6675 Fax: (787) 882-1300
Sra. Olga Menéndez, Director

SIERVAS MISIONERAS DE LA SANTÍSIMA TRINIDAD
P.O. Box 30213
Ponce, PR 00734-0213
(787) 843-1910 Fax: (787) 840-5020
Sister Isolina Ferre, Director

SIGMA LAMBDA BETA
Pontificia Universidad Católica de Puerto Rico
2250 Avenida Las Américas, #625
Ponce, PR 00717-0777
(787) 841-2000 ext. 324
Coral González, Vice Pres. of Student Affairs
Web: www.pucpr.edu

SINDICATO PUERTORRIQUEÑO DE TRABAJADORES. INC.
41 Buenos Aires
Ponce, PR 00731
(787) 843-6850 Fax: (787) 843-6835
Roberto Pagan, President

SOCIEDAD AMERICANA DEL CANCER
Division de Puerto Rico
P.O. Box 366004
San Juan, PR 00936-6004
(787) 764-2295 Fax: (787) 764-0553
Dr. Lillian Santos, Executive Director

SOCIEDAD AMERICANA DEL CÁNCER DE PUERTO RICO, INC.
Hospital Doctor Manuel Figueroa
P.O. Box 152
Arecibo, PR 00613-0152
(787) 879-0656 Fax: (787) 879-0656
Diana Núñez Maldonado, Director

SOCIEDAD AMERICANA DEL CÁNCER UNIDAD OESTE, INC.
Prolongación Dr. Vadl. 203
Mayagüez, PR 00680
(787) 833-3320 Fax: (787) 833-3320
Corali Morales Matos, Director

SOCIEDAD CORAL DE PUERTO RICO, INC.
International Federation of Choral Music
P.O.Box 21663
San Juan, PR 00931
(787) 758-9014
Luis Olivieri, Executive Coordinator
Email: coral8000@aol.com

SOCIEDAD CRISTIANA DE SERVICIOS MÚLTIPLES
P.O. Box 25100
San Juan, PR 00729-5100
(787) 876-7715
José Velásquez, President

SOCIEDAD DE ECOLOGÍA Y CIENCIAS AMBIENTALES
Pontificia Universidad Católica de Puerto Rico
2250 Avenida Las Américas, #625
Ponce, PR 00717-0777
(787) 841-2000 ext. 324
Coral González, Vice Pres. of Student Affairs
Email: Soc.Ecologia.Ambientales@pucpr.edu
Web: www.pucpr.edu

SOCIEDAD DE EDUCACIÓN Y REHABILITACIÓN (SER) DE PUERTO RICO
Affiliate of Fondos Unidos de Puerto Rico
P.O. Box 360325
San Juan, PR 00936-0325
(787) 767-6710 Fax: (787) 758-0950
Sra. Nilda Morales, Executive Director

SOCIEDAD DE HONOR DE ESTUDIANTES DE COMERCIO
Pontificia Universidad Católica de Puerto Rico
2250 Avenida Las Américas, #625
Ponce, PR 00717-0777
(787) 841-2000 ext. 324
Coral González, Vice Pres. of Student Affairs
Web: www.pucpr.edu

SOCIEDAD DE INVESTIGACIÓN CIENTÍFICA, INC. (SODEINC)
P.O. Box 33060 Veterans Plaza Station
San Juan, PR 00933-0060
(787) 641-7582 x10148 Fax: (787) 641-8359
Blanca Lebrón, Executive Director

SOCIEDAD DE RECURSOS HUMANOS GERENCIALES
Pontificia Universidad Católica de Puerto Rico
2250 Avenida Las Américas, #625
Ponce, PR 00717-0777
(787) 841-2000 ext. 324
Coral González, Vice Pres. of Student Affairs
Email: SRHG@pucpr.edu
Web: www.pucpr.edu

SOCIEDAD ESPELEOLÓGICA DE PUERTO RICO, INC.
Apartado 31074, 65 Inf. Station
Río Piedras, PR 00929
(787) 767-0687 or (787) 783-7688
Alberto Rodríguez, President

SOCIEDAD PARA LA GERENCIA DE LOS RECURSOS HUMANOS
Inter American Univ. of Puerto Rico, Ponce
104 Parque Industrial Turpó, Rd. 1
Mercedita, PR 00715-1602
(787) 284-1912 x2092 or (787) 841-0110
Fax: (787) 841-0103
Dilia Rodríguez, Director
Email: drodrigu@ponce.inter.edu
Web: http://ponce.inter.edu/nhp/contents/
OrganizacionesEstudiantiles.html

SOCIEDAD PRO NIÑOS SORDOS DE PONCE
Affiliate of Fondos Unidos de Puerto Rico
Pámpanos Station
Box 8343
Ponce, PR 00732-8343
(787) 840-3011 Fax: (787) 848-0143
Sr. Pedro Galarza, Director

SOCIEDAD PUERTORRIQUEÑA DE AYUDA AL PACIENTE CON EPILEPSIA
Affiliate of Fondos Unidos de Puerto Rico
Antiguo Hospital Ruiz Soler, Calle Marginal
Bayamón, PR 00959
(787) 782-6200 Fax: (787) 782-3991
Srta. Gelitza Falero, Director

SOCIEDAD UNIVERSITARIA DE BIENESTAR ESTUDIANTIL (SUBE)
Inter American Univ. of Puerto Rico, Ponce
104 Parque Industrial Turpó, Rd. 1
Mercedita, PR 00715-1602
(787) 284-1912 x2092 or (787) 841-0110
Fax: (787) 841-0103
Dilia Rodríguez, Director
Email: drodrigu@ponce.inter.edu
Web: http://ponce.inter.edu/nhp/contents/
OrganizacionesEstudiantiles.html

SOCIETY FOR HUMAN RESOURCE MGMT.
University of Puerto Rico, Cayey
Calle Antonio Barcelo
Cayey, PR 00736
(787) 738-2161 Fax: (787) 745-7817
Juan Aguayo, President
Email: shrm-cuc@hotmail.com

TALLER DE TEATRO
Pontificia Universidad Católica de Puerto Rico
2250 Avenida Las Américas, #625
Ponce, PR 00717-0777
(787) 841-2000 ext. 324
Coral González, Vice Pres. of Student Affairs
Web: www.pucpr.edu

TALLER SALUD, INC.
Affiliate of Fondos Unidos de Puerto Rico
P.O. Box 192172
San Juan, PR 00919-2172
(787) 764-9639 Fax: (787) 764-9639
Carmen M. Guzmán, Director
Email: tsalud@ipr.net

TERCERA IGLESIA PRESBITERIANA
P.O. Box 3901
Aguadilla, PR 00605
(787) 882-2075
Alicia Medina, Executive

TESORO DE VIDA
Calle A Final-Bda. Morales
Caguas, PR 00725
(787) 746-6272
Juana Medina de Clara, Director

TRABAJADORES UNIDOS DE LA AUTORIDAD METROPOLITANA DE AUTOBUSES (TUAMA)
Ave., de Diego 784
Río Piedras, PR 00921
(787) 781-7405 or (787) 781-0052
Fax: (787) 783-0345
Wilfredo Gotai, President

TRAVELERS AID DE P.R. (AYUDA AL VIAJERO)
Airport Station, P.O. Box 38017
Carolina, PR 00937-1017
(787) 791-1034 Fax: (787) 791-1054
Sra. Wanda Colón de González, Director

TRI- BETA
Pontificia Universidad Católica de Puerto Rico
2250 Avenida Las Américas, #625
Ponce, PR 00717-0777
(787) 841-2000 ext. 324
Coral González, Vice Pres. of Student Affairs
Email: TriBeta@pucpr.edu
Web: www.pucpr.edu

UNIÓN DE CUBANOS EN EL EXILIO
Puerto Rican Branch
P.O. Box 361074
San Juan, PR 00936-1074
(787) 781-2698 Fax: (787) 781-2698
Beatriz Gallo, President

UNIÓN DE PERIODISTAS
P.O. Box 364302
San Juan, PR 00936-4302
(787) 781-8500 Fax: (787) 749-4839
Israel Rodríguez, Secretary Treasurer

UNIÓN DE TRABAJADORES DE LA AUTORIDAD DE CARRETERAS (UTAC)
P.O. BOX 11085 - Fernández Juncos Station
San Juan, PR 00910
(787) 723-0550
Néstor Gasparini Torres, President

UNIÓN GASTRONÓMICA DE PUERTO RICO
P.O. Box 13037
San Juan, PR 00908-3037
(787) 725-2030 Fax: (787) 725-2033
Rangel Meléndez, President

UNIÓN INDEPENDIENTE AUTÉNTICA DE ACUEDUCTOS Y ALCANTARILLADO
Calle Mayagüez, #49
San Juan, PR 00917
(787) 763-4004 Fax: (787) 759-7840
Héctor René Lugo, President

UNIÓN INDEPENDIENTE DE EMPLEADOS AUTORIDAD DE EDIFICIOS PÚBLICOS
Calle Cádiz #1214
Puerto Nuevo, PR 00920
(787) 781-6975 Fax: (787) 792-0030
Federico T. Montalvo, President
Email: osabcpt@prtc.net

UNIÓN INDEPENDIENTE DE TRABAJADORES DE AEROPUERTO
Altos San Agustin
Calle Marginal, #25
Río Piedras, PR 00924
(787) 751-3460 Fax: (787) 751-3460
Manuel Ortiz Pérez, President

UNIÓN INDEPENDIENTE EMPLEADOS TELEFÓNICOS
RR5 Box 4691, Carretera 167 Km. 19.8
Bayamón, PR 00957
(787) 730-3333 Fax: (787) 730-0300
Alfonso B. Rosa, President

UNIÓN NACIONAL DE TRABAJADORES DE LA SALUD
Calle 42 SE, #1000
Reparto Metropolitano
Río Piedras, PR 00921
(787) 764-6612 Fax: (787) 765-7408
José M. Rodríguez Báez, President

VETELBA
Pase de Diego, #159
Arecibo, PR 00612
(787) 817-2976 or (787) 846-6152
Fax: (787) 817-2976
Elisabeth Gonzales, Director

VICENTITA DELIZ
P. O. Box 345
Quebradillas, PR 00678
(787) 895-2840 Fax: (787) 895-0021
María Pérez Nieves, Director

VILLA DEL RECUERDO
Calle Andrómeda #730
Rio Piedras, PR 00926
(787) 761-5954
Leonor Pérez, Director

VOLUNTARY SERVICE OPTOMETRIC ASSOCIATION
Inter American University of Puerto Rico
School of Optometry, P.O. Box 191049
San Juan, PR 00919-1049
(787) 765-1915 Fax: (787) 767-3920
José Colón, Director
Email: jcolon@inter.edu
Web: www.optonet.inter.edu

Y.M.C.A. DE PONCE
Affiliate of Fondos Unidos de Puerto Rico
Urb. Santa María , Calle C. Urb. Santa María
Ponce, PR 00731
(787) 843-1870 Fax: (787) 843-1811
José A. Ortiz, Director

Y.M.C.A. DE SAN JUAN
Affiliate of Fondos Unidos de Puerto Rico
P.O. Box 360590
San Juan, PR 00936-0590
(787) 728-7200 Fax: (787) 728-0643
Sra. Vivian Dávila, Director

ZETA PHI BETA
Pontificia Universidad Católica de Puerto Rico
2250 Avenida Las Américas, #625
Ponce, PR 00717-0777
(787) 841-2000 ext. 324
Coral González, Vice Pres. of Student Affairs
Web: www.pucpr.edu

RHODE ISLAND

ASOCIACIÓN HISPANA DE BALONCESTO DE RHODE ISLAND/ HISPANIC BASKETBALL ASSOCIATION OF RHODE ISLAND (HBA)
645 Elmwood Ave.
Providence, RI 02907
(401) 784-4622 Fax: (401) 467-6530
Bruno Luki, Treasurer

CENTER FOR HISPANIC POLICY & ADVOCACY (CHISPA)
Affiliate of NCLR
421 Elmwood Ave.
Providence, RI 02907
(401) 467-0111 Fax: (401) 467-2507
Víctor Capellán, Executive Director
Email: chispa2@juno.com

CENTER FOR THE STUDY OF RACE AND ETHNICITY IN AMERICA
Brown University
Box 1886
Providence, RI 02912
(401) 863-3080 Fax: (401) 863-7589
Fayneese Miller, Director

CENTRO PARA LA DEFENSA
421 Elmwood Ave.
Providence, RI 02907
(401) 467-0111
Ernesto Figueroa

CITY HALL OF PAWTUCKET
137 Roosevelt Ave.
Pawtucket, RI 02860
(401) 728-0500 Fax: (401) 723-8620
James Doyle, Mayor

DEPARTMENT OF PORTUGUESE AND BRAZILIAN STUDIES
Brown University
Box 0
Providence, RI 02912
(401) 863-3042 Fax: (401) 863-7261
Prof. Onesimo Almeida, Director
Email: armanda_silva@brown.edu

DIOCESE OF PROVIDENCE
Hispanic Affairs
One Cathedral Sq.
Providence, RI 02903-3695
(401) 278-4500 Fax: (401) 278-4548
Aida Hidalgo, Director for Hispanic Affairs
Email: hmop@intap.net

ESL BILINGUAL OFFICE
330 Harbor Side Blvd.
Providence, RI 02905
(401) 456-9297 Fax: (401) 456-1790
Fran Mossberg, Director

FEDERACIÓN DE ESTUDIANTES PUERTORRIQUEÑOS
P.O.Box 1930
Brown University
Providence, RI 02912
(401) 863-4314
Nelson Sánchez, Director

HELPLINE OF TRAVELERS AID SOCIETY
Llamenos/United Way
177 Union St.
Providence, RI 02903
(401) 351-6500 Fax: (401) 421-7410
Marion S. Avarista, President
Web: www.travelersaid.com

HOLY SPIRIT CATHOLIC COMMUNITY
1030 Dexter Street
Central Falls, RI 02863
(401) 723-5326 Fax: (401) 722-0224
Robert Perron, Pastor

IGLESIA BAUTISTA HISPANA EL CALVARIO
747 Broad St.
Providence, RI 02907
(401) 461-7507 Fax: (401) 785-8277
Francisco Litardo, Pastor

IGLESIA CATÓLICA ESPÍRITU SANTO
472 Atwells Ave.
Providence, RI 02909
(401) 421-3551 Fax: (401) 421-3557
Ignacio Battaglia, Pastor

IGLESIA CATÓLICA NUESTRA SRA. DEL MONTE CARMELO
12 Spruce St.
Providence, RI 02903
(401) 274-2113 Fax: (401) 453-1221
Raymond P. Luft, Pastor

IGLESIA CATÓLICA SAN CARLOS
178 Dexter St.
Providence, RI 02907
(401) 421-6441 Fax: (401) 454-4986
Rev. John Randall, Pastor

IGLESIA CATÓLICA SAN JOSÉ
854 Providence St.
West Warwick, RI 02893
(401) 821-4072 Fax: (401) 821-2408
Charles Browning, Pastor

IGLESIA CATÓLICA SAN JOSÉ
193 Walcott St.
Pawtucket, RI 02860
(401) 724-9190
Charles B. McDermott, Pastor

IGLESIA CATÓLICA SAN JUAN BAUTISTA
69 Quincy Ave.
Pawtucket, RI 02860
(401) 722-9054 Fax: (401) 724-3514
Joel Lecuivre, Pastor

IGLESIA CATÓLICA SAN LUIS
82 Cumberland street
Woonsocket, RI 02895
(401) 762-1100
Roger Houle, Pastor

IGLESIA EVANGÉLICA HISPANA
235 Dexter St.
Pawtucket, RI 02860
(401) 726-4414 Fax: (401) 726-4414
Julio Filomeno, Pastor

IGLESIA PENTECOSTAL EL CALVARIO
P.O. Box 29158
Providence, RI 02909
(401) 421-9078
Salvador Vargas, Pastor

IMMIGRATION & REFUGEE SERVICES
1 Carter St.
Providence, RI 02907
(401) 467-7200 Fax: (401) 467-6310
Jerry Noel, Director
Email: OIRS6@EOL.COM

INSTITUTO INTERNACIONAL
División Educativa, Project Persona
645 Elmwood Ave.
Providence, RI 02907
(401) 781-4238 or (401) 461-5940
Fax: (401) 467-6530
William Shuey, Executive Director

JUANITA SÁNCHEZ COMMUNITY FUND
1 Union Station
Providence, RI 02903
(401) 274-4564 Fax: (401) 331-8085
Anna Cano Morales, Program Associate
Email: annacm@rifoundation
Web: www.rifoundation.org

LATIN AMERICAN STUDENTS ORG.
P.O.Box 1930, Brown University
Providence, RI 02912
(401) 863-2120 x3789 Fax: (401) 863-1184
Ana Escrogima and Moises Cascante
Email: LASO@Brown.edu

PAWTUCKET SER
Affiliate of SER-Jobs for Progress Nat'l, Inc.
101 Main St., #302
Pawtucket, RI 02860
(401) 724-1820 Fax: (401) 724-8490
Lissa Dreyer, Executive Director
Web: www.sernational.org

PROGRESO LATINO
626 Broad St.
Central Falls, RI 02863
(401) 728-5920 Fax: (401) 724-5550
Patricia Martínez, Executive Director
Email: progreso@loa.com

PROJECT HOPE PROYECTO ESPERANZA
400 Dexter St.
Central Falls, RI 02863
(401) 728-0515 Fax: (401) 728-2330
John Barry/Estella Carrera, Exec. Dir./Director

PROVIDENCE ADULT LEARNING CENTER
160 Broad Street, 2nd Floor
Providence, RI 02903
(401) 331-0766 Fax: (401) 274-2539
Patricia Bellart, Contact

PROVIDENCE COMMUNITY ACTION PROGRAM (PRO-CAP)
16 Borinquen St.
Providence, RI 02905

(401) 273-2000 Fax: (401) 273-2007
Frank Carbishley, Director

**PUERTORRIQUENOS UNIDOS, INC.
(UNITED PUERTORICANS, INC.)**
P.O. Box 8168
Warwick, RI 02888
(401) 737-0751
Mrs. Lydia Perez, President

REFORMA
Rhode Island Chapter
University of Rhode Island
Rodman Hall, 94 W. Alumni Ave., #2
Kingston, RI 02881
(401) 874-4641 Fax: (401) 874-4964
Mike Havener, State Coordinator
Email: mhavener@uri.edu
Web: http://clnet.ucr.edu/library/reforma

RHODE ISLAND PROJECT AIDS
232 W. Exchange St.
Providence, RI 02903-4110
(401) 831-5522 Fax: (401) 454-0299
Mr. Miguel Rojas, Outreach Coordinator

ST. MICHAEL CHURCH
239 Oxford St.
Providence, RI 02905
(401) 781-7210 Fax: (401) 461-6164
Raymond Malm, Pastor

STATE E.E.O. OFFICE
1 Capitol Hill
Providence, RI 02908
(401) 222-3090 Fax: (401) 222-6378
Vincent Egliozzi, Director

VETERANS ADMINISTRATION MEDICAL CENTER
830 Charlestone Ave.
Providence, RI 02908
(401) 273-7100 Fax: (401) 457-3370
James Cody, Temp. Director

SOUTH CAROLINA

ACERCAMIENTO HISPANO / HISPANIC OUTREACH, INC.
Affiliate of NCLR
P.O. Box 25277 Columbia, SC 29224-5277
5808 E Shakespeare Rd.
Columbia, SC 29223
(803) 714-0085 Fax: (803) 714-0474
Irma Santana, Executive Director

DIOCESE OF CHARLESTON
Hispanic Affairs
P.O. Box 487
Hardeville, SC 29927
(609) 692-8992 Fax: (609) 338-0793
Sr. Guadalupe Stump, RSM, Director for Hispanic Ministry
Email: slsrsm1@aol.com

HISPANIC-AMERICAN WOMEN'S ASSOC.
115 Brigadoon Court
Greer, SC 29650
(864) 848-3792
María Eugenia Narvaes, Executive Director
Email: AHAM@webtv.net

SOCIEDAD HONORARIA HISPÁNICA
300 Albemarle Rd.
Charlestown, SC 29407
(843) 556-3620 Fax: (843) 556-7404
Maxwell R. Mowry, Director

TELAMON CORPORATION
South Carolina Housing Services Division 8
184 W. Evans St., P.O. Box 12413
Florence, SC 29501
(843) 676-1055 Fax: (843) 676-1086
Jackie Wilson, Supervisor
Email: jwilson@telamon.org
Web: www.telamon.org

South Carolina Office 10
P.O. Box 1102, 400 Lexington Ave.
Kingstree, SC 29556
(843) 354-5708 Fax: (843) 354-5749
Wayne Rogers, Director
Email: wrogers@telamon.org
Web: www.telamon.org

South Carolina Office 2
127 Greenville St. SW
Aiken, SC 29802

(803) 648-9037 Fax: (803) 649-9447
Nancy Pennington, Case Manager
Email: tcsc02@esc.ttrc.doleta.gov
Web: www.telamon.org

South Carolina Office 4
1804-C Savannah Hwy.
Charleston, SC 29407
(843) 766-1545 Fax: (843) 766-3260
Deborah Johnson, Regional Manager
Email: djohnson@telamon.org
Web: www.telamon.org

South Carolina Office 5
912 Evans St.
Florence, SC 29501
(843) 667-4664 Fax: (843) 667-4671
Anita White, Regional Mananger
Email: awhite@telamon.org
Web: www.telamon.org

South Carolina Office 6
583 Amelia St. NE
Orangeburg, SC 29115
(803) 534-6444 Fax: (803) 534-6037
Patricia Crawford, Case Manager
Email: pcrawford@telamon.org
Web: www.telamon.org

South Carolina Office 7
P.O. Box 5291, 134 Garner Rd., #A
Spartanburg, SC 29304
(864) 573-8783 Fax: (864) 573-6342
Carmen Bowers, Regional Manager
Email: cbowers@telamon.org
Web: www.telamon.org

South Carolina State Office 1
P.O. Box 12217, 1413 Calhoun St., 2nd Fl.
Columbia, SC 29201
(803) 256-7411 Fax: (803) 256-8528
Bárbara Coleman, State Director
Email: bcol507581@aol.com
Web: www.telamon.org

SOUTH DAKOTA

DAKOTA HISPANIC COMMUNITY CENTER
302 S Lewis Ave
Sioux Falls, SD 57103
(605) 339-7662 Fax: (605) 339-7662
Jeanne Stoakes Rubio, Co-Project Coordinator
Email: dakchicano@ll.net

DIOCESE OF RAPID CITY
Hispanic Affairs
P.O. Box 678
606 Cathedral Dr.
Rapid City, SD 57709-0678
(605) 343-3541 Fax: (605) 348-7985
Sr. Margaret S. Simonson, Chancellor
Email: chncllr@enetis.net

DIOCESE OF SIOUX FALLS
Hispanic Affairs
1220 E. 8th St.
Sioux Falls, SD 57103
(605) 338-8126 Fax: (605) 338-0419
Rev. John Rader, Hispanic Ministry Coordinator

MIRGRANT AND SEASONAL FARMWORKERS PROGRAM
South Dakota Office
221 S Central
Pierre, SD 57501
(605) 224-0454 Fax: (605) 224-8320
Bill Podhradska, State Director
Email: bpodhradska@tie.net

TENNESSEE

CENTER FOR LATIN AMERICAN AND IBERIAN STUDIES
Vanderbilt University
Box 1806, Station B
Nashville, TN 37235
(615) 322-2527 Fax: (615) 322-2305
James Lang, Director
Email: antilng@ctrvax.vanderbilt.edu

DIOCESE OF MEMPHIS
Hispanic Affairs
5825 Shelby Oaks Dr.
Memphis, TN 38134
(901) 343-1284 Fax: (901) 373-1269
Deacon Curtiss J. Talley, Dir. for Multicultural Min.
Email: ctalley@cdom.org

DIOCESE OF NASHVILLE
Hispanic Affairs
10682 Old Nashville Hwy.

Smyrna, TN 37167
(615) 459-3046
Rev. Richard Gagnnon, Dir. for Hispanic Ministry

HISPANIC MINISTRY
Apostolado de la Diócesis Católica de Knoxville
119 Dameron Ave.
Knoxville, TN 37917
(423) 637-4769 Fax: (423) 971-3575
Jack Kramer, Director
Email: LaCosecha@yahoo.com

RAINBOW/PUSH COALITION
Chattanooga Chapter
P.O. Box 6221, 2118 Raulston St.
Chattanooga, TN 37404
(423) 624-6822
Johny Holloway, Executive Director
Web: www.rainbowpush.com

SOCIEDAD HONORARIA HISPÁNICA
Tennessee Chapter
Christian Brothers High School
5900 Walnut Grove Rd.
Memphis, TN 38120
(901) 682-7801 Fax: (901) 682-7815
Patricia Freire, Chairperson

SOCIETY OF HISPANIC PROFESSIONAL ENGINEERS (SHPE)
Tennessee Professional Chapter
P.O. Box 4042
Oak Ridge, TN 37831
(423) 241-3432 (w) or (423) 457-2476 (h)
Fax: (423) 241-4283
Rafael G. Rivera, Chapter President
Web: www.shpe.org

TELAMON CORPORATION
Dayton Migrant Head Start Center 3
P.O. Box 707, 5312 Dayton Mountain Hwy.
Dayton, TN 37321
(423) 570-9808 Fax: (423) 570-9812
Vicki Chacón, Director
Email: vchacon@usit.net
Web: www.telamon.org

Newport Migrant Head Start Center 4
P.O. Box 769
Newport, TN 37822
(865) 674-8472/8473 Fax: (865) 674-8474
Pauline Raines, Director
Email: praines@usit.net
Web: www.telamon.org

Tennessee State Head Start Office 1
9050 Executive Park Dr., #220-A
Knoxville, TN 37923
(865) 694-3285 Fax: (865) 694-3293
J. Davis, Director
Email: jdavis2@usit.net
Web: www.telamon.org

Unicoi Migrant Head Start Center 2
P.O. Box 9, 551 Mocking Bird Ct.
Unicoi, TN 37692
(423) 743-2028 or (423) 743-6282
Fax: (423) 743-5496
Silvia Fregoso, Director
Email: sfregoso@usit.net
Web: www.telamon.org

TEXAS

ADAIR MARGO GALLERY
415 E. Yandell Dr.
El Paso, TX 79902
(915) 533-0048 Fax: (915) 496-8482
Adair Margo, President
Email: adair@adairmargo.com
Web: www.adairmargo.com

ADELANTE, U.S. EDUCATION LEADERSHIP FUND
8415 Datapoint Dr., #400
San Antonio, TX 78229
(210) 692-1971 Fax: (210) 692-1951
Ruben Garcia III, Assist. Executive Director

ADVOCACY INC.
Central Texas Regional Office
7800 Shoal Creek Blvd., Suite 171-E
Austin, TX 78757
(512) 454-4816 Fax: (512) 302-4936
Roberta Rosenberg-Roque, Regional Manager
Web: www.advocacyinc.org

East Texas Regional Office
7457 Harwin Drive, Suite 100
Houston, TX 77036
(713) 974-7691 Fax: (713) 974-7691

Mary Faithfull, Regional Manager
Web: www.advocacyinc.org

Main Office
7800 Shoal Creek Blvd., # 171-E
Austin, TX 78757
(512) 454-4816 or (800) 252-9108
Fax: (512) 323-0902
Jim Comstock-Galagan, Executive Director
Email: infoi@advocacying.org
Web: www.advocacyinc.org

North Texas Regional Office
1420 West Mockingbird Lane #450
Dallas, TX 75247-4932
(214) 630-0196 Fax: (214) 630-3472
Betty Black, Regional Manager
Web: www.advocacyinc.org

South Texas Regional Office
504 East Dove Suite A
McAllen, TX 78504
(956) 630-3013 Fax: (956) 630-3445
Belinda Garza, Regional Manager
Web: www.advocacyinc.org

West Texas Office
1001 Main St. #200
Lubbock, TX 79401-3200
(806) 765-7795 or (800) 880-4456
Fax: (806) 765-0496
Peggy Durán Klenclo, Regional Manager
Web: www.advocacyinc.org

ALAMO AREA COUNCIL OF GOVERNMENTS
8700 Tesoro Dr., #700
San Antonio, TX 78217
(210) 362-5200 Fax: (210) 225-5937
Laura Jane Stephens, Coordinator
Email: mail@aacog.dst.tx.us
Web: www.aacog.dst.tx.us

ALAMO CITY IMAGE
National Image, Inc.
118 Dobbs
San Antonio, TX 78237
Jesús O. Calvillo, President
Web: www.nationalimageinc.org

**ALCOHOL/DRUG EVALUATION
EDUCATION & COUNSELING**
Avalos García & Associates
4101 San Jacinto #110
Houston, TX 77004
(713) 528-2155 Fax: (713) 528-0435
Miguel García, President

ALCOHOLICS ANONYMOUS
Dallas Inter group
6162 E Mockingbird Ln., #213
Dallas, TX 75214
(214) 905-0770 or (214) 823-3200
Norman Surtees, Volunteer
Email: :aa@dallas/aa.org
Web: www.dallas/aa.org

ALPHA PSI LAMBDA, INC.
Southern Methodist Univ.- Delta Chapter
P.O. Box 75-0436
Dallas, TX 75275-0436
(214) 768-4400
Nery Franco, President
Web: http://alpha-psi-lambda.org/zeta/

**AMERICAN ASSOCIATION OF HISPANIC
CERTIFIED PUBLIC ACCOUNTANTS (CPAS)**
Dallas Chapter/ Mir, Fox & Rodriguez, P.C.
2777 Stemmons Freeway, #998
Dallas, TX 75207
(214) 634-8100 Fax: (214) 634-8181
Juan Torres, Chapter President
Email: jtorres@mfrgroup.com
Web: www.aahcpa.org

**AMERICAN ASSOCIATION OF HISPANIC
CERTIFIED PUBLIC ACCOUNTANTS (CPAS)**
Houston Chapter/Mir, Fox & Rodriguez, P.C.
1900 One Riverway
Houston, TX 77056
(713) 622-1120 Fax: (713) 961-0625
Juan M. Padilla, Chapter President
Email: jpadilla@mfrpc.com
Web: www.aahcpa.org

National Office
100 N. Main St., #406
San Antonio, TX 78205
(203) 255-7003 Fax: (203) 259-2872
Ismael Martínez, President
Email: aahcpa@netscape.net
Web: www.aahcpa.org

AMERICAN G.I. FORUM OF THE U.S.
612 Half League Rd. #5
Port Lavaca, TX 77979
(361) 552-3058 or (361) 552-7602
Humberto Grimaldo, Local Commander

AMERICAN GI FORUM OF THE U.S.
2619 Perez St.
San Antonio, TX 78207
(210) 433-6301
Father Peña, Chaplain

4522 Castenon
Corpus Christi, TX 78416
(361) 853-1803 (h) or (361) 852-8874 (w)
Fax: (361) 852-0079
Tina Cruz, Secretary-Women

**AMERICAN G.I. FORUM OF THE U.S.
NATIONAL VETERANS OUTREACH
PROGRAM (NVOP)**
National Headquarters
206 San Pedro, #200
San Antonio, TX 78205
(210) 223-4088 Fax: (210) 223-4970
Carlos Martínez, President & CEO
Email: giforum@txdirect.net

AMIGOS DE LAS AMÉRICAS
National Headquarters
5618 Star Ln.
Houston, TX 77057
(800) 231-7796 or (713) 782-5290
Fax: (713) 782-9267
Mario Molina, Vice-Pres./CFO
Email: info@amigoslink.org
Web: www.amigoslink.org

AMIGOS DEL VALLE, INC.
Affiliate of NCLR
1116 Conway Ave.
Mission, TX 78572
(956) 581-9494 Fax: (956) 581-2210
Amancio J. Chapa, Jr., President & CEO
Email: mcantu@amigos.vt.com

**AMIGOS EN AZUL (AUSTIN HISPANIC
POLICE OFFICERS ASSOCIATION)**
715 E. Eighth St.
Austin, TX 78701
(512) 444-5411
Joe Múnoz, President
Web: http://www.ci.austin.tx.us/empassoc/
eaamigos.htm

ARCHDIOCESE OF SAN ANTONIO
Hispanic Affairs
P.O. Box 28410
2718 W. Woodlawn Ave.
San Antonio, TX 78228-0410
(210) 734-2620 Fax: (210) 734-2758
Sr. Therese San Miguel, OSF, Director of
Educational/Formation Services
Email: tsanmiguel@archdiosa.org

**ARLINGTON HISPANIC CHAMBER OF
COMMERCE**
302 S. Center St., #400
Arlington, TX 76010
(817) 461-8815 Fax: (817) 795-9499
Greg Vaquera, President
Email: info@hispanic-chamber.org
Web: www.hispanic-chamber.org

ARRIBA!
Pepsico Inc.-Frito-Lay Inc.
7701 Legacy Dr.
Plano, TX 75024
(972) 334-5815 Fax: (972) 334-4847
Nick Adame, President

ARTE PÚBLICO PRESS
Univ. of Houston MD Aderson Library
4800 Calhoun Rd.
Houston, TX 77204-2174
(713) 743-2841 Fax: (713) 743-2847
Marina Tristán, Assistant Director
Email: mtristan@uh.edu
Web: www.arte.uh.edu

ARTISTAS
2622 Florence St.
Dallas, TX 75204
(214) 821-5687
Anita Cisneroz, Director

**ASOCIACIÓN PARA LA EDUCACIÓN
TEOLÓGICA HISPANA (AETH)**
100 East 27st.

Austin, TX 78705
(512) 708-0660 Fax: (512)708-0670
Dr. Eldin Villafañe, Chair Person
Email: Office@aeth.org
Web: www.aeth.org

ASOC. PRO SERVICIOS SOCIALES, INC.
Affiliate of NCLR
406 Scott St.
Laredo, TX 78040
(956) 724-6244 Fax: (956) 724-5458
Alberto Luera, Executive Director

ASSOCIATED CATHOLIC CHARITIES
3400 Montrose Boulevard Suite 400
Houston, TX 77006
(713) 524-0182 Fax: (713) 524-1904
Magalis Candler, Supervisor
Email: acc.dam@hem.org
Web: www.acc.org

**ASSOCIATION FOR THE ADVANCEMENT
OF MEXICAN AMERICANS, INC. (AAMA)**
National Headquarters
6001 Gulf Frwy. Bldg. B-1-#102
Houston, TX 77023
(713) 926-2953 or (713) 926-4756
Fax: (713) 926-8035
Gilbert Moreno, President & CEO

Project Heart/Drug Abuse
204 Clifton St.
Houston, TX 77011
(713) 926-9491 Fax: (713) 926-2672
Gilbert Moreno, President & CEO

**ASSOCIATION OF LATINO SOCIAL WORK
EDUCATORS**
Worden School of Social Service
Our Lady of the Lake University, 411 SW 24th St.
San Antonio, TX 78207-4689
(210) 431-3906 Fax: (210) 431-4028
Juliette Silva, Ph.D., President
Email: herns@lake.ollusa.edu
Web: www.ollusa.edu/alswe/alswehome

**AUSTIN ASSOCIATION OF HISPANIC
FIREFIGHTERS**
ACM Office, P.O. Box 1088
Austin, TX 78767
(512) 403-9749
Randy Moreno, Secretary
Email: smkbuster@aol.com
Web: http://www.ci.austin.tx.us/empassoc/
eaaahf.htm

**AUSTIN HISPANIC CHAMBER OF
COMMERCE**
823 Congress Ave., #1330
Austin, TX 78701
(512) 476-7502 Fax: (512) 476-6417
Dianne Galaviz, Ph. D., President
Email: carol@hispanicaustin.com
Web: www.hispanicaustin.com

**AUSTIN LATINO LESBIAN AND GAY
ORGANIZATION (ALLGO)**
1715 E. 6th St., #112
Austin, TX 78702
(512) 472-2001 Fax: (512) 472-6301
Martha Duffer, Executive Director
Email: allgoinc@aol.com
Web: http://members.tripod.com/--allgo

AVANCE, INC.
National Headquarters
301 S. Frio St., #380
San Antonio, TX 78207
(210) 270-4630 Fax: (210) 270-4612
Dr. Gloria Rodríguez, President
Web: www.avance.org

AVANCE-FAMILY SUPPORT & EDUC. PROG.
Rio Grande Valley Office
1205 Galveston
McAllen, TX 78501
(956) 618-1642 Fax: (956) 618-1698
Raquel Oliva, Executive Director
Email: _avance-rgv_@avance.org
Web: www.avance.org

Houston Office
4289 Dacoma
Houston, TX 77092
(713) 812-0033 Fax: (713) 912-9829
Sylvia García, Executive Director
Email: sgarcia_hou@avance.org
Web: www.avance.org

AVENIDA GUADALUPE ASSOCIATION
Affiliate of NCLR
1327 Guadalupe St.
San Antonio, TX 78207
(210) 223-3151 Fax: (210) 223-4405
Roger Carrillo, Director

**BEE COUNTY AREA HISPANIC CHAMBER
OF COMMERCE**
1400 W. Corpus Christi St., #15
Beeville, TX 78102
(512) 358-8686 Fax: (512) 358-8787
Katherine Cantu Ramires, President
Email: kathyr@dbs.tech.com

BILINGUAL THEATER CORPORATION
P.O. Box 8196
Corpus Christi, TX 78468
(361) 993-8898 Fax: (361) 993-3217
Joseph Rosenberg, Artistic Director
Email: 112173.27.7@compuserve.com

**CALDWELL COUNTY HISPANIC CHAMBER
OF COMMERCE**
108 W. Olive St.
Lockhart, TX 78644
(512) 376-2585 Fax: (512) 258-0285
Alfonso Sifuentes, President

**CÁMARA DE COMERCIO HISPANA DE
AMARILLO (CACHA)**
P.O. Box 1861
Amarillo, TX 79105
(806) 379-8800 Fax: (806) 376-7873
Antonio Rentería, President

**CAMERON COUNTY HISPANIC CHAMBER
OF COMMERCE**
455 La Mancha
Brownsville, TX 78521
(956) 544-1538 Fax: (956) 544-1598
Adam Arredondo, Chair

CAPITOL CITY IMAGE
National Image, Inc.
6508 Clubway Lane
Austin, TX 787-3727
(512) 251-7528 or (512) 470-5097 (cell)
Ricardo Nieto, President
Web: www.nationalimageinc.org

CASA ARGENTINA DE HOUSTON
4740 Ingersoll, #212
Houston, TX 77027
(713) 622-2212
Myriam Marin, President

CASA DE PROYECTO LIBERTAD
113 N. 1st St.
Harlingen, TX 78550
(956) 425-9552 Fax: (956) 425-8249
Rogelio Núñez, Executive Director
Email: nrogelio@aol.com

**CENTER FOR DEVELOPMENT,
EDUCATION AND NUTRITION FAMILY
RESOURCE (CEDEN)**
1208 E. 7th St.
Austin, TX 78702
(512) 477-9017 Fax: (512) 477-9205
Susan Berliner, Interim Director
Email: ceden@bga.com
Web: www.main.org/ceden

CENTER FOR HEALTH POLICY DEV., INC.
6905 Alamo Down Pkwy.
San Antonio, TX 78238
(210) 520-8020 Fax: (210) 520-9522
Charlene Doria-Ortiz, Executive Director
Email: chpd@ix.netcom.com

**CENTER FOR MEXICAN AMERICAN
STUDIES**
University of Texas at Austin
Mail Code F9200
Austin, TX 78712
(512) 471-4557 Fax: (512) 471-9639
Dr. David Montejano, Director
Email: cmas01@uts.cc.utexas.edu
Web: www.utexas.edu/depts/cmas/

**CENTEX HISPANIC CHAMBER OF
COMMERCE**
501 Franklin Ave., #806
Waco, TX 76701
(254) 754-7111 Fax: (254) 754-3456
Joe Rodríguez, Executive Director
Email: cthcc@hot1.net

CENTRO AZTLAN
5115 Harrisburg Blvd.
Houston, TX 77011
(713) 926-8771 Fax: (713) 926-8771

Eduardo Castillo, Notary Public
Email: hcsaztlan@pdq.net

CENTRO CULTURAL MEXICANO
Dallas Office
2917 Swise Ave.
Dallas, TX 75204
(214) 824-9981 Fax: (214) 821-9103
Clara Borja Hinojosa, Director

CENTRO CULTURAL MEXICANO EN EL VALLE DE TEXAS
307 S. Broadway
McAllen, TX 78501
(956) 972-1223 Fax: (956) 972-0350
María Del Carmen Austin, Director
Email: mexcultura@aol.com

CENTRO CULTURAL MEXICANO PASO DEL NORTE
El Paso Office
910 E. San Antonio
El Paso, TX 79901
(915) 533-3644 Fax: (915) 532-7163
Dolores Limonge, Executive Director

CENTRO DE SALUD FAMILIAR LA FÉ, INC.
Affiliate of NCLR
608 S. Saint Vrain St.
El Paso, TX 79901-3007
(915) 534-7979 Fax: (915) 534-7601
Salvador Balcorta, Executive Director
Email: balcorta@mail.htg.net

CHICANO FAMILY CENTER
7524 Ave. E
Houston, TX 77012
(713) 923-2316 Fax: (713) 923-4243
Elena Vergara, Executive Director

CHICANO STUDIES PROGRAM
University de Texas at El Paso
500 W University Ave. / Graham Hall, #104
El Paso, TX 79968-0563
(915) 747-5462 Fax: (915) 747-6501
Dennis Bixler-Márquez, Director
Email: chicstds@utep.edu
Web: www.utep.edu/chicano

CHICANO/LATINO FILM FORUM
400 Post Road Dr.
Austin, TX 78704
(512) 707-7988
René Rentería, Director
Email: LatinoFilmForum@aol.com
Web: http://members.aol.com/LatinoFilmForum/

CHICANOS AGAINST MILITARY INTERVENTION IN LATIN AMERICA
Dallas Chapter
224 Sunset
Dallas, TX 75208
(214) 942-2531
Perfecto Del-Gado, Executive Director

CHICANOS UNIDOS-CAMPESINOS INC.
216 E. Ave. D
Muleshoe, TX 79347
(806) 272-4233
Alberto Daniel, President

CHILDREN OF THE AMERICAS
P.O. Box 140165
Dallas, TX 75214
(214) 823-3922 Fax: (214) 823-7991
W. O. Mills III, President

COALITION OF HISPANIC-AMERICAN STUDENTS (CHISPAS)
P.O. Box 532
Prairie View, TX 77446
(936) 857-4494 Fax: (936) 857-2255
Marcia Shelton, Advisor
Email: marcia_shelton@tvanu.edu

COLONIAS DEL VALLE, INC.
Affiliate of NCLR
P.O. Box 764
1203 East Farguson St.
Pharr, TX 78577
(956) 787-9903 Fax: (956) 782-1016
Aída Gonzáles, Executive Director

COMMISSION AND VISITORS BUREAU
1201 N. Shoreline Blvd.
Corpus Christi, TX 78401
(361) 881-1888 Fax: (361) 887-9023
Tom Miskala, President

CORPORATE HISPANICS NETWORK
P.O. Box 2197
Houston, TX 77252
(281) 920-6061 Fax: (281) 293-1650
Rick Otero, Director

CORPUS CHRISTI HISPANIC CHAMBER OF COMMERCE
615 Upper N. Broadway, #870
Corpus Christi, TX 78477
(361) 887-7408 Fax: (361) 888-9473
Manuel Ugues, President
Email: cchcc@ciris.net
Web: www.cchispanicchamber.org

CREATIVE ACADEMIC ACHIEVEMENT/ PRO-SUCCESS LEARNING CENTER
618 N McColl; P.O. Box 164
McAllen, TX 78504
(956) 682-3436 Fax: (956) 687-6062
Aguie Peña, Chair.

CRISIS INTERVENTION OF HOUSTON, INC.
Affiliate of United Way
P.O. Box 130866
Houston, TX 77219-0866
(713) 527-9864 Fax: (713) 527-0435
Maggie Rincón, Hispanic Coordinator
Web: www.crisishotline.org

CULTURAL ARTS COUNCIL OF HOUSTON & HARRIS COUNTY
3201 Allan Pkwy., #250
Houston, TX 77019
(713) 527-9330 Fax: (713) 630-5210
Lucy Dabney, President
Web: www.cachh.org

DALLAS CONCILIO OF HISPANIC SERVICES ORGANIZATIONS
Affiliate of NCLR
2914 Swiss Ave.
Dallas, TX 75204
(214) 818-0481 Fax: (214) 818-0485
Linda Coria, Director of Programs
Email: clcoria@swbell.net

DALLAS HISPANIC LEADERSHIP
Alumni Ass
1224 Middle Cove Dr.
Plano, TX 75023
(214) 464-2832 Fax: (214) 464-8913
Pearl Garza Fracchia, Chairwomen
Email: pgfracch@swbell.net

DENTON HISPANIC CHAMBER OF COMMERCE
2412 Olz North Rd. Bldg., 104
Denton, TX 76209
(940) 383-2901 Fax: (940) 483-1939
Mariella Cudd, Chairwomen

DENVER HARBOR SENIORS
6402 Market St.
Houston, TX 77020
(713) 672-6395 Fax: (713) 672-5831
Martha González, Executive Director

DIOCESAN AIDS MINISTRY
2900 Louisiana
Houston, TX 77002
(713) 526-4611 Fax: (713) 526-1546
Gabriela Aguada, Outreach Coordiantor
Email: acc.dam@hem.org
Web: www.acc.org

DIOCESE OF AMARILLO
Office of Hispanic Affairs
2300 N. Spring St.
Amarillo, TX 79107-7258
(806) 383-2261 Fax: (806) 383-2266
Rev. Arturo Meza, Vicar for Hispanic Ministry

DIOCESE OF AUSTIN
Off. of Hispanic Ministry, Pastoral Center
1625 Rutherford Ln.
Austin, TX 78754-5105
(512) 873-7771 Fax: (512) 873-8338
Rev. Albert Ruiz
Email: albertruiz@austindiocese.org

DIOCESE OF BEAUMONT
Hispanic Affairs
P.O. Box 3948
703 Archie St.
Beaumont, TX 77704
(409) 838-0451 Fax: (409) 838-4511
Sr. Pilar Dalmau, acj, Director for Hispanic Ministry
Email: pdalmau@dioceseofbmt.org

DIOCESE OF BROWNSVILLE
Hispanic Ministry Office
1910 E. Elizabeth St.
Brownsville, TX 78522
(956) 542-2501 Fax: (956) 542-6751
Luis Zuñiga
Email: dobsynod1@aol.com

DIOCESE OF CORPUS CHRISTI
Hispanic Affairs
1200 Lantana St.
Corpus Christi, TX 78407
(512) 589-6501
Rev. Bobby Dunn, Director for Hispanic Affairs

DIOCESE OF DALLAS
Pastoral Planning and Diocesan Networks
P.O. Box 190507
3725 Blackburn St.
Dallas, TX 75219-0507
(214) 528-2240 x330 Fax: (214) 523-2429
Lynn Rossol, Director
Email: lrossol@cathdal.org

DIOCESE OF EL PASO
Hispanic Ministry Office
499 St. Matthews
El Paso, TX 79907
(915) 595-5063
Sr. Asunto Labrado, Director

DIOCESE OF FORT WORTH
Hispanic Pastoral Services
800 W. Loop 820 S.
Fort Worth, TX 76108-2919
(817) 560-3300 x258 Fax: (817) 244-8839
Andrés Aranda, Director
Email: aaranda@fwdioc.org

DIOCESE OF GALVESTON-HOUSTON
Hispanic Affairs
2403 E. Holcomb Blvd.
Houston, TX 77021
(713) 741-8727 Fax: (713) 747-9206
Jorge A. Delgado, Director for Hispanic Ministry
Email: jdelgado@diocese-gal-hou.org
Web: www.diocese-gal-hou.org

DIOCESE OF LAREDO
Laredo Pastoral Center
1901 Corpus Christi St.
Laredo, TX 78044
(956) 727-2140 Fax: (956) 727-2777
Serapio Hernández, Dir. for Hispanic Ministry

DIOCESE OF LUBBOCK
Hispanic Affairs
P.O. Box 98700, 4620 4th St.
Lubbock, TX 79416
(806) 828-5108 Fax: (806) 792-2953
Rev. Msgr. Antonio González, Chancellor

DIOCESE OF SAN ANGELO
Hispanic Ministry Office
9158 Hwy. 227 South
Abilene, TX 76909
(915) 597-2324 Fax: (915) 456-1390
Noe Rocha, Director

DIOCESE OF TYLER
Hispanic Ministry Office
1015 ESE Loop 323
Tyler, TX 75701-9663
(903) 534-1077 x44 Fax: (903) 534-1370
Rev. Luis Larrea, MFE
Email: llarrea@dioceseoftyler.org

DIOCESE OF VICTORIA
Hispanic Affairs
2116 Leon Dr.
Pt. Lavaca, TX 77979
(361) 552-3664
Deacon Al Calzada, Hispanic Ministry Coord.

EAGLE PASS HISPANIC CHAMBER OF COMMERCE
P.O. Box 3040
Eagle Pass, TX 78853
(830) 757-2704 Fax: (830) 757-2703
Arturo C. Cosme, President

EL PASO HISPANIC CHAMBER OF COMMERCE
2829 Montana, #B100
El Paso, TX 79903
(915) 566-4066 Fax: (915) 566-9714
Cindy Ramos-Davidson, President & CEO
Email: marcella@htg.net
Web: www.ephcc.org

EL PASO MUSEUM OF ART
One Arts Festival Plaza
El Paso, TX 799021
(915) 532-1707 Fax: (915) 532-1010
Becky Duval Reese, Director

EL VALLE CENTER, PROJECT P.O.D.E.R.
530 S. Texas, #J
Weslaco, TX 78596
(956) 969-3611 Fax: (956) 969-8761
Yvette Hinojosa, Executive Director
Email: valley@tfepoder.org
Web: www.tfevalleycenter.org

ELADIO R. MARTÍNEZ LEARNING CENTER
Affiliate of SER-Jobs for Progress National, Inc.
4500 Bernal Dr.
Dallas, TX 75212
(214) 689-1670 Fax: (214) 689-1726
Rosa Peña, Principal
Web: www.sernational.org

ESPERANZA, PEACE & JUSTICE CENTER
922 San Pedro
San Antonio, TX 78212
(210) 228-0201 Fax: (210) 228-0000
Graciela Sánchez, Executive Director
Web: www.esperanzacenter.org

FORT WORTH HISPANIC CHAMBER OF COMMERCE
1327 N Main St.
Fort Worth, TX 76106
(817) 625-5411 Fax: (817) 625-1405
Richard Navarrete, President
Email: fwhcc@onramp.net
Web: www.fwhcc.org

FORT WORTH SER-JOBS FOR PROGRESS, INC.
Affiliate of SER-Jobs for Progress National, Inc.
3030 W. Central Ave.
Fort Worth, TX 76106
(817) 624-3260 Fax: (817) 624-3765
Terry Meza, Executive Director
Web: www.sernational.org

GRAND PRAIRIE HISPANIC CHAMBER OF COMMERCE
114 North East 4th St.
Grand Prairie, TX 75050
(972) 642-2621 Fax: (972) 642-4116
Marcie Delgado, Chair

GRAND PRAIRIE SER-JOBS FOR PROGRESS, INC.
Affiliate of SER-Jobs for Progress National, Inc.
405 Stadium Dr.
Grand Prairie, TX 75050
(972) 237-9300 Fax: (972) 237-7915
Sandra Banks, Executive Director
Email: grandprairieser@hotmail.com
Web: www.sernational.org

GREATER DALLAS HISPANIC CHAMBER OF COMMERCE
4622 Maple Ave., #207
Dallas, TX 75219-1001
(214) 521-6007 Fax: (214) 520-1687
Frank Cortéz, President
Email: gdhcco@gdhcc.com
Web: gdchcc.com

GREATER HISPANIC CHAMBER OF COMMERCE OF CORNAL COUNTY
P.O.Box 311715
New Braunfels, TX 78131
(830) 606-1805 Fax: (830) 606-7930
Mike Cruz, Chairman
Email: ghccnbtx@aol.com

GREATER HOUSTON PARTNERSHIP
1200 Smith #700
Houston, TX 77002-4309
(713) 651-2100 Fax: (713) 844-0200
Jim Kollaer, Director

GREATER VICTORIA HISPANIC CHAMBER OF COMMERCE
P.O. Box 2552
Victoria, TX 77902-2552
(361) 572-6525
María Martínez Moreno, Treasurer

GUADALUPE COMMUNITY CENTER
Affiliate of United Way
1801 W. Durango
San Antonio, TX 78207
(210) 226-6178 Fax: (210) 226-9188
Elizabeth Sánchez, Director

GULF COAST COUNCIL OF LA RAZA, INC.
Affiliate of NCLR
2203 Baldwin Blvd.
Corpus Christi, TX 78405
(361) 881-9988 Fax: (361) 881-9994
María Luisa Garza, Executive Director

HARLINGEN HISPANIC CHAMBER OF COMMERCE
P.O. Box 530967
Harlingen, TX 78553
(956) 421-2400 Fax: (956) 364-1879
Alma Colleli, President

HARLINGEN INFORMATION & SOCIAL SERVICES ORGANIZATION
Affiliate of NCLR
802 N. Commerce
Harlingen, TX 78550
(956) 423-5200
Antonio Ramírez, President

HISPANIC ASSOC. OF AT&T EMPLOYEES
5501 LBJ Parkway
Dallas, TX 75240
(972) 778-2419 or (972) 778-2775
John Guerra, President

HISPANIC ASSOCIATION OF COLLEGES & UNIVERSITIES (HACU)
National Headquarters
8415 Datapoint, #400
San Antonio, TX 78229
(210) 692-3805 Fax: (210) 692-0823
Antonio R. Flores, President
Email: hacu@hacu.net
Web: www.hacu.net

HISPANIC BUSINESS STUDENT ASSOCIATION
c/o Student Activities Nº 295 Texas Union
P.O. Box 7338
Austin, TX 78713-7338
(512) 471-3779 Fax: (512) 471-8711
Omar Ríos, President

HISPANIC CHAMBER OF COMMERCE OF GREATER BAYTOWN
1300 Rollingbrook Dr., #504
Baytown, TX 77521
(281) 422-6908 Fax: (281) 422-6908
Rubén de Hoyos, President
Email: hccdb1@netzero.net
Web: www.baytownhcc.com

HISPANIC CLUB
Tarrant County College
4801 Marine Creek Pkwy.
Fort Worth, TX 76179
(817) 515-7210 Fax: (817) 515-7007
Paul W. Sexton, Advisor
Email: paul.sexton@tccd.net

HISPANIC CONTRACTORS ASSOCIATION DE TEJAS
6006 Melwood Dr.
Austin, TX 78724
(512) 477-8194 Fax: (512) 477-2778
Frank Fuentes, President

HISPANIC EMPLOYEE INITIATIVE FORUM
Texas Instruments
7839 Churchill Way, MS: 3991
Dallas, TX 75251
(972) 917-5767 Fax: (972) 917-6132
Ludy Ortega, Chair

HISPANIC ENTREPRENEURS RECRUITERS ORGANIZATION & SERVICES (HEROS)
14927 James Rivewr Lane
Houston, TX 77084
(281) 859-0564 or (281) 859-2636
Rosemary Acosta-Clark, President

HISPANIC HERITAGE CLUB
PO Box 2007
8060 Spencer Hwy.
San Jacinto College Central Campus
Pasadena, TX 77501-2007
(281) 476-1877 Fax: (281) 476-1823
Rosie Flores, Director

HISPANIC JOURNALISM ASSOCIATION
230 Reed McDonald Bldg.
College Station, TX 77843-4111
(409) 845-4611 Fax: (409) 845-5408
Ed Walraven, Director

HISPANIC NATIONAL BAR ASSOCIATION (HNBA)
901 Main St., #3100
Dallas, TX 75202-3789

(214) 651-5544 Fax: (214) 200-0754
Rubén De León, Vice Pres. – External Affairs
Email: deleonr@hayboo.com
Web: www.hnba.com

Region XII (AR, LA, OK, TX)
106 S. St. Mary's St.
San Antonio, TX 78205-3603
(210) 299-3579 Fax: (210) 299-0145
Yuri Calderón, Regional President
Email: ycalderon@bracepatt.com
Web: www.hnba.com

HISPANIC ORGANIZATION OF POSTAL EMPLOYEES (H.O.P.E.)
Housten Chapter
P.O. Box 475
Housten, TX 77201-0475
(713) 869-8063
Narcissus G. López, President
Email: nglopez100@aol.com
Web: www.community.dallasnews.com/dmn/hopehispanic

HISPANIC PASTORAL CENTER
Catholic Diocese of Galveston-Houston
2403 Holcombe Blvd.
Houston, TX 77021-2098
(713) 741-8727 Fax: (713) 747-9206
Pedro A. Moreno, Director

HISPANIC PRESIDENTS COUNCIL
Texas A&M University
Multicultural Service Dept. MSC - #137
College Station, TX 77843-1121
(979) 845-4551 Fax: (979) 862-2640
Emily Santiago, Advisor

HISPANIC STUDENT ASSOCIATION
Baylor University
P.O. Box 97056
Waco, TX 76798
(254) 710-2371
Jessica Sánchez, Sponsor

HISPANIC STUDENT ASSOCIATON
Human Relation Office-Baylor University
P.O. Box 97053
Waco, TX 76798
(254) 710-6939
Paul Beverly, Coordinator-Multi-Cultural

HISPANIC STUDENT ORGANIZATION
Galveston College
4015 Ave. Q
Galveston, TX 77550
(409) 763-6551 Fax: (409) 762-9367
María Eliaz/Beatriz González, Co-Advisors

HISPANIC WOMEN'S NETWORK OF TEXAS (HWNT)
Dallas Chapter
P.O. Box 516411
Dallas, TX 75251
(972) 864-5516 or (214) 467-0123
Teresa Moreno, President
Email: spdracer@concentric.net
Web: www.concentric.net/~spdracer/hwnt.html

HOUSING OPPORTUNITIES OF HOUSTON, INC.
Affiliate of NCLR
2900 Woodridge, #300
Houston, TX 77087
(713) 644-8488 Fax: (713) 644-8489
Polk Curtiss, President

HOUSTON AREA ASSOCIATION FOR BILINGUAL EDUCATION
Affiliate of TABE and NABE
P.O. Box 7994
Houston, TX 77270
(713) 864-8941 Fax: (713) 861-9036
Amelia Cárdenas-Aguilar, President

HOUSTON COMMUNITY SERVICES
Affiliate of NCLR
5115 Harrisburg
Houston, TX 77011
(713) 926-8771 Fax: (713) 926-8771
Edward M. Casillo, Executive Director

HOUSTON ESPERANZA
Affiliate of NCLR
P.O. Box 230457
Houston, TX 77223
(713) 926-2794 Fax: (281) 481-2360
Paul Ramírez, President

HOUSTON HISPANIC CHAMBER OF COMMERCE
2900 Woodridge Dr., #312

Houston, TX 77087
(713) 644-7070 Fax: (713) 644-7377
Richard R. Torres, President

HOUSTON HISPANIC FORUM
3315 Sul Ross
Houston, TX 77098
(713) 522-8077 Fax: (713) 522-6249
Jenny R. Castañeda, President
Email: hhf@neosoft.com
Web: www.hispanicforum.org

IMAGE
National Image, Inc.
607 N. Hamilton
San Antonio, TX 78207
(210) 842-7715 (Mobile) Fax: (210) 224-7592
Johnny Zepeda, Regional Director
Web: www.nationalimageinc.org

IMAGE DE AUSTIN
National Image, Inc.
PO Box 685331
Austin, TX 78768
(512) 345-7567 (h) or (512) 916-5636 (w)
Fax: (512) 345-756788 (h)(512) 916-5613 (w)
María García, Chairperson & Chapter President
Web: www.nationalimageinc.org

IMAGE DE BEJAR
National Image, Inc.
206 San Pedro Suite 101
San Antonio, TX 78205
(210) 922-0910
Diane M. DeLeon, President
Web: www.nationalimageinc.org

IMAGE DE FORT WORTH
National Image, Inc.
2401 Summit View Drive
Bedford, TX 76021
(817) 285-0404 (H) or (214) 665-7257 (W)
Fax: (817) 285-7081 (HFAX)(817) 665-6648 (WFAX)
Olivia Rodríguez Balandrán, National Image, Inc., Vice-Chairperson Chapter President
Email: Balandran.Olivia-R@epa.gov
Web: www.nationalimageinc.org

IMAGE DE SAN ANTONIO
National Image, Inc.
P.O. Box 28532
San Antonio, TX 78228
(512) 345-7567
Mary Espíritu, President
Web: www.nationalimageinc.org

IMAGE STATE DE TEXAS
National Image, Inc.
P.O. Box 28532
San Antonio, TX 78228
(512) 345-7567
Mary Espíritu, President & San Antonio Chapter President
Web: www.nationalimageinc.org

INFORMATION REFERRAL RESOURCE ASSISTANCE, INC. (IRRA)
Affiliate of SER-Jobs for Progress Natl., Inc.
618 N. Mccoll St.
McAllen, TX 78502
(956) 682-3436 Fax: (956) 687-6062
Agueda Peña, Executive Director
Web: www.sernational.org

INSTITUTE OF CHICANO CULTURE
4370 Highway 6, North, Suite 217
Houston, TX 77084
(713) 866-8856 Fax: (281) 550-2422
Antonio González, Exec. Director
Email: chicanoinstitute@aol.com

INSTITUTE OF LATIN AMERICAN STUDIES ASSOCIATION
Universtly of Texas, Austin
Sid Richardson Hall 1.310
Austin, TX 78712
(512) 471-3065 Fax: (512) 471-3090
Nicolás Schumway, Executive Director
Email: ilas@uts.cc.utexas.edu
Web: http://lanic.utexas.edu/ilas/

INSTITUTO CULTURAL MEXICANO
Houston Office
10103 Fondren Rd.
Houston, TX 77096
(713) 772-4435 Fax: (713) 772-6238
Valentina Vial, Executive Director

San Antonio Chapter
600 Hemisfair Plaza
San Antonio, TX 78205

(210) 227-0123 Fax: (210) 223-1978
Felipe Santander, Director

INTER-AMERICAN CHAMBER OF COMMERCE (ICC)
510 Bering Dr., #300
Houston, TX 77057-1400
(713) 975-6171 Fax: (713) 975-6610
Fan Dorman, President & CEO
Email: icc@neosoft.com

INTERCULTURAL CANCER COUNCIL
1720 Dryden, Suite C
Houston, TX 77030
(713) 798-4617 Fax: (713) 798-3990
Carlotta V. Handcock, Project Coordinator,
Center for Cancer Control Research
Email: handcock@bcm.tmc.edu;
ico@bcm.tmc.edu

INTERCULTURAL DEVELOPMENT RESEARCH ASSOCIATION (IDRA)
5835 Callahan Rd., #350
San Antonio, TX 78228
(210) 444-1710 Fax: (210) 444-1714
Dr. María R. Montecel, Executive Director
Email: contact@idra.org
Web: www.idra.org

INTERNATIONAL ASSOC. OF HISPANIC MEETING PROFESSIONALS (IAHMP)
242 St. Cloud
Friendswood, TX 77546
(281) 992-9639 Fax: (281) 992-2555
Margaret G. González, President
Email: MGVRagency@aol.com

INTERNATIONAL LATINO FOUNDATION
7301 RR 620 N., #155/200
Austin, TX 78726
(512) 266-8690 Fax: (512) 266-8832
Ernesto Chavarría, Chairman & CEO

KLEBERG HISPANIC CHAMBER OF COMMERCE
111 N. Fifth
Kingsville, TX 78363
(361) 592-2708 Fax: (361) 592-8540
Maggie Salinas, President

LA GLORIA DEVELOPMENT CORP.
Affiliate of NCLR
615 Cadena
El Cenizo, TX 78046
(956) 791-3034 Fax: (956) 791-6997
Juan Idrogo, President

LA PEÑA
227 Congress Ave., #300
Austin, TX 78701
(512) 477-6007 Fax: (512) 477-0758
Veronica Péérez, Executive Director

LA ROSA - THE ROSE
P.O. Box 16042
Houston, TX 77222-6042
(713) 699-3974 Fax: (713) 697-3367
Candelaria Pérez, Director

LA SOCIEDAD HISPANA CULTURAL
Our Lady of the Lake University
411 SW. 24th St. FH 214
San Antonio, TX 78207-4666
(210) 434-6711x 272
Maribel Larraga, Director

LA VOZ DEL ANCIANO
6303 Forest Park, #268-A
Dallas, TX 75235
(214) 352-1700 Fax: (214) 352-1075
Teresa Longoria, Director
Email: lavoz22@veriomail.com

LAREDO HISPANIC CHAMBER OF COMMERCE
P.O.Box 790
Laredo, TX 78042-0790
(956) 722-9895 Fax: (956) 791-4503
Miguel Conchas, President & CEO
Email: chamber@surfus.net
Web: www.laredochamber.com

LATINA/O LEADERSHIP OPPORTUNITY PROGRAM
Chicano Studies Program
UT El Paso, 500 W. University
El Paso, TX 79968
(915) 747-5462 Fax: (915) 474-6501
Carlos Ortega, Coordinator

LATINO AMERICAN STUDIES ASSOCIATION
Student Activities
One Main St.
University of Houston-Downtown
280 South
Houston, TX 77002
(713) 221-8573
Tom Corti, Director of Student Activities

LATINO LEARNING CENTER, INC.
3522 Polk Ave.
Houston, TX 77003
(713) 223-1391 Fax: (713) 222-2338
Frank Orozco, Executive Director
Web: www.latinolearning.org/

LATINO USA
University of Texas, Austin
Communication Building B, 3.142
Austin, TX 78712
(512) 475-6767 Fax: (512) 471-3700
Kate Dearborn, Director
Email: kdearborn@mail.utexas.edu

LEAGUE OF UNITED LATIN AMERICAN CITIZENS (LULAC)
221 N. Kansas St., #1200
El Paso, TX 79901
(915) 577-0726 or (915) 584-3722
Fax: (915) 577-0914
Rick Dovalina, President
Web: www.lulac.org

National Executive Committee
3700 Buffalo Speedway, Suite 700
Houston, TX 77098
(713) 624-1000 or (713) 617-4766
Fax: (713) 624-1099
Enrique Dovalina, National President
Email: rickdova@flash.net

National Executive Committee
7051 Brownleaf
San Antonio, TX 78227
(210) 674-1045 Fax: (210) 725-1483
Jason Arce, National Youth President
Email: smtp:cmorales@1pgate1.kelly.af.mil

LEARN, INC.
Affiliate of NCLR
P.O. Box 93358
2161 50th St.
Lubbock, TX 79412
(806) 763-4256 Fax: (806) 763-0791
Eddie Anaya, Executive Director

LUBBOCK HISPANIC CHAMBER OF COMMERCE
P.O. Box 886
Lubbock, TX 79408
(806) 762-5059 Fax: (806) 763-2124
Ester Sepeba, President

LULAC-NATIONAL EDUCATIONAL SERVICE CENTERS, INC. (LNESC)
2220 Broadway
Houston, TX 77012
(713) 641-2463 Fax: (713) 641-2484
Rose Ann Blanco, Director
Web: www.lulac.org

MAGIC VALLEY IMAGE
National Image, Inc.
141 Reynosa Street
Mercedes, TX 78570
(956) 565-1615 (H) or (956) 514-2223 (W)
Yolanda C. Molina, President
Web: www.nationalimageinc.org

MCALLEN HISPANIC CHAMBER OF COMMERCE
200 S. 10th St., #500
McAllen, TX 78501
(956) 928-0060 Fax: (956) 928-0073
Javier Rodríguez, Chairman
Email: hccrgv@borderguide.com

MEXIC-ARTE MULTICULTURAL WORKS
P.O. Box 2632
Austin, TX 78768
(512) 480-9373 Fax: (512) 480-8626
Silvia Orosco, Director

MEXICAN AMERICAN CULTURAL CENTER
3115 W. Ashby
San Antonio, TX 78228
(210) 732-2156 x101 Fax: (210) 732-9072
Sr. María Elena González, President
Email: macc@maccsa.org

MEXICAN AMERICAN LEGAL DEFENSE AND EDUCATIONAL FUND (MALDEF)
Houston Program Office
4401 Lovejoy, #23
Houston, TX 77003
(713) 928-6789 Fax: (713) 921-8504
Patricia Cabrera, Director
Web: www.maldef.org

San Antonio Regional Office
140 E. Houston St., #300
San Antonio, TX 78205
(210) 224-5476 Fax: (210) 224-5382
Albert H. Kauffman, Regional Counsel
Email: maldefsa@aol.com
Web: www.maldef.org

MEXICAN AMERICAN STUDENTS ORGANIZATION (MASA)
Howard College
1001 Birdwell Ln.
Big Spring, TX 79720
(915) 264-5127
Laura Peña, Advisor

MEXICAN AMERICAN UNITY COUNCIL, INC.
National Headquarters
2300 W. Commerce St., #300
San Antonio, TX 78207
(210) 978-0500 Fax: (210) 978-0547
Gilberto Ramón, Chair of the Board

MEXICAN STUDENT ASSOCIATION
University of Texas at El Paso
P.O. Box 634 Box 90
El Paso, TX 79968
(915) 747-5584
Juan Vásquez, President

MEXICAN-AMERICAN CULTURAL CENTER
National Headquarters
3115 W. Ashby Place
San Antonio, TX 78228
(210) 732-2156 Fax: (210) 732-9072
María E. González, RSM, President
Email: macc@maccsa.org
Web: www.maccsa.org

MEXICAN-AMERICAN DEMOCRATS OF TEXAS (MAD)
National Headquarters
400 S. Zang Blvd., #804
Dallas, TX 75208
(214) 943-8683 Fax: (214) 943-8296
Roberto Alonzo, Chairman

MEXICAN-AMERICAN NETWORK OF ODESSA, INC. (MANO)
1609 West 10th St.
Odessa, TX 79763
(915) 335-0250 Fax: (915) 337-6266
Iris Correas, Executive Director
Email: manoinc@nwol.net

MI ESCUELITA PRESCHOOL, INC.
Affiliate of SER-Jobs for Progress
National, Inc.
4231 Maple Ave.
Dallas, TX 75219
(214) 526-0220 Fax: (214) 526-0243
Carolyn Strickland, Director
Web: www.sernational.org

MIDLAND COLLEGE HISPANIC STUDENT ASSOCIATION
Midland College
3600 N. Garfield
Midland, TX 79705
(915) 685-4544 or (915) 685-4701
Tommy Ramos, Student Activities

MIDLAND HISPANIC CHAMBER OF COMMERCE
P.O. Box 11134
Midland, TX 79702
(915) 682-2960 Fax: (915) 687-3972
David Díaz, Executive Director
Email: mhcc@powr.net
Web: www.midlandhcc.com

MIGRANT HEALTH PROMOTION - PROMOVIENDO VIDAS SALUDABLES
Texas Office
P.O. Box 337
Progreso, TX 78579
(956) 565-0002 Fax: (956) 565-0136

MINORITY BUSINESS DEVELOPMENT AGENCY (MBDA)
Dallas Office/U.S. Dept. of Commerce
1100 Commerce St., #7B23
Dallas, TX 75242-0790

(214) 767-8006 or (214) 767-8001
Fax: (214) 767-0613
Raquel Suniga, Business Dev. Specialist
Email: RSuniga@mbda.gov
Web: www.mbda.gov

MIS PRIMEROS SUEÑOS
National Office/ Dallas
8204 Elmbrook, #235
Dallas, TX 75247
(214) 267-1622 Fax: (214) 267-1626
John Honaman, Executive Director
Email: info@nshmba.org
Web: www.nshmba.org

MISSION CENTER
1913 Fletcher
Houston, TX 77009
(713) 227-6371 Fax: (713) 224-0611
Dorcus Byrd, Administrator

MONEY MANAGEMENT INTERNATIONAL
6100 Bandera Rd., #800
San Antonio, TX 78238
(210) 543-1500 Fax: (210) 543-1507
Rudy Cavazos, Jr., Regional Manager
Web: www.mmintl.org

MOVIMIENTO ESTUDIANTIL CHICANO AZTLAN (MECHA)
University of Texas, El Paso
Graham Hall 104, 500 W. University
El Paso, TX 79968
(915) 747-5462 Fax: (915) 747-6501
Dennis Bixler-Marquez, Director
Email: jaragonutep@cs.com
Web: www.mecha.utep.edu

MOVIMIENTO ESTUDIANTIL CHICANO DE AZTLAN (MECHA)
Incarnate Word College
4301 Broadway - Box 127
San Antonio, TX 78209
(210) 829-6077 Fax: (210) 829-6096
Robert Sosa, Director

MULTI CULTURAL EDUCATION AND COUNSELING TO THE ARTS (MECA)
1900 Kane St.
Houston, TX 77007
(713) 802-9370 Fax: (713) 802-9403
Alice Valdéz, Director
Email: meca@neosoft.com
Web: www.multiculturalarts.org

NATIONAL ASSOCIATION FOR HISPANIC ELDERLY
El Paso Office/Project Ayuda
5959 Gateway W. Blvd., #212
El Paso, TX 79925
(423) 778-7825 Fax: (423) 778-7301
Cecilia I. Luna, Project Coordinator
Email: cluna@aol.com

Laredo Office/Project Ayuda
1311 Garfield St., #5
Laredo, TX 78043
(956) 727-8035 Fax: (956) 726-3148
Consuelo Salazar, Project Coordinator
Email: mcg1220@aol.com

San Antonio Office/Project Ayuda
2300 W. Commerce, #106
San Antonio, TX 78207
(210) 226-3806 or (210) 226-5478
Fax: (210) 224-2591
Eva Trevino, Project Coordinator

NATIONAL ASSOCIATION OF HISPANIC FIREFIGHTERS
National Headquarters
8204 Elmbrook Rd.
Dallas, TX 75228
(214) 631-0025 Fax: (214) 320-8712
Salvador Morales, President

NATIONAL ASSOCIATION OF HISPANIC JOURNALISTS (NAHJ)
Region 5
P.O. Box 2171
San Antonio, TX 78297
(210) 250-3000 Fax: (210) 250-3150
Nora López, Region Director
Email: noralopez@aol.com
Web: www.nahj.org

THE NATIONAL ASSOCIATION OF HISPANIC PRIESTS OF THE USA
6550 Fannin, #2117
Houston, TX 77030
(713) 795-4321 Fax: (713) 795-0320
Rev. José Gómez, President

Email: info@ansh.org
Web: www.ansh.org

NATIONAL ASSOCIATION OF LATINO ELECTED & APPOINTED OFFICIALS
Houston Office
4920 Irvington Blvd., #B
Houston, TX 77009
(713) 697-6400 Fax: (713) 694-2229
Héctor de León, Regional Director
Email: hdeleon@naleo.org
Web: www.naleo.org

NATIONAL BUSINESS ASSOCIATION
National Headquarters
5151 Beltline Rd #1150
Dallas, TX 75240
(800) 456-0440 Fax: (972) 960-9149
Pat Archibald, President
Email: www.nationalbusiness.org

NATIONAL CENTER FOR FARMWORKER HEALTH
National Headquarters
1770 FM 967
Buda, TX 78610
(512) 312-2700 Fax: (512) 312-2600
E. Roberta Ryder, Chief Executive Officer
Web: www.ncfh.org

NATIONAL COUNCIL OF LA RAZA (NCLR)
San Antonio Office
115 E. Travis, #320
San Antonio, TX 78205
(210) 212-4454 Fax: (210) 212-4459
Claríssa Martinez, Director
Web: www.nclr.org

NATIONAL HISPANIC BUSINESS ASSOC.
National Headquarters
1712 E. Riverside Dr., #208
Austin, TX 78741
(512) 495-9511 Fax: (512) 495-9730
Anissa Gonzales, President
Email: nhba@nhba.org
Web: www.nhba.org

NATIONAL HISPANIC INSTITUTE (NHI)
National Headquarters
P.O. Box 220
Maxwell, TX 78656
(512) 357-6137 Fax: (512) 357-2206
Ernesto Nieto, President
Email: callnhj@ad.com or NHIinfo@aol.com

NATIONAL LATINO CHILDREN'S INST.
Affiliate of NCLR
320 El Paso St.
San Antonio, TX 78207
(210) 228-9997 Fax: (210) 228-9972
Rebeca M. Barrera, Executive Director
Email: nlci@nlci.org
Web: www.nlci.org

NATIONAL LATINO PEACE OFFICERS ASSOCIATION (NLPOA)
Greater Dallas Chapter
P.O. Box 226411
Dallas, TX 75222-6411
(877) 657-6200
Gilbert Cerda, Past President
Email: nlpoa@aol.com
Web: www.nlpoa.com

Houston Metro Chapter
P.O. Box 53384
Houston, TX 77052
(877) 657-6200
Alfred Postel, Chapter President
Email: alfredpostel@yahoo.com
Web: www.nlpoa.com

San Antonio Chapter
1047 Victoria Crossing
San Antonio, TX 78245
(877) 657-6200
Adrian Garcia, National President
Email: nlpoa@aol.com
Web: www.nlpoa.com

Southeast Harris Chapter
P.O. Box 660
Pasadena, TX 77501
(877) 657-6200
Raul Garivey, Chapter President
Email: rgarivel@houstonisd.org
Web: www.nlpoa.com

Tarrant County Chapter
P.O. Box 4507
Fort Worth, TX 76164

(877) 657-6200
Adrián García, National President
Email: nlpoa@aol.com
Web: www.nlpoa.com

Texas Chapter
P.O. Box 7865
Houston, TX 77270
(877) 657-6200
Adrián García, National President
Email: nlpoa@aol.com
Web: www.nlpoa.com

NATIONAL ORGANIZATION FOR MEXICAN-AMERICAN RIGHTS (NOMAR)
P.O. Box 681205
San Antonio, TX 78268-1205
(210) 520-1831 or (817) 561-5551
Fax: (210) 520-1831
Dan J. Solís, Chairman
Email: NOMAR1@express-news.net

NATIONAL ORG. OF PROFESSIONAL HISPANIC NATURAL RESOURCES CONSERVATION SERVICE EMPLOYEES
P.O. Box 6567
Forth Worth, TX 76115
(817) 509-3292 or (817) 249-6476
Fax: (817) 509-3338
Rafael J. Guerrero, President
Email: rguerrero@stw.nrsc.usda.gov
Web: www.nhq.nrsc.usda.gov/HISPANIC/

NATIONAL SOCIETY OF HISPANIC MBAS
Austin Chapter
3 Vinshire Dr.
Austin, TX 78733
(512) 263-2001 ext. 103 (w)
or (214) 267-1622 (Nat'l Office)
Fax: (512) 263-5828 (w)
or (214) 267-1626 (Nat'l Office)
Sylvia del Bosque, Chapter President
Email: austin@nshmba.org or eli@itgq.com
Web: www.nshmba.org

Chicago Chapter
8204 Elmbrook, #235
Dallas, TX 75247
(714) 522-9664 (w) or (214) 267-1622 (Nat'l Office)
Fax: (214) 267-1626 (Nat'l Office)
Robert Escalante, Chapter President
Email: chicago@nshmba.org
Web: www.nshmba.org

NATIONAL SOCIETY OF HISPANIC MBAS (CONTINUED)
Dallas/Fort Worth Chapter
8204 Elmbrook, #235
Dallas, TX 75247
(214) 267-1622 (Nat'l Office)
Fax: (214) 267-1626 (Nat'l Office)
Giovani Ehrhardt, Chapter President
Email: dallasfortworth@nshmba.org
Web: www.nshmba.or

Denver Chapter
8204 Elmbrook, #235
Dallas, TX 75247
(214) 267-1622 (Nat'l Office)
Fax: (214) 267-1626 (Nat'l Office)
Blanca Cadavid, Chapter President
Email: denver@nshmba.org
Web: www.nshmba.or

Detroit Chapter
8204 Elmbrook, #235
Dallas, TX 75247
(214) 267-1622 Fax: (214) 267-1626
Daisy Ortiz Cirihal, Chapter President
Email: detroit@nshmba.org
Web: www.nshmba.org

Houston Chapter
8204 Elmbrook, #235
Dallas, TX 75247
(713) 656-8645 (w) or
(214) 267-1622 (Nat'l Office)
Fax: (214) 267-1626 (Nat'l Office)
Martha Salinas, Chapter President
Email: houston@nshmba.org
Web: www.nshmba.org

Los Angeles Chapter
8204 Elmbrook, #235
Dallas, TX 75247
(214) 267-1622 (Nat'l Office)
Fax: (214) 267-1626 (Nat'l Office)
Miguel Figueroa, Chapter President
Email: losangeles@nshmba.org
Web: www.nshmba.org

Miami Chapter
8204 Elmbrook, #235
Dallas, TX 75247
(214) 267-1622 (Nat'l Office)
Fax: (214) 267-1626 (Nat'l Office)
Maurice Pinto, Chapter President
Email: miami@nshmba.org
Web: www.nshmba.org

Orange County Chapter
8204 Elmbrook, #235
Dallas, TX 75247
(714) 522-9664 (w)
or (214) 267-1622 (Nat'l Office)
Fax: (214) 267-1626 (Nat'l Office)
Michael Valencia, Chapter President
Email: orangecounty@nshmba.org or
jaime.vasquez@pepsi.com
Web: www.nshmba.org

Phoenix Chapter
8204 Elmbrook, #235
Dallas, TX 75247
(214) 267-1622 (Nat'l Office)
Fax: (214) 267-1626 (Nat'l Office)
Joe Losada, Chapter President
Email: phoenix@nshmba.org
Web: www.nshmba.org

San Antonio Chapter
8204 Elmbrook, #235
Dallas, TX 75247
(214) 267-1622 (Nat'l Office)
Fax: (214) 267-1626 (Nat'l Office)
Roland Moreno, Chapter President
Email: sanantonio@nshmba.org
Web: www.nshmba.org

San Francisco Chapter
8204 Elmbrook, #235
Dallas, TX 75247
(408) 970-5974 (w) or
(214) 267-1622 (Nat'l Office)
Fax: (408) 988-1655 (w) or
(214) 267-1626 (Nat'l Office)
Eliud Landin, Chapter President
Email: sanfrancisco@nshmba.org
Web: www.nshmba.org

San Juan Chapter
8204 Elmbrook, #235
Dallas, TX 75247
(214) 267-1622 Fax: (214) 267-1626 (Nat'l Off.)
Alberto Giménez, Chapter President
Email: sanjuan@nshmba.org
Web: www.nshmba.org

Washington D.C. Chapter
8204 Elmbrook, #235
Dallas, TX 75247
(202) 314-7210 (w) or (214) 267-1622 (Nat'l Off.)
Fax: (214) 267-1626 (Nat'l Office)
Albertina Ponce, Chapter President
Email: washingtondc@nshmba.org
Web: www.nshmba.org

NEIGHBORHOOD CENTERS/RIPLEY HOUSE
4410 Navigation Blvd.
Houston, TX 77011
(713) 923-2661 Fax: (713) 921-8504
Rebecca Castillo, Program Coordinator
Email: rebecca.castillo@neighborhood-centers.org
Web: www.neighborhood-centers.org

NETTIE LEE BENSON LATIN AMERICAN COLLECTION
University of Texas, Austin
Sid Richardson Hall 1.109
Austin, TX 78713-8916
(512) 495-4520 Fax: (512) 495-4568
Laura Gutiérrez-Witt, Head Librarian

NUESTRA CLINICA DEL VALLE
1203 E. Ferguson
Pharr, TX 78577
(956) 787-0787 Fax: (956) 787-2021
Lucy Ramírez, Executive Director
Email: hchcc@hiline.net

THE OFFICE OF BILINGUAL EDUCATION
University of Texas, Austin
Curriculum & Instruction Sanchez Bldg. #406
Austin, TX 78712
(512) 471-3919 Fax: (512) 471-5550
George Blanco, Student Advisor

OFFICE OF MINORITY HEALTH INITIATIVES & CULTURAL COMPETENCY
1100 W. 49th St.
Austin, TX 78756

(512) 458-7629 Fax: (512) 458-7713
Eva Holguin, Executive Assistant

PARENT INVOLVEMENT & COMMUNITY EMPOWERMENT INITIATIVE
Texas Education Agency
1701 N. Congress Ave.
Austin, TX 78701
(512) 475-3488
Dr. Carol Francois, Associate Commissioner
Email: dblue@tmail.tea.state.tx.us
Web: www.tea.state.tx.us

PORT ARTHUR HISPANIC CHAMBER OF COMMERCE
3046 Procter St., #A
Port Arthur, TX 77642
(409) 983-2019 Fax: (409) 983-2031
Edna González, Executive Director
Email: admin@gthcc.org

PROJECT AYUDA
Affiliate of Nat'l. Assn. of Hispanic Elderly
1110 South Alamo
San Antonio, TX 78207
(210) 226-3806 Fax: (210) 224-2591
Eva Treviño, Project Coordinator

PROJECT ESPERANZA (HOLISTIC SVCS.)
Maple Plaza II 5415 Maple Ave., #422
Dallas, TX 75235
(214) 630-0114 Fax: (214) 630-0345
Laura Koster, Executive Director
Email: lkoster@projectesperanza.org
Web: www.projectesperanza.org

PROYECTO ORGANIZATIVO SIN FRONTERAS
201 E. Ninth Ave.
El Paso, TX 79901
(915) 532-0921 Fax: (915) 532-4822
Carlos Marentes, Executive Director

REFORMA
ARRIBA (Southeast Texas) Chapter
1103 Hackney
Houston, TX 77023
(713) 923-6827
Diana Morales, Chapter President
Email: dmorales@hpl.lib.tx.us
Web: http://clnet.ucr.edu/library/reforma

El Paso Chapter
El Paso Public Library, 9321 Alameda
El Paso, TX 79907
(915) 858-0905 Fax: (915) 860-8017
Margie Sánchez, Chapter President
Web: http://clnet.ucr.edu/library/reforma

President's Office
1901 Running Brook Dr.
Austin, TX 78723
(512) 929-7958 Fax: (512) 929-3510
Oralia Garza de Cortés, President
Email: odgc@aol.com
Web: http://clnet.ucr.edu/library/reforma

Rio Trinidad Chapter
Dallas Public Library
4100 Cedar Springs
Dallas, TX 75219
(214) 670-1359 Fax: (214) 670-5703
Corinne Hill, Chapter President
Email: chill@lib.ci.dallas.tx.us
Web: www.geocities.com/athens/forum/4406/index.html

San Antonio Chapter
Our Lady of the Lake University
411 SW 24th St.
San Antonio, TX 78207
(210) 434-6711 ext. 8165 Fax: (210) 436-1616
Linda Payne-Button, Chapter President
Email: paynl@lake.ollusa.edu
Web: www.geocities.com/lajefa_99.geo/

RIO GRANDE CITY CHAMBER OF COMMERCE
601 E. Main St.
Rio Grande City, TX 78582
(956) 487-3024 Fax: (956) 716-8560
Héctor Solís, President
Email: ahfolis@aol.com

RIO GRANDE VALLEY AREA HEALTH EDUCATION CENTER
Affiliate of NCLR
3516 E. Expressway 83, #108
Weslaco, TX 78596

(956) 969-3195 Fax: (956) 969-3378
Candace Delgado, Coordinator

THE RODRÍGUEZ ACADEMY OF DANCE
9403 Richmond Ave.
Houston, TX 77063
(713) 780-1796 Fax: (713) 780-0798
Rogelio Rodriguez, Owner

SAN ANGELO MUSEUM OF FINE ARTS
One Love St.
San Angelo, TX 76903
(915) 653-3333 Fax: (915) 658-6800
Howard Taylor, Director
Email: samfa@airmail.net

SAN ANTONIO HISPANIC CHAMBER OF COMMERCE (SAHCC)
603 Navarro, #100
San Antonio, TX 78205
(210) 225-0462 Fax: (210) 225-2485
Heriberto Herrera, President
Email: admin@sahcc.org
Web: www.shcc.org

SAN JACINTO GIRL SCOUTS
3110 Southwest Frwy.
Houston, TX 77098
(713) 292-0300 Fax: (713) 292-0330
Mary Vietek, Executive Director

SAN MARCOS HISPANIC CHAMBER OF COMMERCE
P.O. Box 1051
San Marcos, TX 78667
(512) 353-1103 Fax: (512) 353-2175
Richard Garza, President
Email: smhcc@latino.net
Web: sanmarcoshispanic.com

SEGUIN-GUADALUPE COUNTY HISPANIC CHAMBER OF COMMERCE
P.O. Box 1154
Seguin, TX 78156
(830) 379-3151 Fax: (830) 372-3151
Bruno Martínez, President
Email: shcc@axs4u.net

SER CHILD DEVELOPMENT CENTER
Affiliate of SER-Jobs for Progress National, Inc.
1525 W. Mockingbird Ln., #300
Dallas, TX 75235
(214) 637-8307 Fax: (214) 637-8313
Alice Escobar, Executive Director
Email: serchild@swbell.com
Web: www.sernational.org

SER-JOBS FOR PROGRESS NATIONAL, INC.
National Headquarters
100 Decker Dr., #200
Irving, TX 75062
(972) 541-0616 Fax: (972) 650-0842
James Parfonf, Director of Network Operations
Web: www.sernational.org

SER-JOBS FOR PROGRESS OF SAN ANTONIO, INC.
Affiliate of SER-Jobs for Progress National, Inc.
1499 Hillcrest
San Antonio, TX 78228
(210) 438-0586 Fax: (210) 438-8058
Linda Rivas, Executive Director
Web: www.sernational.org

SER-JOBS FOR PROGRESS OF SOUTHWEST TEXAS, INC.
Affiliate of SER-Jobs for Progress National, Inc.
4605 Maher Ave.
Laredo, TX 78041
(956) 724-1844 Fax: (956) 724-1831
Efraín Sánchez, Executive Director
Web: www.sernational.org

SER-JOBS FOR PROGRESS OF THE TEXAS GULF COAST, INC.
Affiliate of SER-Jobs for Progress National, Inc.
6565 Rookin St.
Houston, TX 77074
(713) 773-6000 Fax: (713) 773-6010
Jesse Castañeda, Executive Director
Email: serjesse@neosoft.com
Web: www.sernational.org

SOCIETY OF HISPANIC PROFESSIONAL ENGINEERS (SHPE)
Austin Professional Chapter
P.O. Box 2630
Austin, TX 78768
(512) 933-6181 or (512) 280-9496 (h)
Fax: (512) 280-2670
Dr. Kimberly Pacheco, Ph.D., Chapter President
Email: ra5607@email.sps.mot.com
Web: www.shpe.org

Dallas Professional Chapter
P.O. Box 59614
Dallas, TX 75229
(817) 460-2242 (h) Fax: (817) 460-2242
Rogelio Rodríguez, Chapter President
Email: royfrod@flash.net
Web: www.nationwide.net/~shpedfw/

Houston Professional Chapter
P.O. Box 271704
Houston, TX 77277-1704
(281) 890-4566 (w) or (713) 692-3405 (h)
Fax: (281) 890-3301
Griselda Mani, Chapter President
Email: gmani@coade.com
Web: http://reg5.shpe.org/Houston

Texas Bay Area Professional Chapter
P.O. Box 590091
Houston, TX 77259-0091
(281) 587-6824
Juan Anaya, Chapter President
Web: http://reg5.shpe.org/tbac

Texas Tech University
College of Engineering
P.O. Box 42013 - MS 3111
Lubbock, TX 79409
(806) 742-3451 Fax: (806) 742-3493
Lloyd Heinze, Advisor

University of Texas, Austin
College of Engineering, ECJ - 2.102
Austin, TX 78712
(512) 471-7112 Fax: (512) 232-2448
Claudia Sosa, President
Email: shpe@ccwf.cc.utexas.edu
Web: www.marconi.me.utexas.edu/~shpe

University of Texas, El Paso
College of Engineering
500 W. University
El Paso, TX 79968
(915) 747-5460 or (915) 747-6945
Fax: (915) 747-5616
María Cercado, President

SOCIETY OF MEXICAN AMERICAN ENGINEERS AND SCIENTISTS (MAES)
San Antonio Chapter
P.O. Box 17993
San Antonio, TX 78217
(210) 977-2847 Fax: (210) 977-2159
Reynaldo Treviño, Treasurer

Southwest Texas State University
Physics Department
601 University Dr. New Science Building #280
San Marcos, TX 78666
(512) 245-2131
Carlos Gutiérrez, Advisor

Texas A&M University
Computing Services Center
Mail Stop 1237 - MSC 217
College Station, TX 77843-3142
(409) 845-1037
Keith Marrocco, President

University of Texas, El Paso
College of Engineering, 500 W. University
El Paso, TX 79968-0517
(915) 747-5460 Fax: (915) 747-5616
Elsa Villa, Advisor
Web: www.eng.utep.edu/

SOUTH TEXAS VETERANS HEALTH CARE SYSTEM
Audie Murphy Division (136P)
7400 Merton Minter Blvd.
San Antonio, TX 78284-5700
(210) 617-5300x5662 Fax: (210) 617-5195
Linda Mejía Dávila
Email: linda.davila@med.va.gov

SOUTHSIDE LOW-INCOME HOUSING DEVELOPMENT CORPORATION
Affiliate of NCLR
P.O. Box 9323
El Paso, TX 79995
(915) 544-5962 Fax: (915) 544-5725
Carmen Félix, Executive Director

SOUTHWEST KEY PROGRAM
3000 South IH-35, #410
Austin, TX 78704
(512) 462-2181 Fax: (512) 462-2028
Juan J. Sánchez, Executive Director
Email: nduran@swkey.org

SOUTHWEST VOTER REGISTRATION EDUCATION PROJECT (SVREP)
Texas Office
403 E. Commerce #220
San Antonio, TX 78205
(210) 222-0224 Fax: (210) 222-8474
Antonio González, President
Email: SVRP@aol.com

SPARKS HOUSING DEVELOPMENT CORP.
Affiliate of NCLR
106 Payton
El Paso, TX 79927
(915) 852-2245 Fax: (915) 852-1737
Irma Pérez, Executive Director

STAY, INC.
700 S Zarzamora #103
San Antonio, TX 78207
(210) 433-9307 Fax: (210) 435-0711
Óscar Hernández, Director

STUDENT ALTERNATIVES PROGRAM, INC.
Affiliate of NCLR
P.O.Box 15644
San Antonio, TX 78212
(210) 227-0295 Fax: (210) 227-7879
Eduardo Gutiérrez, Chairman

SU CLÍNICA FAMILIAR
Affiliate of NCLR
4501 S. Expressway 83
Harlingen, TX 78550
(956) 428-4345 Fax: (956) 428-2901
Elena Marín, Executive Director
Email: su.clinica@acces.gov

SUCCESS SCHOLARSHIP FOUNDATION
P.O. Box 22926
Houston, TX 77227-2926
(713) 236-4740 or (713) 525-2121
Fax: (713) 236-0247
Dr. B. Veronica Villarreal, Founder
Email: BVilla2038@aol.com
Web: www.successscholars.org

TEATRO DALLAS
1925 Commerce St.
Dallas, TX 75201
(214) 741-6833 Fax: (214) 741-6735
Cora Cardona, Artistic Director

TEJANO CENTER FOR COMMUNITY CONCERNS, INC. (TCCC)
Administrative Office/Affiliate of NCLR
2950 Broadway
Houston, TX 77017
(713) 644-2340 Fax: (713) 641-1853
Richard Farías, President & CEO

7937 Mendez St.
Houston, TX 77029
(713) 673-1080 Fax: (713) 673-1304
Richard Farías, President & CEO

TEJANO DEMOCRATS
Austin Chapter
P.O. Box 334
Austin, TX 78767
(512) 833-8252
Lisa Guerrero, Chair
Email: info@tejanodemocrats.org
Web: www.tejanodemocrats.org

Bexar County Chapter
770 Clearview
San Antonio, TX 78228
(210) 434-4060
Tomás Larralde, Chair
Email: info@tejanodemocrats.org
Web: www.tejanodemocrats.org

Coastal Bend Chapter
4841 Cheryl
Corpus Christi, TX 78415
(512) 853-3058
Joseph Barrientos, Chair
Email: info@tejanodemocrats.org
Web: www.tejanodemocrats.org

Dallas/Fort Worth Chapter
442 W. Northgate Dr.
Irving, TX 75062
(214) 717-5342
René Castilla, Chair

Email: info@tejanodemocrats.org
Web: www.tejanodemocrats.org

Dallas/Fort Worth Chapter
3810 Frontier Ln.
Dallas, TX 75214
(214) 827-8989
Bill Callejo, Chair
Email: info@tejanodemocrats.org
Web: www.tejanodemocrats.org

Dallas/Fort Worth Chapter
312 Trinidad Court
Benbrook, TX 76126
(817) 249-6467
Susan Tedechi, Chair
Email: info@tejanodemocrats.org
Web: www.tejanodemocrats.org

El Paso Chapter
1701 Radford St.
El Paso, TX 79903
(915) 566-1810
Adela Licona, Chair
Email: info@tejanodemocrats.org
Web: www.tejanodemocrats.org

Harris County Chapter
608 Joyce
Houston, TX 77009
(713) 699-9716
Mary Almendárez, Chair
Email: info@tejanodemocrats.org
Web: www.tejanodemocrats.org

Headquarters
P.O. Box 684734
Austin, TX 78768-4734
(512) 916-9732 Fax: (512) 916-9732
Lisa Guerrero, Chair
Email: info@tejanodemocrats.org
Web: www.tejanodemocrats.org

Hidalgo County Chapter
1024 W. Schunior
Edinburg, TX 78539
(210) 383-6862
Marissa Marmolejo, Chair
Email: info@tejanodemocrats.org
Web: www.tejanodemocrats.org

La Joya Chapter
P.O. Box 97
La Joya, TX 78560
(210) 585-9791
Billy Leo, Chair
Email: info@tejanodemocrats.org
Web: www.tejanodemocrats.org

Odessa Chapter
2349 W. Berry
Odessa, TX 79763
(915) 337-3413
Richard Abalos, Chair
Email: info@tejanodemocrats.org
Web: www.tejanodemocrats.org

South Austin Chapter
4905 Allison Cove
Austin, TX 78741
(512) 385-2491
Dennis Garza, Chair
Email: info@tejanodemocrats.org
Web: www.tejanodemocrats.org

Uvalde Chapter
P.O. Box 110
Uvalde, TX 78802
(210) 278-7822
Kissie Reyes Mendeke, Chair
Email: info@tejanodemocrats.org
Web: www.tejanodemocrats.org

TEJANO ENTERTAINERS & MUSIC ASSOC.
1603 Babcock Rd., # 140
San Antonio, TX 78229
(210) 342-1059 Fax: (210) 342-1119
Rudy R. Trevino, President
Web: www.temawards.com

TEXAS ALLIANCE FOR MINORITIES IN ENGINEERING, INC. (TAME, INC.)
University of Texas, Austin
College of Engineering, ECJ 10.324
Austin, TX 78712-1080
(512) 471-6100 Fax: (512) 471-6797
Archie L. Holmes, Executive Director
Email: archieholmes@mail.utexas.edu
Web: www.tame.org

TEXAS ASSOC. FOR BILING. EDUCATION
16031 Oak Grove
San Antonio, TX 78255
(210) 433-5561 or (210) 695-9107 (h)

Fax: (210) 695-9520
Manuel Ruiz III, President
Email: mannie@aol.com
Web: www.tabe.org

TEXAS ASSOCIATION OF COMMUNITY DEVELOPMENT CORPORATIONS (TACDC)
700 Lavaca St., #120
Austin, TX 78701
(512) 457-8232 Fax: (512) 479-4090
J. Reymundo Ocañas, Executive Director
Email: info@tacdc.org
Web: www.tacdc.org

TEXAS ASSOC. OF MEXICAN-AMERICAN CHAMBERS OF COMMERCE (TAMACC)
National Headquarters
823 Congress Ave., #1414
Austin, TX 78701
(512) 708-8823 or (800) 322-3562
Fax: (512) 708-1808
Dr. Ray Leal, President & CEO
Email: info@tbc.tamacc.org
Web: www.tamacc.org

TEXAS ASSOC. OF MEXICAN-AMERICAN COLLEGE STUDENTS (TAMACS)
Terran County Collage SE Campus
2100 SE. Parkway
Arlington, TX 76017
(817) 515-3763 Fax: (817) 515-3562
Josue Muñoz, Faculty Sponsor
Email: josue.munoz@tccd.net
Web: www.tccd.net

TEXAS COUNCIL FOR EDUCATIONAL EXCELLENCE
13306 Somersworth
Houston, TX 77041
(713) 446-4376
Ramón F. Hernández, Executive Director
Email: rfh@quepasa.com

TEXAS ENTERPRISE FOR HOUSING DEV., INC.
Affiliate of NCLR
3316 N Stewart Rd.
Mission, TX 78572
(956) 585-4447 Fax: (956) 585-4447
Reyes L. Cortéz, Executive Director

TEXAS FIESTA EDUCATIVA PROJECT PODER
1017 N. Main Ave., #207
San Antonio, TX 78212
(210) 222-2637 Fax: (210) 222-2638
Yvette Hinojosa, Executive Director
Email: poder@tfepoder.org
Web: www.tfepoder.org

TEXAS MIGRANT COUNCIL, INC.
Affiliate of NCLR
P.O. Box 2579
5215 McPhearson Ave.
Laredo, TX 78014
(956) 722-5174 Fax: (956) 726-0907
Óscar L. Villareal, Chief Executive Officer

TEXAS TALENT MUSICIANS
1149 East Commerce St., Suite 105
San Antonio, TX 78205
(210) 222-8862 Fax: (210) 222-1029
Robert Ariano, President
Email: ttm@icsi.net
Web: www.tejanomusicawards.com

TOMÁS RIVERA POLICY INSTITUTE
Texas Office
P.O. Box 8047
Austin, TX 78713-8047
(512) 471-2872 Fax: (512) 471-2873
Rodolfo de la Garza, Vice President of Research
Email: info@trpi.org
Web: www.trpi.org

UNION BAPTIST ASSOCIATION
2060 N Loop West, #100
Houston, TX 77018
(713) 957-2000 Fax: (713) 957-0320
Jorge Camacho, Church Consultant
Email: scainuba@flash.net
Web: www.ubahouston.org

UNITED LATIN AMERICAN MEDICAL STUDENTS
UT Health Science Center at San Antonio
7703 Floyd Curl Dr.
San Antonio, TX 78284
(210) 567-2654 Fax: (210) 567-2644
Sylvia Fernández, Ph.D., Director

UNITED STATES-MEXICO BORDER HEALTH ASSOCIATION
National Headquarters
5400 Sancrest Dr., #C-5
El Paso, TX 79912
(915) 581-6645 Fax: (915) 833-7840
Piedad Huerta, Communications Officer
Email: huertap@usmbha.org
Web: www.usmbha.org

UNITED STATES-MEXICO CHAMBER OF COMMERCE
Southwest Chapter
P.O. Box 50178
Dallas, TX 75250-0178
(214) 747-1996 Fax: (214) 747-1994
Patricia Snirch, Executive Director
Email: swusmcoc@swbell.net

VECINOS UNIDOS
Affiliate of NCLR
3603 N. Winnetka Ave.
Dallas, TX 75212
(214) 761-1086 Fax: (214) 761-0838
Rosa López, Director

WESLEY COMMUNITY CENTER, INC.
1410 Lee St.
Houston, TX 77009
(713) 223-8131 Fax: (713) 225-3449
Ruth Palmer, Executive Director
Email: info@wesleyhousehouston.org
Web: www.wesleyhousehouston.org

WILLIAM C. VELÁSQUEZ INSTITUTE
Texas Office
403 E. Commerce #260
San Antonio, TX 78205
(210) 222-8014 Fax: (210) 222-8474
Antonio González, President

WOMEN AND THEIR WORK, INC.
1717 La Baca St.
Austin, TX 78703
(512) 477-1064 Fax: (512) 477-1090
Chris Cowden, Director
Email: wtw@eden.com

UTAH

BALLET FOLKLÓRICO DE LAS AMÉRICAS
1866 Hill Mar Circle
Salt Lake City, UT 84118
(801) 964-1224 or (801) 969-2862
Albert Bernard, Director

BRIGHAM YOUNG UNIVERSITY
Minority Law Students
239 JRCB
Provo, UT 84602
(801) 378-3739 Fax: (801) 378-5893
David Domínguez, Contact

CENTER FOR ETHNIC STUDENT AFFAIRS
University of Utah
200 SO Central Campus Drive, Room 318
Salt Lake City, UT 84112-9109
(801) 581-8151 Fax: (801) 581-7119
Augustine Trujillo, Director
Email: atruji@saun.saff.utah.edu

**CENTRO DE LA FAMILIA DE UTAH
(INST. OF HUMAN RESOURCE DEV.)**
Affiliate of NCLR
320 West 200 S., #300B
Salt Lake City, UT 84101
(801) 521-4473 Fax: (801) 521-6242
Graciela Italiano Thomas, Executive Director

THE CHURCH OF JESUS CHRIST OF LATTER DAY SAINTS
North Visitors' Center
50 West North Temple
Salt Lake City, UT 84150
(801) 240-4872 or (801) 240-2205
Fax: (801) 2401471
Richard Winwood, Director
Web: www.lds.org

Park City Family Tree Visitors' Center
531 Historic Main St.
Park City, UT 84060
(435) 940-9502 Fax: (435) 940-9503
Vertus Norton, Director
Web: www.lds.org

St. George Utah Visitor Center
490 South 300 East
St. George, UT 84770
(435) 673-5181 Fax: (435) 652-9589
Elder Critchlow, Director

Web: www.lds.org

CLUB PERÚ
562 E. Kensington
Salt Lake City, UT 84115
(801) 483-0664
Juan Mejía, President

COLONIA COLOMBIA DE UATH
3073 W. 8525 S.
West Jordan, UT 84088
(801) 569-1965
José Bravo, Contact

COMMUNITY ACTION AGENCY
257 E Center St.
Provo, UT 84606
(801) 373-8200 Fax: (801) 373-8228
Myla Dutton, Director
Email: foodbank@unitedwayuc.org

DIOCESE OF SALT LAKE CITY
Hispanic Affairs
27 C St.
Salt Lake City, UT 84103-2397
(801) 328-8641 x331 Fax: (801) 328-9680
Misael Mayorga, Director for Hispanic Ministry
Email: misael.mayorga@mail.dioslc.org

ETHNIC STUDIES PROGRAM
University of Utah
380 S 1400 E, #112
Salt Lake City, UT 84112-0310
(801) 581-5206 Fax: (801) 581-8437
Gladys Mixco, Administrative Assistance

FRATERNIDAD HISPANA
3098 West 5685 South
Salt Lake City, UT 84118
(801) 966-7294 Fax: (801) 966-7294
Elizabeth Robertson, Director
Email: hrobertson@utah-inter.net

HERMANOS HISPA AT&T
5425 S. College Dr.
Murray, UT 84123
(801) 269-3411 (w)
Beatriz Jones, President

HISPANIC AMERICAN CHAMBER OF COMMERCE
3860 S. 2300 East, #204
Salt Lake City, UT 84109
(801) 274-9152 Fax: (801) 274-8815
Mark Osterloh, President
Email: haccu@yahoo.com
Web: www.haccu.com

HISPANIC MEDIA SERVICES
P.O. Box 9434
Salt Lake City, UT 84109
(801) 274-8814 Fax: (801) 274-8815
Ana María Fereday, Owner
Web: www.paginasamarillasdeutah.com

HISPANIC PROGRAM MANAGERS
U.S. Forest Service
324 25th St.
Ogden, UT 84401
(801) 625-5401 or (801) 625-5242
Fax: (801) 625-5417
Cindy Quintana, Contact
Email: cquintana@fs.ser.us/r4
Web: www.fs.ser.us/r4

IMAGE
Salt Lake City Chapter
350 S 400 E,#101A
Salt Lake City, UT 84111
(801) 521-6737 Fax: (801) 359-2811
Max Guerra, President

IMAGE DE UTAH
National Image, Inc.
707 W. 2550 NO.
Clinton, UT 84015
(801) 825-8317
Chris J. Martínez, President
Web: www.nationalimageinc.org

INTERNATIONAL SERVICES
Brigham Young University
1351 WSC
Provo, UT 84602
(801) 378-2695 Fax: (801) 378-8760
Enoc FLores, Director
Email: intloff@stlife.byu.edu

LA FRATERNIDAD EL SALVADOR
499 North 200 West, #39
Bountiful, UT 84010

(801) 277-0862 Fax: (801) 467-2567
Ana Wall, President

LEGAL VOLUNTEER IMMIGRATION PROJ.
BighmamYoung University
430 JRCB
Provo, UT 84602
(801) 378-3025 Fax: (801) 378-2188/3595

MULTI CULTURAL STUDENT SERVICES
Brigham Young University
199 ELWC
Provo, UT 84602
(801) 378-3065 Fax: (801) 378-2630
Liana Brown, Director

OUR LADY OF GUADALUPE CHURCH
715 W 300 N
Salt Lake City, UT 84116
(801) 364-2019 Fax: (801) 363-2709
Ken Vialpando, Pastor

REFORMA
Utah Chapter
320 West 200 N., #300B
Salt Lake City, UT 84101
(801) 521-4473 Fax: (801) 521-6243
Juan Lee, Chapter President
Email: juan@la-familia.org
Web: http://clnet.ucr.edu/library/reforma

SALT LAKE CITY COMMUNITY COLLEGE
Admissions/Multi Cultural Affairs
4600 S Redwood Rd
Salt Lake City, UT 84130-0808
(801) 957-4592 Fax: (801) 957-4958
Charlotte Starks, Coordinator
Email: starksch@slcc.edu

Diversity & Equal Opportunity
4600 S Redwood Rd.
Salt Lake City, UT 84123
(801) 957-4561 Fax: (801) 957-2275
Bill Johnson, Director

SOUTH CENTRAL UTAH HISPANIC CHAMBER OF COMMERCE
651 W Columbia Ln.
Provo, UT 81614
(801) 377-6531 Fax: (801) 374 1790
Joseph Madrigal, President

STATE HISPANIC ADVISORY COUNCIL
660 S 200 E Suite 400
Salt Lake City, UT 84111
(801) 238-4568 Fax: (801) 359-5627
Héctor Cando

UNIVERSITY OF UTAH
Diversity in Engineering
2101 MEB
Salt Lake City, UT 84112
(801) 581-3899 Fax: (801) 581-8692
John Zamora, President

UNIVERSITY OF UTAH
Minority Law Caucus
101 College of Law
Salt Lake City, UT 84112
(801) 581-6833 Fax: (801) 581-6897
Sherman Helenise, President

UTAH COALITION OF LA RAZA (UCLR)
National Headquarters
Sorenson Multicultural Center
855 W. California Ave.
Salt Lake City, UT 84104
(801) 972-1888 Fax: (801) 974-2401
Chris Segura, Executive Director

UTAH GOVERNOR'S OFFICE ON HISPANIC AFFAIRS
Dept. of Community and Economic Dev.
324 S. State St., #500
Salt Lake City, UT 84114-2780
(801) 538-8850 Fax: (801) 538-8678
Leticia Medina, Director
Web: www.ce.ex.state.ut.us/hispanic/welcome/htm

UTAH HISPANIC CHAMBER OF COMMERCE
56 East 800 South
Salt Lake City, UT 84111
(801) 531-7776 Fax: (801) 533-8512
Richard Vélez, President

UTAH HISPANIC CHAMBER OF COMMERCE
P.O. Box 1805
Salt Lake, UT 84110
(801) 483-1218 Fax: (801) 359-8108
John Rentería, CEO

Email: oyecomovi@aol.com
Web: www.utahhispanicchamber.com

UTAH REPUBLICAN HISPANICS
2191 South Timothy Way
Boumpiful, UT 84010
(801) 585-7012
Jesse Soriano, State Chair

WEBER STATE UNIVERSITY
Services for Multicultural Students
1116 University Circle
Ogden, UT 84408-1116
(801) 626-7330 Fax: (801) 626-7635
Georgette González, Latin Students Counselor

VERMONT

DIOCESE OF BURLINGTON
Hispanic Affairs
P.O. Box 526
351 North Ave.
Burlington, VT 05401
(802) 658-6110 Fax: (802) 658-0436
Sr. Mary McNamara, Director for Hispanic Ministry

VIRGIN ISLANDS

DIOCESE OF ST. THOMAS IN THE VIRGIN ISLANDS
Hispanic Affairs
P.O. Box 301825
St. Thomas, VI 00803
(340) 774-3166 Fax: (340) 774-5816
Rev. Neil Scantlebury
Email: chancery@islands.vi

VIRGINIA

ABLE LABOR
P.O.Box 6104
Leesburg, VA 20178
(703) 799-8395 Fax: (703) 777-0441
Paul Leach, President

ALIANZA DE MESAS REDONDAS PANAMERICANAS / ALLIANCE OF PAN-AMERICAN ROUNDTABLES
1730 Great Falls St.
McLean, VA 22101
(703) 821-3982 Fax: (703) 448-6014
Teresa A. Weinger, President

ALL SAINTS
9300 Stonewall Rd.
Manassass, VA 22110
(703) 368-4500 Fax: (703) 257-9299
Robert Cilinski, Adminstrator
Web: www.rc.net/arlington/all_saints

AMERICAN ASSOCIATION OF HISPANIC CERTIFIED PUBLIC ACCOUNTANTS
Washinton, D.C. Chapter/ Soza & Co., Ltd.
8550 Arlington Blvd., #300
Fairlax, VA 22031
(703) 560-9477 Fax: (703) 573-9026
Will Soza, Chapter Representative
Email: wsoza@soza.com
Web: www.aahcpa.org

AMERICAN DIABETES ASSOCIATION
1660 Duke St.
Alexandria, VA 22314
(703) 549-1500 ext. 2133 Fax: (703) 549-6294
Josie Graziadio, Diversity Manager
Web: www.diabetes.org

AMERICAN MEDICAL STUDENT ASSOCIATION FOUNDATION (AMSA)
National Headquarters
1902 Association Dr.
Reston, VA 20191
(703) 620-6600 Fax: (703) 620-5873
Paul Wright, Executive Director
Email: michele@www.amsa.org
Web: www.amsa.org

AMERICAN PERUVIAN CHAMBER OF COMMERCE
313 N Glebe Rd., 200A
Arlington, VA 22203
(703) 243-0691 Fax: (703) 243-9559
Rolando Oré, President
Email: washdc@peruchamber.com
Web: www.peruchamber.com

ARLINGTON DANCING COMPANY
4343 Lee Hwy., #505
Arlington, VA 22207

(703) 528-4094 Fax: (703) 228-5813
Simón R. Contreras Velásquez, Director
Email: sr-contreras@yahoo.com

**ARLINGTON UNITED METHODIST
CHURCH / IGLESIA METODISTA
HISPANA UNIDA DE ARLINGTON**
716 S. Glebe Rd.
Arlington, VA 22204
(703) 920-8076 or (703) 979-7527
Fax: (703) 979-7051
Rev. Daniel Mejía, Pastor

ASOCIACION DE DAMAS BOLIVIANAS
1730 Great Falls St.
McLean, VA 22101
(703) 821-3982
Teresa Weinger, Contact

**ASOCIACIÓN SALVADOREÑA
AMERICANA DE VIRGINIA (ASAV)**
859 N. Larrimore St.
Arlington, VA 22205
(703) 538-5909
J. Walter Tejada, President
Email: jtejada@gmu.edu

**ASSOCIATION OF HISPANIC
ADVERTISING AGENCIES (AHAA)**
National Headquarters
8201 Greensboro Dr., #300
McLean, VA 22102
(703) 610-9014 Fax: (703) 610-9005
Daisy Exposito-Ulla, President
Web: www.ahaa.org

CATHEDRAL OF ST. THOMAS MORE
3901 Cathedral Lane
Arlington, VA 22203
(703) 525-1300 Fax: (703) 528-5760
Very Rev. Dominic P. Irace, Pastor

**THE CATHOLIC COMMUNITY OF
BLESSED SACRAMENT**
P.O. Box 226
Harrisonburg, VA 22802
(540) 434-4341 /0849 Fax: (540) 434-0849
Marta Fidalgo de Meza, Spanish Min. Coord.

CENTER FOR CHILD WELFARE
George Mason University
Social Work Programs
4400 University Dr., MS 2E8
Fairfax, VA 22030-4444
(703) 993-1966/1951 Fax: (703) 993-1970
Dr. Nilsa Burgos, Interim Director

**CENTER FOR MULTICULTURAL HUMAN
SERVICES**
701 W. Broad St., #305
Falls Church, VA 22046
(703) 533-3302 Fax: (703) 237-2083
Dennis J. Hunt, Director
Email: CMHS2000@AOL.COM
Web: www.cmhs-2000.com

**THE COALITION OF HISPANIC AGENCIES
AND PROFESSIONALS (CHAPA)**
P.O. Box 4236
Falls Church, VA 22042
(703) 916-9293
Angie Carrera, Secretary

**COLUMBIA BAPTIST CHURCH / IGLESIA
BAUTISTA COLUMBIA**
103 W. Columbia St.
Falls Church, VA 22046
(703) 534-5700 Fax: (703) 536-6757
Rev. Enrique De Paz, Pastor
Web: www.columbia-baptist.org

COMMONWEALTH CATHOLIC CHARITIES
Refugee Unaccompanied Minors Program
P.O.Box 6565
Richmond, VA 23230-0565
(804) 285-5900 Fax: (804) 285-9130
Cathy Brown, Bilingual Worker
Email: comcathric@aol.com

Refugee Unaccompanied Minors Program
302 McClanahan St. SW
Ronaoke, VA 24014
(540) 342-0411 Fax: (540) 342-3307
Director

Refugee Unaccompanied Minors Program
1859-C3 Seminole Trail
Charlottesville, VA 22901
(804) 974-6880 Fax: (804) 285-9136
Kathie Brown, Director

**CULMORE UNITED METHODIST
CHURCH/ IGLESIA METODISTA HISPANA
UNIDA DE CULMORE**
5901 Leesburg Pike
Falls Church, VA 22041
(703) 820-5131 Fax: (703) 820-4386
Rev. Grace Ellen Rice, Pastor

DAMAS ARGENTINAS DEL SUR
8370 Greensboro Dr., #1007
McLean, VA 22102
Ana Eliza, President
Email: capilladelmonte@aol.com

DIOCESAN HISPANIC MINISTRY
811 Cathedral Pl.
Richmond, VA 23220
(804) 359-5661 Fax: (804) 358-9159
Stephan Colecchi, Contact
Web: www.richmonddiocese.org

DIOCESE OF ARLINGTON
Hispanic Affairs
80 N. Glebe Rd.
Arlington, VA 22203
(703) 524-2122 Fax: (703) 524-4261
Rev. Ovidio Pecharromán, Director for Hispanic
Apostolate

DIOCESE OF RICHMOND
Office of the Hispanic Apostolate
811 Cathedral Pl.
Richmond, VA 23220
(804) 359-5661 Fax: (804) 358-9159
Rev. Michael Schmied, Vicar
Elisa Montalvo, Director
Email: emontalvo@richmonddiocese.org

EAST COAST MIGRANT HEAD START PROJ.
4245 N. Fairfax Dr., #800
Arlington, VA 22203
(703) 243-7522 Fax: (703) 243-1259
Geraldine O'Brien, Executive Director
Email: ECMHSP@ECMHSP.ORG
Web: www.ecmshp.org

EL CENTRO CATÓLICO HISPANO
Diocese of Richmond
269 Clearfield Ave.
Virginia Beach, VA 23462
(757) 490-7896 Fax: (757) 518-9638
Sister Bárbara Gerwe, Director
Email: hispanicapostal8@juno.com

FAIRFAX AREA AGENCY ON AGING
12011 Government Center Pkwy., #720
Fairfax, VA 22035-1104
(703) 324-5411 Fax: (703) 449-8689
Carla Pittman, Director
Email: fairfax-aaa@hotmail.com
Web: http://fairfaxva.ux/service/
aaahomepage.html

**FIRST BAPTIST CHURCH OF
WOODBRIDGE**
13430 Millwood Dr.
Woodbridge, VA 22191
(703) 494-4848 Fax: (703) 4970192
Rev. Edwin Clarke, Pastor
Email: eclarke@fbwoodbridge.org
Web: www.fbcwoodbridge.org

FLORIS UNITED METHODIST CHURCH
Floris Neighbors Program
2730 Centreville Rd.
Herndon, VA 20171
(703) 793-0026 Fax: (703) 793-0028
Libby Fielder, Coordinator

**FOUNDATION FOR THE PERFORMING
ARTS**
Wolf Trap
1624 Trap Rd.
Vienna, VA 22182
(703) 255-1920 Fax: (703) 255-1905
Tarrence Jones, President & CEO

GOOD SHEPHERD
8710 Mt. Vernon Hwy.
Alexandria, VA 22309
(703) 780-4055 Fax: (703) 360-5385
Lea Tenorio, Hispanic Ministry Coordinator
Web: www.gs-cc.org

**GREENBRIER BAPTIST CHURCH / IGLESIA
BAUTISTA GREENBRIER**
5401 Seventh Rd., S.
Arlington, VA 22204
(703) 671-6688 Fax: (703) 379-2996
Rev. René Claros, Pastor
Email: REVTENNANT@worldnet.att.net

HIGHER HORIZONS DAY CARE CENTER
5920B Summers Ln.
Baileys Crossroads, VA 22041
(703) 820-2457 Fax: (703) 820-1578
Mary Ann Cornish, Director

**HISPANIC BAR ASSOCIATION OF THE
COMMONWEALTH OF VIRGINIA, INC.**
P.O. Box 531
Arlington, VA 22216
(703) 777-6800 Fax: (209) 885-8238
Alexander Levay, President
Email: hbava@yahoo.com

**HISPANIC BUSINESS FOR YOUTH
FOUNDATION (HBYF)**
8550 Arlington Blvd., #320
Fairfax, VA 22031
(703) 560-1229 Fax: (703) 573-9026
Celestino M. Beltran, President
Email: hbyf@soza.com

**HISPANIC COMMITTEE OF VIRGINIA /
COMITÉ HISPANO DE VIRGINIA**
Arlington Office
2049 N. 15th St. #100
Arlington, VA 22201
(703) 243-3033 Fax: (703) 243-2297
Jorge Figueredo, Acting Director

National Headquarters
5827 Columbia Pke. #200
Falls Church, VA 22041
(703) 671-5666 Fax: (703) 671-2325
Jorge Figueredo, Acting Director

HISPANIC NATIONAL BAR ASSOCIATION
National Headquarters
8201 Greensboro Dr., #300
McLean, VA 22102
(703) 610-9038 Fax: (703) 610-9005
Alexander M. Sánchez, Executive Director
Email: asanchez@hnba.com
Web: www.hnba.com

HISPANOS UNIDOS DE VIRGINIA
Affiliate of NCLR
6269 Leesburg Pike, #202
Falls Church, VA 22044
(703) 533-9300 Fax: (703) 237-3736
Johnny N. Simancas, Executive Director

HOGAR HISPANO
**Catholic Charities of the Diocese of
Arlington**
6201 Leesburg Pike, #307
Falls Church, VA 22044
(703) 534-9805 Fax: (703) 534-9809
Grace Ortiz, Director

HOLY FAMILY
14160 Ferndale Rd.
Dale City, VA 22193
(703) 670-8161 Fax: (703) 670-8323
Silvia Machuca, Head of Hispanic Commitee

**IGLESIA BAUTISTA HISPANA DE
GROVETON**
6511 Richmond Hwy.
Alexandria, VA 22306
(703) 765-2277 Fax: (703) 765-2277
Rev. Carlos A. Oliveros, Pastor

INSURANCE INST. FOR HIGHWAY SAFETY
1005 N. Glebe Rd.
Arlington, VA 22201
(703) 247-1500 Fax: (703) 247-1586
Brian O'Neil, Executive Director
Web: www.highwaysafety.org

INTER-AMERICAN DEVELOPMENT FDTN.
4705 Eisenhower Ave.
Alexandria, VA 22304
(703) 461-7507 Fax: (703) 370-4017
Juan C. Dulanto, Chairman
Email: jdulanto@jccs.com

INTER-AMERICAN FOUNDATION
901 N. Stuart St., 10th Fl.
Arlington, VA 22203
(703) 306-4301 Fax: (703) 306-4369
George Evans, President
Web: www.iaf.gov

**INTERNATIONAL MEDICAL SERVICES FOR
HEALTH (INMED)**
45449 Severn Way, #161
Sterling, VA 20166
(703) 444-4477 Fax: (703) 444-4471
Linda Pfeiffer, President
Email: inmed@ix.netcom.com

Web: www.inmed.org

THE IVY INTER-AMERICAN FOUNDATION
P. O. Box 248
Ivy, VA 22945
(804) 295-4698 Fax: (804) 296-8330
Anabella Jordan , President
Email: ivyinteram@aol.com

**LA HERMANDAD DE SAN MARTÍN DE
PORRES**
5010 Washington Blvd.
Arlington, VA 22205
(703) 312-9341 Fax: 5160179
Rosibel Abogatas, Directora/Fundadora

LATINAS UNIDAS: VOZ Y PRESENCIA
George Mason University
1601 Arlington Blvd., #209
Falls Church, VA 22044
(703) 578-0687 Fax: (703) 578-0687
Luz M. Diago, President

LEADERSHIP AMERICA
700 N. Fairfax St., #610
Alexandria, VA 22314-2040
(703) 549-1102 Fax: (703) 836-9205
Rita Harmon, Presiden & CEO
Email: info@leadershipamerica.com
Web: www.leadershipamerica.com

**LEAGUE OF UNITED LATIN AMERICAN
CITIZENS (LULAC)**
Northeast Region-VA
P.O. Box 6120
Arlington, VA 22206
(703) 979-3319 Fax: (703) 979-3327
J. Walter Tejada, VA State Director
Email: jtejada@gmu.edu
Web: www.lulac.org

**MANA - A NATIONAL LATINA
ORGANIZATION**
Local Chapter of Northern Virginia
7218 Lackawanna Dr.
Springfield, VA 22150
(703) 451-8153 Fax: (703) 451-8153
Corine Scott, Organizing President
Email: hermana2@aol.com
Web: www.hermana.org

MANASSAS BAPTIST CHURCH
8800 Sudley Rd.
Manassas, VA 20110
(703) 361-2146 Fax: (703) 361-0176
Rev. Carlos Tobar, Pastor
Email: ctobar@manassasbaptist.org
Web: www.manassasbaptist.org

MARCELINO PAN Y VINO, INC. (MAPAVI)
P.O. Box 8523
Falls Church, VA 22041
(703) 845-5757 Fax: (703) 845-5765
Rev. José E. Hoyos, President & Founder
Email: marcelinpanyvino@hotmail.comhttp:
www.mapavi.org
Web: www.mapavi.org

**NATIONAL ASSOCIATION OF HISPANIC
FEDERAL EXECUTIVES (NAHFE)**
National Headquarters
P.O. Box 469
Herndon, VA 20172-0469
(703) 787-0291 Fax: (703) 787-4675
Manuel Olivérez, President & CEO
Web: www.nahfe.org

**NATIONAL ASSOCIATION OF MINORITY
MEDIA EXECUTIVES (NAMME)**
1921 Gallows Rd., #600
Vienna, VA 22182-3900
(888) 968-7658
Fax: (703) 893-2414
James A. MossJeanne Fox-Alston, Pres./Exec. Dir.
Email: nammeexecutivedirector@worldnet.att.net
Web: www.namme.org

**NATIONAL CENTER FOR MISSING &
EXPLOITED CHILDREN**
699 Prince St.
Alexandria, VA 22314
(703)235-3900
Email: ncmec.org
Web: www.missingchildren.com

**NATIONAL CONFERENCE OF PUERTO
RICAN WOMEN (NACOPRW)**
DC Chapter
6934-8 Allingham
Alexandria, VA 22315

(703) 313-0729
Vanny Marrero, President

NATIONAL HISPANA LEADERSHIP INSTITUTE
National Headquarters
1901 N. Moore St., #206
Arlington, VA 22209
(703) 527-6007 Fax: (703) 527-6009
Marisa Rivera-Albert, President
Email: NHLI@aol.com
Web: www.nhli.org

NATIONAL HISPANIC CORPORATE COUNCIL (NHCC)
National Headquarters
8201 Greensboro Dr., #300
McLean, VA 22102
(703) 610-9016/0245 Fax: (703) 610-9005
Randy R. Martínez, President
Email: rmartinez@nhcc-hq.org
Web: www.nhcc-hq.org

NATIONAL HISPANIC ENERGY ENVIRONMENTAL COUNCIL
5909-N Coverdale Way 3rd Floor
Alexandria, VA 22310
(703) 922-3429
Bernadette Villanueva, Coordinator
Web: www.nheec.org

NATIONAL ORGANIZATION FOR THE ADVANCEMENT OF HISPANICS (NOAH)
National Headquarters
2217 Princess Anne St., #205-1
Fredericksburg, VA 22401
(540) 372-3437 Fax: (540) 372-3437
Juan O. Chaves, President
Email: noah-va@noah-va.org
Web: www.noah-va.org

NEW AMERICA ALLIANCE (NAA)
8201 Greensboro Dr., #300
McLean, VA 22102
(703) 610-9026 Fax: (703) 610-9005
María del Pilar Avila, Executive Vice President & Chief Staff Officer
Email: pavila@naaonline.org
Web: www.naaonline.org

NORTHERN VIRGINIA FAMILY SERVICE
Corporate Office
100 N. Washington St., #400
Falls Church, VA 22046-4565
(703) 533-9727 Fax: (703) 241-1310
Mary Agee, Executive Director
Web: www.nvfs.org

NUESTRA SEÑORA REINA DE LA PAZ
Social Services Department
2700 S. 19th St
Arlington, VA 22204
(703) 271-9342 Fax: (703) 979-5590
Rosa Williams, Director

OFICINA INTERGRUPAL DEL NORTE DE VIRGINIA
8143 Richmond Hwy., Lower level
Alexandria, VA 22309
(703) 360-5447

OUR LADY OF ANGELS
13752 Mary's Way
Woodbridge, VA 22191
(703) 494-2444 Fax: (703) 494-2444
Father Lange, Pastor

OUR LADY OF LOURDES
830 S. 23rd
Arlington, VA 22202
(703) 684-9261 Fax: (703) 684-9261
Theresa, Secretary
Email: ol@erols.com

OUR LADY QUEEN OF PEACE
2700 S. 19th St.
Arlington, VA 22204
(703) 979-5580 Fax: (703) 979-5590
Rev. Jeff Duaime, Pastor
Email: olqp.office@verizon.net

PARENT EDUCATIONAL ADVOCACY TRAINING CENTER (PEATC)
6320 Augusta Dr., #1200
Springfield, VA 22150
(703) 923-0010 or (703) 569-6200
Fax: (703) 923-0030
Rosalía Fajardo, Hispanic Outreach
Email: partners@peatc.org
Web: www.peatc.org

QUEEN OF APOSTLES
4329 Sano St.

Arlington, VA 22312
(703) 354-8711 Fax: (703) 354-0766
Rev. Ciullo, Pastor

REFORMA
Washington D.C. Metro Area Chapter
3904 Ridge Rd.
Annandale, VA 22003
(703) 697-1636 Fax: (703) 697-3897
Mena Whitmore, Chapter President
Web: http://clnet.ucr.edu/library/reforma

RESTORATION NEW LIFE EVANGELIC CHURCH
3435 Sleepy Hollow Rd.
Falls Church, VA 22042
(703) 237-1082
Luis Alonzo Villatoro, Pastor

SAINT LEO THE GREAT
3700 Old Lee Hwy.
Fairfax, VA 22030
(703) 273-7277 Fax: (703) 273-2371
Father Kelly, Pastor

SAN JOSEPH CATHOLIC CHURCH / IGLESIA CATÓLICA DE SAN JOSÉ
P.O. Box 4126
Hampton, VA 23669
(757) 851-8800 (W) or (757) 851-2402 (H)
José M. González, Contact

THE SAN MARTÍN SOCIETY
P.O. Box 33
McLean, VA 22101
(703) 883-0950 Fax: (703) 883-0950
Cristian García-Godoy, President
Email: CGGodoy@email.msn.com
Web: www.Barnews.com/SanMartin

SANZ SCHOOL, INC.
2930 Patrick Henry Dr.
Falls Church, VA 22042
(703) 237-6200 Fax: (703) 237-5495

SENIOR EMPLOYMENT RESOURSES (SER)
4201 John Marr Dr., #236
Annandale, VA 22003
(703) 750-1936 Fax: (703) 750-0269
Suzanne Allan, Executive Director
Email: sersue@erols.com
Web: www.seniorjobs.org

SOCIAL MINISTRIES OFFICE, OUR LADY QUEEN OF PEACE
2700 S. 19th St.
Arlington, VA 22204
(703) 271-9342/979-5580 Fax: (703) 979-5590
Rosa María Williams, Director

SOCIEDAD LITERARIA VENEZOLANA
4343 Lee Hwy., #505
Arlington, VA 22207
(703) 528-4094 Fax: (703) 228-5813
Simón R. Contreras Velásquez, Director
Email: sr-contreras@yahoo.com

SOCIETY OF HISPANIC PROFESSIONAL ENGINEERS (SHPE)
Washington D.C. Professional Chapter
P.O. Box 3177
Merrifield, VA 22116
(540) 231-9398 (w) or (540) 953-0447 (h)
Fax: (540) 231-3031
Monique Jackson, Conference Co-Chair
Email: mojackso@vt.edu
Web: www.shpe.org

SPANISH FOR EDUCATORS
816 S. Walter Reed Dr.
Arlington, VA 22204
(703) 228-5813 or (703) 228-8000
Fax: (703) 228-5813
Simón R. Contreras Velásquez, Teacher Instructor
Email: sr_contreras@yahoo.com

ST. AGNES
1914 N. Randolph St.
Arlington, VA 22207
(703) 525-116 Fax: (703) 243-2840
Catherine, Office Manager
Email: stagnes1@juno.com

ST. AMBROSE
3901 Woodburn Rd.
Annandale, VA 22003
(703) 280-2991
Father Ley, Pastor

ST. CHARLES BORROMEO
3304 Washington Blvd.
Arlington, VA 22201

(703) 527-5500 Fax: (703) 527-5505
Gary Creedon, Pastor
Email: garycreedon@erols.com

ST. PHILIP
7500 St. Philip Ct.
Falls Church, VA 22042
(703) 573-3809 Fax: (703) 560-8832
Barbara Ostander, Secretary
Email: st.philips@erols.com

ST. RITA
3815 Russell Rd.
Alexandria, VA 22305
(703) 836-1640 Fax: (703) 836-7825
Rev. Dennis Donahue, Administrator

TALLER DE HISTORIA ARGENTINA
P.O. Box 40
McLean, VA 22101
(703) 883-0950 Fax: (703) 883-0950
Cristian García-Godoy, President
Email: CGGodoy@email.msn.com
Web: www.Barnews.com/SanMartin

TELAMON CORPORATION
Virginia HOPE III Housing Office 10
P.O. Box 500, 111 Henry St.
Gretna, VA 24557
(804) 656-8357 Fax: (804) 656-8356
Robert Gilbert, Coordinator
Email: rgilbert@telamon.org
Web: www.telamon.org

Virginia Housing Services Office 8
P.O. Box 444, 120 West Danville St.
South Hill, VA 23970
(804) 447-2744 Fax: (804) 447-7134
Randy Bottoms, Construction Supervisor
Email: rbottoms@telamon.org
Web: www.telamon.org

Virginia Office 1
4913 Fitzhugh Ave. #202
Richmond, VA 23226
(804) 355-4676 or (804) 355-5106
Fax: (804) 335-4647
Sharon Saldarriaga, State Director
Email: ssaldarriaga@telamon.org
Web: www.telamon.org

Virginia Office 12
116 S. Wayne Ave.
Waynesboro, VA 22980
(540) 941-8432 Fax: (540) 941-2402
José Castillo, Regional Manager
Email: jcastillo@telamon.org
Web: www.telamon.org

Virginia Office 2
1332-D Piney Forest Rd.
Danville, VA 24540
(804) 836-9071 Fax: (804) 836-9072
Kathleen Bullano, Regional Manager
Email: kbullano@telamon.org
Web: www.telamon.org

Virginia Office 3
P.O. Box 908
Exmore, VA 23350
(757) 442-2002 or (757) 442-2001
Fax: (757) 442-7392
Pauline James, Regional Manager
Email: pjames@telamon.org
Web: www.telamon.org

Virginia Office 4
405 Bay St.
Lynchburg, VA 24501
(804) 846-4100 Fax: (804) 528-1692
Wanda Jenkins, Regional Manager
Email: wjenkins@telamon.org
Web: www.telamon.org

Virginia Office 5
316 Main St.
South Boston, VA 24592
(804) 572-8993 or (804) 572-8994
Fax: (804) 572-8613
Peggy King, Regional Manager
Email: pking@telamon.org
Web: www.telamon.org

Virginia Office 6
201 E. Atlantic St.
South Hill, VA 23970
(804) 447-7627 or (804) 447-7628
Fax: (804) 447-4629
Rebecca House, Regional Manager
Email: rhouse@telamon.org
Web: www.telamon.org

Virginia Office 7
23 1/2 S. Braddock St.
Winchester, VA 22601
(540) 722-2507 Fax: (540) 722-3366
Gwendolyn Puryear, Regional Manager
Email: gpuryear@telamon.org
Web: www.telamon.org

TEMPLO BAUTISTA DE FAIRFAX
9524 Braddock Rd,
Fairfax, VA 22032
(703) 323-7750 Fax: (703) 323-9041
Troy R. Calvert, Pastor

UNITED COMMUNITY MINISTRIES, INC.
7511 Fordson Rd.
Alexandria, VA 22306
(703) 768-7106 Fax: (703) 768-4788
Sharon Kelso, Executive Director
Email: ucmagency@aol.com

VENEZUELAN DANCING COMPANY
4343 Lee Hwy., #505
Arlington, VA 22207
(703) 528-4094 Fax: (703) 228-5813
Simón R. Contreras Velásquez, President
Email: sr-contreras@yahoo.com

WOMEN'S CENTER OF NORTHERN VIRGINIA
133 Park St. NE
Vienna, VA 22180
(703) 281-2657 Fax: (703) 242-1454
Judith Mueller, Director
Web: www.thewomenscenter.org

YMCA OF METROPOLITAN WASHINGTON
Arlington Branch
3422 N. 13th St.
Arlington, VA 22201
(703) 525-5420 Fax: (703) 525-2148
Ms. Lisbeth May, Hispanic Program Coord.

WASHINGTON

AGING & ADULT CARE OF CENTRAL WASHINGTON
50 Simon St. SE
E. Wenatchee, WA 98802-7727
(509) 886-0700 or (800) 572-4459
Fax: (509) 884-6943

ALCOHOL/DRUG TREATMENT CENTER
165 N 1st
Othello, WA 99344
(509) 488-5162 Fax: (509) 488-0166
Vickí, Office Manager

AMERICAN ASSOCIATION OF HISPANIC CERTIFIED PUBLIC ACCOUNTANTS (CPAS)
Seattle Chapter
1420 Canyon Ave.
Richland, WA 99352
(509) 627-1110
Dante Montoya, Northwest Area Repr.
Email: dante_montoya@msn.com
Web: www.aahcpa.org

AMERICAN CIVIL LIBERTIES UNION OF WASHINGTON
705 2nd Ave. #300
Seattle, WA 98104
(206) 624-2184
Kathleen Taylor, Executive Director
Web: www.aclu-wa.org

AMERICAN GI FORUM
Veterans of all Wars
109 N. 122nd St.
Seattle, WA 98133
(206) 364-5948 (w) Fax: (206) 361-1341
Francisco Ibarra, National Commander
Email: agifnc@aol.com

ARCHDIOCESE OF SEATTLE
Hispanic Affairs
910 Marion St.
Seattle, WA 98104-1299
(206) 382-4825 or (800) 836-2167
Fax: (206) 382-2069
María Esther Bazán, Dir.for Hispanic Affairs
Email: mariaba@seattlearch.org

ASUW MECHA STUDENTS' COMMISSION
University of Washington
207 HUB, FK-30 Box 352238
Seattle, WA 98195
(206) 543-2380
Dyane Haynes, Director

BAILES FOLKLÓRICOS "OLLIN"
Olympia
913 E Dundee Rd. NW
Olympia, WA 98502-4419
(360) 786-8567 Fax: (360) 943-5354
Cathy Shultz Reyes, Business Manager
Email: ballerollin@thurston.net
Web: www.paradisewest.com/

BELLINGHAM FOODBANK
P. O. Box 6056
Bellingham, WA 98227
(360) 676-0392 Fax: 6760410
Vicki Lewenberger, Executive director
Email: bfb@tellcomplus.net

BLESSED SACRAMENT-SEATTLE
5050 8th Ave. NE
Seattle, WA 98105
(206) 547-3020 Fax: (206) 547-6371
Reginald Martin, O.P.
Web: http://www.blessed-sacrament.org

CATHOLIC FAMILY AND CHILD SERVICES
2139 Van Gisen
Richland, WA 99352
(509) 946-4645 Fax: (509) 943-2068
Judy Dirks, Executive Director

CENTRO LATINO SER-JOBS FOR PROGRESS, INC.
Affiliate of SER-Jobs for Progress
National, Inc.
1208 S. 10th St.
Tacoma, WA 98405
(253) 572-7717 Fax: (253) 572-7837
Alfonso Montoya, Executive Director
Email: amontoya@centrolatino-ser.org
Web: www.centrolatino-ser.org

CENTRO MEXICANO DEL ESTADO DE WASHINGTON
2132 Third Ave.
Seattle, WA 98121
(206) 448-8938 Fax: (206) 448-4771
Mari Carmen Yudin, Vice Counsel

CHELAN-DOUGLAS COMMUNITY ACTION COUNCIL
620 Lewis St.
Wenatchee, WA 98801
(509) 662-6156 or (509) 662-6156
Janice, Deputy Director
Email: cdcac@gte.net

CHICANO EDUCATION PROGRAM
Eastern Washington University
526 5th St. M/S 170
Cheney, WA 99004
(509) 359-2404
Carlos Maldonado, Director

CHICANO STUDIES PROGRAM
American Ethnic Studies Dept.
University of Washington, 13521 Padelford Hall
P.O. Box 354380
Seattle, WA 98195
(206) 543-5401 Fax: (206) 616-4071
Erasmo Gamboa, Director
Web: www.washington.edu

CHRIST THE KING
405 N 107th St.
Seattle, WA 98133
(206) 367-1136 Fax: (20) 6365-6915
Father Alberto, Priest

CLUB TANGO OF SEATTLE
2019 Fairview Ave. E. Houseboat "D"
Seattle, WA 98102
(206) 323-2143
Art Hemenway, President

COLUMBIA BASIN CHRISTIAN MINISTRY
313 Fig St.
Moses Lake, WA 98837
(509) 766-2911
Wayne Hawkins, Contact

COMMUNITY HEALTH CENTER LA CLÍNICA
Affiliate of NCLR
P. O. Box 1323
Pasco, WA 99301-1323
(509) 547-2204 Fax: (509) 547-9329
Guillermo V. Castañeda, Executive Director

DIOCESE OF SPOKANE
Hispanic Affairs
P.O. Box 1453

1023 W. Riverside Ave.
Spokane, WA 99210-1453
(509) 358-7315 Fax: (509) 358-7302
Sr. Myrta Iturriaga, SP, Cons. Hispanic Ministry
Email: cathpso@gntech.net

DIOCESE OF YAKIMA
Hispanic Affairs
213 N. Beech
Topenish, WA 98948
(509) 865-4040 Fax: (509) 663-8437
Rev. Argemiro Orozco, Dir. for Hispanic Ministry

Hispanic Ministry Formation
5301-B Tieton Dr.
Topenish, WA 98908
(509) 865-4040 Fax: (509) 663-8437
Sr. María Jesús Ibarra, Director
Email: mybarra@ixpnet.com

DIVISION OF INSTRUCTIONAL PROGRAMS, WASHINGTON STATE
600 S Washington Migrant Education
Old Capitol Bldg.
Olympia, WA 98504
(360) 753-1031 Fax: (360) 664-2605
Richard Gómez, Director
Email: rgomez@ospi.wednet.edu
Web: www.k12.wa.us

EDUCATIONAL INSTITUTE FOR RURAL FAMILIES (EIRF)
Affiliate of NCLR
P.O. Box 2715
720 N. 20th Ave.
Pasco, WA 99302
(509) 547-8826 Fax: (509) 545-6294
Sara Stephens, Executive Director

EL CENTRO DE LA RAZA
2524 16th Ave. South
Seattle, WA 98144
(206) 329-9442 or (206) 329-2974
Fax: (206) 726-1529
Roberto Maestas, Executive Director
Email: elcentro@cartero.elcentrodelaraza.com
Web: www.elcentrodelaraza.com

EPIC-HEADSTART
1901 Rock Island Rd.
E. Wenatchee, WA 98802
(509) 884-2435 Fax: (509) 884-1383
Rosemaria Ariwoola, Center Manger
Email: rosemariaa@epicnet.org

FLAMENCO ARTS NORTH-WEST
3634 48th Ave., SW
Seattle, WA 98116
(206) 932-4067
Marcos Carmona, Director
Email: carmona2@aol.com

FREE METHODIST CHURCH
3800 Dana Rd.
Bellingham, WA 98225
(360) 734-3837 Fax: (360)734-0860
Joanne Fallis, Secretary
Email: info@lightnlife.org
Web: www.lightnlife.org

HEAD START
1305 Kittitas St.
Wenatchee, WA 98801
(509) 662-0317 Fax: (509) 662-0317
Heather, Director
Email: headstart@cdsca.com

HISPANIC CHAMBER OF COMMERCE OF GREATER YAKIMA
Yakima, WA 98907
(509) 248-5123
Daniel E. Enríquez, President

HISPANIC NATIONAL BAR ASSOC. (HNBA)
Region XVI (AK, ID, MT, OR, WA)
1201 Third Avenue Suite 4800
Seattle, WA 98101-3099
(206) 287-3596 Fax: (206) 583-8500
Frederick Rivera, Regional President
Email: rivef@perkinscoie.com
Web: www.hnba.com

HISPANIC POLITICAL ACTION COMMITTEE OF PIERCE CO. (HISPAC)
8728 Francis Folsom St., SW
Tacoma, WA 98498
(253) 584-3296 Fax: (253) 582-6119
Rafael Ojeda, President

IMAGE DE RAINER
National Image, Inc.
9203 3rd Way SE

Olympia, WA 98513
(360) 438-1631 (H)
Gabriel Ramos-Díaz, State President
Web: www.nationimageinc.org

IMAGE DE SEATTLE
National Image, Inc.
P.O. Box 21247
Seattle, WA 98111
(206) 443-3800
Rodolfo F. Hurtado, President
Web: www.nationalimageinc.org

IMMACULATE CONCEPTION
215 N 15th
Mt. Vernon, WA 98273
(360) 336-6622 Fax: (360) 336-5203
Lawrence Minder, Father

IMMIGRATION AND TRANSLATION SVCS.
Track 29 1 W. Yakima Ave. #38
Yakima, WA 98902
(509) 452-7337
Adelina S. Esquivel, President

KENNEWICK LIBRARY
1620 S Union
Kennewick, WA 99338
(509) 783-7878
Phelps Shepard, Director
Web: www.mcl-lib.org

LA TIENDA
4138 University Way NE
Seattle, WA 98105
(206) 632-1796 Fax: (206) 633-5170
Fred Hart, Contact
Email: latienda@msn.com
Web: www.shoplocal.com

LOS ALTEÑOS - LA SOLEDERA FLAMENCA
1003 36th Ave., E
Seattle, WA 98112-4323
(206) 325-2967
Josela del Rey, Maestra

LUTHERAN SOCIAL SERVICES
NW Area
433 Minor Ave. N
Seattle, WA 98109
(206) 694-5700 Fax: (206) 694-5777
Boots Winterstein, Area Director
Email: lssn@aol.com
Web: www.lssnw.org

MIDCOLUMBIA LIBRARIES
Keewaydin Park
405 S Dayton
Kennewick, WA 99336
(509) 586-3156
Phelps Shepard, Director
Web: www.mcl-lib.org

MIGRANT EDUCATION PROGRAM
Yakima Regional Office-ESD 105
33 S 2nd Ave.
Yakima, WA 98902
(509) 575-2885 Fax: (509) 575-2918
Sandra Davis, Executive Director
Email: sandrapd@esd105.wednet.edu
Web: www.esd105.wednet.edu

MIGRANT EDUCATIONAL
Regional Office
205 Stewart Rd.
Mt. Vernon, WA 98273
(360) 424-9573 Fax: (360) 424-9180
Mary Kernel, Director
Email: mkernel@esd189.wednet.edu
Web: www.esd189.wednet.edu/MERO/default.html

MIGRANT STUDENT RECORDS SYSTEM
1110-B South 6th St.
Sunnyside, WA 98944
(509) 837-2712 Fax: (509) 839-9017
Joe Resendez, Director
Email: msrs@wamsrs.wednet.edu
Web: www.wsmsmsrs.org

MOVIMIENTO ESTUDIANTIL CHICANO DE AZTLAN (MECHA)
Eastern Washington University
526th St., M/S 170
Cheney, WA 99004
(509) 359-6200 or (509) 359-6393

NATIONAL ASSOCIATION FOR CHICANA AND CHICANO STUDIES (NACCS)
Eastern Washington University
Chicano Educational Program
Monroe Hall 202, MS-170

Cheney, WA 99004
(509) 359-2404 Fax: (509) 359-2310
Dr. Carlos S. Maldonado, National Director
Web: www.ewu.edu

NATIONAL IMAGE, INC.
Washington State Chapter
7221 196th St., SW, #D-4
Lynnwood, WA 98036
(206) 684-7576 (W) Fax: (206) 470-6937
Fidel Alvarez, Regional Director
Email: fidel.alvarez@ci.seattle.wa.us
Web: www.nationalimageinc.org

NORTHWEST IMMIGRANT RIGHTS PROJECT
121 Sunnyside Ave.
Granger, WA 98932
(509) 854-2100 Fax: (509) 854-1500
Deirdre Mokos, Executive Director

NORTHWEST WOMEN'S LAW CENTER
119 S Main St., #410
Seattle, WA 98104
(206) 682-9552 Fax: (206) 682-9556
June Krumpatick, Paralegal
Email: nwwlc@nwwlc.org
Web: www.nwwlc.org

NUESTRO LUGAR/OUR PLACE
2105 W. Main St. P.O. Box 1394
Moses Lake, WA 98837
(509) 765-1214 or (800) 491-1214
Fax: (509) 766-0269
Patti Youngblood, Director
Email: ourplace@stoptheviolence.net
Web: www.stoptheviolence.net

OFFICE FOR CIVIL RIGHTS
Dept. of Health and Human Services
2201 6th Ave., #900
Seattle, WA 98121
(206) 553-7483 Fax: (206) 615-2297
Carmen Palomera Rockwell, Regional Manager
Email: ocrmail@os.dhhs.gov
Web: www.dhhs.gov

OFFICE OF RURAL & FARMWORKER HOUSING
1400 Summit View Ave. #203
Yakima, WA 98902
(509) 248-7014 Fax: (509) 575-3845
Brien Thane, Executive Director
Email: brient@orfh.org

OKANOGAN FARMWORKERS CLINIC
P. O. Box 1340
Okanogan, WA 98840
(509) 422-5700 Fax: (509) 422-1320
Mary Woodrow, Secretary

OLYMPIA TIMBERLAND PUBLIC LIBRARY
313 8th Ave., SE.
Olympia, WA 98501
(360) 352-0595 Fax: (360) 586-3207
Cheryl Heywood, Director

OUR LADY OF GUADALUPE ROMAN CATHOLIC CHURCH
P.O. Box 308
Granger, WA 98932
(509) 854-1558 Fax: (509) 854-7326
Father Mario Salacar, Contact

PEOPLE FOR PEOPLE-TOPPENISH
P. O. Box 2
Toppenish, WA 98948
(509) 865-5221 Fax: (509) 865-2485
Gracy Sexton, Office Lead Career Development Council
Web: www.pfp.org

PEOPLE OF COLOR AGAINST AIDS NETWORK (POCAAN)
Affiliate of NCLR
607 19th Ave. East
Seattle, WA 98112
(206) 322-7061 Fax: (206) 322-7204
Lupe López, Director
Web: www.pocaan.org

PROFESSIONAL IMMIGRATION SERVICES
P.O. Box 1444
Sunnyside, WA 98944

RADICAL WOMEN
5018 Rainier Ave. S.
Seattle, WA 98118
(206) 722-6057 Fax: (206) 723-7691

RECONOCIENDO LA IDENTIDAD CON
EDUCACIÓN Y SOCIEDAD
Eastern Washington University
526 5th St., M/S 170
Cheney, WA 99004
(509) 359-6860

SACRED HEART PARISH
P. O. Box 548
Brewster, WA 98812
(509) 689-2931 Fax: (509) 689-2931
Winn Webster, Pastoral Associate

SACRED HEART ROMAN CATHOLIC
CHURCH-OTHELLO
616 E Juniper St.
Othello, WA 99344
(509) 488-5653 Fax: (509) 488-5654
Father Tim Hays, Pastor
Email: sacredheart@cbnn.net

SACRED HEART ROMAN CATHOLIC
CHURCH-PROSSER
1905 Highland Dr.
Prosser, WA 99350
(509) 786-1783 Fax: (509) 786-1747
Father Hernández, Contact

SAFEPLACE WOMEN'S SHELTER
P. O. Box 1605
Olympia, WA 98507
(360) 754-6300 or (360) 786-8754
Fax: (360) 786-6377
Gabriella, Latina Advocate

SEA-MAR COMMUNITY HEALTH CENTER
Bellingham
800 E Chestnut #2A
Bellingham, WA 98225
(360) 671-3225 Fax: (360) 671-0000
Sharon Dowes, Executive Director

SEA-MAR COMMUNITY HEALTH CENTER
Mt. Vernon
1400 La Venture
Mt. Vernon, WA 98273
(360) 428-4075 Fax: (360) 428-5813
Mary Lou Martínez, Director

SEATTLE ARTS COMMISSION
312 First Ave. N
Seattle, WA 98109-4501
(206) 684-7171 Fax: (206) 684-7172
Marcia Twasaki, Director
Web: www.ci.seattle.wa.us/

SENIOR INFORMATION & ASSISTANCE
Pasco Senior Center
1315 N. 7th
Pasco, WA 99301
(509) 545-3459 Fax: (509) 545-3427
Philis Lamb, Recreation Specialist

SENIOR SERVICES FOR SOUTH SOUND
222 NW Columbia
Olympia, WA 98501
(360) 586-6181 Fax: (360) 586-7408
Mckencie Sullivan, Executive Director
Email: ssss@olywa.net

SKAGIT COUNTY COMMUNITY ACTION
AGENCY
P. O. Box 1507, 330 Pacific Pl.
Mt. Vernon, WA 98273
(360) 336-6627 Fax: (360) 416-7599
Karen Pernell, Deputy Director
Email: sccaa@fidalgo.net

SKAGIT VALLEY COLLEGE
2405 College Way
Mt. Vernon, WA 98273
(360) 428-1135
Ruth Silverthorne, Director

SOCIETY OF HISPANIC PROFESSIONAL
ENGINEERS (SHPE)
Eastern Washington Professional Chapter
P.O. Box 1393
Richland, WA 99352
(509) 375-1707 Fax: (509) 376-9118 (w)
Joaquin Cruz, Chapter President
Email: cruz3@bmi.net
Web: www.cbvcp.com/bgcbf/shpe

University of Washington
207 Loew, Box 352180
Seattle, WA 98195-2180
(206) 543-5536 or (206) 685-8359
Fax: (206) 685-0666
Gene Magallanes, Director

Email: eugenem@u.washington.edu
Web: www.shpe.org

Washington State University
College of Engineering and Architecture
138 Dana Hall, P.O. Box 642713
Pullman, WA 99164-2713
(509) 335-1584 Fax: (509) 335-9608
Charlena Grimes, Advisor
Email: shpe@eecs.wsu.edu or charz@wsu.edu
Web: www..eecs.wsu.edu/~shpe

SOCIETY OF LATINO ENGINEERS AND
SCIENTIST (SOLES)
Washington State University
Chicana/o Latina/o Student Center
P.O. Box 644011, Wilson #101, MS 4011
Pullman, WA 99164-4011
(509) 335-2616 Fax: (509) 335-6122
Francisco Tamayo, Counselor

SPANISH ASSEMBLY OF GOD
501 W 2nd
Wapato, WA 98951
(509) 877-2377
Levi Serafín, Executive Director

ST. FRANCIS DE SALES ROMAN
CATHOLIC CHURCH
P.O. Box 1089
Chelan, WA 98816-1089
(509) 682-2433
Father Daniel Dufner, Director of Hispanic
Ministry

ST. JOSEPH ROMAN CATHOLIC CHURCH
212 N. Fourth St.
Yakima, WA 98901
(509) 248-1911 Fax: (509) 248-2604
Father Patrick Carroll, Pastor

ST. JOSEPH ROMAN CATHOLIC CHURCH
205 12th St.
Linden, WA 98264
(360) 354-2334 Fax: (360) 354-5889
Father Woody McCallyster, Pastor

ST. JOSEPH ROMAN CATHOLIC CHURCH
520 S Garfield
Kennewick, WA 99336
(509) 586-0864 Fax: (509) 586-3558
Father Manuel Méndez, Associate Pastor
Email: cp1353@3/cities.com
Web: www.cbvp.com/stjocatch

ST. LOUISE CATHOLIC CHURCH
A Parish of the Catholic Archdiocese of
Seattle
141 156th Ave. SE
Bellevue, WA 98007
(425) 747-4450 Fax: (425) 644-3678
Emilio González, Parochial Vicar

ST. MARTIN'S COLLEGE
1300 Pacific Ave SE
Lacey, WA 98503
(360) 491-4700 Fax: (360) 459-4124
Rex Casillas, International Relations
Email: casillas@stmartin.edu
Web: www.stmartin.edu

ST. MARY'S CHURCH
Hispanic Ministry Office
611 20th Avenue South
Seattle, WA 98144
(206) 324-7100 Fax: (206) 329-4596
Guidelia Alejo, Pastoral Associate

ST. PATRICK ROMAN CATHOLIC CHURCH
1320 W. Henry
Pasco, WA 99301
(509) 547-8841 Fax: (509) 547-3604
Msgr. Pedro Ramírez, Pastor

ST. PETER CATHOLIC CHURCH
Yakima Diocese
15880 Summitview Rd.
Kowiche, WA 98923
(509) 678-4164
David Jiménez, Pastor
Email: StPeterA@AOL.com
Web: www.Diocese.net/site/Parish/Yakima/
St_Peter_Apostle

STATE OF WASHINGTON COMMISSION
ON HISPANIC AFFAIRS
National Headquarters
P.O.Box 40924
Olympia, WA 98504-0924
(360) 753-3159 Fax: (360) 753-0199
Onofre Contreras, Executive Director

Email: hispanic@halcyon.com
Web: www.wahispaniccommission.org

UNITED METHODIST CHURCH
304 Ash St.
Grandview, WA 98930
(509) 882-3645
Jim Simpson, Contact
Email: gumc@quicktell.com

UNITED STATES-MEXICO CHAMBER OF
COMMERCE
Northwest Chapter
1301 5th Avenue, Suite 2400
Seattle, WA 98101-2603
(206) 625-0868 Fax: (206) 389-7288
Email: DDSPENCER@stoel.com

UNIVERSITY OF WASHINGTON
Office of Minority Affairs
P.O. Box 355845
Seattle, WA 98195
(206) 685-0774 Fax: (206) 543-2746
Myron Apilado, Director
Email: oma@u.washington.edu
Web: oma.washington.edu

WASHINGTON FARMWORKERS
INVESTMENT PROGRAM
Yakima Valley OIC
815 Fruitvale Blvd.
Yakima, WA 98902
(509) 248-6751 Fax: (509) 575-0482
Gilbert Alaniz, Program Director
Email: galaniz@yvoic.org
Web: www.yvoic.org

WASHINGTON LATINO AIDS COALITION
607 19th Ave.
Seattle, WA 98112
(206) 322-7061 Fax: (206) 322-7201
Edmont Farlivar

WASHINGTON STATE DEPARTMENT OF
ECOLOGY-TOXIC CLEANUP
15 W Yakima Ave., #200
Yakima, WA 98902-3401
(509) 575-2491 Fax: (509) 575-2809
Polly Zehm, Regional Director
Web: www.wa.gov

WASHINGTON STATE MIGRANT
COUNCIL
Administrative Office
105 B South 6th St.
Sunnyside, WA 98944
(509) 839-9762 Fax: (509) 839-7689
Carlos M. Díaz, Executive Director
Email: tknoth@wsmconline.org

WASHINGTON STATE OF CATHOLIC
CONFERENCE
508 2nd Ave. W
Seattle, WA 98119-3928
(206) 301-0556 Fax: (206) 301-0558
Sharon Park, Executive Director
Email: wscc99@aol.com

WASHINGTON STATE UNIVERSITY
The Office Multicultural Student Services
P.O. Box 641062
Pullman, WA 99164-1032
(509) 335-4531 Fax: (509) 335-1525
Steve Nakata, Director
Email: mss@wsu.edu
Web: www.wsu.edu/multicultural/

WHATCOM HISPANIC ORGANIZATION
P. O. Box 5601
Bellingham, WA 98227
(360) 676-8911 Fax: (360) 671-2231
Becky Díaz, President
Email: bdiaz@nascom

WINLOCK UNITED METHODIST
107 Benton
Winlock, WA 98596
(360) 785-4241
Steve Caski, Contact

DIOCESE OF WHEELING-CHARLESTON
Hispanic Affairs
317 Main St.
Bridgeport, WV 26330
(304) 842-2283
Rev. John L. O'Reilly, Director for Hispanic
Ministry

TELAMON CORPORATION
West Virginia Office 2
60 West Sioux Ln.

Romney, WV 26757
(304) 822-4514 Fax: (304) 822-4515
Carol Breighner, Case Manager
Email: wv02@citlink.com
Web: www.telamon.org

West Virginia Office 5
219 W. Race St.
Martinsburg, WV 25401
(304) 264-0971 or (304) 264-0979
Fax: (304) 264-4414
Jeremy Edgell, Regional Manager
Email: jedgell@telamon.org
Web: www.telamon.org

West Virginia State Office 1
129 S. Queen St.
Martinsburg, WV 25401
(304) 263-0916 or (304) 263-0917
Fax: (304) 263-4809
Karen Hoff, State Director
Email: khoff@telamon.org
Web: www.telamon.org

ALPHA SIGMA OMEGA LATINA
SORORITY, INC.
University of Wisconsin, Parkside
4019 Outer Loop Rd.
Kenosha, WI 53144
María Negrón, Chapter President
Email: milagro_aso@hotmail.com
Web: www.uwp.edu/clubs/greeks/aso/
index2.html

ARCHDIOCESE OF MILWAUKEE
Hispanic Affairs
P.O. Box 07912
3501 S. Lake Dr.
Milwaukee, WI 53207
(414) 769-3393 Fax: (414) 769-3408
Pedro Martínez, Director for Hispanic Ministry

AURORA WEIER EDUCATIONAL CTR.
2669 N. Richards St.
Milwaukee, WI 53212
(414) 562-8398 Fax: (414) 562-8494
Emilio López, Executive Director

CENTER FOR LATIN AMERICA
University of Wisconsin, Milwaukee
P.O. Box 413
Garland Hall, #202
Milwaukee, WI 53201
(414) 229-4401
Kristin Ruggiero, Director
Email: ruggiero@uwm.edu

CENTRO DE LA COMUNIDAD UNIDA /
UNITED COMMUNITY CENTER, INC.
Affiliate of NCLR
1028 S. 9th St.
Milwaukee, WI 53204
(414) 384-3100 Fax: (414) 649-4411
Dr. Walter Sava, Executive Director

CENTRO HISPANO, INC.
Affiliate of NCLR
1321 E. Mifflin St., #200
Madison, WI 53703
(608) 255-3018 Fax: (608) 255-2975
Lucía Núñez, Executive Director
Email: centroad@itis.com

COLOMBIA SUPPORT NETWORK
P.O. Box 1505
Madison, WI 53701-1505
(608) 257-8753 Fax: (608) 255-6621
Email: csn@igc.org
Web: www.colombiasupport.net

COUNCIL FOR THE SPANISH SPEAKING INC.
Milwaukee
614 W. National Ave.
Milwaukee, WI 53204
(414) 384-3700 Fax: (414) 384-7622
Filberto Murguia, Executive Director
Email: jimenez@execpc.com

DIOCESE OF GREEN BAY
Hispanic Affairs Office
P.O. Box 23825
Green Bay, WI 54305-3825
(920) 437-7531 x8247 Fax: (920) 437-0694
Rudy Pineda, Director for Hispanic Services
Web: www.gbdioc.org

DIOCESE OF LA CROSSE
Office of Justice and Peace
P.O. Box 4004
3710 East Ave. S.
La Crosse, WI 54601-4004

(608) 788-7700 Fax: (608) 788-8413
Michael Brown

DIOCESE OF MADISON
Hispanic Ministry Office
3577 High Point Rd.
Madison, WI 53744
(608) 821-3092 Fax: (608) 821-3139
Sr. Teresa Ann Wolf, OSB
Email: hispminmad@mcci2000.com

DIOCESE OF SUPERIOR
Hispanic Affairs
P.O. Box 969
1201 Hughitt Ave.
Superior, WI 54880
(715) 392-2937
Richard Lyons, Director of Pastoral Services

ESPERANZA UNIDA, INC.
1329 W. National Ave.
Milwaukee, WI 53204
(414) 671-0251 Fax: (414) 383-7392
Richard Oulahan, Executive Director
Web: www.esperanzaunida.org

HISPANIC CHAMBER OF COMMERCE OF WISCONSIN
816 W. National Ave.
Milwaukee, WI 53204
(414) 643-6963 Fax: (414) 643-6994
Maria Monreal-Cameron, President & CEO
Email: mcameron@hcpw.org
Web: www.hcpw.org

LA CASA DE ESPERANZA, INC.
Affiliate of NCLR
410 Arcadian Ave.
Waukesha, WI 53186
(414) 547-0887 Fax: (414) 547-0735
Anselmo Villareal, Executive Director
Email: lacasa@execpc.com

LA CAUSA, INC.
Affiliate of NCLR
809 W Greenfield Ave.
Milwakee, WI 53204
(414) 647-5960 Fax: (414) 647-4847
David Espinoza, Executive Director

LA COLECTIVA CULTURAL DE AZTLAN
716 Langdon St. 2nd Floor, Red Gym UW-Madison
Madison, WI 53706
(608) 262-5132 Fax: (608) 263-3912
Diana Aguilar, Co-President

LA GUADALUPANA SENIOR CENTER
1028 S. 9th St.
Milwaukee, WI 53204
(414) 384-2301 Fax: (414) 6494411
Walter Sava, Executive Director

LATIN AMERICAN AND IBERIAN STUDIES PROGRAM
University of Wisconsin, Madison
1155 Observatory Dr.
209 Ingraham Hall
Madison, WI 53706
(608) 262-2811 Fax: (608) 265-5851
Francisco Scrano, Director
Email: latam@macc.wisc.edu

LATINO AGING NETWORK
235 W. Galena St.#180
Milwaukee, WI 53212
(414) 289-5950 or (414) 289-6376
Fax: (414) 289-8525
Estaphani Sustien, Executive Director
Web: www.milwaukeecommunity.com/index/shtl

LATINOS UNIDOS
University of Wisconsin, Parkside
Multicultural Affairs, WYLL D182
900 Wood Rd., Box 2000
Kenosha, WI 53141-2000
(262) 595-2496
Carmen Ireland, Staff Advisor
Email: carmen.ireland@uwp.edu
Web: www.uwp.edu/clubs/latinos.unidos/info/info.htm

LATINOS UNITED FOR CHANGE AND ADVANCEMENT, INC. (LUCHA)
P.O. Box 2033
Madison, WI 53701-2033
(608) 278-1037 or (608) 274-9512
Alfonso Zepeda-Capistran, President
Email:
azepedac@facstaff.wisc.edualfonso_z@hotmail.com

Web: caweb.madison.tec.wi.us/class/sugalde-langstroth/lucha/lucha.html

LEAGUE OF UNITED LATIN AMERICAN CITIZENS (LULAC)
Midwest Region-WI
5158 S. 78th Street
Greendale, WI 53129
(414) 297-6717 Fax: (414) 297-7990
Gregorio Montoto, State Director
Email: montotog@milwaukee.tec.wi.us

MILWAUKEE SER-JOBS FOR PROGRESS, INC.
Affiliate of SER-Jobs for Progress Natl, Inc.
1020/30 W. Mitchell St.
Milwaukee, WI 53204
(414) 649-2640 Fax: (414) 649-2644
Abel R. Ortíz, Executive Director
Email: mser@earthlink.net
Web: www.earthlink.net/~mser

NATIONAL LATINO PEACE OFFICERS ASSOCIATION (NLPOA)
Milwaukee Chapter
P.O. Box 370031
Milwaukee, WI 53237
(877) 657-6200
David Murguia, State President
Email: nlpoa@aol.com
Web: www.nlpoa.com

PARTNERS FOR COMMUNITY DEVELOPMENT
901 Superior Ave.
Sheboygan, WI 53081
(920) 459-2780 Fax: (920) 459-2782
Lucio Fuentez, President
Email: lucio@dataplus.net

PUBLIC SERVICE COMMISSION OF WISCONSIN
P.O.Box 7854, 610 N. Whitney Way
Madison, WI 53705-2729
(608) 266-5481 Fax: (608) 266-3957
Linda Door, Chair
Email: pscrecs@psc.state.wi.us
Web: http://www.psc.state.wi.us

RAINBOW/PUSH COALITION
Milwaukee Chapter
6985 N. Darien St.
Milwaukee, WI 53209
(414) 352-3265
Rev. Floyd Taylor, President
Web: www.rainbowpush.org

ROBERTO HERNÁNDEZ CENTER
University of Wisconsin Milwaukee
P. O. Box 413
Milwaukee, WI 53201
(414) 229-6156 Fax: (414) 229-2250
William Vélez, Director
Web: www.uwm.edu/letsci/services/latino.html

UNION PUERTORRIQUEÑA
Old Red Gym
716 Langdon St. 2nd Floor
Madison, WI 53706-1495
(608) 262-4503
Web: www.wisc.edu/msc/

UNITED MIGRANT OPPORTUNITY SERVICES, INC.
Affiliate of NCLR
929 W. Mitchell St.
Milwaukee, WI 53204
(414) 671-5700 Fax: (414) 671-4833
Lupe Martínez, President & CEO

WYOMING

DIOCESE OF CHEYENNE
Hispanic Affairs
P.O. Box 1468
2121 Capitol Ave.
Cheyenne, WY 82003-1468
(307) 638-1530 Fax: (307) 637-7936

HISPANIC ORGANIZATION FOR PROGRESS AND EDUCATION (HOPE)
501 Dartmouth Lane
Cheyenne, WY 82009
(307) 632-4667 Fax: (307) 632-4667
Ann Redman, President
Email: alphredman@msn.com

Hispanic Correspondents in the US (by nation of origin)
Corresponsales hispanos en EUA (por nación de origen)

ARGENTINA

ANSA ITALIAN NEWS AGENCY
Marcelo Claudio Raimon
1285 National Press Bldg.
Washington, DC 20045
(202) 628-3317
Fax: (202) 638-1792
Web: http://www.ansa.it

B.A.E. (BUENOS AIRES ECONÓMICO)
Fabian Doman
6605 McLean Ct.
McLean, VA 22101
(703) 448-9555
(202) 316-7622
Fax: (703) 448-9555
E-mail: domanf@aol.com
Web: http://www.baedigital.com

CLARIN
Ana Barón Supervielle
National Press Bldg., #1271
Washington, DC 20045
(202) 338-5703
Fax: (202) 737-4853
E-mail: abaron8789@aol.com

EDITORIAL ATLANTIDA
Gustavo Sherquis
83-55 Woodhaven Blvd., Apt. 313
Woodhaven, NY 11421
(718) 805-9526
Fax: (718) 805-9527
E-mail: gsherquis@aol.com

EDITORIAL PERFIL
Carlos Lauria
200 East 58th St., #8A
New York, NY 10022
(212) 888-6453
Fax: (212) 421-9344
E-mail: carlosl509@aol.com
Web: http://www.perfil.com

LA NACIÓN
Maria Odonnell
901 National Press Bldg.
Washington, DC 20045
(202) 628-7907
Fax: (202) 333-1053
E-mail: mariaodon@aol.com
Web: http://www.lanacion.com

PAGINA 12
Mónica Flores Correa
75 Livingston St., Apt. 10D
New York, NY 11201
(718) 722-7283

TELAM NEWS AGENCY
Norberto Svarzman
United Nations #C322
New York, NY 11017
(212) 750-6477
Fax: (212) 750-6477
E-mail: nsvarzman@aol.com

BOLIVIA

LA RAZON
6202 Kirby Road
Bethesda, MD 20817
(301) 320-0278
E-mail: larazonusa@aol.com

BRAZIL

JORNAL FOLHA DE SAO PAULO
Carlos Eduardo Lins da Silva
Maria Cecilia de Sa Porto
3409 Glenmor Dr.
Chevy Chase, MD 20815
(301) 656-2019
Fax: (301) 656-0347

**O ESTADO DE SAO PAULO/
AGENCIA ESTADO**
Paulo Sotero Marques
700 13th St., NW #555
Washington, DC 20005
(202) 682-3752
Fax: (202) 682-0718
E-mail: psotero@aol.com

O GLOBO
Jose Meirelles Passos
529 14th St., NW #1251-NPB
Washington, DC 20045
(202) 628-3313
Fax: (202) 347-6481
E-mail: jpassos@compuserve.com

RADIO BANDEIRANTES
Chris Delboni (Sao Paulo)
4849 Connecticut Ave., NW #4628
Washington, DC 20008
(202) 363-5694
Fax: (202) 363-0402
E-mail: delboni@aol.com

TV GLOBO & IDEA TV
Luis Fernando da Silva Pinto
Lauren Silva Pinto
2141 Wisconsin Ave., # L
Washington, DC 20007
(202) 429-2524
Fax: (202) 429-1713
Web: http://www.idea-tv.com

**ZERO HORA/REDE RBS DIARIO DO
COMERCIO**
A. Edgardo Costa Reis
5900 Valerian Ln.
N. Bethesda, MD 20852
(202) 458-6078
Fax: (301) 881-3016

COLOMBIA

CARACOL TV
Ione Molinares
1825 K St., NW #501
Washington, DC 20006
(703) 924-3734
Fax: (703) 924-3734

NOTICIAS DE LA NOCHE TV
Alejandra Balcazar
10217 Tyburn Terrace
Bethesda, MD 20814
(301) 581-9644
Fax: (301) 581-9645
Cell: (301) 332-3661
E-mail: alejabal@aol.com

NOTICIERO CMI TV
Daniel Rocha
1825 K St., NW #501
Washington, DC 20006
(202) 822-8774
Fax: (202) 822-8776

NOTICIERO DE LAS SIETE TV
Daniel Rocha
1825 K St., NW #501
Washington, DC 20006
(301) 681-6743
Cell: (202) 437-7732

EL TIEMPO
Sergio Gomez
1825 K St., NW #501
Washington, DC 20006
(703) 248-6952
Cell: (202) 607-5929

EL PAIS
Alejandra Balcazar
10217 Tyburn Terrace
Bethesda, MD 20814
(301) 581-9644
Fax: (301) 581-9645
Cell: (301) 332-3661
E-mail: alejabal@aol.com

RADIO RCN
Daniel Rocha
1825 K St., NW #501
Washington, DC 20006
(202) 822-8774
Fax: (202) 822-8776
Pager: (301) 940-1036
E-mail: artvinc@aol.com

RCN FM RADIO
Alejandra Balcazar
10217 Tyburn Terrace
Bethesda, MD 20814
(301) 581-9644
Fax: (301) 581-9645
Cell: (301) 332-3661
E-mail: alejabal@aol.com

ECUADOR

EL EXPRESO AND TELE SISTEMA
John Iturralde
26-45 9th St., #605
Astoria, NY 11102
(718) 777-0830
Fax: (718) 777-0830
E-mail: johnfiturralde@aol.com

PANAMA

LA PRENSA NEWSPAPER
Betty Brannan
7729 Brookville Rd.
Chevy Chase, MD 20815
(301) 652-7645
Fax: (301) 652-0629
E-mail: laprensadc@aol.com

PANAMA AMERICA NEWSPAPER
Henry Raymont
2311 Connecticut Ave., NW #207
Washington, DC 20008
(202) 797-2405

PERU

CPN RADIO
P.O. Box 1887
Rockville, MD 20849-1887
(301) 279-9109
Fax: (301) 279-7954
E-mail: kocerha@iamdigex.net

SPAIN

ABC
Pedro Rodríguez
P.O. Box 1277
Falls Church, VA 22041
(703) 841-7368
Fax:(703) 841-7368
Web-site: http://www.abc.es
E-mail: abcwashington@compuserve.com

CATALUÑA RADIO
Montserrat Vendrell
New York, NY 10012
(212) 982-2499
Fax: (212) 982-2499

CINCO DIAS
Lidia Aguirre
301 Elizabeth St. #9D
New York, NY 10012
(212) 219-9875
Fax: (212) 219-9875

EFE
Maria Peña
1252 National Press Bldg.
Washington, DC 20045
(202) 745-7692
Fax: (202) 393-4119
Web: http://www.efe.es

EFE NEWS SERVICES
Rafael Moreno
25 W. 43rd St. #1512
New York, NY 10036
(212) 867-5757
Fax: (212) 867-9074
E-mail: efe@efenews.com

Correspondents: Alejandro Fernandez, Victor Martin, Ana Gerez, Miguel Rajmil Antonio Lafuente

EXPANSION ACTUALIDAD ECONOMICA
Sonia Franco
14 East 60 St., Penthouse
New York, NY 10022
(212) 737-0115
Fax: (212) 319-0707
E-mail: franco@recoletos.es
Web: http://recoletos.es

HOLA
Isabel Junco
5212 Sangamore Rd.
Bethesda, MD 20816
(301) 320-2731
Fax: (301) 320-2731

EL MUNDO
Carlos Fresneda
300 Mercer Apt. 15M
New York, NY 10003
(212) 539-1843

EL MUNDO Y LA REVISTA
Carlos Fresneda
300 Mercer St., #15M
New York, NY 10003
(212) 539-1843
Fax: (212) 539-1845
Web-site: http://www.eltiempo.es

ONDA CERO RADIO
Agustín de Frutos
235 E. 95th St., #21K
New York, NY 10128
(212) 427-7587
Fax: (212) 427-7587
E-mail: ondaony@worldnet.att.net

EL PAIS
Bureau Chief: Javier Valenzuela
1134 National Press Bldg.
Washington, DC 20045
(202) 638-7604/6375
Fax: (202) 628-4788
E-mail: elpais1@nationalpress.com
Web: http://www.elpais.es

EL PAIS
Juan Cavestany
155 W. 68th St., #1110
New York, NY 10023
(212) 873-9146
Fax: (212) 873-9146

EL PERIODICO TIEMPO
Mercedes Hervás
United Nations Bldg.
Press Area #C-320
New York, NY 10017
(212) 755-4172
Fax: (212) 319-8330
Telex: 421081

RADIO COPE
Manuel Angel Gómez
11924 Sloane Ct.
Reston, VA 22091
(703) 689-0750
Fax: (703) 715-9525

RADIO VOZ
Pilar García
888 8th Ave., #12V
New York, NY 10019
(212) 489-8171
Fax: (212) 489-9564
E-mail: cari231@aol.com

RNE
Bureau Chief: Magin Gonzalez
1288 National Press Bldg.
Washington, DC 20045
(202) 783-0768
Fax: (202) 347-0147
E-mail: rne-eeuu@worldnet.att.net

SER
Javier Del Pino
1134 National Press Bldg., NW
Washington, DC 20045
(202) 628-2522
Fax: (202) 628-4788
We: http://www.cadenaser.es

TIEMPO
Gustavo Valverde
425 East 51st St., #8A
New York, NY 10022
(212) 319-8330
Fax: (212) 319-8330 Telex: 421081

TRIBUNA
Rosana Ubanell
7006 Tyndale St.
McLean, VA 22101
(703) 893-7880
Fax: (703) 288-3792
E-mail: raubanell@aol.com

TV-3
Bureau Chief: Ramón Rovira
Producer: Ana Ubeda
1620 I St., NW #150
Washington, DC 20006
(202) 785-0580
Fax: (202) 296-7896
E-mail: tv3w@erols.com

TVE
Chief Correspondent: Jose Pinar
501 Madison Ave., #604
New York, NY 10022
(212) 371-5112
Fax: (212) 758-7390
Producers: Cristina Carrión, Miguel Moreno
E-mail: nyork@tve-us.org

LA VANGUARDIA
Joaquin Luna
4343 Massachusetts Ave., NW
Washington, DC 20016
(202) 362-6785
Fax: (202) 362-6705

LA VOZ DE GALICIA
Jaime Meilán
319 Barrow St., #3B
Jersey City, NJ 07302
(201) 434-2128
Fax: (201) 434-2128
Web: http://www.lavozdegalicia.com

URUGUAY

CANAL 66
Lidia Aguirre
(212) 861-3514
Fax: (212) 861-0588

RADIO NUEVO TIEMPO
Rolan Maza
(301) 283-0806

VENEZUELA

AGENCIA DE NOTICIAS DE VENEZUELA
960-A, National Press Bldg.
Washington, DC 22150
Fax: (202) 347-3327

Hispanic Television Stations (by State)
Estaciones de televisión hispanas (por Estado)

KDRX, CHANNEL 48
Apogeo Co.
4001 East Broadway Rd., #B-11
Phoenix, AZ 85040
Victor Carranza, Gen. Mgr.
(602) 470-0507 Fax: (602) 470-0810

KHRR-TV, CHANNEL 40
Apogeo Co.
2919 East Broadway, Garden Level
Tucson, AZ 85716
Tamara Valenzuela Cabazos, Gen. Mgr.
(520) 322-6888 Fax: (520) 881-7926
Email: tamara@khrr.com

KQBN-TV, CHANNEL 14
Apogeo Co.
2919 East Broadway, Garden Level
Tucson, AZ 85716
Tamara Valenzuela Cabazos, Gen. Mgr.
(520) 322-6888 Fax: (520) 881-7926
Email: tamara@khrr.com

KSWT-TV, CHANNEL 34
Pappas Telecasting
1301 South Third Ave.
Yuma, AZ 85364
Dave Joseph, Gen. Mgr.
(520) 782-5113 Fax: (520) 782-0320
Email: deejaytus@aol.com

KTVW-TV CHANNEL 33
Univision Television Group
3019 E. Southern Ave.
Phoenix, AZ 85040
Myrna Sonora, Gen. Mgr.
(602) 243-3333 Fax: (602) 276-8658
Web: www.univision.net

KUVE CHANNEL 52
Univision Television Group
2301 N Forbes Blvd., #108
Tucson, AZ 85745
Myrna Sonora, Gen. Mgr.
(520) 622-0984 Fax: (520) 622-0984
Web: www.univision.net

GALAVISION CHANNEL 35
Entravision Communications Corp.
41601 Corporate Way
Palm Desert, CA 92260
Tony Billett, Gen. Mgr.

(760) 341-5837 Fax: (760) 341-0951
Email: tbillett@entravision.com
Web: www.entravision.com

K07TA CHANNEL 7
R &C Enterprises
1138 W Church
Santa Maria, CA 93458
Sandy Keefer, Gen. Mgr.
(805) 928-7700 Fax: (805) 928-8606
Email: ktaf-tv@fix.net

K09UF CHANNEL 9
R &C Enterprises
1138 W Church
Santa Maria, CA 93458
Sandi Kifford, Gen. Mgr.
(805) 928-7700 Fax: (805) 928-8606
Email: ktaf-tv@fix.net

K2OFC CHANNEL 20
Sainte Partmers II, LP
300 Main St.
Chico, CA 95928
Juan Carlos Muñoz, Contact
(530) 893-1234 Fax: (530) 893-1266

KABE-TV CHANNEL 39
Univision Television Group, Inc.
3223 Sillect Avenue
Bakersfield, CA 93308
Teresa Ford, Gen. Mgr.
(661) 325-3939 Fax: (661) 325-3971

KBNT-TV CHANNEL 17
Entravision Communications Corp.
5770 Ruffin Rd.
San Diego, CA 92123
Philip Wilkinson, Gen. Mgr.
(858) 576-1919 Fax: (858) 715-1919
Web: www.kbnt-tv19.com

KCSO-TV CHANNEL 34
Sainte Partmers II, LP
142 N 9th St., #8
Modesto, CA 95350
Roberto Castro, Gen. Mgr.
(209) 572-3400 Fax: (209) 575-4547
Email: rcastro@kcso34.com
Web: www.kcso34.com

KCU CHANNEL 15
Telemundo Group, Inc.
2349 Bering Dr.
San Jose, CA 95131
Eduardo Dominguez, Gen. Mgr.
(408) 944-4848 Fax: (408) 433-5921

KDTV CHANNEL 14
Univision Television Group
50 Fremont St., 41st Fl.
San Francisco, CA 94105
Marcela Medina, Gen. Mgr.
(408) 392-6900 Fax: (415) 538-8053

KFTV-TV CHANNEL 21
Univision Television Group
3239 West Ashlan Ave.
Fresno, CA 93722
Maria Gutierrez, Gen. Mgr.
(559) 222-2121 Fax: (559) 222-0917

KJLA
Costa de Oro Television
2323 Corinth Ave
West Los Angeles, CA 90064
Francis Wilkinson, Gen. Mgr.
(310) 943-52888 Fax: (310) 943-5299
Web: www.kjla.com

KMEX-TV CHANNEL 34
Univision Television Group
6701 Center Drive West, 15th Fl.
Los Angeles, CA 90045
Agustíne Martinez, Gen. Mgr.
(310) 216-3434 Fax: (310) 348-3597
Web: www.kmex.com

KMSG-TV, CHANNEL 59
Sanger Telecaster
706 W Herndon Ave.
Fresno, CA 93650
Lisa Nilmeier, Gen. Mgr.
(559) 435-5900 Fax: (559) 435-1448
Email: kmsg59@kmsg59.com
Web: www.kmsg59.com

KSMS-TV CHANNEL 67
Entravision Communications Corp.
67 Garden Ct.
Monterey, CA 93940
Carlos Ramos, Gen. Mgr.
(831) 373-6767 Fax: (831) 373-6700

KSTS CHANNEL 48
Telemundo Group, Inc.
2349 Bering Dr.
San Jose, CA 95131
Eduardo Dominguez, Gen. Mgr.
(408) 944-4848 Fax: (408) 433-5921

KSUV CHANNEL 52
Tri-Caballero
3701 Pegasus Dr. #102
Bakersfield, CA 93308

Lou Vialpando, Gen. Mgr.
(661) 393-0103 Fax: (661) 393-0285
Programming: Spanish Broadcasting/Music Videos

KTAS-TV CHANNEL 33
R &C Enterprises
1138 W. Church Street
Santa Maria , CA 93458
Sandy Keefer, Gen. Mgr.
(805) 928-7700 Fax: (805) 928-8606

KUNA, CHANNEL 15
Gulf California Broadcast Co.
42-650 Melanie Place
Palm Desert, CA 92211-5170
Martin Serna, Gen. Mgr.
(760) 568-6830 Fax: (760) 568-3984

KUVS CHANNEL 19
Univision Television Group
1710 Arden Way
Sacramento, CA 95815
Jorge Delgado, Gen. Mgr.
(916) 927-1900 Fax: (916) 614-1902

KVEA-TV, CHANNEL 52
Telemundo Group, Inc.
1130 Air Way
Glendale, CA 91201
Fernando Lopez, Gen Mgr
(818) 502-5700 Fax: (818) 502-0029
Email: noticiero52@kvea.com
Web: www.kvea.com

KVER-TV CHANNEL 12
Entravision Communications Corp.
41601 Corporate Way
Palm Desert, CA 92260
Tony Billett, Gen. Mgr.
(760) 341-5837 Fax: (760) 341-0951
Email: tbillett@entravision.com
Web: www.entravision.com
Programming: Full-time Spanish station. Univision Affiliate Station.

KWHY-TV CHANNEL 22
Hariscope of LA, Inc.
5545 Sunset Blvd.
Los Angeles, CA 90028
Martin Dugan, Gen. Mgr.
(323) 466-5441 Fax: (323) 603-4226

XEWT-CHANNEL 12
Televisa
637 Third Ave. #B
Chula Vista, CA 91910

Patricia Alvarez, Gen. Mgr.
(619) 585-9398 Fax: (619) 585-9463

XHAS CHANNEL 33
Televisora Alco
135 Civic Center Dr.
National City, CA 91950
Carlos Sanchez, Gen. Mgr.
(619) 336-7801 Fax: (619) 336-7800
Email: xhas33@isat.com

XHBJ-TV CHANNEL 45
Televisa
4141 Jutland Dr. #150
San Diego, CA 92117
Mario Enriquez Mayans, Gen. Mgr.
(858) 490-2500 Fax: (858) 490-2505

XHJK CH 27
TV Azteca
659 Third Avenue, #E
Chula Vista, CA 91910
Socorro Ruiz, Gen. Mgr.
(619) 425-4848 Fax: (619) 426-4370
Email: socorroruiz@ixpres.com

XHTIT CH 21
TV Azteca
659 Third Ave. #E
Chula Vista, CA 91910
Socorro Ruiz, Gen. Mgr.
(619) 425-4848 Fax: (619) 426-4370
Email: socorroruiz@ixpres.com

XHUAA-CHANNEL 57
Televisa
637 Third Ave. #B
Chula Vista, CA 91910
Patricia Alvarez, Gen. Mgr.
(619) 585-9398 Fax: (619) 585-9463

COLORADO

KCEC-TV CHANNEL 50
Entravision Communications Corp.
777 Grant St., 5th Fl.
Denver, CO 80203
Yrma Rico, Gen. Mgr.
(303) 832-0050 Fax: (303) 832-3410
Web: www.entravision.com

KGHB CHANNEL 27
Entravision Communications Corp.
777 Grant St., 5th Fl.
Denver, CO 80203
Yrma Rico, Gen. Mgr.
(303) 832-0050 Fax: (303) 832-3410
Web: www.entravision.com

KMAS-TV CHANNEL 63/67
Telemundo Network
1120 Lincoln St. #800
Denver, CO 80203
Clara Rivas, Gen. Mgr.
(303) 477-3031 Fax: (303) 832-0777

CONNECTICUT

WDMR-TV, CHANNEL 65
Channel 13 Television, Inc.
886 Maple Ave.
Hartford, CT 06114
Lucio Ruzzier, Gen. Mgr.
(860) 956-1303 Fax: (860) 956-6834

Email: channel13@home.com
Programming: Full-time Spanish station.
Telemundo Affiliate Station Station Address: 974
Main St. Springfiend, MA 01105
Tel: (413) 746-6565

WRDM-TV, CHANNEL 13
Channel 13 Television, Inc.
886 Maple Ave.
Hartford, CT 06114
Lucio Ruzzier, Gen. Mgr.
(860) 956-1303 Fax: (860) 956-6834
Email: channel13@home.com

FLORIDA

WEYS CHANNEL 22
TV-Hola
527 Southard St.
Key West, FL 33040
Jaques Combeau, Gen. Mgr
(305) 296-4969 Fax: (305) 296-1669
Programming: 9 AM - 5 PM in Spanish

WLTV CHANNEL 23
Univision Television Group
9405 NW 41st St.
Miami, FL 33178-2301
Thomas Johansen, Gen. Mgr.
(305) 471-3900 Fax: (305) 471-3959
Email: tjohansen@univision.net

WRMD, CHANNEL 57
ZGS Communications, Inc.
2700 W. Martin Luther King Blvd., #400
Tampa , FL 33607
Laura Santos, Gen. Mgr
(813) 879-5757 Fax: (813) 877-4466
Email: tampa57@aol.com

WSCV-TV, CHANNEL 51
Telemundo Group, Inc.
2340 W 8th Ave.
Hialeah, FL 33010
Luis Fernandez-Rocha, Gen. Mgr.
(305) 887-5151 Fax: (305) 889-7700

WTMO, CHANNEL 40
ZGS Communications, Inc.
1650 Sand Lake Rd. #340
Orlando, FL 32809
Laura Santos, Gen. Mgr.
(407) 888-2288 Fax: (407) 888-3486

WVEA CHANNEL 61
Entravision Communications Corp.
2942 West Columbus Dr. #204
Tampa, FL 33607
Lilly Gonzalez, Gen. Mgr.
(813) 879-8861 Fax: (813) 873-7272
Web: www.entravision.com

WVEN-TV CHANNEL 63
Entravision Communications Corp.
5135 Adanson St. #300
Orlando, FL 32804
May Nohra, Gen. Mgr.
(407) 647-0063 Fax: (407) 647-7363
Web: www.entravision.com

WWTU CHANNEL 8
Hispanics Keys Broadcasting
16502 NW 52nd Ave.
Miami, FL 33014

John Baile, Gen. Mgr.
(305) 621-3688 Fax: (305) 621-5181

GEORGIA

CNN EN ESPAÑOL
P.O. Box 155366
Atlanta, GA 30348
Cristina Ruiz
(404) 827-2594 Fax: (404) 878-0030

W67CI-TV, CHANNEL 67
W67CI, Inc.
5901 Goshen Springs Road, #D
Norcross, GA 30071
James Sims, Gen. Mgr.
(770) 447-8888 Fax: (770) 447-1919
Email: sales_bcz@inetnow.net

ILLINOIS

WFBT CHANNEL 46
Weigel Broadcasting
26 N. Halsted St.
Chicago, IL 60661
Peter Zamaya, Gen. Mgr.
(312) 705-2623 Fax: (312) 705-2620

WGBO CHANNEL 66
Univision Television Group
541 North Fairbanks Ct. #1100
Chicago, IL 60611
Bert Medina, Gen. Mgr.
(312) 670-1000 Fax: (312) 494-6487

WSNS-TV, CHANNEL 44
Telemundo Group, Inc.
430 West Grant Place
Chicago, IL 60614
David Cordova, Gen. Mgr.
(773) 929-1200 Fax: (773) 929-4116
Email: dxcordov@telemundo.com

MARYLAND

WMDO-TV CHANNEL 30
Entravision Communications Corp.
962 Wayne Ave. #900
Silver Spring, MD 20910
Rudy Gernica, Gen. Mgr.
(301) 589-0030 Fax: (301) 495-9556

MASSACHUSETTS

WCEA CHANNEL 19
Cuenca Vision
911 Massachusetts Ave.
Boston, MA 02118
Peter N. Cuenca, Gen. Mgr.
(617) 427-6212 Fax: (617) 427-6227
Programming: Sur Affiliate Station; Full-time Spanish station.

WTMU CHANNEL 32
ZGS Communications, Inc.
17 Main St. #203
Watertown, MA 02472
Patricia Domeniconi, Gen. Mgr.
(617) 923-7004 Fax: (617) 923-7005

WUNI-TV CHANNEL 27
Entravision Communications Corp.
33 4th Ave.
Needham, MA 02494
Gary Marder, Gen. Mgr.
(781) 433-2727 Fax: (781) 433-2750
Web: www.wunitv.com

WWDP CHANNEL 46
ZGS Communications, Inc.
17 Main St. #203
Watertown, MA 02472
Patricia Domeniconi, Gen. Mgr.
(617) 923-7004 Fax: (617) 923-7005

NEVADA

KBLR-TV, CHANNEL 39
Summit Media Ltd.
5000 W Oakey #B2
Las Vegas, NV 89146
Scott Gentry, Owner/Gen. Mgr.
(702) 258-0039 Fax: (702) 258-0556
Email: scgent@juno.com

KINC CHANNEL 15
Entravision Communications Corp.
500 Pilot Rd. #D
Las Vegas, NV 89119
Gabriel Quiroz, Gen. Mgr.
(702) 434-0015 Fax: (702) 434-0527

KUVR-TV CHANNEL 68
Pappas Telecasting
940 Matly Lane
Reno, NV 89502
Doug Davidson, Gen. Mgr.
(775) 333-2727 Fax: (775) 327-6868
Email: ddavidson@kren.com

NEW JERSEY

WXTV-TV CHANNEL 41
Univision Television Group
500 Frank W. Burr Blvd. 6th Fl.
Teaneck , NJ 07666
Christina Schwarz, Gen. Mgr.
(201) 287-4141 Fax: (201) 287-9426
Web: www.univision.com

NEW MEXICO

K52BS-TV, CHANNEL 53
Ramar Communications, Inc.
2400 Monroe St. NE
Albuquerque, NM 87110
Dan Myers, Gen. Mgr.
(505) 875-1515 Fax: (505) 889-8390
Email: dmyers@ramarcom.com
Programming: Telemundo Affiliate Station; in Santa Fe: Channel 52.

K59DB-TV, CHANNEL 59
Clear Channel Communications
6320 Zuni SE
Albuquerque, NM 87108
Alfredo Baca, Gen. Mgr.
(505) 265-8331 Fax: (505) 266-3836

KLUZ-TV CHANNEL 41
Entravision Communications Corp.
2725 F. Broadbent Pkwy., NE
Albuquerque, NM 87107

Luis F. Hernandez, Gen. Mgr.
(505) 344-5589 Fax: (505) 344-8714
Email: informe41@aol.com
Web: www.estravision.com

KTEL-TV CHANNEL 53
Ramar Communications, Inc.
2400 Monroe St., NE
Albuquerque, NM 87110
Dan Myers, Gen. Mgr.
(505) 875-1515 Fax: (505) 889-8390
Email: dmyers@ramarcom.com
Programming: Telemundo Affiliate Station; in Santa Fe: Channel 52.

NEW YORK

HITN-TV CHANNEL 75
Hispanic Information Telecommunications Network
449 Broadway, 3rd Fl.
New York, NY 10013
José Luis Rodríguez, Pres.
(212) 966-5660 Fax: (212) 966-5725
Web: www.hitn.org

R-NEWS CHANNEL 9
Time Warner Communications
71 Mt. Hope Ave.
Rochester, NY 14620
Benjamin Herrera, News Anchor
(716) 756-2424 Fax: (716) 756-1673
Programming: Sundays, R-Mundo Noticias en Español

WNET-TV CHANNEL 13
356 W. 58th St.
New York, NY 10019
William S. Baker, Gen. Mgr.
(212) 560-2000 Fax: (212) 582-3297
Programming: 1 Program in Spanish

WNJU-TV CHANNEL 47
Telemundo Group, Inc.
1775 Broadway, Third Fl.
New York, NY 10019
Ramón Pineda, Gen. Mgr.
(212) 492-5600 Fax: (212) 492-5629
Email: redaccion@noticiero47.net
Web: www.noticiero47.com
Programming: Full-time Spanish station. TV Office:
47 Industrial Ave.
Teboro, NJ 07608
Tel: (201) 288-5550

WNPC-TV/FIEBRE LATINA TV SHOW
State University of New York
SUNY New Paltz, SUB 315
New Paltz, NY 12561
Klever Delgado, Pres.
(914) 257-3098 Fax: (914) 257-3099
Email: wnpc@newpaltz.edu

WXTV-TV CHANNEL 41
Univision Television Group
605 3rd Ave., 3rd Fl.
New York, NY 10158
Christina Schwarz, Gen. Mgr.
(212) 455-5400 Fax: (212) 697-4141
Web: www.univision.com

WXXI-TV CHANNEL 21, ¿QUE PASA?
WXXI Public Broadcasting
280 State St.
Rochester, NY 14614
Norman Silverstine, Pres./CEO
(716) 325-7500 Fax: (716) 258-0330

OREGON

K52FQ-YAKIMA CHANNEL 52
Watch TV, Inc.
6107 N. Marine Dr. #6
Portland, OR 97203
Gregory Herman, Gen. Mgr.
(503) 241-2411
Email: watchtvinc@aol.com

K60FX-YAKIMA CHANNEL 60
Watch TV, Inc.
6107 N. Marine Dr. #6
Portland, OR 97203
Gregory Herman, Gen. Mgr.
(503) 241-2411
Email: watchtvinc@aol.com

PENNSYLVANIA

WWSI CHANNEL 62
Council Tree Communications
1341 N Delaware Ave.,
Penn Treaty Bldg., #408
Philadelphia, PA 19125
Terrill Weiss, Gen. Mgr.
(215) 634-8862 Fax: (215) 425-2683
Email: terrillx@bigfoot.com

PUERTO RICO

WAPA-TV-CHANNEL 4
Lyn Television
San Juan, PR 00936-2050
Joe Ramos, General Manager
(787) 792-4444 Fax: (787) 782-4420
Email: albar@coqui.net
Web: www.televicentropr.com

WCEN CHANNEL 64
Encuentro Vision
Bayamón, PR 00960-0310
Rafael Torres Padilla, President
(787) 799-6400 Fax: (787) 799-6444

WIPN CHANNEL 3
Corporación de Puerto Rico para la Difusión Pública
P.O. Box 190-909
San Juan, PR 00919-0909
Jorge Iserni, Gen. Mgr.
(787) 766-0505 Fax: (787) 753-9846
Email: n6@cprdpprstar.net

WIPR CHANNEL 6
Corporación de Puerto Rico para la Difusión Pública
P.O. Box 190-909
San Juan, PR 00919-0909
Jorge Iserni, Gen. Mgr.
(787) 766-0505 Fax: (787) 753-9846
Email: n6@cprdpprstar.net

WKAQ-TV, CHANNEL 2
Telemundo Group, Inc.
383 Roosevelt Ave.
Hato Rey, PR 00918

Luis Roldan, Gen. Mgr.
(787) 758-2222 Fax: (787) 641-2175
Web: www.telemundopr.com

WLII-TV CHANNEL 11, TELE ONCE
Raycom Media
San Juan, PR 00908-1000
Santiago Rubin, Gen. Mgr.
(787) 724-1111 Fax: (787) 721-4685

WMTJ-TV CHANNEL 40
Sistema Universitario Ana G. Mendez
San Juan, PR 00928
José F. Mendez, Jr., Vice Pres.
(787) 766-2600 Fax: (787) 250-8546
Web: www.suagm.edu

WOLE-TV CHANNEL 12
Western Broadcasting Corporation
Mayaguez, PR 00681
Luis A. Morales, Gen. Mgr.
(787) 833-1200 Fax: (787) 831-6330
Email: woletv@caribe.net

WORA-TV CHANNEL 5
Telecinco, Inc.
San Juan, PR 00908-9986
Jose Atoro, Gen. Mgr.
(787) 721-4054 Fax: (787) 724-1554
Email: woratv@att.net

WPRV CHANNEL 13
Arzobispado de San Juan
P.O. Box 1967
San Juan, PR 00902
Juan Miguel Muñiz, Gen. Mgr.
(787) 276-1300 Fax: (787) 276-1307
Programming: Spanish Broadcasting

WSTE CHANNEL 7
Siete Grande Televisión
P.O. Box 15096
San Juan, PR 00902
Wanda Costanzo, Gen. Mgr.
(787) 724-7777 Fax: (787) 725-5870
Email: wcostanzo@supersiete.com
Programming: Spanish broadcasting

WSUR-TV CHANNEL 9
Raycom Media
Lolita Tizol St. #47
Ponce, PR 00731
Modesto Delgado, Gen. Mgr.
(787) 843-0910 Fax: (787) 841-7358
Email: adiaz@raycommedia.com

RHODE ISLAND

WRIW CHANNEL 50
555 Valley St., Bldg. 51
Providence, RI 02908
Reynaldo Almonte, Gen. Mgr.
(401) 272-2558 Fax: (401) 351-0726

TEXAS

K25FW CHANNEL 25
Caballero Television Texas, LLC
3310 Keller Springs Rd. #105
Carrollton, TX 75006
Eduardo Caballero, CEO
(972) 503-6800 Fax: (972) 503-6801
Email: e_caballero@masmusicateve.com
Web: www.masmusicateve.com

K44FO CHANNEL 44
Teleamerica Spanish Network
2909 San Jacinto
Dallas, TX 75204
Enrique Gómez, Gen. Mgr.
(214) 887-1900 Fax: (214) 887-1100
Email: teleamerica44@usa.net

K51BX-TV CHANNEL 51
Entravision Communications Corp.
1220 Broadway, #500
Lubbock, TX 79401
Richard Morton, Gen. Mgr.
(806) 763-6051 Fax: (806) 744-8363

KAJA-TV, CHANNEL 68
KAJA Communications
409 South Staples St.
Corpus Christi, TX 78401
Jim Smith, Gen. Mgr.
(361) 886-6101 Fax: (361) 887-6666
Web: www.kristv.com

KBGS-TV, CHANNEL 51
Paisano Communications, LLC
2001 E Sabine, #208
Victoria, TX 77901
Jerry Benavides, Gen. Mgr.
(361) 573-9176 Fax: (361) 573-9177
Email: kbgstv51@aol.com

KBZO CHANNEL 51
Entravision Communications Corp.
1220 Broadway, #500
Lubbock, TX 79401
Richard Morton, Gen. Mgr.
(806) 763-6051 Fax: (806) 744-8363
Web: www.entravision.com

KFWD-TV, CHANNEL 52
Telemundo Group, Inc.
3000 West Story Rd., Bldg D.
Irving, TX 75038
Wayne Casa, Gen. Mgr.
(972) 255-5200 Fax: (972) 258-1855
Email: kfwdgm@swbell.net

KGBS, CHANNEL 65
Telemundo Affiliate Station
3307 Northland Drive, Suite 175
Austin, TX 78731
Jorge Sanchez, Gen. Mgr.
(512) 926-4108

KGBT-TV CHANNEL 4
Cosmos Broadcasting
9201 West Express, 83
Harlingen, TX 78552
Coby Cooper, Gen. Mgr.
(956) 421-4444 Fax: (956) 421-2318
Email: ccooper@team4news.com
Web: www.team4news.com

KGMM CHANNEL 58
Caballero Television Texas, LLC
3310 Keller Springs Rd., #105
Carrollton, TX 75006
Eduardo Caballero, CEO
(972) 503-6800 Fax: (972) 503-6801
Email: e_caballero@masmusicateve.com
Web: www.masmusicateve.com

KHMM-TV CHANNEL 16
Caballero Television Texas, LLC
3310 Keller Springs Rd. #105
Carrollton, TX 75006

Eduardo Caballero, CEO
(972) 503-6800 Fax: (972) 503-6801
Email: e_caballero@masmusicateve.com
Web: www.masmusicateve.com

KINT-TV CHANNEL 26
Entravision Communications Corp.
5426 N. Mesa St.
El Paso, TX 79912
David Candelaria, Gen. Mgr.
(915) 581-1126 Fax: (915) 585-4613
Email: dcandelaria@entravision.com
Web: www.entravision.com

KLDO-TV, CHANNEL 27
Entravision Communications Corp.
1600 Water St. #C5
Laredo, TX 78040
Terry Elena Lozano, Gen. Mgr.
(956) 727-0027 Fax: (956) 727-2673
Email: telena@entravision.com
Web: www.entravision.com

KMAZ-TV, CHANNEL 48
Lee Enterprises, Inc.
10033 Carnegie
El Paso, TX 79925
Barry Shainman, Gen. Mgr.
(915) 591-9595 Fax: (915) 591-9896
Email: kmaztv@htg.net

KMMA CHANNEL 18
Caballero Television Texas, LLC
3310 Keller Springs Rd., #105
Carrollton, TX 75006
Eduardo Caballero, CEO
(972) 503-6800 Fax: (972) 503-6801
Email: e_caballero@masmusicateve.com
Web: www.masmusicateve.com

KMMB CHANNEL 4
Caballero Television Texas, LLC
3310 Keller Springs Rd. #105
Carrollton, TX 75006
Eduardo Caballero, CEO
(972) 503-6800 Fax: (972) 503-6801
Email: e_caballero@masmusicateve.com
Web: www.masmusicateve.com

KMMD CHANNEL 3
Caballero Television Texas, LLC
3310 Keller Springs Rd., #105
Carrollton, TX 75006
Eduardo Caballero, CEO
(972) 503-6800 Fax: (972) 503-6801
Email: e_caballero@masmusicateve.com
Web: www.masmusicateve.com

KMMW CHANNEL 47
Caballero Television Texas, LLC
3310 Keller Springs Rd., #105
Carrollton, TX 75006
Eduardo Caballero, CEO
(972) 503-6800 Fax: (972) 503-6801
Email: e_caballero@masmusicateve.com
Web: www.masmusicateve.com

KMUM CHANNEL 15
Caballero Television Texas, LLC
3310 Keller Springs Rd. #105
Carrollton, TX 75006
Eduardo Caballero, CEO
(972) 503-6800 Fax: (972) 503-6801
Email: e_caballero@masmusicateve.com
Web: www.masmusicateve.com

KNVO-TV CHANNEL 48
Entravision Communications Corp.
801 N Jackson Rd.
McAllen, TX 78501
Larry Safir, Gen. Mgr.
(956) 687-4848 Fax: (956) 687-7784
Email: seatback@knvo.com

KORO-TV CHANNEL 28
Entravision Communications Corp.
102 N Mesquite St.
Corpus Christi, TX 78401
Araceli de Leon, Gen. Mgr.
(361) 883-2823 Fax: (361) 883-2931
Email: adeleon@entravision.com
Web: www.entravision.com

KQMM CHANNEL 14
Caballero Television Texas, LLC
3310 Keller Springs Rd. #105
Carrollton, TX 75006
Eduardo Caballero, CEO
(972) 503-6800 Fax: (972) 503-6801
Email: e_caballero@masmusicateve.com
Web: www.masmusicateve.com

KTLM-TV CHANNEL 40
Sunbelt Multimedia
3900 N 10th St., 7th Fl.
McAllen, TX 78501
Bill Jorn, Gen. Mgr.
(956) 686-0040 Fax: (956) 686-0770
Email: wjorn@ktlm-tv.com

KTMD-TV, CHANNEL 48
Telemundo Group, Inc.
3903 Stoney Brook Dr.
Houston, TX 77063
Roel Medina, Gen. Mgr./VP
(713) 974-4848 Fax: (713) 974-5875
Email: t48gm@ktmd.com

KTXS CHANNEL 15
Abilene Sweetwater Broarcasting
4420 N. Clack
Abilene, TX 79604
Jackie Rutledge, Gen. Mgr.
(915) 677-2281 Fax: (915) 676-9231
*Programming: Telemundo Affiliate Station
Channel 40 with cable.*

KUVN-TV CHANNEL 23
Univision Television Group
2323 Bryan St. #1900
Dallas, TX 75201
Rebecca Muñoz-Diaz, Gen. Mgr.
(214) 758-2300 Fax: (214) 758-2338

KVAW CHANNEL 16
Hispanic Television Network
2210 Loop 431
Eagle Pass, TX 78852
Ignacio Trujillo, Station Mgr.
(830) 773-3668 Fax: (830) 773-3668
Email: ignacio78852@yahoo.com

KVDA-TV, CHANNEL 60
Telemundo Group, Inc.
6234 San Pedro Ave.
San Antonio, TX 78216
Emilio Nicholas, Jr., Gen. Mgr.
(210) 340-8860 Fax: (210) 341-3962
Email: exnicholas@telemundo.com

KVMM CHANNEL 41
Caballero Television Texas, LLC
3310 Keller Springs Rd. #105

Carrollton, TX 75006
Eduardo Caballero, CEO
(972) 503-6800 Fax: (972) 503-6801
Email: e_caballero@masmusicateve.com
Web: www.masmusicateve.com

KVYE CHANNEL 7
Entravision Communications Corp.
200 S 5th St.
El Centro, TX 92243
Carlos Cisneros, Gen. Mgr.
(760) 337-8707 Fax: (760) 337-8012

KWEX-TV CHANNEL 41
Univision Television Group
411 E Durango Blvd.
San Antonio, TX 78204
Steve Giust, Gen. Mgr.
(210) 227-4141 Fax: (210) 227-0469
Email: sguist@univision.net

KXLN-TV CHANNEL 45
Univision Television Group
9440 Kirby Dr.
Houston, TX 77054
J. Adán Treviño, Gen. Mgr.
(713) 662-4545 Fax: (713) 668-9054

KXTQ-TV, CHANNEL 46
Ramar Communications, Inc.
904 East Broadway
Lubbock, TX 79403
Chuck Heinz, Gen. Mgr.
(806) 747-2555 Fax: (806) 741-1757

KZMM CHANNEL 20
Caballero Television Texas, LLC
3310 Keller Springs Rd., #105
Carrollton, TX 75006
Eduardo Caballero, CEO
(972) 503-6800 Fax: (972) 503-6801
Email: e_caballero@masmusicateve.com
Web: www.masmusicateve.com

XEMP CHANNEL 2
Cox Communications
4909 N McColl Rd.
McAllen, TX 78504
Emmett Wells, Gen. Mgr.
(956) 972-1117 Fax: (956) 972-0476
Email: emmett.wells@cox.com

XERV CHANNEL 9
Cox Communications
4909 N McColl Rd.
McAllen, TX 78504
Emmett Wells, Gen. Mgr.
(956) 972-1117 Fax: (956) 972-0476
Email: emmett.wells@cox.com

XHAB CHANNEL 7
Cox Communications
4909 N McColl Rd.
McAllen, TX 78504
Emmett Wells, Gen. Mgr.
(956) 972-1117 Fax: (956) 972-0476
Email: emmett.wells@cox.com

XHBR CHANNEL 11
Cox Communications
4909 N McColl Rd.
McAllen, TX 78504
Emmett Wells, Gen. Mgr.
(956) 972-1117 Fax: (956) 972-0476
Email: emmett.wells@cox.com

XHIJ-TV, CHANNEL 44
International Communications
5925 Cromo Dr.
El Paso, TX 79912
Sergio Cabada, Gen. Mgr.
(915) 585-6344 Fax: (915) 585-6333

XHPN CHANNEL 3
Cox Communications
4909 N McColl Rd.
McAllen, TX 78504
Emmett Wells, Gen. Mgr.
(956) 972-1117 Fax: (956) 972-0476
Email: emmett.wells@cox.com

UTAH

KEJT, CHANNEL 48
Airwaves, Inc.
2260 Harrison Blvd.
Ogden, UT 84401
John Terrill, Gen. Mgr.
(801) 393-0012 Fax: (801) 393-1105

KSVN CHANNEL 21
Azteca Broadcasting
4215 West 4000 South
Hooper, UT 84315
Alex Collantes, Gen. Mgr.
(801) 292-1799 Fax: (801) 731-4445
*Programming: Univision Affiliate Station; for Salt
Lake City: Channel 66*

KTLE, CHANNEL 51
Airwaves, Inc.
2260 Harrison Blvd.
Ogden, UT 84401
John Terrill, Gen. Mgr.
(801) 393-0012 Fax: (801) 393-1105

VIRGINIA

PAMPASVISION
Pampasvision
8370 Greensboro Dr. #1007
McLean, VA 22102
Ana Eliza

WZDC-TV, CHANNEL 64
ZGS Communications, Inc.
2000 N. 14th St. #480
Arlington, VA 22201
Wendy Thompson, Gen. Mgr.
(703) 522-6464 Fax: (703) 522-2420
Email: telemundo64@mindspring.com

WASHINGTON

KCJT, CHANNEL 17
Hispanavision
713 W. Yakima Ave
Yakima, WA 98902
Ron Bevins, Owner/Gen. Mgr.
(509) 452-8817 Fax: (509) 248-7499
*Programming: Full-time Spanish station.
(Channel 64 with Cable)*

WISCONSIN

W63CU-TV CHANNEL 63
Weigel Broadcasting
809 S. 60th St.
Milwaukee, WI 53214
Peter Zamaya, Gen. Mgr.
(414) 777-5800 Fax: (414) 777-5802

Hispanic Radio Stations (by State)
Estaciones de radio hispanas (por Estado)

ALASKA

KSKA-FM (91.1 MHZ)
Alaska Public Telecommunications, Inc.
3877 University Dr.
Anchorage, AK 99508
Bede Trantina, Programming Director
(907) 561-1161 Fax: (907) 273-9192
*Programming: Sunday-Monday: Spanish programs for
3 hours.Monday-Friday: El Noticiero news in Spanish.*

ARIZONA

KTZR-AM (1450 KHZ)
2761 Country Club Rd.
Tucson, AZ 85716
Mauro García, Gen. Mgr.
(602) 670-1450 Fax: (602) 670-1601

KEUT-AM (1030 KHZ)
1316 E. Broadway
Tucson, AZ 85719
Ruben Herrera, Gen. Mgr.
(520) 294-1030 Fax: (520) 889-8573

KNXN-AM (1470 KHZ)
680 Avenida del Sol
Sierra Vista, AZ 85635
Rufino Cantu, Jr, Pres.
(520) 459-1470 Fax: (520) 459-5418

KCKY-AM (1150 KHZ)
13968 E. Harmony
Coolidge, AZ 83228
Abel Quiñonez, Prog. Dir.
(520) 963-9290/4145
Fax: (520) 723-5961

KASA-AM (1540 KHZ)
1445 W. Baseline Rd.
Phoenix, AZ 85041
Moisés Herrera, Gen. Mgr.
(602) 276-4241 Fax: (602) 276-8119

KNOG-FM (91.1 MHZ)
150 W. 1st St.
Nogales, AZ 85621
Marcos Romero, Gen. Mgr.
(520) 287-5206 Fax: (520) 287-3606

KJAA-AM (1240 KHZ)
Broadcasting Company, Inc.
1181 Radio Tower Rd.
Globe, AZ 85501
Gene Pearsall, Gen. Mgr.
(520) 425-8185 Fax: (520) 425-6741

KXEW-AM (1600 KHZ)
Cactus Broadcasting

889 W. El Puente Ln.
Tucson, AZ 85713
Allen Herman, Gen. Mgr.
(520) 623-6429 Fax: (520) 622-2680

KOHT-FM (98.3 MHZ)
Cactus Broadcasting
889 W. El Puente Ln.
Tucson, AZ 85713
Allen Herman, Gen. Mgr.
(520) 623-6429 Fax: (520) 622-2680

KTZR-AM (1450 KHZ)
Cactus Broadcasting
889 W. El Puente Ln.
Tucson, AZ 85713
Allen Herman, Gen. Mgr.
(520) 623-6429 Fax: (520) 622-2680
Programming: Spanish programming 24 hours a day.

KPHX-AM (1480 KHZ)
Continental Broadcasting Corporation
824 E. Washington St.
Phoenix, AZ 85034
Jonathan Molina, Gen. Mgr.
(602) 257-1351 Fax: (602) 256-0741

KZLZ-FM (105.3 MHZ)
Entravision Radio Group
2959 East Grant Rd.
Tucson, AZ 85716
Soñia Tabanico, Gen. Mgr.
(520) 325-3054 Fax: (520) 325-3495

KNAI-FM (88.3 MHZ)
National Farm Workers Service
3602 West Thomas Rd. #6
Phoenix, AZ 85019
Michael Nowakowski, Gen. Mgr.
(805) 822-5571 Fax: (602) 269-3020

KDAP-AM (1450 KHZ)
Radio Cristiana
P. O. Box 820
Douglas, AZ 85608
Maria Isabel Cantu, Gen. Mgr.
(520) 364-3486 Fax: (520) 364-3483

KSUN-AM (1400 KHZ)
Radio Fiesta, Inc.
714 N. 3rd St.
Phoenix, AZ 85004
Damian Ramirez, Prog. Director
(602) 252-0030 Fax: (602) 252-4211

KRMC-FM (91.7 MHZ)
Radio Manantial
P.O. Box 2520

Douglas, AZ 85608
Warren Griffin, Gen. Mgr.
(520) 364-5392 Fax: (520) 364-5392
*Programming: Spanish Christian
music 24 hours a day.*

KRMB-FM (90.1 MHZ)
Radio Manantial
P.O. Box 2520
Douglas, AZ 85608
Warren Griffin, Gen. Mgr.
(520) 364-5392 Fax: (520) 364-5392
*Programming: Spanish Christian
music 24 hours a day.*

KQTL-AM (1210 KHZ)
Radio Única
2955 E. Broadway
Tucson, AZ 85716
Steve Cabezas, Gen. Mgr.
(520) 628-1200 Fax: (520) 326-4927
Programming: Spanish music 24 hours a day.

KAPR-AM (930 KHZ)
Unicorn Communications
3434 N. Washington Ave.
Douglas, AZ 85607
Salvadoro Ocaño, Gen. Mgr.
(520) 364-4495 Fax: (520) 364-5277

KVVA-FM (107.1 MHZ)
Z-Spanish Radio Network, Inc.
1641 E. Osborn Rd. #8
Phoenix, AZ 85016
Manny Simo, Gen. Mgr.
(602) 266-2005 Fax: (602) 279-2921

KLNZ-FM (103.5 MHZ)
Z-Spanish Radio Network, Inc.
1641 E. Osborn Rd. #8
Phoenix, AZ 85016
Manny Simo, Gen. Mgr.
(602) 266-2005 Fax: (602) 279-2921

KZNO-FM (98.3 MHZ)
Z-Spanish Radio Network, Inc.
67 E. Bafford
Nogales, AZ 85621
Irma Almada, Gen. Mgr.
(520) 761-4977 Fax: (520) 761-4957

ARKANSAS

KZRA-AM (1599 KHZ)
70 N. E. Street #100
Fayetteville, AR 72701
George Hockman, Gen. Mgr.
(870) 512-5128 Fax: (870) 521-4968

KZRA-AM (1599 KHZ)
70 N. E. Street #100
Fayetteville, AR 72701
George Hockman, Gen. Mgr.
(870) 512-5128 Fax: (870) 521-4968

CALIFORNIA

KIGS-AM (620 KHZ)
6165 Highway 198
Hanford, CA 93230
John Pereira, Owner
(559) 582-0361 Fax: (559) 582-3981
*Programming: From 8pm to 9am
Spanish Christian music, the rest of the day
Portuguese broadcasting.*

KSTN-FM (1420 MHZ)
2171 Ralph Ave.
Stockton, CA 95206
Knox LaRue
(209) 948-5786

KWRM-AM (1370 KHZ)
210 Radio Rd.
Corona, CA 91718
Steve Cruz, Gen. Mgr.
(909) 737-1370 Fax: (909) 735-9572

KXSP-AM (1590 KHZ)
6150 Olivas Park Dr.
Ventura, CA 93003
Marylin Woods, Gen. Mgr.
(805) 644-9555 Fax: (805) 644-1966

KMPG-AM (1520 KHZ)
1330 Nash Rd.
Hollister, CA 95023
Adela Martínez, President
(831) 637-7994 Fax: (831) 637-4031

KAFY-AM (970 KHZ)
230 Truxton Ave.
Bakersfield, CA 93301
Mary Helen Barro, Gen. Mgr.
(805) 324-4411 Fax: (805) 327-9459

KBBF-FM (89.1 MHZ)
P.O. Box 7189
Santa Rosa, CA 95407
María Fincher, Gen. Mgr.
(707) 545-8833 Fax: (707) 545-6244

KLFA-FM (93.3 MHZ)
548 East Alisal St.
Salinas, CA 93905
Hector Villalobos, Gen. Mgr.
(831) 757-1910 Fax: (831) 757-9582

KLNA-FM (105.5 MHZ)
1021 Old Sacramento, 2nd Floor
Dunnigan, CA 95814
José Díaz, Gen. Mgr.
(916) 443-5999

KPRZ-AM (1210 KHZ)
9255 Towne Centre Dr. #535
San Diego, CA 92121
Mark Larson, Gen. Mgr.
(800) 873-1210 Fax: (619) 535-1212

KXLM-FM (102.9 MHZ)
200 S. A St. #140
Oxnard, CA 93030
Alfredo Plascencia, Gen. Mgr.
(805) 240-2070 Fax: (805) 240-5690

KOQO-FM (101.9 MHZ)
Affinity Broadcasting
P.O. Box 9420
Fresno, CA 93792
Chris Pacheco, Gen. Mgr.
(559) 490-1019 Fax: (559) 490-5889

KFIG-AM (1430 KHZ)
352 W. Bedford, #118
Fresno, CA 93711
Antonio Rabago, Gen. Mgr.
(559) 449-0374 Fax: (559) 449-0376

KRQK-FM (100.3 MHZ)
American General Media
2325 Skyway Drive
Santa Maria, CA 93455
Rich Watson, Gen. Mgr.
(805) 922-1041 Fax: (805) 928-3069

KMRO-FM (90.3MHZ)
Association for Community Education
2310 E. Ponderosa Dr. #28
Camarillo, CA 93010
Mary Guthrie, Gen. Mgr.
(805) 482-4797 Fax: (805) 388-5202

KGZO-FM (90.9 MHZ)
Association for Community Education
2310 Ponderosa Dr. #28
Camarillo, CA 93010
Mary Guthrie, Gen. Mgr.
(661) 792-9071 Fax: (661) 388-5202

KGEN-FM (94.5 MHZ)
Azteca Broadcasting
P.O. Box 2040
Tulare, CA 93275
Margarita Hernández, Gen. Mgr.
(559) 686-1370 Fax: (559) 685-1394
Programming: Spanish music 24 hours a day.

XEBG-AM (1550 KHZ)
Cadena California, Inc.
1027 10th Ave. #C
San Diego, CA 92101
Mario Enrique Mayans, Director
(619) 696-9902 Fax: (619) 702-5570

XEMM-AM (800 KHZ)
Cadena California, Inc.
1027 10th Ave. #C
San Diego, CA 92101
Mario Enrique Mayans, Director
(619) 696-9902 Fax: (619) 702-5570

XMOR-FM (98.9 MHZ)
Cadena California, Inc.
1027 10th Ave. #C
San Diego, CA 92101

Mario Enrique Mayans, Director
(619) 696-9902 Fax: (619) 702-5570

XLTN-FM 104.5 RADIO LATINA (104.5 FM)
Califormula Broadcasting
1690 Frontage Rd.
Chula Vista, CA 91911
Gabriel Castro, Promotions Director
(619) 575-9090 Fax: (619) 423-1818

XTIM-FM 97.7 LA MEJOR (97.7 FM)
Califormula Broadcasting
1690 Frontage Rd.
Chula Vista, CA 91911
Gabriel Castro, Promotions Director
(619) 575-9090 Fax: (619) 423-1818

KLOQ-AM (1580 KHZ)
Clark Broadcasting
514 East Bellevue Rd.
Atwater, CA 95301
Kelly Leonard, Gen. Mgr.
(209) 358-9723 Fax: (209) 358-9793

KBKO-AM (1490 KHZ)
Clear Channel Communications
414 East Cota Street
Santa Barbara, CA 93101
Richard Marsh, Gen. Mgr.
(805) 965-1490 Fax: (805) 879-8434

KDIF-AM (1440 KHZ)
Clear Channel Communications
1465 A. Spruce St. #A
Riverside, CA 92507
Gilberto Esquivel, Gen. Mgr.
(909) 784-4210 Fax: (909) 784-4213
Programming: Spanish music and news 24 hours a day.

KSPE-FM (94.5 MHZ)
Clear Channel Communications
414 East Cota Street
Santa Barbara, CA 93103
Richard Marsh, Gen. Mgr.
(805) 965-1490 Fax: (805) 879-8434

KNSE-AM (1510 KHZ)
Coronado Four-County Broadcasting, Inc.
8729 E. 9th St.
Rancho Cucamonga, CA 91730
Malú Hernández, Gen. Mgr.
(909) 981-8893 Fax: (909) 981-2032

XEXX-AM (1420 KHZ)
Doble XX
353 Third Ave. #201
Chula Vista, CA 91910
Wally Reid, Director
(619) 427-1420 Fax: (619) 427-6027

KTAP-AM (1600 KHZ)
Emerald Wave Media
104 W. Chapel
Santa María, CA 93458
Augusto Ruiz, Gen. Mgr.
(805) 928-4334 Fax: (805) 349-2765

KIDI-FM (105.5 MHZ)
Emerald Wave Media
104 W. Chapel
Santa Maria, CA 93454
Augusto Ruiz, Gen. Mgr.
(805) 928-4334 Fax: (805) 349-2765

KMXX-FM (99.3 MHZ)
Entravision Communications

626 Main St.
El Centro, CA 92243
Carlos Cisneros, Gen. Mgr.
(760) 352-2277 Fax: (760) 352-1430

KSXX-FM (99.9 MHZ)
Entravision Communications
5301 Madison Ave. #401
Sacramento, CA 95841
Larry Lemanski, Gen. Mgr.
(916) 418-1555 Fax: (916) 418-1565

KCAL-AM (1410 KHZ)
Entravision Communications
1950 S. Sunwest Lane #302
San Bernardino, CA 92408
Paul Petrilli, Gen. Mgr.
(909) 825-5020 Fax: (909) 884-5844
Programming: Spanish music / news 24 hours a day.

KSES-AM (700 KHZ)
Entravision Communications
339 Pajaro Street #E
Salinas, CA 93901
Kim Bryant, Gen. Mgr.
(831) 771-9950 Fax: (831) 771-1052

KRCX-FM (99.9 MHZ)
Entravision Communications
5301 Madison Ave. #401
Gold River, CA 95670
Larry Lemanski, Gen. Mgr.
(916) 858-1090 Fax: (916) 418-1565

KSZZ-AM (590 KHZ)
Entravision Communications
1950 S. Sunwest Lane #302
San Bernardino, CA 92408
Paul Petrilli, Gen. Mgr.
(909) 825-5020 Fax: (909) 884-5844

KRRE-FM (104.3 MHZ)
Entravision Communications
5301 Madison Ave. #401
Sacramento, CA 95841
Larry Lemanski, Gen. Mgr.
(916) 418-1555 Fax: (916) 418-1565

KCVR-AM (1570 KHZ)
Entravision Communications, Corp.
1620 N. Carpenter Rd., D-41
Modesto, CA 95351
Lisa Sunday, Gen. Mgr.
(209) 521-5562 Fax: (209) 529-1528

KZMS-FM (97.1 MHZ)
Entravision Communications, Corp.
1620 N. Carpenter Rd., D-41
Modesto, CA 95351
Lisa Sunday, Gen. Mgr.
(209) 521-5562 Fax: (209) 529-1528
Programming: Spanish music / news 24 hours a day.

KLOC-AM (920 KHZ)
Entravision Communications, Corp.
1620 N. Carpenter Rd., D-41
Modesto, CA 95351
Lisa Sunday, Gen. Mgr.
(209) 521-5562 Fax: (209) 529-1528

KMIX-FM (100.9 MHZ)
Entravision Communications, Corp.
1620 N. Carpenter Rd., D-41
Modesto, CA 95351
Lisa Sunday, Gen. Mgr.
(209) 521-5562 Fax: (209) 529-1528
Programming: Spanish music / news 24 hours a day.

KSSE-FM (97.5 MHZ)
Entravision Inc.
3450 Wilshire Blvd. #820
Los Angeles, CA 90010
David Haymore, Gen. Mgr.
(213) 251-1011 Fax: (213) 251-1033

KACD-FM (103.1 MHZ)
Entravision Inc.
3450 Wilshire Blvd. #820
Los Angeles, CA 90010
David Haymore, Gen. Mgr.
(213) 251-1011 Fax: (213) 251-1033

KBCD-FM (103.1 MHZ)
Entravision Inc.
3450 Wilshire Blvd. #820
Los Angeles, CA 90010
David Haymore, Gen. Mgr.
(213) 251-1011 Fax: (213) 251-1033

KBRG-FM (100.3 MHZ)
Excel Communications, Inc.
Radio Romantica
135 Main Street, 16th Fl., Suite 1650
San Francisco, CA 94105
Mike Murphy, Gen. Mgr.
(415) 362-1170 Fax: (415) 675-7126
Programming: Spanish music / news 24 hours a day.

KLOK-AM (1170 KHZ)
Excel Communications, Inc.
Radio Tricolor
135 Main St. 16th Floor
San Francisco, CA 94105
Mike Murphy, Gen. Mgr.
(415) 362-1170 Fax: (415) 675-7126
Programming: Spanish music /news 24 hours a day.

KOJJ-FM (100.5 MHZ)
El Fantastico
165 N. D. St. #3
Porterville, CA 93257
Jose Aguilar, Gen. Mgr.
(209) 782-1005 Fax: (209) 782-8497

KMXN-AM (1150 KHZ)
First Down Promotions, Inc.
750 Mendocino Ave. #6
Santa Rosa, CA 95401
John Paye, Gen. Mgr.
(707) 544-0147 Fax: (707) 524-3753

KESQ-AM (1400 KHZ)
Gulf Broadcasting
42650 Melani Place
Palm Desert, CA 92211
Martin Serna, Gen. Mgr.
(760) 568-6830 Fax: (760) 568-3984

KUNA-FM (96.7 MHZ)
Gulf Broadcasting
42650 Melani Place
Palm Desert, CA 92211
Martin Serna, Gen. Mgr.
(760) 568-6830 Fax: (760) 568-3984

KQVO-FM (97.7 MHZ)
Hanfson Broadcasting Co. of California
P.O. Box 232
Calexico, CA 92232
Douglas Hanfson, Gen. Mgr.
(619) 357-5055 Fax: (760) 357-4168

KUTY-AM (1470 KHZ)
High Desert Broadcasting
570 E. Ave., Q-9

Palmdale, CA 93550
Daniel Perez, Prog. Dir.
(661) 947-3107 Fax: (661) 272-5688

KTNQ-AM (1020 KHZ)
Hispanic Broadcasting Corp.
1645 N. Vine St. #200
Los Angeles, CA 90028
Gary Stone, Gen. Mgr.
(323) 465-3171 Fax: (323) 461-9973

KLVE-AM (1020 KHZ)
Hispanic Broadcasting Corp.
1645 N. Vine St. #200
Hollywood, CA 90028
Gary Stone, Gen. Mgr.
(323) 465-3171 Fax: (323) 461-9973

KFSA-FM (101.9 KHZ)
Hispanic Broadcasting Corp.
1645 N. Vine St. #200
Hollywood, CA 90028
Gary Stone, Gen. Mgr.
(323) 465-3171 Fax: (323) 461-9973

KRCD-FM (98.3 KHZ)
Hispanic Broadcasting Corp.
1645 N. Vine St. #200
Hollywood, CA 90028
Gary Stone, Gen. Mgr.
(323) 465-3171 Fax: (323) 461-9973

KIQS-AM (1560 KHZ)
HUTH Broadcasting
118 W. Sycamore
Willows, CA 95988
Cal Hunter, Gen. Mgr.
(530) 934-4654 Fax: (530) 934-4656

XHTY-FM (99.7 MHZ)
La Invasora
5030 Camino de la Siesta #103
San Diego, CA 92108
Luis Carlos Astiazaran, Gen. Mgr.
(619) 497-0600 Fax: (619) 497-1019
Programming: Spanish groups 24 hours a day.

KJOP-AM (1240 KHZ)
John H. Pembroke
15279 Hanford Armona Rd., P.O. Box 327
Lemoore, CA 93245
Bob Jones, Gen. Mgr.
(559) 584-5242 Fax: (559) 584-0310

KURS-AM RADIO UNICA (1040 KHZ)
K-1040
296 H St. #300
Chula Vista, CA 91910
Victoria Urtasun, President
(619) 425-2132 Fax: (619) 425-2554
Programming: Spanish news 24 hours a day.

XERCN-AM (1470 KHZ)
La Kaliente
5030 Camino de la Siesta #103
San Diego, CA 92108
Luis Carlos Astiazaran, Gen. Mgr
(619) 497-0600 Fax: (619) 497-1019
Programming: Tropical music 24 hours a day.

KHOT-AM (1250 KHZ)
KZFO Radio La Bonita
4928 E. Clinton Sujte 92.1
Fresno, CA 93727
Dora Del Toro, Gen. Mgr.
(559) 455-0180 Fax: (559) 455-0188

KZFO-FM (92.1 MHZ)
KZFO Radio La Zeta

4928 E. Clinton, Suite 92.1
Fresno, CA 93727
Dora Del Toro, Gen. Mgr.
(559) 455-0180 Fax: (559) 455-0188

KXRS-FM (105.7 MHZ)
Lazer Broadcasting Corp.
3600 Lime St. #126
Riverside, CA 92501
Pedro Gutiérrez, Gen. Mgr.
(909) 925-9000 Fax: (909) 275-5316

KOXR-AM (910 KHZ)
Lazer Corporation
418 W. 3rd St.
Oxnard, CA 93030
Miguel Marquez, Gen. Mgr.
(805) 487-0444 Fax: (805) 487-2117

KKHJ-AM (930 KHZ)
Liberman Broadcasting, Inc.
La Ranchera
5724 Hollywood Blvd.
Hollywood, CA 90028
Leonard Liberman, Gen. Mgr.
(323) 461-9300 Fax: (323) 461-9946

KWIZ-FM (96.7 MHZ)
Liberman Broadcasting
3101 W. 5th St.
Santa Ana, CA 92703
Winnie Coombs, Gen. Mgr.
(714) 554-5000 Fax: (714) 554-9362

KWKW-AM (1330 KHZ)
Lotus Communications
6290 Sunset Blvd., Floor 16th
Hollywood, CA 90028
Jim Kalmenson, Gen. Mgr.
(323) 466-8111 Fax: (323) 465-6210

KLOB-FM (94.7 MHZ)
Marvin Gardens Broadcasting
41601 Corporate Way
Palm Desert, CA 92260
Julio Lucero, Gen. Mgr.
(760) 345-9407

KJAZ-FM (107.7 MHZ)
Merced Radio Partners
1360 W. 18th St.
Merced, CA 95340
Ed Hoyt, Gen. Mgr.
(209) 723-2191 Fax: (209) 383-2950

KIBG-FM (106.3 MHZ)
Merced Radio Partners
1360 W. 18th St.
Merced, CA 95344
Edd Hoyt, Gen. Mgr.
(209) 723-2191 Fax: (209) 383-2950

KRRS-AM (1460 KHZ)
Moon Broadcasting
1410 Neotomas Ave. #104
Santa Rosa, CA 95405
Abel de Luna, Gen. Mgr.
(707) 545-1460 Fax: (707) 545-0112

KLVN-FM (106.5 MHZ)
La Nueva
600 W. Broadway #2150
San Diego, CA 92101
Peter Moore, General Manager
(619) 235-0600 Fax: (619) 744-4300
Programming: Mexican music

KIQI-AM (1010 KHZ)
Oro Spanish Broadcasting Company
2601 Mission St.
San Francisco, CA 94110
Carolina Nuñez, Network News Producer
(415) 695-8164 Fax: (415) 695-1023

XEMO-FM (860 KHZ)
La Poderosa
5030 Camino de la Siesta #103
San Diego, CA 92108
Luis Carlos Astiazaran, Gen. Mgr.
(619) 497-0600 Fax: (619) 497-1019
Programming: Mexican traditional music

XHAMR-FM (94.5 MHZ)
Radio Amor
5030 Camino de la Siesta #103
San Diego, CA 92108
Luis Carlos Astiazaran, Gen. Mgr.
(619) 497-0600 Fax: (619) 497-1019
Programming: Romantic music

KMPO-FM (88.7 MHZ)
Radio Bilingüe, Inc.
5005 E. Belmont Ave.
Fresno, CA 93727
Delia Saldivar, Gen. Mgr.
(559) 486-5174 Fax: (559) 455-5778

KHDC-FM (91.9 MHZ)
Radio Bilingüe, Inc.
161 Main St.
Salinas, CA 93901
Delia Saldivar, Gen. Mgr.
(831) 757-8039 Fax: (831) 757-9854

KTQX-FM (90.1 MHZ)
Radio Bilingüe, Inc.
5005 E. Belmont Ave.
Fresno, CA 93727
Delia Saldivar, Gen. Mgr.
(559) 455-5777 Fax: (559) 455-5778

KMYX-AM (1310 KHZ)
Radio Campesina Bakersfield, Inc.
4600 Ash Rd. #313
Bakersfield, CA 93313
Anthony Chávez, Gen. Mgr.
(661) 837-0745 Fax: (661) 837-1612

KMYX-FM (103.9 MHZ)
Radio Campesina Bakersfield, Inc.
4600 Ash Rd. #313
Bakersfield, CA 93313
Anthony Chávez, Gen. Mgr.
(661) 837-0745 Fax: (661) 837-1612

KRKC-FM (102.1 MHZ)
Radio Delrey
1134 San Antonio Dr.
King City, CA 93930
Bill Gittler, Gen. Mgr.
(831) 385-5421 Fax: (831) 385-0635

KAZA-AM (1290 KHZ)
Radio KAZA
P.O. Box 1290
San Jose, CA 95108
Verónica Yañez, Gen. Mgr.
(408) 881-1290 Fax: (408) 881-1292
Programming: Spanish music between 5 a.m and midnight

KGEN-AM (1370 KHZ)
Radio Popular
P.O. Box 2040
Tulare, CA 93275

Margarita Hernández, Gen. Mgr.
(559) 686-1370 Fax: (559) 685-1394
Programming: Spanish music 24 hours a day.

KBUE-FM (105.5 MHZ)
Radio Qué Buena
5724 Hollywood Blvd.
Hollywood, CA 90028
Leonard Liberman, Gen. Mgr.
(323) 461-9300 Fax: (323) 461-9946
Programming: Spanish music 24 hours a day.

KXEX-AM (1550 KHZ)
Rak Communications
139 W. Olive Ave.
Fresno, CA 93728
Albert R. Perez, Gen. Mgr.
(559) 233-8803 Fax: (559) 233-8871

KLQV-FM (102.9 MHZ)
Romantica
600 W. Broadway #2150
San Diego, CA 92101
Peter Moore, General Manager
(619) 235-0600 Fax: (619) 744-4300
Programming: Contemporary Spanish music

KLAX-FM (97.9 MHZ)
Spanish Broadcasting System
10281 W. Pico Blvd.
Los Angeles, CA 90064
Raúl Alarcón Jr., Gen. Mgr.
(310) 203-0900 Fax: (310) 203-8989

KWAC-AM (1490 KHZ)
Spanish Radio Group
5200 Standard St.
Bakersfield, CA 93308
MIke Allen, Gen. Mgr.
(661) 327-9711 Fax: (661) 327-0797
Programming: Spanish music /news 24 hours a day.

KIWI-FM (92.1 MHZ)
Spanish Radio Group
5200 Standard St.
Bakersfield, CA 93308
Mike Allen, Gen. Mgr.
(661) 327-9711 Fax: (661) 327-0797
Programming: Spanish music /news 24 hours a day.

KCHJ-AM (1010 KHZ)
Spanish Radio Group
5200 Standard St.
Bakersfield, CA 93308
Mike Allen, Gen. Mgr.
(661) 327-9711 Fax: (661) 327-0797
Programming: Spanish programming 24 hours a day.

XHFG-FM (107.3 MHZ)
Stereo 107
5030 Camino de la Siesta #103
San Diego, CA 92108
Luis Carlos Astiazaran, Gen. Mgr.
(619) 497-0600 Fax: (619) 497-1019
Programming: Popular music in Spanish 24 hours

XHRST-FM (107.7 KHZ)
Stereo Sol
870 Wilbur Ave.
San Diego, CA 92109
Greg Reddick, Director
(619) 483-9919 Fax: (619) 483-9918

KSUV-FM (102.9 MHZ)
Tri-Caballero
3701 Pegasus Dr. #102
Bakersfield, CA 93308

Lou Vialpando, Gen. Mgr.
(661) 393-0103 Fax: (805) 393-0286

KRME-FM (97.7 MHZ)
Tri-Caballero
3701 Pegasus Dr. #102
Bakersfield, CA 93308
Lou Vialpando, Gen. Mgr.
(805) 393-0103 Fax: (805) 393-0286

XPRS-AM (1090 AM)
United Latins Corp.
6290 Sunset Blvd. #1700
Hollywood, CA 90028
Tedy Fregoso, Owner
(323) 856-5151 Fax: (323) 464-2668

KJAZ-AM (1390 KHZ)
Z-Spanish Radio Network, Corp. Office
1436 Auburn Blvd.
Sacramento, CA 95815
Homero Campos, Prog. Vice President
(916) 646-4000 Fax: (916) 646-1688
Programming: Spanish music / news 24 hours a day.

KZCO-FM (97.7 MHZ)
Z-Spanish Radio Network, Corp. Office
1436 Auburn Blvd.
Sacramento, CA 95815
Homero Campos, Prog. Vice President
(916) 646-4000 Fax: (916) 646-1688
Programming: Spanish music / news 24 hours a day.

KTGE-AM (1520 KHZ)
Z-Spanish Radio Network, Inc.
517 S. Main St. #201
Salinas, CA 93901
Jose Diaz, Gen. Mgr.
(831) 757-5911 Fax: (831) 757-8015
Programming: Spanish music 24 hours a day.

KRAY-FM (103.5 MHZ)
Z-Spanish Radio Network, Inc.
517 S. Main St. #201
Salinas, CA 93901
Jose Diaz, Gen. Mgr.
(831) 757-5911 Fax: (831) 757-8015
Programming: Spanish transmission 24 hours a day.

KSQR-AM (1240 KHZ)
Z-Spanish Radio Network, Inc.
1436 Auburn Blvd.
Sacramento, CA 95815
Homero Campos, Programming Vice President
(916) 646-4000 Fax: (916) 446-1688
Programming: Spanish music / news 24 hours a day.

KCTY-AM (980 KHZ)
Z-Spanish Radio Network, Inc.
517 S. Main St., #201
Salinas, CA 93901
Jose Diaz, Gen. Mgr.
(831) 757-5911 Fax: (831) 757-8015
Programming: Spanish transmission 24 hours a day.

KGST-AM (1600 KHZ)
Z-Spanish Radio Network, Inc.
1110 East Olive
Fresno, CA 93728
Daniel Crotty, Gen. Mgr.
(559) 292-5478 Fax: (559) 497-1125

KLXM-FM (97.9 MHZ)
Z-Spanish Radio Network, Inc.
517 S. Main St. #201
Salinas, CA 93901
Jose Diaz, Gen. Mgr.

(831) 757-5911 Fax: (831) 757-8015
Programming: Spanish programming 24 hours a day.

KLBN-FM (105.1 MHZ)
Z-Spanish Radio Network, Inc.
1110 East Olive
Fresno, CA 93728
Daniel Crotty, Gen. Mgr.
(559) 292-5478 Fax: (559) 497-1125

KZSL-FM (93.9 MHZ)
Z-Spanish Radio Network, Inc.
517 S. Main St. #201
Salinas, CA 93901
Jose Diaz, Gen. Mgr.
(831) 757-5911
Programming: Spanish programming 24 hours a day

KMMM-FM (107.1 MHZ)
Z-Spanish Radio Network, Inc.
1110 East Olive
Fresno, CA 93728
Daniel Crotty, Gen. Mgr.
(559) 292-5478 Fax: (559) 497-1125

KCVR-AM (1570 KHZ)
Z-Spanish Radio Network, Inc.
La Bonita KCVR Stockton Office
6820 Pacific Ave. #3A
Stockton, CA 95207
Lisa Sunday, Gen. Mgr.
(209) 474-0154 Fax: (209) 474-0316

KLOC-AM (920 KHZ)
Z-Spanish Radio Network, Inc.
La Bonita KLOC Stockton Office
6820 Pacific Ave. #3A
Stockton, CA 95207
Lisa Sunday, Gen. Mgr.
(209) 474-0154 Fax: (209) 474-0316

KTDO-FM (98.9 MHZ)
Z-Spanish Radio Network, Inc.
La Bonita KTDO Stockton Office
6820 Pacific Ave. #3A
Stockton, CA 95207
Lisa Sunday, Gen. Mgr.
(209) 474-0154 Fax: (209) 474-0316
Programming: Music/NewsSpanish 24 hours a day.

KZMS-FM (97.1 MHZ)
Z-Spanish Radio Network, Inc.
La Z Stockton Office
6820 Pacific Ave. #3A
Stockton, CA 95207
Lisa Sunday, Gen. Mgr.
(209) 474-0154 Fax: (209) 474-0316
Programming: Spanish music / news 24 hours a day.

COLORADO

KRMX-AM (690 KHZ)
2829 Lowell Ave.
Pueblo, CO 81003
Dan Ramos, Gen. Mgr.
(719) 545-2883 Fax: (719) 545-2931

KRRU-AM (1480 KHZ)
4211 N. Elizabeth St.
Pueblo, CO 81008
Walter Zegaloff, Gen. Mgr.
(719) 542-4277 Fax: (719) 542-4278

KBZZ-AM (1440 KHZ)
P.O. Box 485
La Junta, CO 81050
Raúl Coates, Gen. Mgr.
(719) 384-5456 Fax: (719) 384-5450

KFTM-AM (1400 KHZ)
Arnold Broadcasting
P.O. Box 430
Ft. Morgan, CO 80701
John Waters, Gen. Mgr.
(970) 867-5674 Fax: (970) 542-1023

KGRE-AM (1450 KHZ)
1020 9th St., #201
Greeley, CO 80631
Ricardo Salazar, Gen. Mgr.
(970) 356-1450 Fax: (970) 356-8522

KDTA-AM (1400 KHZ)
Blink Communications
461 Palmer St.
Delta, CO 81416
Carolin Chairez, Host
(970) 874-4411 Fax: (970) 874-4412

KGNU-FM (88.5 MHZ)
Boulder Community Broadcasting
Association, Inc.
P.O. Box 885
Boulder, CO 80306-0885
Sam Fuqua, Public Affairs Dir.
(303) 449-4885

KBNO-AM (1220 KHZ)
Colorado Communications Corporation
2626 32nd Ave.
Denver, CO 80211
Zee Ferufino, Gen. Mgr.
(303) 458-1419 Fax: (303) 433-6420

KLMR-AM (920 KHZ)
Commonwealth Communications
P.O. Box 890
Lamar, CO 81052
Ubaldo Reyes, Host
(719) 336-2206 Fax: (719) 336-7973

KRZA-FM (88.7 MHZ)
Equal Representation of Media
Advocacy Corporation
528 9th. St.
Alamosa, CO 81101
E.G. Sánchez, Program Director
(719) 589-9057 Fax: (719) 589-9258·
Programming: News, jazz, classical; three hours Latin
American /14 hours Spanish programming weekly.

KMXA-AM (1090 KHZ)
Excl Communications Inc.
5660 Greenwood Plaza Blvd. #400
Englewood, CO 80110
Mike Murphy, Gen. Mgr.
(303) 721-9210 Fax: (303) 721-1435

KJMN-FM (92.1 MHZ)
Excl Communications Inc.
5660 Greenwood Plaza Blvd. #400
Englewood, CO 80110
Mike Murphy, Gen. Mgr.
(303) 721-9210 Fax: (303) 721-1435

KJME-AM (1390 KHZ)
JO-MOR Communications, Inc.
828 Santa Fe Dr.
Denver, CO 80204
Christina Roberts, Gen. Mgr.
(303) 623-1390 Fax: (303) 595-0131

KDJ PUEBLO
KMAS-Telemundo
4211 N. Elizabeth
Pueblo, CO 81008
(719) 543-2424 Fax: (719) 685-9711

K49CJ COLORADO SPRINGS KMAS-TELEMUNDO
732 1/2 Main St.
Manitou Springs, CO 80289
(719) 685-4130

KNKN-FM (107.1 MHZ)
Metropolitan City, Inc.
30 North Electronic Dr.
Pueblo West, CO 81007
Lupe Brown, General Manager
(719) 547-0411 Fax: (719) 547-9301

KPOF-AM (910 KHZ)
Pillar of Fire Group/Alma Temple
3455 W. 83rd Ave.
Westminster, CO 80031
Barry Blue, Prog. Dir.
(303) 428-0910 Fax: (303) 429-0910

KCUV-AM (1150 KHZ)
Radio Unica
1888 Cherman St. #200
Denver, CO 80203
Carlos Villalobos, Gen. Mgr.
(303) 861-1156 Fax: (303) 861-1158

KSLV-AM (1240 KHZ)
San Luis Valley Broadcasting, Inc.
109 Adams St., P.O. Box 631
Monte Vista, CO 81144
Jerry Medina, Spanish Music Dir.
(719) 852-3581 Fax: (719) 852-3583

KVVS-AM (1170 KHZ)
Sanchez Velasco Broadcasting Corp.
1200 Carousel Dr. #124K
Windsor, CO 80550
Verónica Sánchez Velásco, Gen. Mgr.
(970) 686-7709 Fax: (970) 686-7700

CONNECTICUT

WFNW-AM (1380 KHZ)
175 Church St.
Naugatuck, CT 06770
Candiro Cirello, Gen. Mgr.
(203) 723-0678 Fax: (203) 723-7565

WDJZ-AM (1530 KHZ)
175 Church St.
Naugatuck, CT 06770
Candiro Cirello, Gen. Mgr.
(203) 723-0678 Fax: (203) 723-7565
Programming: Spanish information program, 5 hours
of Portuguese programming, very little music.

WLAT-AM (1230 KHZ)
330 Main St.
Hartford, CT 06106
Nonar Viccarrondo, Gen. Mgr.
(860) 524-0001 Fax: (860) 548-1922

WRYM-AM-LA GIGANTE DE CONNECTICUT (840 KHZ)
Hartford County Broadcasting
1056 Willard Ave.
Newington, CT 06111
Barry Kursman, Gen. Mgr.
(860) 666-5646 Fax: (860) 666-5647

WPRX-AM-LA PUERTORIQUEÑISIMA (1120 KHZ)
Nievesquez Corporation
81 West MainSt. #G, 2nd Floor
New Britain, CT 06050
Oscar Nieves, President
(860) 826-4996 Fax: (860) 826-4999

WCUM-AM (1450 KHZ)
Radio Cumbre Broadcasting
1862 State St. Ext.
Bridgeport, CT 06605
Pablo De Jesús Colón, Gen. Mgr.
(203) 335-1450 Fax: (203) 331-9378
Programming:Spanish tropical music 24 hours a day.

DELAWARE

WYUS-AM-LA EXITOSA (930 KHZ)
Del Marva Broadcasting Co.
1666 Blairs Pond Rd.
Milford, DE 19963
Rafael Dosman, Prog. Dir.
(302) 422-2428Fax: (302) 422-3069

DISTRICT OF COLUMBIA

The Hispanic Radió Network, Inc.
La Red Hispana
740 National Press Bldg.
Washington, DC 20045
Barrett L. Alley, President
(202) 637-8800 Fax: (202) 637-8801
UPI Spanish Radio Net
1400 I St. NW, 9th Fl.
Washington, DC 20005
Armando Turll, Prog. Dir.
(202) 898-8148

VOA (INTERNATIONAL)
Voice of America
330 Independence Ave., SW
Washington, DC 20237
Sanford Ungar, Dir.
(202) 619-2538 Fax: (202) 619-0085

FLORIDA

WQBA-AM (1140 KHZ)
2828 Coral Way #102
Miami, FL 33145
Claudia Puig, Gen.,Mgr.
(305) 445-4020 Fax: (305) 441-2454

WQBN-AM (1300 KHZ)
5203 North Armenia
Tampa, FL 33603
Mark Vila, Gen. Mgr.
(813) 871-1333 Fax: (813) 876-1333

WLCC-AM (760 KHZ)
1915 N. Dale Mabry Hwy., #200
Tampa, FL 33607
Joshua Mednick, Gen. Mgr.
(813) 871-1819 Fax: (813) 871-1155

WAFC-AM (590 KHZ)
530 East Alverdez Ave.
Clewiston, FL 33440
Robert Castellanos, Gen. Mgr.
(863) 983-6106 Fax: (863) 983-6109

WRTO-FM (98.3 MHZ)
800 Douglas Annex Bldg.
Coral Gables, FL 33134
Claudia Puig, Gen. Mgr.
(305) 447-1140 Fax: (305) 442-7571

WUNA-AM (1480 KHZ)
749 S. Bluford Ave.
Ocoll, FL 34761
Juan Nieves, Gen. Mgr.
(407) 656-9823 Fax: (407) 656-2092

WTMY-AM (1280 KHZ)
2101 Hernek Place

Sarasota, FL 34235
Michael Craft, Gen. Mgr.
(941) 954-1280 Fax: (941) 955-9062

WRMA-FM (93.7 KHZ)
1001 Ponce De Leon
Coral Gables, FL 33134
Mari Elena Yanza, Gen. Mgr.
(305) 444-9292 Fax: (305) 461-4466

WSIR-AM (1490 KHZ)
665 Lake Howard Dr. SW
Winter Haven, FL 33880
Joe Fisher, Gen. Mgr.
(863) 295-9411 Fax: (863) 401-9365

WRNE-AM (980 KHZ)
312 E. Nine Mile Rd. #27
Pensacota, FL 32514
Robert Hills, Gen. Mgr.
(850) 478-6000 Fax: (850) 484-8080

WWRS-AM (1380 KHZ)
1939 7th Ave. N.
Lake Worth, FL 33461
Max Hopkins, Gen. Mgr.
(561) 585-5533 Fax: (561) 585-0131

WLQY-AM (1320 KHZ)
11645 Biscayne Blvd., Suite 102B
Miami, FL 33181
Richard Santos, Gen. Mgr.
(305) 891-1729 Fax: (305) 891-1583

WKAT-AM (1360 KHZ)
13499 Biscayne Blvd.
Miami, FL 33181
Diego Palacios, Pres.
(305) 949-9528 Fax: (305) 949-4404

WDNA-FM (88.9 MHZ)
4848 SW. 74 Ct.
Miami, FL 33155
Margarita Pelleya, Gen. Mgr.
(305) 662-8889 Fax: (305) 662-1975

WAMR-FM (107.5 MHZ)
2828 Coral Way #102
Miami, FL 33145
Claudia Puig, Gen. Mgr.
(305) 529-6631 Fax: (305) 643-1075

WAFZ-AM (1490 KHZ)
2105 W. Inmokalu Dr.
Inmokalu, FL 33934
Robbie Castellanos, Gen. Mgr.
(941) 658-1490 Fax: (941) 658-6109

WWFE-AM (670 KHZ)
Cadena Sur
330 SW 27th Ave., #207, 2nd Fl.
Miami, FL 33135
Jorge Rodríguez, Gen. Mgr.
(305) 643-1121 Fax: (305) 643-6434

WWCL-AM (1440 KHZ)
Caliente
3345 Palm Beach Blvd.
Fort Myers, FL 33916
Angel Ramos, Gen. Mgr.
(863) 337-1440 Fax: (863) 337-4681

WRMD-AM (680 MHZ)
CGS Broadcasting of Tampa
2700 W. MLK, Jr. Blvd. #400
Tampa, FL 33607
Laura Santos, Gen. Mgr.
(813) 879-5757 Fax: (813) 877-4466

WAVP-AM (1390 KHZ)
La Explosiva WAVP
801 US Hwy. 27 S. #5
Avon Park, FL 33825
Roberto Cubero, Station Mgr.
(941) 452-6162 Fax: (941) 452-1006

WPRD-AM (1440 KHZ)
La Fantastica
222 Hazard St.
Orlando, FL 32804
John Torrado, Gen. Mgr.
(407) 841-8255 Fax: (407) 841-8282

WLAZ-FM (88.7 KHZ)
Hispanic Broadcasting
4540 Curry Ford Rd.
Orlando, FL 32812
Victelio Martinez, General Manager
(407) 208-0333 Fax: (407) 208-0633

WAQI-AM (710 KHZ)
Mambi
800 Douglas Annex Bldg.
Coral Gables, FL 33134
Claudia Puig, Gen. Mgr.
(305) 447-1140 Fax: (305) 442-7571

WCRM-AM (1350 KHZ)
Manna Christian Broadcasting
3448 Canal St.
Fort Myers, FL 33916
Salvador Santana, Gen. Mgr.
(941) 334-1350 Fax: (941) 332-5183

WAUC-AM (1310 KHZ)
La Mejicana WAUC
1310 South Florida Ave.
Wauchula, FL 33873
Victor Gonzales, Gen. Mgr.
(863) 773-5008 Fax: (863) 773-2032

11Q RADIO-AM (1030 KHZ)
Nuestra Gente
P. O. Box 617221
Orlando, FL 32861
J.R. Román, Gen. Mgr.
(407) 294-9038 Fax: (407) 578-5827

WWFE-AM (670 KHZ)
La Poderosa
330 SW 27th Ave. #207
Miami, FL 33135
Jorge Rodríguez, Gen. Mgr.
(305) 541-3300 Fax: (305) 643-6434

WPSP-AM (1190 KHZ)
La Primera
5730 Corporate Way 45th St. #210
W. Palm Beach, FL 33407
Lizeth Diaz, Mgr.
(561) 687-9350 Fax: (561) 687-3398

WONQ-AM (1030 KHZ)
Q Broadcasting
1033 E. Semoran Blvd. #253
Casselberry, FL 32707
Jorge Arroyo, Gen. Mgr.
(407) 830-0802 Fax: (407) 260-6100

WRMQ-AM (1140 MHZ)
Q Broadcasting
1033 E. Semoran Blvd. #253
Casselberry, FL 32707
Jorge Arroyo, Gen. Mgr.
(407) 830-0800 Fax: (407) 260-6100

WFIV-AM
Radio Exitos
1080 Country Blvd.
Kissimmee, FL 34741
Edward Allmo, Gen. Mgr.
(407) 847-4422 Fax: (407) 932-1688

WVCG-AM (1080 KHZ)
Radio One
2828 West Flagler St.
Miami, FL 33135
José Silva, Prog. Dir.
(305) 644-0800 Fax: (305) 644-0030

WACC-AM (830 KHZ)
Radio Paz
1779 N.W. 28 QI
Miami, FL 33142
Federico Cap de Pon, Gen. Mgr.
(305) 638-9729 Fax: (305) 636-3976

WCMQ-FM (92.3 KHZ)
Radio Unica
1001 Ponce de León Blvd.
Coral Gables, FL 33134
Mari Elena Yanza, Gen. Mgr.
(305) 444-9292 Fax: (305) 461-4466

WXDJ-FM (95.7 MHZ)
Radio Unica
1001 Ponce de Leon Blvd.
Coral Gables, FL 33134
Mari Elena Yanza, Gen. Mgr.
(305) 444-9292 Fax: (305) 461-4466

WCMQ-FM (92.3 MHZ)
Radio Unica
1001 Ponce De Leon
Coral Gables, FL 33134
Mari Elena Yanza, Gen. Mgr.
(305) 444-9292 Fax: (305) 461-4466

WNMA-AM (1210 KHZ)
Radio Unica Network
8400 NW 52nd St. #101
Miami, FL 33166
Tomas Castrillon, Gen. Mgr., Producer News Department
(305) 463-5000 Fax: (305) 463-5001

WRAU-FM (106.3 MHZ)
South System Broadcasting, Inc.
1001 Ponce de Leon Blvd.
Coral Gables, FL 33134
Raul Alarcon, Sr., Gen. Mgr.
(305) 444-9292 Fax: (305) 461-4466

WOCN-AM (1450 KHZ)
Union Radio, Inc.
350 NE 71st St.
Miami, FL 33138
Richard Vega, Gen. Mgr.
(305) 749-7280 Fax: (305) 759-2276

WAMA-AM (1550 KHZ)
WAMA Radio Hits
2700 W. Martin Luther King Blvd. #400
Tampa, FL 33607
Laura Santos, Gen. Mgr.
(813) 875-0086 Fax: (813) 875-9262

WSUA-AM (1260 KHZ)
WSUA Broadcasting Corp.
2100 Coral Way
Miami, FL 33145
Madila de Restrepo, Pres.
(305) 285-1260 Fax: (305) 858-5907

GEORGIA

WKZD-AM (1330 KHZ)
1864 Thompson Bridge Rd.
Gainesville, GA 30501
David Puckett, Gen. Mgr.
(770) 531-1330

WTMQ-AM (1270 KHZ)
1804 5th St.
Columbus, GA 36869
Tony Quiñonez, Gen. Mgr.
(334) 480-8883 Fax: (334) 480-8893

CNN RADIO NOTICIAS
P.O. Box 105366
Atlanta, GA 30348
Herb Sierra, General Manager
(404) 827-1222 Fax: (404) 588-6539

WAOS-AM (1460 KHZ/1600KHZ/1130KHZ)
La Favorita, Inc.
5815 West Side Rd.
Austell, GA 30106
Samuel Zamarrón, General Manager
(770) 944-0900 Fax: (770) 944-9794

WAOS-AM (1600 KHZ)
La Favorita, Inc.
5815 West Side Rd.
Austell, GA 30168
Samuel Zamarron, Gen. Mgr.
(770) 944-6684 Fax: (770) 944-9794

WLBA-AM (1130 KHZ)
La Favorita, Inc.
5815 West Side Rd.
Austell, GA 30503
Samuel Zamarrón, Gen. Mgr.
(770) 532-6331 Fax: (770) 532-2672

WAZX-FM (101.9 MHZ)
GA-Mex Broadcasting, Inc.
2460 N. Atlanta St.
Smirna, GA 30080
Humberto Izquierdo, Gen. Mgr.
(770) 436-6171 Fax: (770) 436-0100

WAZX-AM (1550 KHZ 101.9KHZ)
Radio la que Buena
2460 N. Atlanta St.
Smirna, GA 30080
Humberto Izquierdo, Gen. Mgr.
(770) 436-6171 Fax: (770) 436-0100

WPLO-AM (610 KHZ)
Radio Mex
239 Ezzat St.
Lawrenceville, GA 30246
Filiberto Prieto, Gen. Mgr.
(770) 237-9897 Fax: (770) 237-8769

IDAHO

KFTA-AM (970 KHZ)
KFTA Radio
1841 W. Main St.
Burley, ID 83318
Benjamin Reed, Mgr.
(208) 678-2244 Fax: (208) 678-2246
Programming: 24 hours in Spanish.

KKIC-AM (950 KHZ)
624 3rd St. S, P.O. Box 1600
Nampha, ID 83653
Steve Sumner, Gen. Mgr.
(208) 322-8437

KJOY-FM (101.9 MHZ)
KJHY-FM
624 3rd St. S, P.O. Box 1600
Nampa, ID 83751
Steve Sumner, Gen. Mgr.
(208) 322-3437

KWEI-AM (1260 KHZ)
Treasure Valley Broadcasting Co.
556 Hwy., S.95, P. O. Box 791
Weiser, ID 83672
Randy Williamson, Gen. Mgr.
(208) 549-2241 Fax: (208) 549-0112

KWAL-AM (620 KHZ)
Treasure Valley Broadcasting Co.
120 First St.
Osburn, ID 83849
Paul Robinson, Gen. Mgr.
(208) 752-1141 Fax: (208) 753-5111

ILLINOIS

WONX-AM (1590 KHZ)
2100 Lee St.
Evanston, IL 60202
Ken Kovas, Gen. Mgr.
(847) 475-1590

WTAU-AM (1500 KHZ)
3576 B Grand Ave.
Gurnee, IL 60031
Robert Jeffers, Gen. Mgr.
(847) 263-1085 Fax: (847) 263-6455

WLXX-AM (1200 KHZ)
Cid Broadcasting, Inc.
625 North Michigan Ave., 3rd Floor
Chicago, IL 60611
Jim Pagliai, Gen. Mgr.
(312) 738-1200 Fax: (312) 654-0092

WLEY-FM (107.9 MHZ)
150 N. Michigan Ave., #1040
Chicago, IL 60601
Margarita Vasquez, Prog. Dir.
(312) 920-9500 Fax: (312) 920-9515

WMBI-AM (1110 MHZ)
La Esperanza
820 N. La Salle Blvd.
Chicago, IL 60610
Gerson García, Gen. Mgr.
(312) 329-4300 Fax: (312) 329-4468

WTAQ-AM (1300 KHZ)
La Mexicana
6012 Pulaski Rd.
Chicago, IL 60629
María Hernández, Gen. Mgr.
(312) 284-8184 Fax: (312) 284-8134

WOJO-FM (1946 KHZ)
Tichenor Media Systems, Inc.
625 N. Michigan Ave. 3rd Fl.
Chicago, IL 60611
Jim Pagliai, Gen. Mgr.
(312) 649-0105 Fax: (312) 664-2472

WIND-AM (560 KHZ)
Tichenor Media Systems, Inc.
625 N. Michigan Ave. 3rd Fl.
Chicago, IL 60611
Jim Pagliai, Gen. Mgr.
(312) 751-5560 Fax: (312) 664-2472

INDIANA

WXRD-FM (103.9 MGZ)
6405 Olcott Ave.
Hammond, IN 46320
Marty Wilgos, Gen. Mgr.
(219) 756-6100 Fax: (219) 844-6190

WRSW-FM (107.3 MHZ)
P.O. Box 1448
Warsaw, IN 46581
Harbey Miller, Gen. Mgr.
(219) 267-3071 Fax: (219) 267-7784

IOWA

KDMI-AM (1460 KHZ)
2350 NE. 44th Ct.
Delaware Township, IA 50317
Harold Camping, Gen. Mgr.
(515) 262-0449

KANSAS

KIBN-FM (90.7 MHZ)
105 S. Broadway St. 70 S.
Wichita, KS 67202
Antonio Delgado, Gen. Mgr.
(316) 263-8887 Fax: (316) 686-7744

LOUISIANA

WFNO-AM (830 KHZ)
La Fabulosa
111 Veterans Blvd. #1810
Metairie, LA 70005
Elsa Méndez, Gen. Mgr.
(504) 828-9366 Fax: (504) 838-7700

KGLA-AM (1540 KHZ)
Radio Tropical
3521 Industry St.
Harvey, LA 70058
Ernesto Schweikert, Gen. Mgr.
(504) 347-1540 Fax: (504) 347-8491

MARYLAND

WKDV-AM (1460 KHZ)
La Mega
8550 Sixteen St. #100
Silver Spring, MD 20910
Jim Bryan, Gen. Mgr.
(301) 588-1050

WKDL-AM (730 KHZ)
Mega Communications
8121 Georgia Avenue, 10th Floor
Silver Spring, MD 20910
Mary Elena Verdugo, Gen. Mgr.
(301) 588-6200 Fax: (301) 588-6129

WACA-AM (1540 KHZ)
Radio America
11141 Georgia Ave. #310
Wheaton, MD 20902
Alejandro Carrasco, Gen. Mgr.
(301) 942-3500 Fax: (301) 942-7798
Programming: Spanish music and news 24 hours a day.

WACA-AM (1540 KHZ)
Radio America
1141 Georgia Ave. #310
Wheaton, MD 20902
Gladys Orbe Orrala, Gen. Mgr.
(301) 942-3500

WILC-AM (900 KHZ)
WILC Corporation, Radio Borinquen
13499 Baltimore Ave. #200
Laurel, MD 20725
Danny Perez, Founder/Chairman
(301) 419-2122 Fax: (301) 419-2409
Programming: Spanish music /news 24 hours a day.

MASSACHUSETTS

WSPR-AM (1270 KHZ)
195 High St.
Holyoke, MA 01040
Melbi Sanchez, Gen. Mgr.
(413) 536-7229 Fax: (413) 534-5542
Programming: Spanish music /news 24 hours a day.

WCUW-FM (91.3 MHZ)
910 Main St.
Worcester, MA 01610
Joe Cutroni, Gen. Mgr.
(508) 753-1012
Programming: Mostly music, community radio broadcasting in different languages, Spanish broadcasting for a total of 25 hours each week.

WJIB-AM (740 KHZ)
443 Concord Ave.
Cambridge, MA 02138
Bob Bettner, Gen. Mgr.
(617) 868-7400

WRCA-AM (1330 KHZ)
Add Radio Group
552 Massachusetts Ave. #201
Cambridge, MA 02139
Stu Fank, Gen. Mgr.
(617) 492-3300 Fax: (617) 492-2800

WUNR-AM (1600 KHZ)
Champion Broadcasting
160 N. Washington St.
Boston, MA 02114
Sr. Lalli, Gen. Mgr.
(617) 367-9003 Fax: (617) 367-2265

WNNW-AM (1110 KHZ)
Costa Eagle Radio Partners Ltd.
462 Merrimack Ave.
Methuen, MA 01844
Pat Costa, Gen. Mgr.
(978) 686-996 Fax: (978) 687-1180
Programming: Spanish tropical music 24 hours a day.

WHAV-AM (1490 KHZ)
Costa Eagle Radio Partners Ltd.
462 Merrimack St.
Methuen, MA 01844
Pat Costa, Gen. Mgr.
(978) 686-9966 Fax: (978) 687-1180
Programming: News talk in Spanish 24 hours a day.

WLLH-AM (1400 KHZ)
Mega Communications
50 Warren St., P.O. Box 1400
Lowell, MA 01853
Maria Alma, Operating Mgr.
(978) 458-8486 Fax: (978) 452-0980
Programming:Spanish tropical music 24 hours a day.

WAMG-AM (1150 KHZ)
Mega Communications
529 Main St. #200
Charleston, MA 02129
Laurendo Munez, Gen. Mgr.
(617) 242-1800 Fax: (617) 241-0017
Programming: Spanish music

WBPS-AM (890KMZ)
Mega Communications
529 Main St. #200
Charleston, MA 02129
Laurendo Munez, General Manager
(617) 242-1800 Fax: (617) 241-0017

WAMG-AM (1400KHZ)
Mega Comunications
529 Main St. #200
Charleston, MA 02129
Laurendo Munez, General Manager
(617) 242-1800

WACM-AM (1490 KHZ)
Radio Popular
34 Syhan St.
W. Springfield, MA 01089
Pol Gois, Gen. Mgr.
(413) 781-5200 Fax: (413) 734-2240
Programming:Spanish tropical music 24 hours a day.

MICHIGAN

WCAR-AM (1090 KHZ)
WCAR Radio
32500 Park Lane
Garden City, MI 48135
Dino Valle, Accounts Mgr.
(734) 525-1111 Fax: (734) 525-3600
Programming: Saturday from 3-5 pm Spanish programming, Viva la Musica.

WKNX-AM (1250 KHZ)
WKNX Radio
306 W. Genesee
Frankenmuth, MI 48734
Frank Lugo, Prog. Dir.
(517) 652-3265 Fax: (517) 652-4600
Programming: 3 hours of Spanish music daily.

MINNESOTA

KYSM-FM (103.5 MHZ)
New Country
1807 Lee Blvd.
North Mankato, MN 56003
Nino Pérez, Prog. Dir.
(507) 345-4673 Fax: (507) 345-4675
Programming: Spanish program/Sunday 10-11 AM

MISSOURI

KFUO-AM (850 KHZ)
KFUO Radio
85 Founder's Lane
Clayton, MO 63105
Chuck Rather, Prog. Dir.
(314) 725-3030 Fax: (314) 725-2538
Programming:Spanish -Saturday 1:00 PM

NEVADA

KDOL-AM (1280 KHZ)
5000 W. Oakey St. #B-2
Las Vegas, NV 89102
Paul Ruttan, Gen. Mgr.
(702) 258-9007 Fax: (702) 258-9394

KUNV-FM (91.5 MHZ)
4505 Maryland Pkwy.
Las Vegas, NV 89154
Mr. Carlos Galván, Prog. Dir.
(702) 895-3976 Fax: (702) 895-4857

KLAV-AM
1810 Weldon Pl.
Las Vegas, NV 89104
Llsa Lupo, Gen. Mgr.
(702) 796-1230 Fax: (702) 796-4433

KLSQ-AM (870 KHZ)
6767 W. Tropicana Ave.
Las Vegas, NV 89103
José Valle, Gen. Mgr.
(702) 367-3322 Fax: (702) 284-6475

KQLO
884 Freeport Blvd.
Reno, NV 89431
Lariano Chávez, Gen. Mgr.
(702) 355-0788 Fax: (702) 355-1709

KXEQ-AM (1340 KHZ)
225 Linden St.
Reno, NV 89502
Juan Morales, Gen. Mgr.
(702) 827-1111 Fax: (702) 827-2082

KXTO-AM (1550 KHZ)
101 Washington St. #101
Reno, NV 89509
Stanley D. Klein, Gen. Mgr.
(702) 793-1386 Fax: (702) 793-5400

UNIVERSAL BROADCASTING INC. DBA
KQLO Radio Universal
600 N. Center St.
Reno, NV 89501
Liriano Chávez, Gen. Mgr.
(702) 322-0847 Fax: (702) 322-0927

NEW JERSEY

WMIZ-AM (1270 KHZ)
632 Maurice River Pkwy., P.O. Box 689
Vineland, NJ 08360
Carl Himple, Gen. Mgr.
(609) 692-8888 Fax: (609) 696-2568

LA Z (1270 AM)
Clear Channel Communications
632 Maurice River
Vineland, NJ 08360
Jimmy Martinez, Dir.
(856) 696-7111 Fax: (856) 696-2568
Programming: 34 Years in Spanish

WWRV-AM (1330 KHZ)
Radio Vision Christiana Mgmt.
P.O. Box 2908
Paterson, NJ 07509
David Greco, Gen. Mgr.
(973) 881-8700 Fax: (973) 881-8324

WREY-AM (1440 KHZ)
Richard & Anita Arsenault
4369 S. Lincoln Ave.
Vineland, NJ 08360
Richard Arsenault, Gen. Mgr.
(609) 327-4141 Fax: (609) 825-5232

NEW MEXICO

KATK-AM (740 KHZ)
714 N. Canyon St.
Carlsbad, NM 88220
Steve Swayze, Gen. Mgr.
(505) 885-4024 Fax: (505) 887-5691

KFUN-AM (1230 KHZ)
P. O. Box 700 Radio Heights
Las Vegas, NM 87701
Dennis Mitchell, Gen. Mgr.
(505) 425-6766 Fax: (505) 425-6767

KRDD-AM (1320 KHZ)
170 Red Bridge Rd.
Roswell, NM 88201
Juanita Nativaldy, Gen. Mgr.
(505) 623-8111 Fax: (505) 623-8111

KLMA-FM (96.5 MHZ)
108 S. Willow
Hobbs, NM 88240
Ermilo Ojeda, Gen. Mgr.
(505) 391-9650 Fax: (505) 397-9373

KLVO-FM (97.7 MHZ)
300 San Mateo Blvd. NE #1000
Albuquerque, NM 87108
Joe Mahon, Gen. Mgr.
(505) 255-5626 Fax: (505) 889-0619

KCCC-AM (930 KHZ)
930 North Canel
Carlsbad, NM 88220
Elia Esparza, Gen. Mgr.
(505) 887-5521 Fax: (505) 885-5481

KCKN-AM (1020 KHZ)
P.O. Box 670
Roswell, NM 88201
John M. Dunn, Gen. Mgr.
(505) 622-6450 Fax: (505) 622-9041

KKYC-FM (103.1 MHZ)
1000 Sycamore St.
Clovis, NM 88101
Noe Ancaldua, Gen. Mgr.
(505) 762-6200 Fax: (505) 762-8800

KFMQ-FM (106.1 MHZ)
1632 S. 2nd St.
Gallup, NM 87301
Mary Ann Armigo, Gen. Mgr.
(505) 863-9391 Fax: (505) 863-9393

KLVO-FM (97.7 MHZ)
P.O. Box 30925
Albuquerque, NM 87190
(505) 878-0980
Joe McMahon, Gen. Mgr.

KPZA-FM (103.7 MHZ)
619 N. Turner St.
Hobbs, NM 88240
William C. Nolan, Gen. Mgr.
(505) 397-4969 Fax: (505) 393-4310

KNFT-AM (950 KHZ)
P.O. Box 1320, # 5 Racetrack Rd
Silver City, NM 88062
Bill Acosta, Prog. Dir.
(505) 388-1958 Fax: (505) 388-5000

KNUM-FM (95.3 MHZ)
106 SD. Bullard St.
Silver City, NM 88061
George Mesa, Gen. Mgr.
(505) 534-8700

KSSR-AM (1340 KHZ)
2818 Will Rogers Dr.
Santa Rosa, NM 88435
Michael Esquivel, Gen. Mgr.
(505) 472-5777 Fax: (505) 472-5777

KUNM-FM (89.9 MHZ)
Onate Hall, University of New Mexico
Albuquerque, NM 87130
Richard Towne, Gen. Mgr.
(505) 277-4806 Fax: (505) 277-8004

KABQ-AM (1350 KHZ)
Albuquerque Corporation
6320 Zuni Rd. SE
Albuquerque, NM 87108
Patricia Traconif, Gen. Mgr.
(505) 265-8331 Fax: (505) 266-3836

KXKS-AM (1190 KHZ)
Continental Broadcasting Corporation
6320 Zuni Rd. SE
Albuquerque, NM 87108
Patricia Traconif, Gen. Mgr.
(505) 265-8331 Fax: (505) 266-3836

KEXT-FM (104.7 MHZ)
Continental Broadcasting Corporation
6320 Zuni Rd. SE
Albuquerque, NM 87108
Patricia Traconif, Gen. Mgr.
(505) 265-8331 Fax: (505) 266-3836

KRZY-AM (1450 KHZ)
Excl Communications Inc.
3451 Candelaria NE
Albuquerque, NM 87107
Ken Martinez, Gen. Mgr.
(505) 837-1059 Fax: (505) 830-1190

KRZY-FM (105.9 MHZ)
Excl Communications Inc.
3451 Candelaria N.E.
Albuquerque, NM 87107
Ken Martinez, Gen. Mgr.
(505) 837-1059 Fax: (505) 830-1190

KARS-AM (860 KHZ)
KARS Radio
208 N. 2nd St., P.O. Box 860
Belen, NM 87002
Ron Ortega, Prog. Dir.
(505) 864-7447 Fax: (505) 864-2719

KSWV-AM (810 KHZ)
Qué Suave
102 Kause St.
Santa Fe, NM 87501
Jorge González, Gen. Mgr.
(505) 989-7441 Fax: (505) 989-7607

KCRX-AM (1430 KHZ)
Radio Exitos
905 Ave. del Sumbre, P.O. Box 2052
Roswell, NM 88202
Rosendo Casarez, Jr., Pres.
(505) 622-1432

KDCE-AM (950 KHZ)
RLG Broadcasting, Inc.
403 W. Pueblo Dr.
Española, NM 87532
Casey Gallegos, Gen. Mgr.
(505) 753-8131 Fax: (505) 753-8685

KNMX-AM (540 KHZ)
San Miguel Broadcasting Company
304 South Grand Ave.
Las Vegas, NM 87701
Nany Lucero, Gen. Mgr.
(505) 425-3555 Fax: (505) 425-3557

KALY-AM (1240 KHZ)
Sun Media Corporation of New Mexico
P. O. Box 6492
Albuquerque, NM 87197
Gloria Septien, Gen. Mgr.
(505) 243-1952 Fax: (505) 243-5761

NEW YORK

WRTN-FM (93.5 MHZ)
1 Broadcast Forum
New Rochelle, NY 10801
Matt Dutch, Prog. Dir.
(914) 636-1460 Fax: (914) 636-2900

WNYG-AM (1440 MHZ)
404 Route 109
Babylon, NY 11704
Malon Brandt, Gen. Mgr.
(516) 587-4400 Fax: (516) 587-5400

WPAT-FM (93.1 MHZ)
26 W. 56th St.
New York, NY 10019
Carry Davis, Gen. Mgr.
(212) 541-9200 Fax: (212) 541-8535

WHCR-FM (90.3 MHZ)
138th and Convent Ave.
New York, NY 10031
Joe Brown, Gen. Mgr.
(212) 650-7481 Fax: (212) 650-7480

WADO-AM (1280 KHZ)
Heftel Broadcasting
485 Madison Ave. 3rd Fl.
New York, NY 10022
Stephanie MacNamara, Gen. Mgr.
(212) 310-6000 Fax: (212) 888-3694

WCAA-FM (105.9 KHZ)
Heftel Broadcasting
485 Madison Ave. 3rd Fl.
New York, NY 10022
Stephanie MacNamara, Gen. Mgr.
(212) 310-6000 Fax: (212) 888-3604

WJTN-AM (1240 KHZ)
James Broadcasting
P.O. Box 1139
Jamestown, NY 14702
Steve Shulman, Prog. Dir.
(716) 487-1151 Fax: (716) 664-9326
Programming: Bilingual programming, Sunday 7-8 AM

WPAT-AM (930 KHZ)
Multicultural Broadcasting, Inc.
449 Broadway, 2nd Floor
New York, NY 10013
Francisco Martínez, Gen. Mgr.
(212) 966-1059 Fax: (212) 966-9580

WNSW-AM (1430 KHZ)
Multicultural Broadcasting, Inc.
449 Broadway, 2nd Floor
New York, NY 10013
Francisco Martínez, Gen. Mgr.
(212) 966-1059 Fax: (212) 966-9580

WSKQ-FM (97.9 MHZ)
Spanish Broadcasting System
26 West 56th St.
New York City, NY 10019
Carry Davis, Gen. Mgr.
(212) 541-9200 Fax: (212) 333-6542

NORTH CAROLINA

WRRZ-AM (880 KHZ)
P.O. Box 378
Clinton, NC 28329
Dade Denton, Gen. Mgr.
(910) 592-2165 Fax: (910) 592-8556

WSSS-FM (91.9 MHZ)
1200 Murchison Rd.
Fayetteville, NC 28301
Janet Wright, Prog. Dir.
(910) 486-1383 Fax: (910) 486-1964

WETC-AM (540 KHZ)
1604 U.S. 64
Zebulon, NC 27597

Lewis Parish, Gen. Mgr.
(912) 217-9382 Fax: (912) 269-5003

WGOS-AM (1070 KHZ)
6223 Old Mendenhall Rd.
High Point, NC 27263
Lynn Ritchy, Gen. Mgr.
(336) 434-5024

WNOW-AM (1030 KHZ)
Radio Lider
P.O. Box 23509
Charlotte, NC 28227
(704) 332-8764 Fax: (704) 882-1330

OHIO

WERT-AM (1220 KHZ)
Community Broadcasting
P.O. Box 487
Van Wert, OH 45891
Bob Nelson, Gen. Mgr.
(419) 238-1220 Fax: (419) 238-2578
Programming: Spanish programming weekdays 1 hour and Sundays at noon.

WERT-FM (99.7 MHZ)
Community Broadcasting
P.O. Box 487
Van Wert, OH 45891
Bob Nelson, Gen. Mgr.
(419) 238-1220 Fax: (419) 238-2578

WEOL-AM (930 KHZ)
Elyria Lorain Broadcasting
P.O. Box 4006
Elyria, OH 44036
José W. Vásquez, Spanish Prog. Dir.
(440) 322-3761 Fax: (440) 322-1536
Programming: Spanish programming, Saturday 10-12 and Sunday 8-10 AM

WDLW-AM (1380 KHZ)
Latino Media Group
3024 W. 25th St. #149
Cleveland, OH 44113
Angel Ramos, Gen. Mgr.
(216) 344-0521 Fax: (216) 344-0511

WDLW-AM (1380 KHZ)
Victory Radio
P.O. Box 1330
Willoughby, OH 44096
Randy Michael, Gen. Mgr.
(440) 946-1330 Fax: (440) 953-0320
Programming: Spanish programming-weekdays 6-12 PM

WFOB-AM (1430 KHZ)
WFOB Radio
P.O. Box 6
Bowling Green, OH 43402
Silvester Duran, Prog. Dir.
(419) 352-4200 Fax: (419) 353-7290

OKLAHOMA

KTLV-AM (1220 KHZ)
1005 N. Main St.
New Castle, OK 73065
David Inglés, Gen. Mgr.
(405) 387-3688

KAKC-AM (1300 KHZ)
Clear Channel Radio, Inc. La Bonita
5801 East 41st St. #900
Tulsa, OK 74135-5618
Francisco J. Treviño, Representative
(918) 664-2810 Fax: (918) 665-0555

KZUE-AM (1460 KHZ)
La Tremenda
2715 S. Radio Rd.
El Reno, OK 73036
Nancy Galván, Gen. Mgr.
(405) 262-1460 Fax: (405) 262-1886

OREGON

KRTA-AM (610 KHZ)
1257 N. Riverside Ave. #10
Medford, OR 97501
Dean Flock, Gen. Mgr.
(541) 772-0322 Fax: (541) 772-4233

KMUZ-AM (1230 KHZ)
2870 NE Hogan
Gresham, OR 97030
Cshea Walker, Gen. Mgr.
(503) 227-2156 Fax: (360) 835-7593

KWIP-AM (880 KHZ)
La Campeona
1405 East Ellendalle Ave.
Dallas, OR 97338
María Teresa Porras, Prog. Dir.
(503) 623-0245 Fax: (503) 623-6733

KUIK-AM (1360 KHZ)
Dolphing Radio Inc.
P.O. Box 566
Hillsboro, OR 97123
James Derby, Prog. Dir.
(503) 640-3707 Fax: (503) 640-6108
Programming: Spanish Programming-weekends 6-12 PM Sunday 5-10 AM

KWBY-AM (940 KHZ)
Radio Fiesta
1585 N. Pacific Hwy. #G
Woodburn, OR 97071
Donald Coss, Gen. Mgr.
(503) 981-9400 Fax: (503) 981-3561

PENNSYLVANIA

WHOL-AM (1600 KHZ)
1125 Colorado St.
Allentown, PA 18103
Leigh J. Murray, Gen. Mgr.
(610) 434-4801

WURD-AM (900 KHZ)
1080 N. Delaware Ave.
Philadelphia, PA 19025
Rafael Grullón, Gen. Mgr.
(215) 238-1010 Fax: (215) 426-1550

**CLASICA WSSJ1310
(1310 AM)**
Mega Communications
1080 N. Delaware Ave. #500
Philadelphia, PA 19125
Maria del Pilar Morales
(215) 426-1310 Fax: (215) 426-1550

WTEL-AM (860 KHZ)
Radio Tropical
555 Cityline Ave. #330
Bala Cynwyd, PA 19004
Raúl Lahee, Gen. Mgr.
(610) 664-8686 Fax: (610) 667-4515

WLCH-FM (91.3 MHZ)
SACA Broadcasting
30 N. Ann St.
Lancaster, PA 17602
Enid Vazquez-Pereira, Gen. Mgr.
(717) 295-7760 Fax: (717) 295-7759

WPHE-AM (690 KHZ)
Salvation Broadcasting Company
321 W. Sedgley Ave.
Philadelphia, PA 19140
Sarrail Salva, Gen. Mgr.
(215) 291-7532 Fax: (215) 739-1337

PUERTO RICO

WCFI-FM (103.7 MHZ)
Calle Post 252 #236
Lajas, PR 00117-0931
Ramón Rodríguez, Gen. Mgr.
(787) 834-5075 Fax: (787) 831-5345

WENA-AM (1330 KHZ)
Condominio Torrez, P.O. Box 1338
Yauco, PR 00698
Nephtali Rodríguez, Gen. Mgr.
(787) 836-1330 Fax: (787) 267-1340

WHOY-AM (1210 KHZ)
P.O. Box 1148
Salinas, PR 00751
Martín Colón, Gen. Mgr.
(787) 824-2755 Fax: (787) 824-3420

WIAC-AM (740 KHZ)
P.O. Box 9023-916
San Juan, PR 00902-3916
Alan Mejía, Gen. Mgr.
(787) 798-7878 Fax: (787) 798-9613

WIPR-AM (940 KHZ)
P.O. Box 190-909
San Juan, PR 00919
Edgardo Gierbolini, Gen. Mgr.
(787) 766-0505 Fax: (787) 250-8258

WKAQ-AM (580 KHZ)
P.O. Box 364668
San Juan, PR 00936
Huberto Biaggi, Gen. Mgr.
(787) 758-5800 Fax: (787) 763-1854

WKFE-AM (1550 KHZ)
P.O. Box 324
Yauco, PR 00698
Gijo Balls, Gen. Mgr.
(787) 856-1320 Fax: (787) 856-4420

WKJB-AM (710 KHZ)
P.O. Box 1194
Mayaguez, PR 00681
Edward del Toro, Gen. Mgr.
(787) 834-6666 Fax: (787) 831-6925

WKVM-AM (810 KHZ)
415 Calle Alfredo Carbonell
San Juan, PR 00918-2866
Ana Meléndez, Gen. Mgr.
(787) 751-1380 Fax: (787) 758-9967

WPAB-AM (550 KHZ)
P.O. Box 7243
Ponce, PR 00732
Alfonso Jiménez, Gen. Mgr.
(787) 840-5550 Fax: (787) 840-3530

WOSO-AM (1030 KHZ)
P.O. Box 9023940
San Juan, PR 00902-3940
Sergio Fernández, Gen. Mgr.
(787) 724-4242 Fax: (787) 723-9676

WPPC-AM (1570 KHZ)
P.O. Box 9064, Papanos Station
Ponce, PR 00732
Carlos Morales, Gen. Mgr.
(787) 836-1570

WPRM-FM (98.5 MHZ)
P.O. Box 487
Caguas, PR 00726
Carmen Pagán, Gen. Mgr.
(787) 744-3131 Fax: (787) 743-0252

WOBS
218 El Vedado
Hato Rey, PR 00918
Angel Román, Gen. Mgr.
(787) 765-1501 Fax: (787) 765-0241

WSAN-FM (98.9 MHZ)
1058 Ponce De Leon
Santurce, PR 00907
Carlos Colón Ventura, Gen. Mgr.
(787) 860-6767 Fax: (787) 721-6767

WSKN-AM (630 KHZ)
Calle 117 Eleanor Roosevelt #1
San Juan, PR 00918
Reynaldo Royo, Gen. Mgr.
(787) 764-1090 Fax: (787) 764-3460

WUNO-AM (1320 KHZ)
P.O. Box 363222
San Juan, PR 00936
Rubén Sánchez, Gen. Mgr.
(787) 758-1300 Fax: (787) 751-2319

WUPR-AM (1530 KHZ)
P.O. Box 868
Utuado, PR 00761
José Martínez, Gen. Mgr.
(787) 894-2460 Fax: (787) 894-4955

WXEW-AM (840 KHZ)
P.O. Box 100
Yabucoa, PR 00767
Víctor Calderón, Gen. Mgr.
(787) 850-0840 Fax: (787) 850-4055

WXRF-AM (1599 KHZ)
P.O. Box 1770
Guayama, PR 00785
Miguel Díaz, Gen. Mgr.
(787) 866-1590 Fax: (787) 864-4615

WZBS-AM (1490 KHZ)
P.O. Box 7612
Ponce, PR 00732
Rosemy Burtrago, Gen. Mgr.
(787) 844-1490 Fax: (787) 840-2460

WQII-AM (1140 KHZ)
P.O. Box 193779
San Juan, PR 00919-3779
N. Gonzalez-Abreu, Gen. Mgr.
(787) 723-4848 Fax: (787) 723-4035

WABA-AM (850 KHZ)
P.O.Box 188
Aguadilla, PR 00605
Rosa Pellot, Gen. Mgr.
(787) 891-0085 Fax: (787) 882-2282

WAPA-AM (680 KHZ)
134 Romenech Ave.
Hato Rey, PR 00918-3502
Blanco Pi, Gen. Mgr.
(787) 723-1066 Fax: (787) 763-4195

WAVB-AM (1510 KHZ)
PR Hwy. 101, P.O. Box 593
Lajas, PR 00667
Aurea Vélez, Gen. Mgr.
(787) 899-1320 Fax: (787) 899-1320

WBMJ-AM (1190 KHZ)
P.O. Box 367000

San Juan, PR 00936-7000
Janet Luttrell, Gen. Mgr.
(787) 724-1190 Fax: (787) 722-5395

WIPR-FM (91.3 MHZ)
P.O. Box 190-909
San Juan, PR 00919
Edgardo Gierbeolini, Gen. Mgr.
(787) 766-0505 Fax: (787) 250-8258

WKAQ-FM (105.47 MHZ)
P.O. Box 364668
San Juan, PR 00936
Huberto Biaggi, Gen. Mgr.
(787) 758-5800 Fax: (787) 763-1854

WORO-FM (92.5 MHZ)
415 Calle Carbonell
Hato Rey, PR 00918
Ana Meléndez, Gen. Mgr.
(787) 751-1380 Fax: (787) 758-9967

WEGM-FM (92.1 MHZ)
1607 Ponce De Leon Ave. #102
San Turse, PR 00908
Cabo Rojo, Gen. Mgr.
(787) 723-9210 Fax: (787) 723-6673

WEXS-AM (610 KHZ)
P.O. Box 640
Patillas, PR 00723
Enrique García Cruz, Gen. Mgr.
(787) 839-0610 Fax: (787) 839-0960

WLEY-AM (1080 KHZ)
P.O. Box 371300
Cayey, PR 00737
J. H. Conesa, Gen. Mgr.
(787) 738-2776 Fax: (787) 738-7744

WMNT-AM (1500 KHZ)
Delta St. #1305
San Juan, PR 00920
Pedro Barbosa, Gen. Mgr.
(787) 783-8810 Fax: (787) 784-7647

WQBS-AM (870 KHZ)
P.O. Box 1748
Jurcos, PR 00681
Angel Romandez, Gen. Mgr.
(787) 756-8700 Fax: (787) 265-0241

WQQZ-FM (98.3 MHZ)
P.O. Box 980
Quebradillas, PR 00678-0980
José J. Arzuaga, Gen. Mgr.
(787) 895-2725 Fax: (787) 895-4198

WZAR-FM (101.9 MHZ)
P.O. Box 7213
Ponce, PR 00732
José Luis Quintana, Gen. Mgr.
(787) 844-9711 Fax: (787) 723-4195

WIOB-FM (97.5 MHZ)
801 Bosque St.
Mayaguez, PR 00681-1718
Felíx A. Bonnet, Vice-Pres.
(787) 834-1094 Fax: (787) 265-4090

WREO-FM (100.3 MHZ)
P.O. Box 487
Caguas, PR 00726
Carmen Pagán, Gen. Mgr.
(787) 744-3131 Fax: (787) 743-0252

WBRQ-FM (97.7 MHZ)
American National Broadcasting
P.O. Box 9297
Caguas, PR 00726-9297

Fernando Vigil, Pres.
(787) 720-7797 Fax: (787) 746-6162

WPRA-AM (990 KHZ)
American National Broadcasting
P.O. Box 1293
Mayaguez, PR 00681
Edward Toro, Gen. Mgr.
(787) 834-6666 Fax: (787) 831-6925

WIVA-FM (100.3 MHZ)
Arso Radio Corp.
P.O. Box 487
Caguas, PR 00726
Carmen Pagan, Gen. Mgr.
(787) 744-3131 Fax: (787) 743-0252

WNEL-AM (1430 KHZ)
Arso Radio Corp.
P.O. Box 487
Caguas, PR 00726
Carmen Pagán, Gen. Mgr.
(787) 744-3131 Fax: (787) 743-0252

WRIO-FM (101.1 MHZ)
Arso Radio Corp.
P.O. Box 7336
Ponce, PR 00732
Francisco Pagán, Gen. Mgr.
(787) 284-1481 Fax: (787) 744-3131

WNNV-FM (105. MHZ)
Aureo Matos Chaparro
P.O. Box 847
Mayaguez, PR 00681
Dominga Barreta, Gen. Mgr.
(787) 833-2495 Fax: (787) 833-7940

WKSA-FM (101.5 MHZ)
Bestov Broadcasting Inc of PR
P.O. Box 750
Isabela, PR 00662
David Mercado, Gen. Mgr.
(787) 872-2030 Fax: (787) 721-0733

WVJP-AM (1110 KHZ)
Borinquen Broadcasting Co.
P.O. Box 207
Caguas, PR 00726
Bertha Estévez, Gen. Mgr.
(787) 743-5789 Fax: (787) 746-6996

WVJP-FM (103.3 KHZ)
Borinquen Broadcasting Co.
P.O. Box 207
Caguas, PR 00726
Jancel Pereira, Gen. Mgr.
(787) 743-5789 Fax: (787) 746-6996

WIVV-AM (1370 KHZ)
Calvary Evangelistic Mission, Inc.
San Juan, PR 00936-7000
Janet Luttrell, General Manager
(787) 724-1190 Fax: (787) 722-5395

WCMN-AM (1280 KHZ)
Caribbean Broadcasting Corp.
P.O. Box 436
Arecibo, PR 00613
Byron Mitchell, Gen. Mgr.
(787) 878-0070 Fax: (787) 880-1112

WCMN-FM (107.3 MHZ)
Caribbean Broadcasting Corp.
P.O. Box 436
Arecibo, PR 00613
Mandy Alicea, Gen. Mgr.
(787) 878-0070 Fax: (787) 880-1112

WEUC-FM (88.9 MHZ)
Catholic Univ. Service
2250 Ave. Las Americas Suite #529
Ponce, PR 00731-6382
Juan Ricart, Gen. Mgr.
(787) 842-8046 Fax: (787) 841-1028

WEUC-AM (1420 MHZ)
Catholic Univ. Service
2250 Ave. Las Americas Suite #529
Ponce, PR 00731-6382
Juan Ricart, Gen. Mgr.
(787) 842-8046 Fax: (787) 841-1028

WEKO-AM (930 KHZ)
David Ortíz, Inc.
P.O. Box 681, Lolita Antron Bldg.
Cabo Rojo, PR 00623
María Isabel Ortiz, Gen. Mgr.
(787) 851-1236 Fax: (787) 851-7500

WCHQ-AM (1360 KHZ)
Del Pueblo Radio Corp.
P.O. Box 629
Camuy, PR 00627
Joe Cordero, Gen. Mgr.
(787) 898-1360 Fax: (787) 898-6505

WYQE-FM (92.9 KHZ)
Efrain Archilla-Roig
Apt 2-A Gripo 28, P.O. Box 9300
Naguabo, PR 00718
Efrain Archilla, Gen. Mgr.
(787) 720-5880 Fax: (787) 874-9290

WCGB-AM (1060 KHZ)
Grace Ministries International
P.O. Box 248
Juana Díaz, PR 00795
José Rodríguez, Gen. Mgr.
(787) 837-1060 Fax: (787) 260-1060

WNIK-AM (1230 KHZ)
Kelly Broadcasting System Corp.
P.O. Box 556
Arecibo, PR 00613
Raúl Santiago, Gen. Mgr.
(787) 880-2607 Fax: (787) 879-1011

WNIK-FM (106.5 MHZ)
Kelly Broadcasting System Corp.
P.O. Box 556
Arecibo, PR 00613
Raúl Santiago, Gen. Mgr.
(787) 880-2607 Fax: (787) 879-1011

WGDL-AM (1200 KHZ)
Lares Broadcasting Corp.
P.O. Box 872
Lares, PR 00669
Pedro Hernández, Gen. Mgr.
(787) 897-3889 Fax: (787) 897-7821

WMSW-AM (1120 KHZ)
Manati Radio Corp.
537 Miramar Ave.
Arecibo, PR 00612
Achi Vélez, Prog. Dir.
(787) 879-4094 Fax: (787) 817-8004

WTIL-AM (1300 KHZ)
Mayaguez Radio Corp.
P.O. Box 489
Mayaguez, PR 00681
Francisco Acosta, Gen. Mgr.
(787) 834-1290 Fax: (787) 834-9845

WMEG-FM (106.9 MHZ)
La Mega Estación
Edificio Cobian Plaza #102
Prince de León 1607
San Juan, PR 00909
Ismael Nieves, Gen. Mgr.
(787) 723-9210 Fax: (787) 723-6673

WCRP-FM (88.1 MHZ)
Min. Radial Cristo Viene Pronto
P.O. Box 344
Guayama, PR 00785-9905
Carmen Rivera, Gen. Mgr.
(787) 864-3658 Fax: (787) 864-6780

WMTI-AM (1580 KHZ)
Morovis Radio Assoc.
P.O. Box 24
Toa Alta, PR 00954
Pablo Ortega, Gen. Mgr.
(787) 730-5880 Fax: (787) 730-5860

WNOZ-AM (1340 KHZ)
NOS, Inc.
Muñoz Rivera 51 altos
Aguadilla, PR 00605
Luis Ortiz, Gen. Mgr.
(787) 268-4200 Fax: (787) 268-3660

WALO-AM (1240 KHZ)
Ochoa Broadcasting Corp.
P.O.Box 1240
Humacao, PR 00792
Efrain Archilla-Roig, Gen. Mgr.
(787) 852-1240 Fax: (787) 852-1280

WMDD-AM (1480 KHZ)
Pan Caribbean Broadcasting Corp.
P.O. Box 948
Fajardo, PR 00738
Rita Friedman, Gen. Mgr.
(787) 863-0202 Fax: (787) 863-0166

WMIA-AM (1070 KHZ)
Piralio López Stations
P.O. Box 1055
Arecibo, PR 00613
Epifanio Rodríguez, Gen. Mgr.
(787) 878-1275 Fax: (787) 880-3026

WAEL-AM (600 KHZ)
Pirallo Lopez Stations
P.O. Box 1370
Mayaguez, PR 00681
María Del Pilar Pirallo, Gen. Mgr.
(787) 832-0600 Fax: (787) 792-3140

WOYE-FM (94.1 KHZ)
Premedia Broadcasting Group
801 Bosque St., P.O. Box 1718
Mayaguez, PR 00681-1718
Felix A.Bonnet, Vice Pres.
(787) 834-1094 Fax: (787) 265-4090

WIDA-AM (1400 KHZ)
Primera Iglesia Bautista
P.O. Box 188
Carolina, PR 00986
William Lebron, Gen. Mgr.
(787) 757-1414 Fax: (787) 769-4103

WIDA-FM (90.5 MHZ)
Primera Iglesia Bautista
P.O. Box 188
Carolina, PR 00986
William Lebrón, Gen. Mgr.
(787) 757-1414 Fax: (787) 769-4103

WOIZ-AM (1130 KHZ)
Radio Antilles
P.O. Box 561130
Guayanilla, PR 00656
Luis Adán Rodríguez, Gen. Mgr.
(787) 835-3130 Fax: (787) 835-3130

WBQN-AM (1160 KHZ)
Radio Borinquen, Inc.
P.O. Box 1625
Manati, PR 00674
Luis Rivera, Gen. Mgr.
(787) 854-2450 Fax: (787) 854-3738

WORA-AM (760 KHZ)
Radio Cadena Information, Inc.
3822 Marina St.
Mayaguez, PR 00681
Joe Díaz, Gen. Mgr.
(787) 834-0488 Fax: (787) 834-0760

WIOC-FM (105.1 MHZ)
Radio Cadena Informativa, Inc.
P.O. Box 7302
Ponce, PR 00731
Lourdes Pagán, Gen. Mgr.
(787) 848-6610 Fax: (787) 841-6121

WKVN-FM (88.5 MHZ)
Radio Clamor
P.O. Box 40000
Bayamon, PR 00958
Raúl Rozado, Gen. Mgr.
(787) 784-8851 Fax: (787) 795-7026

WLUZ-AM (1600 KHZ)
Radio Luz
P.O. Box 9394
San Juan, PR 00908
Julia M. Acosta, Gen. Mgr.
(787) 785-1600 Fax: (787) 785-2094

WISA-AM (1390 KHZ)
Radio Noreste
P.O. Box 750
Isabela, PR 00662
David Mercado, Gen. Mgr.
(787) 872-2030 Fax: (787) 721-0733

WRSS-AM (1410 MHZ)
Radio Progreso
P.O. Box 1410
San Sebastian, PR 00685
Eurogio Cardona Beltrán, Gen. Mgr.
(787) 896-2121 Fax: (787) 896-5753

WLRP-AM (1460 KHZ)
Radio Raices
P.O. Box 1670
San Sebastián, PR 00685
Alfredo Pérez, Gen. Mgr.
(787) 896-1460 Fax: (787) 896-8100

WRTU-FM (89.7 MHZ)
Radio Universidad de Puerto Rico
P.O. Box 21305, University Station
San Juan, PR 00931-1305
Rafael García Machuca, Prog. Dir.
(787) 763-4699 Fax: (787) 764-1290

WTPM-FM (92.9 MHZ)
Seventh Day Adventists
P.O. Box 1629
Mayaguez, PR 00681
Julio Javier, Gen. Mgr.
(787) 831-9200 Fax: (809) 265-4044

WIAC-FM (102.5 KHZ)
Sistema 102

P.O. Box 9023-916
San Juan, PR 00902
Alan Mejia, Gen. Mgr.
(787) 798-7878 Fax: (787) 798-9613

WPRP-AM (910 khz)
Super Cadena
P.O. Box 7771
Ponce, PR 00732
Carlos Morales Crespo, Gen. Mgr.
(787) 844-0910 Fax: (787) 843-9770

WNRT-FM (96.9 mhz)
La Voz Evangélica de PR
P.O. Box 13324
Santurce, PR 00908
Rev. Moises Flores, Gen. Mgr.
(787) 758-8833 Fax: (787) 758-8833

WIBS-AM (1540 khz)
Wigberto Baez Santiago
P.O. Box 1540
Guayama, PR 00785
Wilberto Vaez Santiago, Gen. Mgr.
(787) 866-1540 Fax: (787) 866-1540

WZNT-AM (93.7 mhz)
Z93
P.O. Box 949
Guaynabo, PR 00970
Hillary Hattler, Gen. Mgr.
(787) 720-5001 Fax: (787) 720-2126

RHODE ISLAND

WRIB-AM (1220 khz)
La Inconfundible
200 Water St.
East Providence, RI 02914
John Pierce, Gen. Mgr.
(401) 434-0406 Fax: (401) 434-0409

WALE-AM (990 khz)
Radio Caribe
1185 North Main St
Providence, RI 02903
Bob Cotoya
(401) 621-9253

WRCP-AM (1290 khz)
La Voz del Continente
1110 Douglas Ave.
North Providence, RI 02904
Joseph Pesare, Gen. Mgr.
(401) 434-0406 Fax: (401) 840-2460

SOUTH DAKOTA

KKQQ-FM (102.3 khz)
111 Main Ave.
Brookings, SD 57006
Tom Couthley, Gen. Mgr.
(605) 692-9125 Fax: (605) 692-6434

TEXAS

KINE-AM-LA TEJANITA (1330 KHZ)
P.O. Box 5445
Corpus Christi, TX 78465
Humberto López, Gen. Mgr.
(361) 855-1330 Fax: (361) 387-5396

XEPZ-AM (1190 KHZ)/ XEROX-AM (800 KHZ)
2211 E. Missouri, E-237
El Paso, TX 79903
Maria E. Mareret, Gen Sales Mgr
(915) 542-2969 Fax: (915) 542-2958

KRVA-AM (1600 KHZ)
5307 E. Mockingbird, #500
Dallas, TX 75206
Bob Proud, Gen. Mgr.
(214) 214-887-9107 Fax: (214) 841-4215

KEPS-AM (1270 KHZ)
P.O. Box 1123
Eagle Pass, TX 78852
Rosa de la Garza, Gen. Mgr.
(830) 773-9247 Fax: (830) 773-9500

KVIV-FM (1340 KHZ)
4900 Montana Ave.
El Paso, TX 79903
Alfonso Cabrera, Gen. Mgr.
(915) 565-2996 Fax: (915) 562-3156

XHIM-FM (105.1 MHZ)
2211 E. Missouri #237
El Paso, TX 79903
María Elena Lazo, Gen. Mgr.
(915) 542-2969 Fax: (915) 542-2958

KPAS-FM (103.1 MHZ)
P.O. Box 371010
El Paso, TX 79937
Algie Folder, Gen. Mgr.
(915) 851-3382 Fax: (915) 851-4360

KLAR-AM (1300 KHZ)
3220 Anna Ave.
Laredo, TX 78044
Héctor Patiño, Gen. Mgr.
(956) 723-1300 Fax: (956) 723-9539

KWEL-AM (1070 KHZ)
1110 E. Scharburoug
Midland, TX 79705
Laustino Quiróz, Gen. Mgr.
(915) 685-1958

KVWG-AM (1280 KHZ)
1581 Oilfield Rd.
Pearsall, TX 78061
Jesús Sifuentes, Gen. Mgr.
(830) 334-4338

KYST-AM (920 MHZ)
7322 SW Fwy. #500
Houston, TX 77074
Cruz Velázquez, President
(713) 779-9292 Fax: (713) 779-1651

KVOU-AM (1400 KHZ)
1400 Batesville Rd.
Uralde, TX 78801
Rue Jaston, Gen. Mgr.
(850) 278-2555 Fax: (850) 278-9461
Programming: Spanish 1 pm-12 midnight.

KWFS-AM (1290 KHZ)
974 Springlake Rd.
Wichita Falls, TX 76307
Jim Perane, Gen. Mgr.
(940) 855-3555 Fax: (940) 855-4041

KBEN-AM (1450 KHZ)
203 S. 4th St.
Carrizo Springs, TX 78834
Noelia S. Herbort, Gen. Mgr.
(830) 876-2210 Fax: (830) 876-5489

KERB-AM (89.5 KHZ)
P.O. Box 553
Ordessa, TX 79760
Peter Almanza, Gen. Mgr.
(915) 333-1227 Fax: (915) 333-3044

KMUL-AM (1380 KHZ)
600 W. 8th St. #486
Muleshoe, TX 79347
Elias Noe Anzaldoa, Gen. Mgr.
(806) 272-4273 Fax: (806) 272-5067

KSEY-AM (1230 KHZ)
700 8th St. #210
Seymour, TX 76301
Tommy Cobos, Gen. Mgr.
(940) 888-2637 Fax: (940) 766-0011

KBIB-AM (1000 KHZ)
Rt. 1, Box 95-C
San Antonio, TX 78124
Pastor Ken Hutcheson, Gen. Mgr.
(210) 914-2083

KLEY-FM (94.1 KHZ)
7800 W. IH 10 #330
San Antonio, TX 78230
Luis Albertini, Gen. Mgr.
(956) 340-1234 Fax: (956) 340-1775

XEAS/XENU/XERT/XERKF/XHPX/XEWL-AM
6044 Gateway Blvd. E. #500
El Paso, TX 79905
Mike Edwards, Gen. Mgr.
(915) 771-0081 Fax: (915) 771-0111

KKPS-FM (99.5 MHZ)
901 E. Pike Blvd.
Weslaco, TX 78596
Danny Fletchar, Gen. Mgr.
(956) 968-1548 Fax: (956) 968-1643

KMFM-FM (104.9 MHZ)
P.O. Box 252
McAllen, TX 78505
Paulino Bernal, Gen. Mgr.
(956) 781-5528 Fax: (956) 686-2999

KRGE-AM (1290 KHZ)
P.O. Box 1290
Weslaco, TX 78596
Henry Garza, Gen. Mgr.
(956) 968-7777 Fax: (956) 968-5143

KBNR-FM (88.3 MHZ)
216 W. Elizabeth
Brownsville, TX 78521
Moisés Flores, Gen. Mgr.
(956) 542-6933 Fax: (956) 542-0523

KMXO-AM (1500 KHZ)
604-N. Second St.
Merkel, TX 79536
Zacarias Serrato, Gen. Mgr.
(915) 928-3060 Fax: (915) 928-4683

KRVA-FM (106.9 MHZ)
5307 E. Mockingbird, #500
Dallas, TX 75206
Bob Proud, Gen. Mgr.
(214) 887-9107 Fax: (214) 841-4215

XHNZ-FM (107.5 MHZ)
2211 E. Missouri #E-237
El Paso, TX 79903
Elena Lazo, Gen. Mgr.
(915) 542-2969 Fax: (915) 542-2958

KERB-FM (106.3 MHZ)
P.O. Box 553
Ordessa, TX 79760
Peter Almanza, Gen. Mgr.
(915) 333-1227 Fax: (915) 333-3044

KITE-FM (95.3 MHZ)
1581 Oilfield Rd.
Pearsall, TX 78061
Jesús Sifuentes, Gen. Mgr.
(830) 334-8900

KBDR-FM (100.5 MHZ)
815 Salinas Ave. #1140
Laredo, TX 78040-8012
Bruce Miller Earle, Gen. Mgr.
(956) 725-1000 Fax: (956) 718-1000

KBMI-FM (97.7 MHZ)
100 S. Bethel St.
Roma, TX 78584
Orion Paulson, Gen. Mgr.
(210) 849-2031 Fax: (210) 849-1701

KCOM-AM (1550 KHZ)
105 N. Sand
Comanche, TX 76442
Bill Cole, Gen. Mgr.
(915) 356-2558 Fax: (915) 356-5757

KELP-AM (1590 KHZ)
6900 Commerce
El Paso, TX 79915
Arnie McLatchey, Gen. Mgr.
(915) 779-0016 Fax: (915) 779-6641

KGLF-AM (1510 KHZ)
P.O. Box 260715
Corpus Christi, TX 78426-0715
Rufino Sendejo, Gen. Mgr.
(512) 387-1510 Fax: (512) 387-4704

KIKZ-AM (1250 KHZ)
105 NW. 11th St.
Seminole, TX 79360
Danny Curtis, Gen. Mgr.
(915) 758-5878 Fax: (915) 758-5878

KHOY-FM (88.1 MHZ)
1901 Corpus Christi
Laredo, TX 78040
Benett Mcbride, Gen. Mgr.
(956) 722-4167 Fax: (956) 722-4467

KIWW-FM (96.1 MHZ)
200 S. 10th. #600
McAllen, TX 78501
José Saldivar, Gen. Mgr.
(956) 631-5499 Fax: (956) 631-0090

KJSA-AM (1140 KHZ)
P.O. Box 638
Mineral Wells, TX 76067
Richard Niblett, Gen. Mgr.
(940) 325-1140 Fax: (940) 328-1747

KLBO-AM (1330 KHZ)
P.O. Box 270
Monohans, TX 79756
Harold Halloway, Gen. Mgr.
(915) 943-2588 Fax: (915) 943-7314

KLTP-FM (104.9 MHZ)
2200 Market #610
Galveston, TX 77550
Gary Stone, Gen. Mgr.
(409) 762-2100 Fax: (409) 762-9283

KSEM-FM (106.3 MHZ)
105 NW. 11th St.
Seminole, TX 79360
Danny Curtis, Gen. Mgr.
(915) 758-5878 Fax: (915) 758-5878

KWCB-FM (89.7 MHZ)
1905 10th St.

Floresville, TX 78114
Cissy González, Gen. Mgr.
(210) 393-6116

KWMC-AM (1490 KHZ)
903 E. Cortinas St.
Del Rio, TX 78840
Alfredo Garza, Gen. Mgr.
(830) 775-3544 Fax: (830) 775-3546

KGBT-FM (98.5 MHZ)
200 S. 10th
McAllen, TX 78501
Pepe Saldivar, Gen. Mgr.
(956) 631-5499 Fax: (956) 631-0090

XHTGS-FM (107.3 MGZ)
505 Houston St.
Laredo, TX 78040
Miguel Villarreal, Gen. Mgr.
(956) 725-1491 Fax: (956) 725-3424

KBBA-AM (1560 MHZ)
A. Lloyd Mynatt
1740 N. 1st St.
Abilene, TX 79603
Caroline Whitaker, Gen. Mgr.
(915) 677-7225 Fax: (915) 672-6669

KHER-FM
Acelga Broadcasting Corporation
P.O. Box 743
Crystal City, TX 78839
Noelia S. Herbort, Gen. Mgr.
(210) 374-2203 Fax: (210) 374-2803

KOPY-FM (92.1 KHZ)
Alice Broadcast Co.
P.O. Box 731
Alice, TX 78333
Mike Smith, Gen. Mgr.
(361) 664-1884 Fax: (361) 664-1886

**KLFB-AM-LA FIESTA
(1420 KHZ)**
Ballard Broadcasting Co.
2700 Marshall St.
Lubbock, TX 79415
Shirley Ballard, Gen. Mgr.
(806) 765-8114 Fax: (806) 763-0428

KEJS-FM (106.5 MHZ)
Barton Company
1607 13th St.
Lubbock, TX 79401
Ernesto Barton, Gen. Mgr.
(806) 747-5951 Fax: (806) 747-3524

KIRT-AM (1580 KHZ)
Bravo Broadcasting Co.
608 S 10th St.
McAllen, TX 78501
Humberto Pedraza, Gen. Mgr.
(956) 686-2111 Fax: (956) 668-0370

KQXX-FM (98.5 MHZ)
Bravo Broadcasting Company
200 S. 10th St. #600
McAllen, TX 78501
José Luis Muñoz, Gen. Mgr.
(956) 631-5499 Fax: (956) 631-0090

KPSO-FM (106.3 MHZ)
Brooks Broadcasting Corporation
304 E. Rice
Falfurrias, TX 78355-3624
Raymond Creeley, Gen. Mgr.
(512) 325-2112 Fax: (512) 325-2112

KHCB-AM-RADIO AMISTAD (1400 KHZ)
Christian Houston Broadcasters
2424 South Blvd.
Houston, TX 77098
Bruce Munsterman, Gen. Mgr.
(409) 744-6343

KNDA-FM (102.9 KHZ)
Christian Ministries of the Valley
2001 Saratoga Blvd
Corpus Christi, TX 78417
Patricia Rodriguez, Gen. Mgr.
(361) 814-1030 Fax: (361) 814-1036

KFLZ-FM (106.9 MHZ)
Cimek Corporation
110 E. Main St.
Bishop, TX 78343
Joe Cisneros, Gen. Mgr.
(361) 584-2532 Fax: (361) 584-3959

KSAB-FM-RADIO PLAZA (99.9 MHZ)
Clear Channel, Inc. Radio Plaza
501 Tupper Ln.
Corpus Christi, TX 78417
Kent Cooper, Gen. Mgr.
(361) 560-5722 Fax: (631)289-5035

KVOP-AM (1400 KHZ)
Cornerstone Radio Holding, LLC
3218 N. Quincy St.
Plainville, TX 79072
Mike Fox, Gen. Mgr.
(806) 296-2771 Fax: (806) 293-5732

KUBR-FM (104.9 KHZ)
La Cristiana
P.O. Box 252
McAllen, TX 78505
Eloy Bernal, Prog. Dir.
(956) 781-5528 Fax: (956) 686-2999

KEDA-AM (1540 KHZ)
D & E Broadcasting Company
510 S. Flores St.
San Antonio, TX 78204
Alberto Dávila, Gen. Mgr.
(210) 226-5254 Fax: (210) 227-7937

KXTG-FM (107.9 MHZ)
El Dorado Communications
1980 Post Oak Blvd. #1500
Houston, TX 77056
Pedro Gasc, Gen. Mgr.
(713) 993-8000 Fax: (713) 968-4499

KEYH-AM (850 KHZ)
El Dorado Communications
1980 Post Oak Blvd. #1500
Houston, TX 77056
Pedro Gasc, Gen. Mgr.
(713) 993-8000 Fax: (713) 968-4499

KQQK-FM (106.5 MHZ)
El Dorado Communications
1980 Post Oak Blvd. #1500
Houston, TX 77056
Pedro Gasc, Gen. Mgr.
(713) 993-8000 Fax: (713) 968-4499

KIMP-AM (960 KHZ)
East Texas Broadcasting
P.O. Box 990
Mount Pleasant, TX 75456
Bud Kitchen, Gen. Mgr.
(903) 572-8726 Fax: (903) 572-7232

KSVE-AM (1150 KHZ)
Entravision Communications Corp.

5426 N. Mesa St.
El Paso, TX 79912
David Candelaria, Gen. Mgr
(915) 581-1126 Fax: (915) 585-4611

KXEB-AM (910 KHZ)
La Fiesta Mexicana
3500 Maple St. #1310
Dallas, TX 75219
Carmen Hernández, Gen. Mgr.
(214) 508-1600 Fax: (214) 787-1910

KELG-AM (1440 KHZ)
Garcia Communications
7524 N Lamar Blvd.
Austin, TX 78752
Joe José García, Gen. Mgr.
(512) 453-1491 Fax: (512) 458-0700

KTXZ-AM (1560 KHZ)
Garcia Communications
7524 N Lamar Blvd.
Austin, TX 78752
Joe José García, Gen. Mgr.
(512) 453-1491 Fax: (512) 458-0700

**KFJZ-AM-LA PANTERA
(870 KHZ)**
Garden City Broadcasting
2214 East 4th St.
Forth Worth, TX 76102
José Vázquez, Gen. Mgr.
(817) 336-7175 Fax: (817) 338-1205

KJBZ-FM (98.1 MHZ)
Guerra Enterprises
902 E. Calton Rd.
Laredo, TX 78041
Belinda Guerra, Gen. Mgr.
(956) 726-9393 Fax: (956) 724-9813

KESS-AM (1270 KHZ)
Hispanic Broadcasting Corporation
7700 John Carpenter Fwy.
Dallas, TX 75247
Jose Valle, Gen. Mgr.
(214) 630-8531 Fax: (214) 689-3818

KAMA-AM (700 KHZ)
Hispanic Broadcasting Corporation
2211 E Missouri #South-300
El Paso, TX 79903
Kathy Clark, Gen. Mgr.
(915) 544-9797 Fax: (915) 544-1247

KBNA-AM (920 KHZ)
Hispanic Broadcasting Corporation
2211 E Missouri #South-300
El Paso, TX 79903
Kathy Clark, Gen. Mgr.
(915) 544-9797 Fax: (915) 544-1247

KLAT-AM (1010 KHZ)
Hispanic Broadcasting Corporation
1415 N. Loop W. #400
Houston, TX 77008
Mark Nasepohl, Gen. Mgr.
(713) 407-0933 Fax: (713) 407-1400

KXTN-FM (107.5 MHZ)
Hispanic Broadcasting Corporation
1777 NE Loop 410 #400
San Antonio, TX 78217
Dan Wilson, Gen. Mgr.
(210) 829-1075 Fax: (210) 804-7825

KOVE-FM (9.33.MHZ)
Hispanic Broadcasting Corporation
1415 N. Loop W. #400

Houston, TX 77008
Mark Nasepohl, Gen. Mgr.
(713) 407-0933 Fax: (713) 407-1400

KLNO-FM (94.1 MHZ)
Hispanic Broadcasting Corporation
7700 John Carpenter Fwy.
Dallas, TX 75247
Jose Valle, Gen. Mgr.
(214) 630-8531 Fax: (214) 689-3818

KBNA-FM (97.5 MHZ)
Hispanic Broadcasting Corporation
2211 E Missouri #South-300
El Paso, TX 79903
Kathy Clark, Gen. Mgr.
(915) 544-9797 Fax: (915) 544-1247

KOVA-FM (104.9 MHZ)
Hispanic Broadcasting Corporation
1415 N. Loop W. #400
Houston, TX 77008
Mark Nasepohl, Gen. Mgr.
(713) 407-0933 Fax: (713) 407-1400

KDXX-AM (1480 KHZ)
Hispanic Broadcasting Corporation
7700 John Carpenter Fwy.
Dallas, TX 75247
Jose Valle, Gen. Mgr.
(214) 630-8531 Fax: (214) 689-3818

KDXX-FM (107.9 MHZ)
Hispanic Broadcasting Corporation
7700 John Carpenter Fwy.
Dallas, TX 75247
Jose Valle, Gen. Mgr.
(214) 630-8531 Fax: (214) 689-3818

KLTN-FM-STEREO LATINO (102.9 MHZ)
Hispanic Broadcasting Corporation
1415 N. Loop W. #400
Houston, TX 77008
Mark Nasepohl, Gen. Mgr.
(713) 407-0933 Fax: (713) 407-1400

KRTX-FM-HOUSE PARTY (100.7 MHZ)
Hispanic Broadcasting Corporation
1415 N. Loop W. #400
Houston, TX 77008
Mark Nasepohl, Gen. Mgr.
(713) 407-0933 Fax: (713) 407-1400

KDXT-FM (106.9 MHZ)
Hispanic Broadcasting Corporation
7700 John Carpenter Fwy.
Dallas, TX 75247
Jose Valle, Gen. Mgr.
(214) 630-8531 Fax: (214) 689-3818

KHCK-FM (99.1 MHZ)
Hispanic Broadcasting Corporation
7700 John Carpenter Fwy.
Dallas, TX 75247
Jose Valle, Gen. Mgr.
(214) 630-8531 Fax: (214) 689-3818

KDOS-FM (107.9 MHZ)
Hispanic Broadcasting Corporation
7700 John Carpenter Fwy.
Dallas, TX 75247
Jose Valle, Gen. Mgr.
(214) 630-8531 Fax: (214) 689-3818

KXTN-AM (1310 KHZ)
Hispanic Broadcasting Corporation
1777 NE Loop 410 #400
San Antonio, TX 78217
Dan Wilson, Gen. Mgr.

(210) 829-1075 Fax: (210) 804-7825

KUKA-FM (105.9 MHZ)
Ideal Media
P.O. Box 589
Alice, TX 78333
Armando Marroquin, Gen. Mgr.
(361) 668-6666 Fax: (361) 668-6661

KXYZ-AM (1320 KHZ)
Infinity Broadcasting
7300 S.W. Freeway #1500
Houston, TX 77074
Alejandro Sánchez, Gen. Mgr.
(713) 472-2500 Fax: (713) 334-5150

KBZO-AM (1460 KHZ)
Intravision Communications
1220 Broadway #500
Lubbock, TX 79401
Richard Morton, Gen. Mgr.
(806) 763-6051 Fax: (806) 744-8363

KBTS-FM (94.3 MHZ)
KBTS, Inc
608 Johnnson St.
Big Spring, TX 79720
John Weeks, Gen. Mgr.
(915) 264-9494 Fax: (915) 267-1579

KUNO-AM (1400 KHZ)
KDOS Ltd.
1301 Horn Rd.
Corpus Christi, TX 78416
Luis Alonso Muñoz, Gen. Mgr.
(361) 560-5866

KPAN-AM/ FM (860 KHZ/106.3 MHZ)
KPAN Radio Stations
218 E. 5th. St.
Hereford, TX 79045
Edward Maldonado, Prog. Dir.
(806) 364-1860 Fax: (806) 364-5814
Programming: Spanish-weekdays 6-8 PM

KRMY-AM-LA CALIENTE (1050 KHZ)
KRMY Radio Station
314 N. 2nd. St.
Killeen, TX 76541
Irwin Martínez, Gen. Mgr.
(254) 628-7070 Fax: (254) 628-7071

KYMI-FM (98.5 MHZ)
KYMI Radio Station
P.O. Box 319
Lamesa, TX 79331
Israel Ibáñez, Gen. Mgr.
(806) 872-6553 Fax: (806) 872-6244

KMIL-AM (1330 KHZ)
Malam Broadcasting Company
P.O. Box 832
Cameron, TX 76520
Joe Smitherman, Gen. Mgr.
(254) 697-6633 Fax: (254) 697-6330

KOZA-AM (1230 KHZ)
Mesa Entertainment
P. O. Box 553
Odessa, TX 79761
Peter Almanza, Gen. Mgr.
(915) 333-1227 Fax: (915) 333-3044

KQLM-FM (107.9 MHZ)
Mesa Entertainment
P.O. Box 553
Odessa, TX 79761
Peter Almanza, Gen. Mgr.
(915) 333-1227 Fax: (915) 333-3044

KTNO-AM (1440 KHZ)
Mortenson Broadcasting Station
3105 W. Arkansas Ln. #82
Arlington, TX 76016
José Alfredo Castillo, Prog. Dir.
(817) 469-1540 Fax: (817) 261-2137

KBOR-AM (1600 KHZ)
La Nueva KBOR, Inc.
1050 McIntosh
Brownsville, TX 78521
Edgar Treviño, Gen. Mgr.
(956) 544-1600 Fax: (956) 544-0311

KTJN-FM (106.3 KHZ)
La Nueva KBOR, Inc.
1050 McIntosh
Brownsville, TX 78523
Hilda Treviño, Gen. Mgr.
(956) 544-1600 Fax: (956) 544-0311

KBOR-FM (105.5 MHZ)
La Nueva KBOR, Inc.
1050 McIntosh
Browsville, TX 78523
Edgar Treviño, Gen. Mgr.
(210) 544-1600 Fax: (210) 544-0311

KQXX-AM (1700 KHZ)
La Nueva KBOR, Inc.
1050 McIntosh Full
Browsville, TX 78523
Edgar Treviño, Gen. Mgr.
(956) 544-1600 Fax: (956) 544-0311

KILE-AM (1560 KHZ)
La Nueva U-16
P.O. Box 386
Port Lavaca, TX 77979
Paul Duenez, Gen. Mgr.
(361) 552-2951 Fax: (361) 552-2953

KIUN-AM (1400 KHZ)
Pecos Radio Company, Inc.
P.O. Box 469
Pecos, TX 79772
Bill R. Cole, Gen. Mgr.
(915) 445-2497

KGBC-AM (1540 KHZ)
Prets Blum Media
P.O. Box 11
Galvenston, TX 77554
Leon Blum, Gen. Mgr.
(409) 744-4567 Fax: (409) 744-4567

KBRN-AM (1500 KHZ)
Radio Cristiana
P.O. Box 252
Mc Allen, TX 78505
Paulina Bernal, Gen. Mgr.
(956) 781-5528 Fax: (956) 686-2999

KVER-FM (91.1 MHZ)
Radio Manantial
4126 N. Mesa
El Paso, TX 79902
Azael de la Garza, Gen. Mgr.
(915) 544-9190 Fax: (915) 544-9193
Programming: Spanish Christian music 24 hours a day.

KCLR-AM (1530 KHZ)
Radio Victoria
1519 34th St. #C
Lubbock, TX 79405
Alfonso Cabrera, Pres.
(806) 763-2133 Fax: (806) 763-5817

KXTQ-AM (950 KHZ)
Ramar Communications
904 E. Broadway St.
Lubbock, TX 79403
Chack Heinz, Gen. Mgr.
(806) 747-2555 Fax: (806) 741-1757

KXTQ-FM (93.7 MHZ)
Ramar Communications
904 E. Broadway St.
Lubbock, TX 79403
Chuck Heinz, Gen. Mgr.
(806) 747-2555 Fax: (806) 741-1757

KOIR-FM-RADIO ESPERANZA (88.5 MHZ)
Río Grande Bible Institute
4300 S. Business Hwy. #281
Edinburg, TX 78539
Jerónimo Disla, Gen. Mgr.
(956) 383-3845 Fax: (956) 380-8156

KRIO-AM-RADIO ESPERANZA (910 KHZ)
Río Grande Bible Institute
4300 S. Business Hwy. #281
Edinburg, TX 78539
Jerónimo Disla, Gen. Mgr.
(210) 383-3845 Fax: (210) 380-8156

KDOS-AM (1490 KHZ)
Rio Grande Media, Inc.
505 Houston St.
Laredo, TX 78040
Miguel Villarreal, Gen. Mgr.
(956) 725-1491 Fax: (956) 725-3424

KZIP-AM (1600 KHZ)
Rodriguez Communications
3639 B Wolflan Ave.
Amarillo, TX 79102
Susie Dobervach, Gen. Mgr.
(806) 355-1044 Fax: (806) 352-6525

KGRW-FM (94.7 MHZ)
Rodriguez Communications
3639 B Wolflan Ave.
Amarillo, TX 79102
Susie Dobervach, Gen. Mgr.
(806) 355-1044 Fax: (806) 352-6525

KSLR-AM (630 KHZ)
Salem Communications
9601 McAllister Frwy. #1200
San Antonio, TX 78216
Mary Dockery, Gral. Mgr.
(210) 344-8481 Fax: (210) 340-1213

KCTM-FM (103.1 MHZ)
Sound Investments Unlimited, Inc.
Route 5, Box 103 FM
Rio Grande City, TX 78582-9805
Gus Valdez, Gen. Mgr.
(956) 487-8224 Fax: (956) 487-6283

KXOX-AM (1240 KHZ)
Stein Broadcasting, Inc.
1801 Hoyt Ln.
Sweet Water, TX 79556
Lily Gutiérrez, Prog. Dir.
(915) 236-6655 Fax: (915) 235-4391
Programming: Spanish-weekdays 7:30-9 PM

KGBT-AM (1530 KHZ)
Tichenor Media System
200 S. 10th #600
McAllen, TX 78501

José Saldivar, Gen. Mgr.
(956) 631-5499 Fax: (956) 631-0090

KTKO-FM (105.7 MHZ)
Treb Broadcasting
P. O. Box 700
Beeville, TX 78102
Val Moreno, Gen. Mgr.
(361) 358-1490 Fax: (361) 358-7814

KSJT-FM (107.5 MHZ)
La Unica Broadcasting Company
209 W. Beauregard Ave.
San Angelo, TX 76903
Armando Martínez, Gen. Mgr.
(915) 655-1717 Fax: (915) 657-0601

KSML-AM-LA ZETA (1260 KHZ)
Wates Broadcasting
118 W. Shepherd St.
Lufkin, TX 75901
Ino Reyes, Gen. Mgr.
(936) 632-8444 Fax: (936) 632-8451

KBNL-FM (89.9 MHZ)
World Radio Network
1620 E. Plum St.
Laredo, TX 78043
Paul Bell, Gen. Mgr.
(956) 724-9090 Fax: (956) 724-9919

KEPX-FM-RADIO MANANTIAL (89.5 KHZ)
World Radio Network
P.O. Box 873
Eagle Pass, TX 78853
Gary Lawson, Gen. Mgr.
(830) 757-0895 Fax: (830) 757-8950

UTAH

KRGQ-AM (1550 KHZ)
P.O. Box 539
Magna, UT 84315
Gene Guthrie, Gen. Mgr.
(801) 364-0199 Fax: (801) 972-3440

KRCL-FM (91 MHZ)
208 West 800 South
Salt Lake City, UT 84101
Donna Land, Dir.
(801) 363-1818 Fax: (801) 533-9136

KSGO-AM (1600 KHZ)
80 S. Redwood Rd. #211
North Salt Lake City, UT 84054
Jesus Tovar, General Manager
(801) 936-9300 Fax: (801) 936-0686

KSVN-AM (730 KHZ)
La Mejicana
4215 W. 4000 S.
Hooper, UT 84315
Alex Collantes, Station Mgr.
(801) 292-1799 Fax: (801) 292-1799

KCPX-AM (1600 KHZ)
Radio Fiesta
1715 West 700 North #200
Salt Lake City, UT 84116
José López, Gen. Mgr.
(801) 364-2898 Fax: (801) 364-2897

VIRGINIA

WPVN-AM
Pampas Broadcasting
8370 Greensboro Dr. #1007

McLean, VA 22102
Ana Eliza

WASHINGTON

KYXE-AM (1020 KHZ)
706 Butterfield Rd., P.O. Box 2888
Yakima, WA 98907
Bob Powers, Gen. Mgr.
(509) 457-1000 Fax: (509) 452-0541

KBSN-AM (1470 KHZ)
2241 W. Main
Moses Lake, WA 98837
Jim Davis, Gen. Mgr.
(509) 765-3441 Fax: (509) 766-0273

KUOW-FM (94.7 MHZ)
P.O. Box 353750
University of Washington
Seattle, WA 98195
Lisa Levi, Prog. Dir.
(206) 543-2710 Fax: (206) 543-2720

KZTA-AM (99.7 MHZ)
P. O. Box 2888
Yakima, WA 98907
Jesús Rosales, Gen. Mgr.
(509) 457-1000 Fax: (509) 452-0541

KBRC-AM (1430 KHZ)
P. O. Box 250
Mt. Vernon, WA 98273
Alberto González, Prog. Dir.
(360) 424-7676 Fax: (360) 424-1660

KWWX-AM (1340 KHZ)
231 N. Wenatchee Ave. #401
Wenatchee, WA 98801
David Herald, Gen. Mgr.
(509) 665-656 Fax: (509) 663-1150

KZHR-FM (92.5 MHZ)
38 E. Main St.
Walla Walla, WA 99362
Robert Bogges, Gen. Mgr.
(509) 525-3162 Fax: (509) 522-2746

KBRO-AM (1490 KHZ)
P.O. Box 1277
Tacoma, WA 98401
Josie Baine, Gen. Mgr.
(360) 377-2325 Fax: (360) 922-3348

KGDC-AM (1320 KHZ)
103 E. Main St.
Walla Walla, WA 99362
Joe Gonzales, Gen. Mgr.
(509) 525-0506

KJOX-AM (930 KHZ)
P.O. Box 2888
Yakima, WA 98907-2888
Robert L. Towers, Gen. Mgr.
(509) 457-1000 Fax: (509) 452-0541

KRCW-FM (96.3 MHZ)
121 Sunnyside Ave.
Granger, WA 98932
Ricardo García, Gen. Mgr.
(509) 854-1900 Fax: (509) 854-2223

KREW-AM (1210 KHZ)
638 Decanter
Sunnyside, WA 98944
Don Benett, Gen. Mgr.
(509) 837-2277 Fax: (509) 837-3777

KVYF-FM (103.3 MHZ)
P.O. Box 1056
Moses Lake, WA 98837
Randy Buroks, Gen. Mgr.
(509) 766-1369 Fax: (509) 766-6001

KZTB-FM (96.7 MHZ)
706 Butterfield Rd., P.O. Box 2888
Yakima, WA 98967
Ed Ramirez, Gen. Mgr.
(509) 457-1000 Fax: (509) 452-0541

KKMO-AM (1360 KHZ)
Hispanic Media Services
4501 Pacific Hwy.
Tacoma, WA 98424
James L. Baine, Gen. Mgr.
(206) 922-3345 Fax: (206) 922-3348

KDNA-FM (91.9 MHZ)
KDNA Radio
121 Sunnyside Ave.
Granger, WA 98932
Ricardo García, Gen. Mgr.
(509) 854-2222 Fax: (509) 854-2223

KRSC-AM (1400 KHZ)
KRSC Radio-AM
180 E. Main
Othello, WA 99344
D.C. Hart, Gen. Mgr.
(509) 488-2791 Fax: (509) 488-3345

KMUZ-AM 1230, LA ZETA (1230 KHZ)
Pacific Northwest Broadcasting Corp.
24 South A St. #C
Washougal, WA 98671
Cshea Walker, General Manager
(360)-835-3400 Fax: (360) 835-7593

WISCONSIN

WBJX-AM (1460 KHZ)
2310 S. Green Bay Rd. #C
Racine, WI 53406
Robert Jeffers, Gen. Mgr.
(414) 635-1460

WYOMING

KGBA-AM (650 KHZ)
1912 Capital Ave. Suite 300
Shaymon, WY 82001
Phil Mercado, Spanish Prog. Dir.
(307) 632-4400 Fax: (307) 632-1818

KGOS-AM (1490 KHZ)
KGOS Radio
West Valley Rd., Route 2 Box 40
Torrington, WY 82240
Henry Prado, Prog. Dir.
(307) 532-2158 Fax: (307) 532-2640
Programming: Spanish-Sunday 12-1 PM

AHHY: 1986-2000. Thematic Index

AHHY: 1986-2000. Índice temático

De las primeras xilografías, al libro, al almanaque, al diario se cumplió un proceso de democratización de la cultura. Hasta fines del siglo XVIII, el diario era todavía un pasatiempo para hidalgos eruditos, pero en el siglo XIX el libro, la revista y el diario provocaron ya el interes casi morboso de las mayorías. Hoy, en el inicio del siglo XXI, los nuevos medios de comunicación sacuden a toda la humanidad

The first two numbers indicate the year of the AH-HY and the following numbers indicate the page number.
Los dos primeros números señalan el año del AH-HY y los siguientes la página.

Information Update

Actualice la información

TIYM Publishing Co., Inc.
6718 Whittier Ave., #130
McLean, VA 22101
Tel: (703) 734-1632
Fax: (703) 356-0787
E-mail: tiym@aol.com

If your organization, agency, or publication has made changes during the past year, or if you know of one that does not appear within this edition, please take a few moments to let us know by filling out the form below. Fax to **(703) 356-0787**, or cut the form along the dotted line, fold as indicated and tape it closed. Don't forget to include the correct postage. You may also visit www.HispanicYearbook.com or www.AnuarioHispano.com and fill out the online form or e-mail the updated information to **tiym@aol.com**. We appreciate your efforts in helping us keep the ANUARIO HISPANO-HISPANIC YEARBOOK as up-to-date and accurate as possible.

Please indicate listing preference:

☐ Career Opportunities for Hispanics: ☐ Federal/State ☐ Private Sector
☐ Minority Business Opportunities
☐ Institution Offering Scholastic Financial Aid
☐ Hispanic Business
☐ Hispanic Organizations
☐ Hispanic Publications
☐ Hispanic Radio Stations
☐ Hispanic TV Stations
☐ Other _____

Agency/ Company/ Organization Name: _____
_____ Date Founded: _____
If it is a ☐ Branch or ☐ Affiliate of a larger organization, What is the name of that organization? _____

Address: _____
City: _____ State: _____ Zip Code: _____
Telephone 1: _____ Telephone 2: _____ Fax: _____
E-mail: _____ Web: _____
Name of the Principal Contact: _____
Title of the Principal Contact: _____
Chief Purpose of the Organization (☐ attached is a separate sheet with a detailed description, or organization brochure): _____

Publication/ Station Name: _____
Circulation: _____ Verified: _____
No. of Members: _____ Most Important Meeting: _____ Date Held: _____
How often is the Publication Produced: _____
Language: ☐ Spanish ☐ English ☐ Other: _____
Other Specifications: _____

Thank you for helping us keep the ANUARIO HISPANO - HISPANIC YEARBOOK up-to-date.

Keep us informed, and we'll spread the word.

Take a few moments to fill out the form on the opposite side of this page to help keep all our readers current with your organization, publication, service or program.

— — — — — — — — — — — — — — — — Fold Here — — — — — — — — — — — — — — — — —

A N U A R I O
H I S P A N O

ANUARIOHISPANO.COM   **HISPANICYEARBOOK.COM**

H I S P A N I C

Y E A R B O O K

— — — — — — — — — — — — — — — — Fold Here — — — — — — — — — — — — — — — —

_____

_____

_____

| Place Postage Here |

TIYM Publishing Co., Inc.
6718 Whittier Ave., #130
McLean, VA 22101
USA

344   Tape Closed Here   AnuarioHispano.**com**